Understanding Scots Law:

An Introduction to Scots Law, Procedure and Legal Skills

Second Edition

Understanding Scots Law:

An Introduction to Scots Law, Procedure and Legal Skills

SECOND EDITION

BY

Christina Ashton
*Former Head of Centre for Law,
Edinburgh Napier University*

David Brand
*Honorary Teaching Fellow in
Law, University of Dundee*

Gordon Cameron
*Senior Lecturer in Law,
University of Dundee*

James Chalmers
*Senior Lecturer in Law,
University of Edinburgh*

Vic Craig
*Professor Emeritus,
Heriot Watt University*

Valerie Finch
*Senior Lecturer in Law,
University of the West of
Scotland*

Alex Gibb
*Lecturer in Law,
Aberdeen College*

Nicholas Grier
*Senior Lecturer in Law,
Edinburgh Napier University*

Dr Nick McKerrell
*Lecturer in Law,
Glasgow Caledonian University*

Alan Reid
*Lecturer in Law,
LRG University of Applied
Sciences, Switzerland.*

Robert Shiels
Solicitor in Scotland

Joe Thomson
*Former Regius Professor of Law
at the University of Glasgow and
Commissioner, the Scottish Law
Commission*

W. GREEN

First edition   2007

Published in 2012 by W. Green, 21 Alva Street,
Edinburgh EH2 4PS
Part of Thomson Reuters (Professional) UK Limited
(Registered in England & Wales, Company No 1679046.
Registered Office and address for service:
Aldgate House, 33 Aldgate High Street, London EC3N 1DL)

www.wgreen.co.uk

Typeset by YHT Ltd, Hillingdon
Printed and bound in Great Britain by CPI Antony Rowe, Wiltshire

No natural forests were destroyed to make this product;
Only farmed timber was used and replanted

A CIP catalogue record for this book is available from the British Library

ISBN 978-0-414-01845-7

Thomson Reuters and the Thomson Reuters logo are
trademarks of Thomson Reuters.

© Thomson Reuters (Professional) UK Limited 2012

All rights reserved. United Kingdom statutory material in this publication is
acknowledged as Crown copyright.

No part of this publication may be reproduced or transmitted in any form or by any
means, or stored in any retrieval system of any nature without prior written permission,
except for permitted fair dealing under the Copyright, Designs and Patents Act 1988, or in
accordance with the terms of a licence issued by the Copyright Licensing Agency in respect
of photocopying and/or reprographic reproduction. Application for permission for other
use of copyright material including permission to reproduce extracts in other published
works shall be made to the publishers. Full acknowledgment of author, publisher and
source must be given.

North East Scotland College
Library +

Telephone: 01224 612138

GENERAL NOTE TO SECOND EDITION

This is a completely revised second edition.

The law is stated as at June 2012.

PREFACE TO FIRST EDITION

This book is intended to be an accessible, comprehensive and concise guide to Scots law. It is designed for BA Law (or equivalents) and HNC/D Legal Services students and the subject areas covered closely reflect the subject matter taught on these courses.

The book is divided into five sections: Introduction to the Scottish legal system; Public law; Scots private law; Procedure; and Legal Skills. The inclusion of the final two sections marks a departure from the traditional approach of guides to multiple areas of Scots law which concentrate solely on the detail of the law itself. Two chapters on procedure have been included to provide introductory material for procedural modules taken as part of an HNC/D in Legal Services. The legal skills chapter seeks to help the reader to understand the legal materials involved in the study of law: legislation and cases. It also contains useful advice about legal problem solving, essay writing skills and passing law exams.

The book contains features designed to aid understanding and to enable students to use it as both an introductory guide and as a revision aid. The chapters convey important concepts and issues and contain a high level of explanation. Each chapter begins with a short overview and a list of outcomes which the reader should achieve by reading the chapter. Key concepts and cases are highlighted throughout the text. At the end of the chapters the following features appear: a chapter summary which consists of key points listed with the relevant legal authority and which is designed to be used as a revision aid; a quick quiz to test the readers' knowledge from reading the chapter; further reading and relevant web links.

The law has been stated as at April 30, 2007 but where possible the authors have tried to take account of future developments since that date. The imminent replacement of District Courts by Justice of the Peace Courts has been noted in the text. The replacement of the House of Lords by the new Supreme Court has not been included as this change is not due to take place until 2009.

Karen Fullerton
Commissioning Editor, W. Green
July 2007

Contents

Paragraph

▶ PART 1: INTRODUCTION TO THE SCOTTISH LEGAL SYSTEM

CHAPTER 1: SOURCES OF SCOTS LAW
Christina Ashton

CHAPTER 2: STRUCTURE OF THE LEGAL SYSTEM
Christina Ashton

► PART 2: PUBLIC LAW

CHAPTER 3: CONSTITUTIONAL LAW
Valerie Finch

CHAPTER 4: THE EU DIMENSION TO THE SCOTTISH LEGAL SYSTEM
Alan Reid

CHAPTER 5: HUMAN RIGHTS LAW
Valerie Finch

CHAPTER 6: CRIMINAL LAW
James Chalmers

▶ PART 3: SCOTS PRIVATE LAW

CHAPTER 7: CONTRACT
Alex Gibb

CHAPTER 8: SALE OF GOODS AND CONSUMER LAW
Nicholas Grier

CHAPTER 9: EMPLOYMENT LAW
Professor Vic Craig

CHAPTER 10: COMMERCIAL LAW
Nicholas Grier

CHAPTER 11: DELICT
Gordon Cameron

CHAPTER 12: PROPERTY
David Brand

CHAPTER 13: TRUSTS
James Chalmers

CHAPTER 14: SUCCESSION
David Brand

CHAPTER 15: FAMILY
Joe Thomson

▶ PART 4: PROCEDURE

CHAPTER 16: CIVIL LITIGATION
Robert Shiels

CHAPTER 17: CRIMINAL PROCEDURE
Robert Shiels

► PART 5: LEGAL SKILLS

CHAPTER 18: LEGAL SKILLS
Dr Nick McKerrell

Table of Cases

Table of Statutes

Acts of the Scottish Parliament

Table of Statutory Instruments

Scottish Statutory Instruments

Table of European Legislation

Regulations

Directives

Chapter 1   Sources of Scots Law

Christina Ashton[1]

▶ CHAPTER OVERVIEW

This chapter is concerned with the development of Scots law and its sources. It starts by **1–01**
examining how Scots law has developed over the centuries and defines what is meant by
public and private law, statute and common law, and civil and criminal law. It examines
how statutes are created by the UK Parliament and the Scottish Parliament and then
discusses how law can be made by the courts. Finally, the lesser sources of law are
discussed—authoritative writers, custom and equity.

✓ OUTCOMES

At the end of the chapter you should be able to: **1–02**

- ✓ understand how Scots law has developed over the centuries;
- ✓ appreciate the differences between public law and private law; between civil law and criminal law; and between common law and statue law;
- ✓ appreciate the different types of bill made by the UK Parliament;
- ✓ identify the process of making an Act of Parliament;
- ✓ understand how subordinate legislation is made and the advantages and disadvantages of using this form of legislation;
- ✓ describe how legislation is made by the Scottish Parliament;
- ✓ identify the circumstances when judicial precedent is binding upon a court;
- ✓ understand the importance of the authoritative writers to the development of Scots law;
- ✓ describe what is meant by custom as a source of law; and
- ✓ understand the meaning of equity.

INTRODUCTION

There are many definitions of what laws are and why society needs them. One view is that **1–03**
law is a system of rules and regulations by which we regulate our lives, so that we have the
most freedom for ourselves while not harming or restricting the freedoms of others. Laws
will try to strike a balance between these two competing needs, since "one man's freedom
is another man's prison".

Laws are also the ways by which a Government controls the population of the country.
Violent or dishonest behaviour is controlled by the criminal law and the State—in the

---

[1] Formerly Head of Centre for Law, Edinburgh Napier University.

form of the Government—administers that law. But the Government also controls many other areas of law, such as in housing law where the standard of house building is quality controlled, and a landlord can only evict a tenant if the correct legal procedure has been carried out. In company law, a new company has to be registered and fulfil certain requirements, and some people are prohibited from being directors. In employment law, there are regulations regarding the amount of redundancy awarded to a worker and employers cannot discriminate against employees on the grounds of race, sex, marital status or disability.

Laws, therefore, affect every aspect of our lives. Each activity is subject to control by the civil or criminal laws, and sometimes by both. Thus, if you travel by public transport, you are conveyed under a contract of carriage. If you buy a newspaper, you enter into a contract of sale with the shopkeeper. At all times you are subject to the criminal law, so you do not leave a bus or train without paying for your ticket and you obey the road traffic laws when you are driving. Each of us is also subject to the civil law of delict, which says that we must not harm anyone else by our actions. For instance, if you jump off the bus without looking and knock an elderly woman over, then you may be liable in damages for negligence if you have caused her injury.

How Scots law has developed

1–04   There are two main types of legal system in the world. The continental, or civilian, system is based on Roman law and is found in European countries. The Anglo-American system is based on English common law, and as the name suggests, is found in England, the United States of America and other countries which were part of the British Empire, such as Australia and Canada.

Scotland has a mixed legal system derived from both Roman law and the English common law. It is said to have more empathy with the civilian systems of law in many respects. However, there is no doubt that the strongest influence for several centuries has been the law of England. Nevertheless, the Scots system retains significant elements of difference which have been protected by the Act of Union 1707 and jealously guarded by the courts since that time.

Until 1707, Scotland and England were two distinct sovereign states which, from 1603, had shared a monarch. Both countries had their own Parliament which made laws quite separately. In 1707, the two parliaments agreed to join together by means of a Treaty of Union—which was ratified by the Scottish Parliament passing the Act of Union with England and then by the English Parliament passing its Act of Union with Scotland. The two parliaments were abolished and a new Parliament of Great Britain was created, sitting in London. Although this meant that there was now only one law-making body between the two countries, it did not mean that Scots law was abolished, since the Treaty, and then the Acts of Union, preserved the status of Scots law and the legal system.

So what was important about this legal system that was preserved by the Treaty? As noted above, it was a mixed system of law, derived from various historical influences. One of the main influences was of course that of English law, particularly before 1296, when Norman noblemen and clergy settled in Lowland Scotland bringing their feudal system of land tenure and justice.

Another great influence at this time was the Church of Rome and its canon law. It is thought that canon law introduced elements of Roman law into Scots law and procedure, which were then becoming established. The idea of the king as "fountain of justice" helped to establish a more uniform system of law; cases were commenced by the issue of a writ or "brieve" in the king's name. This brieve would require an official to carry out an action or investigation.

From 1296 to 1603, Scotland and England were frequently at war and Scotland formed an alliance with France, thus encouraging influence from the Continent. Regular meetings of Parliament were held with the burgesses from the burghs participating in the Parliament; the levying of taxation was made with their agreement. At first, however, the Parliament's main role was as a court of first instance and for appeals. It was not until the reign of James I (1406–37) that Parliament became primarily a legislature.

In the fifteenth and sixteenth centuries, a number of statutes were passed which had effect for centuries. For instance, an Act of 1424 ensured that the poor had access to legal aid, the Prescription Act 1469 established the long negative prescription and the Act of 1573 (c.55) regulated the law of divorce for desertion. The principal civil court, the Court of Session was set up in 1532 and from its proceedings, legal writings called "Practicks" were produced and notes of legal directions; these were the first case reports and helped to set up a more unified system of law. The court was given power to make Acts of Sederunt to regulate the way in which the court operated. The judges were known as Senators of the College of Justice (as they still are today) and initially they sat as a collegiate body. By the beginning of the seventeenth century, however, it appears that the modern form of the court was starting to take shape, with a small number of judges sitting in an "Outer House" hearing cases.

From the Union of the Crowns in 1603 up until 1800, there was a great interest in Roman law and many young Scotsmen studied in France and Holland, bringing back with them the principles of Roman law and using them when they became practitioners and judges in Scotland. Roman law became a major factor in forming Scots law—particularly in the law of obligations and moveable property. In 1617, the General Register of Sasines was set up to record transactions relating to land, helping to ensure that buyers of land in Scotland receive secure title to that land.

From 1655, there was much movement in the legal system with the publication of "institutional writings". These became important sources of law and are discussed in more detail later in this chapter.

The High Court of Justiciary was established in 1672, consisting of five judges from the Court of Session and the Justice-General and Justice-Clerk. The judges were known as Commissioners of Justiciary (now Lords Commissioners of Justiciary) and they dealt with criminal cases in Edinburgh.

The Union of the Parliaments of Scotland and England on May 1, 1707 dissolved the two Parliaments and created a new Parliament of Great Britain. Article XIX of the Union Treaty specified that the Scots law and the Scottish courts should continue. Although the Treaty stated that no causes in Scotland should be heard in the Courts of Chancery, Queen's Bench, Common Pleas, "or any other court in Westminster Hall", this was held not to include the House of Lords and the practice of sending civil appeals to the House of Lords began within a short time of the Union coming into effect.[2]

From 1800, the Napoleonic Wars prevented the travel of Scots students to the Continent and accordingly, English law now became the major influence on Scots law. Two factors contributed to this:

- the House of Lords now heard all Scottish civil appeals; and
- the Westminster Parliament passed all laws.

Both of these institutions were based on English models and were peopled by mainly English-trained lawyers and judges. Concepts of English law were used to decide Scots

---

[2] *Greenshields v Magistrates of Edinburgh* (1710–1711) Rob. 12.

law, thus changing the Scots principles and causing confusion. Growing concern with the decisions made by the House of Lords during the eighteenth and early nineteenth centuries led to the passage of the Appellate Jurisdiction Act 1876, ensuring that at least one of the judges in the House of Lords was Scottish-trained.

In the field of Government of Scotland, the office of Secretary for Scotland was created in 1885 to administer matters such as law and order and education in Scotland and this office became a Cabinet post in 1892. From 1979, the Secretary of State for Scotland belonged to a party which did not have a majority of Scottish seats in the UK Parliament, creating a "democratic deficit" in Scotland; thus it could be said that the Government, as represented by the Secretary of State, did not represent the majority of the electors. The Conservative Government under Margaret Thatcher implemented policies which were not supported by the majority of Scottish electors, e.g. the replacement of household rates with the community charge or "poll tax". There was an impression that the needs of Scotland were not being given due consideration by a Government which drew its support from other parts of the United Kingdom.

The "democratic deficit" led in 1988 to the publication of *A Claim of Right for Scotland* by the Campaign for a Scottish Assembly. This declaration stated that Scotland had a right to decide her own constitution and called for a convention to be set up to devise a scheme for a Parliament or Assembly.[3] The next year the Constitutional Convention was set up, drawing support from a wide range of people and groups. In 1995 the Convention published its final report *Scotland's Parliament, Scotland's Right* and this formed the basis of the Labour Government's proposals in 1997. After a referendum in September 1997 affirmed the support of the Scottish electorate for devolution, the UK Parliament passed the Scotland Act in 1998 and a new system of government came into being in Scotland in May 1999.

CATEGORISING LAW

Distinction between public/private law

1–05 What does the phrase "public/private law" mean? In practical terms, very little. It is a simple method of categorising the various "branches" of law and keeping like subjects together. For instance, Scots private law comprises a number of different areas of law, such as succession, family law, delict and so on. In all of these areas, the involvement of the State is minimal and the cases may involve the breakdown of relationships between individuals or legal persons, such as companies and partnerships.

Where the law relates to the Government of the country or to the relationship between the State and an individual citizen, the law will be termed "public law". This regulates the activities of public authorities such as the courts, Scottish Executive and Scottish Parliament, and local government. Examples of public law topics include constitutional law, criminal law and EU law.

Distinction between civil law and criminal law

1–06 One of the main differences between civil law and criminal law is that there is a different court system for each. A criminal case will be heard in courts which have different procedures, rules of evidence and remedies from a case heard in a civil court. The distinction

---

[3] O. Edwards (ed.), *A Claim of Right for Scotland* (Polygon, 1989).

is, therefore, very important since it affects the outcome of the case for the people concerned.

Many people think of criminal courts when asked to describe what they think a court is. Most people will talk about "prosecuting" someone for damaging their property instead of "suing" them. Many of these misconceptions arise because the media expose us to the criminal legal procedure more often than civil courts. Discussion of the technicalities of a clause in a contract would not make good TV or cinema, but the very human stories of a criminal court can make for riveting viewing.

The criminal law has a separate structure of courts, which deal with issues affecting the liberty of individuals, the punishment of persons found guilty and to a limited extent, the compensation of victims of criminal behaviour. The standard of proof required in a criminal case is very high—"beyond reasonable doubt". This means that if there is some doubt and that doubt is reasonably held, the accused must be acquitted. In Scotland, an accused can only be found guilty if the evidence is corroborated, that is, there are at least two independent sources or witnesses that the accused committed the crime.

It is now very rare for a private prosecution by a victim of a crime. In one of only two in the twentieth century, a woman who had been raped and slashed with a razor was granted a Bill for Criminal Letters. The Lord Advocate then took on the case and the culprits were successfully prosecuted and punished.[4]

A civil case will occur where the relationship between two or more parties breaks down or where the conduct of one party has caused loss to another. Examples of civil actions would occur when a builder fails to complete a house extension, or a dry cleaning firm ruins an item of clothing, or a van driver hits another vehicle. In all of these cases, the person aggrieved may take these people to court if they do not otherwise fulfil the contract or pay compensation for the damage they have caused. In these examples, the criminal law is not involved. However, if the van driver drives off without leaving his name and other details, he will be guilty of an offence and thus it can be seen that an action which otherwise would be only a civil matter can escalate to involve the criminal law.

Distinction between common law and statute law

A further distinction is between common law and statute law. **1–07**

Common law was originally the body of law common to the whole country based on ancient customs and worked out, and built up, in the courts by the process of declaration of rules and their application to cases. Much of the common law has now been superseded by statute law, but it is still very important in Scotland in many areas. For instance, it controls the operation of contract, delict and much of the criminal law.

Statute law is the most important form of law. It is enacted by the United Kingdom and the Scottish Parliaments and it will usually overturn any other type of law except EU law, where special rules and problems exist.

SOURCES OF LAW

Rules and principles of law must have a source, and it is this source which will give the rule **1–08** its authority and binding force. In the Scottish legal system, as in England and Wales, there is in effect a hierarchy of sources of law, whereby legislation takes precedence over case law, which takes precedence over authoritative writings, and so on. If a source is incorporated into a higher source, the original source will lose its authority. Thus, many

---

[4] *H v Sweeney*, 1983 S.L.T. 48.

instances of custom are now incorporated into legislation, and custom is rarely relied upon as a source of law. Similarly, if a decision in a case is subsequently confirmed, or negated, by an Act of Parliament, the legislative provision becomes the legal and binding principle. There are now a myriad of different sources of the law in Scotland. Legislation is passed by the UK Parliament, by the Scottish Parliament, and by the European Union,[5] while case law and other common law sources still play an important part.

Key Concepts

Sources of law:

- legislation;
- judicial precedent;
- authoritative writings;
- custom;
- equity.

LEGISLATION

1–09 Legislation is the most important source of law and arguably the legislation created by the United Kingdom is the highest source of law affecting Scotland. Although with the advent of the Scottish Parliament there is less UK legislation having effect on the Scottish legal system, this form of law is still the most authoritative because of the doctrine of supremacy of Parliament (see Chapter 3, para.3–24). As you will see below, laws made by the Scottish Parliament are subject to certain requirements and the Scotland Act 1998 s.28(7) clearly states that the UK Parliament retains the power to make laws for Scotland. Regarding the laws made by the European Union, the doctrine of supremacy of Parliament is also relevant and the UK Parliament retains the right to make laws for the United Kingdom, while allowing the European institutions to make laws within the context of those areas covered by the various European treaties.

Legislation made by the UK Parliament

1–10 Traditionally, every autumn, or after a General Election, the Queen opens Parliament and announces in the Queen's Speech the Government's legislative plans for the coming parliamentary session. Around 20 pieces of legislation will be announced at this time, but many more Bills will be introduced and passed during the course of the year.

Key Concepts

Generally speaking there are three types of **Bills**:

- a **Private Bill**, which applies to a particular area or person or persons;
- a **Hybrid Bill**, which is a combination of the other two; and
- a **Public Bill**, which has general application.

---

[5] The EU dimension to Scots law is discussed in Chapter 4.

Private Bills concern particular bodies, for instance a local authority or private company where they require powers beyond, or in conflict with, the general law. The procedure for passing these Bills is slightly different from that for a Public Bill. The Committee Stage will consist of hearings, during which the proposers and opponents of the Bill will be given the opportunity to put forward their evidence. Private Bills must be publicised to those who will be affected by its provisions.

Hybrid Bills are those which, on the whole, have general application but they appear to contain particular provisions affecting the interests of particular persons or organisations. For instance, the building of the Channel Tunnel rail link required an Act, which involved a private company being given compulsory purchase powers to buy the land to build the northern end of the tunnel.[6]

Public Bills are, of course, the most important of the three types and they take up the greater part of the legislative programme of Parliament. There are two types of Public Bills—Government Bills and Private Members' Bills.

A *Private Member's Bill* is introduced by an MP or peer who is not a government minister. There are three methods of initiating a Private Member's Bill.

(1) *Ballot*: At the start of each session of Parliament a ballot of backbench MPs is held. The first 20 MPs whose names are drawn out are allocated time to present a Bill. The chances of these Bills becoming law is very small; to have a chance the Bill has to be one of the first seven in the ballot, non-controversial and have cross-party support. On average each year around six Bills presented through the ballot will become law.

(2) *Ten minute rule Bill*: This is a popular way of introducing a Bill to Parliament because of the high profile nature of its timing, just before ministerial question time. In many respects, however, the proposer is not seriously trying to create new law but is trying to highlight the need for change in some aspect of the law. The proposer of the Bill speaks for 10 minutes, then anyone opposed to it speaks for 10 minutes, and then there is a vote. Generally, only one 10 minute rule Bill will become law each session.

(3) *Ordinary presentation Bill*: Here a Bill is introduced to Parliament during the course of the day; there is no particular time given over to it. The Bill is presented formally but the MP does not make a speech when presenting it. Normally, only one Bill will pass into law.

Private Members' Bills serve a useful function. They ensure that backbench MPs are more fully involved in the legislative process. They may change the law when the Government is unwilling to do so, but there is support in the House for such a change. In 2009–2010 (a shorter session because of a general Election) seven Private Member's Bills were passed out of 67 introduced; this compares with 112 introduced in the previous session with five being passed.

A *Government Bill* is prepared by legal draftsmen in the Parliamentary Counsel Office, after consultation with the department proposing the Bill. It will have been considered by a Cabinet Committee and then the Cabinet itself will approve it. Often the Bill will have been the subject of extensive consultation and a draft Bill may be published. Draft Bills are referred to a Commons Select Committee and evidence may be taken from interest groups.

A Bill may be introduced in either House but certain Bills will always be introduced first to the House of Commons; these include Money Bills (i.e. those which seek to raise

---

[6] Channel Tunnel Rail Link Act 1996.

taxation or involve expenditure), controversial Bills, and Bills of constitutional significance. A Bill which starts in the House of Lords will progress through the same stages as in the House of Commons.

Stages of a Bill

1–11

First Reading	This is a formal reading. At the start of business the clerk reads out the short title of the Bill and an order is made for the Bill to be printed. No vote is taken.
Second Reading	This is a general debate about the principles of the Bill—no amendments are allowed at this stage. At the end of the debate the motion is put to the vote. After a Bill has been given a second reading, the House considers any clauses which require a Money Resolution (which will authorise expenditure) or Ways and Means Resolution (which authorises the levying of taxes or other charges). The Public Bill Committee cannot consider these clauses of the Bill until the resolutions have been agreed.
Committee Stage	At committee stage, the Bill is considered clause by clause and amendments are made. There are two types of committee: the Public Bill Committee and the Committee of the Whole House: (1) A Public Bill Committee consists of between 16 and 50 MPs chosen to reflect the political composition of the House. The committee will include the minister in charge of the Bill and usually a front-bench spokesperson from the opposition parties. (2) In a Committee of the Whole House, all of the MPs consider the Bill clause by clause on the floor of the House. This is set up for Bills of constitutional importance, such as the Scotland Bill during 1998 and the House of Lords Bill during 1999. It is also used for Bills which need to be passed quickly, such as the annual Finance Bill. Amendments are voted on as they occur. The Government usually opposes amendments but may support some.
Report Stage	If the Bill has been before a Committee of the Whole House this stage is a formality. Otherwise, this stage informs MPs who were not on the Public Bill Committee of any amendments. The new clauses will be debated and the Government may bring forward further amendments if it had agreed to do so in committee. There is no vote.
Third Reading	This Reading follows on immediately from the Report stage. The Bill is debated as it now stands and a vote taken. No amendments may be taken. It is unusual for a Bill to be lost here.

Once these stages have been completed, the Bill is sent to the other House where the whole procedure is gone through again. The process in the House of Lords is the same, except for three main differences. First, the committee stage is usually a Committee of the Whole House. Second, there is no guillotine motion (see below) and debate is, therefore, unrestricted. Finally, it is possible to make an amendment at third reading.

> **Key Concept**
>
> A Government Bill will pass through five stages in each House—first reading, second reading, committee stage, report stage and third reading.

After both Houses have agreed the Bill, it is sent for Royal Assent and comes into effect, either immediately, or on a date specified in the Act, or on a date to be decided by the minister. The Act will state which of these dates is to be followed. It is not unusual for an Act to be brought into effect in stages.

> **Key Concept**
>
> A new statute will come into effect in one of three ways:
>
> - immediately it receives the Royal Assent;
> - on a date specified in the Act itself; or
> - on a date to be decided by the Minister.

One of the problems with the legislative procedure is the amount of time it takes. This allows opponents of a Bill to lengthen the process further by putting down many amendments. In November 2000, the House of Commons adopted a new system to try to timetable Bills more effectively. The programme motion sets out the amount of time allocated to any stage of a Bill. The motion is agreed by the Government, and the opposition parties, before it is submitted to the House. If the Government and Opposition do not agree the programme motion, the Government may feel compelled to put an allocation of time motion, commonly and colourfully called a "guillotine" motion. This formalises the timetable for the Bill and allows proceedings to be brought to a conclusion once the time allocated has been exhausted. It curtails debate but also prevents consideration of those parts of the Bill not yet reached by the Public Bill Committee or the House.

On occasion, the two Houses will not agree a Bill. If the House of Lords amends a Commons Bill and the Commons does not agree with the amendment, the House of Lords has a stark choice: it may either accept the Commons wording, or it may refuse to change its amendment. In the latter case, the Bill will fall. The Government is at liberty to bring back an identical Bill in the next session of Parliament. If the House of Lords still refuses to accept the Bill without amending it, the Speaker of the House of Commons may sign a declaration and the Bill will proceed to Royal Assent without the consent of the House of Lords. This procedure is controlled by the Parliament Act 1911, as amended by the Parliament Act 1949. One year must have elapsed between the Bill's Second Reading in the Commons in the first session and the Bill being passed by the Commons in the second session. In this way, the power of the House of Lords to block legislation is curtailed.

Normally, if a Bill does not receive the Royal Assent by the time Parliament is prorogued at the end of a parliamentary session, it will fall. In 1998, the House agreed that it may be possible for a Government Bill to be carried forward into the next parliamentary session. The first Bill to be carried forward was the Financial Services and Markets Bill 1998–1999 which was taken forward to the 1999–2000 session after a debate on October 25, 1999.

Delegated legislation

1–12 The considerable detail of how legislation is to work cannot be set out comfortably in a statute; it is, therefore, included in subordinate legislation.[7] This kind of legislation will take the form of statutory instruments or Orders in Council.

> **Key Concept**
>
> **Subordinate legislation** derives its authority from a parent or enabling Act and it must only seek to do what the parent Act allows. If an instrument goes beyond the authority given in the parent Act, it will be ultra vires, literally beyond the powers. Subordinate legislation may, therefore, be challenged in the courts; an Act of Parliament may not be challenged for lack or excess of power.

Advantages and uses of subordinate legislation:

(1) Subordinate legislation saves parliamentary time. There has been a marked increase in the amount of primary legislation passed by Parliament each year and there is always difficulty in finding enough time to pass all of the legislation that the Government and backbench MPs want. The general practice is to enact the policy, and leave it to the Government to fill in the details of how the policy will be implemented.
(2) Subordinate legislation allows the Government to seek advice from experts in the area under consideration, e.g. road traffic laws, food hygiene standards.
(3) This type of legislation is useful in times of emergency when there is no time to enact primary legislation. An example occurred in the late 1980s when radioactive fallout from the Chernobyl nuclear power station in the USSR affected animals grazing on upland pastures in southern Scotland and the Lake District.
(4) It is used to bring a statute, or part of statute, into operation. The parent Act will state whether it is to come into effect on a particular day or whether the Secretary of State is to make a commencement order. This is one of the most common uses of statutory instruments. There may be more than one commencement order for a statute, bringing in different sections at different times.
(5) If an amendment needs to be made in the future, it is the regulation which is amended not the Act itself. Thus, it is easier and quicker to react to changing or unforeseen circumstances.

Disadvantages of subordinate legislation:

(1) Lack of consultation. There is relatively little consultation regarding the content or implementation of statutory instruments, except where technical issues are being implemented.
(2) Inadequate controls. Parliament does not exercise strict control over the implementation of statutory instruments. When a statutory instrument is laid in Parliament, it cannot be amended by an MP, although an MP may ask questions of the minister regarding the effect of the instrument. If there is dissent, the Government will withdraw the instrument, redraft it and re-introduce it. The Joint

---

[7] Also called delegated legislation or secondary legislation.

Committee on Statutory Instruments—which is a joint committee of members of both Houses and is sometimes called the Scrutiny Committee—scrutinises statutory instruments, but only after they have come into effect. The Joint Committee is not able to comment on the merits of the instrument, only whether it was correctly drafted. The Committee will report to the House any instance where the authority of the Act has been exceeded, or there has been an "unexpected or unusual" use of the powers. If there is a defect in the instrument, damage may already have been done since it will have been put into effect. Similarly, although it is possible to challenge a regulation in court as being ultra vires, this can only happen after the regulation has been brought into effect and the damage has been done. In any event, the regulation may have been drafted very widely, making it impossible for any action to be ultra vires.

(3) Lack of publicity. There is little publicity that a statutory instrument has been brought into force. The Statutory Instruments Act 1946 sets out rules for numbering, printing and publication of statutory instruments but many rules and regulations will not come within the terms of the 1946 Act.

(4) Use of skeleton statutes. A skeleton statute is one which gives the briefest detail of policy and leaves the minister to flesh out the detail. This may speed up the process of passing the statute but it has little to do with democracy, since the implementation of detail of the policy is left to ministers and officials.

(5) "Henry VIII" clauses. These give power to a minister to amend a statute by means of an order or regulation; normally changing an Act of Parliament requires a new statute to be passed. Note that this power can apply to any statute, not just the parent Act. Such clauses are very powerful weapons; they are supposed to be used sparingly but their use has increased since the 1970s. An example of a Henry VIII clause is found in s.2(2) of the European Communities Act 1972.

Statutory instruments

Statutory instruments are often known as regulations or rules. The power to make **1–13** instruments will be delegated by an Act of Parliament to a minister. Many statutory instruments must be laid before Parliament. However, they are not scrutinised to any extent; they are laid on the table of the House (literally) for a period of time. If the parent Act has declared that the instrument is to be passed using the *negative resolution* procedure, it will come into effect in 40 days unless either House resolves that it should be annulled. Note that the regulation cannot be amended.

The other main method of laying the instrument is the *affirmative resolution* procedure. Here the instrument requires the approval of Parliament during a debate in the House, which will last for up to 90 minutes. Again, no amendment of the instrument is allowed. If the resolution is not passed, the instrument will be taken back for amendment and resubmission by the department concerned.

Orders in Council

The "Council" referred to here is the Privy Council which advises the Queen on matters of **1–14** national importance and constitutional significance. There are two types of Order in Council. The first is an Order which is made with the authority of the royal prerogative. This kind of Order, made by the Privy Council with the authority of the Queen, does not require the approval of Parliament and is usually reserved for matters of some importance, such as the order to dissolve Parliament. The second type is used by the Government, but does not bypass Parliament. The parent Act will authorise the use of an Order in Council to legislate in some area. Orders in Council were used to transfer powers from Ministers of the UK Government to those of the devolved assemblies.[8]

Legislation of the Scottish Parliament

1–15 The Labour Party elected to Government in May 1997 included a commitment to creating a Scottish Parliament in its manifesto. The Scotland Bill was introduced to the UK Parliament in December 1997 and became law in November 1998. Elections to the new Parliament were held on May 6, 1999 and the new Parliament had its first sitting on May 12. The Queen officially opened the Parliament on July 1, 1999, signalling the transfer of powers from Westminster to the new Parliament and the Scottish Executive.

The Scotland Act 1998 created the Scottish Parliament by devolving certain powers from the UK Parliament to the Scottish Parliament and the Scottish Administration.

Key Concept

Devolution may be defined as a delegation of power from a central body to local bodies. The idea is to allow decisions to be made closer to the people who will be affected.

The UK Parliament retains a number of powers, known as "reserved powers". These are mainly concerned with issues with international impact, for instance defence and foreign affairs, and issues which need to be the same throughout the United Kingdom—such as social security and other benefits and employment laws. The UK Parliament retains the right to legislate for Scotland on any matter. Section 28(7) of the Act clearly states: "This section does not affect the power of the Parliament of the UK to make laws for Scotland." This section reiterates the doctrine of supremacy of the UK Parliament, a doctrine which could not in any case be abandoned by them.[9] A convention, formerly called the Sewel Convention, but now known as a motion for legislative consent, has evolved to ensure that the consent of the Scottish Parliament is sought before the UK Parliament legislates on a matter which is otherwise devolved.

The Scotland Act does not state which powers have been devolved to the Scottish Parliament and Scottish Executive. Rather, the devolved bodies have the power to legislate on any topic not specifically excluded in the Scotland Act. This is called the retaining model of devolution, where everything is devolved except a limited number of exceptions.

Key Concepts

Devolved powers include:

- health;
- education;
- local government;

---

[8] See for instance, Scotland Act 1998 (Transfer of Functions to the Scottish Ministers etc.) Order 1999 (SI 1999/1750).

[9] According to Lord Hope of Craighead in House of Lords debates on the Bill—*Hansard*, HL Vol.592, col.796 (1998).

- social work;
- housing;
- planning;
- police and prisons;
- law and home affairs including criminal and civil law, prosecution system and courts;
- agriculture, fishing and forestry;
- environment;
- natural heritage;
- some aspects of transport, now including railways.

The other model of devolution is called the transferring model and this involves stating the specific areas in which devolved powers may be exercised; anything which is not specified will be retained by the central body. Its main drawback is that the list of statutes devolving power from Westminster must constantly be updated. The power to make laws is contained in s.28, which is read in conjunction with s.29. The latter section sets out the Parliament's legislative competence.

Key Concepts

Limits on the **legislative competence** of the Scottish Parliament:

- the Scottish Parliament may not legislate for another country or territory;
- the Scottish Parliament may not legislate on a matter which is reserved to the UK Parliament as detailed in Schedule 5;
- the Scottish Parliament may not legislate in breach of the restrictions in Schedule 4. This schedule states that certain UK statutes may not be amended or repealed by the Scottish Parliament, e.g. the Act of Union 1707; European Communities Act 1972; Human Rights Act 1998; Scotland Act 1998;
- legislation of the Scottish Parliament must not be incompatible with Convention rights or European Union law;
- the Scottish Parliament may not remove the Lord Advocate from his position as head of the systems of criminal prosecution and investigation of deaths in Scotland.

Reserved matters

Matters on which the UK Parliament alone may make law are detailed in Sch.5 to the Act. **1–16** These "reserved" matters cover a variety of different areas.

Key Concepts

Reserved matters include:

- constitutional matters;
- UK foreign policy;
- UK defence and national security;

- the fiscal, economic and monetary system;
- immigration and nationality;
- energy: electricity, coal, gas and nuclear energy;
- common markets;
- trade and industry;
- employment legislation;
- social security;
- gambling and the National Lottery;
- data protection;
- abortion, human fertilization and embryology, genetics and vivisection;
- equal opportunities.

A new Scotland Bill is likely to be passed in 2012, transferring further powers from Westminster to the Scottish Parliament.

Scrutiny of proposed legislation in Scottish Parliament

1–17 Section 28(1) of the Act states: "The Parliament may make laws, to be known as the Acts of the Scottish Parliament." A proposed statute is a Bill and this will become an Act of the Scottish Parliament (ASP) when it is passed by the Parliament and receives the Royal Assent. The validity of an ASP is not affected by any invalidity in the proceedings and ASPs are to be judicially noticed. This means that the Act does not require that evidence of its existence and contents have to be led in court proceedings.[10]

A Bill may be presented by:

- a member of the Scottish Executive;
- a committee of the Parliament; or
- an individual member.

Executive Bill

1–18 Generally, there is considerable consultation on a Bill before it is presented to the Parliament. There are five stages in the legislative process:

Introduction of the Bill	The Government or Executive makes a statement of legislative competence[11] and submits a memorandum detailing the consultation that took place and the effect of the changes to be enacted. A financial memorandum is also included. The Presiding Officer will make his statement regarding the legislative competence.[12] The Bill is then authorised to be printed and published.
Stage 1	The Bill is sent to the relevant committee where the principles are considered. A report is prepared for the Parliament and a debate and vote is held in the Parliament on the principles.

---

[10] There is an equivalent rule for UK statutes in the Interpretation Act 1978 s.3.
[11] Scotland Act 1998 s.31(1).
[12] Scotland Act 1998 s.31(2).

Stage 2	This is a detailed consideration of each clause. The Bill may be sent to one or more committees for consideration, but one committee will act as the "Lead Committee" drawing all of the comments together. If the Bill confers powers to make subordinate legislation, the Subordinate Legislation Committee must consider and report on these aspects of the Bill. There must be a period of at least 11 sitting days between Stage 1 and Stage 2. The committees will consider any amendments made by any MSP.
Stage 3	After a further lapse of at least 9 sitting days, the Bill moves to Stage 3, where the amended Bill is returned to the Parliament for final discussion and vote.
Submission for Royal Assent	This final stage cannot take place immediately. There must be a period of four weeks from the final vote in the Parliament to the presentation for Royal Assent. This four-week moratorium allows any Law Officer of the United Kingdom or any Minister of the United Kingdom to consider the Bill and its implications. If any of them feel that the Parliament has legislated beyond its competence, then they may refer the matter to the Supreme Court of the United Kingdom under s.33 (Law Officers) or s.35 (Ministers). If the Supreme Court finds that the Bill is outwith the legislative competence, the Bill must be returned to the Parliament for amendment. If the amendment is made and there is no further challenge, the Bill is sent by the Presiding Officer to the Queen for Royal Assent. It is possible for this four-week period to be curtailed if the Law Officers and Secretaries of State indicate that they do not intend to refer the Bill.

Committee Bill

This is a new development in UK Parliamentary affairs and its inclusion indicated the view **1–19** of the Government that MSPs should be more involved in the making of legislation than their counterparts in the UK Parliament.

If a committee has conducted inquiries into an area of law and decided that changes in the law should be made, the committee may report this to the Parliament. If the Parliament agrees, the Scottish Executive then has five "sitting days" to decide whether or not to propose legislation. If the Scottish Executive declines to bring forward a Bill, the Parliament may decide to authorise the drafting of a Bill by adopting the committee's report. The Bill is then introduced to the Parliament with a general debate (Stage 1) and, if approved, it proceeds to committee stage (Stage 2) and then final debate in Parliament (Stage 3). There is no need for the general principles to be considered by a committee at Stage 1. The requirements for legislative competence still apply.

The first Committee Bill was introduced by the Justice 1 Committee in 2001 and was passed as the Protection from Abuse (Scotland) Act 2001.

Member's Bill

1–20 There are two methods for an individual MSP to propose legislation. In the first method, an MSP submits a written proposal to a committee, which may proceed by holding an inquiry into whether such legislation is required. If the committee decides to do so, the Bill proceeds as if it were a Committee Bill. The second method requires the MSP to obtain the support of at least 18 other MSPs.[13] The proposer lodges the Bill with the Parliamentary Clerk. If 18 signatures are received within a month, the Bill will proceed as if it were an Executive Bill. The Presiding Officer gives the usual statement on legislative competence. One of the first Member's Bills was introduced in 2000 by Tommy Sheridan MSP to abolish poindings and warrant sales.[14]

Special Bills

1–21   (1) *Budget Bills*: A Budget Bill is an Executive Bill to authorise payments to be made from the Scottish Consolidated Fund. It may only be introduced by a member of the Scottish Executive.

    (2) *Private Bill*: This is a Bill introduced by an individual, or a body corporate, or an unincorporated association for the purpose of obtaining powers which are in conflict with the general law. At Stage 1 the committee may require additional reports and information, may ask the proposer to advertise the Bill and invite objections. The committee must prepare a report on the need for the provisions and detail any objections to the Bill. The first Private Bill was introduced in June 2002.[15]

    (3) *Emergency Bill*: The first measure to be considered by the Parliament was an Emergency Bill, the Mental Health (Public Safety and Appeals) (Scotland) Act 1999. The procedure is an accelerated one but the Scottish Parliament must first agree to allow the Bill to be treated as an emergency measure. There is no Stage 1 committee scrutiny and Stage 2 committee scrutiny is taken by a Committee of the Whole House. There are no time limits, indeed Standing Orders state that the Bill should complete its parliamentary stages on the same day it is introduced to the Parliament.

Subordinate legislation in the Scottish Parliament

1–22 The Scotland Act 1998 gives power to Her Majesty in Council, Ministers of the Crown and Scottish Ministers to make subordinate legislation. Schedule 7 to the Act states the procedure to be used when enacting subordinate legislation under specific sections of the Act. For instance, subordinate legislation made under s.30 (legislative competence of the Parliament) has to be passed using Type A procedure. This requires an Order in Council to be laid before each House of Parliament and the Scottish Parliament and approved by resolution of each House and the Scottish Parliament.

Where the power to create subordinate legislation is given in a UK statute passed before devolution, and this power has been transferred to the Scottish Ministers, the procedure for scrutiny must be the same in the Scottish Parliament. Thus, if the pre-devolution statute required that subordinate legislation should be passed using the affirmative

---

[13] These 18 MSPs must come from at least half of the political parties or groups in the Parliament.

[14] Abolition of Poindings and Warrant Sales Act 2001.

[15] Robin Rigg, Offshore Wind Farm (Navigation and Fishing) Bill. This Bill ran out of time at the end of the first session of the Parliament and was reintroduced in the second session.

resolution procedure, the Scottish Parliament must use the same procedure to enact post-devolution subordinate legislation.

The Scotland Act also allows the transfer of functions from a UK Minister to the Scottish Ministers, where those functions relate to Scotland.[16] This is done by an Order in Council made with the approval of both Houses of Parliament and the Scottish Parliament.

The Scottish Parliament's role is to scrutinise subordinate legislation, not make it. The content and purpose of subordinate legislation must be within the Parliament's legal powers.

Statutory instruments made under the authority of the provisions of the Scotland Act are known as Scottish Statutory Instruments (SSIs). An instrument is laid before Parliament by lodging it with the Clerk of Parliament at least 21 days before it is due to come into force. The instrument is then referred for consideration to the relevant lead committee and to the Subordinate Legislation Committee. The Subordinate Legislation Committee will decide whether Parliament's attention should be drawn to the instrument because of some procedural or technical irregularity. This committee reports to the lead committee and Parliament within 20 days of the instrument being laid. The lead committee will consider the merits of the instrument.

If an instrument is subject to annulment any member may propose its annulment within 40 days of the instrument being laid.[17] A debate is held, by the lead committee on the annulment motion, lasting up to 90 minutes. The lead committee will report to Parliament and make its recommendation within 40 days of the instrument being laid. A debate may be held by Parliament on the annulment if the committee so recommends.

Byelaws

In addition to statutory instruments made by the Scottish Parliament, another form of subordinate legislation is found in Scotland. This is made by local authorities and certain other public bodies, such as railway authorities, the Ministry of Defence and Scottish Water. The Local Government (Scotland) Act 1973, as amended, governs byelaws for local authorities in Scotland. Byelaws made before the reorganisation of local government in 1996 were to cease to have effect on December 31, 1999[18] although the minister could grant exemption or postpone that date. Generally, byelaws are required to be reviewed every 10 years to ensure they are still needed and up-to-date. **1–23**

Byelaws must satisfy a number of conditions. They must be within the terms of the authorising statute, reasonable and certain. In addition, they must not exercise power for an improper purpose, or make lawful something declared unlawful by general law, or take away any rights specifically given, or be manifestly unjust.

JUDICIAL PRECEDENT

After legislation, judicial precedent, or case law, is the most authoritative source of law. It is judge-made law, created in the course of deciding cases and as such it has to be extracted from the written judgment. This can make its exact meaning more problematic; some judges will be very precise and clear in their written judgments, others will be less explicit. Judicial precedent is sometimes also called stare decisis, literally, to stand by decisions. The **1–24**

---

[16] 1998 Act s.63.
[17] Interpretation and Legislative Reform (Scotland) Act 2010.
[18] Local Government etc. (Scotland) Act 1994 s.59(6).

principle of stare decisis means that a court is bound to follow the law set down in a previous case by a higher court.

Generally, in Scotland it was considered that a single precedent could not bind a court, that there needed to be a series of decisions. The influence of the House of Lords and the increased availability of law reports affected that position, and the principle of judicial precedent, certainly in civil cases, is now more often followed. The doctrine of judicial precedent is not followed slavishly; the previous decision must fulfil two requirements if it is to be binding upon the current case.

Key Concepts

The **precedent** must:

- be "in point"; and
- have been made by a higher court.

In addition to these two requirements, there is also a practical issue: it must be possible to extract the ratio decidendi of the precedent.

The precedent must be in point

1–25 This means that the question of law in the previous case must be the same as the one to be decided now. If the case is in point, then the relationship of the courts is considered to find out whether the precedent is to be considered as binding or not. Although the facts of the two cases will be broadly similar, it is the question of law which is pertinent.

If the precedent is not exactly in point, then the precedent will have persuasive, not binding, force. Persuasive means that the judge may accept the reasoning or not; very often the standing of the judge in the preceding case will affect whether the ratio is followed.

If the precedent is not in point, the judge will distinguish the two cases, by pointing out where the two cases differ.

The position of the court

1–26 There is a hierarchy of courts in Scotland and the question of whether a precedent is binding or not will depend upon the position of the court which made the previous decision, in relation to the one now deciding the question of law. The basic rule is that a court is only bound by another court of higher standing. The decision of a court of equal or lower standing is only persuasive. The Scottish courts will consider the precedents of courts elsewhere in the United Kingdom, but with the exception of decisions of the Supreme Court of the United Kingdom as discussed below, will not be bound by these precedents.

Civil courts

1–27
- *European Court of Justice*: The ECJ does not itself operate a system of judicial precedent, but in all questions of the interpretation of EU law, all UK courts must follow the decisions of the ECJ.
- *Supreme Court of the United Kingdom*: Decisions of the Supreme Court are binding on all Scottish civil courts. A decision of the Supreme Court made in an English

appeal is likely to be binding on the Scottish courts where the issue involves a statute with UK application. However, the Inner House declined to follow such a decision in *McDonald v Secretary of State for Scotland*[19] where the meaning of s.21 of the Crown Proceedings Act 1947 was in issue. The Lord Justice Clerk, Lord Ross, declared that a decision of the English court had "great weight" but was not binding in Scotland.

- *Inner House of the Court of Session*: One Division will normally regard itself as bound by the decision of the other, or its own previous decision. If there is a conflict of precedent, then a Full Bench will be convened to decide the matter and this court may overrule any precedent of either Division, or itself.
- *Outer House of the Court of Session*: A Lord Ordinary is bound to apply the precedents of the Inner House but is not bound by the previous decisions of another Lord Ordinary.[20]
- *Sheriff court*: A sheriff is bound by the same precedents as a Lord Ordinary.

Criminal courts

The doctrine of judicial precedent is less rigid in the criminal courts but, nevertheless, is **1–28** still an important method of guiding judges in the lower courts.

In 2003, the High Court of Justiciary heard two appeals, both relating to the offence of "shameless indecency". The appellants alleged that this offence no longer had a basis in Scots law and that it contravened the principle of certainty of law required by art.7 of Sch.1 to the Human Rights Act 1998. The court overturned a precedent, creating a new one in the first case, which was then applied to the second case.

> *Webster v Dominick*, 2003 S.L.T. 975
> The Crown alleged that the appellant's conduct was "shamelessly" indecent and directed towards girls under the age of puberty. The court decided that the charge of "shameless indecency" no longer had a satisfactory basis in Scots law and such behaviour should be treated as a crime of public indecency. This would be judged on the merits of each case and according to the social standards of the average citizen in contemporary society.

> *Bott v MacLean*, 2003 S.C.C.R. 547
> Here a schoolteacher was accused of the common law crime of shameless indecency by engaging in an inappropriate relationship with a pupil. Since it had just been decided in *Webster v Dominick* that there was no longer a crime of shameless indecency, the appeal was upheld, following the precedent *Webster* set.

Although the point of law may be the same, there may be differing facts, which affect that point of law.

- *High Court of Justiciary as a Court of Appeal*: Basically, it will not be bound by its own decisions. If there is any doubt regarding the precedent, a Full Bench would be convened.
- *High Court of Justiciary (trial court)*: The High Court sitting as a trial court will be bound by the precedents of the appeal court, but not the decision of another Lord of Justiciary.

---

[19] 1994 S.L.T. 692.
[20] *McFarlane v Tayside Health Board*, 1997 S.L.T. 211.

- *Sheriff court*: Until 1987, it was thought that sheriffs were not bound by the decisions of the High Court sitting as a trial court. However, the appeal court held in *Jessop v Stevenson*[21] that the sheriff was bound by the decision of the High Court sitting as a trial court. Sheriffs are, therefore, bound by the High Court decisions, whether these are from the trial court or the appeal court.
- *Justice of the Peace Court (formerly the District court)*: As you would expect, a JP court is bound by the decisions of the High Court of Justiciary sitting as an appeal court or a trial court.

Key Concept

The **ratio decidendi** (reason for a decision) is the point of law on which the previous decision was based.

It can be difficult to find the ratio decidendi of a case and, indeed, sometimes there will be no useful ratio at all. In an appeal court, several judges may have given their opinions but may have arrived at the same conclusion by a different line of reasoning. Thus, finding the ratio of that judicial precedent may be difficult.

Key Concept

Obiter dicta—these are remarks of the judge, which are not essential for the disposal of the case. They tend to be hypotheses indicating what his preferred decision would have been if the facts had been slightly different.

Such remarks are only persuasive; they are never binding. Nevertheless, they can be useful illustrations of how different scenarios would have led to a different decision. Their usefulness will depend on the authority and standing of the judge, for instance an obiter remark by the Lord President will be carefully considered by judges in later cases.

As with all such doctrines, judicial precedent has its advantages and disadvantages. Among the advantages are:

(1) *Certainty*: Lawyers can consult the law reports and determine what the law is on a particular issue and thus be better able to advise their clients on the likely outcome of litigation.
(2) *Consistency*: It is important that there is equality of treatment in the courts, and the use of precedents can assist in ensuring consistency.
(3) *Orderly development*: Judges will extend, or limit, a principle of law established in an earlier case, thus developing that principle in an orderly way. Again, it assists lawyers to advise their clients on the likelihood of a successful outcome.

The disadvantages of the application of the doctrine include:

---

[21] 1987 S.C.C.R. 655; 1988 S.L.T. 223.

(1) *Rigidity*: The lack of flexibility may lead to the law failing to keep up with changes of attitude in society.

(2) *Artificial distinctions*: The precedent applicable to a current case may not be appropriate in the circumstances and the judge may, therefore, feel that it would be unjust to apply it. The judge may then seek to distinguish elements of the two cases in such a way as to draw fine or artificial distinctions between them.

(3) *Difficult to find*: As noted above, it may be difficult to decide what the precedent is, but it may also be difficult to find a precedent among the many thousands of reported cases. The introduction of legal databases will make this task easier and faster.

AUTHORITATIVE WRITERS

Authoritative writers are the writers who first brought the principles of Scots law together **1–29** into one document. They mostly lived in the seventeenth and eighteenth centuries, but their work and their influence upon the law of Scotland cannot be underestimated. Although the scope of their authority has dwindled they are still referred to on occasions when there is no statute or precedent covering the issue of law in question. They are sometimes also referred to as institutional writers because of the way they compiled their works, following the order of the textbooks of Roman law, such as *Justinian's Institutes*. A statement in an institutional writing may be given the same authority as one of the Inner House.

There are seven writers whose influence is considered to have been extensive.

(1) **Sir Thomas Craig of Riccarton** (1538–1608): His work *Ius Feudale* (Feudal Law) is the earliest of the institutional writings, although it was not published until 1655 after his death.

(2) **Sir George Mackenzie of Rosehaugh** (1636–91): Mackenzie was a criminal prosecutor of some notoriety and is credited as the founder of the Advocates' Library, now the National Library of Scotland. He published the *Laws and Customs of Scotland in Matters Criminal* in 1678.

(3) **James Dalrymple, Viscount Stair** (1619–95): Viscount Stair is the most prominent of all the institutional writers. He lived in troubled political times and his law career reflects this. He was Lord President of the Court of Session from 1671 to 1681 before falling out of favour and fleeing to Holland. He returned to Scotland when William of Orange and Mary took the throne in 1688 and he was reappointed Lord President in 1689. His institutional work was first published in 1681 and the *Institutions of the Law of Scotland* began the systematic development of Scots law. Stair based his work on the broad principles found in the customary law, feudal law, Roman law and the law of the Bible.

(4) **Lord Bankton** (1685–1760): Bankton's work *An Institute of the Laws of Scotland* published between 1751 and 1753 compares the Scots law with the English law of the time.

(5) **Professor John Erskine** (1695–1768): Erskine's work *An Institute of the Law of Scotland* is regarded as second to Stair's work in terms of influence upon the Scots legal system. Published after his death, Erskine's *Institute* is the most authoritative statement of Scots law in the eighteenth century, setting out the rules of Scots common law before the impact of legislation and judicial precedent.

(6) **Baron David Hume** (1757–1838): Hume's work deals with the criminal law. The *Commentaries on the Law of Scotland respecting the Description and Punishment of Crimes* was published in 1797.

(7) **Professor George Bell** (1770–1843): Bell published two works of institutional status. The *Commentaries on the law of Scotland and on the Principles of Mercantile Jurisprudence* was published in 1810 and set out the principles of the mercantile law and bankruptcy. The second work *Principles of the Law of Scotland* published in 1829 was originally a student textbook, which was reworked and enlarged.

Custom

1–30   It is less common now for custom to act as a source of new law. Many of the customs which were part of the common law were incorporated into the authoritative writings. For instance, Stair recognised that the udal law of Orkney and Shetland, which regulated the system of land tenure, was enforceable in the Scottish courts.

Equity

1–31   The term "equity" is used in two senses in Scots law.

Equity meaning "fairness" or "reasonableness" or "natural justice"

1–32   The broad meaning of equity in Scotland has allowed Scottish judges to deal with cases in a fair and just manner. It is seen in the remedies available to parties in the courts and in the way the court will give a remedy it deems appropriate, although the party has not asked for it. If a person is in breach of contract, the court may give the remedy of damages to the aggrieved party and require the party in breach to perform the contract. If a contract states that excessive penalties are imposed if the contract is breached, the court may intervene if it appears that these penalties are unjustified.

It can be argued that equity, as a source of new law, is not exhausted. The common law may require a judge to exercise his discretion in interpreting the law. Similarly, a statutory provision may allow a judge to exercise discretion within certain limitation.

Equity referring to the *nobile officium*

1–33   The equitable power of the Court of Session and the High Court of Justiciary, known as the *nobile officium* is a power whereby the court, as a last resort, may declare certain actions to be unlawful or give a remedy where none is otherwise available.

The *nobile officium* of the Court of Session is important for the law of trusts. It may be that a trust condition is so restrictive that the trust is unable to operate. The court may remove the condition.[22] The essence of the *nobile officium* is that the law is allowed to operate in circumstances where a technicality would otherwise prevent it.

> ### Roberts, Petitioner
> ### (1901) 3 F. 779
>
> The petitioner was a bankrupt who had completed all of the requirements needed to discharge his bankruptcy, except for making a certain statutory declaration. He was prevented from doing so because he had become insane. The court dispensed with the declaration to allow him to be discharged.

---

[22] *Gibson's Trustees, Petitioners*, 1933 S.C. 19.

The equitable power may be used to give effect to rights Parliament has obviously intended to give, but the statutory provision is defective.

Wan Ping Nam v German Federal Republic Minister of Justice
1972 J.C. 43

Statutory provisions provided relief for individuals who had been imprisoned pending an extradition hearing. The provision stated that an application could be made to a sheriff court for a writ of habeas corpus, a remedy unknown to Scots law. The court used its declaratory power to give effect to the intention of Parliament.

The High Court of Justiciary has a declaratory power whereby it can declare acts to be criminal. This power is used sparingly.

Khaliq v HM Advocate
1984 J.C. 23

A shop-keeper was found guilty of selling "glue-sniffing" kits to children; the offence was not recognised in Scots law but the High Court decided that it was the type of behaviour considered by the common law to be harmful.

The court also exercised the *nobile officium* to allow an appeal to be heard where this had previously been abandoned. The petitioner's legal adviser had given him inaccurate advice.[23] It is, however, unusual for the High Court to allow a petition to the *nobile officium* to correct errors made by the legal profession.

▼ CHAPTER SUMMARY

DEVELOPMENT OF SCOTS LAW

1. Over the centuries, Scots law has been influenced by many other legal systems but the most significant influence has been that of the English common law.
2. The principal civil court, the Court of Session, was set up in 1532 and legal writings called "Practicks" were produced from its proceedings. These were the first case reports and helped to set up a more unified system of law.
3. In 1617, the General Register of Sasines was set up to record transactions relating to land helping to ensure that buyers of land in Scotland receive secure title to that land.
4. The High Court of Justiciary was established in 1672.
5. The Union of the Parliaments of Scotland and England on May 1, 1707 dissolved the two Parliaments and created a new Parliament of Great Britain. Article XIX of the Union Treaty specified that Scots law and the Scottish courts should continue.
6. The practice of sending civil appeals to the House of Lords began within a short time of the Union coming into effect:

1–34

---

[23] *McIntosh, Petitioner*, 1995 S.L.T. 796.

➤ *Greenshields v Magistrates of Edinburgh* (1710–1711) Rob. 12.

7. From 1800, English law now became the major influence on Scots law. Two factors contributed to this: the House of Lords now heard all Scottish civil appeals; and the Westminster Parliament passed all laws.
8. The position of Secretary for Scotland was created in 1885 to administer matters such as law and order and education in Scotland and this office became a Cabinet post in 1892.
9. The UK Parliament passed the Scotland Act in 1998, which devolved powers to a new Scottish Parliament and Scottish Executive.

SOURCES OF LAW

1. There is a hierarchy of sources of law: legislation; case law; authoritative writings, custom and equity.

LEGISLATION

1. Legislation is passed by the UK Parliament, Scottish Parliament and the European Union.

UK PARLIAMENT

1. There are three types of Bill passed by the UK Parliament—Public Bills, Private Bills and Hybrid Bills. Public Bills are further divided into two types—Government Bills and Private Member's Bills.
2. A Government Bill has to pass through five stages in each House—first reading, second reading, committee stage, report stage and third reading. After both Houses have agreed the Bill, it is sent for Royal Assent.
3. A new statute will come into effect in one of three ways: immediately it receives the Royal Assent, or on a date specified in the Act itself, or on a date to be decided by the Minister.
4. The powers of the House of Lords to veto Bills from the House of Commons were curtailed by the Parliament Acts 1911 and 1949.
5. Subordinate legislation is often used to bring statutes into effect.
6. Examples of subordinate legislation are statutory instruments and Orders in Council.

LEGISLATION FROM THE SCOTTISH PARLIAMENT

1. The Scotland Act 1998 devolved powers to the Scottish Parliament to make laws for Scotland in certain areas. However, the UK Parliament retained ultimate power to make legislation for Scotland:

   ➤ Scotland Act 1998 s.28(7).

2. Bills passed by the Scottish Parliament must be within the Parliament's legislative competence.

3. **The UK Parliament retains powers over reserved matters:**

   ➤ Scotland Act 1998 Sch.5.

4. **Types of Bills in the Scottish Parliament: Executive Bills, Committee Bills and Member's Bills.**
5. **Stages of an Executive Bill: introduction of the Bill, Stage 1, Stage 2, Stage 3, submission for Royal Assent.**

JUDICIAL PRECEDENT

1. **After legislation, judicial precedent made by judges is the most important source of law.**
2. **To be applicable in a case, the judicial precedent must be in point and stated by a court higher or on the same level as the court in which this case is being heard. It must be possible to extract the ratio decidendi of the precedent.**
3. **The ratio decidendi (reason for a decision) is the point of law on which the previous decision was based.**
4. **Obiter dicta are remarks of the judge, which are not essential for the disposal of the case. They tend to be hypotheses indicating what his preferred decision would have been if the facts had been slightly different.**
5. **The doctrine of judicial precedent is less rigid in the criminal courts.**

OTHER MINOR SOURCES OF LAW

1. **Authoritative writers remain an important but limited source of law.**
2. **Authoritative writers mostly lived in the seventeenth and eighteenth centuries and were the first to bring the principles of Scots law together into one document.**
3. **Custom is a less important source of law.**
4. **Equity has two senses in Scots law: "fairness" or "reasonableness" or "natural justice" and referring to the *nobile officium*.**
5. **The *nobile officium* is a power of the Court of Session and the High Court of Justiciary and allows the court, as a last resort, to declare certain actions to be unlawful or give a remedy where none is otherwise available:**

   ➤ *Roberts, Petitioner* (1901) 3 F. 779;
   ➤ *Wan Ping Nam v German Federal Republic Minister of Justice,* 1972 J.C. 43.

6. **Declaratory power of the High Court.**

   ➤ *Khaliq v HM Advocate,* 1984 J.C. 23.

? QUICK QUIZ

SOURCES OF SCOTS LAW

Legislation

- What are the differences between a Private Bill and a Private Member's Bill in the UK Parliament?
- Describe the stages of a UK Bill.
- What are the advantages of using subordinate legislation?
- Define what is meant by the retaining model of devolution.
- What kinds of powers have been reserved to the UK Parliament?
- Why is there a period of four weeks between the Scottish Parliament passing a Bill and it receiving the Royal Assent?

Judicial precedent, authoritative writers and equity

- When will a precedent be binding on a current case?
- Define ratio decidendi and obiter dicta. What is the main difference between the two?
- How important are institutional works to the law today?
- In what circumstances may the *nobile officium* be invoked?

📖 FURTHER READING

The historical development of Scots law is given detailed treatment by Professor David Walker in his text *The Scottish Legal System*, 8th edn (W. Green, 2001).

An account of the legislative powers of the UK Parliament and the Scottish Parliament is contained in Profs Bradley and Ewing, *Constitutional and Administrative Law*, 15th edn (Longman, 2010) and in C.M.G. Himsworth and C.M. O'Neill, *Scotland's Constitution: Law and Practice*, 2nd edn (Bloombury Professional, 2009).

Judicial precedent, and the other sources of Scots law, are discussed by R. White and I. Willock, *Scottish Legal System,* 4th edn (Tottel Publishing, 2007).

🖰 RELEVANT WEB LINKS:

Scottish Executive: *http://www.scotland.gov.uk*
Scottish Parliament: *http://www.scottish.parliament.uk*
UK Parliament: *http://www.parliament.uk*
Scottish courts: *http://www.scotcourts.gov.uk*

Chapter 2 Structure of the Legal System

CHRISTINA ASHTON[1]

▶ CHAPTER OVERVIEW

This chapter will consider how the legal system operates as a broad concept, examining the **2–01** courts and the people who work in the legal profession. The Scottish courts are divided into two distinct and separate systems, each with its own jurisdiction, and indeed as will be seen, its own terminology. The operation of tribunals and ombudsmen in Scotland will also be discussed.

✓ OUTCOMES

At the end of the chapter you should be able to:

- ✓ distinguish between civil and criminal courts;
- ✓ understand the hierarchy of the civil and criminal legal systems;
- ✓ appreciate the sentencing powers of the criminal courts;
- ✓ appreciate what is meant by a "devolution issue";
- ✓ understand why tribunals are important to the legal system;
- ✓ describe how various Ombudsmen work;
- ✓ understand the respective roles of advocates, solicitors and solicitor-advocates;
- ✓ describe the role of the Law Officers for Scotland; and
- ✓ appreciate the role of the Public Defence Solicitors' Office.

CIVIL LEGAL SYSTEM

The civil courts in Scotland deal with disputes between individuals, companies or public **2–02** bodies. The disputes can be in diverse areas of law such as divorce, consumer complaints, personal injury claims, disputes regarding succession or trusts, breach of contract and defamation. The Scottish civil courts are the sheriff court, the Court of Session and the Supreme Court of the United Kingdom. The Court of Session is divided into two distinct parts—the Inner House and the Outer House.

Civil cases are adversarial, meaning that the judge will hear legal argument and evidence from all of the parties and then make a judgment based on the "balance of probabilities". This standard of proof is not as high as is required in criminal cases. Where a case involves the interpretation or validity of EU law, the court in Scotland will suspend the case until a ruling on the matter has been sought from the European Court of Justice. Once that ruling

---

[1] Formerly Head of Centre for Law, Edinburgh Napier University.

has been made, the domestic court will apply it to the facts of the case and make a decision.[2]

Sheriff court

2–03 This is the busiest court in Scotland because it deals with both civil and criminal matters. Since there are 49 sheriff courts around Scotland, it is essentially a local court. Since 1975, Scotland has been divided up into six sheriffdoms.

Key Concepts

The Sheriffdoms:

- Grampian, Highland and Islands;
- Tayside, Central and Fife;
- Lothian and Borders;
- Glasgow and Strathkelvin;
- North Strathclyde; and
- South Strathclyde, Dumfries and Galloway.

Each sheriffdom is headed by a sheriff principal, who is a full-time judge and administers the work of the sheriffdom. He is assisted by a number of sheriffs, around 15 in each sheriffdom, except Glasgow and Strathkelvin where the number is greater to cope with the larger workload. Both sheriffs and the sheriff principal are required to be solicitors, or advocates, of at least 10 years standing and they retire at the age of 70.[3] They are appointed by the monarch on the recommendation of the First Minister, after consultation with the Lord President. The sheriff principal may act as an appeal judge in certain types of action.

Each sheriffdom (except Glasgow and Strathkelvin) is divided into districts. One or more sheriffs will be appointed to sit in the sheriff court in one of these districts, but each sheriff has jurisdiction over all matters occurring anywhere within the sheriffdom. The sheriff court is a "court of first instance", i.e. cases will start and be determined there.

The boundaries of the sheriffdoms can be altered by the Scottish Ministers at any time under the terms of the Sheriff Courts (Scotland) Act 1971.

In late 1999, a crisis hit the legal system as a result of the Human Rights Act 1998 and the Scotland Act 1998.

Starrs v Ruxton
2000 J.C. 208

In this case, an accused man was able to plead that he did not have a fair trial as required by the Convention because the temporary sheriff who heard his case was not considered to be impartial. He was able to argue this because temporary sheriffs were appointed by the Secretary of State for Scotland on the advice of the

---

[2] For more details on the EU dimension to Scots law see Chapter 4.
[3] Judicial Pensions and Retirement Act 1993.

Lord Advocate,[4] held office for short periods of time and could be dismissed at short notice. They did not have security of tenure of office because they depended on the Lord Advocate's "good will" to have their contracts renewed. This was held to be contrary to art.6(1) of the European Convention on Human Rights (ECHR).

As a result of this case, all 126 temporary sheriffs had to be dismissed and a new system put into place. They have now been replaced by part-time sheriffs who hold office for a fixed term and cannot be dismissed without good cause.[5]

Jurisdiction of the sheriff court

The civil jurisdiction of the sheriff court is considerable. There are two aspects to the **2–04** jurisdiction:

(1) jurisdiction over persons; and
(2) jurisdiction because of the subject-matter.

Jurisdiction over persons

The general principle is that a case will be heard by the court which has jurisdiction over **2–05** the defender. The legal maxim is *actor sequitur forum rei*—the pursuer follows the court of the defender. The defender must normally either live in the sheriffdom, or have a place of business there.

The Civil Jurisdiction and Judgments Act 1982 controls jurisdiction in a number of areas. This Act was passed primarily to give effect to the Brussels Convention of 1968, but it has wider scope than the Convention. Its provisions give effect to judgments made by a court in one part of the United Kingdom, as well as courts outside the EU area. A new set of rules for jurisdiction in Scotland was also introduced.

Key Concepts

The main rules under the **1982 Act** are:

- a person may be sued in the court where they are domiciled, i.e. where they have a usual residence;
- if the person has no fixed address, the court with jurisdiction will be where they are personally cited, i.e. handed the summons to appear in court;
- if the matter concerns a contract, the jurisdiction will lie with the court where the contract is to be performed;
- if the matter concerns a delict, the jurisdiction will lie with the court where the wrongful act occurred;

if the matter involves a consumer contract, the consumer may sue the other party in the court where they are domiciled. This is a special rule to protect consumers and ensure that their legal expenses are kept to the minimum.

---

[4] Sheriff Courts (Scotland) Act 1971 s.11.
[5] Bail, Judicial Appointments etc. (Scotland) Act 2000.

If the rules of the 1982 Act do not apply to the matter, the jurisdiction rules are as in the Sheriff Courts (Scotland) Act 1907, as amended.

Key Concepts

Jurisdiction rules under the Sheriff Courts (Scotland) Act 1907:

- the defender resides in the sheriffdom, or has recently done so (within the last 40 days) but has now moved and has no known address in Scotland;
- the defender has a business in the sheriffdom and is personally cited or cited at his place of business;
- the defender is the owner, or tenant, of heritable property situated in the sheriffdom and the case involves that property;

the action is concerned with a contract performed in the sheriffdom and the defender is personally cited there.

Subject-matter of the jurisdiction

2–06 Generally, a sheriff court has unlimited jurisdiction. However, some cases must be sent to a particular court for disposal. For instance, judicial review cases can only be heard in the Court of Session. Actions involving the status of a person, e.g. a declarator of marriage, may also only be heard in the Court of Session.

   The sheriff court has privative jurisdiction, i.e. exclusive jurisdiction over certain matters and an action involving these must be raised in the sheriff court. Examples include actions involving sums of money less than £3,000.

Cases before the sheriff court

2–07 Sheriff courts deal with three types of cases:

Ordinary cause

2–08 These are cases involving sums of money over £5,000, or where another remedy is sought, e.g. recovery of heritable property, divorce, or aliment of children. A record of proceedings is kept so that an appeal can be made. The action is commenced by means of an "initial writ". It is possible for the sheriff to remit an ordinary cause to the Court of Session, if the case is of sufficient importance or difficulty and any of the parties has requested this.

Summary cause

2–09 These mainly involve actions for sums of money between £3,000 and £5,000. Since June 2002,[6] an action of damages for personal injury must be brought as a summary cause. Actions of damages for defamation and actions of aliment are not competent as small claims actions and must be brought as a summary cause. No record is made of the proceedings, other than the notes taken by the sheriff. This will make an appeal more difficult.

---

[6] Act of Sederunt (Summary Cause Rules) 2002 (SSI 2002/132) as amended.

Small claims

This procedure was introduced as a new form of summary cause by the Law Reform **2–10** (Miscellaneous Provisions) (Scotland) Act 1985. It is relatively informal and cost-effective and was devised to help individual citizens to resolve minor disputes where the amount claimed is less than £3,000.

Appeals from the sheriff court

Ordinary cause

An appeal from the sheriff may be made to the sheriff principal, and thence to the Inner **2–11** House of the Court of Session. A further appeal to the House of Lords will be on a point of law only.

Alternatively, an appeal can be made directly to the Inner House from the decision of the sheriff. This is more likely to happen when both parties are determined that they will appeal whatever the decision of the sheriff principal, or where the issue is one of importance and therefore requires a decision from a senior court.

A party will appeal to the sheriff principal where he is trying to keep costs down: an appeal to the Inner House will require representation by an advocate or solicitor-advocate, as well as the local solicitor. There is, therefore, considerable cost.

Summary cause

An appeal from the sheriff to the sheriff principal is allowed on a point of law only. A **2–12** further appeal will lie on a point of law to the Inner House, and thence to the House of Lords.

Small claims

An appeal from the sheriff will be to the sheriff principal on a point of law only. **2–13**

Court of Session

Established in 1532, the Court of Session sits in Parliament House, Edinburgh. Unless the **2–14** matter is privative to the Court of Session, a pursuer may start his case in the sheriff court or the Court of Session. The pursuer will decide which court after asking himself certain questions, such as:

- Is the claim for a large sum of money, say £100,000?
- Is there an important or difficult point of law involved? Do I therefore need an authoritative judgment?
- Do I have enough money to pay the legal fees?

The Court of Session is divided into two Houses—the Inner House and the Outer House. The terms come from when the court was being set up: a group of eminent judges would meet together in an inner room of Parliament House. Individual judges who were less experienced would meet with parties in other rooms of Parliament House—outer rooms. If a party did not like the judgment of the individual judge, he would go to the inner room and ask the group to look again at the matter. Thus, the appellate court known as the Inner House was created.

The main statute, which covers the procedures and composition of the court, is the Court of Session Act 1988. Currently there are 34 judges, of whom only five are women.[7] The retirement age for Senators of the College of Justice, as they are officially known, is 70 years.[8] Two of the judges are permanently seconded to other bodies: one to the Scottish Law Commission as its Chairman and the other to the Scottish Land Court. The most senior judge in the Court of Session is the Lord President, who, along with the second most senior judge, the Lord Justice-Clerk, is appointed by the monarch on the recommendation of the First Minister, who receives recommendations from the Judicial Appointments Board for Scotland. The judges in the Court of Session are appointed by the monarch, on the recommendation of the First Minister, after consultation with the Lord President. The judges will be sheriffs or sheriffs principal of five years' standing, or advocates or solicitors with five years' right of audience in the Court of Session. All of the judges in the Court of Session are also judges in the High Court of Justiciary. The Lord President takes the title of Lord Justice General when sitting in the High Court.

Outer House

2–15 This is a court of first instance, staffed by 21 judges. Cases are heard by a single judge, known as a Lord Ordinary.

Jurisdiction extends to all civil matters, except those which are privative to another court, or when the matter is specifically excluded by statute. Jurisdiction also extends to the whole of Scotland. Under the Civil Jurisdiction and Judgments Act 1982, jurisdiction will be over persons who are domiciled in Scotland.

Certain issues are privative to the Outer House, for instance, a petition seeking judicial review of an administrative decision must be commenced in the Outer House.

It is still possible to seek a jury trial in the Outer House although it is uncommon and is confined to a narrow range of uncomplicated cases, e.g. defamation or action for damages for personal injury. The jury consists of 12 persons.

The normal method of raising an action is to issue a "summons" to the defender; this is essentially a statement of claim and summons the defender to appear in court to answer the claim. If the defender wishes to defend the claim, he will lodge written defences, answering the issues raised in the summons. These will form the basis of the "open record" and the two parties will then agree certain facts and each will answer the allegations made by the other. This process of agreement and answers will result in a "closed record" which is the final document presented to the court. The closed record will have the pursuer's statement of the remedies he seeks (the conclusions), the agreed facts and those facts the pursuer avers (the condescendence), the facts as the defender sees them, the pursuer's pleas-in-law followed by the defender's pleas-in-law. If the case turns only on a question of fact, there will be a proof (trial) before the Lord Ordinary.

The decision of the court on a question of fact is called a "decree"—this may either grant the pursuer's request for remedy, or it may "assoilzie" the defender, i.e. state that he is not liable.

If the case requires a decision on a question of law, then the question of law must first be settled by the Lord Ordinary. The pleas-in-law are considered by the court and an interlocutor will be issued. This will "sustain" the pleas-in-law of one party and "repel" those of the other. If necessary, the interlocutor on the question of law will be applied to the questions of fact. On occasion, the Lord Ordinary will not be able to decide the

---

[7] Maximum Number of Judges (Scotland) Order 2004 (SSI 2004/499).
[8] Judicial Pensions and Retirement Act 1993.

question of law without knowing the facts of the case. The evidence will be heard first before the question of law is decided. This is called "proof before answer".

The other main method of seeking the judgment of the court is to petition the court, e.g. to appoint new trustees or wind up a company. If the petition is opposed, the statement of opposition is called the "answers" and the party opposing is called the respondent.

Inner House

This is basically the appeal court, but it can be a court of first instance in limited cir- **2–16** cumstances, e.g. appeals against the decision of some tribunals and a petition to the *nobile officium*.

The Inner House comprises 11 judges and is divided into two Divisions, simply called the First Division (with six judges) and the Second Division (with five judges). The First Division is headed by the Lord President, the most senior judge in Scotland. The Second Division is headed by the Lord Justice-Clerk, the second most senior judge. If there is a heavy workload, an Extra Division of three judges from the Outer House may be convened; an Extra Division sits very frequently.

For most appeals, only three judges, called Lords of Session, will sit, but if the matter is particularly important or difficult, a bench of five or seven judges may be convened. An appeal will take the form of a "reclaiming motion" or a statutory "appeal". It is unusual for additional evidence to be heard in an appeal; the normal procedure is for the court to consider the legal arguments of the parties. The court may give a decision immediately, with one judge stating the decision and the reasons in an "opinion". If the issue is more difficult, the judges will make "avizandum" meaning that they will retire to consider their decision and give written opinions at a later date. A judge who does not agree with the majority of the bench will give a "dissenting" opinion. The decision of the Inner House will either take the form of "adhering" to the interlocutor of the Lord Ordinary (i.e. dismissing the appeal) or "recalling" the interlocutor of the Lord Ordinary and giving a different one.

Supreme Court of the United Kingdom

The Supreme Court is an appellate court and is the final court of appeal for civil cases **2–17** from Scotland. The court was created by the Constitutional Reform Act 2005 and came into being in 2009 replacing the Appellate Committee of the House of Lords. There are relatively few appeals from Scotland with only 10 or so each year.

There are 12 Justices of whom normally two will be Scottish trained judges.[9] Although it is not a rule that a Scottish judge sits to hear an appeal from Scotland, it is usual for at least one of the five judges to be Scottish.

In an appeal from a decision of the Inner House, the appellant will petition the court asking that the interlocutor of the Inner House be altered. Once the Supreme Court has given its judgment, the matter is returned to the Inner House to apply that judgment. The Supreme Court will normally only hear appeals on important or difficult questions of law, or questions of fact and law.

The Supreme Court may not hear criminal appeals from the High Court of Justiciary but may consider devolution issues under the Scotland Act 1998 for both civil and criminal cases.

---

[9] At the time of writing, these are Lord Hope and Lord Reed.

European Court of Justice

2–18 Although not an appeal court within the Scottish legal system, the European Court of Justice is part of the system for any issues relating to matters covered by the European Treaties. It is a requirement that where such an issue arises in the case before the domestic court, the direction of the ECJ must either be sought, or if a decision already exists on the same issue, that decision must be followed by the domestic court. The ECJ is discussed in Chapter 4.

CRIMINAL LEGAL SYSTEM

2–19 The criminal courts in Scotland are the Justice of the Peace Court, the sheriff court, the High Court of Justiciary as a trial court, and the High Court of Justiciary as an appeal court. In addition, cases may be sent to the European Court of Justice for interpretation of EU law. Prosecutions are brought by the Crown "in the public interest". Reports of crimes and offences are made by the police and other bodies to the procurator fiscal and the Crown Office. Each report has to be considered and a decision made as to whether prosecution "in the public interest" is warranted. Many cases are disposed of by police conditional offers and fiscal fines, and other methods of disposal, leaving around 130,000 cases to be disposed of annually in the Scottish criminal courts. Around 88 per cent of these cases result in a guilty plea or guilty verdict.

Since the Scotland Act 1998 came into force, any cases involving devolution issues may be sent to the Supreme Court for decision.[10]

The criminal jurisdiction of the courts is split into two types of procedure—summary and solemn. Summary jurisdiction falls to the justice of the peace court and the sheriff summary court, where cases are heard "on complaint" by a judge sitting alone. In solemn jurisdiction, the accused appears "on indictment" and faces a judge sitting with a jury of 15 people. Although there are certain crimes and offences which must be heard in a particular court, using either the summary or solemn procedure, it is generally at the discretion of the prosecutor to which court the accused will be directed. In most cases, the procurator fiscal decides whether or not to prosecute an accused person and will decide the venue of the prosecution. In serious cases, the procurator fiscal will consult with the Crown Office in Edinburgh, which is the office of the Lord Advocate, and an advocate-depute will decide whether the prosecution should proceed in the High Court of Justiciary. The procurator fiscal handles summary complaints, while prosecutions on indictment, particularly those before the High Court of Justiciary, will be handled by an advocate-depute appointed by the Lord Advocate.

The Criminal Proceedings etc. (Reform) (Scotland) Act 2007 created a new justice of the peace court within the Scottish Courts Service and reformed the way in which justices are recruited and trained.

The procedure for bringing and conducting prosecutions is covered by the Criminal Procedure (Scotland) Act 1995.

---

[10] See para.2–33 below.

Justice of the Peace courts

The Justice of the Peace court was created after the re-organisation of the criminal justice **2–20** system in 2007.[11] The JP courts replace the district courts which were organised by local councils. The new courts are now part of the Scottish Courts Service.

The JP court deals with minor crimes and offences and is mainly presided over by lay justices of the peace. In Glasgow JP Court, the work is shared between lay justices and legally qualified stipendiary magistrates.

The JP court is a local court, to be found in all local authority areas, except Orkney Council, where the work is done by the sheriff court. The area covered by the court is called the commission area and the justices are appointed to hold a commission for that area alone.

A legal advisor will sit with the justices to advise them on the law. The legal advisor is not, however, involved in making judicial decisions, such as guilt or innocence, or how far mitigating circumstances should affect a sentence.

The work of the court is scrutinised by the Scottish Executive and by the Scottish Parliament. The Scottish Ministers will be responsible for appointing justices after receiving recommendations from the local Justice of the Peace Advisory Committee.

The requirements for appointment as a justice are that they must be under 70 years old. The office is renewable after five years. Most justices are male, over 50 and white. Attempts have been made over the years to try to have a bench which is more representative of the community in which it works. Thus, the number of younger people and women has increased, but the number of justices from ethnic communities is still too low. Justices are required to undergo training at regular intervals and be appraised in their performance.

Stipendiary magistrates are appointed by the sheriff principal and are solicitors or advocates of at least five years' standing. They do not sit with a legal assessor, and they have the same powers of disposal as a sheriff sitting in a summary case. Although all sheriffs principal have power to appoint stipendiary magistrates they are only to be found in Glasgow and Strathkelvin Sheriffdom.

Jurisdiction of the Justice of the Peace court

The court has jurisdiction over any summary case which occurs in its commission area and **2–21** which has been declared by statute to be within its competency. The main statute covering the jurisdiction of the JP court is the Criminal Procedure (Scotland) Act 1995.

The kinds of cases heard by the court are common law offences, e.g. minor assault, breach of the peace, theft, and statutory offences such as parking offences, litter, and minor road offences. The JP court and the sheriff court both hear cases using the summary procedure and the procurator fiscal will decide which court to use.

Key Concepts

Justice of the Peace court or **sheriff court**? The decision is taken on the basis of:

- the seriousness of the offence;
- the sentence which can be imposed;
- whether the sheriff court is very busy; and
- perhaps also on the basis of the proficiency of the justices.

---

[11] Criminal Proceedings etc. (Reform) (Scotland) Act 2007.

The justice has the power to impose up to 60 days' imprisonment and/or a fine up to £2,500. However, it should be noted that some statutes impose a different maximum penalty and the court cannot exceed such penalty. The court also has other types of sentence that can be imposed and these are discussed below.

A stipendiary magistrate has the same sentencing powers as the sheriff, that is, up to 12 months' imprisonment and up to £10,000 fine.

Sheriff court

2–22 The sheriff court is a local court which deals with both civil and criminal cases and, as such, it is the busiest of the courts.

Jurisdiction of the sheriff court

2–23 The jurisdiction is over most criminal offences committed within the sheriffdom. However, there are certain types of cases which are privative (i.e. exclusive) to other courts. For instance, parking and litter offences are privative to the JP court while murder and rape cases may only be heard in the High Court of Justiciary. Thus, many of the cases which come before the sheriff court could have been heard by one of the other courts. The decision to prosecute a case in the sheriff court, or elsewhere, is taken by the procurator fiscal.

Criminal cases are prosecuted using either the summary procedure or solemn procedure. Both the court procedures and the sentencing powers available are different, depending on the type of prosecution procedure used.

Key Concepts

The sheriff court hears two types of criminal procedures:

- summary procedure; and
- solemn procedure.

Summary procedure

2–24 This is used for minor crimes and offences. The case is heard by a sheriff sitting without a jury. A sheriff's powers of disposal are limited by the Criminal Procedure (Scotland) Act 1995 to 12 months' imprisonment and/or a fine up to £10,000.

Solemn procedure

2–25 Here the sheriff will sit with a jury of 15 persons. The accused appears on indictment, charged with a serious offence, such as robbery, serious assault, or a serious motoring offence, and can be sentenced to up to five years' imprisonment and/or an unlimited fine. However, some statutory offences, such as motoring offences, specify a range of sentencing options, and the sheriff is required to implement those. If an accused is found guilty, the sheriff may remit the accused to the High Court for sentence if he believes that his sentencing powers are inadequate for the gravity of the crime.

High Court of Justiciary

The High Court of Justiciary is the senior criminal court and handles both appeal cases **2–26** and trials. It is the last court of appeal for criminal appeals in Scotland, unless the matter of the appeal refers to a devolution issue under the Scotland Act 1998: in this case, the last court of appeal is the Supreme Court of the United Kingdom (formerly the Judicial Committee of the Privy Council).[12]

Trial court

The High Court is a circuit court, sitting in various locations in Scotland, using the local **2–27** sheriff court as its base. This allows the criminal justice system to operate at all levels within a locality, instead of the most serious cases being sent to the court in Edinburgh where all serious civil matters are heard. It further allows the accused to be tried by "his peers" since the jury will be drawn from people on the local electoral register.

Section 2(1) of the Criminal Procedure (Scotland) Act 1995 allows the High Court to sit at such times and in such places as the Lord Justice General may determine.

The court in Glasgow handles around half of the total cases of the High Court and thus sits permanently, as it does in Edinburgh and Aberdeen. In a very exceptional case, the trial of the two men accused of bombing Pan-Am Flight 203 over Lockerbie in 1988, causing the deaths of 270 people, was held in the Netherlands before three judges sitting without a jury.[13] A fourth judge was available in case one of the judges became ill or died. This trial was enabled by an Order in Council made under the United Nations Act 1946.[14]

As a trial court, the High Court is presided over by a Lord Commissioner of Justiciary, who sits with a jury of 15. In a case of particular difficulty or importance, two or more judges may sit with the jury, but this is unusual, having occurred in only a few cases in the last century, e.g. *HM Advocate v McKenzie*.[15]

The territorial jurisdiction of the High Court, as a trial court, is the whole of Scotland together with the territorial waters of Scotland. Certain crimes committed outside Scotland may also be heard, e.g. hijacking by a Scottish national anywhere in the world.

The case jurisdiction of the High Court is only limited by statute. Thus, the High Court could hear a breach of the peace case normally heard in the sheriff or district court, but this would be unusual and wasteful of the court's time. In practice, the court will hear the more serious crimes such as armed robbery and serious assault. Certain crimes are privative to the High Court, i.e. the High Court has exclusive jurisdiction. These are murder, rape and treason. Certain statutory offences must be tried in the High Court, such as offences under the Official Secrets Act 1911.

Cases within the High Court are taken on solemn procedure. The accused is indicted to appear before the court to answer the charge and will often appear from custody. The powers of sentencing available to the High Court are unlimited imprisonment and unlimited fine, although these are, of course, subject to the provisions of a statute. The court may impose only a sentence of life imprisonment on a person convicted of murder although the sentence may contain a recommendation of, say 15 years, imprisonment before the accused is eligible to apply for parole.

---

[12] *Follen v HM Advocate*, 2001 S.C. (P.C.) 105; 2001 S.L.T. 774.
[13] *HM Advocate v Megrahi (No.4)*, 2001 G.W.D. 5–177.
[14] High Court of Justiciary (Proceedings in the Netherlands) (United Nations) Order 1998 (SI 1998/2251).
[15] 1970 S.L.T. 81.

Appeal court

2–28 The High Court of Justiciary is the highest criminal appeal court in Scotland and all appeals must be heard there, whether coming from the district court or the High Court itself. The territorial jurisdiction is the whole of Scotland. There is no right of appeal to the Supreme Court of the United Kingdom.[16]

In criminal cases, the accused may appeal against conviction and/or against sentence, except where the sentence imposed is prescribed by statute, e.g. the mandatory sentence for murder is life imprisonment and a person so convicted may not appeal against that sentence, but may appeal against the conviction. Most appeals are against sentence only (80 per cent).

The system of appeals changed as a result of the Criminal Procedure (Scotland) Act 1995. Originally, any person convicted could appeal and their appeal would be heard by a bench of three judges at the High Court in Edinburgh, sitting as a court of appeal. This meant that there were many appeals made which had no foundation and were unreasonable. Accordingly, the High Court was unable to cope with the volume of appeals and delays in the appeal procedure became extensive.

The new system is a two-stage one whereby the accused states the reasons for appeal, e.g. the sentence is too severe, and these are considered by a single High Court judge, who "sifts" the appeals. If he decides that there are no grounds for appeal, the appellant may appeal that decision to a bench of three judges. If the "sifting" judge decides that there are grounds for appeal, the matter goes before the appeal court. It is possible for the sifting judge to decide that the grounds of appeal stated by the appellant are irrelevant or incompetent, but that there are other grounds for appeal not stated by the appellant. Such a decision would go to the appeal court.

A convicted person may always seek leave to appeal, whether the case has been heard by solemn or summary procedure. In certain circumstances, it is also possible for the prosecution to appeal against the level of sentence where it appears to be too lenient.

There are a number of different methods of appeal.

(1) *Stated case*: This is the method used after summary conviction to appeal against that conviction and/or sentence. The judge will prepare a statement of the facts found proved and will request the High Court to answer questions of law, which the accused or prosecutor wants answered. This kind of appeal is known as a Justiciary Appeal.

(2) *Appeal by Bill of Suspension or Advocation*: After summary conviction, a bill of suspension is used by the accused where appeal by stated case is inappropriate or incompetent. It is most often used if there have been irregularities in the trial procedures. A bill of advocation is used by the prosecutor to appeal against the acquittal of the accused, on the ground of an alleged miscarriage of justice. These bills are very rare.

(3) *Note of appeal*: This is a faster method of appeal, used when the offender wishes to appeal against sentence only. The sentence may be increased or decreased by the High Court.

(4) *Solemn appeals*: There is one ground of appeal for solemn cases—miscarriage of justice. This ground of appeal, called a Criminal Appeal, was clarified by the Criminal Procedure (Scotland) Act 1995 s.106 as amended by the Crime and Punishment (Scotland) Act 1997. The statute allows review by the High Court against a conviction and/or sentence and allows the court to take into account

---

[16] *Macintosh v Lord Advocate* (1876) 3 R. (H.L.) 34.

evidence which was not heard at the original trial and where the jury returned a verdict "no reasonable jury properly directed could have returned". The Lord Advocate may appeal against sentences he considers unduly lenient.[17] Leave to appeal by the trial judge is now required for solemn appeals. The High Court may authorise a re-trial to take place, although it is up to the Crown to decide whether a re-trial should take place. This power is rarely used by the High Court.

(5) *Lord Advocate's Reference*: This applies where an indictment has led to an acquittal or conviction, but has raised a point of law which requires clarification by the court. The decision of the court has no effect on an acquittal. Such references are very infrequent.[18]

Miscarriages of justice

In recent years there have been a number of prominent miscarriages of justice in England **2–29** and Wales. These resulted in a Royal Commission on Criminal Justice in 1991. One of its recommendations was that an independent review authority should be set up to decide whether or not a case should be referred to the Court of Appeal. This decision had previously been taken by the Home Secretary, once all of the normal appeals process had been exhausted. In Scotland, the Secretary of State undertook to consider whether a similar body was needed, and a Committee on Appeals Criteria and Alleged Miscarriages of Justice was set up in 1994, under the chairmanship of Sir Stewart Sutherland.

At that time, the Secretary of State had power to refer the case back to the High Court to be heard as if it were an appeal. The Sutherland Committee reported in 1996 and recommended that an independent body be set up to consider and refer miscarriages of justice. This was rejected by the Conservative Government but a change was forced on the Government during the passage of the Crime and Punishment (Scotland) Act 1997 and an amendment was made to the Criminal Procedure (Scotland) Act 1995 to set up the Scottish Criminal Cases Review Commission

The Commission was set up in 1999 and is independent of Government; its members are appointed by the Queen on the recommendation of the First Minister. At least one-third of the members must be advocates or solicitors of 10 years' standing and at least two-thirds must have experience of the criminal justice system, including the investigation of offences and treatment of offenders. The Commission investigates cases where a miscarriage of justice may have taken place and, if it is of the opinion that a miscarriage of justice may have taken place and it is in the interests of justice, a reference to the High Court of Justiciary may be made. Then the High Court will deal with the reference under the normal appeals procedure.

Verdicts

In Scotland, an accused person may be convicted, or acquitted, or found "not proven". **2–30** This last verdict has the same effect as an acquittal, in that the accused is set free and there is no criminal record kept. However, in some ways it is unsatisfactory since it indicates that the court felt the accused was not wholly innocent, but there was not enough evidence to meet the requirement of "beyond reasonable doubt" which is the standard of proof required in criminal cases. The verdict does not, contrary to popular misconception, allow the prosecution of the person to be reopened if further evidence comes to light in the future. Once a verdict of "not proven" is given, the rule of double jeopardy comes into

---

[17] *HM Advocate v McPhee*, 1994 S.L.T. 1292.
[18] *Lord Advocate's Reference (No.1 of 2002)*, 2002 S.L.T. 1017.

play; this says that a person cannot be tried twice for the same crime. Recent concerns on this rule (after the acquittal of an accused in the "World's End" murder case of Helen Scott and Christine Eadie) led to the passing of the Double Jeopardy (Scotland) Act 2011. The rules for re-trial are very strict and limited to certain very serious cases.

Sentencing powers

2–31 The broad sentencing powers of courts at common law have been described above. However, courts have more sentencing options open to them other than a fine or imprisonment. The courts may also be given statutory sentencing powers for specific offences, such as disqualification from driving where the offender has 12, or more, penalty points on his driving licence.

Options available to the courts include:

- Absolute discharge—under summary procedure, no conviction is recorded. This verdict is especially useful in minor cases where the offender hopes to join the armed forces and a criminal conviction might preclude that.
- Community payback order—introduced in 2011, this replaced the community service order, probation order and supervised attendance order. The CPO addresses the areas of the offender's life that need to change, e.g. alcohol treatment.
- Deferral of sentence, subject to conditions.
- Drug court order—if the offender agrees to this, they will start treatment within 48 hours. Thereafter they will be regularly tested and the court will review their progress at a hearing.
- Restriction of liberty order—which is imposed for up to 12 months on an offender aged over 16 years. The order restricts the offender's movements requiring them to be in a specified place at a specified time, or not to be in a specified place at a specified time. An example would be a football hooligan required to attend at a police station when his team is playing.
- Forfeiture order—this can be imposed on the property of the offender which has been used in committing a crime, e.g. a motor car used as a getaway vehicle, or for the transport of drugs. The order allows the sale of the property.
- Young offenders, i.e. those between 16 and 21 may be sent to a detention centre for a period of four weeks to four months, or a young offender's institution for a period not exceeding that which would have been imposed on an adult.

The vast majority of sentences imposed are fines, particularly in the JP court where these account for 90 per cent of the penalties imposed.

The Crime and Punishment (Scotland) Act 1997 provides for an automatic life sentence to be imposed on offenders over 21 who have previously committed a qualifying offence (such as culpable homicide, attempted murder, rape, robbery with a firearm) and who have been again convicted of a qualifying offence. However, the mandatory nature of this provision is mitigated by a provision whereby the court need not impose the automatic life sentence if it is not in the interests of justice to do so. This appears to give the court discretion in sentencing. The Lord Advocate is given the right to appeal against a decision not to impose the automatic life sentence.

Before sentence is passed on a person who has been found guilty, the court will give that person an opportunity to have their say, in particular to explain why they committed the crime and to put forward any relevant information about their circumstances.

The court will then take certain circumstances into account before passing sentence.

Key Concepts

Factors affecting **sentence**:

- the accused's personal circumstances;
- any criminal record;
- the circumstances of the offence;
- the accused's age if they are under 21;
- whether the accused has served any previous custodial sentence;
- time spent by the accused in custody awaiting trial;
- a plea of guilty;
- any minimum sentence required by law;
- aggravation on grounds of race etc; and
- any guidance or guidelines provided by the High Court.

Alternatives to prosecution

The business of the courts has increased markedly over the years and cases take longer to 2–32 come to court after the decision to prosecute has been taken. In the early 1990s, it was obvious that action would have to be taken before the whole system ground to a halt. The Criminal Justice (Scotland) Act 1987 had introduced the concept of "fiscal fines", whereby cases which could be brought before the district court could be diverted out of the court system by allowing the accused to pay a fine. The idea was that if the fine was paid, there would be no prosecution and the acceptance of the "offer" of the fiscal fine was not recorded as a conviction. This was introduced in 1988 with the fine being set at £25.

In the Criminal Justice (Scotland) Act 1995, all summary statutory offences were made triable in the JP court, thus opening the way to introduce fiscal fines for a larger number of offences. The scale of penalties was also increased up to £100. However, the Criminal Procedure etc. (Reform) (Scotland) Act 2007 has increased the maximum fiscal fine to £500. The result of these provisions has been an increase in the number of fiscal fines and, thus, a decrease in the number of cases before the JP court.

A recent development has been the introduction of a Drugs court in Glasgow as a pilot scheme. The remit of the Drugs court is to act as an alternative method of dealing with prosecutions for drug-related offences. Offenders must agree to accept medical and rehabilitative treatment for their drug problem. Section 42 of the Criminal Justice (Scotland) Act 2003 gives additional sentencing powers to the Drugs Court where an offender has failed to comply with a drug treatment and testing order or probation order. Additionally, specialist courts for domestic abuse cases and youth courts have been the subject of pilot schemes.

"DEVOLUTION ISSUES"

As a result of the Scotland Act 1998, the Scottish Executive is required to ensure that any 2–33 subordinate legislation, or any other actions undertaken by them, are compatible with Convention rights and with EU law.[19] This section of the Act does not apply to the Lord Advocate when his act is done to prosecute an offence, or is done in his capacity as head of

---

[19] 1998 Act s.57(2).

the systems of criminal prosecution and investigation of deaths in Scotland, where such an act would not be unlawful under s.6 of the Human Rights Act 1998. The section protects the prosecuting authorities, when they are found to be prosecuting a violation of a statutory provision which is held to be incompatible with Convention rights. The section also ensures that the Lord Advocate is able to bring a prosecution under UK legislation where the prosecuting authorities in England have been able to do so under the same legislation. This ensures that UK legislation is applied the same way across the United Kingdom.

A person seeking a remedy, after being adversely affected by an Act of the Scottish Executive or an Act of the Scottish Parliament, will bring a "devolution issue" before the courts. The concept of the devolution issue is raised in s.98, which refers the reader to Sch.6 where the devolution issue is defined.

Any alleged breach of the Convention under the Scotland Act will become a devolution issue for the purposes of Sch.6. The validity of an Act of the Scottish Parliament cannot, however, be challenged on the grounds that the proceedings leading to its enactment were invalid.[20]

Key concept

The Scotland Act 1998 para.1 of Sch.6 defines a devolution issue as:

"(a) a question whether an Act of the Scottish Parliament or any provision of an Act of the Scottish Parliament is within the legislative competence of the Parliament
. . .
(d) a question whether a purported or proposed exercise of a function by a member of the Scottish Executive is, or would be, incompatible with any of the Convention rights or with EU law.
(e) a question whether a failure to act by a member of the Scottish Executive is incompatible with any of the Convention rights or with EU law."

Proceedings for the determination of a devolution issue may be instituted by the Advocate General for Scotland or the Lord Advocate, or by a person, who is a "victim" in terms of art.34 of the European Convention on Human Rights, during the course of existing legal proceedings.[21] A devolution issue may, therefore, be raised in any court or tribunal proceedings but para.5 of the Schedule requires that the Advocate General and the Lord Advocate are given intimation that the devolution issue has arisen. Either Law Officer may then become a party to the proceedings, as far as it relates to the devolution issue.

In criminal cases it is possible to raise a devolution issue, but this is subject to time limits. In a case brought on indictment the devolution issue must be raised within seven days of the indictment being served. In summary cases the devolution issue must be stated before the accused has been asked to plead.

When a devolution issue is raised in a tribunal from which there is no appeal, the tribunal must refer the devolution issue to the Inner House of the Court of Session; any other tribunal may choose to do this.[22] Any civil court (except the Supreme Court or the Court of Session sitting with three or more judges) may refer the devolution issue to the

---

[20] 1998 Act s.28(5).
[21] 1998 Act s.100(1).
[22] 1998 Act Sch.6 para.8.

Inner House.[23] Any criminal court (except the High Court of Justiciary sitting with two or more judges) may refer the devolution issue to the High Court of Justiciary.[24] These provisions are designed to ensure that, where necessary, a lower court may refer a devolution issue to a superior court and it will be dealt with by the superior court, not just passed upwards to another court. The superior court may itself refer the devolution issue to a higher court. This applies to the Court of Session convened as a court with at least three judges and the High Court of Justiciary convened with at least two judges. The court to which the reference will be made, in both civil and criminal cases, is the Supreme Court (formerly the Judicial Committee of the Privy Council). This requirement creates for the first time an appeal route from the High Court of Justiciary acting in its appellant capacity.

Once the decision on the reference has been given, the right of appeal against that decision will come into operation. Where the reference has been made under paras 7 or 8 to the Inner House, appeal is to the Supreme Court. Where the reference has arisen under para.9, or the devolution issue has arisen in the ordinary course of proceedings before the High Court of Justiciary as an appeal court, then any appeal requires leave to appeal from the High Court or the Supreme Court and is made to the Supreme Court.[25] Where there is a reference to the Inner House in a case from which there is no appeal to the Supreme Court[26] then appeal may be made to the Supreme Court with the leave of the Inner House or the Supreme Court.[27] The routes for reference and appeal are set out in the table below.

Court in which devolution issue is raised	Court for reference	Appeal
Any tribunal (except those where there is no appeal)	Inner House of Court of Session (para.8)	Supreme Court (para.12)
Civil court, i.e. sheriff court, Outer House of Court of Session	Inner House of Court of Session (para.7)	Supreme Court (para.12)
Criminal court, i.e. Justice of the Peace court, sheriff court, High Court of Justiciary as trial court	High Court of Justiciary as appeal court (para.9)	Supreme Court but only with leave to appeal (para.13(a))
Court of Session, with at least three judges, but not if devolution issue raised under paras 7 or 8	Supreme Court (para.10)	Supreme Court, but only with leave to appeal and if no right of appeal to Supreme Court (para.13(b))
High Court of Justiciary, with at least two judges	Supreme Court (para.11)	Supreme Court, but only with permission to appeal (para.13(a))

---

[23] 1998 Act Sch.6 para.7.
[24] 1998 Act Sch.6 para.9.
[25] 1998 Act Sch.6 para.13(a).
[26] For instance, from the Lands Valuation Appeal Court.
[27] 1998 Act Sch.6 para.13(b).

Where the devolution issue concerns the proposed exercise of a function by a member of the Scottish Executive, then the person making the reference must notify a member of the Scottish Executive that the issue has been raised. The devolution issue may not have arisen in judicial proceedings, but any of the Law Officers may refer the issue of the proposed exercise. Thereafter, no member of the Executive may exercise the function until the matter is disposed of. If a member of the Scottish Executive does exercise the function, the Advocate General or any other person may bring proceedings against the Scottish Executive.

Normally, when a legal provision or action is found to be ultra vires the provision or action is treated as null and void. A court action, to challenge the validity of a provision of an action made under the Scotland Act, will take time to be heard and decided. It is likely, therefore, that the provision may have been implemented before the action is raised, and individuals may have relied upon the provision or action. Any decision of invalidity will be retrospective and may cause difficulty for those who have relied upon it. The Act allows the court to limit the effect of such a decision by removing, or limiting, any retrospective effect of the decision or suspending the effect of the decision, pending its being corrected.[28] The court is required to have regard to the effect the making of an order would have on persons who are not parties to the proceedings and the court must order intimation to the Lord Advocate, and if the matter is a devolution issue, to the appropriate Law Officer.

TRIBUNALS

2–34   The State is involved in more and more areas of our lives, and so disputes will inevitably arise from the application of the numerous rules and regulations made by the Executive. These disputes could be settled in the courts, but they would clog up an already over-crowded legal system. Alternatively, they could be settled by the government department or body which has responsibility for the regulations. The problem envisaged here, was that the body would in effect be policing itself. Neither of these options was considered satisfactory, hence the creation of a new machinery to handle these disputes—tribunals.

Key Concepts

Reasons why tribunals are **necessary in modern society**:

- ordinary courts could not cope with the volume of cases likely to arise;
- there is often no necessity for the formality encountered in a court;
- there may be a need for expert and specialised knowledge which a judge may not have;
- tribunals are cheap to set up and operate;
- judges are required to interpret legislation and are often unable to take into account social principles and policies behind the legislation; and
- the subject-matter of the disputes may be comparatively trifling.

Tribunals are independent adjudicatory bodies set up under statute and occasionally by prerogative. The term "tribunal" is not defined in legislation, but it appears to cover any

---

[28] 1998 Act s.102(2).

person or body of persons who have judicial or quasi-judicial functions. Lord Denning described a tribunal hearing as "more in the nature of an inquiry before an investigating body charged with the task of finding out what happened".[29]

Tribunals are the primary mechanism provided by Parliament for the resolution of certain grievances between the citizen and State, but a few tribunals also cover disputes between citizen and citizen, for instance employment tribunals. Tribunals handle six times the number of cases than the courts and cover a wide range of topics such as benefit appeals, immigration adjudicators, child support appeals and the children's hearings. Many of the tribunals come under the supervisory control of the Administrative Justice & Tribunals Council (formerly the Council on Tribunals).

From the end of the Second World War, tribunals proliferated—mainly because of the setting up of the welfare state. Tribunals were seen as necessary for the benefit of the public and to ensure fair treatment by officials.

In 1957 the Franks Committee[30] reported on the working of tribunals clarifying the place of tribunals within the justice system. The recommendations contained in the Franks Report were largely implemented by the Tribunals and Inquiries Act 1958. Other parts of the report were implemented by means of changes in administrative procedures.

A constant theme of the Franks Report was that there were three characteristics of a tribunal: openness, fairness and impartiality. Openness includes knowledge of the essential reasoning behind decisions and publicity of proceedings. Impartiality refers to the freedom of the tribunal from the interference of the government department. Fairness refers to the adoption of a clear procedure, so that parties know their rights and the case they have to meet.

Key Concepts

A tribunal will have some, but not all, of these **properties**:

- it will make final, legally enforceable decisions;
- it will be independent of any department;
- it will hold a public hearing which is judicial in nature;
- its members will possess the relevant expertise;
- it will give reasoned decisions; and
- it will allow an appeal to the Court of Session or High Court of Justice on a point of law.

Most tribunals are set up by statute and the powers and duties are regulated, either in the statute itself, or in regulations made under the statute.

Reform of the tribunals system

In May 2000, the Lord Chancellor commissioned a review of the tribunal system, to look **2–35** at the strengths and weaknesses of the current system. Led by Sir Andrew Leggatt, the review was the first wide ranging independent review since the Franks Report in 1957 and a consultation document was sent to interested parties, to gather ideas for the review. The

---

[29] *R. v National Insurance Commissioner Ex p. Viscusi* [1974] 1 W.L.R. 646.
[30] *Report of the Committee on Administrative Tribunals and Inquiries*, Cmnd.218 (1957).

consultation document stated that its aim was "to provide a framework for the strategic development of the British system of administrative justice."

The Leggatt Report: *Tribunals for users: One System, One Service* was published in March 2001. The report was problematic for Scottish tribunals, as it covered only UK tribunals, not those based purely in Scotland, such as children's hearings. The most important recommendations were that tribunal users should be able to prepare and present cases themselves and that a Tribunals Service should be created to administer all of the tribunals in a single national system, with regional structure and management. The Tribunals Service started full operation in April 2006 and will provide common administrative support for a number of central government tribunals.

The Leggatt Report also recommended that there should be First-tier tribunals, with appeals on a point of law to an Upper Tribunal and further appeal, again on a point of law, to the Court of Appeal in England, or Court of Session in Scotland.

The Tribunals, Courts and Enforcement Act 2007 abolished the Council on Tribunals and replaced it with the Administrative Justice and Tribunals Council, which has a broader remit to include a more general oversight of administrative justice. This new Council has separate committees for Scotland and Wales.

The Public Bodies Act 2011 allowed the Government to review the need for certain "arm's length bodies" such as the AJTC and, at the time of writing, has indicated that it wishes to abolish the AJTC.

Children's hearing system

2–36   The children's hearing system was introduced in 1971 as a result of the Social Work (Scotland) Act 1968, itself the result of the report of the Kilbrandon Committee of 1964. The Committee's approach, was that children in need of care and juvenile offenders had similar characteristics and, therefore, "a unified welfare-based system which responded to their needs rather than their deeds was required". Children should not normally be brought before the courts, but referred to a new local official, the Reporter to the Children's Panel, to see if there are sufficient grounds for referral and whether compulsory care is necessary. The report emphasised the need for care, and in fact the report referred to the juvenile panel as a "locally based treatment authority". The needs of the child were to be paramount, with the existing concept of punishment being discarded. The children's hearing system is discussed further in Chapter 15.

Key Concepts

Why the **Children's Hearing** is a distinctive tribunal:

- It seeks to find a resolution of problems outwith the court system.
- It works in a fairly informal way, by discussion between the child, the parents and the panel.
- The panel comprises three lay members from the local community and, by law, must include both a man and a woman on the panel.
- If there is a dispute regarding the reasons for referral, this is dealt with away from the panel by the sheriff.

The Children's Hearing (Scotland) Act 2011 is intended to modernise the existing system but it has not, at the time of writing, been brought fully into force.

OMBUDSMEN IN SCOTLAND

Devolution has led to considerable changes in the Ombudsman system in Scotland. In the **2-37** early days of the Scottish Parliament, complaints of injustice caused by maladministration were directed to the Scottish Parliamentary Commissioner for Administration.[31] Maladministration is not defined by statute, but generally it appears to consist of issues such as poor administrative practices, or the wrong application of rules, or giving misleading or inadequate advice, or failing to inform a person of a right of appeal. A person making a complaint, that he has suffered "injustice caused by maladministration", must normally have exhausted the internal complaints procedure of the department, or body, concerned before the relevant Ombudsman will investigate the matter.

The SPCA was also the holder of the office of Parliamentary Commissioner for Administration in the UK Parliament. Section 91 of the 1998 Act required the Scottish Parliament to establish provision for the investigation of complaints and this has now been implemented by the Scottish Public Services Ombudsman Act 2002. This Act establishes a "one-stop shop" to streamline the public sector complaints system, by creating a single Ombudsman to replace the SPCA, the Health Commissioner for Scotland, Local Government Ombudsman and the Housing Association Ombudsman for Scotland.

The SPSO is appointed by the Queen on the nomination of the Scottish Parliament and will be able to accept complaints directly from members of the public. The PCA and SPCA were unable to investigate complaints unless an MP or MSP referred the matter to them. This "MP/MSP filter" was an unnecessary complication to the complaints system, but Members of the two Parliaments had wanted to ensure that they were kept informed of events in their constituencies.

The new system is intended to simplify the complaints procedure in Scotland, by creating just one Ombudsman to oversee a number of different subject areas. Schedule 2 to the 2002 Act lists the bodies which fall within the remit of the SPSO. The list includes the Scottish Parliament and Scottish Administration, the health service bodies in Scotland, local authorities, registered social landlords, a substantial number of Scottish public authorities and a number of cross-border public authorities.[32] More recent additions include universities and colleges, and prisoners.

The Ombudsman has power to conduct an investigation[33] after receiving a complaint from a member of the public, or a request from a listed authority.

(1) *Complaint from a member of the public*: The person must have suffered injustice or hardship in consequence of maladministration, or a "service failure", although the latter will not lead to an investigation involving a family health service provider, or a registered social landlord.[34] The person aggrieved may make the complaint, or may instruct another to act on his behalf.[35] This provision is intended to improve accessibility to the Ombudsman by allowing the person himself, or perhaps his MSP or local councillor, to make the complaint. The legal representatives of a deceased person may make a complaint, if that person suffered maladministration before his death.

---

[31] The Scotland Act 1998 (Transitory and Transitional Provisions) (Complaints of Maladministration) Order 1999.
[32] e.g. Criminal Injuries Compensation Authority, Forestry Commissioners, Sea Fish Industry Authority.
[33] 2002 Act s.2.
[34] 2002 Act s.5(2).
[35] 2002 Act s.9(1).

The complaint must normally be made within 12 months of the aggrieved person being made aware of the maladministration. However, the Ombudsman has discretion to extend this time limit of she deems it appropriate to do so. The complaint may be made in writing, or by electronic means, or, at the discretion of the Ombudsman, orally.[36]

(2) *Request by listed authority*: This is an interesting development in Ombudsman services. Previously an Ombudsman, such as the PCA, could only investigate a public body where a complaint had been received. Sometimes a public body would be criticised but if no complaint had been received there could be no investigation. The Scottish Executive has indicated that this request for an investigation should only be made where the authority has taken all reasonable steps to resolve the problem.

Investigations

2–38 The Ombudsman cannot investigate a number of issues, such as any actions taken by the police or prosecution authorities in the investigation or prevention of crime, the commencement or conduct of civil or criminal proceedings, contractual or commercial transactions of any listed authority (except certain NHS contracts), any issues relating to personnel matters, or the determination of the amount of any rent or service charge.[37]

The Ombudsman has power under s.13 to require any member, officer, or any other person to supply information and produce documents relevant to the investigation. She has the same powers as the Court of Session to require the attendance and examination of witnesses and the production of documents.[38] She may not, however, require the production of papers from the Scottish Cabinet or the UK Cabinet. Any person who obstructs the Ombudsman in her investigation, or commits an act (or fails to do so) which would constitute contempt of court in the Court of Session, may be liable to be sent to the Court of Session to be dealt with. Investigations are to be held in private.

Reports

2–39 The Ombudsman may make a number of reports about her activities.

(1) *Report on a decision not to investigate*: The Ombudsman has discretion as to whether she should investigate a complaint[39]; and may not be compelled to do so. However, if she declines to investigate, she must send a statement of her decision and the reasons for it to the aggrieved person, or their representative, and the listed authority or person alleged to have committed the maladministration.[40]

(2) *Investigation report*: This report must be sent to the persons listed in s.11 and also to the Scottish Ministers.[41] In addition, a copy of the report has to be laid before Parliament. Normally no individuals will be identified in the report, unless the Ombudsman decides that disclosure is in the public interest and the interests of the person in question. The listed authority must make the report available for inspection or purchase and publicise these arrangements.

---

[36] 2002 Act s.10(3).
[37] 2002 Act s.8 and Sch.4.
[38] 2002 Act s.13(4).
[39] 2002 Act s.2(3).
[40] 2002 Act s.11(2).
[41] 2002 Act s.15.

(3) *Special reports*: A special report may be made where the Ombudsman considers that the aggrieved person has suffered injustice, or hardship, and this has not been, nor is likely to be, remedied. This report is laid before Parliament and copied to those who were sent the original investigation report. The provision allowing a special report to be made is intended to encourage compliance with the decision in the Ombudsman original report.

(4) *Annual reports*: The Ombudsman is required to lay a general report before the Parliament on the performance of her functions. She may also lay other reports before Parliament if she thinks these are necessary to publicise an issue.[42]

LEGAL PROFESSION

In Scotland, there were traditionally two branches of the legal profession—solicitors and **2–40** advocates. Members of these branches must be legally qualified and also be a member of the relevant regulatory body. Solicitors may now become solicitor-advocates and these are considered separately below.

> **Key Concepts**
>
> The members of the legal profession in Scotland are:
>
> - advocates;
> - solicitors; or
> - solicitor-advocates.

Advocates

An advocate is a specialist court practitioner who practices "at the Bar", i.e. the bar of the **2–41** court. Each advocate is a member of the Faculty of Advocates. Unlike solicitors, advocates may not practise in a partnership; each advocate practises on "his own account". However, they all subscribe to Faculty Services Ltd, a company set up by the Faculty to assist advocates in collecting their fees and receiving instructions from clients. There are around 460 practising advocates.

Although advocates work mainly in the Edinburgh courts, they appear in other courts in Scotland, particularly the High Court in Glasgow. Until the Law Reform (Miscellaneous Provisions) (Scotland) Act 1990, only advocates had the right to appear before the Superior Courts: now solicitors may apply for this privilege and these are known as solicitor-advocates.

A newly-qualified advocate is referred to as "junior counsel" and after a period of some years' practice, may then apply to become a Queen's Counsel. Not every advocate will apply to "take silk" as it called; many will be content to continue with their practice as a junior counsel to retirement. Junior counsel may be instructed in a case on their own, but if the matter is particularly important, the client may be advised that both senior and junior counsel be retained.

Counsel must be instructed through a solicitor: it is not possible for a client to approach an advocate directly. If there is a meeting between the client and counsel, the solicitor must

---

[42] 2002 Act s.17.

also be present. This is important, since the solicitor is responsible for making the formal instructions to counsel and for paying the advocate's fees from money obtained from the client.

An advocate need not accept instructions from a client, although there is a rule—the cab rank rule—which states that an advocate should take a case unless there are good reasons for not doing so, e.g. the advocate is employed on another case at the same time, or there is a conflict of interest with another client. The cab rank rule is an ancient principle, devised to ensure that a client will always have someone to plead for him in court.

As well as appearing in court, advocates are consulted about matters where the client is uncertain as to his legal grounds. These are called "opinions" and the advocate will draw up their opinion of the legal merits of the case. This will often be used as a method of settling a dispute without going to court. The solicitor will draw up a "Memorial for Opinion of Counsel" stating the facts, asking for the counsel's opinion of the legal principles and enclosing various supporting documents.

Solicitors

2–42 Formerly called "writers" or "law agents" the correct term for these legally qualified persons is solicitor. The profession is regulated by statute and it is currently under review by the Scottish Parliament. The consolidating statute, Solicitors (Scotland) Act 1980, has been amended by various other statutes—Law Reform (Miscellaneous Provisions) (Scotland) Acts of 1980, 1985 and 1990 and the Solicitors (Scotland) Act 1988. These Acts set out the requirements for entry to the profession, as well as regulating how solicitors may carry out their practice.

Although many solicitors will work either in a sole person practice or in partnership, many more are employed by large companies and public authorities. Each solicitor must have a practising certificate and this must be renewed each year. In addition, solicitors must contribute to the Guarantee Fund and be covered by the master policy of professional indemnity, which exists to protect clients from the negligence of a solicitor. The Legal Services (Scotland) Act 2010, when brought fully into force, will allow lay representation in the Court of Session as well as removing certain practising restrictions in respect of licensed legal service providers (so-called "Tesco lawyers").

The regulatory body is the Law Society of Scotland and all practising solicitors must be included on the Roll of Solicitors administered by the Society. The Law Society has a number of functions, including setting the education, training and admission requirements for the profession. The Society ensures that professional standards and discipline are upheld. As mentioned above, it has set up and administers a guarantee fund, which is available to compensate clients if they suffer loss as a result of the dishonesty of their solicitor.

If a client makes a complaint about a solicitor, it will be investigated by the Law Society, who may then refer the matter to the Scottish Solicitors' Discipline Tribunal. Complaints may also be referred to the tribunal by judges, the Lord Advocate, the Scottish Legal Aid Board and other bodies. The tribunal has the power to discipline a solicitor by fining him, or suspending his practising certificate, or requiring him to practice for a period of time as an assistant, or striking his name from the Roll of Solicitors. There is a right of appeal from the tribunal to the Court of Session.

Solicitor-advocates

2–43 These were created by the Solicitors (Scotland) Act 1980, as amended by the Law Reform (Miscellaneous Provisions) (Scotland) Act 1990. A qualified solicitor may be given the right of audience in the Supreme Courts. The solicitor has to satisfy the Council of the

Law Society of Scotland that he has completed the necessary training in pleading, for the court in which he seeks audience, has the necessary knowledge and the necessary experience of proceedings in the sheriff court and that he is a fit and proper person to have the right of audience in the court. Basically, the intending solicitor-advocate must have court practice of at least five years, have undertaken the necessary training, passed written examinations and sat in the court for a minimum number of days. A panel of five solicitors will then consider the application and make a recommendation to the Council of the Law Society.

A solicitor-advocate has the same rights of audience as an advocate, but may not work as a junior to a Queen's Counsel. The Faculty of Advocates took a decision some years ago not to work with solicitor-advocates to try to preserve their monopoly. Clients who retain a solicitor-advocate do not need to retain a solicitor and an advocate, thus saving themselves some legal fees.

Paralegals

In recent years, there has been an increase in the number of paralegals working in the legal **2–44** profession. A paralegal is a person working in the legal environment under the direction of a solicitor. Often the paralegal will also have a legal qualification. Paralegals carry out work which requires sufficient legal knowledge that would otherwise require to be performed by a solicitor. Paralegals tend to be involved in the areas of domestic conveyancing, commercial conveyancing, trust and executry, debt recovery and family law.

LAW OFFICERS FOR SCOTLAND

The Law Officers for Scotland are the Lord Advocate and the Solicitor General for **2–45** Scotland. Additionally, the Scotland Act 1998 created the post of Advocate-General for Scotland, who is the Scottish Law Officer in the UK Government and is responsible for advising the UK Government on matters of Scots law.

The Law Officers (the Lord Advocate and the Solicitor General for Scotland) are political appointments made by the Queen, on the recommendation of the First Minister and with the approval of the Scottish Parliament. Initially, the Lord Advocate was a member of the Scottish Cabinet, but this is no longer the case. Both Law Officers are members of the Scottish Executive. They need not be members of the Scottish Parliament, but may be called upon by the Parliament to give statements and answer questions.

The Lord Advocate is head of the systems of criminal prosecution and investigation of deaths in Scotland, and, as such, exercises powers independently of the Scottish Executive.[43] The Lord Advocate alone decides whether a prosecution will take place and they have control over the procurator fiscal service. Although the Lord Advocate and the Solicitor General for Scotland may themselves prosecute a major crime, it is now unusual for them to do so, instead advocates are appointed by the Lord Advocate to act as "advocates-depute" to prosecute solemn crimes in the High Court.

---

[43] Scotland Act 1998 s.29.

PUBLIC DEFENCE SOLICITORS' OFFICE (PDSO)

2–46 A recent innovation in Scotland was the introduction of the PDSO. On October 1, 1998, a pilot scheme was set up covering the summary courts of Edinburgh District Court and Edinburgh Sheriff Court. The scheme was to test the feasibility of providing criminal assistance through solicitors employed directly by the Scottish Legal Aid Board.[44] The PDSO would comprise no more than six solicitors for a period of five years, working in the summary courts. To ensure a steady flow of clients, the Scottish Legal Aid Board directed that defendants seeking legal aid and whose birthdays fell within the months of January and February would be represented by the PDSO, unless they were granted a waiver to use a private solicitor. This system ran until July 2000 when the PDSO took over 60 per cent of the sheriff court summary duty solicitor scheme.

There are seven offices across Scotland, and the public defence solicitors may take on any case where the accused has legal aid.

▼ CHAPTER SUMMARY

SCOTTISH COURTS IN GENERAL

2–47
1. **There are two types of courts within the Scottish legal system: the civil courts and the criminal courts.**
2. **The busiest court in Scotland is the sheriff court, because it deals with both civil and criminal actions.**

CIVIL LEGAL SYSTEM

1. **The civil courts are the sheriff court and the Court of Session.**
2. **Judgment is made on the balance of probabilities.**
3. **There are 49 sheriff courts and 6 sheriffdoms.**
4. **The sheriff principal is a full-time judge, administers the work of the sheriffdom and acts as an appeal judge in certain types of action.**
5. **Part-time sheriffs were introduced following the finding that the previous system of temporary sheriffs was contrary to art.6(1) of the European Convention on Human Rights:**

   ➢ *Starrs v Ruxton*, 2000 J.C. 208.

6. **Sheriff courts hear three types of cases: ordinary cause (cases for over £5,000); summary cause (cases for between £3,000 and £5,000); and small claims (case for under £3,000).**
7. **The Court of Session is divided into two "Houses"—the Outer House is a court of first instance while the Inner House is essentially an appeal court. The Inner House is divided into two divisions: First Division and Second Division. An Extra Division frequently sits.**
8. **The most senior judge in the Court of Session is the Lord President and the second most senior judge is the Lord Justice-Clerk.**
9. **The highest appeal court for Scotland in civil cases is the Supreme Court.**

---

[44] Legal Aid (Scotland) Act 1986 s.28A, inserted by the Crime and Punishment (Scotland) Act 1997 s.50.

10. The European Court of Justice is not an appeal court, but if an issue arises in relation to the European Treaties the domestic courts must seek the direction of the European Court of Justice, or follow one of its existing decisions.

CRIMINAL LEGAL SYSTEM

1. The criminal courts are the Justice of the Peace court, the sheriff court, the High Court of Justiciary, as a trial court, and the High Court of Justiciary as an appeal court. In addition, cases may be sent to the European Court of Justice for interpretation of European Union law.
2. Prosecutions are brought by the Crown "in the public interest".
3. There are two types of criminal procedure—summary and solemn. Solemn cases are on indictment and heard by a judge and jury. Summary cases are on complaint and heard by a judge sitting alone.
4. Fifteen people sit on a criminal jury.
5. In the Justice of the Peace court the justice has the power to impose up to 60 days' imprisonment and/or a fine up to £2,500. A stipendiary magistrate has the same sentencing powers as the sheriff, that is, up to 12 months' imprisonment and up to £10,000 fine.
7. The Justice of the Peace court and the sheriff court both hear cases using the summary procedure.
8. The sheriff court can hear both summary procedure and solemn procedure.
9. If a case is heard under summary procedure, the sheriff's powers of disposal are limited to 12 months' imprisonment and/or a fine up to £10,000:

   ➢ Criminal Procedure (Scotland) Act 1995.

10. Under solemn procedure a sheriff can impose sentences to up to five years' imprisonment and/or an unlimited fine:

   ➢ Criminal Procedure (Scotland) Act 1995.

11. The High Court of Justiciary is the senior criminal court and handles both appeal cases and trials.
12. Murder, rape and treason are can only be tried in the High Court.
13. The highest court of appeal in Scotland, for criminal cases, is the High Court of Justiciary, although devolution issues may be referred to the Supreme Court.
14. The Scottish Criminal Cases Review Commission investigates possible miscarriages of justice.
15. A criminal court may give one of three verdicts—guilty, not guilty or not proven.

DEVOLUTION ISSUES

1. The Scottish Executive is required to ensure that any subordinate legislation, or any other actions undertaken by them, are compatible with Convention rights and with EU law. A person seeking a remedy, after being adversely affected by an Act of the Scottish Executive or an Act of the Scottish Parliament, may bring a "devolution issue" before the courts:

   ➢ Scotland Act 1998 s.57(2).

2. **A devolution issue is a question whether: an Act of the Scottish Parliament is within the legislative competence of the Parliament; the exercise of a function by a member of the Scottish Executive is incompatible with any of the Convention rights or with EU law; or a failure to act by a member of the Scottish Executive is incompatible with any of the Convention rights or with EU law:**

   ➤ Scotland Act 1998 Sch.6.

3. **The highest court of appeal with regard to a devolution issue is the Supreme Court, in both civil and criminal cases.**

TRIBUNALS

1. **Tribunals cover a wide range of cases between citizens and the State.**
2. **Children's hearings are unique to Scotland and deal with problems affecting children.**

OMBUDSMEN

1. **The Scottish Public Services Ombudsman is a "one-stop shop" for complaints about maladministration by public bodies:**

   ➤ Scottish Public Services Ombudsman Act 2002.

LEGAL PROFESSION

1. **The legal profession has traditionally been divided into two branches: solicitors and advocates.**
2. **Advocates are specialist court practitioners who practice at the Bar. They appear in court and provide opinions. Traditionally only advocates had rights of audience in the supreme courts.**
3. **Solicitors are regulated by the Law Society of Scotland.**
4. **Solicitor-advocates are solicitors who have qualified as solicitor-advocates and who have the same rights of audience as advocates in the supreme courts.**

LAW OFFICERS FOR SCOTLAND

1. **The Law Officers for Scotland are the Lord Advocate and the Solicitor General for Scotland.**
2. **The Lord Advocate is the head of the system of criminal prosecution and investigation of deaths in Scotland.**
3. **The Advocate-General for Scotland is the Scottish Law Officer in the UK Government and is responsible for advising the UK Government on matters of Scots law.**

PUBLIC DEFENCE SOLICITOR'S OFFICE

1. **The Public Defence Solicitors' Office provides free advice and representation in criminal cases to anyone entitled to legal aid.**

? QUICK QUIZ

STRUCTURE OF THE LEGAL SYSTEM

Civil legal system

- Describe the kinds of cases heard in the sheriff court.
- What qualifications must a person have to become a judge in the Court of Session?
- What are the main differences between the Inner House and the Outer House?

Criminal legal system

- Who takes the decision to prosecute a person?
- In summary cases, what factors will a prosecutor take into account when deciding to send a case to the Justice of the Peace court?
- Describe the procedure for appealing against the sentence imposed by the sheriff solemn court.
- What is the difference between a not guilty verdict and a not proven verdict?
- Explain what is meant by the term "devolution issue".

Tribunals

- Why are tribunals necessary in modern society?

Ombudsmen, the legal profession and law officers

- What is the role of the Scottish Public Services Ombudsman?
- Are there any differences between the SPSO's powers and those of the PCA?
- Differentiate between an advocate and a solicitor.
- Who are the Law Officers for Scotland and what is their role in the legal system?

📖 FURTHER READING

Professor Walker's text, *The Scottish Legal System*, 8th edn (W. Green, 2001) gives a fine account of the development of the courts in Scotland. Many cases and materials of relevance are included in A. Paterson, T. Bates and M. Poustie, *The Legal System of Scotland: Cases and Materials*, 4th edn (W. Green, 1999) as well as interesting discussion.

Sheriff A. Stewart, *The Scottish Criminal Courts in Action*, 2nd edn (Bloomsbury Professional, 2007) is entertaining as well as instructive and is particularly useful for students.

🖱 RELEVANT WEB LINKS

Judiciary of Scotland: *http://www.scotland-judiciary.org.uk*
Scottish Courts: *http://www.scotcourts.gov.uk*
Scottish Public Services Ombudsman: *http://www.spso.org.uk*
Administrative Justice and Tribunals Commission: *http://www.ajtc.justice.gov.uk*
Public Defence Solicitor's Office: *http://www.pdso.org.uk*
Scottish Executive: *http://www.scotland.gov.uk/Home*
Law Society of Scotland: *http://www.lawscot.org.uk*
Faculty of Advocates: *http://www.advocates.org.uk*
Society of Solicitor Advocates: *http://www.solicitoradvocates.org*

Chapter 3   Constitutional Law

VALERIE FINCH[1]

► CHAPTER OVERVIEW

3–01 This chapter is concerned with constitutional law, concentrating in particular on the law which operates in Scotland. It starts by examining the concept of a constitution and the nature of the UK constitution. It then examines the specific sources of constitutional law. The chapter then considers the doctrines of the constitution. An account is given of the operation of the institutions of Government, which operate at UK level. The chapter then focuses on Scottish Government, starting with an account of the process of devolution and then considering the powers, composition and procedures of the Scottish Parliament. The chapter then turns to consideration of the Scottish Government and local Government in Scotland.

✓ OUTCOMES

3–02 At the end of this chapter you should be able to:

- ✓ appreciate the nature of the UK constitution;
- ✓ identify the sources of constitutional law;
- ✓ appreciate the importance of the doctrines of the constitution;
- ✓ understand the relationship between the monarch and Parliament;
- ✓ appreciate the agenda for House of Lords reform;
- ✓ understand the relationship between the Scottish Parliament and the UK Parliament.
- ✓ appreciate the powers and composition of the Scottish Parliament;
- ✓ understand the concept of legislative competence; and
- ✓ understand the grounds under which the actions of the Scottish Government may be challenged.

GENERAL NATURE OF THE UNITED KINGDOM CONSTITUTION

3–03 Every country requires a system of law and Government, so that the affairs of the State can be administered. This system of law and Government is generally described as a constitution. The word constitution is often taken to denote a formal legal document which sets out the framework for the Government of the State. The United Kingdom, unlike most other modern democracies, does not have a formal constitution embodied in a single legal document. This does not mean that the United Kingdom has no constitution.

---

[1] Senior Lecturer in Law, University of the West of Scotland.

The wider definition of a constitution is that it encompasses the whole system of Government of a country and will include all of the rules which establish and regulate the Government.

A select committee of the House of Lords was appointed in 2001 to review the workings of the constitution. This committee has defined the constitution as: "the set of laws, rules and practices that create the basic institutions of the State, and its component and related parts, and stipulate the powers of those institutions and the relationship between the different institutions and between those institutions and the individual."[2]

Key Concepts

The **constitution** of the United Kingdom relates to such matters as:

- the rules of government of the State;
- who will be a citizen of the State;
- how the Government will be elected; and
- how the rules can be changed.

Three characteristics of the UK constitution are, that is an unwritten constitution, it is flexible and it is parliamentary rather than presidential.

Written/unwritten constitutions

Most civilised states now have written constitutions. These constitutions have often been **3–04** the result of political upheaval in the State, e.g. a civil war or the attainment of independence. The United Kingdom has had no such radical change in the nature of its Government in modern times and so the need for a written constitution has never arisen. The constitution of the United Kingdom is described as "unwritten" because there is no single constitutional document. This is misleading, because the UK constitution is more written than most. Although there is not a single constitutional document, many of our constitutional rules are found in statutes and cases. In theory, it would be possible to extract all of the principles of constitutional significance from legislation and cases and combine them together in one document and call it the constitution.

There are some advantages in having a written constitution:

(1) The existence of a written constitution would mean that constitutional law could be more easily distinguished from other laws. However, the lack of a written constitution does not mean that the Government of the country is unregulated. A country does not need a written constitution to ensure that the rights of its citizens are protected.
(2) Written constitutions generally allow the courts to declare laws as unconstitutional. The courts in the United Kingdom do not have power to declare an Act of Parliament unconstitutional. As such, that power is not given to the courts, their role is limited to interpreting legislation in order to ensure that the Executive (the Government) does not have too much power.

---

[2] HL 11 (Session 2001/02).

In reality *all* constitutions have both written and unwritten elements. This means that the classification of constitutions into written and unwritten is largely unsatisfactory. No one document can contain all of the rules and procedures necessary for a Government to operate. All constitutions are comprised of written rules and procedures *and* the unwritten habits and practices. The written elements give stability and continuity; the unwritten elements allow for flexibility.

Rigid/flexible constitutions

3–05 To be of use to a nation, the constitution has to be amenable to change to meet the different aspirations of a changing society. A flexible constitution is one which can be changed by the same process as any other law. A rigid constitution is one which can only be changed by means of a special process. Most written constitutions fall into this category. However, the processes used for amending the constitution vary from easy to difficult and thus the degree of rigidity also varies. The constitution may require the consent of other bodies (e.g. the individual states of the USA) or of the people themselves in a referendum, as in the Republic of Ireland.

Some constitutions can be changed by the Legislature alone and others require the involvement of the Legislature and another body. A constitution which requires amendment by both Legislature and another body is called a supreme constitution. Examples of supreme constitutions occur in Australia, Ireland and Denmark. A supreme constitution means that all the organs of State are subordinate to the constitution. Amendments cannot be made without the use of the special process stated in the constitution and no one organ has the power to make these amendments. While a supreme constitution has much to commend it, it does make for difficulties if the amending process is too complex.

The UK constitution is flexible as, in theory, any part of it can be changed by an ordinary Act of Parliament. No matter how radical the change in the law, the courts would be unable to declare the legislation invalid on the ground that it was unconstitutional. The courts must give effect to the will of Parliament, where it is expressed in clear and unambiguous terms.

A flexible constitution has certain advantages:

- it can be adapted to suit political and cultural changes and so is less likely to fall out of date; and
- it can be temporarily set aside in times of national emergency.

There are also obvious dangers in having a flexible constitution:

- individual rights, which have been developed through ordinary legal processes, can be taken away with equal ease; and
- without political restraint, a Government with a large majority could push constitutional amendments through Parliament in order to undermine democracy and entrench its position of power.

Presidential and parliamentary constitutions

3–06 The distinction between a Presidential and a parliamentary Government is that a President will be merely the Head of State and will not sit in the Legislature. In a parliamentary constitution, there will be a Prime Minister who will, invariably, sit in the Legislature and a separate Head of State, such as a monarch. Presidential Executives are found mainly in those countries where the USA has had influence. The great majority of members of a parliamentary Executive, such as the UK Government, do not sit in the Parliament—they are civil servants and other officials. Only the heads of government departments sit in the Parliament. Other members of the Executive and the Judiciary are precluded from sitting as members of the Parliament.

Key Concepts

A **constitution** is the system of Government of a country. It will include all of the rules which establish and regulate the Government.
A constitution may be contained in a **formal document** or derived from a variety of legal sources.
 The constitution of the United Kingdom can be described as an **unwritten** and **flexible parliamentary constitution**.

SOURCES OF CONSTITUTIONAL LAW

The rules relating to the UK constitution can be found mainly in the ordinary sources of **3–07** law, i.e. legislation, judicial precedent, custom and authoritative writings. Acts of Parliament which have constitutional significance have no special legal status, they are ordinary Acts of Parliament subject to the same rules of interpretation and potentially subject to future repeal in the same way as any other Act of Parliament. Judicial precedent, as a source of law, is less important in constitutional law than in many other branches of law. This is because important questions of constitutional law seldom come before the courts. Textbooks are given more respect as a source of law in the field of constitutional law, as there are a number of influential writers. Custom also plays a greater role as many of the rules of constitutional law are not based on any of the more formal sources of law, but are merely based on convention.

Legislation

Although there is not a single document which comprises a constitution of the United **3–08** Kingdom, there are a substantial number of statutes which relate to the system of Government. Some important examples are:

- *The Bill of Rights and Claim of Right 1689*: the Bill of Rights by the English Parliament, and the equivalent Claim of Right by the Scottish Parliament, curbed the powers of the monarch to rule by prerogative right. The two instruments both declared that the monarch could not make laws or raise taxes, without the consent of Parliament.
- *Act of Settlement 1700*: this Act of the English Parliament was incorporated into the Acts of Union 1707. The 1700 Act settled that, on the death of Queen Anne, the protestant heirs of Sophia, Electress of Hanover should succeed to the throne, rather than the heir according to the constitution who was the deposed Catholic King James VII and II. The parliament enacted the statute with Anne's consent to ensure that the "Auld Pretender" could not succeed on her death. The Act also contained some restrictions on the power of the monarch which were complementary to the earlier Bill of Rights and Claim of Right of 1689.
- *Acts of Union 1707*: there were two Acts of Union, one passed by the Scottish Parliament and one by the English Parliament. The two Legislatures ceased to exist

on April 30, 1707 and the new Parliament of Great Britain came into being on May 1, 1707.

Other statutes of constitutional importance include:

- the European Communities Act 1972, which ratified the Treaty obligations signed by the Government for the United Kingdom to become a member of the European Communities on January 1, 1973;
- the Parliament Acts 1911 and 1949, which curtailed the power of the House of Lords to prevent the passage of a Government Bill;
- the Human Rights Act 1998, which incorporated the European Convention on Human Rights into the domestic law of the United Kingdom;
- the Scotland Act 1998, which created the Scottish Parliament and devolved to it the power to legislate over certain matters; and
- the Constitutional Reform Act 2005—establishing the Supreme Court and providing for greater separation of powers.

Although there are a significant number of statutes, which relate to the form and functions of the Government of the United Kingdom, they do not cover all matters of importance. If they were collected together they would not give a clear account of the constitution. The legislation must be considered in conjunction with the other sources.

Case law

3–09 The decisions of the superior courts may declare the law in relation to constitutional matters. Notable decisions include the case of *Entick v Carrington*,[3] in which it was held that a government minister had no power to issue search warrants and warrants for the arrest of those publishing seditious papers, and *Burmah Oil Co. v Lord Advocate*,[4] in which it was held that the Government was obliged to pay compensation where property of a subject had been destroyed.

The courts have no power to question the validity of an Act of Parliament, although there is a duty under the European Communities Act 1972 to disapply an Act of Parliament which clashes with EU law.[5] The courts can, however, mitigate the effect of changes in the law by interpreting Acts where the meaning is unclear or is disputed. Important principles of constitutional law may arise out of the interpretation of statutes.

Common law presumptions of legislative intent

3–10 These are established principles used by the courts when interpreting legislation. These principles are guides to interpretation rather than conclusive rules. One presumption is that an Act is not intended to have retrospective effect, unless there is a clear and unqualified indication that Parliament intended it to have such effect. This principle was applied in the case of *R. v Lambert*.

---

[3] (1765) 19 St. Tr. 1030.
[4] [1965] A.C. 75.
[5] European Communities Act 1972 s.3.

R. v Lambert
[2001] 3 All E.R. 577

A person who had been convicted at trial before the Human Rights Act 1998 came into force claimed on appeal that his rights under the Human Rights Act had been infringed. The House of Lords held that the provisions of the Human Rights Act did not create any rights before the date when it came into force.

Another presumption is that statutes do not bind the Crown unless it is expressly stated or there is a necessary implication. This principle was considered in the case of *Lord Advocate v Strathclyde Regional Council*.

Lord Advocate v Strathclyde Regional Council
1990 S.L.T. 158

The Property Services Agency was carrying out work on the perimeter fence at Faslane nuclear base, which caused some obstruction of the highway. No permission had been sought from, either the roads authority—Strathclyde Regional Council, or the planning authority—Dumbarton District Council. Both authorities took action to have the road cleared. In an appeal to the House of Lords, Strathclyde Regional Council and Dumbarton District Council argued, unsuccessfully, that the rule that statutes do not apply to the Crown, unless there was express provision to that effect, was limited to provisions which would affect prejudicially the property rights, interests and privileges of the Crown. The House of Lords held that the Crown was not bound by any statutory provision unless an intention to be bound was included in the Act by express words or necessary implication.

The principles of interpretation may change and develop over time. There used to be a principle that the courts could not look at *Hansard* (the record of parliamentary debates) in order to discover the intention behind the legislation. It was made clear in the case of *Pepper v Hart*[6] that the courts may now look at *Hansard* in order to ascertain the intention of the person who proposed the legislation.

Royal prerogative

This has been described as the "inherent legal attributes unique to the Crown". Prerogative powers originate from before the Union of the Crowns in 1603. The sovereign then held all executive power and was able to do what he or she wished. Parliament met only when the sovereign called it, and that could be infrequently. During the seventeenth century, the power of Parliament gradually increased and the sovereign's powers were transferred to his ministers and to Parliament itself. Today, most prerogative powers are exercised by the Queen, on the advice of her ministers.

3–11

Prerogative power is a legal source of law and, as such is recognised and enforced by the courts. The exercise of the power is controlled by convention and so, for example, although the appointment of ministers is made by the Queen, she does not choose them but is given their names by the Prime Minister. The Queen signs the formal proclamation

---

[6] [1993] A.C. 593.

62   *Understanding Scots Law*

that Parliament is to be dissolved and a General Election held, but the Prime Minister advises the Queen that he wishes to call an election and the date on which he wishes to be held. Technically, the Queen could refuse his request, but she is unlikely to do so unless she felt the Prime Minister was acting capriciously or that the country was in danger.

In the seventeenth century, the courts and Parliament laid down the limitations of today's prerogative powers. It was held that the king could not act as a judge, he had to dispense justice through his judges.[7] The king could only make laws through Parliament.[8] During this century there were many disputes between the king and Parliament, culminating of course in the Civil War, the beheading of Charles I and expulsion of Charles II. When the monarchy was restored, there was relative calm until Charles II died and his brother James came to the throne. James VII and II was a Roman Catholic and wanted his religion to be the official religion of the country. Parliament resisted this and James was forced to abdicate in 1688 and his sister Mary and her husband, William of Orange, were invited to take the throne. The offer of the throne was made by Parliament in the Bill of Rights 1689, which set out the powers of Parliament and declared that certain uses of the prerogative were illegal. In Scotland, the invitation to take the throne was passed by the Scottish Parliament and called the Claim of Right. Gradually, over the coming years, the right to use the prerogative was transformed from the king to his ministers and Parliament.

Key Concepts

Examples of the **Royal prerogative** include:

- appointment of ministers;
- dissolution of Parliament; and
- power of pardon.

The term "Royal prerogative" denotes attributes of the Crown, which do not apply to ordinary people. It is important to note that, although the prerogative can be abolished or changed by statute, no new prerogative powers can be created. This was established by the decision in *BBC v Johns*,[9] where Lord Diplock gave the leading judgment: "It is 350 years and a civil war too late for the Queen's courts to broaden the prerogative. The limits within which the executive government may impose obligations or restraints on citizens of the UK without any statutory authority are now well settled and incapable of extension."

A prerogative power may, however, be applied to new circumstances.

R. v Home Secretary Ex p. Northumbria Police Authority
[1989] Q.B. 26

The Home Secretary issued CS gas and baton rounds to all police forces in England and Wales. The local police authority objected to this and sought a declaration that the Home Secretary did not have the power to issue such equipment without

---

[7] *Prohibitions del Roy* (1607) 12 Co. Rep. 63.
[8] *The Case of Proclamations* (1611) 12 Co. Rep. 74.
[9] [1965] Ch. 32.

their consent. The court held that the Home Secretary did have such power, this being derived from the Police Act 1964 and the royal prerogative of keeping the Queen's peace. The Home Secretary could "supply equipment reasonably required by police forces to discharge their functions".

Authoritative works

When no other source of law is available, the courts may turn to the works of eminent **3–12** authors who have collected the law into one place. The works of Dicey are of particular importance.[10] Such works, however, never have binding force, they are persuasive only and will only be consulted when no other authority such as statute or case law is available.

Conventions

Conventions are non-legal "rules" of the constitution, which exist because they allow the **3–13** administration of Government to run more smoothly. Conventions usually evolve over a long period of time. They are not entrenched rules. They can develop and change as the habits and practices of Parliament change. They are obeyed because of the implications if they are not. For instance, the convention may relate to a constitutional principle: if the convention is ignored the principle may be put at risk. One example, of such a convention, is that the sovereign will not refuse Royal Assent to a Bill. Technically, she may refuse but this would cause a major constitutional crisis since she would then be going against her Government and Parliament. Queen Anne was the last sovereign to refuse to give a Bill of the Royal Assent, in 1708, when she refused to sign the Scottish Militia Bill.

The office of Prime Minister is based on convention. No statute states that there must be a Prime Minister, yet it is taken for granted that there will be a Prime Minister at the head of the Government. It is now also taken as convention that the Prime Minister will be a member of the House of Commons, not the Lords. The last peer to act as Prime Minister was Lord Salisbury in 1902. In 1962, the Earl of Home (Alex Douglas-Home) disclaimed his peerage and sought a seat in the Commons to continue as Prime Minister.

There is also a convention that each government minister should be a member of the Commons or a peer in the House of Lords. This is to ensure that government policies can be questioned by members of the two Houses. Where a minister is appointed and does not have a seat in Parliament, he must either fight a by-election to enter the Commons or be granted a peerage. In the summer of 1998, Gus McDonald was appointed as a minister in the Scottish Office. He was not an MP and so it was announced that he would be made a life peer later in the year.

When a General Election is held, and the outcome is that the Prime Minister who called the election has lost it, the convention is that he and his Government immediately resign unless he or she believes that a coalition Government may be formed. John Major resigned as Prime Minister on the day after the 1997 election. In 1974, Edward Heath waited three days before resigning, since he had been seeking the support of the Liberal MPs to allow him to carry on. In 2010 the result of the General Election gave no political party an overall majority in the House of Commons and so there was a delay of several days while negotiations took place to establish a coalition Government.

---

[10] A.V. Dicey, *The Law of the Constitution*, edited by E.C. Wade, 10th edn (Macmillan, 1959).

Consequences of a breach of a convention

3–14 Although the breach of a conventional rule does not have legal consequences, there may be political or constitutional implications. For instance, there is a convention that ministers do not make statements that are contrary to government policy. Should a minister do so, he is expected to resign from the Government. In 1982, Nicholas Fairbairn, the Solicitor-General for Scotland, resigned after making comments to the press on a case known as the *Glasgow Rape Case* the day before the Lord Advocate was due to give a statement on the matter to Parliament.

Occasionally, a convention will be deliberately disregarded and lead to drastic consequences. In 1909 and 1910, the House of Lords disregarded the convention that the House of Commons, as the elected chamber, should have the final say in the passing of Bills, particularly Money or Finance Bills. The Parliament Act 1911 was forced through Parliament restating the convention and redefining the relationship between the two Houses.

It can be argued that the rules under which the Government in the United Kingdom operates would be more transparent if conventions were formally written down. However, that would destroy their great usefulness, the ability to adapt and change. New conventions can be created to meet changing circumstances, for example there is a convention known as the Sewell Convention by which the Westminster Parliament will refrain from legislating in relation to Scotland on matters which have been devolved to the Scottish Parliament. Under the convention, the Westminster Parliament will only extend legislation on such matters to Scotland on the request of the Scottish Parliament.

> **Key Concepts**
>
> In the absence of a formal written constitution, the **sources of constitutional law** are the same as those of law in general, namely legislation, judicial precedent and custom.
>
> Although there are **Acts of Parliament** which have constitutional significance they are nevertheless ordinary Acts of Parliament.
>
> **Custom**, in the form of conventions, is an important source of operational rules.

DOCTRINES OF THE CONSTITUTION

Separation of powers

3–15 A system of Government is normally divided into three branches: the Legislature, the Executive and Judiciary. In the United Kingdom, these are represented by Parliament, the political Government and civil service, and the courts. The doctrine of separation of powers states that the functions carried out by each of the branches should be separate and there should be no overlapping or mixing of these functions. The doctrine was stated by the French jurist, Montesquieu, in 1748, who proposed that there should be a separation of the powers of government to ensure that one branch would not become so powerful that it could override the other two.

In the United Kingdom, the doctrine has not been developed to give such defined boundaries as in countries, such as the USA, where the constitutions clearly define the role of each branch of Government and establish the extent to which each branch is influenced and controlled by the others. Indeed, in the United Kingdom there is no significant separation of powers between the Legislature and the Executive, and the main importance of the doctrine is in relation to the independence of the judiciary.

Relationship between the Legislature and the Executive

In the United Kingdom the Legislature and the Executive have common members. For **3–16** instance, by convention, all members of the Government are also members of either the House of Commons or the House of Lords, so that they may be questioned on their policies and actions. There is a limit of 95 on the number of government ministers who may sit in the House of Commons. Since there are between 110 and 120 ministerial posts, it is obvious that some ministers must of necessity sit in the Lords. This ensures that the Government must include the House of Lords in its work.

There are also rules which prevent members of the executive forming too great a portion of the membership of the Legislature. Civil servants, members of the non-departmental public bodies, members of the armed forces and other government agencies are prevented from sitting in the House of Commons by means of the House of Commons Disqualification Act 1975. This is recognition of the importance of keeping the lawmakers separate from those who implement the law.

Until 2003 the Lord Chancellor was a prominent member of all three branches. In the Legislature he acted as the Speaker of the House of Lords. In the Executive, he was a member of the Cabinet and had his own government department. He was also head of the Judiciary in England and Wales, as well as a Lord of Appeal in Ordinary in the House of Lords. The Constitutional Reform Act 2005 increased the independence of the judiciary by reforming the office of Lord Chancellor, and establishing the Lord Chief Justice as head of the judiciary of England and Wales.

One of the functions of Parliament is to pass legislation, but this function is shared with the Executive as government departments may pass subordinate legislation. The Executive controls the Legislature by establishing policy and controlling the Parliamentary schedule; but the Legislature also controls the Executive by exerting its power to prevent legislation being passed and ultimately it can bring about the downfall of a government by passing a vote of no confidence in it. This last occurred in 1979 when James Callaghan's Labour Government was forced to call a General Election. Members of the Government owe their position to the support of their party in Parliament and thus the Governing party can exert influence over the Government.

Independence of the Judiciary

The independence of the Judiciary is arguably the most important part of the doctrine. **3–17** The Lord Chancellor has responsibility under the Constitutional Reform Act 2005 to defend the independence of the judiciary.

Recent constitutional changes have also increased the independence of the Judiciary. Following the incorporation of the European Convention on Human Rights into domestic law by the Scotland Act 1998 and the Human Rights Act 1998, it became apparent that changes would have to be made in order to ensure that the right under art.6, to a trial before an independent and unbiased tribunal, could be sustained.[11] The level of political control over appointment of judges has been reduced by the introduction of a Judicial Appointments Board in Scotland. The Board has 10 members, half from the legal profession and half from commerce and academia.[12] A Judicial Appointments Commission,

---

[11] *Clancy v Caird (No.2)*, 2000 S.C. 441; 2000 S.L.T. 546; 2000 S.C.L.R. 526, Ex Div; *Starrs v Ruxton*; sub nom. *Ruxton v Starrs*, 2000 J.C. 208; 2000 S.L.T. 42, HCJ Appeal.

[12] Bail, Judicial Appointments etc. (Scotland) Act 2000.

for the selection of judges in England and Wales, was established by the Constitutional Reform Act 2005.

Judges need not fear that their salaries may be reduced because they have displeased either the Legislature or the Executive. Judges' salaries are a charge on the consolidated fund and do not require the annual authorisation of Parliament; they are not, therefore, debated in the House. The judges fulfil an important role, in ensuring that the rights of the individual citizen are not infringed by an Executive exceeding its powers. The independence of the Judiciary is thus a check on the power of the Executive.

The functions of the Executive and Judiciary do, however, mingle in some respects. For instance, the Executive may make decisions, which have a judicial element; for example the reporter in a public inquiry has to weigh the competing arguments and come to a decision. Tribunals are administrative authorities but they fulfil a judicial function and are regarded as part of the machinery of justice. In Scotland, the sheriff has administrative duties as well as extensive judicial functions.

The Judiciary and the Legislature are less intermingled. Members of the Judiciary are disqualified from membership of the House of Commons by the 1975 Act. The recent establishment of the Supreme Court achieved a complete separation between the United Kingdom's senior judges and the House of Lords, emphasising the independence of the law lords. In August 2009 the Justices moved out of the House of Lords building (where they sat as the Appellate Committee of the House of Lords) into their own building on the opposite side of Parliament Square. They sat for the first time as a Supreme Court in October 2009.

Judges may not review the validity of an Act of Parliament, although this convention has now been modified by the UK's membership of the European Union, where it is possible for a British court to declare that an Act of the UK Parliament is incompatible with EU law.[13] Under the Human Rights Act 1998 the courts may declare that an Act of Parliament is incompatible with the European Convention on Human Rights, but such a declaration does not mean that they may disapply the Act in question.

On occasions, the Judiciary exercises legislative functions. In Scotland, the Court of Session and the High Court of Justiciary have certain equitable powers, which enable them to declare certain actions to be unlawful or to give a remedy where none is otherwise available. The exercise of the *nobile officium* (equitable power) of the Court of Session allows the law to be implemented in circumstances where a technicality would otherwise have prevented it. The power may also be used, albeit very sparingly, to insert a provision into a statute or document where this provision was accidentally omitted or was unforeseen.

Wan Ping Nam v German Federal Republic Minister of Justice
1972 S.L.T. 220

A member of a ship's crew was accused of a murder, which had been committed while the ship was at sea. When the ship docked at Greenock, the crewman was taken into custody and held pending extradition to Germany where the ship was registered. The relevant extradition statute gave relief to persons so imprisoned by stating that they could apply to the sheriff court for a writ of habeas corpus. This writ, however, is unknown in Scots law and the court therefore invoked the *nobile officium* to give effect to the rights Parliament obviously intended to give.

---

[13] European Communities Act 1972 s.3.

The High Court of Justiciary has a similar equitable power whereby it can declare acts to be criminal. Again, the power is used sparingly although it was seen in *Khaliq v HM Advocate*.

Khaliq v HM Advocate
1984 J.C. 23

A shop-keeper was found guilty of selling "glue-sniffing kits" to children. This offence had not been previously recognised in Scots law, but the High Court of Justiciary decided that it was the type of behaviour considered by the common law to be harmful.

Key Concepts

The concept of **separation of powers,** states that each branch of Government, the Legislature, the Executive and Judiciary, should be separate and have independent status, and no individual should serve in more than one branch.
  Separation of powers is a device to control and prevent the **abuse of power**.

Rule of law

The rule of law is not easy to define, but it could be said to mean that the Government **3–18** must obey the law and should not act beyond the powers granted to it or without lawful authority. The idea of rule of law, was formulated by A.V. Dicey in *The Law of the Constitution* in 1885. He identified three aspects of the British constitution, at that time, which he felt embodied the rule of law:

(1) Absence of arbitrary power.
(2) Equality before the law.
(3) The constitution is the result of the ordinary law of the land.

Absence of arbitrary power

Dicey defined the rule of law as the "absolute supremacy or predominance of regular law **3–19** as opposed to the influence of arbitrary power". It is unclear exactly what he meant by "regular law". Lawful authority normally means authority derived from a statute and it is possible that Parliament will legislate in such a way that the Executive is given very wide discretionary powers, so that virtually any exercise of the power is capable of being considered within the law. The rule of law means that discretionary powers need to be controlled by ensuring that government business is carried on using rules and principles, which restrict the use of discretionary power. An example of abuse of power by the Executive arose in the case of *Congreve v Home Office*.

Congreve v Home Office
[1976] Q.B. 629

In anticipation of a large rise in the cost of television licences many people renewed their licences one month early so that they would obtain their licences at the previous price. The minister decided to revoke any licences which had been prematurely renewed, thus forcing payment of the higher fee. Lord Denning stated that if the minister revoked a licence "without giving reasons, or for no good reason, the courts can set aside his revocation and restore the licence. It would be a misuse of the power conferred on him by Parliament: and these courts have authority—and, I would add, the duty—to correct a misuse of power by a minister of his department."

The classic case on rule of law is the English case of *Entick v Carrington*.[14]

Entick v Carrington
(1765) 19 State T.R. 1030

The King's messengers executed a warrant from the Secretary of State to arrest Entick and to seize his books and papers. However, to do so, they broke and entered his house and took away papers. Entick sued for trespass to his house and goods. The defendants said that the warrant was commonly used and had been executed before without challenge and that the power of seizure was essential to the Government. The court held that since there was no statute or judicial precedent upholding the legality of the warrant, the practice was illegal.

The act of a public authority may be upheld if it was in accordance with the law in the sense that it did not infringe any law. This was seen in *Malone v Metropolitan Police Commissioner*.[15]

Malone v Metropolitan Police Commissioner
[1979] Ch. 344

The tapping of a suspect's telephone was held to be lawful, since it was carried out on the authority of the Home Secretary using the normal procedure. Malone subsequently successfully complained to the European Court of Human Rights that the telephone tapping was a violation of art.8 of the European Convention on Human Rights, the right to respect for private life and correspondence. Legislation was subsequently passed providing legal authority for the interception of communications.[16]

The rule of law will of course be undermined if the Government indulges in breaches of the law. One breach of the doctrine occurred where it appeared that the ill treatment of

---

[14] *Entick v Carrington* (1765) 19 State T.R. 1030 (Court of Common Pleas).
[15] *Malone v Metropolitan Police Commissioner* [1979] Ch. 344.
[16] Interception of Communications Act 1985.

terrorist suspects in Northern Ireland was officially but unlawfully authorised. The issue was raised in the ECHR, which held that the procedures contravened art.3 of the European Convention on Human Rights, in that they amounted to inhuman and degrading treatment, but they did not amount to torture.[17]

It is also important that the Government should comply with judgments of the courts and, in this regard, it is contrary to the principle of the rule of law that the Government should introduce retrospective legislation to mitigate the effects of a decision made against it.

Burmah Oil Co Ltd v Lord Advocate
[1965] A.C. 75

The House of Lords held that compensation should be awarded to the Burmah Oil Co for property which had been destroyed by the British military authorities during wartime, to prevent it falling into enemy hands. The company's success in this case meant that others in a similar position would have a claim against the Government; these claims would have amounted to many millions of pounds, which the Government was reluctant to pay. The War Damage Act 1965 was passed to prevent such compensation being payable. The Act was retrospective in that actions instituted before the Act was passed were to be dismissed by the courts.

The Government has used its legislative powers to pass other statutes which have retrospective effect. One example is the War Crimes Act 1991, which allows charges to be brought for murder, manslaughter or culpable homicide, against a person in the United Kingdom, who was not necessarily a UK citizen at the time of the alleged offence, who committed the offence during the Second World War in Germany or in territory occupied by Germany and where the offence constituted a violation of the laws and customs of war. Retrospective penal legislation of this type may contravene art.7 of the European Convention on Human Rights.

Equality before the law

According to Dicey the rule of law means: "equality before the law, or the equal subjection **3–20** of all classes to the ordinary law of the land administered by the ordinary law courts".

His idea was that officials should not be exempt from the obedience to the law and should comply with the decisions of the courts. Dicey's ideas have been criticised as lacking foresight and indeed accuracy. Even at the time he was writing, certain people had immunity from suit and prosecution, for instance, the monarch, diplomats, MPs and judges. The immunity of the Crown, as opposed to the monarch in her personal capacity, has been changed by the Crown Proceedings Act 1947 and the Crown is now, in normal circumstances, as liable to suit for contract or delict as any ordinary citizen. However, some immunities still exist. Section 10 of the 1947 Act prevents an action for delict, where a member of the armed forces has been killed or injured by another and the Secretary of State has certified that the injury was one attributable to service for the purposes of pension entitlement. This section threw up many injustices and it was put into suspense by the Crown Proceedings (Armed Forces) Act 1987, but it can be revived by the Secretary of State if he thinks it expedient to do so. The immunities of the Crown have largely

---

[17] *Ireland v UK* (1978) E.H.R.R. 25.

disappeared, including in England and Wales, the immunity of a minister from the effects of an injunction.

> ### M v Home Office
> #### [1994] 1 A.C. 377
>
> The Home Secretary was found to be in contempt of court by ignoring an injunction preventing the deportation of a Zairian national who had claimed political asylum. This case however has not been followed in Scotland, where the Court of Session considered that interdicts against the Crown were prohibited by the Crown Proceedings Act 1947 s.21.[18]

There must be open access to the courts, or tribunals, so that a citizen may obtain redress of his grievance. In a civilised society, this also means that access to this redress should not depend on your wealth; a State will assist a complainant who has only modest, or less than modest, wealth to bring their action to court. If this does not happen, then only those with financial resources will have access to justice.

The constitution is the result of the ordinary law of the land

3–21 Dicey placed a lot of emphasis on the fact that the main source of the individual's rights and freedoms was decisions of the courts. Statute law has steadily encroached on the common law in this area and the citizen now has many more explicit rights than Dicey had in mind. The incorporation of the European Convention on Human Rights and Fundamental Freedoms into the domestic law of the United Kingdom, by the Human Rights Act 1998, is an important milestone in the development of civil rights in the United Kingdom, as it provides a set of principles by which to test whether the actions of government are according to law.

Other theories of the rule of law

3–22 In 1959, the International Commission of Jurists compiled the Declaration of Delhi. This declared that the purpose of all law was respect for "the supreme value of human personality". The declaration set out minimum standards, which included representative government, basic human freedoms, the right to a fair trial and an independent Judiciary. This is a wider description of the rule of law than Dicey's and it probably represents what most people think of as the rule of law.

Laws should be open and made known by proper and sufficient publication and publicity. In the United Kingdom it is generally held that "ignorance of the law is no excuse" and that everyone has access to the law. This of course is somewhat unreasonable; there are so many laws, rules and regulations being created by the Executive that it is impossible for the ordinary citizen to know them all. It should also be remembered that many guidelines and rules are not published at all, and so the citizen cannot find out to which rules he is subject.

---

[18] *McDonald v Secretary of State for Scotland*, 1994 S.L.T. 692.

The rule of law and the European Convention on Human Rights

The European Convention on Human Rights and Fundamental Freedoms was incorpo- **3–23** rated into the domestic law of the United Kingdom by the Human Rights Act 1998. One effect of this incorporation is that the jurisprudence of the ECHR is now taken into account by the UK courts. The tests which have been applied by the ECHR, and which are now applied by domestic courts, include a test based on the rule of law.

Key Concepts

Restrictions on qualified convention rights are deemed to be justified, if they meet the following four criteria:

(1) they must be lawful;
(2) they must be intended to pursue a legitimate purpose;
(3) they must be "necessary in a democratic society"; and
(4) they must not be discriminatory.

The test of lawfulness is based on a premise that interference with Convention rights is prima facie unlawful, therefore any interference must be specifically authorised. In giving specific authorisation for an infringement of a right, "the law must indicate the scope of any such discretion conferred on the competent authorities and the manner of its exercise with sufficient clarity, having regard to the legitimate aim of the measure in question, to give the individual adequate protection against arbitrary interference".[19] This is a restatement of Dicey's first principle of the rule of law as, "the absolute supremacy or predominance of regular law as opposed to the influence of arbitrary power".[20]

Key Concepts

The **rule of law** means that government must be conducted according to law. **Dicey** identified three aspects of the British Constitution which were indicative of the rule of law:

(1) absence of arbitrary power;
(2) equality before the law; and
(3) the constitution is the result of the ordinary law of the land.

Supremacy of Parliament

The doctrine of supremacy of Parliament is also called "sovereignty of Parliament". This **3–24** idea refers to the supreme legal and political authority of Parliament to make laws for the United Kingdom. The doctrine, of course, has been modified by the effect of the UK's membership of the European Union. Devolution of legislative power within the United Kingdom also has implications for the doctrine of supremacy of Parliament. An Act of

---

[19] *Malone v UK* (1985) 7 E.H.R.R. 14, para.68.
[20] A.V. Dicey, *The Law of the Constitution,* edited by E.C.S. Wade, 10th edn (Macmillan, 1959), p.202.

Parliament has to be passed by the House of Lords, the House of Commons and receive the Royal Assent. Although an Act may be passed without the consent of the House of Lords, the power to do so derives from the Parliament Acts 1911 and 1949. The House of Commons and the House of Lords acting alone may not pass statutes; the three elements of the "Queen in Parliament" are required for a statute to claim its legitimacy. A resolution of one of the Houses, or a proclamation by the Crown, does not have force of law unless a statute or subordinate legislation is enacted to bring it into law.

Traditional doctrine

3–25 The traditional doctrine of supremacy of Parliament has three aspects:

> (1) Parliament can make or unmake any law it pleases;
> (2) no other body may question the validity of an Act of Parliament; and
> (3) no Parliament can bind its successors.

Parliament can make or unmake any law it pleases

3–26 This aspect of the doctrine states that Parliament is the supreme lawmaker and that there is no matter which cannot be legislated for. However, the proposition is limited by the realities of what Parliament can and cannot do. It is, for instance, possible for Parliament to legislate to ban smoking on the streets of Paris. The reality is that such a law would be neither practicable nor possible. Such a law would be absurd and could not be enforced. Parliament is thus restricted by its territorial jurisdiction, in that it can only make effective laws for those areas it controls. However, Parliament can pass laws so that a person abroad committing a particular offence under UK law may be tried in this country. So in recent years, legislation has been passed making it illegal for a British citizen to engage in procuring children for sexual purposes. The War Crimes Act 1991 is a further example of this type of legislation.

Parliament may extend the boundaries of the State by legislation. So in 1965 the Continental Shelf Act was passed to give the UK sovereignty over the continental shelf out to 200 miles from the coast, or to a half-way mark where the coastal waters of another State intervened. In 1972, the Island of Rockall Act was passed to extend British sovereignty to that small island in the Atlantic Ocean and thus ensure control over any mineral wealth on the surrounding seabed.

Parliament may legislate to extend its own life. During both of the World Wars, Parliament extended its life so as to prevent the holding of a General Election during the war. Parliament has altered the succession to the throne by the Act of Settlement 1700 and again by His Majesty's Declaration of Abdication Act 1936.

No other body may question the validity of an Act of Parliament

3–27 This has been interpreted as meaning that the courts may not question an Act's validity and the courts have indeed shown considerable reluctance to interfere in how a statute has been passed.

British Railways Board v Pickin
[1974] A.C. 765

In this case it was alleged that there had been procedural errors made during the passage of a private Act of Parliament. The courts, however, would not challenge the Act on the basis that it was prima facie valid. The House of Lords held that the respondent was not entitled to examine proceedings in Parliament to show that fraud had occurred and that any question as to the validity of the statute would require to be investigated by "the High Court of Parliament"—in other words by the internal procedures of the two Houses.

The courts will, however, now look at the proceedings in Parliament where they are considering the interpretation of a statute and there is some ambiguity in the terms of the statute and the intention of its proposers. The courts will then look at the Official Record of proceedings in the House, *Hansard*, to determine the words used and their meaning. However, only the words of the proposers of the Bill, whether minister or private member, may be considered.[21]

No Parliament can bind its successors

This element of the doctrine has itself a number of aspects flowing from the supposition **3–28** that the ultimate lawmaker cannot bind itself or its successors, or it will then be subject to some higher law and thus not be the ultimate lawmaker.

Doctrine of implied repeal

A later Act of Parliament will repeal an earlier contradictory statute by implication. The **3–29** courts recognised the principle of implied repeal in *Ellen Street Estates Ltd v Minister of Health*.

Ellen Street Estates Ltd v Minister of Health
[1934] 1 K.B. 590

The case involved the assessment of compensation, for property which had been acquired under a compulsory purchase scheme. The wording of the Acquisition of Land (Assessment of Compensation) Act 1919 s.7 said that the provisions of any Act authorising compulsory acquisition: "shall . . . have effect subject to this Act, and so far as inconsistent with this Act those provisions shall cease to have or shall not have effect."

It was argued that this Act applied to later Acts, in particular to the Housing Act 1925. The Court of Appeal however rejected this argument and held that the 1919 Act had been overridden by the provisions of the later Acts since the terms of the 1919 Act could not control future Parliaments. This meant that the higher rate of compensation authorised by the 1925 Act had to be paid.

---

[21] *Pepper v Hart* [1992] 3 W.L.R. 1032.

Independence statutes

3–30 There must be some limitations to the exercise of this element of the doctrine. For instance, from the 1940s to 1960s, Parliament granted many previous colonies their independence by passing a statute for that purpose. It would be ludicrous to suppose that Parliament now could repeal any of those independence statutes. Parliament had itself acknowledged the reality of this situation. The Statute of Westminster 1931 s.4 enacted that Parliament would not legislate for a dominion unless the dominion so requested and then consented to such legislation. Under the Scotland Act 1998 powers to legislate over certain matters have been devolved to the Scottish Parliament, while other powers have been reserved to the UK Parliament.[22] It is unclear whether the Scotland Act has the same status as the independence statutes.

Statutes with "special status"

3–31 In recent years there has been an increasing recognition of a hierarchy of statutes. In *Thoburn v Sunderland City Council*,[23] Laws L.J. distinguished between ordinary statues and constitutional statutes. He defined a constitutional statute as one that would affect the legal relationship between the individual and the State or would increase or diminish the scope of fundamental rights.

The Acts identified as constitutional statutes are:

- Magna Carta 1215;
- Bill of Rights 1689;
- Acts of Union;
- European Communities Act 1972;
- Human Rights Act 1998;
- Scotland Act 1988; and
- Government of Wales Act 1998.

Such statutes are no longer subject to implied repeal as they protect the special status of constitutional rights. They can only be repealed by express repeal.

The Union with Ireland Act 1801 established the United Kingdom of Great Britain and Ireland and its wording implied that the Union was intended to be permanent. However, after a century of conflict, the Government of Ireland Act 1920 was passed to establish two Parliaments for Ireland—one for Northern Ireland and one for the South. The Irish Free State was subsequently established in 1922, thus finally breaking the terms of the Act of Union 1801. Independence was granted to the southern part of the island by the Ireland Act 1949. This Act also made provision for the future governance and status of Northern Ireland.

Unlike the Irish Union, the Union between Scotland and England still subsists and in Scotland at least is the subject of a belief that the Act of Union 1707 has a special status not found in other statutes. The Treaty of Union set up a new Parliament of Great Britain and appears to state that this Parliament could freely legislate in most areas of law, but acknowledged there would be some areas, which were declared to be fundamental and unalterable. The Treaty was ratified by an Act of each Parliament, first in Scotland, then in England; the English Parliament recognised and agreed the terms of the Treaty and the contents of the Scottish Act. It could, therefore, be said that it agreed that certain parts of

---

[22] For details see Chapter 1.
[23] [2002] EWHC 195.

the Treaty were accepted as being unalterable. However, one of the unalterable provisions was repealed by the Universities (Scotland) Act 1853, which abolished the requirement that University professors should be Presbyterians. Article XIX of the Treaty retained the Court of Session and the High Court Justiciary as the supreme court of Scotland: "subject nevertheless to such regulations for the better administration of justice as shall be made by the Parliament of Great Britain." The courts in Scotland have reserved their judgment on the hypothetical case of Parliament trying to pass legislation, which would seek to abolish the Scottish Supreme Courts.

MacCormick v Lord Advocate
1953 S.C. 396

This case arose out of the use of the royal title "Queen Elizabeth II" in Scotland when there had not been a Queen Elizabeth I. The challenge failed on the ground that a title is no more than that. It carries no great legal significance. However, Lord President Cooper took the opportunity to consider the doctrine of supremacy of Parliament. He described the doctrine as a "distinctively English principle which has no counterpart in Scottish constitutional law". He went on to say:

"Considering that the Union legislation extinguished the Parliaments of Scotland and England and replaced them by a new Parliament, I have difficulty in seeing why it should have been supposed that the new Parliament of Great Britain must inherit all the peculiar characteristics of the English Parliament but none of the Scottish Parliament, as if that happened in 1707 was that Scottish representatives were admitted to the Parliament of England. That is not what was done. Further, the Treaty and associated legislation, by which the Parliament of Great Britain was brought into being as the successor of the expressly reserve to the Parliament of Great Britain powers of subsequent modification, and other clauses which either contain no such power or emphatically exclude subsequent alteration by declarations that the provision shall be fundamental and unalterable in all time coming, or declarations of a like effect."

"I have not found in the Union legislation any provision that the Parliament of Great Britain should be 'absolutely sovereign' in the sense that Parliament should be free to alter the Treaty at will."

The Scottish courts have tended to be reluctant to enter into debate regarding the status of the Treaty of Union.[24]

Robbie the Pict v Hingston (No.2)
1998 S.L.T. 1201

Robbie was charged with failing to pay the toll to cross the Skye bridge. He maintained that the toll was a tax or excise within the meaning of art.XVIII of the Treaty of Union. There was a contravention of the Treaty because the tax was being

---

[24] See, e.g. *Gibson v Lord Advocate*, 1975 S.L.T. 134; *Sillars v Smith*, 1982 S.L.T. 539.

imposed in Scotland in a different way from similar provisions in England, where bridge tolls were only imposed where there was an alternative route which could be taken. On appeal to the High Court of Justiciary, it was held that a road toll was not an excise within the meaning of art.XVIII. However, Lord Coulsfield, giving the Opinion of the Court said that art.XVIII might prohibit a different application of identical legislation between England and Scotland.

International law

3–32   British courts do not recognise international laws as limiting the supremacy of Parliament. International law and domestic law are two separate systems and international law has no status within the United Kingdom, unless and until it is incorporated into UK law by means of legislation. This is called a dualist approach and is contrasted with the monist approach whereby international law is automatically incorporated into domestic law, with no requirements for domestic legislation to be passed. Such international law then takes precedence over the domestic legislation. The monist approach is used in France and Italy.

Ratification of a Treaty by the Government will not incorporate a Treaty into UK law. Legislation is also required. The European Convention on Human Rights is a good example of this. For many years, persons claiming a breach of the Convention in the British courts had no case because the Convention was not part of UK law. The British Government ratified the Convention in 1966 and British citizens could then take a complaint against the UK Government to the ECHR. However, it was not until the European Convention on Human Rights was incorporated into domestic law, by the Scotland Act 1998 and the Human Rights Act 1998 that actions could based on rights under the European Convention on Human Rights could be brought before the UK courts.

If a Treaty is to be ratified by the Government, but does not require to be brought into UK law, the text of it is laid before Parliament before the ratification takes place. This ensures that the Legislature is aware of what the Executive is doing. The courts will not interfere in the ratification process since it is seen as a prerogative of the Crown and not justiciable.

Blackburn v Attorney General
[1971] 1 W.L.R. 1037

The court did not recognise the contents of the EEC Treaty, which was about to be ratified by the Crown, that is the British Government. Lord Denning remarked famously that the courts could not look at the Treaty until it was embodied in a statute.

Where domestic law conflicts with international law, the courts will always implement the domestic law.

Mortensen v Peters
(1906) 8 F. (J.) 93

The Scandinavian captain of a fishing vessel was caught fishing in the Moray Firth and charged with, and convicted of, fishing illegally contrary to bylaws made under the Herring Fishery (Scotland) Act 1889. At the time of the offence, the boat was outside the three-mile limit, in international waters. However, the byelaw prohibited fishing in the whole of the Moray Firth, most of which was in international waters. On appeal, the High Court of Justiciary upheld the conviction; the terms of the legislation were unambiguous and affected everyone including foreigners. This decision has been upheld in other cases, including *Croft v Dunphy PC*[25] where Lord Mac-Millan said:

"Legislation of Parliament, even in contravention of generally acknowledged principles of international law, is binding upon, and must be enforced by, the courts of this country."

Although the courts try to interpret domestic law as not being in conflict with international law, if there is a conflict, the court will uphold the domestic law even if this results in the United Kingdom breaching a Treaty obligation.

Parliamentary supremacy and EU law

The United Kingdom became a member of the EC on January 1, 1973, having ratified the Accession Treaty in 1972 and having implemented it by means of the European Communities Act 1972. Parliament recognised the special status of the EC Treaties in the Act and, in particular, recognised the common requirements and objectives of EU law. **3–33**

The European Communities Act 1972 s.2(1) incorporates all existing EU law into UK law and states:

"(1) All such rights, powers, liabilities, obligations and restrictions from time to time created or arising by or under the Treaties. And all such remedies and procedures from time to time provided for by or under the Treaties, as in accordance with the Treaties are without further enactment to be given legal effect or used in the UK, shall be recognized and available in law, and be enforced, allowed and followed accordingly; and the expression 'enforceable EU right' and similar expressions shall be read as referring to one to which this subsection applies."

Future EU law is given effect by virtue of s.2(4):

"(4) The provision that may be under subsection (2) above includes subject to Schedule 2 to this Act, any such provision (of any such extent) might be made by Act of Parliament, and any enactment passed or to be passed, other than one contained in this Part of this Act, shall be construed and have effect subject to the foregoing provisions of this section ..."

The Act gives power to the Government to amend existing legislation or create new legislation by means of statutory instruments (s.2(2)). This has the beneficial effect of

---

[25] [1933] A.C. 156.

allowing changes to be made quickly. However, some matters may require to be enacted by statute rather than subordinate legislation; for instance, where an EU Directive has to be implemented with retrospective effect, this could only be achieved by passing a statute. Section 3(1) of the Act states that questions of the interpretation of EU law are to be determined: "in accordance with the principles laid down by any relevant decision of the European Court". Thus acknowledging the primacy of the European Court of Justice.

Section 2(1) clearly provides that EU law in existence on January 1, 1973 is to be given effect; this, therefore, provides that if a rule of EU law conflicts with a domestic law made before January 1, 1973, the EU law will prevail. There is no difficulty with this; the principle in fact occurs with the traditional doctrine of implied repeal that a later Act, in this case the European Communities Act 1972, will prevail over a conflicting earlier Act.

The problem occurs when a provision of EU law is inconsistent with a post-1972 Act. The ECJ has always made it clear that it views EU law as supreme over domestic law. This has given rise to difficulties in reconciling the doctrine of supremacy of Parliament with the idea of supremacy of EU law. Where a statute is passed after January 1, 1973 and conflicts with EU law, the British courts endeavour to interpret the statute so as to conform with the EU law. The words in UK statutes are interpreted as widely as possible to achieve consistency.

Where a UK statute cannot be construed in conformity with EU law, EU law must be applied in preference to the UK statute. This principle was asserted by the House of Lords in *R. v Secretary of State for Transport Ex p. Factortame.*

R. v Secretary of State for Transport Ex p. Factortame
[1990] 2 A.C. 85

The EC common fishing policy required that fishing vessels from all member states should have equal access to the fishing grounds. When fishing conservation measures were introduced, a number of Spanish vessels were counted as part of the British quota because their owners had registered as British Companies. The Government introduced the Merchant Shipping Act 1988 to restrict registration so that only those with a genuine connection with the United Kingdom could register as British boats. *Factortame* challenged the regulations as being incompatible with EC law.

The House of Lords held unanimously that: "By virtue of section 2(4) of the European Communities Act 1972, Part II of the Act of 1988 is to be construed and take effect subject to directly enforceable Community rights and those rights are, by section 2(1) of the Act of 1972 to be 'recognised and available in law ...'."

The case then went to the ECJ for a preliminary ruling and, on its return to the House of Lords, Lord Bridge declared: "Whatever the limitation of its sovereignty Parliament accepted when it enacted the European Communities Act 1972 was entirely voluntary. Under ... the Act of 1972 it has always been clear that it was the duty of a UK court, when delivering final judgement, to override any rule of national law found to be in conflict with any directly enforceable rule of community law."

The principle of the supremacy of EU law was further reinforced in *R. v Secretary of State for Employment Ex p. Equal Opportunities Commission*[26] where the provisions of the Employment Protection (Consolidation) Act 1978 were held to be incompatible with

---

[26] [1995] 1 A.C. 1.

art.119 EC and with Council directives. In this case, there was no reference to the ECJ; the British courts decided for the first time without prompting from the ECJ that British statutory provisions were unenforceable.

The political realities of EU membership dictate that so long as the United Kingdom wishes to remain in the EU, the supremacy of Parliament must if necessary give way to the greater authority of EU law. However, the United Kingdom's continued membership of the EU is dependent on Parliament not passing another statute to take the United Kingdom out of the EU. As such then, the doctrine is intact although it depends for its validity not on its legality, but on the political views of the Government of the day.

Key Concepts

The **Westminster Parliament** has supreme political and legal authority to make laws for the United Kingdom.
The traditional doctrine of **supremacy of Parliament** has a number of elements:

- Parliament is the supreme lawmaker in the United Kingdom.
- An Act of Parliament is the highest source of law in the United Kingdom.
- No Parliament can bind it successors.

UNITED KINGDOM PARLIAMENT

Key Concepts

Parliament consists of: 3–34

- the sovereign;
- the House of Lords; and
- the House of Commons.

The monarch

The Queen is a part of Parliament in a formal sense. All Acts of Parliament require the   3–35
approval of the "Queen in Parliament", i.e. they must be passed by both Houses of Parliament and receive the Royal Assent before they can become law. The Queen also summons Parliament, prorogues it at the end of each annual session and dissolves Parliament at the end of its five-year term.

House of Lords

The House of Lords consists of unelected members. They are members either because they   3–36
hold a hereditary peerage, or because they have been appointed by the Crown. There are four main categories of members and, until 1999, the total membership was around 1,200.

The numbers in March 1998 were:

- 759 hereditary peers;
- 26 spiritual peers, e.g. Archbishop of Canterbury, Bishop of London;
- 464 life peers; and

- 26 Law Lords (serving and retired).

Life peers are created under the Life Peerages Act 1958. These are conferred on the recipient for the duration of their life and do not pass to their heir on their death. Life peers tend to be working members of the House and participate in its work.

Reform of the House of Lords

3–37 The first stage of reform was achieved by the House of Lords Act 1999 which removed the automatic right of a hereditary peer to take a seat in the House of Lords. Hereditary peers have not all been banished from the House. In addition to the Earl Marshal and the Lord Great Chamberlain, 90 hereditary peers continue to participate as active members of the House until the reforms are complete. Fifteen of the 90 places are taken by hereditary peers, who are office holders and 75 were elected by a ballot, under which places were allocated to reflect the balance of political parties.

> **Lord Gray's Motion**
> **2000 S.C. (H.L.) 46**
>
> The Treaty of Union included a provision that there would be 16 Scottish peers in the House of Lords. The removal of the right of hereditary peers to participate in the business of the House was, therefore, challenged as being contrary to the terms of the Treaty of Union. The House of Lords Committee of Privileges held, however, that the Treaty of Union did not provide an unalterable restraint on the powers of Parliament.

Hereditary peers who are not members of the House of Lords may stand for election to the House of Commons.

A Royal Commission on the Reform of the House of Lords was established in 1999 to "consider and make recommendations on the role and function of the second chamber, and to recommend the method or combination of methods of composition required to constitute a second chamber fit for that role and those functions".[27] The Royal Commission recommended that the House should have around 550 peers serving a fixed term. The membership should comprise a combination of elected members and members appointed by an independent appointments commission. A Government White Paper in 2001,[28] accepted the Royal Commission's broad framework for the composition of the House, but agreement on the details and the procedures for reform has proved to be difficult to achieve. In a White Paper in 2007 the Government proposed to hold a free vote on House of Lords reform, if re-elected, during the next Parliament.[29] The White Paper proposed a hybrid House of 50 per cent elected members and 50 per cent appointed members, including 20 per cent non party-political and 30 per cent party-political appointments. The Government favoured an election system based on the regions used for elections to the European Parliament, with members being elected for long periods. Regardless of the outcome of the free vote on the composition of the second chamber, the Government made an explicit commitment in its 2005 manifesto to end the right of the hereditary peers to sit in the House of Lords.

---

[27] *Royal Commission on Reform of the House of Lords, A House for the Future* (1999), Cm.4534.
[28] *The House of Lords Completing the Reform* (2001), Cm.5291.
[29] *The House of Lords: Reform* (2007), Cm.7027.

Appointment to the House of Lords

The Prime Minister has the power to decide the overall number of new peers created and **3–38** the balance between the parties. He also appoints party-political peers, in consultation with the other party leaders. Following the recommendations of the Royal Commission on the Reform of the House of Lords, a House of Lords Appointments Commission was established on a non-statutory basis in May 2000.[30] The Appointments Commission is responsible for vetting the nominations of those nominated by the political parties, advising the Prime Minister of any concerns about propriety before the Prime Minister passes on the nominations to the Queen. Non party-political appointments are recommended by the Appointments Commission and the Prime Minister passes on these recommendations to the Queen. The Prime Minister may also nominate up to 10 distinguished public servants on retirement in any one Parliament. The Appointments Commission plays no part in nominating government ministers, the Law Lords or the Lords Spiritual.

A 2007 White Paper recommended the establishment of a Statutory Appointments Commission to recommend people for political-party appointments (on the basis of nominations from the parties) and non party-political appointments (selected directly by the Statutory Appointments Commission). The White Paper recommended that the membership of representatives of the Church of England should continue, but that the number of Lords Spiritual should be reduced.

In 2007 a debate on the proposals was conducted in both Houses. The House of Commons was unwilling to support any proposals except for either a wholly elected chamber or an 80 per cent elected chamber. In response. a 2008 White Paper proposed a directly elected second chamber, smaller than the House of Commons, which would be either entirely elected or 80 per cent elected and 20 per cent nominated. The White Paper also recommended that elections should take place at the same time as general elections with members serving a term of 12 to 15 years. A House of Lords Reform Bill is currently being considered by a Joint Committee.

Key proposals contained in the draft House of Lords Reform Bill include:

- a reformed House with 300 members, each eligible for a single term of three parliaments;
- elections using the single transferable vote (STV), electing a third of members each time with elections normally taking place at the same time as General Elections;
- multi-member electoral districts, to be drawn up independently based on national and county boundaries;
- a continuation of the presence of Bishops of the Church of England in the House of Lords, reducing their number from 26 to 12; and
- a transition staggered over the course of three electoral cycles.

Both the draft Bill and White Paper are clear that the powers of the reformed House of Lords will remain the same, with it continuing to provide scrutiny and expertise, complementing the work of the Commons. It is the Government's intention that the first elections take place in 2015.

---

[30] *Royal Commission on Reform of the House of Lords, A House for the Future* (2000), Cm.4534.

Law Lords

3–39 The Constitutional Reform Act 2005 created a Supreme Court to take over the appellate jurisdiction of the House of Lords. The Constitutional Reform Act prevents Justices of the Supreme Court, and other holders of judicial office, from sitting and voting in the House of Lords while they hold office. Retired holders of high judicial office may continue to be appointed as non-political members of the second chamber.

Powers of the House of Lords

3–40 The House of Lords is one element of the supreme lawmaker and, as such, its members do have the power to introduce legislation. However, this is not done often, except where the Government is introducing a Bill first into the Lords rather than the Commons. This often occurs for legislation that is less contentious. A Bill that purports to raise, or spend, revenue must always start its parliamentary life in the Commons. This is because the Commons is the elected chamber and is subject to the will of the people.

The Parliament Acts of 1911 and 1949 had a marked effect on the powers of the House of Lords. In 1906 a Liberal Government was elected on a mandate to bring about social reform. The Lords was, as it always has been, dominated by the Conservative party and conflict between the two Houses was inevitable. In 1909 the Lords voted against the Finance Bill. This Bill had proposed increases in taxes on income and property to finance old-age pensions and unemployment insurance. The increases would affect members of the Lords particularly. The Government called a General Election, which they won—although with a reduced majority. The Finance Bill was then enacted. The Government decided that the powers of the Lords should be curtailed so that a similar situation could not arise. However, it was obvious that the Lords would not willingly vote to curtail their own powers and so the Prime Minister, Asquith, asked the new King George V to create new Liberal peers so that there would be a Liberal majority. Around 400 new peers would be required. The King agreed provided there was direct electoral support for the proposals. Another General Election was called and the Liberals were returned with their mandate. The Lords then realised that they could not win and did not oppose the Parliament Bill.

The Parliament Act 1949 was proposed by the Labour Government who were elected in the post-war landslide of 1945. The Government had a huge nationalisation programme and decided to extend it to other areas, in particular to the shipbuilding industry. The Lords had indicated that they would be unwilling to allow any such Nationalisation Bill to be passed. The Government then decided to curtail the delaying power further by reducing the two-year period to one year.

Bills which are not subject to the Parliament Acts are:

- Bills prolonging the length of a Parliament beyond five years;
- Private Bills;
- Bills sent up to the Lords less than a month before the end of a session; and
- Bills which start in the Lords.

The Parliament Acts had three main consequences:

- The House of Lords no longer has the power of veto over a Public Bill, except one which tries to extend the life of Parliament beyond five years. The power of veto remains for Private Bills and subordinate legislation.
- The House of Lords was given a delaying power on Public Bills. Where a Bill is passed by the House of Commons, but rejected by the House of Lords in two successive sessions, it may be presented for Royal Assent provided one year has

elapsed between its Commons second reading, in the first session, and its third reading in the same House in the following session.
● Money Bills certified as such by the Speaker may be presented for the Royal Assent, if not passed by the Lords within one month of being sent there by the Commons.

Functions of the House of Lords

(1) *Scrutinising the work of the House of Commons*: The Lords is regarded by many as **3–41** the "Protector of the Constitution". If the Government has a very large majority in the Commons, it can pass any legislation it pleases, since there will be no opposition in the Commons to stop it. The Lords, however, have traditionally taken a more "conservative" view and thus might try to stop legislation which was very radical, e.g. legislation to abolish the monarchy. The Lords also have the power to prevent the Government introducing legislation to extend the life of Parliament.

(2) *Revision of legislation*: The House spends about two thirds of its time on legislation. This is one of the most important roles of the Lords, particularly where a Bill has been "guillotined" in the Commons. This occurs when the Government curtails debate on a Bill to ensure it is not talked out by opponents. There is no guillotine, or closure motion, in the Lords and so there can be a full debate on the implications of the Bill. The Lords may make amendments to the Bill to clarify it, or change its meaning entirely.

(3) *Debates*: Members of the Lords have a wide range of experience and provide a source of independent expertise. The working peers include many former ministers, former MPs, and business people, who have achieved much and are thus able to make worthwhile contributions to debates.

(4) *Select committees*: Members of the House of Lords are also involved in joint committees with the Commons, the most important being the Joint Committee on Subordinate Legislation and European Communities legislation. It also has a number of select committees, which include the Science and Technology Select Committee and the Economic Affairs Committee. A Constitution Select Committee was set up in 2001 "to examine the constitutional implications of all Public Bills coming before the House; and to keep under review the operation of the constitution". The Constitutional Committee began its work with an enquiry into the working of devolution. Ad hoc committees are also set up, from time to time, to examine issues which are outside the remits of the main investigative committees.

House of Commons

At least every five years the membership of the House of Commons changes after a **3–42** General Election. The right to vote, called the franchise, is given to every British citizen, who is at least 18 years old, is resident in the United Kingdom, is not subject to a disqualification and whose name appears on the Electoral Register.

Generally, those entitled to vote are residents of the United Kingdom who are either:

● British citizens;
● citizens of British dependent territories;
● British overseas citizens;
● Commonwealth citizens; or
● citizens of the Irish Republic.

A citizen of the European Union may vote in European Parliamentary elections and local elections, but not General Elections. Those who are disqualified from voting include:

- aliens;
- minors (under 18);
- hereditary peers and peeresses who have seats in the House of Lords;
- prisoners;
- patients in mental hospitals (the insane are regarded as not having the capacity to understand why they are voting and so they do not have the vote—a voluntary mental patient might not have lost the capacity of understanding and may be able to vote by post if they are so registered); and
- overseas voters (a British citizen who resides abroad and has done so for more than 20 years may not vote in UK elections).

Disqualification from membership of the House of Commons

3–43 A person may be elected to sit in the Commons, but be unable to take that seat because of a disqualification. These persons are stated in the House of Commons Disqualification Act 1975 as:

- minors (a candidate must be 21 before he or she can take their seat);
- aliens;
- peers who have seats in the House of Lords;
- clerics (members of the established churches of England, Wales, Scotland and Northern Ireland and Roman Catholic priests are disqualified, but the clergy of other religions are not disqualified);
- psychiatric patients (if a member becomes mentally ill, this has to be reported to the Speaker and after six months, the seat may be declared vacant if the member is still certified as ill);
- bankrupts (a bankrupt may not be elected to the Commons—if a member subsequently becomes bankrupt he or she will have to resign their seat, unless the bankruptcy is cleared within six months);
- prisoners (a person who is sentenced to imprisonment of more than one year or an indefinite sentence (as for murder) is disqualified—no such person may now be nominated as a candidate);
- holders of public office (people who hold certain public offices may not sit, e.g. judges, police, members of the armed forces, civil servants, members of certain boards and tribunals);
- persons convicted of corrupt or illegal practices (these are electoral offences such as bribery, personation); and
- the Advocate-General for Scotland.

Functions of Members of Parliament

3–44 The current electoral system in the United Kingdom means that an MP is elected to represent a constituency. However, most MPs are also elected because they represent a particular political party. The Government is considering changing the voting system to reflect this. The Parliamentary Voting System and Constituencies Act 2011 provides for a referendum on the question that: "At present, the UK uses the 'first past the post system' to elect MPs to the House of Commons. Should the 'alternative vote' system be used instead?"

The Act also includes provisions which make the amendments to the existing electoral legislation that it would be necessary to make to implement the alternative vote system in the event of a "yes" vote in the referendum.

Part 2 of the Act provides that the number of parliamentary constituencies in the United Kingdom will be reduced to 600 representing approximately the same number of voters. This will have the effect of reducing the number of MPs from Scottish constituencies in the UK Parliament.

The functions of MPs are to:

- Check on the activities and power of Government. The Government's own backbench MPs may have more power than those of the opposition.
- Act for constituents in grievances they may have against central or local government. The MP may ask questions of ministers, or lobby for the constituent, or refer the matter to the Parliamentary Ombudsman.
- Represent pressure groups. Many MPs have links with pressure groups such as the trade unions, professional bodies or charities.
- Represent and support the party.
- Work in committees of the House of Commons.

Functions of the House of Commons

The House of Commons does not govern the country. This is done by the central government departments, local authorities and other bodies, which are charged by legislation to perform these functions. **3–45**

The House of Commons is a body which:

- scrutinises proposed legislation brought to it by the Government, individual members and other private bodies;
- questions the actions of government ministers and departments;
- debates various issues and ensures different opinions are heard; and
- checks the financial probity of the Government.

Scrutinising legislation

There are three types of Bills: **3–46**

- Private Bills—which apply to particular areas or persons;
- Hybrid Bills—which apply to particular persons, but which also contain sections which alter the general law of the land;
- Public Bills—which have general application.

Private Bills concern particular bodies, e.g. a local authority or public corporation. The procedure for passing these Bills is slightly different from that for a Public Bill. There is often no (or very little) discussion of the contents of the Bill within Parliament. Hybrid Bills are those which, on the whole, have general application, but also contain particular provisions applying specifically to particular persons. For instance, the building of the Channel Tunnel required an Act, which involved a private company being given compulsory purchase powers to buy the land to build the northern end of the tunnel. Public Bills are the most important of the three types and they take up the greater part of the legislative programme of Parliament. There are two types of Public Bills: Government Bills and Private Members' Bills. The proposal for a Private Member's Bill may come from the MP themself, from a pressure group, or indeed, from the Government.

A Bill may be introduced in either House, but certain Bills will always be introduced first to the House of Commons. These include Money Bills, controversial Bills, Bills of constitutional significance.

Questions

3–47 At the beginning of business on Monday to Thursday each week, ministers are required to answer questions which have been laid down in advance by backbench MPs. The ministers take it in turn to answer questions; usually they will appear every three or four weeks and will answer questions for about an hour. The Prime Minister is the exception to this: he will answer questions for 30 minutes every Wednesday.

Ministers may only be questioned on matters for which they have responsibility. This has caused much confusion in recent years. During the late 1980s, the Thatcher Government introduced reforms of the civil servants, implementing the "Next Steps Initiative" which set up agencies to carry out functions, which were previously carried out by central government departments. These were under the leadership of Agency Chief Executives who had day-to-day control of the agency's functions. The Government decided that any parliamentary questions, which involved the work of an agency, would be passed for answer to the Chief Executive and would no longer be answered on the floor of the House by the minister. This outraged many opposition MPs, but the practice persisted and is still in place. Thus a question, on a matter which is within the remit of an agency, will be sent to the Chief Executive who will reply directly to the MP. The minister will not be involved and the MP will not be able to ask supplementary questions on the floor of the House. The answers are now published in *Hansard* at the end of the day's debate.

The Scott Inquiry into the Arms for Iraq affair in 1992 highlighted that ministers were answering some questions in a dubious manner. Answers are usually prepared for ministers by their civil servants and they are now instructed to be as open and truthful as possible. In particular, an answer should not be given which is literally true, but likely to give rise to misleading inferences.

Key Concepts

A minister should try to answer **questions** where possible, but there are instances when he may decline to do so:

- the question does not relate to the minister's departmental responsibilities;
- they are statements not questions;
- the matter is currently sub judice;
- the matter was asked in the previous three months;
- the cost of finding the answer would be too costly;
- the answer might damage national security;
- the matter involves confidential exchanges between Governments;
- the question relates to commercial or contractual confidentiality.

Debates

3–48 MPs participate in debates on the second readings of Bills, motions to approve some aspect of government policy, motions set down by the opposition parties to challenge government policies, the budget proposals and many other matters. Each day there is an adjournment debate, taking place at the end of the day for 30 minutes. The topic is chosen by a backbench MP, who has competed successfully in a ballot to bring the matter to the attention of a minister and the House.

Select committees

There are some 33 select committees set up for the whole parliamentary session. There are **3–49** 17 departmental select committees, which "shadow" a government department and investigate the workings of the department and its associated public bodies and agencies. Other committees are concerned with the internal workings of the House, e.g. select committees on services and standing orders. Some select committees are very important to the work of the House of Commons. Arguably the most important one is the Public Accounts Committee.

Financial proceedings

A Government cannot function if it is unable to raise and spend revenue. This principle **3–50** was seen at work during the conflict between the House of Commons and House of Lords in 1909–1911, which led to the passage of the Parliament Act 1911, curtailing, inter alia, the power of the House of Lords to delay Financial Bills of the Government.

Key Concepts

The basic rules for **spending and taxing**:

- Legislative approval is required for taxation and expenditure proposals.
- Only the Crown (i.e. a minister) may move such proposals.
- Proposals must originate in the Commons.
- Spending and taxing proposals in a Bill must be approved separately. They are usually voted on after the second reading of the Bill.

The timetable for expenditure proposals has been modified recently. The Chancellor of the Exchequer announced in 1998, that the departmental estimates would be for three years rather than the previous one. The Treasury receives all of the departmental "bids" for funding and allocates the available funds according to government policy. Negotiations for funds go on for several months. Eventually the proposals are set before the House for debate, usually around March of each year. Three days are set aside for the debates, which must be concluded before August 5. Once the estimates are approved, an annual Appropriation Bill is enacted; this usually occurs in late July.

The Budget

The Chancellor of the Exchequer presents his spending plans in March of each year **3–51** together with his plans for raising the money needed to pay for these plans. This is known as the Budget statement and is one of the highlights of the parliamentary year. As soon as the statement is made, the House passes a series of financial resolutions, which authorise the immediate alteration of taxation amounts. These are given interim legitimacy, by the Provisional Collection of Taxes Act 1968, until the Budget proposals are passed in the Finance Act.

Reform of the House of Commons

3–52 In 2009 a select committee on the reform of the House of Commons (The Wright Committee) was established. The Coalition Government has undertaken to implement the committee's proposals which include; giving Parliament control over timetabling its own business, secret ballot elections for select committees and their chairs, a public right to petition for debate in commons time.

POWERS AND PRIVILEGES OF PARLIAMENT

3–53 Parliamentary privilege is the sum of the rights enjoyed by each House of Parliament, and by Members of each House individually. Parliamentary privilege confers rights, which exceed those possessed by other bodies or individuals. The exercise of the rights of privilege is justified, by the fact that they are necessary so that both Houses of Parliament can discharge their functions.

Powers of the House of Commons

Powers of the Speaker

3–54 In order to ensure that debates can be conducted in a reasonably orderly manner, the Speaker has various powers. These powers may also be exercised by a Deputy Speaker, when he is presiding in the House.

- *Calls to Order.* The Speaker will call a Member to order if they deviate from the topic under discussion, or if they persistently interrupt a Member who is speaking or if they use unparliamentary language. Should a Member disregard this call to order, the Speaker may instruct that Member to resume their seat. If this order is disobeyed, the Speaker may request the Member to leave the Chamber for the remainder of that day's sitting. If the Member does not leave, the Speaker may invoke Standing Order No.43, which requires the Member to leave the House and its precincts for the remainder of that day's sitting. If a Member refuses to leave, then they may be named under Standing Order No.44.
- *Naming and suspension.* The Speaker may name a Member who has abused the rules of the House. The most senior government minister present, then moves that the Member be removed. If the motion is agreed to, the Member is suspended for a number of days. Apart from continuing to serve on committees for the consideration of Private Bills, the Member may not enter the Parliament buildings for the duration of the suspension.
- *Suspension of sitting.* If a situation of grave disorder arises in the House, the Speaker may, under Standing Order No.46, adjourn the House without question, or suspend the sitting until a time of his or her choosing. These suspensions are usually only for a short period of time (up to 30 minutes).
- *Expulsion.* Expulsion is the ultimate power available to the House. Members in the past have been expelled for such crimes as perjury, forgery, fraud and corruption. An expelled Member may seek re-election to the House, even by standing in a by-election of the same Parliament that elected him. Expulsions are rare. The most recent was in 1954.
- *Censure.* Members may be admonished by the Speaker standing in their places for unparliamentary conduct.

Parliamentary Standards

The Select Committee on Standards and Privileges was established in 1995. At the same **3–55** time, the office of Parliamentary Commissioner for Standards was created. His responsibilities include that of maintaining the Register of Members' Interests. The Committee drew up a Code of Conduct on Standards and Privileges in 1996.[31] The Code is based on the "Seven Principles of Public Life" set out by the Committee on Standards in Public Life (the Nolan Committee).[32] The principles are as follows.

> **Key Concept**
>
> **Seven principles of public life**: selflessness, integrity, objectivity, accountability, openness, honesty, and leadership.

The 1996 Code of Conduct also includes some new principles, including that MPs should avoid conflicts of interest, maintain the integrity of Parliament, register their interests, act openly with ministers, other Members and public officials and not misuse confidential information. The Select Committee on Standards and Privileges considers the conduct of Members and makes reports on its findings.

Following a controversial scandal over MPs; claims for expenses, the Parliamentary Standards Act 2009 was passed. This Act set up an independent statutory body called the Independent Parliamentary Standards Authority (IPSA). IPSA is responsible for the scope and implementation of the MPs' allowances scheme. It is also responsible for a code of conduct on financial interests and establishing rules for investigations. The Act also created a new criminal offence of knowingly providing false or misleading information in a claim for an allowance. The penalty is imprisonment for up to 12 months or a fine.

Powers over non-members

The powers which may be exercised over non-Members are usually only invoked if there **3–56** has been conduct amounting to contempt. Contempt may be disorderly or disrespectful conduct, words which impugn the character of proceedings of the House, premature publication of Committee proceedings, or obstructing Members or officials in the discharge of their duty.

Power to detain

When there is unruly conduct, within the Parliament buildings, offenders are removed and **3–57** escorted from the premises by the Serjeant at Arms and his staff of doorkeepers. If the disruption was serious, the offenders may be detained in a police custody room on the premises until the House rises at the end of the day. Where the conduct amounted to a criminal offence the offenders may be transferred to police custody.

---

[31] House of Commons, *The Code of Conduct together with the Guide to the Rules Relating to the Conduct of Members*, HC Paper No.637–638 (Session 1995/96).

[32] House of Commons. Select Committee on Standards in Public Life, *First Report*, HC Paper No.637 (Session 1994/95).

Power to compel committee witnesses to attend

3–58 If a select committee witness is unwilling to attend, the committee can order the attendance of a witness at a specified date and time. If the witness does not respond the House may order the Serjeant at Arms to serve a warrant on the witness. The Serjeant, or his appointee, may call on the full assistance of the civil authorities, including the police. The last use of the warrant was in January 1992 when the Maxwell brothers were obliged to attend the Social Security Select Committee, which was investigating the operation of pension funds.

Imprisonment

3–59 The House still retains the power to imprison for a period not exceeding the length of the Parliamentary session. This power has not been exercised for over 120 years. Offenders are ordered to be detained either in one of HM Prisons, or in the custody of the Serjeant at Arms.

Absolute or qualified privilege

3–60 Absolute privilege extends to parliamentary proceedings and prevents any actions with regard to such proceedings. Qualified privilege is afforded to newspaper and media reports of parliamentary proceedings. No action can be taken with regard to the contents of such a report provided that it is fair and accurate and free from malice.

There is no statutory definition of parliamentary proceedings although parliamentary committees have described it as all things done or written by a Member of Parliament as part of their duties or for the purpose of enabling them to carry out their duties. The lack of a clear definition has caused uncertainty. In 2008 the police raided the office of a Conservative MP in the course of an investigation into leaks of information. The MP claimed that the documents which were seized were privileged. An investigation was instituted but was later dropped. In February 2010 it was announced that a number of MPs would be prosecuted in the criminal courts over fraudulent expenses claims. It was held, by Southwark Crown Court, that proceedings in Parliament did not include MPs' claims for expenses and so there was no bar to criminal prosecutions.

A Bill to reform the law and to clarify the extent and application of parliamentary privilege was included in the Queen's speech in May 2010.

Powers of the House of Lords

3–61 There is no established procedure in the House of Lords for sanctions against members who commit contempt. In 2009, following a scandal in which it was alleged that four life peers had accepted money in return for favouring the interests of the donors, the Leader of the House of Lords requested advice from the Committee of Privileges on the sanctions available to the House. The committee decided that the House had the power to suspend members but not to expel them permanently.

THE GOVERNMENT

> **Key Concepts**
>
> **Central Government** consists of:
>
> - the sovereign;
> - the Privy Council;
> - the ministers of the Crown;
> - central government departments;
> - the civil service.

3–62

The sovereign

Succession to the throne is governed by the Act of Settlement 1700. The main principle of succession is that on the death of the monarch, the right to succeed to the throne descends to the heirs of her body.

3–63

There are three rules which are applied:

(1) *Preference for males*. Sons of the monarch rank before daughters, regardless of age.
(2) *Primogeniture*. The oldest son ranks before younger sons.
(3) *Representation*. A child, or other descendant of a person who would have succeeded if he had survived, may succeed in their place, for example the children of the oldest son will rank ahead of the younger sons.

The person who succeeds to the throne must take the coronation oath, declare that he is a faithful protestant and promise to uphold the Church of England and the Church of Scotland. When a monarch dies, his heir succeeds automatically and immediately. Where the heir to the throne is under the age of 18, is ill and incapable, or is absent from the United Kingdom and unable to return when he succeeds to the throne, the royal functions must, according to the Regency Act 1937, be carried out by a regent. A regent can exercise all of the royal powers, except that he must not assent to a Bill altering the succession to the throne. He is also not permitted to assent to a Bill repealing the Scots Act, which protects the status of the Church of Scotland.[33] The regent is usually the next person in line to succeed to the throne who is over the age of 18.

Royal functions can be delegated to Counsellors of State, if the monarch is to be outside the United Kingdom or is suffering from a mental or physical disability which is not sufficiently serious or permanent to justify the appointment of a regent. The Counsellor's of State are the monarch's spouse and the next four persons in line of succession over the age of 18. Counsellors of State may not dissolve Parliament or confer honours.

Privy Council

Privy Councillors are appointed for life, by letters patent issued by the Queen on the advice of the Government. They adopt the title "Right Honourable". They take an oath, which binds them to secrecy on Privy Council business.

3–64

---

[33] Protestant Religion and Presbyterian Church Act 1707.

> **Key Concepts**
>
> Membership of the **Privy Council**:
>
> - Lord President of the Council, a member of the government;
> - all past and present Cabinet ministers;
> - the Speaker of the House of Commons;
> - the Lords of Appeal in Ordinary and the holders of other high judicial offices;
> - the Archbishops of Canterbury and York;
> - leading statesmen from Commonwealth countries.

The quorum of the Privy Council is three members and usually four are summoned to attend. They are selected as being suitable for the business to be dealt with. A larger meeting may be convened for business of state importance, for example approval of the marriage of the heir to the throne. The majority of the business of the Privy Council consists of giving formal effect to acts of the Crown done under the authority of the royal prerogative or of statute. The Council issues proclamations for summoning, proroguing and dissolving Parliament and may issue Orders in Council for a wide range of purposes, including, making delegated legislation, declaring states of emergency.

Ministers of the Crown

Prime Minister and the Cabinet

3–65 The Cabinet is composed of around 20 senior MPs and peers, each holding some important government office or responsibility. There are no set rules for who must be included in a Cabinet, but the Chancellor of the Exchequer, Home Secretary, Defence Secretary and Foreign Secretary are invariably included. The Prime Minister is chosen as a result of either a successful General Election, in which his party is returned as the largest party, or on the resignation of a former Prime Minister, such as occurred in 1990 when Margaret Thatcher was forced to resign by her Parliamentary party. In either event, the party leader must be invited by the Queen to form a Government.

The Prime Minister has huge powers.

Patronage

3–66 The Prime Minister appoints his Cabinet and all of the other ministerial posts. However, his power is not unlimited; he has to try to reconcile the various "wings" of the party and there may be people who have helped him attain his position and, therefore, need to be rewarded. Thatcher's first Government contained ministers who were to the left of the Conservative Party, and she needed to keep the left happy for the sake of party unity.

Dissolution of Parliament

3–67 Until recently the Prime Minister could decide when to call a General Election. The duration of a Parliament is now fixed at 5 years.[34] The Prime Minister can only seek an earlier dissolution if 55 per cent of the Commons votes in favour.

---

[34] Fixed Term Parliaments Act 2011.

Powers relating to the Cabinet

The size and composition of the Cabinet is decided by the Prime Minister alone, as are the **3–68** sizes and composition of Cabinet Committees, which discuss proposed legislation and other matters. The Prime Minister decides when the Cabinet will meet, what will be discussed and what will be written in the minutes. Votes are not often taken in Cabinet; rather the Prime Minister "senses the mood of the meeting" and sums up for the minutes.

Ministerial responsibility

Key Concepts

The term **"ministerial responsibility"** applies in two circumstances: **3–69**

(1) Collective responsibility; the obligation to adhere publicly to government policies.
(2) Individual responsibility; the responsibility of a minister for the actions of his department.

Collective responsibility is the responsibility of the Government as a whole for the decisions it has made and the policies it has carried out. It is particularly important in the Cabinet, where decisions are taken in secret and where the discussions leading to a decision remain confidential.

There are some good reasons for this secrecy:

- It preserves an image of a united Government. Nothing damages a Government more than the impression that it is split on a certain issue. The Major Government was an example of this.
- It suggests a stability, which reassures the money markets.
- It presents a united front in policies, for both friends and enemies of the country, so that they know where the Government stands on particular issues.
- It helps government ministers who are under attack for a particular policy. As the policy has been decided by the Cabinet, all members of the Cabinet must stand by it and the minister who has to implement it.
- It helps to hide mistakes, inefficiency and deceit.

If a minister is unable to accept a decision, he must resign office. Examples of such resignations include Michael Heseltine over the Westland affair and Geoffrey Howe in 1990 over Thatcher's European policy. Most ministers, however, make their protest in Cabinet and then accept the final decision, thus keeping their cabinet post. In recent years it has become more common for ministers unhappy with decisions to "leak" their dissent to the media.

Individual ministerial responsibility is a more complex principle. It refers to the minister's responsibility for the actions of himself as a government minister, those of any junior ministers and those of his civil servants. It does not refer to the actions of a minister in his or her personal capacity. So a minister who has indulged in misconduct, which does not amount to a crime, will not necessarily have to resign, although pressure may be brought by his party to do so because of the embarrassment being caused to the party.

Historically, a minister was responsible for the actions, or inaction, of civil servants and this was feasible because government departments were small and manageable, and ministers could keep a watch on what was happening. The idea was that the civil servants were carrying out the instructions and policies of the minister and, therefore, should be protected from public criticism by them being named as the "culprits". Civil servants are required to work for any Government, and every Government, in an impartial manner, so that the administration of Government will flow smoothly from Conservative Government to Labour Government, and so on.

By the end of the Second World War, however, government departments were larger and their work more diverse. It was impossible for a minister to know the day-to-day operational details within the department. The question of a minister's responsibility was brought up in the Crichel Down Affair in the early 1950s. The Air Ministry acquired farmland in 1938 by compulsory purchase. When it no longer required the land, as a bombing range, the minister transferred it to the Ministry of Agriculture, who transferred it to the Commissioners for Crown Lands, who let it to a tenant. The original owner was prevented from buying the land back (the normal procedure in such cases) or leasing it. Other landowners were similarly affected. An inquiry published in 1954 concluded that civil servants in the Ministry of Agriculture had acted in a high-handed and deceitful manner. There was considerable criticism and the Agriculture Minister, Sir Thomas Dugdale, who resigned taking full responsibility for the mistakes of his officials. Although this appears to be the doctrine working properly, in fact Dugdale had been involved in the decisions and the civil servants had been named in the inquiry report.

After this affair, the Home Secretary stated how the doctrine should work:

Key Concepts

A minister should **protect a civil servant** where the civil servant:

- has carried out an explicit order; or
- has acted in accordance with the minister's policy.

A minister is under **no obligation** to protect a civil servant:

- if he has acted contrary to the minister's orders and without the minister's knowledge.

The Home Secretary, however, stated that the minister would remain "constitutionally responsible to Parliament for the fact that something has gone wrong".

Departments

3–70 Each government department (with the exception of non-political departments such as the Inland Revenue) is headed by a member of the Government. The most important have the title Secretary of State. All Secretaries of State are members of the Cabinet. Other departments are headed by other ministers, not all of whom are in the Cabinet. In recent years, departments have tended to become larger as functions are amalgamated to form departments with wide portfolios. These departments have a Secretary of State, or other senior minister, at their head and other junior ministers responsible for specific functions.

Scottish business at Westminster

The Scottish Office was replaced by the Scotland Office on July 1, 1999, following devo- **3–71** lution and the establishment of a Scottish Executive. Many of the responsibilities of the former Scottish Office were transferred to the Scottish Executive. There is a Memorandum of Understanding and a set of Concordats dealing with the division of functions between the Scottish and UK administrations. There are also more detailed bilateral Concordats between the Scottish Executive and individual UK government departments. The UK Government retains responsibility for a range of issues including employment, fiscal and economic policy, taxation, social security, benefits and pensions.[35] In June 2003 a new Department of Constitutional Affairs was established. This has now been replaced by the Ministry of Justice. The Scotland Office, headed up by the Secretary of State for Scotland, is now part of the Ministry of Justice.

Key Concepts

The **Secretary of State**:

- represents Scottish interests within the UK Government in matters that are reserved to the UK Parliament under the terms of the Scotland Act 1998;
- encourages co-operation between the Parliaments and between the UK Government and Scottish Executive;
- intervenes in relations between UK and Scottish Administrations, if required by the Scotland Act;
- pays grant to the Scottish Consolidated Fund;
- manages other financial transactions; and
- exercises certain residual functions in reserved matters, such as the conduct and funding of elections.

Under s.35 of the Scotland Act the Secretary of State may make an Order prohibiting the Scottish Parliament's Presiding Officer from submitting a Bill for Royal Assent, which he or she has reasonable grounds to believe would be incompatible with:

- any international obligations;
- the interests of defence; or
- the interests of national security.

The Secretary of State may also make an Order under s.35 if he or she reasonably believes that the Scottish Parliament Bill makes modifications to, and would have an adverse effect on, the operation of the law as it applies to reserved matters.

The Advocate-General for Scotland is the principal legal adviser to the Government as regards Scots law. Following devolution, the Lord Advocate and the Solicitor General for Scotland transferred to the Scottish Executive and a new office of Advocate-General was created. The Advocate General for Scotland is a Minister of the Crown and is responsible to Parliament. The Advocate General sits on a number of Cabinet Committees. He is also responsible for the Office of the Solicitor to the Advocate-General for Scotland, which

---

[35] For more details see Chapter 1.

provides legal advice to most UK departments in relation to Scotland. He also exercises statutory functions under the Scotland Act.

Key Concepts

Functions of the **Advocate-General**:

- advising the UK Government on Scots law;
- referring Bills of the Scottish Parliament to the Judicial Committee of the Privy Council for decisions on their competence; and
- raising proceedings in the courts, or the Judicial Committee, on devolution issues. He receives notice of all devolution issues raised in court cases and can intervene in the courts or the Judicial Committee.

Civil service

3–72 The civil service is part of the Executive arm of Government. Its traditional role is to advise ministers on policy matters and, once the policy has been decided, implement that policy. The civil servant is a Crown servant and may enjoy certain of the immunities afforded to the Crown. However, it is now considered that civil servants are responsible to the Government of the day rather that the State and it is to the Government that they owe their loyalty. They are not answerable to Parliament and if required to give evidence before a select committee their answers must reflect the Government's policy because they are deemed to speak on behalf of their minister. If a civil servant were able to speak freely, they might give a view that conflicted with government policy, and this would undermine their professional political impartiality.

In 1968 a report on the working of the civil service was released. The recommendations of the Fulton Report were wide-ranging, but the Government did not implement them all. Changes did occur in the way civil servants were recruited and promoted and a new Civil Services Department was set up to deal with these. The report also recommended that certain functions carried out by civil servants in government departments should be devolved to bodies, which would exist outside the departmental framework while still being subject to ministerial guidance. This part of the report became the starting point for the reforms in the 1980s.

These reforms changed the civil service considerably. Many public utilities and amenities were privatised and replaced by Executive agencies with new management practices. The new structure of Government has been called "the new public management" and it consists of a number of components:

Key Concepts

New public management:

- professional management;
- goals and targets identified and set;
- greater competition;
- decentralisation to smaller units.

One of the most notable features of the reforms was the split between service delivery and the making of policy, which resulted from the Next Steps Initiative, by which many of the functions previously carried out by government departments were transferred to executive agencies.

Executive agencies and civil servants

The main consequence of the reforms was a significant reduction in the number of civil **3–73** servants in the mainstream civil service. The civil service used to have the image of being a uniform service, where staff could move from one department to another on being promoted. Pay grades were universal: a higher executive officer in the Ministry of Defence would be on the same scale as a higher executive officer in the Scottish Office. Conditions of service were also uniform. Now, an Agency Chief Executive can implement pay scales and conditions of service, which he or she considers appropriate. This means that civil servants wishing to transfer back into the mainstream service, so as to become involved in policy making, may have difficulty in doing so without losing seniority or pay.

Further reform of the Civil Service was instituted in 2010 by the Constitutional Reform and Governance Act 2010. Part 1 of the Act provides for:

- A power for the Minister for the Civil Service to manage the civil service, and a parallel power for the Secretary of State in relation to the diplomatic service;
- A requirement for a code of conduct for civil servants which specifically requires civil servants to carry out their duties in accordance with the core civil service values of integrity, honesty, objectivity and impartiality;
- The establishment of a Civil Service Commission with functions in relation to selections for appointments to the civil service and in relation to hearing complaints that the civil service and diplomatic service codes have been breached;
- A requirement for appointments to the civil service to be made on merit on the basis of fair and open competition;
- The Civil Service Commission will publish principles on the application of the fundamental requirement that selections for appointment are made on merit on the basis of fair and open competition, and will investigate complaints under the code of conduct for civil servants.

SCOTTISH PARLIAMENT

The opening sentence of the first section of the Scotland Act 1998 is: "There shall be a **3–74** Scottish Parliament." This Act marked the culmination of a long campaign for major constitutional reform in the United Kingdom. Devolution is the delegation of power from a central Government to local bodies without the relinquishment of sovereignty. The scheme of devolution means that, although there is now a Scottish Parliament, it operates subject to statutory authority from the Westminster Parliament and the extent of it powers is limited.

History of devolution

The concept of a Scottish Parliament is not new. Scotland had its own Parliament until the **3–75** union of the Scottish and English Parliaments in 1707. A number of Acts of the original Scottish Parliament are still in force today. The 1707 Treaty of Union merged the existing Parliaments of Scotland and England. The Treaty provisions included safeguards for the Scottish church and the separate Scottish legal system. The combined Parliament was supposed to be a new Parliament, rather than a continuation of the former English Parliament, however the new Parliament consisted of all existing English MPs and peers. Seats for 45 MPs from Scotland were created in the House of Commons and 16 peers of Scotland became hereditary peers in the House of Lords. The new British Parliament continued to follow the procedures and practices of the English Parliament. A post of Secretary for Scotland was created to look after Scottish interests, but it lapsed in 1746 and was not revived until 1855. The post became a Secretary of State post in 1926 with responsibility for a government department known as the Scottish Office.

During the twentieth century there were a number of campaigns for Scottish independence. In 1973 the Royal Commission on the Constitution recommended a form of legislative devolution for Scotland. Subsequently, the Government put forward legislation to establish a Scottish Assembly. The resulting Act, the Scotland Act 1978, required that 40 per cent of the Scottish electorate had to vote support the Act for it to come into force. A referendum was held in 1979 and the devolution scheme was supported by 52 per cent of those voting. As this was not equal to 40 per cent of those entitled to vote, the scheme was not implemented and shortly afterwards there was a change of political party in Government.

The new Conservative Government of 1979 did not support devolution, but preferred instead to further devolve the administrative Government of Scotland and to allow special treatment of Scottish business in Parliament itself. However, it was not always possible to devote an appropriate amount of Parliamentary time to Scottish business. Scottish legislative changes were often included in UK statutes when separate legislation would have been more suitable. The political pressure for reform continued to grow and a body called the Scottish Constitutional Convention came together in the late 1980s to campaign for devolution. The Scottish Constitutional Convention included some of the political parties in Scotland, local authorities, the churches and many other organisations. Over the next few years several reports were published. Its main demand was for a Scottish Parliament with law-making powers. A devolution policy was included in the Labour Party manifesto for the May 1997 General Election. After election, the Labour Government arranged for a referendum on its proposals, which were set out in a White Paper of July 1997, *Scotland's Parliament*. The referendum was held on September 11, 1997 and produced clear majorities for the two propositions about the creation of a Scottish Parliament and it's having certain tax-varying powers. Following this result, the Scotland Act was passed in Parliament in 1998.

Key Concepts

Under the devolved framework of Government in the United Kingdom, there is now a **Scottish Parliament**. There are also Regional Assemblies in Wales and Northern Ireland.

Devolution is the delegation of power from a central Government to local bodies without the relinquishment of sovereignty.

Relations between UK Parliament and Scottish Parliament

3–76 It is important to remember that the constitutional change, that has occurred in the United Kingdom through the process of devolution, has not created a federal structure but remains unitary. The Scottish Parliament operates as a self-contained and fully functioning Parliament in its own right. Legislation can be passed by the Scottish Parliament without going through the Westminster Parliament. However, the UK Parliament at Westminster retains power to legislate on all matters, both reserved and devolved.[36] There is, however, a convention of devolution that the UK Parliament will not normally legislate on devolved matters without the consent of the Scottish Parliament. It may sometimes be more convenient for Westminster to legislate for the whole United Kingdom, even where some of the subject-matter falls within the Parliament's legislative competence and this Sewel Convention (named after Lord Sewel) provides a means for this to happen.

Any powers which remain with the UK Parliament at Westminster are known as reserved powers. Reserved matters include constitutional matters, foreign policy and taxation.[37]

The powers, which are not designated by the Scotland Act as reserved, are known as residual powers. There is no explicit indication of the extent of the devolved powers, but they include matters such as health, education, social work and planning.

Since the Scottish Parliament is a subordinate body, created by a UK statute, the laws which it enacts are also subordinate. This means that, unlike Acts of the UK Parliament, the Acts of the Scottish Parliament are subject to the scrutiny of the courts and can be declared invalid. There is also the possibility that, in the future, the UK Parliament may legislate to reduce or even remove the powers of the Scottish Parliament.

In 2007 the Scottish Parliament established the Calman Commission, to review the operation of the devolved Scottish Parliament and to make recommendations for future changes. The Commission published its final report in June 2009.

Main conclusions and recommendations:

- The Scottish Parliament should have greater control over the raising of revenue. This could be achieved by sharing responsibility for setting income tax rates with the UK Parliament and through devolution of some taxes.
- Income tax rates in Scotland should be reduced by 10 pence in the pound.
- The Scottish Government should have new borrowing powers.
- Responsibility for the regulation of airguns, the administration of elections, drink driving limits and the national speed limit should be devolved.
- Regulation of health professions and corporate insolvency (currently substantially reserved) should be fully reserved.
- Scottish Ministers should be more involved in decisions and appointments relating to UK bodies such as the BBC.
- There should be better dialogue and communication between the Scottish and UK Parliaments.
- There should a new mechanism to enable the Scottish Parliament to legislate on reserved matters with the consent of the UK Parliament.
- Procedures for Scottish Parliament scrutiny of Bills should be revised.
- Any Promoter of a Bill should make a declaration that it is within the legislative competence of the Parliament. (Currently this only applies to Bills introduced by ministers).

In order to implement the main recommendations of the Calman Commission a Scotland Bill was introduced in 2010. However, the UK Government said it would not pass the bill unless it had prior consent from the Scottish Parliament in the form of a legislative consent motion. Throughout 2010, 2011 and into 2012 while the Bill was under consideration in

---

[36] Scotland Act 1998 s.28(7).
[37] For more details see Chapter 1.

the House of Commons and the House of Lords, negotiations about the details of the provision took place and the Scottish Parliament refrained from passing the legislative consent motion. The UK Government stated that the Parliament of the United Kingdom could pass the Bill in any case. The Scottish Parliament eventually agreed to pass a legislative consent motion when the Bill was in the report stage in the House of Lords in March 2012 following agreement on a number of amendments.

The Bill aims to strengthen the devolution settlement in Scotland, increase the financial accountability of the Scottish Parliament, and renew the policy responsibility split between the UK and Scottish Parliaments.

The Bill allows for:

- an increase in the percentage of its budget the Scottish Parliament will be responsible for raising from around 15 per cent to approximately 35 per cent;
- the replacement of the Scottish variable rate of income tax with a Scottish rate of income tax. Existing rates of income tax for Scottish taxpayers will be reduced by 10 pence, and a new Scottish rate amount will be added on top;
- the devolution of stamp duty land tax and landfill tax;
- a reduction in Scotland's block grant;
- new borrowing powers to be conferred on the Scottish Government;
- the Scottish Parliament to levy new taxes, when they have the agreement of the UK Parliament;
- devolution of responsibility for the regulation of airguns, national speed limits and drink driving;
- a role in appointments in broadcasting and the Crown Estate; and
- a new procedure for Scottish criminal cases that go to the UK Supreme Court.

The Scottish Government is planning to hold a referendum in autumn 2014 to gauge public opinion with regard to further devolution or independence for Scotland.

The Secretary of State for Scotland is a member of the UK Cabinet, and is supported by the Scotland Office, which is responsible for the administration of reserved matters in Scotland. He also acts as the conduit between the UK and Scottish Parliaments and between the Scottish Executive and the UK Government.

Key Concepts

The United Kingdom after devolution is a **unitary system**.
The **UK Parliament** retains power to legislate on all matters.
Certain matters are **reserved** exclusively to the UK Parliament.

3–77 The Scottish Parliament is a creature of statute and is not a sovereign body in its own right. Its powers, functions and duties derive from statute. As a subordinate body it is subject to the control of the Scotland Act and thus to the UK Parliament. A report, *Shaping Scotland's Parliament*, published in January 1999, included comprehensive proposals for the working of the new Parliament. Four key principles were identified:

Key Concepts

Key principles for the Scottish Parliament

(1) **Sharing the power**: The Scottish Parliament should embody and reflect the sharing of power between the people of Scotland, the legislators and the Scottish Executive.
(2) **Accountability**: The Scottish Executive should be accountable to the Scottish Parliament and the Parliament and Executive should be accountable to the people of Scotland.
(3) **Access and participation**: The Scottish Parliament should be accessible, open, responsive and develop procedures which make possible a participative approach to the development, consideration and scrutiny of policy and legislation.
(4) **Equal opportunities**: The Scottish Parliament in its operation and its appointments should recognise the need to promote equal opportunities.

Powers of the Scottish Parliament

Parliament has power to call for witnesses and documents. Anyone who is summoned to attend, or to produce documents, and fails to do so is guilty of an offence punishable by a fine or up to three months' imprisonment.[38] This punishment is not imposed by the Parliament itself, but by the courts. **3–78**

Privileges

MSPs are protected against action in defamation, arising from statements which they make in Parliament.[39] Such remarks are held to be absolutely privileged. The publications authorised by Parliament are also protected by the Scotland Act and other reports of proceedings, which are fair and accurate and made without malice, are protected by the Defamation Act 1996 s.15. MSPs are not entirely exempt from the general law on contempt of court and must, therefore, refrain from discussing matters which are sub judice. However, a limited form of immunity is granted by s.42, whereby proceedings in relation to a Bill, or subordinate legislation, will not be covered by the strict liability rule of the Contempt of Court Act 1981. The Inner House considered the extent of the privilege afforded to the Scottish Parliament and MSPs by the Scotland Act in the case of *Whaley v Lord Watson of Invergowrie*. **3–79**

Whaley v Lord Watson of Invergowrie
2000 S.C. 340

The case was an appeal against a decision of the Lord Ordinary to refuse to grant an interim interdict against a member of the Scottish Parliament, restraining him from promoting, and introducing a Bill to outlaw hunting with dogs. Whaley claimed

---

[38] Scotland Act 1998 s.23.
[39] Scotland Act 1998 s.41.

that the MSP had assistance from a pressure group, the Scottish Campaign Against Hunting with Dogs, which breached the rules relating to members' interests.[40]

The Inner House held, that although the Scottish Parliament was a body created by statute and was subject to the jurisdiction of the courts in the same way as any other statutory body, Parliament was afforded some immunity from court orders by the Scotland Act.[41] This does not mean, however, that the protection against court orders will always apply to individual MSPs. A standards committee decision on an act of an MSP did not bar the courts from considering the matter, or the Crown from investigating and prosecuting a suspected offence. The balance of convenience in the particular case, however, did not favour the grant of interim interdict, as an interdict in these circumstances would have had the effect of preventing the Parliament from considering a Bill which was within its competency.

Composition of the Scottish Parliament

3–80 The Scottish Parliament is unicameral, that is to say it has only one chamber, unlike the bicameral UK Parliament, which includes the House of Commons and the House of Lords. There is no equivalent to the House of Lords in the Scottish Parliament. The Scottish Parliament is made up of 129 elected Members of the Scottish Parliament, known as MSPs. One of the MSPs is elected by the Parliament to serve as the Presiding Officer. There are also two deputy Presiding Officers.

Members of the Scottish Parliament

3–81 The elected representatives in the Scottish Parliament are known as Members of the Scottish Parliament or, more commonly, as MSPs.

MSPs can be elected in two ways:

(1) Seventy-three constituency members are elected, based on the UK Parliament constituencies, using the "first past the post" system.
(2) A further 56 regional members are elected, 7 for each of 8 regions (based on the regions used in the European Parliament elections). These members are elected using the "Additional Member" System. This is a form of proportional representation using party lists, which ensures that each party's representation in the Parliament reflects its overall share of the vote.

Despite the fact that some MSPs are elected to represent a constituency and others are regionally elected members, they all have equal status once they are elected. Elections are normally held every four years. An extraordinary General Election may be held if either Parliament resolves to dissolve itself with a two-thirds majority, or there is no nomination for the office of First Minister within the first 28 days after a vacancy occurring.

The Scottish Parliament is required to meet within seven days of the result of the poll being announced. MSPs may work from the Parliament Headquarters in Edinburgh, but many also have a local office within their constituency or region, where they may hold surgeries. A Member may resign his or her seat by giving notice in writing to the Presiding Officer. Seats will also become vacant if an MSP dies or becomes disqualified. If this causes a constituency seat to become vacant, the vacant seat will be filled by holding a by-

---

[40] Scotland Act 1998 (Transitory and Transitional Provisions) (Members' Interests) Order 1999 art.6.
[41] Scotland Act 1998 s.40(4).

election, unless there is less than six months to the next General Election.[42] If a regional seat becomes vacant there is no by-election. If the Member who resigns was elected as an individual the seat will remain vacant until the next election. If he was returned from a political party's regional list, the next unelected person on the list will take the seat. If there is nobody left on the list to take the seat, the seat remains vacant.

In general, persons who are disqualified from membership of the UK Parliament by the House of Commons Disqualification Act 1975 are also disqualified from membership of the Scottish Parliament.[43] However, there are some differences: citizens of the European Union who are resident in the United Kingdom are not disqualified, neither are peers and peeresses nor priests and ministers of any religious denomination. The Scotland Act makes provision for further disqualifications for the holders of certain public appointments. Members of the UK Parliament are not disqualified from membership of the Scottish Parliament. All MSPs must take the oath of allegiance, usually at the first meeting after a General Election.

Presiding Officer

The Parliament is required to elect a Presiding Officer and two deputies at its first meeting **3–82** after a General Election. They hold office until the next election, which would normally occur at the first meeting of the next Parliament. The Presiding Officer has several roles.

Key Concepts

The **Presiding Officer**:

- chairs the meetings of the Parliament;
- convenes and chairs weekly meetings of the Parliamentary Bureau, where the future business of the Parliament is agreed;
- declares the date of the next General Election;
- chairs the Corporate Body;
- decides on questions raised regarding the meaning of the rules for Parliamentary proceedings;
- represents the Parliament at home and abroad and with such bodies, for example, as the UK Parliament, the Devolved Assemblies, European institutions and Parliaments from across the world; and submits Bills for Royal Assent.

Scottish Executive

The term "Scottish Executive" is the statutory term for the senior ministers of the **3–83** devolved Scottish Government. The Scottish Executive is formed from the party, or parties, holding a majority of seats in the Parliament. The members of the Executive, collectively referred to as "the Scottish Ministers", are:

---

[42] Scotland Act 1998 s.10.
[43] Scotland Act 1998 s.15.

> **Key Concepts**
>
> **Scottish Executive**
>
> ● The First Minister.
> ● The Lord Advocate and the Solicitor-General (also known as the Law Officers).
> ● Other ministers appointed by the First Minister.

First Minister

3–84   The MSPs select a nominee who is then formally appointed by the Queen. He holds office at her Majesty's pleasure and, in theory, could be dismissed by the sovereign. He will cease to hold office as soon as another First Minister is appointed. The First Minister may resign at any time and is required to do so if Parliament passes a vote of no confidence in the Scottish Executive. As head of the Scottish Executive, the First Minister has a direct relationship with the sovereign in appointing ministers and law officers. The First Minister is, in effect, Scotland's counterpart of the Prime Minister in the UK Parliament. He may appoint ministers with the agreement of Parliament and may dismiss them without any requirement for such agreement.[44]

Scottish Law Officers

3–85   There are two Scottish Law Officers, the Lord Advocate and the Solicitor-General for Scotland who are part of the Scottish Executive. They advise the Scottish Executive on legal matters and represent its interest in court. The Lord Advocate is head of the systems of criminal prosecution and investigation of deaths in Scotland. Both are appointed by the Queen on the recommendation of the First Minister, made with the approval of the Scottish Parliament. Since their work is highly specialised, it may not be possible to appoint them from amongst the elected MSPs. If this is the case, they can still participate in the work of the Parliament but cannot vote.

Organisation of the Scottish Executive

First Minister

———

Deputy First Minister

———

Ministers

(Justice, Education and Young People, Enterprise, Transport and Lifelong Learning, Finance and Public Services, Environment and Rural Development, Parliamentary Business, Social Justice, Tourism, Culture and Sport, Health and Community Care)

———

Law Officers

(Lord Advocate, Solicitor-General for Scotland)

---

[44] Scotland Act 1998 s.49.

Scottish Ministers

The members of the Scottish Executive are referred to by the statutory collective term **3–86** "The Scottish Ministers".[45] This term is used for various legal purposes. Where an Act of Parliament conferred a power, or a duty, on a specific minister with regard to what is now a devolved function, such a power or duty is now exercisable by the "Scottish Ministers". This allows any one of them to exercise such powers interchangeably. Legal challenges, such as judicial review of the acts of members of the Scottish Executive, are brought against the "Scottish Ministers", rather than against the specific ministerial office with responsibility for the decision which is being challenged. The term "Scottish Ministers" is also used descriptively and informally to apply to all ministers including junior ministers. The Scottish Ministers are appointed by the First Minister. A minister's portfolio may be covered by one or more committees of the Parliament. The committees' members are chosen with regard to the political parties and groupings in the Parliament. A minister can be called to appear before a committee to explain policies or to participate in inquiries.

Ministers who are not Members of the Scottish Executive are called "Junior Scottish Ministers". All ministers are MSPs. There is no limit to the number of ministers who may be appointed. Ministers are part of two separate organisations: the Scottish Executive (ministers) and the Scottish Parliament (MSPs). A minister cannot sit on a parliamentary committee dealing with a subject for which he or she is minister. At present, it is general practice that no ministers sit on committees.

Major government policy initiatives are announced to the Parliament by the Scottish Executive. Political parties represented within the Parliament may also make statements regarding their own policies during meetings of the Parliament. The Executive often produces policy and consultation documents (similar to the "White" and "Green" Papers produced by the UK Government), which outline the Executive's proposals for legislation. After the consultation has been considered by the Executive, the Executive may introduce a Bill into Parliament. This is known as an Executive Bill. Like all Bills, Executive Bills will be scrutinised by Committees and by the whole Parliament. It is for the Parliament to decide whether proposed legislation should be passed. Once this is achieved, responsibility is then passed back to the Executive, who will draw up a time scale for the implementation of the Act.

Ministerial responsibility

The Scottish Ministerial Code,[46] published in August 1999, defines the doctrine of col- **3–87** lective responsibility, which applies to members of the Scottish Executive, including Deputy Ministers.

Key Concepts

Collective Responsibility

2.1. The Executive operates on the basis of collective responsibility. The internal processes through which a decision has been made should not be disclosed. Decisions reached by the executive are binding on its member.

---

[45] Scotland Act 1998 s.44(2).
[46] *http://www.scotland.gov.uk/Publications* [Accessed May 12, 2012].

> 2.2. Collective responsibility requires that Ministers should be able to express their views frankly in the expectation that they can argue freely in private while maintaining a united front when decisions have been reached. This in turn requires that the privacy of opinions expressed and advice offered within the Executive should be maintained.
> 2.3. Collective Responsibility as defined above also applies to any junior Scottish Ministers who are appointed by the First Minister under the terms of Section 49 of the Scotland Act even though they are not members of the Executive. (This refers to Deputy Ministers).

Parliamentary Bureau

3–88 The Parliamentary Bureau comprises the presiding officer and:

- one representative of each political party represented by more than five members; and
- one representative of any group formed by members who represent a political party with fewer than five representatives.

The main function of the Parliamentary Bureau is to propose the business programme. It allocates time during the meetings of the Parliament for matters such as debates and decision on the general principles of Bills. The membership of each committee is approved by the Parliament on a motion of the Parliamentary Bureau. It refers draft proposals for Bills from MSPs to committees. The Parliamentary Bureau also resolves any questions about committee remits.

Scottish Parliament Committees

3–89 The important role played by committees is a distinctive feature of the Scottish Parliament. The use of committees is one of the methods of furthering the principle that Scottish Parliament should be accessible, open and responsive. The committee procedures ensure that there are opportunities for the general public to participate in the development, consideration and scrutiny of policy and legislation.

Mandatory committees

3–90 Certain committees must be set up by the Scottish Parliament. Procedures, Standards and Finance Committees must be established within 21 sitting days of a General Election. Other mandatory committees must be established within 42 sitting days. Mandatory committees will be established for the entire Parliamentary session.

Key Concepts

Mandatory Committees and their remits

Procedures:	Practice and procedures of Parliament.
Standards:	Members' conduct.
	Members' rights and privileges.
Finance:	Proposals for public expenditure or taxation.
	Responsibilities with regard to Budget Bills.
	Handling of financial business.
Audit:	Accounts laid before Parliament.
European:	Proposals for European Communities legislation.
	Implementation of EC legislation.
	European Communities or European Union issues.
Equal Opportunities:	Matters relating to equal opportunities, including their observance within the Parliament.
Public Petitions:	Admissibility of public petitions and proposals for action is to be taken.
Subordinate legislation:	Any delegated legislation laid before Parliament.
	Proposed powers to make subordinate legislation in Bills.
	General issues about subordinate legislation-making powers.

Subject committees

All committees that are not mandatory committees will be known as subject committees. **3–91** Subject committees may be established to deal with a particular subject by Parliament on a motion of the Parliamentary Bureau. Where a matter falls within the remit of more than one committee, Parliament may identify one as the lead committee for that matter. The lead committee will then take into account the views of the other committees. Although committees are responsible for distinct subject areas, the matters which they consider in relation to their subject area are the same.

Key Concepts

Matters considered by subject committees:

- the need for law reform;
- the policy and administration of the Scottish Administration;
- proposals for legislation before the Scottish or UK Parliaments;
- EC legislation and international conventions; and
- financial proposals of the Scottish Administration.

A committee may introduce Bills relating to its subject area.

Committee meetings

3–92 Meetings will be held in public if the committee is considering:

- proposals for legislation by the Scottish or UK Parliaments;
- EU legislation or international conventions or agreements; or
- the need for law reform.

Scottish Parliament Corporate Body

3–93 The members of the Scottish Parliament Corporate Body are the Presiding Officer and four other MSPs. The Corporate Body is required, because the Scottish Parliament is not a body corporate and cannot hold property, enter into contracts or bring or defend legal actions. The Corporate Body may enter into contracts, charge for goods and services, make investments and accept gifts.[47] The Corporate Body is responsible for the financing of the Parliament and allocation of the budget, the staffing of the Parliament, accommodation and the use and security of Parliamentary facilities. It meets at regular intervals and acts in a politically neutral way.

SCOTTISH PARLIAMENT LEGISLATION

3–94 Section 28(1) of the Scotland Act 1998, provides that the Parliament may make laws, to be known as Acts of the Scottish Parliament. Section 29 sets a limit on that power to legislate. The power to legislate is referred to as "legislative competence". Legislative competence is defined according to five criteria.

Key Concepts

Criteria for legislative competence:

- the Parliament can only legislate for, or in relation to, Scotland;
- it cannot legislate in relation to the "reserved matters" set out in Sch.5 to the Act;
- it cannot modify certain enactments set out in Sch.4 to the Act (which include the Human Rights Act 1998 and certain provisions of the Acts of Union and the European Communities Act 1972);
- its legislation must be compatible with the European Convention on Human Rights and with EU law; and
- it cannot remove the Lord Advocate from his position as head of the system of criminal prosecutions and the investigation of deaths.

The precise boundaries of the Parliament's powers to legislate can ultimately be decided only by the courts.

Proposed Acts of the Scottish Parliament are called Bills. Most Bills are "Public Bills". If they are passed the resulting Act will alter the general laws of Scotland. Private Bills are Bills introduced by private individuals or bodies, seeking powers or benefits in excess of or in conflict with the general law. Private Bills are subject to distinct Rules.

---

[47] Scotland Act 1998 Sch.3 para.4.

Bills may be proposed by:

- the Scottish Executive: these Bills are known as Executive Bills;
- a committee of the Parliament: such Bills are called Committee Bills; or
- an individual member: these Bills are called Members' Bills.

Procedural defects

The validity of an Act of the Scottish Parliament is not affected by any invalidity in the **3–95** proceedings of the Parliament leading to its enactment. Every Act of the Scottish Parliament shall be judicially noticed.

Key Concepts

The **Scotland Act 1998** enables the Scottish Parliament to legislate for Scotland on a wide range of matters.

It may, however, only act within its **legislative competence** as defined in the Scotland Act.

Acts of the Scottish Parliament are either **Public Acts**, which deal with matters of public policy and change the general law, or **Private Acts**, which confer powers or benefits on an individual or an organisation.

PETITIONS

An interesting aspect of the Scottish Parliament's ethos of openness and accessibility to the **3–96** public, is that a member of public may petition the Scottish Parliament on a matter which falls within its legislative competence. A Public Petitions Committee has been established to consider petitions.

Subject-matter of petitions

A petition can make a request for the Parliament to: **3–97**

(1) take a view on a matter of public interest or concern; or
(2) amend existing legislation or introduce new legislation.

There are some restrictions on the subject-matter of petitions.

(1) The Parliament can only amend or introduce legislation within its legislative competence.
(2) The Parliament may not interfere with the executive decisions of other public bodies in Scotland.
(3) Petitions which relate to cases which have been subject to legal or court proceedings, industrial tribunals, appeals procedures, and the like, may not be considered. However, general issues arising out of such cases, such as a petition to change a legal procedure may be considered.
(4) Petitions should be in the public interest.
(5) Petitions should not ask the Parliament to do something unlawful.
(6) The wording of a petition should not amount to a breach of interdict or of commercial confidentiality.

(7) Petitions should not relate to matters that are sub judice (i.e. matters which are the subject of any court proceedings).

(8) Petitions should not include false statements or information. They must be submitted in good faith.

Action prior to submission of petitions

3–98   Before presenting a petition the petitioner should have taken all reasonable steps to resolve the issues by other means. In many cases, representations to the Scottish Ministers should be made in the first instance. At the very least, a petitioner should have sought the assistance of his MSP. The petition should make it clear what action the petitioner wishes the Parliament to take.

The Public Petitions Committee will consider each admissible petition and make a decision on the action to be taken in each case. The Committee may:

(1) agree to take no further action;

(2) forward to another committee of the Parliament, or to another body or person within the Parliament, such as the Presiding Officer, the Parliamentary Bureau or the Scottish Parliamentary Corporate Body for its consideration;

(3) forward to another body or organisation (outwith Parliament), e.g. the Scottish Executive, for consideration and response;

(4) recommend to the Parliamentary Bureau that the petition be debated at a meeting of the Parliament;

(5) invite the petitioner(s) to appear before it;

(6) invite the petitioner(s) to provide additional information; or

(7) take any other action it considers appropriate.

When it has considered the petition, and decided what action to take, the Public Petitions Committee responds formally to the petitioner stating clearly the action which is to be taken or gives notice in cases where no action is to be taken. The Public Petitions Committee monitors the action taken in respect of all petitions submitted to the Parliament. It publishes an annual report, which will provide a summary of its activities.

SCRUTINISING THE WORK OF THE SCOTTISH EXECUTIVE

3–99   As well as scrutinising Executive Bills, there are a number of other ways that all MSPs can examine and question the work of the Executive. The main method of ensuring that the Executive is accountable to the Scottish Parliament is by questioning ministers during sittings of the Parliament. At Question Time, MSPs can ask oral questions of the ministers and First Minister. These questions can be about any matter within the general responsibility of the Scottish Executive. Additionally, MSPs can submit written questions to the Executive. Both oral and written questions and their answers are published and are available to the public.

SCOTTISH GOVERNMENT

3–100   The "Scottish Administration" is the statutory term, which denotes both the political and administrative side of the Scottish Government. The Scottish Administration is made up of four elements: the Scottish Executive, junior ministers, non-ministerial office-holders and civil servants. Rather confusingly, the term "Scottish Executive" is used by the present Scottish Government for the overall devolved administrative system of government in Scotland (including the ministerial Scottish Executive) instead of the statutory term "Scottish Administration".[48] In recent years the term "Scottish Government" has been favoured and the Scotland Bill includes a formal recognition of this change of name.

When the Scottish Executive was established in 1999 the responsibilities previously held by the Scottish Office were divided between the newly-formed Scottish Executive and the Scotland Office. The powers and duties exercised by ministers in the Scottish Office, relating to devolved matters, were transferred to the Scottish Ministers.

CHALLENGES TO ACTIONS OF THE PARLIAMENT OR THE SCOTTISH EXECUTIVE

Although the courts have no power to declare a provision in an Act of the Westminster **3–101** Parliament invalid, the same principle does not apply to Acts of the Scottish Parliament. Acts of the Scottish Parliament are only valid if they are within the legislative competence, which has been devolved by the Scotland Act.[49] Acts of the Scottish Parliament and Scottish subordinate legislation are to be read as narrowly as is required for them to be within competence. An action taken under the Scotland Act, raising an issue of the competence of the Parliament or the executive, is referred to as a "devolution issue". Devolution issues are defined as the following questions:

Key Concepts

Devolution Issues:

- whether an Act of the Scottish Parliament, or a provision within it, is within the legislative competence of the Parliament;
- whether a function is a function of a Scottish Minister or the First Minister or the Lord Advocate;
- whether the exercise of a function by a member of the Scottish Executive would be within devolved competence;
- whether the exercise of a function by a member of the Scottish Executive is or would be incompatible with EU law or Convention rights;
- whether a failure to act by a member of the Scottish Executive is incompatible with EU law or Convention rights; and
- any other question as to whether a function is within devolved competence and any other question arising by virtue of the Act about reserved matters.

A devolution issue may arise in any case, civil or criminal, anywhere in the United Kingdom. Schedule 6 sets out the rules as to which court, or tribunal, may hear the devolution issue and the appropriate rules of the courts in Scotland were amended accordingly.[50] Courts and tribunals elsewhere in the United Kingdom are also detailed in the Schedule.[51]

---

[48] Scotland Act 1998 s.126(6)–(8).
[49] Scotland Act 1998 s.54.
[50] Act of Sederunt (Devolution Issue Rules) 1999 (SI 1999/1345) for civil proceedings and Act of Adjournal (Devolution Issue Rules) 1999 (SI 1999/1346) for criminal proceedings.
[51] Scotland Act 1998 Sch.6 para.1.

As the Lord Advocate and the Advocate General for Scotland have a special interest in ensuring that devolution issues are resolved, the Scotland Act provides that either officer may institute proceedings to determine a devolution issue.[52] Devolution issues can also be raised by parties in any legal proceedings, whether they are proceedings instigated for the specific purpose of determining a devolution issue, or proceedings where the original purpose was the resolution of another matter, but a devolution issue has arisen during the course of the proceedings. Devolution issues may be raised in courts at any level of the hierarchy. This means that in civil cases devolution issues may be raised in the sheriff court, the Court of Session and the House of Lords and in criminal cases devolution issues may be raised in the district court, sheriff court and High Court of Justiciary. If neither the Lord Advocate nor the Advocate General is a party to the legal proceedings, notice must be given to both the Lord Advocate and the Advocate General that a devolution issue is to be raised so that they may participate in the proceedings.

Legal challenges to Acts of the Scottish Parliament

3–102 A challenge to the validity of a provision in an Act of the Scottish Parliament came before the Privy Council in October 2001.

> ### A v Scottish Ministers
> #### 2002 S.C. (P.C.) 63
>
> A had previously challenged the lawfulness of a restriction order, under which he was detained in a hospital after being convicted of homicide. This challenge was unsuccessful and A appealed. He argued that the Mental Health (Public Safety and Appeals) (Scotland) Act 1999 s.1, which had amended the Mental Health (Scotland) Act 1984, was incompatible with the Human Rights Act 1998 Sch.1 Pt I art.5. Article 5 is concerned with the right to liberty. The article includes a list of exceptions to the right of liberty and provides that persons who are of unsound mind may be detained. However in the case *Winterwerp v Netherlands*[53] the European Court of Human Rights held that compulsory detention in a hospital is only lawful where there is medical evidence that it is justified.
>
> The Privy Council dismissed the appeal. They held that the Mental Health (Public Safety and Appeals) (Scotland) Act 1999 s.1 was not outside the legislative competence of the Scottish Parliament. It was not incompatible with art.5 of the European Convention on Human Rights, as there is nothing in that article to the effect that persons of unsound mind may only be detained for the purpose of receiving medical treatment.

The validity of the legal aid regulations came under consideration by the Privy Council in the case of *McLean v Buchanan*. Aspects of the Children's Hearing System in Scotland have also been challenged as devolution issues.[54]

---

[52] Scotland Act 1998 Sch.6 para.4(1).
[53] *Winterwerp v Netherlands* (1979–80) 2 E.H.R.R. 387.
[54] *S v Principal Reporter (No.1)*, 2001 S.C. 977; 2001 S.L.T. 531.

McLean v Buchanan
2002 S.C. (P.C.) 1

In the course of a criminal appeal McLean contended that the inadequate legal aid funding that he and his co-accused had been awarded under the Criminal Legal Aid (Fixed Payments) (Scotland) Regulations 1999, unfairly prejudiced them. He claimed that the inadequacy of legal aid provision was a devolution issue. The regulations were outside the legislative competence as they were incompatible with the right to a fair trial under art.6(3) of the European Convention on Human Rights.

The Privy Council held that the inadequacy of the legal aid funding was not incompatible with McLean's right to a fair trial. In his case, the solicitors and counsel had continued to act even though funding had run out. However, it was noted that in a case where no legal representation was available, as a result of the 1999 Regulations but under his Convention rights a defendant should be afforded representation, then a breach might arise.

Normally when a legal provision or action is found to be ultra vires the provision or action is treated as null and void. However, actions in court to challenge the validity of a provision or action made under the Scotland Act will take time to be heard and decided and, before the case is raised, the provision or action may have been acted upon. This would lead to uncertainty, as people could not rely on the provision in case a retrospective decision of invalidity was made. The Scotland Act, therefore, allows that a court, or tribunal, may remove or limit any retrospective effect of the decision, or suspend its effect for a period to allow correction of the defect, if it decides that provisions are ultra vires.[55] The court is also required to have regard to the effect of an order on persons who are not parties to the proceedings.

Challenges to the validity of Acts of the Scottish Parliament may only be brought by a person who has title and interest to sue. He or she must be able to show that they are directly affected by the Act. Furthermore, the Scotland Act states that a person may not bring any proceedings in a court or tribunal on the ground that the Act is incompatible with Convention rights, unless he would be a victim for the purposes of art.34 of the Convention, if proceedings in respect of the Act were brought before the European Court of Human Rights.[56]

Adams v Scottish Ministers
2003 S.C. 171

Adams brought a petition for judicial review of the Protection of Wild Mammals (Scotland) Act 2002, which rendered mounted foxhunting unlawful. He contended that the Act was partly incompatible with the Human Rights Act 1998 Sch.1 Pt I arts 8 and 14, as it amounted to an infringement of the right to respect for private and family life and was discriminatory. He claimed, therefore, that the Act was beyond the legislative competence of the Scottish Parliament, and was ultra vires. (Adams was a manager of foxhounds, who lived in a house provided in the course of his employment.)

---

[55] Scotland Act 1998 s.102.
[56] Scotland Act 1998 s.100(1).

The petition was dismissed because Adams was held not to qualify as a victim with a right to bring proceedings on the grounds of incompatibility of an Act with Convention rights.[57] In the opinion of the Lord Ordinary, foxhunting did not amount to an activity of private life for the purposes of art.8 of the Human Rights Act. The Act could affect Adams' right to property, but it was within the legislative competence to infringe such a right in order to further the general interest in preventing cruelty to animals.

Investigation of maladministration within the Scottish Parliament

3–103 The Scottish Parliamentary Standards Commissioner Act 2002 created the post of Scottish Parliamentary Standards Commissioner. The Scottish Parliamentary Corporate Body appoints the Commissioner with the agreement of the Parliament. His function is to investigate the conduct of MSPs in order to determine whether a Member of the Parliament has breached:

- a provision of the Code of Conduct;
- the Members' Interests Order;
- any provision in an Act of the Scottish Parliament (asp) that replaces that Order; or
- any provision of the standing orders of the Parliament.

A Code of Conduct for members of the Scottish Parliament was adopted and approved by the Parliament on February 24, 2000. Contravention of the Code of Conduct is an offence.

Key Concepts

Appointment of the Commissioner

The following people are not eligible for the appointment of Commissioner:

- Members of the Parliament;
- staff of the Parliament; and
- any person who has been a Member of the Parliament or a member of staff of the Parliament during the preceding two years.

The Commissioner is required, on receipt of a complaint, to investigate whether a Member of the Parliament has committed the conduct complained of and whether the relevant provisions cover that conduct. The Commissioner may not investigate any other conduct without a specific complaint. The Commissioner can investigate complaints about former Members of Parliament in relation to conduct that took place when they were Members. He can also investigate the conduct of Scottish Law Officers and former Scottish Law Officers, if they are not members of the Parliament.

The standing orders or the Code of Conduct may specify classes of complaints that are to be excluded from the investigation powers of the Commissioner. Nevertheless, excluded

---

[57] Scotland Act 1998 s.100; Human Rights Act 1998 Sch.1 Pt I art.34.

complaints may still be investigated by the Commissioner if the Standards Committee considers this to be appropriate and makes a direction to this effect (s.12).

The Commissioner may give advice on the procedure for making a complaint but may not give advice to a Member of the Parliament or to a member of the public in relation to whether any proposed or previous conduct would constitute a breach of the relevant provisions. The Commissioner must comply with the directions of the Standards Committee. These could include such matters as requiring the Commissioner to ensure that all persons interviewed by them are given a right to have a third party present and are advised of this right. Directions may not be given in relation to a particular investigation, as that would compromise the independence of the Commissioner.

Key Concepts

Investigation process

Stage 1:   Initial consideration by the Commissioner.
Stage 2:   Investigation by the Commissioner and report to Parliament.
Stage 3:   Parliamentary procedures (probably involving Standards Committee).
Stage 4:   The Parliament decides whether to impose sanctions.

Stage 1

A complaint may be dismissed at this stage if the Commissioner considers that it is **3–104** inadmissible. In certain circumstances, he may also report a procedural defect to the Standards Committee who would be able to instruct that the investigation proceed or that the complaint be dismissed.

Stage 2

The investigation by the Commissioner is conducted in private. He may make an interim **3–105** report to the Standards Committee at any time on the progress of an investigation. The Commissioner decides when and how to carry out an investigation. After investigating, the Commissioner reports to the Parliament, on the conclusions which he has reached, but he does not express a view upon what sanctions would be appropriate for any breach of the Members' Interests Order or the Code of Conduct.

Stage 3

The procedures, which are followed after the Commissioner has made his report, are a **3–106** matter for Parliament to decide for itself as it is master of its own procedures. The Standards Committee considers the report of the Commissioner and may conduct their own investigations or require the Commissioner to carry out further investigations. The Standards Committee then reports to the Parliament on the complaint, with any recommendations for actions to be taken where they consider that the complaint should be upheld. The Standards Committee can also investigate the conduct of MSPs where the conduct has been brought to their attention by other means

Stage 4

The Parliament decides whether to accept the Committee's report and if appropriate **3–107** impose sanctions.

Admissibility

3–108 The Scottish Parliamentary Standards Commissioner applies three tests in order to decide whether or not a complaint is admissible:

(1) the complaint must be relevant;
(2) it must comply with certain specified procedural requirements; and
(3) it must warrant further investigation.

Three matters need to be established for a complaint to be relevant:

(1) the complaint must relate to conduct of a Member of the Parliament;
(2) it must be within the jurisdiction of the Commissioner; and
(3) some part of the conduct complained about must relate to a matter that the Commissioner considers may be covered by the relevant provisions.

The third test, that further investigation of a complaint is required, is satisfied when the Commissioner having carried out an initial investigation, decides that there is enough evidence to suggest that the conduct complained about may have taken place

Legal challenges to Acts of the Scottish Executive

3–109 Section 57(2) of the Scotland Act states that a member of the Scottish Executive has no power to make any subordinate legislation, or to do any other Act, so far as the legislation or Act is incompatible with any of the European Convention Human rights. Excesses and abuses of power may be prevented in two ways:

(1) the Scotland Act provides that a Secretary of State may make an order to prevent an action of a member of the Scottish Executive, which the Secretary of State believes is incompatible with an international obligation, other than the ECHR; and
(2) a Secretary of State may also make an order requiring a member of the Scottish Executive to implement an international obligation.

The legality of actions or decisions of the Scottish Executive may also be challenged in the courts, through judicial review procedure. The validity of an action may also be raised in the course of legal proceedings in certain circumstances, for example as a defence to a criminal prosecution. If a court or tribunal finds that an action of the Scottish Executive infringes a Convention right or a principle of European law, or is otherwise ultra vires, the court or tribunal has power to strike down the offending action. The remedies, which may be granted, are the same as those which may be awarded by the court in any other action. Therefore, if the Court of Session finds in favour of the petitioner in relation to a devolution issue, the court may order, reduction, declarator, specific implement or damages.

The Lord Advocate is a member of the Scottish Executive and many of the notable challenges to actions of the Scottish Executive relate to his functions with regard to the Scottish judicial system. Challenges have been brought in relation to such matters as, the procedures for judicial and shrieval appointments, the provision of legal aid, the Childrens' Hearing System and delays in the prosecution of crimes. Where successful challenges have been made, the Scottish Parliament has acted promptly to introduce reforms by measures such as the Convention Rights (Compliance) (Scotland) Act 2001—which dealt with a wide range of procedures, or by specific reforms—such as the Bail, Judicial Appointments etc. (Scotland) Act 2000. Two examples of challenges are given below:

Starrs v Ruxton
2000 J.C. 208; 2000 S.L.T. 42

A prosecution, before Temporary Sheriff David Crowe in Linlithgow Sheriff Court, was challenged on the basis that a temporary sheriff could not be regarded as impartial when his future employment prospects were subject to influence by the Lord Advocate. The Lord Advocate had a key role in the appointment, dismissal and non-reappointment of temporary sheriffs. He is also head of the public prosecution system in Scotland. Temporary sheriffs may be reluctant to reach decisions that may cause the Lord Advocate to look upon them with disfavour. Consequently, temporary sheriffs could not be regarded as sufficiently independent of the Executive to meet the requirements of art.6 that an accused have a fair hearing before an "independent and impartial tribunal". It was held that the independence of a member of a court was to be established by reference to the manner of appointment, the term of office, the guarantees against outside pressure and the appearance of independence. Temporary sheriffs were appointed by the Secretary of State for Scotland,[58] however, the Lord Advocate played an important role in that he decided what appointments were required and advised the Scottish Courts Administration on selection. Appointments were generally for one year only. Appointment as a temporary sheriff was widely regarded as a step towards appointment as a permanent sheriff. Possible hopes of such advancement, as well as the short-term nature of the office, compromised the independence of the temporary sheriff. The absence of security of tenure was the most important factor in casting doubt on the independence of temporary sheriffs. While there was no suggestion that the Scottish Executive had ever acted contrary to the principles of judicial independence, it was necessary that legal guarantees of the independence of the judiciary be in place.

Clancy v Caird (No.2)
2000 S.L.T. 546; 2000 S.C.L.R. 526

An action of damages went to proof before a temporary judge. During *avizandum* the decision in *Starrs v Ruxton* was issued. On the basis of that decision, one of the parties in the damages action sought to raise as a devolution issue, that a temporary judge was not an independent and impartial tribunal. It was held that the appointment and use of temporary judges to hear cases, where the Crown itself was not involved in the claim, did not breach a party's Convention rights. Temporary judges have security of tenure and enjoy the same status and immunities as a permanent judge. The absence of a guarantee of reappointment did not affect a temporary judge's independence. The Lord President decided whether or not to use a temporary judge and had laid down restrictions on the use of temporary judges in potentially sensitive cases, such as judicial review. Though the temporary judge remained in legal practice, there were institutional safeguards such as the judicial oath, and so this factor did not breach art.6.

---

[58] Sheriff Courts (Scotland) Act 1971 s.11.

These two cases brought the issue of judicial appointments into the limelight and caused the Scottish Ministers to recognise the need for a review of the process of judicial appointments. Following a process of consultation, the Justice Minister announced judicial appointment reforms, which include the advertising of all appointments of the Court of Session judges, sheriff principals and sheriffs and an independent Judicial Appointments Board. The Judicial Appointments Board scrutinises candidates' applications and recommends the best person for nomination to the First Minister.[59]

Scottish Public Services Ombudsman

3–110   Under s.91(1) of the Scotland Act 1998, the Parliament is under a duty to make provision for the investigation of maladministration complaints against members of the Scottish Executive, in the exercise of functions conferred on the Scottish Ministers, and against other office-holders in the Scottish Administration. The Scottish Public Services Ombudsman Act 2002 established a Scottish Public Services Ombudsman to deal with complaints against public bodies, which were previously dealt with by:

(1) the Scottish Parliamentary Commissioner for Administration;
(2) the Health Service Commissioner for Scotland;
(3) the Commissioner for Local Administration in Scotland; and
(4) the Housing Association Ombudsman for Scotland.

The Public Services Ombudsman also has responsibility for:

(1) the Mental Welfare Commission's function of investigating complaints relating to mental health; and
(2) complaints against Scottish Enterprise and Highlands and Islands Enterprise.

The Act establishes a standardised set of procedures for dealing with all relevant complaints against a wide range of public authorities. The authorities, which may be subject to investigation by the Public Services Ombudsman, are listed in Sch.2. The list includes 89 different organisations. They fall into six categories:

Key Concepts

Authorities which may be investigated:

- Scottish Parliament and Scottish Administration;
- health service;
- local government;
- housing;
- Scottish public authorities; and
- cross-border public authorities.

---

[59] Bail, Judicial Appointments etc. (Scotland) Act 2000.

Investigations by the Ombudsman

The Ombudsman decides whether to initiate, continue or discontinue an investigation. He **3–111** may take such action in connection with the complaint, or request, as he thinks may be of assistance in reaching any such decision or resolving the complaint, or request.

Matters which may be investigated

The following matters may be investigated: **3–112**

(a) actions taken by, or on behalf of, a listed authority in the exercise of administrative functions of the authority;

(b) actions taken by or on behalf of a health service body or an independent provider;

(c) service failure by a listed authority (except a family health service provider or a social landlord);

(d) actions taken by or on behalf of a family health service provider, in connection with any family health services provided by that provider; and

(e) actions taken by or on behalf of a registered social landlord.

The Ombudsman may only investigate a matter, if a member of the public claims to have sustained injustice or hardship in consequence of the acts which amount to maladministration, or failure to act. The person making the claim is referred to in this Act as the "person aggrieved".

The Ombudsman is not entitled to question the merits of a decision unless there has been maladministration. The Ombudsman must not investigate action taken by, or on behalf of, a member of the Scottish Executive unless the action was taken in the exercise of functions conferred on the Scottish Ministers, or of functions conferred on the First Minister alone. He must not investigate action taken by, or on behalf of, a listed authority which is a cross-border public authority, unless the action taken concerned Scotland and did not relate to reserved matters. He may only investigate action taken in the exercise of the functions of a public nature. He may not investigate when there are other remedies available—such as a right of appeal to a minister or a remedy by way of proceedings in any court of law.

After conducting an investigation, the Ombudsman must send a report of the investigation to the Scottish Ministers and must lay a copy of the report before the Parliament.

Key Concepts

The first Schedule to the Act gives statutory authority to the independence of the Ombudsman, his deputies and his staff. It states that are not to be regarded as servants or agents of the Crown. The Ombudsman, in the exercise of that officer's functions, is not subject to the direction or control of:

(a) any Member of the Parliament;
(b) any Member of the Scottish Executive; or
(c) the Parliamentary corporation.

LOCAL GOVERNMENT IN SCOTLAND

3–113 The structure, function and financing of local government are devolved matters and, as such, are the responsibility of the Scottish Parliament. The current framework for local government in Scotland dates from 1996, when the Local Government etc. (Scotland) Act 1994 was implemented. The Local Government etc. (Scotland) Act 1994 set out provisions for comprehensive reform of the system of local government. Between 1975 and 1996, local government was operated as a two-tier structure consisting of 9 regional councils and 53 district councils on mainland Scotland. There were also three islands councils. This framework was abolished and replaced with a unitary system of local government. The structure of the three island authorities remained unchanged. The 1994 Act also provided for the creation of joint boards, consisting of elected members from constituent councils, with responsibility for overseeing the delivery of police, fire and valuation services.

Structure of local government

Key Concepts

3–114 **Structure**:

* 32 multi-purpose councils (29 councils on mainland Scotland and 3 island authorities);
* 6 joint police boards;
* 6 joint fire boards; and
* 10 valuation joint boards.

The 1996 reorganisation restructured the boundaries and brought most of the services provided by the former regions and districts together into one authority. The unitary councils range in population size, from over 62,000 in the City of Glasgow to only 48,000 in Clackmannan. They also vary considerably in size. Clackmannan is about 300 square miles whereas Highland is about 160,000 square miles. The powers and functions of local authorities, as a whole, were not altered by the 1994 Act. Some of the powers and duties of local authorities to provide particular services, such as education or social work, are contained in separate legislation.

   The Local Government etc. (Scotland) Act 1994 removed responsibility for water and sewerage services from the councils and transferred them to three newly created quangos whose boards were selected by the Secretary of State. These have subsequently combined to form one water authority for Scotland. The Act gave power to the Secretary of State (now the Scottish Ministers) to create joint boards for the provision of a service, where it is considered that the function should be carried out jointly so as to maximise efficiency and economy. The Act also allows councils to set up joint committees for services. Each council retains the responsibility for the service, but it is carried out jointly. Councils may also contract with one another to provide a service, for example it may be cheaper for a small council to contract out the rubbish collection and disposal service to a council which is better placed geographically to provide the service. Alternatively, two or more councils may set up a consortium to provide a service. Councils have resisted setting up joint arrangements, although they have contracted with other organisations for the provision of some services. Joint action for anything other than a very limited range of services is regarded as equivalent to introducing another tier of Government, which would undermine the position of the unitary authorities.

The 1994 Act did not change the way in which councils in Scotland operate. They are made up of councillors who are elected for a three-year term of office. Full meetings of the council establish the policies to be followed. Specific matters are delegated to a range of committees. The functions are carried out by officers, headed by a chief executive and a number of chief officers in charge of departments, which provide either a service, such as housing or education, or provide administrative support to the council itself.

Functions of local government

Key Concepts

Functions: 3–115

Provision of services: Planning, resourcing and direct provision of services including education, housing, local roads, social work, economic development, public protection, planning, leisure and recreation.

Strategic planning: Strategic planning framework, setting objectives based on the needs and priorities of their constituents.

Regulation:

Regulatory functions include: (a) granting licences for such things as the sale of alcohol or the operation of taxis, and (b) registration and inspection functions (e.g. private residential homes); trading standards.

Community leadership

The Local Government Committee has the main responsibility for local government affairs within the Scottish Parliament. There are, however, aspects of the work of local authorities which fall within the remit of a number of other committees, for example education, culture and sport, health and community care, rural affairs and social inclusion, housing and voluntary sector. The 1994 Act gave the Secretary of State for Scotland, and so now the Scottish Ministers, over 100 new powers to make orders and directions in relation to local government.

Throughout the United Kingdom, local councils may only do those things, which are provided in the legislation setting them up. In Scotland, the Local Government (Scotland) Act 1973 is still the source of authority for the powers and duties of councils. Local authorities may only incur expenditure and provide services within the statutory framework. The 1973 Act gave limited power to a local authority to spend money, where the authority considered it to be in the best interests of the inhabitants of their area. This limited power was, however, curtailed by s.164 of the 1994 Act which states that councils may only incur expenditure which is in the interest of their area and will bring "direct benefit" to it.[60] There are further restrictions on the power under s.164, including an obligation to ensure that the direct benefit is commensurate with the expenditure. The

---

[60] See s.83(1) of the Local Government (Scotland) Act 1973 (as amended by s.164 of the Local Government etc. (Scotland) Act 1994).

Scottish Ministers may set a limit on the expenditure that may be incurred under this section. Should a local authority provide services outside the current statutes, it would be acting ultra vires, literally *beyond its powers*, and may be subject to legal challenge in the courts.

Key Concepts

Powers and duties of local authorities.

Mandatory:　　Services which must be provided (e.g. education for school age children).

Permissive:　　Services which may be provided (e.g. economic development).

Discretionary:　A general power to spend a limited amount of money, which will bring direct benefit to the council area.

The Scottish Ministers have powers to control local government finance and expenditure. The Scottish Ministers are responsible for most of the costs of funding local councils. Permission must be sought, before certain expenditure is incurred by a local authority.

▼ CHAPTER SUMMARY

GENERAL NATURE OF THE UK CONSTITUTION

3–116
1. **The constitution of the United Kingdom relates to the rules of Government of the State.**
2. **The UK constitution is unwritten, flexible and parliamentary.**

SOURCES OF CONSTITUTIONAL LAW

1. **Important sources of constitutional law include:**

   ➢ The Bill of Rights and Claim of Right 1689.
   ➢ Act of Settlement 1700.
   ➢ Acts of Union 1707.
   ➢ European Communities Act 1972.
   ➢ Parliament Acts 1911 and 1949.
   ➢ Human Rights Act 1998.
   ➢ Scotland Act 1998.

2. **Presumptions of legislative intent**

   (a) **No retrospective effect without clear intention:**

   ➢ *R. v Lambert* [2001] 3 All E.R. 577.

   (b) **Statutes do not bind the Crown, unless it is expressly stated:**

   ➢ *Lord Advocate v Strathclyde Council*, 1990 S.L.T.158.

(c) *Hansard* may be used to aid interpretation:

> ➤ *Pepper v Hart* [1993] A.C. 593.

3. **Royal prerogative—residual powers of the crown**

   (a) **No new prerogative powers may be created:**

   > ➤ *BBC v Johns* [1965] Ch. 32.

   (b) **An existing power may apply to new circumstances:**

   > ➤ *R. v Home Secretary Ex p. Northumbria Police Authority* [1989] Q.B. 26.

4. **Authoritative works; particularly Dicey.**
5. **Conventions, e.g. Royal Assent for legislation.**

Doctrines of the Constitution

1. **Separation of Powers; Independence of the Judiciary:**

   > ➤ Constitutional Reform Act 2005.

2. **Rule of Law**

   (a) **Absence of arbitrary power:**

   > ➤ *Entick v Carrington* (1765) 19 State T.R. 1030;
   > ➤ *Burmah Oil Co v Lord Advocate* [1965] A.C. 75.

   (b) **Equality before the law;**

   > ➤ *M v Home Office* [1994] 1 A.C. 377.

   (c) **The constitution is the result of the ordinary law of the land.**

3. **Supremacy of Parliament**

   (a) **Parliament can make or unmake any law it pleases:**

   > ➤ War Crimes Act 1991.

   (b) **No other body may question the validity of an Act of Parliament:**

   > ➤ *British Railways Board v Pickin* [1974] A.C. 765.

   (c) **No Parliament can bind its successors:**

   > ➤ *Ellen Street Estates v Minister of Health* [1934] 1 K.B. 590;
   > ➤ *McCormick v Lord Advocate*, 1953 S.C. 396;
   > ➤ *R. v Secretary of State for Transport Ex p. Factortame* [1990] 2 A.C. 85.

United Kingdom Parliament

1. **The monarch.**
2. **House of Lords**

   (a) **Reform:**

   > ➤ House of Lords Act 1999.

    (b) Supreme court:

      ➤ Constitutional Reform Act 2005.

    (c) Powers to delay Public Bills:

      ➤ Parliament Acts 1911 and 1949.

3. House of Commons

    (a) Membership:

      ➤ House of Commons Disqualification Act 1975.

    (b) The functions of the House of Commons are: scrutiny of legislation; questions to ministers; debates; and checks financial probity of the government.

    (c) There are three types of Bill: Private Bills, Hybrid Bills; and Public Bills.

POWERS AND PRIVILEGES OF PARLIAMENT

1. **The Speaker of the House of Commons exercises various powers: Calls to Order; naming and suspension; suspension of sitting; expulsion and censure.**
2. **Powers of the Committee on Standards and Privileges;**

    ➤ Code of Conduct on Standards and Privileges 1996.

    (a) Seven principles of public life: selflessness, integrity, objectivity, accountability, openness, honesty and leadership.

THE GOVERNMENT

1. **The sovereign. Three rules are applied with regard to succession: preference for males; primogeniture and representation.**
2. **Privy Council.**
3. **The Prime Minister has powers of patronage, powers regarding the dissolution of Parliament and powers relating to the cabinet.**
4. **Ministerial responsibility applies in two circumstances: collective Responsibility and individual Responsibility.**
5. **Scottish business at Westminster**

    (a) Scotland Office part of the Ministry of Justice;

    (b) Advocate General;

    (c) Secretary of State for Scotland. The role of the Secretary of State is to: represent Scottish interests in the UK Government; encourage co-operation between Parliaments; intervene in relations between the UK and Scottish Administrations; pay the grant to the Scottish Consolidated Fund; manages other financial transactions; and may make orders under s.35 of the Scotland Act, preventing a Bill which is outside the legislative competence being submitted for Royal assent.

6. **Civil Service.**

SCOTTISH GOVERNMENT

1. **Devolution:**

    ➢ Scotland Act 1998.

2. **Relations between the UK Parliament and the Scottish Parliament. Devolved matters, reserved matters. Sewel Conventions.**
3. **Scottish Parliament. Key principles for the Scottish Parliament are: sharing the power; accountability; access and participation; and equal opportunities.**
4. **Privileges of the Scottish Parliament:**

    ➢ *Whaley v Lord Watson of Invergowrie*, 2000 S.C. 340.

5. **Composition of the Scottish Parliament. The Scottish Parliament is unicameral. It has 129 MSPs one of whom is elected to be the Presiding Officer.**
6. **Scottish Executive;**
    First Minister;
    Lord Advocate and Solicitor-General;
    Other ministers appointed by First Minister.
7. **Ministerial Responsibility:**

    ➢ Scottish Ministerial Code, 1999.

8. **Scottish Parliament Committees. There are mandatory Committees and subject Committees.**

SCOTTISH PARLIAMENT LEGISLATION

1. **Legislative Competence:**

    ➢ Scotland Act 1998.

PETITIONS

1. **Views on matters of public interest.**
2. **Amendments to legislation.**

SCOTTISH ADMINISTRATION

The Scottish administration consists of: the Scottish Executive; junior ministers; non-ministerial office-holders and civil servants.

CHALLENGES TO ACTIONS OF THE PARLIAMENT OR THE SCOTTISH EXECUTIVE

1. **Devolution Issues:**

    ➢ Scotland Act 1998 Sch.6;
    ➢ *A v Scottish Ministers*, 2002 S.C. (P.C) 63.

2. **Maladministration;**

➤ Scottish Parliamentary Standards Commissioner Act 2002.

3. **Legal Challenges to acts of the Scottish Executive:**

➤ Scotland Act 1998 s.57(2);
➤ *Starrs v Ruxton*, 2000 J.C. 208; 2000 S.L.T 42. (Temporary Sheriffs);
➤ *Clancy v Caird (No.2)*, 2000 S.L.T. 546; 2000 S.C.L.R. 526. (Temporary judges).

4. **Scottish Public Services Ombudsman;**

➤ Scottish Public Services Ombudsman Act 2002.

LOCAL GOVERNMENT IN SCOTLAND

➤ Local Government etc. (Scotland) Act 1994.

1. **Functions of local government are: provision of services; strategic planning; regulation and community leadership.**

? QUICK QUIZ

CONSTITUTIONAL LAW

- List three characteristics of the UK constitution.
- Can an Act of Parliament be declared invalid by the courts?
- Give three examples of prerogative powers.
- What are the three branches of Government?
- What three meanings did Dicey ascribe to the principle of the rule of law?
- List three categories of people who are disqualified from voting in parliamentary elections.
- When may a minister decline to answer questions in Parliament?
- List the "Seven Principles of Public Life" set out by the Committee on Standards in Public Life.
- What are the functions of the Advocate-General?
- What is a unicameral Parliament?
- What functions are carried out by the Presiding Officer of the Scottish Parliament?
- What are the four principles which underpin the operation of the Scottish Parliament?
- What function is carried out by the Parliamentary Bureau?
- Give two examples of the mandatory committees, which must be set up by the Scottish Parliament.
- What is a devolution issue?
- Who would consider a complaint from a member of the public against a Scottish local authority?

FURTHER READING

There are two books which give comprehensive and up-to-date accounts of UK constitutional law: A. Bradley and K. Ewing, *Constitutional and Administrative Law*, 15th edn (Addison Wesley Longman, 2010) and H. Barnett, *Constitutional and Administrative Law*, 9th edn (Routledge, London, 2011).

C.M.G. Himsworth and C.R. Munro, *Scotland Act 1998*, 2nd edn (W. Green, 1999). This book provides explanations of the provisions of the Scotland Act 1998 and includes the provisions of the Act.

J. McFadden and M. Lazarowicz, *The Scottish Parliament: An Introduction* (Tottel, 2003). This book gives an account of the operation of the Scottish Parliament.

A more comprehensive account of Constitutional Law in Scotland can be found in C.M.G. Himsworth and O'Neill, *Scotland's Constitution: Law and Practice* (Tottel, 2003), and Munro, *Public Law*, (W. Green, 2007).

RELEVANT WEB LINKS

Internet sources are particularly useful in the context of constitutional law. The following sites are particularly useful:

Houses of Parliament: *http://www.parliament.uk*
UK Online Government Gateway: *http://www.direct.gov.uk*
Statute Law database: *http://www.legislation.gov.uk*
This database contains primary legislation that was in force at February 1, 1991 and primary and secondary legislation that has been produced since that date. Primary legislation is kept up-to-date by applying the effects contained within subsequent legislation. New legislation is added as soon as possible after it has been issued.

Acts of the Scottish Parliament: *http://www.legislation.gov.uk/asp*
This site has all Acts of the Scottish Parliament. It also includes the explanatory notes to the Acts.

Scottish Executive: *http://www.scotland.gov.uk*
Scottish Parliament: *http://www.scottish.parliament.uk*
The Scottish Parliament website is a very useful source of information on the day-to-day operation of the Scottish Parliament. It includes the official report of the meetings of Parliament.

Chapter 4   The EU Dimension to the Scottish Legal System

ALAN REID[1]

▶ CHAPTER OVERVIEW

4–01 This chapter is concerned with the impact membership of the European Union has had upon the Scottish legal system. The chapter discusses the development of the original European Community from the original membership of 6 Member States through to its present membership of 27 in the expanded guise of the European Union. The chapter then discusses the sources of EU law before going on to outline the powers and roles of the various EU institutions. Finally, the chapter discusses the relationship between EU law and national law and the key role played by the Court of Justice of the European Union in this relationship.

✓ OUTCOMES

4–02 At the end of the chapter, you should be able to:

- ✓ appreciate why the European Union was established;
- ✓ identify the main primary and secondary sources of EU law;
- ✓ understand the powers and roles of the main EU institutions;
- ✓ understand the meaning of the terms "supremacy of EU law" and "Direct effect"; and
- ✓ appreciate the key role played by the Court of Justice of the European Union in promoting European integration.

HISTORY OF THE EUROPEAN UNION

4–03 Prevention of a third world war and European economic prosperity were the main reasons for establishment of what is now the European Union. The first attempt to link Europe economically occurred in 1951, when France, Germany, Italy, Belgium, the Netherlands and Luxembourg signed the Treaty of Paris. This Treaty brought into being the European Coal and Steel Community in 1952. This Community fused together the coal and steel making industries of these countries, thus creating an enlarged European internal market for these outputs and minimising the risk of future conflict between the Member States. This Community was to be subject to a "supranational" control mechanism, independent of and superior to the Governments of the Member States. The Treaty of Paris provided for the creation of four autonomous institutions, namely the High Authority, the Council

---

[1] Lecturer in Law, LRG University of Applied Sciences, Switzerland.

128

of Ministers, the Assembly and the European Court of Justice. This Community was so successful that the founding Member States agreed to further sectoral and economic integration. In 1957, two Treaties of Rome were signed, creating the European Atomic Energy Community [Euratom] and the European Economic Community [EEC], which was later renamed as the European Community. Thus, three European Communities were created and in 1965, the Merger Treaty ensured that the three communities shared a single institutional structure.

The first expansion of the European Community took place in 1973, when the United Kingdom, Ireland and Denmark joined. Further expansion took place in the 1980s with the accession of Greece in 1981 and Spain and Portugal joining in 1986. Austria, Finland and Sweden joined in 1995 and in 2004, 10 new members joined the European Union club, in the shape of Cyprus, the Czech Republic, Estonia, Hungary, Lithuania, Latvia, Malta, Poland, Slovakia and Slovenia. Most recently, Bulgaria and Romania joined on the January 1, 2007, bringing the current total membership to 27. In the future, the European Union may expand to include countries such as Croatia, Iceland and Turkey.

The European integration process also deepened during this period of expanding membership. The EEC was always intended to be more than a simple economic grouping. In 1986, the Single European Act was enacted, primarily to re-invigorate the internal market process and greatly expand the European Community's competences to cover such areas as the environment and health and safety. The competences of the three Communities were further expanded by the Treaty on European Union, also known as the Maastricht Treaty, of 1992. In addition, a new three pillar institutional structure was created, to be known as the European Union. This organisation had competence to deal with foreign and security issues and promote action in the field of Justice and Home Affairs. However, action in this area was not supranational in nature but was rather an example of inter-governmental cooperation. Further amendments to the Treaty on European Union took place in 1997 with the signing of the Treaty of Amsterdam and 2001 saw the signing of the Treaty of Nice. The Treaty of Amsterdam renumbered the EC Treaty, renamed the Third Pillar Police and Judicial Cooperation in Criminal Matters and attempted to pave the way for further enlargement through various institutional changes. The Nice Treaty was designed to finish the streamlining process started by Amsterdam, in preparation for the accession of the 10 new Member States in 2004. The Treaty of Paris expired in 2002 with the competences being transferred to the EC Treaty. Further structural changes were outlined in the Treaty Establishing a Constitution for Europe but for political reasons this Treaty never came into force. In particular, the Treaty was rejected by the French and Dutch populations in 2005. Because of these political problems, the European Union's politicians decided to embark on a less ambitious programme of reform. These negotiations led to the drafting of the Treaty of Lisbon. The Treaty proved to be almost as controversial as the Constitution for Europe. The Irish population rejected the Treaty in 2008 in a referendum and was subject to a number of legal challenges in the Czech Republic, Germany and the United Kingdom. However the Irish subsequently voted yes and the various domestic legal actions were disposed of, allowing the Treaty to come into force on December 1, 2009.

The Treaty of Lisbon creates a new legal structure for the European Union, expands the range of EU competences and makes the EU political and legislative processes more democratic.

The legal foundations of the European Union are now set out in three Treaties, namely:

- the Treaty on European Union (TEU);
- the Treaty on the Functioning of the European Union (TFEU); and
- the Charter of Fundamental Rights of the European Union.

Key Timeline

1951 Treaty of Paris—European Coal and Steel Community
1957 Treaties of Rome—Euratom and the European Economic Community
1965 Merger Treaty
1973 First Enlargement—Britain, Ireland and Denmark
1981 Second Enlargement—Greece
1986 Third Enlargement—Spain and Portugal
       Single European Act
1992 Treaty on European Union
1995 Fourth Enlargement—Austria, Finland and Sweden
1997 Treaty of Amsterdam
2001 Treaty of Nice
2002 Expiry of Treaty of Paris
2004 Firth Enlargement—Cyprus, the Czech Republic, Estonia, Hungary, Lithuania,
       Latvia, Malta, Poland, Slovakia, Slovenia
       Treaty Establishing a Constitution for Europe signed
2007 Sixth Enlargement—Bulgaria and Romania
2009 Treaty of Lisbon comes into force
       Herman van Rompuy becomes President of the European Council
       Baroness Ashton becomes High Representative of the EU for Foreign Affairs
       and Security Policy
2010 The Enhanced Cooperation procedure is used for the first time
2011 Croatia signs Accession Treaty

Key Concepts

European Union diagram

Treaty on European Union

Treaty on the Functioning
of the EU

Charter of Fundamental
Rights of the EU

INSTITUTIONS

The modern European Union is served by seven principal institutions: **4–04**

- The European Commission[2] which acts in the interests of the Union;
- The Council of the European Union[3] representing the Member States;
- The European Council,[4] a political entity composed of the Heads of State or Government of the Member States;
- The European Parliament[5] representing the peoples of Europe;
- The Court of Justice of the European Union, the judicial arm of the Union;
- The Court of Auditors, which ensures the integrity of the EU's financial budget[6]; and
- The European Central Bank,[7] which oversees the operation of the Eurozone.

The European Union is assisted by a number of subsidiary bodies, such as the Economic and Social Committee, the Committee of the Regions, the European Investment Bank, the European System of Central Banks and the European External Action Service.

The European institutional structure is not characterised by a rigid separation of powers. There is an independent judiciary, and a separation between legislative and executive functions, with the Parliament and the Council sharing legislative power and the Commission acting as the executive, however the Commission plays a role that is by turns legislative, executive, judicial and administrative. It is the guardian of the Treaties, the initiator and co-ordinator of Union policy and the executive agency of the Union.

The Commission

The Commission currently comprises 27 Commissioners, one for each Member State. **4–05** After 2014, the number of Commissioners will be reduced to two thirds of the number of Member States. Commissioners are chosen on grounds of their general competence and are to act independently of their Member State for the good of the Union. They serve for five-year renewable terms. The process of appointment is as follows.

First, the European Council nominates the President of the Commission by qualified majority, with the Parliament approving the candidate by majority vote. This President-Elect, in conjunction with the Council, then produces a list of Commissioners-nominate. The entire Commission then gains the consent of the Parliament. The European Council then approves the entire Commission, by qualified majority.

The Commission also has a Vice President, who operates under a dual mandate as Vice President of the Commission and as the Council's High Representative of the Union for Foreign Affairs and Security Policy.

The Commission operates in a similar vein to a cabinet in the domestic political system, in that the entire Commission bears collective responsibility for Commission decisions and individual Commissioners are assigned a portfolio of responsibility. The Commission's powers and functions are set out in arts 244 to 250 TFEU and fall into three main categories.

---

[2] Formerly the High Authority.
[3] Formerly the Council of Ministers.
[4] Became an institution by virtue of the Treaty of Lisbon.
[5] Formerly the Assembly.
[6] Became an institution by virtue of the Maastricht Treaty.
[7] Became an institution by virtue of the Lisbon Treaty.

1. Guardian of the Treaties

4–06 By virtue of art.17 TEU, the Commission ensures that EU law is correctly applied by the Member States. Article 258 TFEU allows individuals and companies to complain to the Commission that a Member State is infringing their EU law rights.[8] The Commission will then investigate and may ultimately prosecute Member States on the basis that they have breached their EU law obligations, in particular the good faith (or loyalty) clause of art.4.3 TEU. If the Commission cannot broker a settlement with the Member State(s) concerned, the Commission can refer the matter to the Court of Justice of the European Union.

In the case where the Member State has been taken to court and has failed to comply with the judgment, the Commission may bring the matter again to the court and specify the amount of the lump sum or penalty payment to be paid. The court may then impose a lump sum or penalty payment.[9]

In the situation where a Member State wishes to take another Member State to the Court of Justice of the European Union for failure to fulfil obligations, the Commission plays an important role as mediator.[10]

The Commission also monitors the actions or inaction of the Council, the Parliament and the European Central Bank.

2. Initiator of Union Action

4–07 The Commission is empowered to propose legislation for subsequent adoption by the Council and the Parliament. However, in order to make the European Union more democratic, in addition to the Commission's primary right of initiative, the Council and the Parliament can request that the Commission submit appropriate proposals for legislation. Further, under the Citizens' Initiative, a million citizens from across at least seven Member States can also submit legislative proposals to the Commission.[11]

3. Executive of the Union

4–08 The Commission has its own power of decision which it exercises in the functioning and development of the internal market.

It also administers the customs union, the common agricultural policy, state aids and the common commercial policy. A significant part of its executive function is to manage the Union budget for submission to the Council and administer special funds such as the European Agricultural Guidance and Guarantee Fund, the European Regional Development Fund, the Cohesion Fund and the European Social Fund which form part of the budget.

The Commission also acts as negotiator of international trade and co-operation agreements with third countries, or groups of countries, which the Council then concludes.

The Commission can also act by way of delegated legislative power from the Council and Parliament, under arts 290 and 291 TFEU. This practice of decision-making involves the Commission's legislative activities being supervised by the Council and Parliament under a complex system involving the submission of the Commission's draft implementing measures to committees composed of officials from Member States.

---

[8] An example is case *Commission v Cyprus* C-340/10 [2012] E.C.R. 0.
[9] *Commission v Greece* [2000] E.C.R. I-5047.
[10] TFEU art.259. An example of the Commission's good offices is case *Hungary v Slovakia* C-364/10 [2012] E.C.R. 0.
[11] TEU art.11.4 and EU Regulation 211/2011.

The Council of the European Union

The Council comprises representatives from the Member States at ministerial level, **4–09** authorised to commit the government of that Member State. The wide-ranging remit of the Council's work means that there are 10 different Council configurations and the membership changes, based on the subject matter under discussion. For example, in the field of external relations, the Council meets as the Foreign Affairs Council under the direction of the High Representative of the Union for Foreign Affairs and Security Policy.

The Council's powers and functions are set out in arts 237 to 243 TFEU.

The Council is the European Union's main decision-making institution. In terms of law-making, the Council and the Parliament work together as co-legislators in the vast majority of areas of EU competence.

Depending on the subject under discussion and the voting procedures specified in the Treaties, the Council acts by a simple majority of its members, by a qualified majority or by unanimous decision. The most important (and most complicated) voting procedure is that of Qualified Majority Voting. Under this system, until 2014, each Member State is assigned a set number of votes roughly based on population size and are weighted as follows:

Country	Votes
Austria, Bulgaria, Sweden	10
Belgium	12
Cyprus, Estonia, Latvia, Luxembourg, Slovenia	4
Czech Republic	12
Denmark, Finland, Ireland, Lithuania, Slovakia	7
France, Germany, Italy, United Kingdom	29
Greece, Hungary, Portugal	12
Malta	3
Netherlands	13
Poland, Spain	27
Romania	14
TOTAL	345

In order to pass a proposal, there must be at least 255 votes in favour, with a numerical majority of Member States in favour. In some cases the Treaties may require a two-thirds majority. If doubts exist as to the result, a Member State can request verification that the qualified majority comprises at least 62 per cent of the total population of the Union before the act may be adopted. From 2014, the voting scheme will be amended and simplified. Under this new system, in general, a qualified majority would require 55 per cent of the Member States to be in favour, a numerical minimum of 15 States and for those States to represent 65 per cent of the Union's population. Thus, four large Member States could block a legislative proposal.

The Council's role is to:

● co-ordinate the general economic policies of the Member States;

- conclude international agreements on behalf of the European Union;
- adopt the Union budget, in conjunction with the Parliament;
- take decisions necessary to define and implement the Common Foreign and Security Policy; and
- adopt measures, Regulations and Directives and take decisions in the Area of Freedom, Security and Justice.

The Presidency of the Council is held by each Member State on a six-monthly rotating basis and plays a vital part as the driving force in the legislative and political decision-making process. It organises and chairs all meetings and works out compromises to resolve difficulties. In order to ensure consistency and continuity, the outgoing Member State and the future incumbent Member State work with the present Member State as a Presidency Trio.

The European Parliament

Composition

4–10 The European Parliament presently consists of 754 members representing 501 million citizens in the 27 Member States of the European Union, with a minimum number of MEPS from one Member State being fixed at 6 and a maximum number of 96. The European Parliamentary elections of June 2009 were held under the old Treaty of Nice rules, which set the maximum number of parliamentarians at 751. As a consequence of Lisbon coming into force, 12 Member States gained a number of additional MEPs, whilst Germany should be losing 3 MEPs, however, by EU law, MEPs holding a mandate cannot be deprived of their position during a parliamentary term. Therefore, the net result is that 18 MEPs had to join the Parliament in the period 2009–2014, taking the total number of MEPs to 754, exceeding the limit set out in the Lisbon Treaty and thus requiring a Treaty change to be implemented by the Member States.

Citizens of the European Union are eligible to vote and stand for election (art.22 TFEU and art.39 of the Charter of Fundamental Rights).

Since 1979 the Parliament has been directly elected every five years throughout all the Member States.

The allocation of seats is as follows:

Country	Seats
Cyprus, Estonia, Luxembourg, Malta	6
Slovenia	8
Latvia	9
Ireland, Lithuania	12
Denmark, Finland, Slovakia	13
Bulgaria	18
Austria	19
Sweden	20
Belgium, Czech Republic, Greece, Hungary, Portugal	22
Netherlands	26

Romania	33
Poland	51
Spain	54
Italy, United Kingdom	73 (Scotland has 6 MEPs)
France	74
Germany	99
TOTAL	754

MEPs sit in 9 political groups rather than in national delegations. The Parliament meets in plenary session in Strasbourg, holds its committee meetings in Brussels and has its secretariat in Luxembourg.

The Parliament performs a supervisory role over the EU institutions, and exercises legislative and budgetary power in conjunction with the Council of the European Union.

In terms of supervision, the Parliament can set up temporary Committees of Inquiry and appoint a Parliamentary Ombudsman. It may receive petitions from individuals or companies in the Member States on any matter within the Union's fields of activities. Members of the European Parliament can put written or oral questions to the Commission and to the Council or make recommendations.

The appointment of the Commission, its President and the High Representative for Foreign Affairs by the Council, is dependent upon the Parliament's consent. In general, the Commission is responsible to the European Parliament and the Parliament may require the Commission to resign in the event of a motion of censure being carried.

Originally, the Treaty of Rome allowed the European Parliament to act only in a consultative capacity. Successive Treaty amendments have extended this purely advisory role to one which fully involves Parliament in the legislative process. Under the Lisbon Treaty, the power of decision is now shared jointly by the Council and Parliament (art.14.1 TEU). The extent to which this is exercised is specified within the Treaties depending on the nature of the provision authorising action by the Union for a particular purpose (the legal basis).

Normally, legislation is enacted according to the ordinary legislative procedure, as set out in arts 289 and 294 TFEU.

The Parliament is jointly involved with the Council in the budgetary procedure from the preparation stage, notably in laying down the general guidelines and the type of spending, voting on the annual budget prepared by the Commission and overseeing its implementation.[12]

The Court of Justice of the European Union

The Court of Justice of the European Union is tasked with ensuring that European Union **4–11** law is observed.[13]

After the Treaty of Lisbon, the European Court of Justice is now subdivided into three configurations, namely the Court of Justice, the General Court (formerly the Court of First Instance) and the Civil Service Tribunal.

The Court of Justice consists of 27 judges, one from each Member State. It may sit in

---

[12] TFEU art.314.
[13] TEU art.19.

plenary session, as a Grand Chamber consisting of 13 judges, or in chambers of three or five judges. Its deliberations take place in private and result in a single, collegiate judgment. The working language of the court is French, though documents are translated into all official languages of the Union.

The Court of Justice is assisted by eight Advocates-General whose task it is to examine the cases and deliver reasoned opinions to the court. Both judges and Advocates-General are appointed for a period of six years. The judges are chosen on the basis that their independence is beyond doubt and that they are either qualified to be appointed to the highest judicial offices in their respective countries or are jurisconsults (legal experts including academics) of recognised competence. The appointments process is divided into two stages. First, a panel of seven legal experts, who are either ex-CJEU judges, domestic Supreme Court justices or recognised legal experts, give their opinion on the suitability of the judges-nominate. Upon receipt of this report, the judges-nominate are then appointed by common accord of the Governments of the Member States.

The Court of Justice acts both as a court of first instance and as an appeal court from the General Court and exceptionally, from the Civil Service Tribunal.

The court's functions and powers are set out in arts 251 to 281 TFEU as well as within its own Rules of Procedure.

The court's main areas of jurisdiction are as follows:

(1) Infringement actions against Member States, particularly:

    (a) Commission v Member States (art.258 TFEU)
    (b) Member State v Member State (art.259 TFEU)
    (c) Member State's failure to fulfil a Treaty obligation (art.260 TFEU).

(2) Non-contractual liability of the Community (art.340 TFEU) and Compensation for damage in that event (art.268 TFEU).
(3) The legality of Union action or inaction (Articles 263 and 265 TFEU), with the exception of certain cases heard by the General Court.
(4) Preliminary rulings on the interpretation and validity of EU law at the request of a national court or tribunal (art.267 TFEU and art.19.3.b TEU).

The growth in EU competences, combined with a rapidly increasing membership of the European Union meant that the Court of Justice was struggling under its workload. Thus, the General Court was set up to relieve this workload. Thus, the General Court exercises a wide ranging jurisdiction, as follows:

- Contractual and non-contractual liability of the Union (art.340 TFEU; *FIAMM* [2005]) and compensation for damage in that event (art.268 TFEU).
- Actions relating to European Trade Marks.
- Appeals against decisions of the Civil Service Tribunal, the Community Plant Variety Office or the European Chemicals Agency.
- Direct actions under arts 263 and 265 TFEU, where they are instituted by natural and legal persons, brought by a Member State against the Commission or brought by a Member State against the Council in relation to state aid, dumping or its exercise of implementing powers.
- Arbitration clauses contained in a contract concluded by or on behalf of the Union (art.272 TFEU).

The General Court consists of one judge from each Member State appointed under the same criteria as the Judges of the Court of Justice. It may sit with one judge, in chambers of three or five judges, in a Grand Chamber of 13 judges or in plenary session. It has no permanent Advocates-General, with the task of Advocate-General being carried out by one of 27 judges of the General Court, although it may be assisted by Advocates-General in the future (art.254 TFEU).

In a similar vein, the Civil Service Tribunal was created in 2004 to assist the Court of Justice of the European Union. It commenced its work in 2005. The Tribunal consists of seven judges and hears disputes between the EU institutions, bodies and agencies and their respective employees (art.270 TFEU).

The Court of Auditors

The Court of Auditors was set up in 1975 to control and supervise the implementation of **4–12** the budget. It comprises one full-time member from each Member State among persons who have had relevant auditing experience and whose independence is beyond doubt.

Its powers and functions are set out in arts 285 to 287 TFEU.

The European Council

Originally, the European Council was an informal opportunity for the heads of State or **4–13** Government of the Member States to meet and discuss the political priorities of the European Union. The Treaty of Lisbon elevated the status of the European Council to that of an institution of the European Union and created the permanent post of President of the European Council, with a term of office of two and a half years. The first holder of this office is Herman van Rompuy. Further, the European Council now meets four times a year. The European Council comprises the Heads of State or Government of all 27 Member States, the President of the European Council and the President of the Commission.

The European Council performs a number of important EU functions:

- it provides the Union with the necessary political impetus;
- it represents the European Union externally in relation to the Common Foreign and Security Policy (CFSP) and identifies the strategic interests and objectives of the Union in relation to international issues, including those of defence;
- it can, with Parliament's consent, determine that a Member State has engaged in a serious and persistent breach of the Union's values (art.7.2 TEU);
- it proposes to the Parliament, the nominee for the post of Commission President and appoints the entire Commission, after obtaining the consent of the Parliament;
- it appoints the High Representative for Foreign Affairs (art.18 TEU) who is tasked with implementing CFSP decisions adopted by the European Council and the Council;
- it has the power to agree, in the future, upon the creation of a common defence (art.42.2 TEU);
- it defines strategic guidelines for legislative and operational planning in respect of the Area of Freedom, Security and Justice (art.68 TFEU);
- it considers the employment situation of the Union on an annual basis and may adopt conclusions on this matter (art.148 TFEU);
- it regularly assesses the threats facing the Union, in particular, those of terrorism and natural and man-made disasters (art.222.4 TFEU).

The European Central Bank

4–14 The European Central Bank is the central bank for the Member States of the European Union that have the Euro (€) as their currency. To date, there are 17 countries that have adopted the Euro as their currency. The role of the ECB is to set the monetary policy of the Eurozone. In particular, its role is to maintain the purchasing power of the Euro and as such is tasked with keeping inflation low in the Eurozone, in order to guarantee price stability. To do so, the ECB sets interest rates for the entire Eurozone. The ECB comprises 6 members of the Executive Board plus the 17 governors of the Eurozone member national banks.

Key Concepts

- Supranational institutional system independent from the Member States.
- Seven institutions: Commission, Council of the European Union, European Council, Court of Justice of the European Union, Parliament, Court of Auditors and the European Central Bank.
- European Council is an important political body.
- Separation of powers.
- Parliament is the only directly democratically elected institution.

Sources of Law

4–15 In common with other legal systems, the EU legal system classifies sources of law as being either primary or secondary sources.

Primary sources

4–16 The primary sources of law are the two Treaties that establish the European Union, namely, the Treaty on the Functioning of the European Union and the Treaty on European Union. In addition, by virtue of the Treaty on European Union, the European Union's Charter of Fundamental Rights has the same legal status as the two Treaties.

The secondary sources of law include secondary legislation enacted by the EU institutions, the case law of the Court of Justice of the European Union and recourse to general principles of law.

Secondary sources

4–17 Article 288 TFEU provides that the EU institutions can enact a range of secondary legislation to give further effect to the objectives of the European Union.

Regulations have general application, are binding in their entirety and directly applicable in all Member States. That is, Regulations apply to any number of Member States, individuals or companies, must be completely complied with and become part of the "law of the land" when they are enacted in Brussels and do not require domestic law to be enacted.

Directives are binding as to the result to be achieved, are addressed to Member States only and grant the Member States a discretion in how they implement the Directive's legal obligations through their own legal system. Member States must implement the obligation(s) within a set time limit and failure to do so attracts legal liability on the part of the Member State.

Decisions are binding in their entirety upon those to whom they are addressed.

Recommendations and opinions have no binding force and are of persuasive force only.

The Treaties specify which type of act and which legislative procedure must be adopted to achieve a particular aim of the Union. Secondary legislation must state the reasons on which it is based. If the wrong legal basis has been selected, the legislative measure can be challenged and ultimately annulled.[14]

Case law of the Court of Justice of the European Union

The decisions of the Court of Justice of the European Union are authoritative on all **4–18** aspects of the Treaties, acts of the Institutions and acts of the Member States which arise in conformity with their EU law obligations. Unlike the common law tradition of Anglo-American systems, the civilian nature of Union law based on Continental legal systems does not rely on the doctrine of precedent and this means that the Court of Justice of the European Union is not rigidly bound by its own previous decisions. It may therefore depart from them if it feels the need to adapt or update its case law.[15]

General principles of law

As well as the Treaties, the Court of Justice of the European Union draws on general **4–19** principles of law derived from the legal traditions of the Member States. These general principles can be used by all courts to interpret Union law. They include:

- Proportionality—legislative measures should not go beyond what is necessary to achieve the desired objective.[16]
- Legal certainty—comprising respect for legitimate expectations and the principle that European Union measures should not have retroactive effect.[17]
- Legal Professional Privilege—written communication between independent (not in-house) lawyers and clients are respected.[18]
- Fundamental Human Rights.[19]

---

[14] *Commission of the European Communities v Council of the European Communities* (C-300/89); sub nom. Titanium Dioxide Directive, Re (C-300/89) [1991] E.C.R. I-2867 and *Commission v Council 'Environmental Crimes'* [2005].

[15] *Keck and Mithouard* [1993] E.C.R. I-6097.

[16] *Bela-Mühle v Grows Farm* [1977] E.C.R. 1211.

[17] *Council of the European Communities v European Parliament* (34/86) [1986] E.C.R. 2155 and *Mulder v Minister van Landbouw en Visserij* [1988] E.C.R. 2321.

[18] *Akzo Nobel v European Commission* (C-550/07P) [2010] E.C.R. 0.

[19] *Nold v Commission* (4/73) [1974]. E.C.R. 491.

Key Concepts

Primary Sources of EU law:

- Treaty on the Functioning of the European Union.
- Treaty on European Union.
- Charter of Fundamental Rights of the European Union.

Secondary Sources:

- Secondary Legislation: Regulations, Directives, Decisions, Recommendations and Opinions.
- Case law of the Court of Justice of the European Union.
- General Principles of law.

EUROPEAN LAW AND NATIONAL LAW

4–20 The United Kingdom joined the European Economic Community (as was) in 1973. By acceding to the EEC, the UK Government agreed to limit its sovereign rights in a range of significant competences.

Membership of the EEC was to have a profound and lasting impact upon cherished and long-established constitutional principles such as Parliamentary Supremacy and Parliamentary Sovereignty. Indeed, such concepts have to cede to the European Union concept of the rule of law. The European Union has the legal power to enact legislation in a wide range of areas and once the European Union has enacted a law, the Member States must give effect to that law in their domestic legal systems and must not frustrate the aims and objectives of the European Treaties.

Direct effect

4–21 The European Union legal order creates certain judicially enforceable rights within Member States for the nationals of those states as if they were part of the law of the land. This individual right is known as "Direct Effect" and means that individuals can pursue their EU law rights through their own local courts. Direct effect was not set out in the founding Treaties, but was developed through the case-law of the Court of Justice of the European Union. The three criteria for establishing direct effect are that the provision must be clear and unambiguous in its terms, the obligation must be unconditional, that is, not subject to any qualifications and there must be no need for further implementing or discretionary measures to be taken by either the Member States or the Union institutions.

Treaty articles

4–22 The case of *Van Gend en Loos* established that certain provisions of EU law can give rise to legally enforceable individual rights, which the Member States' courts are obliged to uphold and give effect to.[20]

---

[20] *Van Gend en Loos NV v Nederlandse Administratie der Belastingen* [1963] E.C.R. 1.

> ### Case 26/62 Van Gend en Loos NV v Nederlandse Administratie der Belastingen
> ### [1963] E.C.R. 1
>
> Van Gend en Loos was a Dutch importer of chemicals. The EC Treaty provided that customs duties were to be progressively reduced and eventually abolished between the Member States. The Dutch Government re-classified a range of chemicals such that when Van Gend en Loos attempted to import the chemicals into the Netherlands, it found that it had to pay a higher level of customs duty. The Court of Justice held that the EC Treaty created legal rights for individuals which national courts were bound to protect and uphold.

This type of relationship is known as vertical direct effect, since individuals and the State are in a vertical relationship—the state at the apex and the individual beneath, allowing an individual the right to sue a Member State within his own national court when he considers that it has not complied with its EU law obligations.

Member State

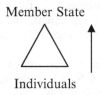

Individuals

The Court of Justice then confirmed in *Defrenne v SABENA* that Treaty articles could also be horizontally directly effective, that is the Treaty imposed obligations on private individuals and private organisations, which could be enforced in national courts.[21] Miss Defrenne successfully sued her employer, the Belgian national airline in her national court for sex-discrimination, in direct violation of the EC Treaty.

Member State

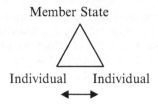

Individual   Individual

Regulations

Regulations generally apply directly within the Member States' legal systems without the **4–23** need for domestic law to be enacted.[22] This direct applicability is different from direct effect. Regulations still have to satisfy the three direct effect criteria, if they are to be successfully utilised in a domestic court case.[23] All that direct applicability means is that

---

[21] *Defrenne v SABENA* [1976] E.C.R. 455.
[22] *Commission v Italy* [1973] E.C.R. 161.
[23] *Marimex* [1972] E.C.R. 1309.

there is no need for further legislation to be enacted by Member States incorporating the provision into national law. A Regulation becomes law when it is published in the Official Journal.

Decisions

4–24 Decisions can be addressed to one or more Member States or one or more individuals. If a Decision is addressed to a Member State and it fulfils the direct effect criteria it can also give rights to individuals.[24]

Directives

4–25 Directives are never directly applicable and were never designed to be. Directives always require some national enacting measure to be introduced. Nevertheless, under certain conditions Directives may be vertically directly effective, on the basis that failure to implement a Directive is a failure to grant citizens of a Member State their rights under EU law.[25] However, vertical direct effect of Directives only arises where:

- the time limit for implementation has expired and the Member State thus loses its discretionary period to implement (*Ratti*)[26];
- the Directive satisfies the three criteria for direct effect; and
- the Member State fails to implement, incorrectly implements or incompletely implements the Directive into national law (*Becker*[27]; *Emmott*[28]).

The granting of vertical direct effect to Directives was a great step forward in advancing the effectiveness of EU law. Member States could no longer take advantage of their own failure to implement. However, individuals could not rely on the terms of an unimplemented Directive against private individuals, that is Directives could not be horizontally directly effective.

Marshall v Southampton Area Health Authority
(152/84) [1986] Q.B. 401

Miss Marshall sued her employer on the basis that she was compelled to retire at 60, five years earlier than her male colleagues. Miss Marshall was successful in her case not on the basis of horizontal direct effect but on the basis that her employer, the local health authority, was in actual fact an emanation of the State, that is a public law authority and hence subject to the rule of vertical direct effect.

The Court of Justice further interpreted the phrase "emanation of the State" as widely as possible to include corporations such as British Gas and the Chief Constable of the Royal Ulster Constabulary.[29] The key test is whether the organisation is acting in a private

---

[24] *Grad* [1970] E.C.R. 825.
[25] *Van Duyn v Home Office* [1974] E.C.R. 1337.
[26] (148/78) [1979] E.C.R. 1629.
[27] [1982] E.C.R. 53.
[28] (208/90) [1991] E.C.R. I-4269.
[29] *Foster v British Gas plc* [1990] E.C.R. I–3313 and *Johnston v Chief Constable of the Royal Ulster Constabulary* [1986] E.C.R. 1651.

capacity or is fulfilling a wider public law duty. If the body is acting in a purely private capacity, then direct effect can not be invoked.

In *Faccini Dori v Recreb Srl*[30] the Court made it clear that Directives could never create horizontal direct effects.

Although Directives do not have horizontal direct effect, this does not mean that individuals are without legal redress. Rather, individuals may enforce their rights under a Directive through the concept of indirect effect or through the *Francovich* principles of State liability.

Indirect effect

The absence of horizontal direct effect for Directives results in discrimination, since there **4-26** is a difference of treatment based simply on the nature of the organisation being sued.

The court thus created an obligation on national courts to interpret national law in such a way as to achieve the aim of the Directive. This concept of indirect effect is based on art.4.3 TEU—the good faith clause.

In the case of *Von Colson und Kamman v Land Nordrhein-Westfalen*[31] the relevant Directive was deemed to be insufficiently clear and precise. The Court of Justice stated that nevertheless the Member State was under an obligation to interpret and apply national law in conformity with the requirements of European law, in so far as it was given discretion to do so under national law.

This obligation to interpret and apply national law so as to give effect to the terms of a Directive even extends to pre-existing national law and applies even where the national law was not enacted with the specific purpose of complying with the European law.[32]

Clearly, there are limits to the appropriateness and usefulness of this interpretative obligation, especially in the situation where national law expressly contradicts the Directive.[33]

The Court of Justice of the European Union has made it clear that indirect effect cannot be used in criminal proceedings.[34]

During the period in which Member States have discretion to implement national law to give effect to the Directive, they must refrain from taking action which undermines the aims and objectives of the Directive and/or the Treaties.[35]

Direct Effect of Recommendations and Opinions

Since Recommendations and Opinions do not produce binding legal effects, they cannot **4-27** produce direct effects (*Grimaldi*[36]).

---

[30] [1994] E.C.R. I-3325.
[31] [1984] E.C.R. 1891.
[32] *Marleasing SA v La Commercial Internacional de Alimentacion SA* [1990] E.C.R. I-4135 and *Litster v Forth Dry Dock Engineering* [1990] 1 A.C. 546.
[33] *Wagner Miret* [1993] E.C.R. I-6911.
[34] *Kolpinghuis Nijmegen* (80/86) [1987] E.C.R. 3969 and *Arcaro* (C-168/95) [1996] E.C.R. I-4705.
[35] *Mangold* (C-144/04) [2006] All E.R. (EC) 383.
[36] (C322/88) [1989] E.C.R. 4407.

> **Key Concepts**
>
> **Direct Effect**
>
> Individuals can pursue their EU law rights through their own local courts. EU law can only be directly effective if it satisfies three criteria:
>
> - the provision is clear and unambiguous in its terms;
> - the obligation is unconditional, that is, not subject to any qualifications; and
> - the obligation must take effect without any further implementing or discretionary measure either by Member States or by Union institutions.
>
> Direct effect can be both vertical and horizontal.
> Directives cannot give rise to vertical direct effect.
> Member States placed under an interpretative obligation.

Member State liability

4-28 The lack of horizontal direct effect for Directives created a legal void since individuals could not directly enforce the obligations of the Directive. The case of *Francovich* provides that, as a last resort, individuals affected by a Member State' failure to fulfil an EU law obligation are entitled to compensation for that breach. *Francovich* declared that three conditions must be satisfied before a Member State could be found liable, namely:

- the Directive must confer rights for the benefits of individuals;
- the content of the rights must be identifiable from the Directive; and
- there must be a causal link between the damage suffered and the breach.

In joined cases *Brasserie du Pêcheur v Germany* and *R v Secretary of State for Transport, Ex p. Factortame*[37] the court expanded the scope of Member State liability to include other areas of EU law where the following conditions are satisfied:

- the rule of law infringed must be intended to confer rights on individuals;
- the breach must be sufficiently serious; and
- there must be a direct causal link between the breach of the obligation resting on the State and the damage sustained by the injured parties.

A breach will be sufficiently serious where the Member State manifestly and gravely disregards the limits of its discretion[38] or completely disregards its EU law obligations.[39]

---

[37] [1996] Q.B. 404.
[38] *R v Ministry of Agriculture, Fisheries and Food, Ex p. Hedley Lomas (Ireland) Ltd* [1997] Q.B. 139.
[39] *Dillenkofer v Federal Republic of Germany* [1997] Q.B. 259.

Supremacy

The EU legal system would be of little practical use if Member States could simply **4–29** circumvent their EU law obligations by passing domestic law that overrides EU law or choose which EU rules they wish to apply. To avoid this problem the Court of Justice declared the supremacy of EU law over domestic law in the case of *Costa v ENEL*.[40]

Costa v ENEL
[1964] E.C.R. 585

Mr Costa challenged a small electricity bill from the Italian State electricity authority, arguing that the Italian legislation nationalising the electricity industry infringed both the Italian Constitution and certain provisions of the EEC Treaty. The Court of Justice held that the Member States had limited their sovereign rights by transferring certain competences to the European institutions and as such they were now prevented from maintaining in force inconsistent domestic law.

The case of *Costa* posed no significant legal problems since in any event the EC law had been enacted after the nationalisation of ENEL. Thus, the normal legal rule that the most recent law overrides earlier law applied in this case. The more problematic issue would be where a later domestic law was enacted and this law contradicted the earlier EC law. Which law would prevail? The Court of Justice of the European Union affirmed that EU law was to take precedence in such a situation in the case of *Simmenthal*.[41] This rule applies even where the offending national law is the domestic Constitution itself.[42]

In the United Kingdom, the European Communities Act 1972, as amended,[43] provides for the supremacy of Union law by accepting the legal effect of EU law in the United Kingdom. In relation to Acts of the UK Parliament, this means that directly applicable Union measures prevail even over future Acts of Parliament, if the latter are inconsistent with EU law. It also means that by ratifying the European Treaties, the United Kingdom, like any other Member State must refrain from enacting legislation inconsistent with EU law and must set aside such law.[44] In relation to the Scottish Parliament, since that Parliament is a devolved institution, with clearly defined and limited legislative competences, the issue of the relationship between EU law and Acts of the Scottish Parliament is much more straightforward: the Scotland Act 1998 provides that the Scottish Parliament cannot enact laws that are incompatible with EU law.[45] Further, the Scottish Ministers are similarly prevented from acting in any way that violates EU law.[46]

Nevertheless, accepting supremacy of EU law has raised difficulties in some Member States over the years, particularly with respect to previously enacted national law or the provisions of a Member State's own constitution. The EU view is that the Member States have permanently transferred their sovereign powers and have thus legally limited their sovereignty on a permanent basis, by virtue of the EU Treaties. This stance is difficult to accept for certain countries, particularly the United Kingdom, Germany and Italy. The

---

[40] [1964] E.C.R. 585.
[41] [1978] E.C.R. 629.
[42] *Internationale Handelsgesellschaft* [1970] E.C.R. 1125.
[43] The 1972 Act has most recently been amended by the European Union Act 2011.
[44] *Factortame (No.2)* [1991] 1 A.C. 603.
[45] 1998 Act s.29(2)(d).
[46] 1998 Act s.57(2).

British view is that the transfer of sovereignty is not a permanent situation and does not alter the concept of Parliamentary sovereignty and supremacy. Rather, the European Communities Act 1972 limits the sovereignty of the UK Parliament until such time as the political will in the United Kingdom changes and the UK Government desires to leave the European Union and thus repeals the European Communities Act 1972.[47] Nevertheless, it is also recognised that the 1972 Act is a "constitutional" piece of legislation and as such cannot be impliedly repealed, that is the 1972 Act would have to be expressly repealed in the case of British exit from the European Union. Until such time, the 1972 Act remains in force and the Executive, the Legislature and the Judiciary are bound by the terms of the EU Treaties to give effect to EU legal obligations.[48]

Key Concept

Supremacy

- The European Union has its own legal capacity, personality and competences.
- Member States have limited their sovereign rights and permanently transferred powers to the European Union.
- Member States cannot validly enact laws or keep in force laws which conflict with the aims and objectives of the European Union.
- The supremacy obligation extends to the Executive, the Legislature and the Judiciary.

Subsidiarity and proportionality

4–30   Subsidiarity is the principle that EU action should only be undertaken where the objectives of the proposed action cannot be sufficiently achieved by Member States and therefore the objectives can be better achieved by the European Union.[49] The operation of the concept of subsidiarity is supervised through the national parliaments of the Member States. The Commission must send all draft legislative proposals to the national parliaments and they then have eight weeks to decide whether the proposal is compliant with the principle. If a third of Member States' parliaments object then the Commission must review its proposal. If the Commission decides to press ahead with the proposal, then half of the national parliaments could object to the proposal at this stage. Ultimately, any controversial legislative proposal that became law would also be subject to the general judicial review procedure under art.263 TFEU.

Further, the Commission is obligated to submit an annual report on the application of subsidiarity to the Council, the European Council and the European and national parliaments.

Proportionality is the concept that EU measures should not go beyond what is strictly necessary, in order to achieve their objectives.

---

[47] *Thoburn v Sunderland City Council* [2002] EWHC 195.
[48] *Köbler v Austria* [2004] Q.B. 848.
[49] Article 5.3 TEU, the Protocol on Subsidiarity and Proportionality and the Protocol on Information for the National Parliaments.

JUDICIAL REVIEW

The Treaties provide for an extensive system of judicial review. The Treaties confer specific **4–31** powers and duties on each of the EU institutions which they must exercise according to EU law:

- Under art.263 TFEU the Court of Justice of the European Union may consider an action for annulment of an act of the institutions.
- Article 265 TFEU provides the means by which an institution's failure to act may be investigated.
- Article 277 TFEU provides a means of indirect review via the "plea of illegality".
- Article 340 TFEU provides for redress in the event of the non-contractual liability of the European Union.

Action for annulment under article 263 TFEU

Article 263 TFEU empowers the Court of Justice of the European Union to review the **4–32** legality of all legally binding secondary legislation, namely Regulations, Directives and Decisions and also acts of the EU institutions that are intended to produce legal effects as regards third parties.[50]

Member States, the Council, the Commission and the European Parliament can challenge these legally binding instruments on four grounds:

- Lack of competence—the EU institutions must act within the limits of their powers.[51]
- Infringement of an essential procedural requirement—normally where the legislative procedure has not been followed.[52]
- Infringement of the Treaties or of any rule of law relating to their application—including a breach of the general principles of law.
- Misuse of powers—the EU institution attempts to achieve an objective other than that for which the original powers were conferred.[53]

The European Central Bank, the Court of Auditors and the Committee of the Regions can also bring a case where they are acting to protect their prerogatives.

Natural or legal persons, known as non-privileged applicants, can also institute an action under art.263 TFEU but are restricted to challenging decisions where they can demonstrate sufficient legal standing.

The most straightforward situation for non-privileged applicants is when an applicant challenges a decision addressed to them, since they will clearly have sufficient standing.

If a decision is addressed to another person or to a Member State, then the non-privileged applicant must show that the act in question is of direct and individual concern to them (*Fiskano v Commission*).[54]

A measure is of direct concern to an applicant when a Member State is given no discretion to act under the disputed provision or when there is no implementing measure required to be acted upon by the Member State and the measure directly affects the legal

---

[50] *Commission v Council (re ERTA)* [1971] E.C.R. 263 and *European Parliament v Council* [1994] E.C.R. I-2067.
[51] *Commission v Council (re ERTA)* [1971] E.C.R. 263.
[52] *Roquette Frères* [1980] E.C.R. 3333 and *Commission v Council Re Titanium Dioxide Waste* [1991] E.C.R. I-2867.
[53] *Giuffrida v Commission* [1976] E.C.R. 1395.
[54] [1994] E.C.R. I-2885.

situation of the individual.[55] Individual concern requires that the applicant prove that they are affected in the same way as if the measure had been addressed to him personally, either alone or as a member of a closed class.[56] In the case of *Plaumann*, Plaumann was an importer of Clementines. The Commission's decisions concerning the importation of Clementines were applicable to all Clementine importers and as such Plaumann was not individually concerned, since it was an open group. It is notoriously difficult to prove individual concern and only a handful of cases have been successful.[57]

These restrictive rules on locus standi for private applicants have been subject to severe academic criticism. Thus, the Lisbon Treaty has relaxed these rules but only in respect of regulatory acts that do not entail implementing measures. For these types of acts, applicants need only display direct concern.

The rules were only liberalised for these types of EU acts in order to avoid the "floodgates" argument—the Member States were concerned that if the rules on standing were relaxed, there would be a concomitant explosion in legal claims being pursued at the Court of Justice of the European Union.

The action for annulment must be brought within two months from the date of publication of the measure, the date of notification to the applicant or two months from the date when the measure came to the attention of the applicant. These dates are enforced very strictly by the court, however, in exceptional circumstances, the applicant may be granted an extension, for example in the case of force majeure (*Bayer*).[58]

In the event of a successful challenge art.264 TFEU provides that the court shall declare the measure void from the very beginning. The court has no power to order the institution concerned to take any particular steps but the institution is required under art.266 TFEU to take the measures necessary to comply with the court's judgment and therefore to endeavour to recreate the situation which would have existed had the measure not been adopted.

The Failure to act under article 265 TFEU

4–33   Actions under art.265 TFEU can be regarded as "the other side of the coin" from actions under art.263 TFEU. While judicial review under art.263 TFEU may annul acts of the institutions, failure to act under art.265 TFEU may be used to compel an institution to fulfil its EU obligations. An action will thus only be available where the applicant can show that such an obligation exists. If the application under art.265 TFEU is upheld, the court will declare that the failure to act is contrary to EU law and art.266 TFEU requires that the institution must "take the necessary measures to comply with the judgment of the Court of Justice of the EU" within a reasonable period of time. If, however, the institution has defined its position but not adopted the disputed measure, it is not possible to bring an action for "failure to act" (*Lütticke*).[59]

The plea of illegality of article 277 TFEU

4–34   This Treaty article provides for a challenge to be made to a Regulation but only where other proceedings have been brought against the applicant and it may only be invoked in the course of proceedings already underway on other grounds. Because of the restrictive nature of locus standi for the action of annulment under art.263 TFEU, the individual

---

[55] *Glencore Grain* [1998] E.C.R. I-2435 and *Bock* [1971] E.C.R. 897.
[56] *Plaumann* [1963] E.C.R. 199.
[57] For example, *Töpfer* [1965] E.C.R. 405; *Piraiki-Patraiki* [1985] E.C.R. 207 and *Codorniu* [1994] E.C.R. I-1853.
[58] [1991] E.C.R. I-5619.
[59] [1966] E.C.R. 19.

may not mount a direct challenge to a Regulation. However, in the course of art.263 TFEU proceedings challenging a Decision, provided he overcomes the admissibility hurdle, he may claim that the original Regulation on which the Decision is based, is illegal. This action has also been held to covers acts of the institutions which produce similar effects to those of Regulations but which do not actually take the form of Regulations (*Simmenthal*).[60]

If the art.277 TFEU plea succeeds, although the Regulation itself will not be annulled, its basis for the Decision in question will be "inapplicable" and the Decision will be void.

Non-contractual liability of the EU under article 340 TFEU

Under this article, individuals can sue the EU institutions in the event of non-contractual **4–35** liability. The term "non-contractual liability" equates to the law of delict in Scotland and refers to circumstances in which a civil wrong has been committed by the EU institutions. The liability of the EU institutions attaches where it can be proved that the EU institutions owed a duty of care and have breached that duty, the applicant has suffered damage and there is a direct causal link between the breach of the duty and the damage sustained.[61]

Key Concepts

- the European Union operates a comprehensive system of judicial review;
- art.263 TFEU strikes down EU secondary legislation;
- individuals can only invoke art.263 TFEU where they can prove sufficient legal standing;
- art.265 TFEU forces the EU institutions to act;
- art.277 TFEU is an indirect method to challenge a Regulation; and
- art.340 TFEU permits individuals to sue the EU institutions in the event of non-contractual liability.

PRELIMINARY RULINGS

It is essential that EU law is consistently and uniformly applied throughout the 27 **4–36** Member States. To that end, art.267 TFEU enables national courts and tribunals to refer questions of EU law that require to be decided in a case pending before them to the Court of Justice of the European Union for a ruling.[62] This procedure has also proved to be the springboard for the development of some of the most fundamental concepts of EU law, such as direct effect and supremacy and can also be used to mount an indirect challenge to the validity of European Union acts.

This preliminary rulings procedure is not an appeal mechanism. Rather, it is a constructive dialogue between the national courts and tribunals and the Court of Justice of the European Union. The national judge is empowered to refer a question of EU law to the Court of Justice of the European Union, to enable him or her to give judgment in the present case. Therefore, the national court case is suspended pending the ruling from the Court of Justice of the European Union.

The Court of Justice of the European Union does not investigate the facts of the case,

---

[60] [1979] E.C.R. 777.
[61] *Stanley Adams v Commission* [1985] E.C.R. 3595.
[62] An example of a reference from Scotland is the case of *Kulikauskas* (C-44/12) January 30, 2012.

nor does it apply the law to the case. It simply clarifies the point of EU law. The judgment is binding on the national court referring the question. The case of *Walter Schmid*[63] clarified the meaning of "court or tribunal" within the Union context. The Court of Justice will only accept references from bodies that fulfil the following criteria:

- is established by law;
- is permanent;
- has compulsory jurisdiction;
- follows an inter partes procedure;
- applies the rule of law; and
- is independent.

Since the procedure is designed to assist the resolution of legal disputes, the Court of Justice of the European Union will not hear hypothetical problems nor will it entertain situations where there is no real dispute between the parties.[64]

The Court of Justice of the European Union is empowered to deliver preliminary rulings on the interpretation of Union law and on the validity of secondary legislation. In common with other constitutional courts, the Court of Justice of the European Union does not have the power to call into question the validity of the founding constitutional texts, that is the Treaty on the Functioning of the European Union and the Treaty of the European Union.

The Court of Justice of the European Union will interpret the Treaties and the secondary legislation of the Union in such a way as to ensure that the aims and objectives of the European Union are secured. This interpretative method is known as the teleological or purposive approach since the court will seek to discover the purpose of the measure in question and in case of ambiguity, the court will attempt to interpret that ambiguity in a way that is most beneficial to the European Union.

The power to declare a Union act invalid is reserved to the Court of Justice of the European Union. National courts cannot declare Union law invalid.[65]

The national court has an absolute and unfettered discretion as to whether it submits a request to the Court of Justice of the European Union, except in the case where the national court is a court of last resort.[66] The highest national courts are under a mandatory obligation to refer EU law questions to the Court of Justice of the European Union. However, this mandatory obligation has been subject to intense debate and has given rise to two competing theories: the abstract theory and the concrete theory. The abstract theory provides that on a literal interpretation of art.267 TFEU, the court of last resort could only ever be the highest constitutional court. Thus, in the Scottish legal system, that court would be the Supreme Court of the United Kingdom, as regards both civil and criminal matters. This is because the question as to whether a Scottish criminal law provision offends against EU law is deemed a devolution issue, which confers jurisdiction upon the Supreme Court. The concrete theory counters that a lower court could become the court of last resort where leave to appeal to the higher court has been refused. Thus, in Scotland, in certain cases, the court of last resort could be the Court of Session or the High Court of Justiciary, where leave to appeal to the Supreme Court has been refused. In any event, the lower court judge(s) seized of the case must weigh up the advantages of sending the preliminary ruling to the Court of Justice of the European Union.

---

[63] [2002] E.C.R. I-4573.
[64] *Foglia v Novello* [1980] E.C.R. 745 and *Schulte* [2005] E.C.R. I-9215.
[65] *Foto-Frost* [1987] E.C.R. 4199.
[66] *Auroux* [2007] E.C.R. I-385 and *Traghetti* [2006] E.C.R. I-5177.

The mandatory nature of the obligation placed upon the highest courts of the Member States has created a number of difficulties. In particular, national judges may resent the imposition of this obligation as an attack on their competence to fulfill their judicial role. At the Union level, this mandatory procedure also created difficulties in that the Court of Justice was in danger of being overwhelmed by the sheer volume of cases being referred. As a result, the Court of Justice declared in *CILFIT*[67] that courts of last instance would not have to refer a question to the Court of Justice if the following criteria were satisfied:

- the question of Union law is irrelevant to the case at issue;
- the point has already been decided by a previous decision of the Court of Justice of the European Union;
- the correct application of Union law is so obvious as to leave no doubt as to the manner in which the matter is to be resolved; and
- the matter is equally obvious to the courts of the other Member States and to the Court of Justice of the European Union.

The court went on to set out the potential problems that could arise if a national supreme court were to decide not to seek for a preliminary ruling in such circumstances:

- EU law is drafted in several different languages all of them equally authentic and binding, so any interpretation by a national court would require a comparison of all different language versions;
- EU law has its own particular terminology, legal concepts do not necessary have the same meaning in Union law as they do in national law; and
- EU law must always be interpreted in context and in the light of the purposes of the treaties as a whole, of the objectives of EU law and the evolution of EU law at that particular time, in other words, interpretation is by the teleological method.

Now that EU law is becoming more and more familiar to national judges, it is not unusual for the national supreme courts to use the doctrine of acte clair and decide cases containing a point of EU law without referring to the court in Luxembourg (*British Fuels v Baxendale*).[68] However, the decision of the national court of last instance not to send a case to Luxembourg will attract the legal liability of the Member State, in situations where the reference to Luxembourg was subsequently actually deemed necessary.[69]

---

[67] [1982] E.C.R. 3415.
[68] [1999] 2 A.C. 52.
[69] See the EU cases of *Köbler v Austria* [2004] Q.B. 848, and *Traghetti* [2006] E.C.R. I-5177 and the English case of *Cooper v HM Attorney General* [2011] Q.B. 976.

> **Key Concepts**
>
> **Preliminary Rulings Procedure**
>
> - Ensures the uniform and consistent application of EU law.
> - Only national courts and tribunals can seek a reference.
> - It is a system founded on mutual cooperation and respect.
> - It is not an appeals procedure.
> - CJEU does not answer hypothetical questions.
> - National courts have discretion to refer.
> - Courts of last instance must refer, except where *CILFIT* conditions exist.
> - Unjustified failure of the court of last instance to refer a case to Luxembourg attracts Member State liability.

▼ CHAPTER SUMMARY

HISTORY OF THE EUROPEAN UNION

4–37
1. **The European Communities were originally established to promote peace and prosperity.**

   ➢ Treaty of Paris 1951, Euratom Treaty 1957, European Economic Community Treaty 1957.

2. **The competences of the European Union have been considerably expanded over the past 60 years, as well as the membership of the Union.**

   ➢ SEA 1986, TEU 1992, Treaty of Amsterdam 1997, Treaty of Nice 2001, Treaty of Lisbon 2009.
   ➢ Treaties of Accession: New members joined in: 1973 (x3); 1981 (x1); 1986 (x2); 1995 (x3); 2004 (x10) and 2007 (x2).

INSTITUTIONS OF THE EUROPEAN UNION

1. **Seven institutions serve the European Union:**

   ➢ Commission, Council of the European Union, European Council, Court of Justice of the European Union, Court of Auditors, European Parliament and the European Central Bank.

2. **Commission:**

   ➢ guardian of the Treaties;
   ➢ represents the interests of the European Union; and
   ➢ the executive of the European Union.

3. **Council of the European Union:**

   ➢ represents the interests of the Member States;
   ➢ shares legislative power with the Parliament; and

➤ increasingly decides matters by Qualified Majority Voting.

4. European Council:

➤ is a political body which gives the European Union the necessary political impetus to drive forward the EU's agenda.

5. Court of Justice of the European Union:

➤ ensures that the law is observed; and
➤ assisted by the General Court and the Civil Service Tribunal.

6. Court of Auditors:

➤ controls and supervises the budget.

7. European Parliament:

➤ supervises the EU institutions;
➤ shares legislative power with the Council of the European Union;
➤ shares budgetary power with the Council of the European Union; and
➤ directly democratically elected representative body.

8. European Central Bank:

➤ issues the Euro banknotes;
➤ sets interest rates in the Eurozone; and
➤ maintains price stability in the Eurozone.

SOURCES OF LAW

1. Primary Sources:

➤ The Treaty on European Union, the Treaty on the Functioning of the European Union and the Charter of Fundamental Rights of the European Union.

2. Secondary Sources:

➤ secondary legislation: Regulations, Directives, Decisions, Recommendations and Opinions;
➤ case law of the Court of Justice of the European Union; and
➤ general principles of law.

EUROPEAN UNION LAW AND NATIONAL LAW

1. Direct Applicability:

(a) Regulations become part of the law of the land without the need for enactment of domestic law:

➤ *Commission v Italy* [1973].

2. Direct Effect:

(a) individuals can enforce their EU law rights in the national court:

➤ *Van Gend en Loos* [1963].

(b) The EU law provision must be clear and unambiguous, the obligation must be unconditional and there must be no need for further implementing or discretionary measures:

➢ *Van Gend en Loos* [1963].

(c) Treaty articles and Regulations may be both vertically and horizontally directly effective:

➢ *Defrenne v SABENA* [1976].

(d) Directives can never give rise to vertical direct effect:

➢ *Faccini Dori v Recreb Srl* [1994].

However, they may create an incidental direct effect:

➢ *CIS Security v Signalson* [1996].

(e) Directives only create direct effects where the time limit for implementation has expired, the criteria for direct effect has been satisfied and the Member State is in default:

➢ *Ratti* [1979]; and
➢ *Emmott* [1990].

(f) Directives can impose liability on "emanations of the State":

➢ *Marshall v Southampton Area Health Authority* [1986].

(g) Member States are under an interpretative obligation to give effect to Directives:

➢ *Von Colson und Kamman v Land Nordrhein-Westfalen* [1984].

(h) Member States can be found liable in damages for a failure to implement a Directive, where the Directive confers rights, the rights are identifiable and there is a causal link between the damage suffered and the breach:

➢ *Francovich* [1991].

3. **Member State liability**
Member States can be found liable for failure to comply with EU law where the rule of law infringed intended to confer rights on individuals, the breach was sufficiently serious and there is a direct causal link between the breach of the obligation and the damage sustained:

➢ *Brasserie du Pêcheur v Germany*; and
➢ *R v Secretary of State for Transport, Ex p. Factortame* [1996].

4. **Supremacy:**

(a) According to the EU view, Member States have permanently transferred their sovereignty, thus they cannot validly create laws that are incompatible with EU law.

(b) In a conflict between EU law and national law, EU law prevails:

➢ *Costa v ENEL* [1964].

(c) Supremacy applies immediately, binds all three branches of the Member State and extends to future parliaments.

(d) The Scottish Parliament is expressly prevented from enacting Scottish law in contravention of EU law:

> ➤ Scotland Act 1998 s.29(2)(d).

(e) The Scottish Ministers are prevented from taking actions in violation of EU law:

> ➤ Scotland Act 1998 s.57(2).

JUDICIAL REVIEW

The European Union operates a comprehensive system of judicial review:

1. Article 263 TFEU is used to challenge EU legislation:

> ➤ individuals must prove direct and individual concern or direct concern only in the case of regulatory acts that do not entail implementing measures.

2. Article 265 TFEU is used to force the EU institutions to take action.
3. Article 277 TFEU is used to indirectly challenge the legality of Regulations.
4. Article 340 TFEU provides for the non-contractual liability of the EU institutions.

PRELIMINARY RULINGS

The preliminary rulings procedure under art.267 TFEU is designed to ensure the uniform and consistent application of EU law in the national courts of the 27 Member States:

1. National courts and tribunals can seek guidance from the Court of Justice of the European Union on issues of EU law.
2. The relationship between the national courts and the Court of Justice of the European Union is not hierarchical and is based on mutual cooperation and respect.
3. The system is not an appeals process.
4. The Court of Justice only concerns itself with relevant and practical questions concerning EU law.
5. National courts have a discretion to refer:

> ➤ *Auroux* [2007].

6. Courts of last instance must refer questions of EU law to the Court of Justice of the EU, unless the matter satisfies the conditions laid out in:

> ➤ *CILFIT* [1982].

7. Where the court of last instance unjustifiably refuses to refer, Member State liability will attach:

> ➤ *Traghetti* [2006];
> ➤ and *Cooper* [2011].

? QUICK QUIZ

THE EU DIMENSION TO THE SCOTTISH LEGAL SYSTEM

- Why was the European Community established?
- What is the European Union?
- How many enlargements have there been and outline which countries joined in each enlargement.
- Identify the seven institutions of the European Union and outline their main functions.
- What does Qualified Majority Voting mean?
- What types of secondary legislation can the EU enact?
- Outline the legal nature of each type of secondary legislation.
- What is meant by the terms, direct applicability, direct effect and supremacy?
- What is the difference between vertical and horizontal direct effect?
- What are the conditions necessary for imposing Member State liability?
- What is meant by the terms subsidiarity and proportionality?
- Under art.263 TFEU, what does direct and individual concern mean?
- Outline the purposes of the Preliminary Ruling Procedure.
- When can national courts legitimately refuse to refer a case to the Court of Justice of the European Union?

📖 FURTHER READING

A.M. Dashwood, B. Rodger, E. Spaventa, and D.A. Wyatt, *Wyatt & Dashwood's European Union Law*, 6th edn (Sweet and Maxwell, 2011).
N. Foster, *Foster on EU Law*, 3rd edn (OUP, 2011).
A.S. Reid, *EU Law Basics*, 4th edn (Sweet and Maxwell, 2010).
E. Szyszczak and A. Cygan, *Understanding EU Law*, 2nd edn (Sweet and Maxwell, 2008).

🖰 RELEVANT WEB LINKS

The European Union Online (the Europa Server): *http://europa.eu*
What's New on Europa: *http://europa.eu/geninfo/whatsnew.htm*
EUR-Lex: *http://eur-lex.europa.eu*
European Parliament: *http://www.europarl.europa.eu*
Council of the EU: *http://www.consilium.europa.eu*
European Council: *http://www.european-council.europa.eu/home-page.aspx*
European Commission: *http://ec.europa.eu*
European Central Bank: *http://www.ecb.int/home/html/index.en.html*
Court of Justice of the European Union: *http://www.curia.europa.eu*
Court of Auditors: *http://www.eca.europa.eu*
European Economic and Social Committee: *http://www.eesc.europa.eu*
Committee of the Regions: *http://www.cor.europa.eu*
BBC Inside Europe: *http://www.bbc.co.uk/news/world/europe*
EU Business website: *http://www.eubusiness.com*

Chapter 5   Human Rights Law

VALERIE FINCH[1]

▶ CHAPTER OVERVIEW

The aim of this chapter is to provide an explanation of the legal protection of human **5–01** rights in Scotland. It starts by explaining the background to the European Convention on Human Rights and the process of incorporation into UK law. Some important general concepts are discussed. The chapter then considers the individual articles which have been incorporated into UK law and some key cases. It then considers the remedies which are available.

✓ OUTCOMES

At the end of the chapter you should be able to: **5–02**

- ✓ understand the principles and purposes of the European Convention on Human Rights and Fundamental Freedoms;
- ✓ appreciate the process of incorporation of the ECHR into UK law;
- ✓ understand the underlying principles of the operation of the principles of the ECHR;
- ✓ distinguish between absolute rights, limited rights and qualified rights;
- ✓ understand the concept of qualified rights—requiring to be according to law, for a legitimate purpose and, so far as is necessary, in a democratic society;
- ✓ understand the nature of the rights conferred under the individual articles; and
- ✓ identify the remedies for infringements of human rights in the United Kingdom.

INTRODUCTION

Whereas constitutional law focuses on the powers of the Government, human rights law is **5–03** concerned with the rights of an individual in relation to the Government. The European Convention on Human Rights and Fundamental Freedoms is a Treaty which was drawn up by the Council of Europe (a body with a wider membership than the European Community), in the aftermath of the Second World War. From 1966 onwards, UK citizens have had the right to take an action against the UK Government to the European Court of Human Rights in Strasbourg. The Human Rights Act 1998 and the Scotland Act 1998 incorporated the European Convention on Human Rights into UK law. The effect of this is that remedies for infringements of Convention rights can now be sought in the UK courts and cases will only need to be taken to the European Court of Human Rights if there is no remedy under UK law.

---

[1] Senior Lecturer in Law, University of the West of Scotland.

THE HUMAN RIGHTS ACT AND THE SCOTLAND ACT

> **Key Concepts**
>
> **5–04**
>
> There are three fundamental principles in the Human Rights Act:
>
> - legislation must be interpreted so as to comply with the Convention;
> - courts and tribunals must take account of the jurisprudence of the European Court of Human Rights;
> - public authorities must act in a manner compatible with Convention rights.

Legislation must be interpreted so as to comply with the Convention

5–05 So far as it is possible to do so, primary legislation and subordinate legislation must be read and given effect in a way which is compatible with the Convention rights.[2] This applies to all cases coming before the courts on, or after, October 2, 2000 *"irrespective of when the activities which form the subject-matter of those cases took place"*. In relation to Scottish Parliament legislation, the Scotland Act states that an Act of the Scottish Parliament is not law, so far as any provision of the Act is outside the legislative competence of the Parliament.[3]

Courts and tribunals must take account of the jurisprudence of the European Court of Human Rights

5–06 This does not mean that the judgments of the European Court of Human Rights are binding precedents.[4] There are principles of interpretation which must be taken into account in deciding whether a judgment, or decision, should have a strong persuasive value.

Public authorities must act in a manner compatible with Convention rights

5–07 This section does not apply where, as the result of primary legislation, the authority could not have acted differently, or where the authority was acting to give effect to a provision in primary legislation, which could not be read as compatible with Convention rights.[5] A public authority is defined as:

(a) a court or tribunal;
(b) any person certain of whose functions are functions of a public nature, (with the exception of parliamentary business).

Additionally, the Scotland Act states that a member of the Scottish Executive has no power to make any subordinate legislation, or to do any other act, so far as the legislation or act is incompatible with any of the Convention rights.[6]

---

[2] Human Rights Act 1998 s.3(1).
[3] Scotland Act 1998 s.29. See Chapter 3.
[4] Human Rights Act 1998 s.2.
[5] Human Rights Act 1998 s.6(1).
[6] Scotland Act 1998 s.57(2). See Chapter 3.

Principles of the European Convention on Human Rights

> **Key Concepts**
>
> The term "Convention rights", as used in the Human Rights Act, means the rights **5–08**
> and fundamental freedoms set out in:
>
> - arts 2 to 12 and 14 of the Convention;
> - arts 1 to 3 of the First Protocol; and
> - art.1 of the Thirteenth Protocol.

Principles of interpretation of the European Convention

The European Convention was intended to apply international standards across diverse **5–09**
jurisdictions. Therefore, when dealing with cases from each jurisdiction, the judges of the
European Court of Human Rights take into account the national laws and culture of the
relevant State. This is done by allowing a "margin of appreciation" when considering
issues, such as whether or not a restriction on a right is reasonable. For this reason, the
courts in the United Kingdom cannot treat cases from Strasbourg as precedents in the
same way as cases from superior UK courts.

Purpose of the Convention

Any interpretation of the terms of the Convention must give consideration to the object **5–10**
and purpose of the Convention. As it is first, and foremost, an instrument for the protection of individuals its provisions should be interpreted so as to make its safeguards
practical and effective.[7] This does not mean that there will be no restrictions whatsoever on
individual rights or liberties, since restrictions will often be justified. The legitimacy of each
restriction on individual rights is considered on its own merits.

Uniform meaning for Convention terms

The Court of Human Rights interprets terms used in the Convention in a manner inde- **5–11**
pendent of their meaning under particular national laws. The court has had to develop its
own meanings for words, whose meanings vary amongst national legal systems. This is in
order to secure consistent application, regardless of the national legal systems from which
a case originates. This is known as the principle of "autonomous meaning". The terminology used under national law is taken into account for clarification. When cases from
the European Court of Human Rights are cited as precedents in UK courts, the courts
need to be aware of the language of the Convention.

Convention as a dynamic and evolving instrument

The Court of Human Rights has repeatedly stressed that the Convention is a living **5–12**
instrument, which must be interpreted in the light of present-day conditions.[8] This means,
that the original negotiations for the development of the Convention and the original
statements of intent are rarely taken into account. The Court of Human Rights is aware of

---

[7] *Loizidou v Turkey* (A/310) (1995) 20 E.H.R.R. 99, para.72.
[8] See *Loizidou v Turkey* (A/310) (1995) 20 E.H.R.R. 99.

developing standards in human rights protection and its decisions take account of these changes in standards.

Convention rights as minimum standards

5–13 Article 53 of the Convention states that the standards for the protection of rights in the Convention are the minimum standards. Where an individual already has a higher level of protection under domestic law, that law will take precedence. Resort to the European Court will only be required where the law of the State concerned has failed to protect an individual's right, when judged against the benchmark of the minimum standard in the relevant article or articles.

Derogation and reservation

5–14 A State may enter a reservation, with regard to a specific article, when it adopts the Convention. It is also possible to derogate from an article at a later date for a specific period. A few Convention rights are absolute and subject to no possibility of derogation. These are the prohibitions on torture, inhuman and degrading punishment, on slavery, and on retroactive criminal offences.[9] The United Kingdom has entered derogations from art.5, when national security so requires.[10]

THE NATURE OF CONVENTION RIGHTS

Key Concepts

5–15 There are three types of Convention rights.

- Absolute rights, such as the right to protection from torture, the prohibition on slavery and the protection from retrospective criminal penalties.
- Limited rights, such as the right to liberty, where the exceptions to the right are set out in the article itself.
- Qualified rights, such as the rights to respect for private and family life, freedom of religion and belief, freedom of expression, and freedom of association, where interference with, is permissible, if the restrictions meet the following four criteria:
  (a) they must be lawful;
  (b) they must be intended to pursue a legitimate purpose;
  (c) they must be "necessary in a democratic society"; and
  (d) they must not be discriminatory.

Lawful restrictions

5–16 Interference with Convention rights is prima facie unlawful, therefore, any interference must be specifically authorised by an identifiable legal rule.

---

[9] ECHR arts 3, 4(1) and 7.
[10] *Brogan v United Kingdom* (A/145-B) (1989) 11 E.H.R.R. 117. For example; a derogation was made under art.15 in relation to the Anti-Terrorism, Crime and Security Act 2001.

Restrictions intended to pursue a legitimate purpose

Any interference with individual rights must have a legitimate objective. The relevant **5–17** objectives are stated in each article. In the case of *Handyside v United Kingdom*[11] the court was satisfied that, although the applicant's rights had been infringed, this was done for the legitimate purpose of the "protection of morals" of a child audience.

Necessity for the restriction

The restriction must not exceed that which is necessary to meet the stated legitimate **5–18** purpose. According to the principle of proportionality, in order to be justified, the extent of the restriction must be sufficient to achieve its aim without restricting individual freedoms any more than is strictly necessary.[12] The law should aim for a fair balance between the rights of individuals, and the needs of the wider community.

Restrictions must not be discriminatory

The Convention does not contain a general prohibition against discrimination per se. **5–19** However, art.14 prohibits discrimination in relation to the rights and freedoms in the Convention. Under the Convention, discrimination is established where a distinction in treatment has no reasonable and objective justification.[13] The concept of discrimination relates specifically to circumstances where restrictions that are reasonable, when applied uniformly, may be unreasonable if applied in a different way to different groups of people.

INDIVIDUAL RIGHTS AND FREEDOMS

Responsibility of the State

Article 1

The High Contracting parties (i.e. the States) shall secure to everyone within jur- **5–20** isdiction the rights and freedoms defined in the Convention.

The State, therefore, is responsible for actions taken by, and on behalf of, the Government and also has a duty to provide adequate protection from any violations of the Convention. This includes an obligation to ensure that the substantive laws and legal procedures are effective. Any action against a State before the European Court of Human Rights is brought on the grounds that the State has failed to fulfil this obligation.

---

[11] *Handyside v United Kingdom* (1976) 1 E.H.R.R. 737.
[12] *Handyside v United Kingdom* (1976) 1 E.H.R.R. 737.
[13] *Belgian Linguistic Case* (1968) 1 E.H.R.R. 252, para.10.

A v United Kingdom
5 B.H.R.C. 137; [1998] 2 F.L.R. 959; [1998] 27 E.H.R.R. 611

A child, whose stepfather had been acquitted of assaulting him, applied to the European Court of Human Rights. It was held that there had been a breach of art.3, because the child had suffered severe beatings. The acquittal of the stepfather demonstrated that English law, as it stood, failed to provide adequate protection for children. The United Kingdom was, therefore, in breach of its duty under art.1 to ensure the protection of those within its jurisdiction.

RIGHT TO LIFE

Article 2

5–21 (1) Everyone's right to life shall be protected by law.
(2) Deprivation of life shall not be regarded as inflicted in contravention of this article when it results from the use of force which is no more than absolutely necessary:
(a) in defence of any person from unlawful violence;
(b) in order to effect a lawful arrest or to prevent the escape of a person lawfully detained;
(c) in action lawfully taken for the purpose of quelling a riot or insurrection.

In addition to this article, art.1 of Protocol 13 states that the death penalty shall be abolished in all circumstances. (This replaces Protocol 6 which abolished the death penalty in peacetime.) There is a wide range of circumstances in which the right to life is important. As well as providing protection against the arbitrary use of force by state officials, art.2 may impose duties upon a State to take positive steps to preserve life. There have been many attempts to extend the meaning of art.2 to encompass areas not perhaps envisaged by the original drafters. A duty has been deemed to exist in circumstances such as use of force by the State, death in custody, protection for individual against imminent threats of violence from others, responsibility to minimise the risk of harm from noxious and potentially lethal pollutants. Article 2 should also be taken into account with regard to denial of health care, withdrawal of medical treatment and deportation or extradition. The State probably does not have a duty under art.2 with regard to the adequacy of social benefits to sustain life, the prevention of abortion or making provision for assisted suicide.

Euthanasia and the withdrawal of medical treatment

5–22 It has been established that it would be a breach of the convention for a State to sanction mercy killing.

Pretty v UK
(2002) 35 E.H.R.R. 1

Diane Pretty, who suffered from motor neuron disease, sought judicial review of a decision that her husband might be prosecuted if he assisted her to die. Her petition was refused by the House of Lords and she took her case to the ECHR which held that art.2 could not be used in this way to guarantee the right to end life.

Hospitals must consider the rights of the individual when they are making decisions about treating patients, but this does not mean that every decision which leads to a loss of life will be unlawful.

A (Children) (Conjoined Twins: Medical Treatment) No.1, Re
(1997) 24 E.H.R.R. 423

It was held that an operation to separate conjoined twins could go ahead, even though the death of one child was the inevitable result of the procedure.

The withdrawal of treatment when a person is in a persistent vegetative state has been held to be justified.

Law Hospital NHS Trust v Lord Advocate
1996 S.C. 301

Following decisions in several English cases,[14] the Court of Session held that the court had power to authorise the discontinuation of life-sustaining treatment. The Lord Advocate issued a statement that no criminal prosecution would follow a decision to withdraw treatment, provided that permission had been granted by a civil court.

There are arguments put forward, to the effect, that legalised abortion is in contravention of art.2, but the domestic law of the United Kingdom has consistently ruled that the legal protection of the person commences at birth.[15]

The responsibility of the State under art.1 also includes a duty to protect the lives of people living within the jurisdiction.

The second paragraph of art.2 permits the use of force by the State, but only where it is strictly necessary.

---

[14] *Airedale NHS Trust v Bland* [1993] A.C. 789.
[15] See *Paton v United Kingdom* (1980) 3 E.H.R.R. 408.

McCann, Farrell and Savage v United Kingdom
(1995) 21 E.H.R.R. 97

The European Court of Human Rights ruled that the action of soldiers, in shooting three Irish Republican Army members in Gibraltar was justified, in the light of the information available to the security forces at the time. The decisions taken by the authorities, however amounted to unlawful action. The operation should have been more tightly controlled, so that the suspected terrorists were not killed. In order to be lawful the action must be proportionate to the circumstances in each case.

As well as the negative obligation on the State not to take actions which cause the death of those in its jurisdiction the State also has a positive obligation to ensure that laws are in place to protect individuals from harm done by other individuals and that the laws are implemented.

Osman v UK
(2000) 29 E.H.R.R. 245

A teacher became obsessed with a pupil and committed some minor offences against him and made death threats. The police were aware of the situation, but took no measures to protect the boy or his family. The teacher murdered the boy's father and another person. The court held that the authorities should have taken steps to protect the boy and his family.

Venables and Thompson v News Group Newspapers Ltd
[2001] 1 All E.R. 908

Venables and Thompson had been convicted of the murder of two-year-old James Bulger when they were 10 years old. When they were due to be released from custody they sought permanent injunctions to prevent the press disclosing their whereabouts or their adult appearance. They based their claim on art.2 and art.3. The press relied on art.10 and argued that injunctions would limit their freedom of expression. Permanent injunctions were granted as a failure to do so could have lead to serious injury or death.

Article 2 has also been held to apply to a wide range of cases, including extradition or deportation, where there is an imminent risk to life, to cases of death in custody[16] and to cases where the identity of a person involved in criminal proceedings has been hidden in order to protect them from retribution.[17]

---

[16] *R. (on the application of Amin) v Secretary of State for the Home Department* [2004] 1 A.C. 653.
[17] *Venables and Thompson v News Group Newspapers Ltd* [2001] All E.R. 908; *R v Lord Saville of Newdigate, Ex p. A* [1999] 4 All E.R. 860.

PROHIBITION OF TORTURE

> ### Article 3
>
> No one shall be subject to torture or to inhuman or degrading treatment or punishment.

5–23

This article protects people from three different types of treatment. Torture involves intense physical suffering and a probability of actual bodily injury. Inhuman treatment may involve mental or physical suffering, of a lesser degree, and degrading treatment is the sort of treatment which arouses feelings of fear, anguish and inferiority. An application to the European Court of Human Rights on the basis of a breach of art.3 was made in the case of *Campbell and Cosans v United Kingdom,* when two mothers claimed that the use of the tawse in Scottish schools was a degrading punishment. The court rejected this argument, but held that there had been a violation of the Convention on other grounds.[18]

> ### Napier v Scottish Ministers
> 2004 S.L.T. 555; 2005 1 S.C. 229; 2004 S.C.L.R. 558; [2004] U.K.H.R.R. 881
>
> A prisoner, who was held on remand in Barlinnie Prison, petitioned for judicial review, claiming that the conditions in which he was held amounted to inhuman and degrading treatment. It was held that to detain a person along with another prisoner in a cramped cell for 20 hours per day, with no sanitation facilities and no activity other than daily walking exercise for 1 hour and a weekly recreation period of an hour and a half was degrading treatment, infringing art.3. He was awarded damages of £2,000.

If the art.3 threshold for degrading treatment is not reached a victim may still have a right to a remedy under art.8, which also covers the integrity of the person. In the more recent case of *Greens, Stanger and Wilson v Scottish Ministers*[19] it was held that the provision of a chemical toilet in a single cell did not amount to treatment which was incompatible with art.3. It was pointed out that, in the *Napier* case it was the cumulative effect of all of the conditions in which he was held and not just the deficienies in the sanitary arrangements that amounted to inhuman and degrading treatment. It was held however that the procedure for emptying the chemical toilets amounted to an infringement of the right to privacy rights under art.8. They were awarded £500 each as just satisfaction

> ### Othman (Abu Qatada) v United Kingdom
> [2012] ECHR 56
>
> The European Court of Human Rights held that there would be no breach of art.3 if Othman was deported from the United Kingdom to stand trial in Jordan. He would not face a "real risk" of ill-treatment contrary to art.3 due to guarantees contained in

---

[18] *Campbell and Cosans v United Kingdom* (1982) 4 E.H.R.R. 293.
[19] 2011 S.L.T. 549.

a Memorandum of Understanding between the United Kingdom and Jordan. The court ruled however, that there would be a real risk that evidence obtained by torture would be used against Othman and this would amount to a flagrant denial of justice which would contravene art.6. The ruling provides important guidance concerning the reliance on governmental assurances against ill-treatment in cases involving extradition and deportation.

PROHIBITION OF SLAVERY AND FORCED LABOUR

Article 4

5–24
1. No one shall be held in slavery or servitude.
2. No one shall be required to perform forced or compulsory labour.
3. For the purpose of this Article the term "forced or compulsory labour" shall not include:
   (a) any work required to be done in the ordinary course of detention imposed according to the provisions of Article 5 of this convention or during conditional release from such detention;
   (b) any service of military character or, in case of conscientious objectors in countries where they are recognised, service exacted instead of compulsory military service;
   (c) any service exacted in case of emergency or calamity threatening the life or well-being of the community;
   (d) any work or service which forms part of normal civic obligations.

In the period following the implementation of the Human Rights Act in the United Kingdom there has been increased awareness of the problems associated with human trafficking and forced labour. Legislation has been introduced to impose penalties for behaviour such as trafficking for the purpose of prostitution and/or the production of obscene or indecent material,[20] and human trafficking for other purposes,[21] The Criminal Justice and Licensing (Scotland) Act 2010 also contains provision for the closure of premises associated with human exploitation which includes trafficking an individual for the purpose of exploitation.[22] Section 47 of the Act introduces a new offence of holding someone in slavery or servitude, or requiring a person to perform forced or compulsory labour. The offence applies to anyone holding a person in such circumstances and the maximum penalty is 14 years imprisonment. Community service orders for offenders are deemed to be lawful under art.4(3)(a), as an order is only imposed if the offender consents to it.[23]

---

[20] Criminal Justice (Scotland) Act 2003 s.22, as amended by s.46 of the Criminal Justice and Licensing (Scotland) Act 2010.
[21] Asylum and Immigration (Treatment of Claimants) Act 2004 ss.4 and 5, as amended by s.46 of the Criminal Justice and Licensing (Scotland) Act 2010.
[22] Criminal Justice and Licensing (Scotland) Act 2010 s.99.
[23] Criminal Procedure (Scotland) Act 1995 s.238(2).

RIGHT TO LIBERTY AND SECURITY

Article 5

Everyone has the right to liberty and security of person. No one shall be deprived of his liberty save in the following cases and an accordance with a procedure prescribed by law:

    (a) the lawful detention of a person after conviction by a competent court;

    (b) the lawful arrest or detention of a person for non-compliance with the lawful order of a court or in order to secure the fulfilment of any obligation prescribed by law;

    (c) the lawful arrest or detention of a person effected for the purpose of bringing him before the competent legal authority on reasonable suspicion of having committed an offence or when it is reasonably considered necessary to prevent his committing an offence or fleeing after having done so;

    (d) the detention of a minor by lawful order for the purpose of educational supervision or his lawful detention for the purpose of bringing him before the competent legal authority;

    (e) the lawful detention of persons for the prevention of the spreading of infectious diseases, of persons of unsound mind, alcoholics, drug addicts or vagrants;

    (f) the lawful arrest or detention of a person to prevent his effecting an unauthorised entry into the country or of a person against whom action is being taken with a view to deportation or extradition.

Everyone who is arrested shall be informed promptly, in a language which he understands, of the reasons for his arrest and any charges against him. Everyone arrested or detained on suspicion of having committed a crime shall be brought promptly before a judge or other officer authorised by law to exercise judicial power and shall be entitled to trial within a reasonable time or to release pending trial. Release may be conditioned by guarantees to appear for trial. Everyone who is deprived of liberty by arrest or detention shall be entitled to take proceedings by which the lawfulness of his detention shall be decided speedily by a court and his release ordered if the detention is not lawful. Everyone who has been the victim of arrest or detention in contravention of the provisions of this article shall have an enforceable right to compensation.

5–25

This article has given rise to a great number of cases, partly because the complexity of the article itself has led to problems of interpretation. It is also an article from which the UK Government has derogated in part, for example with regard to the length of time for which terrorist suspects can be detained.[24] Following a House of Lords decision, to the effect that extended detention of terrorist suspects was unlawful,[25] the Government has brought in new legislation[26] to create a judicial structure under which the activities of suspected terrorists could be restricted and controlled.

---

[24] Anti-terrorism, Crime and Security Act 2001.
[25] *A (FC) v Secretary of State for the Home Department* [2005] 2 A.C. 68.
[26] Prevention of Terrorism Act 2005.

Austin v United Kingdom
2012 (Applications Nos. 39692/09, 40713/09 and 41008/09)

The applicants complained that their restriction within a police cordon (a measure known as "kettling") for up to seven hours during the course of a demonstration in central London amounted to a deprivation of their liberty in breach of art.5 of the Convention. The court found that there had been no deprivation of their liberty within the meaning of art.5.

Detention

5–26 A power of detention does not necessarily mean the same as a power to take someone into custody. Detention is a form of limited or temporary arrest, ranging from simply stopping a person in the street for a few minutes to taking a suspect to a police station to be held in custody. Where a constable believes that a person has information regarding an offence which has been committed, he may require that person to give his name and address.[27] A person who fails to comply with this requirement may be arrested.[28] A constable may also detain a person if he suspects that the person has committed an offence punishable by imprisonment. Reasonable force may be used.[29]

Wilson v Robertson
1986 S.C.C.R. 700

Wilson and another, who had been convicted of theft from vending machines in a club, appealed on the basis that their conviction depended largely on their own alleged admissions during detention. They argued that they had been illegally detained as there were no reasonable grounds for suspecting that they had committed the offences. It was held that there reasonable grounds for the relevant suspicion as a fire exit at the scene of the crime had been interfered with and there was evidence that the accused were nearby. The detention was lawful and the admissions were admissible as evidence.

Arrest

5–27 Arrest, or apprehension, is the most fundamental invasion of the liberty of the individual. Reasonable force may be used to effect an arrest if necessary. Arrests are almost always carried out by police officers.

---

[27] Criminal Procedure (Scotland) Act 1995.
[28] Criminal Procedure (Scotland) Act 1995 s.13(1).
[29] Criminal Procedure (Scotland) Act 1995 s.14.

Key Concepts

Police powers of arrest are derived from three sources of authority:

- a judicial warrant;
- a specific statutory provision; or
- common law.

Reasonable force may be used and it is an offence to resist a lawful arrest or to escape from police custody.[30] When an arrest is being made, under the authority of a statute, the courts expect strict compliance with any conditions under which the power of arrest is exercised.

Wither v Reid
1979 S.L.T. 192

A woman, who had been arrested under the Misuse of Drugs Act 1971, refused to allow a clothing and body search and was charged with resisting arrest. The Misuse of Drugs Act only authorises arrest if an officer reasonably suspects that the person has committed an offence under the Act and that they will abscond if not arrested, or if he has been unable to verify the name and address of the suspect. It was held that the arrest was unlawful, because none of those conditions were met. As the arrest was unlawful the woman was entitled to resist the search.

The usual ground on which an officer may arrest a person is that he has reasonable ground to suspect that the person has committed an offence. The test is rather subjective and usually the courts will be satisfied if the arresting officer honestly believed that the person arrested had committed the offence. The arrest may be unlawful if there were no grounds whatsoever on which to base that belief.

Nicol v Lowe
1990 S.L.T. 543

Nicol and another, having been seen by the police emerging from a driveway late at night, had been arrested and cautioned. They were searched and incriminating articles were found. Nicol argued that his presence in the driveway was an insufficient basis for arrest and search. It was held that the police officers did not have reasonable grounds to suspect that an offence had been committed. The men had not acted suspiciously and the police had not asked the householder whether the men were there lawfully.

---

[30] Police (Scotland) Act 1967 s.41.

Arrest at common law

5–28   There is a general principle in Scots law that a person should not be arrested unless the arresting officer believes that it is necessary, in the interests of justice, so to do. A police officer has power to arrest without warrant where he sees a person committing a crime or if he is informed, by an apparently credible witness that the person has just committed a crime. A person who is seen running away from the scene of a crime, pursued by others, may also be arrested without warrant. The police may also arrest a person if they are threatening danger to members of the public or are behaving in a way offensive to public decency.

Detention on medical grounds

5–29   Article 5(e) permits the lawful detention of persons of unsound mind. Release from detention should only be refused if there is medical evidence establishing that continued compulsory hospitalisation is necessary, or appropriate. The first Act of the Scottish Parliament was the Mental Health (Public Safety and Appeals) (Scotland) Act 1999 which provided for detention to protect the public.

A v Scottish Ministers
2001 S.C. 1

Three people, who had been held in Carstairs under a mental health detention order, sought a review of the 1999 Act on the ground that the Act was incompatible with the right to liberty under art.5. It was held that the right to liberty was not absolute and had to be balanced against the duty imposed on Governments under art.2 of the Convention, to protect life and health.

Complaints about the conditions of detention, rather than the fact of detention, will be considered under art.3 or art.8.

RIGHT TO A FAIR TRIAL

Article 6

5–30   1.   In the determination of his civil rights and obligations and of any criminal charge against him, everyone is entitled to a fair and public hearing within a reasonable time by an independent and impartial tribunal established by law. Judgement shall be pronounced publicly but the press and public may be excluded from all or part of the trial in the interests of morals, public order or national security in a democratic society, where the interests of juveniles or the protection of the private life of the parties so require, or to the extent strictly necessary in the opinion of the court in special circumstances where publicity would prejudice the interests of justice.
        2.   Everyone charged with a criminal offence shall be presumed innocent until proved guilty according to law.
        3.   Everyone charged with a criminal offence has the following minimum rights:

(a) to be informed promptly, in a language which he understands and in detail, of the nature and cause of the accusation against him;

(b) to have adequate time and facilities for the preparation of his defence;

(c) to defend himself in person or through legal assistance of his own choosing or, if he has not sufficient means to pay for legal assistance, to be given it free when the interests of justice so require;

(d) to examine or have examined witnesses against him and to obtain the attendance and examination of witnesses on his behalf under the same condition as witnesses against him;

(e) to have the free assistance of an interpreter if he cannot understand or speak the language used in court.

This article has been the subject of a great number of cases since the Scotland Act came into force. Article 6(1) concerns a general right in relation to both civil rights and obligations and criminal charges. Articles 6(2) and 6(3) are concerned with the rights of persons charged with criminal offences.

Challenges on the basis of delay

Although art.6 includes a right to a trial within a reasonable time, challenges on the basis **5–31** of delay have, on the whole, been unsuccessful as the delays have been held to be justified in the circumstances of the individual cases, or not to have caused a serious infringement of rights.

HM Advocate v Workman
2000 J.C. 383

It was held that delays totalling 3 years, including a period when charges were progressed against two other parties for the same offence, called for an explanation and no satisfactory explanation had been given. However a breach of art.6 had to be assessed on the whole facts and circumstances and not just the length of any delay. The delay for W was not so serious as to amount to a breach of art.6.[31]

Challenges on the grounds of bias

The right to a trial by an independent and impartial tribunal was subject of a series of **5–32** cases in which the impartiality of sheriffs and judges was questioned. It was held that temporary sheriffs, whose appointment could be influenced by the Lord Advocate, could be perceived as lacking independence. Temporary judges, however, given the institutional safeguards of the judicial oath and declinature were held to be sufficiently independent.[32] Partly as a result of these two cases, the procedures for judicial appointment were reformed by the Bail, Judicial Appointments etc. (Scotland) Act 2000 and an independent Judicial Appointments Board was established. Evidence of bias, in the mind of one

---

[31] See also *Crummock (Scotland) Ltd v HM Advocate,* 2000 J.C. 408; 2000 S.L.T. 677; 2000 S.C.C.R. 453; *McLean v HM Advocate,* 2000 J.C. 140; 2000 S.C.C.R. 112; [2000] U.K.H.R.R. 73.

[32] *Starrs v Ruxton,* 2000 J.C. 208; 2000 S.L.T. 42; 1999 S.C.C.R. 1052; *Clancy v Caird (No.2)* 2000 S.L.T. 546; 2000 S.C.L.R. 526. See para.3–17.

member of a tribunal, may be sufficient to call into doubt the impartiality of the whole tribunal.

Hoekstra v HMA

2000 J.C. 391; 2000 S.L.T. 605; 2000 S.C.C.R. 367; [2000] H.R.L.R. 410; [2000] U.K.H.R.R. 578

A decision of the High Court of Justiciary not to allow an appeal against conviction for drug offences was challenged. The bench of three judges was chaired by Lord McLuskey, who had expressed very strong disapproval of the European Convention on Human Rights in a series of newspaper articles. The appeal was, therefore, referred to a differently constituted bench.

In relation to criminal law the basic premise is that the courts, and public authorities, should start from the standpoint that the accused is innocent and that it is for the prosecution to prove their guilt. The question of the right to remain silent and not incriminate oneself was raised in the case of *Brown v Stott*. It had been held previously that the requirement of the Road Traffic Act 1988 to admit who had been driving a car which had been caught speeding, was not compatible with the right under art.6 not to incriminate oneself. The Privy Council overturned this decision on appeal, finding that the Act addressed the problem of drunk driving in a reasonable and proportionate way.[33] In *B v HM Advocate*, it was held that art.6 had been violated when a jury for the trial of an alleged sex offender, was selected from a panel of 22 people, of whom 15 were women.[34] In *Sinclair v HM Advocate*, it was held that the act of allowing evidence from a witness, when the statements had not been made available to the defence, amounted to a breach of art.6 and the conviction was quashed.[35] In the milestone case of *Cadder v HM Advocate*,[36] the Supreme Court held, having regard to the decision of the European Court of Human Rights in *Salduz v Turkey*,[37] that the Crown's reliance on admissions made by an accused who had no access to a lawyer while he was being questioned as a detainee at a police station was a violation of his rights under art.6(1) and art.6(3)(c). The Criminal Procedure (Scotland) Act 1995 was amended to provide for a right to legal representation during police questioning. Following the *Cadder* case the Supreme Court has considered a number of cases clarifying the impact of the *Cadder* decision on criminal procedure in Scotland. In a reference from the Appeal Court of the High Court of Justiciary at the request of the Lord Advocate the Supreme Court considered whether the right to have a lawyer present during questioning by a police officer applies only to questioning when a person is in police custody or to questioning at an earlier stage of an investigation.[38] The Supreme Court held that the principle established in the *Salduz* case does not extend to questioning prior to detention. It was not incompatible with art.6 to use evidence of statements made by the roadside or in a suspected person's home, however it was incompatible with art.6 to use evidence of statements made by a person who was restrained in handcuffs as this amounted to circumstances of detention. Where a suspect

---

[33] *Brown v Stott* (2003) 1 A.C. 681.
[34] *B v HM Advocate*, 2006 S.L.T. 143; 2006 S.C.C.R. 80.
[35] *Sinclair v HM Advocate* [2005] UKPC D2; 2005 1 S.C. (P.C.) 28; 2005 S.L.T. 553; 2005 S.C.C.R. 446.
[36] [2010] UKSC 43.
[37] (2008) 49 E.H.R.R. 421.
[38] *Ambrose v Harris (Procurator Fiscal, Oban) (Scotland), Her Majesty's Advocate v G (Scotland), Her Majesty's Advocate v M (Scotland)* [2011] UKSC 43.

has waived his right to have a lawyer present in circumstances which are voluntary, informed and unequivocal it is not incompatible with art.6 to use evidence of statements made in detention.[39]

Freedom from retroactive criminal convictions or penalties

Article 7

5–33

1. No one shall be held guilty of an offence on account of any act or omission which did not constitute a criminal offence under national or international law at the time when it was committed. Nor shall a heavier penalty be imposed than the one that was applicable at the time the criminal offence was committed.
2. This article shall not prejudice the trial and punishment of any person for any act or omission which, at the time when it was committed, was criminal according to the general principles of law recognised by civilised nations.

This article is intended to protect individuals from arbitrary prosecution. It does not mean that the law cannot be developed by judicial interpretation.

SW v United Kingdom
(1996) 21 E.H.R.R. 363

Two men, who had been convicted on charges of rape upon their wives, claimed that their convictions violated art.7 because, at the date of their actions marital rape was not a criminal offence. It was held that art.7 did not prevent the retrospective application of the criminal law, provided that the development of criminal liability was clearly defined and foreseeable. At the time the two men committed the acts, the removal of immunity from prosecution for rape within marriage could be reasonably foreseen and so the national courts' decisions did not violate art.7.

The High Court of Justiciary has a declaratory power which allows it to declare the ambit of a known crime, or even to criminalise an action which was formerly not know to be criminal. Exercise of this power could give rise to a challenge under art.7. The power was exercised in the case of *Khaliq v HM Advocate*.[40] It was held in *The Scottish Ministers v Mcguffie* that the confiscation of property under Pt 5 of the Proceeds of Crime Act 2002 did not amount to a retrospective criminal penalty.[41]

---

[39] *McGowan (Procurator Fiscal, Edinburgh) v B (Scotland)* [2011] UKSC 54.
[40] *Khaliq v HM Advocate*, 1983 S.C.C.R. 402.
[41] *The Scottish Ministers v Mcguffie*, 2006 S.L.T. 1166.

Right to respect for private and family life one's home and correspondence

Article 8

5–34
1. Everyone has the right to respect for his private and family life, his home and his correspondence.
2. There shall be no interference by a public authority with the exercise of this right except which as is in accordance with the law and is necessary in a democratic society in the interests of national security, public safety or the economic well-being of the country, for the prevention of disorder or crime, for the protection of health or morals, or for the protection of the rights and freedoms of others.

The right to respect for private life, under the Convention, has a much wider meaning than the traditional meaning of privacy in Scotland, where it tends to focus on the right to be protected from intrusion by the press. It also includes the right to live in a manner suited to one's own personal beliefs and inclinations. There will be interference with private and family life, whenever state action has a direct impact on an individual, for example when property is searched. A State may also be in Contravention of art.8 if it does not provide adequate legal safeguards to protect the privacy of individuals, through measures such as data protection legislation.

Respect for private life

5–35 Scots law does not recognise a right of privacy per se, although the privacy of the home is protected by regulation of the police powers of entry and search. There may be situations where the publication of private information may be restrained, for example, publication of information may be prevented where it has been obtained in breach of confidence.[42] The Press Complaints Commission's Code of Practice provides that everyone is entitled to respect for his or her private life, home, health and correspondence. It states that a publication will be expected to justify intrusions into any individual's private life without consent. Publication is justified where it is in the public interest. Public interest is defined as including the detection of crime, the protection of public health and safety and preventing the public from being misled by a statement, or action, by an individual or organisation. An individual whose rights have been infringed may be able to claim that the Code of Practice does not provide an adequate remedy in terms of art.13.

The concept of private life encompasses the physical and moral integrity of the person, including his or her sexual life.[43]

Smith v United Kingdom
[1999] I.R.L.R. 734; (2000) 29 E.H.R.R. 493; (1999) 11 Admin. L.R. 879

Several service men and women sought compensation after they had been dismissed from the armed forces on the grounds of their sexual orientation. Eventually, after an unsuccessful appeal to the House of Lords, the group of service personnel brought a case to the European Court of Human Rights. They contended that the

---

[42] *Quilty v Windsor*, 1999 S.L.T. 346.
[43] *X & Y v Netherlands* (1985) 8 E.H.R.R. 235.

investigations into their private lives constituted an infringement of their right to respect for their private lives under art.8. The investigations had included detailed interviews with them and with their partners on matters relating to their sexual orientation and practices. The ECHR held that the exceptional intrusion into the applicants' private lives, constituted a violation of art.8.

Respect for the person—police powers to search persons

Unless a person has been arrested, there is no power to search them under common law. **5–36** However, in situations of extreme urgency searches carried out before arrest may be excused and the evidence obtained may be used at trial.

Bell v Hogg
1967 J.C. 49; 1967 S.L.T. 290

While investigating a suspected theft of copper, a police officer noticed marks, which he suspected were made by copper, on suspects' hands. Before they were arrested or charged of any offence he asked the suspects to give hand-rubbings on paper. The substance from their hands matched the stolen wire and the four were prosecuted. Objection was taken to the evidence of the rubbings, but it was held that in view of the urgency of preserving evidence, the officer was justified in taking the hand rubbings.

Search before arrest may be authorised by specific statutory provisions.[44] Statutory powers of search must be exercised strictly in accordance with the procedures laid down by the relevant statute.[45] Once a person has been arrested, the police have a power at common law of search, which includes a power to photograph a person, to make a physical examination and to take prints and samples.[46]

Surveillance

In the United Kingdom, surveillance in the interests of national security, may be carried **5–37** out with lawful authority by two organisations. MI5 is the internal security service and MI6 deals with overseas security. The Regulation of Investigatory Powers Act 2000 deals with the regulatory framework of a range of investigatory powers including the interception, acquisition and disclosure of communications data, the use of covert and intrusive surveillance and of human intelligence gathering throughout the United Kingdom. The Regulation of Investigatory Powers (Scotland) Act 2000 is concerned principally with the use of surveillance powers and covert human intelligence sources by the police and the Scottish Crime Squad operating in Scotland. A general principle, under both Acts, is that surveillance will only be authorised if it is necessary and proportionate.

---

[44] For example, Civic Government (Scotland) Act 1982 s.60.
[45] *Normand v McCutcheon,* 1994 S.L.T. 327.
[46] Criminal Procedure (Scotland) Act 1995 s.18.

**HM Advocate v Higgins, HM Advocate v Murphy,
HM Advocate v Scott**
2006 S.L.T. 946; 2006 S.C.C.R. 305

It was held that to set a trap for accused persons by placing them in adjacent cells and then posting officers to eavesdrop was not authorised by the Regulation of Investigatory Powers (Scotland) Act 2000 and was a breach of art.8.

Respect for one's home and family life

5–38 Local authorities now have two specific powers, which enable them to protect the right of the citizen to peaceful enjoyment of his home. Potentially, a failure by a local authority to exercise these powers could lead to a challenge under the Human Rights Act by a person whose private home life is disrupted by the conduct of neighbours. Under the Crime and Disorder Act 1998, a local authority may make an application for an anti-social behaviour order if a person has pursued a course of anti-social conduct, likely to cause alarm or distress to one or more persons outside his household in the authority's area.[47] The Act also gives local authorities powers to evict a tenant if his own conduct, or that of other people at his house, disturbs neighbours.

Power of entry to premises

5–39 Interference with the right of respect for one's home may be authorised by law for the purpose of law enforcement. At common law, a constable is justified in entering premises if they are in close pursuit of a person who has committed, or attempted to commit, a serious crime.[48] A police officer may also enter private premises to quell a disturbance. In an emergency the police officer may force entry, but only after first knocking loudly, stating that it is the police, indicating the nature of the business and demanding admission.[49] Several statutes authorise a police officer to enter premises without a warrant. In each case the police may only take the specific actions which are authorised by the statute. Where the police enter a person's home, without appropriate lawful authority, it will amount to a breach of art.8.[50]

Search of premises

5–40 The police have no general power to search premises without a warrant, unless a person has been arrested on a serious charge and a delay in carrying out a search may defeat the ends of justice.[51]

---

[47] Crime and Disorder Act 1998 s.19.
[48] *Cairns v Keene*, 1983 S.C.C.R. 277.
[49] *Campbell (Sharon) v Vannet*, 1997 S.C.C.R. 787.
[50] *McLeod v United Kingdom* (1999) 27 E.H.R.R. 493.
[51] For example, Civic Government (Scotland) Act 1982 s.60. See *Druce v HM Advocate*, 1992 S.L.T. 1110.

Birse v HM Advocate
2000 S.L.T. 869; 2000 S.C.C.R. 505; 2000 J.C. 503

Birse claimed that a search warrant had violated his rights under art.8, as there was not a proper ground for suspecting that he was in possession of controlled drugs. It was held that, provided that a justice had acted correctly within the provisions of the Misuse of Drugs Act, the granting of a warrant could not breach art.8. The purpose of the search was for the prevention of crime and a warrant to search could be necessary in a democratic society for the purpose of preventing drugs offences.

Respect for one's correspondence

The interception of communications is permitted in a wide range of circumstances. There **5–41** must, however, be clear, specific unambiguous legal authority for any invasion of privacy. In *Malone v United Kingdom* it was held that art.8 had been violated by intercepting telephone conversations, without specific legal authorisation.[52] The law regarding interception of communications was unclear at the time. The interception, acquisition and disclosure of communications data is now regulated by the Regulation of Investigatory Powers Acts.[53] In the case of correspondence of prisoners, it may be difficult to reconcile individual rights to privacy and the legitimate aim of preventing crime.

Campbell v United Kingdom
(1993) 15 E.H.R.R. 137

An inmate of a prison in Scotland, who was serving a life sentence for murder, was involved in several sets of proceedings in the civil courts and two applications to the European Commission. His letters were opened and read by prison authorities. The court held that the opening of general letters to Campbell had been in accordance with the law as there was a legitimate aim of preventing crime or disorder. However, opening letters between a solicitor and his client is not necessary in a democratic society. This was a breach of art.8.

FREEDOM OF THOUGHT, CONSCIENCE AND RELIGION

Article 9

1. Everyone has the right to freedom of thought, conscience and religion: this right **5–42** includes freedom to change his religion or belief and freedom, either alone or in community with others and in public or private, to manifest his religion and belief, in worship, teaching, practice and observance.
2. Freedom to manifest one's religion or beliefs shall be subject only to such limitations as are prescribed by law and are necessary in a democratic society

---

[52] *Malone v United Kingdom* (1985) 7 E.H.R.R. 14.
[53] See *Henderson v HM Advocate, Marnoch v HM Advocate*, 2005 S.L.T. 429; 2005 S.C.C.R. 354 (telephone tapping).

in the interests of public safety, for the protection of public order, health or morals, or for the protection of the rights and freedoms of others.

Key Concepts

Article 9 has three distinct elements:

- Freedom of belief; there is an absolute right to freedom of thought, conscience and religion. This is not limited to religious beliefs, but can be applied equally to moral and political ideologies.
- Right to act in accordance with the belief; the freedom to manifest one's belief establishes a freedom to worship. To teach and to observe religious customs and practices.
- The right to manifest religious beliefs in community with others.

This right is a qualified right and may be restricted for one of the legitimate purposes listed in the article. The cases, which have been brought under art.9, have usually been related to the right to manifest ones religious beliefs.

R. (on the application of Begum) v Denbigh High School Governors
[2006] UKHL 15; [2007] 1 A.C. 100; [2006] 2 All E.R. 487; [2006] 1 F.C.R. 613;
[2006] H.R.L.R. 21; [2006] U.K.H.R.R. 708

A schoolgirl, who was Muslim, wished to wear a jilbab to school, rather than a shalwar kameeze as dictated by the school's uniform policy. She claimed that the school uniform policy amounted to an infringement of her right to manifest her religious beliefs. It was held that the school was justified in banning the jilbab. It had taken immense pains to devise a uniform policy that respected Muslim beliefs and the rules were acceptable to mainstream Muslim opinion.

FREEDOM OF EXPRESSION

Article 10

5–43
1. Everyone has the right to freedom of expression. This right shall include freedom to hold opinions and to receive and impart information and ideas without interference by public authority and regardless of frontiers. This article shall not prevent States from requiring the licensing of broadcasting, television or cinema enterprises.
2. The exercise of these freedoms, since it carries with it duties and responsibilities, may be subject to such formalities, conditions, restrictions, or penalties as are prescribed by law and are necessary in a democratic society, in the interests of national security, territorial integrity or public safety, for the

prevention of disorder or crime, for the protection of health or morals, for the protection of the reputation or rights of others, for preventing the disclosure of information received in confidence, or for maintaining the authority and impartiality of the judiciary.

Article 10 gives only a qualified right to freedom of expression and there is a wide set of circumstances under which freedom of expression may be restricted. However, s.12 of the Human Rights Act states that the courts must pay particular regard to the importance of art.10, when considering journalistic, literary or artistic material.

Defamation

Defamation laws may be perceived as an indirect restriction on freedom of expression. The **5–44** purpose of the law of defamation is to provide a remedy where false statements have harmed the reputation of an individual. The law of defamation could be a threat to free and open debate in Parliament and in judicial proceedings. For this reason, the protection of absolute privilege is given to:

(a) Words spoken in proceedings in the Westminster Parliament.[54]
(b) Statements in the course of judicial proceedings.
(c) Statements made by the Parliamentary Commissioner for Administration.[55]
(d) Statements made in the course of proceedings in the Scottish Parliament.[56]
(e) Publications made under the authority of the Westminster or Scottish Parliament, e.g. official reports of debates, committee papers and radio or television broadcasts of proceedings.

Absolute privilege means that whatever the accuracy of the statement, or the intent with which it was made, no action for defamation can be based on it.

Qualified privilege is given to reports of Parliamentary or judicial proceedings. Qualified privilege applies, where a statement is a fair and accurate report of the proceedings and it is made without malice.[57]

Obscenity

Obscenity laws restrict freedom of expression, but the restrictions will often be held to be **5–45** lawful as being for the legitimate purpose of protecting morals. It was held in the case of *Ingram v Macari* that obscene publications are those which "possess the liability to corrupt and deprave those to whom they are sold and exposed".[58] Under the Civic Government Scotland Act 1982 s.51, it is an offence to display any obscene material where it can be seen by the public. Material is defined as any book, magazine, bill, paper, print, film, tape, disc or other kind of recording (whether of sound or visual images or both), photograph, drawing, painting, representation, model or figure.

---

[54] Bill of Rights 1689.
[55] Parliamentary Commissioner Act 1967 s.10(5).
[56] Scotland Act 1998 s.41.
[57] Defamation Act 1996 s.15.
[58] *Ingram v Macari*, 1983 S.L.T. 61.

Ross (Crawford David) v HM Advocate
1998 S.L.T. 1313

A man was charged with operating computer bulletin board systems which contained visual images and text files of an obscene nature. The accused argued that "text files" did not fall within the definition of "material" provided by the 1982 Act. He was convicted and appealed unsuccessfully. It was held that text files could be considered to be a recording of a visual image and so were included in the definition of obscene material.

It is also an offence under the Civic Government (Scotland) Act to publish, sell or distribute any obscene material, or to keep any obscene material with a view to its eventual sale or distribution.

Rees v Lees
1997 S.L.T. 872

A large quantity of sex articles had been seized from a shop during police raids, but the owner argued that there was no proof that he had "sold" obscene material. He also argued that since the magazines were sealed in clear wrappers, they were not liable to corrupt or deprave. It was held that the word "sells" in the Act included "offers for sale". Obscene magazines and videos visibly displayed, with no warnings or age restrictions, were liable to corrupt and deprave unsuspecting members of the public.

There is a defence of inadvertance. A person will escape conviction if he can prove that he used all due diligence to avoid committing an offence.[59]

Contempt of court

5–46 The law of contempt of court, prevents the reporting of anything which could be prejudicial to court proceedings. Under the Contempt of Court Act 1981 a person who publishes any prejudicial speech, writing, broadcast or other communication in whatever form, which is addressed to the public at large or to a section of the public, may be liable to a penalty.[60]

HM Advocate v News Group Newspapers
1989 S.C.C.R. 156

Following the shooting of a Yugoslavian in Kirkcaldy, two newspapers published articles of a sensational nature relating to the incident. These articles were published the day after the shooting and subsequent to the arrest of a suspect. Both newspapers were held to be in contempt of court. The article in one newspaper was fairly specific in its allegations, implying the suspect was guilty but not naming him. A heavier fine was imposed on that newspaper.

---

[59] Civic Government (Scotland) Act 1982 s.51(4).
[60] Contempt of Court Act 1981.

The 1981 Act lays down a rule of strict liability when proceedings are active, i.e.

- Criminal proceedings; from the time of arrest without warrant, or the time of granting of a warrant of citation, or the time when an indictment or other document specifying the charge is served on the accused.
- Civil proceedings in the Court of Session, or the sheriff court, when the record is closed, or when a motion or application is made.
- In other proceedings, the date when they become active is when the date of a hearing is fixed or a hearing is allowed.
- A case remains active until it is disposed of or abandoned, discontinued or withdrawn.

HM Advocate v Scotsman Publications Ltd
1999 S.L.T 466

Shortly after Mohammed Sarwar, MP for a Glasgow constituency, was charged with electoral fraud, an article was published in the Scotsman newspaper under the headline "Sarwar charge witnesses ask for protection". The article alleged that two witnesses had sought police protection as a result of fears about intimidation. It was held that there had been contempt of court. An ordinary reader was likely to conclude that it was intimidation by Sarwar which was to be feared. There would be a material risk of serious prejudice if any juror had read the article.

DEFENCES

- At the time of publication, or distribution of the publication, the publisher does **5–47** not know and has no reason to suspect that relevant proceedings are active.
- Fair and accurate reports of legal proceedings, held in public, and published contemporaneously and in good faith do not attract the strict liability rule.
- A publication which is a discussion in good faith of public affairs, or matters of general public interest, will not be held to be in contempt if the risk of impeding or prejudicing legal proceedings is merely incidental to the discussion.
- The behaviour of people present at court hearings may also be restricted by the law of contempt of court.

Young v Lees
1998 S.C.C.R. 558

Young was present at the trial of his partner. When she was remanded in custody Young shouted "You guffy" at the sheriff. The sheriff found him in contempt of court. He was sentenced to 60 days' imprisonment.

Freedom of expression is also restricted by offences, such as incitement to racial hatred or religious hatred.[61]

---

[61] Public Order Act 1986 s.17.

OFFICIAL SECRECY

5–48 Under the Official Secrets Act 1989, certain categories of government information are protected from disclosure to the public. This restricts the freedom of speech of Crown Servants and government contractors, in the interests of national security. Crown servants are ministers of the Crown, civil servants, diplomats, police constables and members of the armed forces. The maximum penalty for disclosing protected information is a period of imprisonment of up to two years, or a fine, or both.

FREEDOM OF ASSEMBLY AND ASSOCIATION

Article 11

5–49
1. Everyone has the right to freedom of peaceful assembly and to freedom of association with others, including the right to form and join trade unions for the protection of interests.
2. No restrictions shall be placed on the exercise of these rights other than such as are prescribed by law and are necessary in a democratic society, in the interests of national security, or public safety, for the prevention of disorder or crime, for the protection of health or morals, for the protection of the rights and freedoms of others.

This Article shall not prevent the imposition of lawful restrictions on the exercise of these rights by members of the armed forces, of the police, or of the administration of the State.

The right under art.11, to form and join trade unions, includes the right to choose not to join a trade union.[62] The fact that this is a qualified right was illustrated in the case of *Council of Civil Service Unions v United Kingdom,* in which it was held that a ban on union membership at Government Communications Headquarters was justified in the interests of national security.[63] Scots law does not recognise a right of public protest. People are free to gather together in groups, but the police could disperse them if they were obstructing the passage of others, or if it was deemed likely that a breach of the peace may occur.[64]

Restrictions on the freedom of assembly

5–50 Public processions and assemblies are regulated by the Civic Government (Scotland) Act 1982[65] and the Public Order Act 1986 (as amended by the Criminal Justice and Public Order Act 1994). Local Councils have the power to permit a procession to take place or to prohibit the holding of a procession. Twenty eight days notice must be given prior to a procession taking place. Notice must be given to both the council and the chief constable.[66]

---

[62] *Young, James and Webster v United Kingdom* (1982) 4 E.H.R.R. 38.
[63] *Council of Civil Service Unions v United Kingdom* [1988] 10 E.H.R.R. 269.
[64] *Aldred v Miller*, 1924 J.C. 117.
[65] As amended by the Police, Public Order and Criminal Justice (Scotland) Act 2006.
[66] Civic Government (Scotland) Act 1982 ss.62–63.

Exceptions:

- Processions which are customarily or commonly held.
- The Scottish Ministers may grant exemption from the requirement to give notice to certain types of procession, or the processions of specific organisations.
- The full period of notice may be waived for processions which are organised urgently in response to a particular event.

Conditions

A local authority may impose conditions as to the date, time, and route of processions and **5–51** the duration of assemblies. Notice of the conditions must be given in writing at least two days before the procession or assembly is due to be held. Appeal against a prohibition, or any conditions imposed, may be made to a sheriff on the ground that the council has exceeded its powers under the Civic Government (Scotland) Act.

Police powers to control processions and assemblies

The Public Order Act gives power to a senior police officer, who is present at an event, to **5–52** impose conditions where is a risk of serious public disorder, serious damage to property or serious disruption to the life of the community, or that the purpose of the organisers is to intimidate others. Conditions may be imposed in so far as they are necessary to prevent serious disorder, disruption or intimidation.

Offences

- To hold a procession without permission. **5–53**
- To knowingly fail to comply with conditions.
- To incite others to behave in a manner contrary to the conditions.
- To take part in an unauthorised procession and to refuse to desist when required to do so by a policeman in uniform.

It is a defence for a person to prove that the failure to comply with the conditions arose from circumstances outwith their control.

RIGHT TO MARRY AND FOUND A FAMILY

Article 12

Men and women of marriageable age have the right to marry and to found a family, **5–54** according to the national laws governing the exercise of this right.

This article recognises that states may have different laws relating to capacity to marry and the formalities which may be required. The right to marry and to found a family does not confer a right to end a marriage by divorce. In *Johnston v Ireland* an applicant claimed that his right to marry and found a family was violated by Irish law, which prevented him divorcing his first wife and marrying the woman with whom he lived.[67] Prisoners are entitled to marry, but the right to marry does not extend to the right to conjugal visits whilst in prison.[68]

---

[67] *Johnston v Ireland* (1987) 9 E.H.R.R. 203.
[68] *X v United Kingdom*, No.6564/74, 2 D.R. 105 (1975).

PROTECTION OF PROPERTY

First Protocol Article 1

5–55   Every natural or legal person is entitled to the peaceful enjoyment of his possessions. No one shall be deprived of his possessions except in the public interest and
subject to the conditions provided for by law and by the general principles of
international law.

   The preceding provisions shall not, however, in any way impair the right of a
State to enforce such laws as it deems necessary to control the use of property in
accordance with the general interest or to secure the payment of taxes or other
contributions or penalties.

RIGHT TO EDUCATION

First Protocol Article 2

5–56   No person shall be denied the right to education. In the exercise of any functions
which it assumes in relation to education and to teaching, the State shall respect the
right of parents to ensure such education and teaching in conformity with their own
religious and philosophical convictions.

It has been claimed that a refusal by a school to allow a pupil to wear full-length robes
could amount to a breach of art.3, but it has been held that this would depend on the
circumstances of each case.[69]

Campbell and Cosans v United Kingdom
(1982) 4 E.H.R.R. 165

Two mothers claimed that the use of corporal punishment in Scottish schools was a
violation of art.2. The court rejected the argument that the use of the tawse (belt)
was inhuman and degrading, but accepted that there was a violation of art.2 as
parents were denied the right to education in accordance with their philosophical
convictions.

The use of corporal punishment in all state schools was abolished by the Education (No.2)
Act 1986.

---

[69] *R. (on the application of Begum) v Denbigh High School Governors*. Also known as: *R. (on the application of SB) v Denbigh High School Governors* [2006] UKHL 15; [2007] 1 A.C. 100; [2006] 2 All E.R. 487; [2006] 1 F.C.R. 613; [2006] H.R.L.R. 21; [2006] U.K.H.R.R. 708.

RIGHT TO FREE ELECTIONS

> ### First Protocol Article 3
>
> The High Contracting Parties undertake to hold free elections at reasonable inter-   5–57
> vals by secret ballot, under conditions which will ensure the free expression of the
> opinion of the people in the choice of legislature.

In the case of *Smith v Scott* a formal declaration of incompatibility was made to the effect
that s.3(1) of the Representation of the People Act 1983 was incompatible with art.3 as it
deprived all people serving custodial sentences of the right to vote.[70]

RIGHT TO AN EFFECTIVE REMEDY

> ### Article 13
>
> An effective remedy before a national authority must be secured to those whose   5–58
> rights and freedoms as set forth in the convention have been violated.

Rather than incorporating this article into UK law the Human Rights Act lays down its
own structure for remedies.[71] This is appropriate, as this article gives an individual a right
to take an action to the European Court of Human Rights if an adequate remedy is not
available under domestic law. The action in such a case is against the State itself, whereas
the remedies provided under the Human Rights Act are against the individual public
authority responsible for the infringement of a Convention right.

A failure by a public authority to act in a manner compatible with Convention rights
will render the act ultra vires on grounds of illegality. The Human Rights Act provides
that a person who claims that a public authority has acted (or proposes to act) in a way
which is unlawful, may bring proceedings against the authority in the appropriate court or
tribunal. Alternatively, they may rely on the Convention right or rights concerned in any
legal proceedings. The Scotland Act makes provision for challenge of Scottish Parliament
legislation, which infringes human rights under judicial review procedure. Judicial review
is also available where acts of the Scottish Administration infringe Human Rights.[72]

Under the Equality Act 2006 a Commission for Equality and Human Rights has been
established, to take action in relation to human rights issues throughout the United
Kingdom. The Scottish Commission for Human Rights Act 2006, makes provision for a
separate Scottish Commission for Human Rights to operate on human rights issues which
relate to devolved matters. A Commission on a Bill of Rights was established by the UK
Government on March 18, 2011. The Commission has been given a remit to "investigate
the creation of a UK Bill of Rights that incorporates and builds on all our obligations
under the European Convention on Human Rights, ensures that these rights continue to
be enshrined in UK law, and protects and extend our liberties". It is expected to report by
the end of 2012.

---

[70] *Smith v Scott*, 2007 S.L.T. 137; following *Hirst v United Kingdom* (2006) 42 E.H.R.R. 41.
[71] Human Rights Act 1998 ss.7–9.
[72] See Chapter 3.

▼ CHAPTER SUMMARY

INTRODUCTORY CONCEPTS

5–59   1. Human rights law is concerned with the rights of an individual in relation to the
             Government.
         2. European Convention on Human Rights and Fundamental Freedoms is a Treaty
             drawn up by the Council of Europe.
         3. UK citizens can take an action against the UK Government to the European Court
             of Human Rights.
         4. The Human Rights Act 1998 and the Scotland Act 1998 incorporated the European
             Convention of Human Rights into UK law.
         5. Human Rights Act 1998:

             (a) legislation must be interpreted so as to comply with the Convention;
             (b) courts and tribunals must take account of the jurisprudence of the European
                 Court of Human Rights;
             (c) public authorities must act in a manner compatible with Convention rights.

         6. Scotland Act 1998:

             (a) an Act of the Scottish Parliament is outside the legislative competence of the
                 Parliament if it infringes human rights;
             (b) an act of the Scottish Executive is ultra vires if it infringes human rights.

PRINCIPLES OF THE EUROPEAN CONVENTION ON HUMAN RIGHTS

         1. Convention rights are the rights and fundamental freedoms in:

             ➢ articles 2 to 12 and 14 of the Convention;
             ➢ articles 1 to 3 of the First Protocol; and
             ➢ article 1 of the Thirteenth Protocol.

         2. Interpretation of the European Convention:

             (a) a margin of appreciation is applied to take account of the laws and culture of
                 each State;
             (b) provisions should be interpreted so as to make its safeguards effective;
             (c) the ECHR uses its own meaning for words, regardless of where a case
                 originated;
             (d) the Convention is a living instrument which must be interpreted in the light of
                 present-day conditions;
             (e) the rights in the Convention are the minimum standards.

         3. Convention rights:

             (a) absolute rights;
             (b) limited rights;
             (c) qualified rights, where interference is permissible if the restrictions are: lawful;
                 intended to pursue a legitimate purpose; "necessary in a democratic society";
                 and not discriminatory.

INDIVIDUAL RIGHTS AND FREEDOMS

1. **Article 1 Responsibility of the State:**

   ➢ *A v United Kingdom* [1998] 2 F.L.R. 959; [1998] 3 F.C.R. 59 (1999) 27 E.H.R.R: the United Kingdom was in breach of its duty to ensure the protection of those within its jurisdiction, because the laws to protect children from abuse were ineffective.

2. **Article 2 Right to Life and article 1 of Protocol 13; Abolition of death penalty:**

   ➢ *Pretty v UK* (2002) 35 E.H.R.R. 1: art.2 could not be used to guarantee the right to end life;

   ➢ *A (Children)(Conjoined Twins: Medical Treatment) (No.1), Re* (1997) 24 E.H.R.R.423: an operation to separate conjoined twins could go ahead even though the death of one child was the inevitable result;

   ➢ *Airedale NHS Trust v Bland* [1993] A.C.789: the continuation of treatment when a person is in a persistent vegetative state is not always justified;

   ➢ *Osman v UK* (2000) 29 E.H.R.R. 408: the State has a duty to protect the lives of citizens;

   ➢ *McCann, Farrell and Savage v United Kingdom* (1995) 21 E.H.R.R. 97: reasonable force may only be used where it is strictly necessary.

3. **Article 3 Prohibition of Torture:**

   ➢ *Campbell and Cosans v United Kingdom* (1982) 4 E.H.R.R. 165: the use of the belt in Scottish schools was not a degrading punishment;

   ➢ *Napier v Scottish Ministers*, 2004 S.L.T. 555; 2005 1 S.C. 229; 2004 S.C.L.R. 558; [2004] U.K.H.R.R. 881. Conditions in a Scottish prison amounted to inhuman and degrading treatment.

4. **Article 4 Prohibition of slavery and forced labour.**
5. **Article 5 Right to Liberty and Security:**

   ➢ *Nicol v Lowe*, 1990 S.L.T. 543: police officers may only arrest a person if they have reasonable grounds to suspect that an offence has been committed.

   (a) Article 5(e) permits the lawful detention of persons of unsound mind:

   ➢ *A v Scottish Ministers*, 2001 S.C.1. The Mental Health (Public Safety and Appeals) (Scotland) Act 1999, which provided for detention to protect the public, was not outside the legislative competence, as that the right to liberty had to be balanced against the duty under art.2 to protect life and health.

6. **Article 6 Right to a fair trial:**

   ➢ *HM Advocate v Workman*, 2000 J.C. 383: a delay will not always render a trial unfair;

   ➢ *Cadder v HM Advocate* [2010] UKSC 43: evidence derived from questioning a suspect during detention may only be used if the suspect has legal representation during the questioning;

   ➢ *Starrs v Ruxton*, 2000 J.C. 208; 2000 S.L.T. 42; 1999 S.C.C.R. 1052: temporary sheriffs, whose appointment could be influenced by the Lord Advocate, could be perceived as lacking independence;

   ➢ *Clancy v Caird (No.2)*, 2000 S.L.T. 546; 2000 S C.L.R. 526: temporary judges were held to be sufficiently independent;

> *Hoekstra v HM Advocate (No.3)*, 2000 S.L.T. 605; 2000 S.C.C.R. 367; [2000] H.R.L.R. 410; [2000] U.K.H.R.R. 578. Evidence of bias in the mind of one member of a tribunal, may be sufficient to call into doubt the impartiality of the whole tribunal.

7. **Article 7 Freedom from retroactive criminal convictions or penalties:**

> *SW v United Kingdom* (1996) 21 E.H.R.R. 363; A prosecution under new circumstances will not violate art.7 if it relates to a perceptible evolution of case law;
> *The Scottish Ministers v Mcguffie*, 2006 S.L.T. 1166: the confiscation of property under Pt 5 of the Proceeds of Crime Act 2006, did not amount to a retrospective criminal penalty.

8. **Article 8 Right to respect for private and family life one's home and correspondence:**

> *Smith v United Kingdom*, [1999] I.R.L.R. 734; (2000) 29 E.H.R.R. 493; (1999) 11 Admin. L.R. 879: it was breach of art.8 for the armed forces to carry out intrusive investigations into the private lives of men and women, to ascertain their sexual orientation;
> *Bell v Hogg*, 1967 J.C. 49; 1967 S.L.T. 290: a search may be carried out before a rest if there is a risk of evidence being lost;
> *HM Advocate v Higgins, HM Advocate v Murphy, HM Advocate v Scott*, 2006 S.L.T. 946; 2006 S.C.C.R. 305. To set a trap for accused persons, by placing them in adjacent cells and then posting officers to eavesdrop, was a breach of art.8;
> *McLeod v United Kingdom* (1999) 27 E.H.R.R. 493: where the police enter a person's home without appropriate lawful authority, it will amount to a breach of art.8;
> *Birse v HM Advocate*, 2000 S.L.T. 869; 2000 S.C.C.R. 505; 2000 J.C. 503: a warrant to search premises is necessary in a democratic society, if it is for the purpose of detecting crime;
> *Campbell v United Kingdom* (1992) 15 E.H.R.R. 137: opening letters between a prisoner and his lawyer may be a breach of art.8.

9. **Article 9 Freedom of thought, conscience and religion:**

> *R. (on the application of Begum) v Denbigh High School Governors*. Also known as: *R. (on the application of SB) v Denbigh High School Governors*, [2006] UKHL 15; [2007] 1 A.C. 100; [2006] 2 All E.R. 487: a ban on Muslim religious garments in schools may be justified if the uniform is acceptable to mainstream Muslim opinions.

10. **Article 10 Freedom of expression:**

> *Ingram v Macari*, 1983 S.L.T. 67: obscene publications are those which "possess the liability to corrupt and deprave those to whom they are sold and exposed";
> *Ross (Crawford David) v HM Advocate*, 1998 S.L.T. 1313: text files are included in the definition of obscene material;
> *Rees v Lees*, 1997 S.L.T. 872: the word "sells" in the Civic Government (Scotland) Act includes "offers for sale";
> *HM Advocate v News Group Newspapers*, 1989 S.C.C.R. 156: fines were imposed for contempt of court when newspapers named a suspect.

11. **Article 11 Freedom of assembly and association:**

> ➢ *Council of Civil Service Unions v United Kingdom* [1988] 10 E.H.R.R. 269: a ban on union membership, at Government Communications Headquarters, was justified in the interests of national security.

12. **Article 12 Right to marry and found a family.**
13. **Protocol 1 Article 1 Protection of property.**
14. **Protocol 1 Article 2 Right to education:**

> ➢ *Campbell and Cozens v United Kingdom* (1982) 4 E.H.R.R. 165: the children of parents who had objected to the use of the tawse in Scottish schools, had been deprived of the right to an education in accordance with their philosophical convictions.

15. **Protocol 1 Article 3 Right to free elections:**

> ➢ *Smith v Scott,* 2007 S.L.T. 137: s.3(1) of the Representation of the People Act 1983 was incompatible with Protocol 1 art.3 as it deprived all people serving custodial sentences of the right to vote.

16. **Article 13 Right to an effective Remedy.**

> (a) **an individual may take an action to the European Court of Human Rights if an adequate remedy is not available under domestic law;**
> (b) **the Human Rights Act and the Scotland Act provide remedies in the United Kingdom.**

? QUICK QUIZ

HUMAN RIGHTS LAW

- When was the European Convention on Human Rights and Fundamental Freedoms Incorporated into UK law?
- List the three fundamental principles of the Human Rights Act 1998.
- List four Convention rights from which derogation is not permitted.
- List four examples of qualified Convention rights.
- Explain the four criteria by which infringements of qualified rights are assessed.
- Is it lawful to assist a person to end their own life?
- Give an example of a Scottish case in which it has been held that there has been inhuman and degrading treatment.
- On what grounds may a person be arrested at common law?
- Discuss the significance of the case of *Starrs v Ruxton,* 2000 J.C. 208; 2000 S.L.T. 42
- Do you think that a different decision would be reached in the case of *Khaliq v HM Advocate,* 1983 S.C.C.R.402, if it were to be heard now?
- Name the Act which gives authority to Scottish Police Forces to intercept communications.
- In what circumstances will it be lawful for a school to ban pupils from wearing full length robes?
- Distinguish between absolute privilege and qualified privilege.
- Can a person be prosecuted under the Civic Government (Scotland) Act for displaying obscene materials, if there is no evidence of any actually being sold?

- At what stage will criminal proceedings be classed as active under the Contempt of Court Act 1981?

📖 FURTHER READING

There are several books, which give more in-depth analysis of human rights law as it applies in Scotland.

K. Ewing and K. Dale-Risk, *Human Rights in Scotland; Text Cases and Materials* (W. Green, 2004).

C. Ashton & V. Finch, *Human Rights and Scots Law* (W. Green, 2002).

Murdoch, *A Guide to Human Rights in Scotland*, 2nd edn (Tottel, 2007).

🖱 RELEVANT WEB LINKS

The Ministry of Justice: *http://www.justice.gov.uk*

The Ministry of Justice guidance on human rights: *http://www.justice.gov.uk/human-rights*

Decisions of the European Court of Human Rights: *http://www.echr.coe.int/echr/*

Scottish Judiciary: *http://www.scotland-judiciary.org*

Chapter 6 Criminal Law

JAMES CHALMERS[1]

▶ CHAPTER OVERVIEW

This chapter is concerned with the criminal law. It provides a brief treatment of the nature **6–01** and sources of criminal law, before explaining the "anatomy" of a crime—that is, the different elements which must be established in order to convict a person of a criminal offence. It goes on to outline the major offences recognised by Scots criminal law, before reviewing the principal defences to crime.

✓ OUTCOMES

At the end of the chapter, you should be able to explain and apply the following: **6–02**

- ✓ the "anatomy" of a crime, and the difference between actus reus, mens rea and defences;
- ✓ the definitions of the main offences recognised by Scots law, such as murder, culpable homicide, assault, rape, theft, reset and breach of the peace;
- ✓ the concept of "inchoate" offences (attempt, conspiracy and incitement);
- ✓ the concept of "art and part" (accessory) liability; and
- ✓ the principal defences recognised by Scots criminal law, and the criteria which must be satisfied for each defence to succeed.

THE NATURE OF CRIMINAL LAW

It has been said that criminal law "is a species of political and moral philosophy".[2] That is **6–03** not to say that a philosophical training is required for the study of criminal law, but that the question which criminal law asks is in substance philosophical—what are the conditions under which persons may be held criminally responsible for their actions and, therefore, liable to be punished by the State? The study of criminal law is a study of those conditions.

There are, of course, important underlying philosophical questions regarding the issue of why the State is entitled to hold people "criminally responsible". In other words, why is a State entitled to punish its citizens? However, a basic study of criminal law is not concerned with such issues.[3] Instead, the student approaching criminal law for the first time will (normally) be required to consider how criminal offences are defined, what must

---

[1] Senior Lecturer in Law, University of Edinburgh. I am indebted to Christopher Gane and Fiona Leverick for their comments on an earlier version of this chapter.
[2] George P. Fletcher, *Rethinking Criminal Law* (Little, Brown & Co, 1978), xix.
[3] For a modern discussion, see Nicola Lacey, *State Punishment* (Routledge, 1988), especially Ch.2.

be proven in order to convict a person of a crime, and which defences may exonerate persons from criminal liability. It is these issues with which this chapter is concerned.

SOURCES OF SCOTS CRIMINAL LAW

6–04 Throughout the world, criminal law is normally codified law. Most systems—and certainly almost all Western systems—have a criminal (or "penal") code which lays out the definitions of offences and the conditions under which individuals can be held responsible for committing those offences.

In this respect, however, Scots law is radically different. There is no Scottish criminal code, although an "unofficial draft" of a potential code has been written by a group of academics and was published in 2003.[4] Instead, the predominant part of Scots criminal law is common law, i.e. constructed from judicial decisions in particular cases over the years. There is a great deal of statutory criminal law, particularly in "regulatory" areas such as road traffic and health and safety law, and also misuse of drugs legislation, but almost all major criminal offences have no statutory definition, which must instead be discerned from the decided cases.[5] The one exception to this is the law of sexual offences, which was put into statutory form in 2009 following a review by the Scottish Law Commission.[6] In addition to case law, the Scottish courts often rely on a number of legal writers, particularly (Baron) David Hume, whose nineteenth-century work *Commentaries on the Law of Scotland, Respecting Crimes*[7] is generally considered an authoritative statement of the criminal law as it applied at the time, and is even now frequently relied upon by the courts in the process of ascertaining the modern criminal law.[8]

The case-based nature of Scots criminal law is generally thought to allow for greater flexibility in the development of the criminal law. Historically, the Scottish courts have asserted a power referred to as the "declaratory power"—that is, a power on the part of the High Court "competently to punish ... every act which is obviously of a criminal nature; though it be such which in time past has never been the subject of prosecution."[9]

While this power to "create new crimes" has rarely been exercised explicitly[10]—at least in recent times—the courts have still drawn on the "flexible nature" of the criminal law in more modern cases to address what might be seen as "new problems". So, in *Khaliq v HM Advocate*,[11] the High Court felt able to declare that selling "glue-sniffing kits" to children was the offence of "causing real injury", on the basis that the sellers bore responsibility for any injury caused to the children from their substance abuse, and in *Carmichael v Black; Black v Carmichael*,[12] it was held that to "wheel-clamp" cars which had been improperly parked on private property and demand a fee for their release could be both theft and extortion at common law.

In this way, it has been judicially suggested, the courts have "helped to ensure that Scots

---

[4] Scottish Law Commission, *A Draft Criminal Code for Scotland with Commentary* (2003).

[5] English law is similar in approach, although a much greater part of the "common law" has been altered by, or codified in, statute in England than is the case in Scotland.

[6] Sexual Offences (Scotland) Act 2009. See Scottish Law Commission, *Report on the Law of Rape and Other Sexual Offences* (2009), Scot. Law Com. No.207.

[7] David Hume, *Commentaries on the Law of Scotland, Respecting Crimes*, 4th edn (Bell & Bradfute, 1844), by B.R. Bell, (hereafter cited as "Hume, *Commentaries*").

[8] See also the further reading notes section at the end of this chapter.

[9] Hume, *Commentaries*, i, p.12.

[10] It has not been explicitly relied upon since *Bernard Greenhuff* (1838) 2 Swin. 236.

[11] 1984 J.C. 23.

[12] 1992 S.L.T. 897.

criminal law ... has not been subject to undue interference by overenthusiastic legislators".[13] Against that must be weighed two principled objections. The first principle is that of *legality*: criminal law should be known (or, at least, accessible). Citizens are entitled to know in advance whether or not any conduct on which they intend to embark is criminal—they should not have to wait for the courts to decide that question afterwards. The second principle is, quite simply, *democracy*: many would argue that it is fundamentally inappropriate for the courts to be acting as legislators, and that such questions must be for the Scottish or Westminster Parliaments to address. The question has been hotly debated with respect to the declaratory power in particular.

It would be all but impossible for the declaratory power to be invoked today, due to the provisions of the Human Rights Act 1998 and the European Convention on Human Rights, art.7 of which explicitly states that "no one shall be held guilty of any criminal offence on account of any act or omission which did not constitute a criminal offence under national or international law at the time when it was committed". Some development of the criminal law through judicial decision is, however, probably inevitable and necessary, because it is never possible to anticipate in advance all the problems which the criminal courts might require to address. Provided that any development of the law by the courts is reasonably foreseeable, this will not violate the European Convention on Human Rights.[14]

Any study of criminal law will reveal numerous areas where the law is uncertain or unclear. While the resultant "grey area" may well be frustrating, it should be remembered that it may well be of limited importance in practice. Most cases of crime, which are reported to the police and prosecution authorities, will quite clearly fall within (or quite clearly fall outwith) the definition of a criminal offence. Similarly, while the exact boundary of a criminal offence may be unclear, it will normally still be clear how citizens are expected to behave if they do not wish to fall foul of the law. The lack of a clear boundary is not necessarily unfair, provided that it is not difficult to stay on the right side of the boundary. In that sense, the "grey area" may be more theoretical than real in many cases. That is not to say that the exact definitions of crimes are not important—far from it—simply that the ambiguities which exist may not present as many practical problems as might first appear.

GENERAL PRINCIPLES OF CRIMINAL LIABILITY

The anatomy of a crime

It is normal to regard a criminal offence as being made up of three elements, as follows: **6–05**

    (1) actus reus;
    (2) mens rea;
    (3) the absence of a defence.

The actus reus is probably best understood as the physical element of the crime. Despite the term "actus", it need not necessarily be an action—depending on the crime, it may be constituted by an omission to act or a "state of affairs" (such as being in possession of a controlled drug).

---

[13] *McLay v HM Advocate*, 1994 J.C. 159, per Lord McCluskey at 173. Compare, however, the comments by the same judge in *Lord Advocate's Reference (No.1 of 2001)*, 2002 S.L.T. 466.

[14] See *SW v United Kingdom* (1996) 21 E.H.R.R. 363.

Mens rea is the fault element, which is required for the crime, such as an intention to cause a particular result, knowledge that a particular circumstance exists, or recklessness as to the consequences of one's actions. For some statutory offences, a fault element may not actually be required. This is known as "strict liability", and is discussed further below.[15]

It is important to notice that the word "defence" is used here in a technical sense. In ordinary language, we refer to anything which might result in a person's acquittal as a defence—so in that sense, it is a defence to show (for example) that someone else committed the crime, that the complainer in a theft case consented to the appropriation of his property, or that an accused did not actually possess the mens rea required for the crime. These are simply denials that the prosecution have proved actus reus or mens rea.

The word "defence" is used here to refer to those rules of law which may be pled as a *justification* or *excuse* for the accused's conduct where actus reus and mens rea have both been shown to exist. In this sense, defences include such concepts as self-defence, insanity or necessity. Defences are discussed in full at the end of this chapter.[16]

It is important to note that an accused cannot normally be required to prove anything in a criminal trial. Even where an accused pleads a defence such as self-defence, the most they can be required to do by law is simply to point to *some* evidence suggesting that the defence might apply. The prosecution must then prove beyond a reasonable doubt that the defence does not apply, otherwise the accused is entitled to an acquittal.[17] The only exceptions to this rule at common law[18] are the defences of insanity[19] and diminished responsibility,[20] which must be proved by the accused on the balance of probabilities.[21]

Actus reus

6–06 All crimes require a physical element, referred to as an actus reus. The law does not punish a guilty mind alone. This physical element may include such factors as the conduct of the accused, the circumstances in which that conduct takes place, and the results of that conduct.

Normally, the actus reus will involve some sort of action by the accused—which is relatively unproblematic—but the criminal law also imposes liability for omissions in certain circumstances. This is more problematic, and requires further discussion.

Liability for omissions

6–07 Crimes of omission may be divided into two forms. The first category, sometimes referred to as "pure omissions", are crimes which consist simply of a failure to do something, such as a failure to report a road traffic accident where required by law to do so.[22] Virtually all examples of such crimes are statutory.

The second category may be referred to as crimes of "commission by omission". Omitting to act may amount to the actus reus of a result crime. Where a person is under a duty to act but fails to do so, and this has the effect of causing a particular legally

---

[15] See below, para.6–12.
[16] See below, para.6–63 et seq.
[17] *Lambie v HM Advocate*, 1973 J.C. 53.
[18] Exceptions in statutory offences are extremely common: cf. Andrew Ashworth and Meredith Blake, "The presumption of innocence in English criminal law" [1996] Crim. L.R. 306.
[19] See below, para.6–64.
[20] See below, para.6–20.
[21] *Lindsay v HM Advocate*, 1997 J.C. 19. Both of these defences were put into statutory form by s.168 of the Criminal Justice and Licensing (Scotland) Act 2010, which did not alter the burden of proof.
[22] See Road Traffic Act 1988 s.170.

prohibited result, the person may be guilty of that offence. The most obvious example is a person who fails to prevent a death when they are legally obliged to do so: such a person may be guilty of murder or culpable homicide. Duties to act are only imposed in exceptional cases: under Scots law, a person who walks past a stranger in peril and fails to assist may be morally guilty, but cannot be said to be legally guilty of anything.[23]

There is very little authority on the extent of crimes of commission by omission in Scots law, but it is generally thought that duties to act are recognised in the following circumstances:

(1) *Family relationships.* A parent has a duty to prevent harm coming to their child.[24] It is normally thought, however, that a child has no reciprocal duty towards a parent unless they have assumed responsibility for that person (see (2) below).

(2) *Assumption of responsibility.* A person who assumes responsibility for another must prevent harm coming to that person. In the English case of *R. v Stone and Dobinson*,[25] a man and his partner allowed the man's sister to live with them. The sister, described as "eccentric in many ways", did not eat properly and largely confined herself to her room. Eventually, she became unwilling or unable to leave her bed. Stone and Dobinson made some ineffectual attempts to seek medical assistance but did nothing further, and the sister died. It was held that they had accepted responsibility for her by taking her in, and that their failure to summon medical assistance meant that they were guilty of manslaughter (the English equivalent of culpable homicide).

Responsibility may, in such cases, have been assumed by contract, although it should certainly not be thought that a contract is essential. In *William Hardie*[26] it was held that a man employed as a poor inspector could in principle be held guilty of culpable homicide, if it was shown that his failure to render assistance to a woman who had made an application for poor relief had caused her death.

It has also been suggested that there might be a duty to act where the accused has created a dangerous situation.[27] That is, a person who has created a dangerous situation might be under an obligation to remedy the danger created, even if they were not initially at fault. In the English case of *R. v Miller*,[28] a tramp squatting in an unoccupied house fell asleep while smoking a cigarette, which set fire to his mattress. He then awoke, left the mattress smouldering and moved to another room instead. The house caught fire and he was charged with arson.[29] It was held that he could be held liable for arson on the basis that he had done nothing to remedy the danger caused by his initial act of falling asleep while smoking. However, in the recent case of *McCue v Currie*,[30] where the accused had accidentally dropped a cigarette lighter while breaking into a caravan, causing a fire, the appeal court declined to follow *Miller* and refused to hold the accused guilty of culpable and reckless fireraising. The decision has been criticised because the appeal court seems to

---

[23] *HM Advocate v McClure and Bone* Unreported September 2002, High Court at Stonehaven (observations of Lord Abernethy in his charge to the jury).

[24] *Bone v HM Advocate*, 2006 S.L.T. 164. See also *R. v Gibbins and Proctor* (1918) 13 Cr. App. R. 134; cf. *Paterson v Lees*, 1999 J.C. 159.

[25] [1977] Q.B. 354.

[26] (1847) Ark. 247.

[27] See, e.g. T.H. Jones and M.G.A. Christie, *Criminal Law*, 4th edn (W. Green, 2008), paras 3–11 and 3–12.

[28] [1983] 2 A.C. 161. See also the Scottish case of *Macphail v Clark*, 1983 S.L.T. (Sh. Ct) 37.

[29] Scots law does not use the term "arson". The nearest equivalent offence is fireraising, on which see below, para.6–51.

[30] 2004 J.C. 73.

have misunderstood the basis of *Miller*, treating it as a decision on the interpretation of a specific English statutory provision (which it is not) rather than the application of a general principle about liability for omissions (which it is).[31]

Causation

6–08 In crimes which require a particular result as an element of the actus reus (such as murder or culpable homicide, where the relevant result is the death of the victim), it must be shown that the accused's act (or omission) caused that result. Although much academic and philosophical work has been directed towards developing a theoretical account of causation,[32] the courts have tended to take the view that causation "is essentially a practical question of fact which can best be answered by ordinary common sense rather than by abstract metaphysical theory".[33]

There are two well-recognised doctrines which require special attention, however. The first of these is the doctrine of *taking your victim as you find him* (also referred to as the "thin skull" rule). If A assaults B, and it transpires that B has a weak heart, or an egg-shell skull, and dies as a result, B's special susceptibility to injury is no reason to hold that A has not caused B's death.[34] In the English case of *R. v Blaue*,[35] Blaue stabbed a young woman who later refused a blood transfusion on the ground that she was a Jehovah's Witness and died as a result. While it was accepted that she would not have died had she accepted a blood transfusion, the Court of Appeal held that Blaue's actions were still to be regarded as the cause of her death—an assailant must take his victim as he finds him, religious beliefs and all.

The second doctrine is that of novus actus interveniens (a new intervening cause). If A assaults B, and B later dies, but something new and unforeseeable has happened between the two incidents which can be regarded as a new, supervening cause of B's death, A's assault will not be regarded as the cause of death. This might include extremely poor medical treatment (sometimes referred to as "malregimen"), a new act by a third party, or possibly even the actions of the victim himself. The need for such actions to be unforeseeable before they will break the chain of causation must be emphasised, however—where A supplies a harmful substance (such as glue or a controlled drug) to B knowing that B wishes to abuse that substance, B's actions in abusing the substance will not break the chain of causation between A's original act and any harm sustained by B as a result.[36]

Mens rea

6–09 For all common law crimes, the accused cannot be criminally liable on the basis of the actus reus alone. It is essential that the prosecution also prove mens rea (sometimes referred to as a "guilty mind").

The exact form of mens rea required will depend upon the definition of the particular offence. It is usually expressed in terms of intention, knowledge, or recklessness. Scots law has not paid much attention to how the first two of those terms might be defined, although it is not clear that attempts to define those terms would be particularly helpful. Recklessness is generally defined as an "utter disregard" for the consequences of one's actions,[37]

---

[31] See James Chalmers, "Fireraising By Omission", 2004 S.L.T. (News) 59; M.G.A. Christie, *The Criminal Law of Scotland: Third Edition Supplement* (W. Green, 2005), para.3.34.

[32] See, in particular, H.L.A. Hart and T. Honoré, *Causation in the Law*, 2nd edn (Clarendon, 1985).

[33] *Alphacell Ltd v Woodward* [1972] A.C. 824, per Lord Salmon at 847.

[34] *James Williamson* (1866) 5 Irv. 326; *Bird v HM Advocate*, 1952 J.C. 23.

[35] [1975] 1 W.L.R. 1411.

[36] *Khaliq v HM Advocate*, 1984 J.C. 23; *Lord Advocate's Reference (No.1 of 1994)*, 1996 J.C. 76.

[37] *Cameron v Maguire*, 1999 J.C. 63; *Quinn v Cunningham*, 1956 J.C. 22.

although it is possible that different definitions may apply with respect to different criminal offences.[38]

The (ir)relevance of motive

It is commonly said that motive is irrelevant to culpability: "It is as firmly established in **6–10** legal doctrine as any rule can be that motive is irrelevant to responsibility".[39] This is only true up to a point, however. Motive is, indeed, generally irrelevant to questions of mens rea. If A intends to hit B, he has the mens rea for assault (that is, an intention to attack B) regardless of his motive for doing so. Motivation can, however, be extremely relevant to the question of whether A has a valid justification or excuse for his conduct, such as the defence of self-defence.[40]

Error

An error as to the scope of the criminal law (i.e. a belief that a certain act is *not* criminal) is **6–11** no defence to a criminal charge. Other errors of fact, however, may relieve a person from criminal liability. It is important to distinguish between three types of error in this respect.

First, errors may be irrelevant—for example, if A hits B, it is no defence for him to say that he thought he was hitting C.[41]

Secondly, an error of fact may show that the accused did not in fact have the mens rea required for the crime. For example, the mens rea required for the crime of rape is that the man knew that the woman was not consenting to sexual intercourse, or was reckless as to whether or not she was consenting. It has, therefore, been held that a man who has sexual intercourse with a woman in the belief that she is consenting is not guilty of the common law offence of rape, however unreasonable that belief may be.[42] Where the accused lacks the mens rea for a crime because of an error of fact, it matters not how unreasonable it is— he is still entitled to be acquitted.[43]

Thirdly, errors of fact may provide a foundation for a justificatory or excusatory defence. For example, if A believes (wrongly) that he has grounds for acting in self-defence, and does so, he may be entitled to plead the defence of self-defence.[44] His belief must be reasonable, however.[45]

Strict liability

Although no person can be convicted of a common law offence without proof of mens rea, **6–12** this is not always the case with statutory offences. Some statutory offences may not require proof of any mens rea for conviction. These are referred to as "strict liability" offences.

The question of whether or not an offence requires proof of mens rea for conviction is one of statutory interpretation. It is always presumed that an offence requires mens rea unless the terms of the statute imply otherwise.[46] The statute may make it clear that mens rea is required, by the use of terms such as "knowingly" or "wilfully". In many cases, however, a statutory offence will make no explicit provision as regards mens rea, and the

---

[38] cf. *Allan v Patterson*, 1980 J.C. 57.
[39] A. Norrie, *Crime, Reason and History*, 2nd edn (Butterworths, 2001), p.36.
[40] On the requirements of this defence, see below, para.6–67.
[41] cf. *Roberts v Hamilton*, 1989 S.L.T. 399.
[42] *Jamieson v HM Advocate*, 1994 J.C. 88; *Meek v HM Advocate*, 1983 S.L.T. 280. See further below, para.6–33.
[43] cf., however, *Dewar v HM Advocate*, 1945 J.C. 5.
[44] See further below, para.6–67.
[45] *Owens v HM Advocate*, 1946 J.C. 119.
[46] *Duguid v Fraser*, 1942 J.C. 1; *Sweet v Parsley* [1970] A.C. 132.

courts must, therefore, apply various criteria in order to determine whether the offence is one of strict liability. These criteria were set out in the following case:

Gammon Ltd v Attorney-General of Hong Kong
[1985] A.C. 1

Lord Scarman: "(1) there is a presumption of law that mens rea is required before a person can be held guilty of a criminal offence; (2) the presumption is particularly strong where the offence is 'truly criminal' in character; (3) the presumption applies to statutory offences, and can be displaced only if this is clearly or by necessary implication the effect of the statute; (4) the only situation in which the presumption can be displaced is where the statute is concerned with an issue of social concern, and public safety is such an issue; (5) even where a statute is concerned with such an issue, the presumption of mens rea stands unless it can also be shown that the creation of strict liability will be effective to promote the objects of the statute by encouraging greater vigilance to prevent the commission of the prohibited act."

The fact that an offence is punishable by imprisonment is no bar to it being held to be one of strict liability.[47]

Corporate liability

6–13 It is clearly competent to prosecute a corporation for a criminal offence,[48] and such prosecutions are relatively common where crimes of "strict liability" are concerned. However, more difficulty arises where mens rea is required. Here, it must be shown that a person who was the "controlling mind" of the company themselves possessed the mens rea required for conviction. This can pose difficulties, as the following case demonstrates:

Transco plc v HM Advocate
2004 J.C. 29

Transco, a company responsible for gas supplies, were prosecuted for culpable homicide after four people died in a gas explosion. The charge against Transco alleged that the explosion had resulted from a long series of alleged failures on Transco's part. The court held that because the charge did not allege that any particular individual had the mens rea required for culpable homicide, it did not provide a basis for convicting Transco. It was not possible to "aggregate" the states of mind of different people at different times in order to construct mens rea.

Although, in cases like *Transco*, it may be possible to bring alternative charges such as violations of health and safety legislation,[49] the difficulties encountered in prosecuting companies for culpable homicide (in England, manslaughter) in cases like this has caused

---

[47] *Gammon Ltd v Att-Gen of Hong Kong* [1985] A.C. 1, per Lord Scarman at 17.
[48] Criminal Procedure (Scotland) Act 1995 ss.70 and 143. See also *Purcell Meats (Scotland) Ltd v McLeod*, 1987 S.L.T. 528.
[49] Transco was later convicted of a contravention of ss.3 and 33(1) of the Health and Safety at Work Act 1974, in respect of this incident, and fined £15 million.

concern throughout the United Kingdom. This has resulted in legislation creating a specific offence of corporate homicide which is designed to deal with such cases.[50]

Defences

Even where both actus reus and mens rea can be proven, an accused may be able to argue **6–14** that his conduct is in some way justified or excused. Such a claim will only result in an acquittal if it can be framed in terms of one of the several general defences (such as self-defence or necessity), which are recognised by Scots law. These are discussed in full at the end of this chapter.

> **Key Concepts**
>
> A **criminal offence** is constructed from three elements: (1) the actus reus (the physical element); (2) mens rea (the fault element) and (3) the absence of a defence.
>
> There is **generally no liability for omissions** in the criminal law unless (a) this is explicitly provided for by statute or (b) a person is under a duty to act. Duties to act may arise from family relationships, the assumption of responsibility or (possibly) the creation of a dangerous situation.
>
> Where the actus reus of a crime requires a particular result, it must be shown that the accused caused that result: this is the requirement of **causation**.
>
> Mens rea requirements are usually defined in terms of **intention, knowledge or recklessness**.
>
> Some statutory crimes do not require mens rea: this is known as **strict liability**.
>
> **Corporations** can be criminally liable under Scots law. Where an offence requires mens rea, it must be shown that a person who was the "controlling mind" of the company themselves had that mens rea.

HOMICIDE

Scots law distinguishes between two forms of homicide: murder and culpable homicide.[51] **6–15** (There are also statutory offences of causing death by dangerous driving, by careless driving, by careless driving when under the influence of drink or drugs, and causing death by driving when unlicensed, disqualified or uninsured).[52] The actus reus of both types of homicide is the destruction of a self-existent human life,[53] although the mens rea differs (the definitions of mens rea which apply to each form of homicide are explained below).

The destruction of an unborn child is not homicide under Scots law, because such a child does not have an independent existence.[54] It may, however, be the crime of abortion.[55] The situation is different, however, where injuries are inflicted on an unborn child

---

[50] Corporate Manslaughter and Corporate Homicide Act 2007.

[51] Note also the relevant crimes against international law, which are recognised by the International Criminal Court (Scotland) Act 2001 s.1.

[52] Road Traffic Act 1988 ss.1–3ZB, as amended. Such conduct can, of course, be charged as either murder or culpable homicide if the requirements of those crimes are met: see, e.g. *McDowall v HM Advocate*, 1998 J.C. 194.

[53] Macdonald, *Criminal Law*, 5th edn (W. Green, 1948), p.87.

[54] *Jean McCallum* (1858) 3 Irv. 187.

[55] See generally G.H. Gordon, *Criminal Law*, 3rd edn (W. Green, 2001), by M.G.A. Christie, Vol.II, Ch.28.

who is born alive but subsequently dies as a result of those injuries. Such circumstances are generally thought to be sufficient for the actus reus of homicide.[56]

Culpable homicide is a lesser crime than murder: while murder carries a mandatory sentence of life imprisonment,[57] there is no fixed sentence for culpable homicide and it is not unknown for persons convicted of culpable homicide to walk free from court in some cases.[58] It is, however, competent to pass a sentence of life imprisonment on a conviction for culpable homicide in appropriate cases.[59]

Murder

6–16 The classic definition of murder is that offered by Macdonald:

> "Murder is constituted by any wilful act causing the destruction of life, whether intended to kill, or displaying such wicked recklessness as to imply a disposition depraved enough to be regardless of consequences."[60]

It can be seen from this that there are two alternative forms of the mens rea of murder. A person who causes the death of another is guilty of murder if (i) he intended to kill; or (ii) was "wickedly reckless".

In *Drury v HM Advocate*,[61] it was said that Macdonald's definition was incomplete, and that an intention to kill must (like recklessness) also be "wicked" before the actor can be guilty of murder. Quite what the court meant by "wicked" in this context is unclear, but it seems that an intention to kill will always be regarded as "wicked" unless the defences of provocation or diminished responsibility apply.[62] These are partial defences, which "reduce" murder to culpable homicide, and are discussed below in that context.[63]

Wicked recklessness was defined by Lord Sutherland in *HM Advocate v Hartley* in the following terms:

HM Advocate v Hartley
1989 S.L.T. 135

Lord Sutherland: "That ['wicked recklessness'] sounds a bit archaic. If it does, it is not surprising, because it is a definition which has been in existence for hundreds of years, and has stood the test of time. And basically what it means is simply this. If you act in such a way as to show that you don't really care whether the person you are attacking lives or dies, then that can constitute this degree of wicked recklessness which is required to constitute murder. It may, in the end of the day, come as a considerable surprise to you, and indeed a matter of regret too that your victim dies, but that doesn't alter the fact that you have committed murder, if you have, during the course of the attack, displayed such wicked recklessness as to show that you are regardless of the consequences, that you have no particular interest in whether your victim lives or dies."

---

[56] cf. *McCluskey v HM Advocate*, 1988 S.C.C.R. 629.
[57] Criminal Procedure (Scotland) Act 1995 s.205.
[58] See, e.g. *Burns v HM Advocate*, 1998 S.C.C.R. 281 (sentence of 240 hours community service).
[59] *Kirkwood v HM Advocate*, 1939 J.C. 16.
[60] Macdonald, *Criminal Law*, 5th edn (W. Green, 1948), p.89.
[61] 2001 S.L.T. 1013.
[62] *Gillon v HM Advocate*, 2007 J.C. 24.
[63] The terminology of "reducing" murder to culpable homicide was disapproved in *Drury*, but used in the later case of *Galbraith v HM Advocate (No.2)*, 2002 J.C. 1.

In *HM Advocate v Purcell*,[64] the High Court held that a person could not be said to be "wickedly reckless" unless he had intended to cause some physical injury, meaning that a person who had struck and killed a young boy while driving a car through a pedestrian crossing at high speed, but had not intended to injure any person, could be convicted of culpable homicide but not murder. This does not mean that an intention to cause physical injury is *sufficient* for wicked recklessness, but in the absence of such an intention, wicked recklessness cannot be found proven.

Culpable homicide

There are three forms of culpable homicide which are recognised by Scots law: 6-17

- voluntary culpable homicide (this covers cases where the actor has the mens rea of murder but one of the two partial defences available to murder—provocation or diminished responsibility—applies and "reduces" the crime to culpable homicide);
- unlawful act culpable homicide (this covers cases where the actor has committed another crime which has resulted in death); and
- involuntary culpable homicide (this covers cases where the actor does not have the mens rea of murder, but has been grossly negligent).

Each of these categories will now be considered in more detail.

Voluntary culpable homicide

Where the requirements for the crime of murder have been made out, an accused may   6-18 nevertheless be convicted of culpable homicide if a "partial defence" applies. There are two such partial defences recognised by Scots law: provocation and diminished responsibility.

Provocation

The plea of provocation, if successful, will result in the accused being convicted of culpable   6-19 homicide rather than murder. It is not a complete defence. While evidence of provocation may be considered in mitigation of sentence for any other crime (most commonly assault), it is only in homicide cases that it can have any effect on the offence of which the accused is convicted.

When considering a plea of provocation, a jury must address the following questions.[65]

(1) Was there a recognised provocation? Scots law only recognises two forms of provocation—firstly, provocation by assault (i.e. the deceased assaulted the accused) and secondly, provocation by infidelity. For provocation by infidelity to operate, the accused must have been in a relationship of fidelity (not necessarily marriage, or even a heterosexual relationship).[66] The accused must have discovered that his partner was unfaithful, and killed either the partner or their paramour in consequence of that revelation. Although the defence may, historically, only have applied where the accused caught the parties in the act of infidelity, this is no longer the case, and a simple confession of infidelity will suffice.[67]

---

[64] 2008 J.C. 131. See also *Petto v HM Advocate*, 2011 S.L.T. 1043.
[65] See generally, *Drury v HM Advocate*, 2001 S.L.T. 1013.
[66] *McKay v HM Advocate*, 1991 J.C. 91; *HM Advocate v McKean*, 1996 S.C.C.R. 402.
[67] *HM Advocate v Hill*, 1941 J.C. 59.

Under Scots law as it currently stands, words can never be sufficient to found a defence of provocation.[68]

(2) Did the accused lose his self-control? A person is only entitled to plead provocation if he loses his self-control and kills in the heat of the moment. A person who kills for revenge may not plead the defence.

(3) If the provocation was by infidelity: would an ordinary person, subjected to such provocation, have been liable to react in the same way? Or, if the provocation was by assault, was there a "reasonably proportionate relationship" between the deceased's violence and the accused's response?[69]

If all of these questions are answered in the affirmative (or, strictly speaking given the burden of proof, if the Crown has failed to prove beyond a reasonable doubt that any one of them should be answered in the negative), the defence will succeed and the accused will be convicted of culpable homicide and not murder.

Diminished responsibility[70]

6–20 This partial defence is generally considered to have originated in the 1867 case of *Alexander Dingwall*.[71] In that case, Dingwall—an alcoholic—killed his wife, with whom he was generally on good terms, after a quarrel. He was mentally ill, but not insane. Lord Deas directed the jury that it was open to them to convict Dingwall of culpable homicide rather than murder on the grounds of the "extenuating circumstances" of the case, which they did.

The requirements for the defence are now set out in a statutory provision[72] which largely codifies the decision of five judges in the leading case of *Galbraith v HM Advocate (No.2)*,[73] and are as follows:

(1) The accused must have been suffering from an "abnormality of mind" at the time of the killing. This abnormality can take any form, provided that it is one "recognised by the appropriate science". Prior to *Galbraith*, it was thought that only a "mental disease" qualified (and the defence could, therefore, not be based on a personality disorder), but this is no longer the case.[74] The defence may not, however, be based on the influence of alcohol, drugs or any other substance.[75]

(2) The abnormality of mind must have resulted in "the person's ability to determine or control conduct" being "substantially impaired".[76]

The accused must prove both of these requirements on the balance of probabilities (*not* beyond reasonable doubt).[77] This is an exception to the general rule that the burden of proof in a criminal case is always on the prosecution.

As with provocation, evidence of diminished responsibility can be taken into account in

---

[68] See Macdonald, *Criminal Law*, 5th edn (W. Green, 1948), p.93.
[69] *Gillon v HM Advocate*, 2007 J.C. 24.
[70] See generally *Report on Insanity and Diminished Responsibility* (2004), Scot. Law Com. No.195.
[71] (1867) 5 Irv. 466.
[72] Criminal Procedure (Scotland) Act 1995 s.51B, as inserted by s.168 of the Criminal Justice and Licensing (Scotland) Act 2010.
[73] 2002 J.C. 1.
[74] See *Connelly v HM Advocate*, 1990 J.C. 349 and *Williamson v HM Advocate*, 1994 J.C. 149, both of which were overruled in *Galbraith*.
[75] Criminal Procedure (Scotland) Act 1995 s.51B(3).
[76] Criminal Procedure (Scotland) Act 1995 s.51B(1).
[77] Criminal Procedure (Scotland) Act 1995 s.51B(4).

mitigation of sentence on any charge, but it is only on a charge of murder that it can alter the offence of which the accused is convicted.

Unlawful act culpable homicide

It is thought that any criminal act, which results in death, is always culpable homicide. The **6–21** position is clearly settled in relation to assault, and the leading case is the 1952 decision in *Bird v HM Advocate*.[78]

> ### Bird v HM Advocate
> #### 1952 J.C. 23
>
> Bird believed that a woman had taken money belonging to him. He followed her for half a mile and forcibly restrained her from boarding a passing car, whereupon she collapsed and died. It was later discovered that she had a diseased heart. Lord Jamieson directed the jury that if it was proved that Bird had assaulted the deceased, and that this had caused her death, this was sufficient for a finding of guilty of culpable homicide. It was, therefore, unnecessary to show any mens rea on Bird's part beyond the mens rea which is required for assault. Bird was convicted of culpable homicide, and his conviction was upheld on appeal.

It is clear that this rule extends to any criminal act which involves a foreseeable risk of personal injury—and so, for example, it was applied in *Mathieson v HM Advocate*[79] to find the accused guilty of culpable homicide after he had committed a fireraising, which resulted in the deaths of some occupants of a nearby building. It is not clear, however, whether the rule applies to criminal acts which do not involve a foreseeable risk of injury, although for obvious reasons, a charge of unlawful act culpable homicide based on such an offence would be unlikely.[80]

Involuntary culpable homicide

This crime is committed where the accused causes death through an act which is not **6–22** unlawful (or at least not a basis for a charge of unlawful act culpable homicide) and does so with the mens rea of this form of culpable homicide.

The classic statement of the mens rea of this form of culpable homicide can be found in *Paton v HM Advocate*, where it was said that the mens rea required was "gross, or wicked, or criminal negligence, something amounting, or at any rate analogous, to a criminal indifference to consequences".[81] That is a rather lengthy formulation, and in the more recent case of *McDowall v HM Advocate*,[82] Lord Abernethy directed the jury that if the accused had shown "a complete disregard for any potential dangers which might result" from his actions, that was sufficient mens rea for the crime. In McDowall's subsequent appeal against conviction, it was accepted that this direction was correct.[83]

Because, as noted above, any unlawful act, which results in death, is necessarily culpable homicide, without the need to prove this mens rea, it has been said that this form of

---

[78] 1952 J.C. 23.

[79] 1981 S.C.C.R. 196. See also *Sutherland v HM Advocate*, 1994 S.L.T. 634.

[80] See, however, *Lourie v HM Advocate*, 1988 S.C.C.R. 634.

[81] 1936 J.C. 19, per the Lord Justice-Clerk (Aitchison) at 22.

[82] 1998 J.C. 194.

[83] Lord Abernethy's directions were referred to with approval in *Transco plc v HM Advocate*, 2004 J.C. 29.

culpable homicide "is almost entirely confined to traffic cases".[84] Driving a car (unlike, for example, assaulting someone) is perfectly lawful in itself—but if it is done with complete disregard for the safety of the public and a death results, the driver will be guilty of culpable homicide.

Key Concepts

Murder is committed where a person causes a death while either (a) wickedly intending to kill or (b) acting in a such a way as to display a wicked recklessness of the consequences of his actions.

If a person would otherwise be guilty of murder but successfully pleads either **provocation** or **diminished responsibility**, they will be convicted of **culpable homicide** instead. This form of culpable homicide is referred to as **voluntary culpable homicide**.

Diminished responsibility applies where a person, at the time of the killing, suffered from an abnormality of mind, which substantially impaired his ability, as compared with a normal person, to determine or control his acts.

Provocation applies where a person (a) is subject to a recognised provocation (violence or a revelation of infidelity), which (b) causes him to lose control and kill another person, provided that (c) an ordinary person subjected to such provocation would have been liable to react in the same way.

A person is guilty of **unlawful act culpable homicide** where he commits an unlawful act, which involves a foreseeable risk of physical injury (such as an assault), and this causes a death.

A person is guilty of **involuntary culpable homicide** if he causes a death by acting with a complete disregard for any potential dangers which might result from his actions.

NON-FATAL OFFENCES AGAINST THE PERSON

Assault

Actus reus

6–23   The actus reus of an assault is simply an "attack upon the person of another".[85] This will normally involve force being applied to the victim, often (but not necessarily) resulting in injury. Examples of "attacks" found in the case law include spitting at a person (*James Cairns*),[86] whipping a pony which was being ridden by a boy so that it threw him off its back and injured him (*David Keay*),[87] and setting a dog on a person (*Kay v Allan*).[88] The attack need not, however, involve any actual force being applied to the victim, as the following case illustrates:

---

[84] G.H. Gordon, *Criminal Law*, 3rd edn (W. Green, 2001), by M.G.A. Christie, Vol.II, p.366.
[85] Macdonald, *Criminal Law*, 5th edn (W. Green, 1948), p.115.
[86] (1858) 1 Swin. 597.
[87] (1837) 1 Swin. 543.
[88] (1978) S.C.C.R. Supp. 188. See also *Quinn v Lees*, 1994 S.C.C.R. 159.

Atkinson v HM Advocate
1987 S.C.C.R. 534

Atkinson was convicted of assaulting a shop assistant by coming into the store wearing a mask and jumping over the counter at the assistant. On appeal, it was held that this was sufficient for assault even although it had not been proven that Atkinson had physically touched the shop assistant: "an assault may be constituted by threatening gestures sufficient to produce alarm".

Essentially, then, there are two forms of "attack"—actions which apply force to the victim, and actions which put the victim in fear of an immediate application of force. (Threatening the use of force at some point in the future may, in certain circumstances, be a criminal offence, but it would not be assault.)

An assault may be regarded as "aggravated" (and usually, therefore, will be more severely punished by the courts) by a number of circumstances, such as the use of a weapon (and the type used), the severity of the injury caused, any danger to life (which resulted), or the character of the victim—particularly where the victim is a police officer. There is a specific statutory offence of assaulting, resisting, obstructing, molesting or hindering a constable in the execution of his duty.[89]

Mens rea

The mens rea of assault is "evil intent".[90] To be guilty of assault, therefore, a person must **6–24** intend either to apply force to the victim or to put them in fear of an attack. The use of the word "evil" might be taken to suggest that a particular type of motive must be proven. This is, however, not the case, as the following decision illustrates:

Lord Advocate's Reference (No.2 of 1992)
1993 J.C. 43

A man ["X"] entered a shop, presented an imitation firearm at the shop owner and said "Get the money out of the till and lay on the floor." He fled after noticing that another member of staff was present. He was charged with assault and, as a defence, argued that his actions were a joke, that he had never intended to rob the shop, and, therefore, had no "evil intention". The trial judge directed the jury that if X had in fact been joking, he would have had no evil intention and should therefore be acquitted of assault. The jury acquitted him.

The Lord Advocate referred the point of law involved to the High Court for an opinion. It was held that X's claim that his actions were a joke was irrelevant. Macdonald's statement that "evil intention" was the essence of assault meant only "that assault cannot be committed accidentally or recklessly or negligently". The trial judge had therefore misdirected the jury.

It should be made clear that, although it is no "defence" to say "it was a joke", a person who carries out a joke which unintentionally results in injury will not be guilty of assault,

---

[89] Police (Scotland) Act 1967 s.41.
[90] Macdonald, *Criminal Law*, 5th edn (W. Green, 1948), p.115; *Smart v HM Advocate*, 1975 J.C. 30.

because they do not have the intention to attack which is necessary for the crime. The holding in the *Lord Advocate's Reference* means only that a person who intends to attack another person *as a joke* is guilty of an offence despite their supposedly "humourous" motivation.[91]

Although assault cannot be committed recklessly, the intention may be "transferred". So, if A throws a glass intending to hit B, but misses and hits C instead, he can be found guilty of assaulting C. This is because he intended to assault B, even though he had no intention of assaulting C, the actual victim.[92]

Specific defences

6–25 Although the general defences discussed at the end of this chapter apply equally to assault as to other crimes, there are a number of defences specific to assault, which should be considered at this point.

Reasonable chastisement of children

6–26 A person who uses force to discipline a child may be entitled to plead the defence of "reasonable chastisement". This defence is available only to parents or to persons in loco parentis (i.e. having care of a child in place of a parent). In deciding whether the chastisement used was reasonable, the court will take into account the nature of the punishment, the age, health and sex of the child, and the effect of the punishment on the child.[93] Actions involving a blow to the head, shaking or the use of an implement can never be considered "reasonable".[94]

Consent

6–27 It is generally said that consent is not a defence to assault. The leading authority is *Smart v HM Advocate*:

> ### Smart v HM Advocate
> #### 1975 J.C. 30
>
> Smart was charged with assaulting another man, Wilkie. He admitted that he had assaulted Wilkie, but claimed that Wilkie had consented to a fight. He was convicted of assault, and appealed against his conviction. In upholding the conviction, it was held that any such consent was irrelevant and that Smart was guilty of assault, whether or not Wilkie had consented to the fight.

It appears, however, that consent is a valid justification insofar as socially accepted procedures such as surgery, tattooing and ear-piercing are concerned.[95] Consent may also be a defence to assaults which do not involve injury.[96] It has also been said that "for conduct in a sporting game to be criminal, it would require to be shown to be outwith the normal

---

[91] See also *Quinn v Lees*, 1994 S.C.C.R. 159; *Gilmour v McGlennan*, 1993 S.C.C.R. 837.
[92] *Connor v Jessop*, 1988 S.C.C.R. 624; *Roberts v Hamilton*, 1989 S.L.T. 399.
[93] Criminal Justice (Scotland) Act 2003 s.51.
[94] Criminal Justice (Scotland) Act 2003 s.51(3).
[95] See G.H. Gordon, *Criminal Law*, 3rd edn (W. Green, 2001), by M.G.A. Christie, Vol.II, p.415; *R. v Brown* [1994] 1 A.C. 212, per Lord Templeman at 231.
[96] G.H. Gordon, "Consent in assault" (1976) 21 J.L.S.S. 168.

scope of the sport",[97] which goes some way towards explaining why boxers, etc. are not guilty of assault. The position is more difficult where persons consent to activities which are not "socially accepted" in this way. In the English case of *R. v Brown*,[98] it was held that a group of sado-masochists who used "nails and sandpaper ... in ways that would make a self-respecting carpenter blush"[99] were guilty of assault notwithstanding that all the parties concerned had consented.[100]

Reasonable restraint

Police officers are entitled to use reasonable force in order to arrest or detain persons. If **6–28** such force is excessive, however, they will be guilty of an assault. So, in *Marchbank v Annan*,[101] two police officers engaged in a high-speed chase after a boy who had stolen a car. When the car was forced to a halt, one of the officers used his baton to smash the window, hit the boy on the head, then dragged him out and kicked him on the body two or three times. On his appeal against a conviction for assault, the High Court held that he had gone "far beyond the limit of the force which a police officer is entitled to apply when attempting to apprehend a suspect" and upheld his conviction.

Key Concepts

An **assault** is committed by a person who (a) attacks another person and (b) does so with evil intent. An attack can involve either injuring a person or putting them in fear of immediate injury. The term "evil intent" merely emphasises that assault cannot be committed recklessly; it does not mean that a person must have an "evil motive" in order to be found guilty of assault.

There are three specific **defences** to assault, as follows:

Consent to a fight is not a defence to a charge of assault. However, consent does operate as a defence where socially acceptable practices such as surgery, tattooing or ear piercing and sports are concerned.

The defence of **reasonable chastisement of children** is available to parents (or persons acting in the place of parents) who use reasonable force to discipline children.

A police officer who uses reasonable force to arrest or detain a suspect is entitled to the defence of **reasonable restraint**.

Reckless injury

It is a crime to recklessly cause injury to another person. The mens rea required is an **6–29** "utter disregard" for the consequences of one's actions.[102] It used to be thought that it was necessary to show that the public at large had been endangered by the accused's actions,[103] but this is no longer required.[104] There is, in principle, no limit to the number of ways in which this crime can be committed. Examples include giving a quarter pint of whisky to a

---

[97] *Lord Advocate's Reference (No.2 of 1992)*, 1993 J.C. 43, per the Lord Justice-Clerk (Ross) at 48.
[98] [1994] 1 A.C. 212. cf. *Wilson* [1996] 2 Cr. App. R. 241.
[99] C. Munro, *Studies in Constitutional Law*, 2nd edn (Butterworths, 1999), p.345.
[100] See also *McDonald v HM Advocate*, 2004 S.C.C.R. 161.
[101] 1987 S.C.C.R. 718.
[102] *Cameron v Maguire*, 1999 J.C. 63.
[103] *Quinn v Cunningham*, 1956 J.C. 22.
[104] *HM Advocate v Harris*, 1993 J.C. 150.

seven-year-old child, which rendered the child permanently liable to convulsions (*Robert Brown and John Lawson*),[105] and throwing a bottle out of the fifteenth-floor of a block of flats which struck and seriously injured a passer-by (*RHW v HM Advocate*).[106] In *HM Advocate v Kelly*,[107] Kelly, having tested positive for HIV, had unprotected sexual intercourse with his girlfriend after falsely claiming to her that he was not HIV-positive. She subsequently contracted HIV, and he was convicted of recklessly injuring her.

Reckless endangerment

6–30 It is a crime to recklessly endanger the safety of the public. The mens rea required is, again, an "utter disregard" for the consequences of one's actions.[108] Again, there is in principle no limit to the number of ways in which this crime can be committed. Examples from the law reports include discharging firearms so that bullets might have ricocheted in the direction of a public road (*Cameron v Maguire*),[109] burning straw in a field so as to send smoke over a road, obscuring the vision of passing drivers (*Macphail v Clark*),[110] and allowing a live puma to roam around an Edinburgh public house (*Reynolds v Lockhart*).[111] Persons who have falsely claimed to police officers, prior to being searched, that they have no sharp objects or needles in their possession have also been found guilty of this offence.[112]

It is not clear whether it is a criminal offence to endanger individuals (as opposed to the public at large), but the authorities (particularly the cases on exposing police officers to a risk of injury from needles) suggest that endangering a small number of people, or even a single person, is a criminal offence.

Reckless supply of harmful substances

6–31 In *Khaliq v HM Advocate*,[113] the accused were charged with having "culpably, wilfully and recklessly" supplied what might be referred to as "glue-sniffing kits" to children between the age of 8 and 15 years. The court held that this was a valid charge, although the nature of the crime involved is not exactly clear. It was treated by the court as a form of "causing real injury", but it had not been alleged by the Crown that the children were in fact injured by their use of the "kits", only that their health had been endangered. This seems almost to be a form of reckless endangerment, in that the supplier is held responsible for the danger to the purchaser's health, which is caused by their subsequent use of the substance. In *Ulhaq v HM Advocate*,[114] it was held to be sufficient that the accused had supplied substances such as lighter fluid and glue in their normal containers to adults whom he knew intended to use them for the purposes of solvent abuse. The significance of these cases is that they hold that the "victim's" voluntary act does not break the chain of causation, where the seller knows of their intentions at the time of supplying the substance (or perhaps even where he is reckless as to their intentions). He can, therefore, be held responsible for the consequences of their substance abuse in such cases. If the person to whom a dangerous substance (which may be a controlled drug) is supplied dies as a result

---

[105] (1842) 1 Broun 415. See also *Borwick v Urquhart*, 2003 S.C.C.R. 243.
[106] 1982 S.L.T. 420.
[107] Unreported February 13–23, 2001 High Court at Glasgow.
[108] *Cameron v Maguire*, 1999 J.C. 63.
[109] 1999 J.C. 63.
[110] 1983 S.L.T. (Sh. Ct) 37.
[111] (1977) 41 J. Crim. L. 57.
[112] *Donaldson v Normand*, 1997 J.C. 200. But a person who refuses to say whether they have any sharp objects or needles is not guilty of the offence: *Mallin v Clark*, 2002 S.L.T. 1202.
[113] 1984 J.C. 23.
[114] 1991 S.L.T. 614.

of taking it, the supplier may be guilty of culpable homicide.[115] This does not follow automatically from the fact of death. It will be necessary to prove that they had the mens rea required for that crime (a complete disregard for the consequences of their actions).[116]

In *Lord Advocate's Reference (No.1 of 1994)*,[117] the accused supplied amphetamine to a number of persons, one of whom died as a result of taking the drug. It was held that, by an extension of the principle invoked in *Khaliq* and *Ulhaq*, this could amount to the crime of culpable homicide. It seems that this would be "unlawful act" culpable homicide,[118] based on the initial crime of supplying the controlled substance.

Key Concepts

The crime of **reckless injury** is committed where a person causes injury to another person while acting with an "utter disregard" for the consequences of his actions.

The crime of **reckless endangerment** is committed where a person endangers the safety of the public while acting with an "utter disregard" for the consequences of his actions. This crime may—although the law is unclear—also apply to putting specific individuals in danger as opposed to the public at large.

The crime of **reckless supply of harmful substances** is committed where a person supplies harmful substances to a person knowing that the recipient will abuse the substance to the danger of their health. This crime may be viewed as a special form of reckless endangerment.

SEXUAL OFFENCES[119]

Following a review by the Scottish Law Commission,[120] the Scottish law of sexual offences **6–32** was revised and put into statutory form by the Sexual Offences (Scotland) Act 2009. The 2009 Act is not, however, an entirely comprehensive code of all offences which might be considered "sexual", and some of the other offences discussed in this section are criminal either at common law or by virtue of other legislation. Rape is generally considered to be the most serious of the sexual offences, although it should be observed that it is narrowly defined (being limited to penile-vaginal penetration of a woman by a man), and that other sexual offences can be equally harmful and degrading to the victim.

Rape

At common law, the crime of rape under Scots law was extremely narrow. The actus reus **6–33** consisted of penetration of the vagina by the accused's penis without the woman's consent (other forms of non-consensual intercourse could be indecent assault, but not rape), and the mens rea required was that the accused (a) knew that the woman was not consenting or (b) was reckless as to whether she was consenting.[121] A man who honestly believed that a

---

[115] *MacAngus v HM Advocate*; *Kane v HM Advocate*, 2009 S.L.T. 137.
[116] See above, para.6–22.
[117] 1996 J.C. 76.
[118] See above, para.6–21.
[119] See generally J. Chalmers, *The New Law of Sexual Offences in Scotland* (W. Green, 2010).
[120] See Scottish Law Commission, *Report on the Law of Rape and Other Sexual Offences* (2009), Scot. Law Com. No.207.
[121] *Lord Advocate's Reference (No 1 of 2001)*, 2002 S.L.T. 466.

woman was consenting to sexual intercourse could not be guilty of rape, no matter how unreasonable his belief.[122]

The 2009 Act changes this definition significantly. The actus reus of rape now consists of penetration of the victim's vagina, anus or mouth by the penis of the accused, without the consent of the victim.[123] This means that both men and women can be the victims of rape under Scots law. The mens rea is, unusually, defined in a negative sense: the accused (A) will have the mens rea of the crime if A penetrates the victim (B) "without any reasonable belief that B consents".[124]

Although the offence of rape is restricted to penile penetration, there is a separate offence of "sexual assault by penetration" which covers non-consensual sexual penetration of the victim's vagina or anus "with any part of A's body or anything else".[125] The mens rea of this crime is the same as for rape.

Consent is defined by the 2009 Act as meaning "free agreement",[126] and the Act, in addition, provides a list of circumstances in which consent will be deemed to be absent, including where A has deceived B as to the nature or purpose of the conduct, or where A has induced B to agree by impersonating a person known personally to B.[127]

Other sexual offences under the 2009 Act

6–34   The 2009 Act creates a range of other sexual offences, which are not discussed in detail here. These include sexual assault, sexual coercion, coercing a person into being present during a sexual activity, coercing a person into looking at a sexual image, communicating indecently, sexual exposure and voyeurism.[128] These offences (along with rape and sexual assault by penetration) each have a series of corresponding offences in respect of "young children" and "older children". An older child is one over the age of 13 but under the age of 16, while a young child is one under the age of 13. For the purpose of each of these offences, the absence of consent is not an element of the crime, because children cannot give any valid consent to sexual intercourse. However, the law still recognises that an older child can give a factual consent, meaning that (for example) if an 18 year old has consensual sexual intercourse with a 15 year old, this is the offence of "having intercourse with an older child" under s.28 of the Act and not rape.

The "older children" offences can only be committed by someone who is themselves over the age of 16. Where two "older children" engage in sexual activity with each other, it may be that both commit a criminal offence under s.37 of the Act, but the offences under this section are limited to a narrow range of sexual conduct and not all sexual activity between children is criminal. Where one person is under the age of 16 and the other over, but they are less than two years apart in age, and they engage in consensual sexual conduct, a defence to a charge of a sexual offence may be available, again depending on the type of sexual conduct engaged in.[129]

---

[122] *Jamieson v HM Advocate*, 1994 J.C. 88.
[123] Sexual Offences (Scotland) Act 2009 s.1(1).
[124] Sexual Offences (Scotland) Act 2009 s.1(1)(b).
[125] Sexual Offences (Scotland) Act 2009 s.2.
[126] Sexual Offences (Scotland) Act 2009 s.12.
[127] Sexual Offences (Scotland) Act 2009 s.13.
[128] Sexual Offences (Scotland) Act 2009 ss.3–9.
[129] See s.39 of the Sexual Offences (Scotland) Act 2009.

Indecent assault

Indecent assault "is not a specific crime, it is simply an assault accompanied by circum- **6–35** stances of indecency".[130] Because it is part of the general law of assault rather than a specific sexual offence, indecent assault has been left unchanged by the 2009 Act. It is sometimes suggested that there is a distinction between indecent assault and assault, in that consent is specifically recognised as a defence to the former but not the latter.[131] However, an alternative approach is to say that this is simply a practical distinction rather than a technical one: consent may (although the law is not settled) be a defence to all assaults, which do not involve injury, indecent or otherwise. Conversely, it is unlikely that the Scottish courts would recognise consent as a defence to an indecent assault which did in fact involve the infliction of injury.[132]

Key Concepts

Rape is committed by a person (A) who has sexual intercourse with another person (B) who does not consent, provided that A does not reasonably believe that B is consenting. Sexual intercourse, for these purposes, means penetration of B's vagina, anus or mouth with A's penis.

Incest and related offences

The Scots law governing incest and related offences is found in ss.1–3 of the Criminal Law **6–36** (Consolidation) (Scotland) Act 1995.[133] These provisions create three separate offences, as follows:

- Incest (s.1) is committed by a person who has sexual intercourse with a close relative of the opposite sex. This covers sexual intercourse with ascendants, descendents, aunts, uncles, nieces and nephews. It does not, however, cover cousins or adoptive siblings.
- Intercourse with a step-child (s.2). This section provides that a "step-parent or former step-parent who has sexual intercourse with his or her step-child or former step-child shall be guilty of an offence if that step-child is either under the age of 21 or has at any time before attaining the age of 18 lived in the same household and been treated as a child of his or her family".

Intercourse with a child under 16 by a person in a position of trust (s.3). This section provides that any person of 16 or over who has sexual intercourse with a child under 16, while being a member of the same household as that child, and who is "in a position of trust and authority in relation to that child" is guilty of an offence.

There are four specific defences, which must be proved by the accused on the balance of probabilities if they are to succeed. These are as follows:

---

[130] G.H. Gordon, *Criminal Law*, 3rd edn (W. Green, 2001), by M.G.A. Christie, Vol.II, p.406.
[131] *Smart v HM Advocate*, 1975 J.C. 30.
[132] See *McDonald v HM* Advocate, 2004 S.C.C.R. 161.
[133] These provisions derive from the Incest and Related Offences (Scotland) Act 1986, which repealed the Incest Act 1567. See Scottish Law Commission, *Report on the Law of Incest in Scotland* (1981), Scot. Law Com. No.69.

- that he or she did not know and had no reason to suspect that they were related in this way (a defence to the ss.1 and 2 offences);
- that he or she believed, on reasonable grounds, that the person with whom they had intercourse was over the relevant age (a defence to the ss.2 or 3 offences);
- that he or she did not consent to have sexual intercourse or to have sexual intercourse with that person (a defence to all of the offences); and
- that he or she was validly married to that person (a defence to all of the offences).

It should be noted that all of these offences are limited to (heterosexual) "sexual intercourse". Although this term is not defined in the statute, it appears to be limited to penile-vaginal penetration.

Homosexual offences

6–37 Sexual acts between males were criminal at common law, either as sodomy (a crime which is restricted to anal intercourse), or as shameless indecency. It appears that sexual acts between women are not criminal at common law in Scotland, and the following discussion, therefore, relates only to male homosexual acts.

Although homosexuality was decriminalised in England and Wales in 1967,[134] following the recommendations of the Wolfenden Committee,[135] decriminalisation did not take place in Scotland until 1980.[136]

Initially, homosexual acts were decriminalised provided that they took place in private between two males over the age of 21 (commonly referred to as the "age of consent"). That age was reduced to 18 in 1994,[137] but was nevertheless two years higher than the age of consent for heterosexual intercourse. In 1997, the European Commission on Human Rights ruled that the differing ages of consent for heterosexual and homosexual intercourse in the United Kingdom violated arts 8 (the right to privacy) and 14 (non-discrimination in the enjoyment of rights) of the European Convention on Human Rights.[138] The UK Government subsequently legislated to reduce the age of consent for homosexual intercourse to 16.[139]

Shameless indecency and public indecency

6–38 Until relatively recently, Scots law recognized a crime called "shameless indecency", a controversial offence based on a statement in Macdonald's *Criminal Law* to the effect that "all shamelessly indecent conduct is criminal".[140]

The crime was of importance in three contexts.[141] First, it covered what has been described as "corruption of public morals".[142] This included the supply of indecent materials, the staging of indecent displays[143] and showing indecent material to children[144]

---

[134] Sexual Offences Act 1967 s.1.
[135] *Report of the Committee on Homosexual Offences and Prostitution* (1957), Cmnd.247.
[136] Criminal Justice (Scotland) Act 1980 s.80.
[137] Criminal Justice and Public Order Act 1994 s.145.
[138] *Sutherland v United Kingdom* [1998] E.H.R.L.R. 117.
[139] Sexual Offences (Amendment) Act 2000 s.1(3).
[140] Macdonald, *Criminal Law*, 5th edn (W. Green, 1948), p.150 (and the 1st edn (1866), at p.202). For an extended criticism of this statement, see G.H. Gordon, *Criminal Law*, 3rd edn (W. Green, 2001), by M.G.A. Christie, Vol.II, p.536.
[141] See C.H.W. Gane, *Sexual Offences* (Butterworths, 1992), p.143.
[142] C.H.W. Gane, *Sexual Offences* (Butterworths, 1992), p.146.
[143] *Lockhart v Stephen*, 1987 S.C.C.R. 642 (Sh. Ct); *Geddes v Dickson*, 2000 S.C.C.R. 1007.
[144] *Carmichael v Ashrif*, 1985 S.C.C.R. 461.

(although simply failing to prevent them viewing such material did not suffice).[145] The mens rea required was an intention to corrupt or deprave the person(s) to whom the conduct is directed, or a knowledge that the conduct is liable to corrupt or deprave.[146]

The second form of shameless indecency was indecent exposure ("the exposure of those parts of the person that are usually concealed").[147] This form of the offence could be committed recklessly.[148]

Thirdly, it covered certain forms of sexual relations regarded as "repugnant to society" such as sexual acts short of intercourse by a man with his 16-year-old daughter,[149] sexual intercourse by a man with a foster daughter who was living as a child of the family,[150] or sexual intercourse between a schoolteacher and a pupil.[151]

However, the crime was "abolished" by the appeal court in the following case:

Webster v Dominick
2005 J.C. 65

The appeal court held that there was no such crime as "shameless indecency", which was an improper judicial creation. Instead, there was an offence of "public indecency". This is a public order offence for which it is sufficient that "on an objective assessment, the conduct complained of should cause public offence".

Although some commentators have welcomed *Webster v Dominick* as abolishing the much-criticised offence of shameless indecency,[152] its replacement with "public indecency" is itself open to criticism.[153] First, it is not clear exactly what the actus reus of the new offence is, and the court left open the possibility that it might apply to non-sexual conduct. Secondly, if it is sufficient that the "conduct complained of should cause public offence", this is a low threshold which seems to criminalise a broader range of conduct than the "deprave and corrupt" test which applied to certain forms of shameless indecency. Thirdly, the court did not make it clear what the mens rea requirement of the new crime is. These issues may have to be resolved by the courts in the future.

Key Concept

The offence of **shamelessly indecent conduct** covered three types of behaviour: first, "corruption of public morals"; secondly, indecent exposure and thirdly, certain forms of sexual relations which are regarded as repugnant to society.

That offence, however, no longer exists: it has been replaced by the courts with an offence of **public indecency** which covers conduct objectively liable to cause public offence.

---

[145] *Paterson v Lees*, 1999 J.C. 159.
[146] *Geddes v Dickson*, 2001 J.C. 69.
[147] G.H. Gordon, *Criminal Law*, 3rd edn (W. Green, 2001), by M.G.A. Christie, p.531.
[148] *Usai v Russell*, 2000 S.C.C.R. 57.
[149] *R v HM Advocate*, 1988 S.L.T. 623.
[150] *HM Advocate v K*, 1999 S.C.C.R. 259.
[151] *Batty v HM Advocate*, 1995 J.C. 160.
[152] See, e.g. Juliette Casey, "Offences of Indecency Revisited", 2003 S.L.T. (News) 225.
[153] See James Chalmers and Christopher Gane, "The Aftermath of Shameless Indecency" (2003) 8 S.L.P.Q. 310.

Offences relating to prostitution and brothel-keeping

6–39 Part I of the Criminal Law (Consolidation) (Scotland) Act 1995 contains a number of criminal offences relating to prostitution and brothel-keeping, which were not altered by the Sexual Offences (Scotland) Act 2009. In this context, it should be noted that the actual *act* of prostitution (selling sexual intercourse for money) is not itself criminal. Instead, the statutory offences cover acts such as procuring women to act as prostitutes, running brothels and living off the earnings of prostitution.[154]

PROPERTY OFFENCES

Theft

Actus reus

6–40 The actus reus of theft may be defined as the "appropriation of property without the consent of the owner or custodier".[155] There are therefore three elements to the actus reus:

(1) appropriation;
(2) of property which is capable of being stolen; and
(3) without the consent of the owner or custodier.

The concept of appropriation covers more than simply the physical removal of property (which Hume appeared to consider an essential part of the crime).[156] While such physical removal would certainly suffice, appropriation can take place by other means. It has been said, that "appropriation involves conduct which without authorisation deprives the owner of one or more of those rights, for example possessory rights, which his ownership of the property in question would in the circumstances entail."[157] See the following case:

Carmichael v Black; Black v Carmichael
1992 S.L.T. 897

Black was charged with having committed theft by using "wheel clamps" to immobilise vehicles which had parked on his property in contravention of a warning notice intimating that he would take such action against anyone who parked there without authorisation (and would charge a fee of £45 for the removal of the clamps).

The High Court held that this was a valid charge of theft. The Lord Justice-General (Hope) said: "It seems to me that the act of depriving the motorist of the use of his motor car by detaining it against his will can accurately be described as stealing something from him ... the physical element of appropriation is clearly present, in my opinion, since the purpose and effect of the wheel clamp was to immobilise the vehicle and use of it as a motor car."

---

[154] This offence is restricted to male persons, but a female can be guilty art and part: *Reid v HM Advocate*, 1999 S.C.C.R. 19. It is thought, however, that a prostitute cannot herself (or himself) be guilty of this offence: see Sheriff Gordon's commentary to the S.C.C.R. report.

[155] Macdonald, *Criminal Law*, 5th edn (W. Green, 1958), p.16, as interpreted in *Carmichael v Black; Black v Carmichael*, 1992 S.L.T. 897.

[156] Hume, *Commentaries*, i, p.57.

[157] G.H. Gordon, *Criminal Law*, 3rd edn (W. Green, 2001), by M.G.A. Christie, Vol.II, p.12. It follows that a non-owner, who is lawfully in possession of property, can subsequently steal it: see, e.g. *Elizabeth Anderson* (1858) 3 Irv. 65.

Only "corporeal" (i.e. physical), moveable property can be stolen.[158] "Incorporeal" property (such as a legal right, or intellectual property), or "immoveable" property (land and buildings) cannot be stolen under Scots law.[159] However, if incorporeal property such as information is contained within a physical item (such as a document), that physical item is itself capable of being stolen, and if items which form part of land (such as potatoes in a field)[160] are removed from the land, then such property becomes treated as moveable property and can be stolen. As a matter of practice, Scots law regards electricity as property which is capable of being stolen.[161]

It is not theft if the property is appropriated with the consent of the owner. This probably applies even where the owner's consent has been obtained by fraud (and a charge of fraud, rather than theft, would therefore be appropriate in such a case).[162]

Conversely, if an item of property has *no* owner (as in the unusual case of wild animals), it cannot be the subject of theft.[163] The fact that property has been abandoned or lost does not make it ownerless—Macdonald gives the example of taking property from a lost luggage store, which is clearly theft.[164] A person who appropriates abandoned property may, however, lack the mens rea required for theft, which is discussed below.

Mens rea

The mens rea of theft is based around an intention to deprive the owner of his property, **6–41** but its exact scope is not at present entirely clear. It has always been clear that an intention to deprive the owner *permanently* is sufficient, but it appears that less than this may suffice in certain cases.

First, an intention to deprive *indefinitely* will also suffice—and so, in *Fowler v O'Brien*,[165] where the accused took the complainer's bicycle without his consent and abandoned it in a place where it was only found several days later, it was held that his intention to deprive the complainer "indefinitely" of his property was sufficient mens rea.

Secondly, an intention to deprive *temporarily for a nefarious purpose* is also sufficient. For example, it is theft to appropriate property for the purpose of extorting money from the owner. In *Kidston v Annan*,[166] the complainer had given a television set to the accused in order to get an estimate for repair work. The accused then repaired the television set without authorisation and refused to return it until his bill was paid. The court held that the accused was effectively holding the television set to ransom, and was, therefore, guilty of theft. It is not clear whether "nefarious purpose" is restricted to "criminal purposes" or can include other motives.[167]

Thirdly, it has recently been suggested that an intention to deprive *temporarily* will suffice for the mens rea of theft, even in the absence of a nefarious purpose.[168] If that is true, then it would be possible to describe the mens rea of theft as simply being an

---

[158] Under Scots law, property may be classified into corporeal and incorporeal property, and moveable and immovable property.

[159] As regards immoveable property, see G.H. Gordon, *Criminal Law*, 3rd edn (W. Green, 2001), by M.G.A. Christie, Vol.II, p.20. For incorporeal property, see *Grant v Allan*, 1987 J.C. 71.

[160] *Andrew Young* (1800) Hume, i, p.79.

[161] G.H. Gordon, *Criminal Law*, 3rd edn (W. Green, 2001) by M.G.A. Christie, Vol.II, pp.18–19.

[162] For a review of the complex case law on this point, see G.H. Gordon, *Criminal Law*, 3rd edn (W. Green, 2001), by M.G.A. Christie, Vol.II, pp.38–43.

[163] *Valentine v Kennedy*, 1985 S.C.C.R. 89 (Sh. Ct).

[164] Macdonald, *Criminal Law*, 5th edn (W. Green, 1948), p.17.

[165] 1994 S.C.C.R. 112.

[166] 1984 S.L.T. 279.

[167] See *Milne v Tudhope*, 1981 J.C. 53, per the Lord Justice-Clerk (Wheatley) at 57.

[168] See *Carmichael v Black; Black v Carmichael*, 1992 S.L.T. 897, per the Lord Justice-General (Hope) at 901–902.

"intention to deprive", regardless of the purpose of the deprivation or whether it was intended as temporary or permanent. However, the cases in which this suggestion has been made have all been cases which did in fact involve a nefarious purpose, and it has been suggested that "it is open to doubt whether a bare intention to deprive temporarily will suffice."[169]

It is sometimes suggested that the accused's intention to deprive must be *dishonest*. This is supported by the decision of the High Court in *Kane v Friel*,[170] where Kane was convicted of having stolen a quantity of metal piping and a sink unit, which he claimed to have found lying behind a local shop. On appeal, it was held that the prosecution had to show that his appropriation of the property had been "dishonest", and because the prosecution had not proved that Kane "must have known that the items were property which someone intended to retain", he should not have been convicted of theft. The court's assumption that dishonesty is part of the mens rea of theft is somewhat controversial, because it finds only very limited support in the earlier Scottish decisions.[171]

Key Concepts

The actus reus of **theft** is the appropriation of another person's property without their consent.

Appropriation is not limited to physically removing property from another's possession. It covers any act, which deprives the owner of any of the rights associated with the ownership of property.

The mens rea of theft is an intention to deprive the owner of the property (a) permanently; (b) indefinitely or (c) temporarily for a nefarious purpose. It may be that a simple intention to deprive temporarily is sufficient, but the law is unsettled. From recent authority, it appears also that the intention must be **dishonest**.

Housebreaking

6–42 Scots law recognises a crime of "housebreaking with intent to steal". Housebreaking will frequently involve physically damaging the property in order to gain entry (in which case the accused is probably also guilty of the offences of malicious mischief or vandalism),[172] but any case where "the security of the building has been overcome" is considered housebreaking.[173] So, for example, it would be housebreaking to enter a building by using a stolen key, or picking a lock, or even—as in the case of *Rendal Courtney*[174]—coming into a house down the chimney!

It should be noted that housebreaking is not in itself a criminal offence unless it is done with an intention to steal. For that reason, a charge of "housebreaking with intent to rape" was held irrelevant in *HM Advocate v Forbes*,[175] but the court in that case said that such actions could be charged as a breach of the peace, or possibly attempted rape.

It was observed in *Forbes* that the significance of the crime of housebreaking with intent to steal lies in the fact that attempted theft was not itself an indictable offence until 1887,

---

[169] G.H. Gordon, *Criminal Law*, 3rd edn (W. Green, 2001), by M.G.A. Christie, Vol.II, p.50.
[170] 1997 S.L.T. 1274.
[171] But see *Mackenzie v Maclean*, 1981 S.L.T. (Sh. Ct) 40.
[172] See below, paras 6–49 and 6–50.
[173] Alison, *Principles of the Criminal Law of Scotland* (W. Blackwood, 1832), p.282.
[174] (1743) Hume i, p.99.
[175] 1994 S.L.T. 861.

and the crime, therefore, partially filled a gap left by the non-availability of a charge of attempted theft.

Nowadays, most cases of housebreaking with intent to steal would also be cases of attempted theft, and the question of which charge to use is entirely at the discretion of the prosecutor.

Embezzlement

The crime of embezzlement is closely related to theft. Indeed, because it is possible to **6–43** commit theft of property which is already lawfully in one's possession, it has been said that the distinction between the two crimes is "rather technical than substantial".[176] The distinction between the two offences is not a sharp one and an act may amount to both offences.

If a person is lawfully in possession of the property of another, but is under an obligation to account for that property to the true owner, and he appropriates that property, this will amount to the actus reus of embezzlement.[177] Incorporeal property can be the subject of this crime (unlike the crime of theft), and so it was held in *Guild v Lees* that a club treasurer who had used the club cheque book to pay his electricity bill was guilty of embezzlement.[178] The court observed that this could not have been charged as theft, because the property, which had been appropriated by the accused, was incorporeal (it was technically part of a debt owed by the bank to the club)—but the charge of embezzlement was a valid one.

The mens rea of the offence is a dishonest intention to appropriate the property of another.[179]

Robbery

Robbery may be defined as "theft accomplished by means of personal violence or inti- **6–44** midation".[180] While in the normal case this will involve property being removed from the victim's person by force, this is not an essential element of the crime—and so, for example, it would be robbery to force someone to unlock a safe by threats of violence (assuming property was removed from the safe thereafter).[181]

The violence (or threats of violence) must have been used in order to obtain the property—and so, for example, it is not robbery if violence is used after the property has been appropriated; nor is it robbery if the violence has been used for some other purpose and the appropriation of property thereafter is merely opportunistic.[182] Such cases would be considered as separate offences of assault and theft.

---

[176] *HM Advocate v Laing* (1891) 2 White 572, per Lord Kincairney at 576.

[177] See Macdonald, *Criminal Law*, 5th edn (W. Green, 1948), p.45.

[178] 1994 S.L.T. 68.

[179] *Allenby v HM Advocate*, 1938 J.C. 55.

[180] *Cromar v HM Advocate*, 1987 S.C.C.R. 635, per Sheriff Pirie at 635. This statement appears to be a quote from Gordon's *Criminal Law*: see now G.H. Gordon, *Criminal Law*, 3rd edn (W. Green, 2001), by M.G.A. Christie, Vol.II, p.91.

[181] See Alison, *Principles of the Criminal Law of Scotland* (W. Blackwood, 1832), p.281.

[182] cf. *James Templeton* (1871) 2 Coup. 140.

Extortion

6–45 Extortion may be defined as an attempt "to enforce either legal or illegal demands by illegal means".[183] There are, therefore, two elements to the crime: (a) a demand; and (b) the illegal means which are used to back it up. The demand need not be for the payment of money—in *Rae v Donnelly*,[184] it was a demand that the complainer withdraw her claim for unfair dismissal which she was pursuing before an industrial tribunal.

The more difficult question is this: what constitutes "illegal means" for the purposes of this crime? The issue was explored in the following case:

> ### Carmichael v Black; Black v Carmichael
> #### 1992 S.L.T. 897
>
> Lord Justice-General (Hope): "In my opinion it is extortion to seek to enforce a legitimate debt by means which the law regards as illegitimate, just as it is extortion to seek by such means to obtain money or some other advantage to which the accused has no right at all. Furthermore, the only means which the law regards as legitimate to force a debtor to make payment of his debt are those provided by due legal process. To use due legal process, such as an action in a court of law or a right of lien or retention under contract, or to threaten to do so, is no doubt legitimate. It is not extortion if the debtor pays up as a result. But it is illegitimate to use other means, such as threats which are not related to the use of legal process, or the unauthorised detention of the debtor's person or his property, and it is extortion if the purpose in doing so is to obtain payment of the debt."

Fraud

6–46 The actus reus of fraud consists of three elements: (1) a false pretence; (2) a definite practical result; and (3) a causal link between the pretence and the result.[185]

There is no limit to the type of action which may be a false pretence: obvious examples would include false claims as to one's identity, qualifications or status, or false claims as to the nature or quality of goods. False pretences may take more unusual forms, and so, for example, it was held in *Richards v HM Advocate*[186] that a statement of "present intention as to future conduct" could amount to a false pretence if in fact the actor had no such intention, while in *James Paton*[187] the false pretence consisted of puncturing and inflating with air the skins of bulls who were to be entered in a prize exhibition, and attaching artificial horns to their heads in order to give them a "better and more symmetrical appearance" so that their chances of winning prizes in the exhibition would be increased.

The fraud is not complete unless another party is deceived by it and, therefore, acts in a way which he would not otherwise have done (or refrains from doing something which he would otherwise have done). This represents the second and third elements of the actus reus which were identified earlier—the causal link and the definite practical result. It is not

---

[183] *Alex. F. Crawford* (1850) J. Shaw 309, per Lord Moncrieff at 329, cited with approval in *Carmichael v Black; Black v Carmichael*, 1992 S.L.T. 897, per the Lord Justice-General (Hope) at 900.
[184] 1982 S.C.C.R. 148.
[185] *MacDonald v HM Advocate*, 1996 S.L.T. 723, per the Lord Justice-Clerk (Ross) at 726, approving a statement in Gordon's *Criminal Law*: see now G.H. Gordon, *Criminal Law*, 3rd edn (W. Green, 2001), by M.G.A. Christie, Vol.II, p.129.
[186] 1971 J.C. 29.
[187] (1858) 3 Irv. 208.

necessary that anyone should in fact be prejudiced or suffer loss in order for there to be a definite practical result, as the following case illustrates:

Adcock v Archibald
1925 J.C. 58

Two mine workers were convicted of fraud, in that they had tampered with pins on a coal-mining "hutch" so as to suggest that the coal contained therein had been mined by Adcock (instead of Wilson, another miner) and therefore induce their employers to pay Adcock for having mined the coal. However, the employers operated a minimum wage scheme, and because Adcock and Wilson had both mined less than the relevant amount of coal, they both received the minimum wage—meaning that they were both paid exactly the same amount as if the tampering had not taken place. On appeal, it was held that they had nevertheless been correctly convicted of fraud.

The Lord Justice-General (Clyde) observed that it would be "a mistake to suppose that to the commission of a fraud it is necessary to prove an actual gain by the accused, or an actual loss on the part of the person alleged to be defrauded. Any definite practical result achieved by the fraud is enough." The fact that the employers had calculated the miners' pay on the basis of false information seems to have been a sufficient "definite practical result".

It is essential that the definite practical result has been caused by the false pretence. So, in *Mather v HM Advocate*,[188] Mather was accused of committing fraud by writing a cheque which he knew would not be honoured in payment for nine cattle. It was held that because Mather had obtained delivery of the cattle (the alleged result) *before* writing the cheque (the pretence), the "result" had not been caused by the pretence, and Mather could not be convicted of fraud.

There are two elements to the mens rea of fraud. First, the actor must know that the pretence which he is making is a false one. It seems that recklessness as to the truth of a statement will not suffice for fraud.[189] Secondly, the actor must intend to deceive the victim and thereby achieve the "definite practical result".

Forgery and uttering as genuine

Under Scots law, a person who forges a document (assuming he does nothing with it) does **6–47** not commit a criminal offence at common law (although there is a statutory offence of making counterfeit currency).[190] Forgery only becomes a criminal offence when the forgery is "uttered as genuine": that is, where the actor exposes the document to another person with the intention of deceiving that person and prejudicing someone thereby (usually, but not necessarily, the person whose name is forged).[191] The crime is complete when the document is exposed (or placed in the post to be delivered),[192] and it is not necessary to

---

[188] (1914) 7 Adam 525.
[189] *Mackenzie v Skeen*, 1971 J.C. 43.
[190] Forgery and Counterfeiting Act 1981 s.14.
[191] The requirements of the crime are set out in *John Smith* (1871) 2 Coup. 1, per the Lord Justice-General (Inglis) at 8–10.
[192] cf. *William Jeffrey* (1842) 1 Broun 337.

show either that the actor was successful in his deception or that any person was in fact prejudiced.[193]

The crime of uttering was probably of particular significance when attempted fraud was not itself an indictable crime.[194] Now that this is no longer the case, most cases of forgery and uttering will probably be attempted frauds, but there may be exceptional instances where this crime applies but attempted fraud does not.[195]

Reset

6–48 Reset has been defined as "the receiving and keeping of stolen goods, knowing them to be stolen, with the design of feloniously retaining them from the real owner."[196] By virtue of statute, it also applies to property appropriated by embezzlement or fraud,[197] but the following discussion will refer to "stolen goods" for the sake of clarity of expression.

The actus reus of the crime consists of "receiving and keeping" stolen goods. It is not essential that the actor receives the goods from the actual thief: they may have passed through the hands of others in the interim.[198] The actual thief cannot himself be guilty of reset.[199] It is not reset to acquire the proceeds of stolen property (so where goods are stolen and then sold for cash, it is not reset for a third party to take possession of the money).[200]

While it will normally be essential that a person takes possession of stolen goods in order to be guilty of reset, it has been held that a person may also be guilty of reset by being "privy to the retention" of stolen property,[201] such as by allowing a thief to hide stolen goods in his house,[202] or accepting a ride in a stolen car.[203]

There are two elements to the mens rea of the crime: first, knowledge that the goods are stolen and secondly, an intention to keep them from the real owner (so that a person who intends to return the goods to the owner, or the police, cannot be guilty of reset). Where a person has "wilfully blinded" himself to the fact that goods are stolen, this wilful blindness may be regarded as equivalent to knowledge and therefore sufficient mens rea for the crime, as the following case demonstrates:

Latta v Herron
(1967) S.C.C.R. Supp. 18

Latta, a criminal lawyer, collected weapons. He was informed that a client had firearms for disposal and met the client in a Glasgow alleyway at 11pm at night to purchase them. They transpired to be stolen and he was charged with reset. He denied having known that they were stolen. It was held that even if his claim were true, he had "wilfully blinded himself to the obvious", and that this was sufficient mens rea for reset.

---

[193] *Macdonald v Tudhope*, 1984 S.L.T. 23.
[194] Prior to the Criminal Procedure (Scotland) Act 1887 s.61.
[195] See G.H. Gordon, *Criminal Law*, 3rd edn (W. Green, 2001), by M.G.A. Christie, Vol.II, para.18.35.
[196] Alison, *Principles of the Criminal Law of Scotland* (W. Blackwood, 1832), p.328.
[197] Criminal Law (Consolidation) (Scotland) Act 1995 s.52.
[198] Alison, *Principles of the Criminal Law of Scotland* (W. Blackwood, 1832), p.329.
[199] *Druce v Friel*, 1994 S.L.T. 1209.
[200] cf. *Helen Blair* (1848) Ark. 459.
[201] Macdonald, *Criminal Law*, 5th edn (W. Green, 1948), p.67.
[202] See *HM Advocate v Browne* (1903) 6 F. (J.) 24, per the Lord Justice-Clerk (Macdonald) at 26; Hume, *Commentaries*, i, p.113.
[203] *McCawley v HM Advocate* (1959) S.C.C.R. Supp. 3.

> **Key Concepts**
>
> A person is guilty of **embezzlement** if (a) he is lawfully in possession of property; (b) is under a duty to account to the true owner for that property, and (c) he intentionally appropriates the property.
>
>   **Robbery** is theft accomplished by means of personal violence or intimidation.
>
>   **Extortion** is an attempt to enforce either legal or illegal demands by illegal means.
>
>   The actus reus of **fraud** has three elements: (1) a false pretence; (2) a definite practical result; and (3) a causal link between the pretence and the result. The mens rea required is an intention to deceive the victim (knowing that the pretence is false) in order to achieve the definite practical result.
>
>   Forgery is not itself criminal under Scots law, but passing off a forgery as genuine is the offence of **uttering as genuine**.
>
>   **Reset** is the taking possession of (or being privy to the retention of) stolen goods with the intention of keeping them from the true owner.

Malicious mischief

Damaging—or possibly simply interfering with—the property of another person may **6–49** amount to the offence of malicious mischief. It was formerly thought that the actus reus of this offence extended only to damaging or destroying property, but that view was rejected in the following case:

> **HM Advocate v Wilson**
> 1984 S.L.T. 117
>
> Wilson was charged with having committed malicious mischief by pressing an emergency stop button on a power station generator, causing the loss of £147,000 worth of electricity generation. He argued that the charge was irrelevant, in that it did not allege that there had been any physical damage to the property concerned. The High Court rejected the challenge, holding that interference with property which caused financial loss, was sufficient for the actus reus of malicious mischief, even if there was no physical damage.

Interference with property which does not cause either damage to that property or financial loss, is not malicious mischief.[204] Despite the term "malicious", the mens rea requirement is satisfied by either an intention to cause damage or financial loss, or recklessness as to the possibility of such damage being caused.[205] Nor is it essential that the accused had any "malicious purpose", provided that this basic mens rea requirement of intention or recklessness is met.[206]

---

[204] *Bett v Brown*, 1997 S.L.T. 1310.
[205] *Ward v Robertson*, 1938 J.C. 32.
[206] *Lord Advocate's Reference (No.1 of 2000)*, 2001 J.C. 143.

Vandalism

6–50 Vandalism is a statutory offence under Scots law. Section 52 of the Criminal Law (Consolidation) (Scotland) Act 1995 provides that "any person who, without reasonable excuse, wilfully or recklessly destroys or damages any property belonging to another shall be guilty of the offence of vandalism."[207] When this offence was introduced by statute in 1980, it was admitted by the then Government that it added nothing new in substance to Scots law—because such acts would already amount to malicious mischief—but it was suggested that it was desirable to have a more specific and readily understood offence covering acts of vandalism.[208]

Fireraising

6–51 There are two separate offences of fireraising in Scotland: "wilful fireraising" and "culpable and reckless fireraising". Until very recently, it was thought that the distinction between the two crimes was that they applied to different types of property, and that the crime of "wilful fireraising" applied only to setting fire to houses, corn, coal workings and woods, all of which had been considered capital offences prior to 1887.[209] This had the curious result that intentionally setting fire to other types of property was occasionally charged as "culpable and reckless fireraising" despite it being quite clear that the accused's actions were deliberate.[210]

This unsatisfactory state of affairs was remedied recently by the Full Bench decision in *Byrne v HM Advocate*.[211] *Byrne* makes it clear that both offences can be committed in respect of any type of property—so the actus reus of each offence is simply setting fire to property.

The two offences are distinguished by their different mens rea: "wilful fireraising" is fireraising committed intentionally, and "culpable and reckless fireraising" is fireraising committed recklessly. Recklessness, in this context, means a "complete disregard for any dangers" which might result from one's actions.[212]

Key Concepts

The actus reus of **malicious mischief** is either (a) damaging the property of another or (b) interfering with the property so as to cause financial loss. The mens rea is an intention to cause damage or loss, or recklessness as to the possibility of damage or loss being caused.

A person who "without reasonable excuse, wilfully or recklessly destroys or damages any property belonging to another" is guilty of **vandalism**. There is a considerable overlap between this offence and malicious mischief.

There are two separate offences of fireraising in Scotland. Deliberately setting fire to property belonging to another is **wilful fireraising**; recklessly causing another's property to catch fire is **culpable and reckless fireraising**.

---

[207] As to "reasonable excuse", see *McDougall v Ho*, 1985 S.C.C.R. 199 and *John v Donnelly*, 1999 J.C. 336.
[208] See C.H.W. Gane, C.N. Stoddart and J. Chalmers, *A Casebook on Scottish Criminal Law*, edn (W. Green, 2009), para.15–18.
[209] Capital punishment for wilful fireraising was abolished by the Criminal Procedure (Scotland) Act 1887 s.56.
[210] See *Wither v Adie*, 1986 S.L.T. (Sh. Ct) 32 (setting fire to a man's shoelaces).
[211] 2000 J.C. 155.
[212] *Carr v HM Advocate*, 1994 J.C. 203; *Thomson v HM Advocate*, 1995 S.L.T. 827.

OFFENCES AGAINST PUBLIC ORDER

Breach of the peace[213]

Breach of the peace is a crime of extremely wide scope, and operates as something of a **6–52** "catch-all" offence in Scots law. It is probably popularly thought to cover the sort of conduct which might be described as "drunk and disorderly". While it certainly does cover such activity, it can cover much more besides this. For example, breach of the peace charges have been held to cover "peeping tom" activities,[214] making indecent remarks to young boys in private,[215] and even inconsiderate driving.[216]

Concern has been expressed for some time about the rather vague and wide nature of the offence, and in particular whether this is compatible with the European Convention on Human Rights. The issue was considered by the High Court in the following case:

> ### Smith v Donnelly
> ### 2002 J.C. 65
>
> Pamela Smith was convicted of having committed a breach of the peace by lying on the road in front of a naval base and disrupting traffic as a protest against nuclear weapons. She appealed against her conviction, arguing that the definition of the offence was so wide and unclear that "a citizen could not know with reasonable certainty what actions would breach criminal law", and that the offence was therefore contrary to art.7 of the European Convention on Human Rights, which prohibits retrospective criminal legislation and requires that the criminal law meets basic standards of clarity.
>
> The court rejected Smith's challenge to her conviction. It was said that breach of the peace "is conduct which does present as genuinely alarming and disturbing, in its context, to any reasonable person." The law was sufficiently clear as to be compatible with the Convention.

The *Smith v Donnelly* court left open the question of whether certain charges of breach of the peace, such as that faced by Smith, might breach the right to freedom of expression which is guaranteed by art.10 of the European Convention, as that point had not been argued in the appeal. However, a challenge based on art.10 failed in a later case, where the decision in *Smith v Donnelly* was reaffirmed.[217]

Although it is clear from *Smith v Donnelly* that the actus reus of the crime is "conduct which does present as genuinely alarming and disturbing, in its context, to any reasonable person",[218] it is not clear what mens rea is required for the crime. It may be that it is sufficient to show that the actor should have known that his conduct presented a risk of alarm and disturbance.[219] It is difficult to envisage a case where the actus reus has been proven and yet it has not been proven that the accused should have known of this risk,

---

[213] See generally M.G.A. Christie, *Breach of the Peace* (Butterworths, 1990).
[214] *Raffaelli v Heatly*, 1949 J.C. 101; *MacDougall v Dochree*, 1992 J.C. 154; *Bryce v Normand*, 1997 S.L.T. 1351.
[215] *Young v Heatly*, 1959 J.C. 66. This case was, however, overruled in *Harris v HM Advocate*, 2010 J.C. 245, where the High Court stressed that the crime required a "public element".
[216] *Horsburgh v Russell*, 1994 S.L.T. 942; *Austin v Fraser*, 1998 S.L.T. 106.
[217] *Jones v Carnegie*, 2004 J.C. 136.
[218] *Smith v Donnelly*, 2002 J.C. 65, per Lord Coulsfield at 71.
[219] cf. *Hughes v Crowe*, 1993 S.C.C.R. 320.

which may explain why there has been very little discussion of mens rea in the reported cases on breach of the peace.

Mobbing

6–53   Where a group of people assemble for an illegal common purpose, which causes public alarm, this may amount to the crime of mobbing.[220] The group must be of a reasonable size, although as few as eight persons has been held sufficient.[221] Charges of mobbing appear to be seldom used nowadays, and in the recent case of *Coleman v HM Advocate*, Lord Coulsfield suggested that "far from providing a simple means of dealing with cases of group violence, a charge of mobbing and rioting involves embarking on an area of law which is full of uncertainties and narrow distinctions."[222] For that reason, the prosecution may prefer to bring charges relating to the specific illegal actions of the mob, rather than rely upon the more generalised crime of mobbing.

Key Concepts

Breach of the peace may be defined as "conduct which does present as genuinely alarming and disturbing, in its context, to any reasonable person".

Where a group of people assemble for an illegal common purpose which causes public alarm, this may amount to the crime of **mobbing**.

Offences Against Justice

Attempting to pervert the course of justice

6–54   Attempting to pervert the course of justice is arguably simply a catch-all term for a variety of different offences such as perjury, but in recent years it appears to have become recognised as a crime in its own right.[223] It covers such actions as knowingly making a false statement to the police,[224] escaping from lawful custody,[225] and intimidating witnesses.[226] Wasting the time of the police by falsely reporting a crime is also a criminal offence,[227] although this is generally treated as a specific crime in its own right rather than as an attempt to pervert the course of justice.

Perjury

6–55   A witness in a trial—criminal or civil—who gives false evidence is liable to prosecution for perjury. The mens rea required is knowledge of the falsity of the statement. It is sufficient, however, that the witness makes a statement which he does not know to be true, even if he does not actually know that it is false.[228] It is not necessary to show that the false evidence

---

[220] See generally Scottish Law Commission, *Mobbing and Rioting* (Consultative Memorandum 60, 1984).
[221] *Hancock v HM Advocate*, 1981 J.C. 74.
[222] 1999 S.L.T. 1261 at 1272.
[223] For a full discussion, see G.H. Gordon, *Criminal Law*, 3rd edn (W. Green, 2000), by M.G.A. Christie, Vol.I, pp.29–35.
[224] *Watson v HM Advocate*, 1993 S.C.C.R. 875.
[225] *HM Advocate v Martin*, 1956 J.C. 1.
[226] *Dalton v HM Advocate*, 1951 J.C. 76.
[227] *Kerr v Hill*, 1936 J.C. 71; *Gray v Morrison*, 1954 J.C. 31.
[228] *Simpson v Tudhope*, 1988 S.L.T. 297.

had any effect on the outcome of the trial.[229] A person charged with a crime who gives false evidence in his own defence is guilty of perjury, although a prosecution would be unusual in such a case.[230] Inducing a person to give false evidence amounts to the crime of subornation of perjury.[231]

Contempt of court

Contempt of court takes two forms: first, contempt "in the face of the court" and secondly, the publication of material likely to be prejudicial to court proceedings. It is not, strictly speaking, a criminal offence, but because it is punishable as if it were a crime, it has been suggested that it "may be regarded as virtually a crime".[232]   **6–56**

Contempt in the face of the court can take various forms, such as a failure to appear in court when required, refusing to answer questions, "prevaricating", which in general terms means being evasive in response to questions, or offensive conduct in court (such as conduct which disrupts proceedings).[233]

Contempt by the publication of prejudicial material is now largely governed by the Contempt of Court Act 1981. It is a contempt to publish material "which creates a substantial risk that the course of justice in the proceedings will be seriously impeded or prejudiced."[234] Liability for this form of contempt is strict: there is no need to prove any intention to interfere with the course of justice.[235]

INCHOATE OFFENCES

A person—or group of persons—may form a criminal purpose, but not complete it. Such a purpose may remain "inchoate", or "incomplete" for any number of reasons. The actor may, for example, have tried but failed to fulfil the purpose, changed his mind before completing the scheme, or been prevented from doing so by the police or a third party.   **6–57**

In such circumstances, there may be good reasons for holding that the actor is criminally liable even though the offence has not been "completed". It would clearly be absurd if the police were unable to intervene to prevent a person committing a crime, or were able to intervene but unable to charge them with any offence.

Consequently, Scots law recognises three forms of "inchoate offences": incitement, conspiracy and attempt. It should be noted that these are not crimes in themselves, but are perhaps best understood as modified forms of the complete offence. For example, the inchoate forms of murder are "incitement to murder", "conspiracy to murder" and "attempted murder". It would, strictly speaking, be wrong to simply speak of someone as being guilty of "incitement", "attempt" or "conspiracy".

---

[229] *Lord Advocate's Reference (No.1 of 1985)*, 1986 J.C. 137.
[230] *HM Advocate v Cairns*, 1967 J.C. 37; *Milne v HM Advocate*, 1996 S.L.T. 775.
[231] See Hume, *Commentaries*, i, pp.381–383.
[232] G.H. Gordon, *Criminal Law*, 3rd edn (W. Green, 2001) by M.G.A. Christie, Vol.II, p.749.
[233] See generally C.H.W. Gane, C.N. Stoddart and J. Chalmers, *A Casebook on Scottish Criminal Law*, 4th edn (W. Green, 2009), pp.632–641.
[234] Contempt of Court Act 1981 s.2(2).
[235] Contempt of Court Act 1981 s.1.

Incitement

6–58 A person will be guilty of incitement if it can be shown that he "reached and sought to influence the mind of [another] person towards the commission of a crime".[236] It is irrelevant whether or not the crime is in fact ever carried out.

Conspiracy

6–59 A conspiracy consists of two or more persons agreeing to commit an act, which would be criminal if done by a single individual.[237] The conspiracy is complete when the agreement is made, and it is not necessary to show that any action was taken in furtherance of the conspiracy.[238]

Attempt

6–60 There is explicit statutory provision to the effect that any attempt to commit a crime is itself criminal.[239] Identifying the actus reus of an attempted crime may prove difficult. It must be shown that the accused has "got beyond the stage of preparation into the stage of perpetration".[240] This test—the application of which is a question of fact rather than law—can be rather broad in its application. In *HM Advocate v Camerons*,[241] a husband and wife planned to defraud insurers by staging a fake robbery. It was proven that they had staged the robbery, and that they had reported the theft to their insurance broker—but it was not proven that they had actually made a claim. Nevertheless, the jury convicted them of attempted fraud.

It is often assumed that "attempt" implies an intention to commit the completed crime—and as a matter of the English language, that may well be correct. However, under Scots law, where a person acts with the mens rea which is required for the completed crime, this will provide sufficient mens rea for guilt of the attempted crime. The point is illustrated by the following case:

> **Cawthorne v HM Advocate**
> 1968 J.C. 32
>
> Cawthorne was charged with attempted murder, in that he had shot repeatedly at four persons through a locked door. At the trial, Cawthorne's counsel argued that he could only be found guilty of attempted murder if it was proved that he had intended to kill. This argument was rejected by both the trial judge and the appeal court. The Lord Justice-General (Clyde) observed that "attempted murder is just the same as murder in the eyes of our law, but for the one vital distinction, that the killing has not been brought off and the victim of the attack has escaped with his life. But there must be in each case the same mens rea, and that mens rea in each case can be proved by evidence of a deliberate intention to kill or by such recklessness as to show that the accused was regardless of the consequences of his act whatever they may have been."

---

[236] *Baxter v HM Advocate*, 1998 J.C. 219, per the Lord Justice-General (Rodger) at 221.
[237] Macdonald, *Criminal Law*, 5th edn (W. Green, 1948), p.185. See also *Maxwell v HM Advocate*, 1980 J.C. 40, per Lord Cameron at 43.
[238] See G.H. Gordon, *Criminal Law*, 3rd edn (W. Green, 2000), by M.G.A. Christie, Vol.I, pp.234–235.
[239] Criminal Procedure (Scotland) Act 1995 s.294.
[240] *HM Advocate v Camerons*, 1911 S.C. (J.) 110, per the Lord Justice-General (Dunedin) at 115.
[241] 1911 S.C. (J.) 110.

Impossibility and inchoate offences

Is it a criminal offence to attempt something which is in fact impossible? There was **6–61** formerly some confusion in Scots law on this point, because while it had been held in two cases that there could be no crime of attempted abortion where the woman was not actually pregnant,[242] it had been held in another case that it was attempted theft for a man to try and pick an empty pocket.[243]

The position was settled by a Full Bench in *Docherty v Brown*.[244] In that case, Docherty was charged with attempting to possess a controlled drug with intent to supply. Although he believed that the tablets in his possession were a controlled drug (MDMA, or "ecstasy"), they were in fact laxatives.[245] The court held that the impossibility of what he was trying to do was no defence to the charge, and that the cases which held that there was no crime of attempted abortion, where the woman was not pregnant, had been wrongly decided.

Although *factually* impossible attempts are criminal, *legally* impossible attempts are not. So, if Docherty had known that the tablets in his possession were laxatives, but wrongly thought that it was a criminal offence to sell laxatives, he could not have been convicted of any offence.

The courts have taken the same view of impossibility with regard to conspiracy,[246] and it is thought that the same approach would be taken with regard to incitement if the issue were to arise.

Key Concepts

Scots law recognises three **inchoate** (incomplete) forms of offences: **incitement**, **conspiracy** and **attempt**. These are not offences in themselves, but incomplete forms of other offences.

Incitement consists of attempting to influence another person towards the commission of a crime.

Conspiracy is an agreement by two or more persons to commit a crime.

An **attempt** is committed by a person who has moved from preparation to the stage of perpetrating a crime but does not complete the offence. The mens rea requirement is the same as for the completed offence.

It is no defence to a charge of an inchoate offence that the accused was trying to do something which was **impossible**.

ART AND PART LIABILITY

Where two or more persons participate in carrying out a crime, they are all equally guilty **6–62** of the offence. (There may, of course, be differences in their culpability or level of involvement, which can be reflected in sentencing). Lord Patrick explained the concept in the following case:

---

[242] *HM Advocate v Anderson*, 1928 J.C. 1; *HM Advocate v Semple*, 1937 S.L.T. 48.
[243] *Lamont v Strathern*, 1933 J.C. 33.
[244] 1996 J.C. 48.
[245] A fact which does not appear in the law reports, but was reported in the press: "Accused faces jail over rave laxatives", *Scotsman*, March 21, 1996.
[246] *Maxwell v HM Advocate*, 1980 J.C. 40.

HM Advocate v Lappen
1956 S.L.T. 109

Lord Patrick: "To illustrate this doctrine of the law ... if a number of men form a common plan whereby some are to commit the actual seizure of the property, and some according to the plan are to keep watch, and some according to the plan are to help to carry away the loot, and some according to the plan are to help to dispose of the loot, then, although the actual robbery may only have been committed by one or two of them, every one is guilty of the robbery, because they joined together in a common plan to commit the robbery."

Art and part is a doctrine by which persons who participate in a criminal enterprise may be held liable for the complete offence even though they did not personally execute every part of the enterprise. It is not a crime in itself, but simply a doctrine by which persons may be held guilty of existing criminal offences.

Two conditions must be satisfied for a person to be held guilty of a crime art and part. First, a common purpose must be proven. In *HM Advocate v Welsh and McLachlan*,[247] two men were charged with theft by housebreaking and murdering the occupant of the house. Because it could not be shown which of the men had killed the occupant, and it could not be shown that the men had agreed to use lethal violence as part of the housebreaking, it followed that neither could be convicted of murder.

Secondly, a person must participate in the criminal enterprise in order to be guilty art and part. In *HM Advocate v Kerr*,[248] it was held that an allegation that a man had stood behind a hedge and watched a rape without intervening or calling for assistance could not be sufficient to find him guilty of the rape art and part. The situation would be different where a person was under a legal duty to intervene, such as a policeman who fails to prevent a junior officer assaulting a suspect.[249]

Key Concept

A person may be guilty of a crime **art and part** if, even though he did not carry out every part of the crime himself, he had (a) a **common purpose** with another person or persons and (b) **participated** in the commission of the crime.

GENERAL DEFENCES

6–63   As was noted earlier, we tend in ordinary language to refer to anything which might result in an accused's acquittal as being a "defence". This would include simple denials of actus reus or mens rea (i.e. claims that the accused did not actually commit the prohibited act, or did not do so with a legally culpable state of mind). This section, however, is concerned with defences in the sense of a justification or excuse which the accused offers for his conduct. Scots law recognises a number of "general defences". These are "general" in the sense that they are not specific to particular crimes.

---

[247] (1897) 5 S.L.T. 137.
[248] (1871) 2 Coup. 334.
[249] *Bonar and Hogg v McLeod*, 1983 S.C.C.R. 161.

Mental abnormality

Mental disorder and unfitness to plead

Mental disorder may affect a person's liability to be punished in two distinct ways. For- **6–64**
merly, these were both (confusingly) called "insanity", but that term, which is thought to
be stigmatic and misleading, no longer forms part of Scots law.[250]

First, it may be argued that a person is "unfit for trial". While mental disorder is a
common basis for this plea, it can in fact be made on the basis of any "mental or physical
condition".[251] This plea exists because it would be inappropriate to subject a person to a
criminal trial if they are not able to properly participate in that process. The important
question here is a person's condition at the time of the proposed trial—not at the time of
the alleged offence. Of course, if their condition subsequently improves, then a trial may
take place at a later date. In this context, the court must consider a range of factors set out
in statute, including in particular whether the accused can understand the nature of the
charge against him along with the proceedings as a whole, and whether he can instruct and
communicate with his legal representatives. If the court concludes that the accused is
incapable of "participating effectively in a trial", then the plea of "unfit for trial" must be
upheld.[252] If the plea succeeds, an "examination of facts" may be held. The accused cannot
be convicted at this hearing—the most that can happen is that the court can make a
finding that he "did the act or made the omission constituting the offence"[253]—but he can
be acquitted, which would preclude him being tried for the offence at a future date.

Secondly, where a person is fit to stand trial, they may plead as a defence that they were
not responsible for their conduct because of mental disorder at the time the offence is
alleged to have been committed. This plea—which is broadly equivalent to the old common law plea of insanity but is not given any formal statutory name—requires that a
person be acquitted if they were "at the time of the conduct unable by reason of mental
disorder to appreciate the nature or wrongfulness of [their] conduct".[254] This question is
one of fact. It is not a medical decision, but "is to be judged on the ordinary rules on which
men act in daily life."[255]

This defence must be proven by the accused on the balance of probabilities, which is an
exception to the rule that the burden of proof is normally on the prosecution in a criminal
trial.[256]

Automatism

As has been seen, the defence of insanity applies where there is a "total alienation of **6–65**
reason" caused by mental illness. What is the situation where a person suffers a total
alienation of reason due to an external factor such as a drug? The leading case is *Ross v
HM Advocate*:

---

[250] See Scottish Law Commission, *Report on Insanity and Diminished Responsibility* (2004), Scot. Law Com.
No.195, paras 2.19–2.23.
[251] Criminal Procedure (Scotland) Act 1995 s.53F(1).
[252] Criminal Procedure (Scotland) Act 1995 s.53F.
[253] Criminal Procedure (Scotland) Act 1995 s.55.
[254] Criminal Procedure (Scotland) Act 1995 s.51A(1).
[255] *HM Advocate v Kidd*, 1960 J.C. 61, per Lord Strachan at 70.
[256] Criminal Procedure (Scotland) Act 1995 s.51A(4).

Ross v HM Advocate
1991 J.C. 210

Ross was drinking lager from a can which, unknown to him, had been "spiked" with temazepam and LSD. Within about half an hour, he proceeded to lunge about with a knife, severely stabbing a number of people. He was convicted of a number of counts of assault. On appeal, he argued that he should be acquitted of the charges on the basis that his involuntary intoxication meant that he was not responsible for his actions. The court, in quashing his convictions, held that where an actor has suffered a total alienation of reason—and thus lacks mens rea—he should be acquitted, provided that this was the result of an external factor, which he was not bound to foresee.

Because a total alienation of reason is required, it is not sufficient for a person to say only that their drink was spiked and that they did something which they would not have done sober. So, in *Cardle v Mulrainey*,[257] the accused had attempted to steal a number of cars after drinking a can of lager spiked with amphetamine. He later admitted that he had known what he was doing but did not know why. It was held that, because he had understood what he was doing, the requirement of a total alienation of reason had not been satisfied and the defence could not apply.

The requirement that the total alienation of reason be caused by an external factor which the accused was not bound to foresee means that a person who takes a drug or other substance knowing that it will or is likely to have this sort of effect is not entitled to plead the defence.[258] Such cases are regarded as examples of voluntary intoxication, which is discussed immediately below.

Voluntary intoxication

6–66 It is commonly said that self-induced intoxication is no defence to a criminal charge in Scots law. The leading case is *Brennan v HM Advocate*:

Brennan v HM Advocate
1977 J.C. 38

Brennan drank between 20 and 25 pints of beer, a glass of sherry and took a microdot of LSD. Later that day, he had an argument with his father which resulted in him stabbing his father to death. He argued that his extreme intoxication provided a defence, either because (a) he should be regarded as temporarily insane or (b) it showed that he did not have the mens rea required for murder. The court rejected this argument, holding that (a) a plea of insanity could not be based upon the transient effects of self-induced intoxication and (b) Brennan's actions in getting wholly intoxicated could demonstrate, in themselves, the criminal recklessness which is sufficient mens rea for the crime of murder.

---

[257] 1992 S.L.T. 1152.
[258] See *Ebsworth v HM Advocate*, 1992 S.L.T. 1161; *Finegan v Heywood*, 2000 J.C. 444.

Brennan appears to leave open the question of crimes which require intention or knowledge as mens rea. Should a person who lacks the relevant intention or knowledge for criminal guilt because of their own self-induced intoxication therefore be acquitted? The answer appears to be a clear no. In the subsequent case of *Ross v HM Advocate*, the Lord Justice-General (Hope) stated that where a condition "which has resulted in the absence of mens rea is self-induced ... the accused must be assumed to have intended the natural consequences of his act".[259] Evidence of self-induced intoxication may, therefore, either suffice in itself to show mens rea, or—if it excludes mens rea—will result in a presumption of mens rea being applied. Either way, it will not result in an acquittal.

Involuntary intoxication, by contrast, may provide the basis for a defence of automatism, as discussed earlier.[260]

Key Concepts

A person must be acquitted if by reason of **mental disorder** they were "at the time of the conduct unable by reason of mental disorder to appreciate the nature or wrongfulness of [their] conduct". The test is a legal and not a medical one.

The defence of **automatism** applies where an accused was suffering from a total alienation of reason caused by an external factor, which they were not bound to foresee.

Voluntary intoxication is not a defence under Scots law.

External threats and compulsion

Self-defence (or private defence)

A person who acts in order to protect themselves (or a third party) from a violent attack **6–67** may be entitled to plead self-defence. The requirements for the defence are set out in the following case:

HM Advocate v Doherty
1954 J.C. 1

Lord Keith: "First of all, there must be imminent danger to the life or limb of the accused, to the person putting forward this defence; there must be imminent danger to his life and limb; and, secondly, the retaliation that he uses in the face of this danger must be necessary for his own safety. Those are two fundamental things you will keep in mind, that there is imminent danger to life and limb and that the retaliation used is necessary for the safety of the man threatened ... Again, if the person assaulted has means of escape or retreat, he is bound to use them."

Although Lord Keith refers to "imminent danger to the life or limb of the accused", it is clear that the defence is equally applicable where the accused has acted in defence of a third party.[261] For this reason, some writers prefer to describe the defence as "private

---

[259] 1991 J.C. 210 at 214. See also *Donaldson v Normand*, 1997 J.C. 200.
[260] See above, para.6–65.
[261] *HM Advocate v Carson*, 1964 S.L.T. 21; *Moss v Howdle*, 1997 J.C. 123 at 128–129.

defence" rather than "self-defence", but the latter is the term which is normally used in Scots law.

It can be seen from *Doherty* that there are three requirements for the defence, as follows:

(1) There must be imminent danger to life or limb. A mistaken belief as to such danger will suffice to found the defence, but the mistake must be based on reasonable grounds.[262]

(2) The force used by the actor must be necessary in the circumstances. This means that it is never permissible to use lethal force in response to an attack, which does not place the actor at risk of death, with the exception that a woman may use lethal force to prevent a rape.[263] In general terms, the actor's response must be proportionate to the attack, but it is commonly said that this is not a matter which should be "weighed in too fine scales"—allowance must be made for the fact that the accused acted out of fear and in the heat of the moment.[264] A person who kills using excessive force may be entitled to the partial defence of provocation if the requirements of that defence are met.[265]

(3) There must have been no means of escape or retreat available to the actor. Such means of course, must be reasonable.[266] For example, a person cannot be required to opt for a means of escape (such as leaping out of an upstairs window), which would in itself expose him to serious risk of injury.

Coercion

6–68 A person who is forced to commit a criminal offence by threats may plead the defence of coercion.

Thomson v HM Advocate
1983 S.L.T. 682

The High Court recognised that a defence of coercion could be available where the following factors were present:

(1) Threats of death or serious injury against the accused or a third party. The threats must be of present and not future injury.
(2) The threats must be "of such a nature as to overcome the resolution of an ordinarily constituted person of the same age and sex as the accused."

The reason for requiring that the threats be of present and not future injury is that a person threatened with injury at some point in the future is expected to seek assistance from the police or other appropriate authorities and not to comply with the demands which the threats accompany.

Coercion is probably not available as a defence to a charge of murder.[267] A person who knowingly exposes himself to the risk of being coerced—such as a person who associates

---

[262] *Owens v HM Advocate*, 1946 J.C. 119; *Jones v HM Advocate*, 1990 J.C. 160.
[263] cf. *McCluskey v HM Advocate*, 1959 J.C. 39.
[264] See *HM Advocate v Doherty*, 1954 J.C. 1, per Lord Keith at 4–5.
[265] See above, para.6–19.
[266] *McBrearty v HM Advocate*, 1999 S.L.T. 1333.
[267] See *Collins v HM Advocate*, 1991 S.C.C.R. 898, per Lord Allanbridge at 902.

with a gang or similar organisation, which is known to carry out violent crime—will not be entitled to plead the defence.[268]

Necessity

In circumstances of emergency, a person may feel that it is necessary to break the criminal **6–69** law in order to prevent a "greater evil" occurring. In such a case, that person may be entitled to plead the defence of necessity. For some time, it was not clear whether and to what extent the defence was recognised by Scots law, but doubts on this matter were settled by the 1997 decision in *Moss v Howdle*.[269] From that case and subsequent decisions, it is clear that there are four requirements for the defence to succeed:

(1) There must be an immediate danger to life or of serious injury. So, in *Ruxton v Lang*,[270] the accused drove off in fear of a knife attack despite having drunk too much alcohol to lawfully drive. She was stopped by the police two miles away. It was held that while her initial actions might have been justified by necessity, the "immediate danger" had passed well before she had driven two miles and that the defence was, therefore, unavailable.

(2) The circumstances must have constrained the actor to break the law. If there is a "legal way out", it must be taken. In *Moss v Howdle*, the accused argued that he had broken the speed limit out of necessity because his passenger had shouted out in pain and he wanted to get to a service station area quickly. It was held that, because the prudent course of action would have been to pull over to the side of the road and ascertain what the problem was, Moss's actions in breaking the speed limit could not be regarded as justified by necessity.

(3) The actor must have broken the law *because of* the circumstances of necessity. If he would have acted in the same way regardless of those circumstances, the defence will be unavailable.[271]

(4) The act must have a reasonable prospect of removing the danger.[272]

There is no Scottish authority on whether necessity can ever be a defence to murder, but the English courts have ruled that it is unavailable in such cases.[273]

Key Concepts

A person may plead **self-defence** if, in circumstances of immediate danger, where there is no reasonable means of retreat available, they use reasonable force to defend themselves or a third party.

The defence of **coercion** is available where a person is forced to commit a criminal offence by threats of death or serious injury against that person or a third party, provided that an ordinary person would also have given in to the threats.

---

[268] See the English case of *R. v Sharp* [1987] 3 W.L.R. 1.
[269] 1997 J.C. 123.
[270] 1998 S.C.C.R. 1 (Sh. Ct).
[271] *Dawson v McKay*, 1999 S.L.T. 1328.
[272] *Lord Advocate's Reference (No 1 of 2000)*, 2001 J.C. 143 at [46].
[273] *R. v Dudley and Stephens* (1884) 14 Q.B.D. 273. But cf. *Re A (Children)* [2001] 2 W.L.R. 480.

> The defence of **necessity** is available where a person commits a criminal offence in order to avoid a greater harm occurring, provided that there was immediate danger to life and limb and that there was no "way out" other than committing the offence. The act must have a reasonable prospect of removing the danger.

▼ CHAPTER SUMMARY

GENERAL PRINCIPLES OF CRIMINAL LIABILITY

6–70
1. Scots criminal law is "uncodified", meaning that the principal rules are found in case law rather than in any systematic statutory form. Some offences—including, in particular, sexual offences—are, however, statutory.
2. A criminal offence is comprised of three elements: (1) actus reus (the physical element); (2) mens rea (the fault element); and (3) the absence of a valid defence.
3. There is normally no liability for an omission to act, except where it is imposed by statute. However, a parent has a duty to prevent harm coming to their child, and any person who has assumed responsibility for another person may have a duty to prevent harm coming to them.
4. Some offences are ones of "strict liability", meaning that mens rea need not be proven.
5. A corporate body can be guilty of a criminal offence. If that offence requires mens rea, it must be shown that a person who was the "controlling mind" of the company had that mens rea:
   ➢ *Transco plc v HM Advocate* (2004): a company could not be convicted of culpable homicide, because the charge against it did not allege that any individual who was a "controlling mind" of the company had the necessary mens rea.

OFFENCES AGAINST THE PERSON

1. The offence of murder is committed by a person who causes the death of another and either (a) wickedly intended to kill or (b) was wickedly reckless of the consequences of their actions:
   ➢ *Drury v HM Advocate* (2001) sets out this definition.
2. Where a person would be guilty of murder, but successfully pleads provocation or diminished responsibility, they will be convicted of culpable homicide instead. These are partial defences which do not apply to other crimes.
3. Provocation requires (a) a recognised provocation (violence or infidelity); (b) that the accused lost his or her self-control as a result of that provocation, and (c) [if the provocation was by infidelity] that an ordinary person would have been liable to react in the same way, or [if the provocation was by violence] that there was a "reasonably proportionate relationship" between the deceased's violence and the accused's response:
   ➢ *Drury v HM Advocate* (2001) sets out these criteria.

4. **Diminished responsibility requires (a) that the accused was suffering from an "abnormality of mind" at the time of the killing and (b) that this "substantially impaired" their ability to determine or control their acts:**

   ➢ Section 51B of the Criminal Procedure (Scotland) Act 1995 sets out these criteria.

5. **Culpable homicide may be committed in two other ways: (a) where the accused commits an unlawful act, such as assault, which causes death; or (b) where the accused does any act—lawful or otherwise—with a complete disregard for the consequences of their actions, and death results:**

   ➢ *Bird v HM Advocate* (1952): a man who committed a minor assault on a woman who then died was guilty of culpable homicide despite the death being unexpected: any assault which causes death is, at least, culpable homicide.

6. **The actus reus of assault is an "attack" on another person—whether or not they are injured. The mens rea is "evil intent", although the use of the word "evil" does not mean that any particular motive is required; it simply stresses that intention is required;**

   ➢ *Atkinson v HM Advocate* (1987): assault can be committed by "threatening gestures sufficient to produce alarm"; actual injury is not required.

7. **Consent is generally not a defence to assault:**

   ➢ *Smart v HM Advocate* (1975): because consent is not a defence to assault, it was irrelevant that two men had agreed to a "square go" in a pub car park; assault had still been committed.

8. **It is a crime to recklessly injure a person, or to recklessly endanger the safety of the public.**

SEXUAL OFFENCES

1. **Rape is committed by a person (A) who has sexual intercourse with another person (B) who does not consent, provided that A does not reasonably believe that B is consenting. Sexual intercourse, for these purposes, means penetration of B's vagina, anus or mouth with A's penis:**

   ➢ This crime is now defined in section 1 of the Sexual Offences (Scotland) Act 2009.

2. **The recently recognised offence of public indecency covers conduct objectively liable to cause public offence. The offence of shameless indecency is no longer recognised by the law:**

   ➢ *Webster v Dominick* (2005): this decision "abolished" the offence of shameless indecency and replaced it with a new offence of "public indecency".

PROPERTY OFFENCES

1. **The actus reus of theft is appropriation of corporeal moveable property without the consent of the owner. The mens rea is an intention to deprive; it may be necessary for the intention to be dishonest.**
2. **Housebreaking is not itself an offence in Scots law, but housebreaking with intent to steal is.**
3. **Robbery can be defined as "theft accomplished by means of personal violence or intimidation".**
4. **Extortion can be defined as an attempt "to enforce either legal or illegal demands by illegal means":**

    ➢ *Carmichael v Black; Black v Carmichael* (1992): a person who "wheel clamped" cars and demanded money for their release was guilty both of theft and extortion.

5. **The actus reus of fraud consists of (1) a false pretence; (2) a definite practical result; and (3) a causal link between the pretence and the result. The mens rea consists of (1) knowledge that the pretence is false and (2) an intention to deceive and thereby achieve the definite practical result:**

    ➢ *Adcock v Archibald* (1925): because fraud requires only a "definite practical result", no actual gain or loss is necessary.

6. **Forgery is not itself an offence in Scots law, but it is an offence to utter a forged document as genuine.**
7. **Reset may be defined as "the receiving and keeping of stolen goods, knowing them to be stolen, with the design of feloniously retaining them from the real owner".**
8. **The actus reus of malicious mischief is damaging or destroying property, or interfering with property in such a way as to cause financial loss. Despite the name of the offence, it can be committed either intentionally or recklessly:**

    ➢ *HM Advocate v Wilson* (1984): malicious mischief can be committed by interfering with property in such a way as to cause patrimonial loss, even if the property is not actually damaged.

BREACH OF THE PEACE

1. **The offence of breach of the peace is committed by "conduct which does present as genuinely alarming and disturbing, in its context, to any reasonable person":**

    ➢ *Smith v Donnelly* (2002): established the definition of breach of the peace quoted here, and held that the crime is not so vague as to be incompatible with art.7 of the European Convention on Human Rights.

INCHOATE OFFENCES

1. **Scots law recognises three "inchoate offences": incitement, conspiracy and attempt:**

    ➢ *Cawthorne v HM Advocate* (1968): the mens rea of an attempted crime is the same as for the completed crime. A person can be committed of an attempt without intending to commit the relevant crime.

ART AND PART LIABILITY

1. **Where a person does not wholly commit an offence themselves, but does so along with other people, they may be guilty of the complete offence "art and part". There are two requirements for this: first, a common purpose between the different actors, and secondly, actual participation. Merely watching a crime does not make a person guilty of it.**

DEFENCES

1. **A person must be acquitted if they were "at the time of the conduct unable by reason of mental disorder to appreciate the nature or wrongfulness of [their] conduct":**

    ➢ Section 51A of the Criminal Procedure (Scotland) Act 1995 sets out this definition.

2. **A person will be entitled to the defence of automatism where (a) they were suffering from a total alienation of reason, (b) as the result of an external factor and (c) they were not bound to foresee that factor. Voluntary intoxication is not a defence under Scots law:**

    ➢ *Ross v HM Advocate* (1991): the court recognised the defence of automatism and set out the criteria required for it to succeed.

3. **A person will be entitled to the defence of self-defence if (a) there was imminent danger to life or limb (either their own, or that of another person); (b) the force they used was necessary in the circumstances, and (c) there was no means of escape or retreat available:**

    ➢ *HM Advocate v Doherty* (1954) sets out these criteria.

4. **A person will be entitled to the defence of coercion where (a) they committed a crime as the result of threats of death or serious injury and (b) the threats were "of such a nature as to overcome the resolution of an ordinarily constituted person of the same age and sex as the accused":**

    ➢ *Thomson v HM Advocate* (1983) sets out these criteria.

5. **A person will be entitled to the defence of necessity where they commit a criminal offence in order to avoid a greater harm occurring, provided that there was immediate danger to life and limb and there was no "way out" other than committing the offence. The act must have a reasonable prospect of removing the danger.**

? QUICK QUIZ

General principles of criminal liability

- What are the elements of a criminal offence?
- In what circumstances does the law impose criminal liability for an omission to act?

Homicide

- What is the definition of murder?

- What are the various types of culpable homicide recognised by Scots law? How are these defined?
- What partial defences to murder are recognised by Scots law? How are these defined?

Assault

- It is said that "evil intention is of the essence of assault"—but what does this mean?
- Can you assault a person without physically touching them under Scots law?

Sexual offences

- What is the definition of rape?
- What are the other principal sexual offences recognised by Scots law?

Property offences

- How is theft defined?
- What types of property can be stolen under Scots law?
- Can embezzlement be clearly distinguished from theft?
- What is the meaning of a "definite practical result" in the offence of fraud?
- Is forgery a crime under Scots law?
- What criminal offences exist to protect the physical integrity of property?

Inchoate offences

- What inchoate offences are recognised by Scots law?
- Can it be a crime to attempt the impossible?

Defences

- How are the defences of insanity and automatism differentiated from each other?
- Is voluntary intoxication a defence to a criminal charge?
- What are the requirements for the defence of self-defence?
- What are the differences between the defence of necessity and the defence of coercion?

📖 FURTHER READING

The leading textbook on the criminal law of Scotland is G.H. Gordon's *Criminal Law*, which is now regularly referred to by the courts. The first edition of this book was published in 1967. A third edition (edited by Michael G.A. Christie) was published in two volumes in 2000 and 2001, along with a supplement in 2005. A detailed treatment of criminal defences is available in J. Chalmers and F. Leverick, *Criminal Defences and Pleas in Bar of Trial* (W. Green, 2006). A more recent scholarly treatment of the criminal law in general can be found in P.R. Ferguson and C. McDiarmid, *Scots Criminal Law: A Critical Analysis* (Dundee University Press, 2008).

These are detailed reference works, and students approaching the subject for the first time would be well advised to consult a more concise introduction, such as T.H. Jones and M.G.A. Christie, *Criminal Law*, 4th edn (W. Green, 2008). Two revision guides are available: C. Connelly, *Criminal LawBasics*, 4th edn (W. Green, 2010) and C. McDiarmid, *Criminal Law Essentials*, 2nd edn (Dundee University Press, 2010).

C.H.W. Gane, C.N. Stoddart and J. Chalmers, *A Casebook on Scottish Criminal Law* (4th edn, W. Green, 2009) contains extracts from leading cases and statutory materials, accompanied by detailed commentary. It can be used as a supplement to a more traditional textbook or as a standalone text on the subject.

The Scottish courts will frequently make reference to older works on Scottish criminal law, which are considered (to varying degrees) to be authoritative. The leading work here is (Baron) David Hume's *Commentaries on the Law of Scotland, Respecting Crimes*, 4th edn with Bell's Notes (Bell & Bradford, 1844). (Sir) Archibald Alison's *Principles of the Criminal Law of Scotland* (W. Blackwood, 1832) and *Macdonald's Criminal Law*, 5th edn (W. Green, 1948) are also frequently referred to, but do not have the same high standing as Hume.

RELEVANT WEB LINKS

The Scottish Law Commission (*http://www.scotlawcom.gov.uk*) has undertaken a number of projects on criminal law over recent years, and is expected to continue to do so in the future. The (unofficial) Draft Criminal Code for Scotland is available via its website, where it is published as a consultation paper.

Chapter 7   Contract

ALEX GIBB[1]

▶ CHAPTER OVERVIEW

7–01 This chapter is concerned with the law of contract. It starts by examining the concept of a contract and the creation of legally enforceable obligations. The Scottish concept of promise is discussed, as this is a different type of obligation. The chapter goes on to consider the formality and validity of contracts. Illegal contracts and exclusion clauses are also discussed. The chapter then turns to consider remedies for breach of contract and how contracts are terminated.

✓ OUTCOMES

7–02 At the end of this chapter you should be able to:

- ✓ understand the principles relating to formation of contract;
- ✓ appreciate the difference between void, voidable and unenforceable contracts;
- ✓ identify the requirements of writing in relation to contracts;
- ✓ understand the rules relating to contractual capacity
- ✓ appreciate the effect of error on contracts;
- ✓ appreciate the factors affecting the validity of contracts;
- ✓ understand the enforceability of restricted covenants;
- ✓ understand the law relating to exclusion clauses;
- ✓ identify the remedies for breach of contract and their appropriate use; and
- ✓ understand the different ways in which a contract can be terminated.

INTRODUCTION

7–03 Contracts are all around us. They are part of our everyday lives. Much of the time, we enter into contracts without ever pausing to reflect on the fact that we are entering into a legal relationship, one which could have very significant consequences. We purchase snacks, we travel on the bus, we make use of a range of products and services; all the time we are entering into contracts. For many, the word "contract" has connotations of large-scale transactions or long-term commitments, but actually these types of contracts are the exception rather than the rule. It is important to bear in mind that the "little things" involve contracts too, and are in fact far more common.

At the risk of over-simplification, the basics of all contracts are the same, whatever the

---

[1] This chapter was originally written by Dr Alasdair Gordon, formerly Lecturer in Law, Aberdeen College, and has been updated by Alex Gibb, Lecturer in Law, Aberdeen College.

value of the subject matter. A contract is a binding obligation that can be enforced by the parties to it. Most contracts are not expressed in writing, although there are cases where writing is essential or desirable.

In Scotland, contract law is largely based on common law. Whilst there have been major statutory inroads in certain areas,[2] the basic law of contract has been developed by the courts rather than Parliament. In today's complex society, the trend is towards a higher degree of statutory or regulatory control. In the 1990s, the Scottish Law Commission presented five significant reports on various aspects of contract law that it saw as in need of reform. In that decade, the recommendations from only one of these reports passed into legislation.[3] In 2009 a draft "Common Frame of Reference" was published which seeks to aid the harmonisation of various private law areas across Europe,[4] and at the time of writing, the Commission is again undertaking a significant review of contract law.[5] These projects raise the likelihood of further reforming legislation in the future.

What is a Contract?

A much quoted definition of a contract is "an agreement which creates, or is intended to create, a legal obligation between the parties to it".[6]   **7–04**

Key Concepts

A contract has three **essential elements**:

(1) agreement about the same thing;
(2) at least two contracting parties; and
(3) "legal" obligations.

Unless all three elements are present, the agreement is not a legally enforceable contract.

Agreement about the same thing

In the traditional textbooks, this concept appears under the maxim *consensus in idem*[7] and   **7–05**
lies at the heart of contract law. If there is no real agreement, or the apparent agreement is really about different things, there is no contract. Say, for example, that Alfred owns two cars; a brand new sports car (which he has just purchased) and an old hatchback (which he wants to sell). Benny offers to buy Alfred's "car" for £5,000, with the intention of purchasing the sports car. Alfred accepts, with the intention of selling the hatchback. There is no contract at all here; although both parties might *think* that they have entered into a contract, they have not reached an agreement about exactly the same thing. The essential

---

[2] e.g. Sale of Goods Act 1979.
[3] Contract (Scotland) Act 1997.
[4] C. von Bar et al. (Eds), *Principles, Definitions and Model Rules of European Private Law: Draft Common Frame of Reference*, (Munich: Sellier, 2009).
[5] See, e.g. Scottish Law Commission, *Review of Contract Law: Discussion Paper on Formation of Contract* (The Stationery Office, 2012), Scot. Law Com. D.P. No.154.
[6] W. Gloag, *The Law of Contract*, 2nd edn (Edinburgh: W. Green, 1929), p.8.
[7] Agreement about the same thing.

consensus in idem ("consensus" for short) is lacking. In *Raffles v Wichelhaus*,[8] a cargo was to be transported on a ship *Peerless* from Bombay to England. Unknown to both parties, when the contract was formed, there were two ships of the same name in Bombay harbour, one sailing in October, the other in December. One party had meant the October ship, the other had intended December. There was no consensus, thus no contract.[9]

At least two contracting parties

7–06 Common sense dictates that it is impossible to have a contract between less than two parties. There is no legal upper limit, unless created by statute. All parties to the contract must also have the necessary capacity[10] (legal capability) to enter a contract.

"Legal" obligations

7–07 The agreement must create obligations that the law recognises as appropriate to enforce. The courts will not enforce agreements that are clearly illegal, criminal or immoral. However, there are agreements which are perfectly legal, but which the courts will not uphold. A so-called "social contract", such as a dinner date, is perfectly legal, but if one party fails to turn up, the disappointed host will not be able to take action to compel performance or seek damages. Social workers, counsellors and others whose provide personal or emotional support increasingly make "contracts" with their clients. Such agreements are intended to be moral, not legal, obligations so that the parties are clear as to boundaries and expectations on both sides.

Historically, the courts would not enforce betting and gaming wagers, called *sponsiones ludicrae*[11] or sportive promises. In *Kelly v Murphy*,[12] K was unsuccessful in an action against M, a pools promoter, for the prize money which K was due as winner of the pool. In *Ferguson v Littlewoods Football Pools Ltd*,[13] a syndicate completed pool coupons and gave them to a party who failed to pass them to Littlewoods. If the coupons had been received, a dividend of some £2.5 million would have been payable. The syndicate unsuccessfully sought payment. However, in *Robertson v Anderson*,[14] two friends played bingo together. One of them won the national jackpot. There was a longstanding agreement between the two parties that winnings would be split. This agreement was *not* a gambling debt, as it was collateral[15] to the wager itself. However, more recently the position was put beyond doubt with the passing of the Gambling Act 2005, which came into force in September 2007. The doctrine of *sponsiones ludicrae* has now been abolished,[16] meaning that gaming contracts are enforceable. (It is important to note, however, that the gambling industry is still subject to considerable statutory control.)

There is the occasional problem of the so-called "gentleman's agreement" or honourable understanding. In *Ritchie v Cowan & Kinghorn*,[17] R was unable to pay his creditors, C&K, in full but arranged to pay 10s. (50p) in the £1. C&K gave him a receipt stating that they were accepting his payment "*in full*" but added that it was understood that R would

---

[8] (1864) 2 H. & C. 906.
[9] See also *Mathieson Gee (Ayrshire) Ltd v Quigley*, 1952 S.C. (H.L.) 38.
[10] Considered further below.
[11] Obligations in jest.
[12] 1940 S.C. 96. See also *Robertson v Balfour*, 1938 S.C. 207; *County Properties & Developments Ltd v Harper*, 1989 S.C.L.R. (Sh. Ct) 597.
[13] 1997 S.L.T. 309.
[14] 2003 S.L.T. 235.
[15] Connected to, but separate from.
[16] Gambling Act 2005 s.335.
[17] (1901) 3 F. 1071.

pay the balance "*whenever he is able to do so*". These additional words were an honourable understanding and not legally enforceable.

FORMATION OF CONTRACT

A contract is formed (made) when the parties reach agreement on the essential features of **7–08** the bargain, i.e. when they achieve consensus. Either expressly or by implication, there will be an offer and an acceptance. This could be simply expressed as:
Offer + Acceptance = Contract

Offer

Offers may be made by using words such as "I hereby offer . . .", but often the offer may be **7–09** implied. Getting on to a bus and asking to be taken to a specific destination, is an example of a simple offer. If someone makes an offer, he is signalling an intention to enter into a binding contract. (It is important to contrast this with a willingness to negotiate, explained in the next paragraph.) The offer must come before the acceptance. Equally, there can be no acceptance unless there is an offer that is capable of being accepted. The offer may be made verbally, in writing, or by any other suitable means of communication, such as fax, text message or email. Some contracts require to be formed in writing.[18] If the offer is communicated through any of the above means, this is called an *express* offer. The offer may also be inferred from the actions of the parties, i.e. the offer is not express, but is by *implication*. If a customer goes into a shop, lifts up an item and hands the money to the sales assistant, a valid contract is formed: offer and acceptance are both implied. Equally, a vending machine permanently offers to supply a particular commodity. By placing the appropriate coin in the slot, the consumer implies acceptance. A self-service petrol pump similarly makes an open-ended offer, which is accepted by implication when a customer "helps himself".[19]

Contrast an offer with a willingness to negotiate

A proposal to do business is not the same as an offer. For example, Alison might say to **7–10** Brenda that she is thinking of selling her television for £100. If Brenda says she'll buy it for that amount, is there a contract? The answer is no; Alison was not making an offer, she was only indicating a possible willingness to negotiate. In fact, it is *Brenda* here who has made the offer, by clearly communicating that she will buy the television for £100. It is entirely up to Alison how she wishes to respond to Brenda's offer, including refusing it entirely and keeping the television after all.

Key Concepts

There is one hard and fast rule to which there are no exceptions: **an offer must always come before an acceptance**. To put this another way, no one can accept what is not on offer.

---

[18] Explained below.
[19] See *Chapelton v Barry Urban DC* [1940] 1 K.B. 532 where, in context, a contract was formed when a consumer helped himself from a pile of deck chairs.

Shops, in law, do not offer goods for sale: they merely indicate a willingness to negotiate, quite different from the open-ended offer made by a vending machine. It is confusing, of course, when shops display signs such as "special offer" when, in fact, they are not offering anything. Despite the usage of such terminology, a shop owner does not have to sell any goods against his will and has an absolute right to refuse an offer to buy.

> ### Pharmaceutical Society of Great Britain v Boots Cash Chemists Southern Ltd[20]
> #### [1952] 2 Q.B. 795
>
> Legislation required that listed poisons could only be sold under the supervision of a registered pharmacist. Such a poison had been sold in a self-service store. There was no pharmacist near the shelves where the goods were displayed, but there was a pharmacist at work beside the checkout. The question was—when did the actual sale take place? Was it (a) when the customer took the goods off the shelf; or (b) when the goods were presented at the checkout? The display of goods on the shelf did not comprise an offer. It was the customer who made the offer by taking the goods to the checkout. The sales assistant, as agent for the company, accepted the offer and the contract was thus formed, under the supervision of the pharmacist. B was not in breach of the Act.

Other good examples of willingness to negotiate are advertisements, or illustrations of goods in catalogues. It appears that prices displayed online also fall into this category; in the Singaporean case of *Chwee Kin Keong v Digilandmail.com Pte Ltd*,[21] a seller mistakenly under-priced a product with the result that orders were placed for 1,600 items. The court held that there was no enforceable contract as the buyers had knowingly taken advantage of the seller's mistake; it seems likely that the Scottish courts would take a similar view.

So, how is it possible to tell whether a particular statement is an offer (in which case it can be accepted) or a mere willingness to negotiate (which cannot be accepted)? As a rule of thumb, if the first party publicly communicates a statement that is *non-discriminatory*, that statement is likely to be an offer. The self-service petrol pump offers to supply petrol at the given price to whoever chooses to help himself. A shopkeeper, on the other hand, does not have to sell any item of his stock to a customer if he does not wish to.

Quotation of price

7–11   If a potential supplier of goods or services indicates the price of his commodity in advance, this will normally be taken to be an estimate or quotation, i.e. an indication of willingness to negotiate. In context, however, it could sometimes be taken to be a tender or an actual offer.

---

[20] See also *Fisher v Bell* [1961] 1 Q.B. 394.
[21] (2004) 2 S.L.R. 594.

Harvey v Facey
[1893] A.C. 552

H sent a telegram to F "Will you sell us Bumper Hall Pen?[22] Telegraph lowest cash price." F telegraphed in reply "Lowest price for Bumper Hall Pen £900". H then telegraphed to F "We agree to buy Bumper Hall Pen for £900 asked by you". H received no reply to his telegram, but argued that there was a valid contract. F's telegram was merely a statement of the lowest price at which he might be prepared to sell. It was not an offer to H, nor was it an affirmative reply to the question in H's first telegram.

By contrast, in *Philp & Co v Knoblauch*,[23] K wrote to P, oil-millers, "I am offering today plate linseed for January/February and have pleasure in quoting you 100 tons at 41/3d usual plate terms. I shall be glad to hear if you are buyers and await your esteemed reply". The following day, P telegraphed "Accept hundred January/February plate 41/3d". The telegram was confirmed by letter. K then attempted to recall his original quotation by sending a telegram to that effect. K's original letter/quotation *was* an offer to sell and not merely a statement of the current price. A contract had been formed by P's acceptance telegram. K's subsequent telegram was too late to have any effect.

There are always potential problems since the words "offer", "estimate", "quotation" and "tender" are frequently used loosely in colloquial speech. It is a question of interpretation as to what words actually mean in context.

Expression of intention

An announcement by one party that he has something for sale for which offers may be **7–12** made is normally only an indication of willingness to negotiate. In *Paterson v Highland Ry*,[24] the fact that a railway company had announced reduced rate tickets, for a particular period of time, did not prevent it from withdrawing the concession before the period expired. In *Dawson International plc v Coats Paton plc*,[25] directors of CP agreed to recommend to company members that an offer from DI to buy their shares should be accepted. The recommendation was duly made, but was later withdrawn when a higher bid was received from a third party. DI did not succeed in their claim for damages for breach of contract, since there was no contract. It is not easy to glean precise principles out of the case law.

If a party invites offers, such as is common in the sale of heritable property, he is not bound to accept any offer, even the highest. When property is advertised at a fixed price, this is no more than a willingness to negotiate. A prospective buyer may offer a lower or higher price. A sale by auction is completed by the fall of the hammer, or equivalent. At this point, the auctioneer, as agent for the seller (exposer), "prefers" (accepts) the highest bid (offer). Until that moment, the bidder may withdraw his offer. In *Fenwick v Macdonald Fraser & Co*,[26] it was held that the exposer was similarly free to withdraw his goods before the hammer fell. Occasionally, the so-called "referential" bid may be encountered in sealed

---

[22] "Bumper Hall Pen" was the name of a farm in Jamaica. The case came to the Privy Council by way of appeal.
[23] 1907 S.C. 994.
[24] 1927 S.C. (H.L.) 32. *Mason v Benhar Coal Co* (1882) 9 R. 883, the fact that a company had proposed to issue new shares, did not commit it to do so.
[25] 1993 S.L.T. 80.
[26] (1904) 6 F. 850.

competitive bids, such as an offer to "top" the highest bid by a specified sum, or by a given percentage. Bids of this kind were held to be invalid in *Harvela Instruments Ltd v Royal Trust Co of Canada Ltd*[27] unless the prospective bidders are all given reasonable notice that this method may be employed.

Withdrawal of offer

7–13 An offer can be withdrawn, in most cases, at any time before it is accepted. This is an important feature of offers and the period before acceptance when the offerer is still free to withdraw is traditionally referred to as *locus poenitentiae*.[28]

> ### Key Concepts
>
> If a **time limit** is placed on the offer and that limit passes without an acceptance, the offer automatically lapses. If an offerer undertakes to keep his offer open for a certain time, this undertaking will be binding. This is because, in Scots law, a promise can be a binding obligation and breach of that promise could give rise to a claim for damages.

In *Littlejohn v Hadwen*,[29] the solicitor for the seller of an estate indicated by letter that the potential buyer had an option to purchase which would remain open for ten days. This undertaking was legally binding. If, as in *Effold Properties v Sprot*,[30] the offer simply states that it must be accepted within a certain time, this does not count as an undertaking and the offerer can still withdraw his offer.[31]

How long does an offer last?

7–14 When a time limit is stated, the matter is clear. If the offer is not accepted within the time limit, it automatically falls. If no time limit is stated, the offer remains open for a "reasonable" time.[32] There are times when it is only fair to give the second party some days to consider the offer. Equally, there are occasions when it is obvious that an offer must be accepted promptly.[33]

In the following two cases, the original offer *had* lapsed due to the length of time. In *Wylie & Lochhead v McElroy & Sons*,[34] an offer to carry out certain iron work on a new building had not been "accepted" until five weeks had passed, during which time there had been a considerable rise in the price of iron. In *Glasgow Steam Shipping Co v Watson*,[35] an offer made on August 5 to supply coal had not been "accepted" until October 13, by which time coal had risen substantially in price. By contrast, the court decided in *Murray v*

---

[27] [1986] 1 A.C. 207, HL.
[28] Literally meaning "room for repentance".
[29] (1882) 20 S.L.R. 5.
[30] 1979 S.L.T. (Notes) 84.
[31] In *McMillan v Caldwell*, 1991 S.L.T. 325, it was held that a formal written offer to buy heritable property can be withdrawn verbally, provided the withdrawal reaches the offeree before he accepts.
[32] See, e.g. *Flaws v International Oil Pollution Compensation Fund*, 2001 S.L.T. 897.
[33] e.g. if the subject-matter is raw materials, which have a volatile price movement, or where perishable goods are involved.
[34] (1873) 1 R. 41.
[35] (1873) 1 R. 189.

Rennie and Angus,[36] that an offer dated June 10, to carry out certain mason work, was still open for acceptance on June 21.

Death, insanity and bankruptcy

Provided the offer has not been accepted, it will automatically lapse on the death, insanity or bankruptcy of the offerer, unless the latter was acting purely as an agent for another party. **7–15**

Acceptance of an offer

Key Concepts

If there is no **acceptance** of an offer, there is no contract. An acceptance must "meet" the offer, i.e. there must be consensus. If (and this is quite common) there are new or altered terms or conditions in the so-called acceptance, no contract has yet been formed. What the original offerer has received is confusingly called a "qualified acceptance". Without exception, a qualified acceptance never concludes the process of formation of a contract. **7–16**

The so-called qualified acceptance is really a new offer (or counter offer). A contract is only formed when an offer is met by an "unqualified acceptance", i.e. one in which no new or altered terms are proposed. It is the combination of an offer and an unqualified acceptance that results in the parties reaching consensus.[37]

In *Wolf & Wolf v Forfar Potato Co Ltd* [38] F offered, by telex, to sell a quantity of potatoes to W. The offer was open for acceptance by 5pm on the following day. W sent an "acceptance" by telex the following morning, but it contained new conditions. F telephoned W and informed them that the new conditions were unacceptable. W sent a second telex, still within the time-limit, purporting to accept the terms of the original offer. The court held that there was no contract. The first "acceptance" was actually a counter-offer that killed off the original offer. The original offer could therefore no longer be accepted. W's "acceptance" of the original offer was merely a counter-offer (qualified acceptance), which had never been accepted by F.

The acceptance does not require to repeat the offer word for word. It is sufficient that it shows acceptance of the offer as a whole. Like an offer, an acceptance may be either express or implied. In most cases, express acceptance is required in order to achieve consensus, but sometimes it may be implied, e.g. an order for goods may not require an express acceptance, since acceptance is implied by the act of supplying the goods. Acceptance can also *sometimes* be implied from a failure to reject an offer, but this can only arise if there have been similar dealings between the parties in the past. The law, in general, does not take kindly to contracts being imposed on people against their will.[39]

---

[36] (1897) 24 R. 965.

[37] *Nelson v The Assets Co Ltd* (1889) 16 R. 898. See also *Stobo v Morrisons (Gowns) Ltd*, 1949 S.C. 184.

[38] 1984 S.L.T. 100. Followed in *Rutterford Ltd v Allied Breweries Ltd*, 1990 S.C. 249; distinguished in *Findlater v Maan*, 1990 S.C. 150.

[39] The practice whereby certain unscrupulous traders would send unsolicited goods to persons, and demand payment if the goods were not returned within a specified time, was largely curbed by the Unsolicited Goods and Services Act 1971. Persons who receive unsolicited goods can keep these goods if the sender does not take steps to recover them within a certain period.

Method of acceptance

7–17 A person making an offer is entitled to state the method by which the acceptance should be communicated, e.g. letter, telephone or fax. If the precise method and/or time for acceptance is stated, it must be adhered to. If no special conditions are laid down, acceptance can be given in any competent manner.

Offers to the general public

7–18 As demonstrated earlier, an advertisement is not an offer, merely an indication of a willingness to negotiate. However, there have been rare occasions where the courts have decided that particular advertisements go beyond being mere willingness to negotiate and are really offers to the general public. The most celebrated occasion must be:

> ### Carlill v Carbolic Smoke Ball Co. Ltd
> [1893] 1 Q.B. 256
>
> CSB, through newspaper advertisements, offered to pay £100 to any member of the public who bought a patent preventative "smoke ball" and, having used it according to instructions, contracted influenza. C bought a smoke ball, used it according to instructions and still contracted influenza. She sought payment of £100. CSB refused payment, claiming that there was no contract. They submitted that the advert was no more than a willingness to negotiate and thus could not be accepted. This particular advertisement was held to be an offer to the general public. C had accepted the offer when she bought the smoke ball and used it according to the instructions. There was a contract between CSB and C and she was entitled to her payment of £100.[40]

The reasoning behind this decision was that C did not require to enter into any kind of negotiation. All she had to do was buy and use the so-called preventative. The advertisement was non-discriminatory so it was really an offer.

Withdrawal of acceptance

> **Key Concepts**
>
> 7–19 The general rule is simple. Once an acceptance is given, provided it is final and not qualified, it cannot be **withdrawn**.

The parties are now in a mutually binding contract. However, under the so-called postal rules (below), there is one interesting and illogical quirk in this rule.

---

[40] This case, though very famous, is somewhat of a "maverick". See also *Hunter v General Accident, Fire and Life Assurance Corporation*, 1909 S.C. (H.L.) 30.

THE POSTAL RULES

Offering and accepting

Where parties are negotiating *entirely* by post they rely on an agent, i.e. the postal service, **7–20** to convey offers, counter offers, qualified acceptances and final unqualified acceptances. Over the years, certain common law "rules" have been developed to regulate this situation—but it is always possible for parties to agree their own provisions or even for certain rules to be inferred.

Starting with the obvious—if an offer is posted, it must actually reach the second party (offeree).

Key Concepts

A potential problem arises as to when a posted acceptance actually achieves **consensus**. Under the postal rules, consensus is achieved when the second party posts his acceptance.

This acceptance rule is arguably unsatisfactory, in that the offerer can be in a binding contract without being aware of it; this is because the acceptance could have been posted, but not yet delivered. It has a further knock-on effect: if an offer is open for acceptance within a specified period, acceptance is effective if it is *posted* within that time limit. In *Jacobson Sons & Co v Underwood & Son Ltd*,[41] the offer stated "for reply by Monday 6th". The acceptance was posted on the 6th but it did not arrive until the 7th. The offer *had* been accepted on time, because the reply had been in the hands of the Post Office on the 6th.

Withdrawal of offer

An offerer might post his offer and then have second thoughts and wish to withdraw it. His **7–21** withdrawal is only effective if it reaches the offeree before the acceptance is placed in the post. In *Thomson v James*,[42] J made a written offer to buy an estate from T. Some days later, T posted an acceptance. On the same day on which T posted his acceptance, J posted a letter withdrawing his offer. There was a binding contract since consensus had been achieved when T posted his acceptance. J was too late to withdraw his offer.

Withdrawal of acceptance

From the point of logic, the above rules ought to mean that once an acceptance is posted, **7–22** it is irrevocable since consensus has been achieved. However, there appears to be a quirk in the law, based on an old case of *Countess of Dunmore v Alexander*.[43] A wrote to D, offering her services as a maid-servant. On November 5th, D wrote to A accepting her offer. On the 6th, D changed her mind and wrote to A withdrawing her acceptance. A received both

---

[41] (1894) 21 R. 654.
[42] (1855) 18 D. 1.
[43] (1830) 9 S. 190.

letters at the same time. The court decided that D's withdrawal of acceptance was effective: there was no contract.[44]

Contracts not covered by the postal rules

7–23 In contracts made with overseas parties, if they are made under the Uniform Laws on International Sales Act 1967, the postal rules do not apply, so the contract will only be formed when an acceptance arrives in the office of the offering party.

The postal rules do not apply to communications made by telex, which are treated in the same way as oral communications.[45] An acceptance by telex is effective when it is printed out at the offerer's end. It is assumed that similar rules apply to fax. Modern technology throws up other problems in the use of email and text messages. An email does not come under the postal rules. There is regulation applicable to parties, who are not consumers, requiring the manner of setting up an electronic contract to be set out clearly and unambiguously.[46] This is an area of law that, potentially, will develop further.

PROMISES

7–24 A particular feature of the Scottish law of obligations is the possibility of a binding agreement even when nothing is asked in return. Most contracts contain an element of reciprocity, i.e. both parties will give and take something of value. This is usually referred to as "consideration". The tradition, in English law, is that if there is no element of consideration, the contract is not legally enforceable.[47]

Key Concepts

In Scotland, consideration is not an absolute requirement for an undertaking to be **legally binding**. An obligation to do or give something gratuitously can be as enforceable as any mutual contract. In *Morton's Trustees v Aged Christian Friend Society of Scotland*,[48] M wrote to a new charitable society, offering to provide pensions for elderly people, funded by annual capital payments. The obligation to meet these payments was a binding contract.

In law, however, there is a general presumption against donation. Also, mere verbal promises are not legally enforceable in every case. Under the Requirements of Writing (Scotland) Act 1995[49] writing is required to constitute a gratuitous unilateral obligation, except where undertaken in the course of a business.

---

[44] If the acceptance had reached A before the recall, there would have been a contract. The Scottish Law Commission has recommended the abolition of the postal rules (Scottish Law Commission, *Report on the Formation of Contract: Scottish Law and the United Nations Convention on Contracts for the International Sale of Goods* (1993), Scot. Law Com. No.144).

[45] *Brinkibon Ltd v Stahag Stahl* [1983] 2 A.C. 34.

[46] The Electronic Commerce (EC Directive) Regulations 2002 (SI 2002/2013). Consumers who buy goods and services "at a distance" have important protection under the Consumer Protection (Distance Selling) Regulations 2000 (SI 2000/2334).

[47] *Stilk v Myrick* (1809) 2 Camp. 317.

[48] (1899) 2 F. 82.

[49] Requirements of Writing (Scotland) Act 1995 s.1(2)(a)(ii).

It appears that a true gratuitous *contract*, as distinct from a gratuitous unilateral obligation, does not require to be in writing.[50]

THE REQUIREMENTS OF WRITING

The general rule is that no special formalities are required for parties to enter into a **7–25** contractual obligation. There are, however, exceptions to this general rule and some contracts do require writing for their constitution. Until August 1, 1995, when the Requirements of Writing (Scotland) Act 1995 came into force, there were certain contracts, known as the *obligationes literis*, which required to be expressed in writing.

Under the 1995 Act, this entire area of law was modernised.[51] A written document is required[52] for: (i) creation, variation or extinction of an interest in land[53]; (ii) gratuitous unilateral obligations, unless undertaken in the course of business; (iii) creation of a trust where a person declares himself to be sole trustee of his own property.[54]

Key Concepts

Under the 1995 Act a document is **formally valid if it is subscribed by the granter**. In other words, a simple signature is sufficient formality to make the document binding. Thus most contracts only require the signatures of the parties.

If a document is to be regarded as self proving[55] it requires to be attested. This means it is signed, or the signature is acknowledged, by the granter before one witness aged at least 16, who signs as a witness. If a document is not self proving, i.e. if the signature was not witnessed, an application can be made to the sheriff court to give it self proving status should that be required.

In the case of a basic contract, a signature is required on the last page. Annexations, such as plans or schedules, only require to be signed if the contract relates to land. However, an annexation is only incorporated into any contract if it is referred to in the main document and identified on its face as being the annexation referred to. This rule applies whether the annexation requires to be signed or not.[56]

Personal bar

If a contract requires to be in writing, but is not (or is only partly in writing) and the party **7–26** "loyal" to the defective contract (i.e. who wants it to continue, called the "first party" in the Act) acts, or refrains from acting, with the knowledge and acquiescence of the other party (the "second party"), the latter is said to be *personally barred* from withdrawing from the contract on the grounds of lack of writing. Personal bar will only operate if the

---

[50] This distinction between the two can be obscure. See *Bathgate v Rosie*, 1976 S.L.T. (Sh. Ct) 16.
[51] The old law continues to apply to documents executed before the 1995 Act came into force.
[52] 1995 Act s.1(2).
[53] With the exception of leases of not more than one year's duration.
[54] There are also statutory instances where certain documents (not all of them contracts) require writing, e.g. testamentary documents, life assurance, bills of exchange, hire purchase and regulated credit agreements.
[55] When a document is self proving, its subscription is presumed valid without need for further evidence.
[56] It is easy to overlook this requirement.

position of the first party has been materially affected by his own actings and would be similarly affected if the second party were allowed to withdraw from the contract.[57]

Electronic communication

7–27 The Electronic Communications Act 2000 made provision for electronic communication to be recognised as the equivalent of a written document, including the possibility of electronic signatures. It will be for the court to decide, in a particular case, whether an electronic signature has been correctly used and what weight it should be given. It is open to businesses to contract with each other about how they are to treat each other's electronic communications

VALIDITY OF CONTRACTS

> **Key Concepts**
>
> **7–28** Parties may have a contract which is **ex facie**[58] valid but which, in some way, is **defective**. Depending on the form of the defect, the contract may turn out to be:
>
> - void;
> - voidable;
> - unenforceable.

Void contracts

7–29 A contract is void if, for any reason, true consent[59] is lacking. Strictly speaking, it is illogical to refer to any contract as void. If a contract is void, there is no contract.[60]

Lack of true consent may arise in a number of situations. It might be that one or both of the parties is not recognised in law as having the required capacity to give consent, e.g. young children or insane persons. Lack of consent could also arise where there is serious misunderstanding about the subject-matter of the contract.[61]

If an apparently valid contract is void, for whatever reason, it has no legal effect and must be treated as though it has never existed. The contract will not (indeed, it cannot) be enforced by the courts, and will not confer any rights on the parties. Thus, if Colin purports to sell his bicycle to Daniel and the contract of sale is void (for whatever reason), the bicycle still belong to Colin, even if Daniel has paid full value.

Third parties (those who subsequently become involved) may also be affected if a contract is void. Even though third parties act in good faith, they cannot acquire rights either. If Daniel in the meantime had sold the bicycle to Eddie (the third party) who paid for it and acted in good faith, the bicycle nevertheless still belongs to Colin.[62]

---

[57] A concise account of the various categories of personal bar can be found in A. Gibb & A. Gordon, *Contract Law Basics*, 3rd edn (W. Green, 2009), Ch.2.

[58] On the face of it.

[59] i.e. the element of consensus.

[60] Law is not an exact science, nor is it always logical.

[61] As in *Raffles v Wichelhaus* (1864) 2 H. & C. 906.

[62] Whilst this may seem unfair on the face of it, it should be noted that Eddie can sue Daniel for return of the he has money paid, and equally Daniel can sue Colin to get his money back. No-one (in theory at least) should lose out.

A simple example of a void contract is where the subject-matter is stolen goods, which will always belong to their original owner no matter how much time has elapsed nor on how many occasions they have changed hands.

O'Neill v Chief Constable of Strathclyde
1994 S.C.L.R. 253

One car was exchanged (bartered) for another car which turned out to have been stolen. The car which had *not* been stolen was sold to a third party who took in good faith and for value. Because one stolen car had been involved, the original contract of barter was void. The third party could not acquire rights to the non-stolen car.

Voidable contracts

If a defect in a contract does not strike at the root of the agreement, and so does not **7–30** remove the basic consensus, the contract is not void, merely voidable. A contract could also be voidable because of some defect in its formation, e.g. if a contract for the sale of a house is not in writing. A voidable contract is not invalid and it could still be honoured by the parties to it, or personal bar might operate.

In other words, if a contract is voidable, it is valid until steps are taken to have it set aside or "avoided".[63] The parties have two options: either they can ignore the defect and treat the obligation as fully binding or one of them can use the defect as a means of getting out of the contract.

The right to cancel a voidable contract may be lost in certain cases, such as where the parties cannot restore each other to their former positions, known as restitutio in integrum.[64] The involvement of a third party can also remove the right to avoid a voidable contract. This is because, unlike with a void contract, if goods, property or rights which have changed hands under a voidable contract are subsequently transferred to a third party, that party *does* acquire ownership of them, so long as he has acted in good faith and for value and, at the time of transfer, the original contract has not been avoided. (This is an extremely important difference between the rights acquired under a void contract and under a voidable contract.) The knock-on effect is that the original voidable contract can no longer be cancelled.

For example, say this time Cheryl is selling her bicycle to Donna, but the contract is voidable; Donna will acquire ownership rights to the bicycle, so long as neither party takes step to avoid the contract. Further, if Donna then sells the bicycle to Evelyn, Evelyn will acquire rights and the original contract can no longer be avoided.

Unenforceable contracts

These are contracts that are not necessarily void, nor voidable, but, because of their **7–31** nature, cannot be enforced in the courts. The obvious examples are social agreements, dealt with earlier.

The main reasons for a contract being either void, or voidable,[65] are lack of contractual capacity, error, misrepresentation and illegality.

---

[63] Which basically means "cancelled".
[64] Entire restoration.
[65] Apart from the requirements of writing, considered above.

CONTRACTUAL CAPACITY

7–32 The capacity, i.e. the legal capability, of certain persons to make a contract may be limited either at common law or by statute, because it is considered, for one reason or another, that they cannot give valid consent.

Children and young people

7–33 The Age of Legal Capacity (Scotland) Act 1991 came into force on September 25, 1991. The centuries old division, of young people under the age of majority into pupils and minors, disappeared and a new single tier system took its place.

> **Key Concepts**
>
> Young people **under the age of 16** ("children") have *no* contractual capacity subject to certain exceptions.

"Reasonable transactions" commonly entered into by persons of the child's age and circumstances are valid.[66] These would include children buying items such as sweets, or travelling on a bus. A positive aspect of the 1991 Act is the element of flexibility through age and circumstances, recognising that growing up is a gradual process. A nine-year-old is unlikely to be spending large sums of money, whereas a 15-year-old could have substantial spending power.

> **Key Concepts**
>
> Young people **aged 16 and 17** have full contractual capacity, although transactions which cause them "substantial prejudice" may be set aside on application to the court.

The young person has until age 21 in which to apply for court protection. The court would only set aside a transaction if an adult exercising reasonable prudence would not have entered into it and it has caused, or is likely to cause, substantial prejudice to the applicant.[67] This does not imply that any contract that does not work out as well as expected, can be easily set aside.

Parties might well be ultra-cautious about entering into a transaction with any young person aged between 16 and 17, particularly if buying heritable property. The Act[68] introduces a procedure for making a proposed transaction unchallengeable by application to the sheriff court. The decision of the sheriff is final.

---

[66] 1991 Act s.2(1).
[67] 1991 Act s.3(2).
[68] 1991 Act s.4.

Insane persons

At common law, an insane[69] person has no capacity to contract, although he must pay a **7–34** reasonable price for "necessaries". Traditionally, someone certified insane might have had a curator bonis[70] appointed by the court and all contracts would made through him.

The Adults with Incapacity (Scotland) Act 2000 (as amended) provides a whole new mechanism for regulating this difficult area. A responsible person (referred to as a guardian) can be appointed, whose function is to make decisions relating to the adult's property, financial affairs or personal welfare.[71] Applications for appointment of a curator bonis are no longer competent. Section 1 of the 2000 Act outlines the fundamental principles of the legislation, among which are: that there must be no intervention unless it is for the benefit of the adult and the outcome cannot be achieved in any other way; so far as is possible, the views of the adult must at all times be taken into account; and any intervention must take the least restrictive option.

Intoxicated persons

Intoxication, like insanity, is a question of fact and degree. As a general rule, drunkenness **7–35** is not a ground on which a contract is either void, or voidable, unless the drunkenness has reached the stage where the person has lost his reason and could give no true consent. There is no modern Scottish case in which a contract has been set aside on the grounds of intoxication.[72]

EFFECT OF ERROR ON CONTRACTS

Either or both parties to a contract, may have entered into it under some form of error and **7–36** this may well affect the validity of the contract. In the first instance, errors can be divided into two distinct categories:

- **Errors as to law**: These could arise where one or other of the parties was in error in relation to his rights, or to the legal effect of the contract. The general rule is that an error as to law does not affect the validity of a contract. There is a well-known legal maxim *ignorantia juris neminem excusat*.[73]
- **Errors as to fact**: One or both of the parties may be mistaken as to some fact connected with the contract, e.g. the price of the goods. Errors as to fact can affect the validity of a contract in different ways. What follows, hereafter, is an examination of the legal effect of errors of fact, in different situations.

Error of expression

Errors of expression can arise where there is no doubt what both parties meant but, owing **7–37** to a clerical error of a third party, the written contract is not expressed in the terms originally agreed by the parties. In *Anderson v Lambie*,[74] the owner of an estate, of which a

---

[69] Insanity is not a very precise concept at common law. In law, there is a presumption of sanity. The contrary must be proved or admitted.

[70] One who has a care of goods.

[71] 2000 Act s.57.

[72] For older authorities see *Pollock v Burns* (1875) 2 R. 497 and *Taylor v Provan* (1864) 2 M. 1226.

[73] Ignorance of the law is no excuse.

[74] 1954 S.C. (H.L.) 43. See also *Krupp v John Menzies Ltd*, 1907 S.C. 903; *Aberdeen Rubber Ltd v Knowles & Sons (Fruiterers) Ltd*, 1995 S.L.T. 870.

farm formed part, agreed to sell only the farm. Due to a mistake by his solicitor, the entire estate was conveyed to the buyer. As the disposition[75] did not give effect to the original agreement, the court reduced (nullified) the disposition, so that a correct version could be recorded in its place.

In some ways, this is not so much an error of fact, as a defect in the way in which the contract is expressed. At common law, there is equitable power to deal with such situations by reducing the written document. This requires an Action of Reduction in the Court of Session.

There is a simpler statutory procedure, under the Law Reform (Miscellaneous Provisions) (Scotland) Act 1985,[76] to rectify documents that fail to express what the parties had intended. An advantage of the statutory procedure, is the power given to the court to change the wording of a document. At common law, the court can uphold or reduce a document (or parts of it), but cannot change it. A statutorily rectified document is counted as though it had always been in its rectified state. There is protection of third parties who have acted in good faith in reliance on the document in its original state.

Error of expression can also occur when a person expresses an offer in terms that he did not intend and the incorrect offer is accepted. An example would be quoting a lower price than intended. If the person accepting the offer *knows* that there is a mistake, the contract is probably void. If he does not know of the mistake, the position is less clear and all one can say is that the contract could be voidable in some circumstances.[77]

If there is a faulty transmission of an offer, there will be no contract if the message delivered is substantially different from the original. In these days of fax and email, such problems are less common than they were when telegrams were sent down telegraph lines in Morse code.[78]

Error of intention

7–38 For there to be an error of intention, one or both of the parties must be mistaken as to the nature or subject-matter of the contract which they are entering. This area can be divided into three aspects:

> (1) unilateral error;
> (2) common error; and
> (3) mutual error (incidental and essential).

(1) Unilateral error

7–39 The general rule is that if the error is of one party only, this does not affect the validity of the contract. So, if a person with full contractual capacity freely and willingly pays more for something than it is worth or sells something for less than its true value, the contract cannot be cancelled on these grounds alone, unless he was the victim of fraud or misrepresentation.[79]

Both common error and mutual error, which are dealt with below, are sometimes said to be forms of bilateral error. The latter is a somewhat misleading term as it could be taken to imply that both parties must be in error, which is not always the case. If parties are

---

[75] The deed that conveys heritable property.

[76] 1985 Act ss.8 and 9.

[77] *Seaton Brick and Tile Co Ltd v Mitchell* (1900) 2 F. 550; *Wilkie v Hamilton Lodging-House Co Ltd* (1902) 4 F. 951.

[78] *Verdin Bros v Robertson* (1871) 10 M. 35.

[79] *Stewart v Kennedy* (1890) 17 R. (H.L.) 25; *Spook Erection (Northern) Ltd v Kaye*, 1990 S.L.T. 676.

genuinely at cross-purposes, they need not both be in error. Where both parties are in error, or have so confused the situation that they cannot have achieved consensus, these situations are more accurately classified as errors of intention.

(2) Common error

Common, or shared, error can arise when both parties have made the *same* mistake about **7–40** a matter of fact. To put it another way, they both share the same mistaken belief. If that belief is material and goes to the root of the contract, that contract will be void. A statutory example is where there is a contract of sale of specific goods, e.g. a particular painting, which, unknown to the seller, have perished at the time the contract is made.[80]

Where the common error was really just a matter of opinion, as distinct from an error of fact, the contract will be valid. In *Dawson v Muir*,[81] M sold certain vats to D for £2. Both parties were of the opinion that they were only of scrap value. Subsequently, it was found that they were worth £300. The contract stood.[82]

(3) Mutual error

This refers to a situation where, for reasons good or bad, the parties have misunderstood **7–41** one another. Each party thinks consensus has been achieved, but each has a different perception of what has been agreed. In such a situation, the courts will have to look at the terms of any written contract or the prior negotiations.

Key Concepts

If the **misunderstanding** does not go to the heart or root of the contract, i.e. is "incidental", the contract will stand, unless the error was induced by misrepresentation, in which case, the contract may be voidable. If, however, the error goes to the root of the contract, i.e. is "essential" (of the essence), the contract is void.

Incidental error

This form of error, also known as *error concomitans*,[83] refers to matters that do not go to **7–42** the root of the contract, or are only incidental. Incidental errors do not prevent basic consensus and, therefore, the contract will stand, unless the error was induced by misrepresentation, in which case the contract may be voidable. In *Cloup v Alexander*,[84] the manager of a company of French comedians hired an Edinburgh theatre "for their performances". The comedians subsequently discovered that it was illegal for them to perform in that particular theatre. They were still obliged to pay the rent. The error in this case was an incidental, or collateral, issue, namely what kind of act could be put on in the theatre.

---

[80] Sale of Goods Act 1979 s.6.
[81] (1851) 13 D. 843.
[82] There was a similar result in *Leaf v International Galleries* [1950] 2 K.B. 86, when both buyer and seller mistakenly, but genuinely, believed that a particular painting was a genuine work of John Constable.
[83] Collateral error.
[84] (1831) 9 S. 448.

Essential error

7–43 Where error is of the essence[85] of the contract there is no consensus and this makes the contract void, not merely voidable. Error is said to be essential "whenever it is shown that but for it one of the parties would have declined to contract".[86] Traditionally, essential error occurs in five possible situations, although these should not be regarded as final or watertight.

Subject-matter

7–44 This arises when the parties believe they are in agreement as to which item, or service, forms the subject-matter whereas, in fact, they have different things in mind. One of the classic cases is *Raffles v Wichelhaus*,[87] considered earlier.

Price

7–45 The fact that a price has not been fixed, does not make a contract void as a matter of course. If it has not been fixed (or some clear reference system put in place to ascertain the price), this usually means that the parties are still at the pre-contract stage of negotiation. However, it is possible for both parties to think that a price has been fixed whereas, in fact, they have different prices in mind. In such circumstances, the contract will be void.

If the goods cannot be returned to their original owner, the courts have power both at common law and by statute[88] to fix a reasonable price.

Identity

7–46 In many cases, it matters little with whom a party actually contracts. However, there are times when identity can be of the essence of a contract. There are certainly cases where *delectus personae*[89] applies; common sense indicates that if Frank wants his portrait painted by Gregory, he need not accept a portrait painted by Harold as a substitute (see further below on termination). But, in the case of less personal contracts, what would be the effect of Fiona thinking that she is contracting with Gillian but, in fact, is contracting with Harriet?

Morrison v Robertson
1908 S.C. 332

In this case, a confidence trickster named Telford ("T") introduced himself to M, a cattle dealer, fraudulently claiming to be the son of Wilson, a dairy farmer of good credit, who was known to M. T claimed authority from his father to buy cows from M on "the usual credit terms". M was totally deceived and gave the cows to T without hesitation, on the basis of Wilson's good standing. T had no intention of paying for the cows. He sold them on to a third party, R, who bought in good faith, without knowing that they had been improperly obtained. When M realised that he had been tricked, he made enquiries and found that the cows were in R's possession. The

---

[85] Also known as error *in substantialibus* (in the substantials).
[86] Lord Watson in *Menzies v Menzies* (1893) 20 R. (H.L.) 108.
[87] (1864) 2 H. & C. 906. See also *Scriven v Hindley* [1913] 3 K.B. 564.
[88] Sale of Goods Act 1979 s.8; *Stuart & Co v Kennedy* (1885) 13 R. 221; *Wilson v Marquis of Breadalbane* (1859) 21 D. 957.
[89] Choice of person.

original contract between M and T was void because of the error in M's mind as to the true identity of T. The latter had never owned the cows and could not pass ownership to R, the third party, even though R acted in good faith.

This case should be contrasted with:

MacLeod v Kerr
1965 S.C. 253

K advertised his car for sale. A con-man named Galloway, who told K his name was Craig, responded to the advertisement and agreed to buy the car. He wrote out a cheque and signed it "L Craig" and K gave him the registration document. The chequebook was stolen and the signature was a forgery. A few days later, Galloway, now giving his name as Kerr, sold the car to Gibson, a garage proprietor, who bought in good faith. In an action of multiple poinding,[90] K argued that there had been essential error of identity and that the car still belonged to him. The court held that the car belonged to Gibson, the third party. The original contract between K and Galloway had not been void, merely voidable. When the contract was formed, there was no error in K's mind as to the identity of the person with whom he was contracting: it was the man in front of him, whether he called himself Galloway or Craig. This was *not* a case of essential error as to identity, so *Morrisson v Robertson* was not applied. Even although the original contract had been voidable, it could no longer be set aside, because the third party (Gibson) had acquired rights.

There appears to be no single clear approach that is consistently being taken by the courts when considering whether to protect the third party purchaser or the original seller. There is something of a lack of Scottish authority but, in England, several subsequent cases have favoured the decision reached in *MacLeod*,[91] whilst a more recent case has followed the reasoning of *Morrison*.[92] Perhaps the only conclusion that can be drawn from this is that each case of this type will be decided on its own merits.

Quantity, quality or extent

Some authorities suggest that this is an example of error as to the subject-matter (above) **7–47** rather than a distinct category of its own. In *Patterson v Landsberg & Son*,[93] P, a dealer, bought from a London dealer items of jewellery that appeared to be antique. In fact, they were reproductions. The contract was void. There had been a crucial misunderstanding as to the quality of the goods.

---

[90] A form of action used where the ownership of property is in dispute.
[91] *Phillips v Brooks*, 1919 2 K.B. 243; *Lewis v Averay* [1971] 3 All E.R. 907.
[92] *Shogun Finance Ltd v Hudson* [2003] UKHL 62.
[93] (1905) 7 F. 675.

Nature of the contract

7–48 This category of error can only arise in a written contract. It could arise when a party signs a document that he did not intend,[94] or in a capacity in which he did not intend.

However, the law is not generally sympathetic to individuals who, without being induced by misrepresentation, sign solemn undertakings and subsequently claim not to have understood them.

Royal Bank of Scotland plc v Purvis
1990 S.L.T. 262

A wife signed an undertaking as cautioner[95] for money lent by R to her husband. When he defaulted, R raised an action against the wife for payment of all sums due. The wife claimed she had signed at the request of her husband and that she was unfamiliar with business. Since the wife must have known she was signing a document which gave rise to obligations, the court could not look into what was in her mind when she signed and she was thus bound by it.

Although the courts are unwilling to overturn clear written agreements, it was held in *Smith v Bank of Scotland* [96] that a bank is under a duty to advise a cautioner spouse to take independent advice.

MISREPRESENTATION

7–49 It could be said that misrepresentation is really part of error. It is fairly obvious that, in at least some of the cases already considered, the "misunderstanding" between the parties arose from the conduct or statements of one party to the other. If one party makes such a statement, and that statement is false, this is called a misrepresentation. Clearly, in many cases the party making the false statement does so knowingly, and can be said to be acting fraudulently. However, people also make misrepresentations with less blameworthy mindsets, and indeed a misrepresentation can be made entirely innocently.

Key Concepts

Misrepresentation arises in three distinct situations, which are partly self-explanatory:

- innocent;
- fraudulent;
- negligent.

Misrepresentation can have at least two effects on a contractual situation. First, if the misrepresentation induces an error on the part of the other party, and causes them to

---

[94] *McLaurin v Stafford* (1875) 3 R. 265.

[95] Guarantor.

[96] 1997 S.C. (H.L.) 111; this appeared to bring Scots law into line with the English case of *Barclays Bank plc v O'Brien* [1994] 1 A.C. 180. In fact, Scots law is still developing in this area: *Forsyth v Royal Bank of Scotland plc*, 2000 S.L.T. 1295; *Clydesdale Bank plc v Black*, 2002 S.L.T. 764.

do something they otherwise might not have done, the validity of the contract might be affected. (This is true regardless of whether the misrepresentation has been made innocently, fraudulently or negligently.) Secondly, if the party making the misrepresentation did so either fraudulently or negligently, the misled party might also have the right to claim damages. It is therefore worth noting that genuinely innocent misrepresentation does not give rise to a damages claim.[97]

Innocent misrepresentation

If a person makes a statement, honestly believing it to be true and unaware that it is false, **7–50** the misrepresentation counts as innocent, provided it is not actually negligent. If the error induced by the innocent misrepresentation goes to the root of the contract (i.e. it is an "essential" error as discussed previously), the contract will be void. If the error is non-essential, the contract it will be voidable. Before a contract can be reduced on the grounds of innocent misrepresentation, the misrepresentation must have been more than merely trivial and must have been relied on by the party misled, inducing him to enter the said contract. In addition, the party wishing to reduce must be in a position to give restitutio in integrum.[98] If this is not possible, the contract will generally have to stand.

> ### Boyd & Forest v Glasgow & South Western Railway Co. (No.1)
> 1912 S.C. (H.L.) 93
>
> B, contracting engineers, agreed to build a new stretch of railway track for G. The price was fixed by B at £243,000 based on data provided by G. B subsequently found that the information was materially inaccurate, making the work more difficult and expensive. The original data had been the work of independent surveyors and were accurate. However, G's own engineer disagreed with some of the figures and had altered them in good faith. Despite many problems, B completed the track at a cost of £379,000. B sued G for damages claiming they been supplied with misleading information, inducing them to enter the contract by fraudulent misrepresentation. The House of Lords held there was no fraud. G's engineer had altered the figures only because he honestly believed them to be inaccurate. Any misrepresentation was innocent and no damages could be awarded.

Fraudulent misrepresentation

Like innocent misrepresentation, fraudulent misrepresentation may induce error, making **7–51** the contract void or voidable. (If the error is essential, the contract is void, otherwise it is voidable.) The more relevant question, then, is whether fraudulence can be proven and therefore allow a damages claim to be made. Statements of exaggeration such as might be used in advertising (commonly known as "trade puffs" or *verba jacantia*[99]) are allowed some degree of latitude in practice, since few people take claims such as "good value" or "superior quality" too seriously; although legislation imposes criminal sanctions where

---

[97] *Ferguson v Wilson* (1904) 6 F. 779.
[98] Entire restoration to the original position.
[99] Words thrown about.

there is material misdescription of goods or services.[100] It is not fraud to express a genuinely held opinion, even if it is wrong, although nowadays this could give rise to an action on the grounds of negligent misrepresentation. In *Hamilton v Duke of Montrose*,[101] a statement which had been made about the capability of certain land to sustain a particular number of livestock turned out to be incorrect. There had not been any misrepresentation of fact, merely a statement of opinion. The contract was valid.

Where a statement of opinion, which turns out to be wrong, is made in the course of business and, in context, is reasonably relied on, it may count as a misrepresentation. (Though it is more likely to be counted as negligent than fraudulent.) A statement of pure future intention such as "I am hoping to expand my business over the next five years" is not a misrepresentation since, as a pure future statement, it is neither true nor false. If, however, a future statement relies on some present fact and is unreliable, it is not "pure" and may count as misrepresentation.[102]

Misrepresentation is not fraudulent unless it was known to be untrue and conscious dishonesty must be proved. Mere carelessness is not fraud, but it may amount to negligence. *Bile Bean Manufacturing Co v Davidson*[103] gives a classic example of fraud. B advertised "Bile Beans" as being manufactured from secret ingredients, previously known only to Australian Aborigines. These claims were totally fictitious.

In *Derry v Peek*,[104] directors of a tramways company issued a share prospectus stating that the company had the right to use steam power in its trams. D bought shares on the strength of that statement. In fact, the company was only entitled to use steam power if it was issued with a Board of Trade certificate. The Board declined to issue such a certificate. D failed in his action for damages against the directors of the company, since the court accepted the directors' submission that the statement had been made in the honest belief that it was true, even though the directors had not taken all reasonable care to check their statements.[105]

Reference is made above to the 1912 case of *Boyd & Forest*. Having lost their first action, B raised a second action,[106] this time for reduction of the original contract claiming that G's innocent misrepresentation made it voidable. If B had succeeded in they could have claimed the *actual* cost of the railway. The House of Lords was not convinced that there had been any misrepresentation. Even if there had been, B's claim failed. B had not proved that the alleged misrepresentation had actually induced them to enter the contract.

Today, no contractor would give a fixed price on such a large undertaking. If a similar situation did arise, an action would probably be on the grounds of negligent misrepresentation.

Negligent misrepresentation

7–52 This area of law has developed in more recent times.

---

[100] Consumer Protection from Unfair Trading Regulations 2008.
[101] (1906) 8 F. 1026; *Flynn v Scott*, 1949 S.C. 442.
[102] *British Airways Board v Taylor* [1976] 1 All E.R. 65.
[103] (1906) 8 F. 1181.
[104] (1889) App. Cas. 337.
[105] The law on company prospectuses was changed by statute shortly afterwards.
[106] *Boyd & Forest v Glasgow & South Western Railway (No.2)*, 1915 S.C. (H.L.) 20.

> **Key Concepts**
>
> A representation is **negligent** if the person making it failed to take reasonable care in making the representation *and* he was under a legal duty to do so.

A foundation case is:

> **Hedley Byrne & Co Ltd v Heller & Partners Ltd**
> [1964] A.C. 465
>
> HB were advertising agents. They were asked by Easipower Ltd to arrange advertising. HB enquired into the financial soundness of E by requesting their own bank to write to H&P, bankers to E. H&P stated that E were financially stable enough to honour the contract. The letter from H&P was headed "Confidential. For your private use and without responsibility on the part of this Bank". In reliance on the information, HB placed advertisements. Shortly afterwards, E went into liquidation, leaving HB with a substantial loss. It was clear, from subsequent enquiries, that E had been in financial difficulties when H&P had made their reassuring statement. HB sued H&P, claiming negligent misrepresentation. The case established that bankers owe a duty of care in answering such enquiries where it is clear that recipients rely on them.

Although the case only dealt with a matter of delict, the basic principle was basic extended to contractual matters.[107] To put the matter beyond doubt, the Law Reform (Miscellaneous Provisions) (Scotland) 1985[108] provided that damages for negligent misrepresentation are recoverable in Scotland.

Silence or concealment as misrepresentation

When parties enter a contract, they normally do so after negotiating *at arm's length*. **7–53** Neither party is going to volunteer information, unless he has to. Say Ian is selling an antique vase for £200, and is approached by Jacob who offers to pay this price. However, unbeknownst to Ian, Jacob already has a buyer lined up who is willing to pay £500 for this exact vase. Jacob does not need to disclose this fact to Ian; as a general rule, contracting parties are expected to see to their own interests and satisfy themselves that they are striking a good bargain.[109] Although beyond the scope of this chapter, a buyer frequently has important statutory protection, particularly under the Sale of Goods Act 1979. What follows here is basically the common law position.

If a direct question is put, it must be answered truthfully, otherwise the reply could count as fraudulent. Problems can arise, however, when nothing is said. Can silence count as misrepresentation? In *Gillespie v Russell*,[110] G, a land owner, sought to cancel a lease of mineral rights he had given to R. R had known that the land in question contained a

---

[107] *Esso Petroleum Co v Mardon* [1976] Q.B. 801; *Kenway v Orcantic Ltd*, 1980 S.L.T. 46; *Foster v Craigmillar Laundry Ltd*, 1980 S.L.T. (Sh. Ct) 100.

[108] 1985 Act s.10.

[109] This is sometimes expressed in the maxim caveat emptor (let the buyer beware).

[110] (1856) 18 D. 677; *Royal Bank of Scotland v Greenshields*, 1914 S.C. 259.

particularly valuable seam of coal, but G had been unaware of this fact. The lease was valid as the concealment of such information by R was not fraud.

However, there can be cases in which silence is, in fact, a subtle form of mis-representation, as in *Gibson v National Cash Register Co,*[111] where G ordered two new cash registers. He was actually supplied with two second-hand machines, reconditioned to look like new. This was clearly fraudulent.

A potentially problematic area is where parties are "economical with the truth". In fact, half-truths can be every bit as misleading as complete untruths.[112] A second-hand car dealer might truthfully tell a prospective customer that a particular car has been "thor-oughly checked". But if nothing had been done to cure the many faults discovered by the check, the assurance would be worthless.

Contracts not subject to "arm's length" rule

7–54 Having established the general "arm's length" rule, there may be occasions where parties to a contract *do* require to make full disclosure to one another. Contracts which are not subject to the arm's length rule fall into two main categories:

Contracts uberrimae fidei[113]

7–55 Insurance, or partnership, are the two generally accepted categories. In all insurance contracts, the policy will be voidable if the party insured fails to disclose some material fact, which might affect the risk being undertaken by the insurer, even if the insurer did not ask a specific question relating to it. This is powerfully illustrated by the following case:

> **The Spathari**
> (1925) S.C. (H.L.) 6
>
> D, a Greek ship broker, resident in Glasgow, bought the *SS Spathari*, a Finnish ship at Hull, with the intention of selling her to a syndicate of Greeks at Samos. At the time, Greek vessels had great difficulty in getting insurance. D arranged with B, a Glasgow ship broker, that she would be transferred into B's name, that the latter would register and insure her, ostensibly as owner, until the voyage to Samos was complete. On the voyage, the *Spathari* sank. The insurance company was entitled to refuse payment on account of B's failure to disclose a material fact, namely the "Greek" element of the boat.

Contracts involving a fiduciary relationship

7–56 These are contracts where the parties stand in a relationship of trust to one another, e.g. parent and child, agent and principal, solicitor and client. Common sense indicates that such parties do not contract with each other as strangers. Solicitors have strict professional rules about making contracts with clients, outwith the provision of normal professional services.[114]

---

[111] 1925 S.C. 477.
[112] *Shankland v Robinson*, 1920 S.C. (H.L.) 6.
[113] Of utmost good faith.
[114] *McPherson's Trustees v Watt* (1877) 5 R. (H.L.) 9.

OTHER FACTORS AFFECTING VALIDITY

In the following cases, the validity of the contract is affected, as the consent of one of the **7–57** parties has been improperly obtained.

Facility and circumvention

A contract can be reduced where the party misled, is not insane, but is suffering from **7–58** weakness of mind due to old age or ill health, i.e. there is a "facility". Circumvention is the motive to mislead, falling short of actual fraud. If both factors are present and the party misled suffers some kind of harm, or loss, as a result of the contract, it is voidable. In *Cairns v Marianski*,[115] a frail elderly man was completely under the "command and control" of his son-in-law with whom he lived. The old man was inappropriately persuaded to sign over all his property to his son-in-law. The court reduced the contract.

Undue influence

A contract is voidable if one person is in a position to influence another and abuses this **7–59** position to induce this other party to make the contract to his disadvantage. In *Gray v Binny*,[116] a young man had been left a legacy by his father. His mother, aided and abetted by the family solicitor, unfairly pressurised him to transfer this property to her. Undue influence is most likely to occur in fiduciary relationships, such as parent and child, doctor and patient or solicitor and client, but it could take place in any relationship where there is some element of confidence. There is no need, however, to prove that the weaker party was subject to any facility.

Force and fear

Generally, if a contract is entered into because of force or fear, it is void through lack of **7–60** true consent. The threats may be physical or mental, e.g. "blackmail", and could be made in respect of a near relative as well as to the victim himself. In *Gow v Henry*,[117] a threat to dismiss a workman from his post, without just cause, counted as force and fear. However, a threat to do something legal, such as pursuing a legitimate debt, or asking a dishonest employee to resign rather than call in the police, is not force and fear. In the very old case of *Earl of Orkney v Vinfra*,[118] the Earl commanded V to sign a contract. V refused, but then did so when the Earl threatened to kill him. The contract was void.

Extortion

The general rule is that a contract is neither void, nor voidable, merely on the grounds of **7–61** being a poor bargain. In *McLachlan v Watson*,[119] M took a 10-year lease of a Glasgow hotel under an arrangement which was clearly a poor bargain. M died four years into the lease, but his widow was unsuccessful in her attempts to have it reduced. However, under statute the court has power to re-open and alter or set aside a credit agreement if it deems

---

[115] (1850) 12 D. 919; *MacGilvary v Gilmartin*, 1986 S.L.T. 89; *Anderson v The Beacon Fellowship*, 1992 S.L.T. 111.
[116] (1879) 7 R. 332.
[117] (1899) 2 F. 48. See also *Priestnell v Hutcheson* (1857) 19 D. 495; *Hunter v Bradford Trust Ltd*, 1977 S.L.T. (Notes) 33; *Hislop v Dickson Motors (Forres) Ltd*, 1978 S.L.T. (Notes) 73.
[118] (1606) Mor. 16481.
[119] (1874) 11 S.L.R. 549.

there is an unfair relationship between the parties, e.g. if the rate of interest appears to be extortionate.[120]

ILLEGAL AGREEMENTS

7–62 A contract must be lawful both in its objects and in the way in which it is performed. If either of these elements is not satisfied, the courts will not enforce the agreement. Such agreements are known as *pacta illicita*.[121] It is not necessarily criminal to set up such agreements, but the court will not enforce them, nor award damages in the event of breach. Some of these agreements would more properly be called unenforceable. The general principle is *ex turpi causa non oritur actio*.[122]

Another maxim in this area of law is *in turpi causa melior est conditio possidentis*.[123] Thus, the loss is allowed to lie where it falls, e.g. if a person pays money for an illegal drug, which is not supplied, he will not be able to take legal steps to recover the money from the drug dealer.

However, when the parties are not *in pari delicto*,[124] the court may assist the party who is less blameworthy.

Statutory illegality

7–63 An Act of Parliament can place a limit on the freedom of a person to make a contract. Sometimes it may even declare a certain type of contract to be illegal, making it null and void. However, the courts may give effect to rights which are incidental to the contract, to prevent one party from gaining an unfair advantage over another. In *Cuthbertson v Lowes*,[125] C sold L two fields of potatoes at £24 per Scots acre. This contract was void, as imperial measure was obligatory. Even though the court could not enforce the contract, C was entitled to the market value of the potatoes at the time of harvesting.[126]

Illegality at common law

7–64 A contract is illegal at common law if its purpose is criminal, fraudulent, immoral[127] or contrary to public policy.

Agreements contrary to public policy

7–65 Public policy is notoriously difficult to define. Some agreements are clearly against public policy, e.g. contracting with an enemy alien,[128] or interfering with the administration of justice. Less easy are contracts which seek to restrict a person's freedom to work or to trade, i.e. contracts in restraint of trade, although these are mainly governed now by the Competition Act 1998.

Closely related are restrictive covenants, which are governed by common law. A

---

[120] Consumer Credit Act 1974 ss.140A–140D, inserted by the Consumer Credit Act 2006 ss.19–22.
[121] Illegal agreements.
[122] No action arises out of an immoral situation; *Hamilton v Main* (1823) 2 S. 356.
[123] In an immoral situation, the position of the possessor is the better one; *Barr v Crawford*, 1983 S.L.T. 481.
[124] Equally at fault; *Strongman v Sincock* [1955] 2 Q.B. 525.
[125] (1870) 8 M. 1073.
[126] Contrast *Jamieson v Watt's Trustee*, 1950 S.C. 265.
[127] *Pearce v Brooks* (1886) L.R. 1 Ex. 213.
[128] A person or company from an enemy state in wartime; see, e.g. *Cantiere San Rocco SA (Shipbuilding Co) v Clyde Shipbuilding & Engineering Co Ltd*, 1923 S.C. (H.L.) 105.

restrictive covenant seeks to restrict a person's freedom to work where he pleases, for whom he pleases and in what line of business he pleases.

Key Concepts

The very general common law rule is that contracts in **restraint of trade** or **restrictive covenants** are void unless it can be shown that the restrictions are reasonable, both for the parties to the contract and for the public. The courts will also want to be convinced that the parties are contracting on equal terms.[129]

Agreements between employers and employees

A restrictive covenant seeks to prevent an employee from working in competition with his **7–66** former employer in the future. This may be part of the employee's contract of employment and normally will only take effect when the employment comes to an end. Even if the employee is wrongfully dismissed, the restrictive covenant may still apply. Such covenants are most common in service industries, or where there are trade secrets or sensitive information.

Key Concepts

The courts do not generally take kindly to an individual being **unreasonably restrained** and such an agreement will not be enforced, unless the employer can show that he is protecting his legitimate interests.

- It *is* legitimate for an employer to protect his trade secrets or his customer base.
- It *is not* legitimate to prevent fair competition.

If the courts are asked to uphold a restrictive covenant, it will have to pass the reasonableness test. Thus, the courts will look at all the factors involved, e.g. the type of business, radius or customer area, location and the status of the employee. The courts tend to interpret "reasonable" more strictly in the relationship of employer and employee, than between buyer and seller of a business (considered below). There is a large body of case law, of which only a sample will be given here.

In *Mason v Provident Clothing & Supply Co Ltd*,[130] M was employed as a salesman with P. The company had branches all over England, but M was employed only in a limited area of London. He had agreed that he would not become employed in a similar business within a radius of 25 miles of London and within a period of three years. As M was employed in a relatively minor capacity and, considering the dense population of London, the restraint was far wider than reasonably necessary and was unenforceable.

In *Fitch v Dewes*,[131] F was employed as managing clerk to D, a solicitor. F was well known to D's clients. F had agreed that he would not become engaged in the business of a

---

[129] *Schroeder Music Publishing v Macaulay* [1974] W.L.R. 1308.

[130] [1913] A.C. 724; contrast *The Scottish Farmers' Dairy Co (Glasgow) Ltd v McGhee*, 1933 S.C. 148 and *Rentokil Ltd v Kramer*, 1986 S.L.T. 114.

[131] [1921] 2 A.C. 158.

solicitor, within a radius of seven miles of D's office. This restriction was reasonable and enforceable. D had done no more than attempt to prevent his clients being enticed away from him. On the other hand, in *Dallas McMillan & Sinclair v Simpson*[132] the court refused to prevent an outgoing partner of a firm of solicitors from practising within 20 miles of Glasgow Cross.

An important factor is the right, referred to above, of an employer to protect his trade secrets. A classic modern example is *Bluebell Apparel v Dickinson*.[133] D was a management trainee with B, manufacturers of "Wrangler" jeans. Within a few months, D was in sole charge of one of B's Scottish factories. Shortly afterwards, he intimated that he was taking up a position with rival manufacturer Levi Strauss & Co. The court held that the two year, world-wide restriction in his original contract was reasonable; both companies operated on a world-wide basis, and D was in possession of trade secrets[134] which would be of value to a business competitor.

The courts have no power to change an agreement into which parties have voluntarily entered. Either the agreement stands or falls, as illustrated in *Empire Meat Co v Patrick*.[135] P was manager of a butcher's shop whose customers came mainly from within a one-mile radius. P had agreed that he would not set up business, nor work for another butcher within a five-mile radius of his employer's premises. This restriction was too great and thus entirely unenforceable. A one-mile radius would have been acceptable, but the court had no power to change the agreement.

If there are two parts to the agreement, one of which seems reasonable and the other does not, the court may be prepared to allow one part to stand but to delete ("blue pencil") the other part, provided the two parts are severable, i.e. capable of being separated and standing on their own.[136]

Agreements between buyer and seller of a business

7–67   When a purchaser buys the goodwill of a business, he will usually insist that the seller binds himself not to set up in competition within a certain area and/or time. The courts are more willing in these cases to enforce the agreement, but the test of reasonableness will still apply. The agreements must not cover a longer period of time, nor a wider area of operations, than is necessary. A famous case is *Nordenfelt v Maxim Nordenfelt Guns and Ammunition Co Ltd*.[137] N, the owner of a cannon manufacturing business, sold it to M and agreed not to engage in the making of cannon anywhere in the world for 25 years. As the business was unique and customers few, the restriction was not too wide nor contrary to the public interest, and was enforced.

Joint agreements between manufacturers or traders

7–68   These agreements, although not unknown in common law, are mainly regulated by statute and delegated legislation to protect the interests of the public.

The current law is found in the Competition Act 1998 and articles 101 and 102 of the Treaty on the Functioning of the European Union. Competition law is a subject in its own right and only a few basic comments can be included in this chapter. The 1998 Act

---

132 1989 S.L.T. 454; contrast *Stewart v Stewart* (1899) 1 F. 1158.
133 1980 S.L.T. 157.
134 A trade secret need not necessarily refer to a technical process. It could refer to any confidential information, such as the business of a bank: *TSB Bank plc v Connell*, 1997 S.L.T. 1254.
135 [1939] 2 All E.R. 85.
136 *Mulvein v Murray*, 1908 S.C. 528.
137 [1894] A.C. 535; contrast *Dumbarton Steamboat Co Ltd v MacFarlane* (1899) 1 F. 993.

introduced a requirement to interpret its provisions in the light of the competition law of the European Union. The Act covers, for example, agreements which: fix buying or selling prices; limit production, markets or investment; or which share markets or sources of supply. There is provision for exemption. The Act also set up the Competition Commission, taking the place of the former Monopolies and Mergers Commission.

Solus agreements

These are agreements between the supplier of goods and the distributor, or retailer, under **7–69** which the retailer sells only one brand of goods, in return for which he receives special discounts or privileges. Such *solus*[138] agreements are quite common but, if challenged, must again meet the reasonableness test. The relative bargaining position of the parties might also be taken into account.[139]

EXCLUSION CLAUSES IN CONTRACTS

At an early stage in the chapter, it was emphasised that, before anyone can claim that a **7–70** contract exists, there must be consensus. Sometimes, one of the two parties may have greater bargaining power than the other, and will try to bring conditions into the contract which the other party has no knowledge of, does not fully understand, or does not appreciate the significance of. The party with the greater bargaining power might attempt to incorporate an exclusion (of liability), or an exemption in his own favour by printing appropriate wording[140] on a "ticket", notice or display.

When a ticket is issued upon payment for goods or services, it can be viewed either as a receipt for the money paid, or as a voucher to claim the relevant property or services. The ticket may have conditions printed on it, or it may refer to conditions published elsewhere. Sometimes there will be no ticket issued, but a notice may be displayed on business premises, intended as a written clause in an otherwise unwritten contract. Sometimes, the clause will appear both on a ticket and on a notice.

Key Concepts

The purpose of an exclusion clause is to **exclude or limit liability**, particularly for negligence. Whether or not such a clause is effective depends partly on the nature of the ticket or notice displaying the conditions, and partly as to whether the other party's attention has been properly drawn to it.

Attempts to impose post-formation conditions

New conditions cannot be added after a contract has been formed, unless with the consent **7–71** of both parties. In *Olley v Marlborough Court Ltd*,[141] Mr and Mrs O made a hotel booking. On the wall of their room was a notice "THE PROPRIETORS WILL NOT HOLD THEMSELVES RESPONSIBLE FOR ARTICLES LOST AND STOLEN". They

---

[138] Alone, only.
[139] *Petrofina (GB) v Martin* [1966] Ch. 146; *Esso Petroleum Co Ltd v Harpers Garages (Stourport) Ltd* [1968] A.C. 269.
[140] e.g. "PERSONS ENTER THESE PREMISES AT THEIR OWN RISK".
[141] [1949] 1 K.B. 532; *Thornton v Shoe Lane Parking Ltd* [1971] 2 Q.B. 163.

locked the room and gave the key to the receptionist. A thief obtained the key and stole goods. The hotel management attempted, unsuccessfully, to rely on the notice on the wall. The condition was unknown to Mr and Mrs O until after the contract had been formed and was not part of it.

The nature of the ticket

7–72 For a condition printed on a ticket to be an integral part of the contract the ticket itself must be *more* than just a voucher or receipt. Usually a ticket is an integral part of contracts of carriage (e.g. a train journey) or deposit (e.g. left luggage) and the courts would expect a reasonable person to be aware that such contracts are normally subject to published conditions.

If the ticket is not an integral part of the contract and is merely a receipt or voucher, conditions printed on it will not generally be binding.[142]

Sometimes, even though no notice is given of a specific exclusion, a person may still be bound by it because he is aware of it due to previous dealings between the parties. However, before allowing this, the courts would have to be convinced that the previous dealings had been consistent.[143]

Was attention adequately drawn to the condition?

7–73 Even if the ticket is integral to the contract, the existence of conditions must still be adequately brought to the attention of the customer. If the conditions are not adequately drawn to his attention, the contract itself is still valid but the conditions on the ticket are not binding.[144]

Exclusions at arm's length

7–74 If parties who are in business elect to sign contracts at arm's length, they will be bound by them, subject to "standard form" contracts requiring to be fair and reasonable under the Unfair Contract Terms Act 1977, considered further below. In *Photo Production Ltd v Securicor Transport Ltd*,[145] S agreed to provide security inspection at a factory. One of their employees criminally started a fire in the factory, resulting in a loss of £615,000. The factory owners sued for damages. S successfully relied on a clause in its standard conditions which excluded liability in most situations including acts such as that of its employee.[146]

Signing a ticket

7–75 It would seem that if a person actually signs a ticket, he is presumed to have read and accepted the conditions, unless misrepresentation took place.[147]

---

[142] *Chapelton v Barry UDC* [1940] 1 K.B. 532; *Taylor v Glasgow Corporation*, 1952 S.C. 440.

[143] *McCutcheon v David MacBrayne Ltd*, 1964 S.C. (H.L.) 28.

[144] *Henderson v Stevenson* (1875) 2 R. (H.L.) 71. There was a similar result in *Williamson v North of Scotland Navigation Co*, 1916 S.C. 554, where conditions had been printed on the front of a steamer ticket but in the smallest typeface known. Contrast *Hood v Anchor Line*, 1918 S.C. (H.L.) 143.

[145] [1980] A.C. 827; *Ailsa Craig Fishing Co v Malvern Fishing Co*, 1982 S.C. (H.L.) 14.

[146] Subsequent developments in the area of employer's liability suggest that this position might not be followed nowadays.

[147] *Curtis v Chemical Cleaning & Dyeing Co. Ltd* [1951] 1 All E.R. 631.

> **Key Concepts**
>
> **Summary of exclusions through tickets**
>
> (1) An exclusion clause cannot usually be brought in through the use of a ticket if it is only a voucher or receipt. In contracts of carriage or deposit, parties normally understand that the contract will be subject to certain published conditions.
> (2) If it is more than a mere voucher or receipt, and the person knew that there were conditions but did not read them, he will still be bound by them if they are of the type expected in that kind of contract, subject to the Unfair Contract Terms Act 1977 ("UCTA").
> (3) If the person has actually read the conditions, he will be bound by them (subject to UCTA).
> (4) If he did not know of the conditions, he will only be bound by them (subject to UCTA) if they have been properly brought to his attention. In the light of decided cases, that seems to mean that either the conditions must be clearly printed on the front of the ticket or, if the actual conditions are to be found somewhere else, there must be a clear reference on the front of the ticket that this is the case.

UNFAIR CONTRACT TERMS ACT 1977

The title of this Act is misleading, as it does not cover all unfair contract terms—only **7–76** exclusion clauses. Under UCTA, certain exclusion clauses are declared void whereas others are subject to a test of being "fair and reasonable". The burden of proving that a term is fair and reasonable in its context lies with the business that is seeking to rely on it. UCTA only applies to attempts to exclude liability by businesses. In this situation, "business" includes companies, partnerships, sole traders, professionals, local authorities and government departments. It does *not* include individuals who act in a personal or private capacity.

Part I of UCTA applies to England and Wales, Part II to Scotland and Part III to all of the United Kingdom. The Act applies to the following types of contracts:

- **Contracts in the course of a business**:

    - *Consumer contracts*: where one of the parties deals in the course of a business and the other does not and the goods are of a type normally bought by a consumer.
    - *Standard form contracts*: the contract is only offered, or accepted, on the basis of the party's "standard" conditions. These, in fact, are often consumer contracts but a contract between two businesses can be brought into the provisions of the Act where it is "standard form" (see further below).

- **Contracts for the sale of goods: This includes goods bought under credit or hire purchase agreements.**
- **Contracts for the hire of goods: This would include moveable items, such as a car or television set, but not a lease of heritable property.**
- **Contracts of employment: This also includes contracts of apprenticeship.**
- **Contracts for services: This covers a wide area including services provided by a law agent, accountant, builder, dry-cleaner, car-park owner, bus company, left luggage.**

- **Contracts allowing entry to someone's property**: Included are items such as a ticket for admission to a sports ground, cinema, safari park, museum, swimming pool. Also included are parties who are given permission to enter property, e.g. to carry out repairs.

Certain contracts are, however, excluded from the Act. These include insurance and contracts for the transfer of an interest in land. A condition in a contract to which UCTA applies is void if it relates to exclusion of liability for death or personal injury. The condition is of no effect in other cases unless it was fair and reasonable when the contract was made. The contract itself is not voided, only the purported exclusion.

Unfair Terms in Consumer Contracts Regulations 1999

7–77 The above Regulations[148] came into effect on October 1, 1999 and were subsequently amended.[149] A consumer (a natural person acting outside his trade, business or profession) can avoid a term in a contract for goods or services by showing that it is unfair, contrary to good faith or causes imbalance to his detriment. This goes further than UCTA, which only deals with exclusions of liability.

The basic premise that parties are free to contract at arm's length is not affected. Thus if parties individually negotiate the selling price of a particular item at arm's length, the Regulations do not apply. However, they *do* apply to standard term contracts and to contracts of insurance.

The "battle of forms"

7–78 It is common for businesses when sending an order, i.e. an offer, to do so subject to their own standard pre-printed conditions. A problem could arise when the second party accepts the offer on its own standard form acceptance—but the terms of offer and acceptance do not meet and may even contradict. Sometimes each set of conditions may say that, in the event of a dispute, its terms will rule.

If a dispute arises, there can be major problems, not least whether or not a contract even exists. Usually the courts decide there *is* basic consensus, although that may not always be entirely logical. Frequently, the terms of the contract will be those of the party who "fired the last shot".[150]

REMEDIES FOR BREACH OF CONTRACT

7–79 At this stage, it is assumed that a contract has been validly formed and is free from vitiating factors. Fortunately, the majority of contracts are performed uneventfully, but there will always be some defaulters. When one of the parties to a contract fails to carry out his side of the obligations, he will be considered to be in breach of contract, unless the reasons for his non-performance are recognised as valid in law (e.g. supervening impossibility, considered later).

Breach can arise, in practice, in three different ways: total non-performance, partial performance and defective performance. When a breach arises, the "innocent" party has access to various "remedies" and other measures that seek to resolve the situation. The

[148] SI 1999/2083.
[149] Unfair Terms in Consumer Contracts (Amendment) Regulations 2001 (SI 2001/1186).
[150] *Butler Machine Tool Co v Ex-Cell-O Corporation* [1979] 1 All E.R. 965; followed in *Uniroyal Ltd v Miller & Co Ltd*, 1985 S.L.T. 101.

main remedies and defensive measures are: specific implement and interdict; rescission; retention; lien; and action for payment. In addition, the innocent party will often be entitled to claim damages for any losses he has suffered as a result of the breach.

Specific implement and interdict

An innocent party can ask the court for a decree to make the party in breach fulfil the **7–80** terms of his obligation under the contract. If the action is in the positive, i.e. to make the party in breach do something, the court may award a decree *ad factum praestandum*,[151] ordering the party to "specifically implement" what he agreed to do.

If the action is in the negative, i.e. to stop the party in breach from doing something he agreed not to do, the court may award a decree of interdict. If an employer wanted to prevent a former employee from working for a competitor, in breach of a restrictive covenant, he could use a remedy such as in *Bluebell Apparel v Dickinson*,[152] discussed earlier.

Interdict can never be used to enforce a positive obligation. In *Church Commissioners for England v Abbey National plc*,[153] AN intended to close a branch office. C, the landlords, considered this to be in breach of the lease. However, they were unable to make AN keep the branch open by means of the remedy of interdict. It is, however, possible to specifically implement a positive obligation in a lease to "keep open" certain premises, provided it is not impossible, nor unreasonable.[154]

If the party in breach wilfully fails to obey the decree, whether it be positive or negative, he puts himself in contempt of court, the result of which could be a fine or even imprisonment. In practice, the court will not lightly take these draconian steps.

Under Scots law, specific implement is, in theory, the primary remedy to which an innocent party is entitled in the case of breach of contract. In practice, it is not particularly common. In addition, there are a number of situations where the courts do not consider specific implement as an equitable or suitable remedy and will not grant a decree. The following are the main areas where a court will *not* grant a decree *ad factum praestandum*.

(1) Where the obligation is to *pay a sum of money*. A debtor in default could find himself in contempt of court and thus liable to imprisonment for non-payment. As a matter of public policy, debtors are not normally sent to prison. In Scotland, a creditor can enforce payment by simpler processes, such as action for payment and diligence.

(2) Where a contract involves *personal relationships*, e.g. employment or partnership. If A and B are business partners and B does not wish the partnership to continue, common sense indicates that there is nothing to be gained by A taking B to court and trying to force the issue.[155]

(3) Where the subject-matter of the contract has *no special significance in itself*, such as 100 bags of flour. The remedy for the innocent party would be to rescind[156] the contract, obtain the goods elsewhere and claim damages. An action *ad factum*

---

[151] For the performance of an act.

[152] 1980 S.L.T. 157.

[153] 1994 S.L.T. 959.

[154] *Retail Parks Investments Ltd v The Royal Bank of Scotland plc (No.2)*, 1996 S.L.T. 669; followed in *Highland and Universal Properties Ltd v Safeway Properties Ltd*, 2000 S.L.T. 414.

[155] *Skerret v Oliver* (1896) 23 R. 468 (a minister of a Presbyterian church) and *Page One Records Ltd v Britton (t/a The Troggs)* [1967] 3 All E.R. 822 (the manager of a pop group). Under employment legislation, an employee who has been unfairly dismissed may be awarded reinstatement by an industrial tribunal.

[156] See further below.

praestandum could be appropriate if the contract concerned a specific item, such as a unique painting, as that is said to have a *pretium affectionis*.[157]

(4) Where the contract is *illegal or impossible* to perform, or where the court could not enforce the decree, e.g. if the party in breach is furth of Scotland.

(5) Where, in the opinion of the court, it would be *unjust* to grant such a remedy.

At common law, an interdict can be obtained quite speedily on an interim basis. Although there is no such common law equivalent in the case of specific implement, there are appropriate statutory provisions under the Court of Session Act 1988.[158] In either case, the interim award is at the discretion of the court and without prejudice to its decision at a subsequent hearing.

Rescission

7–81 The innocent party may, in certain circumstances, bring the contract to an end ("rescind" it) without the need to go to court. Clearly, access to this remedy must be restricted, otherwise it would favour "hotheads" who might call off a contract for the most trivial of reasons.

Key Concepts

For **rescission** to be appropriate, the breach must be material and go to the root of the contract. An inappropriate rescission counts as a repudiation and can give rise to a claim in damages.

Wade v Waldon
1909 S.C. 571

Wade, a comedian, better known by his stage name "George Robey", contracted with Waldon to appear in one year's time at a Glasgow theatre. A clause in the contract provided that Wade was to give 14 days' notice before the performance and also to supply publicity material. He failed to do either. Waldon called off the entire contract, although Wade was more than willing to appear at the theatre as agreed. Wade *was* in breach of contract, but it was *not* a material breach and could not justify rescission on Waldon's part. The essence of the contract was Wade's appearing on stage, which he had always been willing to do. Waldon was thus liable in damages, as he had repudiated the contract.

Rescission, then, means the justifiable cancellation of a contract, in response to a material breach or repudiation by the other party. Repudiation is where, without any legal right to do so, a party indicates that he does not intend to perform his part of the obligation.[159]

---

[157] Literally, "price of affection" meaning that it has value in itself.

[158] 1988 Act ss.46 and 47.

[159] These definitions are favoured by the Scottish Law Commission, who also distinguish the often-confused term "resile" as meaning to withdraw from a contract lawfully in circumstances other than breach or repudiation; Scottish Law Commission, *Discussion Paper on Remedies for Breach of Contract* (The Stationery Office, 1999), Scot. Law Com. D.P. No.109, para.1.14.

Repudiation gives the innocent party the option to accept the repudiation as a material breach and rescind the contract, or to affirm the contract and insist upon performance (or do nothing and wait to see what happens).[160]

In any contract, both parties are bound to perform their respective obligations. The implication is that one party cannot insist on performance by the other, if he himself is not willing to carry out his part of the agreement. An employee is entitled to be paid for duties performed, but if he refuses to comply with the requirements of his employment, he cannot expect to be paid.[161] This is the case even if he genuinely (but mistakenly) believes his actions are justified.[162]

If the innocent party rescinds, he cannot then enforce performance of any part of the contract. He can only claim damages. In *Lloyds Bank plc v Bamberger*,[163] the innocent party rescinded and then sought certain interest payments, as specified in the contract. This was not possible since the innocent party had rescinded the entire contract and could not now seek to invoke parts of it. This decision is in line with the established principle of "approbate and reprobate", which means that a party cannot take advantage of one part of a written document and reject the remainder. However, provisions can be built into a contract which keep certain parts of it alive, even if the material parts are rescinded.

The central question with rescission is whether there has been material breach. Total non-performance would always be material, but if the innocent party still wishes the party in breach to perform, obviously he will not rescind as long as he believes that there is life in the contract. Parties may agree between themselves at the outset which breaches would count as material, and in some cases it will be clearly implied. Common sense dictates that a wedding dress would be required in time for a wedding. In such a case, it is said that *time is of the essence* of the contract.

Usually time is not of the essence, unless expressly stated or where circumstances, such as the involvement of perishable goods, make it clearly implied. In contracts for the sale of heritable property, payment of the purchase price on the date of entry is not of the essence.[164]

Parties are not expected to wait indefinitely for contracts to be performed. The normal practice is to issue a "warning" to the other side and, frequently, impose a reasonable time limit for performance.

Particular problems can arise where the breach is one of several stipulations as in *Wade v Waldon* (above) or involves defective performance. Just how defective does performance have to be to count as material breach? At common law, that is not always easy to answer.[165]

Retention

Retention is the withholding of performance by one party until such time as the other **7-82** party performs his obligations in full. Very often, this involves withholding monetary payment, e.g. a tenant may wish to withhold his payment of rent until the landlord carries out his legal duty to make the house habitable. This is useful where the breach is not

---

[160] *White & Carter (Councils) Ltd v McGregor* 1962 S.C. (H.L.) 1; see further discussion below under "anticipatory breach".
[161] *Graham v United Turkey Red Co*, 1922 S.C. 533 (an agent in material breach of his contract was not entitled to commission).
[162] *Blyth v Scottish Liberal Club*, 1983 S.L.T. 260.
[163] 1994 S.L.T. 424.
[164] *Rodger (Builders) Ltd v Fawdry*, 1950 S.C. 483. It is common for the seller to qualify his acceptance, by stating that time is of the essence as regards payment in full at the date of entry.
[165] Sometimes a statute itself may give guidance, such as the Sale of Goods Act 1979 s.15B.

material, or where rescission of the contract is undesirable. Retention, like lien (below), is not so much a remedy as a defensive measure.

There is an important restriction placed on retention in that, generally, it can only be exercised when the payment (or otherwise) being withheld is reciprocal to the obligation not being performed. A clear consequence of this is that in most cases one party cannot withhold payment due under *one* contract because *another* contract has been breached, or because there is a debt of some other kind due. (Although this situation might be remedied under the mechanism of "compensation", considered below.) More complicated is the situation where a contract involves a range of obligations; does failure to perform one obligation by one party justify the withholding of any and all obligations by the other? In *Macari v Celtic FC*,[166] M unsuccessfully argued that he was justified in failing to comply with a residence obligation in his contract because CFC had previously breached their implied obligation of trust and confidence towards him. However, more recently the UK Supreme Court has held that all obligations under a contract should, at least as a starting point, be regarded as reciprocal to one another unless there is a clear indication to the contrary.[167] Whether or not obligations under a contract are reciprocal is a matter that will seemingly be judged on a case-by-case basis.

Lien

> **Key Concepts**
>
> 7–83   **Lien** (pronounced "lean") is the withholding of property which would normally be delivered to the other party. There are two kinds of lien, general and special. The special lien is by far the more common.

A special lien allows a person who has done work on the moveable property of another, or has not been paid the purchase price of goods, to retain possession of that property until he has received the payment due. Say, for example, that Isobel takes her car to Janet's garage for repairs, but ultimately cannot pay the bill; Janet may retain possession of the car until payment is made. This is exercising a right of lien against these "special" or specific goods. Two other points should be noted:

(1) Lien is a possessory right. The car in the above example does not become Janet's property, it is merely in her possession. Furthermore, if Janet were to allow Isobel to take her car away without paying the bill, she cannot later re-exercise the lien.[168]

(2) A special lien can only be exercised against the goods that are specific, or special, to the contract.[169]

Much less common is the general lien, which allows the holder of the article to retain it until a general balance due by the owner of the goods is satisfied. Certain trades and

---

[166] 1999 S.C. 628.
[167] *Inveresk plc v Tullis Russell Papermakers Ltd* [2010] UKSC 19.
[168] *Hostess Mobile Catering v Archibald Scott Ltd*, 1981 S.L.T. (Notes) 125.
[169] For a modern case on lien that provides useful commentary on the subject, see *Wilmington Trust Company & Orix Aviation Systems Ltd v Rolls-Royce plc & IAE Aero Engines AG* [2011] CSOH 151.

professions have the right in law to do this. The courts do not favour extending these categories.

A law agent may retain title deeds and share certificates in his possession, until a client had paid his professional account. In *Paul v Meikle*,[170] Mrs D bequeathed property to her son. The will had been drawn up by M, her solicitor, who was also her creditor in respect of unpaid professional fees extending over many years. M was entitled to retain the will until his fees were paid.[171] When a document, or title deed, subject to a lien is the property of sequestrated debtor, the permanent trustee in the sequestration can require delivery of the document in question.[172]

In practice, it is relatively simple to defeat a lien over a document, where a duplicate or certified copy can be obtained. An accountant does not enjoy a right of general lien, although it is well established that he has right of special lien.[173] A banker has a general lien on bills of exchange, cheques and promissory notes belonging to a customer, provided these have come into his possession in the course of banking transactions. This general lien does not extend to articles left with the bank for safe keeping. An innkeeper has a general lien over a guest's luggage, pending payment of the hotel bill.

Although it is only a defensive measure, lien is common in practice and highly persuasive in making payment forthcoming. It is useful where the innocent party does not wish to rescind, or where it would be pointless to do so because he has, in fact, performed his part of the contract.

Action for payment

The commonest breach of contract is non-payment of money. A short delay in payment is **7–84** not necessarily material breach. There is sometimes a fine line between delay in payment and actual non-payment; thus rescission must not be exercised too hastily. In any event, it would normally be inept to rescind a contract unless parties can be returned to their original positions. Where the contract price is unpaid but goods have been delivered or services performed, the creditor can recover payment by means of a court action.

The Late Payment of Commercial Debts (Interest) Act 1998 has given rights to businesses to charge interest on late payment of money debts, due by other businesses or by bodies in the public sector. Whilst parties can contract out of these provisions, they can only do so *after* the creation of the debt.

Damages

It has been said that under Scots law, wherever there is an established breach of contract, a **7–85** claim for damages is always open. In the oft-quoted words of Lord President Inglis, "It is impossible to say that a contract can be broken, even in respect of time, without the party being entitled to claim damages—at the lowest, nominal damages."[174] Whilst modern authorities perhaps do not accept the position that a right to damages is automatic, is certainly seems that situations where there would not be such a right are rare.

---

[170] (1868) 7 M. 235.
[171] A solicitor's right of lien is well established, being traced back to the old case of *Ranking of Hamilton of Provenhall's Creditors* (1781) Mor. 6253.
[172] Bankruptcy (Scotland) Act 1985 s.38(4).
[173] *Meikle & Wilson v Pollard* (1880) 8 R. 69.
[174] *Webster & Co v Cramond Iron Co* (1875) 2 R. 752.

Key Concepts

The purpose of damages is simple: to compensate the innocent party for his loss and to place him in the position he would have been in had the contract been fully performed, in so far as money alone is capable of doing this.[175]

There are four important points to note about damages.

1. Damages are intended to compensate the innocent party for his loss, not punish the party in breach.
2. The innocent party is expected to take reasonable steps to minimise his loss.
3. Damages can only be claimed for losses actually caused by the breach.
4. Damages can generally only be claimed for direct and foreseeable losses resulting from the breach.

Loss, then, is a logical starting point. To assist in calculating the quantum[176] of damages, it is necessary to determine the innocent party's loss. A well-established method is to compare the innocent party's position as a result of the breach with the position he would have been in had the contract been properly performed.[177] There might, however, be some difficulty in assessing exactly what position the innocent party would have been in had the contract been fully performed. It is usual for this assessment to be made as at the time of the breach itself, but in one English case at least the courts have been willing to consider circumstances arising *after* the breach.[178]

It follows that if no loss is suffered by the innocent party, no damages can be claimed.[179] Although damages are most commonly claimed for financial losses, it is also possible to claim for mere trouble and inconvenience, particularly where no quantifiable financial loss can be proven. In *Webster v Crammond Iron* (quoted above), damages were awarded for breach of contract despite no financial loss being proven. More recently, in *Mack v Glasgow City Council*,[180] M was successful in claiming damages against her landlord based on the trouble and inconvenience she suffered as a result of the flat's damp problem. Indeed, the courts are showing an increasing tendency to award substantial damages even in the absence of quantifiable financial loss being proven, for example due to the disappointment caused when a wedding photographer fails to appear on the arranged day,[181] or when a holiday fails to match the reasonable expectations of the holidaymaker.[182]

The innocent party is expected to take reasonable steps to minimise his loss, otherwise his claim for damages might be restricted to the amount he could have claimed if he had taken such steps. For example, if a party is not supplied with goods, but then delays in purchasing suitable replacement goods elsewhere until the price has risen, his claim for damages will be restricted.[183] However, it should be noted that only "reasonable" steps

---

[175] This passage paraphrases the opinion expressed by Baron Parke in *Robinson v Harman* (1848) 1 Ex. 850.

[176] How much.

[177] *Houldsworth v Brand's Trustees* (1877) 4 R. 369; *Lonedale Ltd v Scottish Motor Auctions (Holdings) Ltd* [2011] CSOH 04.

[178] *Golden Strait Corporation v Nippon Yusen Kubishka Kaisha* [2007] 2 W.L.R 691, HL.

[179] *Wilkie v Brown*, 2003 S.C. 573.

[180] 2006 S.C. 543

[181] *Diesen v Samson*, 1971 S.L.T. (Sh. Ct) 49.

[182] *Jarvis v Swan Tours* [1973] 1 All E.R. 71; *Milner v Carnival plc (t/a Cunard)* [2010] EWCA Civ 389.

[183] *Ireland v Merryton Coal Co* (1894) 21 R. 989.

need to be taken, so if mitigation of loss can only be achieved through very onerous steps being taken by the innocent party, this is not required.[184]

There is also the issue of "causation". Damages can only be recovered for losses actually caused by the breach of contract. In other words, there must be a proven link between the breach and the loss incurred.

Irving v Burns
1915 S.C. 260

B, secretary of a company, engaged Irving to carry out plumber work, although B had no authority to do so. Irving performed his part of the contract, but received no payment since the company was now insolvent. Irving was unsuccessful in an action for damages against B. Even if the latter had been given authority to form the contract, Irving would have received nothing, due to the insolvency. He was thus no worse off as a result of B's conduct.

Losses that are caused by a breach of contract can be very far-reaching. Say, for example, that Karl hires a room at a conference centre from Lenny, for the purpose of hosting a business exposition. He invites a large number of companies to come and display their products, and is confident that the industry buyers will also be particularly interested in his own latest inventions. However, Lenny forgets about Karl's booking, and goes on holiday a few days before the exposition, which consequently does not go ahead. Karl suffers the wrath of many disappointed would-be attendees, his reputation is badly damaged, and he loses the opportunity to secure a buyer for his own innovative products. As a result of these things, his business suffers financial ruin, which causes much tension between Karl and his wife, who eventually leaves him.

Clearly the ramifications of Lenny's breach are vast, but common sense dictates that a limit must be placed on Lenny's liability. So, given the total of Karl's losses, what should Lenny be liable for? Such questions might well be answered by the terms and conditions of the contract (see below), but if they are not, the law must provide a solution.

The general principle is that damages can only be claimed for losses which are a direct and foreseeable result of the breach. Such damages are often referred to as "general" or "ordinary" damages. If there are "knock-on" effects that lead to unusual or special loss, the party in breach is not held liable unless he knew of the special circumstances *at the time the contract was formed*. This basic principle is sometimes referred to as "the rule in *Hadley v Baxendale*",[185] and was applied in the leading Scottish case on this subject.

Balfour Beatty Construction (Scotland) Ltd v Scottish Power plc
1994 S.L.T. 807

B were constructing a concrete aqueduct to carry the Union Canal over a by-pass. This required a long "continuous pour" of concrete. Work on the first stage was almost complete when the electricity supply failed. As a result, the first stage had to be entirely demolished. B claimed special damages of over a quarter of a million pounds against S. In the House of Lords, B lost their case. It would have required a

---

[184] *Gunther v Lauritzen* (1894) 1 S.L.T. 435.
[185] *Hadley v Baxendale* (1854) 9 Ex. 341.

high degree of technical knowledge of the construction industry on the part of S for them to have foreseen the results of an interruption of the electricity supply.

Further illustration is provided by *Victoria Laundry v Newman Industries*,[186] in which N agreed to supply a boiler to V, who required it in order to (a) expand their business and (b) permit them to take up a large government contract. The boiler was delivered late, by which time the government contract had been lost. As N had no way of knowing about the government contract when they agreed to supply the boiler, they were only liable for ordinary or general damages for the foreseeable loss of business and not for any special damages in respect of the lost contract.[187]

Finally, a modern authority demonstrates that it is still difficult, in practice, to claim damages for remote losses. In *Transfield Shipping Inc v Mercator Shipping Inc (The Achilleas)*,[188] the late return of a chartered ship resulted in the subsequent charterer successfully renegotiating his fee due to the lost days, at a cost of over $1.3 million to the ship's owner. The owners sued the first charterers for recovery of this sum, but were awarded only the market rate for the lost days; a sum of $158,000.

LIQUIDATE DAMAGES

7–86 In the cases considered so far, the courts have been required to assess the quantum of damages to be paid. Parties can, however, agree at the outset how much will be paid as damages in the event of a breach taking place. This form of damages is called liquidate damages and is perfectly legitimate and enforceable, *provided* it is a genuine pre-estimate of loss. Confusingly, such a provision in a contract is often called a "penalty clause". This is an unsatisfactory title since, as demonstrated, damages for breach of contract are intended to be compensatory, not penal.

Key Concepts

The name given to the clause is unimportant. What matters is its **actual effect**. Where it is clear that the clause is intended to punish rather than to compensate, it is invalid and unenforceable and the court would assess damages using the usual criteria.

Where there is a genuine liquidate damages clause, whatever it may actually be called, the amount recoverable by the innocent party is restricted to that amount even if the actual loss is larger or smaller than the sum specified.

In distinguishing between penalty clauses and liquidate damages clauses, the courts have frequently had regard to the principles set out by Lord Dunedin,[189] summarised as follows:

(a) the use of the words "penalty" or "liquidate damages" is not conclusive in itself;

---

[186] [1949] 2 K.B. 528.
[187] There was a similar result in *"Den of Ogil" Co Ltd v Caledonian Railway Co* (1902) 5 F. 99.
[188] [2008] UKHL 48.
[189] *Dunlop Pneumatic Tyre Co v New Garage and Motor Co* [1915] A.C. 79.

(b) a penalty punishes; liquidate damages is a genuine pre-estimate of loss;

(c) whether a sum is a penalty or liquidate damages is a question judged at the time of the formation of the contract, not at the time of the alleged breach;

(d) if a sum is clearly extravagant, it will be counted as penal and thus unenforceable;

(e) if the same single lump sum is payable on the occurrence of several different situations, it will be presumed to be penal.

In *Lord Elphinstone v Monkland Iron & Coal Co*,[190] tenants in a mineral lease had undertaken to level and soil-over ground by a certain date under a *"penalty of £100 per imperial acre for all ground not so restored."* The sum was liquidate damages, not a penalty as it was a genuine pre-estimate of loss. By contrast, in *Dingwall v Burnett*[191] a lease of a hotel provided for a "penalty of £50" to be paid in the event of any breach of the lease provisions. The tenant totally non-performed, but maintained that he was only liable to pay the £50 "penalty". The court found that the £50 was a penalty and thus unenforceable. This left the way was open for the landlord to claim a higher amount according to the normal rules for assessing the quantum of damages.

Finally, and very rarely, there could be circumstances in which it is impossible to give a genuine pre-estimate of loss. If this is so, any sum agreed on by the parties will be accepted as liquidate damages, even if in normal circumstances it would appear penal.[192]

It has long been recognised that the law on penalty clauses is in need of modernising. The Scottish Law Commission have made a number of recommendations in this area, perhaps most significantly that agreed damages clauses should be enforceable unless manifestly excessive.[193]

ANTICIPATORY BREACH

It might seem strange for a party to a contract to claim a remedy for breach until a breach **7–87** has actually occurred. However, it is possible that one of the parties could indicate in advance of performance, by his words or actions, that he does not intend to fulfil his obligations. This is known as anticipatory breach.

For example, suppose that in January Katie forms a contract agreeing to perform at Lauren's concert hall in July. In April, Katie says she will not perform; in other words, come July she will be in breach of contract. Lauren would have a choice. She could (1) treat this as a repudiation of the contract, rescind on the grounds of material breach, and claim damages, or (2) she could wait until the time of the performance and see what happens, leaving the contract alive. If Lauren follows option (2), and Katie does indeed fail to perform, Lauren could then sue for damages.

---

[190] (1886) 13 R. (H.L.) 98. See also *Cameron-Head v Cameron & Co*, 1919 S.C. 627.

[191] 1912 S.C. 1097.

[192] *Clydebank Engineering and Shipbuilding Co v Castaneda* (1914) 7 F. (H.L.) 77.

[193] Scottish Law Commission, *Report on Penalty Clauses* (The Stationery Office, 1999) Scot. Law Com. No.171, para.3.10.

> **Key Concepts**
>
> For an **anticipatory breach** to take place, the refusal to give performance must be definite. If one party merely expresses doubts about ability to perform, that is not anticipatory breach.

In some cases, a third option has been exercised by the innocent party: to perform his side of the contractual obligations, and claim for the full contract price. This has proven controversial in practice, as a leading case shows.

> **White & Carter (Councils) Ltd v McGregor**
> 1962 S.C. (H.L.) 1
>
> W supplied street litter bins to local authorities on condition that W could sell advertising space on the bins. One of W's representatives called at M's garage and agreed a new advertising contract for three years. Later in the day, M telephoned W to cancel the contract. W chose to ignore this purported cancellation. They duly prepared the advertisements and displayed them for the three year period. W were held to have been entitled to proceed with the contract and to sue for the contract price, even although M had already intimated that he would not perform his side of the obligation.

The above case is not without its critics and, although a House of Lords appeal on a Scottish case, the verdict was by a 3:2 majority. There has been a significant difference of approach taken in subsequent cases by the English and Scottish courts. In the English case of *Clea Shipping Co v Bulk Oil International (The Alaskan Trader)*,[194] it was held that the innocent party's keeping a ship at anchor off the Piraeus for seven months after an anticipatory breach was wholly unreasonable. In the Scottish case of *Salaried Staff London Loan Co. Ltd v Swears & Wells*,[195] tenants had taken a 34-year lease of premises on an industrial estate but, after the lease had only run for five years, the tenants gave notice that they wished to renounce it. The landlord was entitled to ignore this anticipatory breach. It would seem that in this area cases will continue to be considered on their own merits.[196]

TERMINATION OF CONTRACT

> **Key Concepts**
>
> **7–88** The parties to a contract have reciprocal rights and duties, i.e. they are both debtor and creditor to one another. A "debt" is not only an obligation to pay money; it can equally be a duty to perform.

---

[194] [1984] 1 All E.R. 129.
[195] 1985 S.C. 189.
[196] *Miller Fabrications Ltd v J&D Pierce (Contracts) Ltd* [2010] CSIH 27.

If Mike agrees to sell a camcorder to Norman, we have the following situation: Mike is Norman's debtor, in so far as Mike is due to deliver the camcorder to Norman. Mike is also Norman's creditor, in so far as Mike is entitled to be paid by Norman. Equally, Norman is Mike's debtor, as he is due to pay for the camcorder, but Norman is also Mike's creditor because he is entitled to have the goods delivered. (This may seem confusing at first, but it is actually quite simple!)

When these reciprocal arrangements are satisfied in full, the contract is terminated by performance. There are other ways in which a contract might be ended, such as by rescission (considered above), but there are a number of situations that are of particularly significance in so far as they do not give rise to a damages claim. It is these situations that are covered here.

Performance

This is the most common way of ending a contract. Partial performance does not count as **7–89** performance, but there is a legal maxim de minimis not curat lex,[197] which means that very minor discrepancies are not suitable issues for litigation, nor valid grounds for rescission.

Frequently the missing element of performance is payment. Work is done, or goods are delivered, but payment is not forthcoming. Payment should be made in the proper manner, usually at the creditor's place of business or his residence. A creditor can insist (unless agreed to the contrary) on being paid in legal tender, which under the Coinage Act 1971 (as amended) is:

- £1 or £2 coins up to any amount;
- 20p and/or 50p coins up to a maximum of £10;
- 10p and/or 5p coins up to a maximum of £5; and
- bronze up to a maximum of 20p.

In Scotland, no Bank of England notes are legal tender. Scottish clearing banks have the historic right to issue their own bank notes, but they are not legal tender either, even in Scotland. Certain "special issue" coins, such as £5 crowns, are given the status of legal tender.

Payment by credit or debit card is not legal tender, though widely accepted, subject to conditions or limits. Payment by cheque is only conditional payment of a debt. If the cheque is accepted, the money debt is extinguished, but it is revived if the cheque is dishonoured.[198] In *Charge Card Services*,[199] it was held that payment by a credit, or charge card, counts as absolute and not conditional payment.

Acceptilation

A debtor may have non-performed or part performed, or even defectively performed his **7–90** part of the obligation, yet the creditor is prepared to accept this as though it was full performance. Giving discount is a common form of acceptilation.

---

[197] The law does not concern itself with trifles.
[198] This is known as a resolutive condition; it is worth noting that recently many businesses have implemented a policy of refusing to accept payment by cheque, due to the risk of them not being honoured.
[199] [1988] 3 All E.R. 702.

Novation

7–91 A creditor and debtor may expressly agree that the debtor will substitute a new obligation for the one originally undertaken. For example, Mel orders a bag of red apples from Nikki. However, Nikki only has green apples in stock, so she offers these as a substitute. If Mel is happy to do so, she can accept this "new" obligation in place of the original. She does not have to, as a debtor has no right to substitute a new obligation unilaterally. It is important that the original obligation is expressly discharged, as there is a general presumption in law against novation. Thus, there is always the danger that the debtor will find himself with two obligations to perform.

Delegation

7–92 Delegation is a form of novation. It involves the substitution of a new debtor, as distinct from a new obligation. It requires the express consent of the creditor and would be inappropriate in a contract involving *delectus personae*.[200] To reiterate an example given earlier in this chapter, if someone has arranged for his portrait to be painted by a famous artist, he is unlikely to accept that "debt" being contracted out to a third party. There is a general rule that in contracts of agency, an agent has no implied authority to delegate the performance of his duties. This is summed up in the maxim *delegatus non potest delegare*.[201] There are some notable exceptions. It is well recognised that a solicitor may delegate the searching of public registers to a professional searcher. Similarly, an architect may delegate measurement of final plans to a surveyor.[202]

Confusion

7–93 Confusion, occasionally known as "combination", operates where the same person in the same capacity becomes both creditor and debtor in an obligation. A person cannot be his own debtor. If he finds himself in such a position, the debt is normally extinguished. Examples are not common in practice, but there is one of relevance in the case of tenancy. Imagine that Oliver is the tenant of a flat owned by Pete. Pete decides to sell the flat, and Oliver buys it. Clearly, the contract of lease comes to an end as Oliver will not have to pay himself rent.

Compensation

7–94 This can be traced back to the Compensation Act 1592. If one party is both debtor and creditor to the other party, he can offset one claim against the other, reducing or extinguishing the amount due.

For example, if Olga owes Petra £500 and Petra owes Olga £200, Olga need only pay Petra the net sum of £300. However, compensation can only operate if certain conditions are fulfilled:

- Compensation must be pleaded in an action for recovery of the debt. It does not automatically reduce or extinguish the debt. Thus, in the above example, Petra would be entitled to sue Olga for £500. Olga would plead compensation of £200, so the court would grant decree for £300.
- Unless both debts arise out of the same contract, or one of the parties is bankrupt, the debts must both be liquid.

---

[200] Choice of person.
[201] The one to whom delegation has been made cannot delegate.
[202] *Black v Cornelius* (1879) 6 R. 581.

- There must be *concursus debiti et crediti*.[203] This concept has already been explored in relation to retention, above.

Prescription

Not all rights last forever (although some do, such as the right to recover stolen property). **7–95** Many rights come to an end after a certain period of time, i.e. they "prescribe". Most obligations under contract prescribe after five years (called short negative prescription) and this includes the right to payment.[204]

It is essential that the period of time is unbroken. If there is interruption, the running of the period goes back to "zero" and starts again. An interruption can take place by a "relevant claim"[205] or a "relevant acknowledgement".[206]

Prescription is of ancient origin. The modern law is found in the Prescription and Limitation (Scotland) Act 1973 as amended.

Impossibility

A valid contract may be formed, but subsequent or supervening events outwith the power **7–96** of both parties make it impossible to perform.

Key Concepts

The obligation must be **literally impossible to perform**, not merely inconvenient or more expensive. In addition, the impossibility must not be due to the fault of the non-performing party.

In *The Eugenia*,[207] it was known that part of a ship's voyage, namely the Suez Canal, was a war zone, but the charterer ordered her to proceed by that route. The ship was detained in the canal, but the charterer could not escape damages. It was he who had been instrumental in causing the supervening event. The court conceded that performance was now impossible, but damages were still awarded.

A common example of impossibility is *rei interitus*,[208] where the subject matter of the contract is destroyed. In *Taylor v Caldwell*,[209] a music hall had been hired for a concert. After the hire had been agreed, the hall was badly damaged by fire. This was not due to the fault of the owner. The contract was terminated, without damages being payable.

In a contract for the sale of heritable property, the risk (as distinct from the ownership) passes to the buyer as soon as there is an agreement to buy. This rule applies even although the buyer has not taken entry, paid the price nor been given a legal title.[210]

---

[203] Concurrence of debt and credit.
[204] Certain other rights, e.g. relating to land, are subject to the long negative prescription of 20 years. Also, certain rights may be acquired by positive prescription, but this is not relevant to termination of contract.
[205] Creditor raises a court action or refers the matter to arbitration.
[206] Debtor has shown signs of performing, or has admitted in writing that the obligation still exists.
[207] [1964] 2 Q.B. 226.
[208] Destruction of a thing.
[209] (1863) 3 B. & S. 826.
[210] *Sloans Dairies Ltd v Glasgow Corporation*, 1977 S.C. 223. The Scottish Law Commission has recommended the statutory reversal of the common law rule (Scottish Law Commission, *Report on the Passing of Risk in Contracts for the Sale of Heritable* Property (HMSO, 1990) Scot. Law Com. No.127), but no legislative action has been taken.

Sometimes subjects are not literally destroyed but, to all intents and purposes, the effect is the same. This is known as "constructive" destruction, as in *London and Edinburgh Shipping Company v The Admiralty*,[211] where a ship had been very badly damaged but had not actually sunk.

It might be impossible for a contract to be performed due to the condition of one of the parties. An example would be breakdown of health, as in *Robinson v Davidson*.[212]

The fact that a contract has become more expensive or more difficult does not make it impossible to perform. In *Davis Contractors v Fareham Urban District Council*,[213] a builder had agreed to construct 78 houses within 8 months for a fixed sum. Due to shortages of labour and material, bad weather and inflation, the builder found himself substantially out of pocket. However, as performance was not impossible, the contract was not terminated.[214]

If the impossibility is due to the substantial neglect or default of one of the parties, the possibility of damages would be open. However, the courts will not grant a decree *ad factum praestandum* where an obligation is impossible.

Illegality

7–97 The rule here is simple. If a valid contract is formed, but a subsequent change in the law, or political circumstances such as outbreak of war, make performance illegal, the contract is at an end.[215] Indeed, it may be a criminal offence to continue with performance. If a contract is illegal when formed, it is void ab initio[216] and does not require to be terminated, although the court may have to adjudicate on the relative positions of the parties.

Frustration

7–98 Frustration[217] can terminate a contract which is valid and could be performed, but subsequent events outwith the control of either party have made the result of performance materially different from what the parties originally had in mind.

The concept of frustration can be well illustrated by the two "coronation cases", which arose from the postponement of the coronation of Edward VII due to his illness. In *Krell v Henry*,[218] a contract was formed for the hire of rooms to overlook the procession. It was possible for the contract to be performed, i.e. the hiring of the room, but the outcome (looking at the London traffic instead of the procession) would have been so radically different as to frustrate the contract. By contrast, in *Herne Bay Steam Boat v Hutton*,[219] there was a contract for the hire of a pleasure boat to watch the review of the fleet off Spithead by the King. Although the King was unable to attend, the fleet was present and it was possible to enjoy the outing; the contract was not frustrated.

In *Jackson v Union Marine Insurance*,[220] a contract of charterparty[221] provided for a ship to proceed from Liverpool to Newport and pick up a cargo of iron for San Francisco. On her way to Newport, the ship grounded on a sandbank. It took several months to

---

[211] 1920 S.C. 309; *Tay Salmon Fisheries v Speedie*, 1929 S.C. 593; *Mackeson v Boyd*, 1942 S.C. 56.
[212] (1871) L.R. 6 Exch. 269; *Condor v Barron Knights* [1966] 1 W.L.R. 87.
[213] [1956] A.C. 696.
[214] Most building contracts routinely allow for rises in costs due to materials, wages, or inflation.
[215] *Fraser & Co Ltd v Denny, Mott & Dickson Ltd*, 1944 S.C. (H.L.) 35.
[216] From the beginning.
[217] From the Latin *frustra* (in vain).
[218] [1903] 2 K.B. 740.
[219] [1903] 2 K.B. 683.
[220] (1874) L.R. 10 C.P. 125.
[221] Hire of a ship.

recommission her. Meanwhile, the charterer had put his goods on another ship. The original charterparty was frustrated. It would have been possible for the original ship to proceed to San Francisco, but the outcome would have been very different, due to the long delay.

By contrast, it should be noted that frustration, like impossibility, does not terminate a contract merely because performance has become more expensive. Where a ship bound for Britain had to take the longer route round the Cape of Good Hope, due to the sudden closure of the Suez Canal in 1956, the charterparty was not frustrated.[222]

Recovery of monies

In the case of frustration, impossibility or illegality, it is possible that money may have **7–99** been paid in advance. This falls to be paid back, not under the law of contract but under an action for repetition (repayment) known as the *condictio causa data causa non secuta*.[223] In *Cantiere San Rocco SA v Clyde Shipbuilding and Engineering Co*,[224] a Scottish company had agreed to supply engines to an Austrian company, payment to be by instalments. One instalment had been paid, but no engines were supplied as the outbreak of the First World War made performance illegal. After the war, the Austrian company was able to recover the deposit.

▼ CHAPTER SUMMARY

WHAT IS A CONTRACT?

1. **An agreement between at least two parties which creates a legally enforced 7–100 obligation.**
2. **Parties must achieve consensus, i.e. full agreement on the main terms:**
   - ➤ *Raffles v Wichelhaus* (1864): parties had different subject-matter in mind, contract void through lack of consensus.
3. **Obligations must be legally enforceable—thus social agreements, wagers, immoral or criminal agreements are excluded:**
   - ➤ *Kelly v Murphy* (1940) and *Ferguson v Littlewoods Pools* (1997): gambling contracts unenforceable;
   - ➤ *Robertson v Anderson* (2003): but an agreement to share bingo jackpot enforceable.

FORMATION OF A CONTRACT

1. **Consensus is achieved when an offer is made and an acceptance is given.**
2. **Offer always comes before acceptance.**
3. **Offer may be express or by implication:**
   - ➤ *Chapelton v Barry UDC* (1940): invitation to "help yourself" was, in context, an offer.

---

[222] *Tsakiroglou & Co Ltd v Noblee Thorl GmbH* [1962] A.C. 93.
[223] Action applicable when consideration has been given and consideration has not followed.
[224] 1923 S.C. (H.L.) 105.

4. **Willingness to negotiate is not an offer and cannot be accepted.**
5. **There are no hard and fast rules as to how to differentiate between offer and willingness to negotiate—although a non-discriminatory statement is more likely to be an offer. Shops do not offer goods for sale, they merely indicate a willingness to trade:**

   ➢ *Pharmaceutical Society of GB v Boots Chemists* (1952): shop displays are not offers.

6. **A firm quotation may count as an offer whereas an estimate does not—however, it is important to look at the context as well as the wording:**

   ➢ *Harvey v Facey (1892):* expression of willingness to negotiate not an offer.

7. **An expression of intention is normally only a willingness to negotiate.**
8. **Normally an offer may be withdrawn before it is accepted, although there are cases where this may not be possible if there is an undertaking to keep the offer open for a specified time:**

   ➢ *Littlejohn v Hadwen* (1882): example of an undertaking to keep an offer open for a specified period.

9. **If no time limit, the offer remains open for a reasonable period. What is reasonable is a question of circumstance and fact:**

   ➢ *Wylie & Lochhead v McElroy & Sons* (1873): reasonable time limit.

10. **An offer lapses on death, insanity and bankruptcy of the offerer.**
11. **Until an offer is accepted, there is no contract.**
12. **Qualified acceptance is really a new offer, which, in turn, is open for acceptance:**

    ➢ *Wolf & Wolf v Forfar Potato Co Ltd* (1984): counter-offer kills off the original offer.

13. **Person making an offer is entitled to state the method of acceptance. Normally, acceptance is given in the same manner as the offer, e.g. telephone or letter.**
14. **Usually an advertisement is not an offer, although there have been occasional exceptions to this rule:**

    ➢ *Carlill v Carbolic Smoke Ball Co* (1983): advertisement (exceptionally) deemed to be an offer, capable of acceptance by general public.

15. **Once final acceptance is given, that acceptance cannot be withdrawn (but see comment on postal rules).**

THE POSTAL RULES

1. **Where parties negotiate entirely by post (and this does not include fax, email or text) the postal rules apply, unless agreed otherwise:**

   ➢ Electronic Commerce (EC Directive) Regulations 2002.

2. **Posted offer must actually reach the second party.**
3. **Acceptance is valid when it is posted to the offerer, not when he receives it:**

   ➢ *Jacobson v Underwood* (1894): incorrectly addressed letter still concluded a contract, as letter posted within time for acceptance.

4. **If offerer wishes to withdraw his offer, withdrawal must reach the second party before he posts acceptance:**

   ➤ *Thomson v James* (1855): acceptance and withdrawal of offer received simultaneously by second party—contract had been completed when acceptance posted and purported withdrawal was too late.

5. **There is a quirk in the law indicating that there might be circumstances where an acceptance sent by post can be withdrawn—it would be unwise to rely on this quirk:**

   ➤ *Dunmore v Alexander* (1830): dubious case suggesting that it may be possible to withdraw an acceptance made by post, if withdrawal arrives at the same time as acceptance.

6. **The postal rules do not generally apply to contracts made with overseas parties.**

PROMISES

1. **In Scotland, a promise may be enforceable, even although nothing is required in return:**

   ➤ *Morton's Trustees v Aged Christian Friend Society* (1899): undertaking to make gift was binding.

2. **There is a general presumption in law against donation.**
3. **Unless it is made in the course of business, a gratuitous unilateral obligation requires to be made in writing:**

   ➤ Requirements of Writing (Scotland) Act 1995.

4. **A gratuitous contract (as distinct from a gratuitous unilateral obligation) does not require writing. The distinction between the two is not always clear.**

THE REQUIREMENTS OF WRITING

   ➤ Requirements of Writing (Scotland) Act 1995.
   ➤ Electronic Communications Act 2000.

1. **Most contracts are not written (although there are times where writing is advantageous).**
2. **Some contracts, such as unilateral gratuitous obligations (except in the course of a business) and contracts referring to land, require writing.**
3. **A document is formally valid if subscribed by the granter.**
4. **A witness signature is only required if the document is to be made self proving.**
5. **Even if a contract requires writing and this is overlooked, subsequent conduct of the parties may personally bar the parties from withdrawing.**

VALIDITY OF CONTRACTS

1. **Defect in a contract makes it potentially void, voidable or unenforceable.**
2. **Contract is void, i.e. does not exist, if there is no true consent. Consent might be lacking due to lack of capacity (see below), absence of consensus or other "essential" error.**

3. **If contract is void, a third party can never acquire rights, even if acting in good faith;**

    ➤ *O'Neill v Chief Constable of Strathclyde* (1994): example of third party not acquiring rights.

4. **Contract is voidable if there is a defect that does not strike at the root of the contract.**
5. **Voidable contract stands, until steps are taken to have it cancelled.**
6. **Right to cancel a voidable contract may be lost if parties cannot be restored to original positions, or if personal bar has operated.**
7. **Possible for a third party, acting in good faith, to acquire rights under a voidable contract.**
8. **Some contracts are unenforceable, such as social agreements or wagers.**

CONTRACTUAL CAPACITY

➤ Age of Legal Capacity (Scotland) Act 1991.

1. **Young people under 16 have no contractual capacity, but can enter reasonable transactions for persons of their age and circumstances.**
2. **Young people aged 17 and 18 have full capacity, but transactions that cause "substantial prejudice" may be set aside by the court.**
3. **Contract with a 17 or 18 year old may be declared unchallengeable by application to the court.**
4. **At common law, an insane person has no contractual capacity. There are statutory provisions for the protection of persons incapable of managing their own affairs:**

    ➤ Adults with Incapacity (Scotland) Act 2000.

5. **Contract cannot be cancelled merely because one of the parties was drunk, unless he had completely lost his reason (no modern case where such a plea has been accepted).**

EFFECT OF ERROR ON CONTRACTS

1. **Ignorance of the law is not valid reason for cancelling a contract. All other errors are of fact, some of which may affect the validity of a contract.**
2. **Error of expression—where the parties knew what they meant but the written version of the contract fails to represent their intentions accurately. Common law and statutory provisions for overcoming this difficulty:**

    ➤ *Anderson v Lambie* (1954): more land than had been agreed mistakenly conveyed (error of expression). Court able to rectify error at common law;
    ➤ Law Reform (Miscellaneous Provisions) (Scotland) Act 1985.

3. **Unilateral error—a person of full capacity, not the subject of fraud or misrepresentation makes a bad bargain—does not affect the validity of a contract.**
4. **Common error—where the parties make the same mistake. As in the case of unilateral error, the contract stands;**

    ➤ *Dawson v Muir* (1851): both parties made same mistake as to value of items (common error)—contract stood.

5. Mutual error—where the parties (for whatever reason) misunderstand one another—may permit the contract to be cancelled. If error trivial, or collateral to the contract, either its validity will not be affected or, at worst, it may be voidable:

    ➢ *Cloup v Alexander* (1831): there was an error as exactly what kind of performances could be offered in a theatre—but the main contract (lease of theatre) stood.

6. If error is essential, i.e. goes to the root of the contract, there is no consensus and contract is void. Essentials include the subject matter, price, identity of the parties (in some cases), quality, quantity or extent or the nature of the contract:

    ➢ *Raffles v Wichelhaus* (1864): essential error as to the subject matter—contract void;
    ➢ *Morrison v Robertson* (1908): essential error as to the identity of other party rendered contract void. Contrast *MacLeod v Kerr* (1965) where seller of car willing to contract with person in front of him. Peterson was impostor—contract only voidable (but no longer possible due to third party rights).

Misrepresentation

1. **Misrepresentation may be innocent, fraudulent or negligent, rendering a contract void or voidable.**
2. **Statement is innocent if made in the honest belief of its truth and is not made negligently. No damages awarded:**

    ➢ *Boyd & Forrest v Glasgow & SW Railway* (1912): genuine opinion, even if wrong, counted as innocent misrepresentation.

3. **Fraudulent misrepresentation implies an intention to deceive:**

    ➢ *Bile Bean Co v Davidson* (1906): classic example of fraudulent misrepresentation.

4. **Representation is negligent where a party failed to take reasonable care and under a duty to do so. As in the case of fraud, damages may be awarded:**

    ➢ *Hedley Byrne v Heller & Partners* (1964): groundbreaking case on duty of care;
    ➢ Law Reform (Miscellaneous Provisions) (Scotland) Act 1985.

5. **Occasionally, silence or concealment counts as misrepresentation:**

    ➢ *Gillespie v Russell* (1856): not necessarily fraud merely to conceal information;
    ➢ *Gibson v National Cash Register Co* (1925): reconditioned cash registers sold as new counted as fraudulent misrepresentation.

6. **Parties to a contract negotiate "at arm's length". Exceptions are contracts of utmost good faith (e.g. insurance) or involving a relationship of trust:**

    ➢ *The Spathari* (1925): famous case underlining the need for full disclosure in contracts of insurance.

OTHER FACTORS AFFECTING VALIDITY

1. **Sometimes validity of a contract may be affected where the consent of one of the parties is improperly obtained.**
2. **The most commonly cited examples include facility and circumvention, undue influence, force and fear and extortion:**

    ➢ *Cairns v Marianski* (1850): classic case on facility and circumvention;
    ➢ *Gray v Binny* (1879): undue influence of a mother on her son;
    ➢ *Earl of Orkney v Vinfra* (1606): force and fear (sign a contract or die)—contract void;
    ➢ *McLachlan v Watson* (1874): contract will not be set aside merely because it is a bad bargain.

ILLEGAL AGREEMENTS

1. **Illegal contracts include agreements whose purposes are criminal, fraudulent, immoral or contrary to public policy.**
2. **Courts will not enforce such agreements although they may assist the party who is least blameworthy. This is most likely in cases of statutory illegality.**
3. **Contracts in restraint of trade are void unless the restrictions are reasonable and not contrary to public policy.**
4. **Whether restrictive covenant is enforceable will depend not only on its being reasonable but also on nature of the restriction, size and type of business, time factor and geographical extent:**

    ➢ *Mason v Provident Clothing* (1913): nation-wide restraint on former employee too wide and unenforceable;
    ➢ *Dallas, McMillan v Sinclair v Simpson* (1989): restrictive covenant of 20 miles radius of Glasgow Cross unenforceable;
    ➢ *Bluebell Apparel v Dickinson* (1978): wide ban on working for rival jeans manufacturer enforceable.

5. **Where more than one restriction imposed by an agreement, court may sever one part of the agreement and leave remainder to stand. Court has no power to change an agreement:**

    ➢ *Mulvein v Murray* (1908): court can delete unreasonable parts of restrictive covenant provided remaining clauses severable.

6. **Traditionally, courts more willing to enforce restrictions where parties are buyer and seller of a business:**

    ➢ *Nordenfelt v Maxim Nordenfelt Guns and Ammunition* (1894): in context a 25-year worldwide restriction enforceable.

EXCLUSION CLAUSES IN CONTRACTS

1. **No exclusions of liability can be added after the contract is formed:**

    ➢ *Olley v Marlborough Court Ltd* (1949): unsuccessful attempt to add conditions after contract formed.

2. **Where a ticket is issued, may be a simple receipt or may be an integral part of contract. In some cases, such as contracts of carriage, common practice for the ticket either to contain conditions or refer to rules elsewhere. Even so, conditions must be adequately drawn to the party's attention:**

   ➤ *Williamson v North of Scotland Navigation Co* (1916): minute typeface on ticket could not validly incorporate terms.

3. **Standard form contracts are subject to the Unfair Contract Terms Act 1977.**

Unfair Contract Terms Act 1977

1. **The 1997 does not cover all unfair contract terms—only exclusion clauses and generally covers consumer contracts, including goods and services, hire and admission.**
2. **Regulations, first introduced in 1999, give further consumer protection, allowing contract to be cancelled where it is unfair, contrary to good faith or causes unfair imbalance:**

   ➤ Unfair Terms in Consumer Contracts Regulations 1999.

Remedies for Breach of Contract

1. **Breach of contract occurs where one party fails to fulfil his part of the bargain without justification. Possibility of damages is always open.**
2. **Specific implement allows innocent party to ask court to direct defaulting party to perform. Remedy inappropriate in certain cases such as seeking payment of money or enforcing a personal relationship (such as employment).**
3. **Rescission allows innocent party to call off contract. Can only be exercised where the breach is material:**

   ➤ *Wade v Waldon* (1909): rescission only available where breach material.

4. **Retention is withholding payment of a money debt until such time as the other party performs.**
5. **Lien is retention of moveable property until a debt is paid. Most liens are specific to the goods that form the subject matter of the contract:**

   ➤ *Paul v Meikle* (1868): example of general lien.

6. **Most common breach of contract is failure to pay:**

   ➤ Late Payment of Commercial Debts (Interest) Act (1998).

Damages

1. **Where there is breach of contract, possibility of damages is always open.**
2. **Purpose of damages is compensation for loss, not penalty against the party in breach:**

   ➤ *Irving v Burns* (1915) and *Webster v Cramond Iron* (1875): damages only awarded on actual loss.

3. **Innocent party is expected to take reasonable steps to minimise loss.**
4. **Remoteness of damage: only loss that is direct and foreseeable consequence of the breach can be claimed (The rule in *Hadley v Baxendale*):**

   ➤ *Hadley v Baxendale* (1854): established test for damages as (1) loss naturally arising as result of breach; and (2) loss for special circumstances only if party knew about them when contract made;
   ➤ *Victoria Laundry v Newman Industries* (1949): special circumstances must be known, not implied;
   ➤ *Macdonald v Highland Railway Co* (1873): word PERISHABLE on boxes gave adequate notice of special circumstances.

LIQUIDATE DAMAGES

1. **Parties may agree at the outset that (liquidate) damages payable in the event of breach.**
2. **Liquidate damages will be enforceable if they represent genuine pre-estimate of loss, not a penalty. Words in the contract such as "penalty" or "liquidate damages" are not conclusive in themselves:**

   ➤ *Lord Elphinstone v Monkland Iron & Coal* (1886): liquidate damages enforceable even though described as "penalty";
   ➤ *Dingwall v Burnett* (1912): liquidate damages only enforceable if fair pre-estimate of loss.

ANTICIPATORY BREACH

1. **If it is clear that one party will not perform, other party has choice of rescinding the contract immediately, on the grounds of material breach, or he can wait and see what happens.**
2. **If one party merely expresses doubt as to ability to fulfil contract, this is not anticipatory breach:**

   ➤ *White & Carter (Councils) Ltd v McGregor* (1962): where breach anticipated, innocent party may elect to proceed with his part of contract.

TERMINATION OF CONTRACT

1. **Most contracts are terminated by performance:**

   ➤ Coinage Act 1971.

2. **Performance of a contract may be delegated, with the express permission of the other party.**
3. **Contracts can be terminated by acceptilation, confusion, compensation, novation and prescription:**

   ➤ Compensation Act 1592;
   ➤ Prescription and Limitation Act 1973.

4. **Contract can be frustrated by supervening impossibility, destruction of subjects, subsequent illegality or change in circumstances:**

➤ *Taylor v Caldwell* (1863): contract impossible to perform due to destruction of property;

➤ *Fraser & Co v Denny Mott & Dickson* (1944): declaration of war made performance of contract illegal;

➤ *Krell v Henry* (1903): postponement of Coronation frustrated contract of hire to view procession. Contrast *Herne Bay Steam Boat v Hutton* (1903);

➤ *Jackson v Union Marine Insurance* (1874): long delay counted as frustration of contract of charterparty.

? QUICK QUIZ

CONTRACT LAW

- What is the distinction between an offer and a willingness to negotiate?
- Explain "error of expression".
- Distinguish contracts void and voidable.
- Outline the circumstances in which essential error might void a contract.
- Distinguish innocent and fraudulent misrepresentation.
- Outline the provision of the Unfair Contract Terms Act 1977.
- Explain specific implement, rescission, retention and lien.
- Outline the "Rule in *Hadley v Baxendale*".
- Explain liquidate damages.
- Explain acceptilation, novation and delegation.
- Outline how a contract can be "frustrated".

📖 FURTHER READING

The leading textbook is W. McBryde, *The Law of Contract in Scotland*, 3rd edn (W. Green, 2007) which is scholarly, detailed and authoritative. It is not a book for beginners. At the opposite end of the scale is A. Gibb and A. Gordon, *Contract Law Basics*, 3rd edn (W. Green, 2009) which gives a foundation treatment and is useful for revision.

The two textbooks written for student consumption are H. MacQueen and J. Thomson, *Contract Law in Scotland*, 2nd edn (Tottel Publishing, 2007) and G. Black, *Woolman on Contract*, 4th edn (W. Green, 2010).

Reference can also be made to the *Stair Memorial Encyclopaedia*, particularly under the heading "Obligations" and to *Gloag and Henderson, The Law of Scotland*, 12th edn (W. Green, 2007).

A useful resource book is John A.K. Huntley, *Contract Cases and Materials*, 2nd edn (W. Green, 2003).

Occasionally, courts might still refer to *Gloag on Contract*, 2nd edn (W. Green, 1929) which is a monumental work of scholarship, although now obviously dated.

Chapter 8   Sale of Goods and Consumer Law

Nicholas Grier[1]

▶ CHAPTER OVERVIEW

8–01 This chapter contains three discrete sections: sale and supply of goods and services; hire of goods; and consumer credit. As all of these comprise such an important part of business, it is important that there are fair rules which protect consumers from unscrupulous sellers, lessors or lenders, but which allow sellers, lessors or lenders rights against consumers who may be acting improperly themselves. The law pays particular attention to consumers, who, in general, have less grasp of their legal rights than do businessmen.

✓ OUTCOMES

8–02 At the end of this chapter you should be able to:

- ✓ understand the implied terms applicable to contracts of sale and supply of goods and services;
- ✓ recognise the differences in the law between commercial contracts and consumer contracts;
- ✓ appreciate the significance of the main terms of such contracts;
- ✓ understand the duties of sellers towards buyers;
- ✓ understand the rights of sellers against buyers;
- ✓ recognise the duty of care owed by sellers to purchasers and users of their products or services;
- ✓ identify the criminal liability of sellers or suppliers who mislead their customers;
- ✓ understand the implied terms applicable to contracts of hire of goods;
- ✓ appreciate the significance of the main terms of such contracts;
- ✓ understand the duties of lessors towards hirers;
- ✓ understand the rights of hirers against lessors;
- ✓ know the main rules relating to the licensing of those who provide credit;
- ✓ understand the main forms of credit agreement;
- ✓ recognise the main exemptions from the credit consumer legislation; and
- ✓ be aware of consumers' rights in regulated agreements.

---

[1] Senior Lecturer in Law, Edinburgh Napier University.

SALE AND SUPPLY OF GOODS

The need for legislation

Traditionally, the sale of goods was regulated by the old Roman law maxim of caveat **8–03**
emptor—let the buyer beware.

While this maxim was certainly clear, it was not always very fair, particularly for purchasers (especially ordinary consumers) who were being taken advantage of by unscrupulous sellers. It provided no incentive, other than the loss of future business, to sellers to treat purchasers fairly, and it gave purchasers few rights. The law has been modernised to remedy this, and now purchasers are given substantial protection by various Acts of Parliament, the best known being the Sale of Goods Act 1979. Various other Acts serve to clarify the responsibilities and rights of the seller and purchaser towards each other.[2]

The Sale of Goods Act 1979 ("SOGA")

SOGA is the main legislation for the sale of goods. It provides a sensible and fair set of **8–04**
rules to apply to the normal process of buying and selling goods.

Definitions

Key concepts

Goods means corporeal moveables. In Scotland, this means physical, tangible and transportable assets, including things growing on, or in, land—SOGA s.61.

Goods covers such things as food, furniture, books, clothing, and electrical equipment, but does not include money—except in the context of antique coins and banknotes.

Services, land and buildings are not goods and SOGA does not apply to them.

Ascertained goods are existing and specific goods selected by, or for, the buyer, as, say, when a customer selects some apples at a greengrocer's, or when the greengrocer himself selects the apples for the customer. *Unascertained* goods are goods not specially selected or identified by, or for, the buyer, but which are available to the buyer for purchase. *Appropriation* is the term used to describe the process of selecting, setting aside or otherwise identifying the goods for the buyer, with the buyer's assent.

Goods do not need to exist at the time of sale: if the goods have yet to be obtained or manufactured, they are called *future goods*.[3]

A *sale* is defined in SOGA s.2 as a contract by which the seller transfers, or agrees to transfer, the property in goods to the buyer for a money consideration, called the price. Swaps and barters are not, therefore, covered by SOGA.

Property means the right of ownership, sometimes also known as "title". Ownership is

---

[2] For example, the Unfair Contract Terms Act 1977, the Sale and Supply of Goods Act 1994, the Consumer Credit Act 1974, the Consumer Protection Act 1987 and the Unfair Terms in Consumer Contracts Regulations 1999, Consumer Protection (Distance Selling) Regulations 2000, the Electronic Commerce Regulations 2002, the Price Marking Order 2004 and the Consumer Protection from Unfair Trading Regulations 2008.

[3] SOGA s.5.

different from possession. A person may own a wheelbarrow, but if he lends that wheelbarrow to a friend the friend has possession, but not ownership.

A contract of sale of goods may be *absolute* or *conditional*.[4] An absolute contract of sale is one where the property is transferred without anything needing to be done first. A conditional sale is one where the property in the goods will not be transferred until some condition is fulfilled. Where the transfer of the property is to take place at a future time, or subject to the fulfilment of some condition, the contract is not a contract of sale, but an *agreement to sell*.[5] An agreement to sell turns into a sale once the requisite time has elapsed, or the condition has been fulfilled.[6]

Breach of contract occurs where a term of the contract is broken by one of the parties to the contract. If a term of the contract is broken by the seller, the buyer is entitled to claim damages for his loss[7], and if it is a very serious breach of a term (known as a "material" breach) the buyer is entitled to reject the goods (i.e. to return them to the seller) and to treat the contract as repudiated (i.e. to refuse to recognise the continued existence of the contract).[8] If he rejects the goods, he will normally seek to have the cost of the goods refunded to him.

A *material* breach is, as stated above, a significant or serious breach as opposed to a trivial or minor breach of a term of the contract. The word "material" is explained in SOGA s.15B(2), where it states that in a consumer contract (to be explained later), any breach by the seller of a term in the contract as to the quality of the goods or their fitness for the purpose for which they were supplied is a material breach.[9] Within SOGA s.15B(2) there are other occasions which are deemed to be material breaches. If a seller sells his goods by description, or if he displays a sample of his goods, there is an assumption that the actual goods will indeed entirely correspond with the seller's description or that the bulk of the goods will correspond with the sample shown to the consumer. If this is not the case, the consumer buyer may treat the goods' deficiencies as a material breach of a term of the contract, and is therefore entitled to reject the goods and claim his money back. Note that SOGA s.15B applies only within Scotland, and that s.15B(2) only applies to consumers, not to commercial purchasers.

A *consumer contract* is defined in the Unfair Contract Terms Act 1977 ("UCTA") as one where: (a) either the seller or the buyer is a consumer (i.e. someone not dealing, or holding himself out as dealing, in the course of a business) and the other party is dealing in the course of a business; and (b) the goods, which form the subject of the contract, are goods that are of a type ordinarily supplied for private use or consumption.[10]

Risk is the term used to denote the exposure of the goods to the danger of loss or damage. From the moment a buyer accepts the risk in goods transferred, or to be transferred to him, he bears the risk of the loss or destruction of the goods; where the risk lies with the seller, he will be responsible for maintaining the goods up to the moment of transfer of risk to the buyer.

Damages is the term used to describe the amount the court may award to cover the difference in value between the value of the contract, if it had taken place properly, and what the actual value turned out to be. In the context of a seller's breach of contract, it is the estimated loss to the buyer directly and naturally resulting, in the ordinary course of

---

4   SOGA s.2(3).
5   SOGA s.2(5).
6   SOGA s.2(6).
7   SOGA s.15B(1)(a).
8   SOGA s.15B(1)(b).
9   SOGA s.15B(2)(a).
10   UCTA s.25(1).

events, from the breach.[11] Damages, in general, aim to restore or bring the claimant to the position he ought to be in if the contract is performed properly, but damages are not meant to be penal (i.e. a form of punishment for failure to honour the contract). Damages will normally amount to the cost of repair or upgrading to the expected standard, or the value of the loss occasioned by the seller's delay or failure to deliver the goods. If the delivered goods are rejected because they are defective, the damages are calculated on the basis of non-delivery.[12] Interest is usually allowable as part of the damages. Where there is loss to the buyer as a result of the delay or fault, any damages claimed are: (a) only available to the buyer and not to others who may be affected by the faulty goods; and (b) may only be claimed against the seller. However, under common law, unless the buyer has specifically drawn the seller's attention to matters which are important to the buyer (such as the need for the supplied goods to be ready by a certain date, because some other matter was dependent on the goods being ready), the seller will only be liable for any reasonably foreseeable loss arising out of the seller's delay or fault.[13]

Express and implied terms

Key concepts

In contracts of sale there are usually *express* terms, which are ones clearly spelled out, and *implied* terms, which are automatically deemed to be in the contracts unless they are specifically disapplied. Even so, the attempt to contract out of the implied terms may, in certain circumstances, be declared void by the courts. The implied terms are as follows:

8–05

(a) Unless the contract of sale specifically says so, a stipulation as to the time of payment for the goods is not deemed to be "of the essence of the contract" (i.e. a material matter which will entitle the seller to claim that the contract has been breached).[14]
(b) The seller has the right to sell the goods.[15] So if the goods turn out to be stolen, the buyer may sue the seller for breach of this right, notwithstanding any intervening circumstances. This took place in *McDonald v Provan of Scotland St Ltd*[16] (a car-dealer had sold a car which consisted of parts of two cars welded together: one of those cars had originally been stolen, which meant that the dealer did not have the right to sell the stolen part).
(c) Up to the moment when the property is to pass to the buyer, there is no charge or encumbrance over the goods, or if there is, it must be disclosed to the buyer.[17] A "charge or encumbrance" is a term of English law and means that some-one else has some right or interest in the goods, thus preventing their sale.

---

[11] SOGA s.53A(1).
[12] SOGA s.53(3).
[13] *Hadley v Baxendale* (1854) 9 Ex. 341, Ex. Ct.
[14] SOGA s.10(1).
[15] SOGA s.12(1).
[16] 1960 S.L.T. 231.
[17] SOGA s.12(2)(a).

(d) Irrespective of the time that the property is to pass, the buyer will enjoy quiet possession of the goods, except to the extent of any disclosed charge or encumbrance.[18] In *Niblett Ltd v Confectioners Materials Co*,[19] the buyers found that the labelling on tins purchased from the seller infringed a recognised trademark whose owners wished to assert their rights and whose interests the seller had ignored. The labels had to be removed and the buyers successfully sued the sellers for breach of the requirement of "quiet possession".

(e) Where either from the terms of the contract, or from the circumstances surrounding the contract, it is apparent that the seller or a disclosed further person does not have full title (i.e. ownership or the right to sell), provisions (a), (b), (c) and (d) above continue to apply but the seller or other disclosed further person will only be liable to the extent of what he has not disclosed. [20]

Unless it is made clear by the seller to the buyer that the seller is only transferring such (limited) title as he may have, [21] any attempt to contract out of s.12 of SOGA (i.e. paragraphs (a) to (e) above) is automatically void under UCTA s.20(1)(a).

(f) Under s.13 goods sold by description will correspond with their description.[22] The bulk of goods should correspond with any sample (as well as with their description if appropriate)[23] and even if a buyer selects his goods, his purchase may, if necessary, still be a sale by description if the buyer has relied on a description.[24]

(g) Under s.14 where goods are sold in the course of a business (but not necessarily otherwise), the goods supplied must be of "satisfactory quality".[25] "Satisfactory" is defined as meeting the standard that a reasonable person would regard as satisfactory, taking account of the description of the goods, the price (where relevant) and all other relevant circumstances.[26] "Quality" means the state and condition of the goods,[27] taking into account the fitness for the purpose for which the goods were supplied, the goods' appearance and finish, freedom from minor defects, safety and durability.[28] In *Clegg v Anderson*[29] the purchaser of a new, and very expensive ocean-going yacht was entitled to expect that it be "perfect or nearly so" but in *Thain v Anniesland Trade Centre*[30] the fact that a car was second-hand, relatively cheap and had high mileage meant that the purchaser should not have expected such high quality. However, if defects or unsatisfactory matters are especially drawn to the buyer's attention,[31] or where the buyer examines the goods and he ought to have noticed the defects, or in the case of a

---

[18] SOGA s.12(2)(b).
[19] [1921] 3 K.B. 387, CA.
[20] SOGA s.12(3), (4), and (5).
[21] SOGA s.12(3).
[22] SOGA s.13(1), *Farrans Construction Ltd v RMC Ready Mixed Concrete (Scotland) Ltd* [2004] CSOH 51.
[23] SOGA s.13(2).
[24] SOGA s.13(3).
[25] SOGA s.14(2).
[26] SOGA s.14(2A).
[27] SOGA s.14(2B).
[28] SOGA s.14(2B)(a) to (e).
[29] [2003] 1 All E.R. (Comm) 721.
[30] 1997 S.L.T. (Sh. Ct.) 102.
[31] *Bartlett v Sidney Marcus Ltd* [1965] 1 W.L.R. 1013.

sample, if a reasonable examination of the sample would have made the defects apparent, the protection afforded by SOGA s.14(2) as to satisfactory quality is withdrawn.[32] When the contract in question is a consumer contract, the "relevant circumstances" referred to in s.14(2A) additionally extend to any advertising and labelling, thereby requiring that goods conform to what their producers or retailers say to consumers about those goods.[33]

(h) Where the buyer explains to the seller the purpose for which the goods are being bought, the goods must be reasonably fit for that purpose (even if that purpose is not the usual use for those goods) unless circumstances show that the buyer was not relying on the seller's skill and judgment in satisfying that purpose, or where it was unreasonable of him to rely on the seller's skill and judgment.[34] In *Griffiths v Peter Conway Ltd*,[35] a purchaser contracted dermatitis as a result of wearing a tweed coat. She then sued the seller on the grounds that the coat was not fit for purpose. It was established that the purchaser's skin was exceptionally sensitive and that it was unreasonable of her not to have told the seller of her particular sensitivity. She thus failed in her claim. A further feature of this rule is that it applies to any seller of any goods in the course of a business, even if the goods in question are not those normally sold by the seller.[36]

(i) The above terms apply to a seller's agents in the course of the seller's business, and to agents for sellers not in the course of business,[37] unless the buyer knows, or has been clearly told, that the seller is not in the course of business.[38]

(j) Under s.15, where there is a sale by sample, the bulk will correspond with the sample in quality and the goods will be free from any defect making the quality of the goods unsatisfactory, which would not be apparent on a reasonable examination of the sample.[39]

The exclusion of implied terms

It is not possible, in any contract of sale to which SOGA applies, to contract out of SOGA **8–06** s.12[40] except, as stated above, where someone who does not have full title openly discloses his title as being less than full[41] or discloses all charges.[42] In that latter case a disclosed holder of a charge may destroy the buyer's possession of the goods.[43] It is also not possible to contract out of the provisions of SOGA ss.13 to 15 (referred to in paragraphs (f) to (j) above) in a consumer contract,[44] though it is possible to do so in a commercial, or non-consumer, contract if the relevant contracting-out clause is "fair and reasonable" as defined in UCTA s.24. This states that in defining fair and reasonable, regard should be had to the circumstances known to, or which ought reasonably to have been known to the

---

[32] SOGA s.14(2C). For the extent of a "reasonable" examination, see *Murdo Donald MacDonald v Robert & Elizabeth Pollock* [2012] CSIH 12.
[33] SOGA s.14(2D).
[34] SOGA s.14(3), *Ashington Piggeries v Christopher Hill Ltd* [1971] 1 All E.R. 847, HL.
[35] [1939] 1 All E.R. 685, CA.
[36] *London Borough of Southwark v Charlesworth* (1983) 2 Tr. L.R. 93, DC.
[37] *Murdo Donald MacDonald v Robert & Elizabeth Pollock* [2012] CSIH 12.
[38] SOGA s.14(5).
[39] SOGA s.15. *Godley v Perry* [1960] 1 All E.R. 36.
[40] UCTA s.20(1).
[41] As, for example, when a liquidator is selling an insolvent company's assets.
[42] A "charge" means a right over the goods in favour of a creditor. These are rare in Scotland.
[43] SOGA s.12(4), (5).
[44] UCTA s.20(2).

parties at the time the contract was made. Reference may also be made to UCTA Sch.2, which lays down various guidelines as to: (a) the abuse of any strength of bargaining power; (b) the effect of any inducements to accept the contracting out clause; (c) normal business practice in the trade concerned or between the parties; (d) the practicality of compliance with any condition without which liability would be excluded; and (e) whether the goods were specially made or adapted to the buyer's particular order.

Further exclusion clauses

8–07 Under the Unfair Terms in Consumer Contracts Regulations 1999 ("UTCCR"), where consumers are required to enter into contracts, where the opportunity for individual negotiation of specific terms is not available (as in contracts for such goods as mobile phones, etc.), consumers will not be bound where a non-negotiable term is "unfair".[45] Unfairness is judged by the criteria of being contrary to the requirements of good faith, being significantly in favour of the non-consumer party to the contract, and being detrimental to the consumer[46]—although the courts are also required to take account of the nature of the goods and services referred to in the contract and to all the circumstances attending the conclusion of the contract.[47] The seller, or supplier, must ensure that each written term of the contract is expressed in plain language intelligible to the consumer.[48] If a term is ambiguous or unclear, the term will be construed in favour of the consumer.[49]

Formation of contracts of sale

8–08 Contracts of sale may be made verbally, in writing, by a combination of these means or may be inferred from the actions of the parties to the sale.[50] In any event, the implied terms, referred to above, are deemed to be part of the contract of sale (except where variation of the implied terms is both agreed by the parties and permissible, which in the case of consumer contracts it may not be). As with all contracts, there must be *consensus in idem* (agreement on the same matters), a buyer and a seller, both with the necessary legal capacity, a price (which in the absence of any other agreement must be reasonable under the circumstances[51]) and goods (present or future) to be transferred along with the property[52] in the goods. Where specific goods have perished, without the knowledge of the seller, before or at the time that the contract is made, there are clearly no goods so the contract is void[53] and no contract of any sort exists. Where there is an agreement to sell specific goods, and the goods subsequently perish through no fault of the buyer or seller before the sale takes place, the agreement is avoided, the seller has no obligation to deliver the goods[54] and any money the buyer had given to the seller for the now perished goods has to be returned to the buyer. This rule does not apply in the case of unascertained goods, since the seller ought to be able to produce more (unperished) goods from his warehouse.

---

[45] UTCCR reg.8.
[46] UTCCR reg.5(1).
[47] UTCCR reg.6(1).
[48] UTCCR reg.7(1).
[49] UTCCR reg.7(2).
[50] SOGA s.4.
[51] SOGA s.8. *Glynwed Distribution Ltd v S. Koronka & Co*, 1977 S.L.T. 65.
[52] "Property" is the word used to mean the right of ownership (sometimes also known as "title") to the goods.
[53] SOGA s.6.
[54] SOGA s.7.

When does the buyer get the property in the goods?

This depends whether or not the goods are unascertained.   **8–09**

Key concepts

Where there is a contract for unascertained goods, no property in the goods is transferred to the buyer unless and until the goods are ascertained. He only obtains title to them once they have been appropriated for his benefit—SOGA s.16, *Hayman & Son v McLintock*.[55]

Where the goods are specific or ascertained, the property in the goods passes to the buyer when the parties intend the property to pass. This is established by the terms of any written or oral contract, the conduct of the parties and any other circumstances—SOGA s.17.

Where it is unclear when the parties intended the property to pass, SOGA s.18 has set up five rules which may be used to establish the intention of the parties. These are as follows:

(1) Where there is an unconditional contract for the sale of specific goods in a deliverable state, the property passes to the buyer when the contract is made, irrespective of any delay in the time of payment or delivery.[56]

(2) Where there is a contract for the sale of specific goods, and the seller has yet to put the goods into a deliverable state, the property does not pass until the goods are in a deliverable state and the buyer has been informed of the fact.[57]

(3) Where there is a contract for the sale of specific goods in a deliverable state, but the goods need to be measured in order to ascertain the price, the property does not pass until the measurement has taken place and the buyer has been informed of the fact.[58]

(4) When goods are supplied on approval, or on sale or return, the property passes when the buyer tells the seller of his approval (or by another action adopts the sale). However, if the buyer does not signify his approval or acceptance but retains the goods without notice of rejection, beyond any specified period for rejection, the property will pass at the end of that period. If there is no specified period, the property will pass after the expiry of a reasonable time.[59]

(5) Where there is a contract for the sale of unascertained, or future goods, by description, and where goods of that description and in a deliverable state are "unconditionally appropriated" to the contract (i.e. irrevocably set aside for the contract without there being any outstanding conditions which have first to be fulfilled) by the seller with the buyer's agreement, or by the buyer with the seller's assent, the property in the goods passes to the buyer when the goods are appropriated.[60] The assent may be given expressly or by implication (i.e. through the actions of the parties) and may take place either before, at or after the appropriation. Unconditional appropriation may also take place where the seller

---

[55] 1907 S.C. 936.
[56] SOGA s.18 Rule 1.
[57] SOGA s.18 Rule 2.
[58] SOGA s.18 Rule 3.
[59] SOGA s.18 Rule 4.
[60] SOGA s.18 Rule 5(1).

delivers the goods to the buyer, or to someone on the buyer's behalf, such as a carrier, without reserving to himself the right to dispose of the goods.[61] Where there is a contract for the sale of a specified quantity of unascertained goods in a deliverable state, which forms part of a bulk agreed upon by the parties, and where, for some reason, the bulk is reduced from its original quantity, but the buyer is the only remaining person due to receive goods from that bulk, the remaining quantity of the goods is to be taken as appropriated to the contract and the property therein passes to the buyer.[62]

These five rules apply where there is no contrary indication in the contract. However, under SOGA s.20A, buyers of unascertained goods in an identified bulk (as, for example, cargo of some commodity such as grain in a ship) and who have paid for those goods, will be treated as owners in common of the bulk to the extent of their paid-for, but undivided, share of the bulk.[63] If the paid-for, but undivided, shares of the bulk of all the owners exceed the actual quantity of the bulk, each owner's share is reduced proportionately.[64] Each owner is deemed to have consented to the delivery of the other owners' shares to their owners, and, unless they agree otherwise, no buyer of the goods has any obligation to compensate any other buyer of goods out of that bulk.[65]

Retention of title

8–10 There is nothing to prevent the seller retaining a right of disposal until the fulfilment of some condition.[66] This is known as retention of title.

When does risk pass?

> **Key concept**
>
> Unless there is some agreement to the contrary, the normal rule in a commercial contract is that the risk in the goods remains with the seller until the property is transferred to the buyer, irrespective of the date of delivery to the buyer—SOGA s.20(1).

In *Pignataro v Gilroy*[67] the buyer acquired bags of rice but failed to uplift them from the seller's premises. When the bags were stolen from those premises the buyer had to bear the loss.

As exceptions to the general rule above, if there has been any delay in the delivery of the goods, and the delay is attributable to one of the parties to the contract, the goods are at the risk of the party at fault, to the extent of the loss which arose as a result of the fault),[68] and secondly, sellers and buyers acting as custodiers, or carriers, cannot rely on the above

---

[61] SOGA s.18 Rule 5(2).
[62] SOGA s.18 Rule 5(3).
[63] SOGA s.20A(1)–(3).
[64] SOGA s.20A(4).
[65] SOGA s.20B(3).
[66] SOGA s.19, *Armour v Thyssen Edelstahlwerke AG* [1991] 2 A.C. 339.
[67] [1919] 1 K.B. 459, KBD.
[68] SOGA s.20(2), *Demby Hamilton & Co Ltd v Barden* [1949] 1 All E.R. 435.

general rule to avoid the duty to take adequate care of the goods while goods are in their care or in transit.[69]

If the sale is a consumer contract, the goods always remain at the seller's risk until they are delivered to the consumer.[70]

Transfer of title

Key concept

If someone obtains goods, which he does not own, and sells those goods without the authority or consent of the owner, the buyer gets no better right to the property than the person purporting to sell the goods—SOGA s.21(1).

8–11

This means that if a thief sells stolen goods, the buyer may be required to hand the goods back to the true owner and sue (if he can) the thief for the value of the goods that he had to relinquish. This rule is disapplied where the owner's own conduct prevents him from objecting to the seller's right to sell the goods.[71] This rule is also disapplied where goods are being sold following an attachment, or other court order, or where agents are acting on the owner's behalf even though the owner had withdrawn his authority.[72]

Under SOGA s.23, where a seller of goods has a voidable title (i.e. a title that could be challenged, as when a seller sells goods obtained by fraud), but that title has not been reduced at the time he sells the goods to a buyer, the seller may transfer title to the goods to a buyer who buys in good faith and without notice of the seller's defect in title.[73] This arose in the case below.

Macleod v Kerr
1965 S.C. 253; 1965 S.L.T. 358, IH (1 Div)

Kerr sold his car to a rogue named Galloway who paid for the car with a stolen cheque. Galloway promptly sold the car to Macleod. Shortly after the sale to Macleod, Galloway's cheque in favour of Kerr was dishonoured. Kerr discovered that Macleod had the car, so he sued Macleod to get his car back. It was held that because Macleod had bought the car in good faith and without notice of Galloway's defect in title, Macleod should retain the car. Galloway's title could have been reduced at the time when the cheque was dishonoured, but unfortunately from Kerr's point of view, that time had not been reached before Galloway had sold the car to Macleod. Kerr's only remedy was to sue Galloway (if he could find him), and Macleod was able to retain the car, as his circumstances fell entirely within the wording of s.23. If this seems unfair to Kerr, it was his choice to accept a cheque from Galloway: a wiser person might have insisted on cash or a banker's draft.

---

[69] SOGA s.20(3).
[70] SOGA s.20(4).
[71] SOGA s.21(1).
[72] SOGA s.21(2). Attachment is a court-approved process whereby a creditor seizes a debtor's assets.
[73] SOGA s.23.

Section 23 only applies in the context of a voidable title. Where the contract is void from the beginning, because, for example, the seller does not have contractual capacity, s.23 does not apply and the original owner will be able to retrieve his goods from the person possessing the goods.

In the context of hire purchase, where someone buying a car on hire purchase from a finance company, tries to sell that car to a purchaser (other than a car dealer) buying it in good faith without notice of the finance company's interest in the vehicle, the purchaser may obtain good title to the vehicle.[74] The exception relating to car dealers arises from the perception that car dealers are well able to look after their own interests without the extra benefit of consumer protection.

When a seller has sold goods to a buyer and received payment for the goods, but the goods remain in the hands of the seller, if the seller inadvertently, or fraudulently, transfers or delivers the goods to a new buyer, buying in good faith and without knowledge of the fact that the goods belong to the first buyer, the new buyer gets good title to the goods.[75] The first buyer is then entitled to sue the seller for damages for non-delivery.

Sometimes a seller will deliver goods to a buyer but will retain the ownership of those goods, usually until he has been paid (commonly known as "retention of title"). If the buyer then delivers, or transfers, the goods to a sub-buyer who buys the goods in good faith and without notice of any rights of the original seller, the sub-buyer obtains good title to the goods.[76] In *Archivent Sales and Development Ltd v Strathclyde Regional Council*,[77] a seller delivered goods to a contractor carrying out work at a school. The contractor sold on the goods to the school, despite not having paid the original seller who had attempted to safeguard his position with a retention of title clause. As the goods had been transferred to the school's owners (Strathclyde Regional Council), which had acquired the goods in good faith and without knowledge of the rights of the original seller, the seller was unable to assert his claim to the goods against the Council. Accordingly s.25(1) limits the applicability of retention of title clauses. This rule does not, however, apply in the context of conditional sale agreements regulated under the Consumer Credit Act 1974 s.25, or in the context of acquisitions by car dealers (referred to above).

How is the contract of sale to be carried out?

8–12

> **Key concept**
>
> It is the duty of the seller to deliver the goods and the duty of the buyer to accept the goods and to pay for them, all in accordance with the terms of the contract for the sale of the goods—SOGA s.27.
>
> Unless the contract says otherwise, delivery and payment are concurrent, and both parties should be ready to perform their parts of the contract simultaneously.

---

[74] Hire-Purchase Act 1964 ss.27–29.
[75] SOGA s.24.
[76] SOGA s.25(1).
[77] 1985 S.L.T. 154; 27 B.L.R. 98, OH.

There are varied and pragmatic rules to govern such matters as where delivery is to take place,[78] the delivery of more or less goods than had been requested,[79] delivery by instalments[80] and delivery to carriers, where generally delivery to the carrier is deemed to be delivery to the buyer; but in each of these events the precise details may be varied by agreement between the parties, and if the buyer is a consumer, delivery of the goods to the carrier is not delivery of the goods to the buyer.[81]

Where the seller delivers goods to the buyer, the buyer must be allowed a reasonable time to examine the goods to see if they conform to the contract, or to see if the bulk of the goods matches previously seen samples.[82] He is not held to have accepted the goods until he has been afforded these opportunities for examination, even if he has signed an acceptance receipt.[83] In a consumer contract, a consumer is not deprived of this right, even if apparently made to do so by the terms of his contract.[84]

The buyer is held to have accepted the goods where he tells the seller he has done so,[85] or where he treats the goods in a manner which is inconsistent with the ownership of the seller, for example, where he uses them as security for some other transaction. Subject to the next paragraph, if a buyer retains the goods for a reasonable time without telling the seller that he is rejecting them, he is deemed to have accepted the goods.[86] If the buyer asks the seller to repair the goods, the request does not signify acceptance[87]; and even if the goods are delivered to someone else through a sub-sale the buyer may still be entitled to reject the goods within a reasonable time.[88] Where the goods are units within a bigger, but ultimately indivisible set of goods, as, e.g. one print within a narrative series of prints all within a limited edition, the acceptance of the one item is deemed to be an acceptance of all the items.[89]

The buyer's right of rejection and other rights

SOGA s.15B allows the buyer to claim damages where the seller is in breach of any express **8–13** or implied terms of the contract, and in addition, if the breach is material, the buyer may reject the goods. If the buyer is a consumer, a material breach means a breach of any term (express or implied) relating to the good's quality, fitness for purpose, conformity with their description or, in the case of a sample, correspondence with their bulk. If rejection is not possible (because, say, he has told the seller that he has accepted the goods), or the breach is not material, the buyer's remaining remedy under SOGA s.15B, assuming the claim is justified, is damages arising out of the loss directly and naturally resulting from the breach of the contract.[90] Unless the terms of the contract say otherwise, it is permissible to have partial rejection, where the buyer is entitled to reject all of an entire consignment of goods, but instead chooses to keep the satisfactory goods and reject the unsatisfactory

---

[78] SOGA s.29.
[79] SOGA s.30.
[80] SOGA s.32.
[81] SOGA s.32(4).
[82] SOGA s.34.
[83] SOGA s.35(2).
[84] SOGA s.35(3).
[85] SOGA s.35(1)(a).
[86] SOGA s.35(4).
[87] SOGA s.35(6)(a). See also *J & H Ritchie Ltd v Lloyd (Scotland) Ltd* [2007] UKHL 9; [2007] 1 W.L.R. 670; [2007] 2 All E.R. 353.
[88] SOGA s.35(6)(b).
[89] SOGA s.35(7).
[90] SOGA s.53A.

goods.[91] If a buyer legitimately rejects goods, he is not bound to return them to the seller unless the terms of the contract of sale say otherwise. He must, however, intimate his rejection to the seller.[92] If the buyer, after a reasonable time, delays or refuses to accept the goods when he should properly do so, the buyer is liable to the seller for the cost of storage and care of the goods.[93]

If the buyer is a consumer, the time for rejection is now up to six months from the period of delivery.[94] Under SOGA s.48B the buyer may require the seller to repair the goods if they are faulty, or to replace them within a reasonable time and with minimal inconvenience and expense to the buyer. As a further option, the buyer can insist on the price being lowered instead.[95] These remedies are subject to safeguards for the seller to allow him reasonable time to effect repairs or replacements,[96] or to allow him to prove that the goods conformed to requirements in the first place.[97]

Other rights for the buyer

8–14 Where the seller neglects or refuses to deliver the goods to the buyer, the buyer may claim damages for non-delivery.[98] Equally, in the case of a contract of sale of specific or ascertained goods, the buyer may petition for specific implement to enforce delivery of the goods.[99] This means that the court pronounces an order compelling the seller to perform his part of the contract.

If a seller has provided a guarantee, either from himself or the manufacturer, the guarantee must be in plain intelligible English and comes into effect at the time of delivery of the goods. It also allows the consumer to sue the manufacturer directly without involving the retailer.[100]

The seller's rights

8–15 Where a seller has not been paid (the "unpaid seller") he is entitled to retain the goods until payment, even if the property in the goods has transferred to the buyer, while in the event of the insolvency of the buyer, he may also stop any goods that are in transit to the buyer.[101] Where some of the goods have been delivered by the unpaid seller to the buyer, but the remainder has not, the unpaid seller may withhold delivery of the remainder pending payment. The unpaid seller also has a right of resale,[102] subject to intimation to the buyer giving him a reasonable time within which to make payment. These rights may be set aside by the terms of the contract, as where an arbitration clause takes effect. Where the unpaid seller is no longer in possession of the goods, or they are still in transit to the buyer as above, he may raise an action for the price,[103] or claim damages for non-acceptance where the buyer ought properly to have accepted and paid for the goods.[104]

---

[91] SOGA s.35A.
[92] SOGA s.36.
[93] SOGA s.37.
[94] SOGA s.48A(3).
[95] SOGA s.48C.
[96] SOGA s.48D.
[97] SOGA s.48A(3).
[98] SOGA s.51.
[99] SOGA s.52.
[100] Sale and Supply of Goods to Consumer Regulations 2002 (SI 2002/3045) reg.15.
[101] SOGA s.39(1)(a) and (b).
[102] SOGA s.39(2).
[103] SOGA s.49(1).
[104] SOGA s.50.

Delictual liability

Problems with SOGA s.14 and the duty of care

> **Key concept**
>
> If a seller sells goods whose defects cause injury to the buyer, the seller may claim damages from the seller under SOGA s.53A.

8–16

What the buyer can sue for is the estimated loss directly and naturally arising in the ordinary course of events from the breach[105] and any consequential losses where those cause damage to the buyer personally or to his property. However, under SOGA only the buyer may sue only the seller for the goods' defects and there is no remedy under SOGA for a victim if he was not the buyer of the goods. So if a buyer buys a present for his uncle, and the uncle is injured by the present, the uncle has no remedy against the seller under SOGA.

However, where a victim, whether a buyer or not, suffers injury from defective components in manufactured goods, he may instead be able to raise an action against the producer of the goods under the Consumer Protection Act 1987 ("CPA"), which provides for liability for defective products. Although there are some permissible defences open to a producer under CPA s.4, it is not possible for a producer to contract out of the liability provisions of CPA s.7, though it is possible for a victim to be contributorily negligent. Where this arises, any damages payable by the producer will be abated to the extent of the victim's own negligence.[106]

The liability of producers

Producers may try to evade liability by claiming that they were not the manufacturers of a **8–17** harmful product. Accordingly producers, if they are not the manufacturers themselves, may be held liable where they unreasonably delay or refuse to identify who the true producer is,[107] although this rule does not apply where goods are supplied other than in the course of a business, in order to protect the parties in private transactions.[108] Businesses that produce their "own brand" products, such as supermarkets, are treated as if they were producers themselves unless they make it clear who the actual manufacturer is.[109] Importers bringing in goods from outside the European Union are treated as constructive producers.[110] The word "product" does not include buildings, though it does include items fitted into buildings.[111] There is no requirement to prove that a producer is negligent in order to assert a claim: it is enough to prove that the product was defective, i.e. that its safety is not such as persons generally are entitled to expect,[112] and safety in this context applies to property as well as to personal injury or death.[113]

---

[105] SOGA s.53A.
[106] CPA s.4, referring to the Law Reform (Contributory Negligence) Act 1945 and the Fatal Accidents Act 1976 s.5.
[107] CPA s.2(3).
[108] CPA s.4(1)(c).
[109] CPA s.2(2)(b).
[110] CPA s.2(2)(c).
[111] CPA s.46.
[112] CPA s.3(1).
[113] CPA s.3(1).

Protection for the manufacturer and the "state of the art" defence

8–18 There are safeguards in CPA s.4 to protect the producer:

    (a) where the goods are manufactured in compliance with EU safety rules;
    (b) where the products were used without the producer's authority (as when the products have been stolen);
    (c) where the products have not been supplied in a commercial transaction;
    (d) where the fault is attributable to some other producer's misuse of the products;
    (e) where the fault lies in the overall design which is not of the producer's making;
    (f) where the defect did not exist in the product at the relevant time;
    (g) where the state of the art defence applies.

The most significant safeguard is the "state of the art" defence in CPA s.4(1)(e): that the defect was such that given the state of scientific and technical knowledge at the time, a similar producer of similar products would also have been unaware of the defect.

Prohibition on small claims and on claims for pure economic loss

8–19 Under CPA damages are available solely for personal injury or damage to property (including land), though to discourage small claims, only claims where the damages would amount to more than £275 will be entertained by the court.[114] CPA s.5 prohibits claims for pure economic loss, since those could be instead be dealt with under SOGA ss.14 or 53A. Claims under the CPA may be made only up to 10 years after the product was supplied, and within 3 years of the later of the date of the injury or damage (subject to certain exceptions).[115]

Criminal liability

8–20 In addition to the civil law protection for the consumer outlined above, there is a large body of criminal law designed to protect the consumer. The main acts dealing with this matter are the Consumer Protection from Unfair Trading Regulations 2008 and much of the CPA, though there are many others which have an important part to play such as the Weights and Measures Act 1965, the Competition Act 2002, the General Product Safety Regulations 2005 and the Misleading Marketing Regulations 2008.

    What follows next is merely an overview of some of the better known legislation.

Consumer Protection from Unfair Trading Regulations 2008

8–21 These regulations prohibit "unfair commercial practices". A commercial practice is "any act, omission, course of conduct, representation or commercial communication (including advertising or marketing) by a trader, which is directly connected with the promotion, sale or supply of a product to or from consumers, whether occurring before, during or after a commercial transaction (if any) in relation to a product" (reg.2(1)). A commercial practice is unfair if it contravenes the requirements of professional diligence, and materially distorts or is likely to materially distort the economic behaviour of the average consumer with regard to the product (reg.3(3)). "Professional diligence" is "the standard of special skill and care which a trader may reasonably be expected to exercise towards consumers which

---

[114] CPA s.5(4).
[115] CPA Sch.2, amending the Prescription and Limitation (Scotland) Act 1973.

is commensurate with either (a) honest market practice in the trader's field of activity, or (b) the general principle of good faith in the trader's field of activity (reg.2(1)).

A commercial practice is also unfair if it is a misleading action (see reg.5), a misleading omission (see reg.6), aggressive (see reg.7) or listed in Sch.1 to the Act (reg.3(4)). The regulations provide a wide range of matters that would be taken into account when deciding which of these categories of unfair commercial actions apply. In essence traders are expected to behave openly and honestly and to treat consumers fairly, and if they fail to do so, they may be prosecuted under the regulations. The effect of this is to outlaw sharp practice, and to prohibit misleading sales promotions. The Office of Fair Trading and local authority trading standards officers are required to enforce these regulations and are given extensive powers to enable them to do so. There are various statutory defences to protect innocent traders where they undertook due diligence to prevent offences occurring (reg.17) or the fault was due to another (reg.16). There are slightly similar rules to protect traders from other traders' misleading advertisements in the Business Protection from Misleading Marketing Regulations 2008.

Producers' breaches of consumer safety may result in prosecution.[116] Under the CPA it **8–22** is a defence to prosecution for breach of consumer safety requirements to state that the accused reasonably believed that the goods were not being used or consumed in the United Kingdom, or that at the time of offering the goods for sale in the course of his business as a retail trader he neither knew, nor had reasonable grounds for believing, that the goods failed to comply with the safety requirement, or that he did not offer the goods as new and that those buying the goods intended to buy the goods in their imperfect state.[117] The Secretary of State has power to make regulations to provide for consumer safety and this is normally done in consultation with retail organisations, manufacturers and the Health and Safety Commission.[118] Adherence to these regulations is naturally advantageous to the accused facing prosecution.[119] Under such regulations there may be, initially, prohibitory notices and warning notices in order to dissuade the producer or seller from selling the unsafe goods,[120] but if these are insufficient, suspension notices may be served on anyone selling goods which may be in breach of the safety regulations.[121] Where the enforcement authority has made a mistake and there is no contravention the enforcement authority is required to compensate the supplier of the goods.[122] It is open to the relevant authorities to seize and forfeit the accused's goods where they fail to comply with the required standards.[123]

Misleading price indications under CPA Part III

Under Part III of the CPA, it is a criminal offence for a person to give misleading **8–23** information to consumers about the prices at which goods, services, accommodation or other facilities may be available.[124] CPA s.21 indicates that a price indication is misleading if it fails to state what a consumer might reasonably expect it to cover, if it suggests that the price is less than it actually is, if it fails to include additional charges or if it fails to detail facts or circumstances which have a bearing on the price, thus ensuring that it is

---

[116] CPA s.10.
[117] CPA s.10(4).
[118] CPA s.11(5).
[119] CPA s.10(3).
[120] CPA s.13.
[121] CPA s.14.
[122] CPA s.14(7).
[123] CPA s.17.
[124] CPA s.20(1).

difficult for the consumer to compare prices. Part III extends to the provision of services, including banking, insurance, foreign currency transactions, electricity, parking and caravan residence.[125] CPA does not, however, apply to contracts of employment, investment services or the sale of new homes.[126] There are defences to Part III: that the accused has complied with non-statutory codes of practices in the relevant industry (such codes having been drawn up in conjunction with the Secretary of State and/or the Director of Fair Trading[127]); that the information is contained in newspaper articles, as opposed to advertisements within newspapers, and is not actionable under the CPA[128]; that publishers of advertisements in newspapers are not liable if they did not know and had no grounds for suspecting that the advertisements were misleading[129]; and that the indication as to prices for goods, services, accommodation or facilities did not relate to the availability from the accused of any of those goods and services, etc. as the accused had merely been recommending a price at which the providers of those goods and services, etc. could offer them, that price being reasonable under the circumstances—even if some providers chose not to follow that price so that it appeared to be a misleading price.[130] The accused may also use the due diligence defence in a similar manner to the one referred to above.[131]

There are provisions for enforcement by authorised officers of the relevant bodies,[132] enabling the officers to make test purchases,[133] search and seize goods and papers,[134] but also to pay compensation where they have failed to obtain a conviction.[135]

HIRE OF GOODS

8–24 This section is concerned with the law relating to hire of goods and starts by considering the various definitions needed for an understanding of this area of law, and defines the various rights that are deemed to apply to all contracts of hire.

A hire of goods differs from a sale of goods in that during a hire the owner (known during the hire as the lessor) retains ownership of the goods and the hirer merely has the use or possession of the goods, in exchange for regular payments known as rent. At the end of the period of hire, possession reverts to the owner. The law relating to hire is partly covered by the common law but mostly by the Supply of Goods (Implied Terms) Act 1973, the Supply of Goods and Services Act 1982 ("SGSA"), the Consumer Credit Act 1974 ("CCA"), the Unfair Contract Terms Act 1977 ("UCTA"), the Unfair Terms in Consumer Contracts Regulations 1999 ("UTCCR") and the Consumer Credit Act 2006 ("CCA 2006") which amends, in some respects, the earlier Consumer Credit Act.

---

[125] CPA s.22.
[126] CPA s.23.
[127] CPA s.25(2).
[128] CPA s.24(2).
[129] CPA s.24(3).
[130] CPA s.24(4).
[131] CPA s.39.
[132] CPA s.27.
[133] CPA s.28.
[134] CPA s.29.
[135] CPA s.34.

Regulated hire agreements

While the common law regulates contracts of hire generally, a hire agreement involving a **8–25** consumer (which term denotes ordinary consumers, sole traders and partnerships, but not limited companies or limited liability partnerships)[136] enduring for more than three months, and requiring the consumer/hirer to make payments amounting of any value, is known as a *regulated consumer hire agreement*.[137] This means that the hirer is entitled to the protection of CCA. This protection does not apply in the case of hires to high net worth individuals[138] and businesses.[139] Apart from these exceptions, the terms of the hire must be properly and clearly set out on appropriately designed forms[140] which in turn must be properly drawn up and executed in accordance with the regulations of CCA.[141] All regulated hire agreements must be in writing, with copies made available to the hirer,[142] clearly explaining both parties' rights. Failure to follow the correct procedure and wordings on all documentation may invalidate the hire or delay the enforcement of the lessor's rights of repossession by requiring the lessor to apply to the court.[143] There is judicial control of any such attempts at repossession by the use of time orders, giving the hirer time to pay, or even reducing or discharging the sum the hirer is due to pay, all on the principle of fairness to the consumer.[144] Prior to the hire, the hirer is entitled to cancel the agreement during a cooling-off period of five days, if there have been face to face negotiations prior to the signing of the hire agreement and if the hire agreement has been signed somewhere other than at the lessor's (or his agent's) premises[145]; following cancellation, the goods must be returned to the lessor and any hire payments returned to the hirer.[146] There are detailed rules to deal with default by the hirer, requiring notices to be sent to the hirer explaining his default and giving him the opportunity to remedy it[147] and other rules to cover early repayment[148] and the termination of the agreement.[149]

Hire agreements which are not regulated hire agreements are covered by SGSA (see next paragraph) and by the terms of the hire agreement itself.

The effect of the Supply of Goods and Services Act 1982

Broadly speaking, SGSA implies into contracts of hire, including regulated consumer hire **8–26** agreements, many of the same terms that are applied to contracts of sale under SOGA, so that there are implied terms that the hirer has title to lease the goods[150] and that the hirer may enjoy quiet possession of the goods.[151] As with SOGA, there are rules to ensure that goods hired on the basis of a description conform to that description,[152] that goods hired

---

[136] CCA 1974 s.189(1).
[137] CCA 1974 s.15.
[138] CCA 2006 s.3.
[139] CCA 2006 s.4.
[140] CCA 1974 s.60.
[141] CCA 1974 s.61.
[142] CCA 1974 s.63.
[143] CCA 1974 s.65.
[144] CCA 1974 ss.126–136.
[145] CCA 1974 s.68.
[146] CCA 1974 s.67–72.
[147] CCA 1974 ss.87–89.
[148] CCA 1974 ss.94–97.
[149] CCA 1974 ss.98–104.
[150] SGSA s.11H(1)(a).
[151] SGSA s.11H(2).
[152] SGSA s.11I.

on the basis of a sample conform to the bulk,[153] and that the goods are of satisfactory quality and fit for their purpose.[154]

The liability of the lessor

8–27 It is expected that the hired goods will be serviceable for the duration of the hire, but if repairs are necessary these should be at the lessor's expense, except where the hire agreement says otherwise or where the repairs are necessary because of the hirer's fault. Where the hired goods cause damage to people or property, the lessor is liable under the Consumer Protection Act 1987 in the same manner as a supplier under a contract of sale (see previous section at paragraph 8–17). He also may suffer the same civil and/or criminal penalties as a supplier, should the hired goods derogate from the required standard of safety that can be expected. The lessor cannot contract out of the provisions of UCTA relating to the lessor's liability for personal injury or death arising out of the hired goods,[155] and any other exclusion clauses will only be acceptable where they are "fair and reasonable".[156] Any consumer hire agreement on standard terms, which has not been individually negotiated with the hirer, may be set aside by the courts (in the same manner as contracts of sale) if the contract is significantly one-sided in favour of the non-consumer party to the contract (i.e. the lessor) and if there is an element of lack of good faith.[157]

The liability of the hirer

8–28 The hirer must pay his hire charges or rent as contracted or, in the absence of a specified rate, at a reasonable rate. In a regulated hire agreement the rates in any event would have to be properly detailed. If the goods are faulty the hirer is normally entitled to deduct a reasonable sum to reflect his inability to use the hired goods satisfactorily. The hirer is under a duty of care to look after the goods properly in the manner that a prudent and sensible person would look after his own property. He would not be responsible for fair wear and tear, but he would be responsible if he wore the goods out through overwork or overuse.[158]

CONSUMER CREDIT

8–29 The Consumer Credit Act 1974 ("CCA") (as amended by the Consumer Credit Act 2006) was introduced in order to: (a) provide a coherent set of rules regulating the provision of credit; (b) set up a licensing system so that only authorised credit dealers could provide credit; and (c) set out a framework for the proper and fair provision of credit.

Licensing requirements

8–30 Under CCA s.21 only licensed traders, lenders or credit brokers may carry on the business of consumer credit and consumer hire. Under CCA s.147 only licensees may carry out the business of credit brokerage, debt-adjustment, debt administration, debt-counselling, debt-collecting or the operation of credit reference or information agencies (known collectively as ancillary credit business). However, an occasional or "one-off" loan, made by

---

[153] SGSA s.11K.
[154] SGSA s.11J.
[155] UCTA s.16(1)(a).
[156] UCTA s.16(1)(b).
[157] UCTTR reg.4(1).
[158] Bell's *Principles*, para.141

someone not in the course of a business, does not normally require the credit-provider or arranger to be licensed[159] and certain bodies such as local authorities are exempt from the licence requirement.[160] There are two types of licence, these being a "standard" licence (the more usual) and a "group" licence.[161] All businesses carrying on licensable credit business, other than those operating through group licences, must obtain a standard licence, and each company within a group, as with a bank and its subsidiaries, must obtain a separate standard licence. Licences will only be issued if the Director General of Fair Trading, who supervises the operation of CCA, is satisfied that the licensee is fit to hold a licence. His criteria take into account not only the licensee's business name (lest there be any confusion with any other business of a similar name and nature), but also its compliance and its employees' compliance with the requirements of CCA.[162] There is a public register of licensees, and penalties for carrying on a licensable credit business without a suitable licence.[163] An unlicensed person will not be able to enforce the terms of any regulated agreements against the debtor.[164]

The protection afforded to the consumer

Who is a "consumer"?

In the context of CCA, a consumer is an individual wishing to enter a credit arrangement **8–31** of any amount.[165] Individuals in this context means private persons, partnerships of private persons, unincorporated clubs, charities and societies,[166] except where these individuals are high net worth individuals (those earning over £150,000 a year and/or have capital of over £500,000)[167] or are acting as businesses.[168] Incorporated bodies, such as limited companies, do not count as individuals, except in the context of a joint hire to an individual and a limited company under CCA s.185(5).

The meaning of "credit"

Credit is a cash loan and any other form of financial accommodation, cash here meaning **8–32** money in any form.[169] The wording is deliberately wide so that most forms of credit will be caught by the legislation—in the interests of the consumer.

Ombudsman

The Financial Services Ombudsman may now be asked by consumers to investigate and **8–33** pronounce on disputes between consumers and those providing or advising on credit.[170]

---

[159] CCA 1974 s.189(2).
[160] CCA 1974 s.21(2).
[161] CCA 1974 s.22(1).
[162] CCA 1974 s.25.
[163] CCA 1974 ss.39 and 147.
[164] CCA 1974 s.40(1) and (2) as amended by the Consumer Credit Act 2006.
[165] CCA 1974 s.8(2).
[166] CCA 1974 s.189(1).
[167] CCA 1974 s.16A.
[168] CCA 1974 s.16B.
[169] CCA 1974 s.9(1).
[170] Financial Services and Markets Act 2000 s.226A.

Regulated agreements

8–34   Regulated agreements are any agreements that are regulated by CCA, of which the most common are described below. It is possible to have some credit arrangements that feature several different types of arrangement, in which case they are known as multiple agreements.

Consumer credit arrangement

8–35   A personal credit arrangement is any agreement between a debtor and a creditor for credit of any amount.

Hire-purchase

8–36   Hire-purchase is treated as a form of credit as, in effect, it spreads the cost of acquiring goods over a period of time by means of regular hire payments followed by an option to purchase.[171] During the period of hire, and under the terms of the hire-purchase agreement, the consumer is still liable for any damage and for any repairs necessary. If the consumer fails to maintain his monthly payments, the finance company is entitled to repossess the goods and sell them to defray its loss. Where the goods are repossessed, CCA lays down careful rules to ensure that the consumer is treated fairly in respects of the payments he has already made. Hire-purchase agreements are regulated by CCA ss.9(3) and 15(1)(a). They are treated as consumer credit agreements for fixed sum credit.

Running account credit (CCA s.10(1)(a))

8–37   This is a facility whereby the borrower may borrow such amount as the creditor is willing to lend. In the absence of any restriction to the contrary, the borrower will be entitled to borrow from the account and make payments into that account.

Fixed sum credit (CCA s.10(1)(b))

8–38   This is a less flexible arrangement than a running account credit. With fixed sum credit a sum of money is borrowed in one amount or in instalments. Both of these are extensively used by banks when offering loans to customers. They may be contrasted with overdrafts which are specifically exempt from CCA by virtue of CCA s.74.

Restricted use agreement (CCA s.11)

8–39   In this situation the credit may only be used for one purpose, as opposed to an unrestricted use agreement which may be used for any purpose. Restricted use agreements are common in hire-purchase agreements where the credit is provided for the one use only, such as the purchase of a car. A restricted use agreement enables the creditor to monitor the debtor's use of the credit more closely, in return for which the creditor may be able to offer a lower interest rate.

Debtor-creditor-supplier agreement (CCA s.12)

8–40   This is an agreement between a debtor (usually a customer), a creditor (usually a finance company) and a supplier (often a retailer). A common example of this is a credit card such as Visa or American Express. If a customer buys a computer from a supplier using his credit card, he pays for the computer with the credit facility offered by the credit card

---

[171] CCA 1974 s.189(1).

company. The credit card company pays the supplier, and the customer will find the cost of the computer on his next statement from the credit card company. He has to pay the amount due on his statement plus any interest if due. The advantage to the supplier is that it knows it will get paid, since a cheque from the customer might not be honoured; the advantage to the customer is that he can buy the computer quickly and if the supplier defaults, under CCA s.75 the customer has a joint and several claim against both the supplier and the credit card company, albeit that the credit card company may then be indemnified by the supplier.

Connected lender liability

The protection afforded the customer under s.75 is known as connected lender liability. **8–41** This rule does not apply where the claim relates to an item whose cash price from the supplier is less than £100 or is greater than £30,000. The particular advantage of CCA s.75 is that where the supplier goes into liquidation, the consumer can still claim against the credit card company should he need to do so. The case of *Office of Fair Trading v Lloyds TSB Bank plc*[172] established that s.75 applies to the purchase of goods and services by credit card from suppliers outside the United Kingdom. Section 75A covers the situation where a consumer uses a "linked credit agreement" which is where the supplier of the goods or services is insolvent, the creditor has used the services of the supplier to provide the finance for the consumer, and the credit supplied is greater than £30,000 but less than £60,260.

Credit token agreements (CCA s.14)

This is a regulated agreement which applies to such forms of credit as storecards. The **8–42** credit token does not need to be limited to the one outlet (as with a storecard that only provides credit for the one shop) though that is its common use.

Where a debtor allows someone else to use his credit token, he is liable for any loss to the creditor arising from that use,[173] but when the credit token is used by an unauthorised person, the debtor is liable up to the sum of £50 to the creditor.[174] If the debtor finds his credit token has been stolen or otherwise lost and immediately informs the credit token provider of his loss, liability does not arise.[175]

Credit agreements exempt under CCA (mostly under CCA s.16)

Certain credit agreements are specifically exempt from the consumer credit legislation. **8–43** These are:

(a) normal trade credit agreements (excepting hire purchase agreements, land purchase agreements and agreements secured by a pledge) for a fixed sum repayable in no more than four payments within a period of a year and for a running account credit agreement (subject to the same exceptions as above) repayable in one lump sum within a designated period—as in a Gold Card or Diners Club card;

(b) land transactions repayable in no more than four repayments;

(c) mortgage lending for the acquisition of land or the securing of a loan upon land;

---

[172] [2007] UKHL 48.
[173] CCA 1974 s.84(2).
[174] CCA 1974 s.84(1).
[175] Consumer Credit (Credit Token Agreements) Regulations 1983.

(d) low cost credit, where the cost of the loan is not greater than base rate plus 1 per cent or 13 per cent, whichever is the higher;

(e) loans for certain insurance policies, usually to pay the premiums on property insurance or mortgage protection policies;

(f) credit agreements for the financing of exports from or imports into the United Kingdom;

(g) consumer credit arrangements where the creditor is a housing authority and where the agreement is secured by a standard security on a house;

(h) hiring of gas, electricity or water meters.

All other agreements, covered by CCA and not exempt, are "regulated agreements".

General rules for regulated agreements

8–44 CCA operates to ensure that any advertising carried out by consumer credit businesses is accurate and intelligible, complete with "health warnings" alerting the borrower or hirer, to the penalties arising from non-fulfilment of his requirements.[176] The annual percentage charge for credit ("APR") must be clearly visible and not include hidden charges. Quotations are similarly closely regulated.[177] Canvassing or soliciting of customers must be fairly done, and may only take place off trade premises under very restricted circumstances.[178] All agreements regulated by CCA have to follow certain specified forms and procedures,[179] one of which is a "cooling-off" period during which time the debtor may change his mind.[180] The debtor is permitted to cancel an agreement within five days of either receiving a copy of the executed agreement (where it was signed off trade premises)[181] or the date when he received notice of the debtor's rights of cancellation intimated to him under CCA s.64. If the agreement is deemed to be unfair by the court, the court has a wide range of remedies for the debtor or anyone guaranteeing his debts.[182]

Notwithstanding the above, CCA s.74 excludes four types of agreement from the above rules, these being:

(a) non-commercial agreements (i.e. one-off non-business loans);

(b) current account overdrafts;

(c) loans in connection with debts due after a death (such as a loan by a bank to pay inheritance tax due by the deceased's estate); and

(d) small agreements for restricted use credit for the provision of credit of less than £50 (in certain circumstances this is reduced to £35).

With all regulated agreements (other than those exempted by CCA s.74), the creditor may not enforce his rights unless he has notified the debtor of his intention to do so by means of a default notice.[183] In the process of enforcing his rights, or should the debtor choose to object to the enforcement, the matter may come before the courts, which may grant a time

---

[176] CCA 1974 ss.43–47.
[177] CCA 1974 ss.52–54.
[178] CCA 1974 ss.48–51.
[179] CCA 1974 ss.60–66.
[180] CCA 1974 s.68.
[181] CCA 1974 s.67(a).
[182] CCA 1974 ss.140A and 140B.
[183] CCA 1974 s.87.

order for payment[184] or in the case of hire purchase, a return order or a transfer order.[185] This will normally be a method of allowing the debtor time to pay off his debts by instalments or to remedy any breach.[186] Any lapse by the creditor in the provision of all the necessary forms and documentation for the agreement may make the creditor's application for enforcement invalid, or delay it until the documentation is correct.

Under CCA ss.98–104 termination of regulated agreements may only be done in accordance with the strict provisions of the Act.

Pawnbroking

Strict rules apply to pawnbrokers and their documentation with regard to the pawning of **8–45** goods. The pawnbroker must give each customer a copy of the pawn agreement, a notice of his cancellation rights and a receipt for the pawned goods.[187] The pawn will be redeemable within a period of six months, or such longer period as may be agreed,[188] or the goods will pass to the pawnbroker who may sell the goods after intimation to the customer,[189] If after the sale of the goods, there is a surplus after repayment of the loan and interest and expenses, the surplus is repayable to the customer.[190] If the sale proceeds are less than the sum due, the balance remains outstanding from the customer to the pawnbroker.[191]

Unfair relationships

An unfair relationship is a credit transaction which the court decides is unfair to the **8–46** borrower. The court, at its discretion, may rewrite the transaction so that a fairer contract subsists. Grounds for deeming a credit transaction unfair would be unreasonable rates of interest, the borrower's current financial pressures and any other relevant facts about the borrower. If a borrower alleges that the relationship is unfair, it is for the creditor to prove that it is not.[192]

▼ CHAPTER SUMMARY

SALE AND SUPPLY OF GOODS

1. **The main statute regulating the sale and purchase of goods in the United Kingdom 8–47 is:**

   ➢ The Sale of Goods Act 1979.

2. **The Sale of Goods Act 1979 implies various terms into all contracts of sale. These terms protect both seller and purchaser. They are as follows:**

   ➢ The seller has the right to sell the goods (Sale of Goods Act 1979 s.12(1)).

---

[184] CCA 1974 s.129.
[185] CCA 1974 s.133.
[186] CCA 1974 s.129.
[187] CCA 1974 s.114.
[188] CCA 1974 s.116.
[189] CCA 1974 s.121.
[190] CCA 1974 s.121(3).
[191] CCA 1974 s.121(4).
[192] CCA 1974 ss.140A–D.

> There is no charge or encumbrance over the goods (Sale of Goods Act 1979 s. 12(2)(a)).
> The buyer will enjoy quiet possession of the goods (Sale of Goods Act 1979 s.12(2)(b)).
> The seller will not be liable for the charge or encumbrance if the charge or encumbrance is disclosed (Sale of Goods Act 1979 s.12(3), (4) and (5)).
> Unless specified otherwise, the time of payments for the goods is not of the essence of the contract (Sale of Goods Act 1979 s.10).
> Goods sold by description will correspond with their bulk (Sale of Goods Act 1979 s.13).
> Goods sold must be of satisfactory quality (Sale of Goods Act 1979 s.14(2)).
> Goods must be reasonably fit for purpose (Sale of Goods Act 1979 s.14(3)).
> The above terms also apply to agents for the sellers in the course of the sellers' business (Sale of Goods Act 1979 s.14(5)).
> The bulk will correspond with any sample (Sale of Goods Act 1979 s.15).

(a) **Breach of certain implied terms, such as the right to receive good title, the right to expect goods to comply with their description, the right to satisfactory quality and fit for purpose, and the right to expect the bulk of goods to conform to a sample, will make the seller liable to the buyer.**

> Sale of Goods Act 1979 ss.12–15.

(b) **Breach by the seller of these implied terms entitles a purchaser to various remedies, including the return of his money or damages:**

> *Rowland v Divall* (1923): the buyer of a stolen car successfully reclaimed the price of the car from the seller;
> *Niblett Ltd v Confectioners Materials Co* (1929): labels on tins infringed a recognised trademark; the buyers successfully sued the sellers for breach of the requirement of "quiet possession";
> *Clegg v Anderson* (2003): a buyer of a new and expensive yacht was entitled to expect that it should be "perfect or nearly so";
> *Thain v Anniesland Trade Centre* (1997): the buyer of a cheap second-hand much-used car is not entitled to expect the quality of the car to be particularly high;
> *Griffiths v Peter Conway Ltd* (1939): a buyer of a tweed coat did not explain her unusually sensitive skin to the seller and could not complain that the coat was therefore not fit for purpose.

3. **Depending on the extent of the seller's breach, the buyer may reject the goods within a reasonable time and claim his money back and/or claim damages (Sale of Goods Act 1979 s.15B), or have the goods repaired (Sale of Goods Act 1979 s.48B):**

(a) **Partial rejection is possible under Sale of Goods Act 1979 s.35A.**

(b) **Damages is a sum of money that represents the loss to the person making the claim:**

> Sale of Goods Act 1979 s.53A.

(c) **You can usually only recover damages for what is reasonably foreseeable:**

> *Hadley v Baxendale* (1854).

4. **The Unfair Contract Terms Act 1977 and the Unfair Contract Terms in Consumer Contracts Regulations 1999 particularly protect consumers from unfair terms and practices by sellers acting in the course of a business.**

5. The time that the buyer gets title to the goods depends on whether the goods are ascertained or unascertained:

> Sale of Goods Act 1979 s.16.

and on when the parties intend title to pass:

> Sale of Goods Act 1979 s.17.

there are special rules to help establish what the parties' intentions were if they are not otherwise specified:

> Sale of Goods Act 1979 s.18.

6. (a) If a seller tries to sell something which is not his to sell, the purchaser gets no better title than the seller has:

> Sale of Goods Act 1979 s.21.

(b) If a seller has a voidable title, and that title is not reduced by the time of sale to a purchaser who buys in good faith without notice of the defect in title, the purchaser may keep the goods:

> Sale of Goods Act 1979 s.23;
> *Macleod v Kerr* (1965).

(c) A purchaser acquiring goods in good faith without notice of a pre-existing retention of title clause may also keep them:

> Sale of Goods Act 1979 s.25;
> *Archivent Sales and Developments Ltd v Strathclyde Regional Council* (1985).

7. (a) An unpaid seller may stop the delivery of any goods in transit (SOGA s.39), or withhold delivery of unsent goods. He has a right of resale if necessary (s.39).

(b) If the goods are delivered but not paid for, an unpaid seller may sue for the price of the goods (Sale of Goods Act 1979 s.49) or claim damages for non-acceptance (Sale of Goods Act 1979 s.50).

8. (a) Consumers are protected by Part I of the Consumer Protection Act 1987 because it gives a remedy to people injured using producers' products even if those people were not purchasers of the products.

(b) The Consumer Protection Act 1987 also covers damage to people's property. Claims must be in excess of £275 and made within 10 years of the acquisition of the product.

(c) Consumer Protection Act 1987 Part III protects consumers where products are unsafe, and Part III prevents producers issuing misleading price information.

9. (a) Producers may invoke various defences, amongst them being the state of the art defence under Consumer Protection Act 1987 s.4. This states that a producer is not liable for defects which were not knowable at the time the product was made.

(b) Other defences are that the product was in conformity with EU safety standards at the time of manufacture, that the product was used without the producer's authority, that the product was not supplied in a commercial transaction, that some other producer had misused the product, that the fault lay in the design and not the product itself, and that the defect did not exist in the product at the time of the injury or damage.

10. **Retailers may be convicted under the Consumer Protection from Unfair Trading Regulations 2008 if they indulge in unfair commercial practices.**

HIRE OF GOODS

1. **A hire is the use by a hirer of some object asset by a lessor in exchange for rent or other hire charges.**
2. **Hire is regulated by the common law and by:**

   ➤ Supply of Goods and Services Act 1982;
   ➤ Unfair Contract Terms Act 1977;
   ➤ Consumer Credit Act 1974 as amended by the Consumer Credit Act 2006.

3. **The protection extended by these acts extends to all hires save to hirers who are high net worth individuals or businesses.**
4. **The main type of hire is a regulated consumer hire agreement which provides extensive protection for the hirer. Further protection for the hirer is provided by:**

   ➤ Supply of Goods and Services Act 1982.

5. **The Consumer Protection Act 1987 makes the lessor liable for injury or damage arising out of the hired item.**
6. **The common law requires the hirer to be responsible for the rent and to look after the hired item carefully.**

CONSUMER CREDIT

1. **The provision of credit to consumers is closely regulated to ensure that consumers are treated fairly.**
2. **The main piece of legislation is:**

   ➤ Consumer Credit Act 1974.

3. **The Consumer Credit Act 1974 requires those who provide credit to consumers, or provide advice about credit to consumers, to be licensed to do so.**
4. **Most types of credit provision to consumers are "regulated agreements". This means that there are complex procedural rules to ensure that consumers are aware of the terms under which credit is being provided to them. These procedural rules must be followed very closely.**
5. **Consumer Credit Act 1974 s.75 applies to debtor-creditor-supplier agreements. Where the creditor is not also the supplier of the goods, the creditor is jointly and severally liable for breaches of contract or misrepresentations made by the supplier. It is for the creditor in an unfair relationships to justify the terms on which he is lending to the debtor.**

   ➤ Consumer Credit Act 1974 s.171.

? QUICK QUIZ

SALE OF GOODS AND CONSUMER LAW

Where possible, try to produce references to the relevant sections of the Act and relevant cases.

Sale and supply of goods

- What are the 10 implied terms of any contract to which the Sale of Goods Act 1979 applies?
- At a minimum, what is needed for a contract for sale in terms of the requirement of the Sale of Goods Act 1979?
- When does the buyer get property in the goods?
- What happens when someone tries to sell goods that he does not own?
- And what happens when someone tries to sell goods that he does own but which he obtained fraudulently?
- What are the buyer's main rights if there is a breach of the seller's duties to him?
- What are the seller's rights if the buyer fails to pay for the goods?
- How does the Consumer Protection Act 1987 protect consumers?
- Under that Act, producers are not necessarily always liable for defective products. When are they not liable?
- What is the effect of the Trade Descriptions Act 1968?

Hire of goods

- What types of hires are not covered by the Consumer Credit Act?
- What is the point of all the requirements needed in a regulated hire agreement?
- What is the duty of the lessor to the hirer?
- What is the duty of hirer to the lessor?

Consumer credit

- Why is the legislation about consumer credit necessary?
- What is the purpose of licensing the provision of credit and the provision of advice about credit?
- The Consumer Credit Act is very strict about the provision of copies of agreements, cooling off periods, the correct documentation being in place and other safeguards for consumers. What happens if these rules are not followed?
- Why is it a good idea to purchase expensive goods and holidays on credit cards?
- How does the law protect a consumer who finds himself locked into an extortionately high interest rate?

FURTHER READING

Cusine and Forte, *Scottish Cases in Commercial Law*, 2nd edn (Butterworths, 2000).
Davidson and MacGregor, *Commercial Law in Scotland*, 2nd edn (W. Green, 2008), Ch.1.
Ervine, *Consumer Law in Scotland*, 3rd edn (W. Green, 2004).
Gloag and Henderson, *The Laws of Scotland*, 13th edn (W. Green, 2012).
Goode, *Consumer Credit, Law and Practice* (Looseleaf), (Butterworths).

Understanding Scots Law

Thomas and Ervine, *Encyclopaedia of Consumer Law* (Sweet & Maxwell, looseleaf updated regularly).

📖 RELEVANT WEB LINKS

http://www.direct.gov.uk/en/Governmentcitizensandrights/Consumerrights/index.htm
This is the BIS's website for consumers, consumer credit and the Sale of Goods Act 1979.

http://www.bis.gov.uk/assets/biscore/consumer-issues/docs/c/10-1255-consolidation-simplification-uk-consumer-law
This is a consultation paper outlining suggested reforms to consumer law.

Chapter 9 Employment

PROFESSOR VIC CRAIG[1]

► CHAPTER OVERVIEW

This chapter is concerned with employment law. It starts by looking at the contract of **9–01** employment and the terms and conditions of employment. The chapter then discusses termination of the contract, wrongful and unfair dismissal and redundancy payments. The chapter concludes by considering discrimination in the workplace.

✓ OUTCOMES

At the end of this chapter you should be able to: **9–02**

- ✓ appreciate the nature of a contract of employment;
- ✓ understand the rules surrounding the formation of a contract of employment;
- ✓ identify the main terms and conditions of employment;
- ✓ identify, and understand, the terms that can be implied into a contract of employment;
- ✓ understand the ways in which a contract of employment can be terminated;
- ✓ understand the rules governing unfair dismissal;
- ✓ appreciate the general principles relating to redundancy; and
- ✓ understand the concept of discrimination in the workplace.

THE CONTRACT OF EMPLOYMENT

Introduction

An understanding of employment law requires a general awareness of: **9–03**

(a) the basic legal principles of contract law and delict[2];
(b) statute law; and
(c) the common law;

and how (b) and (c) relate to each other.

Although the relationship of employment is regulated by both statute and common law, the bulk of modern employment is statutory and is dealt with by employment tribunals.

Generally, the common law develops incrementally, while more radical policy changes in the law regulating the employment relationship are the result of Parliamentary

---

[1] Professor Emeritus, Heriot Watt University.
[2] See Chapters 7 and 11.

intervention, in the form of statutes or regulations made by government departments and approved by Parliament.

The effect of this hybrid, or dual, approach to employment law in the United Kingdom, is to require at least an understanding of the principles of contract law and the legislative rules created by Parliament which have, over recent years, attempted to moderate employer power by creating basic or minimum rights for employees. These rights are often referred to as "a floor of rights", in the expectation that enlightened employers will offer more advantageous provisions, usually as a result of collective bargaining. Unlike in continental legal systems, the collective agreement in the United Kingdom does not automatically create rights and duties for employers and employees throughout an industry, or sector of an industry. Collective agreements, therefore, do not have any binding, normative, or standard-setting effect; in the United Kingdom such a role is played by statute.

However, like in many areas of industry and society, the law of the European Union plays an important part in shaping employment law rights. Some articles of the Treaty on the Functioning of the European Union (TFEU) create directly enforceable rights—without the need for domestic legislation—for all citizens of the European Union. In the field of employment law, the most notable example is art.157 which provides for equal pay for men and women.

Courts and employment tribunals

9–04 Another result of the hybrid system, is that some employment law disputes are dealt with by the ordinary courts. For example, if an employee acts in breach of his contract by disclosing confidential information, his employer may raise an action in the ordinary court; or an employee may sue for his wrongful dismissal in the ordinary court. Generally, actions for breach of contract whether brought by the employer or the employee must be brought in the ordinary courts and not the specialist employment tribunals.[3]

On the other hand, statutory employment rights are capable of being enforced only through the employment tribunals, which are given an exclusive jurisdiction.

In Scotland, where a case is complicated a party may receive legal aid to assist in presenting his case.[4] Complaints usually (in equal pay claims the period is six months beginning on date the employment ended) have to be presented to the Employment Tribunals Office within three months of the right being infringed, although this can be extended. The three-months' time limit is generally strictly enforced by the tribunal, so that complaints can be dealt with while recollections are fresh, without the need for detailed documentation and to allow the system to operate as speedily as possible.

Disputes about the following may be heard only by employment tribunals:

- National Minimum Wage and access to records;
- maternity, paternity and adoption leave and pay and the right to return to work;
- redundancy payments;
- sex, race, age, religion, sexual orientation and disability discrimination;
- time off and holiday pay;
- unfair dismissal;
- unlawful deductions from wages;

---

[3] cf. Employment Tribunals (Extension of Jurisdiction) (Scotland) Order 1994. The main effect of this Order is to permit actions for breach of contract, for example where an employer does not pay wages in lieu of notice, to be raised in the employment tribunal, but an employer is not permitted to raise a breach of contract against an employee although he may make a counter-claim in response to an action raised by an employee. And see para.9–21.

[4] Advice and Assistance (Assistance by Way of Representation) (Scotland) Regulations 2001.

- equal pay (strictly such claims may also be raised in the ordinary courts but seldom are);
- appeals against health and safety improvement, prohibition and non-discrimination notices;
- failure to consult employee representatives on business transfers or redundancy;
- action short of dismissal on grounds of union membership, or non membership;
- exclusion from trade unions;
- refusal of employment on grounds of union membership;
- the subjection of a worker to a detriment for exercising certain rights to time off, carrying out health and safety rights and functions and making public interest disclosures;
- written particulars of terms of employment;
- written statement of reasons for dismissal; and
- payment by Secretary of State where an employer is insolvent.

Identifying the contract of employment

For many years, the most important distinction in employment law was the contract of **9–05** employment (or service) at one end of the spectrum and the contract for services at the other. Essentially, the distinction was between the paid servant, or employee, on the one hand and the independent businessman/woman on the other hand. The distinction was and in some respects still is, important for a variety of reasons. Many of the important legal rights contained in the Employment Rights Act 1996—the main source of individual employment rights—are given only to those who have a contract of employment or a contract of apprenticeship.

Only relatively recently have other types of contracts under which work is done become significant for employment law. Statutes, such as the Sex Discrimination Act 1975, the Race Relations Act 1976 and the Disability Discrimination Act 1995 (whose provisions are now in the Equality Act 2010) conferred protection on the ever increasing group of economically active persons known as "workers". This concept is wider than the concept of "employee". A worker means an individual who has entered into a contract of employment or "any other contract ... whereby the individual undertakes to perform personally any work or services for another party to the contract" who is not a client, or customer, of any profession or business carried on by the individual.[5]

However, there have recently been created "agency workers", who provide their services through the medium of an agency to a third party. For example, a typist (A) may enter a contract with an employment agency (B), which when work becomes available will assign him/her to work for different businesses (C, D, E). Some statutes now expressly apply to employees, workers and agency workers[6]; and agency workers are now given special rights by the Agency Workers Regulations 2010.

Control and other tests

Important rights like unfair dismissal, redundancy pay and notice of termination are **9–06** restricted to those who have contracts of employment and it is still necessary to be able to identify that contract and to distinguish it from others. At one time, if the employer could tell the individual what to do and how to do it, there would exist a contract of employment. This was sometimes referred to as the "control test".

---

[5] Employment Rights Act 1996 s.230.
[6] e.g. the Working Time Regulations 1998.

Performing Right Society v Mitchell and Booker
[1924] 1 K.B. 762

The Performing Right Society, which protects copyright in music on behalf of its composers, sued Mitchell and Booker who owned a dance hall. The Society argued that the band, which played in the dance hall, had played music without receiving the composer's or the Society's permission. If the band were employed under contracts of employment then Mitchell and Booker would be vicariously liable for their breach of the composer's right. On the other hand, if they were independent musicians they themselves could be liable for breaching the composer's right in his music. In the event, having examined the degree to which the members of the band were under the control of the dance hall owners, the court came to the conclusion that they were indeed employed under contracts of employment by the owners of the dance hall. The dance hall owners could specify the type of music to be played at particular times, so that it was fair to conclude they directed, not just the ends, but also the means of performing the contract.

However, the simple control test was not suitable for more developed and sophisticated types of employment. As a result, the courts began to relax the control test, so that it was sufficient if an employer could merely direct a person's individual skill.[7] Similar difficulties were experienced with the advent of professionally qualified staff.[8]

In other circumstances, the courts have adopted what has become known as the "organisation test" or "integration test" which allows the courts to look at whether the services or work done under the contract, is done as an integral part of the employer's activities or organisation.[9]

Multiple and variable test

9-07   Recently, courts and tribunals have developed a more flexible test that can be used to deal with many sorts of employment—the "multiple and variable" test. It permits the court to take into account a multiplicity of different factors, or criteria, and give a particular factor or criterion emphasis or weight according to the circumstances. The test may have the advantage of being universal and flexible, but it does have the disadvantage of making it difficult to predict what is the type of relationship in marginal cases.

Key Concepts

The following may be regarded as **factors** which are **relevant** in determining whether or not there is a contract of employment:

- **Control**—The criterion of control is clearly still an important one, although it is no longer the decisive criterion.
- **Provision of equipment**—The extent to which the person doing the work has to provide equipment at his or her own expense is significant. Generally, incurring a

---

[7] *Stagecraft v Minister of National Insurance*, 1952 S.C. 288.
[8] *Cassidy v Minister of Health* [1951] 2 K.B. 343.
[9] *Whittaker v Minister of National Insurance* [1967] 1 Q.B. 156.

large capital outlay to acquire equipment to perform a task, is more readily associated with a contract for services rather than a contract of employment.

- **Hire of helpers**—If the task cannot be done by the individual, but requires the individual worker to hire additional helpers, that would also suggest it is not a contract of employment; a contract of employment is a contract under which there is personal performance by the workman/woman.
- **Financial risk**—If the contract involves a degree of financial risk and requires exercising responsibility for the management of the work of the contract, it suggests it is not a contract of employment, but more likely to be a contract for services.
- **Opportunity to profit**—An opportunity to profit from the sound management of the contract will more readily be associated with a contract for services.
- **Label or name of contract**—Frequently, the parties to a contract, in an attempt to remove doubt as to the type of contract, will give the contract a particular name However, the name the parties give a contract will not be conclusive, because the existence of a contract of employment is a matter for a court or tribunal to decide and cannot be determined by the name or "label" the parties give to the contract.
- **Change of status**—On the other hand, where the parties have genuinely intended to change the status of the contract, the courts will bear this in mind in determining the relationship between the two parties.
- **Income tax and National Insurance**—Seldom will the fact that the employer does, or does not, deduct income tax or pay National Insurance contributions as if the person was an employee be of much significance. In many cases, whether income tax or National Insurance contributions should be deducted at source, is the issue which has raised the question of the status of the individual. How income tax is collected is of little significance.
- **Mutuality of obligation**—Is the employer required to provide work when it is available and is the individual required to do it when it is provided.
- The status of workers is frequently resolved by having regard to the issue of "mutuality of obligation".

O'Kelly v Trusthouse Forte plc
[1983] I.C.R. 728

O'Kelly and others worked as casual waiters on a regular basis for banquets contracted to Trusthouse Forte. In many cases, the banquets would take place in the same venues and when banquets were to be held preference would be given to staff like O'Kelly and work allocated to them. However, there was no obligation on Trusthouse Forte to give work to staff like O'Kelly when the work was available, nor was there any obligation on staff like O'Kelly to do the work when it was offered to them. For that reason, the court concluded there was insufficient mutuality of obligation for there to be a contract of employment.

Nethermere (St Neots) Ltd v Taverna
[1984] I.C.R. 612

Nethermere St Neots (Nethermere) manufactured trousers in a factory where they employed about 70 operatives, who were undoubtedly employees and from whose wages they deducted income tax and National Insurance contributions. Nethermere also made use of the services of a number of home-workers, from whose remuneration such deductions were not made. Mrs Taverna started as a home-worker in January 1978; her work consisted of mainly putting pockets into trousers for which she used a machine provided by the appellants. She worked between five and seven hours each day although she had no fixed hours of work. The garments were delivered to her daily and sometimes twice a day. In the year 1979–1980 she did not work for 12 weeks; in the year 1980–1981 she did not work for 9 weeks. The arrangement came to an end in July 1981. During the period she worked in 1981 she worked in every week of the year. She was paid weekly, according to the garments that she completed.

   The court accepted that there was a regular course of dealing between parties for years under which the garments were supplied daily to the home-workers, worked on, collected and paid for. The mere fact that the home-workers could fix their own hours of work, take holidays and time off when they wished and vary how many garments they were willing to take on, or sometimes to take none on a particular day, were factors for consideration in deciding whether or not there was a contract of service. The fact that the home-workers could decide how much work to do subject to making it worthwhile for the van driver's time in collecting it, could be read as an obligation on operatives like Mrs Taverna to take a reasonable amount of work. Conversely, there was an obligation on the company to provide a reasonable share of work for each home worker, with the result that home-workers were employees.

The importance of mutuality of obligation and personal performance, has been emphasised by the House of Lords in the following decision.

Carmichael v National Power plc
[2000] I.R.L.R. 43

Mrs Carmichael and Mrs Leese were employed as station guides at the Blyth Power Stations. Their jobs involved conducting visitors on tours of the power stations and the advertisement to which they responded prior to appointment explained that visits were normally two hours long and could be at any time during the day. Employment was to be on a "casual as required basis" at a certain hourly rate. Mrs Carmichael and Mrs Leese were appointed after interview and were told that National Power had noted that they were "agreeable to be employed" on a "casual as required" basis. They signed a pre-typed letter that stated "confirming acceptance of this offer" and they were paid for the hours they worked. When they did work, they had to follow instructions of National Power in relation to first aid responses, uniform and the quality of the tours. National Power claimed that they did not have contracts of employment.

   The House of Lords held that there was no evidence to support the inference that there was an intention to create an employment contract which subsisted when Mrs Carmichael and Mrs Leese were not actually working.

The Lord Chancellor (Lord Irvine of Lairg) stated:

"[There were] no provisions governing when, how or with what frequency guide work would be offered; there were no provisions for notice of termination on either side; the sickness, holiday and pension arrangements for regular staff did not apply; nor did the grievance and disciplinary procedures. Significantly ... in 1994 ... Mrs Carmichael was not available for work on seventeen occasions and Mrs Leese on eight. No suggestion of disciplining them arose. The objective inference is that when work was available they were free to undertake it or not as they chose. This flexibility of approach was well suited to their family needs. Just as the need for tours was unpredictable so also were their domestic commitments. Flexibility suited both sides ... The arrangement turned on mutual convenience and goodwill ... Mrs Carmichael and Mrs Leese had a sense of moral responsibility to [National Power] but ... no legal obligation."

Where there is a triangular relationship between the worker, an employment agency and end-user or a host organisation, the nature of the relationship between the worker and the agency or the host organisation is not to be decided by looking only at the written contracts, but by considering all the evidence including the conduct of the parties. Thus, where an employment agency arranges for a worker to provide their services to a client of the agency (host organisation), it is permissible for a tribunal to hold that the worker has an implied contract of employment with the host organisation.

Dacas v Brook Street Bureau (UK) Ltd
Court of Appeal, 2004 E.W.C.A Civ 217

Dacas was registered as a temporary worker with Brook Street Bureau Ltd, an employment business, which assigned her to work exclusively as a cleaner at a hostel run by Wandsworth Council. The written terms and conditions between Dacas and Brook Street Bureau Ltd provided that the agreement "shall not give rise to a contract of employment". Dacas worked exclusively for the Council for over four years until she was dismissed. Dacas took the view that she had been an employee of either the Council or Brook Street Bureau Ltd and claimed unfair dismissal. The employment tribunal held that Dacas's written contract with Brook Street Bureau Ltd was not a contract of employment, and there was no contract between Dacas and the Council, the host organisation.

The Court of Appeal held that although the construction of the contractual documents is important, it is not necessarily determinative of the nature of the contract and the tribunal should not have focused on the express terms of the written contracts entered into by Brook Street Bureau Ltd with (a) Dacas and (b) the Council, but should have considered whether a contract of employment between Dacas and the Council could have been implied through their conduct over time.

In *James v London Borough of Greenwich*,[10] the EAT observed that the key feature in a triangular relationship is that the end user cannot insist on the agency providing a particular worker and that when the arrangements between the three parties are genuine and actually represent the actual relationship between the parties, as is likely to be the case where there was no pre-existing contract between the worker and the end user, it will be a rare case for there to be evidence to allow an employment tribunal to imply a contract between the worker and the end-user. The Court of Appeal endorsed the approach of the EAT emphasising that a contract of employment between the worker and the host organisation may be implied only where necessary to give business reality to the situation. The approach of the EAT in *James* has been followed by the EAT in Scotland in *Wood Group Engineering (North Sea) Ltd v K.A. Robertson*.[11] In *Autoclenz Ltd v Belcher*[12] the Court of Appeal has emphasised that to determine the nature of a contract a tribunal has to discover the actual legal obligations of the parties and that will require an examination of all the evidence including written terms as well as how in practice the parties conducted themselves. The Supreme Court approved such an approach so that an express right for a worker to delegate performance to another did not prevent the creation of a contract of employment where that right was designed to prevent such a contract conflicted with reality and practice.[13]

Apprenticeship contracts

9–08 The contract of apprenticeship attracts the benefits of modern employment legislation, and the Employment Rights Act 1996 s.230(2) states that a contract of employment also means a contract of apprenticeship. In short, any statute that confers rights on a person with a contract of employment also protects a person with an apprenticeship contract.

The primary duty of the employer under an apprenticeship contract is to instruct the apprentice in the trade or profession concerned. In *Edmonds v Lawson*,[14] Lord Bingham of Cornhill stated:

> "A contract of apprenticeship is in law a contract with certain features peculiar to itself. It is for instance less readily terminable by the employer than the ordinary contract of employment ... [I]t is a synallagmatic contract in which the master undertakes to educate and train the apprentice in the practical and other skills needed to practise a skilled trade or profession and the apprentice binds himself to serve and work for the master and to comply with all reasonable directions. These mutual covenants are in our view cardinal features of such a relationship."

A modern apprenticeship to which the individual learner, an employer and a government sponsored training provider are parties may still have the essential elements of an apprenticeship contract: *Flett v Matheson*.[15] While a trainee's contract may be a contract for training and not of employment[16] a person can be a trainee and an employee.[17]

---

[10] [2007] I.R.L.R. 168.
[11] (EAT Case No.0081/06).
[12] [2010] I.R.L.R. 70.
[13] *Autoclenz Ltd v Belcher* [2011] I.R.L.R. 820, SC.
[14] [2000] I.R.L.R. 391.
[15] [2006] EWCA Civ 53.
[16] *Daley v Allied Suppliers* [1983] I.R.L.R. 14.
[17] *Oliver v JP Malnick & Co* [1983] I.R.L.R. 456.

Company directors

Generally, executive directors of limited companies will have contracts of employment, **9–09** sometimes referred to as "service agreements" with the company. If the director is truly an employee with a contract of employment with the company, he will be protected against unfair dismissal and redundancy. The director will be entitled to have salary and certain other debts due by the company protected and, in the event of the liquidator being unable to pay even these preferred debts, an employee will be entitled to receive payments such as arrears of wages, holiday pay, notice pay and redundancy pay, direct from the National Insurance Fund.[18]

It is, therefore, important to determine whether or not a director is an employee of the company, having regard to all the relevant facts. If an individual had a controlling shareholding, that is certainly a fact which is likely to be significant in all situations and in some cases it might prove to be decisive. However, it is only one of the relevant factors and certainly is not to be taken as determinative without considering all the relevant circumstances. Other relevant matters include:

- how and for what reasons the contract had come into existence;
- whether the contract was genuine or a sham;
- the degree of control exercised by the company over the shareholder/employee;
- whether there were directors other than, or in addition to, the shareholder/employee;
- whether the shareholder/employee was, in reality, answerable only to himself and incapable of being dismissed.

A controlling shareholder may be an employee of the company, and whether a director is an employee of the company depends on all the circumstances and the size of the shareholding is merely one of those circumstances, and this is not in any way conclusive.[19]

Public employment

Many people work in the public sector, but that fact alone does not affect their status as **9–10** employee. What it may mean, however, is that their terms of employment are not merely those set out in their contracts of employment, but have to be read as being supplemented by certain principles of the general law.

Vine v National Dock Labour Board
[1957] A.C. 488

At the relevant time, in order to obtain employment in the nationalised dock industry, dockers had to be on the National Dock Register. Mr Vine had his name removed from the National Dock Register with the result that he was unable to obtain employment as a docker. However, the legislation set down the procedure which might lead to a docker's name being removed from the Register. However, according to the legislation removal of a docker's name from the register could only be done by the National Dock Labour Committee. The court held his name had been removed unlawfully and without proper authority from the Register of Dockers. In law, that was a nullity and resulted in his "dismissal" as a docker being invalid.

---

[18] Insolvency Act 1986 s.386; Employment Rights Act 1996 s.182.

[19] *Secretary of State for Trade & Industry v Bottrill* [1998] I.R.L.R. 120; *Fleming v Secretary of State for Trade & Industry* [1997] I.R.L.R. 682; *Secretary of State for Business, Enterprise and Regulatory Reform v Neufeld* [2009] I.R.L.R. 475, CA.

Another important aspect of employment in the public sector, is that where the employment is regulated by public law, an employee may be entitled to (through requesting the Court of Session to judicially review a decision affecting his employment and) argue that a dismissal is not merely a breach of his contract or terms of employment, but that it is illegal and therefore a legal nullity.[20]

European directives and employees of the State

9–11 Employees of the State or organisations which are "emanations of the state", for example, local government employees, are entitled to enforce against their employer the provisions of EU directives.[21] However, a directive may only be relied on in this way if it is unconditional and sufficiently precise in its language to allow a domestic court to apply it.

Civil servants, technically, do not have contracts of employment, but are generally brought within the framework of modern employment law by provisions which deem them to have contracts of employment.[22]

The correct approach is to regard the civil servant as having a contractual relationship with the Crown, but one which can be determined at pleasure by the Crown without penalty.[23]

Key Concepts

Historically, the most important distinction in employment law was the **contract of employment** (or service) at one end of the spectrum and the **contract for services** at the other.

Statutes confer protection on the ever increasing group of economically active persons known as "**workers**"—a concept wider than the concept of "employee".

Formation of the contract of employment

9–12 Generally, the legal rules relating to the formation of the contract of employment are found in the law of contract.[24]

The general rule,[25] is that the parties may enter into a contract of employment any way they choose. It is possible to create a contract of employment in any of the following ways or by a mixture of them: entirely by a written agreement: entirely oral; by implication through the actings and conduct of the parties. However, it is clearly advisable that a contract of employment be entered into in writing.

---

[20] See *Malloch v Aberdeen Corporation*, 1973 S.L.T. 253.

[21] See *Marshall v Southampton & South West Hampshire Area Health Authority (No.1)* (C152/84) 42696 [1986] I.C.R. 335.

[22] See Employment Rights Act 1996 s.191 and the Trade Union and Labour Relations (Consolidation) Act 1992 s.273(1).

[23] See *Kodees Waaran v Attorney General of Ceylon* [1972] W.L.R. 456.

[24] See Chapter 7.

[25] Exceptions relate to merchant seamen (Merchant Shipping Act 1995); company directors (Companies Act 1985); no strike clause in collective agreements (Trade Union and Labour Relations (Consolidation) Act 1992).

Written statement of particulars

An employer must give to each employee a written statement of the particulars of **9-13** employment.[26] However, this does not require the contract of employment—or even particular parts of it—to be in writing but merely that certain information is given by the employer, in writing, to his employees. Therefore, a failure to issue a written statement of particulars of employment will have no effect on the validity of any contract, which might exist between the employer and the employee.[27] On the other hand, many employers and employees will accept that the written statement of particulars is at least prima facie evidence of the contract. However, since the statement is not a contract, but merely a unilateral document issued by the employer to his employee, either party is free—in the context of a dispute about the contract—to argue that the written statement differs from the contract.

A written statement of particulars of employment must include the following:

- name of employer;
- name of employee;
- date employment with employer began and date continuous employment began if different taking into account employment with associated employers and previous business owners;
- scale, rate or method of calculating, and intervals of, remuneration and how it is paid;
- terms about hours of work including normal working hours;
- terms about holidays/pay and entitlement to accrued holiday pay on termination;
- terms about incapacity for work including sick pay provision;
- terms about pensions;
- notice requirements;
- job title or brief description of the work;
- where job is not permanent, the likely period or the period of a fixed term contract;
- the place of work or if the employee is required to work in different places, that shall be stated as well as the address of the employer;
- any collective agreements which affect the terms of employment and the parties to such collective agreements; and
- where the employee is required to work outside the United Kingdom for more than a month, the period of time, the currency of remuneration, any additional remuneration and benefits payable, and terms about return to the United Kingdom.

A written statement must also: (a) specify any disciplinary rules and procedures applicable to the employee, or refer to a document which does so and which is reasonably accessible to the employee; (b) indicate the person to whom an employee can apply if he is dissatisfied with a disciplinary decision, or if he has a grievance related to his employment; and (c) if there are appeals to higher levels of management.

The written statement must generally be given not later than two months after the employee begins employment. It may be given in instalments, provided all are given within two months of the employee starting work and some (including the names of the employer and employee and terms about remuneration, holidays, job title and place of work) must be included in a document given to each employee. The particulars of any other matters

---

[26] Employment Rights Act 1996 Pt I, giving effect to Directive 91/533.
[27] See *British Steel Corporation v Dingwall*, 1976 S.L.T. 230.

may be contained in a document to which the employee is referred; the document must be reasonably accessible to the employee.

Changes to terms of employment must be given not later than one month after the changes have occurred, or before the employee is to leave the United Kingdom (if that is earlier).

The employee's remedy is to apply to an employment tribunal, which may correct or complete a statement or, if no written statement has been issued, issue a statement which ought to have been issued. However, there is no provision for the tribunal to enforce any of the particulars against an employer or for declaring what meaning is to be given to a written statement. A tribunal can only amend the written statement to ensure it corresponds with what has been agreed between the employer and employee and for that purpose it must identify the terms of the contract.[28]

The written statement is not a contract; it is a unilateral document issued by the employer to the employee and it merely represents the terms of employment which the employer believes to be in existence at the time it is issued and it is not possible to alter the terms of the contract merely by issuing a new written statement.[29]

Written contracts of employment

9–14 Where the contract of employment is entirely in writing, it may be difficult to introduce evidence that it does not accurately represent the contract, or to show the contract contains additional terms which are not set out in writing. This particularly applies where the contract has been set out in a formal document. As a result of the provisions of the Contract (Scotland) Act 1997, where a document appears to comprise all the express terms of a contract, it shall be presumed, unless the contrary is proved, that the document does comprise all the express terms stated. However, extrinsic oral, or documentary, evidence is admissible to prove that the contract does include additional express terms.

Collective agreements

9–15 As a result of the practice of settling terms and conditions of employment through collective agreements, it is important to understand the precise legal relationship between a collective agreement and the individual employee's relationship with his employer.

Definition

9–16 A collective agreement is:

> "any agreement or arrangement made by or on behalf of one or more trade unions and one or more employer or employers' associations and relating to one or more of the following matters specified below:
>
> (a) terms and conditions of employment or the physical conditions in which any workers are required to work;
> (b) engagement or non-engagement or termination or suspension of employment or the duties of employment of one or more workers;
> (c) allocation of work or the duties of employment between workers or groups of workers;
> (d) matters of discipline;

---

[28] *Southern Cross Healthcare Co Ltd v Perkins* [2011] I.R.L.R. 247.
[29] *System Floors (UK) Ltd v Daniel* [1982] I.C.R. 54.

(e) a worker's membership or non-membership of a trade union;

(f) facilities for officials of trade unions; and

(g) machinery for negotiation or consultation, and other procedures, relating to any of the above matters, including the recognition by employers or employers' associations of the right of a trade union to represent workers in such negotiation or consultation or in the carrying out of any such procedures."[30]

Legal effect of collective agreements

The legal status of a collective agreement reflects the historical development of industrial **9–17** relations in the United Kingdom, whereby neither side of industry has wanted their agreements to be subject to adjudication by the courts—the voluntarist approach to industrial relations.

Collective agreements are entered into on the grounds that they do not create legally enforceable contracts between the trade union and the employer. Indeed that common law position is now endorsed by statute which provides that a collective agreement shall be not be a legally enforceable contract unless: (1) it is in writing; and (2) it contains an express provision that it is intended to be a legally enforceable contract,[31] and it is most exceptional to find such a provision in a collective agreement in the United Kingdom.

Incorporation of collective agreements

However, terms of the collective agreement (like those dealing with wages, hours of work **9–18** and other conditions of employment) may be incorporated into the contract of employment between the employer and employees, and this results in certain terms of collective agreements giving rise to legal rights and duties between the employer and those employees into whose contracts of employment the collective agreement has been introduced or incorporated.

Incorporation comes about by an express or implied reference to the collective agreement, in the contract of employment. The principle of incorporation is set out in the following case.

NCB v Galley
[1958] 1 W.L.R. 16

Galley's contract of employment indicated that he accepted employment on "terms negotiated from time to time with the trade unions". Although his own contract of employment made no mention of overtime or weekend working, his employer, the National Coal Board, negotiated collectively with the relevant trade unions from time to time and, in one such negotiation, it was agreed that employees like Galley could be required to do a reasonable amount of overtime, when requested by the mine manager. When Galley was rostered for overtime, he refused to do it on the grounds that it was not in his contract of employment. The court held that his contract of employment was that he would work on such terms as were negotiated from time to time with the trade unions, and as the trade unions and the employer had negotiated a collective agreement, whereby employees could be required to work

---

[30] Trade Union and Labour Relations (Consolidation) Act 1992.

[31] See s.179 of the Trade Union and Labour Relations (Consolidation) Act 1992.

overtime, his contract had incorporated these collectively agreed terms. Galley, therefore, was in breach of his contract by refusing to work the rostered overtime.

Once a collective agreement has been incorporated into the contract of employment, its terms remain in force and effective between the employer and the employee until a new collective agreement is arrived at, or until the individual employee and employer agree to other terms.

Gibbons v Associated British Ports
[1985] I.R.L.R. 376

Gibbons' contract of employment provided that his "wages and conditions of service shall be in accordance with national or local agreements for the time being in force". In 1970 a collective agreement regarding wages was arrived at and in 1982 a collective agreement provided that Gibbons would have a six-day guaranteed week payment, but would lose his nightshift working allowance. In 1984 Gibbons' employers gave notice to the trade union that the six day guarantee payment was to be withdrawn. The trade unions responded by saying that they would then terminate the 1970 collective agreement regarding wages and the employers argued that if they did so, Gibbons' wages would then become regulated by a national agreement which made no provision for rates of pay or any six day guarantee payment. The court held that the six day guarantee payment had been incorporated into Gibbons' contract and it was not affected by the trade union terminating the 1970 collective agreement itself. It could be removed or altered only by a new collective agreement or by Gibbons agreeing to its removal or alteration.

That a collective agreement expressly provides that it shall not be legally binding between the employer and the trade union, is of no relevance to the issue of whether a term originating in a collective agreement can become legally binding once incorporated into a contract of employment.[32] However, a term in the collective agreement will only be incorporated into the contract of employment if it is apt for inclusion in an individual contract.[33] The touchstone for incorporation of a collective agreement's terms is whether the term impacts on the working conditions of the employee. If it does it is likely to be apt for incorporation.

Malone v British Airways plc
[2011] I.R.L.R 32, CA

Collective agreements between British Airways plc (BA) and the trade union Unite made provision for the number or complement of cabin crew and an issue arose as to whether BA could reduce the number of crew on particular flights. The contract of employment of Malone expressly provided for the incorporation of the collective agreement but BA argued that the terms about crew complement were not apt for

---

[32] *Marley v Forward Trust Group Ltd* [1986] I.R.L.R. 369.
[33] *Kaur v Rover Group Ltd* [2005] I.R.L.R. 40, CA.

incorporation into individual contracts of employment. The Court of Appeal held that the task (to determine whether a collective agreement is apt for incorporation) for the court or tribunal is to decide what the parties must have intended the term to mean. In this case although the size or number of the crew had some impact on the working conditions of the crew that had to be set against the fact that making the crew size individually enforceable would have had "disastrous consequences" for BA and if the parties had thought about it at the time of negotiation (of the term in the collective agreement) they would have said it was not intended to permit some crew members to bring a flight to a halt by refusing to work with a reduced complement.

Only in special circumstances will trade union representatives, who negotiate a collective agreement, be regarded as agents acting on behalf of the members (principals). The facts of *Edwards v Skyways Ltd*[54] were special in that the trade union representatives had been expressly authorised by employees, like Edwards, to conclude bargains on behalf of the group of employees with the employer.

Key Concepts

Collective agreements are entered into on the grounds that they do not create legally enforceable contracts between the trade union and the employer(s).

Incorporation comes about by an express or implied reference to the collective agreement, in the contract of employment and results in the incorporated term taking on the legally binding quality of a contractual term.

TERMS AND CONDITIONS OF EMPLOYMENT

This section deals with the main terms and conditions of employment; some of these are **9–19** entirely contractual or entirely statutory, while others are in part contractual and in part statutory. Thus, the relationship between an employee and his employer today is a complex one, involving a mixture of express and implied,[35] contractual and statutory obligations and rights.

Wages

Entitlement to wages will normally be dealt with by an express term of the contract,[36] and **9–20** the written statement must give particulars of the scale or rate of remuneration or the method of calculating remuneration.

Where an employee is hourly paid and the number of hours for the week or month is specified in the contract, the employee is entitled to wages for that number of hours at the agreed rate, whether or not he actually works the specified amount. Where the contract is for piecework (where wages are in accordance with output) the employer is required to

---

[34] [1964] 1 All E.R. 494.
[35] See Chapter 7.
[36] cf. *Thomson v Thomson's Tr.* (1889) 16 R. 333.

provide a steady supply of work, unless there is an established custom of a particular trade that the obligation to pay wages while the worker is idle may be suspended.[37]

A unilateral reduction of wages by an employer allows the employee to continue the contract and sue for damages.

Rigby v Ferodo Ltd
[1987] I.R.L.R. 516

Ferodo Ltd told its employees that it was going to reduce their wages, but Rigby and other employees refused to agree with their decision. However, the House of Lords confirmed that there is no principle of law, that any breach which the innocent party is entitled to treat as a repudiation of the contract, brings the contract to an automatic end. It was clear in this case that Rigby and his fellow employees had not accepted the employer's repudiation of the contract as bringing it to an end, with the result that it had no effect on the terms of their contract with the employer. They were able to claim successfully that they were still entitled to be paid the (unreduced) wages as stated in their contracts of employment.

Late payment of wages may be a repudiation of the contract.

Hanlon v Allied Breweries
[1975] I.R.L.R. 321

Mrs Hanlon worked as a barmaid and received her wages late on two consecutive occasions. Her reaction was to rescind her contract. The tribunal held that she was entitled to do so because the employers, by their conduct, had indicated that they were not seriously intending to perform their obligations to Mrs Hanlon. This case must, however, be regarded as unusual and turning on its own facts.

Unless there is an express term to the effect, generally, the contract of employment does not require payment of wages or salary of an employee who is unable to work through sickness or injury. In 1982, however, Statutory Sick Pay (SSP) was introduced. The provisions are now contained in the Social Security Contributions and Benefits Act 1992. The SSP system requires employers to act as a paying agent on behalf of the State and disputes about entitlement to SSP are dealt with not by employment tribunals but by HM Revenue and Customs with appeals to the First-tier Tribunal (Tax Chamber). Employers pay an amount fixed by statute, for a maximum of 28 weeks to employees who are sick for four consecutive days. SSP is in addition to any contractual rights and cannot be limited or excluded by any agreement.

Until the Wages Act 1986, a manual worker could insist upon being paid in cash and any non-cash payment, for example by cheque or by credit transfer, was regarded as void. However, the 1986 Act repealed that rule and the practice today is to include in the contract of employment an express term dealing with how wages will be paid.

The Wages Act 1986 also revised the law regarding deductions from wages (and any payments the worker is required to make to the employer) and the current rules are now

---

[37] See Bell's Principles s.192 and *Devonald v Rosser & Sons* [1906] 2 K.B. 728.

contained in Part II of the Employment Rights Act 1996 which applies to "workers" as well as "employees".

Section 13 of the 1996 Act provides that "an employer shall not make a deduction from wages of a worker unless (a) the deduction is required or authorised to be made by virtue of a statutory provision[38] or a relevant provision of the worker's contract or (b) the worker has previously signified, in writing, his agreement or consent to the making of the deduction". Thus, a deduction is lawful only if it is required by statute or the worker has before any deduction is made (a) agreed to it in writing or (b) has had written notice of the existence of the unwritten contractual term, giving the employer a right to make the deduction. However, where an employer has a contractual right to transfer an employee to work which is less well paid, a fall in the wages to which the employee becomes entitled is not a deduction from wages.

Hussman Manufacturing Ltd v Weir
[1998] I.R.L.R. 288

Weir had been employed for 12 years by Hussman Manufacturing Ltd on night-shift duty, when his employers decided to alter their shift system and he was moved to a day-shift rota and paid at the day-shift rate. He carried on working under protest and complained to an employment tribunal that his employers had made an unlawful deduction from his wages.

The EAT held that an employer, who moved an employee from a night-shift to a day-shift and reduced his salary to the day-shift rate, had not made an unlawful deduction from the employee's wages.

There are special rules for retail workers. Section 18 of the Employment Rights Act 1996 provides that where an employer of a worker in retail employment makes a deduction on account of cash shortages or stock deficiencies, the deduction shall not exceed 10 per cent of the gross amount payable on that day.

However none of the above rules applies to the following:

- deductions to recover an overpayment of wages or expenses;
- deductions as a result of statutory disciplinary proceedings;
- a deduction the employer is required to make by law and to pay the amount over to a public authority;
- deductions agreed to in writing by the worker which the employer is required to pay over to a third person, an amount notified by that person (e.g. trade union subscriptions and payments to provident and benefit funds);
- deductions on account of the worker having taken part in a strike or other industrial action; or
- deductions agreed to in writing by the worker to satisfy a court or tribunal order requiring the payment to be made by the worker to the employer.[39]

---

[38] e.g. income tax or National Insurance contributions.
[39] ERA 1996 s.14.

Definition of wages

9–21	For the purpose of Part II of the Employment Rights Act wages are "any sums payable to the worker in connection with his employment including fee, bonus, commission, holiday pay or other emolument referable to his employment whether payable under his contract or otherwise".[40] The definition also includes various statutory payments, like statutory sick pay and statutory maternity, paternity and adoption pay. However, the following payments are excluded:

- advances of wages or loans;
- expenses incurred by the worker in carrying out his employment;
- pensions, allowances, gratuities, in connection with retirement or as compensation for loss of office;
- payments referable to redundancy; and
- payments to the worker otherwise than in his capacity as a worker.

In *Delaney v Staples*[41] the House of Lords held that as pay in lieu of notice is made in respect of a period after the contract had been brought to an end it could not be regarded as wages for the purpose of Part II of the Employment Rights Act 1996. Accordingly, while non-payment of pay in lieu of notice is a breach of contract it is not an unlawful deduction from wages under the Employment Rights Act. An alternative to paying an employee in lieu of notice, is to place the employee on "garden leave" during the period of notice. This means that the contract of employment continues during the notice period, and should the employer fail to pay wages there will be an unlawful deduction from wages, because the contract of employment does not come to an end until the garden leave has expired.

A worker can present a complaint in the employment tribunal that his employer has made an unlawful deduction from wages, and if the tribunal upholds the complaint, it shall order the employer to pay to the worker the amount of any deductions.

Employees are entitled to receive a written itemised pay statement containing particulars of:

- the gross amount of wages or salary;
- the amounts of any variable and fixed deductions and the purposes for which they are made;
- the net amount of wages payable; and
- where different parts of the net amount are paid in different ways, the amount and method of payment of each part-payment.[42]

If an employer fails to give an employee an itemised pay statement, the employee may refer the matter to an employment tribunal, which can order the employer to pay to the employee the aggregate of any un-notified deductions.

---

[40]	ERA 1996 s.27.
[41]	[1992] I.C.R. 483.
[42]	ERA 1996 ss.8, 9.

> **Key Concepts**
>
> **Deductions from wages** may generally only be made with the worker's written consent, or by statutory authority.
>
>   **Retail workers** have additional protection for deductions for cash or stock shortages.

National Minimum Wage

Until the National Minimum Wage Act 1998, there was no general protection against low **9–22** pay. The 1998 Act with the National Minimum Wage Regulations 1999 introduced a scheme to ensure a minimum level of pay across all industry. The scheme applies to employees, workers and agency workers. Those who are 16 and 17 receive a development rate and there are different rates for apprentices, those between 18 and 20 and those 21 and over. The Secretary of State may refer matters including the level at which the Minimum Wage is set to the Low Pay Commission.[43] The rate is expressed as an hourly rate and the current rates are: £6.08 for those 21 and over, £4.98 for 18–20 year olds and £2.60 for apprentices.

   In order to decide whether the appropriate rate is paid, it is necessary to determine the pay reference period, the total pay received and the total hours worked during that period. The pay reference period is one month or other shorter period; accordingly the reference period for workers paid weekly is a week, for those paid daily one day and for those paid at longer intervals, e.g. two months, is one month.[44] The total pay is the gross pay, which includes all commission, bonuses and gratuities paid through the payroll, but does not include benefits in kind like luncheon vouchers and use of company car.[45] Accommodation provided by the employer is taken into account but up to the maximum of £32.27 per week.[46] Special shift rates are excluded.

   The hours to which the appropriate hourly rate is applied vary depending on whether it is time work (where the worker is paid according to the hours worked), salaried work (where the worker is paid for a basic number of hours per year for which he gets an annual salary paid in 12 equal monthly instalments or 52 equal weekly instalments), output work (where the worker is paid for the number of units of work completed) or unmeasured work (where there are no specified hours but the worker is required to work when needed or work is available).[47] Briefly for "time work" a worker is entitled to be paid the appropriate rate while required to be working or travelling during normal working hours except while on rest breaks; for "salaried work" a worker is entitled to be paid while required to be working or travelling during normal working hours but also while on rest breaks or holidays if part of minimum contractual hours, but not for hours when entitled only to less than half normal pay (for example while on paid sick leave); for "output work" workers are entitled to the appropriate rate either for all hours worked or a "fair" rate for each item or task completed; for "unmeasured work" a worker is entitled to the appropriate rate either for the hours in a "daily average agreement" or absent such an agreement for every hour worked.

---

[43] National Minimum Wage Act 1998 s.6.
[44] National Minimum Wage Regulations 1999 reg.10.
[45] 1999 Regulations regs 8, 9.
[46] 1999 Regulations reg.36.
[47] 1999 Regulations regs 3–6.

> **Key Concepts**
>
> **Time work**: hours done in reference period.
>   **Salaried work**: basic hours, plus any hours for which the worker received extra payments.
>   **Output work**: hours required to produce a certain number of pieces made at mean hourly output rate, or the actual hours in the reference period.
>   **Unmeasured work**: hours in a "daily average" agreement or the actual hours in the pay reference period.

Enforcement

9–23 Employers are required to keep records to show that the worker is paid the National Minimum Wage and a worker has the right to see such records.[48]

Enforcement of payment of the National Minimum Wage is by the Inland Revenue issuing of an Enforcement Notice on an employer, and by a worker making a complaint to an employment tribunal that there has been an unlawful deduction from wages under Part II of the Employment Rights Act 1996.[49] Where such a complaint is made, it is presumed the worker qualified for the Minimum Wage and that he/she was were paid less than that wage.[50]

Hours of work and holidays

9–24 Until the Working Time Regulations 1998, generally employers and employees were free to make such contractual arrangements as they wished regarding hours of work and holidays. Following the Working Time (Amendment) Regulations of 2003 many previously excluded groups of workers and sectors of industry have been brought within the Regulations including transport and doctors in training, but subject to some modifications.

The Regulations apply to employees, workers and agency workers, but in some cases certain groups are partly excluded, for example domestic servants and workers who set their own hours (managers and executives), and protection to other workers may be reduced if certain conditions are met.

Regulation 21 contains many special circumstances in which the Regulations do not apply or are modified, for example where:

(a) place of work and residence or places of work distant from each other;
(b) security and surveillance require permanent presence;
(c) there is a need for continuity of service and production;
(d) there is a foreseeable surge of activity; and
(e) where there are exceptional events or accidents.

"Working time" means any period during which the worker is working, at the employer's disposal and carrying out his activity or duty, any period during which the worker is receiving relevant training and "any additional period which is to be treated as working

---

[48] 1999 Regulations reg.3.
[49] National Minimum Wage Act ss.19–22.
[50] National Minimum Wage Act ss.17, 18.

time ... under a relevant agreement"[51] so that if an employer, and employee, are in doubt about whether such an additional period is to be treated as working time, they are able to enter an agreement by which that uncertainty is removed. In *Sindicato de Medicos de Assistencia Publica (SIMAP) v Conselleria de Sanidad y Consumo de la Generalidad Valenciana*[52] the European Court of Justice held that time spent on call by doctors must be regarded as working time where their presence at the health centre is required. The fact that doctors can sleep while their services are not required, is immaterial if they are required to be on the employer's premises to provide their services when required.[53] Nor is it lawful to pay a reduced rate of pay for on-call hours[54] and where a worker on call was required to remain at or within a very short distance of her home which was within her place of work the whole time she was on call constituted working time[55] and the extent to which a worker is likely to be called out while on call is irrelevant.[56]

Maximum working week

A worker's average working time—including overtime—shall not exceed 48 hours for each **9–25** seven day period.[57] The only exceptions permitted from the 48-hour limit are in respect of:

- domestic servants;
- workers whose working time "is not measured or predetermined or can be determined by the worker himself" for example, executives, family workers and religious celebrants; and
- where the worker has agreed in writing to exceed 48 hours.[58]

Night work

Night work is work done between 11pm and 6am and generally a night worker's hours **9–26** shall not exceed an average of eight hours in a 24-hour period.[59] The limits on night work are excluded in many cases when certain conditions apply and may be excluded, or modified, by collective or workforce agreement.[60]

Rest periods

There are exceptions for shift workers (reg.22), but generally a worker is entitled to a daily **9–27** rest break of 11 consecutive hours and a weekly rest period of not less than 24 hours. Where a worker's working day is more than six hours, he is entitled to an uninterrupted rest break of not less than 20 minutes.[61]

---

[51] 1998 Regulations reg.2(1).
[52] [2000] I.R.L.R. 845.
[53] *Laudeshauptstadt Kiel v Jaeger* [2003] I.R.L.R. 804, ECJ.
[54] *Dellas v Premier Ministre* [2006] I.R.L.R. 225, ECJ.
[55] *MacCartney v Oversley House Management* [2006] I.R.L.R. 514, EAT.
[56] *Hughes v Graylyn's Residential Home* EAT/0159/08.
[57] 1998 Regulations reg.4. The limit for those between 15 and 18 years is 40 hours: reg.5A.
[58] 1998 Regulations regs 4, 19, 20.
[59] 1998 Regulations reg.6. But see the limits and exceptions for 15–18 years old: regs 6A, 27, 27A.
[60] 1998 Regulations regs 21, 23.
[61] 1998 Regulations reg.12; reg.12 is subject to exceptions in reg.21: see *Martin v Southern Health and Social Care Trust* [2010] I.R.L.R. 1048, NICA.

Annual leave

9–28 A worker is entitled to four weeks' paid annual leave,[62] and this cannot be modified or excluded by collective or workforce agreement and except where the employment is terminated, there can be no payments in lieu. However, since 2009, to this basic entitlement there has been added a further 1.6 weeks and the maximum entitlement is now 28 days and unlike entitlement to the basic four weeks leave, entitlement to the additional leave can be carried forward to the next leave year.[63] It is not permissible to roll up or incorporate holiday pay into an hourly or weekly rate, as payment should be made at the time the holiday is taken.[64] While the Court of the European Union (CJEU) in *Pereda v Madrid Movilidad SA*[65] has held that a worker who is unable to take annual leave because he is on sick leave is entitled to postpone it if need be to the following leave year giving effect to this in domestic law has produced difficulties because the decision in *Pereda* seems to contradict reg.13(9) which prohibits the carrying forward of leave not taken and payment in lieu thereof except on termination of the employment. Thus in *NHS Leeds v Larner*[66] the EAT has held that there is a right, on termination, to payment in lieu of leave accrued but not taken in the year of termination but also in a previous leave year. However, in *Fraser v Southwest London St George's Mental Health Trust*[67] another EAT has held, adopting the "use it or lose it" approach that leave not claimed in the relevant leave year is lost but it is questionable whether this comports with the decision of the CJEU in *Pereda*.

Enforcement and remedies

9–29 There are three ways in which the Regulations can be enforced:

(1) breach of certain regulations (e.g. regs 4(2), 5A(4), 6A) is an offence;
(2) actions for damages in the ordinary court for breach of statutory duty; and
(3) complaints to an employment tribunal under reg.30.

Time-off rights

9–30 Statute now provides that employees are entitled to time off for certain purposes. On some occasions time off is with pay, while on other occasions it is unpaid time off.

Trade union duties and activities

9–31 An official of an independent trade union, recognised by an employer, is entitled to paid time off to carry out his *duties* as an official connected with negotiations with his employer and concerned with the receipt of information and consultation (and for training associated therewith), relating to redundancies and business transfers. An employee is also entitled to unpaid time off to take part in the *activities* of a recognised trade union. In each case, the amount of time off to which an employee is entitled is such time off as is reasonable, with regard to the guidance given by the Code of Practice issued by ACAS and

---

[62] 1998 Regulations reg.13.
[63] 1998 Regulations reg.13A.
[64] *Robinson-Steele v RF Retail Services Ltd* [2006] I.R.L.R. I–2531, CJEU. But the principle has been relaxed provided the incorporation of the holiday pay is transparent and the subject of a clear agreement with the worker: *Lyddon v Englefield Brickwork Ltd* EAT/0301/07, [2008] I.R.L.R. 198.
[65] [2009] I.R.L.R. 959.
[66] [2011] I.R.L.R. 894.
[67] EAT/0456/10, [2012] I.R.L.R. 100.

complaints that an employer has not permitted time-off, lie to an employment tribunal.[68] Time off for union learning representatives was introduced in 2003.[69]

Public duties

Employees who hold certain public offices, e.g. Justices of the Peace, or are members of **9–32** certain public bodies, e.g. local authorities and statutory tribunals, are entitled to reasonable time off without pay to perform their public duties.[70] Jury service is treated by s.85 of the Criminal Procedure (Scotland) Act 1995 and jurors are entitled to expenses for loss of wages and benefits.

Finding work

An employee with two years' service, and who is under notice of redundancy, is entitled to **9–33** reasonable time off with pay, (a maximum of half a week's pay) to look for other work or to arrange training for new employment.[71]

Maternity, paternity, adoption and parental leave, and flexible working

Periods of time off supported by rights to statutory payments for varying periods and at **9–34** different rates in some cases are now available, and in certain conditions employees have the right to request contractual changes for childcare.[72] Briefly, the position is as follows:

(1) *Maternity*: Regardless of length of service all employees are entitled to 26 weeks' ordinary maternity leave (OML) followed by 26 weeks' additional maternity leave (AML) for women who have accumulated 26 weeks' continuous employment by the 14th week before their expected week of childbirth (EWC). A woman who has 26 weeks' employment (with the employer) is entitled to statutory maternity pay (SMP) for a maximum of 39 weeks which is at 90 per cent of earnings for the first 6 weeks and at a flat rate of £128.73 (if less than the 90 per cent of earnings) for the remainder.[73] The right to return to work is also secured. Both employees and agency workers are entitled to paid time off to attend ante-natal care appointments on advice of a doctor, nurse or midwife.[74]

(2) *Paternity*: After 26 weeks' employment by the 15th week before EWC the biological father or the husband (or partner)[75] of the child's mother is entitled to 2 weeks' ordinary paternity leave (OPL), either on the birth of a child provided the leave is taken for the purpose of caring for the child or supporting the mother and the employee has responsibility for the upbringing of the child. The leave must be taken within 56 days of the birth and is with pay at the rate of £124.88 per week or 90 per cent of earnings if less than that. Since April 2011 additional paternity leave (APL) is available to an employee (or an agency worker) with at least 26 weeks' continuous employment, to care for the child if the child's mother was

---

[68] Trade Union and Labour Relations (Consolidation) Act 1992 ss.168, 170.
[69] Trade Union and Labour Relations (Consolidation) Act 1992 s.168A.
[70] ERA 1996 s.50.
[71] ERA 1996 s.52.
[72] Detailed discussion is not possible here, but see the Employment Rights Act 1996 Pt VIII Ch.I (maternity leave), Ch.II (parental leave) and Maternity and Parental Leave Regulations 1999, as amended by the Employment Act 2002 and Regulations made there-under, and the Employment Act 2002 ss.1–4 (paternity and adoption leave and pay) and s.47 (flexible working) and Regulations made there-under.
[73] The Regulations require notices and responses to be given at particular times.
[74] ERA 1996 ss.55, 57ZA.
[75] Same sex partners are included.

entitled to SML, SMP or maternity allowance but has started work again and has as a result lost the right to maternity pay. During the period of APL there is a right to additional paternity pay which is also at the rate of £124.88 or 90 per cent of earnings if less than that. The right to return to work is secured as for a woman returning from OML.

(3) *Adoption*: After 26 weeks' employment by the date of being notified[76] of a match for adoption, an individual (or where the adoption is by a couple one of the couple[77]) is entitled to 26 weeks' ordinary adoption leave (OAL) followed by 26 weeks' additional adoption leave (AAL) with the same rights to return to work as a woman on OML or AML.[78] During OAL employees are entitled to statutory adoption pay (SAP) at the same rates as those which operate for paternity and maternity pay.

(4) *Flexible working*: The right to a flexible working pattern was introduced by the Employment Act 2002 s.47, as part of the family friendly approach to employment. The right is available to an employee/parent (which includes mother, father, adopter, guardian or foster parent or a person married to, or the partner of, such a person and has the responsibility for the child's upbringing) of a child under 17 (or 18 if disability living allowance is in payment) and has at least 26 weeks' continuous employment. It entitles the employee to apply to an employer for changes regarding their: (a) time/hours of work; (b) place of work as between home and place of business; and (c) other terms as regulations may specify. Only one application (which must be in writing) per year is permitted, but the employer's right to refuse is limited to the following: (a) additional costs; (b) detriment to customer demand; (c) quality performance; (d) inability to reorganise work among other staff or recruit other staff; (e) insufficiency of work; or (f) planned structural changes. The right is enforced by complaint to the employment tribunal, which can order reconsideration of the request and make an award of compensation.

Domestic incidents

9–35 Employees are entitled to a reasonable amount of time off during working hours to deal with a domestic incident,[79] for example,

- when a dependant falls ill, is injured or dies, or to arrange care for such a dependant;
- where the care arrangements for such dependant unexpectedly ends; or
- where the employee's child is involved in an unexpected incident at school.

Employee representatives

9–36 An employee who is a representative for purposes of redundancy, business transfer consultation or information and consultation is entitled to reasonable paid time-off to perform his duties or to act as a candidate in an election of representatives.[80]

---

[76] Notification must be by an approved adoption agency.
[77] The other member of the couple may be entitled to paternity leave and pay.
[78] The Regulations require notices and responses to be given at particular times.
[79] ERA 1996 s.57A.
[80] ERA 1996 s.61; Information and Consultation of Employees Regulations 2004 reg.27.

Safety representatives

Safety representatives appointed by a recognised trade union and elected representatives **9–37** of employee health and safety, are entitled to such time off with pay as is reasonable in accordance with the HSC Code of Practice to perform their functions and to receive training.[81]

Study and training

Employees who are between 16 and 18 years of age and not in full-time education are **9–38** entitled to reasonable time off with pay, to undertake study or training which leads to a relevant qualification.[82]

Other contractual terms and duties

As indicated earlier, the contract of employment contains many implied terms. It is **9–39** tempting to think of the implied duties of the contract of employment as specific or discrete. However, the underlying obligation in the relationship today may be expressed simply as an obligation on both parties not to act in such a way that is likely to, or calculated to, destroy or seriously damage the trust and confidence on which the employment relationship is ultimately based. The generality of the duty of trust and confidence is illustrated by the following two cases.

> ### Malik v B.C.C.I. SA
> ### [1997] I.R.L.R. 462
>
> The House of Lords held that an employer could be in breach of the implied duty of trust and confidence by operating his business in a dishonest and corrupt way and an employee who was unable to secure employment in the future, as a result of having worked for such an employer, is entitled to damages for that loss.
> Lord Nicholls of Birkenhead stated:
>
> "Employers may be under no ... implied contractual term of general application, to take steps to improve their employees' future job prospects. But failure to improve is one thing, positively to damage is another. Employment, and job prospects, are matters of vital concern to most people. Jobs of all descriptions are less secure than formerly, people change jobs more frequently, and the job market is not always buoyant. Everyone knows this. An employment contract creates a close personal relationship, where there is often a disparity of power between the parties. Frequently, the employee is vulnerable. Although the underlying purpose of the trust and confidence term is to protect the employment relationship, there can be nothing unfairly onerous or unreasonable in requiring an employer who breaches the trust and confidence term to be liable if he thereby causes continuing financial loss of a nature that was reasonably foreseeable."

---

[81] Safety Representatives and Safety Committee Regulations 1977; Health and Safety (Consultation with Employees) Regulations 1996.
[82] ERA 1996 s.63A(1).

TSB Bank plc v Harris
[2000] I.R.L.R. 157

Harris was unaware that customer complaints had been made against her. When Miss Harris sought another employment, the TSB were approached for a reference. The reference stated that 17 complaints had been made against her, of which 4 were upheld and 8 were outstanding, and as a result of that reference the new employers refused to engage Miss Harris. When Miss Harris discovered that there had been so many complaints against her, in respect of which she was given no opportunity to comment or explain, she resigned and claimed a constructive dismissal. The employment tribunal held that the employers were in breach of the implied term of trust and confidence in providing a reference which made mention of previously unregistered complaints and was misleading and potentially destructive of the employee's career in financial services. That decision was upheld by the Employment Appeal Tribunal, on the grounds that where an employer undertakes to give a reference in respect of an employee, there is an implied contractual obligation to ensure that it is a fair and reasonable reference, and a failure to do so may be a breach of the implied term of trust and confidence. While referring to previously lodged complaints was nothing more than true and accurate, that was not necessarily a reasonable and fair reference.

Other examples of the duty of trust and confidence being breached are: (a) using derogatory nicknames towards or harassing an employee[83]; (b) altering an examiner's marks in way that amounted to an affront to the examining professor's integrity[84]; (c) in giving a reference for a former colleague employee misrepresenting her status or seniority[85]; (d) an employer's unilateral variation of a contract by imposing changes on a football coach's authority to select the team without prior discussion.[86]

Where one party to the contract is in breach of the implied duty of trust and confidence the other party has a choice of remedies. He can accept the repudiatory breach and rescind the contract and sue for constructive dismissal or he can affirm the contract and sue for damages for any continuing loss. He cannot however rely on the other party's breach to withhold performance of a particular term as the Court of Session has held that the duty of trust and confidence is all pervading and not the counterpart of any particular term requiring performance by the other party.[87]

Nonetheless, having underlined the generality of the obligations on both the employer and employee, it is convenient to categorise the implied duties of the employee under the following headings:

Obedience

9–40 An employee must carry out the instructions given to him by his employers for the purpose of performing his contract, provided it does not involve the employee doing an act that is illegal or immoral. Thus, an employee who was employed as a petrol pump attendant was

---

[83] *Parsons v Bristol Street Fourth Investments Ltd*, EAT/501/07.
[84] *Bournemouth Higher Education Corporation v Buckland* [2010] I.R.L.R. 445, CA.
[85] *Bryan v Skills Solutions Ltd* ET/2400252/08.
[86] *McBride v Falkirk Football and Athletic Club* [2011] I.R.L.R. 22, EAT.
[87] *Macari v Celtic Football and Athletic Club Ltd* [1999] I.R.L.R. 787, IH.

entitled to refuse to falsify the sales records at a time when the business was to be put up for sale, because it would have resulted in him performing an illegal and immoral act.[88]

An employee is not required to perform an act which is outside the scope of his contract. Thus, it has been held that a shepherd was entitled to refuse instructions to tend cows.[89] However, an employee is expected to be flexible and co-operative in emergency situations.[90]

The scope of the contract may also be limited in terms of place and time.

Johnstone v Bloomsbury Health Authority
[1991] I.R.L.R. 118

Dr Johnstone, employed as a junior doctor by the health authority, was required by his contract to work a standard working week of 40 hours and additional availability on-call up to an average of 48 hours a week. Dr Johnstone contended his long working hours affected his health. The following statement of Sir Nicolas Browne-Wilkinson is probably an accurate reflection of law:

"There was in the contract of employment no incompatibility between Dr Johnstone's duty on the one hand and the authority's right, subject to the implied duty as to health on the other hand. The implied duty did not contradict the implied term of the contract. There must be some restriction on the authority's rights. In any sphere of employment other than that of a junior hospital doctor an obligation to work up to 88 hours per week would be rightly regarded as oppressive and intolerable. The authority's right to call for overtime under (the contract) was not an absolute right but must be limited in some way. Therefore notwithstanding (the express term in the contract) the authority could not lawfully require the plaintiff to work so much overtime in any week as it was reasonably foreseeable would damage his health."

In some cases, the contract does not make clear where the place of employment is and this has to be determined by looking at all the facts and circumstances.[91] In other cases, the contract will include a term allowing the employer to move the employee from one place of work to another. However, a right to transfer an employee from one place of work to another, is itself subject to the implied qualification that the employer will not use the right in such a way as to make it impossible for the employee to perform his contract.

United Bank Ltd v Akhtar
[1989] I.R.L.R. 507

There was a term in Mr Akhtar's contract of employment which allowed the bank to transfer him to any place of business which the bank had in the United Kingdom, either permanently or temporarily; the contract also provided that the bank may

---

[88] *Morrish v Henlys (Folkestone)* [1973] 2 All E.R. 137; and *Pagano v HGS Ltd* [1976] I.R.L.R. 9.
[89] *Moffat v Boothby* (1884) 11 R. 501.
[90] *Smith v St Andrew Ambulance* [1973] N.I.R.C. Unreported July 12, 1973 (ambulance driver); *Sim v Rotherham B.C.* [1986] I.C.R. 897 (school teacher).
[91] *O'Brien v Associated Fire Alarms Ltd* [1968] 1 W.L.R. 1916: O'Brien's place of work was "the Liverpool area" and he could not, therefore, be required to work in Barrow-in-Furness.

make a contribution to the employee's removal costs. The bank, in reliance on this term, required Mr Akhtar to move from one town in the Midlands to another, without indicating whether the move would be temporary or permanent and without indicating whether they would make a contribution to Mr Akhtar's removal costs. Initially, Mr Akhtar was given only a weekend's notice, which the bank later extended to almost a week. The court came to the conclusion that although the employer appeared to have an unfettered discretion to transfer Mr Akhtar from one place to another, it could not use that contractual term in such a way as to make it virtually impossible for Mr Akhtar to perform his contract. It is clear, therefore, that even an express mobility clause in a contract of employment has to be operated in such a way that it is not virtually impossible for the employee to comply with it.

The scope of the contract is also limited by the implied understanding that employees will not be required to undertake unforeseen and unreasonable risks in carrying out the contract.[92] In *Ferrie v Western District Council*[93] an employee was entitled to refuse to clean ponds in remote locations, where the ponds were deep and steep-sided and presented a serious risk to non-swimmers like Mr Ferrie, who might drown in the event of him slipping or falling into the pond while carrying out the cleaning operation. Instructions must be given in a way that does not undermine trust and confidence. In *Wilson v Racher*,[94] the employee had demonstrated a degree of disobedience to his employer, but the court came to the conclusion that this was provoked by the employer's lack of respect for the employee, by humiliating him in front of others.

Employee's duty of careful performance

9–41 An employee must perform his contract with reasonable care. The principle is exemplified in:

Lister v Romford Ice and Cold Storage Ltd
[1957] A.C. 555

Romford Ice Cold Storage Ltd employed Mr Lister senior and Mr Lister junior (father and son). The son drove a lorry and the father acted as the driver's assistant. When Lister senior was giving manoeuvring instructions to his son, he was injured as a result of his son's careless driving. In accordance with the normal rules of vicarious liability Lister junior's employers, Romford Ice and Cold Storage Company Ltd, were liable to Mr Lister senior for his injuries. Romford Ice and Cold Storage Ltd called upon their insurance policy and their insurers duly made payment to Lister senior. However, relying on their subrogation clause in the contract of insurance, the insurers then insisted that Romford Ice and Cold Storage Company Ltd used their right to require Lister junior to perform his contract with reasonable care, to recover from Lister junior the payments the insurance company had to make to Lister senior. The House of Lords reaffirmed the principle that an employee who breaches his contract by performing his obligations without reasonable care, is required to indemnify the employer for any loss which follows.

---

[92] *Burton v Pinkerton* (1867) L.R. 2 Ex. 340.
[93] [1973] I.R.L.R. 162.
[94] [1974] I.R.L.R. 114.

Employee's duty of fidelity

This implied duty binds an employee to protect his employer's business in the form of **9–42** commercial assets and trade secrets and other confidential information and is relevant to the freedom of an employee to take on secondary, or part-time, employment.[95] At its simplest, it requires the employee to use all reasonable means to advance his employer's business and, secondly, to refrain from doing anything which would injure his employer's business.

Competition

There is no general rule that an employee may not deal in commodities in which his **9–43** employer deals, or is prohibited from working for a competitor of his employer in his own time. It depends on the work the employee does.[96]

Trade secrets and confidential information

The duty of fidelity and loyal service requires that an employee protects and does not **9–44** abuse or disclose his employer's trade secrets, or confidential information. Even after the contract of employment has come to an end, a diluted form of this duty continues.

Faccenda Chicken v Fowler
[1986] I.C.R. 297

Fowler left his employment with Faccenda Chicken to set up in competition. There was no restrictive covenant in Fowler's contract of employment and Faccenda Chicken, therefore, could rely only on Fowler's implied duty not to disclose or use confidential information after the contract came to an end. The information which the employer claimed to be confidential in this case, included the names and addresses of customers and their requirements, the most convenient routes for delivery vehicles and customers' preferences for delivery days and times and the price structure used for particular customers. The Court of Appeal held that while an ex-employee must not disclose secret processes of manufacture or other truly confidential information, the obligation of the ex-employee did not extend to information which was confidential only in that, had it been disclosed during the contract, it would have breached the implied duty of fidelity.

Key Concepts

The factors which are relevant to determining whether or not information is truly confidential include:

- the nature of the job;
- the nature of the information;
- can it be equated with a trade secret;

---

[95] *Graham v Paton,* 1917 S.C. 203; *Faccenda Chicken v Fowler* [1986] I.C.R. 297; and see *Sanders v Parry* [1967] 1 W.L.R. 753.

[96] *Hivac v Park Royal Scientific Instruments Ltd* [1946] Ch. 169.

> - has the employer stressed the confidentiality of the information during the period of employment; and
> - can the confidential information be isolated from other general information to which an employee is exposed in the course of employment?
>
> In Scotland a similar approach has been adopted.[97]

Of course an employee will develop his own skills and knowledge while in employment and they become part of the employee's own "stock in trade", which he is allowed to use in developing his career and earning potential.[98]

Restrictive covenants

9–45 Often employers seek to protect their legitimate interests like business connections, knowledge of customers and confidential information by inserting into contracts of employment restrictive covenants. A covenant which prevents an employee from competing with his employer is regarded as a *pactum illicitum* and will be unenforceable unless it is necessary to protect a legitimate interest of the employer. The mere exclusion of competition by an ex-employee is not, itself, a legitimate interest and in order to be enforceable a restrictive covenant must protect confidential information or trade connections.[99] However, even then for the covenant to be enforceable it must be reasonable and in the public interest.

Reasonableness can be determined by having regard to the time of the restriction, the area to which it applies and the job function to which it relates.

> ### Bluebell Apparel v Dickinson
> #### 1980 S.L.T. 157
>
> Dickinson's contract of employment provided that he would not, for two years after the termination of his employment, perform any services for any competitors anywhere in the world. Having regard to the nature of the jeans industry and the confidential information to which Mr Dickinson had access, the court upheld the validity of the covenant. The court noted the covenant was necessary to protect trade secrets in a world-wide industry. It remarked that "prohibition against disclosing trade secrets is worthless unless accompanied by a restriction upon the employee possessed of secrets against entering the employment of rivals".

Similarly, in *Cyrus Energy Ltd v Stewart*,[100] the difficulty in policing covenants restraining solicitation and having business dealings was recognised by continuing an interdict against future employment by likely competitors.

The covenant must not be against the public interest, which generally requires access to services in a free market.[101]

---

[97] *Harben Pumps (Scotland) Ltd v Lafferty*, 1989 S.L.T. 752, OH.
[98] *United Sterling v Mannion* [1974] I.R.L.R. 314; and see *Exchange Communications Ltd v Masheder* [2009] CSOH 135.
[99] *A & D Bedrooms v Michael*, 1984 S.L.T. 297.
[100] [2009] CSOH 53.
[101] *Bull v Pitney Bowes* [1967] 1 W.L.R. 273.

TERMINATION OF THE CONTRACT AND WRONGFUL DISMISSAL

Notice

Unless the contract is for a fixed period, the contract of employment can be ended by **9–46** either party giving notice of termination. If the contract makes no provision (express or implied) for termination by notice the common law provides that either party may terminate the contract by giving reasonable notice of termination.[102] What is reasonable depends on the circumstances of the case, including the seniority of the employee and how long it is likely to take him to find other work or the employer to find a replacement.

The Employment Rights Act 1996 provides for minimum periods of notice. Provided an employee has been continuously employed for a month or more he is entitled to the period of notice specified in the Act and any contractual term which deprives the employee of that right is void.[103] The length of minimum notice to which an employee is entitled, depends on the length of his continuous employment and for every year of continuous employment an employee is entitled to one week's notice, until the maximum of 12 weeks is reached. Such a sliding scale does not apply to the notice the employee is required to give; under the Act an employee is not required to give more than one weeks' notice, but his contract of employment will often require that he gives more.

The statutory rights to minimum notice are deemed to be incorporated into all contracts of employment so that the remedy for their breach is an action for breach of contract, in practice for wrongful dismissal where the breach is by the employer and wrongful resignation where the breach is by the employee.[104]

The rights to minimum notice are not applicable to fixed term contracts on the view that the date of termination is determined at the time the contract is entered into but in order to prevent employers avoiding the need to give adequate notice of termination s.86(4) of the Employment Rights Act 1996 provides that where a contract is for a fixed period of one month or less the provisions of s.86(1) & (2) apply to an employee who has three months' continuous employment thereby preventing employers from using a succession of fixed term contracts each for a period of less than a month.

Partnership dissolution

Many employees are employed by partnerships. In Scots law there are two kinds of **9–47** partnerships. The first and most common type is that regulated by the Partnership Act 1890 which recognises that a partnership possesses a quasi-legal personality distinct from the personalities of the partners themselves, but lacks the distinct legal personality of a limited company.[105] The dissolution of such a partnership will operate to terminate contracts of employment between the firm and employee. However, where the partnership continues, contracts of employment with the firm are deemed to include an implied term that the death, resignation or assumption of a partner, or partners, will be accepted by the firm's employees.[106] Since 2001, it has been possible to form a limited liability partnership under the Limited Liability Partnerships Act 2000. Where such a partnership is the employer, the contract of employment is with the body corporate whose legal personality is not affected by any change in the partners who make it up.

---

[102] *Forsyth v Heathery Knowe Coal Company* (1880) 7 R. 887.
[103] Employment Rights Act 1996 s.86(3).
[104] *Westwood v Secretary of State for Employment* [1985] I.C.R. 209.
[105] Partnership Act 1890 s.4(2).
[106] *Berlitz School of Languages v Duchene* (1903) 6 F. 181; and see *Rose v Dodd* [2005] I.C.R. 1776, CA dealing with the position in England.

Winding up, receiverships and administration orders

9–48 Where companies are wound up, the effect on the contracts of employment depends on the nature of the winding up and the circumstances surrounding it, but generally a court order which winds up a company (a compulsory winding up order) operates as notice of termination of the contracts of employment between the company and its staff.[107] On the other hand, a resolution to voluntarily wind up a company, may operate to terminate contracts of employment depending upon the facts and circumstances of each case.[108] It may be necessary therefore to distinguish a compulsory winding up to cease business and insolvency[109] from a voluntary winding up, merely to facilitate a take-over or business reconstruction.[110]

Frustration

9–49 The contract of employment may become impossible to perform or "frustrated".[111] The death of either party frustrates the contract of employment,[112] as does the serious or protracted illness of either party. Where the illness of the employee is concerned, a great deal depends on the circumstances of the employment and the nature of the illness as well as the prospect of recovery. In *Marshall v Harland & Wolff Ltd*,[113] the following factors were stated to be relevant:

- terms of the contract;
- the nature of the employment and its expected duration if no illness;
- nature of illness and prospects of recovery;
- period of past employment;
- possibility of acquisition of statutory rights by the replacement employee; and
- continued payment of wages during absence.

Other factors include the length of previous employment, future duration of employment, the employer's need for the work to be done and for a replacement, the employer's actions including dismissal or a failure to dismiss, contractual terms as to sick pay.[114]

Being sent to prison, or interned, may result in the contract being frustrated although again it will depend on the length of the sentence and the nature of the employment, and bail conditions which prevent an employee attending work will not necessarily frustrate the contract.[115]

---

[107] *Day v Tait* (1900) 8 S.L.T. 40.
[108] *Ferguson v Telford, Grier and McKay & Co.* [1967] I.T.R. 387.
[109] *Reigate v Union Manufacturing Company (Ramsbottom) Ltd* [1918] 1 K.B. 592.
[110] *Midland Counties Bank Ltd v Attwood* [1905] 1 Ch. 357.
[111] See Ch.7.
[112] *Hoey v McEwan and Auld* (1867) 5 M. 814.
[113] [1972] 2 All E.R. 715.
[114] *Egg Stores (Stamford Hill) Ltd v Leibovici* [1977] I.C.R. 260; *Williams v Watsons Luxury Coaches* [1990] I.C.R. 536).
[115] *Four Seasons Health Care Ltd v Maughan* [2005] I.R.L.R. 324, EAT.

F.C. Shepherd & Co. Ltd v Jerrom
[1986] I.R.L.R. 358.

The contract of an apprentice who, during his apprenticeship had been convicted of conspiracy to assault and affray, which resulted in him being given a borstal sentence, was frustrated after he had served 39 weeks in borstal.

Lawton L.J. stated: "The apprentice's criminal conduct was deliberate but it did not have by itself any consequences on the performance of the contract. What affected the contract was the sentence of borstal training which was the act of the judge and which he (the apprentice) would have avoided if he could have done . . ." In this case the facts did frustrate the contract.

A contract can also be frustrated by becoming illegal and this has meant that where an employee becomes legally disqualified from performing certain work, his contract may be brought to an end by frustration. Therefore, where a contract of employment requires the employee to hold a valid qualification, a relatively short period of legal disqualification can result in the contract being frustrated.[116]

Rescission

The general rule is that one party cannot bring to an end his contractual obligations **9–50** merely by repudiating the contract, or breaking it in a material or fundamental way. Repudiation merely allows the innocent party to rescind the contract, but while in employment law there are exceptions, repudiation of the contract by a unilateral wage reduction did not itself terminate the contract.

Rigby v Ferodo Ltd
[1988] I.C.R. 29

Ferodo Ltd gave its employees notice that it was going to reduce wage rates, but Rigby and other employees refused to agree. When his wage was reduced Rigby sued for the difference, but Ferodo argued that the notice to reduce the wages should be construed as a 12-week notice to terminate the contract of employment with the offer of a new contract containing the reduced wage rate.

Lord Oliver stated: "There was no reason in law or in logic why, leaving aside the extreme cases of outright dismissal or walk out, a contract of employment should be on any different footing from any other contract, regarding the principle that an unaccepted repudiation was a thing writ in water and of no value to anybody."

Wrongful dismissal

Wrongful dismissal is the term which denotes dismissal in breach of contract and is to be **9–51** contrasted with unfair dismissal, which is primarily concerned with the reasonableness of the employer's actions. Although in unfair dismissal the question as to whether an

---

[116] *Tarnesby v Kensington & Chelsea & Westminster Area Health Authority* [1981] I.R.L.R. 369—doctor's registration being temporarily suspended; *Dunbar v Baillie Brothers*, 1990 G.W.D. 26-1487—HGV driver, losing licence following a heart attack.

employer has broken the contract in dismissing the employee will be relevant, it is only one of all the circumstances the employment tribunal is required to take into account.

Remedies

9–52 Exceptionally wrongful dismissal by a body exercising statutory powers may sometimes be challenged by judicial review, by which an employer's action in dismissing an employee may be declared "unlawful"; the primary remedy is damages.

Scots law regards the contract of employment as a contract involving the provision of personal services—a personal relationship based on mutual trust and confidence. One result of this is that the common law provides that the remedy of specific implement is not available,[117] and this rule is now enshrined in s.236 of the Trade Union and Labour Relations (Consolidation) Act 1992 which provides:

> No court shall, whether by way of—
>
> (a) and order for specific performance or specific implement of a contract of employment, or
> (b) an injunction or interdict restraining breach of threatened breach of such a contract,
>
> compel an employee to do any work or attend at any place for the doing of any work.

The result is that where a breach involves a resignation or dismissal, without giving the notice required by the contract, the courts will generally not grant any order whose effect would be to compel the continuation of the employment relationship.

In England, the courts have restrained a wrongful dismissal by the granting of an injunction and the Scottish courts have followed this trend. Examples of the Scottish courts being prepared to grant interdicts to restrain a dismissal are found in *John Anderson v Pringle of Scotland*[118] and *Peace v City of Edinburgh Council*.[119] However, in each of these cases the Court of Session was not restraining the act of dismissal itself rather it was merely ensuring that the procedures or mechanisms (which might eventually lead to dismissal) were carried out in accordance with the contract of employment. Also in neither case was it clear that there was a breakdown in the underlying and essential duty of trust and confidence. However, in England, the courts have focused on whether damages would be an adequate remedy rather than trust and confidence when considering granting an injunction: compare the decisions in *Gryf-Lowczowski v Hitchingbrooke Healthcare NHS Trust*[120] and *Mezey v South West London and St Georges Mental Health NHS Trust*[121] with *Lakshmi v Mid Cheshire Hospitals NHS Trust*.[122]

Damages

9–53 The most common remedy for wrongful dismissal is an action of damages. If the contract is for a fixed term, damages will, subject to the employee's duty to mitigate, include the salary and other benefits which the employee would have received if the contract had run its full course. If the contract could have been lawfully ended by the employer giving

---

[117] *Murray v Dumbarton County Council*, 1935 S.L.T. 239.
[118] [1998] I.R.L.R. 64.
[119] [1999] I.R.L.R. 417.
[120] [2006] I.C.R. 425, QBD.
[121] [2007] I.R.L.R. 244, CA.
[122] [2008] I.R.L.R. 956, QBD.

notice, the damages will compensate the employee for what he would have received in salary and other benefits during the period of notice. By restricting the loss to the period of the contract or the notice it required, the court is giving effect to the right of the party in breach to perform the contract in the least burdensome way.

Morran v Glasgow Council of Tenants
[1998] I.R.L.R. 67

Morran was dismissed in breach of his contract. If his contract had been performed by the employers, he would have received either four weeks' notice of termination or pay in lieu of notice. In fact he received neither and argued that if he had been given four weeks' notice he would have had enough continuous employment to claim unfair dismissal. He, therefore, claimed damages for loss of the right to claim unfair dismissal.

Held, that in an action for damages for breach of the contract, an employee is entitled to recover damages which will put him in a position he would have been in had the employers fulfilled their contractual obligation. Where, as here, the contract gives the employer the option of terminating by giving due notice or making a payment in lieu thereof the least burdensome way for them is to dismiss the employee and make a payment in lieu of notice. If the employers had dismissed the employee with pay in lieu of notice, his employment would still have terminated before he had the necessary service to claim unfair dismissal.

The approach of the Court of Session in *Morran* accords both with the Court of Appeal in *Harper v Virgin Net Ltd*[123] and the EAT in *Wise Group v Mitchell*.[124]

Addis v Gramophone Company Ltd[125] has long been regarded as precluding an award of damages in respect of the manner of dismissal including injury to the employee's feelings. However, in *Malik v BCCI*[126] the House of Lords has distinguished *Addis* and has held that an employee is entitled to damages for the financial loss he suffered (through, for example, not being able to find other employment) as a result of the employer being in breach of the implied duty of trust and confidence by, for example, running his business in a dishonest and corrupt way. Thus "stigma" damages may now be awarded for loss of reputation caused by such a breach of contract. However, there is still no entitlement to damages for injury to feelings or anxiety for wrongful dismissal.[127]

---

[123] [2005] I.C.R. 921.
[124] [2005] I.C.R. 896. And see *Edwards v Chesterfield Royal Hospital NHS Foundation Trust* [2011] UKSC 58 endorsing the least burdensome rule in relation to wrongful dismissal.
[125] [1909] A.C. 488. See also para.9–39.
[126] [1997] I.R.L.R. 462.
[127] *Johnson v Unisys Ltd* [2001] I.R.L.R. 279, HL.

Johnson v Unisys Ltd
[2001] I.C.R. 480, HL

Johnson seeking to rely on the decision in *Malik* alleged that the manner in which his employer dismissed him had breached the implied duty of trust and confidence and this (the manner of dismissal) resulted in him having a breakdown and difficulty in finding other employment.

Held (by a majority) that the duty of trust and confidence related to the continuation or preservation of the employment relationship and did not apply to the manner of dismissal. Johnson's claim for damages failed.

However, in the later case of *Eastwood v Magnox Electric plc*[128] the House of Lords restricted its decision in *Johnson* to the manner of dismissal in holding that *Johnson* did not apply to the carrying out of a disciplinary procedure and the Supreme Court in *Edwards v Chesterfield Royal NHS Trust*[129] has confirmed the distinction in holding (by a majority) that even where the manner of, or the procedure for, dismissal is the subject of an express contractual term no damages may be awarded for loss suffered as a result of a breach of a term in the contract of employment as to the manner of dismissal unless the loss precedes and is independent of the dismissal. It was Edwards' case that the panel which concluded he had been guilty of misconduct had been improperly constituted but as this was not independent of the dismissal his case was caught by the *Johnson* exclusion. As the Supreme Court itself recognised in *Edwards* drawing the line between losses caused by the manner of dismissal and losses which precede dismissal and are independent of it presents difficulty!

Pay in lieu of notice

9–54 In Scots law, the employer has an implied right to terminate the contract by paying wages and giving other contractual benefits due to the employee in lieu of notice. It follows that where an employer does this in the ordinary case, no action for damages will lie, because no breach of contract will have occurred. Unless the conduct of the employee justifies summary dismissal, an employer who dismisses without notice or without paying in lieu of notice will be liable in damages to the employee for a sum equivalent to wages in lieu of notice and the employee may sue for such, in either the ordinary courts or more usually an employment tribunal.

Key Concepts

The contract can be **terminated** by:

- notice of termination;
- dissolution or winding up of a partnership or company;
- impossibility or illegality of performance (frustration); or
- rescission following repudiation.

The remedy for **wrongful dismissal** is almost always damages.

---

[128] [2004] I.C.R. 1064.
[129] [2011] UKSC 58.

UNFAIR DISMISSAL

Unfair dismissal, describes a dismissal which is contrary to certain standards of reason- **9–55**
ableness or other rules of law. These are currently contained in the Employment Rights
Act 1996, the Transfer of Undertakings (Protection of Employment) Regulations 2006 and
the Trade Union and Labour Relations (Consolidation) Act 1992 (TULRCA), as supplemented by the provisions of any relevant ACAS Code of Practice. Unfair dismissal is
concerned with the employer's reason and motives for dismissal and how it is carried out;
it is dealt with exclusively by employment tribunals and may lead to orders of reinstatement, re-engagement or compensation.

To be protected against unfair dismissal, generally an employee must have been continuously employed for a period of two years at the effective date of termination.[130] The
main exceptions to this are: dismissal for union membership/non-membership and dismissal for participating in union activities at an appropriate time[131]; dismissal for family
reasons including pregnancy[132]; dismissal for asserting a statutory right[133]; dismissal for
certain health and safety reasons[134]; dismissal for making a qualifying disclosure[135]; dismissal in breach of the Working Time Regulations 1998[136]; dismissal in breach of the
National Minimum Wage Act 1998[137]; and dismissal of employee representatives elected to
consult on redundancies and the transfer of an undertaking.[138] In such special cases, no
continuous employment is required before a complaint may be lodged.

Until the Employment Equality (Age) Regulations 2006, employees lost the right to
complain of unfair dismissal when they reached the non-discriminatory normal retiring
age for the position they held or, in any other case, the age of 65.[139] The upper age limit of
65 has been repealed by the 2006 Regulations.[140]

Generally, an employee cannot contract out of the statutory right not to be unfairly
dismissed or to complain to an employment tribunal.[141] However, there are two important
exceptions to this:

(1) where there has been agreement following action by an ACAS conciliation officer;
and
(2) where the employee has entered into a settlement or compromise agreement
having received independent advice which may be from a qualified lawyer,
competent trade union official/member or a competent advice centre worker.

Other employees who are excluded from unfair dismissal law are:

(1) those employed in the police service[142];

---

[130] Employment Rights Act 1996 s.108. The qualifying period was raised from one year to two years in 2012 for
employment beginning on or after April 6, 2012.
[131] TULRCA s.152.
[132] Employment Rights Act 1996 s.99.
[133] ERA 1996 s.104.
[134] ERA 1996 s.100.
[135] ERA 1996 s.103A.
[136] ERA 1996 s.101A.
[137] ERA 1996 s.104A.
[138] ERA 1996 s.103(1).
[139] ERA 1996 s.109.
[140] ERA 1996 s.109 was repealed by reg.49(1) of the 2006 Regulations.
[141] Employment Rights Act 1996 s.203.
[142] ERA s.200.

(2) members of the armed forces[143];

(3) certain civil servants, except those employed for the purposes of the security services.[144]

Continuous employment

9–56 Continuous employment is a statutory concept whose existence depends on the provisions contained in Employment Rights Act 1996 ss.210–219.

The rules relating to continuous employment may be summarised as follows:

(1) Periods of continuous employment are made of weeks that count.
(2) Except where there is a strike or lock out, a week which does not count breaks continuity and the employee has to start accumulating continuity all over again.
(3) Once employment with an employer has begun, it is presumed to be continuous unless the employer proves otherwise.
(4) The following weeks count as continuous employment:
  (a) a week during the whole or part of which the employee's relations are governed by a contract of employment;
  (b) a week in which the employee is incapable because of sickness or injury;
  (c) a week during which the employee is absent on account of a temporary cessation of work (for example a break between two fixed term contracts) or an arrangement whereby continuity is maintained;
  (d) a week of absence because of pregnancy where a woman has exercised her statutory right to return to work;
  (e) a week which occurs between dismissal and re-engagement or which occurs in the period of statutory notice the employee should have received.

Where there is a change of employer for example where a business, undertaking or a commercial contract has been transferred, employment with the transferor counts along with employment with the transferee. Where an employee transfers to an employer who is an "associated employer" of the other employer, the employment with both employers counts towards continuous employment.[145]

Dismissal

9–57 "Dismissal" is defined by ss.95 and 96 of the Employment Rights Act 1996, and if an employee cannot prove that he or she has been "dismissed" in accordance with the definition, the case is bound to fail.

Where the employer, with or without notice, terminates the contract of employment, the employee is dismissed. Where a letter communicates dismissal, the dismissal does not take effect until the employee has read the letter or has had a reasonable opportunity of doing so, although an employee cannot avoid being dismissed by deliberately not reading the

---

[143] ERA ss.191, 192.
[144] ERA s.193.
[145] ERA s.218. Employers are associated, where one is a company that the other controls, or where two or more are companies controlled by a third person: *Merton LBC v Gardiner* [1980] I.R.L.R. 472. And see ERA s.231.

letter. Even unambiguous words of dismissal can be withdrawn, if uttered in the heat of the moment; but the withdrawal must be almost immediate.[146]

Being told by an employer to "resign or be dismissed" is a dismissal even where the employee resigns.[147]

Where an employee is employed on a contract for a limited term, (or until the occurrence of a particular event) the expiry of that contract without its renewal is a dismissal of the employee.[148] Thus, if an employee is employed on a contract which is from January 1, 2006 until December 31, 2006, he is dismissed if the contract is not renewed on its expiry. Of course the dismissal may be fair, but it is nevertheless a dismissal.

Where a contract is terminated by the employee, with or without notice, but in circumstances such that they are entitled to terminate without notice by reason of the employer's conduct, there is also a dismissal—referred to as a "constructive dismissal".

The test for whether an employee is entitled to terminate the contract without notice is contractual, and it is not enough for the employee merely to show that the employer's conduct had been unreasonable in some way.[149] The employer's actions must go to the root of the agreement, or show that the employer no longer wishes to be bound by one or more of its essential terms.

In order to establish that he has been constructively dismissed, an employee must also show that the breach—at least in part—was what caused him to leave.

Reason for dismissal

In the normal case once the employee has satisfied the tribunal that he has been "dismissed" the onus transfers to the employer to show that the dismissal was for a potentially fair reason. These are set out in s.98(2) of the Employment Rights Act 1996. Assuming the employer can do this, the tribunal then considers whether the employer has acted reasonably. Where the employee has less than two years' employment (the qualifying period for ordinary unfair dismissal claims) and is claiming that he has been unfairly dismissed for one of the special reasons mentioned later, the onus is on the employee to prove that he was dismissed for that specific reason. **9–58**

Fair reasons are:

(1) Related to the capability or qualifications of the employee for the work he is employed to do. Capability and qualifications are widely defined; the former includes skill, aptitude, health and mental capacity while the latter includes technical, academic and professional qualifications. The issue of capability must be resolved by reference to the work the employee was doing at the time of dismissal. **9–59**

Shook v London Borough of Ealing
[1986] I.R.L.R. 46, EAT

Shook had a contractual term which allowed her employer to transfer her to any work for which her qualifications were appropriate. On her dismissal,

---

[146] *Martin v Yeoman Aggregates Ltd* [1983] I.C.R. 314.
[147] *Sheffield v Oxford Controls Ltd* [1979] I.R.L.R. 199.
[148] Employment Rights Act 1996 s.95, as amended by the Fixed Term Employees (Prevention of Less Favourable Treatment) Regulations 2002.
[149] *Western Excavations ECC Ltd v Sharp* [1978] I.C.R. 221; *GGHB v Pate*, 1983 S.L.T. 90.

she argued that she was not incapable of doing all the kinds of work that her contract required. Her employers had, therefore, not shown their reason for her dismissal was related to her capability for the work she was employed to do.

The EAT held it was not necessary for the employer to show Shook was incapable of doing all the tasks which the employer was entitled by law to call upon her to discharge. In this case, however widely her contract was construed, her incapability related to her performance of her duties under her contract, even although her performance of all of them may not have been affected.

There is a distinction between the reasons set out in Employment Rights Act 1996 s.98(2)(a) (capability) and (2)(b) (conduct) and the reasons in s.98(2)(c) (redundancy) and (d) (breach of statute). According to the EAT the former two are couched in terms of "relation" whereas the latter two are couched in terms of actuality.

(2) Related to the conduct of the employee. Although statute does not state expressly, it is implied that there must be a connection between the conduct and the employee's responsibilities to his employers. This is sometimes referred to as the "conduct in context test". *Thomson v Alloa Motor Co. Ltd*[150] indicates that the conduct must in some way reflect on the employer/employee relationship. Thus, damage caused to employer's property when a learner driver was leaving the garage forecourt after her duties had ended (which did not involve driving), was not a reason related to her conduct. However, acts of misconduct including criminal activities away from work can have a sufficient connection with the employment relationship to relate to the conduct of the employee; this would particularly be the case where dishonesty was involved and the employee had responsibility for money or property, or where the employee held a senior (management) position.[151]

(3) The redundancy of the employee. "Redundancy" is legally defined in s.139(1) of the Employment Rights Act to mean, a reduction in the needs of the business for employees to do work of a particular kind or a cessation (temporary or permanent, actual or expected) of the business, completely or in the place where the employee is employed. This is dealt with in more detail later.

(4) Contravention of a statutory enactment, either by the employer or employee, if the employee's employment were to be continued. This would apply to the continued employment of a doctor whose registration had been terminated, or an employee who required to have a work permit but whose permit had expired.

(5) Some other substantial reason (SOSR) justifying the dismissal of the employee from the position they held. This reason is frequently pleaded as an alternative to conduct, particularly where the employer is unsure of overcoming the "conduct in context test". It usually involves establishing that the particular ground will have a negative impact upon the employer's business. It has been successfully pleaded in the following situations:

---

[150] [1983] I.R.L.R. 403.
[151] *Norfolk County Council v Bernard* [1979] I.R.L.R. 220.

- criminal conviction unconnected with work (*Singh v London Country Bus Services Ltd*)[152];
- personality clashes resulting from disclosures of private life (*Treganowan v Robert Knee & Co. Ltd*)[153];
- reaction of best customer against conduct of employee (*Scott Packing & Warehousing Ltd v Patterson*)[154]; *and*
- sexual proclivities of an employee which made parents less likely to send their children to the camps (*Saunders v Scottish National Camps Association*).[155]

There will be SOSR for a dismissal where business conditions require the employer to introduce changes in conditions, or terms of employment, which employees refuse to accept, so long as it can be shown that there are pressing business needs constituting the reason for the introduction of the changes. In such circumstances, an employer would be justified in dismissing those employees who refused to accede to the new conditions.[156]

Statute also provides:

(1) that the dismissal of an employee to accommodate the return of a woman from maternity, adoption or additional paternity leave or from medical suspension is for SOSR (Employment Rights Act 1996 s.106); and

(2) where there has occurred a transfer of a business or a service provision change and there is an economic, organisational or technical reason entailing changes in the workforce of the transferee, or transferor, either before or after transfer or change, the dismissal of an employee shall be for SOSR (Transfer of Undertakings (Protection of Employment) Regulations 2006 reg.7).

Admissible evidence

Contrary to the position in cases involving alleged wrongful dismissal, in unfair dismissal **9–60** employers are restricted to producing evidence of which they were aware at the time they took the decision to dismiss. Thus, information or evidence of misconduct which comes to light after the decision to dismiss has been taken, cannot be relied on by the employer to show the reason for the dismissal, or that its conduct in dismissing the employee was reasonable.[157]

Is dismissal fair?

The next question is whether the employer has acted reasonably and shown a sufficient **9–61** reason for dismissing the employee.[158] In considering the issue of reasonableness, it is recognised that there is a "band" of reasonable responses to the employee's conduct, of which one employer might reasonably take one view and another quite reasonably take another. Ultimately, it is for the tribunal as an industrial jury to decide whether the employer's decision fell within this band. It is not for the tribunal to substitute its views for those of the employer.[159] A tribunal which seeks to avoid the band of reasonable response

---

[152] [1976] I.R.L.R. 176.
[153] [1975] I.C.R. 405.
[154] [1978] I.R.L.R. 166.
[155] [1981] I.R.L.R. 277.
[156] *Hollister v NFU* [1979] I.R.L.R. 238.
[157] *Devis & Sons Ltd v Atkins* [1977] I.C.R. 662.
[158] Employment Rights Act 1996 s.98(4).
[159] *Iceland Frozen Foods Ltd v Jones* [1983] I.C.R. 17.

approach, and substitute their views for those of the employer, commits an error of law.[160]

> ### Key Concepts
>
> - Employee must prove they have been dismissed.
> - Employer must prove reason for dismissal is one recognised by s.98.
> - Whether a dismissal is fair depends on whether it falls within the bands of reasonable responses.
> - The employment tribunal must not simply substitute its own view of whether the employer acted reasonably.

Employment Act 2002

9–62 The Employment Act 2002 had a major effect on fairness of dismissals. It sought to encourage workplace resolution of disputes by requiring employers and employees to follow certain statutory disciplinary and grievance procedures. However, the 2002 Act and the regulations made thereunder resulted in much litigation about whether the statutory procedures had been complied with and were not regarded as effective and were repealed in 2008.

Special situations

9–63 What has been stated above applies to dismissal for the ordinary reasons, namely: conduct, capability, redundancy, breach of statute and some other substantial reason. However, special rules exist for some special categories of dismissal and these are discussed now.

Industrial action and lock-outs

9–64 Where the industrial action is official (broadly this means that the action has been authorised by the employee's trade union) or where the dismissal is during a lock-out, the position is regulated by s.238 of TULRCA, and, provided the employee has at least two years' continuous employment, an employment tribunal may only entertain an application if one, or more, relevant employees has not been dismissed. Where the action is unofficial, employees who are dismissed while taking part have no right to claim unfair dismissal, even if other employees who also took part were not dismissed.[161]

Protected industrial action

9–65 Where an employee takes part in protected industrial action (action for which the trade union has immunity under TULRCA s.219) dismissal will be unfair if one of three conditions is satisfied. First, where the dismissal took place within 12 weeks of the start of the action. Secondly, where the dismissal took place out-with the 12-week period, but the employee had stopped taking part in the action before the 12-week period ended. Thirdly, where the dismissal is out-with the 12-week period and the employee is still taking part in it, but the employer has failed to take reasonable procedural steps to resolve the dispute.[162]

---

[160] *Post Office v Foley* [2000] I.R.L.R. 827.
[161] TULRCA s.237. However, excluding the right to claim unfair dismissal does not apply where dismissal is for certain reasons—see TULRCA ss.237(1A) & 238(2A).
[162] TULRCA s.238A.

An employee dismissed while taking protected industrial action does not require a period of continuous employment to make a claim.[163]

Union membership and activities

Individual employees receive certain rights to allow them to join and to participate in the **9–66** activities of an Independent Trade Union (ITU). Thus, ss.152 and 153 of the TULRCA provide it is unfair to dismiss (or select for redundancy) an employee who:

(a) is or proposes to become a member of an ITU;
(b) has taken part or proposes to take part in the activities of an ITU at an appropriate time;
(c) is not a member of any trade union or of a particular trade union; or
(d) has refused to become or remain a union member.

It is also unfair to dismiss an employee who refuses to pay a sum, or suffer deduction from wages, in lieu of membership. In the case of the dismissal of a non-union member, a third party (for example, the trade union itself) may be "sisted" or joined as a respondent in the proceedings against the employer. There is no qualifying period for such dismissals.

Union recognition dismissals

Until the Employment Relations Act 1999 an employer could not be compelled to **9–67** recognise a trade union for collective bargaining purposes. The 1999 Act has introduced such a right (see TULRCA Sch.A1) and special rules now make it unfair to dismiss employees in connection with union recognition. It is unfair to dismiss employees who seek to obtain, support or prevent union recognition or the ending of bargaining arrangements, or who vote or seek to influence the way others vote in a ballot about union recognition.[164] It is also unfair to select employees for redundancy in a discriminatory way, if the reason for their selection was one concerned with union recognition.[165] There is no qualifying period for such dismissals.

Health and safety dismissals

The present provisions are to be found in Employment Rights Act 1996 s.100 where it is **9–68** declared that dismissal of an employee for any of the following reasons will be unfair:

(a) carrying out health and safety duties by an employee designated by the employer to carry out such duties (for example a safety officer);
(b) carrying out functions as health and safety representative or safety committee member;
(c) taking part in consultations with the employer as a representative of employee safety or seeking election to such a post;
(d) where there are no safety representatives, or safety committee, or it is not reasonably practicable to use them and the employee reasonably believes these circumstances were harmful to health or safety;

---

[163] TULRCA s.239.
[164] TULRCA Sch.A1 para.161.
[165] TULRCA Sch.A1 para.162.

(e) leaving the place of work in circumstances of danger, which the employee reasonably believed to be serious and imminent and which they could not reasonably be expected to avert;

(f) taking appropriate steps to protect themselves or others (including members of the public).

There is no qualifying period for the above provisions.

Asserting a statutory right

9–69 It is unfair to dismiss an employee if the reason was one of the following:

- he brought proceedings against the employer to enforce a statutory employment right; or
- he alleged that the employer had infringed a statutory employment right.[166]

It is not necessary to show that the employee actually had the right in question, so long as the claim to the right is made in good faith. There is no qualifying period but the provision only applies to certain statutory rights, namely those described in s.104(4) of the Employment Rights Act 1996. They include:

- rights conferred by the Employment Rights Act 1996, which can be enforced by employment tribunals;
- the right conferred by s.86 of the Employment Rights Act 1996 (to minimum notice of termination);
- rights conferred by ss.68, 86, 146, 168, and 170 of the TULRCA (i.e. deductions from pay, union activities and time off);
- rights conferred by the Working Time Regulations 1998; and
- rights conferred by the Transfer of Undertakings (Protection of Employment) Regulations 2006.

Dismissals on the transfer of an undertaking

9–70 Until 1981 employees who worked in businesses that were sold, or acquired, by another employer could find that the person who acquired the business did not wish to employ the existing workforce at all. To remedy this situation, the EC Acquired Rights Directive was adopted. The Directive was implemented in the United Kingdom by the Transfer of Undertakings (Protection of Employment) Regulations (TUPE) 1981. The 1981 Regulations have been revoked and replaced by the Transfer of Undertakings (Protection of Employment) Regulations 2006. The Regulations do essentially two things for employees, who work in businesses which are sold or transferred to a new owner (the transferee) or where there has been a service provision change, for example where an employer's activities or part of them have been contracted out to a contractor (or transferee). First, unless the employee objects, the contractual rights and duties that the employees enjoyed with the old owner/employer (the transferor) are automatically transferred and become binding on the transferee (reg.4). Secondly, in order to complement this transfer of contracts, the dismissal of an employee because of the transfer or service provision change (or a reason connected with the transfer or service provision change) is unfair (reg.7(1)). An employee who is dismissed because of the transfer or service provision change, or for a

---

[166] Employment Rights Act 1996 s.104.

reason connected with the transfer or service provision change has the right to complain of unfair dismissal so long as the normal qualifying period for unfair dismissal is satisfied. However, it is a defence for the employer to show that the dismissal was for an economic, technical or organisational reason entailing changes in the workforce (reg.7(2)). In such a case, the dismissal is deemed to have been either for redundancy, or for a substantial reason such as to justify the dismissal of the employee and whether it is fair or unfair, will depend upon whether the employer has in other respects acted fairly in dismissing the employee.

Pregnancy and family leave

By s.99 of the Employment Rights Act (which is not dependent on a period of continuous **9–71** employment) a dismissal is unfair if the reason or the principal reason for it is prescribed by the Maternity and Parental Leave Regulations 1999.

Regulation 20 of these Regulations provides that an employee who is dismissed (or selected for redundancy) is unfairly dismissed if: (a) the principal reason for the dismissal (or selection for redundancy) is specified in the regulation; or (b) the principal reason for the dismissal is that the employee is redundant and alternative employment has not been offered in accordance with reg.10 of the Regulations.

> Regulation 10 specifies the following as reasons which make the dismissal (or selection for redundancy) automatically unfair:
>
> (a) the pregnancy of the employee;
> (b) the employee has given birth to a child and dismissal ends her maternity leave;
> (c) because of a legal requirement or a recommendation under a Health and Safety Code of Practice, the employee was suspended from work on the ground that she was pregnant, had recently given birth or was breast-feeding;
> (d) she took, sought to take or availed herself of the benefits of, ordinary maternity leave;
> (e) she took or sought to take—
> (i) additional maternity leave;
> (ii) parental leave;
> (iii) time off for family emergencies;
> (f) she declined to sign a workforce agreement relating to maternity, parental or family emergencies;
> (g) performed (or proposed to perform) any functions or activities as a representative or candidate in relation to such a workforce agreement.

Similar, but not as comprehensive protection, is now extended to employees who take adoption or paternity leave by the Paternity and Adoption Leave Regulations 2002.

Whistle-blowing

The effect of s.103A of the Employment Rights Act 1996 is to make it unfair to dismiss an **9–72** employee who makes any disclosure of information which in the reasonable belief of the person making it tends to show one or more of the following:

(a) a criminal offence has been committed;
(b) someone is failing to comply with a legal obligation;

(c) a miscarriage of justice has occurred or may occur;

(d) the health and safety of any individual is likely to be endangered;

(e) the environment is likely to be damaged; or

(f) information regarding any of the above is likely to be deliberately concealed.

However this is not a "whistle-blowers' charter", in that dismissal is unfair only where the disclosure is made to certain people, i.e. an employer, a legal adviser, a Minister of the Crown who has appointed an employer, or a person designated by the Secretary of State (see the Public Interest (Prescribed Persons) Order 1999 (SI 1999/1549)).[167]

Other special cases

9–73 Employees and workers are also protected from dismissal or termination of employment in connection with their rights under the Working Time Regulations and the National Minimum Wage Act and in relation to tax credits. It is also unfair to dismiss employees who are trustees of an occupational pension scheme, or employee representative for the purposes of consultation on redundancy or the transfer of an undertaking.[168] There is no qualifying period in any of these cases.

Remedies for unfair dismissal

9–74 The Employment Rights Act 1996 (ss.111–132) creates a framework of remedies for unfair dismissal. The primary remedy is supposed to be re-employment (either re-instatement or re-engagement), but this has not been the case in practice. There is also a right to compensation where either the tribunal refuses to order re-employment or the employee does not seek this remedy. Compensation is made up of two elements—the basic award and the compensatory award. There is also a right to an additional award, where the tribunal has ordered re-employment and this has not been complied with by the employer and in some cases the basic award must be at least the minimum prescribed by statute.[169]

Reinstatement and re-engagement

9–75 An order of reinstatement is an order of the tribunal requiring the employer to treat the complainant in all respects as if he had not been dismissed.[170] Alternatively, a tribunal can make an order (of re-engagement) on such terms as it may decide that the complainant be engaged by the employer, or by a successor employer, or by an associated employer, in employment comparable to that from which they were dismissed or other suitable employment (see the Employment Rights Act 1996, s.115(1)).

There is a clear order of priorities as regards re-employment. First, the tribunal must consider reinstatement and only if this is not ordered, should it consider re-engagement and on what terms. In conducting this exercise the tribunal must consider the following:

(a) the wishes of the complainant;

(b) whether it is practicable for the employer to comply;

(c) where the complainant caused or contributed to the dismissal, whether it would be just to make the order (see the Employment Rights Act 1996 s.116(1)).

---

[167] Employment Rights Act 1996 ss.43C–43F.

[168] Employment Rights Act 1996 ss.102, 103, 104A.

[169] Employment Rights Act 1996 s.120.

[170] Employment Rights Act 1996 s.114(1).

Where the employer fails to comply with the order, the tribunal can make an additional award of between 26 and 52 weeks' pay.

Compensation

A complainant's compensation is made up of two elements—a basic award and a compensatory award. **9–76**

The basic award

The basic award is calculated by reference to the period, ending with the effective date of **9–77** termination (EDT), during which the employee has been continuously employed, by starting at the end of that period and reckoning backwards the number of years of employment and allowing:

(a) one-and-a-half weeks' pay for each year in which the employee is over 41;
(b) one week's pay for each year in which the employee was between 22 and 41; and
(c) half a week's pay for each year of employment under 22.[171] The maximum number of years that can be taken into account is 20 and the maximum amount of a week's pay is currently £430.[172]

In cases of dismissal for union membership or activities, or for carrying out duties of: (1) a health and safety representative; (2) a representative in connection with the Working Time Regulations; (3) a trustee of an occupational pension scheme or (4) an employee representative in cases of consultation for redundancies or transfers of an undertaking there is a minimum basic award of £5,300.[173]

Compensatory award

Section 123(1) of the Employment Rights Act declares that the amount of the compen- **9–78** satory award will be such amount as the tribunal considers just and equitable in all the circumstances having regard to the loss sustained by the complainant in consequence of the dismissal, in so far as that action is attributable to action taken by the employer. The award is subject to a statutory maximum that is currently £72,300.

The principles for calculation of the compensatory award were first discussed in *Norton Tool Co Ltd v Tewson*[174] where the most important heads of loss were stated to be as follows:

(a) *Immediate loss of wages*: This is compensation for actual loss of wages and other benefits from the date of dismissal to the date of the hearing.
(b) *Future loss*: Where the complainant is still out of work at the date of the hearing, the tribunal can make an award to cover future loss of wages.
(c) *Loss of pension rights*: The sum here might be substantial, particularly where the complainant contributed to an occupational pension scheme and remains unemployed.
(d) *Loss arising from the manner of the dismissal*: An employee has no general right to compensation for the distress caused by dismissal or for injury to feelings.

---

[171] Employment Rights Act 1996 s.119(2).
[172] Employment Rights Act 1996 s.227.
[173] Employment Rights Act 1996 s.120.
[174] [1972] I.C.R. 501.

(e) *Loss of statutory protection*: There may be occasions where the loss of service-related rights, such as the right to long notice and the right to claim unfair dismissal itself, can be compensated under this head.

Interim relief

9–79 In certain cases, by virtue of s.128 of the Employment Rights Act 1996, (union membership dismissals, health and safety and working time cases, employee representative dismissals and dismissals for making a protected disclosure) employees can apply to an employment tribunal for interim relief. This is an order that the employee's contract, if terminated, will continue in force as if it had not been terminated and, if not terminated, that it will continue in force, in either case until the complaint is settled or determined by the tribunal. The continuation covers pay and other benefits such as pensions and seniority rights and for determining the period of continuous employment.

Key Concepts

Ordinarily an employee is not protected against unfair dismissal until they have **two years' continuous employment**.

In specific situations whether a dismissal is unfair, does **not** depend on the **reasonableness** of the employer's actions.

The **remedies** for unfair dismissal are reinstatement, re-engagement and compensation and exceptionally interim relief.

REDUNDANCY PAYMENTS

9–80 The system for compensating employees for loss of employment, on account of redundancy, was first introduced by the Redundancy Payments Act 1965.

General principles

9–81 The provisions relating to redundancy payments are now contained in the Employment Rights Act 1996, Pt XI. Provided an employee has two years' continuous employment, he becomes entitled to a redundancy payment on being dismissed for redundancy, or after a spell of lay-off or short time.[175] However, selecting an employee for redundancy or the terms on which a redundant employee is offered alternative employment frequently raise discrimination law issues and these are considered later in this chapter.

Dismissal

9–82 Dismissal is defined in the same way as in the law of unfair dismissal (see para.9–57) and there are special provisions relating to redundancy during maternity leave.[176] Additionally the definition includes implied termination[177] so that where in accordance with an enactment or rule of law (a) an act on the part of an employer or (b) an event affecting an employer (including an individual employer's death) operates to terminate the contract of

---

[175] Employment Rights Act 1996 ss.135, 155.
[176] Maternity and Parental Leave Regulations 1999 reg.10.
[177] Employment Rights Act 1996 ss.136, 137.

employment, that act or event shall be taken to be a termination of the contract by the employer.[178] The result is that certain circumstances, which would otherwise be regarded as a frustration of the employment contract, are deemed to be dismissals thereby preserving the employee's right to claim a redundancy payment. For redundancy payments law, a lock-out will not support a constructive dismissal and where an employee is under notice of redundancy and wishes to leave before the expiry of the employer's notice, his notice must be in writing and given during the "obligatory period" as defined by the Employment Rights Act 1996 s.136(4).

Where an employee volunteers for redundancy, there are two possible analyses: (1) he agrees to be dismissed, in which case he is entitled to a redundancy payment; or (2) the contract is ended by mutual consent, in which case there is no dismissal and he is not entitled to a payment. Thus where an employee "volunteers" for redundancy, there is a dismissal provided the causative act (to bring the employment to an end) is that of the employer alone, so that where employees applied for early retirement and the employer accepted their applications there was no dismissal but rather termination by mutual consent.[179]

An employee laid off, or on short-time, may serve notice on his employer that he intends to terminate the employment and claim a redundancy payment. Unless the employer can show that full time employment is to be resumed, the employee will become entitled to a redundancy payment.[180]

Redundancy

For purposes of redundancy payments, the definition of redundancy is set out in s.139 of **9–83** the Employment Rights Act 1996. An employee is dismissed by reason of redundancy if the dismissal is attributable wholly or mainly attributable to the following:

(a) the fact that his employer has ceased or intends to cease, (i) to carry on the business for the purposes of which the employee was employed by him or, (ii) to carry on that business in the place the employee was employed; or

(b) the fact that the requirements of that business, (i) for employees to carry out work of a particular kind or, (ii) for employees to carry out work of a particular kind in the place the employee was employed have ceased or diminished either permanently or temporarily.

There are thus two "limbs" to the definition of redundancy. The first is where the employer ceases the business for the purpose of which the employee was employed, either completely or at the place the employee has been employed. The second deals with whether the requirements of the business for employees to do "work of a particular kind" have ceased or diminished. Whether a "business" ceases is a question of fact and the judicial approach is illustrated by:

---

[178] Employment Rights Act 1996 s.136(5).
[179] *Humber & Birch v Liverpool University* [1989] I.R.L.R. 165.
[180] Employment Rights Act 1996 ss.135, 147.

Melon v Hector Powe Ltd
1981 S.L.T. 74, HL

A company (Hector Powe Ltd) owned a factory at which men's suits were made for sale in the company's retail outlets. They sold the factory and its equipment to another company (Executex Ltd) which made suits for sale in the retail market generally. The employees remained and did the same kind of work (making suits) working for Executex, but the House of Lords held that this resulted in there being the transfer of assets of the business but not the transfer of a business. Making suits for dedicated retail outlets also owned by the factory, was a different type of business from making suits for sale to any wholesaler for onward retail sales. Hector Powe Ltd had ceased to carry on the business of making suits for its own retail outlets when it sold the factory and its equipment to Executex Ltd.

In the definition of redundancy, the place the employee is employed is important. To establish the place of employment and the kind of work for which there is a reduced requirement, until recently the contractual test was applied.[181] The contractual test required consideration of whether, under the contract of employment, the employee could be required to work at a place different from that where he/she worked at the time of dismissal.

The "contractual" approach, to determining what is the employee's place of employment, has now been expressly rejected by the EAT and the Court of Appeal.[182] In *Bass Leisure Ltd v Thomas* it was held that the question of the place of employment concerns the extent or area of a single place and not the transfer from one to another. The only relevant contractual terms, are those which define the place of employment and its extent, but not those terms which allow for the transfer of the employee from one place to another.

Requiring employees to work different hours will generally not mean that an employee who is dismissed, because he is unwilling or unable to work the new hours, is dismissed for redundancy. The critical question, is whether the change in working hours is such that it can be said that the requirements of the business to do work of a particular kind has ceased or diminished.[183]

Archibald v Rossleigh Commercials Ltd
[1975] I.R.L.R. 231

Archibald had been employed as a night shift mechanic whose hours of work were from 10pm to 8am six nights a week. When the employer decided that it would no longer keep the premises open 24 hours a day, Archibald was offered work as a day mechanic, but refused and claimed a redundancy payment. The employment tribunal upheld his claim, because the employer's requirement for employees to do work of a particular kind which the applicant was employed to do—work of a night mechanic—had ceased. The tribunal pointed out that his duties were different from those of the day shift, in that Archibald was required to attend to emergencies which arose during the night; it was not merely a change of the time at which the work was done.

---

[181] *Haden Ltd v Cowen* [1982] I.R.L.R. 314.
[182] *Bass Leisure Ltd v Thomas* [1994] I.R.L.R. 104; *High Table Ltd v Horst* [1997] I.R.L.R. 513.
[183] *Johnson v Nottinghamshire Combined Police Authority* [1974] I.C.R. 170, CA.

To determine whether the requirements of the business, for employees to do work of a particular kind have ceased, it may be necessary to distinguish an employee's skills or abilities from other attributes and the critical issue in each case is: "Have the requirements for work of a particular kind ceased or diminished?" and that requires a careful examination of the work the employer requires to be performed.[184]

The dismissal of one employee to accommodate, and prevent the dismissal of another redundant employee, is also to be regarded as a dismissal on the grounds of redundancy. The concept known as "bumping" means that an employee whose job continues, may, nevertheless, be seen to have been dismissed by reason of redundancy. The reason for this is because the definition of redundancy contained in s.131(1)(b) of the Employment Rights Act 1996 does not expressly require that the redundant employee be an employee who is employed on the particular kind of work the requirements for which have ceased or diminished.[185]

Where an employee is dismissed by reason of redundancy, his entitlement to a redundancy payment may be lost if he refuses an offer of suitable alternative employment made by his employer or an associated employer.[186] The offer need not be in writing; it may be a collective one (or advertised on a notice board), but it must be made before the end of the prior contract and must begin within four weeks of the end of prior contract. If the employment offered is not suitable the employee is entitled to receive a redundancy payment.

Whether alternative employment offered is suitable, and whether the employee's refusal is reasonable, requires a consideration of all facts and circumstances.

Cahuc, Johnson & Crouch v Allen Amery Ltd
[1966] I.T.R. 313

The three employees were previously employed in Hackney, London E2 and were offered, but refused, alternative employment in EC1. The employment tribunal held that the offer was unsuitable, because each employee lived very close to the old premises, but the new premises involved a bus journey of at least 40 minutes. One employee had a widowed mother whom she had been able to look after while she worked at the old premises, but would not be able to do so at the new ones. The tribunal observed

> "The third factor ... was the inconvenience and the time in travelling. It is manifest that it is a great advantage to have a job which does not involve travel in London. If she accepted the offer it would take about 40 minutes in each direction. There is no need to underline the inconveniences of waiting for and the difficulty of catching buses in rush hours, bad weather etc ... We find ... the offer was not of suitable employment in relation to the employees."

---

[184] *Sartin v Co-operative Retail Services Ltd*, 1969 VII K.I.R. 382.
[185] *Murray v Foyle Meats Ltd* [1999] I.R.L.R. 562, HL.
[186] Employment Rights Act 1996 s.141.

Bruce v NCB
[1967] I.T.R. 159

As the alternative employment offered to Bruce, who was a diabetic, would have involved him working three shifts instead of two, his routine would be sufficiently disturbed to allow him to reasonably reject the offer.

Where the employer has given notice of termination, but the employer justifiably terminates for misconduct of the employee, entitlement to a redundancy payment depends on whether an employment tribunal thinks it is just and equitable to make a payment.[187]

Once the employee has proved he has been dismissed and that he is not excluded from entitlement, an employee can rely on the presumption that the reason for dismissal is redundancy.[188]

To preserve his entitlement the claimant must, within six months: (1) agree and receive a payment; (2) serve written notice of claim on ex-employer; (3) refer entitlement to an employment tribunal; or (4) present unfair dismissal claim.[189]

Exclusions

9–84 The main exclusion operates in relation to domestic servants related to the employer and employed in a private household.[190]

Payments

9–85 Payments are calculated in accordance with statutory rules which apply a formula consisting of: (i) the length of the employee's continuous employment prior to the relevant date (which is usually the date the notice of termination expires); (ii) the employee's week's pay; and (iii) the age of the employee.[191] The week's pay is subject to a variable statutory limit, currently £430. Additionally, an employment tribunal may order an employer to compensate an employee for financial loss the employee incurs as a result of non-payment of a redundancy payment.[192]

Key Concepts

Redundancy is a legal concept.

To be entitled to a redundancy payment an employee must have been dismissed, or kept on a short time, or laid off and have **two years' continuous employment**.

Refusing an offer of suitable employment can result in loss of entitlement to a redundancy payment.

---

[187] Employment Rights Act 1996 ss.140, 143.
[188] Employment Rights Act 1996 s.163(2).
[189] Employment Rights Act 1996 s.164(1).
[190] Employment Rights Act 1996 s.161(1).
[191] Employment Rights Act 1996 s.162(1), (2).
[192] Employment Act 2008 s.7(2).

DISCRIMINATION

Until the passage of the Equality Act 2010 discrimination in employment was regulated by **9–86** many discrete provisions enacted over the years in order to comply with European law, beginning with the Equal Pay Act 1970 and culminating with the most recent Employment Equality (Age) Regulations 2006. The law regarding discrimination on the grounds of gender (including gender re-assignment), pregnancy and maternity, marital status and civil partnership, race, disability, sexual orientation, religion and belief and age is now dealt with by the Equality Act 2010 which, insofar as is practicable, deals with the different strands or grounds of discrimination by adopting common concepts, definitions and ter-minology and by introducing an overarching Code of Practice on Employment (2011) which deals with all strands of discrimination except equal pay for which there is a separate Code of Practice on Equal Pay (both effective from April 2011). The 2010 Act also sees the demise of the separate agencies of the (Equal Opportunities Commission (EOC), the Commission for Racial Equality (CRE) and Disability Rights Commission (DRC) and their replacement by the Equality and Human Rights Commission (EHRC). The 2010 Act is principally a consolidating and harmonizing statute but it has introduced some important changes particularly in the field of disability discrimination. European law has also required UK law to regulate discrimination in other fields of employment but these regulations are contained in separate legislation dealing with part time employees, fixed term contract workers and agency workers and these are dealt with at the end of this chapter.

The protected characteristics

What previous legislation regarded as "grounds"—on which discrimination was generally **9–87** unlawful—are replaced by "protected characteristics" namely: (1) age; (2) disability; (3) gender re-assignment; (4) marriage and civil partnership; (5) pregnancy and maternity (6) race; (7) religion or belief; (8) sex; and (9) sexual orientation.[193]

In some cases what is meant by a protected characteristic requires little explanation. Thus, the protected characteristic of sex refers to a male or female of any age and age is defined by reference to a person's age group.[194] Other protected characteristics are more strictly defined.

Thus a person who is proposing[195] to undergo, is undergoing or has undergone a process (or part of a process) to re-assign his or her sex by changing the physiological or other attributes of sex has the protected characteristic of gender re-assignment and a reference to a transsexual is a reference to a person who has the protected characteristic of gender re assignment; the process does not require to be under medical supervision.[196]

While the Court of Session had expressed the view that the phrase "on the ground of sex" in the Sex Discrimination Act 1975 did not include discrimination on the ground of sexual orientation[197] such discrimination has been rendered unlawful in employment since 2003.[198] Sexual orientation means a person's orientation towards persons of: (a) the same sex; (b) the opposite sex; and (c) either sex; accordingly gay men, lesbians and bisexual as well as heterosexual people are covered by the definition and according to the EHRC Code

---

[193] Equality Act 2010 s.4.
[194] Equality Act 2010 ss.5, 212.
[195] This is essentially a question of fact but see EHRC Code of Practice (2011), paras 2.21–2.28.
[196] See EHRC Code of Practice (2011), paras 2.21–2.31.
[197] *Ministry of Defence v Macdonald* [2001] I.R.L.R. 431, IH.
[198] Employment Equality (Sexual Orientation) Regulations 2003.

of Practice[199] sexual orientation discrimination includes discrimination connected with manifestations of a sexual orientation for example places they visit or their appearance.

Race includes colour, nationality as well as ethnic or national origins and the definition may be extended to include "caste" without the need for primary legislation.[200] A group can be defined by reference to its ethnic origins if it constitutes a separate and distinct community which is commonly associated with a common racial origin; an ethnic group must regard itself and be regarded by others as a distinct community by virtue of certain characteristics.[201] "Origins" requires focus on one's descent[202] and "national origins" is not limited to nationality; neither the Scots nor the English are distinct ethnic groups but have different national origins[203] and place of birth is not identical to national origins.[204]

Religion means any religion and a lack of religion and belief is broadly defined to mean "any religious or philosophical belief" or lack of such belief. While a belief must be genuine and not merely an opinion or viewpoint based on the present state of information available and be about a substantial and weighty aspect of human life with a certain level of cogency worthy of respect in a democratic society, it may include a belief in man-made climate change and the environment.[205]

A person has the protected characteristic of marriage and civil partnership if the person is married or is a civil partner and marriage covers any formal union which is recognised by law in the United Kingdom as a marriage[206] and reference to a civil partnership means a civil partnership under the Civil Partnership Act 2004 even if registered or recognised by the laws of other countries[207] but it does not include people who are single or divorced or have had there civil partnership dissolved or are unmarried but in a cohabiting relationship.

Whether a person has the protected characteristic of disability is complex. A person has a disability if: (a) he has a physical or mental impairment; and (b) the impairment has a substantial and long term adverse effect on his ability to carry out normal day to day activities and a reference to a person who has a particular protected characteristic is a reference to a person who has a particular disability and reference to persons who share a protected characteristic is a reference to persons who have the same disability.[208] This definition is further refined by provisions[209] to the effect that: (1) mental impairment includes an impairment resulting from a mental illness but the mental illness is no longer required to be "clinically well recognised"; (2) long term effect means an impairment has lasted or likely to last 12 months or life; (3) an impairment which has ceased to have substantial adverse effect is treated as continuing if its effect is likely to recur; (4) severe disfigurement has substantial adverse effects[210]; (5) progressive conditions which are likely to impair day-to-day activities, are to be regarded as impairments with substantial adverse effects, even although they are not yet in an advanced stage; (6) cancer, HIV infection and

---

[199] EHRC Code of Practice (2011), para.2.66 et seq.
[200] Equality Act 2010 s.9.
[201] *Mandla v Lee* [1983] I.R.L.R. 209, HL regarding Sikhs; and see *CRE v Dutton* [1989] I.R.L.R. 8, CA. regarding Romanies and travellers. Cf. *Dawkins v Department of the Environment* [1983] I.R.L.R. 284, CA that Rastafarians are not a separate ethnic group but probably now protected on the grounds of belief.
[202] *R v Governing Body of JFS* [2010] I.R.L.R. 136, SC.
[203] *BBC Scotland v Souster* [2001] I.R.L.R. 150, CS.
[204] *R v Secretary of State for Defence* [2006] I.R.L.R. 934, CA.
[205] *Grainger plc v Nicholson* [2010] I.R.L.R. 4, EAT.
[206] Equality Act 2010 s.8.
[207] Civil Partnership Act 2004 s.1 and Sch.20; and see the EHRC Code of Practice (2011).
[208] Equality Act 2010 s.6.
[209] Equality Act 2010 Sch.1.
[210] But see Equality Act 2010 (Disability) Regulations 2010 excluding tattoos and body piercings.

multiple sclerosis are each a disability and (7) one must judge the adverse effects of an impairment by ignoring medical treatment or use of a prosthesis (except spectacles).[211]

However, certain conditions are excluded from the definition of disability. Thus, addiction to alcohol, nicotine or any other substance does not amount to an impairment, nor does a tendency to set fires, steal, physical or sexual abuse of other persons, exhibitionism or voyeurism.[212] It is not relevant to consider how an impairment was caused,[213] and the correct approach of an employment tribunal is to consider what a person cannot do (or can only do with difficulty) as opposed to what he or she can do.[214] An impairment is measured in terms of normal day-to-day activities. Under the Disability Discrimination Act 1995 these had to be considered under the following specific and exclusive headings:

- mobility;
- manual;
- manual dexterity;
- physical co-ordination;
- continence;
- memory, powers of concentration, learning and understanding;
- perception of risk of physical danger;
- ability to lift/carry everyday things; and
- speech, hearing, sight.

These headings are no longer specified by the Equality Act 2010 but will—along with any other relevant factors—still act as a guide for employment tribunals[215] in determining whether a person meets the statutory definition.[216]

Anything that is done by most men or most women is a normal day-to-day activity and the fact that putting rollers in hair is an activity carried out almost exclusively by women does not prevent it being a normal day-to-day activity.[217] What a person does at work if it includes normal day-to-day activities is relevant[218] and although work of a particular form is not a normal day to day activity something a person does only at work may be classed as normal if it is common to different types of employment so that carrying out an assessment or examination can be a normal day-to-day activity[219] but there are enough people working night shift for working at night to be a normal day-to-day activity.[220]

---

[211] Also see *Kapadia v London Borough of Lambeth* [2000] I.R.L.R. 699, CA.

[212] Equalty Act (Disability) Regulations 2010 Part 2.

[213] See *Power v Panasonic UK Ltd* [2003] I.R.L.R. 141, EAT; *Millar v Inland Revenue Commissioners* [2006] I.R.L.R. 112, IH.

[214] *Leonard v Southern Derbyshire Chamber of Commerce* [2001] I.R.L.R. 19, EAT; *Goodwin v Patent Office* [1999] I.R.L.R. 4, EAT.

[215] The questions are for the employment tribunal and not for doctors: *Vicary v British Telecommunications Plc* [1999] I.R.L.R. 680, EAT.

[216] See EHRC Code of Practice (2011), Appendix 1, paras 11, 12.

[217] *Ekpe v Commissioner of Police of the Metropolis* [2001] I.R.L.R. 605, EAT.

[218] *Law Hospital NHS Trust v Rush* [2011] I.R.L.R. 611, IH.

[219] *Paterson v Commissioner of Police of the Metropolis* [2007] I.R.L.R. 763, EAT. Cf. *Chief Constable of Lothian and Borders Police v Cumming* [2010] I.R.L.R. 109, EAT.

[220] *Chief Constable of Dumfries and Galloway Constabulary v Adams* [2009] I.R.L.R. 612, EAT.

The common provisions:

Direct discrimination

9–88   Direct discrimination occurs where A, because of a protected characteristic, treats B less favourably than he treats or would treat others[221] and this now includes discriminating against a person because he or she associates with a person who has—or is perceived to have—a protected characteristic[222]. Thus to refuse employment to a person not because the applicant is, for example, gay or of a particular religion or belief but because he or she associates with people who have those protected characteristics is direct discrimination. It would make no difference if the applicant's associates were in fact not gay or of a particular religion. Generally for there to be direct discrimination there has to be a comparator, either real or hypothetical, whose circumstances are not materially different from the person complaining of discrimination. The exception is in relation to pregnancy and maternity in respect of which special provisions are made.[223]

Except with regard to the protected characteristic of age an act of direct discrimination may not be defended by pleading the act was a proportionate means of achieving a legitimate aim, or, in short, justified in some way. Thus it may be lawful to require an employee to retire at a particular age if the employer can show that it was to facilitate retirement with dignity rather than force an assessment of a person's performance as he or she gets older and in order to promote a collegiate culture within a partnership where the partners had agreed in their partnership agreement that partners would retire at 65.[224]

Occupational requirements

9–89   However, while direct discrimination cannot generally be defended by pleading the act was to achieve a legitimate aim there are certain exclusions and for certain jobs having a protected characteristic may be a genuine occupational requirement, that is to say that in order to perform the job effectively possessing or not possessing a protected characteristic is necessary and applied in a proportionate way.

Previous to the Equality Act 2010 different genuine occupational qualifications applied depending on the ground of discrimination.[225] Now the Equality Act provides in more general terms[226] that no contravention of particular provisions of the Act[227] occurs if A applies to B a requirement to have a particular characteristic if A shows that having regard to the nature or the context of the work: (a) it is an occupational requirement; (b) the application of which is a proportionate means of achieving a legitimate aim; and (c) the person to whom A applies it (B) does not meet the requirement (or A has reasonable grounds for not being satisfied that B meets it). There are modifications for requirements relating to transsexual persons and married persons or who have a civil partner, in respect

---

[221] Equality Act 2010 s.13, but note that direct discrimination on grounds of age is not unlawful if it is a proportionate means of achieving a legitimate aim, it is not unlawful to treat a person who is not disabled less favourably than one who is disabled or in the context of sex discrimination to afford special treatment to a woman in connection with pregnancy or childbirth.; and see s.18 regarding pregnancy and maternity.

[222] Whether a person can claim associative discrimination on the grounds of someone else's pregnancy has been referred to the CJEU: *Kulikaoskas v Macduff Shellfish* [2011] I.C.R. 48.

[223] Equality Act 2010 s.18.

[224] *Seldon v Clarkson Wright and Jakes* [2012] UKSC 16, SC; and see the decisions in *Petersen v Berufungsausschuss fur Zahnarzte fur den Bezirk Westfalen Lippe* [2010] I.R.L.R. 254 and *Wolf v Stadt Frankfurt am Main* [2010] I.R.L.R. 244 in which the ECJ takes a generous approach to justifying age discrimination. And see the examples in EHRC Code of Practice (2011), paras 3.36–3.41.

[225] Compare the Sex Discrimination Act 1975 s.8 with the Race Relations Act 1976 s.5.

[226] See Equality Ac 2010 Sch.9.

[227] See Sch.9 para.1(2).

of employment for the purposes of an organized religion and employment by an organization that has an ethos based on religion or belief and to allow the combat effectiveness of the armed forces.[228]

Indirect discrimination

This occurs where A applies to B a provision, criterion or practice (PCP) which is discriminatory in relation to a relevant protected characteristic of B and a PCP is discriminatory in relation to a protected characteristic of B if: (a) A applies or would apply it to persons with whom B does not share the characteristic; (b) it puts, or would put,[229] persons with whom B shares the characteristic at a particular disadvantage[230] when compared with persons with whom B does not share it; (c) it puts or would put B at that disadvantage; and (d) A cannot show it is a proportion means of achieving a legitimate aim.[231] The concept of indirect discrimination now applies with uniform language to all the protected grounds except pregnancy and maternity but of course a pregnant or new mother would be able to claim indirect discrimination relying on the protected characteristic of sex because the Government view is that any PCP which disadvantages pregnant women or new mothers is disadvantageous to women generally and therefore covered by indirect sex discrimination. A full explanation of the issues involved in, and examples of, indirect discrimination are found in Chapter 4 of the EHRC Code of Practice (2011). **9–90**

Indirect discrimination involves the identification of a "pool" of people to which the PCP is, or would be, applied in order to determine whether those who share B's protected characteristic suffer a particular disadvantage. There is no hard and fast rule as to the selection of an appropriate pool[232] and much depends on the nature of the alleged discriminatory act but the pool must be one which suitably tests the discrimination complained of.[233] Thus in *Pike v Somerset County Council*[234] a teacher who had been full time returned to work but in a part time capacity after ill health early retirement. Under the rules of the pension scheme her part time employment was not pensionable because she was already in receipt of her pension but that would not have been the case if she had returned in a full time capacity and she claimed indirect sex discrimination on the ground that the pension scheme rule disadvantaged more women than men. Contrary to the decision of the Employment Judge, the EAT and the Court of Appeal held the correct pool excluded pre-retirement teachers as they were "uninterested" in the post-retirement rules which just did not apply to them. The correct pool was those who had returned to employment after retirement and when that pool was considered the disadvantaged group was the part timers and the advantaged group the full timers; in the post retirement pool about 15 per cent more women than men were in non pensionable employment while 38 per cent more men were advantaged.

It is a defence to a claim of indirect discrimination if the employer can demonstrate that the PCP is a proportionate means of achieving a legitimate aim and what is required of an

---

[228] Sch.9 paras 1(3), 2, 3 & 4. And see EHRC Code of Practice (2011), Ch.13.

[229] It therefore allows a claim to be made by someone to whom a PCP has not yet been applied but to whom it would be applied for example in the event of his applying for promotion or an appointment.

[230] According to the EHRC Code of Practice on Employment (2011), para.4.9: "disadvantage" is to be widely construed to include denial of any opportunity or choice.

[231] Equality Act 2010 s.19.

[232] And it may be there is not always a single suitable pool: per Sedley L.J. in *Grundy v British Airways plc* [2008] I.R.L.R. 74. Cf. *Allonby v Accrington & Rosendale College* [2011] I.R.L.R. 364, CA.

[233] *Rutherford v Secretary of State for Trade and Industry (No 2)* [2006] I.C.R. 785, HL; *Grundy v British Airways Corporation plc* [2008] I.R.L.R. 74, CA; *Somerset County Council v Pike* [2009] EWCA Civ 808, CA.

[234] [2009] EWCA Civ 808.

employer has been the subject of much judicial discussion but an employer has to show the PCP is to achieve a legitimate aim notwithstanding its discriminatory effect[235] or that there is an objective balance between the discriminatory effect of the PCP and the reasonable needs of the person who applies it; and although the principle of proportionality requires the employment tribunal to take into account the reasonable needs of the business, it has to make its own judgment on a fair and detailed analysis of the working practices and business considerations but that is not the same as considering whether the employer's views are within the range of views that are reasonable in the circumstances.[236] While cost may be a relevant factor there are conflicting views as to whether cost alone may be relied on to defend a PCP. In *Cross v British Airways plc*[237] the EAT relying on the jurisprudence of the ECJ held that cost alone could not be relied on to show a proportionate means of achieving a legitimate aim but more recently in *Woodcock v Cumbria Primary Care Trust*[238] another EAT has held to the contrary.[239] In respect of the protected characteristic of religion an employer refused to allow a Muslim security guard to leave work to attend Friday prayers at a mosque. His employer's contract with the client at the site the employee worked required that security guards to remain on site at all times and there was a prayer room on the site which the employee could use; also the employee was given the option of working Saturdays or Sundays but he was not prepared to work at weekends and resolved the issue by taking Fridays as holidays. The EAT held the tribunal in dismissing the claim had properly considered the balance between the discriminatory effect of the PCP and the reasonable operational needs of the business.[240] In *London Underground Ltd v Edwards (No 2)*[241] it was held that the employers had failed to show new rostering arrangements which required employees to start earlier were a proportionate means of achieving a legitimate aim because they could have made arrangements which would not have been damaging to their business plans but which would have accommodated the reasonable needs of the few employees like Ms Edwards who had young families.

Combined discrimination

9–91 Where a person is discriminated against because of two prohibited characteristics for example by being black *and* a woman and not simply because she was black *or* a woman arguably she is not protected because the ground of discrimination was the combination of two characteristics—sex and race.[242] Scope to deal with such dual discrimination is contained in the Equality Act 2010[243] but the provision is not yet in force.

Harassment

9–92 Previously harassment was treated separately by the different statutory provisions. Now all of the protected characteristics are treated uniformly by the Equality Act 2010[244] which provides that a person (A) harasses another (B) if A engages in unwanted conduct to a

---

[235] *Hardys and Hanson v Lax* [2005] I.R.L.R. 726, CA.
[236] *Hampson v Department of Education and Science* [1989] I.R.L.R. 69, CA.
[237] [2005] I.R.L.R. 423, EAT.
[238] [2011] I.C.R. 143, EAT.
[239] And see *Cherfi v G4 S Security Services Ltd* EAT/0379/10.
[240] *Cherfi v G4 S Security Services Ltd* EAT/0379/10.
[241] [1997] I.R.L.R. 157, EAT.
[242] See the discussion in *Bahl v Law Society* [2004] I.R.L.R. 799, CA. Cf. *Ministry of Defence v DeBique* [2010] I.R.L.R. 471, EAT.
[243] Equality Act 2010 s.14.
[244] Equality Act 2010 s.26 and see the EHRC Code of Practice (2011), Ch.7.

relevant protected characteristic[245] that has the purpose or effect of: (i) violating B's dignity; or (ii) creating an intimidating, hostile, degrading, humiliating or offensive environment for B and in deciding whether conduct has such an effect a tribunal must take into account: (a) the perception of B; (b) the circumstances of the case; and (c) whether it is reasonable for the conduct to have that effect, thereby preventing successful claims by overly sensitive people. Also A harasses B if A engages in any unwanted conduct of a sexual nature that has the purpose or effect of (i) or (ii) above or if A or another person engages in unwanted conduct of a sexual nature or conduct that is related to gender re assignment, the conduct has the purpose or effect of (i) or (ii) above and because of B's rejection of, or submission to the conduct A treats B less favourably than A would treat B if B had not rejected or submitted to the conduct. Only with regard to this latter provision is a comparative approach necessary; in all other respects it is not necessary to show another employee was treated more favourably.

The Protection from Harassment Act 1997, which was primarily introduced to protect against "stalking", also applies in the employment field and an employer can be vicariously liable for employees who contravene the Act.[246]

Victimisation

The Equality Act 2010 provides[247] victimisation occurs where A subjects B to a detriment **9–93** because B does, or A believes B has done or may do, "a protected act" which is defined to be: (a) bringing proceedings under the Act; (b) giving evidence or information for such proceedings; (c) doing any other thing for purposes of or in connection with the Act; (d) making an allegation that A or another person has contravened the Act.

What discrimination is unlawful for employers?

Chapter 1 of the Equality Act 2010 makes many types of discriminatory conduct unlawful **9–94** for employees, job applicants, and contract workers as well as for police officers, partners, advocates, office holders and some public appointments. In relation to employment it is unlawful for an employer to discriminate—directly[248] or indirectly[249]—against a person in relation to the following:

(a) the arrangements he makes for determining who should be offered employment, for example the recruitment and selection process;

(b) the terms on which he offers employment, for example requiring that the jobholder works full time;

(c) by refusing to offer employment, for example rejecting a job applicant;

(d) in the way he affords access to promotion, training, transfer, benefits, facilities or services; or

(e) by dismissing (including the non-renewal of a limited term contract and constructive dismissal) or subjecting a person to some other detriment.

---

[245] Pregnancy and civil partnership are not relevant characteristics but harassment on those grounds would be covered by the protected characteristics of sex and sexual orientation.

[246] Note that the definition of harassment in the Protection Against Harassment Act is different and, in some respects, wider than that in the Equality Act 2010 and can apply to, for example, acts of bullying which are not motivated by gender, race etc; there has to be at least two incidents of harassment before breach of the 1997 Act occurs. See *Majrowski v Guy's & St Thomas's NHS Trust*, 2006 UKHL, 34; *Green v DB Group Services (UK) Ltd*, 2006 EWHC 1898, QB.

[247] Equality Act 2010 s.27.

[248] See the examples and explanations in EHRC Code of Practice (2011), Ch.3.

[249] See the examples and explanations in EHRC Code of Practice (2011), Ch.4.

It is also unlawful for an employer to victimise[250] an applicant for employment or an employee in relation to (a), (b), (c), (d) or (e) above or to harass[251] an applicant or an employee and this includes the case where a third party (who is not also an employee) has harassed an employee in the course of the employee's employment provided the employer knows the employee has been harassed on at least two occasions.[252]

Disability discrimination

9–95 While the provisions relating to direct discrimination, indirect discrimination, victimisation and harassment as discussed above apply equally to the protected characteristic of disability there are particular provisions of the Equality Act which apply only to disability, namely: (1) discrimination arising from disability and (2) the duty to make reasonable adjustments.

Under the provisions of the Disability Discrimination Act 1995 it was unlawful for an employer, for a reason which related to a disability, to treat a disabled person less favourably than a person to whom that reason did not apply and the employer could not show that the treatment was justified.[253] Contrary to the views of the Court of Appeal[254] the House of Lords in *Malcolm v London Borough of Lewisham*[255] held that the appropriate comparator in cases of disability related discrimination is a non-disabled person who is otherwise in the same circumstances as the disabled person. The result of *Malcolm* was that where a disabled person was dismissed, for example for sickness absence, the comparator was a non-disabled person who had also been absent and if such a person would also have been dismissed the disabled person would not have been treated less favourably for a reason related to his disability. The *Malcolm* test made it much more difficult for a disabled person to show he had been treated less favourably. The Equality Act 2010 now avoids the difficulty left by *Malcolm* by removing the need to show less favourable treatment and provides A discriminates against a disabled person (B) if A treats B unfavourably because of something arising in consequence[256] of B's disability and A cannot show it is a proportionate means of achieving a legitimate aim, provided A knew or could reasonably have known of B's disability. Unlike both direct discrimination and indirect discrimination this form of disability discrimination does not require a comparative exercise.

The duty to make reasonable adjustments applies to applicants (including those who have indicated they may be applicants) and employees.[257] The duty is threefold, namely where a provision, criterion or practice (PCP), a physical feature of premises (for example of a building or its lay out) or a failure to provide an auxiliary aid puts a disabled person at a substantial disadvantage in comparison with persons who are not disabled the employer must take such steps as it is reasonable to have to take to avoid that disadvantage or provide the auxiliary aid.[258] However the duty only arises if the employer knows or could reasonably be expected to know the applicant or the employee has a disability.[259] For the purpose of considering whether an employer has a duty to make a reasonable adjustment a

---

[250] See EHRC Code of Practice (2011), Ch.11.
[251] See EHRC Code of Practice (2011), Ch.7.
[252] Equality Act 2010 s.39. This protects employees against discrimination or harassment by, for example, customers or self-employed people engaged by their employer.
[253] Disability Discrimination Act 1995 s.3A(1).
[254] *Clark v TDG Ltd (t/a Novacold)* [1999] I.C.R. 951, CA.
[255] [2008] I.R.L.R. 700, HL.
[256] See the examples in EHRC Code of Practice (2011), Ch.5.
[257] And see the Equality Act 2010 Sch.8.
[258] Equality Act 2010 s.20.
[259] Equality Act 2010 Sch.8 para.20; and see the EHRC Code of Practice (2011), Ch.6.

PCP has to be given a wide interpretation and may include the job description itself and the liability of a person who cannot fulfil it to be dismissed just as much as it applies to the employer's arrangements for deciding who gets a job or how much he is paid.[260] The duty may, depending on the circumstances, require an employer to create a new role for a disabled person.[261] Consulting with the disabled person in advance of making an adjustment is strictly not required but is advisable as, if the employer, through a lack of consultation, fails to appreciate the adjustment that is required his lack of knowledge will not excuse his failures.[262] Where the claim is one of an employer failing to make reasonable adjustments it is vital that the employment tribunal adopts the correct process of identifying: (1) the PCP applied by the employer; (2) the physical feature of the premises; (3) the identity of the non disabled comparators (where appropriate); and (4) the nature and extent of the substantial disadvantage suffered by the claimant and unless the tribunal has gone through that process it cannot judge if any proposed adjustment is reasonable because it will be unable to say what adjustments were reasonable to prevent the PCP or the feature placing the disabled person at the substantial disadvantage.[263]

The circumstances will be relevant but generally reasonable adjustment will require consideration of the practicability of an adjustment, the financial cost and disruption to the employer's business, the employer's resources and the availability of help from public or other funds.[264]

Previous legislation contained a list of examples of adjustments that may be required of an employer and although the Equality Act 2010 itself does not do so similar examples are now contained in the EHRC Code of Practice (2011).[265]

Enforcement and remedies

Enforcement of the obligations of employers under the Equality Act 2010 may be by the **9–96** Equality and Human Rights Commission or by complaints made by individuals respectively.

The Commission may enforce the obligations on employers (and others), by way of conducting formal investigations,[266] issuing of unlawful act notices,[267] taking action where there is persistent discrimination[268] and in respect of discriminatory advertisements and instructions or pressure to discriminate.[269] The Commission also has powers to draw up and issue Codes of Practice containing practical guidance to employers, on how to avoid discrimination and any such Code is admissible in employment tribunal proceedings[270] and Codes have been issued in respect of sex, race and disability discrimination. The

---

[260] *Archibald v Fife Council* [2004] I.R.L.R. 651, HL.
[261] *Chief Constable of South Yorkshire Police v Jelic* [2010] I.R.L.R. 744, EAT.
[262] *Tarbuck v Sainsbury Supermarkets Ltd* [2006] I.R.L.R. 664, EAT.
[263] *Environment Agency v Rowan* [2008] I.R.L.R. 20, EAT.
[264] See the EHRC Code of Practice (2011), paras 6.28, 6.29.
[265] See the EHRC Code of Practice (2011), para.6.33, which includes adjusting premises, allocating some of the disabled person's duties to another, transferring the disabled person to an existing vacancy, altering the disabled person's hours of work or training, assigning the disabled person to another place of work, allowing absence for treatment or re habilitation, arranging training or mentoring, acquiring or modifying equipment, modifying manuals and procedures for testing or assessment, providing a reader or interpreter or other supervision or support, allowing period of disability leave, employing a support worker and adjusting redundancy selection criteria.
[266] Equality Act 2006 s.20.
[267] Equality Act 2006 s.21.
[268] Equality Act 2006 ss.24, 24A.
[269] Equality Act 2006 s.111.
[270] Equality Act 2006 s.115.

Commission also has responsibility for promotion of human rights and has a wide power to conduct inquiries into equality, diversity and human rights matters.

The remedy for an individual, is to apply to an employment tribunal within three months of the act complained of, although this may be extended if the tribunal considers it just and equitable to do so[271] and, in the event of the complaint being upheld, the tribunal may grant any or all of the following remedies:

(1) a declaration of the rights of the parties;
(2) an award of compensation which may include a sum in respect of injury to feelings and interest;
(3) a recommendation that the employer takes action for the purpose of obviating or reducing the effect of any act of discrimination.

An important tool for a person who believes that they have been the victim of unlawful discrimination, is the questionnaire procedure. This allows such a person to serve on the employer a statutory questionnaire, in which certain questions may be addressed to an employer (or prospective employer). While there is no obligation on the employer to respond to the questionnaire, any response is admissible in tribunal proceedings and if an employer's responses are absent, evasive or delayed, a tribunal may draw an inference that an act of discrimination has been committed.[272]

"Vicarious" liability

9–97 Liability for an act of discrimination committed by an employee in the course of his employment falls on the employer. Strictly, it is not vicarious liability, rather a provision which deems the employer also to have done the employee's act.[273] Thus, the Equality Act provides that anything done by a person in the course of his employment, shall be treated for the purposes of this Act as done by his employers as well as by him, whether or not the act is done with the employer's approval or knowledge, although it is a defence if an employer can show that he took reasonably practicable steps to prevent the employee doing such an act, e.g. by drawing up and applying a policy to eliminate discriminatory acts and behaviour and by disciplining those who contravene it.[274] However, the approach of tribunals to what is or is not in the course of employment has been generous.

> **Chief Constable of the Lincolnshire Police v (1) Stubbs, (2) Taylor And (3) The Chief Constable Of The North Yorkshire Police**
> [1999] I.R.L.R. 81
>
> Constable Deborah Stubbs and Sergeant Walker were police officers and, while working together, incidents occurred which resulted in Stubbs complaining that she was being sexually harassed by Walker. One of these incidents occurred when Stubbs went for a drink at a pub after work with several fellow officers including Walker and a subsequent incident with Walker, which also took place in a pub after an office leaving party. She complained that acts of sexual discrimination (harassment) alleged to have been committed by Walker were in the course of his

---

[271] Equality Act 2006 s.123.
[272] Equality Act 2006 s.138.
[273] *Chief Constable of Bedfordshire Police v Liversage* [2002] I.R.L.R. 5651, CA.
[274] Equality Act 2006 s.109.

employment, for which the Chief Constable would be vicariously liable. Held: what happened between Stubbs and Walker occurred in circumstances that were "an extension of their employment". In this particular case although the incidents did not occur at the employer's premises, they were nevertheless, social gatherings involving officers from work either immediately after work or for an organised leaving party. The incidents, therefore, came within the concept of course of employment as explained by the Court of Appeal in *Tower Boot Company v Jones*.[275] It would have been different if the acts had taken place during a chance meeting.

Part-time workers

Prior to the passing of the Part-time Workers (Prevention of Less Favourable Treatment) **9–98** Regulations 2000, it had been possible for women and married persons to argue that treating part-time employees less favourably than full-time employees constituted either indirect sex or marital status discrimination. Thus, by excluding part-time employees from promotion or training opportunities an employer could commit an act of sex discrimination, on the grounds that fewer women than men, or fewer married persons than unmarried persons, would work full-time in order to be able to apply for promotion or a training opportunity.

Giving effect to Directive 1997/81, the Part-time Workers (Prevention of Less Favourable Treatment) Regulations 2000 have, since July 2000, enabled less favourable treatment of part-time workers to be challenged without the need for indirect sex discrimination to be established.

Fixed term contracts

Directive 1999/70, with effect from July 10, 2001, requires: (1) that fixed term contract **9–99** workers shall not be treated less favourably than comparable permanent workers, solely because they have a fixed term contract, unless different treatment is justified on objective grounds; and (2) that successive fixed term contracts shall be justified on objective grounds or be regulated in terms of duration or the number of renewals. Regulations have been introduced to give effect to the Directive. With effect from July 10, 2002, it is unlawful to treat fixed term employees less favourably than those on permanent contract.[276]

Agency workers

To give effect to Directive 2008/104 on temporary agency work the Agency Workers **9–100** Regulations 2010 require that temporary workers supplied to an employer/hirer by an agency receive the same basic terms and conditions as employees or workers doing the same job but recruited directly by the employer/hirer.[277] However "basic terms and conditions" are restricted to terms about pay, hours of work and annual leave and while pay is widely defined it expressly excludes certain payments including occupational sick pay, pensions, redundancy pay, payments in respect of maternity, paternity or adoption leave and any payment which is not directly attributable to the amount or quality of work done by a worker and is given to encourage loyalty or reward long term service so that an agency worker is not entitled to incremental seniority bonuses or bonuses paid for example

---

[275] [1997] I.C.R. 254. Also see *Canniffe v East Riding of Yorkshire Council* [2000] I.R.L.R. 555, EAT.
[276] Fixed Term Employees (Prevention of Less Favourable Treatment) Regulations 2002.
[277] Agency Workers Regulations 2010 reg.5.

at Christmas time to directly recruited staff.[278] However, entitlement to equality of basic terms is dependent on the agency worker being employed for 12 (normally consecutive) weeks in the same role and with that same employer/hirer although provision is made for gaps or breaks in the 12-week period to be discounted, for example where a break is not more than 6 weeks or for the purpose of maternity, paternity adoption leave or as a result of a strike at the hirer's establishment.[279] However, this right is modified in relation to pay if the agency worker has a permanent written contract with the agency which entitles him to 50 per cent of his normal pay during any periods between assignments if no work is provided.[280]

An agency worker may not be treated less favourably than a comparable worker directly recruited by the hirer in respect of collective facilities or amenities like canteen or child care or transport facilities unless the difference in treatment is justified on objective grounds.[281] An agency worker is also entitled to be informed by the hirer of any vacancies so that the agency worker has the opportunity of applying for a permanent position with the hirer.[282]

Remedies

9–101 For breach of the Part-time Workers Regulations or the Fixed Term Employees Regulations a tribunal may (1) grant a declaration of rights (2) award compensation (but not for injury to feelings) and (3) recommend the discriminator takes specified steps to obviate the adverse effect on the complainant of a matter to which the complaint relates.[283] The agency worker's remedy in respect of entitlement to basic conditions is against both the agency and the hirer depending on which is responsible for the breach of the regulations.[284] However, only the hirer is liable for treating the worker less favourably in respect of the provision of collective facilities or amenities.[285] Enforcement is by way of complaint to an employment tribunal which can (1) grant a declaration of rights, (2) order payment of compensation and (3) make a recommendation that the respondent takes specified steps to obviate or reduce the adverse effect on the complainant of any matter to which complaint relates.[286]

Equal pay

9–102 The Equal Pay Act 1970 (EPA) was enacted to ensure equal pay for men and women doing work of equal value. The short title states that it is "An Act to prevent discrimination, as regards terms and conditions of employment between men and women" and is concerned with contractual terms of employment including, but not limited to, those concerning pay. The 1970 Act was repealed by the Equality Act 2010 which in Chapter 3 now contains the relevant statutory provisions which are supplemented by the Code of Practice on Equal Pay (2011). Every contract of employment contains an equality clause.[287] The Act applies to employees and those who hold a personal or public office and only gives equality of pay between men and women in the same employment, but this is

---

[278] Agency Workers Regulations 2010 reg 6(3).
[279] Agency Workers Regulations 2010 reg.7.
[280] Agency Workers Regulations 2010 regs 10, 11.
[281] Agency Workers Regulations 2010 reg.12.
[282] Agency Workers Regulations 2010 reg.13.
[283] Part-time Workers Regulations 2000 reg.8(7); Fixed Term Employees Regulations 2002 reg.7(7).
[284] Agency Workers Regulations 2010 reg.14.
[285] Agency Workers Regulations 2010 regs 12(1), 13(1).
[286] Agency Workers Regulations 2010 reg.18.
[287] Equality Act 2006 s.66.

generally defined to include a comparator who is employed by the claimant's employer or an associate and the claimant and the comparator work at the same establishment or at a different establishment provided common terms apply either generally or between the claimant and the comparator.[288]

The three entitlements

A woman (or a man) is entitled to equal pay with a man (or a woman) in the following **9–103** three situations:

> (1) where the man and the woman are engaged on "like work" (s.65(1)(a));
> (2) where the man and the woman are engaged on "work rated equivalent", namely where a job evaluation study has been carried out in respect of the work (s.65(1)(b)); and
> (3) where the man and the woman are engaged on in "work of equal value (s.65(1)(c)).

However, when comparison is being made between the pay of a woman and the pay of a man, in order to ensure transparency in the pay scheme each individual item of the contract has to be compared. However, as to what that "term" is has been considered in *Redcar and Cleveland Borough Council v Degnan*,[289] so that the proper approach is not merely to compare each individual element of remuneration, but to aggregate all payments to work out an hourly rate.

Like work

This occurs where a woman and a man do work which is of the same, or a broadly similar **9–104** nature and if there are any differences in the things that the man and the woman do, they must not be of practical importance in relation to terms and conditions of employment.

Work rated equivalent

This occurs when a woman's job, and that of the man, have been given an equal value in **9–105** terms of the demands made on the worker under several headings like effort, skill, decision-making, etc. in a job evaluation study, or where the woman's job and the man's job would have been given equal value if the evaluation had not been done on a "sex-specific system".

Equal value

This is a flexible route to equal pay and may only be used where men and women are not **9–106** engaged on like work or where there has been no proper job evaluation study undertaken. This permits a woman who is employed, e.g. as a cook or a kitchen assistant to compare her pay, and other contractual conditions, with those of male workers employed as, for example, joiners, plumbers, engineers or accountants.

---

[288] Equality Act 2006 ss.72, 79.
[289] [2005] I.R.L.R. 615, CA.

Material factor defence

9–107 An employer faced with an equal pay claim may defend it by showing that the difference in pay is genuinely due to a material factor between the woman's case and the man's.[290] Provided the difference is genuine and is due to a factor other than sex the defence will be effective.

> ### Strathclyde Regional Council v Wallace
> #### [1998] I.R.L.R. 146
>
> Wallace and others were female teachers who did the same work as male principal teachers, but were paid at a lower rate and not given the opportunity of promotion. The Council could not create new promoted posts because of restraints imposed by Government. As a result, the appellants were doing the work of principal teachers without having been promoted to that grade and without receiving the salary commensurate with it. Relying on the Equal Pay Act, (now the Equality Act 2010) these un-promoted female teachers sought equal pay with male principal teachers. An employment tribunal held that the Council had not shown that the difference was genuinely due to a material difference which was not the difference of sex.
>
> Held: Provided that there is no element of sexual discrimination, an employer can establish a defence under what is now s.69 of the Equality Act 2010 by identifying the factors which he alleges have caused the disparity, proving that those factors are genuine and proving further that they were causally relevant to the disparity in pay complained of.

Remedies

9–108 The majority of equal pay claims are raised in the employment tribunal, but such claims may also be raised in the form of breach of contract actions in the ordinary court. Where a woman's claim to equal pay is upheld, her contract is modified with regard to the future.[291] With regard to the period before the claim is upheld, the tribunal may award arrears of remuneration or damages.[292]

European Union law

9–109 In the field of sex discrimination, art.157 of the Treaty on the Functioning of the European Union (previously art.141 of the Treaty of Rome) states, inter alia, that "each member state shall ... ensure and subsequently maintain the application of the principle that men and women should receive equal pay for equal work". This obligation is amplified by the Equal Pay Directive (75/117) and the Equal Treatment Directive (76/207) prohibits discrimination in conditions of employment including dismissal. Article 157 creates rights which can be enforced by individuals against employers and overrides any contrary domestic law.

In order to enforce any right conferred by art.157, an employee should still raise the case by way of a complaint to an employment tribunal or an ordinary court, which must then hear the complaint under the relevant provisions of the Equality Act by ignoring or "disapplying" any provision of that Act which is contrary to art.157.[293]

---

[290] Equality Act 2006 s.69.
[291] Equality Act 2006 s.66(2).
[292] Equality Act 2006 s.132.
[293] *Biggs and Barber v Staffordshire County Council* [1996] I.R.L.R. 209.

> **Key Concepts**
>
> UK law now makes it unlawful for an employer to **discriminate** on the following grounds:
>
> - sex, pregnancy, marital status, trans-sexualism and sexual orientation;
> - race, national and ethnic origins and nationality;
> - disability;
> - religion or belief;
> - being a part-time worker, an agency worker or fixed-term employee; or
> - age.
>
> **Direct discrimination** is less favourable treatment of an employee simply because of their sex, race, etc.
>
>   **Indirect discrimination** occurs where the same criterion is applied to all but impacts adversely on members of one race, sex, etc. who cannot meet the criterion and is not a proportionate means of achieving a legitimate aim.

▼ CHAPTER SUMMARY

THE CONTRACT OF EMPLOYMENT

1. Breaches of contract must be brought before the ordinary courts, while enforcement of statutory rights is dealt with by employment tribunals.   9–110
2. There are differences between employees, workers and agency workers.
3. Factors which are relevant in determining whether there is a contract of employment are: control; provision of equipment, hire of helpers, financial risk, opportunity to profit; label or name of contract; change of status; income tax and national insurance; and mutuality of obligation.
4. The status of workers is frequently resolved by having regard to the issue of "mutuality of obligation":

   ➤ *O'Kelly v Trusthouse Forte plc* [1983] I.C.R. 728;
   ➤ *Nethermere (St Neots) Ltd v Taverna* [1984] I.C.R. 612;
   ➤ *Carmichael v National Power plc* [2000] I.R.L.R. 43;
   ➤ *Dacas v Brook Street Bureau (UK) Ltd*, Court of Appeal, 2004 E.W.C.A. Civ 217.

4. Any statute that confers rights on a person with a contract of employment also protects a person with an apprenticeship contract.
5. Whether a director is an employee of the company depends on all the circumstances and the size of the shareholding is merely one of those circumstances.
6. A contract of employment can be created: entirely by a written agreement: entirely oral; by implication through the actings and conduct of the parties.
7. An employer must give an employee a written statement of the particulars of employment, but this is not a contract—it represents the terms of employment, which the employer believes to be in existence at the time it is issued.
8. Collective agreements are entered into on the grounds that they do not create legally enforceable contracts between the trade union and the employer(s).

9. Incorporation of a collective agreement can be by an express or implied reference or statement in the contract of employment to it and results in the incorporated term taking on the legally binding quality of a contractual term.

TERMS AND CONDITIONS OF EMPLOYMENT

1. Wages are "any sums payable to the worker in connection with his employment including fee, bonus, commission, holiday pay or other emolument referable to his employment".
2. Deductions from wages may generally only be made with the worker's written consent or by statutory authority.
3. Retail workers have additional protection for deductions for cash or stock shortages.
4. Protection against low pay was created by the national minimum wage:

    ➢ National Minimum Wage Act 1998;
    ➢ National Minimum Wage Regulations 1999.

5. The hours to be used in arriving at the hourly rate vary depending on whether it is: time work; salaried work; output work; or unmeasured work.
6. A worker's average working time shall not exceed 48 hours for each seven-day period. A worker is entitled to 28 days' paid annual leave:

    ➢ Working Time Regulations 1998.

7. Periods off work with rights to statutory payments are available in relation to: maternity; paternity; adoption and parental leave.
8. There is a right to a flexible working pattern in certain circumstances:

    ➢ Employment Act 2002 s.47.

9. There is an obligation on both employer and employee not to act in such a way that is likely to destroy or seriously damage the trust and confidence on which the employment relationship is ultimately based.
10. An employee must carry out the instructions given to him by his employers for the purpose of performing his contract, provided it does not involve the employee doing an act that is illegal or immoral.
11. An employee must perform his contract with reasonable care:

    ➢ *Lister v Romford Ice and Cold Storage Ltd* [1957] A.C. 555.

12. There is an implied duty that requires an employee to use all reasonable means to advance his employer's business and to refrain from doing anything which would injure his employer's business.
13. An employee has a duty to protect and not abuse or disclose his employer's trade secrets or confidential information. Factors relevant to whether information is confidential include; the nature of the job; the nature of the information; whether it could be equated with a trade secret; whether the employer stressed the confidentiality of the information during the period of employment; and whether the confidential information could be isolated from general information to which an employee is exposed in the course of employment?
14. Employers can seek to protect their legitimate interests by inserting restrictive covenants into contracts of employment.
15. To be enforceable, a restrictive covenant must protect confidential information or trade connections and must be reasonable and in the public interest.

TERMINATION OF THE CONTRACT AND WRONGFUL DISMISSAL

1. **A contract of employment can be terminated by: notice of termination; dissolution or winding up of a partnership or company; impossibility or illegality of performance (frustration); or rescission following repudiation.**

2. **An employer has an implied right to terminate the employment contract by paying wages and giving other contractual benefits due to the employee in lieu of notice.**

3. **Wrongful dismissal denotes dismissal in breach of contract and is to be contrasted with unfair dismissal, which is primarily concerned with the reasonableness of the employer's actions.**

4. **The most common remedy for wrongful dismissal is an action of damages.**

5. **Where a breach involves a resignation, without giving the notice required by the contract or a dismissal without notice, the courts will generally not grant any order whose effect would be to compel the continuation of the employment relationship.**

6. **It is possible for an interdict to be granted to restrain a wrongful dismissal.**

UNFAIR DISMISSAL

1. **Unfair dismissal is a dismissal which is contrary to certain standards of reasonableness or other rules of law:**

   ➢ Employment Rights Act 1996;
   ➢ Transfer of Undertakings (Protection of Employment) Regulations 2006;
   ➢ Trade Union and Labour Relations (Consolidation) Act 1992.

2. **To be protected against unfair dismissal, generally an employee must have been continuously employed for a period of two years at the effective date of termination:**

   ➢ Employment Rights Act 1996 s.108.

3. **Constructive dismissal is where a contract is terminated by the employee in circumstances such that they are entitled to terminate without notice, by reason of the employer's conduct.**

4. **To establish constructive dismissal, it is not sufficient for the employee to show that the employer's conduct was unreasonable. The employer's actions must go to the root of the employment contract or show that the employer no longer wished to be bound by one or more of its essential terms. The employee must also show that the breach was what caused him/her to leave.**

5. **To establish unfair dismissal the employee must show that they have been dismissed and then the onus transfers to the employer to show the dismissal was for a fair reason. The tribunal then considers whether the employer has acted reasonably.**

6. **Fair reasons relate to the employee's: capability/qualifications; conduct; redundancy; contravention of statute by either party; or some other substantial reason:**

   ➢ Employment Rights Act 1996 s.98(2).

7. **Employers are restricted to producing evidence of which they were aware at the time they took the decision to dismiss.**

9. **Special categories of dismissal include: industrial action and lock-outs; protected industrial action; union membership and activities; union recognition dismissals; health and safety dismissals; asserting a statutory right; dismissals on the transfer of an undertaking; pregnancy and family leave; whistle-blowing and other special cases.**

10. **Remedies for unfair dismissal are: reinstatement; re-engagement; and compensation.**

REDUNDANCY PAYMENTS

1. **Provided an employee has two years' continuous employment he becomes entitled to a redundancy payment on being dismissed for redundancy or after a spell of lay-off or short time:**

   ➢ Employment Rights Act 1996 Pt XI.

2. **A dismissal is a redundancy if it is wholly or mainly attributable to: the employer ceasing the business for the purpose of which the employee was employed, either completely or at the place the employee has been employed; or the requirements of the business for employees to do "work of a particular" have ceased or diminished:**

   ➢ Employment Rights Act 1996 s.139.

3. **Refusing an offer of suitable employment can result in loss of entitlement to a redundancy payment.**

DISCRIMINATION

Legislation deals with discrimination on grounds of: (1) sex, trans-sexualism, sexual orientation, pregnancy and marital status; (2) race, colour, ethnic and national origins and nationality; (3) disability; (4) religion; (5) age; (6) being part-time workers; and (7) being fixed term contract employees.

1. **The Equality Act:**

   (a) **Direct discrimination occurs where an employer treats (or would treat) a person less favourably than a person on the grounds of a protected characteristic.**

   (b) **Generally, positive discrimination, which means the more favourable treatment of a person on grounds of sex in order to overcome the fact that his or her sex is under-represented in a work group, is not permitted.**

   (c) **Indirect sex discrimination occurs where the same criterion is applied to all, but impacts adversely on members of one group who cannot meet the criterion and is not a proportionate means of achieving a legitimate aim.**

2. **Disability**

   (a) **A disability is "a physical or mental impairment which has a substantial and long-term adverse effect on a person's ability to carry out normal day-to-day activities".**

3. **Less favourable treatment of part-time workers can be challenged without the need for indirect sex discrimination to be established:**

   ➢ Part-time Workers (Prevention of Less Favourable Treatment) Regulations 2000.

4. **It is unlawful to treat fixed term employees less favourably than those on permanent contract:**

   ➢ Fixed Term Employees (Prevention of Less Favourable Treatment) Regulations 2002.

5. **After 12 weeks' employment an agency worker is entitled to the same basic terms and conditions as a similar worker or employee directly recruited by the hirer/host organisation.**

6. **A woman (or a man) is entitled to equal pay with a man (or a woman): where the man and the woman are engaged on "like work"; where the man and the woman are engaged on "work rated equivalent", namely where a job evaluation study has been carried out in respect of the work; and where the man and the woman are engaged on in "work of equal value":**

> ➢ Equality Act 2010 ss.64–66.

? QUICK QUIZ

EMPLOYMENT LAW

- What formalities are necessary to create the contract of employment?
- How do courts identify the contract of employment? List four criteria the courts often take into account. What is meant by "mutuality of obligation"?
- What is the legal status of a Written Statement of Particulars issued under the Employment Rights Act 1996? List six things it must contain.
- What is a collective agreement and how can it become a contract between the union and the employer?
- What is meant by, and what is the result of, incorporation of a collective agreement?
- List two duties on the employee that are implied into the contract of employment.
- What are the main entitlements under the Working Time Regulations?
- List three situations in which employees are entitled to paid leave.
- Explain what a wrongful dismissal is and how it differs from an unfair dismissal.
- What is the main remedy for wrongful dismissal?
- What is meant by the least burdensome performance rule?
- List two situations in which an employee is deemed to be dismissed for unfair dismissal.
- List three reasons which an employer can prove to support an unfair dismissal.
- Which court or tribunal can deal with unfair dismissal complaints?
- What are the remedies for unfair dismissal?
- How does the law define indirect sex discrimination?
- List the areas in which the law makes it unlawful for an employer to discriminate against employees.
- Is an agency worker who has been employed by a hirer for 12 weeks entitled to receive the same productivity bonus and Christmas bonus as a directly recruited worker doing the same job?

Chapter 10   Commercial Law

► CHAPTER OVERVIEW

10–01 Commercial law is a broad category of law, which has no agreed definition and comprises several different discreet areas of law. This chapter discusses the following subject areas: agency, partnership, company law, commercial instruments, diligence and bankruptcy.

✓ OUTCOMES

10–02 At the end of this chapter you should be able to:

- ✓ understand when a principal is liable for the acts of his agent;
- ✓ understand the duties owed by an agent to his principal;
- ✓ recognise the duties owed by a principal to his agent;
- ✓ understand the advantages and disadvantages of partnerships;
- ✓ understand the relation of the partners to each other and to their partnership;
- ✓ understand the distinction between a partnership and a limited partnership;
- ✓ discern the main advantages and disadvantages of trading through a limited company;
- ✓ appreciate the significance of the separate legal personality of the company;
- ✓ understand the principal rules applying to the formation, management and dissolution of a company;
- ✓ be aware of the importance of the rules relating to directors' duties;
- ✓ understand the main features of guarantees;
- ✓ understand the purpose and use of bills of exchange;
- ✓ understand the common law of insurance;
- ✓ be aware of the significance of the terms of "disclosure" and "warranty";
- ✓ understand the main forms and purpose of diligence;
- ✓ understand the process of sequestration;
- ✓ be aware of how the trustee can maximise the bankrupt's estate for the benefit of his creditors; and
- ✓ know how the estate is divided up between the creditors.

---

[1] Senior Lecturer in Law, Edinburgh Napier University.

AGENCY

In business, it is not always easy for a business to find its potential clients, so it will arrange **10–03** for someone to introduce clients to it. An example of this is a travel company, which pays a fee to a travel agent for every customer the travel agent introduces to it. Alternatively, someone might want something done for him which he cannot do himself, because he lacks the requisite skill. He can then hire an agent to do it for him. An example of this would be a businessman who hires an accountant to negotiate with the Inland Revenue on how much tax he should pay.

An agent, therefore, is a person who acts on behalf of a principal (in the above examples, the travel company or the businessman), bringing the principal into a legal relationship with a third party (in the above examples, the customers or the Inland Revenue), but without himself necessarily being involved in that relationship.

In effect, there are two contracts in agency, one between the agent and the principal, and one between the principal and the third party. Normally, but not exclusively, the agent is rewarded by means of a commission or fee from the principal.

Traditionally the law on agency in Scotland is to be found in the Institutional Writers (Bell in particular). However, there are certain areas of agency law where the Commercial Agents (Council Directive) Regulations 1993 ("CA(CD)R") apply. These are discussed at the end of this section.

Key concept

An agent is a person who acts on behalf of a principal, bringing the principal into a legal relationship with a third party, but without himself being involved in that relationship.

Constitution of agency

There are different ways in which an agency may be set up, but the main ways are: **10–04**

    (a) agency by express appointment;
    (b) agency by implied appointment;
    (c) agency by ratification;
    (d) agency of necessity;
    (e) agency by holding out.

Agency need not be constituted in writing, though commercial agents are entitled to obtain from their principals, and principals from their agents, a statement of the terms on which they will do business with each other.[2]

For a contract of agency to exist, the parties must have legal capacity and must exist. Where the principal does not exist, but legal obligations arise, as in a contract made by a director of an as yet unformed company, the purported agent (in this case the purported director) will himself be liable for the obligations arising out of the contract unless the contract says otherwise.[3]

---

[2] CA(CD)R reg.13.
[3] Companies Act 2006 s.51.

> ## Phonogram Ltd v Lane
> [1982] Q.B. 938; [1981] 3W.L.R. 736, CA (Civ Div)
>
> Lane borrowed money to set up a company, which was going to manage a pop group called "Cheap, Mean and Nasty". He never got round to founding the company. The lender asked for its money back. Lane claimed that it was his company that had borrowed the money, but as the company was not yet in existence, he was held liable for the money.

Agency by express appointment

10–05 The deliberate appointment of an agent by a principal, together with the grant of authority to act on the principal's behalf, whether constituted by written contract or not, is known as agency by express appointment.

Agency by implied appointment

10–06 An agency may arise through the actings of the parties, even though there has been no express appointment. In *Barnetson v Petersen Brothers*[4] a shipbroker was held to have been employed to act as agent for the shipowners, by virtue of his actions on their behalf to which they had not objected. Agency may also be implied by operation of law: for example, a partner acts as agent for his partnership.[5]

Agency by ratification

10–07 The agency agreement need not pre-date the agent's actions: an agent might carry out an act for a principal who was unaware that the agent had acted for him, but on the principal's awareness of the act, the principal may ratify (i.e. retrospectively authorise) the act, either by a positive action or by his conduct. Six conditions are required for ratification:

  (a) the agent must act as agent, and must have intimated to the third party that he was acting as agent, and not on his own account[6];
  (b) the principal must exist at the time of the act[7];
  (c) the principal must have the requisite legal capacity to carry out the act, so that a contract struck at by the Age of Legal Capacity (Scotland) Act 1991 would not be binding on a child;
  (d) the principal must be informed of all the material circumstances underlying the act that the agent has carried out on his behalf[8];
  (e) the principal must ratify the agent's act within any specified timescale[9];
  (f) the act must itself be legal.[10]

---

[4] (1902) S.L.T. (Sh.Ct.) 63; 1902 5 F. 86.
[5] Partnership Act 1890 s.5.
[6] *Keighley Maxted & Co v Durant* [1901] A.C. 240, HL.
[7] *Tinnevelly Sugar Refining Co v Mirrlees, Watson* (1894) 2 S.L.T. 149, IH (1 Div).
[8] *Suncorp Insurance and Finance v Milano Assecurazioni SpA* [1993] 2 Lloyd's Rep. 225, QBD (Comm).
[9] *Goodall v Bilsland*, 1909 S.C. 1152; 1909 1 S.L.T. 376, IH (1 Div).
[10] *Bedford Insurance Co Ltd v Instituto de Resseguros do Brasil* [1985] Q.B. 966; [1984] 3 W.L.R. 726, QBD (Comm).

Agency of necessity

An agency of necessity arises where an agent carries out vital acts for a principal without **10–08** receiving instructions. This is also known as *negotiorum gestio*. With the advent of satellite communication it is now rare for agencies of necessity to arise, except in extreme climatic conditions or in a state of war. It occasionally arises where people are too ill to issue instructions, so that others are forced to act on their behalf.[11]

Agency by holding out

This arises either when a principal takes no steps to contradict the impression that an **10–09** individual is his agent, or positively encourages that impression. If a third party relies on that impression, it would be unfair of the principal to reverse that impression, particularly if in the meantime the third party has acted to his detriment, as where a purported managing director of a company instructed certain works, but the company subsequently refused to pay for them on the grounds that the director lacked authority and was not the managing director. The company was found liable for the cost of the works.[12]

The Liability of the principal for the agent and his acts

Limitation of the agent's authority

> **Key concept**
>
> Normally an agent will act within the limits of the authority imposed on him by his **10–10** principal and the principal will, therefore, be liable for all the agent's acts, as he also will be if he ratifies the agent's acts.[13]

However, where an agent oversteps those limits, sometimes in the perceived best interests of the principal, or even sometimes for his own benefit, the principal may still be found liable where the agent is performing acts that similar agents in the agent's position would perform and the third party has no reason to query either the existence, or extent, of the agent's authority. In *Panorama Developments (Guildford) Ltd v Fidelis Furnishings Fabric Ltd* a company secretary, without authority from his employers, hired a car having indicated to the hirers that he would be using it on business. His employers were found liable for the car hire.[14]

Apparent or ostensible authority

This arises where a principal suffers a state of affairs to exist, or a course of dealing to be **10–11** perpetuated, over a period of time which gives the outside world the apparent impression that the principal has given the agent the authority to act as he does, and that, therefore, the principal should be liable for the agent's actions. In *International Sponge Importers Ltd v Watt & Sons*[15] an agent of ISI received payments for ISI directly from his clients. Although this was an unusual commercial practice, this was permitted by ISI. When he

---

[11] *Fernie v Robertson* (1871) 9 M.437.
[12] *Freeman & Lockyer v Buckhurst Park Properties (Mangal) Ltd* [1964] 2 Q.B. 480; [1964] 2 W.L.R. 618, CA.
[13] Bell's *Commentaries*, I, 540.
[14] [1971] 2 Q.B. 711; [1971] 3 W.L.R. 440, CA.
[15] [1911] A.C. 279; 1911 S.C. (H.L.) 57, HL.

then failed to hand the payments over to ISI, ISI was not able to claim the payments from the clients on the grounds that ISI had previously given the agent authority to receive the payments instead. The overall principle of apparent/ostensible authority stands, unless it would be very unlikely that any principal would approve a particular unauthorised and, by normal business standards, unconventional, act. In *British Bata Shoe Co Ltd v Double M Shah Ltd*[16] a cashier within British Bata persuaded gullible clients to make payment by way of blank cheques for goods the clients had acquired. The clients should have queried this exceptional and unconventional behaviour, which no sensible employer would have authorised. Apparent authority also arises where an agent performs actions which are appropriate for his position.[17] In addition, where an agent (a) exceeds his authority, but (b) acts in such a way that a third party has no reason to suspect that the agent is exceeding his authority and (c), the principal has not intimated the agent's limits of authority to the third party, the principal may be liable for the agent's unauthorised act, as in *Watteau v Fenwick*,[18] where a brewery owner was responsible for the actions of one of his publicans, even though the publican had expressly been prohibited from carrying out one of those particular actions, namely the purchase of cigars. As the cigar salesman had not been made aware of the prohibition, the brewery owner was still liable for the publican's actions. Normally, when a third party knows that the agent is not authorised to carry out a certain act, the principal will not liable for his agent's unauthorised actions, but, controversially, in a case where the third party did know the agent lacked the relevant authority to carry out an act, but where the agent gave the impression that the principal would approve the agent's actions, the principal was found liable for not contradicting that impression at an early stage.[19]

Common law duties of a principal to his agent

10–12 A principal is expected to remunerate his agent properly and, in the absence of any express agreement, at the normal rate for the work involved. He should also relieve him of any liability, which the agent may have incurred in the principal's business. The contract of agency should clearly specify the conditions under which remuneration will be payable. In *Menzies, Bruce-Law and Thomson v McLennan*,[20] the agent, as required, found a purchaser for a seller's brewery; the sale collapsed but the agent was still entitled to his fee as his contract was to find a purchaser, not to guarantee that the purchaser would complete the contract.

If an agency is to be a sole agency the principal should say so.[21] If an agent is not paid when he should be, or his expenses are not refunded, he has a right of retention of any asset of the principal's which he may have in his hands.[22]

[16] 1980 S.C. 311; 1981 S.L.T. (Notes) 14, OH.
[17] *Panorama Developments (Guildford) Ltd v Fidelis Furnishings Fabric Ltd* [1971] 2 Q.B. 711; [1971] 3 W.L.R. 440, CA.
[18] [1893] 1 Q.B. 346, QBD.
[19] *First Energy (UK) Ltd v Hungarian International Bank* [1993] 2 Lloyd Rep. 194; [1993] B.C.L.C. 1409; [1993] B.C.C. 533, CA.
[20] (1895) 22 R. 299; (1894) 2 S.L.T. 451, IH (1 Div).
[21] *Lothian v Jenolite Ltd*, 1969 S.C. 111; 1970 S.L.T. 31, 2 Div.
[22] *Glendinning v Hope & Co*, 1911 2 S.L.T. 161, HL; (1911) S.C. (H.L.) 73.

Non-disclosure by the agent of the principal

When an agent sets up a contract between his named and disclosed principal and a third **10–13**
party, the agent is not party to the contract. This means that the principal is liable on the
contract and the agent is not.[23] However, when the principal is undisclosed but the agent
explains that he is acting under the principal's express authority, the agent will be liable if
he refuses to reveal the identity of the principal. Without this rule the third party would
have no remedy against anyone.[24] When the agent is acting as an apparent principal,
though in reality for an undisclosed principal, the agent will normally be liable for the
same reason, but both the agent and the principal may be liable if the third party discovers
who the real principal is, in which case he may choose to sue either the agent or the
principal,[25] but having made his choice, may not change it.[26] If it would not have been, in
practice, difficult to establish who the principal is, the agent would not be liable.[27]

The liability of the agent to the principal

Common law duties and liabilities of the agent

The agent is required to adhere to the terms of any contract between him and the prin- **10–14**
cipal. If he fails to carry out instructions with proper skill and care he will be liable, as
when a haulier managed to load his principal's goods onto the wrong ship, which subsequently sank.[28] The agent should not disclose confidential information to others.[29] The
agent should not exceed the limits of his authority and when he does so, and the principal
becomes liable to the third party, the agent in turn will be liable to the principal for the
principal's loss.[30]

Fiduciary duty

> **Key concept**
>
> The principal duty of an agent to his principal is known as his fiduciary duty. This is **10–15**
> the duty to act in good faith in the best interests of the principal, without obtaining any
> benefit other than what is permitted and authorised by the principal and without letting
> any conflict of interest arise.

Examples of conflicts of interest include when the director of a fishing company received a
secret commission for giving business to a particular firm, and which he failed to disclose,[31]
and when a lawyer quietly arranged for the sale of properties to a business controlled by
his brother, without disclosing his own interest in his brother's business.[32]

In conflict of interest cases, the only cure, apart from not letting it arise, is for the agent

---

[23] Bell, *Commentaries,* I, 540.
[24] *Gibb v Cunningham & Robertson,* 1925 S.L.T. 608, OH.
[25] *Ferrier v Dods* (1865) 3 M. 561.
[26] *David Logan & Son Ltd v Schuldt* (1903) 10 S.L.T. 598.
[27] *Armour v T L Duff & Co,* 1912 S.C. 120; 1911 2 S.L.T. 394, IH (2 Div).
[28] *Gilmour v Clark* (1853) 15 D. 478.
[29] *Liverpool Victoria Friendly Society v Houston* (1900) 3 F.42.
[30] *Milne v Ritchie* (1882) 10 R. 365.
[31] *Boston Deep Sea Fishing Co. Ltd v Ansell* (1888) L.R. 39 Ch.D. 339. CA.
[32] *McPherson's Trustees v Watt* (1877) 5 R. (H.L.) 9.

fully to disclose his interest and seek the consent of the principal for his course of action. The consent may be supplied retrospectively.

Duty not to delegate without permission

10–16 An agent is not permitted to delegate his tasks without the permission of the principal, except where it is normal for the particular profession or trade to do so. This rule derives from the Roman law maxim, *delegatus non potest delegare* (he who has been chosen for a task may not delegate that task to someone else).

Duty to account

10–17 An agent is under a duty to account to his principal for all his transactions on behalf of the principal.[33] All matters pertaining to the principal must be disclosed to him.

Breach of warranty

10–18 This is where an agent does not have the principal's authority to carry out the transaction and so the transaction does not take place. This can render the agent liable to the third party for the loss arising from not having the principal as a party to the contract, or for the loss arising out of the agent's misrepresentation, as where an auctioneer did not have the authority to sell a particular horse, and the would-be purchaser successfully sued the auctioneer for not being able to deliver the horse to him.[34]

Termination of agency

Key concept

10–19 Agency terminates by various means, including:

(a) an express provision in the contract of agency;
(b) the death, or insanity, of either the principal or agent;
(c) the bankruptcy or liquidation of the principal or indeed the agent.

If a principal wishes to ensure that he cannot possibly be liable for the actings of his agent, after termination of the agency agreement, in an ideal world he intimates to all his customers that the agent is no longer his agent. In a large commercial organisation this is clearly impossible, and making public announcements about the termination of agencies may give customers the wrong impression. An alternative, still often used in partnerships, is to publish a notice in the Edinburgh Gazette intimating that a former partner is no longer a partner (and by implication an agent) of the firm.

Commercial agents

10–20 The regulations in CA(CD)R prescribe certain standard rules applicable to contracts of agency giving certain agents standard commercial rights and to some extent protecting them from unscrupulous principals. The regulations only apply to independent contractors (i.e. not employees) and they only apply where the agents deal in, or sell, the

---

[33] *Simpson v Duncan* (1849) 11 D 1097.
[34] *Anderson v Croall & Sons Ltd* (1903) 11 S.L.T. 253; (1903) 11 S.L.T. 453, IH (2 Div).

principal's goods, not services. They do not apply to one-off transactions, nor to the situation where an agent acts for an undisclosed principal. They do not apply to company directors, individual partners in a partnership, insolvency practitioners, unpaid commercial agents, and certain other specialist agents in the financial markets.

Although agents and principals are given some freedom to derogate from the requirements of CA(CD)R, most of the regulations in CA(CD)R are unalterable and will override the common law of agency.[35] The main provisions of CA(CD)R allow commercial agents the right to remuneration at a reasonable rate, and the right to fair notice of termination with compensation for premature termination.[36] In return the agent has to accept duties of confidentiality and sensible restraint of trade provisions, and act dutifully and in good faith for the principal who in turn must act dutifully and in good faith towards the agent, having suitably provided him with the necessary information to carry out his tasks.

PARTNERSHIP

A person may run a business on his own, in which case he is known as a sole trader. As a **10–21** sole trader, he is responsible for his own profits and losses, and does not share them with anyone. Because being a sole trader is a precarious position, it is common for two or more businessmen to join together so that they can enjoy the benefit of each other's skills, capital and clients. When they do this, they may either set up a partnership together, or they may set up a registered company. A partnership is less formal than a registered company, but the partners are more at risk of personal bankruptcy than are the members of a company. This section deals with the law relating to partnership and the following section deals with companies.

The advantages and disadvantages of partnership

There are certain advantages and disadvantages to partnership, which should be con- **10–22** trasted with the advantages and disadvantages of limited companies (referred to in the next section).

Key concepts

The benefits of being a partner in a partnership are:

- colleagues with whom to share losses as well as profits;
- the ease and informality of setting up a partnership;
- rights of management in the partnership;
- privacy in respect of the partnership's accounts;
- colleagues to help share the burden of running the business.

All these are subject to any agreement between the partners otherwise.

---

[35] *Roy v M R Pearlman*, 1999 S.C. 459; 2000 S.L.T. 727, OH.
[36] *Lonsdale (t/a Lonsdale Agencies) v Howard & Hallam Limited* [2007] UKHL 32.

In practice, the main benefit is the absence of any requirement to publish accounts, thereby preventing competitors, customers and employees knowing the extent of the partnership's profits or losses.

Key concepts

The disadvantages of being a partner in a partnership are:

- the risk to each partner of personal liability, without limit, for the entire debts of the partnership;
- the difficulty of raising a loan against the value of any assets other than heritage (i.e. land and buildings).

In practice, the main disadvantage of a partnership is that each partner is jointly and severally liable for the debts of the partnership, (i.e. each partner is liable for the entire debt, not just a proportional share, subject to a right of reimbursement from the other partners). This means that the partners could potentially personally be sequestrated (made bankrupt) in the event of the insolvency of their partnership.

The law of partnership is derived from the old common law, and the Partnership Act 1890 ("PA") codified and standardised what had generally been understood to be the law relating to partnerships. The PA established a number of standard and widely accepted rules that apply to all partnerships, whilst leaving it open to individual partnerships to have other terms if they wish to do so, usually by means of a partnership agreement. However, some partnerships do not bother with a partnership agreement, and in these cases, the PA gives guidelines to ascertain whether there is a partnership at all, to clarify what happens on the termination of the partnership, and to decide how to divide the profits and losses between the partners. In addition, it lays down rules for the relation of partners to each other and to outsiders. The PA steps in where there is no partnership agreement[37] or the partnership agreement is silent on any particular point.[38] PA s.1 defines partnership as "the relation which subsists between persons carrying on a business in common with a view of profit". "Persons" covers all legal personae, including registered companies. The word "firm" in the PA means a partnership, and the name under which the partnership practises is known as the firm name. The choice of firm name must not be contrary to the provisions of The Company and Business Names (Miscellaneous Provisions) Regulations 2009 (SI 2009/1085). A list of a firm's partners' names must be available at its place of business.

The persons involved in a partnership must be carrying on a business, so that a mere association, not involving business, does not qualify as a partnership. The business must be in common. This means that where one person performs one activity, and another a different and unconnected activity, there would be no partnership. Finally the partners must be operating with "a view of profit". This does not say that the partnership must make a profit; it must merely intend to do so.

---

[37] *Starrett v Pia,* 1968 S.L.T. (Notes) 28, OH.
[38] *Popat v Shonchhatra* [1997] 1 W.L.R. 1367; [1997] 3 All E.R. 800, CA.

The separate legal personality of a partnership

> **Key concept**
>
> In Scotland a firm has a separate legal personality in its own right.[39]
> This means that a partnership may own assets in its own right, and those assets belong to the partnership and not to the individual partners.

10–23

Any creditor suing a partner in his personal capacity may not carry out diligence against the partnership assets, though the creditor could carry out diligence against the partner's personal share in the partnership.

Rules for determining the existence of a partnership

The significance of being a partner is that not only is a partner normally entitled to the partnership's profits, but he will also be liable for the partnership's losses. It is, therefore sometimes advantageous for someone to claim he is not a partner, and hence not liable for any partnership losses, when in reality he should be liable. In the absence of a partnership agreement, the following criteria, as delineated in PA s.2, are used to establish the existence of a partnership: **10–24**

(a) joint tenancy, or joint ownership, irrespective of any profits engendered by the joint tenancy or ownership, does not of itself mean that a partnership is in existence[40];

(b) the sharing of gross returns (as opposed to net profits), even out of any common property, does not of itself mean that a partnership is in existence[41];

(c) the receipt by a person of a share of the profits of a business is *prima facie* evidence that that person is a partner in the business. However, mere receipt of a share of the profits does not automatically mean in every circumstance that the recipient is a partner. Five instances are provided by s.2(3) where receipt of a share of the profits does not make the recipient a partner, these being:

   (i) the repayment of a debt out of the profits of a business[42];

   (ii) where an employee is rewarded by a share of the profits[43];

   (iii) where the recipient is a dependent of a former partner and receiving by way of an annuity a portion of the business's profits[44];

   (iv) where a lender lends money to a business and the contract for the loan, which must be in writing and signed by all the parties thereto, states that the interest rate is to vary according to the business's profits[45]; and

   (v) where the recipient is paid an annuity or receives some other benefit out of the profits of the business in consideration of the sale by him of the goodwill of the business.[46]

---

[39] PA s.4(2).
[40] PA s.2(1).
[41] PA s.2(2).
[42] PA s.2(3)(a).
[43] PA s.2(3)(b).
[44] PA s.2(3)(c).
[45] PA s.2(3)(d).
[46] PA s.2(3)(e).

Relations of partners to persons dealing with them

Liability for partners' acts

10–25 Each partner is an agent for the firm, and providing the partner is acting in the ordinary course of his firm's business, his actions bind the firm.[47] Where the partner does not in fact have the authority to act in a particular transaction, and the person with whom he is dealing either knows that the partner does not have authority for the transaction, or does not know or believe that the partner is a partner, the transaction will not bind the partnership.[48]

When a partner signs a document on behalf of the partnership he binds the partnership by that document,[49] even if his fellow partners have not authorised him to do so[50] unless the other party knows of his lack of authority.[51] If the contracting party's belief in the authority of the partner was unjustified, in view of the partner significantly departing from the normal course of business[52] or carrying out an act that is clearly personal rather than one in the normal course of business,[53] the partnership will also not be bound.

Should a partnership be sued and be unable to meet a decree, normally the debt should be satisfied out of the partnership assets first, and thereafter by the individual partners personally. However, PA s.4(2) states that where there is a decree or diligence levelled against a firm, the creditor may, nevertheless, in addition or alternatively proceed directly against any partner he chooses. That partner in turn is entitled to relief pro rata from the firm and the other partners. Partners in a firm are jointly and severally liable for the debts of the firm arising while they are partners: if they die while still partners, their estates then become liable in their stead.[54]

Misappropriation of property by partners

10–26 Where an individual partner, or the whole firm, in each case apparently acting within the course of his or its business, receives money from a third party and misapplies it, the firm is liable for the loss.[55] However, if an individual partner, acting as a trustee, improperly misuses trust property in the firm's business or on account of the partnership, he alone of the partners remains liable for the misapplied property, though any other partner who is aware of the breach by the partner/trustee may still be liable if he has been notified of the partner/trustee's breach, and the property itself may still be recovered from the partnership if it is still in its hands.[56]

Holding out persons as partners

10–27 Where a partnership "holds out" someone as a partner, or does not contradict the impression that someone is a partner even when he is not, the partnership as a whole will be liable to anyone who gives credit to the firm in the belief that the purported partner is indeed a partner.[57]

---

[47] PA s.5.
[48] PA s.5.
[49] PA s.6.
[50] *Mercantile Credit Co Ltd v Garrod* [1962] 3 All E.R. 1103, QBD.
[51] PA s.8.
[52] PA s.7; *Paterson Bros v Gladstone* (1891) 18 R. 403.
[53] *Fortune v Young*, 1918 S.C. 1; 1917 2 S.L.T. 150, IH (2 Div).
[54] PA s.9.
[55] PA s.11.
[56] PA s.13.
[57] PA s.14.

Any admission or representation by a partner made in the ordinary course of business about partnership matters may be evidence against the firm.[58]

The converse of this is that a notice to any one partner about any partnership matter is deemed to be notice to the firm as a whole, so that other partners cannot claim that are not liable merely because one of their fellows had failed to communicate the matter to them.[59]

Vicarious liability of partners

The firm is vicariously[60] liable for any wrongful act or omission of a partner in the ordinary course of business.[61] However, where one partner injures another in the course of business, as when one fisherman hurt another with a boathook in *Mair v Wood*,[62] no vicarious liability attaches to the partnership. **10–28**

The liability of new and retiring partners

An incoming partner is not liable for any debts of the partnership arising from before he became a partner[63]; a retiring partner remains liable for the debts arising during the period of his partnership.[64] Where a retiring partner has not properly notified third parties of his retirement, he may still be liable as if he were still a partner,[65] but notice in the *Edinburgh Gazette* serves as notice of retirement to those who have not had dealings with the firm. **10–29**

The relations of partners to one another

It is normal for prospective partners to draw up a partnership agreement. In the absence of an express agreement, agreement may be inferred from the partners' course of dealing.[66] Partnership property is assumed to be owned by the partnership and each partner is entitled to a *pro indiviso* share, which means that while he may not be easily able to realise partnership property, and creditors cannot effect diligence on the partnership property as a whole if their claim is against the partner in his private capacity, he is entitled on the sale of the partnership property to his proportion of the sale proceeds.[67] PA s.24 outlines the normal rules that will apply to partnerships, unless disapplied or varied by the partnership agreement, such as: equal division of profits and losses; repayment of partnership expenses; loans to the partnership other than the contribution of partnership capital; interest on the capital; the right to share in the management of the partnership; the prohibition on remuneration for acting in the partnership business; the requirement for the consent of all partners for the adoption of a new partner; the use of the majority vote in deciding partnership business—except in the context of changing the partnership business which attracts a unanimous vote; and the accessibility of the partnership books. Partners are in a fiduciary relationship both with each other and with their partnership, so that at all times they must act in good faith in the best interests of the partnership as a whole, without taking any unauthorised advantage of their position.[68] **10–30**

---

[58] PA s.15.

[59] PA s.16.

[60] This means that the firm has to accept its responsibility for those acting on its behalf, even if it does not necessarily approve of those actions.

[61] PA s.10. See *Dubai Aluminium Co Ltd v Salaam* [2002] UKHL 48, [2003] 2 A.C. 366; [2002] 3 W.L.R. 1913.

[62] 1948 S.C. 83; 1948 S.L.T. 326, IH (1 Div).

[63] PA s.17(1).

[64] PA s.17(2).

[65] PA s.36(1).

[66] PA s.19.

[67] PA s.20.

[68] *Finlayson v Turnbull*, 1997 S.L.T. 613, OH.

PA s.25 states that no partner may be expelled by mere majority of votes, unless the partnership agreement permits this. PA s.26 permits retirement at will, subject to any agreement to the contrary.

There is a duty on all partners to render proper and true accounts and to provide true information to each other.[69] Partners must account to the partnership for any profit deriving from the partnership[70] and no partner may compete with his firm.[71] Where a partner assigns his interest in the firm to a third party, the third party has no right of management of that partner's share of the business; instead it merely entitles the assignee to the share of the profits.[72] It is common for a partnership agreement to prohibit assignation without the consent of the other partners.

Dissolution of the partnership

10–31 A partnership is dissolved either by the means specified in the partnership agreement, or in the absence of a partnership agreement, by one of the methods stated in PA s.32, these being the expiry of a designated term, the completion of the undertaking for which the partnership was set up, or by one partner giving notice to the other of his intention to dissolve the partnership. The death, or bankruptcy, of any partner may also cause the partnership to be dissolved[73] unless the partnership agreement says otherwise. Should the partnership be carrying on an illegal activity, it will be dissolved.[74] Under PA s.35, the court may dissolve the partnership if the partnership cannot be dissolved by any consensual method, in particular, on the occasion of the insanity of a partner, the permanent incapacity of a partner, the misconduct of a partner—such that his misconduct would materially affect the carrying out of the partnership business, breach of the partnership business such that the other partners cannot practicably carry on business with him, the partnership making a loss, or where the court considers it just and equitable to dissolve the partnership. Notwithstanding dissolution, the partners remain liable for the debts of the partnership until creditors have been informed of the dissolution of the partnership,[75] so it is in the partners' interests to notify the dissolution of the partnership as soon as possible: there are mechanisms to permit this.[76] The partners retain some rights to deal with partnership property even after the dissolution of the partnership, but only for the purpose of winding up the affairs of the partnership.[77] The partnership assets are sold, or otherwise used, to pay the partnership debts, but any surplus remaining after repayment of creditors is divided between the partners on the basis outlined in the partnership agreement or such other basis as may be agreed.[78] Where the partnership has been dissolved, because of the fraud of one or more of the partners, the innocent partners are entitled to redress from the fraudulent partners.[79] They are also entitled to be indemnified, by the fraudulent partners, for any liabilities of the partnership incurred by the fraudulent partners, but which had to be paid by the partnership or the innocent partners.

Where a partner dies or retires and the partnership business continues for a while after dissolution, as part of the winding up of the partnership, the dead partner's estate, or the

---

[69] PA s.28.
[70] PA s.29.
[71] PA s.30; *Pillans Bros v Pillans* (1908) 16 S.L.T. 611, OH.
[72] PA s.31.
[73] PA s.33.
[74] PA s.34.
[75] PA s.36.
[76] PA s.37.
[77] PA s.38.
[78] PA s.39.
[79] PA s.41.

retiring partner, is entitled to his share of the profits or to interest at five per cent, unless there is an option available to other partners to buy the dead or retired partner's share.[80]

Once the partnership assets have been realised, the partnership debts are repaid, first to creditors, then to each partner in respect of advances, next to each partner in respect of his capital and, finally, the balance is divided up between the partners in the same proportion as profits have been divided up.[81]

If the partnership becomes insolvent, the Bankruptcy (Scotland) Act 1985 applies to its sequestration.

Limited partnerships

A partnership is not the same as a limited partnership. Limited partnerships are regulated **10–32** by the Limited Partnerships Act 1907, and share characteristics of both limited companies and partnerships. They are registered in the same manner as limited companies, though under their own legislation. In a limited partnership there is a limited partner, who contributes some capital, whose liability to the partnership is limited to that amount of capital and no more (s.4(2)), but who takes no part at all in the management on pain of becoming personally liable (s.6(1)); and there is the general partner who bears all the risk (s.4(2)) and depending on the terms of the partnership agreement keeps some profit, less the sums due to the limited partner. Limited partnerships are much used in farming and by certain types of venture capitalists who wish to limit their liability for the debts of the businesses in which they are investing. It should be noted that a limited partnership is not the same as a limited liability partnership, discussed at the end of the next section.

COMPANY LAW

The major benefit of the limited company

The major drawback of being a sole trader is his unlimited liability for his debts, and the **10–33** risk of bankruptcy if his business fails to prosper. The same is true of being a partner in a partnership, in that he is jointly and severally liable for the debts of his partnership.

These two forms of trading may be contrasted with trading through a registered limited liability company.

Key concept

With a limited liability company, the investors in that company (the members) know in advance that their liability to the company is limited to what they have invested, or are prepared to invest in it. This means that their liability is capped and that although at worst they may lose their investment, they are not personally liable for the company's debts.

This section discusses the law relating to registered companies.

---

[80] PA s.42.
[81] PA s.44.

The principal advantages of limited liability companies

10–34 Although there are other types of business that have limited liability, such as the limited liability partnership (discussed at the end of this section) and there are companies which do not have limited liability, also discussed later, the main advantages of the limited liability company, relative to sole traders and partnerships, are as follows:

(a) companies have a legal personality separate from those who are employed by it, those who manage it and those who own it;

(b) there is no restriction on the maximum number of members a company may have, though all companies must have a minimum of one member;

(c) it is possible to be a member of a company without being involved in the management of a company;

(d) a member is not normally liable for the debts of a company beyond the fully paid up value of the shares that he owns plus any premium on those shares, unless:

    (i) the member has, by a separate undertaking, guaranteed the company's debts;

    (ii) the company is a guarantee company, in which case he may have to honour his guarantee if the company becomes insolvent;

    (iii) the company is an unlimited liability company;

    (iv) the member has been involved in certain fraudulent activities involving the company;

(e) the knowledge that their members' liability is limited makes companies and their directors more likely to undertake enterprises than they would if members' liability were unlimited. Although this does mean that a company's creditors bear the risk of the company's default, it also means that entrepreneurs are encouraged to set up businesses, thus creating employment and wealth opportunities.

(f) directors, on the whole, are given considerable freedom to manage their companies, and, provided they behave reasonably competently, honestly and within the permitted limits of the law, are generally able to avoid personal liability for any unfortunate business decisions they make;

(g) companies may grant security over their assets (including moveable assets) by way of a floating charge; this enables them quickly to raise finance with which to exploit a commercial opportunity;

(h) companies may raise funds by offering their shares for sale;

(i) a successful company may offer its shares for sale to the public through a recognised investment exchange, such as the London Stock Exchange, thus creating significant opportunities for wealth, both for entrepreneurs and investors;

(j) some company directors enjoy the status of being a company director;

(k) in theory, a company may continue indefinitely without ever having to be reconstituted (this being known as "perpetual succession"); even if its members and directors change, the company still remains in existence.

The principal disadvantages of being a limited company

10–35 (a) company must disclose its accounts and other details on a regular basis—thus revealing information to competitors, creditors and employees;

(b) most companies' accounts need to be audited at some cost and inconvenience;

(c) companies must be formed in a prescribed manner; there are costs incurred in incorporation and in complying with the requirements of company law generally;

(d) it may be difficult for an investor to withdraw his capital from his company;

(e) although directors are not normally responsible for their company's debts, in certain instances, such as insolvency, the directors may find themselves liable for the company's debts despite the separate legal personality of the company;

(f) creditors (in particular banks) of small companies often demand personal guarantees from the members or directors, thus removing one of the principal advantages of being a limited company, namely the freedom from liability for the company's debts.

Many of the above points apply to limited liability partnerships as well. This will be discussed at the end of this section on company law.

The legislation applicable to companies

Companies are regulated primarily by: **10–36**

(a) Companies Act 2006 ("CA 2006");
(b) Insolvency Act 1986 ("IA") as amended by the Enterprise Act 2002;
(c) Company Directors Disqualification Act 1986 ("CDDA").

The separate legal personality of a company

The separate legal personality of a company has been well established by three cases.   **10–37**

Salomon v A Salomon & Co Ltd
[1897] A.C. 22, HL

Salomon was entitled to be paid a debt due to him from his own company, even though he owned most of the shares in that company and was the managing director, and was entitled to secure the debt by a debenture enabling him to be repaid ahead of other creditors.

Lee v Lee's Air Farming Ltd
[1961] A.C. 12; [1960] 3 W.L.R. 758, PC (NZ)

The director, and majority owner, of the company was entitled to contract in his personal capacity as an employee with his own company.

MacAura v Northern Assurance Co Ltd
[1925] A.C. 619, HL

A timber grower transferred the ownership of some timber to a limited company, which he controlled. The timber remained insured in his own name. The timber subsequently was destroyed by fire and he tried to claim on the insurance policy. The insurers successfully refused the claim as he no longer owned the timber.

These three cases indicate that the company is legally separate from its owners, its directors and its employees, and has a legal personality in its own right.

Lifting the veil

10–38 Although the law, as just indicated, recognises that a company is a separate legal entity from its owners, managers or employees, there are occasions under common law and under statute where this principle is eroded. This is known as "lifting the veil of incorporation" and enables the court to look at the underlying details of the company. Three well-known cases under common law where this has arisen are:

Daimler Co Ltd v Continental Tyre and Rubber Co Ltd.[82] For public policy reasons in wartime, a predominantly enemy-owned company was barred from claiming for a debt due to it by a British company.

Gilford Motor Co Ltd v Horne.[83] Horne could not avoid the terms of a restrictive covenant by claiming that he was working for a company, which was not bound by the restrictive covenant.

Woolfson v Strathclyde Regional Council.[84] The corporate veil should only be lifted where special circumstances exist indicating that it is a "mere façade" concealing the true facts. Cases where a "mere façade" has been held to exist include *Re. H*[85] and *Trustor AB v Smallbone (No.2)*.[86]

Personal liability under statute

10–39 There are certain occasions, under statute, where the law will look at the underlying reality of the company, or may treat the members or, as the case may be, the directors of the company as liable for the debts of the company. Some of these occasions are as follows:

(a) Insolvency Act 1986 s.122(1)(g) (known as the just and equitable grounds)—a quasi-partnership company was wound up following the breach of faith between former partners who had subsequently incorporated their business[87];

(b) Insolvency Act 1986 s.213—fraudulent trading by a member or officer of a subsequently insolvent company makes that person liable for the company's debts[88];

(c) Insolvency Act 1986 ss.212 and 214—misfeasance (breach of duty to the company), or wrongful trading by directors of subsequently insolvent companies, makes them liable for the company's debts[89];

(d) CA 2006 s.767—the directors of a public limited company trading without a trading certificate from the Registrar of Companies may be liable for the company's debts.

Subsidiaries

10–40 In principle a holding company has no liability for its subsidiaries' debts.[90]

Types of company

10–41 The two main types of company are private companies and public companies. There are, in turn, several different types of private company:

[82] [1916] 2 A.C. 307, HL.
[83] [1933] Ch. 935, CA.
[84] 1978 S.C. (H.L.) 90; 1978 S.L.T. 159, HL.
[85] [1996] 2 All E.R. 291, CA.
[86] [2001] 1 W.L.R. 1177; [2001] 3 All E.R. 987, Ch. D. Both these cases involved frauds.
[87] *Ebrahimi v Westbourne Galleries Ltd* [1973] A.C. 360; [1972] 2 W.L.R. 1289, HL.
[88] *Morphitis v Bernasconi* [2001] 2 B.C.L.C. 1.
[89] *Re Produce Marketing Consortium Ltd (No.2)* [1989] B.C.L.C. 520.
[90] *Southard and Co Ltd, Re* [1979] 1 W.L.R. 1198; [1979] 3 All E.R. 556, CA (Civ Div).

(a) unlimited company (rarely used, for the members are personally responsible for the company's debts; no accounts need be published);
(b) guarantee company (commonly used for charities; members are liable for the company's debts up to a guaranteed amount);
(c) private limited company limited by shares (by far the most common).

Certain small companies do not need to provide audited accounts or publish full accounts. The principal features of a public company (commonly known as a "plc") are that:

(a) it has a minimum authorised capital of £50,000 and each share must be paid up to the extent of one quarter, plus any premium;
(b) the company law rules relating to public companies are considerably stricter and require more disclosure of information and accounts than as is the case with private companies;
(c) a public company could, if it wished, offer its shares to the public.

There is a common misconception that all public companies offer their shares to the public. Some public companies do offer their shares to the public. However, many public companies do not do so: they are merely "public" companies because the more stringent capital requirements and the letters "plc" give the company a credibility and status that it might not otherwise have. However, if a company does wish to offer its shares to the public, it must be a public company to do so, for private companies may not issue their shares to the public.[91]

Companies that wish to offer their shares to the public generally do so on the London Stock Exchange (in which case their securities are said to be "listed" on the Stock Exchange), or on some other recognised market such as the Alternative Investment Market. In either case, the companies concerned have to comply with the rigorous disclosure requirements of each market.

Corporate disclosure

All companies must disclose information about themselves at the Register of Companies. **10–42** Failure to send certain documents, such as accounts, to the Registrar of Companies within strict time limits may result in prosecution. Members may also find out about their companies through receiving their annual accounts and directors' reports and may attend shareholders' meetings. There are many complex rules relating to the accounts and capital of a company: these must be followed closely and the accounts and any changes to the company's capital must be properly disclosed to the members and the Registrar of Companies.

The incorporation of a company

At present, in order to incorporate a company, various forms need to be sent to the **10–43** Registrar of Companies. These forms indicate the name of the company, the type of company, the first members, the directors, the company secretary if applicable, the registered address, the company's initial capital, a statement confirming the intention of the first members to set up the company (known as the memorandum of association) and the articles of association.

---

[91] CA 2006 s.755.

> **Key concepts**
>
> A company's articles of association are its internal constitution, detailing how shares may be transferred, directors appointed, meetings held, the rules attaching to different classes of shares, etc.

Most companies' articles are based on standard model articles to be found at the Companies House website. Companies may prepare their own articles if they wish to do so to suit their particular requirements (e.g. *Bushell v Faith*,[92] where weighted voting was declared to be acceptable), providing that the alteration does not contravene any other rule of law. Companies should stay within the limits imposed on themselves by the articles of association, and there are mechanisms to enable members of a company to force the directors to adhere to the company's own rules as laid out therein.[93]

Equally, members, on joining a company, must accept the terms of the articles, as they form part of the effective contract between the member and the company, as to the terms on which the members hold their shares in the company.[94] Classes of shareholders are able to protect their own interests, by the rule that states that only the members of those classes may vote on any change to their rights; it is not usually possible for non-class members to rewrite the class-members' rights.[95] If the members generally do not like the wording of the articles, they may change the articles by means of a special resolution of the members.[96]

The management of a company

Directors

10–44   A company is managed by its directors. They are given authority to deal with the general commercial and administrative affairs of the company, subject to some powers of management (such as altering the articles) being retained by the members. It is possible to be a member and a director simultaneously. As directors know better than anyone what is taking place within their company, there are extensive rules, both under common law and under statute, (i) to ensure that directors manage their companies properly, (ii) to prevent directors taking unauthorised advantage of their position within the company unduly to benefit themselves, and (iii) to ensure that anything that may benefit the directors personally is properly disclosed and approved by the other directors, or in some cases, the members.[97] Directors have a statutory duty to act in the way that they consider, in good faith, would be most likely to promote the success of the company for the benefit of the members as a whole, and in doing so they should have regard to the following matters: the likely consequences of any decision in the long term; the interests of the employees; the need to foster the company's business relationships with suppliers, customers, and others; the impact of the company's operations on the community and the environment; the desirability of the company maintaining a reputation for high standards of business conduct; and the need to act fairly between the members.[98] Where they fail to do so, they

---

[92] [1970] A.C. 1099; [1970] 2 W.L.R. 272, HL.
[93] CA 2006 ss.39–41.
[94] CA 2006 s.33, *Hickman v Kent and Romney Marsh Sheepbreeders Association* [1915] 1 Ch. 881, Ch. D.
[95] CA 2006 s.630. Much depends on the wording of the rights attaching to each class.
[96] CA 2006 s.21.
[97] CA 2006 s.170–231.
[98] CA 2006 s.172.

may be required to make good any loss to the company or repay any unauthorised profit[99] and there are mechanisms to enable a shareholder to bring an action against a director for breach of the director's duties to the company.[100] Directors owe a duty of care[101] to the company and will be required to make good any losses to the company arising out of their negligence.[102]

Relief for directors who breach their duties to the company

Under CA 2006 s.1157 where a director has breached his duty to the company, it is open to **10–45** the courts to relieve him of some or all of his liability provided he has acted honestly and reasonably.[103]

Liability of directors to creditors of the company

Normally a director is not personally liable to creditors of the company, even when the **10–46** director has acted negligently, provided he has acted through the company.[104] But where a director instructs or carries out a fraud through his company he cannot avoid personal responsibility for his fraud, as far as his company's creditors are concerned, by claiming that, since he acted through his company, only his company should be liable.[105] Directors of insolvent companies may also be required to make good any losses to the company under IA ss.212–216.

Disqualification of directors

Directors who abuse their status as directors, or who commit certain criminal acts, may be **10–47** banned as directors for up to 15 years by the Company Directors Disqualification Act 1986, when their conduct as a director merits disqualification.

Company secretary and auditor

The *company secretary* ensures that the company complies with all its legal requirements, **10–48** such as organising meetings and sending documents to the Registrar of Companies. The company secretary is often an accountant, lawyer or chartered secretary.

The *auditor* is required to check the company's accounts before they are lodged with the Registrar of Companies. Their report on the accounts should state that the accounts present a "true and fair" view of the company's financial state.

Company borrowings

A company may borrow just like any other legal person. The common name for the **10–49** document outlining the terms of a loan to a company is a debenture or bond. A company may grant charges over its property as security for the loan. The main types of charge are a standard security (known in England as a mortgage) or a floating charge. Such charges must be registered with the Registrar of Companies within 21 days of their creation.[106] If they are not registered in time, the charge is void against the liquidator, administrator or

---

[99] *Boston Deep Sea Fishing Co Ltd v Ansell* (1888) L.R. 39, Ch. D 339.
[100] CA 2006 ss.265–269. Such an action is known as a derivative claim.
[101] CA 2006 s.174. For explanation of the concept of the duty of care, see para.11–05.
[102] *Dorchester Finance Co. Ltd v Stebbing* [1989] B.C.L.C. 498, Ch. D.
[103] *D'Jan of London Ltd, Re* [1993] B.C.C. 646; [1994] 1 B.C.L.C. 561, Ch. D (Companies Ct).
[104] *Williams v Natural Life Health Foods Ltd* [1998] 1 W.L.R. 830; [1998] 2 All E.R. 577, HL.
[105] *Standard Chartered Bank v Pakistan National Shipping Corporation* [2003] 1 A.C. 959, HL.
[106] CA 1985 s.410, CA 2006 s.886.

any creditor of the company.[107] This means that the charge-holder, usually a bank, is then not able to enforce its security and it ceases to be placed at an advantage compared to the other creditors of the company. The whole purpose of a charge is to ensure that the charge-holder has a right to the charged assets in priority to other creditors, should the company become insolvent.

Whereas a standard security gives the charge-holder a right over land and buildings owned by the company and specifically charged in favour of the charge-holder, a floating charge is (usually) a charge over all the assets of a company (not just land and buildings) to the extent that they are not already subject to some other charge. These assets may change from time to time and the charge, in a sense, hovers or floats over all those assets, however constituted, until the company defaults on its obligations under the original loan. If the company defaults, the floating charge then attaches[108] to all the assets in the company at the time, and the charge-holder, depending on the type of floating charge, then can appoint either a receiver (for pre-Enterprise Act 2002 charges) or an administrator (for post-Enterprise Act 2002 qualifying floating charges[109]). The receiver or administrator, as the case may be, then takes over the management and disposal of the assets. Receivership and administration are both discussed shortly.

Shares

10–50 A share is a unit of ownership in a company owned by a shareholder, and is commonly designated as having a nominal or notional (but not market) value of £1.00. The nominal value of a share is the amount that must be paid by a shareholder to subscribe for a share from the company in order to avoid any further liability to the company. The ownership of shares is commonly evidenced by a share certificate. Shareholders are usually entitled, amongst other things, to a dividend out of the company's profits (if declared), a right to vote at meetings, to see the accounts and directors' report and to a return of capital on solvent liquidation of the company. A company may have many different classes of shares, such as non-voting shares or preference shares, each with differing rights and obligations. The total nominal value of the company's shares is known as its share capital. Under what is known as the capital maintenance rule, the share capital is supposed to be a fund of last resort for the benefit of the creditors (sometimes known as "the creditors' buffer") and funds may only be extracted from the company's share capital following complex procedural rules. These rules restrict the reduction of the company's capital, financial assistance for the purchase of a company's shares, certain dividend payments and repurchase, or redemption, of a company's shares except under certain tightly controlled circumstances designed, at least in theory, to protect creditors.

Shareholders' meetings

10–51 Most large companies have annual general meetings ("AGMs") at which the directors explain the accounts and discuss the future direction of the company. Other meetings are known as extraordinary general meetings ("EGMs"). The members may vote on any resolutions that require their assent, such as changes to the company's articles or name. General meetings are designed to make directors accountable to the members. Members may vote on resolutions, the type of resolution varying according to the significance of the issue:

---

[107] CA 1985 s.410, CA 2006 s.889.

[108] This converts the floating charge into a fixed charge. The process is also known as crystallisation of the floating charge.

[109] More properly known as qualifying floating charges.

(a) special resolutions require the approval of 75 per cent of the voting members and 21 days' notice: they are used for major matters relating to the capital of the company or its constitution;

(b) ordinary resolutions require a bare majority and 14 days' notice and are used for most other decisions;

(c) ordinary resolutions with special notice of 28 days: these are used if the members at a general meeting wish to dismiss a director or an auditor.

In private companies it is permissible to have written resolutions, thus avoiding the inconvenience of holding general meetings.

Corporate insolvency

Liquidation

> **Key concept**
>
> A liquidator is a person who is appointed, either by the creditors or the members, to wind up the company, in other words, to sell the company's assets, or otherwise turn the company's assets into cash which is then divided up between the creditors, and if any surplus remains, between the members.

10–52

A winding up may be either compulsorily ordered by the court,[110] because of the company's inability to pay its debts,[111] or because it would be just and equitable to do so,[112] or voluntarily agreed upon by the members.[113] A members' voluntary liquidation means that the company is solvent and can pay its debts in full; a creditors' voluntary liquidation anticipates that the company is insolvent, in which case preferential creditors are paid first, in full if possible, then ordinary creditors if there are sufficient funds to distribute to them. Where assets are subject to a charge, such as a standard security, or a floating charge, the liquidator is only entitled to deal with the surplus, if any, of the value of the assets over the extent of the standard security and/or the floating charge. A liquidator follows substantially the same rules as does a trustee in sequestration and has the same powers to swell the company's assets by setting aside antecedent transactions, and to equalise diligence, all with the same view to maximising the sums due to the creditors.[114] It is open to him to reduce gratuitous alienations,[115] unfair preferences,[116] extortionate credit transactions[117] and certain floating charges, which may have been granted in order to defraud creditors.[118] Where directors have misapplied company assets,[119] or where fraudulent

---

[110] IA s.122.
[111] IA s.122(1)(f).
[112] IA s.122(1)(g).
[113] IA ss.84–116.
[114] See paras 10–111 to 10–117.
[115] IA s.242.
[116] IA s.243.
[117] IA s.244.
[118] IA s.245.
[119] IA s.212.

trading,[120] wrongful trading,[121] or trading through a phoenix company[122] have been taking place, the liquidator may apply to the court to make the directors accountable to the company.

Receivership

Key concept

Receivership is a mechanism by which a secured creditor enforces his rights against a company under a floating charge.

Receivership for pre-Enterprise Act 2002 floating charges

10–53   The receiver, once appointed, has various options by way of recouping the loss due to the floating charge holder: for example he may keep the company trading until the debt is repaid; or he may sell the company or parts of it. The receiver's primary interest is to repay the floating charge holder, and while he must be mindful of other interests, such as other creditors, he is ultimately working for the benefit of the floating charge holder. In so doing, he will gather in the assets caught by the floating charge, and out of these he must pay certain preferential creditors[123] with rights in priority to the charge holder's rights. A receiver may not seize assets that belong to a third party, such as goods that are leased. A receiver's interest will also be postponed to any pre-existing fixed charges over the company's assets.

The anomalous position of a floating charge over heritage

10–54   If the company subject to a floating charge owns land, the floating charge on crystallisation effectively turns into a fixed charge over that land. However, following the controversial case of *Sharp v Thomson*,[124] technically where there is an unrecorded disposition of land, but the purchasers have already paid the price on the basis of concluded missives, the receiver's right to the land is defeated by the purchasers' beneficial right to the heritage.[125]

Ranking of floating charges

10–55   Floating charges rank in date order of priority unless there is a ranking agreement to the contrary[126]. As indicated above, floating charges will automatically be postponed to prior-ranking fixed charges (of which standard securities in practice are by far the most common) unless again there is a ranking agreement to the contrary.

---

[120] IA s.213.

[121] IA s.214.

[122] IA s.216. This is where a new company is set up with substantially the same name and business as a previously insolvent company. If the new company becomes insolvent, the directors may be found liable for the new company's debts.

[123] IA s.60.

[124] 1997 S.C. (H.L.) 66; 1997 S.L.T. 636, HL.

[125] Changes to the practice of buying and selling land in Scotland make it very unlikely that this would happen. The decision in this case has been much criticised.

[126] CA 1985 s.464(1).

The defeat of the receiver

A receiver may not be able to exercise his rights under a floating charge if the floating **10–56** charge was not properly registered[127] or was improperly granted.[128]

The effect of the Enterprise Act 2002

This Act limits the operation of receivership as delineated above to floating charges cre- **10–57** ated before the implementation of the Enterprise Act, plus a few other very specialised floating charges, which still retain the use of receivership. With effect from September 15, 2003 floating charge holders having the benefit of a new type of floating charge, known as a "qualifying floating charge", and created after that date, must appoint administrators instead of receivers.[129] If a qualifying floating charge holder is concerned about the financial state of the company, which granted the charge, the qualifying floating charge holder may immediately proceed to appoint an administrator. The administrator will have to act primarily to try to maintain the company as a going concern, which failing, the administrator will try to benefit all creditors generally, which in turn failing, the admin- istrator will try to secure the interests of the secured creditors.[130] It is hoped, by these means, that some companies which otherwise would have collapsed will stand a better chance of being saved. In addition, a sum of money, known as the "prescribed part", is set aside by the administrator for the benefit of unsecured creditors.[131]

Administration

> **Key concept**
>
> Administration is a method of attempting to preserve an ailing company as a going **10–58** concern, in the interests of all the company's creditors generally.

During administration, a company's affairs are run by an insolvency practitioner and the directors demit office. During administration a company is insulated from its creditors and no steps may be taken by creditors to enforce their rights against the company. Admin- istration is designed to ensure a more satisfactory resolution of a company's financial difficulties than the drastic steps of liquidation or receivership. Administration may take place at the instance of the company, the directors, or its creditors.

Limited liability partnerships

Limited Liability Partnerships ("LLPs") were introduced into the United Kingdom by the **10–59** Limited Liability Partnerships Act 2000 ("LLPA"). LLPs share many features of com- panies, such as:

    (a) the separate legal identity of the LLP[132];

---

[127] CA 1985 s.410, CA 2006 s.886.
[128] IA s.245.
[129] IA 1986 Sch.B1.
[130] IA 1986 Sch.B1 para.3.
[131] IA 1986 s.176A(3)(a).
[132] LLPA s.1(2).

(b) requirements of registration with the Registrar of Companies[133];
(c) the uniqueness of the LLP's name[134];
(d) the need for a registered office[135];
(e) the ability to grant floating charges[136];
(f) disclosure of accounts and other documentation[137];
(g) insolvency provisions[138];
(h) members acting properly in the course of the business of the LLP are not normally liable for the debts of the LLP (as with directors of companies);
(i) members' risk is limited to their investment in the capital of the LLP, and no more.

Other features of LLPs are that:

(a) the owners of the LLP are known as "members" (not partners or shareholders). Some members are called "designated members" and they have the task of ensuring that the LLP documentation complies with all necessary LLPA legislation.[139] Members may not transfer their membership in the way that shareholders transfer their shares. Membership is, therefore, not tradeable;
(b) each member is an agent for the LLP[140];
(c) IA s.214A provides that where an LLP has gone into insolvent liquidation, under certain circumstances, the liquidator may apply to the court for an order to make a member return to the LLP any assets (including salary) improperly withdrawn from the LLP in the past two years (the "clawback" provision);
(d) the capital maintenance rules do not apply to LLPs;
(e) LLPs do not have a partnership agreement, or memorandum and articles of association, but they normally will have some internal document which will lay out the rights and duties of the members between themselves. If there is no such document, paras 7 and 8 of the Limited Liability Partnership Regulations 2001 provide a standard set, rather in the same manner as the Partnership Act 1890 does for partners;
(f) LLPs are not obliged to have AGMs or any other members' meetings.

The significant benefit of an LLP is that an LLP is able to keep some of its internal arrangements secret (as with a partnership), while the members have the benefit of limited liability (as with a limited company). The main disadvantage is the requirement to publish accounts.

CAUTION AND GUARANTEES

10–60 It is common in domestic, or business, life for one person to guarantee payment or performance for another. For example, a father might guarantee his daughter's overdraft, or a holding company a subsidiary's company's debts. Sometimes in construction projects

---

[133] LLPA ss.2 and 3.
[134] LLPA Sch. Pt I.
[135] LLPA Sch. Pt II.
[136] CA 1985 s.462.
[137] Limited Liability Partnerships Regulations 2001 (SI 2001/1090) Pt II.
[138] The Limited Liability Partnerships (Scotland) Regulations 2001 (SSI 2001/128) Pt III.
[139] LLPA ss.4–6.
[140] LLPA s.6.

a bank or insurance company will guarantee, for a fee, the construction company's payments. A guarantee is a form of security that borrowed money will be repaid or that some obligation will be performed. This section explains the law on such guarantees.

Caution

Caution (pronounced "kay-shun") is the Scots legal term for a guarantee. The term is now **10–61** slightly falling into disuse, except in the context of "lodging caution" which is where the court orders that a party to a court action lodges funds, either in the form of cash or an insurance policy (sometimes known as a "bond of caution"), to cover his opponent's costs. Another use of the word is when a trustee in sequestration, or a liquidator, produces a bond of caution which could be used to indemnify the body of creditors, should the trustee or liquidator default.

The more common term for caution, nowadays, is guarantee. With a guarantee there must be a debtor who is due money, or required to fulfil some other obligation ("the principal debt") for a creditor, who in turn seeks reassurance by way of a guarantee from the guarantor that if the debtor defaults, the guarantor will make good any loss to the creditor. The guarantee is ancillary to the principal debt, so that if the debt is extinguished, so too is the guarantee.

A guarantee is only a *ius in personam* (right against a person) and, therefore, gives the creditor no better rights in the guarantor's assets than any other creditor in the event of the guarantor's insolvency. It is, therefore, not as useful as a *ius in rem* (right against a thing), such as a standard security over a house (in England known as a mortgage), but it is still better than no security at all.

The form of the guarantee

It may be unwise not to have a guarantee in writing, but it is not illegal: it merely leads to **10–62** problems of proof. However, where a guarantee is gratuitous (i.e. no fee is charged for the granting of the guarantee) and is not given in the course of business, it must be in writing.[141] Other guarantees do not need to be in writing, though it is clearly prudent to have them in writing.

There is no standard wording for guarantees (except for certain guarantees regulated under the Consumer Credit Act 1974), though most bank guarantees will normally state the extent of the guarantor's liability, his requirement to pay any interest and expenses and the duration of the guarantee. Commonly there will be a clause giving warrant for preservation and execution, thus enabling the bank to carry out summary (i.e. immediate) diligence against the guarantor. Prudent guarantors will insist on only being liable for a fixed sum, or a fixed proportion of the total sum and no more (known as "benefit of division"), as opposed to being jointly and severally liable (which means that the guarantor could be liable for the entire guarantee if the other guarantors default). They will also wish to ensure that the guarantee relates only to a specific transaction, as opposed to all of the debtor's transactions generally. If there are several guarantors, and one of them is discharged without the others being discharged or without their consent, then all of the guarantors are discharged, unless the guarantee says otherwise.[142]

Prescription applies to guarantees.[143] This means that if the guarantee is not enforced within five years of the liability arising, the creditor cannot enforce it.

---

[141] Requirements of Writing (Scotland) Act 1995 s.1(2)(ii).
[142] Mercantile Law Amendment (Scotland) Act 1856 s.9.
[143] Prescription and Limitation (Scotland) Act 1973 s.6.

The guarantor's rights against the debtor

10–63 Under the common law, if a guarantor has to honour a guarantee, the guarantor is allowed a right of relief against the debtor—for what it is worth. If a debtor is unable to pay his debt to his creditor so that a guarantee has to be honoured, the debtor is generally in no position to repay the guarantor. But if at a later date the debtor, say, inherits some money, the guarantor may still claim against the debtor (assuming the claim has not prescribed).[144] If a guarantor has had fully to honour a guarantee, the creditor must, on request, assign the benefit of any security or other rights (such as diligence) he may have against the debtor in favour of the guarantor, so that the guarantor can the better enforce his right of relief against the debtor.[145]

The *contra proferentem* rule

10–64 If there is ambiguity in the wording of a guarantee, and if one party (usually the stronger party, the creditor) is seeking to rely on the ambiguity of the wording to favour his own interests, the wording is construed in a manner that is contrary to the interest of the person drawing up the contract of guarantee.[146]

Misrepresentation

10–65 With the exception of spousal guarantees, as indicated below, where a debtor induces a guarantor by misrepresentation (providing incorrect information) to sign a guarantee, the guarantee is still valid and the guarantor merely has a right of action against the debtor, though this may be of little benefit to him.[147] A creditor's failure to reveal information about the debtor to the guarantor does not invalidate a guarantee, since it is up to the guarantor to satisfy himself that it is safe to offer a guarantee for the debtor's debts to the creditor[148]; but if the guarantor actually asks the creditor for information about the debtor (either in writing or orally) and the creditor misrepresents the position, either fraudulently or innocently, to the guarantor's disadvantage, he is released from the guarantee.[149] In practice, nowadays it is likely that any creditor given such a request would say that the guarantor must make his own enquiries.

Guarantees for a spouse's debts

10–66 Notwithstanding the important English case of *Royal Bank of Scotland v Etridge*,[150] which requires elaborate procedures to ensure that a guarantor is fully aware of what he is guaranteeing, this case is not part of Scots law and the Inner House—in the leading case of *Royal Bank of Scotland v Wilson*[151]—expressly stated that the English case expects more of a bank than Scots law requires. In Scotland, it would appear sufficient that the creditor should, in good faith, believe that the guarantor has had the benefit of legal advice.[152] The law, therefore, is different between the two countries. For a guarantor to succeed in proving that the creditor had acted in bad faith, the guarantor would need to prove that

---

[144] *Smithy's Place Ltd v Blackadder & McMonagle*, 1991 S.L.T. 790; 1991 S.C.L.R. 512, OH.
[145] *Thow's Trustees v Young* (1910) S.C. 588; 1 S.L.T. 134; 47 S.L.R. 323.
[146] *Aitken's Trs. v Bank of Scotland*, 1944 S.C. 270; 1945 S.L.T. 84, IH (2 Div).
[147] *Young v Clydesdale Bank* (1889) 17 R. 231, IH (1 Div).
[148] *Royal Bank of Scotland v Greenshields* (1914) S.C. 259; 1914 1 S.L.T. 74, IH (1 Div).
[149] *Royal Bank of Scotland v Ranken* (1844) 6 D.1418.
[150] [2002] A.C. 773, HL.
[151] 2004 S.C. 153; 2003 S.L.T. 910.
[152] It is generally considered that a test case would be required to clarify the exact extent of the spouse's liability in Scotland.

the debtor had misrepresented the position to the guarantor and that the creditor took advantage of that position. From a practical point of view, a creditor should recommend to the guarantor that he take independent legal advice, but in the absence of anything drawn to the creditor's attention about the quality or extent of that advice, or evidence of misrepresentation by the debtor, the creditor should be entitled to rely on the guarantee.

Termination of the guarantee

Once the principal debt is repaid, the guarantee is discharged. But where the debt is discharged on the debtor's bankruptcy, the guarantee still continues in existence[153] and, indeed, will almost certainly be called upon. The benefit of a guarantee may be assigned, unless there is some term in the guarantee forbidding this, and providing that the assignation is intimated to the guarantor. During the course of the guarantee the creditor is not permitted to make the guarantor's position worse than the position he had accepted when he entered into the guarantee.[154]   **10–67**

The death of the debtor prevents any further liability under the guarantee, but the guarantor remains liable for whatever he may have contracted for up to that point.[155] The death of the guarantor transfers the guarantor's liability to his estate, unless the guarantee says otherwise.

NEGOTIABLE INSTRUMENTS

Key concept

Negotiable instruments are a method, using signed documents, of transferring funds from one person to another, other than by using cash or by modern methods of electronic transfer. Unlike the transfer of other incorporeal moveables, there is no requirement of assignation, and under most circumstances, the person acquiring a negotiable instrument in good faith and for value gets good title to the instrument.   **10–68**

The word "negotiable" means that a bill may be transferred from one person to another as if it were cash, so that the paper instruction of one person to pay another becomes almost as good as handing cash over in payment for goods. The law relating to negotiable instruments mostly involves bills of exchange, Treasury bills, cheques and promissory notes.

The benefits of bills of exchange

Alan buys goods costing £10,000 from Ben on February 1. Unfortunately Alan cannot pay for the goods on that day, but Charles is due to pay Alan £10,000 on March 1. If Ben was willing to wait for the money, Alan could draw up a bill of exchange that would state that instead Charles was to pay Ben £10,000 on March 1. Charles would accept the bill, that is, acknowledge that he would have to pay the bill on the due date, and forward it to Ben. Ben then has an entitlement to £10,000 from Charles. Furthermore, as the bill is a free-standing obligation in its own right irrespective of the underlying transaction, if Ben's   **10–69**

---

[153] Bankruptcy (Scotland) Act 1985 s.60.
[154] *Huewind Ltd v Clydesdale Bank plc*, 1996 S.L.T. 369; [1996] 5 Bank. L.R. 35, IH (2 Div).
[155] *Woodfield Finance Trust (Glasgow) Ltd v Morgan*, 1958 S.L.T. (Sh.Ct) 14; (1958) 74 Sh. Ct. Rep. 9.

goods turned out to be faulty and Alan refused to accept them, the bill of exchange would still be valid and Charles would have to honour the bill of exchange. Alan would then have to sue Ben for the faulty goods instead, but Charles could not withhold payment.

If Ben needs his money now, rather than waiting a month for it, Ben may sell or "negotiate" the bill to David. David might buy the bill for, say, £9,800, the discount of £200 reflecting Ben's need for cash now, the risk of Charles defaulting on payment, and the loss of a month's interest on £10,000. David could sell the bill to Edward. Even if Edward had defrauded David to obtain the bill, Edward could still sell the bill on to Francis, who, provided he bought the bill from Edward in good faith without notice of there being anything wrong with the bill, and provided the bill was on the face of it valid, could nevertheless ultimately receive payment from Charles.

Negotiation of a bill is not quite the same as transfer: in general, when a bill is transferred, the recipient does not necessarily get good title (i.e. undisputed ownership of the right to payment) to the bill that he has received, whereas with negotiation, the recipient does get good title.

Bills of exchange, while not used as much as they used to be, are still a significant part of banking business. This section is no more than a very simplified synopsis of a very technical area of banking law and practice.

The nature of a bill of exchange

10–70 A bill of exchange is essentially an instruction by one person (in the following example "Alan Armour") to a second person ("Charles Campbell") that Charles should pay a specified sum to a third person ("Ben Buchan") at a specified date. The Bills of Exchange Act 1882 ("BOE") s.3 states as follows:

> A bill of exchange is an unconditional order in writing, addressed by one person to another, signed by the person giving it, requiring the person to whom it is addressed to pay on demand or at a fixed or determinable future time a sum certain in money to or to the order of a specified person, or to a bearer.

Here is an example:

Bill of exchange for £10,000 Edinburgh, February 1, 2012

To Charles Campbell,

At thirty (30) days after date, pay Ben Buchan or order the sum of ten thousand pounds Sterling, for value received.

(Signed) Alan Armour
1 Perth Avenue,
Galashiels

The person who instructs the order, Alan, is known as the *drawer* of the bill. He must sign the bill or it is invalid. Signing the bill works in two ways: it serves as proof of the instruction to the person paying the bill, Charles, but it also makes the drawer, Alan, liable at a later date if the bill is dishonoured (i.e. not paid when it should be).

The person who receives the order or instruction to pay the bill, Charles, is known as the *drawee*. The process of ordering the payment of the bill is known as *drawing a bill*. When a bank pays a cheque, it is acting as a drawee by receiving its customer's order to pay the money to the customer's intended recipient.

The intended recipient of the money on payment, Ben, is the *payee*. When the bill is first drawn, the payee's name will be stated (unless it is made payable to bearer) and the payee will expect to receive payment. If, however, Ben as payee negotiates the bill to someone else, David, Ben loses his entitlement to payment and the new holder of the bill, David, becomes the next payee.

Bearer means any person who is bearing the bill, i.e. has it in his possession. Where a bill is made out to bearer, the bill may be transferred by delivery.[156]

A *holder* is similar to a bearer in that he is a person who is *holding* the bill of exchange, or in other words who has it in his possession, but in addition he is normally entitled to payment on it, particularly if he is a *holder in due course*. Holders are discussed in greater detail later. Bills may not be made out to holder.

The amount payable is stated to be "a sum certain in money".[157] This means exactly what it says, so that the figure stated must be calculable (if there is interest due) and payable in money as opposed to any other commodity.

There must be no conditions attached to the bill, or it will lose its status as a bill.[158] The date of payment must be fixed, or at least determinable.[159] It is common to have bills payable in periods of 30 days, but it is possible to have a bill payable on demand, or on sight or presentment. But a time bill, which gives a specific date, may only be paid on or after that date.

Indorsement

When a bill that is payable *or order* (as in the above example) is negotiated, the practice is **10–71** for the payee to sign his name on the back of the bill. The words *or order* signify that the payee may choose an alternative recipient of the payment. Signing the bill is known as *indorsement* and, when followed by delivery to the recipient, is an effective negotiation of the bill.[160] In turn the recipient (the *indorsee*) may wish to transfer the bill to someone specific, in which case he too will indorse his name and add the words "Pay AB" and hand the bill to AB, the new indorsee. This is known as *special indorsement*[161] and limits the transferability of the bill to AB alone, though AB may negotiate it further if he wishes to do so. It is possible to restrict the transfer by ascribing the indorser's name and adding "Pay AB only", thus making it a *restrictive indorsement*.[162] The bill then ceases to be negotiable to anyone other than AB. If the bill is made payable to bearer, there is no need for signatures; all that is required is delivery.[163] An order bill ought to be indorsed to show who the intended indorsee is, but if none is specified, the bill then becomes *blank indorsed* and is treated as a bearer bill.[164] If a blank indorsed bill is stolen, the thief may easily obtain payment—which is why bearer bills are rare. The recipient of a blank indorsed bill

[156] BOE s.31(2).
[157] BOE s.9.
[158] BOE s.3(2).
[159] BOE s.11.
[160] BOE s.31(3).
[161] BOE s.34(2).
[162] BOE s.35(2).
[163] BOE s.31(2).
[164] BOE s.34(1).

can protect himself by signing his name (or any other indorsee's name) above the indorser's signature, thus converting the blank indorsement into a special indorsement.[165]

A person who indorses a bill has to accept the fact that by indorsing the bill he may have to compensate the indorsee (or subsequent indorser) should the bill not be paid.[166] He may not subsequently assert that he is not liable on the bill on the grounds that the drawer's signature or any previous indorsers' signatures were forged or irregular,[167] or that he did not have good title to the bill anyway.[168]

Acceptance by the drawee of the bill

10–72 For a bill of exchange to be effective on a practical basis, the drawee must know that he has to pay the bill to the payee. He does this by accepting the bill, when it is first sent to him by the drawer.[169] He formally writes on the bill the word "accepted" along with his name. This is not necessary for cheques or promissory notes. The drawee's acceptance of the bill results in his redesignation as an *acceptor*, and he will normally then forward the bill to the payee. Without acceptance, the bill may be less valuable, because acceptance is a formal acknowledgment of the drawee's awareness of his duty to pay. It is possible to give a qualified acceptance,[170] though a wise payee will refuse it as he is entitled to do,[171] since the condition imposed under the qualification might be something beyond his immediate control.

A drawee may refuse or be unable to accept the bill. This is known as *dishonour by non-acceptance* and it makes the drawer who signed the bill liable instead.[172] This is because it is possible that the drawer has no dealings with the drawee and is effectively trying to defraud the drawee, or mislead the payee into believing that the drawee will pay the payee; alternatively the drawee does not have the funds to honour the bill. Where the drawee is a fictitious person, or someone without contractual capacity, the drawer will be trying to negotiate a bill that has no underlying obligation on a drawee to pay. In this case, the drawer will become liable for it.[173]

If a holder has negotiated the unaccepted bill to subsequent indorsers, each of them, along with the drawer. is potentially liable to the ultimate holder of the bill,[174] though the holder must first notify the dishonour to the drawer and to each indorser[175] and those who are not notified will not be liable.[176]

Assuming the bill is accepted, when the time for payment comes the bill will have to be re-presented to the acceptor by the payee or the ultimate holder for payment. However, if the acceptor then refuses to pay the bill further steps will be required. These will be discussed shortly.

---

[165] BOE s.34(4).
[166] BOE s.55(2)(a).
[167] BOE s.55(2)(b).
[168] BOE s.55(2)(c).
[169] BOE s.17.
[170] BOE s.19(2).
[171] BOE s.44(1).
[172] BOE s.43(2).
[173] BOE s.5(2).
[174] BOE s.43(2).
[175] BOE s.48.
[176] BOE s.48.

The holder in due course

The holder

As stated above, the first person due to receive payment under a bill is the payee. Where **10–73** the payee negotiates the bill to someone else, either by indorsement and delivery, or by delivery if the payee is a bearer, the person holding the bill is known as the holder.

Holder for value

A holder for value is a person who has either paid to acquire a bill of exchange himself, or **10–74** a prior holder has paid for it.[177]

Holder in due course

A holder in due course is in the happy position, as indicated earlier, of being well protected **10–75** and well able to obtain payment under the bill, provided the following conditions are satisfied under BOE s.29(1):

(a) the bill must be complete and regular on the face of it, so that as far as can be seen it contains all the essential requirements of a properly drawn up bill;
(b) the bill is not overdue;
(c) the holder is unaware of any previous dishonour of the bill, either by non-acceptance or non-payment;
(d) the holder must have acquired the bill in good faith for value;
(e) the holder must have been unaware of any defect in title in the previous holder who negotiated the bill to him.

If all these criteria are satisfied, the holder becomes a holder in due course and may obtain a better title to the bill than the person who negotiated the bill to him, even if somewhere in the course of the bill's progress it has been obtained fraudulently.

Presentment for acceptance

If the bill is dishonoured, as a result of the non-acceptance of the bill by the drawee, the **10–76** holder in due course may claim against the drawer and any indorsers.[178]

Presentment for payment

The holder will normally present an accepted bill for payment to the acceptor, who will **10–77** pay the bill.[179] If the payment is not made, it is said to be *dishonoured by non-payment*, thus making the drawer and/or indorsers liable instead.[180] The holder must give notice of dishonour to the drawer and each indorser[181] who can then be sued for non-payment if necessary.[182] Inland bills may and foreign bills must be *protested*, which is a formal procedure before a notary public[183] and which is public notice of the failure of the acceptor to pay.[184]

---

[177] BOE s.27(1) and (2).
[178] BOE s.43(2).
[179] BOE s.54.
[180] BOE s.47.
[181] BOE s.48.
[182] BOE s.57.
[183] A notary public is a lawyer who is authorised to confirm the authenticity of certain documents.
[184] BOE s.51.

The effect of forgery

10–78 Forgery of a signature on a bill renders the person whose signature has been forged free from liability,[185] but this does not necessarily mean that the bill itself is void: it merely means that the person whose signature has been forged is not liable. A holder in due course may still be able to claim on the bill, particularly against any indorsers whose signatures are not forged—since indorsers may not refuse to pay a bill on the grounds that the drawer's signature, or any previous indorsement, is a forgery,[186] and against acceptors, who also may not refuse to pay a bill on the grounds that the drawer's signature is forged.[187] He will also be protected where the payee is non-existent or fictitious, since such a bill is treated as a bearer bill and can be presented for payment.[188] Where the drawee's signature as acceptor is forged, the drawer and indorsers would be liable, although the drawee would not be.[189]

Alteration

10–79 Where a bill is materially altered, without the consent of all those party to it, it becomes voidable. The person who altered it without authority will remain liable on it, along with any subsequent indorsers.[190] A holder in due course, who is unaware of the alteration because it is not easily noticeable on the face of it will, however, be able to claim on the bill.[191] Where the alteration is immaterial the bill remains valid. Immaterial alterations are such acts as crossing a cheque[192] or inserting a date.[193]

Discharge of bills

10–80 Bills are discharged when they are paid by the acceptor.[194] Where the holder and the acceptor are the same person, as may occasionally happen in commercial matters, the bill is also discharged. If the drawer is found liable on the bill, payment of the bill does not discharge it, since the drawer may have a right of relief against some other person.[195] A bill may be renounced by the holder, who may choose not to enforce payment, but if so, this must be clearly and unconditionally expressed in writing.[196] A holder may also cancel a bill under BOE s.63.

Prescription

10–81 Bills of exchange, cheques and promissory notes prescribe after five years, in accordance with the Prescription and Limitation (Scotland) Act 1973 s.6(1) and Sch.1 para.1(e).

---

[185] BOE s.24.
[186] BOE s.55(2).
[187] BOE s.54(2).
[188] BOE s.7(3).
[189] BOE s.55(1)(a).
[190] BOE s.64(1).
[191] BOE s.64(1).
[192] BOE s.77.
[193] BOE s.12.
[194] BOE s.59.
[195] BOE s.59(2).
[196] BOE s.62.

Cheques

A cheque is a bill of exchange, payable on demand, drawn on a banker.[197] The drawer is **10–82** the person writing the cheque, the drawee is the bank and the payee is the person to whom the money will be paid. Acceptance does not arise in the context of cheques. Cheques are paid on demand, though it is possible to have a post-dated cheque. Crossing a cheque means that the funds to be paid out on the cheque may only be paid to the payee's bank account, and the payee cannot obtain cash from the drawer's bank account.[198] A special crossing is one where the crossing, by two parallel lines, contains the name of the bank to which payment must be made. This is rare in domestic banking. More common is a general crossing, which consists of two parallel lines and the words "A/C Payee", "Account Payee" or "Account Payee only" and in theory this requires payment to the payee's bank account only[199] and makes the cheque untransferable to anyone else.[200] If a bank does pay in cash a cheque with such a crossing on it to someone who has, say, stolen the cheque, the bank will have to reimburse the true owner.[201] A cheque that is crossed "not negotiable" may be transferred, but the transferee obtains no better title than the transferor,[202] and could, therefore, lose the normal protection of being a holder in due course.

Protection for banks

If a bank, in good faith and without negligence, pays a cheque into a bank account in **10–83** accordance with its crossing, the bank is treated as if it had paid the cheque to the true owner of the cheque, which means that even if the cheque has been stolen the drawer's account may still be debited,[203] even if the cheque was not transferable in terms of BOE s.81A. Equally, where a bank, in good faith and without negligence, receives a cheque for a customer and pays it into his account, and thereafter takes from the customer's account any sums due to the bank, if it transpires that the customer did not have title to the cheque, the bank will not be liable to the true owner of the cheque, merely because it received payment via its customer.[204] This is true even if the cheque is not transferable.[205]

In practice what normally happens with a stolen cheque is that the victim of the theft will tell the drawer to stop the cheque in order to prevent payment.

Indorsement of cheques

Most cheques nowadays are pre-printed with crossings already on them, thus making it **10–84** difficult to indorse cheques. Much of the old law about indorsement of cheques is, therefore, in practice obsolete.

On the rare occasions where a holder in due course presents an indorsed and uncrossed cheque for payment, if the banker pays out cash to the holder in good faith and in the ordinary course of business, the holder may receive payment and the drawer's account will

---

[197] BOE s.73.
[198] BOE s.79(2).
[199] BOE s.80.
[200] BOE s.81A(1).
[201] BOE s.79(2).
[202] BOE s.81.
[203] BOE s.80.
[204] Cheques Act 1957 s.4(1). For an example of a bank acting negligently and being found liable under this section, see *Middle Temple v Lloyds Bank* [1999] 1 All E.R. (Comm.) 193.
[205] Cheques Act 1957 s.4(2).

be debited.[206] This is true even if the payee's indorsement has been forged, since the bank cannot be expected to check every indorsement for forgery.[207]

Expiry of cheques

10–85 As a matter of banking practice and by convention, cheques are said to become "stale" after six months and will need to be re-issued.

Promissory notes

10–86 The law relating to promissory notes may be found at BOE ss.83–89. A promissory note is an unconditional undertaking by one person to another, in writing, that on a fixed or determinable time he will pay a certain sum of money to another person (the payee), or to someone else as instructed by the payee. Promissory notes can be negotiated in the same manner as bills of exchange, and nearly all of BOE applies to promissory notes as it does to bills of exchange, save that the provisions relating to presentment for acceptance and presentment for payment do not apply. Promissory notes may be protested and summary diligence may proceed as with bills of exchange.

INSURANCE

10–87

> **Key concept**
>
> A contract of insurance arises where one person ("the insurer") in consideration of a payment, known as a premium, takes on the financial or other consequences (known as risk) associated with an uncertain event that may befall another person ("the insured") or his assets at or before a future date, certain or uncertain, whereby the insurer is required to pay money to or make good any loss to the insured on the occasion of the uncertain event.

The law applicable to insurance

10–88 Insurance is mostly governed by the common law, though the Marine Insurance Act 1906 restated and codified much of the common law in a statutory form, albeit purely for marine insurance purposes. This Act is often referred to for guidance because it contains much of the best practice that insurance policies should follow. Insurance contracts are carefully worded, and the insurer's liability often depends on whether the situation, giving rise to a claim, falls within the ambit of the words that have been chosen. Commercial insurance is not covered by the Unfair Contract Terms Act 1977, but consumer insurance is covered by the Unfair Terms in Consumer Contracts Regulations 1999. Also in the context of consumer insurance, most insurers adhere to the insurance industry's voluntary codes, the Statement of General Insurance Practice and the Statement of Long-Term Insurance Practice. In commercial contracts of insurance, insurers and policy holders depend on the common law and, where appropriate, the Marine Insurance Act 1906. Where an insurance policy combines an investment element, the Financial Services and Markets Act 2000 applies in respect of the investment element.

---

[206] BOE s.60.
[207] Cheques Act 1957 s.1.

The insurance industry, generally, is regulated by the Financial Services Authority. This section does not deal with the regulatory side of the insurance industry.

Complaints about the business and practices of insurance companies, may be dealt with by the Financial Ombudsman Service. The Ombudsman is an independent agency with the power to investigate and settle disputes, particularly disputes between consumers and insurers.

Life assurance policies may be written in trust for the family of the insured (Married Women's Policies of Assurance (Scotland) Act 1880).

The terms of the insurance contract

In order to effect an insurance contract, the person who wants to have the benefit of the insurance policy, the "proposer", completes a proposal form issued by the insurance company (the insurer as above). The proposal forms, which are commonly standardised, outline the terms on which insurance companies do business. The proposer's completion of the proposal form is an offer to the insurance company, which the insurance company will accept or reject depending on the information given. Typically the insurance company will conditionally accept the offer, subject to payment of the first premium and clarification of any outstanding points. Once the proposer's proposal is accepted, and an insurance policy issued by the insurance company, the proposer becomes known as the "policyholder". The period of insurance usually starts from acceptance of payment of the first premium, though exceptionally it may start beforehand if agreed between the parties. There is no liability if there is no contract (in *Canning v Farquhar* (1886), Canning fell off a cliff; at the time his first premium had been tendered but not accepted, and without acceptance of the premium there was no contract and no liability for the insurers). **10–89**

Uberrimae fidei and the duty of disclosure

Key concept

The principle on which insurance proposals operate is that of *uberrimae fidei*, meaning "the utmost good faith". **10–90**

If a proposal form asks a question, it must be answered truthfully and fully and all material facts must be disclosed. "Material" is defined in the Marine Insurance Act 1906 s.12(2): "Every circumstance is material which would influence the judgment of a prudent insurer in fixing the premium or determining whether he will take the risk."

The Spathari
1925 S.L.T. 322

The proposer deliberately concealed the underlying Greek ownership of a ship, thus breaching his duty to provide all material facts in the utmost good faith.

The duty of utmost good faith means that it is not enough for the proposer to rely on the phrase "to the best of my knowledge and belief", where a little more research or common sense might disclose information which would be material to the insurer.

Further material matters that need to be disclosed often include previous convictions (unless they are deemed to be spent under the Rehabilitation of Offenders Act 1974), the occupation of the insured, any dangerous hobbies of the insured, previous losses which were the subject of a claim and the state of the insured's health.

Matters which generally are not considered material are such matters as diminish the insurer's risk, facts that are deemed to be common knowledge, facts about the law, facts which the insurance company checks for itself and facts that would not be relevant to a claim. Sometimes there is doubt as to whether or not something is material, and it would appear that in England the test of materiality is that of the reasonable insurer,[208] but in Scotland, in the context of life assurance only, the test is that of the reasonable insured.[209] As regards non-life assurance, the test would appear to be that of the reasonable insurer.[210]

Continuing duty of disclosure

10–91 Although, in principle, there is no continuing duty of disclosure, if the insurance contract states that a material change in circumstances must be disclosed to the insurer, that must indeed be done or the policy will fall. In any case, each time the policy renewal notice appears with a request for a new payment of the premium, there is a new contract formed, albeit on the same basis as before, so that the duty to disclose arises on each occasion of the renewal of the policy.

It is a disputed question whether disclosure to an agent amounts to disclosure to the insurance company. It would appear that where the proposer had disclosed information to an agent in good faith and without intention to defraud, the insurance company still had to honour the policy despite the fact that the agent, unbeknownst to the proposer, had misrepresented the true position, as in *Bawden v London, Edinburgh and Glasgow Assurance Co.*[211] This can be contrasted with another case, *Newsholme Bros v Road Transport and General Insurance Co Ltd*,[212] where the agent inserted inaccurate information on the proposal form. In this case, the proposer knew of the inaccuracy but signed it anyway. The agent was held in this case to have acted for the proposer and not for the insurance company, and the insurance company was able to avoid the contract for misrepresentation.

Warranties

10–92 A warranty is: (a) a form of promise by the insured that a certain act will be done, or continue to be done, or as the case may be, will not be done, or that some condition will be fulfilled; or (b) a confirmation that a particular state of affairs does or does not exist. Warranties about the past do not carry forward to the future unless the wording says otherwise. Warranties do not need to be material: the important point is that if the insured is required to warrant something, however trivial, if the insured does not carry out the undertaking in the warranty, or if the act referred to in a warranty about the past did not take place in the manner stated, the insurer incurs no further liability with effect from the date of the breach of the warranty.[213]

---

[208] Reasonable, in this context, means a normal insurer, acting prudently and sensibly in the normal course of business and not expecting its customers to have more than usual commercial awareness.

[209] Reasonable, in this context, means a normal insured person, acting prudently and sensibly and not expected to have more than usual commercial awareness.

[210] *Life Association of Scotland v Foster* (1873) 11 M. 351, affirmed in *Hooper v Royal London General Insurance Co Ltd*, 1993 S.C. 242; 1993 S.L.T. 679, 2 Div; 1993 S.C. 242; 1993 S.L.T. 679, 2 Div.

[211] [1892] 2 Q.B. 534, CA.

[212] [1929] 2 K.B. 356; (1929) 34 Ll. L. Rep. 247, CA.

[213] Marine Insurance Act 1906 s.33(3).

The effect of a warranty may be seen in *Dawsons Ltd v Bonnin*,[214] where a proposer warranted on a proposal form that a vehicle was kept in a stone building in central Glasgow. The vehicle was later burnt in a fire in a wooden garage elsewhere in Glasgow, and it was held that the breach of the warranty avoided the contract. It does not matter how material the warranty may be: what is significant is whether or not the warranty has been carried out, has been or is being observed, or was or is correct. So if a clause is described as a warranty, it must be observed to the letter.

The contra proferentem rule and the wording of contracts generally

The rule in insurance contracts is that the meaning of the words used in such contracts is **10–93** their normal everyday meaning, unless there is a clear indication that some other technical meaning is used instead. If there is ambiguity in the contract, and the insurance company is trying to rely on the ambiguity of the wording of the contract to avoid liability, the construction of the wording will be interpreted contrary to the interest of the insurance company that drew up the contract. As a matter of practice, insurance contracts have gradually become easier to understand, partly through the influence of such bodies as the Plain English Campaign, partly through the *contra proferentem* rule, and partly because of the inadequate wording of earlier contracts, which resulted in liability for the insurance company. In *Harris v Poland* (1941),[215] an elderly lady had taken out insurance for "loss" of her jewels "by fire". Before going on holiday, she carefully hid her jewels in some old newspaper and under some unlit coal in her grate. On her return she felt cold and absentmindedly lit the fire, thus damaging her jewels. She claimed for the loss by fire of her jewels and was duly successful. Had the policy said "self-induced loss" the insurer would not have been liable.

But where the wording is clear, and the insured fails to do what he is supposed to do, such as intimate a claim in time, or take reasonable precautions, there is no liability.

Insurable interest

Since the passing of the Life Assurance Act 1774, the insured must have an insurable **10–94** interest in the thing, or person, insured. This means that the interest must be a genuine family, business or other close personal connection. There must be a genuine insurable interest held by the insured in the insured property.

MacAura v Northern Assurance Co Ltd
[1925] A.C. 619 HL

MacAura insured, in his own name, growing timber which was actually owned by a limited company. When it burnt down, he claimed the insurance proceeds in his own name, but was refused because the timber was owned by the company and he personally had no insurable interest in the growing timber.

Causation

The peril that is insured against must be the proximate or direct cause of the loss giving **10–95** rise to the claim.

---

[214] [1922] 2 A.C. 413; 1922 S.L.T. 444.
[215] [1941] 1 K.B. 462; (1941) 69 Lloyds Law. Rep. 35, KBD.

Leyland Shipping Co Ltd v Norwich Union Fire Insurance Society
[1918] A.C. 350, HL

A marine policy excluded liability relating to damage from enemy action. An insured ship was torpedoed by a German submarine and was towed to Le Havre. It was not allowed to berth there lest it sank and blocked the harbour. It was towed to a spot outside the harbour where it later grounded and sank. The insurers avoided liability on the grounds that the proximate cause was the torpedoing by the enemy, not the grounding.

Miscellaneous terms in insurance policies

10–96 In an indemnity policy the policy-holder may not make a profit on the claim: he should recover his loss and no more. But it is possible to contract that in the event of a specified event happening, the value of which may be hard to estimate in advance, an agreed sum will be paid out for a total loss, even if in fact this may be more or less than the actual value of the loss. This is known as an *agreed value policy*.

An *excess clause* requires the policy-holder to pay, say, the first £100 of a claim. This discourages frivolous claims and may enable the policy holder better to retain a no-claims bonus, whereby the cost of the premiums diminish the longer the holder goes without having a claim.

Over-insurance is where an insured is paying premiums for a higher rate of insurance than the insured property is worth, perhaps because the property has depreciated. In the event of loss, it is the actual extent of the loss that will be paid, and the insured will have effectively been wasting his money by over-insuring. *Under-insurance* is where an asset is insured for less than its true worth, often because the cost of the premiums is too high for the policy-holder. When a claim takes place, the insurer only pays out to the value of the sum insured, which may be much less than the value of the asset. *Average* is the term for the calculation of the extent of the insurer's liability in the event of under-insurance and partial damage. If an asset is valued at £20,000 but is insured for £16,000, and £8,000 worth of damage occurs, the insurance company pays a proportion of the loss: in this case it would only pay sixteen-twentieths of £8,000, being £6,400. The balance of the loss must be borne by the owner.

Contribution occurs where there is more than one insurer for the same asset. Unless the terms of the insurance policies are identical, this can result in long and complicated battles over liability.

Subrogation is where an insurance company steps into the shoes of its insured, and raises an action against the person who has injured the insured, especially if the insured has already received payment from the insurance company. The insurance company may then try to recover damages from the person who injured the insured.

Assignation of policies is a normal procedure, particularly for life policies, whereby the benefit of the proceeds of a life policy is transferred to someone else. Assignation must be accompanied in Scotland by intimation to the insurance company.[216]

Third-party insurance arises mostly in the context of vehicle insurance where it is compulsory.[217] Third-party insurance covers damage to other vehicles or people.

Life assurance policies are designed to pay out a sum of money on the death of the insured within a particular period. *Endowment assurance policies* are a combination of

---

[216] Transmission of Moveable Property (Scotland) Act 1862.
[217] Road Traffic Act 1972 s.143.

insurance and investment: the premiums that the policy holder pays are invested in such a manner that not only will the policy pay out a fixed sum on death within the pre-determined period (the insurance element), but will also pay out a sum at the end of the period which is the proceeds of the invested sums plus the reinvested returns on the invested premiums. In this way the assurance policy provides both protection for the insured and a savings vehicle.

There are certain occasions where insurance is compulsory: for example employers (other than the Government and local authorities) must be insured under the Employers' Liability (Compulsory Insurance) Act 1969.

Some drivers, illegally, drive when they are not insured. If they cause an accident, the Motor Insurance Bureau, a body set up by the main insurance companies, acts as their insurance company and may pay out any claims made by victims of accidents involving uninsured drivers.

DILIGENCE

Key concept

Diligence is the collective term for various forms of debt enforcement. If a debtor fails to pay sums due to a creditor, a creditor ultimately pay be able to use the various forms of diligence to force the sale of some of the debtor's assets (attachment), to take money from the debtor's bank account (arrestment), to sell assets of the debtor's in the hands of a third party (arrestment), to seize some of his earnings (earnings arrestment), to prevent the debtor selling any heritage (inhibition) and to seize his heritage (adjudication for debt). The technicalities of the procedure for carrying out these diligences, and their complex interaction with insolvency, are not discussed here. The court officials who carry the diligences on behalf of the creditor are known as sheriff officers or, for Court of Session business, messengers at arms.

10–97

Authority for diligence

Diligence usually takes place following a decree from the courts in the creditor's favour. **10–98** The courts will grant "warrant" (i.e. permission) for diligence to take place. It may also take place by means of "summary diligence" (i.e. without a warrant from the courts) which is applicable when a debtor has previously consented in a document of debt (for example, a loan agreement or a guarantee) to diligence being carried out against him. Confusingly, certain creditors, such as local authorities and HMRC, are permitted to commence diligence without a court decree. This is known as "summary warrant for diligence" and is only applicable for outstanding council tax, business rates, tax or duty. Diligence carried out against a human debtor must be preceded by a charge, which is a notice delivered to the debtor by sheriff officers or messengers at arms indicating that if the debt is not paid within 14 days, diligence may take place.[218] Human debtors must also be given a copy of a debt information and advice package, which is a booklet providing debt advice.

---

[218] Bankruptcy and Diligence etc (Scotland) Act 2007 s.209.

Diligence-stoppers

10–99 A human debtor who is subject to diligence may apply to court for a time to pay order, allowing the debtor time to pay the relevant debt.[219] This has the effect of stopping the diligence proceeding. Other methods of stopping diligence include sequestration, entering a protected trust deed, or being subject to a debt arrangement scheme. In all the forms of diligence outlined hereafter there are substantial opportunities for debtors who believe that the diligence is either incompetent or unduly harsh to go to court to cause the diligence to be suspended, restricted or cancelled.

Attachment

10–100 Attachment is where the creditor is able to seize the debtor's assets from his place of business and have them sold at auction. There are restrictions on the type of assets that may be sold: for example, the tools of the debtor's trade may not be sold.[220] Depending on the circumstances, a sheriff may grant an exceptional attachment order, which enables the debtor's non-essential assets to be seized from the debtor's own dwellinghouse.[221] A separate form of attachment, known as money attachment, takes place when cash may be uplifted from a debtor's business and remitted to the creditor.[222]

Arrestment

10–101 This is where assets in the hands of a third party may be seized by the creditor.[223] If the assets are in the form of corporeal moveables, the creditor may prevent the third party returning the assets to the debtor, and providing the creditor has obtained decree in an action of furthcoming, the creditor may take away the assets from the third party's premises and sell them to recover his debt. If the assets constitute money in a bank, the bank, after a period of fourteen weeks, should release the money to the creditor.

Earnings arrestment

10–102 A creditor's wages may be arrested in the hands of his employer.[224] The employer deducts a certain sum from the wages and remits it to the creditor. A current maintenance arrestment is similar but the money is paid to an ex-spouse, usually for the benefit of the debtor's children.

Inhibition

10–103 This diligence causes the debtor's name to be registered in the Register of Inhibitions and Adjudications. Once his name is registered there, it is almost impossible for him to sell any heritage without the consent of the inhibiting creditor. This is because the inhibiting creditor has the right to reduce (i.e. set aside) the purchaser's title.[225]

---

[219] Debtors (Scotland) Act 1987 ss.5–11.
[220] Debt Arrangement and Attachment (Scotland) Act 2002 s.11.
[221] Debt Arrangement and Attachment (Scotland) Act 2002 s.47.
[222] Bankruptcy and Diligence etc. (Scotland) Act 2007 Pt 8.
[223] Debtors (Scotland) Act 1987 Pt IIIA.
[224] Debtors (Scotland) Act 1987 s.46.
[225] Bankruptcy and Diligence etc. (Scotland) Act 2007 Pt 5.

Adjudication

Although rare, this enables a creditor ultimately to obtain a debtor's property after a **10–104** period of 10 years.[226] Alternatively, if within that period the debtor sells his property, the adjudicating creditor is entitled to receive payment out of the sale proceeds.

Diligence on the dependence

Under limited circumstances, a creditor may carry out diligence on a debtor even before **10–105** court action has been raised against the debtor.[227] This is permissible if the debtor is either likely shortly to be insolvent or likely to dissipate his assets following the threat of court action.

BANKRUPTCY

Bankruptcy is a legal mechanism for allowing insolvent persons to put a limit on their **10–106** indebtedness so that they can start afresh in business, or indeed in life generally, while giving some redress to creditors. The average return for creditors throughout Scotland is about 20p in the £1.00.

In Scotland, the technical name for the process of bankruptcy is "sequestration".

The law on bankruptcy is primarily regulated by the Bankruptcy (Scotland) Act 1985 ("BSA"). This was substantially amended by the Bankruptcy and Diligence etc. (Scotland) Act 2007 ("the 2007 Act").

The meaning of "bankruptcy"

A bankrupt, in ordinary speech, is a person who is insolvent and cannot pay his creditors. **10–107** A bankrupt may not be a company director, nor hold certain public offices such as Member of Parliament. The terms of many employment contracts state that bankruptcy is grounds for dismissal, particularly if the employee is dealing with commercially sensitive matters.

In Scottish legal parlance, the bankrupt is referred to as the *debtor*.

The process of making a debtor bankrupt, and having his affairs dealt with by an insolvency practitioner[228] or the Accountant in Bankruptcy is known as *sequestration*. The person who looks after the affairs of the debtor is known as the *trustee in sequestration*. The trustee in sequestration will either be the Accountant in Bankruptcy or a designated insolvency practitioner. There are other methods of dealing with a debtor's estate, which do not involve sequestration or indeed insolvency: these include such processes as protected trust deeds and compositions and will be dealt with in due course.

Bankruptcy applies to all legal personae (i.e. human beings, partnerships, limited partnerships, trusts, associations and clubs, and certain corporate bodies),[229] but not to registered companies or limited liability partnerships. The equivalent of bankruptcy for those bodies is liquidation.

Bankruptcy is a large and complex subject, and this text does not pretend to do more than give an overview of the major issues and procedures. In particular, it does not deal with the insolvent estates of deceased persons, with bankruptcy involving an overseas

---

[226] Adjudications Act 1672.
[227] Debtors (Scotland) Act 1987 Pt IA.
[228] An insolvency practitioner is a specialist accountant or lawyer who deals with bankruptcies, liquidations, etc.
[229] BSA s.6.

dimension, nor with the effect of confiscation orders under the Proceeds of Crime Act 2002.

Sequestration

> **Key concepts**
>
> **10–108** Sequestration is the formal process whereby the debtor's estate is put into the hands of a trustee who will then manage, or dispose of, the debtor's assets in accordance with the rules of bankruptcy.
>
> The proceeds therefrom are then distributed among the debtor's creditors.
>
> The overall process is supervised and monitored by the Accountant in Bankruptcy.

The Accountant in Bankruptcy

10–109 The Accountant in Bankruptcy ("AB") is an official whose task is to oversee the practice of sequestration in Scotland. The Accountant in Bankruptcy supervises the insolvency practitioners who act as trustees in sequestration, or otherwise carry out bankruptcy work, and the Accountant in Bankruptcy may be appointed trustee in any sequestration. If either debtors, or their trustees, commit any criminal acts, the Accountant in Bankruptcy may report them to the Lord Advocate for further proceedings.

The outline of sequestration

10–110 The outline of sequestration is as follows:

(1) either the debtor applies for an award of sequestration from the Accountant in Bankruptcy, or a qualified applicant (see later) petitions the sheriff court for the debtor's sequestration;

(2) the award of sequestration of the debtor's estate is duly granted;

(3) as part of the award, a trustee is appointed;

(4) if it is worthwhile the trustee convenes a first statutory meeting of creditors, on which occasion his appointment is usually confirmed; commissioners may also be appointed to assist him;

(5) the trustee is vested in the debtor's estate, ingathers all the debtor's assets, investigates any relevant antecedent transactions and equalises any diligence;

(6) the trustee then distributes the assets, or the proceeds thereof, amongst the creditors, taking account of secured and preferential creditors before unsecured creditors;

(7) once the estate is divided up between the creditors, the sequestration is terminated, the debtor discharged and the trustee discharged.

Who may petition for sequestration?

Methods of sequestration

There are two main methods of sequestrating a debtor. The first method, for debtors only, **10–111** is a debtor application for sequestration to the Accountant in Bankruptcy.[230] The second method is by petition to the sheriff court.

Debtor applications to the Accountant in Bankruptcy

> **Key concept**
>
> Debtor applications come in three forms: the standard debtor application,[231] a low **10–112** income low asset debtor application[232]; and the certification debtor application.[233] At the time of writing there are proposals for further forms of debtor application.[234]

A standard debtor application may be made by the debtor provided the following conditions are satisfied: (a) the total amount of his debts (including interest) at the date of the petition is not less than £1,500; (b) an award of sequestration has not been made against the debtor in the preceding five years; and either (c) the debtor is apparently insolvent or is unable to pay his debts, or (d) he has granted a trust deed which could not be converted into a protected trust deed because of creditors' objections.[235]

A low income low asset application (known as a LILA application) resembles a standard debtor application except that instead of (c) or (d) above applying, the debtor satisfies the requirements of s.5A of the 1985 Act. These requirements are that the debtor's weekly income does not exceed 40 times the national minimum wage from time to time, the debtor does not own any land, and that the total value of the debtor's assets does not exceed £10,000 with no one asset being worth more than £1,000.[236]

A certification debtor application merely requires that the debtor obtains a certificate from an insolvency practitioner or other authorised official[237] certifying that the debtor has had the significance of his sequestration explained to him and that he is unable to pay his debts as they fall due. The certificate is valid for 30 days and must be sent to the Accountant in Bankruptcy within that period.[238]

---

[230] BSA s.5(2)(a).

[231] BSA s.5(2).

[232] BSA s.5A.

[233] BSA s.5(2B)(c)(ib).

[234] These may be seen on the website of the Accountant in Bankruptcy.

[235] The trust deed will be deemed to be approved by the notified creditors, unless within the relevant period the trustee has received notification in writing from a majority in number or not less than one third in value of those creditors that they object to the trust deed (the Protected Trust Deed (Scotland) Regulations 2008 (SSI 2008/143) reg. 9(2).

[236] Bankruptcy (Scotland) Act 1985 (Low Income, Low Asset Debtors etc.) Regulations 2008 (SSI 2008/81).

[237] For example, money advisers in Citizens Advice Bureaux. See the Bankruptcy (Certificate for Sequestration) (Scotland) Regulations 2010 (SSI 2010/397) reg.3(1)(b).

[238] Bankruptcy (Certificate for Sequestration) (Scotland) Regulations 2010 (SSI 2010/397).

Sequestration by petition to the sheriff court

Key concept

10–113 | The second method of sequestration is by petition to the sheriff court by a creditor or by a trustee under a voluntary trust deed.

A petition for the sequestration of a debtor may be presented by a permitted petitioner, which in practice constitutes either: (a) one or more qualified creditors[239] owed not less than £3,000 by the debtor, but in this case there is the additional requirement that the debtor must be apparently insolvent; or (b) the trustee appointed under a voluntary trust deed granted by or on behalf of the debtor for the benefit of his creditors but only if: (i) the debtor has failed to comply with his obligations under the trust deed or with the trustee's reasonable instructions; or (ii) if the trustee avers that it would be in the best interests of the creditors that an award of sequestration be made.[240] A qualified creditor must provide the debtor with a debt advice and information package.[241] A petitioning creditor must produce evidence of the debt that he is owed,[242] and evidence of the apparent insolvency of the debtor.[243] *The meaning of "apparent insolvency"*

Key concept

10–114 | This is explained in BSA s.7 and is caused by (amongst other grounds):

(a) the debtor's sequestration in Scotland or bankruptcy in England, Wales or Northern Ireland;
(b) written notice by the debtor to his creditors that he cannot pay his debts in the ordinary course of business;
(c) the granting of a trust deed for creditors;
(d) the non-payment of a debt within 14 days of receiving a charge;
(e) failure to pay a debt or debts amounting to £750 or provide security for that figure within a period of three weeks following a demand for that sum in a statutorily prescribed form.[244]

Apparent insolvency ceases when the debt is repaid, or when the debtor obtains his discharge.

---

[239] For the meaning of qualified creditor, see BSA s.5(4).
[240] BSA s.5(2)(b)(iv) and (2C).
[241] BSA s.5(2D).
[242] BSA s.11(1), (5); *Clydesdale Bank plc v Grantly Developments*, 2000 S.L.T. 1369.
[243] BSA s.11(5); *Drummond v Clunas Tiles & Mosaics Ltd*, 1909 S.C. 1049.
[244] *Advocate General for Scotland v Zaoui*, 2001 S.C. 448.

Grant of award of sequestration

> **Key concept**
>
> In a debtor application to the Accountant in Bankruptcy, the Accountant in Bankruptcy will normally grant the award assuming the paperwork is correct.[245] In a petition to the sheriff court, the court may grant the award if satisfied as to the grounds therefor: the sheriff may grant the award,[246] refuse it,[247] or continue the case for up to 42 days to allow further time for payment.[248]

10–115

Date of sequestration

The importance of the date of sequestration is that this is the date from which the debtor's **10–116** period of sequestration runs (normally one year), and it may also affect the viability of antecedent transactions. When a debtor applies to the Accountant in Bankruptcy, his date of sequestration will be the date of the award.[249] Where a creditor, or a trustee under a trust deed, presents the petition to the sheriff court, the debtor's date of sequestration is the date of the grant of warrant of citation under BSA s.12(2) requiring the debtor to appear before the court to explain why he should not be sequestrated.[250]

Notice of sequestration

Assuming the award is granted, either by the Accountant in Bankruptcy or the sheriff, as **10–117** the case may be, the Accountant in Bankruptcy or the sheriff clerk intimates the award to the Register of Inhibitions and Adjudications.[251] This means that as from the date of registration of the award the debtor is prohibited from selling his heritable assets. If the appointed trustee is not already the Accountant in Bankruptcy, his appointment must be intimated to the Accountant in Bankruptcy.[252]

Recall of sequestration

It is possible to recall of an award of sequestration, provided the petition for the recall is **10–118** either made within 10 weeks of the date of sequestration,[253] or at any time: (a) where the debtor has either repaid in full all his debts or given adequate security for them[254]; (b) where a majority of the creditors dwell outside Scotland and it would be more convenient to have the debtor's estate dealt with elsewhere[255]; or (c) where there are other awards of sequestration or bankruptcy proceeding elsewhere.[256]

---

[245] BSA s.12(1).
[246] BSA s.12(3).
[247] BSA s.12(3A).
[248] BSA s.12(3B).
[249] BSA s.12(4)(a).
[250] BSA s.12(4)(b).
[251] BSA s.14.
[252] BSA s.14(1)(b).
[253] BSA s.16(4).
[254] BSA s.17(1)(a).
[255] BSA s.17(1)(b).
[256] BSA s.17(1)(c).

The preservation of the debtor's estate

10–119 The trustee is appointed to safeguard the debtor's estate. The debtor must send the trustee a list of his assets and liabilities.[257] Using the list, the trustee will then prepare a preliminary statement of the debtor's affairs, which should indicate whether there is likely to be any payment of a dividend to the debtor's creditors.[258] The list and the statement are sent to the creditors at least four days before the first statutory meeting of creditors,[259] assuming a meeting is called: there may be no demand for a meeting or no point in having one. The list and statement must still be sent to the creditors for their information.

The first statutory meeting of creditors

10–120 The trustee must normally convene a meeting of the creditors within 60 days of the date of sequestration.[260] The creditors will then confirm the appointment of the trustee.[261] If the Accountant in Bankruptcy is the initial trustee, and no meeting is called, or if a meeting is called but no voting creditor attends, or if no trustee is confirmed, the Accountant in Bankruptcy or her nominee is appointed the trustee.[262] At the first statutory meeting the creditors may elect committee members, known as commissioners, to advise the trustee.[263] Their role is to supervise the process of realisation of the debtor's estate and to inspect the trustee's intromissions.

The trustee

10–121 The trustee is said to be *vested* in the debtor's estate, backdated to the date of sequestration.[264] This means that the debtor no longer has any title to the assets in the estate, and equally that the trustee may sign documents such as dispositions and validly transfer title.[265] The trustee has considerable powers to dispose of the debtor's estate. His duties are set out in BSA s.3, one of them being reporting to the Accountant in Bankruptcy any actions by the debtor which may be criminal in nature.[266]

Not all assets of the debtor are vested in the trustee: the trustee has limited rights over the debtor's earnings or over property which is required for the upkeep and aliment of his family.[267] Assets held by the debtor in trust for another do not vest in the trustee.[268]

A particular issue has arisen where a debtor, before sequestration, concludes missives for the sale of heritage, but the purchaser has not registered his title at the time of sequestration. To protect the purchaser's position, as regards heritage, the trustee may not complete title to any heritable estate in Scotland vested in the trustee before the expiry of a period of 28 days beginning with either: (i) the day the certified copy of the order of the sheriff granting warrant to cite the debtor is recorded in the Register of Inhibitions; or (ii) the day the certified copy of the determination of the Accountant in Bankruptcy is

---

[257] BSA s.19.
[258] BSA s.20(1).
[259] BSA s.20(2).
[260] BSA s.21A.
[261] BSA s.24(1).
[262] BSA s.23(3A) and s.25A(1), (2).
[263] BSA s.30.
[264] BSA s.31(8).
[265] BSA s.3(1).
[266] BSA s.3(3).
[267] BSA s.33(1)(a).
[268] BSA s.33(1)(b).

recorded in the Register of Inhibitions.[269] Once that 28-day period is passed, the trustee may register his title.

The position of acquirenda

Acquirenda are capital assets that the debtor acquires after the date of sequestration, and **10–122** are deemed to vest in the trustee.[270] This would apply to such assets as a legacy or bonus shares.[271] Where the debtor has any change in his financial circumstances, he is obliged to tell the trustee of these facts, and failure to do so is a criminal offence.[272] A particular difficulty is the fact that people dealing with the debtor once he is sequestrated may not necessarily be aware of the debtor's sequestration. Technically it is for the trustee to deal with the debtor's assets, and not for the debtor, and any dealings by the debtor at this stage may be set aside by the trustee. BSA ss.9 and 9(ZA) provide that under very restricted circumstances an innocent purchaser, dealing with the debtor in good faith, for value and genuinely unaware of the debtor's sequestration, may nevertheless have the benefit of his dealings with the debtor without the trustee being able to set aside the dealings.

The debtor's earned income

The debtor's earnings do not vest in the trustee. However, if a debtor is earning enough, **10–123** the sheriff may, if necessary, order that such of his earnings as are not required to aliment his family should be applied to the trustee for the benefit of the creditors.[273] The payment order granted by the sheriff may require the debtor to continue to make payments even after the end of his sequestration.[274]

Swelling the debtor's estate

A major task of the trustee is to maximise the extent of the debtor's estate by examining **10–124** transactions carried out by the debtor in the period leading up to the sequestration or, as the case may be, the apparent insolvency of the debtor. Such transactions are often known as antecedent transactions. Antecedent transactions may be reduced by the trustee,[275] and certain others,[276] such a process being known hereinafter as a "challenge". Following a successful challenge, the recipient of an antecedent transaction will be required, under certain circumstances, to return the assets or their value to the debtor's estate, and the assets or their cash equivalent will then be added to the pool of assets distributable to the creditors generally.

Certain of the following antecedent transactions may be challenged both under statute and under common law. Although the common law provisions do still exist and are valid, in practice nowadays only the statutory rules are used, mainly because they are much easier for the challenger to operate. This chapter only deals with the statutory law. The common law is admirably explained in the article by Mackenzie referred to in the "Further Reading" section of this chapter.

The challengeable antecedent transactions are as follows:

---

[269] BSA s.31(1B).
[270] BSA s.32(6).
[271] *Accountant in Bankruptcy* v *Halifax plc*, 1999 S.C.L.R. 1135.
[272] BSA s.32(7).
[273] *Brown's Trustee* v *Brown*, 1995 S.L.T. (Sh.Ct) 2; 1994 S.C.L.R. 470, Sh. Pr.
[274] BSA s.32(2XA).
[275] BSA s.34(1)(b).
[276] BSA s.34(1)(b).

(a) gratuitous alienations[277];
(b) the recalling of a capital sum on divorce[278];
(c) unfair preferences[279];
(d) excessive pension contributions[280];
(e) diligence carried out within certain periods relative to the date of sequestration, or the onset of apparent insolvency[281];
(f) extortionate credit transactions.[282]

Reduction of gratuitous alienations under statute

10–125 A gratuitous alienation is the Scots term for a gift, the transfer of an asset for no value or less than full value, or the renunciation of a claim or a right.[283] It is not unusual for a debtor to give away his assets rather than let his creditors, or the trustee, seize them. To prevent this abuse a gratuitous alienation is challengeable by any challenger[284] where any of (a), (b) or (c) below have taken place, together with (d):

(a) the sequestration of the debtor's estate[285];
(b) the granting of a trust deed which subsequently is protected[286];
(c) the death of the debtor and the sequestration of his estate within 12 months of his death[287];
(d) the alienation took place on a relevant day.[288]

A relevant day is the day that the alienation became completely effectual (for example, a standard security is only effectual on registration in the Register of Sasines or Land Register, not on execution), but it also depends on who the recipient is. If the recipient is an associate of the debtor, the relevant day is any date within a period of five years prior to the date of sequestration, the granting of the trust deed or the death of the debtor.[289] An associate is defined in the BSA s.74 as effectively a close relation, an employer or employee, a partner or a company of which the debtor is a director. If the recipient is not an associate, the period is of two years' duration only.

There are exemptions to the above rule. If the recipient can establish any of the following, the alienation will not be reduced:

(a) at the time of the alienation, or at any other time after the alienation, the debtor's assets were greater than his liabilities[290];
(b) the alienation was made for adequate consideration[291];

---

[277] BSA s.34.
[278] BSA s.35.
[279] BSA s.36.
[280] BSA ss.36A–36F.
[281] BSA s.37 and Sch.7 para.24.
[282] BSA s.61.
[283] BSA s.34(2)(a).
[284] BSA s.34(1).
[285] BSA s.34(2)(b)(i).
[286] BSA s.34(2)(b)(ii).
[287] BSA s.34(2)(b)(iii).
[288] BSA s.34(2)(c).
[289] BSA s.34(3)(a).
[290] BSA s.34(4)(a).
[291] BSA s.34(4)(b).

(c) the alienation was a birthday, Christmas or some other conventional gift (such as a wedding present), or was made for a charitable purpose to someone who was not an associate of the debtor, and it was reasonable to have made the alienation.[292]

Where a recipient has sold a gratuitously alienated asset to a third party, who acquired it in good faith and for value, the third party is not required to deliver the asset back to the trustee. The recipient instead would have to pay the value of the alienated asset back to the sequestrated estate. This is permitted by the wording of the BSA s.43(4) which allows the court to grant a decree of reduction, or order restoration of property to the debtor's estate or other redress as may be appropriate. It would appear from the case *Short's Trustee v Chung*[293] that reduction or restoration is the preferred remedy and only where those are impossible, or inappropriate, will some other form of redress be allowed.

If a recipient of a gratuitous alienation receives an asset from the debtor for less than adequate consideration, he still has to return the asset to the debtor's estate, even though he may have paid some money for it, and he may claim against the estate as a creditor in respect of what he did pay—but only as a postponed creditor.[294]

The term "adequate consideration" was considered in *MacFadyen's Trustee v MacFadyen*,[295] where it was held that consideration is to be given its normal meaning, namely that something of material or significant financial value is paid.

Recalling a capital sum paid on divorce

If a debtor paid a capital sum to his/her spouse as part of his/her divorce settlement, and if **10–126** at the time the debtor was either absolutely insolvent or became so as a result of the payment, and within five years: (a) was sequestrated; (b) granted a trust deed which becomes protected; (c) died and within 12 months his/her estate was sequestrated; or (d) dies and within 12 months a judicial factor was appointed over his/her estate, the court may make an order recalling the order for the repayment of the capital sum to the estate.[296]

Unfair preferences

Unfair preferences arise when a debtor wishes to place certain creditors in a better position **10–127** than other creditors, usually because the debtor hopes to retain the creditors' continued goodwill after his/her bankruptcy. It is sometimes done by giving a creditor a security for an unsecured debt or by repaying a favoured creditor long before payment is due. Under BSA s.36(1), an unfair preference may be challenged if the preference was created not more than six months before: (a) the date of sequestration of the debtor's estate; or (b) the granting of a trust deed which becomes protected.

Under BSA s.36(2), there are certain transactions which are exempt from challenge, these being:

(a) a transaction in the ordinary course of business;
(b) a payment in cash for a debt that was due to be paid, unless the transaction for which the cash was paid was collusive with the purpose of depriving other creditors of funds;

---

[292] BSA s.34(4)(c).
[293] 1991 S.L.T. 472; 1991 S.C.L.R. 629, IH (2 Div).
[294] BSA s.51(3)(c).
[295] 1994 S.C. 416; 1994 S.L.T. 1245, IH (Ex Div).
[296] BSA s.35.

(c) a transaction in which each party undertook reciprocal obligations, either simultaneously or over a period of time, unless as in (b) it was collusive;

(d) the granting of a mandate by a debtor authorising an arrestee to pay over arrested funds to the arresting creditor.

Assuming the challenge is successful the court will reduce the transaction and the subject of the transaction will be returned to the estate,[297] unless some other redress may be more appropriate,[298] always providing that the rights of third parties acquiring assets, originally the subject of the unfair preference, in good faith and for value, are protected.[299]

It would appear that collusion (see (b) above) requires the involvement of both parties to the collusion. In *Nordic Travel Ltd v Scotprint Ltd*,[300] the creditor, knowing that the debtor was insolvent, wanted payment in cash. Although this might have appeared collusive, it was not so, because the transaction in question was in the ordinary course of business and a payment in cash does not automatically imply collusion.

The reciprocal obligation exemption (sometimes known as the *nova debita* exemption) is unobjectionable, because the estate is simultaneously losing an asset, but receiving some other equally valuable asset or benefit. Accordingly, the estate is not diminished overall.[301]

Excessive pension contributions

10–128 A debtor might well be tempted to pay large quantities of his money into a pension fund to be held until his retirement. This is now struck at by BSA ss.36A–36F. These subsections state that the courts may reduce excessive payments into the debtor's pension fund and substitute reasonable payments thereto instead.[302]

Equalisation of diligence

10–129 Diligence is the process whereby a creditor, usually with the benefit of a court judgment or certain instruments of debt, may if necessary instruct messengers at arms (for the Court of Session) or sheriff officers (for the sheriff court) to enforce the creditor's rights of payment in terms of the carefully controlled procedure laid down in the Debtors (Scotland) Act 1987 and the Debt Arrangement and Attachment (Scotland) Act 2002. The law treats all creditors carrying out diligence within 60 days before sequestration as having each carried out their diligence on the same day. All the seized assets are pooled and the trustee divides up the assets *pari passu* (i.e. on a proportional basis) amongst all the creditors.[303]

Extortionate credit transactions

10–130 Under BSA s.61 where the terms on which a debt requires to be repaid are deemed to be extortionate, the court, on the application of the trustee, may set aside the transaction in whole or in part or otherwise, at its discretion, vary the transaction. The creditor would then be required to return any excessive payments to the trustee. It is for the creditor to prove that the terms of the transaction are fair and not extortionate. The transaction in question must have been entered into within three years of the date of sequestration.

[297] *Balcraig House's Tr v Roosevelt Property Services*, 1994 S.L.T. 1133, OH.
[298] BSA s.36(5).
[299] BSA s.36(5).
[300] 1980 S.C. 1; 1980 S.L.T. 189, IH (1 Div).
[301] *Nicoll v Steelpress (Supplies) Ltd*, 1992 S.C. 119; 1993 S.L.T. 533, IH (Ex Div).
[302] BSA s.36B.
[303] BSA s.37.

Management of the estate

The trustee will carry out, as necessary, the above methods of swelling the estate, but he **10–131** may also either close down the business[304] if he thinks it appropriate, or with the advice and consent of the commissioners, the creditors and the courts as the case may be, continue the debtor's business to raise more funds with which to pay creditors or may raise court actions.[305] Commonly, the trustee proceeds to sell as much of the debtor's estate as he is permitted to sell, including if necessary the debtor's home, which, if done, must be done within three years.[306] Where the debtor has heritage over which there is a standard security, either the heritable creditor or the trustee may sell the heritage, but each must account to the other so that the heritable creditor receives his debt in full and the surplus, if any, is handed to the trustee.[307] The trustee must have regard to the rights of the debtor's spouse and children[308] and if the debtor or his family believe that the sale of the family home is premature, they may apply to the court for a delay in the sale.

Examination of the debtor

Sometimes it is necessary for the debtor to be examined in public or in private, before the **10–132** trustee or before a sheriff.[309] The advantage of a public examination is that the presence of creditors, the panoply of the law and cross-examination in the atmosphere of a court room may put pressure on the debtor to reveal what he ought to reveal.

Creditors' claims

Creditors must supply their vouched claims (and indeed will generally already have done **10–133** so if they attended the first meeting of creditors), which will, if accepted, entitle them to draw a dividend from the debtor's estate.[310] Where the trustee rejects a claim, there are procedures available for the creditor to appeal to the sheriff.[311] Where a creditor is both due money to a debtor and is due money from a debtor, he may exercise set-off, but only in respect of debts arising before the date of sequestration.[312]

Distribution of estate

The debtor's estate, once fully ingathered, is distributed to the various creditors in the **10–134** following order of priority[313]:

    (a) the outlays and remuneration of the trustee;
    (b) where the debtor has died, his deathbed and funeral expenses and the expenses of administering his estate;
    (c) where a creditor has petitioned for sequestration, the creditor's expenses;
    (d) preferred debts (to be discussed shortly);
    (e) ordinary debts (i.e. unsecured creditors' debts);

---

[304] BSA s.18(2)(g), (h).
[305] BSA s.39.
[306] BSA s.39A.
[307] BSA s.39(4).
[308] BSA s.40.
[309] BSA ss.44–47.
[310] BSA ss.48–50.
[311] BSA s.49(6).
[312] *Taylor's Tr v Paul* (1888) 15 R. 313.
[313] BSA s.51(1).

(f) interest on preferred debts and on ordinary debts;

(g) any postponed debt.

A *preferred* debt is one of the debts in Pt I of Sch.3 to the BSA and covers certain debts, mostly due to employees.

Ordinary debts include the general body of debts due to creditors.

A *postponed* debt is either a loan from the debtor to his business, where his business is a partnership, or a loan made to the debtor by his spouse, or the value of an asset that formed part of a gratuitous alienation which was challenged by the trustee.[314]

It is unusual for an estate to be quickly divided: some bankruptcies take some months to be sorted out and the creditors receive small payments over a period of time. Frequently, there are insufficient assets for all creditors to be repaid in full and the ordinary creditors only receive a percentage of what they are due. The trustee's accounts require to be exhibited to the commissioners and the Accountant in Bankruptcy.[315]

If at the end of the day there is any surplus, it is returned to the debtor or his successors.[316]

The debtor

10–135 After one year the debtor is automatically discharged[317] unless the trustee, or a creditor, applies to the court to have the debtor's period of bankruptcy extended by up to a further two years.[318] Once the debtor is discharged, he is free to be a company director again and to hold public office. He may, however, still be subject to payment orders as referred to earlier.[319]

Until the debtor is discharged he is subject, under pain of prosecution,[320] to various requirements to inform the trustee of any concurrent proceedings elsewhere and to co-operate with the trustee generally. If he has been an unco-operative debtor, or his behaviour leading up to and during the period of his sequestration merits it, he may be made subject to a Bankruptcy Restrictions Order, or agree to accept a Bankruptcy Restrictions Undertaking.[321] This means that his name is contained on a register for up to 15 years and it will limit his ability to hold public office, be a company director or borrow money. There are criminal penalties for breach of these Orders or Undertakings.

The discharge of the trustee

10–136 The trustee may apply for his discharge once he has made his final division of the estate, and assuming the Accountant in Bankruptcy is satisfied with the trustee's accounts and all other documentation including his sederunt book (his record of all transactions and accounts), he will in due course receive his certificate of discharge.[322]

---

[314] BSA s.51(3).
[315] BSA s.53.
[316] BSA s.51(5).
[317] BSA s.54(1).
[318] BSA s.54(4).
[319] BSA s.32(2XA).
[320] BSA s.67.
[321] BSA ss.56A–56H.
[322] BSA s.57.

Alternative methods of dealing with debtors' estates

Compositions

A composition is where the creditors agree to discharge a debtor in exchange for part **10–137** payment of their debts. If this is done judicially it is known as a general composition. The proposed terms are offered to the commissioners, which failing, the Accountant in Bankruptcy and, if approved, to the creditors. A dividend of at least 25 pence in the pound must be payable to the creditors if the composition is to proceed. A two-thirds majority (in value) of the creditors must approve the composition and the sheriff is asked to consider and approve the composition. If approved by him, the composition proceeds according to its terms.[323] If the debtor defaults on his undertakings in the composition, creditors may resume their actions against him.

Trust deeds for creditors

A trust deed for creditors was originally a method whereby a debtor could convey to a **10–138** trust such of his estate as could be agreed upon by all the creditors. The trust would then be administered by the trustee, for the creditors. Much depends on the wording of the trust deed, the co-operation of the debtor, and the willingness of the creditors. A trust deed's major failing is that any creditor who does not accede to the trust deed is not bound by it, and may continue with action against the debtor. As this may be vexatious for the other creditors, ordinary trust deeds are rarely used: what is much more popular and effective is a closely similar *protected trust deed* which more effectively safeguards the remaining creditors and the debtor from the predations of the non-acceding creditor.

The protected trust deed

If a trust deed fulfils certain conditions specified in BSA Sch.5, including the requirement **10–139** to transfer to a trust the debtor's entire estate (though not necessarily his dwellinghouse) with the exception of vital necessities for himself and his family, the trust deed may be *protected*. The other conditions are that all known creditors, to whom intimation of the proposed trust deed has been made, must, to the extent of a majority in number or at least a third in value, positively object in writing to the terms of the trust deed within five weeks. If the absence of sufficient objections, the trust will be protected and the protected trust deed registered with the Accountant in Bankruptcy.

Debt arrangement schemes

As a potential alternative to bankruptcy, this Act provides a structure to enable a person **10–140** to settle his debts over a period of time. A debtor in financial difficulties may obtain advice from a specialist *money adviser* in the setting up of a *debt payment programme*. Once approved by the debtor's creditors, the debtor may not obtain any further credit but an approved *payments distributor* will distribute the debtor's funds (including some of the debtor's wages) to his creditors. A debt payment programme acts as a diligence stopper and will be a bar to sequestration.

---

[323] BSA Sch.4.

Compositions

10–141 It is possible for a debtor to come to a voluntary arrangement with his creditors. This is known as a "composition" (Sch.4) but they are little used. Unless over a majority in number and one third in value of the creditors reject it, and provided it offers the creditors a payment of at least 25p in the £, it will be accepted.[324]

▼ CHAPTER SUMMARY

AGENCY

10–142
1. **There are five main ways of constituting a contract of agency:**
   - ➢ agency by express appointment;
   - ➢ agency by implied appointment;
   - ➢ agency by ratification;
   - ➢ agency of necessity;
   - ➢ agency by holding out.

2. (a) **Agency by express appointment arises when the agent and principal expressly agree the terms of their appointment.**
   (b) **With agency by implication, the actions of the principal towards the agent indicate that the principal is content to have the agent as his agent:**
   - ➢ *Barnetson v Petersen Brothers* (1902).

3. **Agency by ratification arises where the principal subsequently approves the agent's acts. The principal needs to be fully informed of what he is ratifying.**
4. **Agency of necessity arises when the principal is unable to communicate his instructions:**
   - ➢ *Fernie v Robertson* (1871).

5. **Agency by holding out arises when a principal gives the impression that the agent is authorised to act on the principal's behalf, even if that authority has not actually been given:**
   - ➢ *Freeman & Lockyer v Buckhurst Park Properties (Mangal) Ltd* (1964).

6. (a) **The principal is liable for the acts of the agent generally:**
   - ➢ Bell's *Commentaries*, I, 540.

   (b) **The principal may also be liable where the agent acts within the agent's apparent or ostensible authority:**
   - ➢ *International Sponge Importers v Watt* (1911).

   unless the agent's action are beyond normal commercial practice:
   - ➢ *British Bata Shoe Co Ltd v Double M Share Ltd* (1980).

7. **Where a principal is undisclosed, the agent will normally be liable to any third party unless the principal is revealed or could easily be established. The third party may then elect to sue either the principal or the agent.**

---

[324] 2007 Act s.21.

8. (a) **An agent owes a duty of skill and care to his principal:**

   ➢ *Gilmour v Clark* (1853)

   (b) **An agent also owes a fiduciary duty to his principal:**

   ➢ *Boston Deep Sea Fishing v Ansell* (1888).

9. **An agent may be liable to a third party for breach of warranty of authority to act on the principal's behalf:**

   ➢ *Anderson v Croall & Sons* (1903).

10. **The Commercial Agents (Council Directive) Regulations 1993, provide various safeguards for commercial agents. These will override the common law.**

PARTNERSHIP

1. (a) **The key advantage of running a business as a partnership is the non-disclosure of accounts.**
   (b) **The key disadvantage is partners' joint and several liability for the partnership debts.**

2. **Partnership is regulated by the Partnership Act 1890, which supplies a standard set of rules from which partners may derogate if they wish.**

3. **A partnership has its own legal personality:**

   ➢ Partnership Act 1890 s.4(2).

4. **There are extensive rules for establishing whether or not a partnership is in existence:**

   ➢ Partnership Act 1890 s.2.

5. **Each partner is an agent for the firm and the firm is liable for his acts in the course of the firm's business:**

   ➢ Partnership Act 1890 ss.5 and 6.

6. **The firm is liable for any wrongful acts committed in the course of business by a partner:**

   ➢ Partnership Act 1890 s.10.

7. **The normal rules that apply to the management of the partnership are outlined by Partnership Act 1890 s.24.**

8. (a) **Partners owe a fiduciary duty to the partnership:**

   ➢ *Finlayson v Turnbull* (1997).

   (b) **Partners must not compete with their partnership:**

   ➢ *Pillans Bros v Pillans* (1908).

9. (a) **Partnerships may be dissolved at will:**

   ➢ Partnership Act 1890 s.3.

   (b) **or partnerships may be dissolved by the courts:**

   ➢ Partnership Act 1890 s.35.

10. **Partners remain liable for the partnership debts, until all the creditors have been told of the dissolution of the partnership:**

    ➢ Partnership Act 1890 s.36.

COMPANY LAW

1. **Companies are regulated by the Companies Act 2006.**
2. **The main advantages of limited companies are that they have their own legal personality, and the members are not responsible for their companies' debts, except to the extent of the capital they have contributed.**
3. **The main disadvantages of limited companies are that most companies' accounts have to be audited and published, and that all companies have to conform to stringent legal, and sometimes expensive, procedures for their formation, management and winding up.**
4. **The three main cases for the separate legal personality of the company are:**

    ➢ *Salomon v A Salomon & Co Ltd* (1897).
    ➢ *Lee v Lee's Air Farming Ltd* (1961).
    ➢ *MacAura v Northern Assurance Co Ltd* (1925).

5. **Notwithstanding the separate legal personality of the company, the "corporate veil" may be lifted to make the members or directors liable for the company's debts, either under common law or under statute. But provided a director acts through his company, he will not generally be personally liable to creditors;**

    ➢ *Williams v Natural Life Health Foods Ltd* (1998).

6. **To incorporate a company, various forms must be completed and sent to the Registrar of Companies along with the company's memorandum and articles of association.**
7. **The articles of association are the company's constitution and members have to abide by their terms:**

    ➢ *Hickman v Kent and Romney Marsh Sheepbreeders Association* (1915).

8. **Directors manage the company, but are still subject to certain restraints imposed by the company's articles and the views of shareholders.**
9. **(a) Directors owe various duties to their company, the most important being the duty to promote the success of the company (Companies Act 2006 s.172).**
   (b) The duty of skill and care (Companies Act 2006 s.174):

    ➢ *Dorchester Finance Co Ltd v Stebbing* (1989).

   (c) and various other statutory duties designed to ensure that directors run their companies in a proper manner.

10. **A share is a unit of ownership in a company, commonly with a nominal value of £1.00.**
11. **Shareholders may meet to review the directors' performance at annual general meetings and to pass important resolutions affecting the constitution of the company.**
12. **Liquidation is the turning of all the company's assets into cash, so that the cash may be divided up between the creditors. It is regulated by the Insolvency Act 1986.**

13. Receivership is where a floating charge-holder exercises his right to appoint a receiver, who tries to recoup the sums due by the company to the charge-holder.

14. Administration is when an administrator tries to rescue a failing company if he can, and if he cannot, either to pay the all the creditors or just repay the secured creditors.

15. Limited liability partnerships have many of the features of companies and some of the features of partnerships.

CAUTION AND GUARANTEES

1. Guarantees are a form of security to ensure that a debt is paid, or an obligation fulfilled by the guarantor if the debtor, or obligant, fails to perform.

2. Guarantees do not have to be in writing unless they are gratuitous and not in the course of business (Requirements of Writing (Scotland) Act 1995 s.1(2)(ii)) or required under the Consumer Credit Act 1974.

3. Guarantees are subject to the *contra proferentem* rule:

   ➤ *Aitken's Trs v Bank of Scotland* (1944).

4. Where a debtor misrepresents his own solvency to a guarantor, the guarantor is still liable to the creditor:

   ➤ *Young v Clydesdale Bank* (1889), *Royal Bank of Scotland v Greenshields* (1914).

5. Where the creditor misrepresents the position to the guarantor, the guarantor is not liable:

   ➤ *Royal Bank of Scotland v Ranken* (1844).

6. In spousal guarantees, provided the creditor acts in good faith, it is probably sufficient for a creditor to assume that the guarantor has received the benefit of independent advice:

   ➤ *Royal Bank of Scotland v Wilson* (2004).

NEGOTIABLE INSTRUMENTS

1. A bill of exchange is an unconditional order in writing, addressed by one person to another, signed by the person giving it, requiring the person to whom it is addressed to pay on demand or at a fixed or determinable future time a sum certain in money to or to the order of a specified person, or to a bearer:

   ➤ Bills of Exchange Act 1882 s.3.

2. The person who writes the bill is the drawer. The person who pays the bill is the drawee. The person who receives the money is the payee. The drawee will acknowledge his duty to pay the bill by accepting the bill, whereupon he is also known as the acceptor.

3. (a) If the drawee refuses to accept the bill, this is known as dishonour by non-acceptance and makes the drawer liable:

   ➤ Bills of Exchange Act 1882 s.43(2).

(b) **If the drawee, having accepted the bill and thereby having become the acceptor, later refuses or is unable to pay the bill, the bill is dishonoured by non-payment and the drawer and any indorsers become liable:**

> Bills of Exchange Act 1882 s.47.

4. (a) **Indorsement is signing of the payee's name on the back of the bill to make it negotiable to a recipient known as the indorsee:**

> Bills of Exchange Act 1882 s.31(3).

(b) **The indorsee may add his own signature, thus making the bill payable to some other indorsee. There are various different types of indorsement such as special indorsement, restrictive indorsement and blank indorsement.**

5. **A payee indorsing a bill, or a subsequent indorser indorsing a bill, takes the risk that if the bill is not met the endorsee may sue the payee, or indorser as the case may be, for having negotiated a bill that has not been paid.**

6. **A holder in due course is deemed to have good title to a bill, even if at some stage there has been fraud, provided the bill is complete and regular on the face of it, the bill is not overdue, the holder is unaware of any previous dishonour of the bill, the bill was acquired in good faith and for value and the holder was unaware of any defect in title in the previous holder who negotiated the bill to him:**

> Bills of Exchange Act 1882 s.29(1).

7. (a) **Forgery of a signature on a bill does not render the person whose signature has been forged liable:**

> Bills of Exchange Act 1882 s.24.

(b) **The bill itself may still be valid if the holder is a holder in due course.**

8. **A cheque is a bill of exchange payable on demand drawn on a banker:**

> Bills of Exchange Act 1882 s.73.

9. **Crossing a cheque with the words "a/c payee" within two lines (as most cheques are nowadays) means that the cheque can only be paid into a bank account:**

> Bills of Exchange Act 1882 s.80.

10. **If a bank, in good faith and without negligence, pays a crossed cheque into a bank account the bank is treated as if it had paid the cheque to the true owner of the cheque:**

> Cheques Act 1957 s.4(1).

INSURANCE

1. **Insurance law is mostly governed by the common law, but the Marine Insurance Act 1906 provides useful guidance.**
2. **The duty of disclosure is paramount, and disclosure must be made uberrimae fidei (in the utmost good faith):**

> *The Spathari* (1925) where the Greek ownership was not revealed.

3. **The significance of disclosure is that proper disclosure enables the insurer to fix the correct premium:**

   ➢ Marine Insurance Act 1906 s.12(2).

4. **Warranties must be followed to the letter:**

   ➢ *Dawsons Ltd v Bonnin* (1922)—vehicle not stored where it should have been.

5. **The *contra proferentem* rule acts to the advantage of the weaker party to the contract:**

   ➢ *Harris v Poland* (1941)—elderly lady's jewels, stored in her coal grate, were insured against "loss by fire".

6. **The insured must have an insurable interest in the person or property insured:**

   ➢ *Macaura v Northern Assurance Co Ltd* (1925)—timber insured in the insured's name, but actually owned by a separate company.

7. **The peril insured against must be proximate cause of the loss:**

   ➢ *Leyland Shipping Co Ltd v Norwich Union Fire Insurance Society* (1918)—ship sunk by enemy torpedo rather than by grounding on a sea bank.

8. **Insurance is obligatory under certain circumstances, such as third party insurance for drivers.**

DILIGENCE

1. **Diligence is the process whereby creditors may enforce payment by debtors of their debts.**
2. **There needs to be authority ("warrant") from the court, from the sheriff or from the debtor himself for diligence to take place. Diligence on the dependence is permitted when a creditor fears that the debtor may shortly become insolvent.**
3. **Attachment is the process of seizing a debtor's non-essential assets from his place of business. Under limited circumstances exceptional attachment is permitted, which is the seizing of non-essentials items from the debtor's home. Money attachment is the seizing of cash in the debtor's business premises:**

   ➢ Debt Arrangement and Attachment (Scotland) Act 2002;
   ➢ Bankruptcy and Diligence etc. (Scotland) Act 2007.

4. **Arrestment is the seizing of the debtor's assets in the hands of a third party. To complete the arrestment an action of furthcoming is needed. If what is seized is money in a bank account, after 14 weeks the bank should automatically release the money to the creditor:**

   ➢ Debtors (Scotland) Act 1987.

5. **Earnings arrestment is the seizing of some of the debtor's wages to pay his creditors:**

   ➢ Debtors (Scotland) Act 1987.

6. **Inhibition is a method of preventing the debtor selling any of his heritage unless he repays the inhibiting creditor:**

   ➢ Bankruptcy and Diligence etc. (Scotland) Act 2007 Pt 5.

7. **Adjudication for debt is a method either of obtaining the debtor's heritage for non-payment of a debt, or of ensuring that the debtor's heritage may only be sold with the creditor's consent and repayment:**

    ➢   Adjudications Act 1672.

BANKRUPTCY

1. **Sequestration is the proper term for the process of bankruptcy in Scotland.**
2. **The debtor himself may apply to the Accountant in Bankruptcy for an award of sequestration. A creditor or a trustee of a protected trust deed, within certain parameters, may petition the sheriff court for the debtor's sequestration. As part of the application or the petition it may be necessary to establish that the debtor is apparently insolvent.**
3. **Apparent insolvency is carefully defined:**

    ➢   Bankruptcy (Scotland) Act 1985 s.7.

4. **(a) Following a successful application to the Accountant in Bankruptcy the award is usually granted. Following a petition for sequestration, a trustee is appointed. The trustee may be the Accountant in Bankruptcy. Normally a creditors' meeting in called with 60 days, at which the appointment of the trustee is confirmed:**

    ➢   Bankruptcy (Scotland) Act 1985 s.24.

    (b) The trustee is vested in the debtor's estate:

    ➢   Bankruptcy (Scotland) Act 1985 s.32.

5. **The trustee will gather in the estate of the debtor for eventual disbursement to the creditors. In doing so, he will revisit any antecedent transactions and try to swell the estate so that the creditors can be paid as much as possible. This can include selling the debtor's home and any other major assets the debtor has.**
6. **These antecedent transactions are:**

    (a) Gratuitous alienations:

    ➢   Bankruptcy (Scotland) Act 1985 s.34.

    (b) Recalling of capital sums on divorce:

    ➢   Bankruptcy (Scotland) Act 1985 s.35.

    (c) Unfair preferences:

    ➢   Bankruptcy (Scotland) Act 1985 s.36.

    (d) Diligence within certain time periods:

    ➢   Bankruptcy (Scotland) Act 1985 s.37.

    (e) Extortionate credit transactions:

    ➢   Bankruptcy (Scotland) Act 1985 s.61.

7. **There are complex rules particularly for gratuitous alienations depending on the recipient of the alienation, the purpose of the alienation, the solvency of the debtor at**

the time of alienation and the date of the alienation. **Similar rules apply to unfair preferences.**

8. **(a) Capital assets, to which the debtor becomes entitled during the period of his bankruptcy, are known as acquirenda and fall to the estate:**

    ➢ Bankruptcy (Scotland) Act 1985 s.32.

    (b) The debtor may also be required to pay sums out of his income to his creditors:

    ➢ Bankruptcy (Scotland) Act 1985 s.32.

9. **When the trustee has gathered in as much money as he will, in order, pay himself, the preferential creditors, the ordinary creditors, in each case in full if possible and proportionately if not.**
10. **Usually after one year the debtor is discharged.**
11. **There are other methods of dealing with debtors in financial difficulties, such as compositions, protected trust deeds and debt arrangement schemes.**

? QUICK QUIZ

COMMERCIAL LAW

Agency

- What does an agent do?
- What are the main ways an agency agreement is set up?
- What is required for agency by ratification?
- When is the principal liable for the agent's actions?
- And when is the principal not liable for the agent's actions?
- What is apparent or ostensible authority?
- What are the duties an agent owes his principal?
- What is the law relating to undisclosed principals?
- How do the Commercial Agents (Council Directive) Regulations 1993 protect agents?

Partnership

- What are the advantages and disadvantages of running a business through a partnership?
- What is the definition of a partnership?
- What are the rules for establishing whether or not a partnership is in existence?
- If a partner is told by his fellow partners not to enter a contract, but does so anyway, is the partnership liable for the contract?
- Is a partnership bound by a contract beyond the normal course of business?
- If a partnership is sued, may the creditor also claim against the partners individually?
- Once a partner has retired, is he still liable for his partnership's debts?

Company law

- What is the proper name for the investors in a company?
- What is the name of the people who carry out the following tasks for a company:
  - Management?

- Checking the accounting?
- Dealing with the legal paperwork?

- What are the different types of company?
- What are the main differences between a private company and a public company?
- What is the benefit of separate legal personality, and what does the phrase "lift the corporate veil" mean?
- What are the three leading cases for separate legal personality?
- What is the leading case for a director's freedom from liability to creditors provided he acts through the company?
- What is a floating charge?
- What is the purpose of shareholders' meetings?
- What is the difference between liquidation, receivership and administration?

Caution and guarantees

- For what purposes are guarantees used?
- When do guarantees have to be in writing?
- If the debtor lies to the guarantor, does the guarantor still have to pay the creditor?
- Can a guarantor be made to pay the creditor where the creditor has lied to the guarantor?
- What is the current legal position with a guarantee by one spouse for the other?
- Does the death of a guarantor extinguish his liability to the creditor?

Negotiable instruments

- What is the definition of a bill of exchange?
- What is the purpose of a bill of exchange?
- In a bill of exchange, which person is the drawer, the drawee, the payee and the acceptor?
- What is indorsement and how is it done?
- If the drawee refuses to accept the bill of exchange, who is liable for it?
- If the acceptor is unable to pay the bill of exchange, who is liable for it?
- What is so advantageous about being a holder in due course?
- What are the requirements for being a holder in due course?
- How does a cheque differ from a bill of exchange?
- What is the effect of crossing a cheque?

Insurance

- What Act of Parliament aids the interpretation of insurance contracts, but is not a definitive source of the law?
- What does uberrimae fidei mean and to what does it apply?
- Why is it necessary for an insurer to know all the details about the insured?
- What is the significance of a warranty? Name an important case about a warranty.
- What is meant by insurable interest?
- What does the *contra proferentem* rule do? Why does the rule exist?
- How does the requirement that the insurance company only needs to meet claims that follow directly from the peril insured against benefit insurance companies?
- When is insurance obligatory?

Diligence

- What is the purpose of diligence?
- What is needed before diligence may be commenced?
- What are the main types of diligence?
- What sort of diligence is carried out against assets in the debtor's own home?
- What sort of things may not be subject to attachment?
- How may you carry out diligence before raising an action against a debtor?
- Why might you wish to do this?

Bankruptcy

- What is the purpose of sequestration?
- How can the debtor apply for his own sequestration? To whom does he apply?
- If a creditor wishes to make a debtor bankrupt, where must he lodge his petition for the debtor's sequestration?
- On what grounds may a creditor petition for the debtor's sequestration?
- What is meant by apparent insolvency?
- What is the function of the trustee?
- Does the trustee have the right to deal with all the debtor's assets?
- The trustee can challenge antecedent transactions carried out by the debtor. There are six different types. What are they?
- What happens if the debtor receives a large inheritance during the period of his bankruptcy? What is he supposed to do with it?
- How can the debtor be forced to apply some of his income towards his creditors?
- What can the trustee do with any land and buildings owned by the debtor?
- Narrate the trustee's order of payment to the debtor's creditors and others.
- For how long is a debtor deemed to be bankrupt?
- There are some other methods of dealing with debtors who are in financial difficulties. What are they?

📖 FURTHER READING

All the topics in the above chapter are discussed in much greater detail in the following three publications:

Davidson and MacGregor, *Commercial Law in Scotland*, 2nd edn (W. Green, 2008), Ch.2.

Gloag and Henderson, *The Law of Scotland*, 13th edn (W. Green, 2012).

Stair Memorial Encyclopaedia: The Laws of Scotland (LexisNexis, 1986).

For more specialist writing, see also:

N. Grier, *Company Law*, 3rd edn (W. Green, 2009).

Cowan, *Scottish Debt Recovery: a Practical Guide* (W. Green, 2011). This is particularly helpful on diligence and bankruptcy.

McKenzie, "Gratuitous Alienations and Unfair Preferences on Insolvency" (1993) 38 J.L.S.S. 141.

🖱 RELEVANT WEB LINKS

The Accountant in Bankruptcy has an excellent website: *www.aib.gov.uk*

This contains a great deal of useful information on the practicalities of bankruptcy and diligence, as well as having links to the current version of the Bankruptcy (Scotland) Act 1985.

Chapter 11   Delict

GORDON CAMERON[1]

▶ OVERVIEW

This chapter provides a basic insight into civil liability for delict. It starts with a brief **11–01** explanation of governing principles, before considering, in greater detail, the basic requirements that must be met for liability in negligence to arise. Damages and defences are also discussed in this section. There is then a brief explanation of vicarious liability, before going on to cover in outline liability for breach of statutory duty. Finally, the essential elements of a small selection of intentional delicts are outlined and explained.

✓ OUTCOMES

At the end of the chapter you should be able to: **11–02**

- ✓ explain the meaning of delict and the aims of the principal remedies;
- ✓ understand the basic criteria for recognising a duty of care in different situations;
- ✓ understand the basic requirements of causation;
- ✓ determine whether particular losses are reparable or not;
- ✓ identify potential defences;
- ✓ appreciate different liability requirements;
- ✓ understand the basic elements of assault and harassment;
- ✓ understand the basic elements of nuisance and trespass;
- ✓ understand the basic elements of defamation and the defences available; and
- ✓ predict whether a given set of facts will give rise to a remedy.

INTRODUCTION

Delict is a branch of the law of obligations concerned with civil wrongs. While contractual **11–03** obligations arise from agreement between the parties, delictual obligations arise from wrongdoing and are imposed by law. A civil wrong occurs when there is an unjustifiable invasion of a person's reparable interest. The delinquent, that is the wrongdoer, comes under an obligation to repair the wrong. Delict therefore, is concerned with righting wrongs.

There is a variety of reparable interests, but the most important, in the sense of being the ones most likely to be invaded, are interests in physical health and property. Wrongful invasions may be repaired by legal remedies. If property has been damaged, or injury caused, then the remedy sought will most likely be damages. If the case is established, the

---

[1] Senior Lecturer in Law, University of Dundee.

wrongdoer will come under an obligation to make reparation, that is to pay a sum in damages.

There are, however, other ways of repairing wrongs, the most important of which is interdict. An interdict is a court order issued to prevent a wrong from occurring or to put an end to a continuing wrong, such as a state of affairs amounting to nuisance or persistent trespass. Nuisance is a wrongful invasion of a proprietor's interest in comfortable enjoyment of heritable property. Trespass is an unjustifiable and temporary intrusion on a proprietor's right to exclusive possession of property. An interdict is a court order, that recognises the wrongdoer's obligation to abate a nuisance or, in the case of trespass, it recognises a negative obligation to desist from intruding on the proprietor's right.

The principles under which the law operates differ according to the remedy sought. The governing principle of reparation, at common law, is *damnum injuria datum*: that is, loss caused by a wrong. The term reparation refers to damages. Thus, in a claim for damages it is necessary for the pursuer to demonstrate *culpa* on the part of the defender. *Culpa* means fault so, in a damages claim, the defender must be proved to have been at fault. Usually, this means that the defender must be shown to have been negligent, but *culpa* takes other forms, so intentional fault may be shown where harm follows from deliberate actions done in the knowledge that harm would result or harm may be done maliciously. For intentional fault to be established, it is not necessary to show that harm to the victim was the object of the defender's conduct. Motive is, in the general case, irrelevant in delictual liability. Motive is only relevant in the relatively limited circumstances in which malice is required for liability. Where remedies other than reparation are sought, it is, in general, sufficient to show that a wrong is being done, or that there are reasonable grounds for its apprehension, in which case interdict may be awarded with no requirement to prove fault.

It is important to note that the requirement to prove fault belongs to the common law. Where liability arises under statute, other requirements for liability may be imposed so, for example, there is no need to show fault where liability arises under the Animals (Scotland) Act 1987. Liability under this statute is strict, meaning there is no burden on the pursuer to prove fault. Under other legislation, for example the Occupiers' Liability (Scotland) Act 1960, the statutory duty is to take reasonable care, so liability under this statute depends upon proof of negligence. Legislation may also provide for specific statutory remedies so, for example, a person who suffers harassment may seek a non-harassment order under the Protection from Harassment Act 1997.

NEGLIGENCE

11–04 Here we are concerned with claims for damages, in circumstances where harm has been caused unintentionally. Negligence, broadly, means a failure to take care in circumstances where care is required. Claims for damages grounded on negligence arise where one party can attribute harm suffered to the carelessness of another. Since most delictual claims arise out of accidents, usually in the workplace or on the roads, negligence may be seen as by far the most important element in delict.

Key concepts

For a valid claim in negligence:

- It must first be established that the defender owed the pursuer a duty of care. Without a pre-existing duty, there can be no valid claim.

- Next, it must be shown that the duty was breached. The duty of care needs content and pursuers must aver exactly what standard of care was incumbent on the defender and the way in which the defender's actions fell short of this standard.
- It must then be shown that the harm was caused by the defender's breach.
- If all these requirements are satisfied, it may then be necessary to consider whether all losses are reparable or whether there are some that are too remote.

Each of these points will be considered below.

The duty of care

Lord Dunedin stated: "Negligence *per se* will not make liability, unless there is first of all a duty which there has been failure to perform through that neglect".[2] We need, therefore, to be able to determine when a duty arises and to whom it is owed. The starting point for this enquiry is Lord Atkin's neighbourhood principle from *Donoghue v Stevenson*.[3]   **11–05**

Donoghue v Stevenson
1932 S.C. (H.L.) 31

"The rule that you are to love your neighbour becomes in law, you must not injure your neighbour; and the lawyer's question, Who is my neighbour? receives a restricted reply. You must take reasonable care to avoid acts or omissions which you can reasonably foresee would be likely to injure your neighbour. Who then, in law, is my neighbour? The answer seems to be- persons who are so closely and directly affected by my act that I ought reasonably to have them in my contemplation as being so affected when I am directing my mind to the acts or omissions which are called into question."

A duty of care will arise, whenever some conduct is contemplated which carries a risk of harm to others or to their property. The duty is owed to persons who will likely be affected in the event that the risk materialises.

Proximity

It can be seen that a duty of care is not owed to the whole world, but only to those persons whom you can reasonably foresee as being likely to be affected by your conduct. It is not sufficient for the existence of a duty to say that a person should have foreseen that somebody might have been harmed. It is necessary to find that harm to the pursuer in particular, or to a class of persons of which the pursuer is a member, was foreseeable to the defender. For example, a motorist owes a duty of care to other road users and pedestrians in the immediate vicinity. Where a duty is owed to a class of persons the membership of that class must be definite or at least reasonably well defined. There is a need for some element of proximity between the parties, before a duty can be said to arise. Proximity may   **11–06**

---

[2] *Clelland v Robb*, 1911 S.C. 253, 256.
[3] 1932 S.C. (H.L.) 31.

be understood as drawing the parties together so that one should have the other within his or her contemplation.

The requirement of proximity is well demonstrated in the case of *Hill v Chief Constable of West Yorkshire*.[4]

Hill v Chief Constable of West Yorkshire
[1989] A.C. 53

The police were negligent in the process of apprehending the Yorkshire Ripper, Peter Sutcliffe. Had a better job been done on the investigation Sutcliffe might have been in custody before claiming his final victim, Jacqueline Hill. The mother of Jacqueline Hill sued for damages, but was unsuccessful. While it was foreseeable to the police that women in the Leeds area were in danger, so long as the Ripper remained at large, there was no relationship of proximity between the police and Jacqueline. As a woman, she was a member of a class too widely drawn for a duty of care to be owed. Moreover, there was nothing about Jacqueline that could have identified her as being in particular danger and so the harm that befell her was not something that the police ought reasonably to have contemplated. She was, therefore, owed no duty of care.

Novel circumstances

11–07 Courts have recognised the existence of duties in many circumstances and, generally, where personal injury or property damage is caused by a person who ought to have contemplated such harm—either to the pursuer in particular or to a limited class of persons of which the pursuer is a member—then a duty will normally be recognised. On the other hand, where a claim arises in novel circumstances, that is in a situation where there is no clear precedent for holding that a duty is owed, courts have some discretion in deciding whether to recognise a duty.

The governing authority for recognising a duty in novel circumstances is *Caparo Industries plc v Dickman*.[5]

Caparo Industries plc v Dickman
[1990] 2 A.C. 605

Caparo established a three part test for recognising a duty. First, harm to the pursuer must be reasonably foreseeable; second there must be a close degree of proximity between the parties; third it must be fair, just and reasonable for the court to recognise a duty.

The final part of the *Caparo* test gives courts scope for denying the existence of a duty on policy grounds. Although it is not always made explicit, courts may allow or deny the existence of a duty for reasons of policy. For example, the court in *Hill v Chief Constable of West Yorkshire* took the view that it would be undesirable to expose the police to

---

[4] [1989] A.C. 53.
[5] [1990] 2 A.C. 605.

potential civil liability in the circumstances, as this might have a detrimental effect on the process of criminal investigation.

The *Caparo* test has been applied in a number of subsequent cases, notably in *Gibson v Chief Constable of Strathclyde*.[6] In this case police officers had assumed control over a collapsed road bridge. When the officers left the scene without any warning of the danger left in place, a car drove off the bridge. It was held that a duty of care was owed by the police to the occupants of the car. Persons travelling on this particular stretch of road fell within a small and sufficiently well defined class for a duty to be owed them. Moreover, by assuming control in an emergency the police officers were in a sufficiently proximate relationship with motorists using this road. The policy argument that had applied in *Hill*, did not apply in this case where the police were not conducting a criminal investigation, but were exercising a very different function in taking control over hazardous road conditions. *Hill v Chief Constable of West Yorkshire* was, therefore, distinguished. The recognition of a duty of care was, in the circumstances, fair, just and reasonable. The *Caparo* test was applied in *McFarlane v Tayside Health Board* to hold that the defenders breached a duty of care owed to the pursuers when the result of a vasectomy was negligently reported to a patient as successful. The vasectomy had failed and the McFarlanes conceived a fifth child. In *Mitchell v Glasgow City Council* Mitchell was a council tenant whose difficulties with a violent neighbour led to the Council calling the neighbour to a meeting at which he was threatened with eviction. Following the meeting the neighbour killed Mitchell with an iron bar. *Caparo* rules were applied to hold that the Council owed Mitchell no duty to warn him the meeting was to take place.

Key concepts

- Duties of care are not owed to the whole world. Duties are owed to identifiable persons or persons within a well defined class. There must be proximity between pursuer and defender.
- In novel circumstances where there is no precendent the *Caparo* test is used to determine whether a duty arises.

Foreseeability of harm

A duty of care will only arise in respect of foreseeable harm that is reasonably likely to materialise if sufficient care is not taken. Thus in *Muir v Glasgow Corporation*[7] while an employee of the Corporation did owe a duty of care to children in premises of which she was in charge, the duty was not breached when some children were scalded by hot water spilling from a tea urn that was carried down a corridor. The view was taken, in the House of Lords, that this was not an event which the employee could have contemplated.   **11–08**

Some risks are so slight, that no duty arises in respect of them. In *Bolton v Stone*[8] a neighbour was hit by a cricket ball which was struck so effectively that it left the cricket ground altogether. This was not the first time a ball had left the ground. It was established in evidence that balls had been struck beyond the ground 6 times in the previous 30 years. On this basis, while the injury that occurred was a possibility, it was not probable and the

---

[6] 1999 S.C. 420.
[7] 1943 S.C. (H.L.) 3.
[8] [1951] A.C. 850.

defendants were entitled to ignore the risk. On the other hand in *Lamond v Glasgow Corporation*,[9] liability did arise when the pursuer was struck by a golf ball when walking down a public path. On average 6,000 balls were struck onto the path per annum so the event was not only possible, but probable. The defenders were under a duty to guard against this foreseeable event and, having taken no precautions they were in breach.

Nature of harm

11–09 A duty of care only arises in respect of the type of harm that is foreseeable, so if property damage is foreseeable and personal injury occurs then there will be no duty since there was only a duty to guard against property harm. The defender is not liable for consequences that are not the foreseeable results of his conduct. This will not, however, enable liability to be avoided where the harm that occurs is greater than could have been foreseen, but is, nevertheless, of the foreseeable type or where the precise chain of events that led to the harm was unforeseeable. This was established in *Hughes v Lord Advocate*[10] in which a boy was severely burned when a paraffin lamp left unattended by workmen, was knocked over by the boy and his friend as they investigated an open manhole. The paraffin vaporised before igniting making the injuries more severe than might have been anticipated. In addition, the pursuer takes his victim as he finds him. In *McKillen v Barclay Curle*[11] a duty of care in respect of personal injury was breached and the pursuer suffered a broken rib. The defenders were liable for this, but they were also liable for the consequent reactivation of the pursuer's tuberculosis. This was an unforeseeable consequence of their neglect, but it was still personal injury and the defenders were accordingly liable.

The standard of care

11–10 The question, how much care, or what particular precautions ought to have been taken for the duty to have been fulfilled is addressed by determining the standard of care. There is no absolute standard, the degree of care required will vary according to the circumstances and depends upon the interaction of elements of the risk. One is the likelihood of harm, the other is the potential magnitude of harm. In other words, how probable is it that harm will follow and if it does, how badly will people be injured or what will be the extent of property damage? The highest degree of care is required where there is a high probability of severe injury or major property damage. A less exacting standard of care may be required where the risk of harm is relatively low and harm, if it materialises will not be so serious. Greater care will be required if the probability of harm is relatively low, but any harm will be serious or if there is a high probability of less serious harm.

In *Latimer v AEC Ltd*[12] an employee was injured when he slipped on a factory floor. There had been a flood making the floor slippery and sawdust had been spread to make it safe. The injury occurred on an uncovered part of the floor. The plaintiff argued that the factory should have been closed down, but it was held that, given the small danger to which he was exposed when weighed against the expense and disadvantage of closing the factory, the defendants had done all a reasonable employer would have done in the circumstances. Therefore, there was no breach of duty.

The standard of care in all cases is that of the reasonable person in the circumstances. This is an objective standard so no account is taken of the individual characteristics of the

---

[9] 1968 S.L.T. 291.
[10] 1963 S.C. (H.L.) 31.
[11] 1967 S.L.T. 41.
[12] [1953] A.C. 643.

defender. Thus, in *Nettleship v Weston*[13] it was held that the standard of care incumbent on a learner, was no different from that expected of an experienced driver. To succeed in a claim, the pursuer must show that the defender exercised less care than would have been exercised by the reasonable person in the defender's position: e.g. the reasonable builder; the reasonable neurosurgeon; the reasonable bus driver and so on.

Individual characteristics of the victim, on the other hand, may be relevant. In *Paris v Stepney Borough Council*[14] an employee who was blind in one eye, lost his sight completely in an accident at work. Had he been provided with safety goggles he would have been protected. It was not at the time standard practice to provide safety goggles for the work carried out by the plaintiff and so, had the same injury occurred to one of his workmates it is unlikely that the defendants would have been found in breach of duty. However, because the risk was of especially severe harm to the plaintiff, a higher standard of care was owed him and his employers were liable.

A deviation from standard practice may indicate breach of duty, but not necessarily. The pursuer in *Brown v Rolls Royce*[15] maintained that his employers ought to have provided a barrier cream, which would have protected him against dermatitis. The provision of this cream was standard practice in the industry. The claim was successfully defended. Rolls Royce had sought expert advice in the process of reaching the decision that the cream was not to be provided. They had been advised that the cream would have been ineffective. Having given the matter serious consideration, they had acted as a reasonable employer in the circumstances and so were not in breach of the duty of care they owed the pursuer. Had they neglected, even to have considered provision of the cream, the result might have been different.

The pursuer must specify particular precautions, that ought to have been taken by the defender, to demonstrate how the defender's conduct fell short of the standard. In *Argyll & Clyde Health Board v Strathclyde Regional Council*[16] the essence of the pursuers' case was that the defenders had failed to maintain a water pipe which burst flooding the pursuers' premises. The case failed, because the pursuers' pleadings did not stipulate what maintenance should have been undertaken. Thus there was inadequate specification of the standard of care and the defenders were not given proper notice of the case against them.

Key concepts

- A duty will only arise in respect of foreseeable harm that will probably result if sufficient care is not exercised.
- The degree of care to be exercised, varies according to the circumstances.
- The standard of care is that of the reasonable person in the position of the defender.

Causation

In any claim for damages it is necessary to prove that the loss was caused by the wrong. **11–11** Causation is, therefore, relevant whatever the form taken by *culpa*, but for convenience it is considered here in the context of negligence. There are two elements in the test of

---

[13] [1971] 2 Q.B. 691.
[14] [1951] A.C. 367.
[15] 1960 S.C. (H.L.) 22.
[16] 1988 S.L.T. 381.

causation. First, the breach must be the factual cause of the harm: that is the *causa sine qua non*. The pursuer must be able to say that "but for" the breach the harm would not have resulted.

There are claims that have failed, because it has not been shown that the breach caused the harm.[17]

Barnett v Chelsea and Kensington Hospital Management Committee
[1969] 1 Q.B. 428

A hospital doctor breached a duty, when he failed to see a patient who presented at the hospital during the night with violent vomiting. Following the death of the patient, the claim for damages against the hospital failed, because the patient had arsenic poisoning and would have died anyway. Therefore, the doctor's breach did not cause the harm.

Establishing factual causation is not sufficient for liability. It is also necessary to establish legal causation. In addition to being the *causa sine qua non,* the breach must also be the direct, immediate or effective cause of the harm: that is the *causa causans*. Where harm does not follow immediately on the breach, something may occur which breaks the chain of causation between the factual cause and the legal cause and if the chain is broken, then there is no legal causation and no liability. A novus actus interveniens will break the causal chain. Novus actus interveniens simply means new intervening act. To break the chain this intervening act must be something unforeseeable and independent of the breach.

Consider the following example. As a result of A's negligence, B is injured at work and she is taken to hospital in an ambulance. C is a drunk driver who pulls out in front of the ambulance. B dies in the crash. But for A's negligence, B would not have been in the ambulance and so would not have died. A's negligence is the factual cause of B's death. A's negligence is not, however, the legal cause. The effective cause of death is C's conduct and not A's breach. C's behaviour is not a foreseeable consequence of A's breach, it is a novus actus interveniens, which breaks the causal chain between A's breach and B's death. C, not A, is liable for B's death.

Key concepts

- The breach must be both the factual and legal cause of the harm.
- The causal chain is broken by a novus actus interveniens, occurring between the factual cause and the immediate cause.
- To break the causal chain a novus actus interveniens must be some act or event independent of the breach, rather than a foreseeable consequence of it.

Damages

11–12 The purpose of damages is to repair the loss suffered by the pursuer. The court will seek to restore the pursuer, financially, to the position he or she would have been in had the wrong not occurred. This is known as effecting *restitutio in integrum*. Except in relatively rare

---

[17] *Barnett v Chelsea and Kensington Hospital Management* [1969] 1 Q.B. 428.

circumstances, damages are not intended to penalise the defender. Where liability is established in respect of property harm, the sum of damages will be the cost of repairing or replacing the property.

Where the harm is personal injury, then the pursuer will recover damages in the form of *solatium* in respect of pain and suffering, any disability or impairment incurred and in respect of diminished life expectancy where applicable. He or she may also recover sums in respect of consequential or derivative economic losses such as loss of earnings, outlays and reasonable expenses. Compensation for economic, that is financial losses make up the patrimonial part of the claim. Under the Administration of Justice Act 1982 s.8 a sum of damages may be awarded to pay for relatives' services in looking after the pursuer. Under s.9, of the same Act, relatives may claim a sum in respect of services that the pursuer is no longer able to provide as a consequence of their injuries. This claim is raised under s.6 of the Damages (Scotland) Act 2011 where the victim has died. When the victim dies his or her claim for losses incurred up to the date of death passes to the executor. Future loss of earnings will normally form the major part of the victim's claim, but this claim is lost on death, instead the victim's closest relatives have two types of claim under s.4 of the Damages (Scotland) Act 2011. First, immediate family and any relative actually supported by the victim have a patrimonial claim for loss of support. This effectively replaces the victim's claim for loss of future earnings. Secondly, immediate family members have a *solatium* claim for "loss of society". The elements making up this claim are: distress and anxiety over the suffering of the deceased before death; grief and sorrow caused by the death; and the loss of the benefits of the deceased's company and guidance.

Solatium then, can be seen to refer to intangible forms of loss. *Solatium* is also available in respect of affront to honour and feelings. In *Stevens v Yorkhill Hospital NHS Trust*[18] an award of damages in this form was made to the pursuer, in respect of the unauthorised removal at post mortem and retention of her month old daughter's brain.

In summary, there are different forms of loss that are reparable through damages. The first is patrimonial loss, meaning losses to a person's *patrimonium* or estate. Financial and property losses come under this head. Second, losses for which *solatium* is available are of two types. *Solatium* is available in respect of pain and suffering. It is also available in respect of affront to honour and feelings.

Key concepts

- Damages are available in respect of patrimonial loss.
- Damages in the form of *solatium* are available in respect of pain, suffering and other intangible losses.
- Damages in the form of *solatium* are also available in respect of affront to honour and feelings.

Remoteness

Some losses are too remote from the breach of duty to be recoverable in damages. A line **11–13** has to be drawn between reparable losses and those that are too speculative or remote. For example, through careless driving A knocks B off his motorbike. B suffers a broken leg. This causes him pain and suffering and lost wages for six weeks. It also means B is unable to take a week's holiday he had planned, with consequent loss of enjoyment. Moreover,

---

[18] 2006 S.L.T. 889.

the holiday was B's only chance to meet his perfect partner who goes home at the end of the week to Tierra del Fuego, never again leaving that island. B becomes lonely and depressed, turns to alcohol and dies young with cirrhosis of the liver.

In the long term we can see that A's careless driving has ruined B's entire life. A cannot, however be obliged to repair all these losses. Subject to the observations made above on *Hughes v Lord Advocate* and *McKillen v Barclay Curle*, the rule is that A is liable to pay damages only in respect of reasonably foreseeable losses. This has been discussed recently in *Simmons v British Steel plc*.[19] In this example A would be liable to pay damages in the form of *solatium*, for pain and suffering and also economic costs associated with the injury: that is the loss of wages. It is most unlikely that A would be liable for the lost chance to go on holiday and A would certainly not be liable for the other losses that flow from this.

Personal injury and associated financial costs, ought to have been within A's contemplation as foreseeable consequences of driving undertaken without due care. Some consequent inconvenience to the victim would also be within A's contemplation, although A would not contemplate specifically that the victim would miss a holiday. The victim's failure to enter into a loving relationship, and eventual alcoholism and untimely demise, are not consequences that A ought to have had within his reasonable contemplation, they are not foreseeable consequences and are, therefore, too remote to be reparable.

Financial harm

11–14 The circumstances under which a duty of care arises to avoid causing purely financial harm are strictly limited. Purely financial interests are not, generally, reparable interests in delict. Economic losses ought normally to be pursued in contract or unjustified enrichment.

Three types of financial harm or economic loss may be identified. These are derivative economic loss, secondary economic loss and pure economic loss. Derivative economic losses are recoverable in delict subject to remoteness. Financial harm is derivative when it is consequent on harm to a reparable interest. Hence, the requirement to pay damages in respect of financial costs associated with personal injury or property damage. Secondary economic losses are not recoverable.

Financial harm is secondary when it is consequent on a breach of duty owed to a different party. In *Dynamco v Holland & Hannen & Cubitts*[20] a contractor severed a power cable in breach of a duty owed to the owners of the cable, the electricity supply company. *Dynamco* were unable to recover the financial losses suffered from the break in production consequent on interruption of the power supply. Dynamco's loss was secondary to the primary loss which was to the property of the electric company. Accordingly, the factory owners were unable to recover damages from the negligent party.

Pure economic loss is financial harm that is not associated with any other form of harm, such as personal injury or property damage. Damages in respect of purely financial losses are of course normal in contract and unproblematic in the intentional delicts such as fraud, inducing breach of contract or conspiracy, but the idea that there could be liability for such losses caused negligently took some time to develop. A duty of care, to avoid pure economic loss, will only arise where there is some special relationship of proximity between the parties. Such duties have been recognised in a very limited number of contexts.

[19] 2004 S.C. (H.L.) 94.
[20] 1971 S.C. 257.

Negligent misstatement

Duties of care to avoid pure economic loss may be recognised in two ways. Such a duty **11–15** may arise in the context of negligent misstatement. The classic example of negligent misstatement is where a banker carelessly represents a client as being creditworthy when in fact this is not the case. A party who advances credit to the client, relying on the banker's skill and judgment, may stand to lose substantial sums if the client becomes insolvent. This indeed is what happened in the first case in which the House of Lords recognised that there might, in principle, be a duty of care owed by the bank, *Hedley Byrne v Heller and Partners*. While it was held that a duty might be owed where the bank had assumed responsibility for the financial interests of the party seeking advice, there was no liability in that case since the advice had been given explicitly "without responsibility". The current governing authority on the point is *Henderson v Merrett Syndicates Ltd*.[21] The defender must have assumed responsibility for the financial interests of the pursuer; the defender must know that the pursuer is relying on the professional expertise of the defender; a disclaimer, that is a statement excluding liability, will prevent a duty of care from arising.

Assumptions of responsibility do not require a positive statement to that effect. In *Smith v Eric S Bush* it was held that assumptions of responsibility may be inferred from the relationship between the parties, from conduct, or the terms of any contract between the parties. This view was affirmed in *Royal Bank of Scotland Ltd v Bannerman, Johnstone Maclay*,[22] in which it was held that an assumption of responsibility could be inferred when a statement is made in the knowledge that the recipient is reliant upon its having been made with professional skill. While the party making the statement may avoid undertaking a duty of care by use of a disclaimer, that disclaimer will be subject to the test of reasonableness in s. 16(1) of the Unfair Contract Terms Act 1977. This means that if it is not reasonable in the circumstances to allow the defender to exclude a duty of care, the disclaimer will be given no effect. An example is found in *Bank of Scotland v Fuller Peiser*.[23] Mrs Mackay wanted to buy a hotel. To do this, she required to borrow money from the bank. Before purchase, she had the hotel valued by a firm of surveyors. The surveyors negligently over-valued the hotel. The bank lent the money for the purchase taking a standard security over the property. When Mrs Mackay defaulted on the loan, the bank called in the security. The proceeds of the sale of the hotel did not cover the sums outstanding on the loan. The bank sued the surveyors to recover their losses. Did the surveyors owe the bank a duty of care in respect of economic losses arising from their negligent misstatement? The surveyors had known that the bank would rely on their expertise, but they had inserted a disclaimer into their contract with Mrs Mackay, to the effect that they "accepted no responsibility to any party other than the client". Was this disclaimer effective to prevent a duty of care to the bank arising? The disclaimer was subjected to the reasonableness test in the Unfair Contract Terms Act. In circumstances where the parties were of equal bargaining power, the term was held to be reasonable. The bank had the resources to instruct an independent survey had they wished. Accordingly, no duty of care was owed the bank by the surveyors.

Where there is no assumption of responsibility this does not necessarily mean there is no duty. In the absence of an assumption, *Caparo* rules may be applied to determine whether a duty of care may be recognised.

---

[21] [1995] 2 A.C. 145.
[22] 2003 S.C. 125.
[23] 2002 S.L.T. 574.

Key concepts

- Derivative economic loss is reparable.
- Secondary economic loss is not reparable.
- Pure economic loss caused negligently is reparable only where a duty to avoid it is recognised either under *Henderson v Merrett* rules or *Caparo v Dickman* rules.

Duty of solicitors to disappointed beneficiaries

11–16 A duty of care not to cause financial harm has been recognised in the context of negligence in the drafting of wills. In *White v Jones*,[24] the House of Lords followed an earlier ruling in the Court of Appeal and held that a solicitor owed a duty of care to persons who would have benefited under a will, had it not been for the solicitor's negligence. This was affirmed in Scots law in *Holmes v Bank of Scotland*.[25] The principles that operate are no different from those applicable in negligent misstatement.

Junior Books liability

11–17 A defect in heritable property, which is not dangerous and which does not harm other property, arising for example, through a negligently performed contract, is not property damage, but pure economic loss. When damages are sought to put right any such defect, the remedy should be pursued in contract. Exceptionally, however, damages may be available in delict. This may prove useful where the pursuer has had no contract with the negligent party. This is a special form of liability for pure economic loss which arises from *Junior Books v the Veitchi Co Ltd*.[26]

Junior Books v the Veitchi Co Ltd
1982 S.C. (H.L.) 244

Junior Books contracted with Ogilvie Builders for refurbishment of their premises. Junior Books nominated Veitchi as a subcontractor to lay the floor. The floor when laid was defective. Junior Books sought damages to cover the costs of having the floor lifted and replaced. The action was successful. In order to recover damages in such circumstances, there are strict requirements that must be met. The parties must be linked by a series of contracts operating concurrently. In this case, Junior Books' contract with Ogilvie was operating at the same time as Ogilvie's contract with Veitchi. The defender must know the identity of the pursuer and must also know that the pursuer will suffer economic loss as a result of negligent performance of the defender's contract with the linking party, in this case Veitchi's contract with Ogilvie.

Mental harm

11–18 While in the context of employment an employer is under a duty of care not to cause stress to employees, the aspect of mental harm, with which we are concerned here, is psychiatric damage arising from some horrific, or frightening event caused by the defender's

---

[24] [1995] 2 A.C. 207.
[25] 2002 S.L.T. 544.
[26] 1982 S.C. (H.L.) 244.

negligence. Psychiatric damage must be in the form of some recognised condition. In *Simpson v ICI*[27] post traumatic stress disorder, was held to be a condition that enabled the rules on psychiatric harm to be brought into play.

In addressing the question whether a duty of care is owed in respect of psychiatric harm, the first stage in analysis is to determine whether the pursuer is a primary or secondary victim. A primary victim is a person who has suffered mental injury as a result of being in some immediate bodily danger. A secondary victim is a person who has been in no such danger themselves, but who has suffered mental injury as a result of witnessing something that has happened to another person, that other person being the primary victim. The distinction is important, because the rules that apply are quite different.

On the authority of *Page v Smith*,[28] primary victims are able to recover damages, provided it can be shown that their condition has resulted from breach of a duty owed to them to avoid causing personal injury. Thus, with primary victims, psychiatric harm is treated simply as a form of personal injury. Secondary victims, by contrast, will not succeed, unless they satisfy a number of special proximity requirements.

In the case of secondary victims, the governing principle, laid down in *Bourhill v Young*,[29] is that no duty will be owed to any victim unless psychiatric harm is a reasonably foreseeable consequence of the defender's negligence. This rule operates in conjunction with three proximity requirements that were laid down in the Hillsborough disaster case, *Alcock v Chief Constable of South Yorkshire*.[30] Where the pursuer is a secondary victim, they must show close ties of love and affection to the primary victim. The secondary victim must be present at the event or its immediate aftermath. The secondary victim must have perceived the event directly, it is not sufficient if the event has been viewed on television, heard about on the radio or where the pursuer has been informed of the event by another party.

In applying these requirements, the courts have taken a restrictive approach to liability. Many actions brought by secondary victims have failed, because there has been no link between the secondary and primary victim sufficient to suggest close ties of love and affection. While such ties can be presumed in the cases of, for example, parent and child or spouses, with other relationships, such as those between brothers in law, the strength of the relationship requires to be proved.

The present rules on recovery of damages by secondary victims are not thought to be satisfactory. The courts have, in cases such as *Salter v UB Frozen and Chilled Foods* and *Anderson v Christian Salvesen,* demonstrated a little flexibility in allowing persons who were not themselves in danger to recover as primary victims.

Key concepts

- In claims for damages for psychiatric harm it is first necessary to determine whether the pursuer is a primary or secondary victim.
- A primary victim will recover damages if a duty owed him or her to avoid personal injury is breached.
- Secondary victims must satisfy *Alcock* rules before damages will be recoverable.

---

[27] 1983 S.L.T. 601.
[28] [1996] A.C. 155.
[29] 1942 S.C. (H.L.) 78.
[30] [1992] 1 A.C. 310.

Contribution

11–19 A claim for damages can be defended on grounds that the harm was attributable, not only to the defender's negligence, but was at least partly the fault of the pursuer. Where the pursuer's fault is established this has the effect of reducing the sum of damages awarded by a proportion to reflect the pursuer's contribution. The court must determine the total amount that would have been payable, had there been no contribution, then apportion blame. The rules are set out in the Law Reform (Contributory Negligence) Act 1945.

Volenti non fit injuria

11–20 Volenti, where established, is a complete defence to an action for damages. Volenti non fit injuria, means no harm is done to one who is consenting. Volenti can be a difficult defence to establish. It will only operate where it can be shown that the injured party has knowingly and willingly consented to run a risk. This defence was successful in *Morris v Murray*,[31] in which two friends took off in a light aircraft following a period of heavy drinking. The claim brought by the injured passenger against the pilot's estate failed. The plaintiff had knowingly assented to the risk of flying with a drunken pilot. The same point would not apply to a passenger who gets into a car with a drunk driver. This is because the defence of volenti is disapplied from situations involving road vehicles by s.149 of the Road Traffic Act 1988.

VICARIOUS LIABILITY

11–21 Vicarious liability means that where a person causes harm wrongfully in the course of their employment, the employer may be sued in addition to the person at fault, even though the employer is personally blameless. If liability is established, the employer will then be liable to pay damages. Any such sum paid may in principle be recovered by the employer from the delinquent employee, but in practice the employee may not be in a position to meet any such demand. Vicarious liability also arises in the contexts of agency and partnership.

Employers cannot be held liable for every delict committed by employees. For vicarious liability to arise, the delictual act or omission must be connected in some way with employment. The most recent authoritative formulation of a test for vicarious liability is the sufficient connection test established by the *House of Lords in Lister v Hesley Hall Ltd*.[32] In that case a local authority was held vicariously liable, when a warden of a care home was found to have abused children in local authority care. It can be seen that vicarious liability operates, not only in respect of negligence, but also for intentional wrongs.

The sufficient connection test means that every case has to be determined on its own circumstances. Prior to *Lister*, courts sought to draw distinctions according to rules laid down in *Kerr v NCB*. In this approach, courts have had to distinguish between unauthorised acts done within the scope of employment, for which the employer would be vicariously liable, and acts outwith the scope of employment altogether, for which there was no vicarious liability. This was always a difficult distinction to draw and the case law tends to show a strong inclination towards findings of vicarious liability. The reason is that vicarious liability gives pursuers a defender worth suing. Employers are, in general, more likely than employees to have the funds or the insurance to meet a claim for damages.

---

[31] [1991] 2 Q.B. 6.
[32] [2001] 2 W.L.R. 1311.

Despite *Lister* the *Kirby* rules appear not to have been completely superseded and legal argument may still proceed on the question of whether an act is within the scope of employment.

STATUTORY LIABILITY

Acts of Parliament may impose their own liability regimes. Liability may be absolute **11–22** meaning that a breach of statutory duty will entail liability with no possibility of a defence. More often, liability is strict meaning that pursuers do not have to prove fault, but there are nevertheless defences that may be established.

An example of strict liability is found in the Consumer Protection Act 1987 s.2(1) which makes producers liable where "any damage is caused wholly or partly by a defect in a product". A further example is found in the Animals (Scotland) Act 1987.

Some Acts stipulate that no civil liability is to arise from a breach. An example is found in s.47 of the Health and Safety at Work Act 1974. Where an Act is silent on whether civil liability arises from breach of a statutory duty, it becomes necessary to determine Parliament's intention by construing the provision. Courts will consider the whole Act, the pre-existing law, the scope and purpose of the Act and for whose benefit the duty was intended.

Cutler v Wandsworth Stadium Ltd
[1949] A.C. 398

A bookmaker raised an action for damages claiming the operators of a dog track were in breach of s.11(2) of the Betting and Lotteries Act 1934. This provision imposed on the operators a duty to make space on the track available for bookmakers. In the House of Lords, the view was taken that the purpose of the provision was to regulate the way in which places of amusement were to be managed for the public benefit, rather than for the benefit of individual bookmakers. Accordingly, the breach of duty did not make the operators civilly liable to bookmakers.

Liability for animals

Section 1 of the Animals (Scotland) Act 1987, imposes liability on the keepers of dan- **11–23** gerous animals and foraging animals. The keeper of an animal will normally be the owner or person in possession of the animal. Section 5 clarifies situations where the identity of the keeper might otherwise have been unclear so, for example s.5(1)(a) provides that where an animal is owned by a child under the age of 16, the keeper is the person with actual care and control of the child. Under s.5(2)(b) where an animal is abandoned, the person with ownership or possession at the time of abandonment, remains the keeper until some other person acquires the animal.

Liability under the Act extends to two types of harm, caused by two different groups of animals: first, animals that are likely to attack persons or livestock; and second, animals that are likely to cause property harm by foraging. The keeper is strictly liable in the event that a dangerous animal severely injures, or kills, persons or other animals. Provided the requirements of s.1 are met, there is no burden on pursuers to show *culpa*. Section 1(3)(a) extends the coverage of the Act, not only to dangerous animals, but also to dogs of whatever breed. The keeper is also strictly liable in the event that a foraging animal, such as a sheep, horse or pig causes material damage to property.

There is no liability under the Act if a foraging animal causes injury, or a dangerous animal, or dog, causes property harm, so liability under the Act will not arise where somebody is bitten by a sheep or their vegetable patch is dug up by a dog. In such cases, it will be necessary to seek reparation under the common law. An example of the application of the Act is found in *Fairlie v Carruthers*.[33] The pursuer had been knocked to the ground by the defender's retriever and injured. Her claim based on the Act failed, because the injury was not the result of an attack, but an accident caused by a dog being boisterous. The claim grounded on the common law also failed, as no negligence on the part of the defender could be proved.

Defences available under the Act are provided in s.2. For example it is a defence if the injury or damage is wholly attributable to the fault of the pursuer. The defence of volenti non fit injuria is made available in s.2(1)(b).

Occupiers' liability

11–24 Section 2 of the Occupiers' Liability (Scotland) Act 1960, imposes on the occupiers of land or premises a duty to take reasonable care to avoid injury or damage "in respect of dangers which are due to the state of the premises or to anything to be done or omitted to be done on them." Thus, there is a statutory duty to take reasonable care to ensure that land and buildings are kept in a safe condition. The coverage of the Act extends, however, under s.1(3)(a), to fixed or movable structures including vessels, vehicles and aircraft. Accordingly, any injury suffered by a passenger due to some defect in the bus, plane or other mode of transport will give rise to liability under the Act provided negligence can be established.

In determining to whom a duty is owed, the common law continues to apply by virtue of s.1(2) thus the duty is owed to persons whose presence on the property is foreseeable and is not restricted to persons with a right to be on the land. The duty extends to trespassers, provided their presence is foreseeable. The party upon whom the duty is imposed is the occupier. For purposes of the Act this may be the owner, but if the premises are let, or are in the control of some other party. then the occupier will be the person with effective control such as the tenant. If property is unoccupied during building work, then the builder with control of the premises will be the occupier.

Liability under the Act may be excluded by use of a disclaimer in the form of a contractual or non-contractual notice, but such disclaimers will normally be subject to the test of reasonableness in the Unfair Contract Terms Act and any attempt to exclude liability, for death or personal injury, will be void under s.16 of that Act.

Since the Act requires reasonable care to be taken, it is necessary for pursuers to prove negligence. The fact that harm has occurred, is not sufficient for liability. If a building is locked or a danger is fenced, for example, any person who has broken into the building or climbed the fence, before encountering the danger, will be hard put to establish liability. Moreover, the defence of volenti non fit injuria available under s.2(3) means that where someone has had to overcome an obvious hurdle to get to a danger, they may be deemed to have consented to the risk, provided they are of a sufficient age where they ought to have appreciated there might be a risk.

---

[33] 1996 S.L.T. (Sh Ct) 56.

> ### Devlin v Strathclyde Regional Council
> #### 1993 S.L.T. 699
>
> A 14-year-old boy died while playing a game of tig on the roof of a school building. A duty of care was owed to the boy and his friends whose presence on the roof was foreseeable. However, since they had had to climb a wall and use a drainpipe to get up onto the roof, it was held that the occupiers were not in breach of their duty. The boys were old enough to appreciate the dangers of playing on a roof and so were deemed to have consented to the risk. Had the roof been accessible to a three-year-old who had fallen from it, then the result might well have gone a different way.

Where there is negligence by the defender, but the pursuer is old enough to appreciate the risk he or she undertakes there may be a reduction in damages for contributory negligence. Thus, in *McLeod v British Railways Board*,[34] an award of damages of £250,000 was reduced to £200,000 when a 12-year-old boy spent nine months in hospital with burns after falling on power cables carrying 25,000 volts. His contribution to the harm was assessed at 20 per cent.

ASSAULT AND HARASSMENT

Damages are available in civil law for assault. The same act may, therefore, incur both **11–25** criminal and civil liability. There is a difference in the standard of proof. In a criminal action guilt must be established beyond reasonable doubt, whereas in a civil case proof can be established on the balance of probabilities. The latter is a lower standard of proof, so there may be cases in which a civil action would succeed where a criminal conviction will fail. *Mullan v Anderson No.2*[35] is an example in which a man who had been found not proven on a murder charge was found civilly liable to the family of the victim whom he had killed with a knife.

Clearly assault may be established by a physical attack. However, it is important to note that physical contact is not a necessary requirement for liability. Some older authorities such as *Cock v Neville*,[36] show that threats and abuse are sufficient to found a claim for damages. *Tullis v Glenday*[37] and *Ewing v Earl of Mar*[38] both demonstrate that damages are available where a person has been spat at, the latter case showing that immediate fear of hostile or objectionable physical contact is actionable. The defender had ridden his horse at the pursuer. Assault then, encompasses not just objectionable physical contact, but also affront to dignity more generally. Self defence affords a defence to an action, but the defender must show that the force used was proportionate to the violence or threat of violence used by the pursuer. Provocation is not a complete defence, but damages may be reduced to reflect any degree of provocation. In *Ross v Bryce*[39] damages were reduced by 50 per cent to reflect the fact that the pursuer had provoked the assault through verbal abuse and kicking the defender's dog.

Where a person apprehends harassment, then technically it remains competent to seek

---

[34] 2001 S.C. 534.
[35] 1997 S.L.T. 93.
[36] (1797) Hume 602.
[37] (1834) 13 S. 698.
[38] (1851) 14 D. 314, 330.
[39] 1972 S.L.T. (Sh. Ct.) 76.

caution for lawburrows. This means that the delinquent must lodge a sum of money in court, which will be forfeit in the event that the terms of the lawburrows are breached. This, however, is an ancient remedy and nowadays a victim of harassment is much more likely to seek protection under the Protection from Harassment Act 1997. Sections 8–11 of this Act apply in Scotland. The Act confers upon every individual the right not to be harassed. While harassment is not statutorily defined, in order to be actionable under the Act, the behaviour complained of must amount to a course of conduct, so the Act provides no remedy in respect of one-off events with the sole exception of domestic abuse. Non-domestic abuse on a single occasion may, however, amount to assault giving rise to an action for damages at common law.

Damages are available under the Act in respect of anxiety and any financial loss, where harassment is established. Employers may be held vicariously liable where harassment takes place at work as was the case under the equivalent English provisions in *Majrowski v Guy's and St Thomas's NHS Trust*.[40] An interdict or a non-harassment order may be sought from the court where future harassment is apprehended. These remedies are mutually exclusive, the court will not award both and will not award a non-harassment order if an interdict would suffice. Breach of a non-harassment order is a criminal offence, punishable by fine or imprisonment or both. The police have powers of arrest without warrant. Section 8(4) provides that an action brought under the Act may be defended on grounds that: the conduct was authorised by law; was pursued for purposes of detecting crime; or was, in the particular circumstances reasonable.

Key concepts

- Assault is not restricted to offensive physical contact, but includes threats of such contact and offences to dignity.
- Self-defence affords a defence to a claim, but the force used must be proportionate.
- Provocation is not a defence, but may serve to reduce damages.
- Harassment involves a course of offensive conduct except in cases of domestic abuse where a single instance will give rise to a claim.

NUISANCE

11–26 The reparable interest protected by the law of nuisance, is the right to comfortable enjoyment of heritable property free from serious disturbance, substantial inconvenience or material harm. Nuisance, therefore, is concerned with interferences with people's use of land. This may mean their homes, but industrial and commercial premises are also protected as is agricultural land.

Classically the law of nuisance has been invoked where premises have been rendered unusable, or at least unpleasant by smoke or smells, noise, heat or vibration from engines or building operations. More recently, nuisance has been invoked in cases where there has been some positive action resulting in the withdrawal of support from a building, as in *Kennedy v Glenbelle*,[41] which concerned the removal of a supporting wall in a ground floor flat in a tenement building. Where nuisance is established, damages are available not only

---

[40] [2006] UKHL 34.
[41] 1996 S.C. 95.

in respect of physical harm to property, but injury to health and economic harm is also reparable. It must be remembered that the restrictions on the recovery of damages for economic loss, that apply where such loss is caused negligently, are not applicable in cases where the loss is caused intentionally, that is through deliberate action rather than as the consequence of a failure to take care.

In *Shanlin v Collins*,[42] the pursuer was awarded damages in respect of nervous debility suffered as a long term consequence of her neighbour's dogs barking. In *The Globe v North of Scotland Water Authority*,[43] the pursuers were allowed to go to proof before answer, in an action brought to recover business losses, when road works outside a pub premises persisted over a period of nine months. Damages are also available to compensate for diminution in the value of premises consequent upon nuisance.

Nuisance gives rise to an obligation to effect abatement. It may also give rise to an obligation to make reparation. Interdict may be sought to end a continuing state of affairs amounting to nuisance, or to prevent prospective nuisance from arising. Where the claim is for interdict, the pursuer must establish nuisance. Where the claim is for damages, the pursuer must establish nuisance plus *culpa*.

Establishing nuisance

The criteria on which nuisance is established, is that a situation is more than the com- **11–27** plainer ought reasonably to tolerate in the circumstances. This is known as the *plus quam tolerabile* test for nuisance. This mechanism derives from a dictum of Lord President Cooper in *Watt v Jamieson*,[44] which serves as a definitive statement on Scots common law nuisance.

> ### Watt v Jamieson
> #### 1954 S.C. 56
>
> "If any person so uses his property as to occasion serious disturbance or substantial inconvenience to his neighbour or material damage to his neighbour's property, it is in the general case irrelevant to plead merely that he was making a normal and familiar use of his own property. The balance in all such cases has to be held between the freedom of a proprietor to use his property as he pleases and the duty on a proprietor not to inflict material loss or inconvenience on adjoining proprietors and adjoining property; and in every case the answer depends on considerations of fact and degree ... The critical question is whether what he was exposed to was *plus quam tolerabile* when due weight has been given to all the surrounding circumstances of the offensive conduct and its effects."

In determining whether harm is sufficiently intolerable, to amount to nuisance, courts have regard to a variety of factors. All relevant circumstances will be taken into account, since it must be remembered that a state of affairs is only ever a nuisance in the particular circumstances. In all cases, the harm must be shown to be material, trivial disturbances will not count as nuisance. The extent, nature and duration of the harm or disturbance must be established. Not all neighbourhoods are the same, a degree of disturbance that is normal and not sufficient to amount to nuisance in the centre of Glasgow, might be

---

[42] 1973 S.L.T. (Sh Ct) 21.
[43] 2000 S.L.T. 674.
[44] 1954 S.C. 56.

intolerable in a village in the Outer Isles. It will be harder to establish, say noise nuisance in a noisy neighbourhood, but even though noise may be a feature of a given locality, this does not entitle anybody to make a material increase in existing levels of disturbance.

The law seeks to protect the reasonable occupier of premises, so if it can be shown that the pursuer is unduly sensitive, this will tend against a finding of nuisance. This was the case in *Simpson v Millar*,[45] in which the occupier of a tenement flat complained of disturbance from a baker's dough mixing machine on the ground floor. Some of the evidence was inconclusive, but the noise and vibration from the machine was found, by some witnesses, to be imperceptible and the pursuer was adjudged to be of an especially nervous disposition. The claim failed. The courts may also have regard to the broader social value of both the activities interfered with and complained of. Finally, the ability of pursuers to take simple protective measures to minimise disturbance and of defenders to remedy matters may be relevant factors for consideration.

While reasonable behaviour does not afford a defence, the reasonableness, or otherwise, of the defender's land use and conduct is a factor that may have a strong bearing on the outcome, when the *plus quam tolerabile* test is applied. Malicious use of property, with the intention of spiting a neighbour, may give rise to an action *in aemulationem vicini,* in which the burden of proving malice falls on the pursuer.

A finding of nuisance is sufficient to entitle the complainer to interdict. The terms of interdict must be framed narrowly, so that defenders will normally be allowed to continue activities, but not in such a way as to give rise to nuisance. This may be effective in prompting defenders to apply remedial measures. Where there is some overwhelming public interest in allowing an activity to continue, pending remedial measures then a final decree of interdict may be postponed. This happened in *Webster v Lord Advocate*.[46] Preparations for the Edinburgh Tattoo created a noise nuisance, but the operation of the interdict was postponed to allow the tattoo to go ahead.

Key concepts

- The right to comfortable enjoyment of property free from serious disturbance, substantial inconvenience or material harm is protected by the law of nuisance.
- Nuisance is established where the disturbance, inconvenience or harm to the victim is more than reasonably tolerable in the circumstances.
- Interdict is the primary remedy.
- Damages in actions grounded on nuisance may be available not only in respect of physical harm but also for injury to health and economic loss.
- Culpa is not required for an interdict, but in an action for damages it is necessary to prove *culpa*.

Establishing culpa

11–28 Where damages are sought, *culpa* must be proved in addition to establishing nuisance. Proof of *culpa* was only finally established as a necessary requirement for a successful claim in damages grounded on nuisance by the House of Lords in *RHM Bakeries (Scotland) Ltd v Strathclyde Regional Council*.[47] The relevant forms of *culpa*, in an action

---

[45] (1923) 39 Sh. Ct. Rep. 182.
[46] 1985 S.C. 173.
[47] 1985 S.C. (H.L.) 17.

for damages grounded on nuisance, are intention and recklessness. To quote Lord President Hope in *Kennedy v Glenbelle, culpa* may be relevantly averred in terms of: "a deliberate act done in the knowledge that harm would be the likely result".

Claims for damages are most likely to arise where there has been actual physical harm to property, such as resettlement of a building following a withdrawal of support or where premises have been flooded. The question may arise, whether a claim for damages should be grounded upon either nuisance or negligence. The answer will depend on the form in which it is intended to aver *culpa*. Following Lord President Hope's discussion on *culpa* in *Kennedy v Glenbelle,* damages for harm arising from a failure to take care, in circumstances where care is required, ought to be pursued according to the ordinary rules of negligence. In such a case, it will be necessary to aver a duty of care and breach of that duty. Where harm arises from deliberate conduct carried out in the knowledge that harm to neighbouring property would result, then the action may proceed according to the rules of nuisance. Nuisance must first be established. A deliberate act, done in the knowledge that harm would result, is an intentional or reckless act. Knowledge is viewed constructively, that is the court is less concerned with the individual defender's state of knowledge regarding harmful consequences, than with what the reasonable defender ought to have known. This point is apparent in *Kennedy v Glenbelle*, but was confirmed in the subsequent case of *Anderson v White*.[48]

Culpa in nuisance may also be established where a state of affairs in the control of defenders is allowed to persist, despite the defender's knowledge of continuing harm. This is another slant on intentional wrongdoing. In *Powrie Castle Properties v Dundee City Council*,[49] the pursuers were able to recover the costs of making the gable end of a building watertight. The council had had an adjoining building demolished. The contractors had failed to proof the exposed gable against the elements and the pursuers' property had suffered ingress of water. The defenders had been made aware of this state of affairs, but had taken no action.

Finally, if especially hazardous works are instructed and neighbouring property is damaged, then defenders cannot evade liability on the basis that they instructed a competent contractor to carry out the operation. This aspect of *culpa* in nuisance can be seen in *Noble's Trustees v Economic Forestry*.[50]

TRESPASS

The view, that there is no such thing as trespass in Scots law is a myth. Landowners have the **11–29** right to exclusive possession of property and where it is anticipated that this right will be invaded, then interdict is available to prevent unjustifiable intrusions. Trespass refers to temporary intrusions: permanent intrusions such as a wall that extends onto a neighbour's land are encroachments. Damages for trespass will not be available, unless there is some form of tangible loss incurred. In practice, where damages have been sought, the harm tends to have been caused by straying animals and rules on liability for animals have been applied.

Interdict may be awarded, where there is reasonable apprehension that trespass will occur in the future, and will be refused where there are no grounds to anticipate a future occurrence. For example in *Hay's Trustees v Young*,[51] a neighbour had trespassed in order to gather evidence for a court case. Since there was no reason to anticipate a repeat trespass

---

[48] 2000 S.L.T. 37.
[49] 2001 S.C.L.R. 146.
[50] 1988 S.L.T. 662.
[51] (1877) 4 R. 398.

interdict was refused. Interdict is personal and only effective against named persons. This means that it can be used by employers to prevent occupation of company premises during an industrial dispute, since they will be able to identify their workforce by name, but in general interdict is only truly effective in respect of identifiable repeat trespassers.

The scope for protecting property against trespass has become limited with the coming into force of the Land Reform (Scotland) Act 2003. This Act provides everybody with statutory rights of access to land. Section 1 provides two distinct rights. The first is to be on land for specified purposes of recreation, educational activities or commercial enterprises. The second is the right to cross land. These rights only exist to the extent that they are exercised responsibly.

Some types of land are excluded from statutory access rights under s.6 and certain activities are excluded under s.9. The Act has a significant effect on the law of trespass. In any action for interdict, it will have to be established whether the alleged trespass is an exercise of statutory rights or not. Under s.28 the sheriff has power to determine questions regarding the exercise of these rights and it may be doubted whether interdict, at common law, will be granted without the statutory mechanism for determining access rights having first been employed.

Key concepts

- The right to exclusive possession of property is protected by the law of trespass.
- Interdict will only be available where there is reasonable apprehension of future trespass.
- Land is now subject to access rights under the Land Reform (Scotland) Act 2003.

DEFAMATION

11–30   The reparable interest in honour and reputation is protected by the law of defamation. Defamation normally consists in objectionable words, written or spoken, that have the effect of damaging reputation. In determining whether the words complained of are defamatory reference is often made to a dictum of Lord Atkin in *Sim v Stretch*[52]: "Would the words tend to lower the plaintiff in the estimation of right thinking members of society generally?" Thus, if a person is wrongly described as corrupt, or a thief, or a child molester, that would be defamatory. Lord Atkin's dictum has the disadvantage that it doesn't work terribly well where bodies, such as corporations, partnerships or unincorporated associations are defamed yet such bodies do have reputations which they are quite entitled to protect at law.

A statement may be defamatory on the face of it or it may bear a defamatory meaning. This is known as innuendo. A newspaper article reporting that a portrait by Raeburn has been stolen from the law school and that the Dean has ample hanging space on his living room wall might be read to suggest that the Dean had stolen the painting. It would be for the Dean to contend that the article contained a defamatory innuendo and the question to be addressed is that laid down in *Duncan v Associated Scottish Newspapers*[53] by Lord Anderson: "what meaning would the ordinary reader of the newspaper put upon the paragraph which the pursuer complained of?"

---

[52] [1936] All E.R. 1237.
[53] 1929 S.C. 14.

To be defamatory words must be seriously intended or heard or understood to be so. For this reason vulgar abuse and sarcasm are not actionable though a course of such behaviour might amount to harassment. Words spoken in the heat of the moment in the course of an argument similarly are either not actionable or may invoke the old defence of *in rixa*. Where words are defamatory the pursuer may seek damages. *Solatium* may be granted for affront and, where there is financial loss, for example where the reputation of a business has been defamed, there may be a patrimonial award also. Interdict is an important remedy in defamation to prevent words from being published or spread further.

Defences

A defamatory statement is by definition a false statement and is presumed to be made **11–31** maliciously. An action may therefore be defended on the grounds that the statement is true. It is for the defender to prove truth, not for the pursuer to prove falsity. This defence is known as *veritas*, it is called justification in English law. Where it is comment rather than fact that is objected to, the relevant defence is fair comment. To say that the food served in a restaurant is under-cooked and that service is slow are statements of fact, These statements are either true or they are not though there is a question of degree in both cases. Stating that the restaurant offers a terrible night out is comment. It is a statement of opinion based on the facts of under cooked food and slow service. So long as the comment is based on facts truly stated; so long as sufficient facts are given to allow readers to draw their own conclusions whether comments are justified; and provided the issue is a matter of some public interest, comments are defensible. Considerable freedom is given to comment made on matters of public interest, This includes reviews as well as news articles. Comments may be scathing, they do not have to be reasonable. Of course, the defender may be called upon to prove the truth of the alleged facts and if unable to do so the defence will fail.

Some statements enjoy absolute privilege. Where this applies any action for defamation is irrelevant. Thus witnesses, cannot be sued for anything said in evidence in court. Absolute privilege covers anything said in Parliament whether Westminster or Edinburgh, the proceedings of parliamentary committees and most participants in legal proceedings but not the parties to a civil action. Qualified privilege arises where a person makes a statement in response to a duty to do so and the statement is made to a person with an interest in receiving the statement. The duty may be social or moral, it does not have to be a legal duty. If a potentially defamatory complaint is made against a person this will be protected by qualified privilege, but only where the complaint is addressed through the proper channels, for example through a complaints or grievance procedure at work or to the police if the allegation involves crime. Qualified privilege is not a complete defence, it has the effect or removing the presumption of malice, principally because there is a better explanation why the statement was made at all, that is in pursuance of a duty. Where qualified privilege applies the pursuer must prove the defender acted with malice. This can be established in two ways. Either the defender acted maliciously out of spite which may be hard to prove or, the defender did not believe in the truth of the allegation. In *Fraser v Mirza*[54] a police officer was awarded damages against a person who had accused the officer of racially motivated behaviour. The accusation had been made in a letter of complaint to the officer's chief constable and so it was protected by qualified privilege. The court found that the defender had no honest belief in the truth of his accusation and had therefore acted maliciously.

The *Reynolds* defence operates to protect the publication of stories where there is a

[54] 1993 S.C. (H.L.) 27.

considerable public interest in being informed. This defence originates in *Reynolds v Times Newspapers*.[55] This case was brought by the former Toiseach of the Republic of Ireland, the offending article had published details of the reasons for his resignation. The newspaper sought some protection against being sued for defamation in respect of political information that was of clear and immediate public interest. What has emerged is a defence of responsible journalism. It has been affirmed by the House of Lords in *Jameel v Wall Street Journal*[56] that where the defence applies it cannot be overturned by proof of malice. In *Reynolds* Lord Nicholls established a list of the factors to be taken into consideration in determining whether the defence applies. These factors include the seriousness of the allegations and the tone in which they are reported. Are allegations reported as such or are they presented as established fact? The defender may have to demonstrate the steps taken to verify the information and the reliability of the source. It may help if the article is presented in a balanced way, if the pursuer has been approached for comment and if his or her side of the story is also reported. This defence operates to protect the publication of material which ought to be in the public domain, but where perhaps it has not been possible or there has not been time to establish the absolute truth of all the material.

Liability in defamation arises every time a defamatory allegation is published or repeated. Liability moreover may arise when defamation is innocent. The classic case for innocent defamation is *Hulton v Jones*,[57] This case involved the serialisation in a periodical of a fictitious story in which one Artemus Jones engaged in immoral behaviour. Specifically he went to France with a lady who was not his wife. The real Artemus Jones was a barrister on his way to becoming a judge. He convinced the court that readers of the periodical would understand the story as referring to him and was awarded substantial damages. Whether this defamation was really innocent is open to question since Jones had previously been employed at the same periodical that published the story. Some protections are now in place for the benefit of those with little or no responsibility for the dissemination of defamatory statements. Section 1(1) of the Defamation Act 1996 provides a defence that one is not the author, editor or publisher of a defamatory statement, took reasonable care in the circumstances and did not know or have reason to believe that they caused or contributed to publication of a defamatory statement. The same Act makes provision for the hapless journalist or newspaper editor who has indeed defamed somebody by providing for an offer of amends to be made to the victim under s.2. Amends are made by correcting the statement, publishing an apology and paying compensation. Legal proceedings end where the offer is accepted although the Act does provide for enforcement. Where the offer is rejected the fact that the offer has been made will serve as a defence precluding the use of other defences.

Key concepts

- Defamatory words are capable of damaging the victim's reputation.
- Defamatory words are presumed to be false, but an action may be defended if the defender proves they are true.
- Objectionable comments or opinions may be defended as fair comment.
- Certain occasions are granted absolute privilege.

---

[55] [2001] 2 A.C. 127.
[56] [2006] UKHL 44.
[57] [1910] A.C. 20.

- Qualified privilege arises when the statement is made under a duty to do so to a relevant person.
- The effect of qualified privilege is to cast on the pursuer the burden of proving malice.
- Where a statement is in the public interest the Reynolds defence may apply where the defender has acted responsibly.
- The Defamation Act 1996 provides a defence for those disseminating statements without responsibility for doing so.
- The Act also provides for an offer of amends to be made to the victim.

▼ CHAPTER SUMMARY

DELICTUAL OBLIGATIONS

1. A delict is a civil wrong consisting of an unjustifiable interference with a reparable **11–32** interest.
2. Delictual obligations arise from wrongdoing. The obligation is to repair the wrong.
3. Wrongs may be repaired by remedies, principally through damages (reparation) or preventing through interdict.
4. Liability for reparation falls under the general principle: *damnum injuria datum.*
5. In claims for reparation, at common law, *culpa* must be proved. Culpa means fault.
6. *Culpa* takes different forms and may be divided broadly into negligence (unintentional fault) and intentional fault.
7. Intentional fault refers to conduct undertaken deliberately in the knowledge that harm would result. Harm need not be the object of the conduct, since motive is not usually relevant.
8. Conduct is negligent where the harm that results is the foreseeable consequence of insufficient care.
9. In claims for interdict, it must be established that a wrong is being done or is apprehended. It is not necessary to prove *culpa.*
10. In claims brought under statute, different requirements for liability may be imposed according to the provisions of the particular Act.

NEGLIGENCE

1. There will be no liability, unless the harm has been caused by a breach of a duty of care and the loss is not too remote.
2. Duties of care are owed to persons whom one ought to think about as being likely to be affected by one's conduct:

   ➢ *Donoghue v Stevenson* (1932): establishes neighbourhood principle.

3. Duties of care are owed only where there is some element of proximity between the parties. Duties are owed only to individuals or to persons within a definite or reasonably narrowly drawn class:

   ➢ *Hill v Chief Constable of West Yorkshire* (1989): example of a case in which no duty was owed for lack of proximity between the parties.

4. **In novel circumstances no duty will be recognised unless the requirements in *Caparo* are satisfied:**

   ➤ *Caparo Industries v Dickman* (1990): harm to the pursuer must have been reasonably foreseeable; there must be a close degree of proximity between the parties; it must be fair just and reasonable to recognise a duty of care. These requirements were satisfied in *Gibson v Chief Constable of Strathclyde* (1999).

5. **A duty will only arise in respect of foreseeable harm that will probably result if sufficient care is not exercised:**

   ➤ *Muir v Glasgow Corporation* (1943): no liability arose where the harmful event was not foreseeable;
   ➤ *Bolton v Stone* (1951): no liability arose where the harmful event was improbable;
   ➤ *Hughes v Lord Advocate* (1963): even though the harm is of greater extent than could have been foreseen, where harm results from breach of duty there will still be liability provided the harm is of the type that was foreseeable;
   ➤ *McKillen v Barclay Curle* (1967): breach of a duty to avoid personal injury will create liability for the full extent of personal injury even though it is greater than could have been foreseen.

6. **The degree of care to be exercised varies according to the circumstances.**
7. **The standard of care is that of the reasonable person in the position of the defender:**

   ➤ *Argyll & Clyde Health Board v Strathclyde Regional Council* (1988): pursuers must specify precisely the care that should have been taken;
   ➤ *Nettleship v Weston* (1971): the standard of care for a learner driver is no different from that expected of an experienced driver;
   ➤ *Latimer v AEC* (1953): there is no breach where the defender has acted as a reasonable person in the defender's position would have done;
   ➤ *Brown v Rolls Royce* (1960): a failure to follow standard procedures is not necessarily evidence of a breach of duty;
   ➤ *Paris v Stepney Borough Council* (1951): more care must be exercised in respect of especially vulnerable persons.

8. **The breach must be both the factual and legal cause of the harm.**
9. **The causal chain is broken by a novus actus interveniens occurring between the factual cause and the immediate cause.**
10. **To break the causal chain, a novus actus interveniens must be some act or event independent of the breach rather than a foreseeable consequence of it:**

    ➤ *Barnett v Chelsea & Kensington Hospital Management Committee* (1969): even though the duty was breached there was no liability since the breach was not the cause of death.

11. **Damages are available in respect of patrimonial loss.**
12. **Damages in the form of *solatium* are available in respect of pain and suffering.**
13. **Damages in the form of *solatium* are also available in respect of affront to honour and feelings:**

    ➤ *Stevens v Yorkhill Hospital NHS Trust* (2006): example of a case in which *solatium* was awarded for affront.

14. **Damages are not available for losses that are too remote:**

> *Simmons v British Steel plc* (2004): the law on this point is clarified and foreseeability is established as the criteria for remoteness.

15. **Derivative economic losses are recoverable in damages provided they are not too remote.**

16. **Secondary economic loss is not recoverable in damages:**

> *Dynamco v Holland & Hannen & Cubitts* (1971): example of secondary loss.

17. **Pure economic loss may be recoverable in a contractual claim or in a claim based on intentional harm. It is recoverable in a claim based on negligence provided either *Henderson* or *Caparo* rules are satisfied.**

> *Henderson v Merrett Syndicates Ltd* (1995): sets out the requirements for a duty of care to avoid causing financial harm by negligent misstatement;
> *Royal Bank of Scotland plc v Bannerman, Johnstone Maclay* (2003): an assumption of responsibility may be inferred from a statement made in the knowledge that the maker's professional skill will be relied upon, by the party to whom it is addressed;
> *Bank of Scotland v Fuller Peiser* (2002): the reasonableness test in Part 2 of the Unfair Contract Terms Act 1977 is applied to a disclaimer seeking to avoid a duty of care arising in respect of a statement;
> *White v Jones* (1995): establishes that a solicitor instructed to draft a will, owes a duty of care to beneficiaries to avoid financial loss;
> *Junior Books v The Veitchi Co Ltd* (1982): sets out the requirements for a duty of care owed by sub-contractors to the owners of buildings to avoid financial harm arising from defective work where the parties are linked by a series of contracts operating concurrently. This is a special form of liability for pure economic loss not determined by *Henderson* or *Caparo* rules on the duty of care.

18. **In claims for damages for psychiatric harm it is first necessary to determine whether the pursuer is a primary or secondary victim:**

> *Page v Smith* (1996): where a duty to a primary victim to avoid causing personal injury is breached there will be liability for psychiatric harm;
> *Alcock v Chief Constable of South Yorkshire* (1992): sets out the requirements for liability towards secondary victims.

19. **Where the pursuer has contributed to the harm through their own negligence, then damages will be reduced by a sum to reflect the pursuer's contribution:**

> Law Reform (Contributory Negligence) Act 1945 s.1.

20. **Volenti non fit injuria, is a complete defence which operates when the pursuer has knowingly assented to undertake the risk of harm.**

VICARIOUS LIABILITY

1. **Where a delict is sufficiently connected with the defender's employment the defender's employer will be vicariously liable in damages:**

> *Lister v Hesley Hall Ltd* (2001): establishes the "sufficient connection" test for vicarious liability.

STATUTORY LIABILITY

1. **If a statute imposes absolute liability for breach of duty, then there is no scope for a defence.**
2. **If a statute imposes strict liability for breach of duty, then there is no onus on pursuers to prove *culpa*, but defences may be available.**
3. **A statute may stipulate that there is to be no civil liability in the event of a breach of duty.**
4. **Where a statute is silent on whether civil liability arises from breach of duty, then the Act will have to be construed to determine whether it was Parliament's intention that civil liability should arise.**

   ➢ *Cutler v Wandsworth Stadium* (1949): claim for breach of statutory duty failed because the duty was not imposed for the benefit of the pursuer.

5. **Liability under the Animals (Scotland) Act 1987 is strict.**
6. **The person liable under the Act is the keeper of the animal.**
7. **The Act covers injury or death of a person, or other animal, caused by a dangerous animal or dog.**
8. **The Act also covers material property damage caused by foraging animals.**
9. **Defences are provided in s.2 of the Act.**
10. **Where the Act is not applicable, liability for harm done by animals must be established according to the common law.**

    ➢ *Fairlie v Carruthers* (1996): demonstrates that liability under the Act does not apply where injury is caused by a dog, who does not attack, but is merely boisterous.

11. **Liability under the Occupiers' Liability (Scotland) Act 1960 depends on proof of negligence.**
12. **The person liable under the Act is the occupier, that is the person with effective control.**
13. **The common law operates to determine to whom a duty is owed.**
14. **The Act covers not only land and buildings, but fixed and moveable structures such as oil rigs or vehicles and vessels.**
15. **Liability under the Act may be excluded by use of a disclaimer, but any disclaimer is subject to provisions in Part 2 of the Unfair Contract Terms Act 1977.**
16. **Volenti non fit injuria affords a defence under the Act:**

    ➢ *Devlin v Strathclyde Regional Council* (1993): occupiers need only take the precautions that would be taken by a reasonable occupier and persons of an age to appreciate the risk, may be deemed to have consented to the risk of harm;
    ➢ *McLeod v British Railways Board* (2001): where there is a breach of duty, but the pursuer is old enough to appreciate the risk damages may be reduced for contributory negligence.

ASSAULT AND HARASSMENT

1. **In civil cases proof may be established on the balance of probabilities.**
2. **Since *solatium* is available for affront, liability in a case of assault does not require physical contact:**

> *Cock v Neville* (1797): threats and abuse are sufficient to found a claim for damages.

3. **A course of conduct, amounting to harassment, is actionable under the Protection from Harassment Act 1997.**
4. **In cases of domestic abuse a single event is sufficient to invoke the Act.**
5. **Remedies under the Act include damages and non-harassment orders.**

NUISANCE

1. **The right to comfortable enjoyment of property, free from serious disturbance, substantial inconvenience or material harm is protected by the law of nuisance.**
2. **Damages in actions grounded on nuisance may be available, not only in respect of physical harm, but also for injury to health and economic loss:**

> *Shanlin v Collins* (1973): damages for nervous debility;
> *Globe v North of Scotland Water Authority* (2000): relevant claim for damages in respect of loss of business.

3. **Nuisance is established where the disturbance, inconvenience or harm to the victim is more than reasonably tolerable in the circumstances:**

> *Watt v Jamieson* (1954): *plus quam tolerabile* mechanism for establishing nuisance introduced.

4. **Factors to consider in determining whether nuisance is established include: the materiality, nature and extent of the harm; the nature of the locality; the sensitivity of the victim or land use invaded; the social value of the land uses invaded and complained of; and the ability of either party to take protective or remedial measures.**
5. **Malicious use of property with the aim of harming a neighbour, may give rise to a claim *in aemulationem vicini*.**
6. **The terms of interdict are drawn narrowly, so as not to restrict the conduct of the defender any more than is necessary to prevent nuisance.**
7. **In an action for damages it is necessary to establish nuisance and prove *culpa*.**

> *RHM Bakeries (Scotland) Ltd v Strathclyde Regional Council* (1985): established *culpa* as the necessary basis for liability in damages;
> *Kennedy v Glenbelle* (1996): a relevant averment of *culpa* is: a deliberate act done in the knowledge that harm would be the likely result;
> *Anderson v White* (2000): knowledge is viewed constructively;
> *Powrie Castle Properties v Dundee City Council* (2001): *culpa* is also established where a defender allows a state of affairs to continue in the knowledge that it is causing harm.

TRESPASS

1. **The right to exclusive possession of property is protected by the law of trespass.**
2. **Interdict will only be available where there is reasonable apprehension of future trespass:**

> *Hay's Trustees v Young* (1877): interdict refused because no grounds to apprehend repeat trespass.

3. **Damages are not available in respect of bare trespass.**
4. **Land is now subject to access rights under the Land Reform (Scotland) Act 2003.**
5. **In claims for interdict it will be necessary to determine whether trespassers are in fact exercising statutory rights of access.**

DEFAMATION

1. **The reparable interest in honour and reputation is protected by the law of defamation:**

   ➢ *Sim v Stretch*: Lord Atkin's test for defamation: "Would the words tend to lower the plaintiff in the estimation of right thinking members of society generally?"

2. **A defamatory meaning may be contained in an innuendo:**

   ➢ *Duncan v Associated Scottish Newspapers*: Lord Anderson's test for innuendo: "what meaning would the ordinary reader of the newspaper put upon the paragraph which the pursuer complained of?"

3. **Defences: Veritas: The defender offers to prove the truth of the statement.**
4. **Fair comment: the comment is on a matter of public interest and based on facts truly stated.**
5. **Absolute privilege: any action for defamation is irrelevant.**
6. **Qualified privilege: where applicable the pursuer has to prove malice on the part of the defender.**

   ➢ *Fraser v Mirza*: malice established where an accusation was made with no belief in its truth.

7. *Reynolds* **defence of responsible journalism**
8. **Section 1(1) defence in Defamation Act 1996 that defender is not the author, editor or publisher of the statement**
9. **Offer of amends under s.2 Defamation Act 1996.**

? QUICK QUIZ

DELICT

- What are the four essential requirements for a successful action for damages in respect of harm caused negligently?
- In novel circumstances what authority must be applied to determine whether a duty of care should be recognised?
- In which cases would you find rules that will tell you whether full damages are recoverable, where a breach of a duty to avoid causing personal injury has resulted in more extensive injuries than could have been foreseen?
- If a duty of care to avoid personal injury is breached and the harm that results is property damage will there be liability for negligence?
- What is a novus actus interveniens?
- What is necessary before a duty of care to avoid financial loss can be held to arise in respect of negligent misstatement?

- In cases involving psychiatric harm, what is the difference between primary and secondary victims?
- Name the defence where the pursuer has knowingly undertaken a risk of harm.
- If you are injured by a person who is carrying out her duties for her employer whom should you sue?
- Is liability for breach of a statutory duty always strict?
- What is the effect of provocation on liability for assault?
- Is it possible to obtain both an interdict and a non-harassment order under the Protection from Harassment Act 1997?
- What must be shown in order to establish nuisance?
- Which Act may serve to complicate attempts to interdict trespassers?
- Is it defamatory to say that a person is (a) a wife beater (b) a college lecturer (c) a homosexual?
- If the leader of the conservatives calls the First Minister a big fat numpty in the Edinburgh Parliament, could he sue her for defamation?
- What advice would you give a newspaper editor who has inadvertently defamed an advocate.

📖 FURTHER READING LIST

G. Cameron, *Delict Law Basics*, 4th edn (W. Green, 2011).
W.J. Stewart, *Delict*, 4th edn (W. Green, 2004).
J.M. Thomson, *Delictual Liability*, 4th edn (Tottel, 2009).
F. McManus and E. Russell, *Delict*, 2nd edn (DUP, 2011).

Chapter 12   Property

DAVID BRAND[1]

► CHAPTER OVERVIEW

12–01 This chapter is concerned with the law of property. It starts by explaining general concepts in property. Corporeal and incorporeal moveable property and securities over these types of property are examined, followed by the various aspects of landownership. Leases and securities over heritable property are then discussed. The chapter concludes with an outline of a typical conveyancing transaction.

✓ OUTCOMES

12–02 At the end of this chapter you should be able to:

✓ understand the general concepts of property law;
✓ distinguish between corporeal and incorporeal moveable property and under-stand how rights and security rights are created in such property;
✓ appreciate the historical basis of land law and how registration is of fundamental importance;
✓ understand the extent and incidents of landownership and the restrictions on the use of land;
✓ appreciate the essentials of leases, the obligations on landlords and tenants and the remedies for breach of these;
✓ understand the nature and effect of securities over heritable property; and
✓ identify the various steps required in the sale and purchase of a house.

INTRODUCTION

12–03 As in all legal systems, property law forms a large area of Scots law. It covers rights and obligations in relation to land, moveable items and intangible items such as intellectual property. The right of peaceful enjoyment of property, subject to certain controls in the public interest, is recognised in human rights legislation.[2] This chapter provides a general overview of Scottish property law. It does not cover, in any detail, the transmission of property rights, which is the subject of conveyancing, although it provides an outline of a typical conveyancing transaction.

The two main historical sources of Scottish property law are Roman law and feudal law. Roman law remains the foundation of much of the modern law, particularly the law on

---

[1] Honorary Teaching Fellow in Law, University of Dundee.
[2] European Convention on Human Rights Protocol 1 art.1.

moveable property. The influence of feudal law has waned over the centuries, and the last remaining aspects of feudalism were abolished on November 28, 2004. Scottish property law is substantially different from English property law. The law is based on both statutory and common law sources and there is no codification of the law.

When the Scottish Parliament was established after devolution, the first Scottish Executive chose land law reform, and the abolition of the feudal system in particular, as one of its key reforms in order to symbolise a new, modern Scotland. Accordingly, an extensive programme of land reform legislation was undertaken resulting in several Acts which, amongst other matters, abolished the feudal system, introduced a right to roam over land, reformed burdens over land and improved the law on tenements.[3] These substantial changes to Scottish land law are ongoing with Bills before the Scottish Parliament at the time of writing to amend the law on long leases and update the system of registration of title to land. Accordingly, Scottish land law has changed substantially over the past few years.

General Concepts

Ownership and lesser property rights

The term "property" can be used in two different ways. It can be used to mean the actual **12–04** physical thing which is owned such as a house, a car or an iPod. It can also be used to signify the right of ownership of something or some less extensive right of ownership. The owner of a house has a property right in that house, the right of ownership. If there is a mortgage over the house, the lender of the mortgage will have a security over the house, which is also a lesser property right. It is possible, therefore, for more than one property right to exist in the same thing or item of property.

The most complete property right is ownership. Property in this sense is known as *dominium* in Roman law. Property in the second sense of the thing owned is known as a *res* in Roman law.

These extensive but restricted rights which ownership confers are sometimes known as a bundle of rights. They are known as *iura in re propria*, rights in a property which a person owns. Other property rights which are less extensive than ownership, such as the right of a lender of a mortgage with a security over a house or a tenant, are usually referred to as subordinate rights. They are known as *jura in re aliena*, rights in a property which another person owns.

The classic definition of property, in the sense of ownership, in Scots law is "the right of using and disposing of a subject as our own, except in so far as we are restrained by law or paction (i.e. agreement)".[4] The first part of this definition states what most people understand as property. The subject, or thing, is owned by a person to do with as they please. The second part qualifies this by making it clear that this right is not absolute. The law imposes restrictions on the exercise of the right of ownership and the owner may agree to restrict that right. For instance, an owner cannot use the subject in a way which causes a nuisance to neighbours, or for a purpose which requires planning permission. These are restrictions on absolute ownership which the common law or specific statutes impose on

---

[3] Abolition of Feudal Tenure etc. (Scotland) Act 2000, Title Conditions (Scotland) Act 2003, Land Reform (Scotland) Act 2003, Agricultural Holdings (Scotland) Act 2003.

[4] Erskine II, ii, 1.

an owner. In addition, an owner may agree to a restriction on the absolute use of the subject, for instance by granting a neighbour a servitude right of access over the subject.[5]

Classification of property

12–05 Property can be classified in various ways:

- heritable and moveable;
- corporeal and incorporeal;
- fungible and non-fungible.

Classification is important because various property rules relating to transfer, rights in security and succession depend on how a property is classified. There are different rules on these matters for different types of property.

Heritable and moveable[6]

12–06 The most important classification is whether a property is heritable or moveable. Most heritable property is classified as heritable because of its nature and broadly covers, land and buildings, or anything attached to the land. Rights connected with land and buildings, such as servitudes and leases, are also heritable. All other property is moveable, which is by its nature capable of being moved, such as furniture and cars. Rights connected with moveables, such as a right to sue under contract or delict, are also moveable rights.

This classification of property into heritable or moveable derives from the old law of intestate succession in Scots law, which had different rules on who would succeed to the property of a deceased where there was no will. Under the principle of *primogeniture* the land, i.e. heritable property, went to the heir-at-law who was the eldest son. This was abolished by the Succession (Scotland) Act 1964, although the distinction between heritable and moveable property is still important in relation to legal rights.[7]

Some types of property are clearly heritable or moveable. Land and buildings are obviously heritable, as are trees. When trees are cut down as timber, the timber is clearly moveable. Cows grazing in a field are obviously moveable. The grass on which the cows are grazing is growing out of the ground and is acceding to, or attached to, the soil. Natural fruits of the land, which require no constant cultivation, including grass, are regarded as heritable by nature and remain so until severed from the land.[8] An exception to this rule is made of industrial growing crops, which are classified as moveable although physically growing from the soil and acceding to the land. These crops, such as barley, wheat, and potatoes, require cultivation and are classified as moveable.[9]

This principle of property, where something growing accedes to where it is growing, is known as accession by fruits. The principle also applies to growing things in moveables and, therefore, young unborn animals accede to their mothers.[10]

This classification is not completely straightforward, however, as property may become heritable not by its nature but by accession. This is where moveable property converts to heritable property by attachment to the land. Accession will occur in such circumstances

---

[5] See Restrictions on landownership, para.12–49 et seq. below.
[6] In England the terms are real and personal property, which are almost synonymous with heritable and moveable property.
[7] See Chapter 14 on Succession.
[8] Erskine II, ii, 3.
[9] Erskine II, ii, 4.
[10] *Lamb v Grant* (1874) 11 S.L.R. 672.

as, for example, where a substantial summerhouse is erected on land and becomes part of that land,[11] or where a fireplace is built into a room in a building on land. What was originally moveable converts to heritable under the principle of accession. The question of whether a moveable item has converted to become a heritable item, can be a difficult one and is a problem area in the sale and purchase of houses and other properties. It is generally known as the law of fixtures and is discussed more fully below.

Corporeal and incorporeal

Property is corporeal if it is tangible and can be seen or touched, for example, furniture or **12–07** jewellery. Incorporeal property is intangible, and includes items such as shares in a company or an insurance policy. A share certificate or insurance policy document is tangible and corporeal, but the right itself is intangible and incorporeal. These examples are moveable, but both heritable and moveable property can be either corporeal or incorporeal. Land is corporeal heritable property and rights relating to land, such as a lease or a servitude, are incorporeal heritable property.

Fungible and non-fungible

A fungible property is property which disappears when used but can be replaced by a **12–08** similar property, such as milk or money. A non-fungible property is one which cannot be replaced readily and has an inherent value, such as a work of art. In other words, fungible property is non-specific whereas is non-fungible is specific.

Ownership and possession

Possession is an important concept in both heritable and moveable property. One of the **12–09** incidents of unrestricted ownership is the right to exclusive possession and the ability to prevent others from interfering with it. An owner of land is entitled to be free from persons trespassing or encroaching on the land.[12] In the law of heritable property the operation of prescription, whereby land held on a good title for the appropriate period of time, usually 10 years, is free from challenge by anyone claiming title to that land, is fundamental.[13] Possession is also important in moveable property. There is a presumption that the possessor of goods is the owner in the absence of evidence to the contrary.[14] This gives some weight to the popular phrase "possession is nine tenths of the law". Possession can be either natural or civil.[15] Natural possession is where the possessor actually occupies the land or retains the goods personally. Civil is where the possession is by another on behalf of the owner. For instance, if a person owns a house and actually lives there, this is natural possession by the owner, but if the owner leases the house to a tenant and the tenant lives there, this is civil possession by the tenant.

What constitutes possession itself may not be straightforward. The classic definition states "there must be an act of the body which is the detention and holding; and an act of the mind which is the inclination or affection to make use of the thing obtained".[16] This means that there are two elements, which are, an act of body, which means there must be a physical element of actual retention and holding the property, and an act of mind, which means the mental intention to possess property for oneself. It is possible to have one

---

[11] *Christie v Smith's Exr.*, 1949 S.C. 572.
[12] See Incidents of landownership, para.12–41 et seq. below.
[13] See Prescription, para.12–35 below.
[14] Stair II, i, 42, *Prangnell-O'Neill v Skiffington*, 1984 S.L.T. 282.
[15] Erskine Inst. II, ii, 22.
[16] Stair II, i, 17.

element without the other. A person can have actual physical retention of the property, without intending to keep it as their own. The property may be held on behalf of someone else, such as a friend or employer, and in this case there is no legal possession, only custody. It is also possible to have possession of a property without a legal right, as where a thief is in possession of stolen goods and is intending to keep them. This satisfies both elements of possession.

Real rights and personal rights

12–10 There is an important fundamental distinction in property rights between real rights and personal rights. A real right is enforceable against anyone at all, whereas a personal right is enforceable only against a particular person or persons. Personal rights are created by an agreement, or contract, between parties. Many types of personal rights and corresponding obligations can arise from the contract. These will be enforceable by the parties to the contract against each other, but not against third parties. A real right is enforceable against third parties. To take the example of a sale of a house, when houses are sold and transferred to the seller, the first stage is usually the missives. These are letters which constitute the contract for the sale and purchase of the house. When the missives are completed there are several steps required before the house transfers to the seller and the seller becomes the owner but, in the meantime, there is a completed enforceable contract. At this stage, the purchaser remains the owner. The seller could sell to someone else and transfer ownership to that person. The purchaser would then have to sue the seller for breach of contract. This would be on the basis of the personal right under the missives. Once all the steps to transfer ownership have been completed, and the document transferring the title to the purchaser has been registered in the appropriate register, the purchaser becomes the new owner and obtains a real right to defend that right of ownership against anyone.

Real rights are created in different ways for different types of property. Normally this involves two stages. The first stage will be an agreement, or contract, between the parties. In the case of the house, as it is heritable property, this is the missives stage, when the contract for the sale and purchase is concluded. This gives rise to a personal right only. The next stage is a public act by registering the document of transfer of title in the appropriate public property register, either the General Register of Sasines or the Land Register. This second stage of recording in the public property register creates the real right.[17]

There is normally a two-stage process with moveable property also. In the transfer of corporeal moveables, the first stage is the agreement, or contract, between the parties, and the second stage which creates the real right is the delivery of the moveables.[18]

Co-ownership

12–11 Both heritable and moveable property can be owned by more than one person. There is a distinction between:

- joint property;
- common property; and
- common interest.

---

[17] See Registration, para.12–34 below.
[18] See Corporeal moveable property, para.12–17 et seq. below.

Joint property

This is where two or more persons own a property as an individual whole. This is known **12–12** as *pro indiviso,* or undivided ownership, and the property is said to vest in the owners *pro indiviso.* The joint owner cannot dispose of the right during lifetime or on death by a will, and when the ownership is surrendered or the person dies, that right of ownership accresces, or is added to, the other joint owner or owners. Examples of this type of ownership include an unincorporated association, such as a club, where the members of the club own the club's property jointly and a club member will be a joint owner but will cease to be so on ceasing to be a member, or trust property, where the trustees own trust property jointly.[19]

Common property

Common property is much more widespread than joint property. This is where two or **12–13** more persons own a property and each owner has an individual share of the property. This can be disposed of during the co-owner's lifetime, or under a will or according to the rules of intestate succession on death.[20] A co-owner can also divide their share or grant a security over it. If a co-owner wishes to dispose of their share and the other co-owner or co-owners refuse, it is open to apply to the court under an action of division and sale to have the court order that the whole property be sold and the proceeds divided amongst the co-owners.[21]

The usual example of co-ownership is a husband and wife owning their home as common property. It is usually said that their title is in joint names, but this does not mean that the property is joint property. If one spouse wished to sell and the other does not, there are protection provisions in actions of sale and division.[22]

The general common law rule for management of common property is that all co-owners must consent to the management of the property. This includes any alterations, improvements or repairs to the property.[23] Accordingly, one co-owner can veto the proposals of all the others. In the case of essential repairs, it is possible for one co-owner to instruct these and recover the appropriate share of the cost from the other co-owners.[24] There are now specific statutory rules for common property in tenements.[25]

Common interest

Common interest is a right which an owner of property has in respect of property owned **12–14** by another by implication of law. This right acts as a restriction on what the owner of the property can do with the property, as certain actions may affect the property of the other person. In a tenement building, in the absence of provision in the title deeds, a ground floor flat owner will own the section of the external gable wall enclosing the flat.[26] An upper-floor flat owner will have a right of common interest in that section of the gable wall, as the wall supports the upper flat. The ground-floor flat owner cannot do anything which adversely affects the right of common interest of support, such as putting in a new window which destabilises the gable wall.

---

[19] See Chapter 13 on Trusts.
[20] Unless there is a survivorship destination—see Chapter 14 on Succession.
[21] *Upper Crathes Fishings Ltd v Bailey's Exrs,* 1991 S.L.T. 747.
[22] Matrimonial Homes (Family Protection) (Scotland) Act 1981 s.19.
[23] *Rafique v Amin,* 1997 S.L.T. 1385.
[24] *Deans v Woolfson,* 1922 S.C. 221.
[25] See Law of the tenement, para.12–40 below.
[26] See Law of the tenement, para.12–40 below.

Common interest occurs mainly in the law of the tenement, which is discussed below, but can occur in other situations, such as where owners of a river have a common interest in the water of the river.[27]

Other types of property rights

Liferents

12–15 A liferent is a special type of property right. It is the right to the use of, or income from, a property during the lifetime of the person who has the right, known as the liferenter, or some other period set out in the deed constituting the liferent. It applies to both heritable and moveable property. The liferenter is not entitled to the capital of the property, known as the fee, which belongs to the person known as the fiar. The fiar is the owner of the property, but will not have complete ownership of the property until the liferent comes to an end. During the liferent, the liferenter must not do anything to the detriment of the capital of the liferented subjects. Liferents are classed as either proper or improper liferents and alimentary liferents are an important type of improper liferent.

An example of a liferent is where a married man dies and does not want to leave all his estate to his wife, but wishes it to go to his children. In the past this used to be a fairly common situation. What happens is that a will is made leaving his estate to his widow in liferent and to his children in fee. The widow then has the benefit of the income from the estate during her lifetime, and on her subsequent death the whole estate passes to the children.

Occupancy rights of a non-entitled spouse

12–16 A new type of property right was introduced under the Matrimonial Homes (Family Protection) (Scotland) Act 1981. This is an occupancy right in relation to a matrimonial home. This is intended to give protection to either a husband or wife where only one of the married couple owns the home in which they live. That person, known as the non-entitled spouse, is given occupancy rights which allow the spouse to continue to reside in the home and to re-enter and reside if he or she is not living there. Spouses have automatic occupancy rights under the 1981 Act. This was extended to registered civil partners under the Civil Partnership Act 2004. The 1981 Act makes provision for cohabiting couples who are not married to apply to the court for occupancy rights.

Key Concepts

"**Property**" can be used to mean two different things. It can be used to signify the right of ownership of something or it can be used to mean the actual thing which is owned.
Property can be **classified** in various ways:

- heritable and moveable;
- corporeal and incorporeal;
- fungible and non-fungible.

---

[27] See Water rights, para.12–46 below.

Most **heritable** property is classified as heritable because of its nature and broadly covers land and buildings, or anything attached to the land. All other property is **moveable**, which is by its nature capable of being moved.

Corporeal property is tangible and can be seen or touched. **Incorporeal** property is intangible.

Fungible property is non-specific. It can be replaced by similar property. **Non-fungible** property is specific. It cannot readily be replaced and has an inherent value.

The right to exclusive **possession** is an incident of unrestricted ownership. In heritable property, prescription, whereby land is held on a good title for a certain period, is fundamental. In moveable property there is a presumption that the possessor of goods is the owner.

A **real right** is enforceable against anyone at all, whereas a **personal right** is enforceable only against a particular person or persons.

In **co-ownership** there is an important distinction between:

- joint property;
- common property; and
- common interest.

CORPOREAL MOVEABLE PROPERTY

Acquisition

Corporeal moveable property can be acquired in one of two ways. These are original **12–17** acquisition and derivative acquisition. Original acquisition is where an item of property has never had an owner before it is acquired, or the owner has lost the right of ownership. It also includes property which has been newly created and did not previously exist. Derivative acquisition is where the acquisition is by transfer from the existing owner to a new owner. There are different rules for each type of acquisition.

Original acquisition

Original acquisition can be divided into four categories: **12–18**

- occupation;
- accession;
- specification;
- confusion and commixtion.

Occupation

Moveable property which has never been owned by anyone becomes the property of the **12–19** person who acquires it with the intention of becoming the owner.[28] Such property is known as *res nullius*. Most items of corporeal moveable property are owned by someone, but some are not, such as pebbles or shells on a beach or wild animals, birds or fish. These can be acquired by the first person to take control of them. Certain wild creatures cannot

---

[28] Stair II, i.33.

be acquired in this way, such as salmon and royal birds, which belong to the Crown, or protected species, such ospreys or badgers.[29]

Once such property is in the control of a person, that person remains the owner and the property cannot be legally removed. In the case of wild creatures, however, if the creature escapes, then it returns to its wild ownerless state. Some time may be allowed for these to be recaptured before they become *res nullius* again.[30] Domestic animals and creatures with a homing instinct, such as bees and pigeons, cannot be acquired by occupation.[31]

Similarly, property which has been owned by someone cannot be acquired by occupation. Ownership will remain with that person, even if that owner has lost possession. Lost or abandoned property cannot be acquired by occupation. If the owner of lost property retains the intention of keeping the property, ownership will be retained. If property is abandoned or long lost with the owner resigned to the loss, the property belongs to the Crown as part of the royal prerogative.[32] This includes treasure trove which does not belong to the finder.[33] The finder of lost or abandoned property is under a statutory duty to take reasonable care of the property, and report the finding or deliver the property to the police within a reasonable time of finding.[34] The Chief Constable has a discretion to give the property to the finder.[35]

> ### Lord Advocate v University of Aberdeen
> ### 1963 S.C. 533
>
> A team of students from Aberdeen University were on a field trip to St Ninian's Isle in Shetland and discovered eighth-century treasure hidden underground. The University appropriated the treasure and took it to its museum in Aberdeen. The Lord Advocate, on behalf of the Crown, sued for delivery of the treasure. The University argued that the treasure was governed by udal law, which is a relict of the time when Shetland and Orkney belonged to Norway, and part of that law still applies in Shetland and Orkney. Under udal law, the finder of treasure would keep part of it. The Inner Division of the Court of Session held that Scots law applied, not udal law, and the Crown owned the treasure.

Accession

12–20   Accession is more common where moveable property accedes to heritable property and converts from being moveable to being heritable by attachment.[36] However, it is possible for there to be accession of moveables to moveables. This can occur naturally, as when animals have offspring. The owner of the animal becomes the owner of the offspring.[37] It can also take place with incorporeal moveable property, as when interest accumulates on a bank account. The owner of the bank account is entitled to the interest on the account.

---

[29] Wildlife and Countryside Act 1981; Protection of Badgers Act 1992.
[30] *Anderson v Valentine*, 1985 S.C.C.R. 89.
[31] Stair II, i.33.
[32] Erskine Inst.II, i, 12.
[33] *Lord Advocate v University of Aberdeen*, 1963 S.C. 533, the "*St Ninian's Isle Treasure Case*".
[34] Civic Government (Scotland) Act 1982 Pt VI.
[35] 1982 Act s.70(i)(b).
[36] See Fixtures, para.12–38 below.
[37] *Lamb v Grant* (1874) 11 S.L.R. 672.

Specification

Specification concerns property, which is newly created from component materials and **12–21** cannot revert back to its original components. When grapes are made into wine, or corn into flour, it is not possible to turn the wine back into grapes or the flour back to corn. When such a new entity is created, the person who creates the new entity will become the owner of the new entity, provided the creator has acted in good faith. This applies whether or not the creator provided the component materials.[38]

It is essential that a new entity comes into existence and the component parts cannot be separated back to their original state.[39] If they can, the component parts will belong to their original owners. In one case, where the front part of one car and the rear part of another had been welded together, it was held that specification could not take place because the two parts could be separated again.[40] It is also essential that the creator acted in good faith because the doctrine is an equitable one.[41]

The owner or owners of the original component materials may be entitled to compensation for the cost of the materials.[42]

International Banking Corporation v Ferguson, Shaw & Sons
1910 S.C. 182

A company bought oil in good faith from another company who had no right to sell, as it belonged to a different company. The purchasing company paid for and received the oil and manufactured lard, which the company sold. The true owners succeeded in an action to recover the cost of the oil.

Confusion and commixtion

Confusion and commixtion occur when materials of the same kind are mixed together. **12–22** Confusion applies to liquids and commixtion to solids. If the constituent liquids or solids are not the same and a new liquid or solid is created which cannot be separated, the principle of specification will apply. Where the constituents are of the same kind, the liquid or solid is owned in common in shares corresponding to the amount and value of the contribution to the whole.[43]

Derivative acquisition or transfer

Derivative acquisition is transfer of ownership to a new owner from an existing owner. **12–23** Corporeal moveable property can be transferred in various situations such as gift, exchange, sale or loan. The rules on security for a loan are examined later.[44] There are two basic essentials for derivative acquisition to operate—intention and delivery. Erskine states:

---

[38] Stair, Inst.II, i, 41.
[39] *North-West Securities Ltd v Barrhead Coachworks Ltd*, 1976 S.C. 68, per Lord McDonald at 72.
[40] *McDonald v Provan (of Scotland Street) Ltd*, 1960 S.L.T. 231.
[41] Bell Princ. 1298.
[42] *International Banking Corporation v Ferguson, Shaw & Sons*, 1910 S.C. 182.
[43] Stair, Inst.II, i.37.
[44] See Rights in security over moveable property, para.12–26 et seq. below.

"Two things are ... required to the conveyance in this matter: First, the intention or consent of the former owner to transfer it upon some just or proper title of alienation, as sole gift, exchange, etc: Secondly, the actual delivery of it, in pursuance of that intention."[45]

As previously noted,[46] the first stage of intention set out in an agreement only creates a personal right. The second stage of delivery is required to create a real right of ownership enforceable against the world.[47] It is generally not possible for someone other than the owner to transfer a good title to a property by mere delivery, without the owner consenting to, or intending to, transfer the property.[48] Similarly, owners cannot transfer a more extensive right than their own.[49] For instance, if a thief sells stolen goods to a buyer who does not know the goods are stolen, the buyer does not get a good title to the stolen goods, which can be recovered by the owner. The buyer will only be able to sue the thief, for what that may be worth.

It is important to note here that, in the field of sale of goods, these general rules have been modified by statute under the Sale of Goods Act 1979. Under this Act it is possible in certain circumstances for title to goods to be transferred without delivery. It is also possible for a contract to provide that title is reserved to a seller notwithstanding delivery of goods to the purchaser until the price has been fully paid.

The intention to transfer will usually be set out in writing in a form of agreement. Delivery can be actual, constructive or symbolic. Actual delivery is where the property is physically handed over to the acquirer, or the agent of the acquirer, or physical control is handed over, for instance by means of a key.[50] Constructive delivery occurs when a third party is holding property on behalf of the original owner and is instructed by the original owner to hold the property on behalf of the acquirer.[51] Symbolic delivery occurs when the property, or control of the property, cannot be physically handed over and a symbol of this is handed over instead. The main example of this is a bill of lading, which is a document of title to goods which are in transit by ship.[52]

Inglis v Robertson & Baxter
(1898) 25 R. (H.L.) 70

Goldsmith owned whisky in a bonded warehouse in Glasgow. The warehouse held this on behalf of him or his assignees and Goldsmith had a warrant to this effect. Goldsmith borrowed money from Inglis and endorsed and delivered the warrant to Inglis. This was not intimated to the warehouse keepers. In a dispute between Inglis and the creditors of Goldsmith it was held that as there had been no intimation to the third party holding the whisky, the real right to the whisky remained with Goldsmith.

---

[45] Erskine Inst.II, I, 18.
[46] See Real rights and personal rights, para.12–10 above.
[47] Lord President Inglis in *Clark v West Calder Oil Co* (1882) 9 R. 1017 at 1024.
[48] This principle is known as *nemo dat quod non habet*.
[49] *The Scottish Widows Fund v Buist* (1876) 3 R. 1078, dealing with incorporeal moveable property.
[50] *West Lothian Oil Co Ltd v Mair* (1892) 20 R. 64.
[51] *Inglis v Robertson & Baxter* (1898) 25 R. (H.L.) 70.
[52] *Hayman v McLintock*, 1907 S.C. 936.

> **Key Concepts**
>
> **Original acquisition** is where ownership is acquired independent of the ownership of another. It can be divided into four categories:
>
> - occupation;
> - accession;
> - specification;
> - confusion and commixtion.
>
> **Derivative acquisition** is transfer of ownership to a new owner from an existing owner. The two basic essentials of derivative acquisition are intention and delivery.

INCORPOREAL MOVEABLE PROPERTY

Incorporeal moveable property is property which is the subject of commercial and mercantile law such as shares in a company or insurance policies, and the creation of such property rights is governed by mercantile law. In addition, there are special laws in relation to rights arising from original and creative works in cultural, scientific or business areas, known as "intellectual property". **12–24**

As with corporeal moveable property, the general rule is that there are two requirements for the transfer of incorporeal moveable property. Unlike corporeal moveable property, incorporeal moveable property is intangible and cannot be physically delivered to transfer ownership. The two requirements to transfer are assignation and intimation. Certain incorporeal moveable property cannot be transferred at all. Rights which are personal to a particular person, under the doctrine known as *delectus persona*, cannot be transferred, for instance a contract of employment.

An assignation is the transfer of ownership from the assignor to the assignee. Technically, an assignation need not be in writing[53] but, in practice, it usually is. Some types of assignation, for instance policies of assurance, need to have a certain form as laid down by statute.

Delivery of the assignation gives the assignee an effective personal right, but the assignee will not obtain a real right against third parties unless there is intimation. There are various forms of intimation set out by statute[54] and various equivalents of intimation, for instance the debtor acknowledging the assignee's right.

The effect of assignation is that the assignee takes the place of the assigner and succeeds to all the rights and obligations of the assigner. The assignee will have no greater right than the assigner and, if there is a defect in the rights of the assigner, this defect will pass to the assignee.[55] There is one exception to this rule. If there is a latent trust of which the assigner is unaware, and the assignee takes in good faith and for value, the assignee will not be affected by the latent trust.[56]

---

[53] Requirements of Writing (Scotland) Act 1995 s.11.
[54] Transmission of Moveable Property (Scotland) Act 1862.
[55] *Scottish Widows' Fund v Buist* (1876) 3 R. 1078.
[56] *Redfearn v Somervail* (1830) 1 Dow 50.

Intellectual property rights

12–25 Intellectual property rights are incorporeal moveable rights, which relate to original and creative works in cultural, scientific or business areas. This is a complex and expanding area of law. The main types of intellectual property are:

- patents;
- copyright;
- trade marks; and
- designs.

Patents give the creator of an invention a monopoly in respect of the manufacture and use of the invention. The main statutory provisions are the Patents Acts 1977 and 2004.

Copyright can exist in certain types of literary, dramatic, musical or artistic work and covers visual, aural and written forms. Copyright gives an exclusive right to make copies and reproduce the work of the author. The main statutory provision is the Copyright, Designs and Patents Act 1988.

Trade marks are graphical signs, which distinguish the goods or services of one undertaking from another. They enable the public to identify a particular business with the trade mark. Protection of trade marks is achieved by registration. The main statutory provision is the Trade Marks Act 1994.

Designs are similar to copyright and are shapes, which can be either functional or aesthetic. Certain designs may be registered. The main statutory provision is the Copyright, Designs and Patents Act 1988.

Key Concepts

Incorporeal moveable property, is property which is the subject of commercial and mercantile law, such as shares in a company or insurance policies.

Rights in incorporeal moveable property are transferred by assignation plus intimation.

Rights arising from original and creative works in cultural, scientific or business areas are known as **intellectual property** rights, and include:

- patents;
- copyright;
- trade marks; and
- designs.

RIGHTS IN SECURITY OVER MOVEABLE PROPERTY

12–26 One of the uses of property is to use it as security to obtain something else, usually a loan of money. Both heritable and moveable property can be used for this purpose. It is common place, when a house is purchased, for a bank or building society loan to be obtained to help finance the purchase and the house itself is used as a heritable security. Jewellery, or other valuable moveable property, can be taken to a pawn-shop and handed over in exchange for a loan of money. In such cases, the property acts as security for the debt and gives the holder, the creditor, a preferential right over an unsecured creditor in the secured property. In the event of the granter of the security, the debtor, becoming insolvent, a secured creditor generally has a right to sell the secured property and be paid before the unsecured creditors.

If properly constituted, the right is a real right in security enforceable against the world. A right in security is only an accessory right to secure the performance of an obligation, usually repayment of a loan, and once the obligation has been performed the creditor must return the secured property to the debtor, or grant an appropriate discharge. The right in security is redeemable and must be redeemed on performance of the obligation.

Rights in security can arise by agreement or by operation of law. Some rights are governed by common law and some by statute. There are different rules for the constitution of rights in security over different types of property. Generally, security rights over moveable property require delivery.

Securities over corporeal moveable property

Securities over corporeal moveable property, which require delivery, can arise by agreement known as pledge or by operation of law known as liens. Securities which do not require delivery are hypothecs and floating charges. **12–27**

Pledge

A pledge is a simple contractual form of security. The owner of the corporeal moveables, the pledger, agrees with the lender, the pledgee, usually to borrow a sum of money. In exchange for the money, the pledger delivers the property to the pledgee. On repayment of the debt, the pledgee is bound to return the property to the pledger. Pawnbroking is a good example of a pledge, although there are special rules for pawnbroking under the Consumer Credit Act 1974.[57] **12–28**

Delivery is an essential element in pledge. Delivery may be actual, constructive or symbolic.[58]

Liens

A lien is a security right, which arises by operation of law and results from the creditor being in possession of the property belonging to the debtor. A lien can be special or general. A special lien is the right of a creditor to retain a specific item of property until the debt incurred in relation to that property has been repaid. This will often occur when something is handed over for repair. Until the repair bill is paid, the item will not be handed back and the special lien exercised. **12–29**

A general lien is the right of a creditor to retain property of the debtor, in possession of the lender, until all the general debts due by the debtor have been settled, whether relating to that property or not. These liens relate to particular trades and four are generally recognised. A factor has a general lien over all goods, bills, money or documents of the principal, which have come into the factor's possession during the employment of the factor.[59] This includes advances made to the principal, salary and commission, and any liabilities incurred on behalf of the principal.[60] The banker has a general lien over all negotiable instruments belonging to customers, which have come into possession of the bank in business transactions as opposed to mere deposit.[61] An innkeeper has a general

---

[57] 1974 Act ss.114–122.
[58] See Derivative acquisition or transfer, para.12–23 above.
[59] Bell Princ. 456.
[60] *Glendinning v Hope*, 1911 S.C. (H.L.) 73.
[61] Bell Princ. 1451.

lien over luggage of a guest for the amount of the hotel bill.[62] Certain items, such as clothes, are excluded.[63] A solicitor has a general lien over all papers belonging to a client, including title deeds, wills and share certificates, for unpaid bills and expenses made in the ordinary course of business.[64]

Hypothecs

12–30 Hypothecs give a creditor a right in security without delivery to the creditor in certain situations. The hypothec may be conventional or legal. A conventional hypothec arises by agreement. They are rare and are confined to maritime law.[65] A legal hypothec arises by operation of law. There are certain maritime hypothecs which give a right in security over a ship, including a right to seamen in respect of unpaid wages and the master in respect of properly incurred wages.[66] A solicitor has a hypothec over costs or property recovered in a court action for expenses incurred in the court action.[67] A landlord has a hypothec over certain corporeal moveable property belonging to the tenant. This used to apply to all types of leases but was recently abolished in relation to residential leases and agricultural leases and is now restricted to commercial leases. [68]

Floating charges

12–31 Floating charges were introduced in Scotland in 1961[69] and can be created over heritable or moveable property.[70] They can only be used by companies. The charge does not attach to a company's assets until an event, such as the winding-up of the company, causes the charge to crystallise and attach to all the assets of the company.

Securities over incorporeal moveable property

12–32 The rules for creation of a security over incorporeal moveables which cannot be delivered, follow those for transfer of incorporeal moveables and require assignation in security and intimation. In relation to company shares, a valid right in security requires a share transfer form and registration of this form with the company, subject to the right to transfer back to the debtor when the debt is repaid. Securities can also be granted over intellectual property, although no intimation is possible in respect of such property. There are specific rules regarding this.

Key Concepts

A **right in security** is only an accessory right to secure the performance of an obligation; once the obligation has been performed, the creditor must return the secured property to the debtor or grant an appropriate **discharge**.

Securities over corporeal moveable property, which require delivery, can arise by agreement known as **pledge** (a simple contractual form of security) or by operation

---

[62] Bell Princ. 1428.
[63] *Sunbolf v Alford* (1838) 2 M. & W. 248.
[64] Bell Princ. 1438.
[65] Bell Princ. 456.
[66] Merchant Shipping Act 1995 ss.39 and 40.
[67] Solicitors (Scotland) Act 1980 s.62.
[68] Bankruptcy and Diligence etc. (Scotland) Act 2007 s.208(3).
[69] Under the Companies (Floating Charges) (Scotland) Act 1961.
[70] For Heritable property, see para.12–80 et seq. below.

of law known as **liens** (special or general). Securities which do not require delivery, are **hypothecs** (conventional or legal) and **floating charges** (in the case of companies).

Historical background

The two key features of landownership in Scotland throughout the centuries have been the **12–33** feudal system and registration in a public land register. The feudal system in Scotland dates back to the twelfth century and a public land register was first introduced in 1617.[71] Registration is discussed in the next section. As noted in the introduction to this chapter, abolition of the feudal system was chosen as a symbolic major reform by the first Scottish Executive following devolution in 1999, and was welcomed by the new Scottish Parliament without opposition. Under the Abolition of Feudal Tenure etc. (Scotland) Act 2000 the feudal system was finally abolished on November 28, 2004.[72]

Feudalism was introduced into Scotland as a social, political and economic system.[73] The fundamental principle of feudalism was that all land derives from the Crown as ultimate feudal superior. Originally, the King granted land to his nobles in the return for services to the King. These services were originally military service in the far off days of constant warfare. Land was not granted to the nobles outright, but was feued, or transferred, to them on a tenure, a type of holding of land, in return for the services, known as a *reddendo*. The nobles, in turn, were able to grant land to lesser mortals who actually worked on the land by subfeuing the land to them, again on a tenure in return for a *reddendo*, which might be agricultural services. The person who granted or feued the land was known as the superior and the person who received the land was known as the vassal.

The superior retained a right of ownership in the land as it was not granted outright, and this right enabled the superior to claim and receive the *reddendo*. This right of ownership was known as *dominium directum*. The right of ownership of the vassal, who received the land to use but without outright ownership, was known as *dominium utile*. This meant that every time there was a grant of land and land was feued, or more correctly subfeued, there was a new link in a chain of ownership stretching back to the Crown as ultimate feudal superior. This ultimate ownership of the Crown was known as *dominium eminens*. Therefore, from the Crown down to the person actually occupying and using the land, there was a feudal chain of ownership with a person being at the same time the vassal of the superior who had subfeued to them, and the superior of the vassal to whom they, in turn, had subfeued.

Originally, under the feudal system there were different types of tenure and *reddendo*, but by the twentieth century there was virtually only one type of tenure, feu farm, and one type of *reddendo*, feuduty, or payment of money. Over the centuries substantial reform took place. The feudal system which was abolished in 2004 was very different from the original one and many of the features of feudalism had long since gone. In particular, since the mid-eighteenth century it was possible to transfer land not by subfeuing, but by

---

[71] Registration Act 1617.

[72] 2000 Act s.1.

[73] See generally Reid, *The Law of Property in Scotland* Butterworths, (1996), paras 41–113 (written by Professor G. Gretton); Gordon and Wortley, *Scottish Land Law* (W. Green, 2009), Chs 2 and 3.

substitution without the consent of the superior.[74] This was where a vassal transferred land, not by subfeuing, whereby the vassal would become the superior of the vassal who granted the land, but instead by stepping out of the feudal chain with the person granted the land becoming the new vassal of the original vassal's superior. Thus, instead of creating an additional new link in the feudal chain, the link was replaced by a substitute link.

Two further features of the feudal system were that it was commonplace for a superior to insert feuing conditions, usually known as real burdens, in the title of the vassal when granting the land. These related to such matters as restrictions on the use that vassals could make of the land, to protect the amenity of the neighbouring land.[75] If such conditions were properly constituted, a superior would retain the right to enforce these conditions against the vassal. This could be done on the basis of simply being the superior, even if the superior had no other connection with the land. To back up enforcement, it was usual to insert in the title of a vassal a right of irritancy, which gave the ultimate power to a superior to take back the land if the vassal failed to observe the feuing conditions.

Major reforms of the feudal system took place in recent times, until final abolition in 2004. Under the 2000 Act all superiorities were abolished and *dominium utile* became full *dominium,* or outright ownership.[76] All feuduties were extinguished,[77] with certain provisions for payment of compensation to superiors,[78] and irritancies were abolished.[79] Former superiors can only enforce real burdens if the new rules in the Title Conditions (Scotland) Act 2003, which came into force on the same day, are satisfied.[80]

Key Concepts

The two key historical features of landownership are the **feudal system** and **registration** in a public land register.

The feudal system was finally abolished in 2004 by the Abolition of Feudal Tenure etc. (Scotland) Act 2000.

There are two public land registers in Scotland. The Register of Sasines, which dates back to 1617, and the new Land Register, which was introduced in 1979.

Registration

12–34 The key feature of landownership in Scotland, which still remains, has been the need for registration in a public property register to complete a good title to land. Since 1617, a system of registration has existed in Scotland and the registration of a title to land has been necessary to complete a real right in the land. Most rights in land, whether they be outright ownership of land or a more restrictive property right such as a right in security, require the title to such right to be in writing and the title deed to be registered.[81] The

---

[74] Tenures Abolition Act 1746.
[75] See Restrictions on landownership, para.12–49 et seq. below.
[76] 2000 Act s.2.
[77] 2000 Act s.7.
[78] 2000 Act s.8.
[79] 2000 Act s.53.
[80] See Real burdens, para.12–54 et seq. below.
[81] On the requirements of writing in deeds relating to interests in land, see generally the Requirements of Writing (Scotland) Act 1995.

Register of Sasines[82] was introduced in 1617[83] and was the basis of the system of land registration in Scotland for well over 300 years. Although the system was not perfect it did work remarkably well. By the latter half of the twentieth century, however, it was felt that the system was becoming outmoded and a new system of land registration was introduced in 1979 with a new register, the Land Register. Over a long period of time all land in Scotland will be registered in the Land Register with the advantages that register brings.

The system of registration introduced in 1617 with the Register of Sasines is a system in which the register is a register of deeds only, not a register of title. The title to land does not flow from the register itself but from the deed. The deed acts as a public notice that the person has registered a particular title deed but, if that title deed is faulty, the register does not cure the defect. In contrast, the Land Register is a register of title where the title flows from the register itself and the Land Register does guarantee title. Once a title deed has been registered in the Land Register and the Keeper of the Register issues a land certificate, the land certificate is a guarantee that the holder has title to the land and this is backed up with a state guarantee so that the holder will be indemnified against any adverse action against the title.

On the face of it, the Register of Sasines was seen to be a poor system of registration as a person cannot get a title which is free from challenge after registration. The system is fortified, however, by the operation of positive prescription. This is examined in the next section. The basic principle is that, if a person has a title to land which is not obviously defective and possesses the land for the appropriate prescriptive period, then the title becomes free from challenge. This system of registration in the Register of Sasines plus the operation of positive prescription lasted until the introduction of the Land Register in 1979. As it will be many years before the new system of land registration applies to all land in Scotland, it is the way many titles to land in Scotland are still held.

One other drawback to the system of registration in the Register of Sasines, apart from the lack of a guarantee of title, is inadequate description of the land in the register. There are various formal requirements for a title deed before it will be accepted in the Register of Sasines. These include the need for a description of the subjects. Many sasine title deeds do not contain plans of the subjects.[84] Those that do are often inaccurate. The subjects are also described in words in the deed. These words are all too often vague or ambiguous. For instance, it may be impossible to tell where the physical boundaries are situated. The operation of positive prescription may help[85] but all too often the position is unsatisfactory. The requirement for an accurate plan of the subjects would be a distinct improvement. This was one of the reasons for introducing a new system of land registration in 1979.

The Land Registration (Scotland) Act 1979 introduced a new system of land registration which is gradually being extended throughout Scotland. Land in Scotland was divided into operational areas[86] and the provisions in the Act were introduced to these areas between 1979 and 2003.[87] At present, land is only registered in the new Land Register on a sale, not for instance where it is gifted or subject to a security. It will be some time in the future before all land in Scotland is registered in the Land Register.

When land is first registered in the Land Register, the Keeper examines the title deeds to

---

[82] Sasine means the act of giving and taking possession of land.
[83] Registration Act 1617.
[84] No record of plans attached to deeds was kept at Register House prior to 1924 and plans were only automatically recorded from 1933.
[85] See Prescription, para.12–35 below.
[86] 1979 Act s.30.
[87] The final areas in the Highlands and Islands were declared operational from April 2003.

be satisfied that the person registering the title is the owner of the specified land. Once satisfied, the title is registered and a land certificate is issued which will have a plan attached. This will be an ordinance survey plan and will accurately delineate the boundaries of the land.

The certificate has four sections:

- property section, detailing the property and referring to the plan;
- proprietorship section, stating who the owner is;
- charges section, detailing any securities over the property;
- burdens section, setting out the burdens which affect the property.

The effect of registration of title is that the title is guaranteed and indemnity will be paid if a subsequent problem arises with the title.[88] If the Keeper anticipates a potential problem as there is some doubt as to certain aspects of the title of the person seeking to register, for instance a doubt as to whether a piece of land forms part of the subjects actually owned by the person seeking to register, it is open to the Keeper to exclude indemnity from part of the title.[89]

It is also open to the Keeper to rectify the Land Register by altering the register in certain circumstances.[90] This is a problem area, as the purpose of the Land Register is to guarantee title and the guarantee will be undermined if the register can be altered after a title has been registered and a land certificate issued.[91]

A further problem with registration generally arose recently following the case of *Sharp v Thomson*[92] Prior to that case it was accepted that registration in the appropriate register was essential to create a real right and that any earlier stage, such as the delivery of the title deed by a seller to a purchaser, would not create a right greater than a personal right.[93]

Sharp v Thomson
1997 S.C. (H.L.) 66

The Thomsons purchased a flat from a company, Albyn Construction Ltd. The first stage of a contract for the sale, the missives was concluded. The company had a floating charge over its whole property including the house sold to the Thomsons. Due to a departure from normal conveyancing practice the document transferring the title to the Thomsons, the disposition was delivered late and then not registered straight away. Before the disposition was registered, the company went into receivership and the floating charge "crystallised" over the assets. The question was who received the house? Scottish land law is clear that the receivership should take precedence over the Thomsons as the disposition was not recorded and that was the decision of the Inner House of the Court of Session. The House of Lords, however, reversed this, apparently because the result was manifestly unjust. The actual reason for their decision is not entirely clear but can be explained by the

---

88 1979 Act s.12.
89 1979 Act s.12(2).
90 1979 Act s.9.
91 See generally the series of cases leading to *Short's Trs v Chung*, 1999 S.L.T. 751.
92 1997 S.C. (H.L.) 66.
93 *Gibson v Hunter Homes Design Ltd.* 1976 S.C. 23.

interpretation of the provisions in the relevant legislation on floating charges. This decision seems to go against a fundamental principle of Scottish land law and has been subject to much criticism.[94]

Subsequent to *Sharp v Thomson* it was hoped that this deviation from the principle that registration is essential to create a real right would only apply to situations involving a company receivership. This was confirmed in the case of *Burnett's Tr. v Grainger*,[95] where there was a failed attempt to extend this deviation to the sequestration of an individual. In this case a house was purchased, missives concluded, and the disposition delivered but not registered by the purchaser. The seller was then sequestrated, that is made bankrupt, and the trustee in sequestration of the seller registered his title before the disposition was belatedly registered by the purchaser. The Sheriff Principal held that the House of Lords decision in *Sharp v Thomson* also applied to a sequestration. His decision was overturned by the Inner House of the Court of Session, which ruled that the decision in *Sharp v Thomson* did not apply to a trustee in sequestration situation and this was upheld by the House of Lords.

The problems raised by the case of *Sharp v Thomson* and other aspects of the new system, such as rectification of the Register, highlighted the fact that the new system has various shortcomings. This led the Scottish Law Commission to undertake a complete review of the registration system. The Commission issued a Report in 2010.[96] In December 2011 the Scottish Government introduced the Land Registration etc. (Scotland) Bill 2011 into the Scottish Parliament. At the time of writing the Bill has commenced its course through the Scottish Parliament, but it is anticipated that the changes to the current system will not come into force until 2014 at the earliest. The Bill makes detailed changes to improve the current system, makes provision for the use of electronic conveyancing and electronic registration and provides for a speeding up of the process for eventual completion of the Land Register containing all land in Scotland.

Key Concepts

The **Register of Sasines** is a register of deeds only, not a register of title and title is not guaranteed. The **Land Register** is a register of title where the title flows from the register itself and the Land Register does guarantee title.

Prescription

Prescription may be positive or negative. The function of positive prescription is to create **12–35** rights in land or render existing rights unchallengeable. The function of negative prescription is to extinguish rights which have not been exercised. Both types of prescription have existed under the common law and there was a statute on prescription as early as 1617.[97] The main statute dealing with the modern law of prescription dates from 1973.[98]

---

[94] See for example—"Jam today: Sharp in the House of Lords", 1997 S.L.T. (News) 79.
[95] 2004 S.C. (H.L.) 19.
[96] Scottish Law Commission *Report on Land Registration* (2010), Scot. Law Com. No.222.
[97] Prescription Act 1617.
[98] Prescription and Limitation (Scotland) Act 1973.

The most important changes over the years have been to the length of the various prescriptive periods.

The two main periods of negative prescription set out in the 1973 Act are known as the short negative prescription and the long negative prescription. The former is a period of five years[99] and the Act sets out various rights such as the right to receive payment of rent under a lease which will be extinguished if not exercised during the period.[100] The latter is a period of 20 years[101] and includes such rights as a servitude right of way which will be similarly extinguished if not exercised during the period.

Positive prescription operates to create a right or to fortify an existing right. The operation of positive prescription alongside the system of registration of a deed in the Register of Sasines ensures that the registration system functioned effectively for many years. For positive prescription to operate a person must have a suitable title to an interest in land and have had suitable possession of that interest for the appropriate prescriptive period. The 1973 Act sets out the nature of the title and possession which is required.[102] Positive prescription usually applies to the right of ownership of land but also applies to other rights such as servitudes,[103] recorded leases[104] and salmon fishings.[105]

The title must be ex facie valid, that is valid on the face of it and not forged.[106] It need not be in good faith. The possession must be for the appropriate period and openly, peaceably and without judicial interruption.[107] Openly simply means that the right has been possessed in an obvious and unsecretive way. Peaceably simply means that there has been no dispute over the possession and without judicial interruption means that the possession has not been challenged by some court or similar action.[108]

The appropriate period is 10 years for most interests including the right of ownership,[109] 20 years for rights in respect of the foreshore and salmon fishings,[110] and also in respect of recorded leases,[111] positive servitudes and public rights of way.[112]

Key Concepts

The function of **positive prescription** is to create rights in land or render existing rights unchallengeable. The function of **negative prescription** is to extinguish rights which have not been exercised.

---

[99] 1973 Act s.6.
[100] 1973 Act Sch.1.
[101] 1973 Act s.7.
[102] 1973 Act s.1.
[103] 1973 Act s.3.
[104] 1973 Act s.2.
[105] 1973 Act s.1(2).
[106] 1973 Act s.1.
[107] 1973 Act s.1.
[108] The appropriate actions are set out in s.4.
[109] 1973 Act s.1.
[110] 1973 Act s.1(5).
[111] 1973 Act s.2.
[112] 1973 Act s.3.

Extent of landownership

If a person owns heritable property or land, various questions arise as to the extent of that **12–36** landownership. What exactly is the physical extent of the landownership? What are the actual property rights that go with ownership of the land? To what extent is an owner of land restricted in the use and enjoyment of the land? The first two questions are now dealt with under the headings *Physical extent of landownership* and *Incidents of landownership* and the third under the following section *Restrictions on landownership*.

Physical extent of landownership

The physical boundaries of land with neighbouring land will be determined by the title **12–37** deeds. In an ideal world, all titles to land will have an accurate plan attached which clearly sets out where the physical boundaries are. This is one of the aims of the Land Register introduced in 1979 whereby all title deeds of all land in Scotland will have an ordinance survey plan showing the physical boundaries. This will not happen for some considerable time, however.[113] Meantime, many title deeds registered in the Register of Sasines do not have accurate plans or have no plans at all.[114] The question of where the boundaries are must be determined by a construction of the wording in the title deeds. All too often the wording is vague or ambiguous in such titles and boundary disputes are not uncommon.

Where the description in the title deeds is referred to as a "bounding" description this will normally contain specific details of the boundaries and will be sufficient to accurately identify the actual boundaries. Where there is an ambiguity, prescription may establish the extent of the land and where the boundaries are. If a landowner has a recorded title, which on the face of it could be interpreted as including the boundary the landowner claims is the true boundary and the landowner possesses the land contained by that boundary peaceably, openly and without judicial interruption for the prescriptive period of 10 years,[115] that boundary will normally become the legal boundary. The position is not straightforward, however, and this whole area is a problem one for conveyancers.

Landownership is theoretically from "the heavens to the centre of the earth".[116] This means that a landowner owns the airspace above the land and the ground strata below. This allows a landowner to prevent encroachment into the airspace by such things as overhanging branches of a neighbour's tree[117] or a tower crane.[118] This right is subject to limitations. A landowner cannot prevent aeroplanes flying overhead. There is statutory provision to allow aeroplanes to fly over property at a reasonable height.[119] Further upwards, there are statutes dealing with space exploration and outer space.[120] Below the ground there are also restrictions. Certain precious metals belong to the Crown under a statute dating back to 1424,[121] as do petroleum and natural gas.[122] The coal and the right to mine for it vest in the British Coal Authority.[123] Other minerals are included with landownership but the right of ownership to these can be severed.

---

[113] See Registration, para.12–34 above.
[114] No record of plans attached to deeds was kept at Register House prior to 1924 and plans were only automatically recorded from 1933.
[115] Prescription and Limitation (Scotland) Act 1973 s.1; see Prescription, para.12–35 above.
[116] The latin maxim is *a coelo usque ad centrum.*
[117] *Halkerston v Wedderburn* (1781) Mor. 10495.
[118] *Brown v Lee Construction Ltd*, 1977 S.L.T. (Notes) 61.
[119] Civil Aviation Act 1982.
[120] For example, the Outer Space Act 1986.
[121] Royal Mines Act 1424.
[122] Petroleum Act 1998.
[123] Coal Industry Act 1994.

Halkerston v Wedderburn
(1781) Mor. 10495

Wedderburn's garden in Inverness had elm trees in it. The branches of the elm trees grew to overhang his neighbour, Halkerston's property. Halkerston was annoyed and went to court. The court decided that Wedderburn was bound to prune his trees so that they would not overhang Halkerston's property. Although not actually decided in the case itself, this case is usually taken as authority for a neighbour's right to remove an encroachment of branches of trees.

In a tenement, in the absence of provisions in the title deeds, ownership extends vertically to the mid-point of the joist separating upper and lower individual flats.[124] Ownership of the air space above the roof or the highest point of a sloping roof belongs to the ground floor flat owner.

Fixtures

12–38 Ownership of land includes ownership of any buildings on the land under the principle of accession. When moveable items are attached to a building or land these items may convert to become heritable and part of the building or land by accession. The law on this is known as the law of fixtures.

Prior to 1876, Scots law on fixtures seemed simple and straightforward but a case decided in that year has complicated the position.[125]

Brand's Trustees v Brand's Trustees
(1876) 3 R. (H.L.) 16

Mining machinery was introduced onto land leased by a tenant for use in the tenant's business. The tenant died and the question was who owned the mining machinery? Prior to this case it was generally understood that the position in Scots law was that, if moveables were introduced onto land and were removable, they did not become a fixture and that the intention of the parties was a relevant factor. The machinery in dispute was removable. The case was decided by the House of Lords with three English judges sitting. These judges assumed that the law on fixtures was the same in Scotland and England and applied English law in their decision. English law was different. It provided that mining machinery was a trade fixture which belonged to the landlord on the tenant's death unless previously removed. Accordingly, they decided that the machinery belonged to the landlord. The intention of the parties was irrelevant.

It appears that there are usually three essentials before an item of moveable property will accede to heritable property. These are:

- physical attachment;
- functional subordination;
- a degree of permanency.

---

[124] See Law of the tenement, para.12–40 below.
[125] *Brand's Trs v Brand's Trs* (1876) E.R. (H.L.) 16.

There must be some degree of physical attachment. The greater the physical attachment the more likely accession has taken place. For instance, wallpaper attached to a wall will accede but a picture loosely attached by a picture hook will not. In between these extremes a painting on a panel which could be removed without damage but which exposed a bare wall was held to remain moveable.[126] The weight of an item may make it a fixture, as with a two ton summer house.[127]

Functional subordination is where the use of the moveable item is subordinated to the use of the heritable property. For instance, if storage heaters are attached to a heritable property the function of these is to heat the heritable property and they become fixtures, even though they are relatively easy to remove.[128]

There must be some degree of permanency before a moveable item becomes a fixture. This will vary according to circumstances but the attachment must be more than temporarily. If any change is made to the item to make it fit in a building or if the building is adapted to take the item such as laying special foundations, this will be a strong indication of permanency.[129]

In addition to these three essentials, there are other factors which may be relevant. Whether an item can be removed without destruction of the item itself or damage to the land or building may be important. If it can, it is more likely to be regarded as moveable, but if it cannot, then it may well be a fixture.[130]

The intention of the parties would seem to be a relevant factor but the case of *Brand's Trs v Brand's Trs* in 1876 ruled that it is not. However, a later case appears to allow some room for the deemed intention of the parties to be relevant.[131]

Even though the item has become a fixture by accession, there may be a right to remove the fixture in certain circumstances. This right to remove applies to certain trade fixtures which the tenant has introduced for business use[132] and certain agricultural fixtures in agricultural holdings.[133] It is not clear whether tenants can remove domestic or ornamental fixtures, as is the case in England.[134]

Crown rights

Various rights of property vest in the Crown as sovereign. These Crown rights are known **12–39** as *regalia*. *Regalia* are divided into two types, *regalia majora* and *regalia minora*. The former are held by the Crown in trust for the public and cannot be sold. This means that such rights are, in practice, public rights. The latter originally belonged to the Crown but could be disposed of by the Crown by sale or other means and are now under the control of the Crown Estate Commissioners.

The *regalia majora* are the right to navigate, moor temporarily and fish for white fish in relation to the sea, the foreshore and tidal navigable rivers. The foreshore is that part of the beach which lies between the high and low water marks of the spring tides. In addition, the public have a right of access for recreation to the foreshore under the common law.

The *regalia minora* are the right to certain precious metals under the Royal Mines Act 1424, treasure and lost property, salmon fishings and the foreshore itself.

---

[126] *Cochrane v Stevenson* (1891) 18 R. 1208.
[127] *Christie v Smith's Ex.,* 1949 S.C. 572.
[128] *Assessor of Fife v Hodgson,* 1966 S.C. 30.
[129] *Scottish Discount Co v Blin,* 1985 S.C. 216.
[130] *Dowall v Miln* (1874) 1 R. 1180.
[131] *Scottish Discount Co v Blin,* above.
[132] *Syme v Harvey* (1861) 24 D. 202.
[133] Agricultural Holdings (Scotland) Act 1991 s.18.
[134] *Spyer v Phillipson* (1931) 2 Ch. 183.

Law of the tenement

12–40 A tenement is a building comprising two or more flats which are divided from each other horizontally. It is a widespread type of building in Scotland and rules regarding the ownership of different parts of a tenement developed at common law. These rules regarding ownership were subject to the overriding common interest in the whole tenement of all the owners. The individual titles of flats in many tenements contain specific provisions in relation to the common parts of a tenement. In the absence of such provisions, or where they are unclear or not comprehensive, the common law of the tenement applied, prior to the introduction of statutory provisions under the Tenements (Scotland) Act 2004.[135] The common law rules were not entirely satisfactory and this Act was introduced to improve the position as part of the major updating of Scottish land law. The provisions came into force on November 28, 2004, the day the feudal system was abolished and when the Title Conditions (Scotland) Act 2003 also came into force. The Act replaces the common law rules but the new rules remain "default" rules. If the individual titles contain specific provisions, these will continue to apply.

> **Rafique v Amin**
> 1997 S.L.T. 1385
>
> There were provisions in the title deed of flats in a tenement property which purported to alter the common law of the tenement in respect of common property. It appears that the drafting did not achieve all that was intended. There was a dispute as to the rights of the proprietors of the flats. It was held that one proprietor had an absolute right of veto to prevent alterations to the common property.
>   Lord Justice-Clerk Ross (at 1387f): "It is somewhat ironical that if, instead of making these elaborate provisions regarding common property, the granter had allowed the more usual law of the tenement to prevail, many of these difficulties [in this case] would not have arisen."

The 2004 Act sets out who owns the individual parts of a tenement.[136] The *solum,* the ground on which the tenement is built, and adjacent ground belongs to the owner of the ground or basement flat, or where more than one, the *solum* below the individual flat and adjacent ground. The internal walls in flats are owned by the individual flat-owners; external walls are owned in sections by the flat owners whose flat they enclose and walls dividing flats are owned to the mid-point. Similarly, floors/ceilings are owned to the centre line of the joist. The roof and roof space within the roof is owned by the top floor flat owner, or where more than one, the section above the individual flat. The airspace above the roof belongs to the owner of the *solum,* following the principle that ownership extends from the centre of the earth to the heavens.[137] There is a new provision where there is a sloping roof. The airspace above the slope up to the highest point belongs to the top floor flat owner.[138] Previously, it was an encroachment to build a dormer window into this airspace.[139]

The close, comprising the common passage, stairs and landings, is the common property

---

[135] *Rafique v Amin*, 1997 S.L.T. 1385.
[136] Tenements (Scotland) Act 2004 ss.2 & 3.
[137] See Physical extent of landownership, para.12–37 above.
[138] 2004 Act s.2(7).
[139] *Watt v Burgess's Trs* (1891) 18 R. 766.

of all the flat owners, excluding any main door flat owners. This includes the *solum* below and the roof above the close. The position is the same with lifts. They are common property unless they serve one flat only. The ownership of other pertinents, such as pipes, chimneys and fire escapes, is determined by a service test. If they serve one flat only they are owned by that flat owner but if they serve more than one flat they are owned in common by the owners of the flats which they serve.

The right of common interest is re-stated in statutory form. Flat owners have a positive duty to maintain parts of a tenement which provides shelter or support for the tenement, unless this is unreasonable taking account of the age and condition of the tenement and the cost of maintenance.[140] They also have a negative duty not to do anything which would or would be likely to impair the shelter or support or interfere with the natural light enjoyed by any part of the tenement.[141]

Repairs to a tenement were a problem area under the common law. Decisions on whether repairs were necessary to the common parts of the tenement required the consent of all the flat owners. If a repair was essential it was probably the position that one owner could instruct the repair and recover from the others.[142] In some cases the local authority could issue a repairs notice in respect of such repairs [143] and this is still the case. Another problem was that responsibility for certain repairs was unfair. For instance, a top floor flat owner was solely responsible for repairs to the roof above his or her flat.

To improve the position on repairs the 2004 Act introduces a Tenement Management Scheme which applies in the absence of provisions in the titles of the flats in the tenement. This provides for repairs to scheme property which includes the common property in the tenement plus significant parts of the tenement including the *solum*, roof and load bearing walls.[144] In general, decisions regarding repairs to scheme property are taken by a simple majority with each flat owner having one vote.[145]

Key Concepts

Physical boundaries of land with neighbouring land will be determined by the title deeds. Landownership is theoretically from "the heavens to the centre of the earth".

When moveable items are attached to a building or land, these items may convert to become heritable and part of the building or land by accession under the law of **fixtures**. For this to happen there must be:

- physical attachment;
- functional subordination;
- a degree of permanency.

Various rights of property vest in the Crown as sovereign. These **Crown rights** are known as *regalia majora* and *regalia minora*.

---

[140] 2004 Act s.8.
[141] 2004 Act s.9.
[142] *Deans v Woolfson*, 1922 S.C. 221.
[143] Housing (Scotland) Act 1987 s.108.
[144] 2004 Act Sch.1 rule 1.
[145] 2004 Act Sch.1 rule 2.

> The individual titles of flats in many tenements contain specific provisions in relation to the common parts of a tenement but in the absence of provisions or where the provisions are unclear or not comprehensive the **law of the tenement** under the Tenements (Scotland) Act 2004 will apply.

Incidents of landownership

12–41 Landownership includes the right to exclusive possession of the land and to use and enjoy the land. Exclusive possession includes the right to prevent trespass and encroachment. The right to use and enjoy the land includes the right of support, certain rights in water, certain game and fishing rights and the right to be free from nuisance. These are sometimes collectively known as incidents of landownership.

Exclusive possession

12–42 A landowner has the right of exclusive possession of the land and can exclude others from the land. This possession will be natural possession where the landowner physically occupies the land personally. It is open to the landowner to give the right of actual physical possession to someone else, e.g. a tenant under a lease. Where this happens the possession by the tenant will be civil possession of behalf of the landlord landowner.

This right of exclusive possession is subject to various statutory restrictions whereby certain people are given the right to enter land in the public interest, for instance, gas board officials under the Gas Act 1995 and health and safety inspectors under the Health and Safety at Work etc. Act 1974. These restrictions are relatively uncontroversial, but substantial inroads into a landowner's right of exclusive possession were introduced under the controversial Land Reform (Scotland) Act 2003.

Subject to these qualifications and those under the 2003 Act, it follows from this right of exclusive possession that a landowner can prevent trespass or encroachment on the land.

Trespass and encroachment

12–43 Trespass is where a landowner's right of exclusive possession is encroached by the temporary intrusion of someone on the land. However, trespass is not by itself recognised as a crime in Scotland.[146] There is very little a landowner can do against a single act of trespass. The landowner can ask the trespasser to leave but cannot use force unless the trespasser threatens violence to person or property.[147] Trespass by itself is not a civil wrong either but, if damage is caused, the trespasser may be sued. It may be possible to obtain an interdict against trespass but this may not be granted if the trespass is trivial[148] or if repetition of the trespass is not expected.[149]

A landowner can endeavour to prevent trespass by notices, alarms or barbed wire but a duty of care is owed in delict to trespassers, which would prevent the use of such things as booby-traps.[150] A guard dog is permitted but there are rules on control and warnings.[151]

---

[146] See generally Gordon, *Criminal Law*, 3rd edn (W. Green, 2001), 15.43.
[147] *Wood v North British Railway Co* (1899) 2 F. 1.
[148] As with a straying pet lamb, in *Winans v Macrae* (1885) 12 R. 1051.
[149] *Hay's Trs v Young* (1877) 4 R. 398.
[150] Occupiers' Liability (Scotland) Act 1960 s.1(1).
[151] Guard Dogs Act 1975.

It is not trespass to enter on land in an emergency such as a fire, pursuit of a criminal or to avoid danger.[152]

The right of a landowner to prevent someone accessing his or her land is further restricted by the public right of access to land introduced under the Land Reform (Scotland) Act 2003.[153]

Encroachment is where a landowner's right of exclusive possession of the land including the airspace above the land is interfered with. Encroachment into airspace has already been noted.[154] Encroachment can also take place on or below ground. If roots from a neighbour's tree grow into land, this is an encroachment on that land. If the owner of minerals under a landowner's land extracts these without permission or express title to do so, this will also be an encroachment.

Like trespass, the usual remedy against encroachment is interdict.

Public access rights

Under the Land Reform (Scotland) Act 2003 Pt 1, new rights of public access to land have **12–44** been introduced which are often referred to as "the right to roam". Section 1 of the Act confers statutory access rights on land to everyone. These allow the public to be on land for specified purposes or to cross land. These purposes must be recreational, educational or commercial, provided it is one which could also be non-commercial, such as acting as a mountain guide.

Certain land is excluded from these rights.[155] These include buildings, school grounds, sports fields, building sites and land on which crops have been sown or are growing. Also excluded is sufficient land adjacent to houses to allow a reasonable measure of privacy. This is not precisely defined and has resulted in several high profile cases on how much land to exclude the public from is reasonable.[156] A further exclusion is where land has been open to the public on payment of a fee. This is intended to exclude tourist attractions.

These rights of access must be exercised responsibly by those using them[157] and landowners must manage their land responsibly to take account of these rights of the public.[158] Landowners are specifically prohibited from taking action to prevent exercise of these rights such as putting up notices, obstructions or leaving animals at large.[159] Enforcement powers are given to local authorities.[160]

A Scottish Outdoor Access Code has been drawn up by Scottish Natural Heritage, as provided for in the 2003 Act, and approved by the Scottish Parliament. This sets out in detail how rights of access should be exercised responsibly.

Right of support

Land would collapse if it was not supported. Support is necessary from below and also **12–45** from surrounding land to prevent collapse or subsidence. It is a natural right of a landowner to receive such support and any operations beneath the land or on neighbouring land which cause surface damage will lead to a claim for damages. It is not necessary to

---

[152] Bell Princ. 956.
[153] See Public access rights, para.12–44 below.
[154] See Physical extent of landownership, para.12–37 above.
[155] 2003 Act s.6.
[156] See, especially, *Gloag v Perth and Kinross Council*, 2007 S.C.L.R. 530.
[157] 2003 Act s.2.
[158] 2003 Act s.3.
[159] 2003 Act s.14.
[160] 2003 Act Ch.5.

prove negligence.[161] Such a right of support arises automatically by law. In other situations a right of support may be implied in all the circumstances. An automatic right of support only arises in respect of the land itself and not buildings on the land, but such a right may be implied. This question usually arises when minerals are excavated under the land.

> ### Angus v National Coal Board
> ### 1955 S.C. 175
>
> This case concerned an action of damages brought after an agricultural worker died due to subsidence in a field where he was working and under which a colliery company had formerly worked coal.
>
> Lord Justice-Clerk Thomson (at 181): "The right of support is an incident of property ... The owner, in virtue of his ownership, has the right to have his land left in its natural state and he enjoys that right *qua* owner. If the owner's right of support is breached, he becomes entitled to damages for surface damage without requiring to establish negligence."

The right to work minerals may be reserved by a previous owner, usually the superior. In such cases a right of support of buildings will be implied where the buildings were already on the land at the time of reservation,[162] where there was an obligation imposed in the title to erect buildings when the reservation was made[163] or where the erection of buildings was clearly foreseen at the time of reservation.[164]

If buildings are damaged as a result of operations by a neighbouring landowner this may constitute a nuisance.[165]

Various statutes make provision for loss of support or damage. For instance, the Coal Mining Subsidence Act 1991 provides for remedial work to be paid by British Coal where subsidence to land or buildings is caused by the loss of support due to their mining operations.

Water rights

12–46 The law on water rights is established under the common law, although there are various statutory provisions which affect the position, such as those on control of pollution. The Crown has extensive rights in water, particularly the sea, sea lochs and tidal rivers as part of the Crown *regalia*.[166] This section deals with landowners who have water as part of the land they own. Water can be running water, such as rivers and streams, or still water, such as a loch or a bog.[167] Running water is ownerless. Still water which lies on the surface of land or water which percolates through the ground belongs to the owner of the land. This can be extracted by a well and can be used for manufacturing purposes even if it would

---

[161] *Angus v National Coal Board*, 1955 S.C. 175 at 181.
[162] *Caledonian Railway Co v Sprot* (1856) 2 Macq. 449.
[163] *North British Railway Co v Turners Ltd* (1904) 6 F. 900.
[164] *Neill's Trs v William Dixon Ltd* (1880) 7 R. 741.
[165] *Lord Advocate v The Reo Stakis Organisation Ltd*, 1982 S.L.T. 140.
[166] See Crown rights, para.12–39 above.
[167] Stair states "running waters are common to all men, because they have no bounds; but water standing, and capable of bounds, is appropriated", Inst II.i.5.

otherwise flow to a stream.[168] Such water can be discharged onto a lower landowner's land if it naturally flows that way, but not in a polluted state.[169]

Lochs are either sea lochs or fresh water lochs. A sea loch is equated to the sea and belongs to the Crown.[170] For other lochs, if the loch is completely surrounded by a landowner's own property the landowner has full rights of ownership in the loch. Where a loch is surrounded by land belonging to different landowners, these landowners own the loch, with the right to sail on it and catch fish other than salmon in it, in common. The bed of the loch, the *alveus*, is owned by each landowner adjacent to their land up to the centre of the loch.

The rights in rivers and streams depend on whether they are navigable or non-navigable. If a navigable river is tidal, the Crown owns the *alveus*[171] but the public have a right to navigate and fish the river, and to moor boats temporarily on the river.[172] If the navigable river is non-tidal, the banks and the *alveus* to the mid-point of the river are owned by the riparian owners, those owning land up to the banks of the river. This is subject to the public's right of navigation. There is also a common interest in the flow of the water and a riparian proprietor cannot do anything to interfere with the quality of the water or the amount of the flow. The riparian owners must not interfere with the public right of navigation.[173] The question of whether a river is navigable and the extent of the right of navigation can be a matter of dispute.[174]

> ### Orr Ewing & Co. v Colquhoun's Trustees
> ### (1873) 4 R. (H.L.) 116
>
> The owner of land on both banks of a river constructed a bridge across the river. Two of the piers were built in the water. From time immemorial, small vessels had used the river to get from the River Clyde to Loch Lomond. Objection was taken to this artificial structure in the river. The Inner House of the Court of Session held that the river was a public navigable river and no one had a right to erect structures on the bed of the river. The House of Lords reversed this decision and held that, while the public may have a right of navigation in a non-tidal navigable river, the proprietors of the *alveus* are entitled to erect structures on it unless the structure so erected would actually interfere with and obstruct navigation.

Where a river is non-navigable, the riparian owners own the banks and the *alveus* to the mid-point of the river. The riparian owners have a common interest in the water and can use their section of it for sailing and other activities, subject to the same restrictions which prevent interference with the quality or flow of water. Each owner can take water from the river for drinking or washing even if this diminishes the flow, but not for any commercial purpose, unless there is no change to the flow or quality of the water.

---

[168] *Milton v Glen-Moray Glenlivet Distillery Co* (1898) 1 F. 135.
[169] *Montgomerie v Buchanan's Trs* (1853) 15 D. 853.
[170] See Crown rights, para.12–39 above.
[171] See Crown rights, para.12–39 above.
[172] *Crown Estates Commissioners v Fairlie Yacht Slip Ltd*, 1979 S.C. 156.
[173] *Orr Ewing & Co v Colquhoun's Trs* (1877) 4 R. (H.L.) 116.
[174] See, e.g. *Wills' Trs v Cairngorm Canoeing & Sailing School Ltd*, 1976 S.C. (H.L.) 30. It was held that a one-way right of navigation existed where logs had been floated down a river to the sea from time in memorial.

Fishing and game rights

12–47 The right of ownership includes the right to fish in lochs, rivers and streams belonging to the landowner. Tidal navigable rivers and lochs belong to the Crown and the public has a right to fish, other than for salmon, in these. If there is more than one owner of a river, each riparian owner has the right to fish to the mid-point of the river. The riparian owners must fish from their own side, but may cast their rods across the mid-point. The right to fish does not include salmon unless this is separately owned, as salmon fishing forms part of the *regalia minora* of the Crown. Salmon fishing is regulated by statute, principally under the Salmon and Freshwater Fisheries (Consolidation) (Scotland) Act 2003.

Certain animals are classed as game under various statutes and these include hares, rabbits, pheasants and grouse.[175] A landowner has the right to kill game on the land. It is possible and common to lease shooting rights. The right belongs to the owner, not the occupier and a tenant does not have the right unless specifically leased to the tenant. There are also various statutory provisions aimed at preventing poaching, including the Night Poaching Act 1828 and the Poaching Prevention Act 1862.

Freedom from nuisance

12–48 A landowner is entitled to be free from actions and behaviour by other landowners which interfere with the enjoyment of the land. Such conduct may constitute a nuisance under the common law and is considered in the next section on restrictions on landownership.

Key Concepts

Landownership includes various **incidental rights** which are:

- exclusive possession and the right to be free from trespass and encroachment;
- water rights;
- support;
- fishing and game rights;
- freedom from nuisance.

Restrictions on landownership

12–49 Although theoretically an owner of land is unrestricted in the use and enjoyment of the land, there are various restrictions on this use. These restrictions are imposed for the benefit of other landowners and for the public generally. They exist to limit the activities of a landowner which may be detrimental to neighbours or the public generally, to regulate property which may be owned or used in common and to give landowners certain rights to another's land. These restrictions may be imposed by law or may be agreed by the owner. When agreed by the owner they are usually inserted in the owner's title as title conditions and are generally known as real burdens and servitudes.

Real burdens and servitudes are interrelated but have different origins, as servitudes derive from Roman law and real burdens were developed in the nineteenth century as a practical necessity when property was sold. The law under the common law was complex and uncertain in parts, particularly in relation to real burdens. There were various areas of difficulty, such as entitlement to enforce real burdens and the ability to extinguish a real

---

[175] Wildlife and Countryside Act 1981 and other Acts.

burden. There were some, but insufficient, statutory provisions. The Title Conditions (Scotland) Act 2003 simplifies and modernises the law on real burdens and servitudes to a large extent, although some problems remain. The law on real burdens created after the Act came into force is clear and coherent, but the position relating to real burdens created before then is not free from difficulty. Real burdens and servitudes are examined in some detail below.

The 2003 Act deliberately uses the term "title conditions" and details the type of conditions covered by the Act. This encompasses both real burdens and servitudes and includes others such as conditions in long leases.

Restrictions at common law and by statute

There are restrictions imposed by law on the use and enjoyment of land. This is both under **12–50** the common law and extensively by statute. The restrictions under the common law are sometimes referred to as the law of neighbourhood, as the underlying principle is that a landowner cannot use land in such a way as to interfere with a neighbour's use and enjoyment of their land. If such interference is regarded as unlawful, it amounts to a nuisance which is a delictual wrong.

Nuisance

A nuisance can be caused to the public generally as well as to neighbours. **12–51**
Nuisance is defined as:

> "Whatever obstructs the public means of commerce and intercourse ... Whatever is noxious or unsafe, or renders life uncomfortable to the public generally, or to the neighbourhood; whatever is intolerably offensive to individuals, in their dwelling houses, or inconsistent with the comfort of life".[176]

Various factors are taken into account to ascertain whether or not a nuisance has been committed, including the nature of the harm suffered and the nature of the conduct causing the harm. There are not many recent cases on nuisance, probably as there are many statutory provisions which deal with conduct which may also be a common law nuisance.[177]

Webster v Lord Advocate
1984 S.L.T. 13

The owner of a flat adjacent to and overlooking Edinburgh Castle esplanade sought an interdict against nuisance by noise caused by the erection of scaffolding for the Edinburgh Military Tattoo and the Tattoo itself. It was held that the Tattoo itself was not a nuisance but the noise from the erection of steel scaffolding was, although the interdict was postponed for six months to allow the Tattoo to proceed and allow a system of scaffolding erection to be considered which did not involve a nuisance.

---

[176] Bell Princ. 974.
[177] One recent case is *Webster v Lord Advocate*, 1984 S.L.T. 13.

The usual remedy against a nuisance is an interdict. If damage has been caused, it will be necessary to establish blame before damages can be recovered.[178]

Spite

12–52 Another common law restriction which is rarely but sometimes established is where the conduct of a landowner is regarded as spiteful[179] and is for no other purpose than to cause harm to neighbours. Older cases deal with such matters as erecting a wall on a boundary to block out a neighbour's light[180] but, in a relatively recent case, shutting off a water pipe which supplied the pursuer and ran through the defender's garden was held to be within the doctrine.[181]

Statutes

12–53 Many statutes impose restrictions on the use of land in various ways. These include legislation on town and country planning, building control, the countryside, public health, housing and civic government, health and safety at work and environmental matters. In all these statutes in these areas and many more there is some restriction on the use a land-owner can make of land.

Real burdens

12–54 A real burden is defined in the Title Conditions (Scotland) Act 2003 as:

> "An encumbrance on land constituted in favour of the owner of other land in that person's capacity as owner of that other land."[182]

It is an obligation in respect of the land which is inserted in the title to that land for the benefit of another landowner. If it is properly constituted it will be enforceable against the owner of the burdened land for the time being by the owner of the other land for the time being and is said to "run with the land". Often these burdens have been inserted long ago but they remain enforceable against the burdened proprietor by the benefited proprietor.

Historical background—feudal and non-feudal burdens

12–55 Under the feudal system, it was usual for the superior to insert real burdens in the title of the vassal to restrict the use of the land by the vassal. This originally served a useful purpose in the days before there were any statutes dealing with such matters as planning restrictions, development control and pollution. These burdens acted as a social control on land which would otherwise be uncontrolled. If a superior retained other land in the vicinity it was in the superior's interest that land in the community was properly regulated. In the modern era, feudal burdens caused problems as superiors were still able to enforce these burdens even when they had disposed of all their property in the neighbourhood. Just by being the superior entitled the superior to enforce the burden.

Real burdens could also be created in transfers which were not feudal transfers by subinfeudation but ordinary transfers by substitution. Such burdens are non-feudal burdens.

---

[178] *RHM Bakeries (Scotland) Ltd v Strathclyde Regional Council*, 1985 S.L.T. 214.
[179] The Latin term is *aemulatio vicini*.
[180] e.g. *Ross v Baird* (1827) 7 S. 361.
[181] *More v Boyle*, 1967 S.L.T. (Sh. Ct) 38.
[182] 2003 Act s.1(1).

Under the Abolition of Feudal Tenure etc. (Scotland) Act 2000, feudal burdens have been abolished and only non-feudal burdens remain. Certain non-feudal burdens have been converted into non-feudal burdens.

Types of real burden

Real burdens can be affirmative, which involves a positive obligation, for instance to build **12–56** and maintain a boundary wall, or negative, which involves refraining from certain actions, for instance to refrain from using a house for commercial purposes.[183] There may also be an ancillary burden to either of these.[184]

Real burdens can be praedial or personal. Praedial is the usual type of real burden and requires a benefited and burdened land.[185] The burden must be for the benefit of the land itself or a community of land and not simply for the owner of the land. Such a benefit would be a personal benefit and not a real benefit. The whole concept of a real burden is that it is for the benefit of whoever happens to be the owner of that land for the time being, which will change from time to time. The 2003 Act, however, introduced a new type of non-praedial burden, known as a personal real burden, which appears a contradiction in terms.

These were introduced for limited situations.[186] They are real burdens in the sense that they can be enforced against anyone, but they are personal to a particular benefited proprietor only and there is no benefited land. For instance, one type of personal real burden is a conservation burden. This type of burden can be created to preserve the architectural, historical or other special characteristics of land in favour of a conservation body such as Scottish Natural Heritage, which will have the sole right to enforce the burden, whether or not they own land in the vicinity of the burdened land.[187]

The two main types of praedial real burdens are community burdens and neighbour burdens. Community burdens are defined in the 2003 Act. This is where a burden is imposed on a common scheme of two or more units of land, and each of the owners is both a benefited and burdened proprietor. A typical example is burdens in a tenement of two or more flats which regulate matters relating to the tenement building, and where each flat owner has to comply with the burden and can enforce it against the other flat owners.

A neighbour burden is not defined in the 2003 Act but is where a burden has been placed in a piece of land for the benefit of the neighbour only. A typical example is where an owner of a house sells off part of his or her garden and imposes burdens on the use of the garden ground which is sold, such as limiting any house built on the ground to one storey. This burden will be enforceable by the owner of the original house only and has a "one way" effect.

Other types of praedial real burden under the 2003 Act are facility burdens, service burdens[188] and manager burdens.[189] These burdens are less common than community and neighbour burdens, which are the most important type.

---

[183] Title Conditions (Scotland) Act 2003 s.2(1)(a) and (b).
[184] 2003 Act s.2(2).
[185] *Praedium* means another piece of land.
[186] There are eight types set out in the Title Conditions (Scotland) Act 2003 s.1(3).
[187] 2003 Act ss.38–42.
[188] 2003 Act s.122.
[189] 2003 Act s.63.

Creation of real burdens

12–57 Real burdens are inserted in the title of the burdened proprietor by the benefited proprietor, usually when the land is being transferred for the first time, or can appear in a separate deed of conditions

Until the 2003 Act was passed, the rules for the creation of real burdens were set out in the common law. One of the criticisms of real burdens under the common law was a lack of transparency. The existence of a real burden was not as clearly defined as it might be and it was frequently not entirely clear who had the right to enforce the burden. Under the 2003 Act, the rules for creation were largely re-enacted with three additional rules to make it easier to find out details of new real burdens after they are created.

The leading case of *Tailors of Aberdeen v Coutts*[190] sets out the requirements of a real burden under the common law.

Tailors of Aberdeen v Coutts
(1840) 1 Rob. App. 296

This dispute involved a disposition by the Tailors of Aberdeen to George Nicol of part of Bon Accord Square in Aberdeen. Nicol undertook a number of obligations including, in particular, an obligation to build houses and to pay two thirds of the cost of forming and enclosing the central square. Nicol then became insolvent and the subjects were sold and conveyed to Coutts. The essential question was whether the obligations imposed on Nicol in the disposition were enforceable against Coutts. The court's judgment sets out in detail the requirements for the constitution of real burdens.

These are:

- clear intention to burden the land not the person;
- acceptable purpose;
- expressed in clear terms;
- registered in the Register of Sasines (or Land Register).

These rules are more or less re-enacted under the new rules for creation in ss.3–6 of the 2003 Act. These can now be more accurately stated as:

- the burden must be praedial for the benefit of the land, excepting community burdens which must be for the benefit of the community and personal real burdens which must be for the benefit of a specified person;
- the burden cannot be illegal;
- the burden cannot be contrary to public policy, such as an unreasonable restraint on trade;
- the burden cannot be repugnant with ownership;
- the burden cannot impose a monopoly;
- the burden must be set out in a constitutive deed and be registered.

---

[190] (1840) 1 Rob. App. 296.

Various other cases under the common law have clarified aspects of these rules. It is unsurprising that a burden must be for an acceptable purpose and not be illegal, contrary to public policy, impose a monopoly or be repugnant with ownership. An example of the last aspect would be an attempt to prevent a landowner having the right to lease the land. An unsuccessful attempt to create a monopoly was discussed in *Aberdeen Varieties v James F Donald (Aberdeen Cinemas) Ltd.*[191]

It is also not unsurprising that a real burden must be in clear and unambiguous terms. There is a presumption that landownership is free from restriction and any restriction is strictly construed *contra proferentem*, that is against the person wishing to apply the restriction. Examples of wording rejected as too vague and ambiguous by the courts include a restriction against any building "of an unseemly description" in *Murray's Trustees v St Margaret's Convent Trustees,*[192] and a prohibition against any operations the superior "may deem objectionable" in *Meriton Ltd v Winning,*[193] although the court did consider that the wording may be appropriate in certain circumstances. In *Anderson v Dickie,*[194] a purported real burden was inserted in a title deed to impose conditions on part of the ground attached to a mansion house. The wording referred to "the ground occupied as the lawn". This was held to be too imprecise wording for the constitution of a real burden. Under the Act, it is provided that the real burden must be set out in a constitutive deed which will usually be in the individual title deeds themselves but may be in a separate deed of conditions. If it is not, the burden will only be personally binding on the original parties and will not become real and run with the land.[195]

The three new rules apply to all new real burdens created after the Act came into force.

First, a new real burden must be specifically named in the deed which creates it as a "real burden" or a particular type of burden, such as a "community burden".[196] This makes it easier to identify the burden when examining the deed. Secondly, the deed must specify both the burdened and benefited land.[197] This prevents problems in identifying who exactly is entitled to enforce the burden. Thirdly and most importantly, the burden must be registered in the title of both the burdened and benefited land. Previously, the burden was only registered in the title of the burdened land and this dual registration will make the position much more transparent.

Enforcement of real burdens

A validly created real burden exists as a restriction on the burdened land and can be **12–58** enforced against the owner of the burdened land by the owner of the benefited land. Enforcement is not automatic and the owner of the burdened land must satisfy certain requirements before the burden can be enforced. The right to enforce non feudal burdens under the common law was problematic as it is possible to have an implied right to enforce as well as an express right.

It is not possible to have an implied right to enforce new real burdens under the 2003 Act. One of the new requirements for the creation of a valid real burden is the need to specify the benefited land or community, if it is a community burden. This means that the person who has the right to enforce is expressed in the real burden. The problem of implied rights of enforcement in real burdens created prior to the Act remains.

---

[191] 1939 S.C. 488.
[192] 1907 S.C. (H.L.) 8.
[193] 1995 S.L.T. 76.
[194] 1915 S.C. (H.L.) 74.
[195] *Wallace v Simmers*, 1960 S.C. 255.
[196] 2003 Act s.4(2)(a) and (3).
[197] 2003 Act s.4(5).

Under the common law, it is necessary to have both a title and an interest to enforce a real burden. This is repeated in the 2003 Act which provides in s.8(1) that a real burden is enforceable by any person who has both a title and interest to enforce it. Prior to the abolition of the feudal system, only superiors had these automatically.

Under the common law, only the owner of the benefited property was in a position to satisfy these requirements to enforce. This was extended in the Act under s.8(2) to include a tenant of the owner of the benefited property and the non-entitled spouse of the owner.

As regards title, there is no problem with real burdens created after the Act because they require the benefited property to be named and the burden must be registered in the title of both the burdened and benefited property. The title to enforce is clearly expressed. It is also possible to have an express title to enforce under the common law and this presents no difficulty. The person who originally inserted the real burden in the title and the successors to the title of that person will have this. The difficulty lies in the possible existence of an implied title to enforce under the common law.

This implied right to enforce is known was a *ius quesitum tertio* which, if established, gave a neighbouring proprietor the right to enforce a real burden without an express title to do so. This is in addition to the proprietor with an express right to enforce. The law on this was developed in the leading case of *Hislop v MacRitchie's Trs*[198] and was complex and not entirely clear.

If the title creating the real burden was one of a number of titles granted to neighbouring landowners by the same person and all of these titles had the same real burdens, known as a common scheme, and there was clear reference to this common scheme or a mutuality of community interest amongst the landowners, then each landowner was able to enforce the real burdens against each other. This law was subsequently developed in further cases, notably *JA Mactaggart & Co v Harrower*,[199] but the position remained uncertain and imprecise. It created practical difficulties for a burdened proprietor who might not know who exactly was able to enforce the burden in their title. Implied rights could extend to a number of proprietors which potentially could be quite large and all these proprietors might be able to enforce.

Implied rights to enforce real burdens are abolished under s.49 of the Act, but the common law rules on implied rights are replaced with new statutory implied rights in respect of existing real burdens under ss.52–54. The rules established in *Hislop* are abolished but are largely re-enacted. The new implied rules have been subject to criticism and uncertainty in this area will continue.

Hislop v MacRitchie's Trustees
(1881) 8 R. (H.L.) 95

One side of a square was feued in separate feus for the erection of detached villas. There were conditions in each of the separate title deeds which were similar but there was no uniformity, other than the distance back from the street and the conditions were adapted to suit each house. There was no reference to a common feuing plan. The House of Lords held that this did not constitute any right in a third party to enforce the feuing conditions.

Lord Watson (at 102): "The fact of the same condition appearing in feu charters derived from a common superior, coupled with a substantial interest in its

---

[198] (1881) 8 R. (H.L.) 95.
[199] (1906) 8 F. 1101.

> observance does not appear to me to be sufficient to give each feuar a title to enforce it. No single feuar can, in my opinion, be subjected in liability to his co-feuars, unless it appears from the titles under which he holds his feu that such similarity of conditions and mutuality of interest among the feuars either had been or was meant to be established."

As regards interest, under the common law there is a need to have a patrimonial interest to enforce the burden except for superiors whose interest is implied. A patrimonial interest means that the property of the person concerned is affected by the burden and would suffer detriment if it is not enforced. It is possible to have an interest at some point which is subsequently lost due to a change in circumstances. Section 8(3)(a) of the Act provides the statutory requirement which is now necessary for an interest to enforce. It states that such an interest exists if failure to comply would result in material detriment to the value or enjoyment of ownership. This may seem straightforward but a controversial case on this was decided in 2008.

Barker v Lewis
2008 S.L.T. (Sh. Ct.) 17

There was a small rural development of five houses near St Andrews. The development was regulated by real burdens which included a restriction on the properties being used as a domestic dwelling house only. The proprietors of one house started using their house for a bed and breakfast business and the neighbours objected. It was decided that material detriment must amount to substantial inconvenience or annoyance and the neighbours had not shown this.

This seems a higher standard than was the case under the common law. In a subsequent case, it was confirmed that the standard was a high one but this high standard was demonstrated by the neighbours in that case.[200]

The final point to note on enforcement of real burdens is who is liable for the burdens? Affirmative burdens can only be enforced against the owner of the burdened property under s.9(1). Negative and ancillary burdens can also be enforced against a tenant or other occupier under s.9(2). If the burdened property is divided, all parts are liable for the burdens.

Variation, discharge and extinction of real burdens

Under the common law, it was virtually impossible prior to 1970 to vary or discharge a **12–59** real burden without the consent of the benefited proprietor who was often a superior. A variation of discharge was normally effected by a deed known as a minute of waiver, but payment was frequently demanded before a waiver was granted. This position was improved by the introduction of the Lands Tribunal for Scotland under the Conveyancing and Feudal Reform (Scotland) Act 1970. Part of the remit of this new tribunal is to hear applications from burdened proprietors to vary or discharge real burdens and other title conditions. The position was amended by the Title Conditions (Scotland) Act 2003.[201]

---

[200] *Kettlewell v Turning Point Scotland*, 2011 S.L.T. (Sh. Ct.) 143.
[201] See Variation and discharge by the Lands Tribunal, para.12–65 below.

After the 2003 Act, it is still possible to agree a minute of waiver or to make application to the Lands Tribunal. In addition, new ways of varying or discharging a real burden are introduced. Statutory provision is made for a real burden to be extinguished where acquiescence or negative prescription has taken place.

Acquiescence is a form of personal bar and applies when a real burden is breached without any objection by the person entitled to complain. Under the common law, a benefited proprietor could lose an interest to enforce a real burden by acquiescence.[202] The Act introduces a statutory rule on acquiescence for all real burdens which now exists along with the common law position.[203] If the burdened proprietor has incurred material expenditure and there is no objection in a period of 12 weeks, there is a presumption of consent and statutory acquiescence has occurred.

The 2003 Act also introduces a new negative prescription provision.[204] If a real burden is breached without challenge for a period of five years, it is extinguished to the extent of the breach.

There are special provisions made for either variation or discharge of community burdens.[205]

Many existing real burdens were created a considerable time ago and are of no relevance today. To remedy this, the 2003 Act introduces what is known as the "sunset rule".[206] If a real burden is more than 100 years old, the burdened proprietor known as "the terminator"[207] can intimate an intention to register a notice of termination on the benefited proprietor. If the benefited proprietor does nothing the notice can be registered and the burden discharged. If the benefited proprietor wishes to have the burden renewed and continued there must be an application to the Lands Tribunal which will decide whether to renew or discharge.[208]

Servitudes

12–60 A servitude is defined as a "burden on land or houses, imposed by agreement—express or implied—in favour of owners of other [land]".[209]

A servitude is similar to a real burden. If properly constituted it runs with the land. Although a real burden must appear in the title of the land, a servitude may be express in the title or implied. The benefited proprietor in servitudes is usually referred to as the owner of the dominant tenement[210] and the burdened proprietor is referred to as the owner of the servient tenement. A servitude only requires passive observance. For instance, if the servitude relates to access, there is no obligation to maintain the surface of the access in good condition. Servitudes must be positive which permit the owner of the dominant tenement to do something, such as exercise access over the servient tenement. Prior to the 2003 Act, it was possible to have a negative servitude which allowed the owner of the dominant tenement to prevent the owner of the servient tenement from doing something. Such servitudes were very similar to negative real burdens. Accordingly, the 2003 Act

---

[202] *Ben Challum Ltd v Buchanan*, 1955 S.C. 348.
[203] 2003 Act s.16.
[204] 2003 Act s.18.
[205] 2003 Act ss.32–37.
[206] 2003 Act ss.19–23.
[207] 2003 Act s.9(2).
[208] 2003 Act s.81(1)(b).
[209] Bell Princ. 979.
[210] Tenement in this sense means an interest in property not a block of flatted property.

prohibits the creation of negative servitudes[211] and converts existing negative servitudes into negative real burdens[212]

There are several essentials before servitude can be created. There must be two different tenements or interests in land owned by two different persons.[213] The land concerned must be neighbouring or reasonably adjacent if not actually contiguous. As with real burdens, the benefit must be for the land itself and the person who is the owner of that land for the time being and not the owner personally. Prior to the 2003 Act, the servitude had to be a known servitude or analogous to an existing servitude. Various attempts to extend the list were unsuccessful.[214] There is no such requirement for new servitudes under the 2003 Act.[215]

The list of main servitudes includes:

- right of way or passage over the burdened land;
- *aquaeductus*, the right to run water over or under the burdened land;
- *aquaehaustus*, the right to draw water from a source in the burdened land;
- pasturage, the right to feed cattle or sheep on the burdened land;
- stillicide, the right to let water run from buildings onto to burdened land;
- light and prospect which are negative servitudes which prevent building on the burdened land over a certain height or interfering with light or a view.

Creation of servitudes

Servitudes can be created in three ways: **12–61**

- express grant or reservation;
- implied grant or reservation;
- prescription.

A servitude may be expressly created by either granting to another when the title to that land is given or reserving to oneself when the title is given. In the former case the benefit of the servitude is for the grantee and in the latter it is for the granter. In either case the servitude is created by agreement. It is also possible to have a separate agreement constituting the servitude. It is not necessary for the deed in which the servitude appears to be recorded. No precise form of wording is required[216] and use of the word "servitude" is not required.[217]

Under the 2003 Act, a positive servitude must be in writing and registered in the title of both the benefited and burdened properties.[218]

A servitude may be implied, either as a grant or a reservation if the title deed omitted to include a servitude expressly and the servitude is necessary for the reasonable enjoyment of the property. For instance, if part of an owner's land has been sold and a servitude of access over the land sold is not reserved and the remaining land cannot be accessed and is

---

[211] 2003 Act s.79.
[212] 2003 Act s.80.
[213] Therefore, a public right of way is not a servitude. See *Ayr Burgh Council v British Transport Commission*, 1955 S.L.T. 219.
[214] See, for example, *Neill v Scobbie*, 1993 G.W.D. 13–887.
[215] 2003 Act s.76; see, for example, *Compugraphics International Ltd v Nikolic*, 2011 S.L.T. 955.
[216] *Axis West Developments Ltd v Chartwell Land Investments Ltd*, 1999 S.L.T. 1416.
[217] *Moss Bros Group plc v Scottish Mutual Assurance plc*, 2001 S.L.T. 641.
[218] 2003 Act s.75.

"landlocked", a servitude right of access may be implied.[219] There have been various cases on what is necessary for reasonable enjoyment.[220]

Ewart v Cochrane
(1869) 4 Macq. 117

The implied servitude sought in this case was a right to use a certain drain leading from the Cochranes' tanyard to a cesspool on land belonging to Ewart. The House of Lords held that an implied servitude was essential to the enjoyment of the property.

Murray v Medley
1973 S.L.T. (Sh. Ct) 75

The implied servitude sought in this case was a right to use a water pipe which ran under a building and piece of land sold by Murray to Medley and serving both Medley's property and property retained by Murray. The sheriff held there was no implied servitude right.

A servitude can be created by prescription by use continually for 20 years openly, peaceably and without judicial interruption under statute.[221]

Extinction of servitudes

12–62 Servitudes can be extinguished in a number of ways. These are by express discharge or renunciation; the two separate tenements coming into ownership of one person; negative prescription after 20 years where the servitude has not been exercised[222]; acquiescence where, for instance, an access has been blocked for some time; a change of circumstances where, for instance, a particular building which was the subject of the servitude has been demolished or by the Lands Tribunal.

Wayleaves and public rights of way

12–63 Wayleaves are pipeline servitudes which are granted in favour of utility companies under various statutes. They allow the utility company, for example, Scottish Gas, to enter onto property to lay and maintain service pipes. The statutes contain various provisions regarding reinstatement of the ground and relative matters.

A public right of way is different from, but has similar effect to a servitude right of way. It is also different from the public access rights introduced under the Law Reform (Scotland) Act 2003, discussed above. Under the common law, a public right of way can be created to give members of the public a right of way from one public place to another.

---

[219] Although whether this implied right of access is strictly a servitude has been questioned recently. See *Bowers v Kennedy*, 2000 S.L.T. 1006.
[220] Contrast *Ewart v Cochrane* (1869) 4 Macq. 117 and *Murray v Medley*, 1973 S.L.T. (Sh. Ct) 75.
[221] Prescription and Limitation (Scotland) Act 1973 s.3.
[222] Prescription and Limitation (Scotland) Act 1973 s.7.

They can be over public or private land and can be created expressly, which is rare, or by positive prescription for 20 years.[223]

Public rights of way only require a burdened property, unlike servitudes which also require a benefited property. The right of way must be between two public places. It only allows access and does not confer other rights. As with servitudes, the use must be as of right and not by permission or tolerance. The public use must be substantial, must be continuous and uninterrupted and be exercised along the whole route.[224] What is substantial use will depend on the nature of the right of way. The route may be in a populous area or in a remote one. The use may vary according to the season, for example, where it leads to a beach.

Like servitudes, public rights of way must be exercised in the least burdensome way to the landowner and they can be extinguished by prescription if not used for 20 years.[225]

Extinction and variation and discharge of title conditions by the Lands Tribunal

Title conditions generally can be extinguished in one of five ways: **12–64**

- express discharge or variation;
- prescription;
- consolidation;
- compulsory purchase;
- variation or discharge by the Lands Tribunal.

Express discharge is where the parties agree to discharge or vary the condition in some form of agreement. There are also specific statutory procedures relating to community burdens.[226] The long negative prescription will operate to extinguish a servitude which has not been exercised for 20 years.[227] Consolidation is where the ownership of the burdened and benefited land comes into single ownership. Compulsory purchase has the legal effect of extinguishing conditions in the title. In addition to extinction on these four grounds, it has been possible since 1970 to apply to the Lands Tribunal for Scotland to either vary or discharge a title condition.

Variation and discharge by the Lands Tribunal

Prior to 1970, unless a benefited proprietor lost an interest to enforce a title condition, it **12–65** was impossible for a burdened proprietor to have a title condition varied or discharged without the consent of the benefited proprietor. There was no action a benefited proprietor could take unilaterally. The usual way to get a condition in the title varied was to ask the benefited proprietor for a minute of waiver which the benefited proprietor may or may not have granted. If granted, it was usually done so in exchange for a payment.[228] In 1970, the Lands Tribunal for Scotland was set up and one of its functions is to adjudicate on applications to vary or discharge title conditions which are referred to as land obligations in the Act.[229]

The Lands Tribunal can hear an application by a burdened proprietor to vary or

---

[223] Prescription and Limitation (Scotland) Act 1973 s.3(3).
[224] *Cumbernauld & Kilsyth District Council v Dollar Land (Cumbernauld) Ltd*, 1993 S.C. (H.L.) 44.
[225] Prescription and Limitation (Scotland) Act 1973 s.8.
[226] See Extinction of real burdens, para.12–59 above.
[227] See Prescription, para.12–35, and Extinction of servitudes, para.12–62 above.
[228] The original method of changing title conditions was by a charter of *novodamus*.
[229] Conveyancing and Feudal Reform (Scotland) Act 1970 s.1(2).

discharge an obligation which is enforceable by a benefited proprietor. Land obligations include such title conditions as real burdens, servitudes and leasehold conditions in recorded leases. Certain types of obligations are specifically excluded from the operation of the provisions of the Act such as mineral obligations.[230] Obligations created within two years of the application are also excluded.[231] There is now only one ground on which a variation or discharge can be made.[232] This is that it is reasonable to grant the variation or discharge,[233] having regard to various factors such as a change in the character of the property or neighbourhood.[234]

The Lands Tribunal has power to add or substitute any provision which appears to be reasonable as a result of the variation or discharge of an obligation.[235] In this event, the applicant can either accept this or opt for the status quo. There are provisions for awarding compensation to the benefited proprietor for either substantial loss or disadvantage resulting from the variation or discharge or to make up for any reduction in the consideration paid to the benefited proprietor due to the existence of the obligation.[236]

Unopposed applications are now granted automatically.[237]

Key Concepts

Restrictions on landownership are imposed for the benefit of other landowners and the public generally. These are:

- restrictions at common law and by statute;
- real burdens;
- servitudes.

Under the common law unlawful interference with a neighbour's use and enjoyment of land is a **nuisance** which is a delictual wrong. Many statutes impose restrictions on the use of land in various ways.

A **real burden** is an encumbrance on land constituted in favour of an owner of other land as owner. There are various types of real burdens. The Title Conditions (Scotland) Act 2003 has reformed the law.

The requirements of a real burden are:

- clear intention to burden the land not the person;
- acceptable purpose;
- expressed in clear terms;
- registered in the Register of Sasines or Land Register.

Under the Title Conditions (Scotland) Act 2003 for new burdens the words "real burden" must be used, the burden must identify the burdened and benefited land,

---

[230] 1970 Act Sch.1.
[231] 1970 Act s.2(5).
[232] 1970 Act s.1(3)(a), (b) and (c).
[233] Title Conditions (Scotland) Act 2003 s.98.
[234] 2003 Act s.100.
[235] 2003 Act s.90(11).
[236] 2003 Act s.90(7).
[237] 2003 Act s.97.

and the real burden must be registered in the title of both the benefited and burdened land.

A person wishing to enforce a real burden must have a title and an interest to enforce. Third parties may have an implied right to enforce a burden created before the Title Conditions (Scotland) Act 2003 came into force.

It will be possible to terminate a real burden which is more than 100 years old.

A **servitude** is a burden on land imposed by express or implied agreement in favour of owners of other land. They are enforceable against anyone.

Servitudes must be positive and can be created by:

- express grant or reservation;
- implied grant or reservation;
- prescription.

Title conditions generally can be varied or discharged in various ways, including application to the Lands Tribunal.

There is a **public right of access** to most land which must be exercised responsibly.

LEASES

A lease is a contract between a landlord, usually the owner, and a tenant to use or possess **12–66** land or other heritable subjects for a certain period in return for a rent, usually money. It is an ancient legal concept and old statutes as far back as the fifteenth century are still in force.

There are three distinct types of lease. These are:

- residential leases;
- agricultural leases and crofts; and
- commercial and industrial leases.

Residential leases can be in either the public or private sector and there is considerable legislation controlling this area, which is frequently changing.[238] Similarly, agricultural leases and crofts are subject to considerable statutory controls which are under review at the time of writing.[239] Commercial and industrial leases, however, are largely free from specific statutory control[240] and depend on the contractual terms of the lease. In all types of lease the common law and general statutes on leases applies in the absence of specific legislation.

With the exception of leases for less than one year, a lease must be in writing.[241] Until 2000 there was no limit on the length of the lease. Since 2000, a lease cannot be longer than

---

[238] See particularly the Housing (Scotland) Acts 1987, 1988, 2001, 2006 and 2010.

[239] Agricultural Holdings (Scotland) Acts 1991 and 2003, Agricultural Holdings (Amendment)(Scotland) Bill 2011; Crofters (Scotland) Act 1993, Crofting Reform etc. (Scotland) Act 2007 and Crofting Reform (Scotland) Act 2010.

[240] Exceptions are the Tenancy of Shops (Scotland) Act 1949 and 1964.

[241] Requirements of Writing (Scotland) Act 1995 ss.1 and 2.

175 years.[242] At the time of writing, there is a Bill in the Scottish Parliament which will convert certain long leases into ownership.[243]

Essentials of a lease

12–67 There are four essentials for a contract of lease:

- two separate parties;
- heritable subjects;
- a period;
- a rent.

As a lease is a contract the parties must agree on its terms and these parties must be two separate legal persons. It is not possible for a legal person to be both landlord and tenant.[244]

The subjects must be heritable, otherwise the contract will be for hire not a lease. The subjects must be properly identified in the lease. It is possible to lease fishing rights or rights to shoot game separate from the land where the fish and game are situated.

The period of the lease, known as a term or ish, must be definite or ascertainable. It cannot be for a period more than 175 years.[245] Where there is agreement between the parties on all the essentials of a lease but no period has been specified the law will imply a period of one year or a shorter period if consistent with the other terms of the lease.[246]

There must be a rent, which will normally be a sum of money paid periodically throughout the term of the lease. If there is no rent there will be no lease, only a licence to occupy.

Real rights in leases

12–68 As a lease is a contract, at common law it is only personally binding and will not bind the successors of a landlord, rendering the tenant vulnerable to ejection by a successor of the landlord. To remedy this defect, the Leases Act 1449 was introduced and is still on the statute book today. If the requirements of the Act are satisfied, the tenant in a lease has a real right which is enforceable against the landlord and the landlord's successors. The requirements of the Act are:

- if the lease is for more than a year it must be in writing;
- the subjects must be land, thus excluding leases of fishing or shooting game;
- a rent;
- an ish;
- the tenant must occupy personally;
- the landlord's title must be registered.

It is also possible to acquire a real right in a lease if the lease is registerable and has been registered in the Register of Sasines or Land Register.[247]

---

[242] Abolition of Feudal Tenure etc. (Scotland) Act 2000 s.67.
[243] Long Leases (Scotland) Bill 2012.
[244] *Kildrummy Estates (Jersey) Ltd v Inland Revenue Commissioners*, 1991 S.C. 1.
[245] Abolition of Feudal Tenure etc. (Scotland) Act 2000 s.67.
[246] *Shetland Islands Council v BP Petroleum Development Ltd*, 1990 S.L.T. 82.
[247] Registration of Leases (Scotland) Act 1857 as amended by the Land Tenure Reform (Scotland) Act 1974.

Security of tenure

The protection of obtaining a real right under the Leases Act 1449 or by registration of a **12–69** lease ensures that a tenant will not be forced to vacate the subjects before the end of the term of the lease. In certain types of leases there are statutory provisions to give tenants security of tenure beyond the end of the period of the lease.[248] In addition, if no notice to quit is served by a landlord on a tenant before the end of the period of lease, the lease will renew for a period of one year or a shorter period if the original period was shorter under the principle of tacit relocation.

Assignation and subletting

The general principle is that a tenant cannot assign a lease to a new tenant without the **12–70** consent of the landlord due to the operation of the doctrine *delectus persona,* meaning the landlord personally knows and accepts the particular tenant. The right to assign with consent is often inserted in a lease, but unless this is worded to say that consent will not be unreasonably withheld, a landlord will retain the right to accept or reject a particular new tenant.[249]

If an assignation does take place, the assignee is substituted for the original tenant and when the assignation is intimated to the landlord the original tenant ceases to have any rights or liabilities in respect of the lease.

Similarly, subletting is not possible unless the landlord agrees. Where it take place the original lease remains in force with all the rights and liabilities of the landlord and tenant intact and a new lease between the original tenant and the subtenant is created. There is no contractual relationship between the landlord and the subtenant unless the landlord is a party to the sublease.

Obligations of a landlord

A landlord must: **12–71**

- give full and undisturbed possession to the tenant for the full period of the lease;
- provide the subjects in reasonable condition for their use;
- keep the subjects in repair.

Once the tenant is in possession, the landlord must not take any action to prejudice the tenant's possession[250] but the obligation is only in respect of deliberate actings.[251]

---

[248] e.g. under the Housing (Scotland) Acts 1987, 1988 and 2001 and the Agricultural Holdings (Scotland) Act 1991.
[249] *Lousada & Co Ltd v JE Lessel (Properties) Ltd,* 1990 S.C. 178.
[250] *Golden Sea Produce Ltd v Scottish Nuclear plc,* 1992 S.L.T. 942.
[251] *Chevron Petroleum (UK) Ltd v Post Office,* 1987 S.L.T. 588.

> ### Golden Sea Produce Ltd v Scottish Nuclear plc
> #### 1992 S.L.T. 942
>
> Owners of a fish hatchery business leased a site at Hunterston A Power Station for their business. The lease included a right to use the waste heated cooling water from the power station. A large stock of fish died from pollution by chlorine in the water pumped from the power station and used by the tenants. It was held that the landlords were under an implied obligation not to do anything which adversely affected the tenants' operations under the lease.

The subjects must be provided in a suitable condition for their use[252] but, if let for commercial purposes, it is the responsibility of the tenant to ensure that the proposed use is permitted under planning legislation.[253]

Under the common law, if a lease is an urban as opposed to a rural lease, that is one which is not for agricultural purposes, a landlord must keep the subjects in a tenantable and habitable condition throughout the period. They must be kept wind and water tight. A landlord must be aware of the need for repair before there will be a liability.

A tenant must:

- enter into occupation and occupy and use the subjects;
- use the subjects only for the purposes for which they are let;
- take reasonable care of the subjects;
- pay the rent when due.

It is in the landlord's interest that the tenant actually occupies and uses the subjects for the period of the lease. If a tenant does not, a landlord may recind the lease for breach of contract.[254] In commercial leases it is usual to insert what are known as "keep open" or "keep trading" clauses to ensure that the tenant continues to occupy and trade from the commercial premises and such clauses will be enforceable by the courts.[255]

A tenant cannot use the subjects for a different purpose than that agreed in the lease.[256]

A tenant must take reasonable care of the subjects and this obligation continues until the lease comes to an end.[257]

A tenant must pay the rent on time.

Remedies for breach of terms of a lease

12–72 As a lease is a contract, both the landlord and tenant will have the usual contractual remedies available to them for breach of contract. These are interdict, specific implement, recission and damages. In addition, both the landlord and tenant have further remedies.

A landlord will have the usual remedies of a creditor for recovery of debt if the tenant fails to pay the rent, including summary diligence.

A landlord may be able to irritate the lease. An irritancy means that the lease comes to a premature end and the tenant's rights are extinguished. An irritancy can be legal or

---

[252] *Kippen v Oppenheim* (1847) 10 D. 242.
[253] *Ballantyne v Meoni*, 1997 G.W.D. 29–1489.
[254] *Blair Trust Co v Gilbert*, 1940 S.L.T. 322.
[255] *Retail Parks Investment Ltd v Royal Bank of Scotland*, 1996 S.L.T. 669 and subsequent cases.
[256] *Bayley v Addison* (1801) 8 S.L.T. 379.
[257] *Fry's Metals Ltd v Durastic Ltd*, 1991 S.L.T. 689.

conventional. A legal irritancy is implied by law and occurs at common law if a tenant does not pay rent for two years. There are also legal irritancies in legislation on agricultural holdings and crofts.[258] A conventional irritancy is where the lease has a specific term allowing this to happen. There are statutory controls on conventional irritancies.[259]

A landlord cannot physically eject a tenant even if in breach of the lease and must raise an action of removing.

In addition to the normal contractual remedies, a tenant may be entitled to retain rent until a breach is remedied or to an abatement of rent.

Termination and tacit relocation

A lease will terminate in the following events:

12–73

- end of the period,
- irritancy,
- recission by the landlord or tenant,
- renunciation by both parties,
- total destruction of the subjects,
- death of the tenant if granted for the tenant's lifetime.[260]

A lease will not terminate at the end of the period unless a notice to quit has been given by the landlord to the tenant before the end of the period. The period of notice may be agreed in the lease but there are minimum periods laid down by statute for particular types of lease.[261]

If a landlord fails to give notice to quit, the lease will be renewed under the principle of tacit relocation for a further period of one year or, if the original period was less than one year, the same period.

Key Concepts

A **lease** is a contract between a landlord and a tenant to use or possess land or other heritable subjects for a certain period in return for a rent.

If a lease is for more than a year it must be in **writing.**

A tenant can acquire a **real right** under the Leases Act 1449 or by registering the lease if it is registrable.

It is a general principle that a tenant cannot **assign** or **sublet** without the consent of the landlord.

If there is a **breach of terms** of a lease, both the landlord and tenant have the usual contractual remedies. In addition, a landlord may **irritate** the lease and bring it to a premature end. A landlord cannot physically **eject** a tenant but must raise an action of removing.

A lease will continue by **tacit relocation** if no notice to quit is given.

---

[258] Agricultural Holdings (Scotland) Act 1991 s.20 and Crofters (Scotland) Act 1993 s.5.
[259] Law Reform (Miscellaneous Provisions) (Scotland) Act 1985 ss.4–7.
[260] For succession to leases see Chapter 14 on Succession.
[261] For example, Sheriff Courts (Scotland) Act 1907.

SECURITIES OVER HERITABLE PROPERTY

12–74 The most common use of heritable securities is in relation to mortgages, where a lender gives money to help a borrower to finance the purchase of a house or other property which is secured by a standard security over the property.

A heritable security comprises two elements, a personal obligation and a security over the heritable property. The personal obligation binds the borrower/debtor to repay the full amount of the loan and means that the lender/creditor can go against all the assets of the borrower in the event of default. The security over the heritable property gives the lender a real right in security and a first charge over the property. If default occurs, the lender can sell the property and recover the amount of the loan before any other creditors.

Standard securities

12–75 Since 1970, a heritable security must be in the form of a standard security.[262] A standard security can be granted over any interest in land which is capable of being owned or held as a separate interest and to which a title can be registered in the Register of Sasines or the Land Register.[263] A standard security can be used to secure obligations to pay money or, less usually, to do something.[264] The debt may be a present, future or contingent debt.[265] A standard security can be granted by the debtor or a third party. A standard security is registered in the Register of Sasines or the Land Register. A standard security by a company must also be registered in the Companies Charges Register within 21 days of creation.[266]

Form

12–76 A standard security can be in one of two forms, either A or B.[267] In form A, the debtor's personal obligation is included in the standard security and, in form B, the personal obligation is constituted in a separate deed. The 1970 Act sets out a number of standard conditions which are automatically incorporated into every standard security.[268] These deal with the debtor's rights and obligations and the powers of the creditor. With the exception of the power of sale and foreclosure, these can be varied by agreement between the debtor and creditor.[269]

Ranking

12–77 If there is more than one security over the same heritable property, the question of ranking is relevant. The general common law rule is that ranking depends on the date of registration of the security. A security registered earlier in time has prior ranking. If an earlier security secures future borrowing, a later security which is registered and intimated to the earlier security holder will limit the prior ranking to the amount advanced as at the date of

---

[262] Conveyancing and Feudal Reform (Scotland) Act 1970 s.9.
[263] 1970 Act s.9(8)(b), Land Registration (Scotland) Act 1979 s.29(1).
[264] 1970 Act s.9(8)(c).
[265] 1970 Act s.9(8)(c).
[266] Companies Act 1985 s.410.
[267] 1970 Act s.9(2) and Sch.2.
[268] 1970 Act Sch.3.
[269] 1970 Act s.11(3).

intimation.[270] The creditors and the debtor can adjust the ranking by agreement in a ranking agreement.[271]

Assignation and transmission, restriction and discharge

A standard security may be assigned in whole or in part.[272] Both the creditor and debtor **12–78** can assign.

On the death of the debtor, the liability is heritable in succession but, if the security subjects when realised do not pay off the debt, the balance must be paid from the remainder of the estate.

On the death of the creditor, a standard security is moveable except for the calculation of legal rights.

If the debtor is sequestrated, the heritable subjects vest in the trustee,[273] but the trustee can only sell with the consent of the creditor unless sufficient money is obtained to settle all debts secured by heritable securities.[274]

A part of the security subjects may be released from the heritable security.[275] If there is a part payment, a form of partial discharge and deed of restriction is used. If there is no payment, a deed of restriction only is used.[276] A standard security is extinguished by payment of the debt in full or performance of the obligation secured. It is normal for the security to be formally discharged by registering a discharge in the Register of Sasines or Land Register.[277]

Default

A creditor has various remedies available when the debtor is in default. The default will **12–79** usually be a failure to make the required payments to the creditor, but may be a failure to comply with other requirements of the standard security, such as keeping the property in good repair, or where the proprietor of the security subjects becomes insolvent.[278]

The creditor's remedies are[279]:

- sale;
- entering into possession;
- carrying out repairs;
- foreclosure.

In a sale the creditor must advertise the sale which may be by private bargain or public roup and has a duty to obtain the best price which can be reasonably obtained.[280]

If a creditor enters into possession, the creditor may uplift rents or lease the subjects but may be subject to certain liabilities.[281]

Foreclosure is where a creditor has been unable to sell at a price sufficient to satisfy the

---

[270] *Union Bank of Scotland v National Bank of Scotland* (1886) 14 R. (H.L.) 1.
[271] 1970 Act s.13(3)(b).
[272] 1970 Act s.14 and Sch.4.
[273] Bankruptcy (Scotland) Act 1985 s.31(1).
[274] 1985 Act s.39(4).
[275] 1970 Act s.15.
[276] 1970 Act Sch.4.
[277] 1970 Act s.17 Sch.4.
[278] 1970 Act Sch.3 para.9(1)(a), (b) and (c).
[279] Under Standard Condition 10 in Sch.3.
[280] 1970 Act s.25.
[281] See *David Watson Property Management Ltd v Woolwich Equitable Building Society*, 1992 S.L.T. 430.

debt and the court grants a decree to enable the creditor to take title to the security subjects.[282]

Before a creditor can exercise the remedies on default, certain procedures must be followed. When standard securities were introduced in 1970, three alternatives were provided. These are serving a calling up notice, serving a default notice or petitioning the court for authority to exercise the creditor's remedies under s.24 of the 1970 Act. Recent developments have changed the position. In relation to residential property, under the Mortgage Rights (Scotland) Act 2001, the debtor or proprietor of the security subjects or certain persons living with the debtor or proprietor could apply to the court to suspend the creditor's rights to allow the debtor more time to make arrangements to repay the loan if this was reasonable. The 2001 Act is largely replaced by the Home Owner and Debtor Protection (Scotland) Act 2010 which has the aim of giving more protection to debtors, particularly in the current depressed property market. The 2010 Act provides that in relation to residential property, all creditors must apply to the court before their remedies can be exercised and demonstrate that they have taken reasonable steps to avoid repossession.

In *Royal Bank of Scotland plc v Wilson*,[283] the Supreme Court held that where the debtor has defaulted, a calling up notice is essential. This now means that for standard securities over all properties a calling up notice must be served and for standard securities over residential properties a s.24 warrant is also required in most cases.

Floating charges

12–80 A floating charge is a security which can be created over heritable or moveable property by companies. It is an English concept which was introduced into Scotland in 1961.[284] It is not a fixed charge when created but becomes a fixed charge when it "crystallises" and attaches to the company's assets. Until it attaches, the company is free to dispose of its assets without the consent of the holder of the floating charge. A floating charge attaches when the company goes into liquidation[285] or a receiver is appointed under the floating charge.[286] A floating charge does not attach to all company assets.[287]

A floating charge must be in writing and must be registered in the Companies Charges Register within 21 days of creation.[288] It is not registered in the Register of Sasines or the Land Register, but must be registered in the new register, the Register of Floating Charges.[289]

Floating charges usually contain ranking clauses prohibiting subsequent securities of any type, in which case the floating charge will rank prior to any subsequent charge. Fixed charges created before the crystallisation of a floating charge rank prior to the floating charge. Where there is more than one floating charge, ranking is determined by order of registration.

Floating charges are extinguished when the debt is paid in full.

---

[282] 1970 Act s.28.
[283] 2010 S.L.T. 1227.
[284] Companies (Floating Charges) (Scotland) Act 1961.
[285] Companies Act 1985 s.461(1).
[286] Insolvency Act 1986 ss.53(7) and 54(6).
[287] See *Sharp v Thomson*, 1997 S.C. (H.L.) 66.
[288] Companies Act 1985 ss.410 and 420.
[289] Bankruptcy and Diligence etc. (Scotland) Act 2007 s.38.

> **Key Concepts**
>
> A **heritable security** which is registered in the Register of Sasines or Land Register gives the creditor a **real right** in security over the heritable subjects.
>
> A heritable security must be in the form of a **standard security**. There are two types of standard security which are **Form A** which includes a personal obligation and **Form B** where the personal obligation is in a separate deed. Certain **standard conditions** are automatically incorporated into all standard securities.
>
> **Ranking** of securities depends on the date of registration of the security.
>
> A creditor has various **remedies** available when the debtor is in **default** including sale, entering into possession, carrying out repairs and foreclosure.
>
> A **floating charge** is a security which can be created over heritable or moveable property by companies. It must be in writing and it must be registered in the Companies Charges Register within 21 days. It must also be registered in the new Register of Floating Charges. It only becomes a fixed charge when it "crystallises" and attaches to the company's assets.

A TYPICAL CONVEYANCING TRANSACTION

Conveyancing is the process of transferring rights in property. This is beyond the scope of this chapter but a brief outline of a typical conveyancing transaction involving the sale and purchase of a house may be helpful. There are various steps in this process: **12–81**

- pre-contract;
- contract;
- examination of title and conveyancing;
- settlement;
- registration.

Pre-contract

Before the contract stage is reached, both the purchaser and seller have certain steps to take which are usually facilitated by their solicitor. The first step for a person who wishes to purchase a house is to sort out the finance to establish how much can be afforded. This will usually be determined by the amount of the potential purchaser's savings and how much he or she can borrow, taking account of his or her employment and income position, and ongoing liabilities. Most people are unable to buy a house outright and a mortgage from a bank, building society or other lender will be required. This will be secured by the lender taking out a standard security over the house. It is sensible to establish how much you can borrow before looking at houses in your price range. **12–82**

It is usual for a seller to use the services of an agent to sell his or her house. This will frequently be done by a solicitor, although separate estate agents can be employed. The agent will make the necessary arrangements for marketing the property including valuing the property to determine the asking price. Since December 1, 2008, it is essential that a Home Report is available to potential purchasers when a house is marketed for sale. This has three parts. These are a single survey of the property, including a valuation carried out by a chartered surveyor; an energy report; and a property questionnaire. At this stage, it is wise for the seller's solicitor to check the title of the sale property and initiate any enquiries relating to the property which may be required.

Contract

12–83 Once a house is on the market for sale it is open to potential purchasers to make an offer to purchase the property. Prior to the introduction of Home Reports, a potential purchaser would often arrange a survey of the house to establish its value and the condition of the house, as it would not be sensible to buy a house without a survey. Alternatively, it is always open to a potential purchaser to make an offer on condition that a satisfactory survey is obtained, which condition must be satisfied before a binding contract is concluded. Now a Home Report with its single survey is available to any potential purchaser. However, this survey may not be acceptable to the potential purchaser or the lender of a potential purchaser who is providing finance for the proposed purchase. In this case an independent survey may be obtained. In Scotland, contracts for the sale and purchase of houses and other properties are almost always made by what are known as missives. Instead of drawing up a bilateral contract between the seller and purchaser when a sale is agreed, potential purchasers are free to make an offer for the house. This should be a formal offer from the purchaser's solicitor with detailed conditions of purchase included. If the offer is to be accepted, the seller's solicitor will issue a letter of acceptance. Usually this acceptance will not be an outright acceptance but will be subject to certain qualifications or conditions. This means that until both the seller and purchaser agree all the conditions there is no concluded contract. Once all the conditions are agreed, the letters which pass between the purchaser's and seller's solicitors form the concluded contract and are referred to as the missives.

Before submitting an offer, a purchaser will usually arrange a survey of the house to establish its value and the condition of the house. It would not be sensible to buy a house without a survey. It is open to a purchaser to make an offer subject to obtaining a satisfactory survey, which must be satisfied before the contract is concluded. A seller may or may not accept a particular offer from a potential purchaser. Frequently, if there are a number of potential purchasers who wish to make an offer for the property, a closing date is set by the seller. This means that all the offers have to be lodged by a specified time when they will be considered by the seller.

Examination of title and conveyancing

12–84 When the contract is concluded the examination of title and conveyancing stage takes place. This is the process whereby the purchaser's solicitor ensures that the title of the house is in order and the seller is able to transfer a good title to the purchaser. The seller's solicitor first sends the title deeds to the purchaser's solicitor for examination. This process will differ depending on whether the title is registered in the Register of Sasines or the Land Register. The seller's solicitor must satisfy him or herself that everything is in order and may raise various queries with the selling solicitor which the selling solicitor will investigate and confirm. At the same time, the seller's solicitor will prepare the legal document which transfers the title to the house from the seller to the purchaser. This is known as a disposition. The terms of this disposition are approved by the seller's solicitor and the disposition is signed by the seller to be ready for delivery at settlement.

If the purchaser is obtaining a mortgage, the purchaser's solicitor will usually act for the lender and prepare the necessary documentation required by the lender. This will involve preparing a standard security over the house which the purchaser signs. Once the seller's solicitor is satisfied that everything is in order with the title and the necessary documentation is prepared and signed, settlement can take place on the date agreed in the missives.

Settlement

Settlement is when the purchaser and seller implement their obligations under the missives **12–85** to enable the transfer of the house to take place. The purchaser's solicitor hands over the purchase price of the house to the seller's solicitor. In exchange, the seller's solicitor hands over the keys of the house to enable the purchaser to take possession and also hands over the disposition signed by the seller, which transfers the title to the purchaser.

Registration

Following settlement, the seller has received the proceeds of sale and the purchaser has **12–86** received possession of the house and the document transferring the title. It is essential that the purchaser's solicitor registers the disposition transferring the title straight away. If there is a mortgage, the standard security by the purchaser in favour of the lender is registered at the same time. As discussed above,[290] registration is essential to obtain a real right in heritable property and various problems could arise if registration is delayed. This completes the conveyancing transaction.

Once all these steps have been taken the sale and purchase of the house has been completed. This is an outline only of the process which is more detailed than set out here.

▼ CHAPTER SUMMARY

GENERAL CONCEPTS

1. **Property can mean either the right of ownership or the actual thing owned.**   **12–87**
2. **Property can be classified in several ways—heritable or moveable; corporeal or incorporeal and fungible or non-fungible.**
3. **Heritable property is land and buildings or anything attached to the land. Moveable property is all other types of property.**
4. **Accession by fruits means something growing accedes to where it is growing. Natural fruits of the land not requiring constant cultivation are heritable until severed from the land but industrial growing crops are moveable.**
5. **Moveable property can accede to heritable property as a fixture:**

   ➢ *Christie v Smith's Executor* (1949): A substantial summerhouse becomes part of the house.

6. **Corporeal property is tangible and incorporeal property is intangible.**
7. **Fungible property can be replaced by similar property and non-fungible property can not be readily replaced and has an inherent value.**
8. **An owner of land has exclusive possession and can prevent others from interfering with this.**
9. **There is a presumption that the possessor of goods is the owner.**
10. **Possession requires a physical element of holding the property and an intention to possess for one's self.**
11. **A real right is enforceable against anyone but a personal right is only enforceable against a particular person or persons.**
12. **Normally two stages are required before a real right is created.**
13. **Both heritable and moveable property can be owned by more than one person.**

---

[290] See Registration, para.12–34 above.

14. Joint property is where two or more persons own a property as an individual whole; common property is where two or more owners own an individual share; common interest is where an owner has a right in another person's property.

CORPOREAL MOVEABLE PROPERTY

1. Original acquisition of this type of property is where property is acquired independent of the ownership of another. There are four categories—occupation, accession, specification and confusion and commixtion.
2. Derivative acquisition is the transfer of ownership from the existing owner to a new owner.
3. Occupation is acquiring ownership of property which has never been owned by anyone.
4. Lost or abandoned property cannot be acquired by occupation:

   ➤ *Lord Advocate v University of Aberdeen* (1963): 8th century treasure found by students belonged to Crown.
   ➤ Civic Government (Scotland) Act 1982.

5. Accession is where animals have offspring and the owner of the animal becomes the owner of the offspring:

   ➤ *Lamb v Grant* (1874): The owner of an animal owns that animal's offspring.

6. Specification is where a new property is created from component materials and cannot be converted back. The creator is the owner if in good faith:

   ➤ *McDonald v Provan (of Scotland Street) Ltd* (1960): two stolen parts of car welded together could be separated so no specification.
   ➤ *International Banking Corporation v Ferguson, Shaw & Sons* (1910): Where new substance created in good faith the creator owns this but has to pay compensation for cost of components.

7. Confusion is the mixture of the same liquids together and commixtion is the mixture of the same solids together. The mix is owned by the contributors in common, according to contribution.
8. There are two essentials for derivative acquisition—intention and delivery.
9. Intention is usually in an agreement. Delivery can be actual constructive or symbolic:

   ➤ *Inglis v Robertson & Baxter* (1898): A warehouse keeper received no intimation of transfer so no real right created.

INCORPOREAL MOVEABLE PROPERTY

1. The creation of incorporeal moveable property is governed by commercial and mercantile law.
2. There are two essentials to transfer incorporeal moveable property—assignation and intimation.
3. Intellectual property rights are a special type of incorporeal moveable property relating to original and creative works in cultural scientific or business areas.

4. There are four types of intellectual property—patents, copyright, trade marks and designs

RIGHTS IN SECURITY OVER MOVEABLE PROPERTY

1. A right in security is only an accessory right to secure performance of an obligation.
2. A security over corporeal moveable property may require delivery—a pledge is created by agreement and a lien by operation of law.
3. Hypothecs and floating charges which apply to companies do not require delivery:

   ➢ Companies (Floating Charges) (Scotland) Act 1961.

LANDOWNERSHIP

1. The two key features of land ownership in Scotland were the feudal system and registration in a public land register.
2. The feudal system was abolished on November 28, 2004:

   ➢ Abolition of Feudal Tenure etc. (Scotland) Act 2000.

3. A system of registration has existed in Scotland since 1617 when the Register of Sasines was introduced:

   ➢ Registration Act 1617.

4. The system of registration of deeds in the Register of Sasines which does not guarantee title is being replaced gradually by the system of registration of title in the Land Register which does guarantee title:

   ➢ Land Registration (Scotland) Act 1979.

5. Registration is essential to create a real right.
6. A problem has arisen recently in relation to company receiverships which undermines this principle but is confined to receiverships:

   ➢ *Sharp v Thomson* (1997): A receivership does not take precedence over an owner with an unregistered title.
   ➢ *Burnett's Trustees v Grainger* (2004): Priority of registration does apply in sequestrations.

6. Positive prescription creates rights in land or renders existing rights unchallengeable, negative prescription extinguishes rights which have not been exercised.
7. Negative prescription takes place after either 5 or 20 years.
8. A title will not be challengeable if it is valid on the face of it and there is appropriate possession for the appropriate period, usually 10 years:

   ➢ Prescription and Limitation (Scotland) Act 1973.

9. The physical boundaries of land with neighbouring land are determined by the title deeds. Where this is ambiguous prescription may determine where the boundaries are.
10. Landownership is theoretically from the heavens to the centre of the earth.

    ➢ *Halkerston v Wedderburn* (1781): Overhanging branches can be removed.

11. **Moveable property can accede to heritable property as a fixture if there is physical attachment, functional subordination and a degree of permanency:**

    ➤ *Christie v Smith's Executor* (1949): A substantial summer house becomes part of a house.

12. **The intention of the parties is important in accession, despite a leading case:**

    ➤ *Brand's Trustees v Brand's Trustees* (1876): The House of Lords ruled that intention is not relevant but subsequent cases have doubted this.

13. **The Crown has certain rights of two types—*regalia majora* which are held in trust for the public and regalia minora which can be sold by the Crown Estate Commissioners.**

14. **There is a default law under the Tenements (Scotland) Act 2004 which applies to tenements if there is no provision in the title deeds:**

    ➤ *Rafique v Amin* (1997): Where there are no or incomplete specific provisions in the titles, the default law will apply to tenements; in this case, the common law.

15. **Ownership of the various parts of a tenement is detailed in the Act as individual or common property with a right of common interest for the other proprietors. Repairs to most part of the tenement building require the consent of a majority only of flat owners.**

16. **A landowner has the right of exclusive possession of the land but many officials have a right to enter under specific Acts.**

17. **Trespass is not a crime in Scotland and a single act of trespass is difficult to prevent.**

18. **Encroachment is infringement of a landowner's air space or below ground.**

19. **A landowner has a right of support of land from below and from surrounding land to prevent collapse or subsidence:**

    ➤ *Angus v National Coal Board* (1955): Damages were payable when agricultural worker died due to subsidence in field.

20. **The sea, sea lochs and tidal rivers are part of the Crown *regalia*.**

21. **Still surface water belongs to the landowner; a loch surrounded by land belonging to different landowners is owned in common.**

22. **The public has a right to navigate navigable rivers:**

    ➤ *Orr Ewing & Co v Colquhoun's Trustees* (1873): A landowner could not prevent navigation by building a bridge.

23. **Riparian owners own a non-navigable river to the mid-point and have a common interest in the flow of water.**

24. **The right of ownership includes the right to fish in lochs, streams and rivers and to kill game, although certain wildlife is protected:**

    ➤ Wildlife and Countryside Act 1981.

25. **A landowner is entitled to be free from interference with the enjoyment of the land from other landowners.**

26. **Landowners' use and enjoyment of land can be restricted at common law, under statute and by agreement.**

27. **Under the common law it is a nuisance to interfere unlawfully with land:**

   ➤ *Webster v Lord Advocate* (1984): Noise from the erection of scaffolding for the Edinburgh Military Tattoo constituted a nuisance.

28. **Many statutes impose restriction on the use of land in various ways.**
29. **A real burden is an obligation in respect of land inserted for the benefit of another landowner and is enforceable by whoever owns the other land.**
30. **Following abolition of the feudal system the law on real burdens and also servitudes was updated:**

   ➤ Title Conditions (Scotland) Act 2003.

30. **Real burdens can be affirmative (positive) or negative and praedial (with benefited and burdened land) or personal.**
31. **The two main types of praedial burdens are community burdens which benefit all the owners of four or more units of land and neighbour burdens for the benefit of a neighbour only.**
32. **Under the common law a valid burden must have a clear intention to burden the land not the person, be for an acceptable purpose, be expressed in clear terms and be registered in the Register of Sasines or Land Register:**

   ➤ *Tailors of Aberdeen v Coutts* (1840): The court set out the requirements for the constitution of real burdens.

33. **The 2003 Act restated these requirements and added three others for transparency. The term real burden or a particular type must be used in the constituting deed; the deed must specify both the burdened and benefited land and the burden must be registered in the title of both the burdened and benefited land.**
34. **A person wishing to enforce a real burden must have both a title and interest to enforce. An implied right to enforce may exist where neighbouring landowners are affected by the real burden:**

   ➤ *Hislop v MacRitchie's Trustees* (1881): The rules for the third party implied rights were explained by the court.

35. **A real burden may be terminated under the sunset rule if more than 100 years old.**
36. **A servitude is a burden on land in favour of an owner of other land and runs with the land.**
37. **A servitude must be positive and has several essentials—two different tenements or interests in land owned by two different persons; the land must be neighbouring and the benefit must be for the land itself not the person:**

   ➤ Title Conditions (Scotland) Act 2003.

38. **Servitudes can be created by express grant or reservation, implied grant or reservation and by prescription.**
39. **Servitudes can be extinguished in various ways—by express discharge or renunciation; by the two tenements coming into the ownership of one person; by negative prescription after 20 years; by acquiescence; by change of circumstances and by the Land Tribunal:**

   ➤ Prescription and Limitation (Scotland) Act 1973.
   ➤ Conveyancing and Feudal Reform (Scotland) Act 1970.

40. **Title conditions including real burdens and servitudes can be extinguished in various ways—express discharge or variation; prescription; consolidation; compulsory purchase and variation or discharge by the Land Tribunal.**

41. **The Land Tribunal was set up in 1970 to enable application for variation or discharge of a title condition which was not possible previously unless both the benefited and burdened proprietor agreed:**

   ➤ Conveyancing and Feudal Reform (Scotland) Act 1970.
   ➤ Title Conditions (Scotland) Act 2003.

42. **The public have a general right of access to land for recreational and educational purposes and to cross land. This must be exercised responsibly and certain land is excluded from this right:**

   ➤ Land Reform (Scotland) Act 2003.

LEASES

1. **A lease is a contract between a landlord, usually the owner, and a tenant to use heritable property for a certain period in return for a rent.**
2. **There are three types of lease—residential leases, commercial and industrial leases and agricultural leases and crofts.**
3. **A lease must be in writing and cannot be for more than 175 years:**

   ➤ Requirements of Writing (Scotland) Act 1995.
   ➤ Abolition of Feudal Tenure etc. (Scotland) Act 2000.

4. **The four essentials for a contract of lease are two separate parties, heritable subjects, a period and a rent.**
5. **If the landlord's title is registered and the tenant occupies personally there is a real right in a lease which is binding on successors of a landlord. This gives the tenant security of tenure for the period of the lease:**

   ➤ Leases Act 1449.

6. **A tenant cannot assign or sublet a lease without the consent of the landlord.**
7. **A landlord must give full and undisturbed possession to the tenant for the full period of the lease, provide the subjects in reasonable condition for the use and keep the subjects in repair:**

   ➤ *Golden Sea Produce Ltd v Scottish Nuclear plc* (1992): A landlord was not permitted to allow waste heated cooling water from a power station to pollute water and cause fish to die in property which was tenanted.
   ➤ *Kippen v Oppenheim* (1874): A house which was infested with cockroaches and other bugs, had an offensive smell and was damp was not fit for habitation.

8. **A tenant must enter into occupation and occupy and use the subjects, use the subjects only for the purposes for which they are let, take reasonable care of the subjects and pay the rent when due:**

   ➤ *Blair Trust v Gilbert* (1940): A farmer could not occupy a house as he was in prison and could not be a tenant.

9. **A landlord cannot physically eject a tenant but must raise an action of removing.**
10. **In addition to the usual contract remedies on breach, a landlord maybe able to irritate the lease and the tenant maybe entitled to retain the rent or to an abatement of rent.**

11. A lease will terminate at the end of the period or on the following events—irritancy; rescission by the landlord or tenant; renunciation by both parties; total destruction of the subjects or the death of the tenant.

12. A lease will not terminate at the end of the period unless a notice to quit is given but will continue for a further period of one year or the period of the lease, if less then one year.

SECURITIES OVER HERITABLE PROPERTY

1. The most common type of heritable security is a mortgage which is secured by a standard security over the property. This gives the creditor a real right in security over the subjects when registered, in addition to the personal obligation.

2. A heritable security must be in the form of a standard security:

   ➢ Conveyancing and Feudal Reform (Scotland) Act 1970.

3. A standard security can include the personal obligation or the personal obligation can be in a separate document. All standard securities incorporate standard conditions.

4. If there is more than one security over the same heritable property the order of ranking is dependent on registration.

5. A standard security can be assigned, restricted or discharged.

6. A creditor has various remedies available when a debtor defaults. Default occurs in three situations—where a calling up notice has been served but not complied with, where the debtor has failed to comply with other requirements and where the proprietor of the security subjects is insolvent.

7. On default the creditor has the remedies of sale, entering into possession, carrying out repairs and for closure.

8. In relation to residential property, all creditors must apply to the court before their remedies can be exercised and demonstrate that they have taken reasonable steps to avoid repossession:

   ➢ Home Owner and Debtor Protection (Scotland) Act 2010.

9. A floating charge is a security which can be created over heritable or moveable property by companies.

10. A floating charge must be in writing and will soon require to be registered in a new Register of Floating Charges:

    ➢ Bankruptcy and Diligence etc. (Scotland) Act 2007.

11. A floating charge only becomes a fixed charge when it crystallises and attaches to the company's assets.

? QUICK QUIZ

Property law

- What is the classic definition of "property"?
- Against whom is a real right enforceable?
- Why is possession important in heritable and moveable property?
- What is common interest?
- Original acquisition can be divided into which four categories?
- Is the feudal system still operating?
- What is the difference between the Register of Sasines and the Land Register?
- Who owns the air space above the roof of a tenement?
- What rights of access to land do the public have?
- State the four requirements of a real burden under the common law and the changes under the Title Conditions (Scotland) Act 2003.
- Who can enforce a real burden?
- What is the difference between a real burden and a servitude?
- What are the four essentials of a lease?
- What is the effect of the Home Owner and Debtor Protection (Scotland) Act 2010 ?
- What is the purpose of a Home Report?

📖 FURTHER READING

The following titles would be of assistance:

D.A. Brand, *Property LawBasics* (W. Green, 2009).

D.L. Carey Miller, *Corporeal Moveables in Scots Law*, 2nd edn (W. Green, 2005).

D.J. Cusine and R. Rennie, *Standard Securities*, 2nd edn (W. Green, 2002).

W.M. Gordon & S. Wortley, *Scottish Land Law*, 3rd edn (W. Green, 2009).

W.M. Gloag & R.C. Henderson, *The Law of Scotland*, 12th edn (W. Green, 2007).

G. Gretton and K. Reid, *Conveyancing*, 4 edn (W. Green, 2011).

G. Gretton & A.J.M. Steven, *Property, Trusts and Succession* (Tottel, 2009)

T. Guthrie, *Scottish Property Law*, 2nd edn (Tottel, 2005).

A. McAllister, *Scottish Law of Leases*, 3rd edn (Butterworths, 2002).

R. Paisley, *Land Law* (W. Green, 2000).

Chapter 13   Trusts

JAMES CHALMERS[1]

▶ CHAPTER OVERVIEW

This chapter is concerned with the law of trusts. It starts by explaining the concept of the **13–01** trust as it is recognised in Scots law. The chapter goes on to explain how trusts are created and administered, and sets out the duties, powers and potential liabilities of trustees. It then considers how trust purposes may be varied and how trusts may be brought to an end (terminated).

✓ OUTCOMES

At the end of the chapter, you should be able to explain and apply the following: **13–02**

- ✓   what a trust is and how one can be created;
- ✓   how trusts are administered;
- ✓   the general duties and powers of trustees;
- ✓   the rule against auctor in rem suam (conflict of interest);
- ✓   the potential liabilities of trustees to beneficiaries and third parties;
- ✓   the rules and procedures for varying trust purposes; and
- ✓   the means by which a trust may be terminated.

THE TRUST CONCEPT

A trust may be most easily understood as a tripartite relationship, involving three roles: **13–03**

- the truster (the person who creates the trust and is the owner of the trust property before its creation);
- the trustee (who is the owner of the trust property after the trust is created and is responsible for administering the trust); and
- the beneficiary (the person for whose benefit the trust property is held by the trustee).

In other words, a trust is created when one person (the truster) transfers property to a second person (the trustee) who is then under an obligation to apply the property for the benefit of a third person (the beneficiary).

It is possible for there to be more than one truster, trustee or beneficiary, and it is

---

[1] Senior Lecturer in Law, University of Edinburgh.

possible for one person to hold more than one of those roles (except that a sole trustee cannot be a sole beneficiary).

Trust property is owned by the trustee.[2] However, if the trustee becomes insolvent, the trust property is not available to satisfy the claims of his creditors.[3] Nor is it available to satisfy the claims of the truster's creditors. In this fashion, it forms a separate "patrimony" from the property which the trustee owns personally.[4] This "insolvency effect" is the most important—and often the most useful—feature of the trust.[5] The trust can *itself* become insolvent and be sequestrated, however.[6]

Consequences of a trust

13–04 The trust is a versatile device and its use is not restricted to any one particular context. Seven useful features of the trust may be noted:

- it can divorce the right to benefit from property, from the right of ownership of that property;
- it can divorce the right to benefit from property, from the control and administration of that property;
- it can split the right to benefit from property between two or more individuals;
- it can place restrictions on the right to benefit from trust property, or lay down conditions which must be fulfilled before an individual is entitled to become owner of that property;
- it can be used to postpone a decision on who is to benefit from that property;
- it can be used to place property in the hands of persons who are regarded as more appropriate to administer it than the truster—perhaps because they are better qualified to do so, or are able to devote more time to the role; and
- as noted earlier, trust property is protected from the insolvency of either the truster or the trustee.

Why create a trust?

13–05 Trusts may be created for any number of reasons. Some of the more common are as follows:

- *Protection of the incompetent or the vulnerable.* A truster may wish to set up a trust for a beneficiary who is legally incapable of managing property, or whom the truster believes would not manage the property sensibly.
- *Trusts for the benefit of the public.* A truster may set up a trust fund to be applied to specified public purposes.
- *Collective investment purposes.* Trusts provide a convenient means of administering collective investment schemes (such as pension funds), which allow for professional management and diversification of investment to a degree which would not normally be available to individual investors.

---

[2] See *Sharp v Thomson*, 1995 S.C. 455, per the Lord President (Hope) at 474–475 (decision reversed on other grounds at 1997 S.C. (H.L.) 66).
[3] *Heritable Reversionary Co. Ltd v Millar* (1892) 19 R. (H.L.) 43.
[4] For the "patrimony" theory, see K.G.C. Reid, "Patrimony not Equity: the trust in Scotland" (2000) 8 E.R.P.L. 427; G.L. Gretton, "Trusts Without Equity" (2000) 49 I.C.L.Q. 599.
[5] See G.L. Gretton, "Constructive Trusts" (1997) 1 Edin. L.R. 281, 287–288.
[6] *Bain, Petr* (1901) 9 S.L.T. 14.

- *Tax efficiency*. Manipulation of ownership and control by means of the trust device may be used by a truster in order to minimise liability to taxation.
- *Executors*. The executors in a deceased's estate are (for most purposes) trustees on the estate.

Classifications of trusts

Trusts are frequently classified in various ways. The following are the most important **13–06** classifications:

Public and private trusts

The distinction between public and private trusts is of considerable importance. It has **13–07** been summarised as follows:

> "A private trust is a trust designed to benefit a specified individual or a specified group of individuals ... A public trust on the other hand is one that is set up for the benefit of the public in general, or of a specified class of the public in general."[7]

A number of consequences flow from this distinction. The most important consequence relates to the power of the Court of Session to sanction variation of trust purposes, as the relevant law is entirely different depending on whether the trust is private or public.[8] In addition, the courts generally adopt an approach of "benignant construction" towards public trusts,[9] accepting relatively vague statements of purpose as sufficient to create a valid trust,[10] and stepping in to provide machinery to give effect to those purposes where the truster has failed to do so.[11] The Lord Advocate also has the power to take court action, in the public interest, to enforce the purposes of a public trust.[12]

Inter vivos and mortis causa trusts

An inter vivos trust takes effect during the truster's lifetime; a mortis causa (or "testa- **13–08** mentary") trust takes effect on the truster's death. A person who is appointed executor under a will may, therefore, be regarded as a trustee for most purposes.[13]

Charitable trusts

Charity law is not part of the law of trusts, but many charities take the form of trusts. **13–09** Charitable bodies are subject to a regulatory scheme which has recently undergone major reform. The current scheme, which is not discussed further here, can be found in the Charities and Trustee Investment (Scotland) Act 2005.[14]

---

[7] K. McK. Norrie and E.M. Scobbie, *Trusts* (W. Green, 1991), 17–18.
[8] See below, para.13–68 et seq.
[9] See generally W.A. Wilson and A.G.M. Duncan, *Trusts, Trustees and Executors*, 2nd edn (W. Green, 1995), paras 14–47 et seq.
[10] See below, para.13–21.
[11] See J. Chalmers, *Trusts: Cases and Materials* (W. Green, 2002), paras 12–10 to 12–12.
[12] *Aitken's Trs v Aitken*, 1927 S.C. 374, per Lord Ashmore at 387.
[13] For further discussion, see W.A. Wilson and A.G.M. Duncan, *Trusts, Trustees and Executors*, 2nd edn (W. Green, 1995), Ch.31.
[14] For background, see *Charity Scotland: The Report of the Scottish Charity Law Review Commission* (W. Green, 2001).

Discretionary trusts

13–10 It is commonly said that Scots law does not recognise a special category of "discretionary trusts".[15] Nevertheless, a truster is entitled to confer discretion upon his trustees as to exactly who should benefit from a trust (e.g. by creating a trust for "charitable purposes" and leaving his trustees to decide exactly which charities should benefit). There are limits, however, to how wide a discretion a truster may confer upon his trustees in such cases. This question is discussed further below.[16]

Trusts created voluntarily and those created by legal implication

13–11 Trusts are normally created voluntarily by the truster, and it is this type of trust with which this chapter is primarily concerned. It is possible, however, for trusts to be created by implication of law. Both forms of creation are discussed in the next section.

Key Concepts

A **trust** is created when one person (the truster) transfers property to a second person (the trustee), who is then under an obligation to apply the property for the benefit of a third person (the beneficiary).

It is possible for there to be more than one truster, trustee or beneficiary.

The trustee is the owner of trust property.

Trust property is protected from the insolvency of either the truster or the trustee.

Trusts may be either **private trusts** (for the benefit of individuals or a specified group of individuals) or **public trusts** (for the benefit of the general public or a specified class of the public).

Trusts may be also be either **inter vivos** (taking effect during the truster's lifetime) or **mortis causa** (taking effect on the death of the truster).

While trusts are normally created **voluntarily**, they may also be created **by implication of law**.

CREATION OF A TRUST

Who can create a trust?

13–12 The law does not place any specific restrictions on the type of person who may create a trust. The general rules of legal capacity apply, and, therefore, children under 16—who normally have no legal capacity to enter into any transaction—cannot normally be trusters.[17] Where a truster is insolvent at the time of the trust's creation, or was rendered insolvent by its creation, the trust may be challenged as a gratuitous alienation[18]—but this is an issue of insolvency law and is not specific to the law of trusts in any way.

---

[15] See, e.g. K. McK Norrie and E.M. Scobbie, *Trusts* (W. Green, 1991), p.23.
[16] See below, para.13–21.
[17] Age of Legal Capacity (Scotland) Act 1991 ss.1(1)(a) and 2(1).
[18] See generally, Bankruptcy (Scotland) Act 1985 s.34; Insolvency Act 1986 s.242; D.W. McKenzie Skene, *Insolvency Law in Scotland* (T&T Clark, 1999), Ch.30.

What property can be subject to a trust?

Again, there are no specific restrictions on the type of property which may be subject to a **13–13** trust. It is, therefore, commonly said that "any property which can be alienated can be the subject of a trust".[19] Even that statement may be too restrictive—it has been held in England that where a person holds property which he is legally incapable of alienating (perhaps because he is bound by contract not to do so), he can nevertheless declare *himself* to be trustee of that property.[20] There would seem to be no good reason why the Scottish courts would not take the same view.

How to create a trust

Trusts may be divided into two types—those created voluntarily and those created by legal **13–14** implication. There are different rules governing the creation of each type of trust (and, indeed, a number of different types of legally implied trust, each of which is created in a different way). The following section deals with the creation of voluntary trusts; legally implied trusts are dealt with later in this chapter.[21]

How to create a trust: voluntarily created trusts

Two requirements must be satisfied for the creation of a voluntary trust. There must be (a) **13–15** a declaration of trust and (b) a transfer of property from the truster to the trustee.

Declaration of trust

In order to create a trust, A must transfer property to B accompanied by a declaration that **13–16** B is to apply the property for specified purposes. No "special or technical" form of words is required.[22]

The crucial question is this: did A (i) intend to make an outright gift of the property to B, coupled with a recommendation as to how the property should be applied, but ultimately leaving it up to B as to what he chose to do with the property—in which case no trust is created—or (ii) intend to bind B to apply the property to specified purposes, thus creating a trust? The following two cases illustrate the distinction:

> ### Barclay's Exr. v McLeod
> ### (1880) 7 R. 477
>
> Mr Barclay died, leaving all his property to his wife. His will stated that it was his "anxious desire" that "as soon after my death as is convenient", his wife should execute a will dividing one-half of her property at the time of her death amongst certain relatives, specified by Mr Barclay. His wife later died without ever having executed any will.
>
> It was argued that, because Mr Barclay had transferred property to Mrs Barclay while specifying certain purposes to which that property was to be applied, she held that property in trust and her executor was, therefore, required to distribute that property in accordance with Mr Barclay's wishes. This argument was rejected. Mr Barclay's "anxious desire" was no more than a recommendation.

---

[19] W.A. Wilson and A.G.M. Duncan, *Trusts, Trustees and Executors*, 2nd edn (W. Green, 1995), para.2–18.
[20] *Don King Productions Inc v Warren* [1999] 3 W.L.R. 276; *Swift v Dairywise Farms* [2000] 1 W.L.R. 1117.
[21] See below, para.13–27 et seq.
[22] *Macpherson v Macpherson's CB* (1894) 21 R. 386, per Lord McLaren at 387.

Macpherson v Macpherson's CB
(1894) 21 R. 386

Robina Young died in 1893, leaving money "to Katherine Alexandrina Macpherson, for the benefit of herself and her sister Jane Macpherson". (Jane Macpherson was mentally incapable and reliant on others for her care). There was some doubt about the meaning of this provision in Miss Young's will, and a special case was presented to the Court of Session.

It was held that the words "for the benefit of" were quite clear—this was not an absolute gift to Katherine, but instead a gift to Katherine in trust for the benefit of herself and her sister.

While words such as "in trust" or "on behalf of" will normally be sufficient to create a trust, they will only have that effect "if the circumstances of the case are consistent with that interpretation".[23]

No special formalities are required for the declaration of trust—and so, therefore, the declaration may be verbal—except in the following three cases, where a written document subscribed by the truster is required[24]:

- "a trust whereby a person declares himself to be sole trustee of his own property or any property which he may require"[25];
- a trust of an interest in land (except where created by court decree, statute or rule of law)[26];
- a mortis causa trust (i.e. one created by a will).[27]

Transfer of property

13–17 A trust will not be effective until the trust property is transferred to the trustee. It has been observed that the requirement of a transfer of property is necessary to prevent fraudulent misuse of the trust device:

Allan's Trs v Inland Revenue
1971 S.C. (H.L.) 45

Lord Reid: "I reject the argument ... that mere proved intention to make a trust coupled with the execution of a declaration of trust can suffice. If that were so, it would be easy to execute such a declaration, keep it in reserve, use it in case of bankruptcy to defeat the claims of creditors, but, if all went well and the trustee desired to regain control of the fund, simply suppress the declaration of trust."

---

[23] *Style Financial Services Ltd v Bank of Scotland (No.2)*, 1998 S.L.T. 851, per Lord Gill at 865. See also *Gillespie v City of Glasgow Bank* (1879) 6 R. (H.L.) 104, per Lord Cairns LC at 107 (there is no magic about the word "trust").

[24] See Requirements of Writing (Scotland) Act 1995 s.2(1). Witnessing is not essential for validity, but it is desirable because a properly witnessed document will have "self-proving" status (i.e. it will be presumed to have been signed by the granter). See s.3 of the 1995 Act for the relevant formalities.

[25] Requirements of Writing (Scotland) Act 1995 s.2(a)(iii).

[26] Requirements of Writing (Scotland) Act 1995 s.2(b).

[27] Requirements of Writing (Scotland) Act 1995 s.2(c).

While the property may be transferred to the trustee by physical delivery, that is not essential. First, some types of property (heritable and incorporeal property) cannot, for obvious reasons, be transferred in this way. Secondly, it is possible to transfer ownership in corporeal moveable property without actually moving the property—in *Milligan v Ross*,[28] a woman executed a deed of trust in which she transferred furnishings and household goods to trustees for the benefit of herself, her husband and her daughter. The trust deed was delivered to the trustees and registered in the Books of Council and Session. Mrs Milligan remained in possession of the property. It was held that these actions were sufficient for delivery and that a valid trust had been created.

The law relating to the transfer of property is not specific to the law of trusts, but is of general application and is discussed elsewhere in this book.[29]

Problem of the truster as trustee

It is possible for a truster to declare himself to be sole trustee of his own property. In such a case, there can obviously be no question of delivery between the truster and the trustee. As an alternative to the transfer of property, therefore, intimation to the beneficiaries of their rights under the trust is required for the trust's creation.[30] Intimation to an agent (such as a solicitor or accountant) or to a parent (where the beneficiary is a child) will normally be sufficient.[31]

13–18

Where there are multiple beneficiaries under a trust, intimation to one of the beneficiaries will suffice.[32] Such a course should only be followed with caution, however: in *Clark's Trs v Inland Revenue*,[33] C took out seven assurance policies which he purported to hold for seven different beneficiaries. There was one single proposal form and the initial premiums were paid by one single cheque. Despite this, it was held that these were seven separate trusts and intimation to one of the beneficiaries was insufficient to bring the other six trusts into effect.

The intimation must take place simultaneously with, or subsequent to, the execution of the declaration of trust.[34] If it takes place before the declaration of trust, it is merely an expression of an intention to create a trust and is not legally effective. Furthermore, a declaration of trust cannot be made unless there is actually a trust fund in existence:

> ### Clark Taylor & Co. Ltd v Quality Site Development (Edinburgh) Ltd
> #### 1981 S.C. 111
>
> C sold bricks to Q under a contract which stated that if Q resold, or otherwise disposed of the bricks before Q had paid C for them, Q would hold the proceeds of the disposal in trust for C until payment had been made. It was held that this contract could not in itself create a trust, as there was no trust fund in existence at the time the contract was made—the proceeds of disposal were not received until a later date.

---

[28] 1994 S.C.L.R. 430.
[29] See above, Ch.12.
[30] *Allan's Trs v Lord Advocate*, 1971 S.C. (H.L.) 45.
[31] *Kerr's Trs v Inland Revenue*, 1974 S.L.T. 193, per Lord Fraser at 201.
[32] *Allan's Trs v Lord Advocate*, 1971 S.C. (H.L.) 45.
[33] 1972 S.L.T. 190.
[34] *Kerr's Trs v Inland Revenue*, 1974 S.L.T. 193.

Validity of the trust purposes

13–19 The declaration of trust must specify the purposes of the trust in order to be effective. Trust purposes may be invalid for three reasons. First, they may be void from uncertainty. Secondly, they may be overly wide and, therefore, ineffective. Thirdly, they may be illegal. Each of these categories will be dealt with in turn.

Purposes void from uncertainty

13–20 Purposes will be void from uncertainty if it is impossible to establish their meaning. An example is provided by the following case:

> **Hardie v Morison**
> (1899) 7 S.L.T. 42
>
> David Hardie's will directed his trustees to use his estate for the purposes of establishing "a shop in which one of the objects is the sale of books dealing with the subject of free thought."
>   Lord Kincairney: "I think that a bequest for the promotion of free thought is void from uncertainty, from want of any recognised or determinate meaning of that term … In carrying out this trust it would not be possible to determine what class of books was intended."

By contrast, in *McLean v Henderson's Trs*,[35] it was held that a bequest "for the advancement and diffusion of the science of phrenology" was valid. It was observed that "the expression phrenology denotes a known, although not a flourishing, branch of science".

Overly wide purposes

13–21 It is not essential (and in many cases it would not be possible) for a truster to specify, down to the last detail, how his trustees should distribute or apply his property. He may confer a degree of discretion on his trustees to make that decision:

> **Crichton v Grierson**
> (1828) 3 W. & S. 329
>
> Lord Lyndhurst LC: "a party may, in the disposition of his property, select particular classes of individuals and objects, and then give to some particular individual a power, after his death, of appropriating the property, or applying any part of his property, to any particular individuals among that class whom that person may select and describe in his will."

(Although Lord Lyndhurst is dealing here with mortis causa trusts—those created on death—the same principle is applicable to inter vivos trusts.)

Two issues arise from Lord Lyndhurst's statement of principle. First, there must be a selection of a "particular individual" (or individuals) as trustee(s). Secondly, the truster

---

[35] (1880) 7 R. 601.

must select a "particular class" of individuals and objects. The trustees must then exercise their discretion as to who (or what) within that "particular class" is to benefit from the trust.

The first issue—the selection of a "particular individual" is unproblematic in inter vivos trusts, as it is impossible to create such a trust without appointing trustees. It may be problematic, however, in mortis causa trusts. In such cases, the trustees named in the testator's will may have died before the testator or may decline office—or the testator may simply fail to name an executor in his will. While in such cases, the courts may appoint an executor-dative or judicial factor to administer the deceased's estate, these persons are not entitled to exercise discretion in carrying out trust purposes.[36] In such cases, therefore, the trust purposes will be invalid as being overly wide, and the trust will fail. This is illustrated by the following case:

Angus's Exrx. v Batchan's Trs
1949 S.C. 335

Anne Angus's will directed that, after certain specific legacies had been paid, the residue of her estate should be given to charity. She did not nominate a trustee or executor. It was held that this bequest was, therefore, invalid:

Lord President (Cooper): "No encroachment has yet been tolerated on the basic requirement that a testator must make his own will, and that, when he makes it by designating a class and a person to choose within that class, the designation of both must be his own act, express or plainly implied. To allow a testator to confine himself to designating the class, while deliberately leaving the choice of the individual beneficiaries to anyone who may anyhow acquire a title to administer the estate is, in my opinion, to authorise that testator to delegate the power to test ... A *mortis causa* declaration of charitable benevolence is not a will."

Secondly, the "particular class" must be specified by the trustee. The test for this is "whether or not the [trustee] has described the class he means to benefit with sufficient accuracy as to enable a reasonable man to know who the persons are that he meant to benefit, leaving it only to the trustees to select among those who form that class the particular recipients of his bounty."[37]

It has been held, therefore, that it is insufficient to give property to trustees "to be disposed of ... in such manner as they may think proper"[38] or "in such way or ways as my trustees shall deem best".[39] By contrast, a direction that the residue of a testator's estate should be disposed of "among any poor relations, friends or acquaintances of mine" was held to be valid.[40]

A more difficult question arises where a truster uses a vague form of words such as "public purposes" or "charitable purposes".[41] A special status is given to the words

---

[36] *Angus's Exrs v Batchan's Trs*, 1949 S.C. 335; *Vollar's J.F. v Boyd*, 1952 S.L.T. (Notes) 84.

[37] *Salvesen's Trs v Wye*, 1954 S.C. 440, per Lord Carmont at 444.

[38] *Sutherland's Trs v Sutherland's Tr.* (1893) 20 R. 925.

[39] *Allan and Others (Shaw's Trs)* (1893) 1 S.L.T. 308.

[40] *Salvesen's Trs v Wye*, 1954 S.C. 440.

[41] As to the even more difficult situation, which arises where such terms are combined (e.g. a bequest to "charitable and religious purposes"), see W.A. Wilson and A.G.M. Duncan, *Trusts, Trustees and Executors*, 2nd edn (W. Green, 1995), paras 14–100 to 14–117.

"charitable purposes", which are valid without any further specification.[42] "Educational purposes" is probably sufficiently specific.[43] By contrast, "benevolent purposes" and "public purposes" are not.[44] "Religious purposes" is not sufficiently specific unless the relevant religion is specified.[45]

Illegal purposes

13–22 There are four types of purpose which will be held invalid due to illegality, which are as follows[46]:

- criminal purposes;
- directly prohibited purposes;
- purposes which are *contra bonos mores*; and
- purposes which are contrary to public policy.

Each of these will be dealt with in turn.

(i) Criminal purposes

13–23 There is an almost total absence of authority on this issue, and it is doubtful that it is of much practical importance. It is clear, however, that a trust for criminal purposes is void. The following English case illustrates the point:

> ### Bowman v Secular Society Ltd
> ### [1917] A.C. 406
>
> Charles Bowman left the residue of his estate to the Secular Society Limited, the principal purpose of which was "to promote ... the principle that human conduct should be based upon natural knowledge, and not upon super-natural belief." It was argued that these purposes would necessarily involve committing the criminal offence of blasphemy and that the bequest to the Society was therefore void. The House of Lords held that such conduct was not necessarily blasphemous, and that the bequest was, therefore, valid. It was accepted that if carrying out the purposes of the Society did amount to blasphemy, the bequest would have been for a criminal purpose and therefore unenforceable.

(ii) Directly prohibited purposes

13–24 There are three forms of trust purpose which are directly prohibited by statute, as follows:

    (a) *Entails*.[47] An entail is a device, which was historically used to keep heritable property in the same family indefinitely. The owner would normally be obliged to

---

[42] *Turnbull's Trs v Lord Advocate*, 1918 S.C. (H.L.) 88; A. Mackenzie Stuart, *The Law of Trusts* (W. Green, 1932), 112.

[43] *Brough v Brough's Trs*, 1950 S.L.T. 117. cf. *Harper's Trs v Jacobs*, 1929 S.C. 345.

[44] *Caldwell's Trs v Caldwell*, 1920 S.C. 700, per Lord Skerrington at 702 ("benevolent purposes"); *Blair v Duncan* (1901) 4 F. (H.L.) 1 ("public purposes").

[45] *Grimond v Grimond's Trs* (1905) 7 F. (H.L.) 90; *Bannerman's Trs v Bannerman*, 1915 S.C. 398.

[46] *Bowman v Secular Society Ltd* [1917] A.C. 406, per Lord Dunedin at 434.

[47] See generally Scottish Law Commission, *Report on Abolition of the Feudal System* (1998), Scot. Law Com. No.168, paras 9.8–9.17.

pass the property to his eldest son on his death, and the son on to his eldest son, and so on. This device came to be seen as economically and socially disadvantageous and was gradually restricted by statute. The creation of entails was finally prohibited in 1914,[48] and any entails which continued to exist until recently were finally brought to an end by the Abolition of Feudal Tenure etc. (Scotland) Act 2000.[49]

(b) *Successive liferents.*[50] Successive liferents are similar to entails, but can be used in relation to moveable property. A truster might, for example, direct that the trustee is to receive a liferent of the property and hold the fee in trust for his (the trustee's) eldest son, who is then to receive a liferent of the property and hold the fee in trust for his eldest son, and so on. While successive liferents can still be created, their duration is now restricted by statute. If a person, who was not alive or *in utero* (conceived but unborn) at the time the deed was executed becomes entitled to a liferent interest under the deed, they become the absolute owner of the property.[51] This applies unless they are not yet of full age, in which case they will become the absolute owner upon reaching that age.[52]

(c) *Excessive accumulations of income.* A truster may not create a trust where the trust income is simply added to the trust fund and not spent for longer than certain periods of time. The applicable period of time is generally 21 years, but there are a number of other possibilities depending on the applicability of certain rather complex statutory provisions.[53]

(iii) Purposes which are *contra bonos mores*

Trust purposes may be invalid as being *contra bonos mores* (described by Lord Dunedin in **13–25** *Bowman v Secular Society Ltd* as "offence against what may be termed the natural moral sense"[54]). This head of invalidity has most commonly been used to hold that conditions attached to bequests in wills are invalid. The cases may be divided into three categories, as follows:

(a) *Conditions relating to living arrangements.* In *Fraser v Rose*,[55] a testator left money to his (adult) daughter on the condition that she should leave her mother within four weeks of his death and never live with her again. It was held that the condition was invalid and that the daughter should take the bequest free of the condition.

(b) *Conditions relating to marriage.* A condition that a person may only take a benefit under a trust, if they remain unmarried is generally thought to be invalid.[56] However, it is competent to establish a trust to provide financial support for a person for as long as they remain unmarried, and so in *Sturrock v Rankin's Trs*, a provision which was "not a condition in restraint of marriage, but simply a

---

[48] Entail (Scotland) Act 1914.
[49] See ss.50–52 of the 2000 Act.
[50] On the concept of liferent and fee generally, see Ch.12.
[51] Law Reform (Miscellaneous Provisions) (Scotland) Act 1968 s.18.
[52] "Full age" for these purposes is the age of 18: Age of Majority (Scotland) Act 1969 s.1.
[53] Trusts (Scotland) Act 1961 s.5 and the Law Reform (Miscellaneous Provisions) (Scotland) Act 1966 s.6. See generally, W.A. Wilson and A.G.M. Duncan, *Trusts, Trustees and Executors*, 2nd edn (W. Green, 1995), Ch.9.
[54] [1917] A.C. 406 at 434.
[55] (1849) 11 D. 1466. See also *Grant's Trs v Grant* (1898) 25 R. 929.
[56] *Aird's Exrs v Aird*, 1949 S.C. 154. A condition that the beneficiary should not marry a specified individual appears to be valid: *Forbes v Forbes's Trs* (1882) 9 R. 675.

provision for unmarried daughters who, in the view of the testator, had no other means of support"[57] was held to be valid. The distinction is a narrow one.

(c) *Conditions relating to religion.* A truster may provide that a person may only benefit under a trust if he adheres (or refrains from adhering) to a particular religion.[58] However, a condition that a beneficiary must promise to maintain a particular faith for the rest of his life before taking a benefit would probably be invalid as being *contra bonos mores*.[59]

Where a condition is held invalid, the beneficiary will normally take the benefit without being required to comply with the condition.

(iv) Purposes which are contrary to public policy

13–26 While "public policy" is a recognised ground of invalidity, the term is a misleading one. In this context, it refers to a very narrow doctrine, which is that if trust purposes "are unreasonable as conferring neither a patrimonial benefit upon anybody nor a benefit upon the public or any section thereof, the directions are invalid."[60] The following two cases provide examples of such invalidity:

McCaig's Trs v Kirk-Session of United Free Church of Lismore
1915 S.C. 426

In her will, Catherine McCaig directed that her trustees should convert the McCaig Tower in Oban into a private enclosure, and should erect bronze statues within the tower of members of her family, each of which was to cost not less than £1,000. The trustees were to be bound in all time coming not to sell the tower and statutes. It was held that these purposes were invalid as conferring no benefit on any person: the incidental benefit, which might be received by workmen in constructing the enclosure, was insufficient.

Sutherland's Tr. v Verschoyle
1968 S.L.T. 43

A testatrix directed in her will that her trustees should purchase a house "of a certain size and dignity" in St Andrews to exhibit and preserve for perpetuity her "valuable art collection". In actual fact, the "collection" was unlikely to attract any scholarly or public interest, and many of the items were simply copies. It was held that her directions were invalid, as they conferred no benefit either on particular individuals or the general public.

There are two exceptional cases, however, where trust purposes may be valid despite the fact that they do not confer any benefit upon particular individuals or the general public. These are trusts for memorials (provided they are not unreasonable or extravagant),[61] and

---

[57] (1875) 2 R. 850, per Lord Gifford at 854.
[58] *Blathwayt v Baron Cawley* [1976] A.C. 397.
[59] *Innes's Trs v Innes*, 1963 S.L.T. 353, per Lord Carmont at 358.
[60] *Aitken's Trs v Aitken*, 1927 S.C. 374, per Lord Sands at 381.
[61] *Lindsay's Exr. v Forsyth*, 1940 S.C. 568, per the Lord Justice-Clerk (Aitchison) at 572.

trusts for the maintenance of particular animals.[62] Trusts for the benefit of a class of animals, or the prevention of cruelty to animals, are regarded as conferring a benefit upon the general public.[63]

How to create a trust: legally implied trusts

Resulting trusts

A resulting trust will arise where the purposes of an existing trust fail to dispose of all the **13–27** trust property. In such a case, the trustees will be deemed to be holding the trust property in a resulting trust for the benefit of the truster, or his representatives. This is probably not, strictly speaking, a special form of trust, but simply a "term implied by law into all [voluntarily created] trusts".[64] However, it arises in special circumstances and for that reason is normally treated separately in the textbooks.

A resulting trust may arise in two principal types of case. First, the trust purposes may be void or impossible to fulfil.[65] Secondly, the trust purposes may not exhaust the full trust estate, as in the following case:

> ### Anderson v Smoke
> (1898) 25 R. 493
>
> Mr Anderson created a trust for the benefit of his son, to be administered by his two daughters as trustees. Upon the death of the son, only half of the fund had been spent. It was held that the trustees were not entitled to keep the money for themselves, but should return it to Mr Anderson's heirs.

Fiduciary fees

A fiduciary fee is a special kind of trust, created where A purports to transfer property to B **13–28** in liferent and to B's children in fee, despite B having no children at the time.[66] Such a transfer cannot be effective in its own terms, as it would leave the fee in an "ownerless" state. To avoid this problem, B will be deemed in such cases to hold the property as a kind of trustee, for himself in liferent and his children in fee.[67] This device is now largely obsolete, although still technically competent. If such an arrangement were desired nowadays, it would be normal to explicitly create a trust rather than rely upon this doctrine.

---

[62] *Flockhart's Trs v Bourlet*, 1934 S.N. 23. See further K. McK Norrie, "Trusts for Animals" (1987) 32 J.L.S.S. 386.

[63] *Aitken's Trs v Aitken*, 1927 S.C. 374, per Lord Sands at 381; A. Mackenzie Stuart, *The Law of Trusts* (W. Green, 1932), pp.69–71.

[64] G.L. Gretton, "Constructive Trusts" (1997) 1 Edin. L.R. 281 at 309.

[65] See, e.g. *Templeton v Burgh of Ayr*, 1910 2 S.L.T. 12. Or, exceptionally, unascertainable: see *Thomas v Tennent's Trs* (1868) 7 M. 114.

[66] On liferent and fee generally, see Ch.12.

[67] Trusts (Scotland) Act 1921 s.8.

Constructive trusts

13–29 Scots law (in stark contrast to English law) only recognises constructive trusts to a very limited extent—if, indeed, these are recognised at all. It is commonly thought that a constructive trust will be created in two situations, as follows[68]:

(a) *Where a person in a fiduciary position gains an advantage by virtue of that position.* An example is provided by the following case:

> **Cherry's Trs v Patrick**
> 1911 2 S.L.T. 313
>
> Mr Patrick, a wholesaler, supplied goods to Mr Cherry's business. Upon Mr Cherry's death, he was appointed a trustee on Mr Cherry's estate. The trustees continued to run the business and Mr Patrick continued to supply goods to it. It was held that this amounted to Mr Patrick taking a benefit from his fiduciary position, and that he was, therefore, obliged to return the benefit received to the trust.

It is commonly asserted that Mr Patrick held the benefit received from his dealings on a constructive trust,[69] although the court does not explicitly refer to the concept of "constructive trust" at any point.[70]

(b) *Where a person who is a stranger to an existing trust is to his knowledge in possession of property belonging to the trust.* Although the existence of this type of constructive trust in Scots law has been asserted on a number of occasions,[71] supporting authority is slim if not non-existent.[72]

There is no doubt that a person in position (a) or (b) is under an obligation to repay the benefit received. However, it has been argued that this has nothing to do with any doctrine of constructive trust.[73] The question of whether or not a trust has been created would only be of importance if the alleged "constructive trustee" had become insolvent, as the existence of a trust would protect the trust funds from the claims of his other creditors. In cases not involving insolvency, the result is the same, whether or not it is reached by the creation of a constructive trust.

> **Key Concepts**
>
> There are no specific restrictions on the persons who may create a trust, or the type of property which may be subject to a trust. The general rules of property and legal capacity apply.

---

[68] The classification is from W.A. Wilson and A.G.M. Duncan, *Trusts, Trustees and Executors*, 2nd edn (W. Green, 1995), para.6–61.

[69] See, e.g. K. McK Norrie and E.M. Scobbie, *Trusts* (W. Green, 1991), p.55.

[70] G.L. Gretton, "Constructive Trusts" (1997) 1 Edin. L.R. 281 at 294.

[71] W.A. Wilson and A.G.M. Duncan, *Trusts, Trustees and Executors*, 2nd edn (W. Green, 1995), paras 6–65 to 6–68; K. McK Norrie and E.M. Scobbie, *Trusts* (W. Green, 1991), p.54.

[72] cf. *Huisman v Soepboer*, 1994 S.L.T. 682, discussed by G.L. Gretton, "Constructive Trusts" (1997) 1 Edin. L.R. 281 at 300.

[73] G.L. Gretton, "Constructive Trusts" (1997) 1 Edin. L.R. 281.

A **voluntarily created trust** is created by (a) a **declaration of trust** accompanied by (b) a **transfer of property** from the truster to the trustee.

Where the truster and the trustee are the same person, there can be no transfer of property. In such cases, **intimation to the beneficiaries** of their rights under the trust is required for the creation of the trust.

Trust purposes may be **invalid** for the following reasons:

- they may be too uncertain (i.e. the truster's meaning cannot be ascertained);
- they may be overly wide;
- they may be illegal as being:
  - contrary to the criminal law;
  - directly prohibited (entails, accumulations of income and successive liferents);
  - *contra bonos mores* (an offence against the "natural moral sense"); or
  - contrary to public policy (if they confer no benefit upon any person).

A **resulting trust** is a type of legally implied trust. It will arise where the purposes of an existing trust fail to dispose of all the trust property. In such a case, the trustees will hold the remaining property in trust for the original truster or his representatives.

A **constructive trust** will be created where:

- a person in a fiduciary position gains an advantage by virtue of that position; or
- a person who is a stranger to a trust is to his knowledge in possession of property belonging to the trust.

In such cases, the constructive trustee will be required to communicate the relevant property to the trust estate. There is some doubt as to whether this is, strictly speaking, actually a form of trust.

OFFICE OF TRUSTEE

Who can be a trustee?

The law does not generally place any specific restrictions on the type of person who may **13–30** act as trustees. The general rules of legal capacity apply, and, therefore, children under 16—who normally have no legal capacity to enter into any transaction—cannot normally be trustees.[74] Bankruptcy or insolvency is not normally a barrier to acting as a trustee.[75] A person may be both truster and trustee.

There are, however, specific statutory restrictions on the type of person who may act as a trustee in certain types of trust, particularly charitable trusts.[76]

---

[74] Age of Legal Capacity (Scotland) Act 1991 s.9(f).
[75] See A.J.P. Menzies, *The Law of Scotland Affecting Trustees*, 2nd edn (W. Green, 1913), paras 77 and 913 and cases cited there.
[76] Charities and Trustee Investment (Scotland) Act 2005 s.69. See also Pensions Act 1995 ss.3–6 and 29–30 (pension trusts); Finance Act 1989 Sch.5 para.3(3)(c) (employee share ownership trusts) and the Inheritance Tax Act 1984 Sch.4 para.2(ii).

Appointment and acceptance of the original trustees

13–31 Trustees will generally be appointed in the trust deed. They may be named as individuals, or identified ex officio (as the holder of an office). For example, the trust deed in *Parish Council of Kilmarnock v Ossington's Trs*[77] stated that one of the trustees would be "the chairman of the Parochial Board of the parish of Kilmarnock". Essentially, any description which is sufficient to identify the relevant individual is enough—*in Martin v Ferguson's Trs,*[78] a testator's will stated that "I wish my estate to be managed by the same trustees as my brother", and that was held to be sufficient.

The trustee must accept office. No trustee can be forced to accept office against his will.[79] No particular form of acceptance is required—and, indeed, acceptance need not necessarily be express but can be inferred from actions, as the following case demonstrates:

> ### Ker v City of Glasgow Bank
> ### (1879) 6 R. (H.L.) 52
>
> Ker was named as trustee in a deed. He never formally accepted office, and never attended a meeting of trustees. However, he did sign a transfer of railway stock in favour of the trust "as trustee". It was held that this was sufficient to amount to an implied acceptance of office.

Appointment or assumption of new trustees

13–32 Trustees always have a power to assume additional trustees unless this is excluded by the terms of the trust deed.[80] In a private trust, if there is no remaining trustee(s) (perhaps because all the original trustees have resigned or died), the truster has a "radical right" to appoint new trustees.[81] It is possible for a trust deed to be drafted, so as to confer a wider power upon the truster to appoint new trustees, or even to confer such a right upon third parties.[82]

The court has a statutory power to appoint trustees where there is no power to assume additional trustees under the trust deed, or where a sole trustee is or has become insane or incapable, or has been absent from the United K for six months or has disappeared for that period.[83] The court may also appoint new trustees at common law in exceptional cases. This power has been used where two trustees were unable to work together and the appointment of a third was required to resolve the deadlock.[84]

---

[77] (1896) 23 R. 833.
[78] (1892) 19 R. 474.
[79] *Vestry of St Silas Church v Trs of St Silas Church*, 1945 S.C. 110, per the Lord Justice-Clerk (Cooper) at 121 (referring to ex officio trustees, but the point is of general application).
[80] Trusts (Scotland) Act 1921 s.3.
[81] *Lindsay v Lindsay* (1847) 9 D. 1297.
[82] See, e.g. *Morison, Petr* (1834) 12 S. 307 and 547.
[83] Trusts (Scotland) Act 1921 s.22.
[84] *Aikman, Petr* (1881) 9 R. 213; *Taylor, Petr*, 1932 S.C. 1.

Resignation of trustees

13–33 Trustees always have a power to resign office unless the trust deed provides otherwise.[85] However, a sole trustee is not entitled to resign unless new trustees[86] are appointed, and a trustee who has accepted any legacy, bequest or annuity given on condition of accepting the office of trustee is not entitled to resign unless he is explicitly given the power to do so by the trust deed. Alternatively, he may apply to the court for authority to resign. If the court grants such authority, it may impose conditions relating to the repayment of the legacy accepted by the trustee.[87]

Removal of trustees

13–34 The court has a statutory power to remove a trustee in the following cases[88]:

- where the trustee is insane;
- where the trustee is "incapable of acting by reason of physical or mental disability";
- where the trustee has been absent from the United Kingdom continuously for at least six months; and
- where the trustee has disappeared for at least six months.

In the first two of these cases, the court is obliged to remove the trustee.[89] In the last two cases, it has a discretion as to whether or not to do so.

The court also has a common law power to remove a trustee for misconduct in office, as in the following case:

> ### Stewart v Chalmers
> ### (1904) 7 F. 163
>
> Thomas Chalmers and Robert Stewart were both trustees under Peter Stewart's will. Stewart was also law-agent to the trust. A third trustee resigned, leaving Chalmers and Stewart as the only trustees. Stewart wrote to Chalmers regarding the investment of the trust funds, and Chalmers replied: "As your position and mine as trustees are now equal, I am to insist on half fees for all business to be done by you for this trust. On hearing that you agree to this condition, I will consider the question of investing the trust funds.'

The beneficiaries petitioned the Court of Session to remove Thomas Chalmers from his position as trustee. The court held that Chalmers' conduct had been "quite indefensible", and granted the petition.

The power will only be exercised in exceptional circumstances: for example, a conflict of interest does not automatically warrant removal.[90]

---

[85] Trusts (Scotland) Act 1921 s.3(a).
[86] cf. *Kennedy, Petr*, 1983 S.L.T. (Sh. Ct) 10 (holding that it is sufficient to appoint a single trustee).
[87] For these restrictions, see the Trusts (Scotland) Act 1921 s.3.
[88] Trusts (Scotland) Act 1921 s.23.
[89] This is clear from the language of the statute: see also *Tod v Marshall* (1895) 23 R. 36.
[90] *Earl of Cawdor, Petr.*, 2006 S.L.T. 1070.

Death of a trustee

13–35 Where one of several trustees dies, his share in the trust property passes automatically to the other trustees.[91] The position is more complex where a sole trustee dies. In such cases, the title remains with the sole trustee "and has to be taken out of him by process of conveyancing."[92]

Key Concepts

Trustees may be **appointed** by any description, which is sufficient to identify the relevant individual. They must **accept** office; they cannot be forced to do so. Acceptance may be either express or implied.

Trustees always have the power to **assume additional trustees** unless this is excluded by the terms of the trust deed. The court has the power to **appoint additional trustees** in certain cases.

Trustees always have a power to **resign office** unless the trust deed provides otherwise.

The court has the power to **remove** trustees who are insane, incapable, have been absent from the United Kingdom or who have disappeared for at least six months, or who have misconducted themselves in office.

DECISION-MAKING BY TRUSTEES

13–36 As a general rule, trust decisions may validly be made by a majority of trustees.[93] There are two exceptions to this rule:

- The trust deed may state that the appointment of the trustees is "joint". In this case, decisions must be taken unanimously to be effective.
- The truster may appoint a sine qua non trustee. Without the consent of this trustee, "no act of administration shall be effectual".[94]

Importance of a quorum

13–37 The "quorum" is both:

- the minimum number of trustees who must participate in trust decision-making for any decisions taken to be valid; and
- the minimum number of trustees who must participate in a trust action (e.g. signing contracts on behalf of the trust) for such actions to validly bind the trust, unless the trustees have appointed an agent (who may be one of their own number) with the authority to bind the trust.

---

[91] *Gordon's Trs v Eglinton* (1851) 13 D. 1381.

[92] A.J.P. Menzies, *The Law of Scotland Affecting Trustees*, 2nd edn (W. Green, 1913), para.153. For the procedure required, see W.A. Wilson and A.G.M. Duncan, *Trusts, Trustees and Executors*, 2nd edn (W. Green, 1995), paras 20–09 et seq. and 22–05 et seq.

[93] *McCulloch v Wallace* (1846) 9 D. 32. One-half of the body of trustees is insufficient: *Neilson v Mossend Iron Co* (1885) 12 R. 499.

[94] John McLaren, *The Law of Wills and Succession as Administered in Scotland*, 3rd edn (Bell, 1894), para.1656.

Unless the trust deed provides otherwise, the quorum is a "majority of the trustees accepting and surviving".[95] It should be noted that a trustee who dissents from a decision is, nevertheless, obliged to take any steps which are necessary to give effect to that decision,[96] and a trustee who does not participate in a contract made by the trust may, nevertheless, be personally liable on that contract.[97] If a dissenting trustee believes that the decision of the majority is in breach of trust, it is open to him to take an action for interdict, or declarator, accordingly. Alternatively, he can resign as a trustee, assuming that he has power to do so under the trust deed.

All trustees have a right to be consulted in trust decision-making. A failure to consult a trustee will render a decision taken by the remaining trustees void.[98] Third parties are, however, protected in such a situation by two factors: (a) the personal liability of trustees who make contracts on behalf of the trust[99] and (b) s.7 of the Trusts (Scotland) Act 1921, which states that a deed which bears to be granted by trustees but is "in fact executed by a quorum of such trustees in favour of any person other than a beneficiary or co-trustee" shall not normally be challengeable for lack of consultation or other irregularity of procedure.[100]

A trustee may lose his right to be consulted, as in the following case:

Malcolm v Goldie
(1895) 22 R. 968

One of five surviving trustees left Scotland to reside in Australia. The remaining trustees, acting on the basis that the emigrant trustee "is now resident in Australia and has ceased to act", assumed two new trustees. The proposal to assume the two new trustees was not intimated to the emigrant trustees. The validity of this assumption was later challenged.

It was held that, if the remaining trustees knew that the emigrant trustee was resident in Australia, and did not intend to come back, "to give notice of the meeting would be a mere futile formality", and that the failure to do so did not render the assumption invalid.

Modern advances in communications might mean that this case would be decided differently today.

Can the courts interfere in the trustees' exercise of discretion?

The courts will not normally interfere with decisions taken by trustees except in very **13–38** limited circumstances:

---

[95] Trusts (Scotland) Act 1921 s.3(c).

[96] *Lynedoch v Ouchterlony* (1827) 5 S. 358.

[97] *Cuninghame v City of Glasgow Bank* (1879) 6 R. (H.L.) 98. On the personal liability of trustees under contract generally, see below, para.11–64.

[98] *Wyse v Abbott* (1881) 8 R. 983.

[99] See below, para.13–66.

[100] The effect of this section on transactions involving heritable property is not entirely clear and it is best practice to insist that all trustees sign any relevant deeds: see G.L. Gretton, "Problems in Partnership Conveyancing" (1991) 36 J.L.S.S. 232, 235.

> ## Board of Management for Dundee General Hospital v Bell's Trs
> ### 1952 S.C. (H.L.) 78
>
> Lord Reid: "If it can be shown that the trustees considered the wrong question, or that, although they purported to consider the right question, they did not really apply their minds to it or perversely shut their eyes to the facts or that they did not act honestly or in good faith, then there is no true decision and the Court will intervene."

Trustees who are given a discretion to act must exercise it. They cannot simply refuse to apply their minds to the issue,[101] and the court will not exercise the discretion for them.[102] Trustees are not obliged to give reasons for their decisions.[103]

> ### Key Concepts
>
> Trust decisions may validly be made by a **majority** of trustees.
>
> A **quorum** is a majority of the trustees unless the trust deed provides otherwise. This is the minimum number of trustees who must participate in decision-making for any decisions taken to be valid, and the minimum number of trustees who must participate in a trust action (such as signing contracts) for such actions to validly bind the trust.
>
> All trustees have a **right to be consulted** in trust decision-making. A failure to consult a trustee may render a decision void.
>
> The courts will not **interfere with decisions taken by trustees,** unless it can be shown that they have not properly applied themselves to their duties, or have not acted honestly or in good faith.

DUTIES OF A TRUSTEE

General duty of care

13–39 Trustees must, in all cases, exercise due care in their dealings with the trust estate. The standard of care required in that of the "ordinary prudent man".[104] This is an objective standard, and a trustee who fails to live up to this standard will be liable for any loss caused by this breach of the duty of care even if he has acted in good faith and to the best of his abilities.

Where a person is appointed as a remunerated trustee, on the basis that they have held themselves out as being particularly skilled in some way (perhaps skill in relation to investment matters), they may be liable for failing to exercise the higher standard of care which this skill would suggest.[105]

---

[101] *Train v Buchanan's Trs*, 1907 S.C. 517, per the Lord President (Dunedin) at 524–525.
[102] *Earl of Stair's Trs* (1896) 23 R. 1070, per Lord McLaren at 1074.
[103] *Scott v National Trust* [1998] 2 All E.R. 705. See also *Board of Management for Dundee General Hospital v Bell's Trs*, 1952 S.C. (H.L.) 78, per Lord Normand at 85.
[104] *Raes v Meek* (1889) 16 R. (H.L.) 31.
[105] See the English case of *Bartlett v Barclays Bank Trust Co. Ltd (No.1)* [1980] Ch. 515.

Duty not to delegate the trust

Trustees must take responsibility for trust decision-making themselves and cannot dele- **13–40**
gate this responsibility to a third party.[106] This does not mean, however, that they are
bound to undertake every act of trust administration personally. Instead, they are entitled
to employ agents when a person of reasonable prudence would do so.[107] Trustees are not
liable for losses caused by the negligence of fraud of an agent whom they legitimately
appoint,[108] unless they have failed to exercise due care in the selection or supervision of the
agent.[109]

Duty to secure trust property

A trustee is responsible for ingathering and securing trust property: **13–41**

> "It is the duty of a trustee to take possession of the estate, and to have it transferred
> into the name of the trustees to the extent that no individual trustee or third party can
> use it for other than trust purposes. If he allows trust estate to remain in the hands of
> a third party, or of the law agent, without reducing it into the possession of the trust,
> he incurs the risk of personal liability if it should be lost."[110]

Investment duties

When trustees hold the trust estate for any period of time, they must consider investing the **13–42**
estate to protect its value.

> ### Melville v Noble's Trs
> (1896) 24 R. 243
>
> Trustees left a substantial trust fund on deposit-receipt with a bank for 19 years
> without considering the question of investment. If it had been invested properly, a
> return of 3 per cent per annum could have been received. It was held that they were
> liable to make up this 3 per cent return personally.

If the trustees in *Melville* had addressed their minds to the question of investment, and
concluded honestly and reasonably that leaving the money on deposit-receipt was the best
course, they could not have been liable for any loss.[111]

Trustee investment was, until recently, subject to fairly restrictive statutory rules,
although the truster could give the trustees wider powers by drafting the trust deed
appropriately. Trustees now, however, have a general power to "make any kind of
investment of the trust estate".[112] In exercising this power, they must consider whether the
investment is a suitable one, and consider the need for diversification of the trust

---

[106] *Scott v Occidental Petroleum (Caledonia) Ltd*, 1990 S.L.T. 882.
[107] *Hay v Binny* (1861) 23 D. 594, and see Trusts (Scotland) Act 1921 s.4(1)(f) (power to appoint factors and law
agents normally implied in all trust deeds).
[108] *Thomson v Campbell* (1838) 16 S. 560.
[109] *Carruthers v Carruthers* (1896) 23 R. (H.L.) 55.
[110] A. Mackenzie Stuart, *The Law of Trusts* (W. Green, 1932), 200. See also *Forman v Burns* (1853) 15 D. 362.
[111] See *Manners v Strong's J.F.* (1902) 4 F. 829.
[112] Trusts (Scotland) Act 1921 s 4(1)(ea), as inserted by the Charities and Trustee Investment (Scotland) Act 2005
s 93(2).

investments. They must also obtain and consider proper advice, except where they reasonably consider that such advice is unnecessary or inappropriate.[113]

The problem of "ethical" investment

13–43 In taking investment decisions, trustees must act in the best interests of the trust beneficiaries. They are not entitled to disregard those interests in favour of other considerations, as the following case demonstrates:

> ### Cowan v Scargill
> [1985] Ch. 270
>
> A mineworkers' pension scheme was established under statute. There were 10 trustees, 5 of which were appointed by the National Union of Mineworkers. The NUM trustees objected to the investment plan, on the basis that it involved investment overseas and investment in energies in competition with coal, both of which conflicted with NUM policy. The other trustees sought a declaration that the NUM trustees were in breach of their duties as trustees by demanding that investment decisions be made in accordance with NUM policy. The declaration was granted.

This decision does not necessarily prevent trustees from taking into account what might be termed "ethical" considerations in making investment decisions. Given the wide range of investments which are often open to trustees, if a trustee has a choice between investment A and investment B, which appear to be equally good investments, from the point of view of maximising the funds available for distribution to the beneficiaries, he cannot be criticised for choosing to select investment A over investment B, on the basis of ethical factors.[114] What he may not do, is to subordinate the interests of the beneficiaries to those ethical factors (unless, of course, the trust deed empowers him to do so).

Duty to take advice

13–44 It was noted earlier that trustees must administer the trust-estate to (at least) the standard that a man of ordinary prudence would exercise in the management of his own affairs. The man of ordinary prudence, of course, recognises that he is not an expert in all matters and must seek professional advice in appropriate cases. The following case demonstrates the importance of this duty:

> ### Martin v City of Edinburgh District Council
> 1988 S.L.T. 329
>
> Edinburgh City Council was responsible for the administration of 58 trusts. In 1984, the Labour Party won a majority of seats on the council and put into effect a policy of withdrawing, for ethical reasons, investments held by those trusts in South Africa. A

---

[113] Trusts (Scotland) Act 1921 s.4A, as inserted by the Charities and Trustee Investment (Scotland) Act 2005 s.94. There is also a common law duty to take advice: see below, para.13–44.

[114] See *Harries v Church Commissioners for England* [1992] 1 W.L.R. 1241, per Nicholls V.C. at 1247–1248.

councillor brought an action for declarator, that the council had acted in breach of its duty as a trustee.

Lord Murray: "I conclude that the pursuer has proved a breach of trust by the council in pursuing a policy of disinvesting in South Africa without considering expressly whether it was in the best interests of the beneficiaries and without obtaining professional advice on this matter ... the trustees acting on behalf of the council misdirected themselves in failing to comply with a prime duty of trustees, namely, to consider and seek advice as to the best interests of the beneficiaries, and so they are in breach of trust."

Although trustees must take advice, they are not obliged to follow it (provided that they have concluded it is in the best interests of the beneficiaries not to do so). To simply rubber-stamp the advice of professional advisers would be to improperly delegate the trust.[115] This duty is most important in relation to investment matters but is not confined to such issues.

Duties regarding existing debts and obligations

While it is unusual for an inter vivos trust to have existing debts and obligations, these will **13–45** exist as a matter of course in mortis causa trusts. In such cases, trustees are required to pay off the debts of the deceased, but are not personally liable for those debts. If the deceased's liabilities exceed his assets, then his estate may be sequestrated.[116]

A trustee on a mortis causa trust (normally an executor) cannot be compelled to pay an ordinary debt until six months have expired from the date of death.[117] This rule prevents one creditor obtaining an advantage over another, by taking acting immediately upon a debtor's death before other creditors become aware of the fact.[118] If an executor pays any debts (or legacies) before the expiry of the six month period, he does so at his own risk and may be liable to make up the shortfall if the estate proves to be insolvent.[119]

Duties regarding new debts and obligations

In most cases, in order to discharge their duties, trustees will have to enter into contracts **13–46** with third parties. The general rule is that they incur personal liability in respect of any such contracts, unless they explicitly contract out of such liability.[120] They are, of course, entitled to be reimbursed from the trust-estate for such expenses as they properly incur in the discharge of their duties as trustees.[121]

---

[115] *Martin v City of Edinburgh District Council*, 1988 S.L.T. 329, per Lord Murray at 334.
[116] Bankruptcy (Scotland) Act 1985 s.5.
[117] Act of Sederunt, February 28, 1662. Certain debts such as funeral expenses are regarded as "privileged" and can be paid immediately.
[118] See *Sanderson v Lockhart-Mure*, 1946 S.C. 298, per Lord Patrick at 300.
[119] See, e.g. *Murray's Trs v Murray* (1903) 13 S.L.T. 274.
[120] See below, para.13–66.
[121] See below, para.13–50.

Duty to keep accounts

13–47 Trustees must keep accounts, which detail their dealings with the trust estate.[122] Where a trustee has failed to keep proper accounts, he is theoretically liable to a "strict accounting": "that is, he is given the benefit only of such items as the beneficiaries care to admit".[123] A beneficiary has a right to see the trust accounts and supporting documentation.[124]

Exceptionally, the truster may be regarded as having excluded any duty to keep accounts, as in the following case:

Leitch v Leitch
1927 S.C. 823

The defender's father-in-law made over the whole stock on a small farm to her, as her sole and exclusive property for behoof of herself and her family. Some years later, the pursuer—the defender's daughter—took an action of accounting against her mother, claiming £1,000 in lieu of production of accounts.

Lord Sands: "In the circumstances of the present case I think it extremely improbably that, when the arrangement was entered into, there was any thought in anybody's mind of division among the children in equal shares, or anything of that kind. The defender was left with a large young family to struggle through with . . . the idea that it was contemplated that she should keep trust accounts appears to me to be fantastic."

It was held that the action was ill-conceived and should be dismissed.

Duty to pay the correct beneficiaries

13–48 A trustee must pay out funds to the correct beneficiaries. If a trustee pays out funds to the wrong beneficiaries, "he is held in law still to have the money"[125] and is obliged to make payment to the correct beneficiary out of his own funds. A trustee is protected from liability for improper distribution in a number of specific cases, as follows:

- theft or embezzlement of the trust estate (provided the trustee is not himself at fault)[126];
- a true beneficiary may be personally barred from bringing a claim against the trustees, if he is himself at fault at causing the trustees to pay out to the wrong party[127]; and
- trustees who wrongly distribute property, because they are unaware of the existence of an illegitimate child are protected by statute.[128]

---

[122] *Ross v Ross* (1896) 23 R. (H.L.) 67. The duty exists at common law, but is recognised in statute: Prescription and Limitation (Scotland) Act 1973 Sch.3 para.e(i).

[123] *Polland v Sturrock's Exrs*, 1975 S.L.T. (Notes) 76, per Lord Guthrie at 76 (quoting A. Mackenzie Stuart, *The Law of Trusts* (W. Green, 1932), 220).

[124] *Murray v Cameron*, 1969 S.L.T. (Notes) 76; *Nouillan v Nouillan's Exrs*, 1991 S.L.T. 270.

[125] A. Mackenzie Stuart, *The Law of Trusts* (W. Green, 1932), 221.

[126] *Jobson v Palmer* [1893] 1 Ch. 71.

[127] *Buttercase & Geddie's Tr. v Geddie* (1897) 24 R. 1128, per Lord Kinnear at 1134.

[128] Law Reform (Miscellaneous Provisions) (Scotland) Act 1968 s.7 (as amended by the Law Reform (Parent and Child) (Scotland) Act 1986).

There is some doubt as to whether trustees who wrongly distribute the estate, due to an honest and reasonable error, are liable for improper distribution.[129] However, a trustee in this position is entitled to apply to the court to be relieved from liability for breach of trust,[130] which may render this question somewhat academic.

Where the trustees distribute trust property in error, they may be entitled to recover the property by means of the *condictio indebiti*.[131]

Key Concepts

Trustees have the following duties:

- The duty to **exercise due care** in their dealings with the trust estate. The standard of care required is that of the "ordinary prudent man".
- The duty **not to delegate the trust** and to take responsibility for trust decision-making themselves.
- The duty to **secure trust property**.
- The duty to **invest the trust estate** if they hold it for any period of time. Investments entered into by trustees must be both **authorised** (permitted under the trust deed or by statute) and **proper** (not exposing the trust deed to excessive risk).
- The duty to **take advice** where it is prudent to do so, particularly in relation to investment matters.
- The duty to **meet trust debts and obligations**.
- The duty to **keep accounts**.
- The duty to **pay the correct beneficiaries**.

Rule Against Auctor in Rem Suam

Auctor in rem suam may be translated as "actor in his own cause". This rule prohibits a **13–49** trustee from placing himself in a position where his position as trustee and his interests as an individual conflict.

The consequences of breaching the rule are severe. If a trustee enters into a transaction in breach of the rule, the transaction is voidable, regardless of whether he was acting in good faith or whether or not the transaction was a fair one.[132] If he profits from a breach of the rule, he must hand over those profits to the trust-estate, regardless of whether the trust-estate has in fact suffered any loss.[133]

The rule has three main consequences[134]:

- Trustees may not enter into transactions with the trust estate.[135]

---

[129] See J. Chalmers, *Trusts: Cases and Materials* (W. Green, 2002), para.6.27.
[130] Trusts (Scotland) Act 1921 s.32. See below, para.11–61.
[131] *Armour v Glasgow Royal Infirmary*, 1909 S.C. 916. See J. Chalmers, *Trusts: Cases and Materials* (W. Green, 2002), paras 6.28–6.29. On the *condictio* generally, see Chapter 8.
[132] *Aberdeen Railway Co. v Blaikie Bros* (1854) 1 Macq. 461.
[133] *Hamilton v Wright* (1842) 1 Bell 574.
[134] See K. McK Norrie and E.M. Scobbie, *Trusts* (W. Green, 1991), 128–133.
[135] *University of Aberdeen v Town Council of Aberdeen* (1876) 3 R. 1087.

- Trustees may not use their position to obtain a personal advantage (e.g. if a trustee is given a discretion, he may not exercise it in his favour).[136]
- Trustees may not charge fees for work done for the trust.[137]

A trustee, may, however, be *auctor in rem suam* where this is sanctioned in the trust deed. So, for example, it is not unusual for trust deeds to provide that a trustee may provide professional services (such as legal services) to the trust and be appropriately remunerated for this. The sanction should normally be express, but may be implied, as in the following case:

Sarris v Clark
1995 S.L.T. 44

James Clark executed a will in November 1985 bequeathing his whole property equally among his wife and his three children. His wife was named as one of his executors under his will. In December 1985, he entered into a contract of copartnery in his wife regarding their business as farmers. Upon his death, his wife was placed in a position whereby, as one of the executors, she was involved in negotiations to give up the tenancies of the holdings in exchange for payment. It was argued that the eventual agreement was voidable, because she had acted in breach of the *auctor in rem suam* principle. The court held that, in the circumstances, Mr Clark could be regarded as having impliedly sanctioned his wife being *auctor in rem suam*, as this was an inevitable consequence of the arrangements he had entered into.

A trustee may also be *auctor in rem suam* if this is sanctioned by the beneficiaries.[138]

Where a trustee enters into a transaction in breach of the *auctor rem suam*, this is voidable and may be challenged by the beneficiaries.[139] The beneficiaries may elect either to have the transaction reduced (if the parties can be restored to their original position),[140] or to require the trustee to communicate any benefit received from the transaction to the trust.[141]

Key Concepts

A trustee may not be *auctor in rem suam*. This means that he may not place himself in a position where his interests as trustee and interests as an individual conflict. The rule has three main consequences:

- trustees may not enter into transactions with the trust estate;
- trustees may not use their position to obtain a personal advantage; and
- trustees may not charge fees for work done for the trust.

---

[136] *Inglis v Inglis*, 1983 S.C. 8.
[137] *Home v Pringle* (1841) 2 Rob. 384.
[138] *Bruckner v Jopp's Trs* (1887) 14 R. 1006.
[139] *Fraser v Hankey & Co.* (1847) 9 D. 415. As to the situation where a *former* trustee enters into such a transaction, see J. Chalmers, *Trusts: Cases and Materials* (W. Green, 2002), para.8.32.
[140] See *Sarris v Clark*, 1995 S.L.T. 44, per the Lord Justice-Clerk (Ross) at 49.
[141] See, e.g. *Hamilton v Wright* (1842) 1 Bell 574.

A trustee may, however, be *auctor in rem suam* if this is **sanctioned** in the trust deed or by the beneficiaries.

A transaction entered into in breach of this principle is **voidable** and may be challenged by the beneficiaries.

TRUSTEE'S RIGHT TO REIMBURSEMENT

It is implicit in every trust deed that the trustee is entitled to "receive out of the trust estate **13–50** all the proper charges and expenses incurred by him in the execution of the trust".[142] Trustees are, of course, entitled to apply the trust funds directly to payments, which are necessary for the trust—they are not required to pay such expenses out of their pocket and claim reimbursement later.[143]

Much of the case law concerning the right to reimbursement, is concerned with the issue of whether trustees who initiate or defend court actions are entitled to be reimbursed for their expenses from the trust estate.[144] As a general rule, they are entitled to be reimbursed unless they have "acted unreasonably or recklessly, or otherwise than in accordance with their duty".[145] Where the court action is lost by the trust, trustees will generally be personally liable for the other party's expenses,[146] but will be entitled to pay those expenses out of the trust estate, unless they have acted improperly in bringing or defending the action.

Key Concept

A trustee is entitled to be **reimbursed** for any expenses properly incurred in administering the trust.

POWERS OF A TRUSTEE

Trustees may not do any act in furtherance of the trust purposes, unless they have the **13–51** power to perform such an act (e.g. a power to sell the trust estate; a power to pay debts, etc.) Trustees' powers may be divided into three categories, as follows:

- powers granted in the trust deed;
- powers conferred by statutory provisions; and
- common law powers which may be granted upon an application to the court.

---

[142] A. Mackenzie Stuart, *The Law of Trusts* (W. Green, 1932), p.358.

[143] *Cunningham v Montgomerie* (1879) 6 R. 1333.

[144] For a review of the case law, see J. Chalmers, *Trusts: Cases and Materials* (W. Green, 2002), paras 10.12–10.19.

[145] *Gibson v Caddall's Trs* (1895) 22 R. 899, per the Lord President (Robertson) at 892.

[146] *Mulholland v Macfarlane's Trs*, 1928 S.L.T. 251; *Jeffrey v Brown* (1842) 2 Shaw 349.

Powers granted in the trust deed

13–52 It has been said that the trust deed "is the foundation and the measure of the powers of the trustees".[147] The trust deed may confer powers upon the trustees either explicitly or implicitly.

It was formerly common to list the powers of the trustees at length in the trust deed, but that is now normally unnecessary due to s.4 of the Trusts (Scotland) Act 1921,[148] under which certain general powers are implied in all trust-deeds. Nevertheless, the trust-deed must be examined in all instances to determine which powers it confers upon trustees (and also whether it excludes any of the powers which are otherwise implied under s.4 of the 1921 Act).

Powers conferred by statutory provisions

13–53 Section 4 of the Trusts (Scotland) Act 1921, as amended by later legislation, contains a list of general powers, which all trustees have unless to so act would be "at variance with the terms or purposes of the trust".[149] The principal powers conferred by this section are as follows:

- to sell the trust estate or any part thereof;
- to grant leases of the trust estate or any part thereof;
- to acquire or invest in heritable property;
- to appoint factors and law agents and pay them suitable remuneration;
- to uplift, discharge, or assign debts due to the trust estate;
- to grant all deeds necessary for carrying into effect the powers vested in the trustees; and
- to pay trust debts without requiring the creditors to constitute such debts.

Trustees may, of course, only exercise these powers if to do so would further the purposes of the trust.

Occasionally, some of these powers may be specifically excluded by the trust deed. In such cases, the trustees may petition the court under s.5 of the 1921 Act for power to do the relevant act. The court may grant the power if it is "satisfied that such act is in all the circumstances expedient for the execution of the trust". Section 5 was applied in the following case:

---

[147] *Goodsir v Carruthers* (1858) 20 D. 1141, per Lord Ardmillan at 1145.
[148] See below, para.13–53.
[149] For the meaning of this phrase, see *Marquess of Lothian's C.B.*, 1927 S.C. 579, per Lord Blackburn at 587–588.

Tod's Trs, Petrs
1999 S.L.T. 308

Under a 1929 trust deed, the trustees held property including a large country house ("Tirinie House") in trust for the purpose of providing professional persons with rest and a change of air. It was initially successful but began to run at a loss during the 1990s and was closed. At the time of the court case, the house was in a deteriorating condition and the trustees had limited funds available to maintain it. The trustees, on the view that the trust had failed, sought permission to sell the house so that the value of the trust estate could be preserved, while it was determined what should be done with the trust estate. In the "very unusual" circumstances, the court granted the power.

Certain special trustees (such as trustees in bankruptcy) have additional powers, which are granted under statute.[150]

Common law powers with court application

Aside from s.5 of the 1921 Act, the court cannot normally grant additional powers to trustees.[151] In exceptional cases, however, where it would be impossible to fulfil the trust purposes without additional powers being granted, the court may be able to intervene, as in the following case: **13–54**

Anderson's Trs
1921 S.C. 315

Mr Anderson was a farm tenant. In his will, desiring that his nephew should carry on the farm, he directed his trustees to hold the lease of the farm and the stock in trust for his nephew until he attained the age of 21, whereupon the whole residue of the estate (including the lease and stock) should be conveyed to his nephew. After Mr Anderson's death, the landlord decided to sell the farm, but gave the trustees the option of purchasing it. The trust-deed did not, however, confer upon the trustees any power to purchase heritage. The trustees petitioned the *nobile officium* of the court for authority to purchase the farm. It was held that, in the exceptional circumstances of the case, where the trust purposes would be wholly frustrated unless the power was granted, authority to purchase the farm should be given.

Key Concepts

The trust deed is the principal source of trustees' powers, although **there are a number of powers which are conferred by statute upon all trustees,** unless they are "at variance with the terms or purposes of the trust". The principal statutory powers are as follows:

---

[150] See generally the Bankruptcy (Scotland) Act 1985. See also the Married Women's Policies of Assurance (Scotland) (Amendment) Act 1980 s.2(2), and the Judicial Factors Act 1849 s.7.

[151] *Berwick* (1874) 2 R. 90, per the Lord President (Inglis) at 92; *Scott's Hospital Trs*, 1913 S.C. 289, per the Lord Justice Clerk (Macdonald) at 290–291.

- to sell the trust estate or any part thereof;
- to grant leases of the trust estate or any part thereof;
- to acquire with trust funds any interest in residential accommodation "reasonably required to enable the trustees to provide a suitable residence for occupation by any of the beneficiaries";
- to appoint factors and law agents and pay them suitable remuneration;
- to uplift, discharge, or assign debts due to the trust estate;
- to grant all deeds necessary for carrying into effect the powers vested in the trustees; and
- to pay trust debts without requiring the creditors to constitute such debts.

If one of these powers is excluded by the trust deed, the trustees may **petition the court** for authority to exercise it.

In exceptional cases, the court may be able to grant **further powers** to trustees, if this is necessary in order to avoid an **impossibility** in fulfilling the trust purposes.

LIABILITIES OF A TRUSTEE

Liability to beneficiaries

13–55 Where a trustee has committed, or appears likely to commit a breach of trust, various remedies may be open to the beneficiary, as follows:

Remedies for breach of trust

13–56 The principal remedies for breach of trust are court actions for: (a) interdict; (b) damages and (c) accounting. Depending on the circumstances, it may also be appropriate to petition the court for the removal of an offending trustee,[152] or even to report the matter to authorities such as the police.

(a) Interdict

13–57 Where a trustee proposes to do something, which a beneficiary believes to be a breach of trust, the beneficiary is entitled to seek an interdict. An interdict is a court order prohibiting a person from doing a specified act. If the breach of trust has already taken place, interdict is useless and will not be granted.

(b) Damages

13–58 Where a breach of trust has caused a loss to the trust estate, a beneficiary may take a court action to require the offending trustee to make up the loss in damages.[153] It is a defence for the trustee(s) to show that the loss would have occurred even if the breach had not taken place, as in the following case:

---

[152] See above, para.13–34.
[153] As to whether the terminology of "damages" is appropriate, cf. *Tibbert v McColl*, 1994 S.L.T. 1227.

Millar's Trs v Polson
(1897) 24 R. 1038

A trustee became aware that his co-trustee, Elliot, had not banked £150, which belonged to the trust. Over a period of months, he took no action to recover the money, and Elliot eventually became insolvent. In his defence, he argued that Elliot had always been incapable of repaying the money and that court action would have been fruitless. The court accepted his evidence on this point and held that he was not liable to make good the loss of £150.

Where a trustee has committed multiple breaches of trust, some profitable and others not, he may not set off the profit on one breach against the loss on another in order to minimise his liability in damages.[154] Set off may, however, be allowed if the multiple breaches are part of a single scheme—as in the English case of *Bartlett v Barclays Bank Trust Co. Ltd (No.1)*,[155] where trustees improperly made two speculative property investments, one of which made a profit and the other of which made a loss.

(c) Accounting (count, reckoning and payment)

A beneficiary may also bring an action of "count, reckoning and payment" (commonly **13–59** referred to as an action for accounting), calling upon the trustee to produce trust accounts and to make up any shortfall.[156] This should generally have the same practical result as an action for damages. However, it has two advantages in appropriate cases. First, it may provide a means of ascertaining the amount of any loss where this cannot be otherwise done. Secondly, it may remain available where an action for damages is barred by prescription.[157]

Protecting trustees from liability

Trustees may receive some protection from liability for breach of trust through an **13–60** immunity clause in the trust deed or one of the statutory provisions contained in ss.30–32 of the Trusts (Scotland) Act 1921.

(a) Immunity clauses

An attempt is sometimes made to protect trustees from liability for breach of trust by **13–61** inserting an immunity clause into the trust deed stating (for example) that they will not be liable for errors or neglect of management. It has traditionally been said that such clauses will protect trustees from liability for negligence, but not for liability from gross negligence.[158] However, this view has been thrown into doubt by a recent English case[159]:

---

[154] A. Mackenzie Stuart, *The Law of Trusts* (W. Green, 1932), 375.
[155] [1980] Ch. 515.
[156] On the duty to keep accounts, see above, para.13–47.
[157] See *Hobday v Kirkpatrick's Trs*, 1985 S.L.T. 197. cf. *Ross v Davy*, 1996 S.C.L.R. 369.
[158] *Lutea Trs Ltd v Orbis Trs Guernsey Ltd*, 1997 S.C.L.R. 735; K. McK Norrie and E. M. Scobbie, *Trusts* (W. Green, 1991), p.148. This does, of course, raise the question of whether it is actually possible to distinguish between these two forms of negligence.
[159] See further Scottish Law Commission, *Discussion Paper on Breach of Trust* (2003), Scot. Law Com. D.P. No.123, Part 3.

Armitage v Nurse
[1998] Ch. 241

A trust-deed provided that trustees would not be liable for any errors short of "actual fraud". It was argued that this clause could not be effective. Millet L.J. held that the clause was effective. He concluded the earlier Scottish cases, which suggested that such clauses did not exclude liability for gross negligence, were simply interpretations of the particular clauses under consideration in those cases, and did not lay down any rule that it was impossible to exclude liability for gross negligence. Where the language of a clause clearly did exclude liability for anything short of actual fraud, there was no reason not to give effect to it. Any change in the law—which might well be desirable—had to be a matter for Parliament.

(b) Statutory protections

13–62 There are three principal statutory protections from liability under the Trusts (Scotland) Act 1921.

13–63 **(i) Trustees who have acted "honestly and reasonably"**. The main statutory protection is found in s.32, which allows the court to relieve a trustee from personal liability for a breach of trust if he "has acted honestly and reasonably" and "ought fairly to be excused". It must be noted that a trustee who has acted honestly and reasonably is not *automatically* entitled to be relieved of the consequences—this is a matter which is in the discretion of the court, which may be faced with the awkward task of apportioning a loss between two blameless parties.

However, where a trustee has acted honestly and reasonably, it will normally be assumed that it is fair to grant relief.[160] The fact that the trustee has acted on legal advice is relevant, but will not automatically result in relief being granted.[161] The court may grant partial rather than full relief if this is felt appropriate.[162] It has been suggested that a non-gratuitous (remunerated) trustee is never entitled to claim relief under this section,[163] but this is probably incorrect, although the court will be less willing to grant relief to such a trustee.[164]

13–64 **(ii) Trustees who have committed a breach of trust with the beneficiary's consent**. Under s.31 of the 1921 Act, if a trustee has committed a breach of trust at the instigation or request or with the written consent of a beneficiary, the court is entitled to apply or of any part of that beneficiary's interest in the trust estate to indemnify the trustee.

For s.31 to operate, the beneficiary must have been aware of the facts which made the proposed action a breach of trust, although it is not necessary for the beneficiary to know that it was legally a breach of trust.[165] A beneficiary who has instigated, or consented to, a breach of trust may be personally barred from bringing any action against the trustee, but s.31 may still be important in such cases by affording some protection to the trustee if another beneficiary brings an action.

---

[160] *Perrins v Bellamy* [1898] 2 Ch. 521, per Kekewich J. at 528; affirmed [1899] 1 Ch. 797.
[161] *Marsden v Evans* [1954] 1 W.L.R. 423.
[162] See, e.g. *Re Evans* [1999] 2 All E.R. 777.
[163] A. Mackenzie Stuart, *The Law of Trusts* (W. Green, 1932), 382–383.
[164] See J. Chalmers, *Trusts: Cases and Materials* (W. Green, 2002), para.9.31.
[165] See *Cathcart's Trs v Cathcart* (1907) 15 S.L.T. 646; *Henderson v Henderson's Trs* (1900) 2 F. 1295; *Re Somerset* [1894] 1 Ch. 321.

(iii) Trustees who have lent money on security of heritable property. Section 30 of **13–65** the 1921 Act states that a trustee shall not be liable for breach of trust, by reason of having made a loan on the security of property provided that: (a) a proper valuation was obtained; and (b) the amount of the loan did not exceed two-thirds of the valuation. This protection would have been of considerable importance historically, because loans on the security of heritable property in Scotland were one of the very few implied powers of investment which trustees had at common law. It is unlikely to be of much practical importance today.

Liability to third parties

Trustees will commonly, in order to discharge their responsibilities as trustees, enter into **13–66** contracts with third parties. As a general rule, they are personally liable on such contracts "unless there is an agreement express or implied that the trust estate only is to be held bound".[166]

This point is generally only of importance if the trust fund is or becomes insolvent. Consequently, many of the reported cases on personal liability arose in the context of the disastrous collapse of the City of Glasgow Bank in 1878. It appears that many trust funds included stock in the bank, which was subject to heavy calls. (For example, the trust fund in *Cunningham v Montgomerie*[167] included £1,000 of stock, on which calls of £27,500 were made). In these cases, the trust estate was frequently insufficient to meet the calls, leaving the trustees personally liable for the shortfall.

The rationale for the personal liability rule is that the trustees are supposed to know the state of the trust estate and are warranting its sufficiency to persons with whom they make contracts.[168] For this reason, trustees will generally not be personally liable on a contract with the solicitors to the trust or with a co-trustee, because such persons themselves know the state of the trust.[169]

In order to exclude personal liability, it is not sufficient to show that the third party knew that he was contracting with a trustee.[170] There must be an agreement that the trustee is not to be personally liable. Where a person signs a contract "as trustee", this will generally be taken as indicating such an agreement.[171] The mere use of the word "trustee" is not sufficient, as this may be intended only to describe or identify the signatory.[172]

Third parties who acquire trust property

Where a trustee, acting in breach of trust, sells trust property to a third party, that third **13–67** party will acquire a good title to the property provided that he purchased the property in good faith and for value.[173] Where a third party acquires trust property in bad faith or gratuitously, his title may be reduced.[174]

Third parties also receive further protection by way of s.2 of the Trusts (Scotland) Act 1961.[175] Under this provision, where a trustee enters into a transaction which purports to

---

[166] A. Mackenzie Stuart, *The Law of Trusts* (1932), 358. See *Brown v Sutherland* (1875) 2 R. 615.

[167] (1879) 6 R. 1333.

[168] *Cullen v Baillie* (1846) 8 D. 511, per Lord Fullerton at 522.

[169] *Ferme, Ferme and Williamson v Stephenson's Tr.* (1905) 7 F. 902 (solicitors); *Cullen v Baillie* (1846) 8 D. 511 (co-trustee).

[170] *Mackenzie v Neill* (1899) 37 S.L.R. 666, per Lord Kincairney at 667.

[171] *Gordon v Campbell* (1842) 1 Bell 428.

[172] *Thomson v McLachlan's Trs* (1829) 7 S. 787; *Lumsden v Buchanan* (1865) 3 M. (H.L.) 89.

[173] Hume, *Lectures* (1821–1822) (G.C.H. Paton, ed., Stair Society, Vol.17, 1952), Vol.IV, 315.

[174] *Macgowan v Robb* (1864) 2 M. 943; *Thomson v Clydesdale Bank* (1893) 20 R. 50.

[175] Note also the Succession (Scotland) Act 1964 s.17 (protection of persons acquiring title via an executor).

be an exercise of any of the first six general powers of trustees which are implied by s.4 of the 1921 Act, the validity of that transaction may not be challenged by any person on the ground that the act was at variance with the terms or purposes of the trust.[176] This protection is very strong, because such a transaction cannot be challenged on the ground of bad faith. It is intended to limit any need for trustees to seek court approval before entering into a transaction involving the exercise of one of those implied powers.

Key Concepts

Where a trustee has committed or appears likely to commit a breach of trust, the following remedies may be open to the beneficiaries:

- interdict (a court order preventing the trustee from doing a particular act);
- an action for damages; and
- an action for accounting (a combination of an action to produce accounts and for payment of any shortfall in the trust funds).

Trustees may be protected from liability by **immunity clauses** in the trust deed, providing that they are not to be liable for negligence.

Trustees who commit a breach of trust, but who have acted **honestly and reasonably** may apply to the court to be relieved from the consequences of their breach of trust.

Trustees who commit a breach of trust at the request of, or with the consent of, a beneficiary may apply to the court to be **indemnified** by that beneficiary's interest in the trust estate.

Trustees will be **personally liable to third parties** on contracts which they make on behalf of the trust, unless they have contracted out of such liability.

Third parties who acquire trust property **in good faith and for value** will receive a good title to the property even if the trustee was acting in breach of trust.

VARIATION OF TRUST PURPOSES

13–68 A trust, by its very nature, severely limits the manner in which the property, which is subject to it, may be held and applied. The relevant limitations have, of course, been selected by the truster, and doubtless because, when establishing the trust, he considered that they would represent the most appropriate and expedient set of rules for governing the trust.

Circumstances change, however, and what appears appropriate when the trust is established may cease to be appropriate with the passage of time. For example:

- Changes in the law of taxation, or in the investment climate, may mean that the trust property is no longer being managed in the most effective way possible.
- A public trust may be established for a purpose which is subsequently satisfied by government action without the expenditure of the trust funds, or which the trustees

---

[176] The relevant powers are the powers to sell, lease, excamb (swap) or borrow money on the security of the trust estate (or any part thereof), to invest the trust estate or to acquire heritable property. See Trusts (Scotland) Act 1921 s.4(1)(a)–(eb) (as amended).

manage to fulfil without expending all of the trust capital. Alternatively, there may be insufficient funds to give effect to the trust purposes.

- A testator may, in a will, have left money to an institution which no longer exists or never existed.
- Some or all of the beneficiaries in a private trust may decide amongst themselves that they would prefer the trust to be administered differently.

It is not, of course, open to the truster (unless the trust is revocable)[177] to amend the terms of the trust in such cases. That would be to defeat the very essence of the trust, which is that the truster has alienated his property and put it beyond his control. So what scope exists for varying the terms of the trust?

The answer differs according to whether the trust is private or public.[178] Each type of trust will be dealt with in turn.

Private trusts

At common law, variation of the terms a private trust was competent if all the beneficiaries **13–69** consented to the variation.[179] The obvious practical problem, with this approach, is that not all the beneficiaries may be capable of consenting. For example, the beneficiaries may include children, or the trust deed may even make provision for persons who have not yet been born (and who may never be). A second problem is that if the trust includes an alimentary liferent, the alimentary beneficiary cannot lawfully renounce that liferent.

The Court of Session did have a very limited jurisdiction at common law to authorise variation (or termination) without all the necessary consents being obtained, such as where the trust would become unworkable without additional powers being granted, or where the trustees were only prevented from obtaining the consent of all the beneficiaries by virtue of the fact that unborn children who were, in fact, unlikely ever to be born, would be entitled to benefit under the trust.[180] This inflexibility gave rise to some concern,[181] and was eventually addressed by the Trusts (Scotland) Act 1961.

Section 1 of the 1961 Act enables the court to give consent to a variation on behalf of:

(a) any person who is incapable of consenting by reason of nonage or other disability;

(b) any person who is not currently a beneficiary but may become one on the happening of a future event or on a particular date, unless that person is currently ascertained and is capable of assenting; or

(c) any unborn person.

The court is not entitled to approve the arrangement on behalf of any person "unless it is of the opinion that the carrying out thereof would not be prejudicial to that person".[182] As to what amounts to prejudice, see the following case[183]:

---

[177] See below, para.13–75.
[178] On this distinction generally, see above, para.13–07.
[179] See A. Mackenzie Stuart, *The Law of Trusts* (W. Green, 1932), p.346.
[180] See A. Mackenzie Stuart, *The Law of Trusts* (W. Green, 1932), pp.254–259 and pp.349–353; *Coles*, 1951 S.C. 608; *McPherson's Trs v Hill* (1902) 4 F. 921.
[181] See Law Reform Committee for Scotland, *Ninth Report: The powers of trustees to sell, purchase or otherwise deal with heritable property; and the variation of trust purposes* (1960), Cmnd.1102.
[182] Trusts (Scotland) Act 1961 s.1(1).
[183] For further discussion, see J. Chalmers, *Trusts: Cases and Materials* (W. Green, 2002), para.12.06.

Pollok-Morris, Petrs
1969 S.L.T. (Notes) 60

P established a trust for the benefit of his wife, lawful issue, mother and two sisters. It proved to be unlikely that there would be any children of his existing marriage and he and his wife adopted a child. Approval was sought for a variation so that adoptive children and their issue would fall within the class of beneficiaries. The court refused to approve the proposed variation on behalf of any unborn children.

Lord President (Clyde): "If the group of persons among whom the estate may be divided is increased to include some other person not originally in it, that does, in my view, constitute a possible prejudice to those in the group and makes it impossible for this Court to hold that the carrying out of this arrangement would not be prejudicial . . . ".

It does not follow that, simply because a proposed variation is shown not to be prejudicial, that the court will necessarily grant approval.[184] Instead, the court has a discretion, as to whether or not to grant consent and will take into account the intention of the truster (although this is not conclusive),[185] and all other relevant circumstances including the relative benefits which the various parties would gain from the variation. The question of whether those benefits are fairly distributed is clearly relevant.[186]

Public trusts

13–70   There are two mechanisms available for varying the terms of a public trust. These are first, the common law *cy-prés* jurisdiction, and secondly, variation under s.9(1) of the Law Reform (Miscellaneous Provisions) (Scotland) Act 1990. Variation under s.9(1) of the 1990 Act is only possible where the trust has already taken effect in some form; it is not possible where it is impossible to give any effect to the terms of the trust (but in such cases, *cy-prés* will be available).[187] *Cy-prés* is available whether or not the trust has taken effect, but much stricter criteria must be met for the *cy-prés* jurisdiction to be available.

The criteria which must be satisfied in order for the court to sanction variation are, therefore, different depending on whether we are concerned with a case of "initial failure" (where it was never possible to give effect to the trust) or "subsequent failure" (where the trust was initially given effect to but later failed).[188]

Initial failure

13–71   Variation in such cases must be under the *cy-prés* jurisdiction. In such cases, two factors must be established for variation to be permissible:

- a "general charitable intention" on the part of the truster; and
- failure of the trust purposes (impossibility).

---

[184] *Lobnitz, Petr*, 1966 S.L.T. (Notes) 81.
[185] *Goulding v James* [1997] 2 All E.R. 239. cf. *Re Steed's Will Trusts* [1960] Ch. 407.
[186] See *Lobnitz, Petr*, 1966 S.L.T. (Notes) 81.
[187] See J. Chalmers, *Trusts: Cases and Materials* (W. Green, 2002), para.12.18.
[188] For cases on the distinction, see *Davidson's Trs v Arnott*, 1951 S.C. 42; *Lindsay's Trs v Lindsay*, 1948 S.L.T. (Notes) 81; *Cuthbert's Trs v Cuthbert*, 1958 S.L.T. 315.

In determining whether the truster had a "general charitable intention", the court must ask whether his object was "to establish a charity for the benefit of a certain class with a particular mode of doing it? Or was the mode of application such an essential part of the gift that it is not possible to distinguish any general purpose of charity?"[189] The distinction is illustrated by the following case:

Hay's J.F. v Hay's Trs.
1952 S.C. (H.L.) 29

A testatrix directed in her will that her trustees should maintain a mansion-house "under the style and designation of 'The Hay Memorial' " as a hospital on Shetland. The funds available under the trust-deed were insufficient to maintain the house for this purpose. The trustees applied to the court for a variation of the trust purposes under the *cy-prés* jurisdiction. Held, that *cy-prés* was not available as no general charitable intention existed. It was clear that the use of the house as the "Hay Memorial" was an essential part of the testatrix's intention. If this was not possible, there was no general purpose of charity to fall back on.

(If, as in *Hay's J.F.*, the purpose of a testamentary trust proves impossible to fulfil, but *cy-prés* is unavailable, the relevant part of the testamentary estate will normally fall into intestacy and the relevant rules of intestate succession will apply.)[190]

Where a testator leaves money to a supposed charitable organisation, which never in fact existed, the court will normally find a general charitable intention.[191] Where the institution did in fact exist, but is now defunct, the court will normally not find such an intention,[192] although this distinction has been criticised.[193]

Impossibility may be established by, for example, showing that there are insufficient funds available in the trust estate to carry out the trust purposes,[194] or where property has been left to an organisation for a specific purpose, that the specified organisation is unwilling to accept the property.[195] The fact that the trust purposes cannot be given effect to immediately, does not amount to impossibility,[196] nor does the fact that they may be attended with some difficulty.[197]

---

[189] *Burgess' Trs v Crawford*, 1912 S.C. 387, per Lord Mackenzie at 398.
[190] On those rules, see Chapter 14.
[191] See, e.g. *Tod's Trs v The Sailors' and Firemen's Orphans' and Widows' Society*, 1953 S.L.T. (Notes) 72 ("The Society for Old and Infirm Officers of the Mercantile Marine").
[192] See, e.g. *Laing's Trs v Perth Model Lodging House*, 1954 S.L.T. (Notes) 13.
[193] K. McK Norrie and E.M. Scobbie, *Trusts* (W. Green, 1991), 180–182.
[194] See, e.g. *Tait's J.F. v Lillie*, 1940 S.C. 542.
[195] See, e.g. *National Bible Society of Scotland v Church of Scotland*, 1946 S.L.T. (Notes) 26.
[196] cf. *Templeton v Burgh of Ayr*, 1910 2 S.L.T. 12.
[197] *Scotstown Moor Children's Camp*, 1948 S.C. 630.

Subsequent failure

13–72 In cases of subsequent failure, it is not necessary to establish a general charitable intention on the part of the truster. It is only necessary to establish impossibility (in which case the *cy-près* jurisdiction may be invoked)[198] or one of the statutory grounds under s.9(1) of the Law Reform (Miscellaneous Provisions) (Scotland) Act 1990, which are as follows:

(a) that the purposes of the trust, whether in whole or in part—

    (i) have been fulfilled as far as it is possible to do so; or

    (ii) can no longer be given effect to, whether in accordance with the directions or spirit of the trust deed or other document constituting the trust or otherwise;

(b) that the purposes of the trust provide a use for only part of the property available under the trust;

(c) that the purposes of the trust were expressed by reference to—

    (i) an area which has, since the trust was constituted, ceased to have effect for the purpose described expressly or by implication in the trust deed or other document constituting the trust; or

    (ii) a class of persons or area which has ceased to be suitable or appropriate, having regard to the spirit of the trust deed or other document constituting the trust, or as regards which it has ceased to be practicable to administer the property available under the trust; or

(d) that the purpose of the trust, whether in whole or in part, have, since the trust was constituted—

    (i) been adequately provided for by other means; or

    (ii) ceased to be such as would enable the trust to become a recognised body [a charity]; or

    (iii) ceased in any other way to provide a suitable and effective method of using the property available under the trust, having regard to the spirit of the trust deed or other document constituting the trust.

In cases involving small public trusts (those having an annual income not exceeding £5,000) where one of these conditions is satisfied, the trustees may vary the purposes of such a trust, transfer its assets to another public trust, or amalgamate it with one or more public trusts without the necessity of court application, by following procedures laid down in statute and regulations,[199] provided that the Lord Advocate does not object. In addition, charitable trusts are now able to take advantage of a procedure whereby they can submit a "reorganisation scheme" to the Office of the Scottish Charity Regulator for approval.[200]

It may also be possible to use the *cy-près* jurisdiction to amalgamate two or more trusts on the grounds of expediency, without any need to show impossibility.[201]

---

[198] In *RS Macdonald Charitable Trust Trs v Scottish Society for the Prevention of Cruelty to Animals*, 2009 S.C. 6, the court went further, permitting cy-prés to be invoked on the basis of "strong or compelling expediency". It is not clear why the application in that case was not made under the statutory grounds discussed here.

[199] Law Reform (Miscellaneous Provisions) (Scotland) Act 1990 s.10; Public Trusts (Reorganisation) (Scotland) (No.2) Regulations 1993 (SI 1993/2254).

[200] Charities and Trustee Investment (Scotland) Act 2005 s.39; Charities Reorganisation (Scotland) Regulations 2007 (SSI 2007/204).

[201] See *Mining Institute of Scotland Benevolent Fund, Petrs*, 1994 S.L.T. 785; *Clutterbuck, Petr*, 1961 S.L.T. 427; J. Chalmers, *Trusts: Cases and Materials* (W. Green, 2002), para.12.38.

What can the court do once the variation jurisdiction is triggered?

Once the criteria for variation have been met, the court may approve a scheme for the **13–73** variation of the trust. In doing so, the court will adhere to the "principle of approximation". This means that the objects of the varied trust must "approximate as closely as may be" to those which were originally selected by the truster.[202] See the following case:

> ### Glasgow Royal Infirmary v Magistrates of Glasgow
> ### (1888) 15 R. 264
>
> A society raised funds to provide a fever hospital in Glasgow. The local authority later established a fever hospital without use of those funds. The trustees sought approval for a *cy-prés* scheme. It was suggested by the Infirmary that the funds should be used to provide a home for nurses, while other parties to the case suggested that it should be used to provide warm clothing for fever convalescents on leaving the hospital. The court approved the latter suggestion, holding that this was closest to the original purposes of the trust.

Where the trust purposes were originally confined to a particular locality, the court will seek to maintain this connection.[203] The court will not sanction a variation, whereby the trust funds will be used to provide services or facilities which government agencies are obliged to provide.[204]

As part of variation, the court may transfer trust funds to another body,[205] widen the class of persons who are entitled to benefit from the trust,[206] or extend the powers of the trustees.[207]

---

[202] *Stranraer Original Secession Corporation*, 1923 S.C. 722, per the Lord President (Clyde) at 725.

[203] *Glasgow Royal Infirmary v Magistrates of Glasgow* (1888) 15 R. 264.

[204] *Governors of Jonathan Anderson Trust* (1896) 23 R. 592. This does not apply to services provided at governmental discretion: *Campbell Endowment Trust*, 1928 S.C. 171.

[205] See, e.g. *Clyde Industrial Training Ship Association*, 1925 S.C. 676.

[206] See, e.g. *Trs of Carnegie Park Orphanage* (1892) 19 R. 605.

[207] *McCrie's Trs*, 1927 S.C. 556.

Key Concepts

In some cases, it may be desirable to **vary the purposes** of a trust.

In **private trusts**, the basic principle is that variation is possible with the consent of all the beneficiaries. Where a person who is or may be a beneficiary is unable to consent to a variation, the court may consent on their behalf provided that it is satisfied the variation would not be **prejudicial** to that person.

Where it has never been possible to give effect to the terms of a **public trust** (**initial failure**), the court may apply *cy-prés* to vary the terms of the trust provided that a **general charitable intention,** on the part of the truster, can be shown and that it is **impossible** to give effect to the trust purposes.

Where it has been possible initially to give effect to the terms of a public trust (cases of **subsequent failure**), *cy-prés* may be applied if it has become **impossible** to give effect to the trust purposes. It is not necessary to show a general charitable intention in such cases. Variation may also be possible under s.9 of the Law Reform (Miscellaneous Provisions) (Scotland) Act 1990 if the trust purposes have become in some way inappropriate—s.9 lays down criteria which must be satisfied for variation under this section.

Where grounds for variation of a public trust have been established, the court may **vary the purposes** of the trust, **transfer trust funds** to another body, or **extend the powers** of the trustees.

Termination of a Trust

13–74 This section considers the circumstances in which a trust may be brought to an end. There are three principal ways in which this may happen:

- revocation by the truster;
- termination by the trustees; and
- termination by the beneficiaries.

Revocation by the truster

13–75 Because a mortis causa trust is not effective until the testator's death, it is always open to the testator to revoke his will and prevent the trust from even taking effect.[208] It is possible, however, for a person to contractually bind themselves to include certain provisions in their will, in which case they will be barred from revoking those provisions.[209]

An inter vivos trust is only irrevocable if the following conditions are satisfied:

- there must be an ascertained beneficiary (if the only ascertained beneficiary is the truster himself, the trust remains revocable)[210]; and
- the beneficiary must have a *jus quaesitium* (an "immediate beneficial interest"[211]). If the truster only intended to confer a testamentary benefit on the beneficiary (i.e. a benefit in the event of the truster's death), then this is a testamentary provision and

---

[208] C. de B. Murray, *The Law of Wills in Scotland* (W. Green, 1945) 45.
[209] *Paterson v Paterson* (1893) 20 R. 484.
[210] *Bertram's Trs v Bertram*, 1909 S.C. 1238.
[211] W.A. Wilson and A.G.M. Duncan, *Trusts, Trustees and Executors*, 2nd edn (W. Green, 1995), para.11–03.

is revocable.[212] If the beneficiary's interest is contingent on a particular event taking place, then the trust is revocable,[213] unless all that is required is that the beneficiary survive to a specified date.[214]

If these conditions are not satisfied, the truster is entitled to revoke the trust. The question may arise indirectly—e.g. if the truster becomes insolvent, his creditors may seek to have the trust revoked, so that the trust property can be applied to payment of his debts, or if the trustee dies, a question may arise as to whether the trust property formed part of his estate at the time of his death.

If the truster was insolvent at the time of the trust's creation, or was rendered insolvent by its creation, the creation of the trust may be challengeable by his creditors as a gratuitous alienation.[215]

Termination by the trustees

The trustees may bring the trust to an end by fulfilling the trust purposes and distributing **13–76** the trust estate. Trustees are entitled to receive a discharge before leaving office, which should generally be granted by the person entitled to the residue of the trust estate.

Termination by the beneficiaries

There are two relevant principles here, as follows: **13–77**

- all the beneficiaries in a private trust may, acting together, compel the termination of a trust; and
- a beneficiary who has acquired a right in fee to property is entitled to insist that the trustees pass the property to him absolutely (the *Miller's Trustees* principle).

Termination by consent of all the beneficiaries

If all the beneficiaries in a private trust consent to the termination of a trust, the trustees **13–78** must comply, unless the trust includes any alimentary rights (because these cannot be renounced except with the permission of the court),[216] or where termination would prejudice the proper administration of the trust, as in the following case:

---

[212] *Bertram's Trs v Bertram*, 1909 S.C. 1238.
[213] *Bulkeley-Gavin's Trs v Bulkeley-Gavin's Trs*, 1971 S.C. 209 (benefit contingent on the wholesale nationalisation of land).
[214] *Robertson v Robertson's Trs* (1892) 19 R. 849.
[215] On gratuitous alienations generally, see D.W. McKenzie Skene, *Insolvency Law in Scotland* (1999), Ch.30.
[216] See the Trusts (Scotland) Act 1961 s.1(4).

> ## De Robeck v Inland Revenue
> ### 1928 S.C. (H.L.) 34
>
> In his will, D's husband left his estate to trustees for certain purposes. The heritable estates were found to be heavily mortgaged, and considerable death duties applied. To avoid a forced sale, the trustees elected to pay these duties by 16 half-yearly instalments. At a later date, a question arose as to whether, for taxation purposes, D was to be treated as to owner of the estate—which she would have been if she was entitled to insist that the trust be terminated. It was held that, while the payments were ongoing, D was not entitled to insist on termination, because that would have prejudiced the legitimate arrangement which the trustees had entered into regarding payment of death duties.

The Miller's Trustees principle

13–79 According to the case of *Miller's Trs v Miller*,[217] a beneficiary who has acquired a right in fee to property is entitled to insist that the trustees transfer the property to him absolutely, even if they have instructions to the contrary.

> ## Miller's Trs v Miller
> ### (1890) 18 R. 301
>
> In his will, Sir William Miller directed his trustees to manage certain property for the benefit of his son John Miller. He directed that the property was to vest in him once he reached the age of 25, or upon marriage if he married between the ages of 21 and 25. The trustees were to pass the property to him once he reached the age of 25.
>
> John Miller married after reaching the age of 21 and requested that the trustees pass the trust property to him. The Court of Session held that the trustees were obliged to pass it to him, notwithstanding the directions in his father's will.

It should be noted that, if the trust deed had simply stated that the estate would not vest in the beneficiary until he attained the age of 25, he would not have been entitled to lay claim to it until he reached that age. If the trustees were to pay it over to him before the property had vested in him, they would be acting to the potential prejudice of whoever was to become entitled to the estate if he had died without reaching that age.

The trustees may be entitled to refuse to transfer the property, if this would prejudice the proper administration of the trust (as in *De Robeck v Inland Revenue*, discussed above), or if it would prejudice other trust purposes—as in *Graham's Trs v Graham*,[218] where the trustees might have required to use the capital which was being claimed by one beneficiary in order to make annual payments to other beneficiaries.

---

[217] (1890) 18 R. 301.
[218] (1899) 2 F. 232.

Key Concepts

Trusts may be **terminated** in a number of ways.
By the **truster**:

- Because a **mortis causa** trust does not take effect until the testator's death, it is normally open to the testator to revoke his will at any time before his death and prevent the trust ever taking effect.
- An **inter vivos** trust may be revoked by the truster unless (a) there is an ascertained beneficiary (other than the truster himself) and (b) that beneficiary has an "immediate beneficial interest".

By the **trustees**: the **trustees** may terminate a trust by fulfilling the trust purposes and distributing the trust estate.
By the **beneficiaries**:

- In a private trust, all the beneficiaries acting together may compel the termination of a trust.
- A beneficiary who has acquired a right in fee to property is normally entitled to insist that the trustees pass the property to him absolutely.

▼ CHAPTER SUMMARY

THE TRUST CONCEPT

1. A trust involves three roles: a truster, trustee and a beneficiary. 13–80
2. The truster is the person who sets up the trust; the trustee is the person who owns and administers the property; the beneficiary is the person for whose benefit the property is administered.
3. These are roles rather than persons: the same person can hold more than one of these roles, and there can be more than one person in each role.
4. There are various practical advantages to the trust device, mainly because it allows a separation of benefit from property from the control of that property. Some of these advantages could be achieved by other legal devices, but the one unique advantage of the trust is that it protects against insolvency: if the trustee is made bankrupt, the trust property cannot be used to pay off his debts:

    ➢ *Heritable Reversionary Co Ltd v Millar* (1892): if a trustee becomes insolvent, the trust property which he holds, cannot be used to satisfy the claims of his creditors.

PUBLIC AND PRIVATE TRUSTS

1. Trusts may be either public or private: that is, for the benefit of the public as whole (or a specific section of the public), or for a defined group of individuals.

CREATING A TRUST

1. **A trust is created by (a) declaring the trust and (b) transferring property from the truster to the trustee. Trusts can also be created by "legal implication" in some circumstances:**

   ➢ *Allan's Trs v Lord Advocate* (1971): to create a trust, delivery of the property, or some equivalent to delivery, is essential.

2. **Where the truster and trustee are the same person, there must be some "equivalent of delivery" to create the trust. This will normally take the form of intimating the rights created by the trust to the beneficiaries.**

3. **In order to be valid, trust purposes must not be (a) too uncertain; (b) too wide or (c) illegal:**

   ➢ *Bowman v Secular Society* (1917): a trust for criminal purposes will be invalid;
   ➢ *McCaig's Trs v Kirk-Session of United Free Church of Lismore* (1915): a trust to create a private enclosure with inordinately expensive statutes was invalid because it conferred no benefit on anyone.

TRUST ADMINISTRATION

1. **Trust decision-making is by a majority of trustees, unless the trust deed provides otherwise.**

DUTIES AND POWERS OF TRUSTEES

1. **Trustees have a number of general duties which are implied by law. The most important of these is to exercise due care in their dealings with the trust estate.**

2. **Trustees are also under a duty not to delegate the trust (that is, to take responsibility for decision-making themselves); to secure trust property; to invest trust property; to take advice where appropriate; to meet trust debts and obligations; to keep accounts, and to pay the correct beneficiaries:**

   ➢ *Leitch v Leitch* (1927): where a truster had set up the trust in such a way that it was "improbable" that he could have expected the trustee to keep trust accounts, there was no duty on her to keep them;
   ➢ *Melville v Noble's Trs* (1896): trustees who failed to invest trust property were liable personally to pay the money that could have been earned if it had been invested.

3. **Trustees must not be *auctor in rem suam* (actors in their own cause). This means they must not put themselves in a position where their personal interests are in conflict with their position as trustee. Specifically, this means: (a) they cannot contract with the trust estate; (b) cannot obtain a personal advantage from their position as trustee; and (c) cannot charge for work done for the trust:**

   ➢ *Cherry's Trs v Patrick* (1911): where a trustee made money by contracting with the trust, this was improper and he was obliged to return the benefit he received;

➢ *Cowan v Scargill* (1985): pension fund trustees could not use their position to further the aims of the National Union of Mineworkers, but had to restrict their considerations to the best interests of the beneficiaries.

4. **A trustee may be *auctor in rem suam* if this is sanctioned in the trust deed or by the beneficiaries:**

➢ *Sarris v Clark* (1995): sanction in the trust deed can be implicit. Because it was an inevitable consequence of the arrangements Mr Clark had entered into in his will and elsewhere that his wife would be *auctor in rem suam*, he could be regarded as having impliedly sanctioned this.

5. **The powers of a trustee may be set out in the trust deed, or the trustee may rely on general powers, which are set out in section 4 of the Trusts (Scotland) Act 1921. These general powers may, however, be excluded by the terms of the trust deed:**

➢ Trusts (Scotland) Act 1921, section 4: sets out various general powers, which all trustees have unless they would be "at variance with the terms and purposes of the trust".

REMEDIES FOR BREACH OF TRUST

1. **Where trustees are in breach of trust or plan to do something which would be a breach, the principal remedies open to the beneficiaries are (a) interdict (a court order which prohibits a person from a specific act); (b) an action for damages or (c) an action for "accounting":**

➢ *Armitage v Nurse* (1998): an "exemption clause" which said that trustees were not liable for anything other than "actual fraud" was held by the English courts to be effective.

TRUSTEES' LIABILITY TO THIRD PARTIES

1. **If trustees enter into contracts on behalf of the trust, they are personally liable on these contracts unless there is an agreement to the contrary. Signing contracts "as trustee" is enough to imply such an agreement.**

VARIATION OF TRUSTS

1. **The purposes of a private trust may be varied by consent of all the beneficiaries. Where a beneficiary is unable to consent, the court may be asked to consent on their behalf. The court cannot do this unless satisfied that the variation would not be "prejudicial" to that person:**

➢ Trusts (Scotland) Act 1961 s.1: where a beneficiary (or potential beneficiary) is unable to consent to a proposed variation of a private trust, this section gives the court a discretionary power to consent on their behalf.

2. **The purposes of a public trust may be varied by way of a court application. Where the trust is a small one, it may be possible to avoid the need for a court application by following alternative statutory procedures.**

3. **Where it has never been possible to give effect to the purposes of a public trust, an application for variation must be under the *cy-prés* jurisdiction. It must be shown that (a) the truster had a "general charitable intention" and (b) that the purposes set out in the trust are impossible.**

   ➢ *Hay's J.F. v Hay's Trs.* (1952): where Ms Hay wished her trustees to maintain a mansion-house as a hospital named the "Hay Memorial", but there were insufficient funds to do this, there was no "general charitable intention". This is because it was clear that the use of the house as the "Hay Memorial" was an essential part of her intention.

4. **Where it has been possible to give effect to the purposes of a public trust, an application for variation may be made under the broader grounds set out in statute**:

   ➢ Law Reform (Miscellaneous Provisions) (Scotland) Act 1990 s.9: makes statutory provision for the variation of the purposes of a public trust.

TERMINATION OF TRUSTS

1. **A trust may be terminated primarily by (a) the trustees fulfilling the trust purposes and bringing the trust to an end or (b) by the beneficiaries acting together to compel its termination.**

? QUICK QUIZ

TRUSTS

Basic concepts and the creation of a trust

- What is a trust? How may trusts be classified?
- Who owns trust property?
- How is a voluntary trust created?
- What types of legally implied trust are recognised by Scots law?
- What restrictions does Scots law place on the validity of trust purposes?

Trustees and trust management

- On what grounds may a trustee be removed from office by the court?
- When will the court interfere in the discretion of trustees?
- Must trust decisions be taken unanimously?
- What general duties does the law impose on trustees?
- What are the obligations of trustees in relation to investment matters?
- What is meant by the rule against *auctor in rem suam*?
- What are the sources of trustees' powers?

Trustees' liabilities

- When a trustee has been in breach of trust, what remedies are open to the beneficiaries?
- How may trustees be protected from liability for breach of trust?
- Are trustees personally liable on trust contracts?

Variation of trust purposes

- What requirements must be satisfied before the terms of a private trust can be varied? To what extent is the court involved in this process?
- In what circumstances may the terms of a public trust be varied?

Termination of a trust

- In what ways may a trust be terminated?

📖 FURTHER READING

The leading textbook on the Scottish law of trusts is W.A. Wilson and A.G.M. Duncan's *Trusts, Trustees and Executors*, 2nd edn (W. Green, 1995). It is a detailed reference work, but is generally unsuitable for someone who is approaching the subject for the first time. Reference is sometimes also made to a number of older textbooks, particularly A. Mackenzie Stuart's *The Law of Trusts* (W. Green, 1932). Mackenzie Stuart's book is brief and readable, but must be treated with some caution given developments in the law of trusts since it was published.

There are relatively few student textbooks on the subject, although substantial coverage can be found in G.L. Gretton and A.J.M. Steven, *Property, Trusts and Succession* (Tottel, 2009). The most recent book on trusts alone is a cases and materials book: J. Chalmers, *Trusts: Cases and Materials* (W. Green, 2002), on which this Chapter draws heavily. There is one textbook: K. McK. Norrie and E.M. Scobbie, *Trusts* (W. Green, 1991). Although it is now over 10 years old, there have been few major developments in the law of trusts over that period and it is still a very useful introduction to the subject. R.R.M. Paisley, *Trusts LawBasics* (W. Green, 1999) is a very brief introduction to the subject.

Reference may also be made to J. McLaren, *The Law of Wills and Succession as Administered in Scotland, Including Trusts, Entails, Powers and Executry*, 3rd edn (Bell, 1894) and A.J.P. Menzies, *The Law of Scotland Affecting Trustees*, 2nd edn (W. Green, 1913). These are very detailed works, which may be of use for researching particular points, but are too dated to be relied upon in themselves.

Two articles which provide useful analyses of the theory of the trust in Scots law should be specifically mentioned: K.G.C. Reid, "Patrimony not Equity: the trust in Scotland" (2000) 8 E.R.P.L. 427; and G.L. Gretton, "Trusts Without Equity" (2000) 49 I.C.L.Q. 599.

🖱 RELEVANT WEB LINKS

The Scottish Law Commission (*http://www.scotlawcom.gov.uk*) currently regards the reform of the law of trusts as a long-term project and has published nine discussion papers and one report on various aspects of the law of trusts between 2003 and 2011.

Chapter 14   Succession

DAVID BRAND[1]

▶ CHAPTER OVERVIEW

14–01 This chapter is concerned with the law of succession. After emphasising the importance of the Succession (Scotland) Act 1964 and the function of private international law in succession, the preliminary matters of proof of death and survivorship are examined. The concept of legal rights is considered, followed by the fundamental difference between intestate and testate succession. Various specific aspects of testate succession are considered next. The steps involved in executry administration are outlined and the chapter concludes with an outline of possible reform of the law.

✓ OUTCOMES

14–02 At the end of this chapter you should be able to:

- ✓ identify the preliminary matters which must be considered in winding up the estate of a deceased person;
- ✓ appreciate the significance of legal rights in succession;
- ✓ explain the fundamental difference between intestate and testate succession;
- ✓ understand how an intestate estate will be distributed;
- ✓ understand the rules affecting the validity, revocation and interpretation of wills;
- ✓ understand the other rules affecting the terms of wills; and
- ✓ identify the various steps involved in executry administration.

INTRODUCTION

14–03 The law of succession governs the distribution of property belonging to a person who has died. Accordingly, with the exception of those few people who die leaving nothing, the law of succession affects everyone. The law deals with a range of matters. It deals with who is entitled to succeed to the property of the deceased person who has made no provision which expresses their wishes as to who is to inherit. This is known as the law of intestate succession. It also deals with the situation where the deceased has left a will, or some other testamentary writing or evidence of intention, as to who they wish to inherit their property. This is known as testate succession and the person leaving the will is known as the testator. Testate succession deals with such matters as the formal requirements for the validity of a will or other testamentary writing, whether the testator had the requisite legal capacity to make a will and the limitations on the testamentary freedom of testators to

---

[1] Honorary Teaching Fellow in Law, University of Dundee.

leave property as they wish. The law of succession also requires to deal with the administrative process of transferring the property of the deceased to those entitled to inherit, known as the beneficiaries. This is carried out by the executor of the deceased and the administration of a deceased's estate is known as an executry.

Scots law on succession was radically altered by the Succession (Scotland) Act 1964, particularly in relation to intestate succession. Prior to this Act, intestate succession to heritable and moveable property was different. The Act changed this and, for most purposes, the same rules apply to both heritable and moveable property. The Act also introduced prior rights for surviving spouses on intestacy and altered the rules for the administration of a deceased's estate.

Subsequent to the 1964 Act, the Scottish Law Commission examined the law of succession in some detail, in the latter half of the 1980s, and issued a report in 1990[2] recommending a range of reforms.[3] Little action was taken on these recommendations until amendments to the existing law were made by the Civil Partnership Act 2004 and the Family Law (Scotland) Act 2006. These amendments gave the same rights on intestacy to registered civil partners as spouses and give a cohabitant of the deceased the right to apply to the court for a discretionary share of the estate if it is intestate. The Scottish Law Commission re-examined the law of succession recently and issued a new Report in 2009.[4] The Scottish Government has indicated that it intends to proceed to formal consultation on this but no time scale has been set out.

In this chapter the following matters are considered:

- proof of death and survivorship;
- legal rights;
- intestate succession;
- testate succession;
- revocation of wills;
- will substitutes;
- interpretation of wills;
- legacies;
- vesting and accretion;
- executry administration; and
- reform.

PRIVATE INTERNATIONAL LAW

Private international law is important in relation to questions of succession. It governs **14-04** situations where the laws of more than one country may apply to particular circumstances in order to determine which is the appropriate law to apply. For instance, if an English person who lived in Scotland dies leaving a house in France, does the succession law of England, Scotland or France apply to determine who inherits the house? The rules relating to such matters are complicated.[5]

The basic position in Scotland is that if a person dies domiciled in Scotland, Scots law of succession will apply to that person's moveable property, wherever it is situated. Scots law will also apply to any immoveable property situated in Scotland, as the general rule in

---

[2] Scottish Law Commission, *Report on Succession* (1990), Scot. Law Com. No.124.
[3] See Reform, para.14–74 below.
[4] Scottish Law Commission, *Report on Succession* (2009), Scot. Law Com. No.215.
[5] See Beaumont and McEleavy, *Anton's Private International Law*, 3rd edn (W. Green, 2011).

private international law is that the law of the country where immoveable property is situated applies to that property. It follows that if a person who is not domiciled in Scotland dies, leaving immoveable property in Scotland, Scots law applies to that property.

Domicile, therefore, has an important effect in private international law. Domicile, however, is a difficult concept. A person will have a domicile of origin and may acquire a domicile of choice. "The central idea is that it is the place where [he] has made his home."[6] However, simple residence in a place is not sufficient to establish domicile.[7]

The classification of a property as moveable or immoveable also has an important effect in private international law and the law which determines how a particular property is classified is governed by the country where the property is situated.[8] It should be noted, that the concept of "heritable and moveable" in Scots law is not exactly the same as that of "immoveable and moveable".[9]

Key Concepts

If a person dies **domiciled** in Scotland, Scots law of succession will apply to that person's moveable property wherever it is situated.

If a person who is **not domiciled** in Scotland dies leaving immoveable property in Scotland, Scots law applies to that property.

PROOF OF DEATH AND SURVIVORSHIP

Proof of death

14–05   In most cases, the fact of death and the date and time of death can be readily ascertained, although modern medical ethics can produce difficulties in relation to brain death as opposed to physical death. There can be no inheritance unless death is proved and an executor must state the precise date and place of death to enable an estate to be administered. If this is challenged, the executor must prove this.[10]

Death is usually evidenced by an extract from the Register of Deaths and such an extract is deemed "sufficient evidence of the death" under the Registration of Births, Deaths and Marriages (Scotland) Act 1965,[11] although not conclusive. Problems can occur with deaths in foreign countries where foreign registration procedures are inadequate. Problems can also occur where no body is found, as a death certificate cannot be issued without a doctor viewing the deceased's body.[12]

---

[6] Beaumont and McEleavy, *Anton's Private International Law*, 3rd edn (W. Green, 2011), see para.7.13 et seq. on The Concept of Domicile.

[7] Beaumont and McEleavy, *Anton's Private International Law*, 3rd edn (W. Green, 2011), see para.7.13 et seq. on The Concept of Domicile.

[8] *MacDonald v MacDonald's Exr*, 1932 S.C. (H.L.) 79.

[9] See Chapter 12 on Property.

[10] Currie, *Confirmation of Executors*, 8th edn (1995), paras 7.10–7.12.

[11] 1965 Act s.41(3).

[12] 1965 Act s.24.

Presumption of death

At common law there was no provision for presuming a person to be dead after dis- **14–06** appearance for a certain period of time. The common law presumed that a person lived to an extreme old age[13] in the absence of proof of death. Such proof required to be beyond reasonable doubt to rebut the presumption.[14]

Since 1881[15] there has been statutory provision on presumption of death. The current law is set out in the Presumption of Death (Scotland) Act 1977. Under this Act any person having an interest can raise an action to have a person declared legally dead. This applies in two main situations:

- where a person is thought to have died, e.g., in a plane crash;
- where a person has not been known to be alive for seven years, e.g. a person disappearing without any contact with anyone.

Proof is on the balance of probabilities. In the first situation the date of death will be either the actual date of death, if proved, or the end of a period of time within which it is not certain when the person died. In the second situation, it will be at the end of the day seven years after the person was known to have been alive.[16]

The court can decide any question relating to any interest in property resulting from the death.[17] The court decree dissolves the missing person's marriage, if married, but the estate will be divided as if the person was married.

If a missing person reappears, or is proved to have died at a different date from that in the decree, any person with an interest can apply to have the decree varied or recalled by a variation order.[18] In order to protect those who have acquired rights by the original court decree, a variation order does not automatically affect any property rights acquired under the decree. If such a variation order is made within five years of the decree, the court can make an order which it "considers fair and reasonable in all the circumstances" which includes restitution in cash or kind.[19] A variation order cannot affect any income already received, or the title of a third party acquiring in good faith and for value.[20]

Proof of survivorship

A beneficiary must survive the deceased in order to inherit. This must be proved on the **14–07** balance of probabilities.[21] "Survivance is in every case a matter of proof, and … when a claimant whose claim depends on proof of survivorship is unable to establish the fact of survivorship, his claim necessarily fails."[22] There is no period of time required and a few seconds of survivorship is sufficient. In practice, to avoid difficulties where a person dies and a beneficiary of that person, for example, a spouse, dies at the same time or within a short time thereafter, it is usual in wills to specify a period of time for survivorship. Thirty days is the most common period specified.

Where more than one person died, and it was impossible to determine who had died

---

[13] Stair states 80 or 100 years—Inst. VI xlv 17.
[14] See, e.g. *Secretary of State for Scotland v Sutherland*, 1944 S.C. 79.
[15] Presumption of Life Limitation (Scotland) Act 1891.
[16] 1977 Act s.2.
[17] 1977 Act s.3(1).
[18] 1977 Act s.4(1).
[19] 1977 Act s.5(3).
[20] 1977 Act s.5(2).
[21] *Lamb v Lord Advocate*, 1976 S.L.T. 151.
[22] Lord Justice-Clerk Cooper in *Drummond's Judicial Factor v Lord Advocate*, 1944 S.C. 298 at 302.

first, there were no presumptions under the common law to assist. This could have unfortunate results in such common calamities.

Ross's Judicial Factor v Martin
1955 S.C. (H.L.) 56

Two sisters left identical wills leaving everything to each other, whom failing a charity. They died together in their home due to a gas leak and it was not clear who had died first. Neither could be proved to have survived the other and the whom failing part of the will could not be applied. Their estates went to their relatives under the law of intestacy, instead of the charity which they wished to benefit.[23]

The Succession (Scotland) Act 1964 reformed the law. The general rule is that where two persons have died in circumstances indicating that they died simultaneously, or that it is uncertain who survived whom, it is presumed that the younger survived the elder.[24] There are two exceptions. First, where the persons were husband and wife, it is presumed that neither survived the other, thus retaining the common law position.[25] Secondly, where the elder left a legacy to the younger whom failing a third party and the younger dies without a will, the elder is presumed to have survived for the purpose of that legacy only.[26]

Under inheritance tax law, parties to a common calamity are deemed to die simultaneously, which avoids a double charge to tax.[27]

Postumous children

14–08 Where a deceased person has left a child conceived but not born, such a child may be treated as having been born and having survived the deceased for the purposes of succession.[28] Two conditions must be satisfied. First, the child must be born alive and not stillborn. Secondly, the rule cannot be invoked to benefit a third party, as with a trust, but only the child directly.[29]

Entitlement to inherit

14–09 A person who would otherwise inherit in an estate may be debarred from doing so for certain reasons. These reasons do not include incapacity, as a person who is incapax due to mental incapacity, or is under the age of 16 is entitled to inherit and the property concerned will normally be held by a guardian of the incapax, or the parent or guardian of a child.

The relevant reasons are either the heir is regarded as unworthy or the children are adopted. It used to be the case that illegitimate children could not inherit, but this no longer applies.

---

[23] See also *Mitchell's Executrix v Gordon*, 1953 S.C. 176.
[24] 1964 Act s.31(1)(b).
[25] 1964 Act s.31(1)(a).
[26] 1964 Act s.31(2).
[27] Inheritance Tax 1984 s.4(2).
[28] *Cox's Trs v Cox*, 1950 S.C. 117.
[29] *Elliot v Joicey*, 1935 S.C. (H.L.) 57.

The unworthy heir

An unworthy heir is the term usually applied to a beneficiary who has unlawfully killed the **14–10** deceased. The rule in Scots law, which prevents an unworthy heir inheriting, appears to derive from both statute and the common law and seems to be based on principles of public policy.

An old statute, the Parricide Act 1594, deals with the killing of parents and grand-parents, but the scope of the Act is not clear and it has never been used to disinherit someone in any reported case.

The rule applies to both murder and culpable homicide[30] but a criminal conviction is not essential. The unworthy heir is not regarded as predeceasing the deceased, but is simply ignored in the distribution of the deceased's estate.[31]

Burns v Secretary of State for Social Services
1985 S.L.T. 351

A woman was provoked by her husband's violence. She had been assaulted by him over a period of years and she had suffered numerous injuries. She stabbed him and he died. She pled guilty to culpable homicide. Her claim for a widow's allowance was disallowed, as she had deliberately killed her husband.

The Forfeiture Act 1982 enables the court to modify this forfeiture rule in appropriate circumstances, but is given no power to modify the effects of the 1594 Act. The court can modify the rule where it is satisfied that it is just to do so, having regard to the conduct of the offender and the deceased and other relevant circumstances.[32] A court can only modify and not completely exclude the rule, but the modification can be virtually a complete exclusion. In one case, the killer of the deceased in extenuating circumstances received 100 per cent of the heritable estate and 99 per cent of the moveable estate.[33]

Adopted children

Prior to 1964, adoption did not affect the succession rights of adopted children. They **14–11** retained a right of inheritance in their natural parents' estates, but not in their adopted parents' estates. This position was reversed under the Succession (Scotland) Act 1964.[34] There are special rules relating to the relationship of the adopted person with brothers and sisters and their descendents.[35]

Illegitimate children

At common law an illegitimate child was regarded as *filius nullius*, nobody's child, and had **14–12** no right to inherit from anyone.[36] Various statutory reforms dating from 1926 gradually

---

[30] *Burns v Secretary of State for Social Services*, 1985 S.L.T. 351.
[31] *Hunter's Exrs, Petitioners*, 1992 S.L.T. 1141.
[32] 1982 Act s.2(2).
[33] *Cross, Petitioner*, 1987 S.L.T. 384.
[34] 1964 Act s.23(1).
[35] 1964 Act ss.24(1) and 24(1A).
[36] Erskine Inst. III. x. 8, *Clarke v Carfin Coal Co* (1891) 18 R. (H.L.) 63.

reduced this discrimination[37] until final abolition of the status of illegitimacy under the Family Law (Scotland) Act 2006.[38]

Key Concepts

Death is usually evidenced by an extract from the Register of Deaths.

Statutory provisions on **presumption of death** provide that a person can be declared legally dead in two situations:

- where a person is thought to have died;
- where a person has not been known to be alive for seven years.

A beneficiary must **survive** the deceased in order to inherit. No period of time is necessary. This must be proved on the balance of probabilities.

An unworthy heir **may not inherit**.

Adopted children inherit from their adopted parents and not their natural parents. Illegitimate children can inherit.

LEGAL RIGHTS

14–13 Legal rights have existed in Scots law for several centuries to protect spouses and children from disinheritance. It is not possible to completely exclude a spouse and children from inheritance by making a will which omits them. Legal rights apply in both testate and intestate succession. Strictly speaking, legal rights are not rights of succession, but are debts due by the deceased estate.[39] If claimed, they are paid out of the net moveable estate after deduction of debts and funeral expenses and also after deduction of prior rights in an intestate estate.[40]

Until recently, legal rights could only be claimed by spouses and children. Cohabitants have no such rights and neither do stepchildren. Illegitimate and adopted children can claim legal rights.[41] Where a child has predeceased the deceased, the children or remoter descendents of that child can claim under the doctrine of representation.[42] Legal rights have now been extended to registered civil partners.[43]

Legal rights are not paid out automatically in the administration of a testate estate; they must be claimed. The right to claim is extinguished after 20 years by the long negative prescription.[44] They are paid out of the moveable estate only, but there is no right to claim specific assets as part of the right. An estate, therefore, must be divided into heritage and moveables for the purpose of calculating legal rights. It follows that it is possible for a

---

[37] Starting with the Legitimacy Act 1926.
[38] 2006 Act s.21.
[39] Lord Watson in *Naismith v Boyes* (1899) 1 F. (H.L.) 79 at 81.
[40] See Prior rights, para.14–19 et seq. below.
[41] See Illegitimate children, para.14–12 et seq. and Adopted children, para.14–11 above.
[42] See para.14–15 below.
[43] Civil Partnership Act 2004 s.131.
[44] Prescription and Limitation (Scotland) Act 1973 s.7 and Sch.1 para.2(f).

person to reduce, or defeat, a potential legal rights claim by converting assets from moveables to heritage in their lifetime, although this has practical limitations.[45]

In legal rights, the amount payable depends on who has survived the deceased:

- where both a spouse or civil partner and children (or remoter issue) survive, the spouse or civil partner gets one third of the moveable estate, the children get one third and the remaining one third is the free estate, which is distributed according to the provisions of the will or rules of intestate succession;
- where a spouse or civil partner only survives, the amount is one half and the other half is free estate;
- where children (or remoter issue) only survive, the amount is one half and the other half is free estate.

Election

It is not possible to take both a provision under a will and claim legal rights. A spouse, **14–14** civil partner or child must choose between accepting what is left to them in a will or reject this and claim legal rights, presumably on the basis that more will be received. This is known as the doctrine of approbate and reprobate in Scots law.

Representation

Prior to 1964, if a child predeceased the deceased and left children, these grandchildren **14–15** had no right to legal rights. The 1964 Act altered this by providing for representation.[46] If a deceased has a child who predeceases him or her leaving grandchildren or remoter issue, such issue have the same right to legal rights as the child would have had by surviving the deceased.

Where there is more than one person claiming legal rights, there are rules as to how the legal rights fund is divided. If all those claiming are related in the same degree to the deceased, division is per capita, or by head. For instance, if there are four grandchildren they will each receive one quarter of the legal rights. If all those claiming are not related in the same degree to the deceased, the division is *per stirpes*, or by branch. For instance, if there is one child living and another child who predeceased leaving two children, i.e. grandchildren, the child of the deceased will receive one half of the legal rights and the grandchildren will receive one half between them, i.e. one quarter each.

Collation

If a child of the deceased wishes to claim legal rights and has received advances of **14–16** moveable property during the lifetime of the deceased, the doctrine of collation applies. Collation is the adding back of the advances to the legal rights fund, which is then divided amongst the children. The purpose of this doctrine is to treat children equally in the division. It only applies in legal rights. There must be more than one person claiming legal rights as a child before the doctrine operates.[47] Where the claimant is representing a predeceasing child, advances made to both the claimant and the predeceasing child must be collated.

Not all advances require to be collated. The following advances are excluded:

---

[45] Another device would be to use up assets to purchase an annuity, which would cease on death. Trusts can also be used to limit legal rights claims.
[46] 1964 Act s.11.
[47] *Coats' Trs v Coats*, 1914 S.C. 744.

- an advance made which is clearly intended by the deceased to be in addition to a claim to legal rights;
- a loan to a child, which is a debt due to the deceased's estate;
- remuneration for services rendered;
- money used for the education and maintenance of a child.[48]

Discharge of legal rights

14–17 Legal rights can be formally discharged, either during the lifetime of the deceased or after the death. Legal rights can be discharged unilaterally, but a discharge of legal rights of a child requires the consent of the child or remoter issue concerned.[49]

Where the discharge is during the deceased's lifetime, the granter of the discharge is treated as dead, which increases the proportional share of any other legal rights claimants. Where the discharge is after the death, the share affected by the discharge falls into the free estate and the share of any other legal rights claimant is unaffected.

M, Applicant
2007 S.L.T. (Sh Ct) 25

The wife of an 81-year-old man suffering from Alzheimer's Disease died without making provision for him in her will. This was done deliberately as she wanted all her estate to go directly to their children. The husband had a potential claim for legal rights which had to be resolved before her estate could be distributed. The three children successfully applied under the Adults with Incapacity (Scotland) Act 2000 for an intervention order allowing them on behalf of their father to renounce his legal rights.

Key Concepts

Legal rights protect spouses, civil partners and children from disinheritance. They apply in testate and intestate succession. They are paid out of the net moveable estate only.

If both a spouse or civil partner and children survive, the amounts are one third of the net moveable estate to the spouse or civil partner, one third to the children and one third to free estate payable to the beneficiaries under the will or intestacy.

If either the spouse or civil partner only or children only survive, they amount to one half of the net moveable estate.

Grandchildren or remoter issue can represent a child who predeceases the testator.

Legal rights can be discharged during the lifetime of the testator or after the death.

---

[48] Ersk. Inst. III, xi, 24.
[49] 1964 Act s.12.

INTESTATE SUCCESSION

Intestacy occurs where there is no will or other testamentary provision relating to a **14–18** deceased's estate. Intestacy can be total or partial where part of the estate is not disposed of. Partial intestacy may be deliberate, although this is unusual, or as a result of a failure of part of a will. If a will fails in part or completely, this is known as artificial intestacy. In practice, most intestacies occur where the deceased died without leaving a will. This is an unfortunate but frequent occurrence as many people do not bother to make wills. The rules of intestacy attempt to set out how society generally would expect someone to dispose of their estate, which may or may not be what the deceased would have wanted.

The rules of intestate succession were radically reformed by the Succession (Scotland) Act 1964. Prior to this Act there were different rules for heritable and moveable property, with heritable property going exclusively to the oldest male heir under the principle known as *primogeniture*. The 1964 Act applies to most property but not to titles, coats of arms and honours. There is now no distinction between entitlement to heritable and moveable property, although the distinction remains important in relation to legal rights. The 1964 Act improved the position on intestacy for spouses, with the introduction of prior rights which are paid first out of the net intestate estate. The 1964 Act also altered the order in which relatives of the deceased are entitled to succeed.

The order of succession in the 1964 Act sets out six stages to be followed in distributing an intestate estate. These are:

- payment of debts[50];
- prior rights—right to dwelling house[51];
- prior rights—furniture and plenishings[52];
- prior rights—cash right[53];
- legal rights;
- free estate.[54]

Prior rights

Prior rights are only payable on intestacy, either total or partial. If an intestacy is partial, **14–19** they are only payable out of the intestate part of the estate. Initially, a surviving spouse was the only person entitled to prior rights. Cohabitants and children were and remain excluded. Under the Civil Partnership Act 2004, this right is extended to registered civil partners.[55] Prior rights are extinguished after 20 years, under the long negative prescription.[56] The value for calculating prior rights is the value as the date of death.[57]

---

[50] See Assets and debts, para.14–69 et seq. below.
[51] 1964 Act s.8(1).
[52] 1964 Act s.8(3).
[53] 1964 Act s.9.
[54] 1964 Act s.2.
[55] Civil Partnership Act 2004 Sch.28 para.1(1).
[56] Prescription and Limitation (Scotland) Act 1973 s.7 and Sch.1 para.2(f).
[57] 1964 Act s.9A.

Dwelling house

14–20 A surviving spouse or civil partner has a right to the deceased's dwelling house, or one of them if more than one, or a cash equivalent depending on the value of the house. A dwelling house includes a part of a building occupied as a separate house and any garden or amenity ground attached.[58]

This prior right applies to a house owned by the deceased or tenanted by the deceased.[59] Tenancies covered by the Rent Acts are excluded, as are tenancies which terminate on the death of the deceased.[60] Also excluded are a house which forms part only of a single tenancy[61] and a house which is used for a business, where the value of the whole estate would be likely to be substantially diminished by disposing of the house separate from the business.[62]

The surviving spouse or civil partner must have been ordinarily resident in the house for the prior right to operate.[63] It is not relevant whether or not the deceased was ordinarily resident in that house. If the surviving spouse or civil partner was ordinarily resident in more than one house, a choice must be made within six months of the date of death as to which one is taken as a prior right.[64]

The upper value for a house which can be taken as a prior right was set at £15,000 under the 1964 Act and has been increased periodically by statutory instrument. The current figure has recently increased substantially from £300,000 to £473,000 from February 2012.[65] If the house is valued at over £473,000 the surviving spouse or civil partner will receive a cash equivalent of £473,000.[66] In practice, where this happens it is usual for the surviving spouse or civil partner to make up the difference to enable the house to be taken. The value of the house is taken after deduction of any heritable debts, such as a mortgage over the house. Any disagreement as to the value is determined by arbitration.[67]

Furniture and plenishings

14–21 The surviving spouse or civil partner has a right to the furniture and plenishings of a dwelling house where normally resident at the date of death. Furniture and plenishings include "garden effects, domestic animals, plate, plated articles, linen, china, glass, books, pictures, prints, articles of household use and consumable stores",[68] but this list is not exhaustive. Articles and animals used for business purposes, money, securities and heirlooms are all excluded.[69]

The current upper limit is £29,000.[70] A surviving spouse or civil partner is entitled to furniture and plenishings up to that value. If the total value exceeds £29,000, items up to that value must be chosen. The furniture and plenishings must come from one house only. If there is more than one house in which the surviving spouse or civil partner was normally resident at the date of death, the spouse or civil partner must choose within six months of

---

[58] 1964 Act s.8(6)(a).
[59] 1964 Act s.8(6)(d).
[60] 1964 Act s.36(2).
[61] 1964 Act s.8(2)(a).
[62] 1964 Act s.8(2)(b).
[63] 1964 Act s.8(4).
[64] 1964 Act s.8(1).
[65] Prior Rights of Surviving Spouse and Civil Partner (Scotland) Order 2011 (SSI 2011/436).
[66] 1964 Act s.8(1)(b).
[67] 1964 Act s.8(5).
[68] 1964 Act s.8(6)(b).
[69] 1964 Act s.8(6)(b).
[70] SSI 2011/436.

the date of death from which house they will be taken.[71] The furniture and plenishings need not be taken from the same house which was chosen for the right to the dwelling house.

Cash right

A surviving spouse or civil partner has a right to a sum of cash in addition to the right to **14–22** the house and furniture and plenishings, but this cash right only arises after the other two rights have been satisfied. The sum is currently a maximum of £50,000 if the deceased is survived by children or remoter issue, or £89,000 if the deceased is not.[72] The cash right is paid out proportionately from the heritable and moveable estate.[73] Interest is payable on the cash sum from the date of death until payment,[74] at a rate fixed by the Secretary of State from time to time. It is currently seven per cent.[75]

If the intestacy is partial only and the spouse or civil partner has been left a legacy in the testate part of the estate, other than a legacy of a dwelling house or of furniture and plenishings taken as prior rights, the value of that legacy as at the date of death must be set off against the cash right and will reduce it accordingly.[76]

Free estate

Prior rights will exhaust the whole estate in many cases. If not, legal rights are calculated **14–23** and satisfied next. If there is any estate left after satisfaction of prior rights and legal rights, this is known as the free estate and is divided under the rules set out in the 1964 Act. The Act lays out the following order of succession[77]:

- children;
- parents and brothers and sisters provided there is at least one from each class— each class taking one half;
- brothers and sisters where there is no surviving parent;
- parents where there is no surviving brothers or sisters;
- spouse or civil partner;
- uncles and aunts, both paternal and maternal;
- grandparents, both paternal and maternal;
- brothers and sisters of grandparents;
- remoter ancestors;
- the Crown as *ultimus haeres*, ultimate heir.[78]

Each successive class of relatives is examined until there is someone entitled to inherit and succession stops at that class. Each class must be exhausted before the next class is examined. Representation is applied in all classes, except parents and spouses or civil partners.[79] Issue includes issue however remote, with no distinction between legitimate and illegitimate relationships.[80]

---

[71] 1964 Act s.8(3).
[72] SSI 2011/436.
[73] 1964 Act s.9(3).
[74] 1964 Act s.9(1).
[75] Interest on Prior Rights (Scotland) Order 1981 (SI 1981/805).
[76] 1964 Act s.9(1) and (6)(b).
[77] 1964 Act s.2.
[78] 1964 Act s.7.
[79] 1964 Act s.5.
[80] See Illegitimate children, para.14–12 above.

Where there is more than one person with a right of succession, the division is per capita, by head, if they are related in the same degree to the deceased or *per stirpes*, by branch, if they are not related in the same degree to the deceased. For example, if a person dies leaving no children and three grandchildren, the grandchildren are in the same degree of relationship to the deceased. Division is by head and they would get one-third each. If there was one child and two grandchildren who were the children of a child who died before the deceased, the child and grandchildren are not in the same degree of relationship to the deceased. Division is by branch. The child would get one half. The other half, which would have gone to the predeceasing child had they survived is divided between their own two children. These grandchildren get one quarter each.

Collaterals of the whole blood, who have two parents in common, exclude collaterals of the half blood who have only one parent in common.

As prior rights are satisfied before legal rights, a surviving spouse or civil partner may be better off if an estate is intestate where the estate has been left to the spouse or civil partner under a will and the deceased left children who intend to claim legal rights. This is because the whole estate going to the spouse or civil partner will have legal rights taken off first, whereas if there was no will, prior rights which might cover the whole estate go to the spouse or civil partner first before legal rights apply. This means that he or she may be better off by refusing to take under the will and making the estate intestate. The question arises whether it is possible to do this and this has been held to be competent.[81]

Kerr, Petitioner
1968 S.L.T. (Sh. Ct) 61

Mr Kerr died leaving all his estate to his wife in a will. He had a daughter who claimed her legal rights. Mrs Kerr renounced her rights under the will and Mr Kerr's estate fell into intestacy. Prior rights were payable first and Mrs Kerr was better off than she would have been under the will, because legal rights of one third of the moveable estate would have been deducted. The court held she was entitled to do this.

Discretionary rights for cohabitants

14–24 Under recent reform of family law, it is now possible for a cohabitant of a deceased person to apply to the court for a discretionary payment from the deceased's estate if it is intestate.[82] Cohabitants include opposite and same sex couples and the court will consider various factors in determining whether the claimant is to be regarded as a cohabitant for this purpose.[83] These include the period of cohabitation, the nature of the relationship and the nature and extent of any financial relationship between the cohabitant and the deceased. If the court considers that the claimant is a cohabitant, it can award a capital sum or a transfer of property. In determining this, the court considers the size of the estate, any benefit received by the claimant and the nature of claims on the deceased's estate. The court cannot award more than a spouse or civil partner would receive. A claim has to be made within six months of the death. There have been a few reported cases on this to date.[84]

---

[81] *Kerr, Petitioner*, 1968 S.L.T. (Sh. Ct) 61.
[82] Family Law (Scotland) Act 2006 s.29.
[83] 2006 Act s.25.
[84] See, for example, *Savage v Purches*, 2009 S.L.T. (Sh. Ct.) 36.

Key Concepts

Intestacy occurs where there is no will or other testamentary provision relating to a deceased's estate.

Prior rights are only payable on intestacy, either total or partial. The only person entitled to prior rights is a surviving spouse or civil partner of the deceased.

There are three types of prior rights, which are satisfied in the following order:

- dwelling house up to a value of £473,000;
- furniture and plenishings up to the value of £29,000;
- cash up to £89,000 if the deceased left no children, or £50,000 if the deceased left children.

Prior rights will exhaust the whole estate in many cases. If not, **legal rights** are calculated and satisfied next. If there is any estate left after satisfaction of prior rights and legal rights this is known as the **free estate** and is divided under the rules set out in the 1964 Act.

A cohabitant can apply to the court for a **discretionary share** in an intestate estate.

Testate Succession

The law of testate succession governs situations where the deceased has left a will or other **14-25** testamentary writing. If a will is valid and disposes of all of the estate of a deceased, it will be given effect and the rules of intestate succession will not apply. As already noted,[85] it is not possible to avoid claims for legal rights by making a will. If a will disposes of part only of a deceased's estate, that part of the estate will be distributed according to the will and the remaining estate will fall into intestacy and be distributed accordingly.

A testamentary writing is one which is intended to dispose of a person's estate after his or her death.[86] They are usually, but not always, in the form of a formal will. Testamentary intention can also be established in other writings. It is sensible, however, to have a formal will drawn up by a solicitor who is qualified and experienced in such matters. Some people endeavour to make homemade wills and there are various will forms available for such do-it-yourself wills. These can cause problems if not completed correctly, which practice indicates is often the case.

There can be more than one testamentary writing which, taken together, form the complete testamentary position. Formal additions or alterations to wills are known as codicils. Where a will has trust provisions, such as leaving property to beneficiaries who are under age and, therefore, the property is to be held by trustees until they reach a certain age, it is sometimes known as a trust disposition and settlement.

The validity of wills and other testamentary writings depends on a number of factors which are usually grouped together under the headings of essential and formal validity, but fall into three areas:

---

[85] See Legal Rights, para.14–13 et seq. above.
[86] It derives from the Latin *testare* which means to verify.

- intention to test;
- capacity;
- formal validity.

Intention to test

14–26 A will does not require a set form of words, but it must be clear that the person making the will, known as the testator, has the intention to test, that is to make a testamentary writing. If it is intended as instructions[87] or notes[88] for a future will, it will be ineffective. This may not be entirely clear, especially if there is an indication in an informal writing that the writer intends to make a formal will in the future. In such cases, the wording must be examined to establish whether there is testamentary intention in the current writing.[89]

Capacity

14–27 A person must be aged 12 or older to have capacity to make a will.[90] A person must also be of sound mind to make a will. This means that a person must know the nature and effect of the will. If a person suffers from a mental illness, which normally prevents this, but has lucid intervals and it can be shown that the will was made during such a lucid interval, the will will be valid.[91] Conversely, a normally sane person can temporarily become of unsound mind due, for instance, to alcohol or drugs which will render the person incapable of making a will.[92]

> ### Nisbet's Trs v Nisbet
> ### (1871) 9 M. 937
>
> Major Nisbet was resident in a mental institution for many years before he died. Two months before he died he made a will. There was medical evidence that he was in a lucid interval at the time the will was made. It was held that he "had become of a sound and disposing mind to the effect of being able to execute the deed".

If a person is partially insane, for instance, is suffering from certain delusions and these delusions have influenced the person in making the will, the will may be invalid.[93] "If the testator is not generally insane, the will must be shown to have been the outcome of the special delusion ... The delusion must be shown to have been an actual and compelling influence."[94]

Eccentricity is different from mental incapacity and, if a will is challenged, it must be proved that the testator has no mental capacity to make a will before it will be set aside.[95] This was clearly shown in a somewhat bizarre case.

---

[87] *Munro v Coutts* (1813) 1 Dow 437.
[88] *Colvin v Hutchison* (1885) 12 R. 947.
[89] *Rhodes v Peterson*, 1971 S.C. 56.
[90] Age of Legal Capacity (Scotland) Act 1991 s.2(2). Interestingly, a person must be aged 16 or over to act as a witness under ss.2(1) and 9 of the same Act. In England, with limited exceptions, the age is 18.
[91] *Nisbet's Trs v Nisbet* (1871) 9 M. 937.
[92] *Laidlaw v Laidlaw* (1870) 8 M. 882.
[93] *Sivewright v Sivewright's Trs*, 1920 S.C. (H.L.) 63.
[94] Viscount Haldane in *Sivewright v Sivewright's Trs*, 1920 S.C. (H.L.) 63 at 64.
[95] *Morrison v Maclean's Trs* (1862) 24 D. 625.

Morrison v Maclean's Trs
(1862) 24 D. 625

Colonel Alexander Maclean died aged 80. He left a will and two codicils which directed that his estate was to be invested to pay an annuity to his housekeeper and to educate poor boys named Maclean. He left nothing to his relatives. His nearest relative raised an action to have the will reduced on the ground that Maclean was insane. There was evidence that he was given to obscene and rambling conversations and claimed to have no relatives. He said that he had been fed when young from an eagle's nest. (There was, in fact, evidence to support this.) The court held there was no proof of insanity, even if the will might have been morally objectionable to some people, particularly the testator's relatives.

A will made by a person who is not of sound mind is void and has no effect. A will which has been made in circumstances which amount to either facility and circumvention or undue influence is voidable. This means that the will is valid but, if challenged, may be set aside.

Facility and circumvention

Facility is where a person has a weakness of mind which does not amount to insanity. This is usually due to illness or old age. Where such a facile person makes a will due to circumvention, which is pressure by someone seeking to influence the terms of the will, such a will may be successfully challenged. Both elements of facility and circumvention must be present. They have been described as being present where "a person is in such a mental state that he is unable to resist pressure, and ... someone else can mould and fashion his conduct as he pleases".[96] **14–28**

It is a matter of degree whether a person is sane, facile or insane. Facility can take a number of forms. "A man may be weak and facile from want of judgement or reason ... [or] from mere nervousness and incapacity to resist solicitation".[97] Other forms include illness and bereavement[98] and alcoholism.[99] Similarly, circumvention can occur in different circumstances, such as taking a facile person to a solicitor's office where she will simply sign what she is asked to sign,[100] or where a facile person is afraid of a relative.[101]

Pascoe-Watson v Brock's Ex
1998 S.L.T. 40

Mrs Brock died of cancer and alcohol abuse in 1994. She left a will made in 1993 in which most of her estate was left to a Mrs Ritchie. Mrs Brock's cousin, Mrs Pascoe-Watson, was left £5,000 but was the main beneficiary in an earlier will which was revoked by the 1993 will. Mrs Pascoe-Watson was unhappy and raised an action to have the will reduced on the ground that Mrs Brock was facile due to dependence

---

[96] Lord Justice-Clerk Alness in *Gibson's Ex. v Anderson*, 1925 S.C. 744 at 790.
[97] Lord Justice-Clerk Inglis in *Morrison v MacLean's Trs* (1862) 24 D. 625 at 635.
[98] *Munro v Strain* (1874) 1 R. 522.
[99] *Pascoe-Watson v Brock's Ex.*, 1998 S.L.T. 40.
[100] *Wheelans v Wheelans*, 1986 S.L.T. 164.
[101] *Cairns v Marianski* (1850) 12 D. 1286.

on alcohol and Mrs Ritchie had used circumvention to make her change her will. She argued that Mrs Ritchie has dominated Mrs Brock and turned her against her family and friends and that Mrs Brock became dependent on Mrs Ritchie to supply her with whisky after her housekeeper refused to do so. It was held that the deceased's state of mind was facile, due to the dependence on alcohol and influence of Mrs Ritchie, and there were sufficient circumstances to infer circumvention.

Undue influence

14–29 Undue influence is where a person has abused a position of trust for personal benefit. A will made in such circumstances may be successfully challenged. The difference between undue influence and facility and circumvention is that the former does not require some weakness of mind in the testator.[102]

There are various relationships in which the doctrine may apply. The most obvious are a parent and child,[103] solicitor and client[104] and doctor and patient.[105] Other less obvious relationships, such as an art dealer and customer, have been included[106] and the list is not closed.

In some cases, both facility and circumvention and undue influence are present,[107] or at least pleaded,[108] and the distinction between the two can be blurred, although they are distinct.[109]

Honeyman's Exrs v Sharp
1978 S.C. 223

A widow gifted four valuable paintings to an art dealer. She had known him for seven years and it was alleged that she had been unduly influenced by him. When the gift was challenged it was argued that undue influence was irrelevant in such circumstances. It was held that where there is a relationship of adviser and advised and the advised places trust and confidence in the adviser, breach of trust for the benefit of the person in whom the trust is confided can constitute undue influence.

Formal validity

14–30 It is obvious that a will or testamentary writing must have some formal requirements to prevent any possibility of fraud because of the importance of the consequences of a will. All legal documents have certain requirements to fulfil to ensure their validity, which may vary depending on the type of legal document. If a will does not comply with these formalities, it will be invalid.[110]

---

[102] Lord President Clyde in *Ross v Gosselin's Exrs*, 1926 S.C. 325 at 334.
[103] This can operate both ways—parent influencing child, e.g. *Allan v Allan*, 1961 S.C. 200 or child influencing parent, e.g. *Grant's Exrs v Grant*, 1999 G.W.D. 36-1772.
[104] *Stewart v MacLaren*, 1920 S.C. (H.L.) 148.
[105] *Radcliffe v Price* (1902) 18 T.L.R. 466.
[106] *Honeyman's Exrs v Sharp*, 1978 S.C. 223.
[107] *Ross v Gosselin's Exrs*, 1926 S.C. 325.
[108] *Boyle v Boyle's Ex.*, 1999 S.C. 479; *Gaul v Deerey*, 2000 S.C.L.R. 407.
[109] *Horne v Whyte*, 2005 G.W.D. 28-525.
[110] *Williamson v Williamson*, 1997 S.L.T. 1044.

A will must be in writing[111] and the formal requirements are different for wills made before and after August 1, 1995 when the Requirements of Writing (Scotland) Act 1995 came into force. A verbal agreement cannot affect the terms of a will.[112]

Williamson v Williamson
1997 S.L.T. 1044

Mrs Williamson made a will in 1988. One of the witnesses to her signature on her will was a solicitor, David Carment Reid Wilson. Instead of signing his normal signature, "David C R Wilson", Mr Wilson signed, "David C R Williamson". The will was held to be invalid, as it had not been witnessed properly. If the will had been signed and witnessed after August 1, 1995, when the 1995 Act came into force, the will would have been valid although not probative.

Prior to 1995

A will executed before 1995 was valid if in one of two forms: **14–31**

- formally attested;
- holograph.

Formally attested wills

A formally attested will is a will which is signed by the testator and witnessed. Various **14–32** requirements for signing, also referred to as execution, have existed over the years and the most recent changes prior to 1995 were made in 1970.[113] Three elements were required to formally attest a will. First, the will had to be subscribed, or signed at the bottom, on every page by the testator. Second, two witnesses had to see the testator sign or acknowledge an already made signature.[114] Third, the witnesses had to sign on the last page and the witnesses had to be designed, or described sufficiently to identify them. It was usual for the date and place of signing to be added, normally in the clause at the end called the testing clause, but this was not essential.

The witnesses needed to be aged 16 or over, have legal capacity and know the testator, although an introduction from a reliable person was sufficient. It did not invalidate the process if the witness was a beneficiary in the will, although this was not advisable. The witnesses were required to sign without any delay and if they signed after the testator died, the will was invalid.[115]

There were various rules covering such matters as alterations to the will before signature and signature on behalf of a blind person or someone unable to write, known as notarial execution.[116] Certain minor defects in the execution could be cured by a statutory process.[117]

The advantage of a formally attested will was that it was probative, or self proving. This means that there was no other requirement to establish the validity of the will.

---

[111] Requirements of Writing (Scotland) 1995 Act s.1(2)(c).
[112] *McEleveen v McQuillan's Executrix*, 1999 S.L.T. (Sh. Ct) 46.
[113] Conveyancing and Feudal Reform (Scotland) Act 1970 s.44.
[114] *Lindsay v Milne*, 1995 S.L.T. 487.
[115] *Walker v Whitwell*, 1916 S.C. (H.L.) 75.
[116] Conveyancing (Scotland) Act 1924 s.18.
[117] Conveyancing (Scotland) Act 1874 s.39.

Holograph wills

14–33 A holograph will was valid if it was either in the testator's own handwriting and signed at the end of the last page, or written by some other person or typed or printed and the testator wrote in his or her own handwriting the words "adopted as holograph" followed by his or her signature.[118] Witnesses were not required. However, such a will was not probative. To enable an estate to be wound up by the process of confirmation,[119] the will had to be proved to be the will of the testator. This was done by obtaining affidavit evidence that the writing and signature on the will were those of the testator.[120]

Form of signature

14–34 The signature of the testator was the surname and a Christian name, abbreviated Christian name or the initial of the Christian name. In certain circumstances, as in correspondence with family or friends, a shortened name such as "Connie"[121] or "Mum"[122] was sufficient. An incomplete signature was invalid.[123] The testator must have actually signed. It would invalidate a signature and a will if the testator's hand was guided, as opposed to supported above the wrist.[124]

> ### Rhodes v Peterson
> #### 1972 S.L.T. 98
>
> Mrs Rhodes died in 1969. She left a will made in 1965 and had written a holograph letter to her daughter in 1966 which read, "I want you to have 63 Merchiston and all the contents, the furniture, linen, silver and all my treasures etc. ... ". She had signed it, "lots of love, Mum". It was held that the letter expressed testamentary intention and was sufficiently signed.

Post 1995

14–35 Under the Requirements of Writing (Scotland) Act 1995 a will must be in writing.[125] It will be formally valid if subscribed by the testator.[126] It is no longer necessary to sign a will on every page, or have the signature witnessed to be valid. It must be signed on every sheet, however, which could be folded up into, say, four pages.[127] The rules relating to holograph documents including wills are specifically abolished by the Act.[128]

A will which complies with these formalities will be valid, but will not be probative or self-proving. As already noted, however, an estate cannot be wound up by the process of confirmation[129] if the will is not probative without an additional court process. In such

---

[118] In an unusual case, a will was upheld as valid where the words "adopted as holograph" were typed— *McBeath's Trs v McBeath's Trs*, 1935 S.C. 471.
[119] See Executry administration, para.14–67 et seq. below.
[120] Succession (Scotland) 1964 s.21.
[121] *Draper v Thomason*, 1954 S.C. 136.
[122] *Rhodes v Peterson*, 1972 S.L.T. 98.
[123] *Donald v McGregor*, 1926 S.L.T. 103.
[124] *Noble v Noble* (1875) 3 R. 74.
[125] 1995 Act s.1(2)(c).
[126] 1995 Act s.2.
[127] See *Baird's Trs v Baird*, 1955 S.C. 286.
[128] 1995 Act s.1(3)(b).
[129] See Executry administration, para.14–67 et seq. below.

cases after 1995, it is necessary to apply to the court for a decree, or certificate, that the subscription of the testator is self-proving on production of affidavit evidence relating to the handwriting.[130] It is much easier, therefore, to ensure the will is self-proving at the time it is made. This is the normal practice of solicitors in preparing wills.

A will is self-proving after 1995 if it is signed by the testator on every page and is witnessed by one witness[131] who signs on the last page.[132] The rules regarding signature and the process of witnessing are very similar to those prior to 1995.[133] There are similar provisions for signature on behalf of a person who is blind or unable to write.[134]

If a will contains a minor defect in the way it is signed, it may be possible to apply to the court to retrospectively validate the will.[135]

Davidson v Convy
2003 S.L.T. 650

Agnes Bessie Sim died and left an unsealed envelope on which she had written "My Will" and signed her signature underneath. Inside the envelope was a single sheet of paper which was written in her handwriting and disposed of her whole estate. The court held that the envelope and sheet of paper taken together constituted a valid testamentary writing.

Mutual wills

A mutual will is a will by more than one person in one will document which is executed by **14–36** both parties. They were popular at one time, particularly with married couples who wanted to leave a will in identical terms, but they are not popular now. There is a general presumption that a mutual will is simply two different wills in one document, but there can be problems in relation to the revocability or otherwise of such wills.[136] They are not recommended.

Informal writings

Formal wills often include a provision that future informal writings may be incorporated **14–37** as part of the will. Such provisions normally refer to future informal testamentary writings subscribed by the testator. Such provisions need to be carefully worded and the informal writing needs to be properly linked to the will.[137] Similarly, but less frequently, later writings may adopt earlier writings.[138] Such informal writings can cause difficulties and are not always recommended. It is much better to make a formal codicil or a new will where minor changes to a will are required.

---

[130] 1995 Act s.4.
[131] After 1995, two witnesses are no longer required.
[132] 1995 Act s.3(1)(a) and (2).
[133] 1995 Act s.7.
[134] 1995 Act s.9.
[135] Requirements of Writing (Scotland) Act 1995 s.4.
[136] See Revocation of wills, para.14–39 et seq. below.
[137] *Waterson's Trs v St. Giles Club*, 1943 S.C. 369.
[138] *Craik's Exrs v Samson*, 1929 S.L.T. 592.

Codicils

14–38 If a will is to be amended in some minor respect, a codicil is frequently used. This amends the terms of the will in certain respects and the remainder of the will still applies. The two documents are taken together to indicate the intention of the deceased. It is possible to have more than one codicil but it is often better to make a new will instead.

Key Concepts

The law of **testate** succession governs situations where the deceased has left a will or other testamentary writing.

The **validity** of wills and other testamentary writings depends on a number of factors which fall into three areas:

- intention to test;
- capacity;
- formal validity.

A person must be aged 12 or older to have **capacity** to make a will and must be of sound mind. A will may be challenged where it has been made under circumstances amounting to **facility** and **circumvention** or **undue influence**.

A will must be in **writing**.

A will executed **before 1995** was valid if in one of two forms:

- formally attested;
- holograph.

A will executed **after 1995** need not be witnessed for validity. It must be signed on every sheet. It must be signed on every page and witnessed by one witness to be self-proving.

REVOCATION OF WILLS

14–39 A will is not effective until the testator dies. A person can, and some people do, change a will as often as they wish. Even if a will states that it is irrevocable, this cannot bind the testator and the will can be revoked. If a person contracts with someone that they will leave a will in certain terms, the position is different. As this is a contract the testator will be bound.[139] There would be nothing to prevent the testator disposing of the assets covered by the contract during their lifetime, however, as the contract would only take effect on death. In a mutual will,[140] there may be a contractual term not to revoke the will without the consent of the other party to the will.[141]

Revocation of a will may be express or implied.

---

[139] *Paterson v Paterson* (1893) 20 R. 484.
[140] See Mutual wills, para.14–36 above.
[141] *Dewar's Trs v Dewar's Trs*, 1950 S.L.T. 191.

Express revocation

A will may be expressly revoked in two ways. These are: **14–40**

- making a new will;
- destruction of the will.

A new will

If a testator makes a new will, the will usually contains a clause revoking all previous wills **14–41** and testamentary writings. If properly worded, revocation will take place but care is required in the wording. The term "testamentary writings" is wider than "wills" and where a later will contained a clause revoking "all wills previously executed by me", this did not revoke a valid bequest of a stamp collection, which was not in a will.[142] If there is more than one earlier will care is required to correctly identify which will is being revoked.[143]

Destruction of a will

If a testator physically destroys a will or instructs an agent to do so and this is done, the **14–42** will no longer exists and is revoked by the express action of the testator. The testator must deliberately intend to destroy the will and destruction while insane, drunk or in a fit of rage is insufficient for revocation.[144] The destruction may not be complete destruction, but some symbolic act such as cutting off a seal[145] or cutting out clauses on a copy of a will with a written explanation.[146] There must be express instruction to an agent to destroy and instructing a solicitor to make a new will does not imply an instruction to destroy an earlier will.[147]

> ### Bruce's Judicial Factor v Lord Advocate
> ### 1969 S.C. 296
>
> Mr Bruce made a will in 1945. In 1949 he instructed his solicitors to make a new will which disposed of all his estate and revoked all previous testamentary writings. He did not expressly instruct his solicitors to destroy the 1945 will. When he died the solicitors were still holding the 1945 will but the 1949 will could not be found. It was held that the 1949 will was presumed to have been intentionally destroyed by Mr Bruce and the 1945 will regulated the disposal of his estate.

If a will is accidentally destroyed or lost, an action known as "proving the tenor" is required to allow the will's provisions to be proved and the will to be given effect. The onus is on the party wishing the will to be reinstated to prove that the testator did not intend to destroy it and what the terms of the will were.[148]

---

[142] *Clark's Exrs v Clark*, 1943 S.C. 216.
[143] *Gordon's Exs v MacQueen*, 1907 S.C. 373.
[144] *Laing v Bruce* (1838) 1 D. 59.
[145] *Nasmyth v Hare's Trs* (1821) 1 Sh. App. 65.
[146] *Thomson's Trs v Bowhill Baptist Church*, 1956 S.L.T. 302.
[147] *Bruce's Judicial Factor v Lord Advocate*, 1969 S.C. 296.
[148] *Morrison v Morrison*, 1992 G.W.D. 23-1350.

Where part of a will has been destroyed by the testator deleting part of it, proof is required that there was no intention to revoke the deleted words,[149] as where a married woman deleted her married name in her will, as she was reverting to her maiden name.[150]

Implied revocation

14–43 A will may be impliedly revoked in two ways. These are:

- making a new will;
- birth of children to the testator in certain circumstances.

A new will

14–44 Where a new will does not contain an express revocation of previous wills and testamentary writings, an earlier will may be revoked by implication. The general rule is that in such a case both wills must be read together to establish the intention of the testator.[151]

The position has been clearly stated that "it is a well established principle of the law of Scotland that where a person deceased has left various writings, probative in themselves, for disposing of his or her property, they are to be understood as constituting one testamentary settlement in so far as they have not been revoked and are not inconsistent with each other."[152]

If the terms are inconsistent, the later will may revoke the earlier. For instance, if a will made in 2004 leaves someone a legacy of £5,000 and a later will is made in 2006 which leaves that same person a legacy of £10,000, the £10,000 legacy revokes the £5,000 legacy and will apply. The onus of proof is on the person seeking to establish implied revocation.[153]

Birth of children to the testator

14–45 If a testator has a child subsequent to making a will, the will may be impliedly revoked on the principle that it is presumed that the testator would not want to omit the child from the testamentary provision.[154] The principle does not apply automatically, but is a rebuttable presumption. The only person who can rely on the presumption is a child born after the will.[155] The presumption can be rebutted by proof that the testator deliberately intended to omit to benefit the child.[156]

It should be noted that a will is not impliedly revoked on the marriage or divorce of the testator.[157]

---

[149] *Pattison's Trs v University of Edinburgh* (1888) 16 R. 73.
[150] *Fotheringham's Trs v Reid*, 1936 S.C. 831.
[151] *Duthie's Exrs v Taylor*, 1986 S.L.T. 142.
[152] *Stoddart v Grant* (1852) 1 Macq. 163.
[153] *Mitchell's Administratrix v Edinburgh Royal Infirmary*, 1928 S.C. 47.
[154] *Greenan v Courtney*, 2007 S.L.T. 355.
[155] *Stevenson's Trs v Stevenson*, 1932 S.C. 657.
[156] *Stuart-Gordon v Stuart-Gordon* (1899) 1 F. 1005.
[157] Unlike the position in England.

Revival of revoked wills

If a later will which revoked an earlier will is revoked in turn, there is a possibility that the **14–46** earlier will may revive. The case law is divided on this issue, with some cases in favour of revival[158] and others against.[159] If the earlier will has been destroyed, revival is impossible and a clause which revokes previous wills should also authorise their destruction.

Key Concepts

A will is not **effective** until the testator dies. A person can **change** a will as often as he or she wishes.

A will may be **expressly revoked** by making a new will or by destruction of the will.

A will may be **impliedly revoked** by the making of a new will or by birth of children to the testator in certain circumstances.

WILL SUBSTITUTES

The usual way to leave all or part of an estate to beneficiaries and avoid the rules of **14–47** intestate succession applying is to make a will or other testamentary writing. There are other methods to achieve this which are recognised under Scots law. These are generally known as will substitutes, or quasi-wills. These are:

- special destinations;
- life assurance policies;
- nominations;
- gifts in contemplation of death;
- rearrangements after death.

Special destinations

Special destinations take two forms known as a destination-over or a survivorship des- **14–48** tination. Destinations-over, where property is left to one person whom failing another, are now rare.[160] Survivorship destinations, where property is in the name of two (or more) persons and the survivor (or survivors) remain common. They are mainly used in heritable property. The way they operate is that if such a survivorship destination is placed in the title of the property, on the death of the first person the property automatically passes to the survivor without the need for any formal procedures. The usual situation for their use is when a house is bought by a husband and wife, and the title to the house is placed in their joint names and to the survivor.[161]

The revocability of survivorship destinations is a problem area. It is clear that a party to the destination can evacuate or revoke the destination by disposing of their share during their lifetime.[162] On death, whether or not the destination can be revoked, depends on whether or not the destination is regarded as contractual. Normally this depends on who paid for the property. Where one party contributed the whole price, that party will be

---

[158] *Scott's Judicial Factor v Johnson*, 1971 S.L.T. (Notes) 41.
[159] *Elder's Trs v Elder* (1895) 22 R. 505.
[160] Except in wills—see Destinations-over, para.14–60 below.
[161] Although the property is said to be in joint names, it is common property—see Chapter 15.
[162] *Steele v Caldwell*, 1979 S.L.T. 228.

entitled to revoke the destination by a will.[163] Where both parties contributed to the price, or the property was gifted, the destination will be regarded as contractual and a will cannot revoke the destination.[164]

If a destination is revocable on death, it must be properly revoked by a specific reference to the destination and the declared intention on the part of the testator to evacuate it.[165] This is strictly construed.[166] Property which passes under a contractual destination on death is subject to the debts of the deceased.[167]

The operation of survivorship destinations can cause difficulties and unintended results. In particular, if the title is to be changed from joint names and the survivor to a single name, which may happen when a couple split up, great care is needed in the wording to achieve this.[168] If a will is made at the time the property is purchased, there is no need for the destination and potential problems will be avoided.

Gardner's Exrs v Raeburn
1996 S.L.T. 745

Mr and Mrs Gardner bought a house together and the title was put in their joint names with a survivorship destination. They later separated and divorced. As part of the divorce settlement, Mr Gardner paid Mrs Gardiner £40,000 and Mrs Gardner conveyed her one half share of the house to Mr Gardner. When Mr Gardner died his ex-wife claimed that his original one half share of the house passed to her under the survivorship destination. This claim succeeded despite the fact that she had received £40,000. To evacuate the destination in the transfer of the property at the time of the divorce settlement Mr and Mrs Gardner should have jointly conveyed the whole house to Mr Gardner.

The position has been improved when there is a divorce. A divorce or a dissolution of a civil partnership now automatically revokes an unevacuated survivorship destination.[169]

Life assurance policies

14–49 It is possible for a person to take out a life policy on their own life for the benefit of someone else. On death, the proceeds of the policy will be paid direct to the other person and will not form part of the deceased's estate. Certain policies under the Married Women's Policies of Assurance (Scotland) Act 1880 operate in this way.[170]

---

[163] *Brown's Tr. v Brown*, 1944 S.L.T. 215.
[164] *Perrett's Trs v Perrett*, 1909 S.C. 522.
[165] 1964 Act s.30.
[166] *Marshall v Marshall's Ex.*, 1987 S.L.T. 49.
[167] *Fleming's Tr. v Fleming*, 2000 S.L.T. 406, overruling *Barclay's Bank v McGreish*, 1983 S.L.T. 344.
[168] See, e.g. *Gardner's Exrs v Raeburn*, 1996 S.L.T. 745 and *Redfern's Exrs v Redfern*, 1996 S.L.T. 900.
[169] Family Law (Scotland) Act 2006 s.19.
[170] 1880 Act s.4, as amended by the Married Women's Policies of Assurance (Amendment) (Scotland) Act 1980.

Nominations

Nominations relate to money deposited with certain small savings institutions. On death **14–50** the money is paid to the person nominated by the deceased. Nominations are of limited scope with a maximum sum allowed of £5,000.[171]

Gifts in contemplation of death

These gifts are made during the lifetime of the granter to a person on condition that the **14–51** person survives the granter.[172] The gift can be revoked by the granter at any time before they die. Such gifts are rare.

Rearrangements on death

It is possible for all the beneficiaries under a will to rearrange the division of an estate after **14–52** the death.[173] No one can be compelled to take what is due to them under a will or on intestacy. A rearrangement is sometimes effected formally for tax purposes, under what is known as a deed of family arrangement. To be effective for such tax purposes, which may include a reduction of inheritance tax, the deed must be made within two years of the date of death and intimation made to the Capital Taxes Office within six months of the date of the deed.[174]

Key Concepts

Other legally recognised methods of avoiding the rules of intestate succession are known as **will substitutes** or **quasi-wills**. They are:

- special destinations (destinations-over or survivorship destinations);
- life assurance policies (taken out for the benefit of someone else);
- nominations (to a maximum of £5,000);
- gifts in contemplation of death;
- rearrangements after death.

INTERPRETATION OF WILLS

How a will is interpreted, or construed, is obviously important in testate succession. The **14–53** fundamental principle is that the intention of the testator must be interpreted from what has actually been written.[175] Normally extrinsic evidence will not be allowed to ascertain the intention, but it may be in certain circumstances. There are a number of rules of interpretation which can be applied to wills generally, but they are only applied to aid interpretation. The terms of the will itself is the primary means of interpretation.

---

[171] Administration of Estates (Small Payments) Act 1965 ss.2 and 6, Administration of Estates (Small Payments) (Increase of Limit) Order 1984 (SI 1984/539).
[172] *Morris v Riddick* (1867) 5 M. 1036.
[173] *Gray v Gray's Trs* (1877) 4 R. 378.
[174] Inheritance Tax Act 1984 s.142.
[175] e.g. *Fortunato's Judicial Factor v Fortunato*, 1981 S.L.T. 277.

"We must find all the intention of the testatrix within the four corners of the deed which she has legally executed ... It is only if the terms of the deed appear to be in themselves doubtful in their import or legal construction, that it is either necessary or legitimate to affect or explain them by extraneous circumstances."[176]

There are three rules to aid interpretation. These are:

- the will should be read as a whole;
- the will should be interpreted to avoid intestacy;
- words should be given their ordinary meaning.

The will should be read as a whole

14–54 A will should be read as a whole, including later or ancillary codicils or other testamentary writings, to establish the testator's whole intention. Any apparently conflicting intentions should be reconciled as far as possible. Where a later deed refers to a bequest in an earlier deed, which contains no such bequest, the bequest will be given effect.[177] If a later deed conflicts with an earlier one, such as in the amount of a legacy, the later one will be given effect.[178]

> ### Forbes' Trs v Forbes
> #### (1893) 20 R. 248
>
> In an ante nuptial contract of marriage, a husband bound himself to pay his wife a yearly annuity of £100 after he died. In a later will he referred to this contract as providing for payment of a yearly annuity of £150. It was held that the widow was entitled to an annuity of £150.

The will should be construed to avoid intestacy

14–55 A court will do its best to avoid an intestacy where there is a will, on the grounds that intestacy is not what a testator intends. To do otherwise has been referred to as a "counsel of despair".[179] Accordingly, an interpretation which avoids intestacy may be given, even if the usual rules of interpretation are not strictly followed.[180]

> ### Magistrates of Dundee v Morris
> #### (1858) 3 Macq. 134
>
> Trustees were directed in a will to set up a school. No sum was stated for this purpose, but the will did specify the size of the school and the size of the legacy necessary could be worked out. The legacy was held to be valid and not void from uncertainty. The school was built and is now Morgan Academy in Dundee.

---

[176] Lord Justice-Clerk Moncrieff in *Blair v Blair* (1849) 12 D. 97 at 107.
[177] *Grant v Grant* (1851) 13 D. 805.
[178] *Forbes' Trs v Forbes* (1893) 20 R. 248.
[179] Lord McLaren in *MacDuff v Spence's Trs*, 1909 S.C. 178 at 184.
[180] e.g. *McGinn's Executix v McGinn*, 1994 S.L.T. 2, and *Magistrates of Dundee v Morris* (1858) 3 Macq. 134.

Words should be given their ordinary meaning

Words are interpreted to have their ordinary meaning.[181] Where words are used which **14–56** have a technical legal meaning, that technical meaning will normally be applied because they are used in a will.[182]

If the estate or part of the estate is left to a class, such as children or nieces and nephews, the question arises as to when the class is established. The normal rule is that the class is established and identified as at the date of death.[183] Therefore, a legacy left to the nephews and nieces of the testator will include a nephew or niece born after the will was made, but before the testator died. Care is required in properly identifying a class and some words, such as "dependants", have no precise meaning and a legacy to dependants will be void due to uncertainty.[184]

> ### Robertson's Judicial Factor v Robertson
> ### 1968 S.L.T. 32
>
> In a holograph will Miss Robertson made a provision for her nephew and niece "and their dependants". Lord President Clyde stated "In our system of law the word . . . is . . . too vague a description . . . to ascertain what class of persons was intended to be benefited there by." He held the bequest to dependants was void from uncertainty.

Use of extrinsic evidence

Extrinsic evidence can be admitted for a number of purposes: **14–57**

- to translate a will in a foreign language;
- to establish whether a deed is a will;
- to interpret words differently from their ordinary meaning;
- to rebut the presumption against double provision;
- to prove what the testator knew about the property;
- to identify the subject or object of a legacy.

It is obvious that extrinsic evidence in the form of a translation is required to translate a will in a foreign language. Similarly, if a will is in the form of a code, this will be allowed.[185]

Extrinsic evidence may be required to show that a deed is not a will but intended as a draft, or has been revoked.[186] It may also show that the testator lacked capacity, or has been subject to facility and circumvention or undue influence.[187]

Where a word has an ordinary meaning and a possible secondary meaning, extrinsic evidence may be allowed to show that the secondary meaning was intended by the testator. This has been used to interpret the word "children" as including grandchildren.[188]

There is a presumption that two identical legacies in a will is a mistake and only one is payable. This can be rebutted by extrinsic evidence.

---

[181] *Young v Robertson* (1862) 4 Macq. 314.
[182] *Macdonald's Trs v Macdonald*, 1974 S.L.T. 87.
[183] *Gregory's Trs v Alison* (1889) 16 R. (H.L.) 10.
[184] *Robertson's Judicial Factor v Robertson*, 1968 S.L.T. 32.
[185] *Goblet v Beechey* (1829) 3 Sim. 24.
[186] See Revocation of wills, para.14–39 et seq. above.
[187] See Capacity, para.14–27 et seq. above.
[188] *Yule's Trs*, 1981 S.L.T. 250.

If there is a question as to whether or not the testator knew that they owned property bequeathed in their will, extrinsic evidence may be allowed. If a person bequeaths property which is not owned, the normal rule is that this was a mistake and the legacy falls. Extrinsic evidence, however, may show that the testator knew the correct position and deliberately made the legacy. In such a case, the executor must try to acquire the object of the legacy and give it to the legatee. If this is not possible, the value of the object must be paid to the legatee.[189]

If there is an ambiguity as to the subject or object of a legacy, extrinsic evidence may be allowed. This may be used where there is a minor error in identifying the beneficiaries.[190]

Keiller v Thomson's Trs
(1824) 3 S. 279

Mr Thomson died leaving a legacy to "Janet Keiller or Williamson, confectioner in Dundee". There was no such person but there was an Agnes Keiller or Wedderspoon who was married to a confectioner in Dundee. There was also a sister Janet Keiller married to a seaman named Whitton. The court allowed extrinsic evidence, which showed that Mr Thomson had intended the legacy to go to Agnes Keiller.

Mr Thomson was not very good with names and had also left a legacy to "William Keiller, confectioner in Dundee". No such person existed. There was a William Keiller who was a confectioner in Montrose and a James Keiller who was a confectioner in Dundee. The court again allowed extrinsic evidence, which showed that Mr Thomson had intended the legacy to go to James Keiller.[191]

Key Concepts

The terms of the will itself is the primary means of **interpretation**. The three rules to aid interpretation are:

- the will should be read as a whole;
- the will should be interpreted to avoid intestacy;
- words should be given their ordinary meaning.

Extrinsic evidence can also be admitted for a number of purposes.

LEGACIES

14–58 Legacies fall into three main categories. These are:

- specific or special legacies;
- general legacies;
- residue.

---

[189] *Meeres v Dowell's Ex.*, 1923 S.L.T. 184.
[190] *Keiller v Thomson's Trs* (1824) 3 S. 279.
[191] *Keiller v Thomson's Trs* (1826) 4 S. 730.

A specific legacy is a legacy of a specific, identifiable object such as a house or a car. If the object of the legacy no longer exists or no longer belongs to the testator, the legacy will fall under the principle of ademption.[192]

Ogilvie-Forbes' Trs v Ogilvie-Forbes
1955 S.C. 405

Sir George Ogilvie-Forbes made a will in 1952 which gave his daughter a liferent of his mansion house and other land. Before he died, he transferred the mansion house and other land to a company in which he retained a controlling interest. It was held that the transfer to the company meant he no longer owned the mansion house and other land at the time he died and the legacy had adeemed. The daughter did not receive the liferent.

If a specific legacy indicates the source of a particular object, for instance, a sum of money from a certain bank account, this is known as a demonstrative legacy. If there is insufficient money to pay that sum in that bank account at the date of death, the legatee will have a claim against the residue of the estate.

A general legacy is a legacy of a subject which is no different from any other subjects of the same kind and has no specific, individual characteristics. A legacy of a sum of money, also known as a pecuniary legacy, is a typical general legacy.

A legacy of the residue is a legacy of all of the estate that remains after everything else has been deducted. These deductions cover all debts and other expenses, taxes, claims for legal rights and other legacies. Any legacies which have lapsed, or failed, will form part of the residue. If there is no legacy of the residue, the residue will fall into intestacy and be divided accordingly.

Cumulative and substitutional legacies

If there is more than one legacy to the same person, the legacies may be cumulative when **14–59** both will be paid or substitutional when only one will be paid. The intention of the testator may be clearly expressed, but if the intention is not clear, certain presumptions are applied. If a deed contains identical legacies, they are presumed to be substitutional and only one will be paid on the ground that the testator is presumed to have repeated the legacy through forgetfulness. For instance, if a will includes legacies of £500 to a number of people and the same person is mentioned twice, £500 only will be received by that person. This is a presumption only which can be rebutted.[193] If the legacies in the same deed are different they will be presumed to be cumulative and both will be paid. If there is more than one legacy, in more than one deed, they will be presumed to be cumulative whether they are identical or not.[194]

Destinations–over

A destination-over is a provision in a will in favour of one person with the possibility of **14–60** another taking the legacy after or instead of that person. The wording is in the form of a legacy to "X whom failing Y". X is the primary legatee and is known as the institute. Y is

---

[192] *Ogilvie-Forbes' Trs v Ogilvie-Forbes*, 1955 S.C. 405.
[193] *Gillies v Glasgow Royal Infirmary*, 1960 S.C. 438, although the facts were unusual and unusually interpreted.
[194] *Edinburgh Royal Infirmary v Muir's Trs* (1881) 9 R. 352.

known either as a conditional institute or alternative legatee, or as a substitute or second successive legatee. If X dies and does not inherit, in both cases Y will inherit in his or her place. If X does survive and inherit, if Y is a conditional institute he or she will have no further right. If Y is a substitute, however, he or she will take the legacy in turn on surviving the death of X, provided X has not disposed of the subject of the legacy during lifetime or under his or her will.

Whether Y is a conditional institute or substitute depends on the terms of the will[195] or on certain presumptions if the will is not specific. Where the legacy is of heritable property, the presumption is for conditional institution and where it is of moveable property, the presumption is for substitution.[196]

Division of legacies

14–61 Where a legacy is left to a number of legatees, it is presumed that all the legatees will take an equal share if the will does not provide to the contrary. This is known as division *per capita*, by head. The alternative division is *per stirpes,* by branch, which may be important in relation to certain categories of legatees. For instance, if a testator leaves a legacy to the children of a brother and sister, the brother may have two children and the sister have three children. If the division is per capita each of the five children will get one-fifth but if the division is *per stirpes* each of the brothers' children will get one-half of one-half, i.e. one-quarter, and each of the sisters' children will get one-third of one-half, i.e. one-sixth. It is important, therefore, to specifically provide for *per stirpes* division in the will if this is intended, because the presumption is for per capita division.

Children of a legatee

14–62 Where a legacy is made to someone who dies before the testator, that legacy will normally lapse. There is an exception to this rule in certain circumstances when an implied gift to the children of a predeceasing legatee is presumed. This only applies to legatees who are close relatives of the testator. It applies to the testator's own children and remoter descendants including grandchildren[197] and more remote descendants.[198] It also applies to nephews and nieces on the basis that the testator is a parent figure to them. This will be presumed unless it can be shown that the testator was not viewed as such.[199]

Where this presumption applies, such children will take precedence over any conditional institute in a destination-over.[200] The presumption can be rebutted, for instance, where there is separate provision for the children of the legatee.[201]

Conditions attached to legacies

14–63 A will may attach conditions to a legacy. These conditions must be satisfied before the legatee can take the legacy. Certain conditions may be ineffective and, if so, the condition is ignored and the legacy is unconditional. A condition will be ineffective where it is impossible to perform, unlawful or against public policy, such as attempting to prevent

---

195 *Simpson's Trs v Simpson* (1889) 17 R. 248.
196 *Crumpton's Judicial Factor v Barnardo's Homes*, 1917 S.C. 713.
197 *Mowbray v Scougall* (1834) 12 S. 910.
198 *Grant v Brooke* (1882) 10 R. 92.
199 *Knox's Ex. v Knox*, 1941 S.C. 532.
200 *MacGregor's Trs v Gray*, 1969 S.L.T. 355.
201 *Greig v Malcolm* (1835) 13 S. 607.

marriage or cohabitation by the legatee.[202] If the condition is inconsistent with the legacy, it will also be ineffective under the doctrine of repugnancy.[203]

There are three types of conditions:

- potestative;
- suspensive; and
- resolutive.

Potestative conditions are those which require the legatee to do something before the legacy can be taken, such as moving to live with the testator.

A suspensive condition is one where the making over or payment of the legacy is postponed until the condition is fulfilled, such as attaining a certain age. If the condition is not met, the legacy will fall.

A resolutive condition is one where the legacy may lapse if a certain event takes place, for instance if the legatee remarries.

Interest and abatement

Interest is payable on a legacy from the date of death until payment. There is no fixed rate **14–64** of interest and the rate paid should be equivalent to what the estate earned or should have earned during the administration if it was properly administered.[204] It is open to the testator to provide that a legacy is paid without interest.

If there is insufficient estate to pay all the debts and other expenses, any tax and all the legacies, the legacies must be reduced under the doctrine of abatement. The order in which legacies are abated is:

- residuary legacies;
- general legacies equally;
- demonstrative legacies do not abate until the specified fund is exhausted but then abate like general legacies;
- specific legacies.

If the legacies are numbered in a will this will not alter this priority.[205]

Key Concepts

Legacies fall into three main categories. A **specific legacy** is a legacy of a specific, identifiable object. A **general legacy** is a legacy of a subject which is no different from any other subject of the same kind and has no specific, individual characteristics. A legacy of the **residue** is a legacy of all of the estate that remains after everything else has been deducted.

A will may contain a **destination-over** which provides an alternative legatee.

Legacies may be divided either **per capita,** per head or *per stirpes*, per branch.

A will may attach **conditions** to a legacy (potestative, suspensive or resolutive). These conditions must be satisfied before the legatee can take the legacy.

---

[202] *Aird's Exrs v Aird*, 1949 S.C. 154.
[203] *Miller's Trs v Miller* (1890) 18 R. 301.
[204] *Kearon v Thomson's Trs*, 1949 S.C. 654.
[205] *McConnel v McConnel's Trs*, 1939 S.N. 31.

> **Interest** is payable on a legacy from the date of death until payment.
> If there is insufficient estate to pay all the legacies, the legacies must be reduced under the doctrine of **abatement**.

VESTING AND ACCRETION

Vesting

14–65 Vesting takes place in two situations. These are vesting in an executor and vesting in a beneficiary. Vesting in an executor is where the whole estate passes to the executor for the purpose of administration of the estate.[206] It gives the executor the title to administer the property which comprises the estate.[207] Vesting in a beneficiary is a more difficult concept.

A legacy or a share in the testate estate vests in the beneficiary when the beneficiary obtains a completed right to it. Vesting is different from actual receipt or payment. A beneficiary may have a vested right in the benefit of a legacy or share of the intestate estate before receiving possession or payment of the benefit. This enables the beneficiary to dispose of the benefit as part of his or her property either during lifetime or in a will.

There are various rules which apply in vesting. These are:

- the intention of the testator is paramount;
- early vesting is presumed;
- suspensive conditions postpone vesting.

The intention of the testator is, as always, paramount and a will may expressly provide for vesting.

Where the intention is not clear, an interpretation which produces an earlier date of vesting will be presumed. A legacy without any conditions and a share of the intestate estate vest in the beneficiary at the earliest possible date, which is the date of death of the testator.

A suspensive condition in any legacy, which means that the legatee will not get the legacy until the condition is met, postpones vesting. Conversely, a resolutive condition does not postpone vesting, but is said to vest subject to defeasance because the legacy may lapse on the happening of a certain event.

Accretion

14–66 Where there is a legacy in favour of more than one person, each of the legatees will take a proportionate share of the legacy by surviving the testator. A problem arises if one or more of the legatees die before the testator. The question is whether the share of a predeceasing legatee forms part of his or her estate or whether it passes to the surviving legatee or legatees under the principle of accretion. This depends on whether the legacy is joint or several. If it is joint, the legacy remains individual and accresces or passes to the surviving legatee or legatees by accretion. If it is several, it will not accress.

The will may make express provision for this and in the simple case of a legacy to "X and Y" this will be joint and accretion will apply. Conversely, a destination-over will exclude accretion. Accretion will also be excluded if there are what are known as words of

---

[206] Succession (Scotland) Act 1964 s.14(1).
[207] See Executry administration, para.14–67 et seq. below.

severance such as "equally among them" or "in equal shares".[208] If the wording is "equally among them and to the survivors or survivor" then accretion will take place.

Key Concepts

Vesting takes place in two situations. These are vesting in an executor and vesting in a beneficiary. The estate of the deceased vests in the executor for the purpose of administering the estate. Vesting in a beneficiary is different from receipt or payment and is when the beneficiary obtains a completed right. Vesting in a beneficiary may be at the date of death or postponed.

Accretion may apply where there is a legacy in favour of more than one person and one person dies before the testator.

EXECUTRY ADMINISTRATION

When a person dies, the process of winding up the deceased's estate is known as executry **14–67** administration. The first stage is ascertaining the assets and debts or liabilities of the deceased. Then the assets must be ingathered, debts and any tax due paid and the estate distributed to the beneficiaries. The person responsible for this is the deceased's executor. Under the Succession (Scotland) Act 1964, the estate of a deceased vests in the executor by the process of confirmation for the purpose of administering the estate.[209]

Executors

An executor may be appointed by a will, known as an executor-nominate or by the sheriff **14–68** court, known as an executor-dative. An executor is not entitled to payment for acting as executor unless there is a provision in the will for this. A beneficiary may be an executor but cannot derive any personal benefit at the expense of the estate.[210] There is no limit on the number of executors. A majority of the executors is a quorum unless the will provides to the contrary.[211] The executor is only liable for his or her own acts or omissions. If an executor deals with the estate without obtaining confirmation, he or she may be liable for all the debts of the deceased by being what is known as a vitious intromittor.

An executor-nominate is appointed in the testator's will. If the testator fails to appoint an executor or the executor has died or is otherwise unable to act, an executor-dative will be appointed by the sheriff court. A petition is lodged in the sheriff court with a bond of caution from an insurance company guaranteeing that the executor-dative will perform his or her duties honestly.[212] There is a set order for who may be appointed an executor-dative as follows:

- general disponees, universal legatees or residuary legatees;
- the deceased's spouse or civil partner where prior rights exhaust the whole estate;

---

[208] *Paxton's Trs v Cowie* (1886) 13 R. 1191.
[209] 1964 Act s.14(1).
[210] *Clark v Clark's Exs*, 1989 S.L.T. 665.
[211] Trusts (Scotland) Act 1921 s.3(c).
[212] A bond of caution is not necessary where the executor-dative is a spouse and prior rights exhaust the estate. A bond of caution is not necessary for an executor-nominate. The Scottish Law Commission recommends that bonds of caution are abolished. See Scottish Law Commission, *Report on Succession* (2009), Scot. Law Com. No.215.

- the person who is entitled to inherit the free estate[213];
- the deceased's creditors.

Assets and debts

Assets

14–69 The estate of the deceased includes all property belonging to the deceased and certain personal obligations as at the date of death. The property of the deceased extends to all types of property, including the deceased's *pro indiviso* share of property held in common with others.[214] Where there is a special destination, the deceased's share of the property held under the destination forms part of the estate and is taxable but passes automatically under the destination.[215] It does not vest in the executor and confirmation is not required to transfer this asset to the survivor in the destination.

Certain property rights which belong to the deceased, however, will be extinguished on his or her death. A liferent in the sole name of the deceased will come to an end.[216] Occupancy rights under matrimonial homes legislation will also come to an end.[217] A benefit payable on death under an insurance policy on the life of the deceased may not be payable if the deceased committed suicide and there is express or implied provision in the policy to this effect.

Property rights in leases form part of the deceased's estate and vest in the executor on confirmation.[218] Whether the lease comes to an end or not depends on whether it is the landlord or tenant who has died and the terms of the lease. On the death of the landlord the position is straightforward. The landlord owns the property and it forms part of the estate. The tenant will have the right to continue as tenant.[219] If the tenant dies and the lease expressly prohibits transfer on death, the lease will come to an end unless the landlord consents otherwise. If there is no express prohibition on transfer, the executor will transfer the lease to the legatee if the estate is testate or to the person entitled to succeed if the estate is intestate.[220]

A deceased's claim in delict or for patrimonial loss, which is financial loss by damage to earning capacity or property, forms part of the deceased's estate. A deceased's claim for *solatium*, which is pain and suffering, provided it relates to the period between an injury and death, also forms part of the estate.

A deceased's contractual rights will also form part of the estate, unless they are regarded as personal to the deceased, such as a contract of employment.

Debts

14–70 When a person dies, his or her estate is liable for his or her debts. Inheritance to the estate only takes place after payment of debts, funeral expenses and the expenses of winding up the estate. After an executor obtains confirmation, he or she is liable for the debts of the deceased up to the value of the estate. If the estate is insolvent, he or she must proceed to have a judicial factor or trustee in bankruptcy appointed.[221]

---

[213] Under the 1964 Act s.2.
[214] See Chapter 12.
[215] See Will substitutes, para.14–47 et seq. above.
[216] See Chapter 13.
[217] See Chapter 15.
[218] 1964 Act ss.14(1) and 36(2).
[219] Leases Act 1449, see Chapter 12 on Property.
[220] 1964 Act s.16.
[221] Bankruptcy (Scotland) Act 1985 s.8(4).

Debts intimated to the executor within six months of the death rank equally, with the exception of certain limited privileged debts such as funeral expenses which can be paid immediately. If an executor pays out debts or legacies before six months after the death, he or she will be personally liable to a creditor who appears within this six month period. Conversely, if he or she pays out after six months in good faith and a creditor subsequently appears, he or she is not liable.[222]

The order of ranking for debts is:

- expenses of sequestration;
- deathbed and funeral expenses;
- secured debts, such as a standard security over a house;
- preferred debts, such as tax and social security contributions due in the 12 months before death and employees' wages for four months before death;
- ordinary debts.

Moveable debts are paid out of moveable property and heritable debts out of heritable property. Where a debt is secured over a particular asset, such as a loan over a house, the person who inherits the house will take the house subject to the debt, unless the will provides otherwise.

Inheritance tax

Inheritance tax is a debt on the estate. It is chargeable on the value of the deceased's estate **14–71**
at the time of death, after deduction of debts and funeral expenses.[223] The executors and beneficiaries are liable to account for the tax to the estate confirmed or inherited, although the executor is liable first as confirmation cannot be obtained until the executor has accounted to the Capital Taxes Office for inheritance tax. Inheritance tax is paid out of residue unless there is a direction in a will to pay a legacy subject to deduction of inheritance tax.

Confirmation

Confirmation is the process whereby the commissary court confirms the appointment of **14–72**
the executor and authorises administration of the estate as detailed in the inventory of assets prepared by the executor. In most cases an executor must produce confirmation issued by the commissary court to uplift the assets of the deceased in the United Kingdom. The procedures for uplifting assets of the deceased situated abroad can be complicated and depend on the law on administration of estates in the foreign country. An executor must apply for confirmation within six months of assuming possession and management of an estate. Commissary courts form part of most sheriff courts. Applications for confirmation must be made by a solicitor or licensed executry practitioner.

Confirmation is not required where there is a survivorship destination or in respect of certain small sums. Where property is held under a survivorship destination it will pass automatically under the destination.[224] Payment of certain small sums not exceeding £5,000 may be made without production of confirmation in respect of certain savings bank accounts and financial savings certificates, building society deposits and government

---

[222] *Beith v Mackenzie* (1875) 3 R. 185.
[223] Inheritance Tax Act 1984 s.1.
[224] See Special destinations, para.14–48 above.

stock.[225] If an estate is a small estate where the gross amount does not exceed £36,000,[226] a simplified procedure can be adopted in which it is not necessary to employ a solicitor to obtain confirmation and assistance in winding up the estate is given by the commissary court.

Distribution of the estate

14–73 Once the executor has obtained confirmation, the confirmation is exhibited to all the holders of the assets such as banks, insurance companies and company registrars to enable the executor to ingather all the assets. Once all the assets have been ingathered the executor distributes the estate. The order of distribution is:

- debts and funeral expenses and the expenses of administering the estate;
- inheritance tax;
- prior rights if the estate is intestate;
- legal rights;
- legacies;
- residue.

Once the estate has been wound up the executor is formally discharged.

Key Concepts

When a person dies, the process of winding up the deceased's estate is known as **executry administration**. The person responsible for this is the deceased's **executor**.

An **executor-nominate** is appointed under a will. An **executor-dative** is appointed by the sheriff court.

The estate of a deceased vests in the executor by the process of **confirmation** for the purpose of administering the estate. The following steps take place:

- the assets and debts or liabilities of the deceased are ascertained;
- the executor obtains confirmation from the commissary court;
- the assets are ingathered;
- the debts and any tax due are paid;
- the estate is distributed to the beneficiaries.

REFORM

14–74 As noted in the Introduction, the Scottish Law Commission produced a new *Report on Succession* in 2009[227] and the Scottish Government has indicated that it intends to proceed to formal public consultation on this. The aim of the proposed reform is to radically simplify the law to produce rules which are easily understood and reflect the nature of

---

[225] Administration of Estates (Small Payments) Act 1965; Administration of Estates (Small Payments) (Increase of Limit) Order 1984 (SI 1984/539).

[226] Confirmation to Small Estates (Scotland) Act 1979 s.1(3); Confirmation to Small Estates (Scotland) Order 2011 (SSI 2011/435).

[227] Scottish Law Commission, *Report on Succession* (2009), Scot. Law Com. No.215.

family structures in contemporary Scotland. The main recommendations would simplify the law on intestacy and legal rights and extend the rights of cohabitants.

On intestacy, the Commission recommends that prior rights should be abolished. If the deceased dies leaving a spouse or civil partner, that person will inherit the whole estate up to a maximum threshold sum which will be varied from time to time. This sum was envisaged as £300,000 at the time the Report was issued. If the deceased's estate exceeds the threshold sum, any issue will share the excess equally with the surviving spouse or civil partner. If there are no issue, the surviving spouse or civil partner will take the whole estate.

These recommendations on the division of the estate on intestacy are not likely to be too controversial. The recommendations on reform of legal rights are likely to be more controversial. The Commission decided to recommend that a surviving spouse or civil partner should continue to have a claim on the estate, if disinherited. The Commission was undecided, however, on whether disinherited children should always have a claim and sets out two possible options.

Legal rights are replaced by legal share and a legal share will be payable out of all of the estate and not just moveable property only. The Commission recommends that if a surviving spouse or civil partner is disinherited, they will be entitled to a legal share amounting to 25 per cent of what they would have inherited on intestacy. Option 1 in relation to children recommends that children who are disinherited also receive 25 per cent of the share they would have received on intestacy. Option 2 in relation to children gives dependent children only a capital sum based on their maintenance needs. Disinherited non-dependent children no longer have a claim against the estate. It will be interesting to see the reaction to these two options when the consultation process begins and what is enacted ultimately by the Scottish Parliament,

The Report also recommends that cohabitants be entitled to a percentage of what they would have received if they had been the deceased's spouse or civil partner. The appropriate percentage will be determined by considering only the length and quality of the cohabitant's relationship with the deceased.

▼ CHAPTER SUMMARY

1. **Scots law on succession is governed mainly by the Succession (Scotland) Act 1964. 14–75**

PRIVATE INTERNATIONAL LAW

1. **Private international law determines which law applies in relation to succession where there are factors involving other countries.**
2. **If a person dies domiciled in Scotland, Scots law of succession will apply to that person's moveable property wherever situated. If a person who is not domiciled in Scotland dies leaving in moveable property in Scotland, Scots law applies to that property.**

PROOF OF DEATH AND SURVIVORSHIP

1. **A death must be proved before an estate can be administered.**
2. **A person can be declared legally dead in two situations—where a person is thought to have died and where a person has not be known to be alive for seven years:**

> Presumption of Death (Scotland) Act 1977.

3. **A beneficiary must survive the deceased to inherit. No period of time is necessary and proof is on the balance of probabilities.**

4. **In a common calamity a younger person is presumed to survive an elder with two exceptions—husband and wife and where the elder has a will in favour of the younger whom failing a third party:**

> Succession (Scotland) Act 1964.

5. **An unworthy heir cannot inherit:**

> *Burns v Social Services* (1985); Woman provoked by husband killed him and not entitled to widow's allowance;
> Forfeiture Act 1982.

6. **Adopted children have a right of inheritance in their adopted parents' estate and not in their natural parents' estate.**

7. **Illegitimate children used to be disadvantaged but the status of illegitimacy has been abolished:**

> Family Law (Scotland) Act 2006.

LEGAL RIGHTS

1. **Legal rights have existed in Scots law for centuries to protect spouses and children from disinheritance. They apply to testate and intestate estates.**

2. **Legal rights can be claimed by spouses, registered civil partners and children:**

> Succession (Scotland) Act 1964;
> Civil Partnership Act 2004.

3. **Legal rights must be claimed and the right is extinguished after 20 years.**

4. **Legal rights are payable only out of the net moveable estate.**

5. **Where both a spouse or civil partner and children survive, the spouse or civil partner gets one third of the moveable estate, the children get one third and the remaining one third is free estate.**

6. **Where a spouse or civil partner only survives, the amount of legal rights is one half of the moveable estate and the other one half is free estate.**

7. **Where children only survive the amount is one half of the moveable estate and the other half is free estate.**

8. **Free estate is distributed according to the provisions of the will or rules of intestate succession.**

9. **A spouse, civil partner or child must elect between taking a provision under a will and claiming legal rights.**

10. **Children of predeceasing children can represent their parents. The division is per capita if all claiming are in the same degree of relationship to the deceased or *per stirpes* if they are not.**

11. **Certain advances during lifetime must be collated.**

12. **Legal rights can be discharged during lifetime or after death.**

INTESTATE SUCCESSION

1. Intestacy occurs where there is no will. It may be total or partial intestacy.
2. The 1964 Act radically changed the previous law and sets out six stages for distribution of an intestate estate. These are payment of debts; prior right to dwelling house; prior right to furniture and plenishings; prior rights to cash; legal rights and free estate.
3. A surviving spouse or registered civil partner only is entitled to prior rights:

   ➤ Succession (Scotland) Act 1964;
   ➤ Civil Partnership Act 2004.

4. There is a prior right to the dwelling house up to a value of £473,000. The house must be the normal residence of the spouse or civil partner. If there is more than one house a choice must be made.
5. There is a prior right to the furniture and plenishings up to a value of £29,000. If there is more than one house a choice must be made. Furniture and plenishings from a different house may be chosen.
6. There is a prior right to cash after the previous prior rights are satisfied. This will be £89,000 if there are no children or £50,000 if there are.
7. After prior rights, legal rights are paid and the remainder is free estate. The lengthy order of entitlement to succeed to the free estate is set out in the 1964 Act. Each class is exhausted and representation is possible.
8. A surviving spouse or civil partner maybe better off if the estate is intestate as prior rights are paid before legal rights:

   ➤ *Kerr, Petitioner* (1968): Mr Kerr died with a will leaving everything to his wife and his daughter claimed legal rights. Mrs Kerr was allowed to reject the will and take prior rights instead.

9. Cohabitants have a right to apply to the court for a discretionary share of an intestate estate:

   ➤ Family Law (Scotland) Act 2006.

TESTATE SUCCESSION

1. Testate Succession is where the deceased left a will or other testamentary writing.
2. There must be an intention to test, a testator must be aged 12 or over and must be of sound mind:

   ➤ Age of Legal Capacity (Scotland) Act 1991.
   ➤ *Morrison v MacLean's Trustees* (1862): An 80-year-old colonel left a will with unusual provisions but his eccentricity did not amount to insanity.

3. A will may be voidable if the testator was subjected to facility and circumvention or undue influence:

   ➤ *Pascoe-Watson v Brock's Executor* (1998): Mrs Brock was facile due to her dependence on alcohol and a will which changed her main beneficiary from her cousin to a friend was reduced due to the circumvention of the friend.
   ➤ *Honeyman's Executors v Sharp* (1978): a legacy by a widow of four valuable paintings to an art dealer was reduced due to undue influence.

4. **A will must be in writing. There are different provisions for validity of wills made pre and post 1995:**

    ➢ Requirements of Writing (Scotland) Act 1995.

5. **Pre-1995 a will to be valid had to be signed by the testator on every page and witnessed by two witnesses who signed on the last page:**

    ➢ *Williamson v Williamson* (1997): A witness signed the wrong name and the will was invalid.

6. **Signature by the testator and witnesses needs to be a continuous process:**

    ➢ *Davidson v Convy* (2003): a signed envelope containing an unsigned holograph sheet disposing of the estate was held to be a valid will.

7. **Holograph wills were valid but not self-proving.**
8. **Signature by the testator was normally the surname and a Christian name or abbreviation or initial of this, but a shortened name was permitted in certain circumstances:**

    ➢ *Rhodes v Peterson* (1972): In a letter to her daughter which was testamentary Mrs Rhodes validly signed "Mum".

9. **Post-1995 a will only needs to be signed on every page or sheet by the testator for validity.**
10. **A will is self-proving if also witnessed by one witness.**
11. **There are changed provisions in the 1995 Act to allow certain persons to sign a will on behalf of someone who is blind or unable to write.**
12. **A mutual will is a document which contains a will by more than one party. These are not recommended.**
13. **Future informal writings can be incorporated into wills if the will is carefully worded to provide for this.**
14. **A codicil is a document which amends a will in certain respects and is read together with the will.**

REVOCATION OF WILLS

1. **A will can be changed during a person's lifetime.**
2. **A will may be expressly revoked by making a new will or by destruction of the will:**

    ➢ *Bruce's Judicial Factor v Lord Advocate* (1969): Mr Bruce made a will in 1945 and a later will in 1949. When the 1949 will could not be found it was presumed that it was intentionally destroyed and the 1945 will operated.

3. **A will may be impliedly revoked by the making of a new will or by the birth of children to the testator after the will has been made.**

WILL SUBSTITUTES

1. **There are other ways of avoiding intestacy instead of making a will. These are known as will substitutes.**
2. **A survivorship special destination is where heritable property is in the name of two or more persons and the survivor in the title. Such destinations are revocable during**

lifetime. **They are not revocable on death if the destination is contractual by both parties contributing to the price.**

3. **Survivorship destinations can cause problems and must be properly evacuated when evacuation is possible:**

   ➢ *Gardner's Executors v Raeburn* (1996): when Mr and Mrs Gardner split up Mrs Gardner conveyed her one half share of the house in their joint names with a survivorship destination to Mr Gardner instead of both Mr and Mrs Gardner conveying the whole house to Mr Gardner. When Mr Gardner died his one half share of the house was still covered by the survivorship destination and went to Mrs Gardner.

4. **A person can take out a life policy for the benefit of someone else which will be paid directly to that person on death:**

   ➢ Married Women's Policies of Assurance (Scotland) 1880.

5. **A nomination of a sum of money up to £5000 with certain small savings institutions can be paid directly to the nominated person:**

   ➢ Administration of Estates (Small Payments) Act 1965.

6. **Gifts in contemplation of death are now rare.**

7. **It is possible for all the beneficiaries to make a re-arrangement of the division of an estate after death for tax purposes:**

   ➢ Inheritance Tax Act 1984.

INTERPRETATION OF WILLS

1. **A will should be read as a whole:**

   ➢ *Forbes Trustees v Forbes* (1893): when a later will referred to an earlier annuity of £150 which was, in fact, £100 the annuity was held to be £150.

2. **A will should be construed to avoid intestacy:**

   ➢ *Magistrates of Dundee v Morris* (1853): a will provided for the setting up of a school and there were sufficient details to prevent the legacy being void from uncertainty.

3. **In a will words are given their ordinary meaning:**

   ➢ *Robertson's Judicial Factor v Robertson* (1968): a holograph will left provision for the testator's nephew and niece "and their dependants" which was too vague to ascertain who the dependants were.

4. **Extrinsic evidence can be admitted for certain purposes including identification of the subject or object of legacy:**

   ➢ *Keiller v Thomson's Trustees* (1824): extrinsic evidence was allowed where the testator had given the wrong names of the persons he intended to benefit.

LEGACIES

1. Legacies fall into three categories—specific or special legacies, general legacies and residue.
2. A specific legacy is a legacy of a specific identifiable object. If the object of the legacy no longer exists or no longer belongs to the testator the legacy will fall:

   ➢ *Ogilvie-Forbes' Trustees v Ogilvie-Forbes* (1956): a will included a legacy of a liferent of a house which was transferred before the testator died and the legacy fell.

3. A general legacy is a legacy of a subject which is no different from any other subjects of the same kind such as money.
4. A legacy of the residue is a legacy of all the estate that remains after all debts, expenses, specific legacies and general legacies have been deducted.
5. If there is more than one legacy to the same person this may be cumulative when both will be paid or substitutional when only one will be paid, depending on the intention of the testator.
6. A destination-over is a provision in a will in favour of one person whom failing another.
7. The alternative person is either a conditional institute or a substitute. A conditional institute will not take if the primary legatee survives. A substitute will take if the primary legatee has not disposed of the subject during lifetime or in a will.
8. Where the legacy is heritable property, the presumption is for conditional institution. Where the legacy is of moveable property, the presumption is for substitution.
9. Division of legacies may be per capita, by head or *per stirpes*, by branch.
10. Where a legatee is a close relative of the testator there may be an implied gift to that relative's children if the legatee dies before the testator. This only applies to the testator's own children and remoter descendants and the testator's nephews and nieces if the testator is a parent figure to them.
11. A will may attach conditions to a legacy which must be satisfied before the legatee can take the legacy.
12. A potestative condition is one which requires the legatee to do something. A suspensive condition is one where the legacy is postponed until the condition is fulfilled. A resolutive condition is one where the legacy lapses if a certain event takes place.
13. Interest is payable on legacies from the date of death until payment unless the testator provides otherwise.
14. If there is insufficient estate to pay all the legacies the legacies are abated in the following order—residual legacies, general legacies and specific legacies.

VESTING AND ACCRETION

1. Vesting in an executor is where the whole estate passes to the executor for the purpose of administration of the estate.
2. Vesting in a beneficiary is when the beneficiary obtains a completed a right. Vesting is different from actual receipt or payment. Vesting in a beneficiary may be at the date of death or postponed.
3. Accretion takes place in a legacy to more than one person where the share of a predeceasing legatee passes to the surviving legatee or legatees. This happens when the legacy is joint but not where there is a destination-over.

EXECUTRY ADMINISTRATION

1. **The process of winding up the deceased's estate is known as executry administration. The person responsible for this is the deceased's executor.**
2. **An executor maybe appointed by a will, known as an executor- nominate, or by the Sheriff Court, known as an executor-dative.**
3. **The executor first ascertains the assets and debts of the deceased.**
4. **Inheritance tax is a debt on the estate chargeable on the value at the time of death after deduction of debts and funeral expenses:**

   ➢ Inheritance Tax Act 1984.

5. **Confirmation is the process whereby the court confirms the appointment of the executor and authorises administration of the estate as detailed in the inventory of assets prepared by the executor.**
6. **Once the executor has obtained confirmation the estate is ingathered and distributed.**
7. **The order of distribution is—debts and funeral expenses and the expenses of administering the estate; inheritance tax; prior rights if the estate is intestate; legal rights; legacies and residue.**

REFORM

1. **The Scottish Law Commission published a *Report on Succession* in 2009:**

   ➢ Scottish Law Commission, *Report on Succession* (2009), Scot. Law Com. No.215.

? QUICK QUIZ

SUCCESSION

- When can a person be declared legally dead?
- What presumptions apply when two people die simultaneously?
- Who can claim legal rights and when can they be claimed?
- What are the conditions for the prior right to a dwelling house to apply?
- What is known as the "free estate"?
- What are the current limits on value of prior rights?
- The validity of a testamentary writing depends on which three factors?
- What are the essentials for a will to be self-proving after 1995?
- When is a will impliedly revoked?
- Should a survivorship destination be used instead of a will?
- What is the primary means of interpreting a will?
- Legacies fall into which three main categories?
- How is an executor appointed?
- What is the order of distribution of an estate?

📖 FURTHER READING

Gibb, *Succession LawBasics*, 3rd edn (W. Green, 2012).
Gretton & Steven, *Property, Trusts and Succession* (Tottel, 2009).
Hiram, *The Scots Law of Succession*, 2nd edn (Tottel, 2007).
Macdonald, *Succession*, 3rd edn (W. Green, 2001).
Meston, *The Succession (Scotland) Act 1964*, 5th edn (W. Green, 2002).
Stair Memorial Encyclopaedia—Wills and Succession, Vol.25 (Butterworths, 1989).

Chapter 15   Family

Joe Thomson[1]

► CHAPTER OVERVIEW

This chapter is concerned with family law. It begins by examining families, marriage and **15–01** civil partnership followed by parents and children. The chapter then looks at the rules regarding property rights during marriage, civil partnership and cohabitation followed by the particular issue of domestic violence and the family home. It then goes on to consider divorce, dissolution and the termination of non-marital relationships. This is followed by a short section on private ordering where couples reach settlements without the intervention of the courts. There is then a section on adoption. The chapter concludes by discussing the three main state institutions involved in the care and protection of children.

✓ OUTCOMES

At the end of the chapter, you should be able to: **15–02**

- ✓ understand the legal consequences of marriage and civil partnership;
- ✓ appreciate who the law regards as a parent;
- ✓ identify parental responsibilities and rights;
- ✓ understand the separate property rule;
- ✓ appreciate the obligation to aliment a spouse or civil partner;
- ✓ understand children's rights to financial support from parents;
- ✓ appreciate the effect of domestic violence on the property rights of spouses and civil partners;
- ✓ identify the grounds for divorce or dissolution of a civil partnership;
- ✓ appreciate the rules concerning financial provision on divorce or dissolution;
- ✓ appreciate the nature of private agreements made by couples terminating their relationships;
- ✓ understand the rules on adoption; and
- ✓ understand the roles of local authorities, the courts and the children's hearing system where children are in need of care and protection.

FAMILIES, MARRIAGE AND CIVIL PARTNERSHIP

Families take many forms in Scotland today. They include lone-parent households, **15–03** cohabiting opposite sex and same sex couples with or without children, married couples and civil partners. Individuals may enter into a number of these forms in their lifetime as

---

[1] This chapter was originally written by Anne Griffiths, Professor of Anthropology of Law, University of Edinburgh and has been updated by Joe Thomson, formerly Regius Professor of Law at the University of Glasgow and Commissioner, the Scottish Law Commission.

they move from marriage to lone-parenthood, or to a cohabiting relationship, or from cohabitation to marriage or civil partnership. The changing dynamics of family life create a challenge for Scots family law in its approach to the recognition and enforcement of legal rights and duties among family members. What constitutes a "family" for legal purposes may be at odds with social perceptions of what makes a family unit. The law attempts to provide rules which regulate the problems faced by persons in these diverse family structures.

Changing approaches to defining families in terms of marriage

15–04 Traditionally, marriage has had a central role in Scots family law but growing recognition and acceptance of other types of non-marital family units has led to changes in the way that law deals with them. Scots law no longer discriminates against children on the basis of whether or not their parents were married.[2] In *Ghaidan v Godin–Mendoza*[3] the House of Lords accepted that statutes which give rights to opposite sex cohabitants have to be construed as including same sex cohabitants in order to avoid unlawful discrimination under art.13 of the European Convention on Human Rights. In *Telfer v Kellock*[4] the Lord Ordinary (Lady Smith) held that the Damages (Scotland) Act 1976 would have to be interpreted in this way. Scots law is sensitive to developments taking place in the broader European and International community of which it forms part, including international conventions such as the United Nations Convention on the Rights of the Child and the European Convention on Human Rights and Fundamental Freedoms, to which the United Kingdom is a signatory. The latter has now been partially incorporated into UK law by the Human Rights Act 1998 and has brought about change through decisions of the European Court of Human Rights (ECHR) at Strasbourg, which now, through incorporation, may be directly founded upon by UK citizens along with rights under the Convention.

Human Rights Act 1998

15–05 The Human Rights Act does not provide that the Convention shall have effect as part of Scots (and English) law but instead seeks, to give effect in a number of ways to what it defines as "Convention Rights".[5] First, it establishes a "rule of interpretation". Legislation is to be "read and given effect" in a way which is compatible with "Convention rights"[6]; and the Act provides that, in determining questions relating to such rights the courts must "take into account" the jurisprudence established by the Strasbourg Commission and Court.[7] This is so even where the decision would conflict with an earlier decision of a court in the United Kingdom. Secondly, the Act provides that it is unlawful for a "public authority" to act in a way which is incompatible with a Convention right[8]; and s.7 gives "victims" of any such unlawful act the right either to rely on the Convention right in any legal proceedings or to institute legal proceedings against the relevant authority. Thirdly, the Act, whilst recognising the ultimate sovereignty of the Westminster Parliament, provides in s.4 a procedure whereby a court may make a declaration that a statutory provision is incompatible with a Convention right. If it does so, a Minster may (provided that he

---

[2] Law Reform (Parent and Child) (Scotland) Act 1986 s.1(1).
[3] [2004] 3 W.L.R. 113.
[4] 2004 S.L.T. 1290.
[5] Human Rights Act s.1.
[6] Human Rights Act s.3.
[7] Human Rights Act s.2.
[8] Human Rights Act s.6.

considers such action to be necessary to remove the incompatibility and that there are "compelling reasons" for adopting the special procedure laid down by the Act—rather than bringing new legislation before Parliament in the usual way) make an order effecting the necessary changes.[9] Moreover, the Scottish Parliament cannot legislate in a way that is contrary to the Convention: if it does so the legislation could be struck down by the courts as ultra vires the Parliament's legislative competency.

Of key interest in family law are: art.8 dealing with the right to respect for private and family life[10]; art.12 dealing with the right to marry; art.14 dealing with the right not to be discriminated against; and art.6 dealing with the rights to a fair and public hearing in proceedings determining an individual's civil rights and obligations. Over the years the ECHR has expanded the concept of what constitutes a "family" together with the range of persons that fall within its ambit and the rights accorded to them. In *Marckx v Belgium*,[11] the European Court held that the notion of family life under art.8 is not confined to marriage-based relationships but may encompass other de facto ties[12] such as those between an unmarried mother and her child. In *Goodwin v UK*,[13] the court held that the failure to allow a transsexual to marry a person of the sex opposite to their re-assigned gender was not only a breach of art.12, but a failure to respect the applicant's right to private life in breach of art.8. In *Salqueiro da Silva Mouta v Portugal*,[14] the court held that there had been discrimination in violation of art.14 as well as a breach of art.8, where a Portugese court recalled an order granting parental responsibility, including residence, in favour of a father, on the basis of his sexual orientation as a gay person.[15] In *P, C and S v UK*,[16] the court held that a mother's rights under arts 8 and 6 had been breached by the removal of her son straight after birth without being provided with relevant and sufficient reasons for their action and without being given the opportunity to have legal representation.[17]

In some cases, however, discrimination in relation to substantive rights contained in the

---

[9] Human Rights Act s.10. Note discussion of this declaration of incompatibility in *S v Miller (No.2)*, 2001 S.L.T. 1304, where the court declined to make such a finding on the basis that it was now agreed that Scottish Ministers had power under existing legislation to make regulations to provide for representation before a children's hearing.

[10] Immigration is an area where cases have alleged human rights violations under art.8. See *Ahmed v SS for Home Department*, 2002 S.L.T. 1347, OH; *Akhtar v SS for Home Department*, 2001 S.L.T. 1239, OH; *Saini v SS for Home Department*, 2001 S.C. 951, OH.

[11] (1979–80) 2 E.H.R.R. 330.

[12] See also *X, Y and Z v UK* and *Application No.25680/94 I v UK*, European Commission on Human Rights, Information Note No.129.6 where the Commission found the United Kingdom in violation of art.8, in respect of family life, when the Registrar General refused to allow a post-operative female-to-male transsexual, in a stable relationship. to be registered as the father of a child born as a result of artificial insemination, because only a biological man could be regarded as the father for the purposes of registration.

[13] (28957/95) [2002] I.R.L.R. 664. Note that while no judgment of the ECHR has yet found that homosexual partners had a right to marry under art.12, as this matter falls within the "margin of appreciation" of a Member State, in *S v UK* (1986) 47 D. & R. 271 the Commission held that even though a stable homosexual cohabiting relationship did not fall within the definition of "family life", such a relationship might still be a matter affecting *private life*.

[14] 2001 Fam. L.R. 2; (2001) 31 E.H.R.R. 47.

[15] The extent to which this case can be used by members of same sex couples to access other family law rights and liabilities in Scots and English law, is explored in K. Norrie "Constitutional Challenges to Sexual Orientation Discrimination" (2000) 49 I.C.L.Q. 755.

[16] 2002 Fam. L.B. 59.

[17] In this case, the mother had a previous conviction in America for harming one of her children and had been diagnosed with Munchausen's syndrome by proxy. The local authority found out her prior history and took out an order allowing them to remove her son hours after his birth. A care order followed and, within a year, the child had been freed for adoption. See also *S v Miller*, 2001 S.L.T. 531 on children's rights to legal representation before a children's hearing.

Convention, including the right to respect for family life, may be permitted where a State can show that it has a legitimate aim, and there is a reasonable relationship of proportionality between the legitimate aim and the means employed to achieve it. So, for example, in *McMichael v UK*[18] an unmarried father took his case to the European Court on the basis that he had no domestic legal right to obtain custody of his son or to participate in care and adoption proceedings before a children's hearing involving him. He argued that this infringed his right to respect for "family life" under art.8 in a discriminatory manner that was contrary to art.14. His action was unsuccessful. While the European Court in *Marckx v Belgium*[19] held that family life is not confined to marriage-based relationship but may encompass other de facto ties, it ruled that there had been no violation of arts 8 and 14 in *McMichael's Case*. This was because the Government was able to appeal to the proviso contained in art.8(2) which requires any interference with family life to be justified on the basis that it is in accordance with the law and necessary to achieve a legitimate aim in a democratic society. In taking account of this, the European Court has allowed a margin of appreciation to Member States taking on board the political climate at the given time. The court accepted the Government's explanation that the aim of the relevant legislation was to provide a mechanism for identifying "meritorious" fathers who might be accorded parental rights, thereby protecting the interests of the child and the mother. For discrimination to occur under art.14 it must have "no objective and reasonable justification", that is if it does not pursue a "legitimate aim" or there is not a "reasonable relationship of proportionality between the means employed and the aim sought to be realised".[20] The court ruled that in this case, the Government's aim was legitimate and that the conditions imposed on natural fathers for obtaining recognition of their parental role respected the principle of proportionality. There was, thus, an objective and reasonable justification for the difference of treatment complained of.[21] In *B v UK*[22] the court revisited the issue of whether unmarried fathers are discriminated against in the protection given to their relationship with their children by comparison with the protection given to married fathers under English law. It reached the conclusion that the Children Act 1989 did not violate an unmarried father's rights, as, following on from *McMichael*, "there exists an objective and reasonable justification for the difference in treatment between married and unmarried fathers with regard to the automatic acquisition of parental rights."[23] However in *Principal Reporter v K*[24] the Supreme Court held that to deny an unmarried father the right to appear as a relevant person before a children's hearing dealing with his child's case was prima facie a breach of art.8.

Marriage and civil partnership

15–06 It is clear that families and marriage need not go together. Nonetheless, marriage still has important legal consequences for family members, e.g. concerning rights to property and support, parenthood, financial provision on the termination of a relationship and for rights of succession on the death of one of the spouses. Marriage is only open to persons of the opposite sex. Persons of the same sex can register a civil partnership which, with a few very minor differences, has the same legal effects for the partners and their family as marriage.

---

[18] (1995) 20 E.H.R.R 205.
[19] (1979–80) 2 E.H.R.R. 330.
[20] See *Marckx v Belgium* (1979–80) 2 E.H.R.R. 330 at para.33.
[21] *McMichael v UK* (1995) 20 E.H.R.R. 205 at para.98.
[22] [2000] 1 F.L.R. 1.
[23] *B v UK* [2000] 1 F.L.R. 1 at 5.
[24] [2010] UKSC 56.

Who can marry or register a civil partnership?

The law dealing with marriage is set out in the Marriage (Scotland) Act 1977 (as amen- **15–07** ded). It provides that parties are free to marry provided they do not fall within the legal impediments to marriage set out in s.5(4) of the 1977 Act.

The following constitute a legal impediment to a marriage viz where:

- the parties fall within the forbidden degrees of relationship[25];
- one of the parties is, or both are, married or in a civil partnership[26];
- one or both parties will be under the age of 16 on the date of the solemnisation of the intended marriage[27];
- one of the parties is or are incapable of understanding the nature of a marriage ceremony or of consenting to marriage[28];
- both parties are of the same sex.[29]

The law dealing with civil partnerships is set out in s.86 of the Civil Partnership Act 2004. The legal impediments are analogous to those in relation to marriage but, of course, the parties must not be of the opposite sex.

Position of transsexuals and same sex couples

One of the fundamental requirements for marriage is that it takes place between a man **15–08** and a woman. Under s.5(4)(b) of the 1977 Act there is a legal impediment to marriage where parties are of the same sex. In *Bellinger v Bellinger*[30] the House of Lords held that only biological criteria could be used to determine a person's sex. This meant that even after sex realignment surgery transsexuals could not marry in their realigned gender because their sex had not changed for the purpose of marriage. However, the House of Lords recognised that this was a breach of arts 8 and 12. This led to the Gender Recognition Act 2004 under which a post operative transsexual can apply for a full gender recognition certificate. When the certificate is issued, the person's gender becomes for all legal purposes the acquired gender. But if the applicant is married only an interim gender recognition certificate can be issued until the applicant obtains a divorce. The same rule applies where the applicant is a party to a civil partnership; only an interim gender recognition certificate can be granted until the civil partnership is dissolved. The issue of an interim gender recognition certificate is a ground of divorce and dissolution.

---

[25] 1977 Act s.5(4)(a). These are relationships based on consanguinity and affinity as set out in s.2 and Sch.1 of the 1977 Act.

[26] 1977 Act s.5(4)(b).

[27] 1977 Act s.5(4)(c). Note that where such a marriage takes place (which is most unlikely given the fact that birth certificates must be submitted to the registrar) it will be void under s.1.

[28] 1977 Act s.5(4)(d). Lack of capacity to understand, or consent to, marriage may involve, mental incapacity, error (but only as to the identity of the person or the nature of the ceremony and not as to its effects), fraud (but only in so far as it produces the appearance without the reality of consent), marriages entered into under force and fear or duress: 1977 Act s.20A.

[29] 1977 Act s.5(4)(e).

[30] [2004] A.C. 467.

Constitution of regular marriage

Marriage (Scotland) Act 1977

15–09 A regular marriage may be either a religious or a civil marriage.[31] In either case, each party to the marriage must submit to the registrar of the district in which the marriage is to be solemnised a notice of intention to marry, accompanied by a birth certificate, and where either party has previously been married, evidence of the dissolution of the previous marriage.[32] There are special provisions where a party to a marriage intended to be solemnised in Scotland is residing in another part of the United Kingdom or is not domiciled in any part of the United Kingdom and also for marriages outside Scotland where a party resides in Scotland.[33] After receipt of the notice, the registrar, if satisfied that there is no legal impediment, or if so informed by the Registrar General, issues a marriage schedule which is the authority for the solemnisation of the marriage.[34] The schedule may not, however, be issued before the expiry of 14 days from receipt of the notice unless on the written request of a party to the marriage and with the authority of the Registrar General.[35]

Civil marriage

15–10 The marriage must be conducted by an authorised registrar[36] and is normally conducted at the registrar's office,[37] although there is now provision for Scottish Ministers to make regulations extending the range of places where civil marriages may be solemnised with the approval of local authorities.[38] Both parties must be present together with two witnesses who profess to be aged 16 or over.[39] There is no prescribed form of ceremony laid down by the Act, but it generally follows a certain procedure which involves the registrar explaining the nature of marriage in Scots law and asking the parties to declare if they know of any legal impediment to their marriage. The parties are then asked to take each other as husband and wife and to exchange consent to marriage. After they have done so, the registrar declares them to be married and the marriage schedule is then signed by both parties, the witnesses and the registrar. The marriage is then registered.

Religious marriage

15–11 A religious marriage may be solemnised by a minister of the Church of Scotland, a minister, clergyman, pastor or priest of a religious body prescribed by the regulations, or other approved celebrant.[40] The marriage schedule must be produced to the celebrant and the parties to the marriage and two witnesses (professing to be aged 16 or over) must be present. Where the celebrant belongs to the Church of Scotland, or a prescribed religious body, the marriage must be in accordance with a form recognised as sufficient by the

---

[31] 1977 Act s.8.

[32] 1977 Act s.3(1).

[33] 1977 Act s.3(4), (5) and (7).

[34] 1977 Act s.6.

[35] 1977 Act s.6(4).

[36] This is a district, or assistant district, registrar appointed in terms of s.17 of the 1977 Act.

[37] In exceptional cases, e.g. where a person is seriously ill, or suffering from serious bodily injury, and is unable to attend and there is good reason why the marriage cannot be delayed, a registrar may give special dispensation for it to be solemnised elsewhere, e.g. in a hospital. See s.18(4)(b).

[38] 1977 Act s.18A, added by the Marriage (Scotland) Act 2002.

[39] 1977 Act s.19(2).

[40] 1977 Act s.8(1). See also Marriage (Prescription of Religious Bodies) (Scotland) Regulations 1977 (SI 1977/1670).

church or body to which the celebrant belongs.[41] In any other case, the statutory requirement is that the form of solemnisation must include a declaration by the parties, in the presence of each other, the celebrant and the witnesses, that they accept each other as husband and wife and a declaration thereafter that they are husband and wife.[42] After the ceremony, the marriage schedule is signed by both parties, the witnesses and the celebrant. It must then be returned to the district registrar for registration within three days of the ceremony.[43]

Unauthorised celebrant and validity of marriage

It is an offence for anyone, who is not within the classes of person authorised under the **15–12** Act to solemnise marriages, to conduct a marriage ceremony in such a way as to lead the parties to believe that he or she is solemnising a valid marriage, or for the celebrant of a religious marriage to solemnise it without at the time having the marriage schedule, or for either the celebrant of a religious marriage or an authorised registrar to solemnise a marriage without both parties being present.[44] Provided both parties were present at the marriage ceremony *and* the marriage has been registered, its validity is not to be questioned in any legal proceedings on the ground of failure to comply with a requirement or restriction imposed by the Act.[45] This provision does not save a marriage that has never been registered and where no marriage schedule was ever issued.[46] In such a case the marriage is null and void.

Impediments to marriage

At any time before the solemnisation of a marriage any person may submit an objection in **15–13** writing to the registrar.[47] Where the objection relates to a matter of misdescription or inaccuracy the registrar may, with the approval of the Registrar General, make any necessary correction. In any other case he or she must, pending consideration of the objection by the Registrar General, suspend the completion or issue of the marriage schedule or, if a marriage schedule has already been issued for a religious marriage, notify the celebrant of the objection and advise him not to solemnise the marriage.[48] If the Registrar General is satisfied that, on consideration of an objection, there is a legal impediment to the marriage as set out in s.5(4) of the 1977 Act, he must direct the registrar to take all reasonable steps to ensure that the marriage does not take place. If, on the other hand, he is satisfied that there is no legal impediment, he must inform the registrar and the marriage schedule may then be completed and issued, if that has not already been done, so that the marriage may proceed.[49]

---

[41] 1977 Act s.14(a).
[42] 1977 Act ss.14(b) and 9(3).
[43] 1977 Act s.15(2).
[44] 1977 Act s.24.
[45] 1977 Act s.23A.
[46] *Saleh v Saleh*, 1987 S.L.T. 633. But if the place of marriage is outwith Scotland, it has been held that the marriage can be valid even though the parties were not present: *MRA v NRK* [2011] CSOH 101, June 17, 2011(W in Scotland and H in Pakistan exchanged consents over the telephone. Because such a marriage was recognized in Pakistan, not a nullity in Scotland in spite of the parties not being physically present.)
[47] 1977 Act s.5(1).
[48] 1977 Act s.5(2).
[49] 1977 Act ss.5(3) and 6(1); Civil Partnership Act 2004 ss.86 and 123.

Registering a civil partnership

15–14 Each of the intended civil partners must submit to the district registrar a notice of their intention to register a civil partnership. Particulars of the notice are entered into the civil partnership book. The names of the parties and the date on which the registration is to take place are then publicised. The registration can only take place 14 days after these details have been published. If satisfied that there are no legal impediments, the registrar can complete a civil partnership schedule. The civil partnership is formed by registration. The registrar asks the parties to confirm that the particulars set out in the schedule are correct. Each then signs the schedule in the presence of each other, two witnesses who are 16 or over and the authorised registrar. The schedule is then signed by the witnesses and the registrar in the presence of the civil partners and each other. The registrar will then enter the details of the schedule into the civil partnership register.[50] The registration can take place in a registration office or any other place that the registration authority agrees can be the place of registration but, in stark contrast to marriage, it cannot take place in religious premises. Section 95A of the Civil Partnership Act 2004 provides the equivalent to s.23A of the Marriage (Scotland) Act 1977.

Defects and invalidity: effect on marriage and civil partnership

15–15 A marriage or civil partnership will be treated as void, that is as a nullity, where either party is under the age of 16,[51] or falls within the prohibited degrees of relationship.[52] A marriage or civil partnership is null if one of the parties was in a prior subsisting marriage or civil partnership or lacked capacity with regard to understanding or consent, or both parties are of the same sex (marriage) or opposite sex (civil partnership). In addition, a marriage but not a civil partnership may be rendered voidable, that is it remains valid up until the point at which it is challenged, on the ground of incurable impotency.[53] On granting declarator of nullity, the court has the same powers to award financial provision in respect of a void or voidable marriage as it has on granting a decree of divorce.[54]

Irregular marriage

15–16 Only one form of irregular marriage is now recognised by Scots law and that is marriage by cohabitation with habit and repute.[55] This form of marriage arises where a couple set up home together without going through *any* form of ceremony. It operates on the presumption that *tacit* consent to marriage is constituted by the cohabitation as man and wife[56] in Scotland[57] of a couple free to marry who are generally reputed to be husband and wife. The presumption is rebuttable. There are two major hurdles to be overcome in establishing a marriage of this kind, namely (a) satisfying the requirement that the

---

[50] See generally Civil Partnership Act 2004 ss.87–100.

[51] 1977 Act s.1; 2004 Act s.86.

[52] 1977 Act s.2; 2004 Act s.86.

[53] The Scottish Law Commission has recommended the abolition of incurable impotency as a voidable ground of marriage in its *Report on Family Law* (1992), Scot. Law Com. No.135, recommendations 49 and 50. The then Scottish Executive declined this recommendation on the basis that it "provides a facility that would not otherwise be available to a limited number of couples in extreme circumstances", see *Parents and Children: A White Paper on Scottish Family Law* (2000), para.10.10.

[54] Family Law (Scotland) Act 1985 s.17(1).

[55] The other two were declaration *de praesenti* and promise *subsequent copula* both of which were abolished by s.5 of the Marriage (Scotland) Act 1939.

[56] Note that it is not cohabitation per se that gives rise to the presumption, but cohabitation as husband and wife.

[57] See Lord Watson's dicta to this effect in the *Dysart Peerage Case* (1881) L.R. 6 App. Cas. 489 at 537–538.

cohabitation must be for a considerable period,[58] and (b) fulfilling the requirements of habit and repute.[59] There is no minimum period required for cohabitation.[60] To meet the second requirement, not only must the parties behave towards one another as husband and wife but they must also be reputed to be such by third parties. According to *Low v Gorman*[61] "although repute need not be universal it must be general, substantially unvarying and consistent and not divided". The opinion of others comes into play and the weight attached to their opinions varies.[62] It is clear that if parties openly admit that they are not married, then marriage on the basis of cohabitation with habit and repute can never be established. The fact that there was a legal impediment to marriage when the cohabitation began, does not preclude the constitution of marriage by continuance of the cohabitation with repute after the parties become free to marry,[63] though circumstances after the removal of the impediment must be sufficient in themselves to establish the inference of tacit consent.[64] Consent to marriage may be proved by cohabitation with habit and repute where spouses have previously been married to one another and divorced.[65] A declarator of marriage must be sought before the legal rights and obligation that attach to marriage will apply to a marriage constituted by consent following relevant cohabitation with habit and repute.[66]

Marriage by cohabitation with habit and repute has been abolished by s.3 of the Family Law (Scotland) Act 2006. However, persons will still be able to use the doctrine provided the cohabitation began before the date of commencement of the Act, i.e. before May 4, 2006. Indeed, under s.3(3) and (4), post Act cohabitation with habit and repute can still be used in the following situation. A and B go through a ceremony of marriage abroad. They believe that they are validly married but in fact the marriage is invalid under the law of the place where the wedding took place. A is, or becomes, domiciled in Scotland and they live here with the repute that they are married. If B dies domiciled in Scotland, a declarator that they had become married by habit and repute can be obtained if A became aware after B had died that the marriage was invalid.

Key Concepts

Scots law no longer discriminates against **children** on the basis of **whether or not** their parents are **married**.

    Marriage and civil partnership have **important legal consequences** for family members, e.g. concerning rights to property and support, parenthood, financial

---

[58] *Campbell v Campbell* (1866) 4 M. 867.

[59] See *Ackerman v Logan's Executors*, 2002 S.L.T. 37, IH, where the court held that the evidence fell far short of establishing the pursuer's averments of general repute.

[60] See *Kamperman v MacIver*, 1994 S.L.T. 763, where the court held that a period of cohabitation lasting six and a half months after an impediment to marriage was removed was not insufficient.

[61] 1970 S.L.T. 356 at 395.

[62] See *Petrie v Petrie*, 1911 S.C. 360, where the court placed greater weight on the evidence of the man's professional colleagues and relatives, who considered him unmarried, compared with the views of persons such as the cleaner and the postman. See also *Ackerman v Logan's Executors*, 2002 S.L.T. 37, where the parties were considered married by neighbours, customers of the pursuer's shop and members of the various organisations with which the deceased was involved, but not by close family members of the deceased. In weighing the evidence the views of the latter prevailed.

[63] *Campbell v Campbell* (1867) 5 M. (H.L.) 115; *S v S*, 2006 S.L.T. 471.

[64] *Low v Gorman*, 1970 S.L.T. 356.

[65] *Mullen v Mullen*, 1991 S.L.T. 205.

[66] Where such a declarator is granted, the court must, under s.21 of the 1977 Act, state the date on which the marriage was constituted and forward it to the Registrar General for registration.

provisions on the termination of a relationship and for rights in relation to succession on the death of one of the spouses or civil partners.

Parties are free to marry or register a civil partnership provided there are no **legal impediments.**

One of the fundamental requirements for **marriage** is that it takes place between a **man** and a **woman;** one of the fundamental requirements for a **civil partnership** is that it takes place between persons of the **same sex.**

Regular marriage may be either a religious or a civil marriage. A **civil** marriage must be conducted by an authorised registrar—**no prescribed form of ceremony** is laid down by the Act. A **religious** marriage may be solemnised by a minister of the Church of Scotland, a minister, clergyman, pastor or
priest of a religious body prescribed by the regulations, or other approved celebrant. The registration of a **civil partnership** is a **civil ceremony** and cannot take place in religious premises.

There is a form of **irregular marriage** known as **marriage by cohabitation with habit and repute**. This has now been abolished unless the cohabitation began before the commencement of the Family Law (Scotland) Act 2006. There is an exception where a marriage celebrated abroad is discovered to be invalid after the death of one of the parties.

PARENTS AND CHILDREN

Who is a parent?

15–17 A child's first legal relationship is with his or her parents. An essential starting point in the law relating to children and parents is the determination of who is a parent in law as this has important legal consequences. These primarily revolve round parentage as a key prerequisite to establishing parental responsibilities and rights and the principle that a parent is responsible for their children's financial support. In regulating this area, the law has to deal with genetic and social parenthood and the complications that arise from advances in reproductive technology, where a distinction can now be drawn between "natural" parents, who can conceive without the use of medical assistance or technology, and "artificial" or "assisted" parenthood, in which the link between genetic parenthood and social or gestational parenthood may be broken.

Presumptions of paternity and related provisions

15–18 At common law, a woman who gives birth is regarded as the legal mother of the child, regardless of whether she is married to the child's father. Where fatherhood is concerned, the Law Reform (Parent and Child) (Scotland) Act 1986 provides that a man is presumed to be the father of a child "if he was married to the mother of the child at any time beginning with the conception and ending with the birth of the child"[67] even if the marriage is invalid or irregular.[68] Where the presumption arising from marriage does not apply, a man is presumed to be the father of a child if both he and the mother have acknowledged his paternity and he has been registered as the father in any register of birth kept under statutory authority in any part of the United Kingdom.[69] These statutory

---

[67] 1986 Act s.5(1)(a).
[68] 1986 Act s.5(2).
[69] 1986 Act s.5(1)(b).

presumptions of paternity are rebuttable, by proof on a balance of probabilities[70] without corroboration.[71]

Where assisted reproduction has taken place, the Human Fertilisation and Embryology Act 2008 provides rules to establish parentage in law. Unless a child is adopted, the mother is the women who is carrying, or has carried, a child as a result of the placing in her of an embryo or of sperm and eggs.[72] Where pregnancy of a married woman results from the foregoing, but her husband is not the genetic father of the child, he will nevertheless be treated as the father unless it is shown that he did not consent to the procedure.[73] Similarly, where the woman is a party to a civil partnership, her civil partner is to be treated as the child's parent unless it is shown that she did not consent.[74] Where a couple are unmarried or have not registered a civil partnership, the mother's partner can become the child's father (male partner) or second female parent(female partner) if both partners agree.[75] Where these provisions apply, no other person is to be treated as the father or parent of the child.[76] Where a child is the genetic child of one or both of the parties to a marriage, but was carried by a woman other than the wife, and certain other statutory requirements are fulfilled, a court may make a "parental order", declaring that the child is the child of the married couple.[77]

A challenge to any of these presumptions, or statutory rules, may be taken in an action for declarator of parentage or non-parentage raised in either the sheriff court or the Court of Session.[78] A party to such proceedings can be requested to provide a sample of blood, or other fluid, or body tissue for testing; if such a request is refused, the court has a discretion to draw such inference, if any, as seems appropriate (including an adverse inference) taking into account the subject-matter of the proceedings.[79] Where a child lacks capacity to consent, this may be provided by any person having parental responsibility for a child under 16, or care and control of such a child.[80] Where such a person refuses to consent on the child's behalf, the court may request them to do so and may draw an adverse inference where they refuse.

Parental responsibilities and parental rights

However, acquiring the status of parentage does not automatically accord parental **15–19** responsibilities and rights to a parent. Such responsibilities and rights (PRRs) are codified in the Children (Scotland) Act 1995. They supersede any such PRRs under common law.[81] Under the 1995 Act parents are entrusted with statutory responsibilities towards children, and parental rights are given only to enable them to discharge those parental responsibilities. The general statutory responsibilities are:

- to safeguard and promote the child's health, development and welfare[82];

---

[70] 1986 Act s.5(4).
[71] Civil Evidence (Scotland) Act 1988 s.1(1).
[72] 2008 Act s.33(1).
[73] 2008 Act ss.35(1) and 48(1).
[74] 2008 Act ss.42 and 48(1).
[75] 2008 Act ss.36, 37 and 48(1) (male partner) and ss.43, 44 and 48(1) (female partner).
[76] 2008 Act ss.38(1) and 45(1). The donor of the sperm used for treatment under the 2008 Act is not to be treated as the father of the child: see s.41.
[77] 2008 Act s.54.
[78] 1986 Act s.7.
[79] 1986 Act s.70(2).
[80] 1986 Act s.6(2).
[81] 1995 Act ss.1(4) and 2(5).
[82] 1995 Act s.1(1)(a).

- to provide direction and guidance in a manner appropriate to the stage of development of the child[83];
- if the child is not living with the parent, to maintain personal relations and direct contact with the child on a regular basis[84];
- to act as the child's legal representative,
- but only in so far as compliance is practicable and in the interests of the child.[85]

A parent's corresponding rights are:

- to have the child living with him or otherwise to regulate the child's residence[86];
- to control, direct or guide, in a manner appropriate to the stage of development of the child, the child's upbringing[87];
- if the child is not living with him, to maintain personal relations and direct contact with the child on a regular basis[88]; and
- to act as the child's legal representative.[89]

When a child reaches the age of 16 parental responsibilities and rights cease with the exception of the responsibility to give guidance, which subsists until the child reaches 18.[90]

Acquisition of PRRs—mother

15–20 A mother automatically has statutory PRRs in relation to her child, whether or not she is, or has been, married to the father.[91]

Acquisition of PRRs—father

15–21 A father acquires statutory PRRs:

- If he is married to the mother at the time of the child's conception or subsequently.[92]
- If he is unmarried but presumed to be the father of the child because he was registered as the child's father.[93] This rule only applies when the man was registered as the child's father on or after May 4, 2006 when the Family Law (Scotland) Act 2006 came into force.
- If he is unmarried but he and the mother have reached agreement and registered it in the Books of Council and Session under s.4 of the 1995 Act. Note that in this case the mother must not have been deprived of any parental rights by the courts. Once registered, such an agreement can only be revoked by the court.
- If he has applied for a court order under s.11 of the 1995 Act for PRRs.

---

[83] 1995 Act s.1(1)(b).
[84] 1995 Act s.1(1)(c).
[85] 1995 Act s.1(1)(d).
[86] 1995 Act s.2(1)(a).
[87] 1995 Act s.2(1)(b).
[88] 1995 Act s.2(1)(c).
[89] 1995 Act s.2(1)(d).
[90] 1995 Act ss.1(2) and 2(7).
[91] 1995 Act s.3(1)(a).
[92] 1995 Act s.3(1)(b)(i).
[93] 1995 Act s.3(1)(b)(ii).

The 1995 Act also allows persons who do not have PRRs but who have care and control of a child under 16 "to do what is reasonable in all the circumstances to safeguard the child's health, development and welfare, including consent to medical treatment and related procedures where the child is incapable of giving consent and it is not known that the parent would refuse such consent."[94]

Where PRRs are held by more than one person, each person may exercise them separately without the consent of the other, unless a court decree or deed provides otherwise.[95] However, there is still a duty to consult the child under s.6(1). Where both parents are exercising parental rights, the consent of both of them is required before the child can be removed from or retained outside Scotland.[96]

Views of the child

In an attempt to comply with art.12 of the UN Convention on the Rights of the Child, **15–22** where any major decision arises, those exercising PRRs or entrusted with the care and control of children, must have regard to the child's views (if they wish to express them) so far as is practicable.[97] Account must be taken of the age and maturity of the particular child, but there is a rebuttable presumption that a child of 12 or older is of sufficient age and maturity to form such views under s.11(10). This does not preclude a child who is younger, but deemed sufficiently mature, from expressing such views. The 1995 Act also requires that children are given the opportunity of having their views considered in court proceedings affecting them[98] (discussed in greater detail below).

Guardianship

A guardian is a person *other than* a parent who takes on that role in certain circumstances. **15–23** Under the 1995 Act a parent may appoint a "testamentary" guardian or guardians to act in the event of his or her death. As such an appointment is a "major decision" a mature child should be consulted before such an appointment is made. An appointment must be in writing and signed by a parent entitled to act as the child's legal representative.[99] A guardian may also be appointed by the court,[100] or by a testamentary guardian with a view to replacing them in the event of their death.[101] If the appointment is accepted, a guardian acquires full PRRs in respect of the child.[102] Once established, the appointment of a guardian can only be terminated on the death of the child or guardian, by court order (e.g. for bad administration), or on the child reaching 18 (unless the deed provides for earlier termination).[103] Where there is more than one guardian, each may act independently of the others unless the decree or deed of appointment provides otherwise.[104] Where disputes arise between guardians these have to be resolved by the court under a s.11 application (discussed below). The same holds good for disputes between a surviving parent and a guardian.

---

[94] 1995 Act s.5(1).
[95] 1995 Act s.2(2).
[96] 1995 Act s.2(3) and (6).
[97] 1995 Act s.6(1).
[98] 1995 Act ss.11(7) and 16(2).
[99] 1995 Act s.7(1).
[100] 1995 Act s.11(2)(h).
[101] 1995 Act s.7(2).
[102] 1995 Act s.7(2).
[103] 1995 Act s.8(5).
[104] 1995 Act ss.7(5) and 2(2).

Court orders relating to PRRs

15–24 Under s.11 of the 1995 Act the Court of Session or the sheriff court may make an order relating to PRRs, guardianship or administration of a child's property. Such an order includes, but is not limited to:

- a *residence* order, which regulates the arrangements as to the person with whom a child is to live, or the persons with whom they are to live alternatively or periodically[105];
- a *contact* order, which regulates the arrangements for maintaining personal relations and direct contact between a child and a person with whom they are not, or will not be, living[106];
- a *specific issue order*, which regulates any specific question which has arisen or may arise in connection with PRRs or guardianship or the administration of a child's property[107];
- an interdict prohibiting the taking of any step specified therein in the fulfilment of PRRs relating to a child or in the administration of a child's property[108];
- an order appointing a judicial factor to manage a child's property or remitting that matter to the Accountant of Court[109];
- an order appointing or removing a person as guardian of the child.[110]

All these orders can be made on a temporary basis and varied and discharged by the court.

Who can apply?

15–25 Not only are the court's powers extensive but they can be invoked by a wide range of people. These include persons who already have PRRs,[111] persons who have had, but no longer have, PRRs (with three exceptions),[112] and any person, who despite never having had PRRs in respect of the child, claims an "interest".[113] Persons in the last category are very broadly construed and include unmarried fathers, grandparents, step-parents, siblings or other relatives and any anyone else with a connection to, or legitimate concern for, the welfare of the child, e.g. foster carers. It is also open to a child to make an application.[114] Even without a formal application by any of those qualified the court can make an order on its own behalf or on request where this forms part of competent proceedings.[115] Note that where two parents have PRRs, and the court grants any of the specified orders this will only inhibit the exercise of those PRRs to the extent provided for in the order.[116] All other rights may continue to be exercised by either parent without the consent of the other—subject to the exception noted above that deals with the removal or retention of a child habitually resident in Scotland where both parents must consent.

---

[105] 1995 Act s.11(2)(c).
[106] 1995 Act s.11(2)(d).
[107] 1995 Act s.11(2)(e).
[108] 1995 Act s.11(2)(f).
[109] 1995 Act s.11(2)(g).
[110] 1995 Act s.11(2)(h).
[111] 1995 Act s.11(3)(a)(iii).
[112] 1995 Act ss.11(4) and 11A. These are where the applicant lost PRRs in respect of the child as a result of an adoption order or a parental order under s.54 of the Human Fertilisation and Embryology Act 2008 or where the PPRs have vested in a local authority under a permanence order.
[113] 1995 Act s.11(3)(a)(i).
[114] 1995 Act s.11(5).
[115] 1995 Act s.11(3)(b).
[116] 1995 Act ss.3(4) and 11(11).

Overriding principles for making an order

A child's welfare prevails over PRRs, so that a court can only grant an order if the **15–26** requirements of s.11(7) are met. These are that:

- the welfare of the child throughout his or her childhood shall be [the court's] paramount consideration[117];
- children must be given the opportunity to express their views and have them taken into account where sufficiently mature.[118] There is a presumption in favour of children aged 12 or over having such maturity[119];
- there should be minimum intervention, that is, a court should only make an order if it is better for the child to make such an order than to make no order at all.[120]
- In determining what is in the best interests of the child, under s.11(7A) to (7E) of the 1995 Act the court has to consider the effects of any domestic abuse on the child, or on the person who looks after the child, and whether it is appropriate to make an order when there would have to be co-operation between the latter and her abuser.[121]

Under the 1995 Act, the welfare principle does not of itself place any onus on the party seeking a PRR order to establish that this is in the child's best interest. Instead it was held in *White v White*[122] that the "court must consider all the relevant material and decide what would be conducive to the child's welfare".[123] There is no exhaustive list of factors relevant to welfare. Among the most influential are, the maintenance of the status quo in the child's life,[124] the desirability of maintaining contact with both parents[125] and with other family members,[126] and the need for the child to understand her racial or ethnic origin.[127] In applying the welfare principle, courts must be careful to comply with the European Convention on Human Rights. Thus refusal of a PRR application on the basis of a parent's religious affiliation may amount to a breach of the Convention.[128] Similarly, courts must be careful not to discriminate against an applicant on the basis of sexual orientation: sexual orientation is only relevant if it directly affects the child's welfare. The European Court has held that discrimination on the grounds of sexual orientation is a breach of art.14.[129]

In reaching their decisions, courts are explicitly instructed to have regard to the views of the child. This requires intimation to the child in "child friendly" language.[130] Courts may dispense with intimation, on application, where a child is considered too young to present views. However, dispensation does not relieve the court of its ongoing duty to provide a

---

[117] 1995 Act s.11(7)(a).
[118] 1995 Act s.11(7)(b).
[119] 1995 Act s.11(10).
[120] 1995 Act s.11(7)(a).
[121] See, for example, *R v R*, 2010 G.W.D. 23-442.
[122] 2001 S.L.T. 485.
[123] At 491G–H.
[124] *Brixey v Lynas*, 1994 S.L.T. 847; *Breingan v Jamieson*, 1993 S.L.T. 186; *Whitecross v Whitecross*, 1977 S.L.T. 225; *J v C* [1970] A.C. 668.
[125] *Sanderson v McManus*, 1997 S.C. (H.L.) 55. There is no presumption that a young child should be with her mother: it is only as a contributor to the child's welfare that parenthood assumes any significance: *Re B (A child)* [2009] UKSC 5 approving a dictum of Lady Hale in *Re G (Children)* [2006] UKHL 43 at para.37.
[126] *Early v Early*, 1989 S.L.T. 114; 1990 S.L.T. 221.
[127] *Perendes v Sim*, 1998 S.L.T. 1382 at 1384; *Osborne v Matthan*, 1998 S.L.T. 1264.
[128] *Hoffmann v Austria* (1994) 17 E.H.R.R. 293.
[129] *Salgueiro da Silva Mouta v Portugal*, 2001 Fam. L.R. 2. Cf. *X v Y*, 2002 Fam. L.R. 58.
[130] This is done by mean of an F9 form under rules of court made under the 1995 Act.

child with an opportunity to express his views where this is practicable.[131] These views must always be weighed against the child's welfare which prevails. The views of a sufficiently mature child are likely to prevail if they are reasonable and coincide with his or her best interests.[132] Where a child is subject to undue influence less significance may be attached to their views.[133]

Aspects of children's legal capacity

15–27 Parental rights exist to enable parents to fulfil their parental responsibilities towards children. As children mature, Scots law empowers them to make decisions on their own behalf before they become adults at 18.[134] The Age of Legal Capacity (Scotland) Act 1991 provides under s.1(1) that, as a general rule, children under 16 have no legal capacity to enter into any transaction. Transaction is broadly defined to include, unilateral transactions, the exercise of testamentary capacity or of a power of appointment, the giving of any consent having legal effect and the taking of any step in civil proceedings. There are four important exceptions to the general rule that a child under 16 has no legal capacity and that any transaction entered into by such a child is void and unenforceable. These are contained in s.2:

- Children under 16 have legal capacity to enter transactions "of a kind commonly entered into by persons of his age and circumstances" so long as the terms of the transaction are "not unreasonable".[135] The aim of the provision is to recognise the validity of everyday, common transactions of children of differing ages and circumstances. The transaction, however, may still be invalid if its terms are unreasonable.
- Children aged 12 or over can make a valid will[136] and their consent to adoption must be obtained.[137]
- Children under 16 can consent on their own behalf to any surgical, medical or dental procedure where, in the opinion of a qualified medical practitioner, they are capable of understanding the nature and possible consequences of the procedure or treatment.[138] The doctor is not required to acquire parental consent or to establish that the treatment is in the child's best interests. Where a child has sufficient maturity and understanding the question arises as to whether parents can consent to such treatment where the child refuses. Section 15(5)(b) of the Children (Scotland) Act 1995 provides that a parent can *only* act as a legal representative "where the child is incapable of so acting or so consenting on his own behalf". Therefore, it seems that a parent cannot consent when the child is capable of doing so. Where a child is under 16, the court has powers to make a specific issue order under s.11 of the 1995 Act and this could include medical treatment where that is in the child's

---

[131] *Shields v Shields*, 2002 S.L.T. 579. Where a child is initially too young to express views, in long drawn out proceedings the court will remain under a continuing duty to check that the child has not developed views since the start of the case, or changed their mind where they have expressed views in earlier proceedings.

[132] *Fourman v Fourman*, 1998 Fam. L.R. 98.

[133] *Perendes v Sim*, 1998 S.L.T. 1382.

[134] Age of Majority (Scotland) Act 1969.

[135] 1991 Act s.2(5).

[136] 1991 Act s.2(2).

[137] 1991 Act s.2(3).

[138] 1991 Act s.2(4). This provision essentially embodies the decision reached by the House of Lords in *Gillick v West Norfolk and Wisbech Area Health Authority*, which provided that children under 16 could consent to medical treatment without parental approval provided they had reached a certain degree of maturity and understanding.

best interests. In that case, an application may be made by a medical practitioner. Where children are not deemed competent to consent, those with PRRs, or who have care and control over them,[139] may consent on their behalf.

Legal representation

Children under 16 have legal capacity to instruct a solicitor and to sue or defend any civil **15–28** matter in their own name, where they have a "general understanding of what it means to do so".[140] There is a presumption that a person aged 12 or over is sufficiently mature to have such understanding[141] although this does not preclude a younger child from having such capacity if sufficiently mature.

Children aged 16 or over

Children aged 16 or over have full legal capacity. Some protection against transactions to **15–29** their detriment is afforded to children aged 16 or 17 which allows them to apply to court to have a prejudicial transaction set aside until they reach the age of 21.[142] A transaction is prejudicial if an adult exercising reasonable prudence would not have entered into it and if it has caused, or is likely to cause, substantial prejudice to the young person.[143] Certain types of transaction are excluded from this provision. Testamentary acts, consent to an adoption order or to medical treatment, initiating, defending or taking steps in civil proceedings, transactions entered into in the course of the young person's trade or business, or induced by his fraudulent misrepresentation as to his age or other material fact, and transactions ratified by the young person or the court cannot be set aside.[144] Ratification by the court is available only in respect of proposed transactions by persons of 16 or 17 and will not be granted if it appears that an adult exercising reasonable prudence would not enter into the transaction.[145] Ratification must be sought in the sheriff court and the sheriff's decision is final.[146]

Areas not covered by the 1991 Act

The Act does not affect the delictual, or criminal, responsibility of any person.[147] Neither **15–30** does it affect statutory age limits for particular purposes,[148] e.g. voting at 18[149] or the capacity of persons under 16 to receive or hold any right, title or interest.[150]

---

[139] 1991 Act s.5.
[140] 1991 Act s.2(4A), inserted by s.105(4) of the 1995 Act and Sch.4.
[141] 1991 Act s.2(4B).
[142] 1991 Act s.3(1).
[143] 1991 Act s.3(2).
[144] 1991 Act s.3(3).
[145] 1991 Act s.4(1) and (2).
[146] 1991 Act s.4(3).
[147] 1991 Act s.1(3).
[148] 1991 Act s.1(3)(d).
[149] Representation of the People Act 1983 s.1(1).
[150] 1991 Act s.1(3)(e).

Key Concepts

An essential starting point in the law relating to **children and parents** is the determination of who in law is a parent as this has important legal consequences.

A woman who gives birth is regarded as the **legal mother** of the child regardless of whether she is married to the child's father.

Acquiring the status of parentage does not automatically accord **parental responsibilities and rights** to a parent, except where that parent is the mother or the father has married the child's mother or has been registered as the child's father. Such responsibilities and rights are now codified in the **Children (Scotland) Act 1995**.

Where any major decision arises, those exercising **PRRs** or entrusted with the **care and control of children**, must have regard to the **child's views** (if they wish to express them) so far as is practicable.

A parent may appoint a "testamentary" **guardian** or guardians to act in the event of his or her death.

A child's **welfare** prevails over **PRRs**.

As a general rule, **children under 16** have **no legal capacity** to enter into any transaction.

PROPERTY DURING MARRIAGE, CIVIL PARTNERSHIP AND COHABITATION

15–31 Property for couples in Scotland today, not only includes traditional forms of wealth such as land and capital but also forms of "new property" that include wages from employment and benefits associated with such labour, or purchased by it, such as pensions and insurance rights as well as social security benefits.

Marriage, civil partnership and the "separate property" rule

15–32 Where parties marry or register a civil partnership or become cohabitants, the law upholds legal rights and duties, most notably the duty of parents to support their children. Property is generally subject to the separate property rule which provides that marriage or civil partnership shall not of itself affect the property rights of the spouses or civil partners.[151] Nor does it affect their legal capacity.[152] Similarly, cohabitants are treated as separate individuals and the ordinary property rules prima facie apply.

For most families, the most important asset they possess is the home in which they live. Most couples buying a home take title in joint names, but where they do not, it is only the person whose name is recorded in the Land Register who is the legal owner. Where the home is rented, title to occupy is conferred on the tenant by way of a lease; it is only the persons named in the lease who are treated as legal tenants although various protections are extended to family members in certain circumstances.

Exceptions to "separate property" rule

15–33 There are certain exceptions to the general rule that marriage or a civil partnership does not affect the parties' property rights. These include:

---

[151] Family Law (Scotland) Act 1985 s.24.
[152] 1985 Act s.24(1)(b).

- a spouse or civil partner's right to aliment[153];
- provisions under the Matrimonial Homes (Family Protection) (Scotland) Act 1981 and the Civil Partnership Act 2004[154];
- presumption of equal shares in household goods[155];
- presumption of equal shares in money and property derived from any house-keeping allowance[156];
- exception to requirement of delivery where insurance policy in favour of spouse, civil partner and/or children[157];
- right to retain possession of tenancy where spouse or civil partner who is tenant leaves matrimonial or partnership home[158]; and
- right to financial provision on divorce or dissolution, where matrimonial or partnership property is subject to fair sharing between the spouses or civil partners regardless of who owns it.[159]

Aliment

Under s.1(1)(a), (b) and (bb) of the Family Law (Scotland) Act 1985 spouses and civil **15–34** partners are obliged to aliment one another. The obligation is to provide such support, as is reasonable in the circumstances, having regard to the needs and resources of the parties,[160] their earning capacities, and all the circumstances of the case.[161] Among the circumstances of which the court may, if it thinks fit, take account is any support, financial or otherwise, which the payer gives, whether or not under an alimentary obligation, to a person whom he maintains as a dependant in his household.[162] In calculating aliment, conduct is to be left out of account unless it would be "manifestly inequitable to leave it out of account".[163]

Proceedings for aliment may be brought by a spouse or civil partner in the Court of Session or in the sheriff court.[164] They may stand alone, or form part of other proceedings such as divorce, dissolution, separation or those concerning parental responsibilities or parental rights.[165] Where any claim for aliment is made, the court has power to award interim aliment—that is aliment pending the outcome of a court case.[166] There is no fixed scale for aliment and courts generally assess need relative to the lifestyle enjoyed by the parties during the marriage or civil partnership. An action may be raised even where the claimant is living in the same household as the defender.[167] But in this case, it is a defence

---

[153] 1985 Act s.1(1)(a), (b) and (bb).
[154] Civil Partnership Act 2004 ss.101–116.
[155] 1985 Act s.25. There is also a parallel provision for cohabitants in the Family Law (Scotland) Act 2006 s.26.
[156] s.26. There is also a parallel provision for cohabitants in the Family Law (Scotland) Act 2006 s.27.
[157] Married Women's Policies of Assurance (Scotland) Act 1880 s.2; Civil Partnership Act 2004 s.132. In this case, the policy vests in the spouse or civil partner, and his or her representatives, as soon as the policy is effected, without delivery.
[158] 1981 Act s.2(8): 2004 Act s.102(8).
[159] 1985 Act s.9(1)(a).
[160] Defined in s.27 of the Act as including "present and foreseeable" needs and resources. The provision of benefits in kind by an employer amounts to a resource to the employee but not to a cash sum equivalent: *Semple v Semple*, 1995 S.C.L.R. 569.
[161] 1985 Act ss.1(2) and 4.
[162] 1985 Act s.4(3)(a).
[163] 1985 Act s.4(3)(b).
[164] 1985 Act s.2(1).
[165] But note that the opportunity to resolve all such issues in one action is now restricted by the provisions of the Child Support Act 1991.
[166] 1985 Act s.6(1).
[167] 1985 Act s.2(6).

that the defender has made an offer, which it is reasonable to expect the pursuer to accept, to receive that person into his household and to fulfil the obligation of aliment.[168] When assessing the reasonableness of an offer, the court is to have regard to any conduct, decree or other circumstances which appear to be relevant but an agreement by the parties to live apart is not of itself to be regarded as making it unreasonable to expect an offer to be accepted.[169]

Where an award is granted, the court will usually order the making of periodical payments, for a definite or indefinite period.[170] A decree for aliment may be varied or recalled if there has been a material change of circumstances.[171] The making of a maintenance calculation under the Child Support Act 1991 is specifically designated as a material change of circumstances justifying variation of aliment paid to a spouse, or civil partner, as well as to a child.[172] Where parties reach their own agreement as to aliment, any provision which purports to exclude liability for future aliment, or to restrict the right to claim aliment, is of no effect unless it was fair and reasonable in all the circumstances of the agreement when it was entered into.[173] The obligation to aliment a spouse or civil partner terminates on death,[174] or divorce, or dissolution.

Social security and income-related state benefits

15–35 Where couples cohabit, but are unmarried or have not registered a civil partnership, they are under no obligation to aliment one another as the right to aliment only arises through marriage or civil partnership. In such cases, where individuals are in need, they will have to turn to the State for support under public law.[175] This may also be true for married couples, or civil partners where they are on very low incomes. However, eligibility for state benefits is dependent upon meeting certain criteria which may prove hard to establish. Each benefit has its own qualifying conditions, but benefits are in general divided into those that are contributory and those that are non-contributory. Certain social security benefits are only payable to individuals who have paid sufficient National Insurance contributions through deductions from their earnings, which entitle them to make a claim. All other benefits are "non-contributory", since they do not depend on the claimant satisfying a given level of National Insurance contributions. The main income-related benefits are jobseeker's allowance, working families tax credit, housing benefit, council tax benefit and in some cases income support.

Income support

15–36 Income support[176] is a means-tested benefit and provides a weekly cash sum to up a claimant's income to a minimum level as prescribed each year by the Secretary of State. It is available to those who are not in full-time work and are not required to sign on as available for work, e.g. people aged over 60 or who are incapable of work through sickness

---

[168] 1985 Act s.2(8)
[169] 1985 Act s.2(9).
[170] 1985 Act s.3(1)(a).
[171] 1985 Act s.5(1).
[172] 1985 Act s.5(1A).
[173] 1985 Act s.7(1).
[174] But a widow has an independent claim against her husband's estate for temporary aliment after his death. A surviving civil partner does not appear to have this right.
[175] The basic legislative framework for benefits is contained in the Social Security Contributions and Benefits Act 1992 and the Social Security Administration Act 1992.
[176] Income Support (General) Regulations 1987 (SI 1987/1967).

or disability, people who bring up children on their own and people who are unable to work because they are caring for a disabled person.

Aggregation of resources—what is a family?

These benefits are all "income-related", in the sense that they are assessed on the basis of **15–37** the resources available to the individual claimant. Under the Social Security Contributions and Benefits Act 1992, these resources include the resources of the claimant's family. The Act provides:

> "Where a person claiming an income-related benefit is a member of a family, the income and capital of any member of that family shall, except in prescribed circumstances, be treated as the income and capital of that person."[177]

For these purposes "family" is broadly defined to include spouses, civil partners and unmarried couples, with or without children, as well as single parent families including a child or young person.[178] Under s.157(1) of the 1992 Act, unmarried couples are defined as a couple who live together in the same household, as if they were husband and wife or civil partners. Where individuals fall within this definition of family, both entitlement and the amount payable in respect of all benefits are determined by aggregating the claimant's capital and income together with that of family members which may well bring him or her above the cut-off point for benefit. The underlying rationale is that the State should not have to support the claimant if sufficient resources are being brought into the household by another member of the family (even if the claimant does not in fact benefit from them). For this reason the "family" is broadly defined to include unmarried or non-civil partnered couples. Such persons are expected mutually to support one another, rather than rely on the State for support, even although they have no obligations to aliment each other under private law.

Recovery from liable relatives

Where benefit is paid to individuals the State reserves the right to recover the cost of an **15–38** award from those who fall within the category of "liable relatives".[179] Under s.78(6) of the 1992 Act, spouses and civil partners are liable to maintain each other and a parent is liable to maintain his or her children. A former spouse or civil partner is not a liable relative, as the duty to aliment a spouse or civil partner ends on divorce or dissolution.

Aliment for children

Children have a right to financial support from both parents, whether or not the parents **15–39** are or have been married or civil partnered to one another and whether or not they live together or apart. The Family Law (Scotland) Act 1985 sets out the principles for determining what support is owed by parents to their children. This support is also known as aliment. In practice, the provisions of the 1985 Act are rarely invoked where parents share a household with each other and the child, and in cases where the parents live apart, the 1985 Act rules on aliment have largely been eclipsed by the Child Support Act 1991, which has introduced wide-ranging changes throughout the United Kingdom in relation to the child's right to support.

---

[177] 1992 Act s.136(1).
[178] 1992 Act s.137(1).
[179] 1992 Act s.106.

Who is liable for aliment?

15–40 The 1985 Act provides that aliment is owed:

- by a father or mother to his or her child[180]; and
- by any person to a child who has been "accepted" as part of their family, except where the child has been boarded out as a foster child by a local authority or voluntary organisation.[181]

Under the 1985 Act a child is generally defined as a person aged under 18, but may also include a person over the age of 18 but under the age of 25 who is "reasonably and appropriately undergoing instruction at an educational establishment, or training for employment or for a trade, profession or vocation".[182] Under this Act, alimentary liability extends beyond the biological, nuclear family to include step-parents, grandparents and others in contrast with the 1991 Act where liability is restricted to parents having a duty to support their *legal* children.[183] Where aliment is owed to a child, it is generally the person with care of the child who receives any money that is payable to the child. This is because children have limited legal capacity which means that a parent or other adult will be required to administer the child's aliment.

Amount

15–41 Unlike the 1991 Act, there is no fixed amount for aliment. As with spouses, the obligation is to provide such support as is reasonable in the circumstances,[184] having regard to the factors which the courts use to determine the amount of aliment, i.e. the needs and resources of the parties, their earning capacities and generally all the circumstances of the case.[185] Where two or more parties own an obligation of aliment to a child, while there is no order of liability, the court, in deciding how much, if any, aliment to award against those persons, must have regard to the obligation of aliment owed to the child by any other person.[186] Where a child is under 16 the court may also include an amount for the reasonable expenses of the person having care of the child where these are incurred in looking after the child.[187]

Who may raise an action?

15–42 A claim for aliment may be brought by:

- The child [188] A child has full legal capacity aged 16 or over. If under 16 the child will have legal capacity to pursue the action if the child has capacity to instruct a

---

[180] 1985 Act s.1(1)(c).

[181] The 1985 Act s.1(1)(d). A child whom a father once treated as his own child but subsequently discovered to have been fathered by another man has not been "accepted" by him as a child of the family: *Watson v Watson*, 1994 S.C.L.R. 1097.

[182] 1985 Act s.1(5).

[183] Parents in this context include genetic and adoptive parents and persons who are to be treated for all purposes as parents under the Human Fertilisation and Embryology Act 2008.

[184] 1985 Act s.1(2).

[185] 1985 Act s.4(1).

[186] 1985 Act s.4(2). In *Inglis v Inglis*, 1987 S.C.L.R. 608 the court took into account the fact that the uncle and aunt owed an obligation to aliment the child in their action against the father of the child for aliment.

[187] 1985 Act s.4(4).

[188] 1985 Act s.2(4)(a).

solicitor[189]; if 18 or over, the child *must* pursue the action as it is no longer competent for a parent to raise the action on the child's behalf.[190]

- A child's parent or guardian.[191]
- Anyone with whom he lives or who is seeking a residence order in respect of him.[192]
- A child's curator bonis, if incapax.[193]

A woman, whether married or not, may bring an action in respect of her unborn child but no such action can be heard or disposed of until the child is born.[194] An order may be made for the making of alimentary payments of an occasional or special nature, including payments in respect of inlying, funeral or educational expenses.[195] Where the person to be alimented is living in the same house as the defender it is a defence to the action for aliment that the defender is thereby fulfilling his alimentary obligation and intends to continue doing so,[196] and it is also a defence that the defender is making an offer, which it is reasonable to expect the person concerned to accept, to receive that person into his household and thereby fulfil his obligation of aliment.[197] However, that defence is not open in the case of aliment for a child under 16. This is because the question of where a child should live is prima facie an issue in proceedings for a residence order where the child's welfare will be the paramount consideration. Where a child is over 16, the defence stands if the defender had offered a home to the child which it was reasonable to expect the child to accept.[198] In determining whether it was reasonable for the child to accept such an offer, the defender's conduct will be taken into account.[199]

A claim for aliment may be brought in the Court of Session or the sheriff court and, unless the court considers it inappropriate, may be raised as an ancillary matter in various proceedings, e.g. divorce, dissolution and actions in relation to parental responsibilities and rights.[200] It takes the form of periodical payments, whether for a definite or indefinite period or until the happening of a specified event.[201] However, the court can order alimentary payments of an occasional or special nature to meet special needs, which it would be unreasonable to expect the claimant to meet out of a periodical allowance.[202] It can also be varied or recalled on the basis of a material change of circumstances since the date of decree.

---

[189] See s.2(4A) and (4B) of the Age of Legal Capacity (Scotland) Act 1991.
[190] *Hay v Hay*, 2000 S.L.T. (Sh. Ct) 95.
[191] 1985 Act s.2(4)(c)(i).
[192] 1985 Act s.2(4)(c)(iii).
[193] 1985 Act s.2(4)(b).
[194] 1985 Act s.2(5).
[195] 1985 Act s.3(1)(b).
[196] 1985 Act s.2(7).
[197] 1985 Act s.2(8).
[198] 1985 Act s.2(8).
[199] 1985 Act s.2(9).
[200] 1985 Act s.2(1) and (2).
[201] 1985 Act s.3(1)(a).
[202] 1985 Act s.3(1)(b).

Child Support Act 1991

Definition of child and parent

15–43 The Child Support Act 1991[203] creates an administrative scheme, administered by the Child Maintenance and Enforcement Commission (CMEC) for assessing and enforcing maintenance owed by a parent to a "qualifying" child.[204] A child[205] is defined as a person:

- under 16;
- under 19 and in full-time, non advanced education[206]; or
- under 18 and registered for work or youth training while a parent is still claiming child benefit in respect of the child.

15–44 Persons who are, or have been, married or registered a civil partnership do not fall within the definition.[207] A qualifying child is one where one or both parents are non-resident parents,[208] i.e. they do not live with the child. A non-resident parent is a parent not living in the same household as the child, where the child is living with a person with care.[209] A person with care is a person with whom the child has his home, who provides day to day care of the child and who does not fall within certain prescribed categories.[210] A person with care does not require to be an individual, so that a parent can be found liable to contribute to the maintenance of a child in the care of a voluntary agency, although no assessment can be levied against an agency.[211]

Under the Act, each parent of a qualifying child is responsible for that child's maintenance. It is important to note that the definition of parent is limited to "any person who is in law the mother or father of the child".[212] Thus natural and adoptive parents are covered, but not step-parents who have no liability under the Act. It is also important to note that maintenance under the Act is only the responsibility of the non-resident parent. The person with day-to-day care of the child in effect meets his or her responsibility to maintain by looking after the child, and need make no payments to, or for the benefit of, the child. A child is generally cared for by one of his or her natural parents ("the person with care"), who is separated from the other ("the non-resident parent"). However, this is not always the case and where the person with care is not a parent, both parents will qualify as non-resident parents under the Act.

---

[203] As amended.
[204] 1991 Act s.3.
[205] 1991 Act s.55.
[206] Full-time education covers those attending school or a further education college but not universities or similar institutions.
[207] 1991 Act s.55(2).
[208] The term non-resident replaces the original term "absent" parent.
[209] 1991 Act s.3.
[210] 1991 Act s.3(3).
[211] 1991 Act s.44(2).
[212] 1991 Act s.54.

Who can apply for a maintenance calculation?

The person with care or the non-resident parent of a qualifying child may apply to the **15–45** CMEC for a maintenance calculation,[213] to be made in respect of the child. A qualifying child, aged 12 or over, who is habitually resident in Scotland may also apply for a maintenance calculation in his or her own right.[214]

Formula for maintenance calculation

The basic rate of child support maintenance is calculated as a percentage of the non- **15–46** resident parent's gross weekly income[215]:

- 12 per cent if one qualifying child;
- 16 per cent if 2 qualifying children;
- 19 per cent if 3 or more qualifying children.

The basic rate applies provided the non-resident parent's gross income is less than £800 a week. If it is more than £800 the non-resident parent will pay 9 per cent,12 per cent and 15 per cent of that part of his income which exceeds £800 for one, two or more children respectively. The maximum gross weekly income is £3,000 a week. The scheme ignores the income of the person with care and also the income of any partner of the non-resident parent. The amount will be reduced if the non-resident parent has one, or more, children living in his household. These include step-children as well as children conceived with the new partner.

Variation

The non-resident parent can apply for a reduction of the normal maintenance calculation **15–47** in certain circumstances. These are when he is incurring "special expenses",[216] and these include high costs of maintaining contact with the child, long term illness or disability of a child living with him, boarding school costs for a qualifying children and mortgage payments in respect of his former home where the person with care continues to live. The person with care can apply for an increase in the normal maintenance calculation if the non-resident parent has assets in excess of £65K, or has additional income or has diverted income or has a lifestyle inconsistent with his declared income.

Relationship between courts and CMEC

The courts' powers to award aliment to qualifying children have largely been replaced by **15–48** the powers of the CMEC to make maintenance calculations.[217] Thus, it is not competent for a court to make any order which has the effect of awarding aliment in cases where a child support calculation may be made. This means that the courts have no jurisdiction to award aliment under the Family Law (Scotland) Act 1985 if the CMEC has jurisdiction under the 1991 Act. However, they may still make awards in the following cases where the 1991 Act does not apply:

---

[213] The term "maintenance assessment" under the original 1991 Act has been replaced by the term "maintenance calculation".
[214] 1991 Act s.7.
[215] 1991 Act Sch.1.
[216] 1991 Act ss.28A–28F (added by the Child Support Act 1995 ss.1–6, and substituted and amended by the CSPSSA 2000 s.5).
[217] 1991 Act ss.11 and 13.

- where a child over 18 is undergoing education or training[218];
- where a claim is made against a step-parent or any other person who has "accepted" the claimant as part of the family;
- where the non-resident parent is not habitually resident in the UK[219];
- where a child seeks aliment from the person with care (because a maintenance calculation cannot be made in respect of such a person).

In those cases, where there are existing court maintenance orders or pre-1993 agreements for aliment the courts retain power to vary them.[220]

There are three exceptions to the general principle that courts do not have the power to award aliment in cases where a maintenance calculation could be made. These are:

- where the award represents a "top up".[221] This occurs where the non-resident parent has more than enough assessable income to meet the maximum child maintenance allowance under the 1991 Act and the court is satisfied that the circumstances of the case make it appropriate for an award to be made under the 1985 Act;
- where the award is made solely for the purpose of meeting some or all of the expenses incurred by a child in receiving instruction at an educational establishment or undergoing teaching for a trade, profession or vocation[222];
- where the child is disabled and the order is made solely for the purpose of meeting some or all of the expenses due to the disability.[223]

Key Concepts

Property is generally subject to the **separate property rule** that provides that a marriage or civil partnership shall not of itself affect the property rights of the spouses.

Most couples buying a **home** take title in **joint names**, but where they do not, it is only the person whose name is **recorded in the Land Register** who is treated as the owner in law.

Spouses and civil partners are obliged to **aliment** one another, to provide such support as is **reasonable in the circumstances** having regard to the needs and resources of the parties, their earning capacities, and all the circumstances of the case.

Children have a right to **financial support** from **both parents**, whether or not the parents are or have been married to one another and whether or not they live together or apart.

The **Child Support Act 1991** creates an administrative scheme for assessing and enforcing **maintenance** owed by a parent to a "qualifying" child.

---

[218] *Park v Park*, 2000 S.L.T. (Sh. Ct) 65; *Macdonald v Macdonald*, 1998 Fam. L.B. 31–4.
[219] 1991 Act s.44(1).
[220] 1991 Act ss.8(3A) and 4(10).
[221] 1991 Act s.8(6).
[222] 1991 Act s.8(7).
[223] 1991 Act s.8(8).

Domestic Violence and the Family Home

One exception to the general principle that marriage or civil partnership has no effect on **15–49**
the property rights of the spouses or civil partners is provided by the Matrimonial Homes
(Family Protection) (Scotland) Act 1981 (spouses) and ss.101–116 of the Civil Partnership
Act 2004 (civil partners). The rules are identical. However, to save repetition we shall
consider in detail the provisions of the 1981 Act only: this is also the context in which the
law has been developed by the courts.

Only the person who owns property, or holds title to it, is entitled to possess it, occupy it
and alienate it by sale or gift. In principle the person who owns the family home has the
power to evict any other occupants and to interdict them from returning to the premises.[224]
Such rights can cause hardship in the domestic sphere. Particular concern arose in the
1970s after a number of studies showed that domestic violence was a prevalent and
increasing problem.

Studies documenting violence and abuse identified a number of key areas for concern.[225]

- If a violent partner was the sole owner of the home (and most perpetrators of such
  violence are male) then he had the sole right to occupy and thus to eject all other
  inhabitants of the house as he pleased, e.g. as a reprisal for calling out police
  because of assault. If the victim left the house she would have no right to re-enter
  the family home against his will.

This had implications for women, namely:

- that they might be rendered homeless or forced to accept sub-standard accommodation for themselves and their children; and
- that for this reason many women put up with abuse or violence because they did
  not have anywhere suitable to go.

These findings made a great impression on both English and Scottish Law Commissions
and led to legislation. In Scotland this took the form of the Matrimonial Homes (Family
Protection) (Scotland) Act 1981. The Act has two main aims:

(1) to provide a spouse, who has no legal right to live in the home, with that right
    (and to extend this to a limited extent to cohabitants); and
(2) to provide increased protection for spouse and children (and to a limited extent
    cohabitants), who are at risk from domestic violence or abuse.

To achieve these ends, the Act is framed around rights to occupy and to exclude a violent
party from the family home. It confers occupancy rights together with various subsidiary
and ancillary rights and remedies[226] on a spouse who is not the owner or tenant of the
matrimonial home, referred to as a "non-entitled spouse" (NES).[227] The spouse who owns,
is the tenant of, or who is permitted by a third party to occupy the property, is the

---

[224] In *Millar v Millar*, 1940 S.C. 56 a wife who let property gave her husband notice to quit and the court upheld
her action. In *Maclure v Maclure*, 1911 S.C. 200 a husband who was the sole tenant of the family home was
granted an interdict to exclude his drunken wife from the premises.
[225] *Report from the Select Committee on Violence in Marriage*, H.C. Paper No.533 (Session 1974/75) and the
Observations on that report ((1976), Cmnd.6690).
[226] Some of these affect a spouse's ability to enter into property transactions, see s.2 of the 1981 Act.
[227] 1981 Act s.1(1). The parallel provisions for civil partners are ss.101–103 of the 2004 Act.

"entitled spouse" (ES).[228] What counts as a matrimonial home is broadly defined to include:

> "any house, caravan, houseboat or other structure which has been provided or has been made available by one or both of the spouses as, or has become, a family residence ... but does not include a residence provided by a person for one spouse to reside in, whether with any child of the family or not, separately from the other spouse."[229]

Under this definition, parties may have more than one matrimonial home.

Occupancy rights of non-entitled spouse

15–50 A NES has the right: (a) if in occupation, to continue to occupy the matrimonial home; and (b) a right, if not in occupation, to enter into and occupy the matrimonial home. The rights arise through marriage and need not be applied for and they may be exercised together with any child of the family. A child is defined as "any child or grandchild of either spouse, and any person who has been brought up or treated by either spouse as if he or she were a child of that spouse".[230] This definition covers step-children and has no age restriction, so that it covers adult children.

In order to uphold, or enforce, these rights an NES must apply to the court. An NES who has been refused entry to the matrimonial home may exercise the right to enter and occupy the home only with the leave of the court.[231] Either spouse may apply to the court for an order declaring, enforcing or restricting occupancy rights, or regulating their exercise or protecting the rights of the applicant spouse in relation to the other spouse.[232] The court must make an order declaring the rights of the applicant spouse if the application relates to a matrimonial home but in the exercise of its other powers the court has discretion to make such orders as it considers just and reasonable.[233] In reaching its decision it is directed to have regard to all circumstances of the case including the conduct of the spouses, their respective needs and financial resources, the needs of any child of the family, the use of the matrimonial home in relation to any trade, business or profession of either spouse and whether the ES has offered suitable alternative accommodation to the NES.[234] The court can grant interim orders pending a decision on regulation of occupancy rights.[235] It also has the power to grant an NES the possession, or use, of furniture and plenishings in the matrimonial home, where these are owned or hired by the ES.[236]

In order to protect these occupancy rights, the NES is also granted various subsidiary rights under the Act. These include a right to make payment of outgoings,[237] e.g. rent, rates, mortgage payments, and to perform obligations incumbent on the ES (other than non-essential repairs and improvements),[238] to enforce performance of an obligation given

---

[228] 1981 Act s.1(2).
[229] 1981 Act s.22.
[230] 1981 Act s.22.
[231] 1981 Act s.3(1).
[232] 1981 Act s.3(1).
[233] 1981 Act s.3(3).
[234] 1981 Act s.3(3)(a)–(e). Conduct relates to the spouses' conduct in occupying the matrimonial home: *Berry v Berry*, 1988 S.L.T. 650.
[235] 1981 Act s.3(4).
[236] 1981 Act s.3(5).
[237] 1981 Act s.2(1)(a).
[238] 1981 Act s.2(1)(b) and (2).

by a third party to the ES,[239] to carry out essential repairs and to take other steps to protect their occupancy rights.[240] An NES, who wishes to carry out non-essential repairs or improvements, must seek authorisation from the court.[241] The court has power to apportion expenditure between the spouses on anything relating to the matrimonial home.[242] The court also has power to enable non-essential repairs to be carried out and to apportion expenditure where both spouses are entitled.[243]

While the court has a whole range of powers to enforce, restrict and protect the occupancy rights of the NES, it may not make an order that would have the effect of excluding the non-applicant spouse from the matrimonial home. This is because this would be a derogation from the common law rights of the proprietor to occupy his or her own property, which requires a special statutory exclusion order as provided for under s.4 of the 1981 Act.

Exclusion orders

Section 4 of the 1981 Act gives the court power to exclude a spouse whether ES or NES **15–51** from the matrimonial home.[244] Thus either spouse, whether or not in occupation, may apply to the court for an exclusion order suspending the occupancy rights of the other spouse.[245] Under s.4(2) the court must make an order:

> "If it appears to the court that the making of the order is *necessary* for the protection of the applicant or of any child of the family from any conduct *or threatened or reasonably apprehended conduct* of the non-applicant spouse which is *or would be* injurious to the physical *or* mental health of the applicant or child." [Emphasis added.]

But it is also directed under s.4(3)(a) that the court shall *not* make such an order if it would be unjustified, or unreasonable, having regard to all the circumstances including the s.3(3) factors set out above.

In reaching a decision about whether to grant an exclusion order, the court has been directed to consider four questions:

- What is the nature and quality of the alleged conduct?
- Is the court satisfied that the conduct is likely to be repeated if cohabitation continues?
- Has the conduct been or, if repeated, would it be injurious to the physical or mental health of the applicant or to any child of the family?
- If so, is the order sought *necessary* for the future protection of the physical or mental health of the applicant or child.[246]

---

[239] 1981 Act s.2(1) and (2).
[240] 1981 Act s.2(1)(d) and (f).
[241] 1981 Act s.2(1)(e).
[242] 1981 Act s.2(3). In doing so the court must have regard to the respective financial circumstances of the parties.
[243] 1981 Act s.2(4). This extends the common law right of co-owners to carry out only essential repairs without the other party's consent.
[244] The parallel provision for civil partners is s.104 of the 2004 Act.
[245] 1981 Act s.4(1).
[246] These questions were set out in *McCafferty v McCafferty*, 1986 S.L.T. 650 at 656.

Initially the courts took a very restrictive view of s.4[247] but subsequent case law has overridden the earlier decisions.[248] Nevertheless, the court must still consider whether the lesser protection of an interdict regulating the conduct of the non-applicant spouse towards the applicant spouse, would be insufficient or inappropriate when deciding whether or not to make an order.[249] The role of the court under the 1981 Act is to provide protection where one spouse is genuinely causing, or in danger of causing, injury of some kind to the other spouse or child of the family. The injury complained of should, therefore, derive directly from the acts of the defender spouse, and not just be stress or unhappiness generally induced by the breakdown of the marriage.[250]

Other orders

15–52 Where the court grants an exclusion order it *must* grant the following orders:

(a) a warrant for the summary ejection of the non-applicant spouse;

(b) an interdict prohibiting the excluded spouse from entering the matrimonial home without the express permission of the applicant; and

(c) an interdict prohibiting the non-applicant spouse from recovering any furniture or plenishings from the house except with the consent of the other spouse or by further order of the court.

In the case of (a) and (c) the defender spouse can plead that the order is unnecessary. In addition, the court *may* grant certain other orders,[251] including importantly, an interdict prohibiting the other spouse "from entering or remaining in a specified area in the vicinity of the matrimonial home".[252] Under s.14 the court can also make a matrimonial interdict prohibiting the defender from entering or remaining in the matrimonial home, any other residence occupied by the applicant spouse, the place of work of the applicant and any school attended by a child who is in the applicant's care.

Matrimonial interdicts and powers of arrest

15–53 The existing common law remedy of interdict has been strengthened by the introduction in the legislation of particular "matrimonial interdicts". The term is used in the Act to denote an interdict which under s.14(2):

(a) restrains or prohibits any conduct of one spouse towards the other spouse or a child of the family; or

(b) prohibits a spouse from entering or remaining in a matrimonial home or any other residence occupied by the applicant spouse or the applicant spouse's place of work or a school attended by a child in the care of the applicant spouse.[253]

But section 14(2)(b) cannot be used as a method of removing a spouse from the matrimonial home: it can only be granted if ancillary to an exclusion order. Powers of arrest can be attached to these interdicts under the provisions of the Protection from Abuse

---

[247] *Bell v Bell*, 1983 S.L.T. 224; *Smith v Smith*, 1983 S.L.T. 275.

[248] *Colagiacomo v Colagiacomo*, 1983 S.L.T. 559; *Brown v Brown*, 1985 S.L.T. 376 and see *McCafferty*, above.

[249] *Roberton v Roberton*, 1999 S.L.T. 38.

[250] *Matheson v Matheson*, 1986 S.L.T. (Sh. Ct) 2.

[251] 1981 Act s.4(5).

[252] 1981 Act s.4(5)(a).

[253] 1981 Act s.14(1) makes clear that the application can competently be made while the parties are living together as husband and wife.

(Scotland) Act 2001. By s.1(1A) the court must attach a power of arrest to a matrimonial interdict (for civil partners this is known as a relevant interdict) where it is ancillary to an exclusion order.

Third party dealings

The 1981 Act does not confer ownership of the matrimonial home on the NES.[254] This **15–54** means that an ES is free to sell the home. In order to protect the NES in this situation, the Act provides that, as a general rule, the continued exercise by an NES of his occupancy rights is not to be prejudiced by reason only of any dealing by the ES relating to the home and a third party is not by reason of such dealings entitled to occupy the matrimonial home or any part of it.[255] Relevant dealings include the sale or lease of a home.[256] However, there are certain situations in which this general protection does not apply for example where the ES occupies the home by the permission of a third party, or along with a third party,[257] or where the NES has consented to the dealing or renounced his or her occupancy rights.[258] The NES also loses protection where the ES sells to a third party who has acted in good faith *and* has either been presented with a written declaration from the seller declaring that the property is not a matrimonial home,[259] *or* a renunciation of occupancy rights *or* consent to the dealing by the NES.[260]

Transfer of tenancy

Where a matrimonial home is occupied under a lease, the court has power, on application **15–55** by the NES, to make an order transferring the tenancy of the matrimonial home to that spouse.[261]

Cohabitants

The protections afforded to adults under the 1981 and 2004 Acts are dependent upon them **15–56** having marital or civil partnership status. However, domestic violence and abuse is not restricted to married couples or civil partners. For this reason the 1981 Act provides certain more limited protections for cohabiting couples.[262] In order to qualify as a cohabiting couple under s18(1), the parties must be a man and a woman who are living with each other as if they were man and wife, or persons of the same sex who are living together as if they were civil partners. In determining the issue, the court is expressly directed to consider all the circumstances of the case, including the time for which it appears they were living together and whether there are any children of the relationship.[263] Unlike spouses or civil partners, cohabitants do not have automatic occupancy rights but must apply to the court to have them declared. Where an application is made the court has no power to

---

[254] This is also the case in respect of a non-entitled civil partner and the family home; for the parallel regime for civil partners see the Civil Partnership Act 2004 ss.106–107.

[255] 1981 Act s.6(1).

[256] 1981 Act s.6(2).

[257] 1981 Act s.6(2).

[258] 1981 Act s.6(3)(a). Note that the court also has power to dispense with the NES's consents, s.7(1).

[259] In such a case the NES may be entitled to "such compensation as the court in the circumstances considers just and reasonable" under s.3(7).

[260] 1981 Act s.6(3)(e).

[261] 1981 Act s.13. The analogous provision for civil partners is Civil Partnership Act 2004 s.112.

[262] Only ss.2–5(1), 13–18 and 22 apply to cohabiting couples. The provisions relating to dealing under s.6 do not apply.

[263] 1981 Act s.18(2).

make an interim order.[264] This means that a cohabitant who wishes to exclude a violent partner under s.4 of the Act must first raise an action for full occupancy rights, which, due to the procedure involved, may take several months. Where the application is granted the court can only make an order for a limited period of up to six months, initially, that may be extended on application for further six month periods.[265] A major oversight arises under the Act where a home shared by a cohabiting couple is owned or tenanted solely by one partner and it is the *entitled* partner who wishes to exclude the *non-entitled* partner from the home.[266] In such a case this will not be possible as s.18(4) expressly provides that only a non-entitled partner with occupancy rights, or a jointly entitled partner, can apply for a s.4 exclusion order.

Termination of rights under the 1981and 2004 Acts

15–57 Rights under the 1981 Act and the Civil Partnership Act 2004 will cease to exist where:

- the marriage or civil partnership comes to an end by death or divorce or dissolution (except where a transfer of tenancy is concerned)[267];
- the entitled spouse or civil partner ceases to be entitled[268];
- the NES or NECP consents to the dealing or renounces his or her occupancy rights[269];
- the parties do not cohabit for a continuous period of two years, during which the non-entitled spouse, or civil partner, does not occupy the matrimonial or family home[270] or the entitled spouse or civil partner has permanently ceased to be entitled to occupy the home in question and, for a continuous period of two years thereafter, the non-entitled spouse or civil partner has not occupied the home.[271]

Protection From Abuse (Scotland) Act 2001

15–58 This Act extends the range of interdicts to which powers of arrest may be attached. Under its provisions, applicants no longer need to demonstrate any particular personal relationship to an alleged abuser. Instead, the court simply has to find that granting the power of arrest is necessary to protect the applicant from the risk of abuse through a breach of interdict. Those currently excluded from using the 1981, or the 2004 Acts, may use the 2001 Act to have powers of arrest attached to an interdict that has been obtained, or is being sought, to provide protection from abuse. Abuse is defined to cover psychological as well as physical abuse. It includes conduct, which need not be active, and which covers a relatively wide category of behaviour including presence in a specified place or area. Powers of arrest must be attached to matrimonial or relevant interdict when it is ancillary to an exclusion order.

---

[264] *Smith-Milne v Gammack*, 1995 S.C.L.R. 1085.
[265] 1981 Act s.18(1).
[266] See *Clarke v Hatten*, 1987 S.C.L.R. 527. But the entitled partner could seek an interdict at common law and seek a power of arrest under the Protection of Abuse (Scotland) Act 2001.
[267] 1981 Act ss.1(1) and 5(1)(a).
[268] As the NES's rights under the 1981 Act are derived from the ES's rights it follows that where the ES ceases to have such rights those of the NES must fall. However, s.6 proves an exception to this rule.
[269] 1981 Act s.6(3)(a)(i) and (ii) and s.6(3)(e).
[270] 1981 Act s.1(7) and s.101(6B) of the 2004 Act.
[271] 1981 Act s.6(3)(f) and s.106(3)(f) of the 2004 Act.

> **Key Concepts**
>
> One **exception** to the general principle that marriage or civil partnership has no effect on the property rights of the spouses, is provided by the **Matrimonial Homes (Family Protection) (Scotland) Act 1981 and the Civil Partnership Act 2004**. The Acts contain provisions which give a spouse or civil partner the **right to occupy** and to exclude a violent party from the **matrimonial or family home**.
>
> The **1981 Act** also provides limited protections for "cohabiting couples". In order to qualify as a **cohabiting couple** the parties must be a man and a woman who are living with each other as if they were man and wife, or two persons living together as if they were civil partners.

PROPERTY ON DIVORCE, DISSOLUTION AND TERMINATION OF NON-MARITAL RELATIONSHIPS

Grounds for divorce and dissolution

Under Scots law marriage, or civil partnership, cannot be terminated until death,[272] except **15–59** by divorce or dissolution. Where married couples, or civil partners, wish to apply the provisions dealing with financial provision at the end of a relationship, under the Family Law (Scotland) Act 1985, they must get a divorce or dissolution. Divorce is regulated by the Divorce (Scotland) Act 1976 and dissolution by ss.117–122 of the Civil Partnership Act 2004. They provide for divorce or dissolution on the ground that the marriage or civil partnership has broken down irretrievably. Irretrievable breakdown can only be established, if one of the four following conditions is met:

- the adultery of the defender: this condition only applies to divorce. It cannot be used to establish the irretrievable breakdown of a civil partnership;
- the behaviour of the defender is of such a kind that the pursuer cannot reasonably be expected to cohabit with him;
- non-cohabitation for a period of one year, combined with the defender's consent to divorce or dissolution; and
- non-cohabitation for a period of two years.

This means that a pursuer will be unable to obtain a divorce, even where the marriage or civil partnership has in fact irretrievably broken down, if he or she is unable to prove one of the facts above. The court does have power to continue the action if it seems that there is a reasonable prospect of reconciliation,[273] but this power is rarely, if ever, used. Proof is on a balance of probabilities. Decree of divorce on the ground of irretrievable breakdown can be suspended until the pursuer grants the defender a religious divorce.[274]

It is also a ground of divorce or dissolution that since the marriage or registration of a

---

[272] On death a surviving spouse or civil partner is entitled to prior rights and legal rights under the Succession (Scotland) Act 1964 where a spouse or civil partner dies without making a will. Where a deceased spouse or civil partner makes a will, the surviving spouse or civil partner may still claim legal rights if he or she is disinherited or decides to reject any testamentary provision under the 1964 Act. These provisions do not apply to unmarried cohabiting couples. However, a surviving cohabitant can apply for financial provision of the deceased's net intestate estate: see Family Law (Scotland) Act 2006 s.29.

[273] 1976 Act s.2(1).

[274] Divorce (Scotland) Act s.3A.

civil partnership, either party has been issued with an interim gender recognition certificate.

General scheme of financial provision on divorce or dissolution

15–60 Financial provision on divorce or dissolution is governed by the Family Law (Scotland) Act 1985.[275] Orders for financial provision on divorce or dissolution can generally[276] only be made by the court on granting decree of divorce or dissolution or within a period specified by the court on granting decree of divorce.[277] The court is directed, where an application for financial provision has been made, to make such order, if any, as is: (a) justified by the principles set out in s.9 of the Act[278]; and (b) reasonable having regard to the parties' resources.[279] The five principles are:

- fair sharing of net value of matrimonial or partnership property[280];
- redressing imbalance of economic advantages and disadvantages[281];
- fair sharing of child care burden[282];
- adjustment for loss of support[283]; and
- relief of serious economic hardship.[284]

Fair sharing of matrimonial or partnership property

15–61 Matrimonial and partnership property is defined[285] as:

all the property belonging to the spouse or civil partners or either of them at the relevant date which was acquired by them or him (otherwise than by way of gift or succession from a third party)—

(a) before the marriage, or registration, for use by them as a family home or as furniture or plenishings for such a home; or

(b) during the marriage, or partnership, but before the relevant date.

It is crucial to note, that matrimonial, or partnership, property includes all property acquired during the relevant period by *either* or *both* spouses or civil partners (subject to the stated exceptions), regardless of whether one or both parties had legal title to the property in question during the subsistence of the marriage. One of two dates may qualify as the "relevant date"; either the date on which the parties ceased to cohabit,[286] or the date

---

[275] These provisions also apply to actions for declarator of nullity of marriage or civil partnership under s.17 of the 1985 Act.

[276] There are two exceptions. Under s.13(1)(c) periodical allowance can be applied for after divorce or dissolution where no order was made at the time and there has been a change of circumstances since the date of decree. Under s.14 dealing with incidental orders, 9 out of the 11 may be made before, on or after decree of divorce or dissolution is granted to refused.

[277] 1985 Act s.12(1).

[278] 1985 Act s.8(2)(a).

[279] 1985 Act s.8(2)(b).

[280] 1985 Act s.9(1)(a).

[281] 1985 Act s.9(1)(b).

[282] 1985 Act s.9(1)(c).

[283] 1985 Act s.9(1)(d).

[284] 1985 Act s.9(1)(e).

[285] 1985 Act s.10.

[286] 1985 Act s.10(3)(a).

of service of the summons in the divorce or dissolution action,[287] whichever one is the earlier.[288] Parties cease to cohabit only when they cease in fact to live together as man and wife, or civil partners.[289] The fact that parties live together in the same house does not necessarily mean that they are still "cohabiting" for the purposes of the Act.[290]

Pension and other rights

The 1985 Act expressly provides that rights to, or interest in, pension schemes or life **15–62** policies and similar arrangements fall within the definition of matrimonial or partnership property.[291] The proportion of the pension rights which fall into matrimonial or partnership property at the relevant date is calculated according to a formula set out in reg.3 of the Divorce etc. (Pensions) (Scotland) Regulations 1966.[292] This involves an apportionment of the total value of the pension rights over the time of the marriage, according to a formula:

Key Concepts

Pension Apportionment

$$\frac{A \times B}{C}$$

Where: **A** is the value of the pension rights at the "relevant date";
B is the period during the marriage when the party is a member of the pension scheme;
C is the total period of membership of the scheme before the relevant date.

Valuation of pension and other rights is done according to the cash equivalent transfer value (CETV) at the relevant date.[293]

Excluded from definition of matrimonial property

Property will not fall within the definition of matrimonial or partnership property where: **15–63**

- Property is acquired *before* marriage or registration,[294] except (a) where it is acquired for use as a family home,[295] or (b) where property acquired before

---

[287] 1985 Act s.19(3)(b).
[288] 1985 Act s.10(3).
[289] 1985 Act s.27(2).
[290] *Buczynska v Buczynski*, 1989 S.L.T. 558.
[291] 1985 Act s.10(5).
[292] SI 1966/1901 as amended by the Divorce etc. (Pensions) (Scotland) Amendment Regulations 1997 (SI 1997/745).
[293] There was some doubt as to whether the court was obliged in terms of the earlier regulations to use the "cash equivalent" figure in valuing benefits at the relevant date for divorce proceedings raised between August 19, 1996 and December 1, 2000. The Divorce etc. (Pensions) (Scotland) Regulations 2000 (SSI 2000/112) now make it clear that for all divorce actions commencing after December 1, 2000 that it is the cash equivalent value that should be applied.
[294] *MacLellan v MacLellan*, 1988 S.C.L.R. 399.
[295] 1985 Act s.10(4) and (4A).

marriage changes its original form, e.g. is sold and thus through acquiring a new form becomes matrimonial or partnership property.[296]

- Property is inherited, or is a gift from a third party, unless it changes its original form in which case it will become matrimonial property.[297]
- It represents an increase or decrease in value of the matrimonial property since the relevant date.[298] The rule applies whether or not the property is owned by one spouse or civil partner or both of them jointly and does not amount to a "special circumstance" justifying a departure from the norm of fair sharing.[299] However, where a property transfer order is to be made, the date of the valuation of the property to be transferred is no longer the relevant date, but instead the appropriate valuation date. The latter is a date agreed by the parties, but in the absence of such agreement, it is the date on which the property transfer order is made.[300] Where property is jointly owned, the court can also make an order for division and sale so that any increase in value after the relevant date can be divided equally between the parties as joint owners.[301]

Net value

15–64 It is the *net* value of the matrimonial or partnership property that is to be divided, so that any debts incurred during the marriage or civil partnership (or before marriage or registration where these relate to matrimonial or partnership property) that are still outstanding at the relevant date, e.g. mortgage, must be deducted. After the net value of the property has been calculated, it is to be shared fairly, i.e. prima facie equally between the parties.[302]

Special circumstances[303]

15–65 There are special circumstances[304] where the court may depart from the norm of equal sharing. The following are listed in the Act but are not exhaustive[305]:

- the terms of any agreement on ownership or sale[306];
- the source of funds or assets used to acquire the property if not derived from the income or efforts of the parties during the marriage or partnership[307];
- any destruction, dissipation or alienation of property by either party[308];

---

[296] *Davidson v Davidson*, 1994 S.L.T. 506. See also *Jacques v Jacques*, 1997 S.L.T. 963. But note that in some cases it may be subject to departure from the norm of equal sharing, s.10(6).
[297] *Whittome v Whittome (No.1)*, 1994 S.L.T. 114.
[298] In *Wallis v Wallis*, 1993 S.C. (H.L.) 49, the House of Lords held that any increase or decrease in the value of matrimonial property, between the relevant date and the date of divorce, must be left out of account in determining what amounts to fair sharing of the property. However s.10(3A) provides a solution to the *Wallis* problem.
[299] *Wallis v Wallis*, 1993 S.C. (H.L.) 49.
[300] 1985 Act s.10(3A): for an example of the application of this provision, see *Willson v Willson* [2008] CSOH 161.
[301] *Jacques v Jacques*, 1997 S.C. (H.L.) 20.
[302] 1985 Act s.10(1).
[303] 1985 Act s.10(6)(e).
[304] 1985 Act s.10(6).
[305] *Cunniff v Cunniff*, 1999 S.C. 537 at 540.
[306] 1985 Act s.10(6)(a).
[307] 1985 Act s.10(6)(b).
[308] 1985 Act s.10(6)(c).

- the nature of the property and the use made of it and the extent to which it is reasonable to expect it to be realised or divided or used as security[309]; and
- actual or prospective liability for expenses of valuation or transfer in connection with the divorce or dissolution.[310]

It is important to note that although these circumstances might justify departure from equal sharing, they cannot *require* it: where the circumstances cited are of negligible significance, or opposing special circumstances counterbalance each other, then equal division may be allowed to stand.[311]

In reaching a decision as to whether or not special circumstances apply to divert from equal sharing in any particular case, the court is expressly directed to ignore the issue of conduct on the part of either spouse unless it has adversely affected relevant financial sources.[312] Amoral behaviour is not relevant as "special circumstances" per se, but the financial consequences of that behaviour are, e.g. where spouse has gambled away the assets of the marriage.

Economic advantage and disadvantage and contributions

This principle is designed to deal with the situation where one spouse or civil partner (the **15–66** "homemaker") has given up or reduced his or her career prospects to care for the other spouse or civil partner and, possibly the children of the family, while the other spouse or civil partner (the "wage-earner") has continued to work and benefited from this arrangement in terms of earnings and career advancement. In these circumstances, a capital settlement based on equal sharing of the matrimonial or partnership property may not be sufficient to compensate for the long-term economic disadvantage the homemaker may have suffered in terms of career prospects, earnings level, and associated benefits, such as occupational pension rights. For this reason, the 1985 Act provides, in addition to the principle of fair sharing under s.9(1)(a), that

> "Fair account should be taken of any economic advantage derived by either party from contributions by the other, and of any economic disadvantage suffered by either party in the interests of the other party or of the family."[313]

"Economic advantage" means any advantage gained before or during the marriage or partnership, and includes gains in capital, income and earning capacity, while "economic disadvantage" is defined as the converse.[314] "Contributions" are defined to include any contributions made before or after the marriage or registration[315] and expressly cover indirect and non-financial contributions, in particular any such contributions made by looking after the family home or caring for the family.[316]

In practice, the courts have tended to be reluctant to make awards under this section. This is because they are instructed when applying s.9(1)(b) to take into account the extent to which:

---

[309] 1985 Act s.10(6)(d).
[310] 1985 Act s.10(6)(e).
[311] *Jacques v Jacques*, 1997 S.C. (H.L.) 20, per Lord Clyde at 24.
[312] 1985 Act s.11(7)(a).
[313] 1985 Act s.9(1)(b).
[314] 1985 Act s.9(2).
[315] 1985 Act s.9(2).
[316] 1985 Act s.9(2).

    (a) the economic advantages or disadvantages sustained by either party have been balanced by the economic advantages or disadvantages sustained by the other party; and

    (b) any resulting imbalance has been or will be corrected by a sharing of the matrimonial property or otherwise.[317]

It is often successfully argued that either the advantages and disadvantages suffered, or gained by, the spouses or civil partners, have balanced themselves out,[318] or that any imbalance has been sufficiently accommodated through the equal sharing of matrimonial property under s.9(1)(a). The most significant application of this principle has been the award of £100,000 to a wife in addition to a capital sum based on the equal division of matrimonial property.[319]

    Under s.28 of the Family Law (Scotland) Act 2006 a cohabitant[320] viz a man and a woman who are (or were) living together as if they were husband and wife, or two persons of the same sex who are (or were) living together as if they were civil partners can seek financial provision on the breakdown of the relationship to correct any clear and quantifiable economic imbalance that might have resulted from the cohabitation as a consequence of (a) the defender having derived economic advantage from contributions made by the applicant or (b) the applicant having sustained economic disadvantage in the interests of the defender. These provisions have been narrowly construed. In particular the applicant must show that the economic disadvantage she sustained was in the interests of the defender, i.e. that the applicant suffered economic disadvantage in a manner intended to benefit the defender and not simply as a consequence of deciding to cohabit with him[321]. In deciding whether a couple are cohabitants for these purposes, the court is expressly enjoined to consider the length of the period they have been living together, the nature of the relationship and the nature and extent of their financial arrangements.[322]

Fair sharing of child care burden

15–67 Section 9(1)(c) was intended to ensure that the economic burden of child-care is shared fairly between the parties. In practice, this meant that the parent who looked after children aged under 16 received additional financial provision in recognition of the economic burden of child care. Since the Child Support Act 1991 has come into effect, the scope and importance of the principle has been reduced because where maintenance is paid in terms of the formula, this includes an element for support of the parent who cares for the child, but it may still be used to justify an additional capital sum payment[323] or transfer of property order.[324]

    If an economic imbalance can be established a cohabitant can seek financial provision under s.28 of the Family (Scotland) Act 2006 "in respect of any economic burden of caring after the end of the cohabitation, for a child of whom the cohabitants are the parents".[325]

---

[317] 1985 Act s.11(2).

[318] *Adams v Adams (No.1)*, 1997 S.L.T. 144.

[319] See *Wilson v Wilson*, 1999 S.L.T. 249, where a farmer's wife obtained a capital sum in respect of her contribution to running a farm which was not matrimonial property and not, therefore, subject to the rules of fair sharing.

[320] As defined in s.25(1) of the 2006 Act.

[321] *Gow v Grant* [2011] CSIH 25.

[322] 2006 Act s.25(2).

[323] *MacLachlan v MacLachlan*, 1998 S.L.T. 693.

[324] See *Cunniff v Cunniff*, 1999 S.C. 537.

[325] 2006 Act s.28(2)(b).

Adjustment from loss of support

Section 9(1)(d) provides that a spouse, or civil partner, who has been financially dependent **15–68** on the other spouse, or civil partner, to a substantial degree, should be awarded such financial provision as is reasonable to allow them to adjust to the loss of that support on divorce or dissolution, over a period of not more than three years from the date of divorce or dissolution. What the Act clearly envisages is that for many homemakers the three-year period will provide a transitional stage during which they can retrain or re-enter the labour market with a view to reacquiring financial independence. Section 11(4) lists various factors the court should consider when making an award, including the age, health, earning capacity and level of dependence of the party making the claim, together with any intention they have to undergo a course of education or training and the needs and resources of the parties.

Relief of serious economic hardship

Section 9(1)(e) requires the court to award such financial provision as is reasonable to **15–69** relieve a party of serious financial hardship where that is a likely consequence of divorce or dissolution. Although the hardship must stem from the divorce or dissolution itself, and not any other factor such as illness, it does *not* apparently require (like s.9(1)(d)) that the claimant spouse or civil partner be financially dependent on the other spouse or civil partner. In assessing what amounts to "serious" financial hardship, the applicant's access to sources of support other than the spouse, or civil partner, including state benefits, must be considered.[326] It is only in very exceptional circumstances that this principle will be relevant.[327]

Although conduct is generally ignored it is relevant to s.9(1)(d) and (e), not only where it has affected the financial resources of the marriage or civil partnership, but also where it would be manifestly inequitable to leave it out of account.[328]

Financial orders

Section 8(1) of the Act entitles either party to apply for one or more of the following **15–70** orders:

- an order for the payment of a capital sum[329];
- an order for the transfer of property[330];
- an order for a periodical allowance[331];
- a pension sharing order[332];
- an "earmarking order" under s.12A(2) or (3) of the Act[333];
- an incidental order within the meaning of s.14(2) of the Act[334];
- anti-avoidance orders under s.18; and
- enforcement orders under ss.19 and 20.

---

[326] 1985 Act s.11(5)(a) and (d).
[327] The fact that the defender was not alimenting the pursuer immediately before the divorce does not per se prevent her from bringing a claim under this principle: *Haugan v Haugan*, 2002 S.C. 631.
[328] 1985 Act s.11(7)(b).
[329] 1985 Act s.8(1)(a).
[330] 1985 Act s.8(1)(aa).
[331] 1985 Act s.8(1)(b).
[332] 1985 Act s.8(1)(baa).
[333] 1985 Act s.8(1)(ba).
[334] 1985 Act s.8(1)(c).

In dealing with an application for financial provision the court is directed to make such order, if any, as is: (a) justified by the principles set out in s.9 of the Act[335]; and (b) as is reasonable having regard to the parties' resources.[336]

Given that by far the more common ground for divorce or dissolution is irretrievable breakdown, the principal philosophy underlying the Act is that divorce or dissolution should be as far as possible a financial "clean break" between the parties: that is, the former spouses or civil partners should be free to lead separate lives after divorce or dissolution, unrestricted by continuing financial obligations to each other. Marriage and registration are seen as partnerships "wound up" by divorce and dissolution, and ideally, the assets of that partnership should be distributed once and for all on its termination to the former partners in the form of capital, or by a transfer of property. Accordingly, the 1985 Act restricts the making of a periodical allowance award, requiring one spouse or civil partner to continue to maintain the other after divorce or dissolution, to occasions where a capital, or property transfer, award is inappropriate or insufficient to meet the objectives of the Act.[337] Furthermore, the court is given a wide range of powers to make it easier for it to award an equitable clean break settlement, including the power to award capital by instalments[338] and make a property transfer order.[339]

It is important to note that ex-spouses or civil partners cannot expect any clean break from any *children* of the marriage or partnership. While divorce or dissolution may end the legal relationship between the spouses and civil partners, the relationship between parent and child persists, and the court where it has jurisdiction still to do so since the advent of the Child Support Act 1991, will make such award of aliment to children of the marriage, or civil partnership, as is justified in the circumstances, before turning to any question of financial provision for the spouses or civil partners.

The courts may make an order for periodical allowance, only where it can be justified under s.9(1)(c), (d) or (e) and only where a capital sum, or property transfer order would be inappropriate or insufficient to meet the demands of s.9 principles, given the resources available to the parties.[340] It is an order for ongoing support not intended to be used as a method of dividing the parties' capital. It may be awarded for a definite or indefinite period,[341] but in any event ceases to have effect on the death or remarriage or re-registration of the payee.[342] In many marriages or civil partnerships it is difficult to order a capital "clean break" settlement, because there are few or no liquid assets available at the date of divorce or dissolution. However, a spouse or civil partner who has no current access to capital may nonetheless have an expectation of acquiring some at a future date, e.g. under an insurance policy, pension scheme or other investment. Alternatively, the paying spouse or civil partner may have a high enough salary to be able to pay off a capital sum by instalments out of income. The courts are, therefore, given the power to defer the date of payment of the capital sum,[343] and to order payment of capital by instalments.[344] It is important to note that an order for payment of capital by instalments is quite different from an order for payment of a periodical allowance because, although both may be paid out of recurrent income, the amount payable under a capital sum order cannot be varied

---

[335] 1985 Act s.8(2)(a).
[336] 1985 Act s.8(2)(b).
[337] 1985 Act s.13(2)(a) and (b).
[338] 1985 Act s.12(3).
[339] 1985 Act s.12(1).
[340] 1985 Act s.13(2).
[341] 1985 Act s.13(3).
[342] 1985 Act s.13(7).
[343] 1985 Act s.12(4).
[344] 1985 Act s.12(3).

once made. The courts are able to vary the date or method of payment on a material change of circumstances,[345] e.g. if an expected pay-out from an investment fails to materialise or if a job is lost or pay-cut imposed.

An order directing the trustees of a pension scheme to pay all or part of a lump sum due to the member, known as an "earmarking order", can only be made by the court on making a capital sum award and will satisfy, at least in part, the amount so ordered.[346] A pension sharing order can provide that one spouse or civil partner's rights under a specified pension arrangement or state scheme shall be subject to pension sharing for the benefit of the other spouse or civil partner and will specify the percentage value, or the amount to be transferred.[347] Unlike an earmarking order, pension sharing can be activated by the parties themselves, if they enter into a formal agreement in the prescribed form and give intimation to the trustees or managers of the scheme after decree of divorce.[348] Another option open to the courts, and in keeping with the philosophy of a clean break, is to make a property transfer order. The transfer may be stipulated to take place at the date of divorce or at a future specified date,[349] e.g. when a child of the marriage reaches 16.[350]

The court has the power to make one or more incidental orders to assist it in implementing its decision under the s.9 principles.[351] Among the court's powers under s.14(2) are the power to:

- order the sale or valuation of property[352];
- to regulate the occupation of the matrimonial or family home after divorce or dissolution[353];
- to declare the property rights of the spouse or civil partner[354];
- to allocate liability for household outgoings after the divorce or dissolution[355]; and
- to order that security be given in respect of any financial provision ordered.[356]

In general, the court can make any ancillary order which it feels necessary in order to give effect to the s.9 principles.[357] Any incidental order made must be justified under the s.9 principles and be reasonable having regard to the resources of the parties. An incidental order of interest[358] is frequently sought where there is a lapse in time between the date at which payment of a capital sum or transfer of property is ordered, usually the date of divorce, and the date at which the capital is actually paid or the property transferred.

Sometimes a spouse or civil partner seeks to reduce his or her potential liability to make financial payments to the other spouse or civil partner on divorce or dissolution by giving away property or selling assets at below market value, with the intention of reducing the total value of the matrimonial or partnership property or reducing his or her resources at the date of divorce or dissolution. In order to prevent such fraudulent behaviour, the court

---

[345] 1985 Act s.12(4).
[346] 1985 Act s.12A(2).
[347] 1985 Act s.27(1).
[348] 1985 Act s.28(1)(f), WRPA 1999.
[349] 1985 Act s.12(2).
[350] On the date for the valuation of the assets to be transferred, see discussion above para.15–63.
[351] A spouse or civil partner cannot apply for an incidental order under s.14(2) in isolation, but only in connection with an order for financial provision: *MacClue v MacClue*, 1994 S.C.L.R. 933.
[352] 1985 Act s.14(2)(a) and (b).
[353] 1985 Act s.14(2)(d).
[354] 1985 Act s.14(2)(c).
[355] 1985 Act s.14(2)(e).
[356] 1985 Act s.14(2)(f).
[357] 1985 Act s.14(2)(k).
[358] 1985 Act s.14(2)(j).

may, under s.18, set aside or vary the terms of any transaction or transfer of property which had the effect of defeating a claim for financial provision.[359] The court may, in addition, make such order in relation to property as it sees fit.[360] Application may be made under s.18 up to a year after the date of divorce or dissolution.[361] However, transactions or transfers can only be reduced or varied if they have occurred within the previous five years.[362] The court may also order that either spouse or civil partner reveals details of their financial resources.[363] Finally, it should also be noted that until decree of divorce or dissolution is granted, the court has power to award interim aliment to either party.[364]

Key Concepts

Under Scots law **marriage or civil partnership** cannot be terminated until death, except by **divorce or dissolution.**
A divorce or dissolution is granted on the "**irretrievable breakdown of marriage or civil partnership**, where there has been:

- adultery (restricted to divorce);
- behaviour of such a kind that the other party cannot reasonably be expected to cohabit;
- non-cohabitation for a period of one year combined with consent; or
- non-cohabitation for a period of two years.

Matrimonial or partnership property includes all property acquired during the relevant period by **either** or **both** spouses or civil partners (subject to the stated exceptions).
  Unmarried couples (whether opposite sex or same sex) can seek an award of **financial provision** on the breakdown of their relationship under s.28 of the Family Law (Scotland) Act 2006.

PRIVATE ORDERING

15–71 When it comes to dealing with family matters such as childcare, aliment and the distribution of property on the termination of a relationship, not all couples find themselves going to court to have their disputes resolved. Many prefer to reach their own agreements on these issues, and indeed, much of the emphasis behind the Children (Scotland) Act 1995 and the Family Law (Scotland) Act 1985 has been towards enabling parties to reach their own decisions, with less intervention by the courts. In reaching these agreements, parties may resort to mediation, involving an impartial third party, the mediator, who assists couples considering separation or divorce to meet and reach agreement on arrangements

---

[359] 1985 Act s.18(1).
[360] 1985 Act s.18(2).
[361] 1985 Act s.18(1).
[362] 1985 Act s.18(1)(i).
[363] 1985 Act s.20.
[364] 1985 Act s.6.

that need to be made for the future.[365] Among the benefits of parties reaching their own agreements are that they:

- save time and money; and
- may reduce the kind of hostility generated by full open court proceedings.[366]

Minutes of Agreement and Joint Minutes—married couples and civil partners

Where such agreements are made during the marriage or civil partnership or on or after **15–72** divorce or dissolution they are formally referred to in law as Minutes of Agreement (MoA). Where entered into they are usually registered in the Books of Council and Session for preservation and execution, or in the sheriff court books. The purpose of this is not only to maintain a record of agreement but to enable either party to enforce the terms of the deed when the other party is in default. Enforcement is a very important issue. Where an agreement is registered, enforcement can be done by summary diligence which saves time and money. This is because a party can act immediately on the warrant in the document without having to go to court to enforce the terms of the deed.

Sometimes parties will reach agreement only after the divorce or dissolution is already underway in the courts. Disputes about financial provision often commence as defended actions in court, but end up being settled by agreement between the parties. In such cases, settlement can be reached in the form of a Joint Minute of Agreement (JMoA). It is usual to ask the court to interpone authority to a JMoA and to grant decree in terms of the arrangements in the agreement. This has the effect of transforming the parties' private agreement into a binding decree of the court.

Once reached, such agreements whether MoAs or JMoAs are binding and cannot be varied or reduced without the consent of both parties, except in certain limited circumstances.[367] This serves to prevent reappraisal and re-negotiation of matters that have already been dealt with and provides another type of "clean break". Thus parties are free to set their own terms which may be quite different from the kind of settlement that would be reached under the 1985 Act. Once made agreements are binding and enforceable in law[368] (except possibly in the case of children).

Circumstances allowing for variation or reduction

Children

Under s.12 of the Children (Scotland) Act 1995 the court is directed in any matrimonial **15–73** proceeding concerning children under 16 to consider whether any s.11 order should be granted, such as a residence or contact order. Its paramount concern in so doing, must be the welfare of the child.[369] Thus agreements reached by parents concerning their children are not binding on the court and, indeed, any person with an interest may apply at any

---

[365] In Scotland mediators may be volunteers appointed by Family Mediation Scotland or lawyer-mediators who are jointly accredited by the Law Society of Scotland and CALM (Comprehensive Accredited Lawyer Mediators).

[366] Note that the courts in Scotland have power compulsorily to refer parties to mediation where they are involved in divorce, dissolution or child-related disputes. See Ordinary Cause Rules 1993 r.33.22 and Rules of the Court of Session 1994 r.49.23.

[367] Where one of the parties is in material breach it may be open to the other party to rescind the agreement without the other's consent see *Morrison v Morrison*, 2000 Fam. L.B. (42) 6.

[368] However, where parties make a separation agreement and then reconcile, their actings may be held to be consistent with an intention to revoke the agreement and the principles of financial provision under the 1985 Act may be applied. See *Methven v Methven*, 1999 S.L.T. 117.

[369] 1995 Act s.11(7)(a).

time for a s.11 order notwithstanding that an agreement has already been signed about residence or contact.[370] However, in practice where agreements about children have been reached, the court does tend to rubber stamp them. There is now a parenting agreement for Scotland to help parents reach agreement in respect of the care of their children and arrangements for contact, etc after the divorce.

Contractual grounds allowing for reduction or variation

15–74   Once made, variation is limited to the terms of the agreement itself, or to claims that consent was procured on the basis of fraud, misrepresentation, undue influence or force and fear.[371] The latter, require a very high standard of proof and very few contracts have been set aside on this basis.

Variation of periodical allowance to ex-spouse or aliment for children

15–75   While there is some scope for varying contractual provisions on periodical allowance, this is limited in the case of MoAs to cases where parties have made appropriate express provision,[372] or in the case of JMoAs to where there has been a material change of circumstances.[373] However, variation on the grounds of a material change in circumstances is only permissible where the agreement forms part of a court decree. It is also important to note that a material change in circumstances must be actual and not based on a deemed, or hypothetical, change of circumstances brought about, for example, by the granting of decree on the basis of erroneous information.[374]

Statutory challenge under the Family Law (Scotland) Act 1985 s.16

Is it fair and reasonable?

15–76   A statutory ground of challenge provides that an agreement may be set aside where it was not "fair and reasonable at the time it was entered into".[375] This will apply to any term of the agreement whether it relates to capital, income or transfer of property. The jurisdiction of the court to alter agreements under s.16 cannot be ousted and any term of the agreement purporting to do this will be void.[376] The power applies in respect of both MoAs and JMoAs.[377] The test of unfairness applies as at the time agreement was reached and not at any other date. This means that changes in the parties' circumstances *after* agreement has been reached cannot be taken into account, for example, if one spouse acquires unforeseen financial burdens in the shape of a new family after separation.[378]

---

[370] *Horton v Horton*, 1992 S.L.T. (Sh. Ct) 37.
[371] Variation of the terms of a periodical allowance may also take place in certain circumstances where the payer becomes bankrupt. In this event the court may, on or after granting decree of divorce, make an order setting aside or varying any term of the agreement relating to periodical allowance under s.16(3).
[372] 1995 Act s.16(1)(a).
[373] 1995 Act s.13(4) in respect of periodical allowance and ss.5(1) and 7(2) in respect of aliment. See *Watson v Mclay*, 2002 G.W.D. 2-73.
[374] *Bye v Bye*, 1999 G.W.D. 33-1591.
[375] 1985 Act s.16(1)(b).
[376] 1985 Act s.16(4).
[377] *Jongejan v Jongejan*, 1993 S.L.T. 595.
[378] See *Drummond v Drummond*, 1992 S.C.L.R. 473.

Independent legal advice

One of the major issues the court will consider is whether the parties had independent legal **15–77** advice when drawing up the agreement. If such advice was obtained then the courts will normally assume that each party was fully appraised of their legal rights and understood the consequences of entering the particular agreement. However, the presence of legal advice does not necessarily mean the agreement cannot be reduced.[379]

The fact that both parties are advised by the same law agent does not automatically imply that the agreement drawn up was not fair or reasonable because of the conflict of interest.[380]

Unequal division of assets

The mere fact that there has been an unequal division of assets between the parties by **15–78** agreement does not of itself give rise to an inference of unfairness or unreasonableness.[381] In some cases, an unequal division may be accepted by one party against their best interests, because they prefer the certainty of knowing precisely what they are to receive on divorce, rather than the uncertainty of waiting to see what a court settlement might produce at a future date.

An agreement can be reduced or varied under s.16 only either before decree of divorce or dissolution is granted, or within such time thereafter as the court may specify.[382] Thus in most cases, if the s.16 plea is not made at the time of divorce or dissolution the agreement will stand. This can be invidious, given that divorce or dissolution is often a time of turbulence and disruption, and that the full effect of an agreement negotiated under the pressure of this period (which is unlikely to constitute legal duress sufficient to allow reduction) may not become apparent until some time later when the action is barred. Furthermore, in many cases, full details as to the financial position, e.g. the value of pension rights, may only emerge after the divorce. Even where the action is raised in time, the courts are most reluctant to reopen a formal written agreement reached by the parties. This is because of the ordinary principle that parties should be bound to contracts they have entered voluntarily in the interests of certainty for both the parties themselves and third parties. It is submitted that this principle is not as compelling in relation to domestic relationships as commercial ones, something which s.16 already reflects, but perhaps not fully enough. There is something to be said for the concept of a "cooling-off" period within which a s.16 action could be brought by right *after* the divorce or dissolution.

In the meantime, it is strongly advisable to draft any agreement as comprehensively as possible with provision built in for unforeseen material changes in either party's circumstances. Otherwise problems may arise in connection with assets that have not been specifically dealt with in the agreement. In *Atkinson v Atkinson*,[383] for example, the agreement dealt with capital but made no mention of periodical allowance. The court

---

[379] See for example *McAfee v McAfee*, 1990 S.C.L.R. (Notes) 805; *Gillon v Gillon (No.1)*, 1994 S.L.T. 978; *Gillon v Gillon (No.3)* 1995 S.L.T. 678; *Inglis v Inglis*, 1999 S.L.T. (Sh Ct) 59.

[380] *Worth v Worth*, 1994 S.C.L.R. (Notes) 362.

[381] *Gillon v Gillon (No.3)*, 1995 S.L.T. 678. In *Anderson v Anderson*, 1991 S.L.T. (Sh. Ct) 11 the husband, in a fit of remorse at his conduct, made a written gift of his whole share of the matrimonial property to his wife. The court held that even if this was an "agreement" under s.16(1)(b) which was dubious, it was fair and reasonable when entered into as the husband had acted voluntarily and in full knowledge of what he was doing.

[382] 1985 Act s.16(2)(b), see also *Jongejan v Jongejan*, 1993 S.L.T. 595.

[383] 1988 S.C.L.R. 396.

found that it still had jurisdiction to make an order for a sum of periodical allowance.[384] For the avoidance of doubt, it should always be expressly provided that the agreement is to be in full settlement of all future financial claims between the parties arising out of the marriage. Given the limited scope for variation it is therefore essential that the parties get fully informed independent legal advice.[385]

Private ordering for cohabitants

15–79   Cohabitants may also wish to enter into agreements about finance and property. However, the legal status of such agreements is not as settled as those made by married couples,[386] nor is there the same right to have agreements reduced on the basis that they were not fair and reasonable at the time they were entered into, as s.16 of the 1985 Act only applies to married persons and civil partners. Where such agreements are entered into and recognised by the court they will only be subject to reduction under the ordinary principles of contract law. Given that cohabitants have the right under s.28 of the Family Law (Scotland) Act 2006 to financial provision when their relationship comes to an end, it is even more important that cohabitants should be able to have an agreement in relation to the financial and property aspects of their relationship.

Key Concepts

Many couples prefer to make their **own agreements** as to child care, aliment and the distribution of property **on the termination of a relationship**.

Where such agreements are made during the marriage or civil partnership, or, on or after divorce or dissolution, they are formally referred to in law as **Minutes of Agreement**.

Once made agreements are **binding and enforceable in law** (except possibly in the case of **children**).

Variation or **reduction** of such agreements may occur:

- with regard to **children**;
- where there are **contractual grounds** allowing for reduction or variation;
- where variation of **periodical allowance to ex-spouse or civil partner** or **aliment for children** is permitted; or
- following a **statutory challenge** under s.16 of the Family Law (Scotland) Act 1985 (Was it fair and reasonable? Did the parties have independent legal advice?—the mere fact that there has been an **unequal division of assets** between the parties by agreement does not of itself give rise to an inference of **unfairness** or **unreasonableness**.)

---

[384] But compare *Sochart v Sochart*, 1988 S.L.T. 449 where the parties agreed by joint minute that the husband should make the wife a periodical allowance but said nothing about any capital sums. In this case, the terms of the minute were held impliedly to dispose of all financial claims between the parties and so the husband was not allowed to seek a capital sum order from the court payable by the wife.

[385] Where this advice is negligent clients may sue their legal adviser, see *Darrie v Duncan*, 2001 Fam. L.R. 14 and *Dible v The Morton Fraser Partnership*, 2001 Fam. L.R. 15.

[386] They may be subject to the claim that they are unenforceable on the basis of the "illegal purposes" doctrine in contract law although the Scottish Law Commission has recommended that there should be a statutory provision upholding such contracts made between cohabitants, or prospective cohabitants: this recommendation was not implemented in the Family Law (Scotland) Act 2006.

ADOPTION

Introduction

Adoption is the legal process by which the relationship of parent and child is created by a **15–80** court order. The law is to be found in the Adoption and Children (Scotland) Act 2007. By s.28(2) of the 2007 Act the effect of an adoption order is to vest parental responsibilities and rights in relation to the child in the adoptive parents so that the child is treated in law as the child of the adoptive parents and has never been the child of any person other than them.[387] Put another way, the parental responsibilities and rights of the birth parents are extinguished when an adoption order is made and the child's rights are enforceable against the adoptive parents. In particular, after a child has been adopted, the birth parent loses the right to apply for parental responsibilities and rights, including the right to contact.[388] In short, adoption is a radical interference with the rights of children and their birth parents under art.8 and the law must be carefully balanced to prevent a breach of that article. While traditionally considered as a way of providing a home for a baby with a childless couple, adoption is increasingly being seen as providing security for older children who need long term care.

Adoption agencies

It is the duty of every local authority to provide a comprehensive adoption service to meet **15–81** the needs of all those who would be affected by adoption viz the child, the birth parents and the adoptive parents. This service is known as an adoptive agency. The 2007 Act proceeds on the basis that all the preliminary arrangements for an adoption should be made by an adoption agency. There is one exception. A private person can place a child for adoption where the proposed adopter is: (i) the child's parent; or (ii) where the child's parent is a member of a relevant couple, the other member of the couple; or (iii) any other relative of the child.[389] So for example a mother can place her child for adoption by her mother, i.e. the child's grandmother.

The welfare of the child

Section 14(2) and (3) of the 2007 Act provides that where a court or adoption agency is **15–82** coming to a decision relating to the adoption of a child they must consider all the circumstances of the case and regard the need to safeguard and promote the welfare of the child throughout the child's life as the paramount consideration. So far as is reasonably practicable to do so, they must have regard in particular to:

- the value of a stable family unit in the child's development;
- the child's ascertainable views regarding the decision taking into account the child's age and maturity;
- the child's religious persuasion, racial origin and cultural and linguistic background;

---

[387] 2007 Act s.40(1) and (4). There are some exceptions to the principle that on adoption the child is no longer regarded as the child of the birth parents: for example for the purpose of the law of incest and the prohibited degrees of marriage and civil partnership, the adopted child remains the child of the birth parents. However an adoptive parent cannot marry an adopted child but adoptive siblings can marry if they are not related by blood: the same rules apply to civil partnerships. Adoption does not affect the law on nationality and citizenship.

[388] Children (Scotland) Act1995 ss.11(4)(a) and 11A.

[389] 2007 Act s.75(2). On relevant couples see beyond.

- the likely effect on the child, throughout the child's life, of making the adoption order.[390]

Accordingly, at every stage of the adoption procedure when an adoptive agency or a court makes a decision which involves an element of discretion the welfare of the child throughout the child's life is the paramount consideration and the child's views must be fed into the decision making process.

Before placing a child for adoption, the adoption must consider whether or not adoption is the best way to meet the child's needs or whether there is some better, practical alternative.[391]

In placing a child for adoption, the adoption agency must have regard so far as is reasonably practicable to the views of the child's birth parents, guardians and other relatives[392] but the welfare of the child is the paramount consideration.

Only children who are under 18 and have not been married or have registered a civil partnership can be adopted.[393] An adopted child can be adopted again.[394] Where a child is 12 or over an adoption order cannot be made without the child's consent.[395]

Prospective adopters

15–83 A relevant couple can apply to adopt a child jointly. A couple is relevant if its members[396]:

- are married to each other;
- are civil partners of each other;
- are living together as husband and wife in an enduring family relationship;
- are living together as if civil partners in an enduring family relationship.

Each member of the relevant couple must be 21 or over and neither of them must be the child's birth parent.[397]

A spouse or civil partner who is not the child's parent and is 21 or over can adopt the child alone if the court is satisfied that the other spouse or civil partner cannot be found, or that the couple has separated and the separation is likely to be permanent or that the other spouse or civil partner is by reason of ill health incapable of making an application for the order.[398] Where a person is a member of a relevant couple and the other member of the couple is the child's birth parent, then that person can adopt the child alone if 21 or over and the birth parent is 18 or over.[399] A person who is not a member of a relevant couple and is 21 or over can adopt a child alone. If that person is a birth parent before the application can go ahead the court must be satisfied that:

---

[390] 2007 Act s.14(4).
[391] 2007 Act s.14(6) and (7).
[392] 2007 Act s.14(5).
[393] 2007 Act ss.28(6) and 119.
[394] 2007 Act s.28(6).
[395] 2007 Act s.32(1). The court may dispense with the child's consent if satisfied that the child is incapable of giving consent: 2007 Act s.32(2).
[396] 2007 Act s.29(3).
[397] 2007 Act s.29(1).
[398] 2007 Act s.30(4). Where the couple are unmarried or have not registered a civil partnership one of them can apply for adoption if the other is incapable of applying because of ill health: 2007 Act s.30(5). If they are not living together they would not be a relevant couple.
[399] 2007 Act s.30(3). The effect of the adoption order is that the child is treated as the child of the couple concerned and as not being the child of any person other than the adopter and the other member of the couple, i.e. the child's birth parent. The parental responsibilities and rights of the other birth parent are extinguished by the order.

- the other birth parent is dead; or
- the other birth parent cannot be found; or
- by virtue of the Human Fertilisation and Embryology Act 2008 there is no other birth parent; or
- the exclusion of the other birth parent is justified for some other reason.

Applications where a birth parent will adopt the child alone—as opposed to being a member of a relevant couple—will be rare.

Parental consent

By s.31(2)(a) of the 2007 Act an adoption order cannot be made unless the court is **15–84** satisfied that each parent or guardian of the child "understands what the effect of making an adoption order would be and consents to the making of the order (whether or not the parent or guardian knows the identity of the persons applying for the order)". For this purpose, parent means a parent who has any parental responsibilities or parental rights in relation to the child.[400] The agreement of a person who is not the child's parent, for example the child's grandparent, is not required even though that person may have parental responsibilities and rights unless that person is the child's guardian. A mother's consent is ineffective if given less than six weeks after the child's birth.[401]

However under s.31(2)(b) of the 2007 Act the court has the power to dispense with parental consent. First a ground for dispensation must exist. Secondly the court must be satisfied that the parent's consent should be dispensed with on this ground viz that it is the child's welfare to do so.

The grounds are:

(1) The parent or guardian of the child is dead.[402]
(2) The parent or guardian of the child cannot be found or is incapable of giving consent.[403]
(3) The parent or guardian of the child is unable to discharge their parental responsibilities and parental rights.[404] This ground does not exist when the only parental responsibility and right relates to contact. The court must be satisfied that the parent or guardian is unable to discharge the parental responsibilities and rights and is likely to continue to be unable to do so. This ground covers neglect and abuse of the child.
(4) The parent or guardian has no parental responsibilities and rights as a result of a permanence order.[405]
(5) If neither (3) or (4) applies the consent can be dispensed with if "the welfare of the child otherwise requires the consent to be dispensed with".[406] It has been held that this ground only applies in exceptional situations when the child's welfare *requires* the consent to be dispensed with: it is not enough that adoption would be in the child's best interests. As such it is not in breach of the parent or guardian's art.8 right.[407]

---

[400] 2007 Act s.31(15)(a).
[401] 2007 Act s.31(11).
[402] 2007 Act s.31(3)(a).
[403] 2007 Act s.31(3)(b).
[404] 2007 Act s.31(4).
[405] 2007 Act s.31(4) and (5). On permanence orders see beyond.
[406] 2007 Act s.31(3)(d).
[407] *Reference from Dumbarton Sheriff Court* [2011] CSIH 38.

Permanence orders

15–85 By s.80 of the 2007 Act a local authority can apply for a permanence order. This consists of a mandatory provision under which the parental rights to provide guidance and to regulate the child's residence vest in the local authority. However the parent retains the right to refuse to consent to the child's adoption. Before the court can make a permanence order, it must be satisfied either: (a) that no one has the right to have the child living with them; or (b) where there is such a person, the child's residence with that person is or is likely to be seriously detrimental to the welfare of the child.[408] Where the child is 12 or over the order cannot be made without the child's consent.

However, in applying for a permanence order the local authority can request the court for a provision granting authority for the child to be adopted. This cannot be granted without the parent's consent or there are grounds for dispensing with the parent's consent. These are exactly the same as the grounds for dispensing with a parent's consent to an adoption order. But as a permanence order can only be made when the child's residence with the parent is likely to be seriously detrimental to the child's welfare, in most cases grounds will exist to dispense with the parent's consent. If a permanence order is granted with authority to adopt there is no need to obtain or dispense with the consent of the parent to the adoption order itself.

The adoption order

15–86 If the child is the subject of a permanence order with authority for adoption or the relevant parental consents have been obtained or dispensed with, the court can make the adoption order. It must be in the child's best interests to do so, i.e. the welfare principle applies. The court can attach any terms or conditions to the order that it thinks fit.[409] This could be used to allow a child to have continued contact with the child's birth parents or birth family thereby promoting open adoptions for older children.

Key Concepts

- Adoption creates a new legal family for the adoptive child.
- Birth parents lose all their parental responsibilities and rights when the child is adopted.
- Adoption cannot be ordered unless the birth parent consents.
- The parent's consent can be dispensed with if grounds exist.
- The welfare principle governs every stage of the process.

STATE INTERVENTION IN THE LIVES OF CHILDREN: CARE AND PROTECTION

15–87 There are three main institutions in Scotland which are involved where children are in need of care and protection. These are:

- the local authority, who has both duties and powers in relations to children, which are usually exercised by its social work department;

---

[408] 2007 Act s.84(5)(c)(i) and (ii).
[409] 2007 Act s.28(3).

- the courts, who have a significant role in preventing the local authority from taking unfettered action and giving children and parents a right to a judicial hearing; and
- the children's hearings system.

Local authority duties and powers

The Children (Scotland) Act 1995 and the Children's Hearings (Scotland) Act 2011[410] set **15–88** out the framework to support children and their families in the community, emphasising partnership between parents and local authorities. The local authority is generally under a duty to promote social welfare by making available advice, guidance and assistance to persons in the area for which they are responsible.[411] This assistance can take the form of:

- cash, but only in exceptional circumstances[412];
- assistance in kind[413];
- the provision of residential nursing accommodation,[414] home helps or laundry facilities.[415]

Assistance under s.12 is restricted to persons aged 18 or over.[416] This is because the 1995 Act gives local authorities special duties in relation to children[417] in need. In particular, under s.22(1) of the 1995 Act, a local authority is under an obligation:

(a) to safeguard and promote the welfare of children in its area who are in need; and
(b) so far as is consistent with that duty, to promote the upbringing of such children by their families so that the children can be helped within their home environment.

Children "in need" are broadly defined[418] to include:

- children who are unlikely to achieve to maintain a reasonable standard of health or development without local authority assistance;
- children whose health or development is likely to be significantly impaired without such assistance;
- disabled children; and
- children affected by the disability of another member of the family.

In providing child care services, the local authority should, so far as is practicable, have regard to the child's religion, racial origin and linguistic background.[419] In keeping with the policy that children in need should be supported within their families, the Children (Scotland) Act 1995 requires local authorities to prepare and publish plans for the

---

[410] And what remains of the Social Work (Scotland) Act 1968.
[411] 1968 Act s.12.
[412] 1968 Act s.12(3) and (4).
[413] 1968 Act s.12(1).
[414] 1968 Act s.13A.
[415] 1968 Act s.14.
[416] 1968 Act s.12(2).
[417] A child is a person under 18, s.93(2)(a) of the 1995 Act.
[418] 1968 Act s.93(4)(a).
[419] 1995 Act s.22(2).

provision of relevant services within their areas.[420] They are also under a duty to co-operate with other agencies and authorities such as health boards.[421]

Voluntary care

15–89 A local authority *may* provide accommodation for any child within its area if it considers that it would safeguard or promote the child's welfare to do so.[422] However, a local authority *must* provide accommodation for any child,[423] residing or found in its area, if it appears to the local authority that the child requires accommodation because:

- no-one has parental responsibility for the child;
- the child is lost or abandoned;
- the person who has been caring for the child is prevented, whether or not permanently and for whatever reason, from providing the child with suitable accommodation or care.[424]

When providing a child with accommodation, the local authority, so far as practicable, must have regard to the child's views (if the child wishes to express them), taking account of the child's age and maturity.[425] In keeping with the Act's philosophy of keeping children at home, a local authority cannot provide accommodation for a child if any person with parental responsibilities and rights objects *and* is willing and able to provide accommodation for the child.[426] In addition, any such person may remove the child from local authority accommodation at any time. However, s.25(7) provides that if a child is in care *for a continuous period of six months,* a parent has no right to take the child away without the consent of the local authority unless that parent has given *not less than 14 days' notice.* It is important to note that this duty to look after the child arises not only when the child has been accommodated under s.25 of the 1995 Act but also when the child is in local authority accommodation as a result of a supervision order or any other order, warrant or authorisation made under the 2011 Act, as a result of which the local authority has responsibilities in respect of the child.

Children who are in s.25 accommodation are "looked after" children. A local authority has extensive duties to safeguard and promote the welfare of any child "looked after" by them under s.17. Such children include:

- children in s.25 accommodation;
- children taken from the family home under child protection or child assessment orders; and
- children under supervision order(s) made by a children's hearing.[427]

---

[420] 1995 Act s.19.
[421] 1995 Act s.21.
[422] 1995 Act s.25(2).
[423] That is a person under 18.
[424] 1995 Act s.25(1).
[425] A child aged 12 or over is deemed to be of sufficient age and maturity to form a view although this does not preclude younger children from being consulted if they have sufficient maturity s.25(5).
[426] 1995 Act s.25(6)(a).
[427] For full definition see s.17(6).

Before making any decision relating to a looked after child, a local authority must, so far as practicable, have regard to the views of the child and of parents or any person with parental rights and any other relevant person.[428]

Local authority powers

A local authority is empowered to apply to a sheriff court for a range of court orders to **15–90** help the local authority fulfil its obligations in respect of children. These include child protection orders, child assessment orders, exclusion orders and permanence orders.

Child protection orders (CPOs)

Situations can arise where it is necessary to act quickly to protect a child from serious ill- **15–91** treatment by removing the child[429] to a place of safety. Any person can apply to a sheriff for a child protection order (CPO), who *may* make an order if satisfied that:

(a) there are reasonable grounds to believe that a child—

    (i) has been or is being so treated (or neglected) that he is suffering or is likely to suffer *significant harm*; or

    (ii) will suffer such harm if he is not removed to and kept in a place of safety, or if he does not remain in the place where he is then being accommodated (whether or not resident there); *and*

(b) an order ... is necessary to protect that child from such harm (or such further harm).[430]

Where the local authority applies, special provisions apply to ensure that an order is only used where investigation of the child's welfare would otherwise be frustrated.[431] The application must identify the applicant and, where it is practicable, the child concerned. It must state the grounds for the application, supported by evidence.[432] Notice of the application must be given to the reporter and the relevant local authority, if the local authority is not the applicant. The effect of the order is to require any person in a position to do so to produce the child and to authorise the removal of the child to a place of safety[433] (or prevent the child being removed from the place the child is currently being accommodated).[434] It does not transfer parental responsibilities or rights but the sheriff can attach conditions and directions, e.g. regulating contact and the exercise of such rights.[435] This may include medical assessment and treatment although the child's right to refuse such treatment is reserved.[436] The order can provide that the location of the place of safety should not be disclosed to any person in the order.[437] Under a CPO, an applicant's actions

---

[428] 1995 Act s.17(4).
[429] Child is defined as a person under 16 or between the ages of 16 and 18 where a supervision order is in force: 2011 Act s.199(1), (6) and (7).
[430] 2011 Act s.39(2).
[431] 2011 Act s.38(2).
[432] 2011 Act s.37(5).
[433] A place of safety is a residential or other establishment provided by a local authority, a community home, a police station, a hospital or surgery whose management is willing temporarily to receive the child, the dwelling house of a suitable person or any other suitable place the occupier of which is willing to receive the child: 2011 Act s.202.
[434] 2011 Act s.37(2).
[435] 2011 Act s.41.
[436] 2011 Act s.186.
[437] 2011 Act s.40.

in respect of the child are restricted to those acts the applicant believes are necessary to safeguard or promote the welfare of the child.[438]

It is important to note that once the CPO is granted, it must be implemented within 24 hours or it will lapse.[439] If the parents do not successfully challenge the CPO at any earlier stage, the CPO must at latest come to an end on the eighth working days after it was taken, when a children's hearing meets to decide whether grounds of referral exist.[440] However, they have an opportunity to challenge the CPO in the courts at two earlier stages.

Stage one challenge

15–92 After a CPO has been made by the sheriff, an application to a sheriff to set aside or vary the CPO (and/or any directions made) is possible before the commencement of the "initial hearing".[441] Such an application must be determined within three working days. The reporter can arrange a hearing to give advice to the sheriff in relation to the CPO.[442] If the sheriff determines that the conditions for making the CPO are *not* satisfied, the sheriff must recall the order and cancel any directions.[443] If satisfied the conditions for granting the CPO *are* met, the order and any directions should be confirmed or varied, new directions can be granted, and the order continued in force until the full children's hearing on the eighth working day.[444]

If a stage one challenge is made, there is no "initial" hearing and if the CPO is confirmed by the sheriff, the child will be kept in the place of safety with any directions made about contact, etc. maintained, until the eighth working day hearing. At that stage, the normal procedure in relation to children's hearings comes into play.

Stage two challenge

15–93 If *no* "stage one" challenge is made prior to the "initial" hearing then there is a second chance to make an application to recall the CPO within two working days of the "initial" hearing.[445] The options available to the sheriff are the same as in the stage one application for recall, except that an advice hearing need not be convened. If the CPO is continued (with or without variation of the order and/or directions) a full hearing is held on the eighth working day from the implementation of the original CPO as above.

A stage one or two challenge may be made by the child, a relevant person, any person not being a relevant person who has, or recently had, a significant involvement in the child's upbringing, the person who applied for the CPO, the person specified in the order to produce the child, the reporter and any other person prescribed by rules of court.[446] There is no further appeal from the sheriff granting, refusing or continuing a CPO, to the sheriff principal or Inner House. This is appropriate, given the emergency and time-limited nature of the order.

If it is not "practicable" to make an application to a sheriff for a CPO, emergency authorisation for removal can be made by a Justice of the Peace.[447]

---

[438] 2011 Act s.58(1) and (2).
[439] 2011 Act s.54.
[440] 2011 Act s.54.
[441] 2011 Act s.48(3)(a).
[442] 2011 Act s.50.
[443] 2011 Act s.51(5)(a).
[444] 2011 Act 2011 s.51(5)(b) and (c).
[445] 2011 Act s.48(3)(b).
[446] 2011 Act s.48(1) and (2).
[447] Act s.55(1).

Child assessment orders (CAOs)

In order to safeguard and promote the welfare of children, local authority social workers **15–94** may require access to the child in order to make an assessment of the child's needs. If there is reason to suspect that a child is suffering from harm, and the parents refuse to allow the child to be seen or examined, then a local authority can apply to a sheriff for a child assessment order (CAO).[448] This empowers the local authority to see and assess and to have the child examined by medical professionals, without the need to take the more extreme step of removing the child from the home. The order lasts seven days. Note, however, that a local authority can be authorised to remove a child from his or her parents so as to carry out the assessment under the CAO.[449] The order lasts three days.

Exclusion orders

A local authority has power to apply to a sheriff for an order excluding an alleged abuser, **15–95** referred to as the "named person" from a child's[450] family home.[451] Such an order is in line with the tenet that the child's needs should take precedence over those of the adults involved. However, what the legislation attempts to do, rather than provide the court with an unfettered discretion to exclude, is to require the sheriff to balance the interests of the child and adult involved using multiple tests. [452] The onus lies on the local authority to satisfy the court that the conditions set out in s.76(2) are met on proof of a balance of probabilities.[453] The grounds set out for exclusion in that section are almost identical to those required for a CPO, i.e. they involve "significant harm". In determining whether an exclusion order should be made, a sheriff has a duty to consult the child.[454] An exclusion order cannot be made unless the named person has been afforded an opportunity of being heard, or represented before the sheriff, and the sheriff has considered the views of any person on whom notice of the application has been served.[455]

Even where the conditions of s.76(2) are met, a sheriff may not make an exclusion order if it appears unjustifiable or unreasonable to grant the order having regard to all circumstances of the case,[456] or if the named person satisfies the sheriff that it is unnecessary.[457] The factors to be taken into account are much the same as those under s.3(3) of the Matrimonial Homes (Family Protection) (Scotland) Act 1981. Where the order is granted a sheriff may grant an interdict preventing the named person from entering the home and attach powers of arrest to it.[458] Where granted, an exclusion order ceases to have effect six months after being made.[459]

---

[448] 2011 Act s.35(1).
[449] 2011 Act s.35(3).
[450] A child is a person who is under 16 and also includes a person between 16 and 18 who is subject to a supervision requirement, 1995 Act s.93(2)(b).
[451] 1995 Act s.76.
[452] See ss.76–80.
[453] *Russell v W*, 1998 Fam. L.R. 25.
[454] 1995 Act s.16(2) and (4)(b)(i).
[455] 1995 Act s.76(3). But if a sheriff is satisfied that the conditions in s.76(2) are met but that the conditions in s.76(3) are not fulfilled, i.e. the named person has not been heard, the sheriff may grant an interim order.
[456] 1995 Act s.76(10).
[457] 1995 Act s.77(4).
[458] 1995 Act ss.77 and 78.
[459] 1995 Act s.79(1).

Permanence orders

15–96 Under s.80 of the Adoption and Children (Scotland) Act 2007 a local authority can apply to a court for a permanence order. Where the child is 12 or over the order cannot be made without the child's consent.[460] The welfare of the child throughout their childhood is the paramount consideration and the child's views must be taken into account and regard taken of the child's religious persuasion, racial origin and cultural and linguistic back ground[461] Before a permanence order can be made, the court must be satisfied either that there is no one who has the parental right to have the child reside with him or her; or if there is such a person, the child's residence with that person is or would be seriously detrimental to the child's welfare.[462] A permanence order vests the responsibility of providing the child with guidance and the right to regulate his residence in the local authority.[463] But the court can make ancillary provisions, for example vesting other parental responsibilities and rights in the authority, extinguishing such responsibilities and rights in other persons and making arrangements for contact with the child.[464] In the order the court can also grant authority for the child to be adopted, but this cannot be done unless the child's parents agree or there are grounds to dispense with their consent. If authority for adoption is granted it is no longer necessary to have parental consent to the adoption order itself.

The children's hearings system—children who are in need of compulsory supervision orders

15–97 Under the Children's Hearings (Scotland) Act 2011 hearings, comprised of members of children's panels, exist to deal with children under 16 who are in need of compulsory supervision orders.[465] State intervention in this context covers a wide range of circumstances including the neglect and abuse of children, or the commission of offences by children, as well as dealing with children who are "beyond the control of a relevant person" or who fail "to attend school regularly without reasonable excuse". It is the panel members who are public volunteers, whose services are unpaid, and who work on a part-time basis, who make decisions about whether or not children are in need of compulsory supervision orders. Each panel consists of three members, at least one of whom must be male, one of whom must be female, and one of whom acts as chairman.[466] Each local authority has a children's panel made up of members including a Chairman and a Deputy Chairman. Members receive training before they serve on a panel and are required to attend further in-service training sessions to extend their knowledge and skills.

Local authorities play an important part in the hearings system in terms of administration, support, and in implementation of the hearings' decisions. However, cases are referred to a children's hearing by a reporter who draws up the grounds for referral and who is an officer of the Scottish Children's Reporter Administration (SCRA)[467] a national

---

[460] 2007 Act s.84(1).

[461] 2007 Act s.84(4) and (5).

[462] 2007 Act s.84(5)(c).

[463] 2007 Act s.81.

[464] 2007 Act s.82.

[465] 2011 Act s.199. Children over 16 but under 18 in respect of whom a compulsory supervision order remains in force may also come before a hearing. Young persons under 18 who have been prosecuted for offences in the criminal courts may also be remitted to the hearing for disposal rather than being sentenced by the court; the court may also simply seek the advice of the hearing relating to the disposal of such a case under s.49(1) of the Criminal Procedure (Scotland) Act 1995.

[466] 2011 Act ss.5 and 6(3)(a) and (b).

[467] The term "reporter" means the Principal Reporter.

body charged with the management and deployment of reporters throughout Scotland. Reporters (who act independently from local authorities) act as gatekeepers to the system, investigating cases brought to their attention by agencies such as social work departments, schools, and police. After reviewing the situation the reporter decides whether to drop the matter, or to encourage a child and family to work with social services on a voluntary basis, or whether to proceed to a hearing. When a hearing is held it is the panel members who must decide whether or not to discharge the referral, or whether a child is in need of a compulsory supervision order, and if so, what measures if any should be imposed.[468] While panel members make decisions about whether or not a child is in need of a compulsory supervision order, reporters play a central role in the operation of the hearing system for it is they who make the initial decision about whether or not a child should go before a hearing, who organise the timetable and necessary documentation for the hearings, and who have responsibility for ensuring that the legal requirements of the process are met.[469]

Key features of the system

Although a legal forum, every effort is made to encourage children and families to participate in proceedings by dispensing with the kind of legal formalities associated with courts. The determination of the facts is separated out from the disposal of the case by the requirement that no hearing can proceed unless the child and family accept the grounds for referral.[470] In this way the demands of formal legality—requiring determination of the facts with regard to due process—are kept distinct from a disposal of the case. The latter, which is concerned with the welfare and development of the child, is more appropriately placed within the jurisdiction of the panels. In cases of dispute, the hearing can either discharge the referral, or refer the matter to the sheriff court for a finding as to whether the disputed grounds are established.[471]

   This approach, premised on consensus as the starting point for discussion, seeks to avoid the adversarial nature of legal proceedings. It is one that minimises the role of lawyers so that children and families are not subject to confrontation with and intimidation by the kind of legal process that operates in ordinary law courts. In order to maintain confidentiality and protect the privacy of children and families, hearings are conducted in private. Rules of evidence and procedure are much less stringent and while lawyers may be present at a hearing they do not act as advocates speaking on behalf of their clients.

   However, while not intended to operate like a court, the proceedings before children's hearings involve the determination of civil rights and obligations that are subject to the terms of art.6(1) of the European Convention on Human Rights dealing with the right to a fair trial.[472] In *S v Miller*[473] the court held that the fact that a child was referred to a hearing on the ground of having committed an offence, did not mean that the child was being

15–98

---

[468] Under s.83. the hearing has the power to take a wide range of measures including directions as to contact, medical examination and treatment, where the child is to live, movement restrictions and secure accommodation authorisation.

[469] Reporters may, but need not be, legally qualified. Some come from a background in social work or education.

[470] Under s.94(1) and (2) where a child is too young to understand the grounds for referral, or has not in fact understood them after an explanation has been given, the hearing can either discharge the referral or direct the reporter to apply to the sheriff for a finding as to whether the grounds of referral are established.

[471] 2011 Act s.93(2).

[472] Article 6 provides that in determining civil rights and obligations or any criminal charge, everyone is entitled to a fair and public hearing within a reasonable time by an independent and impartial tribunal established by law. In addition, there are specific guarantees that are brought into play by art.6(2) and (3) where someone is charged with a criminal offence.

[473] 2001 S.L.T. 531.

charged with an offence and thus the mandatory protections of art.6(3) did not apply. However, it also held that in every referral a child is entitled to a fair hearing under art.6(1). This means that all documentary information used in the decision-making process must be distributed to all parties, including the child.[474] The right to a fair hearing also raised the issue of a right to legal representation. The court held that the hearings system failed to comply with art.6, due to the statutory unavailability of funding for the legal representation of children at such hearings.[475] It acknowledged that legal representation would not be required in every case involving a referral, but only those cases where a child was unable to represent themselves properly and satisfactorily at the hearing.

In *S v Miller* the court did not set out all the circumstances where a child might require legal representation to enable them to participate effectively in a hearing, but they include:

- cases involving deprivation of liberty, e.g. where secure accommodation might be imposed;
- cases involving particularly vulnerable groups of children, e.g. the very young or those with learning disabilities or special needs;
- hearings involving difficult issues of law or procedure, e.g. a defence of self-defence or provocation in an "offence" referral.

The 2011 Act introduces a child advocacy service to provide children with support and representation[476] and the Legal Aid (Scotland) Act 1986 has been amended so that children may receive legal aid and legal assistance[477].

Where a hearing takes place three overriding principles apply. These are that:

(1) the welfare of the child is paramount[478];
(2) children must be able to express their views and have them taken account where sufficiently mature with a presumption in favour of children aged 12 or over having such maturity[479];
(3) that there should be minimum intervention, that is, that a hearing should only make an order if it is better for the child to make such an order than to make no order at all.[480]

Right of attendance at hearing

Child

15–99 Where a case is referred by the reporter to a children's hearing, the child has the right to attend all stages of the hearing[481] and is obliged to do so.[482] However, a pre-hearing can excuse the child's attendance on the grounds that: (a) in a case concerned with a Sch.1

---

[474] At one time, children and families were not entitled to copies of reports submitted to panel members by social workers and other professionals. The European Court in *McMichael v UK* (1995) 20 E.H.R.R. 205 held that notwithstanding the chairman's obligation to reveal the substance of these reports at the beginning of the hearing, children's hearings were in breach of the European Convention on Human Rights. The rules were amended to provide adults entitled to be at hearings with copies of reports under r.5(3) of the Children's Hearings (Scotland) Rules 1996 Rules, but they did not extend to children.

[475] *S v Miller (No.2)*, 2001 S.L.T. 1304.

[476] 2011 Act s.122.

[477] 2011 Act Pt 19.

[478] 2011 Act s.25(2).

[479] 2011 Act s.27.

[480] 2011 Act s.28(2).

[481] 2011 Act s.78(1)(a).

[482] 2011 Act s.73(2).

offence or a sexual offence, the child's attendance is not necessary for a fair hearing; or (b) attendance of the child at the hearing would place the child's physical, mental or moral welfare at risk; or (c) taking account of the child's age and maturity, the child would not be capable of understanding what happens at the hearing.[483] Where the child fails to attend as requested, a warrant may be issued for their apprehension.[484]

Relevant person

Where a child is brought before a hearing, a relevant person has the right to attend all **15–100** stages of the hearing and is obliged to do so.[485] Relevant persons include[486]:

- a parent or guardian having parental responsibilities or parental rights in relation to the child. It is not sufficient for this purpose that a parent or guardian has only a contact order in his favour;
- a person in whom parental responsibilities and rights are vested by virtue of s.11(2)(b) of the 1995 Act;
- a person in whom parental responsibilities and rights are vested by virtue of s.11(12) of the 1995 Act, i.e. under a residence order;
- a person in whom parental responsibilities and rights have vested by virtue of a permanence order; and
- any other person specified by order made by Scottish Ministers.

Prima facie, the father of a child who does not have parental responsibilities and rights does not qualify as a relevant person. This would appear to be breach of his art.8 right to family life.[487] However, a person must be deemed to be a relevant person if a pre-hearing panel considers that that person has or has recently had a significant involvement in the child's upbringing.[488] Accordingly, the father of a child can be deemed to be a relevant father even though he does not have parental responsibilities and rights if he has in fact played a significant part in his child's life and this may be sufficient to avoid a breach of art.8.

While relevant persons have the right to attend a hearing, they can be excluded so long as it is necessary in the interests of the child, where the hearing is satisfied that it must do so in order to obtain the child's views or because the presence of the relevant person is causing, or is likely to cause, significant distress to the child.[489] In order to maintain an "open" process, the chair must explain the substance of what has occurred during the excluded person's absence on his or her return.[490]

Review, appeal, termination

The child or relevant person may appeal to the sheriff against any decision of a children's **15–101** hearing.[491] This includes both to the making of the compulsory supervision order itself, as well as to any of the measures attached to it. In reaching a decision the sheriff has a duty to

---

[483] 2011 Act s.73(3).
[484] 2011 Act s.123.
[485] 2011 Act ss.78(1)(c)and 74(2).
[486] 2011 Act s.200(1).
[487] *Principal Reporter v K* [2010] UKSC 56.
[488] 2011 Act s.81(3).
[489] 2011 Act ss.76(1)(2) and 77(1)(2).
[490] Act ss.76(3) and 77(3).
[491] 2011 Act s.154(1).

consult the child. Where a sheriff forms the view that the hearing's decision is not justified in all the circumstances the sheriff may[492]:

- require the reporter to arrange a children's hearing;
- continue, vary or terminate the order;
- discharge the child from any further hearing;
- make an interim compulsory supervision order or interim variation of a compulsory supervision order; or
- grant a warrant to secure attendance.

Where an appeal is unsuccessful, the sheriff will confirm the decision of the children's hearing.[493] Where a supervision order is in force it should not continue any longer than is necessary in the interests of the child. If a local authority takes the view that the requirement should cease to have effect, it can refer the case to the reporter for review by a children's hearing, who can terminate the requirement if it sees fit.[494] In any event, a supervision requirement cannot remain in force after a year unless it has been continued as a result of a review by a children's hearing. The child and any relevant person have the right to a review of the requirement.[495] On review, a children's hearing may continue the requirement, vary it or terminate it. When a child reaches 18 any supervision requirement ceases to have effect.[496]

Key Concepts

The three main institutions in Scotland, which are involved where **children** are in need of **care and protection,** are the local authority, the courts and the children's hearing system.

Under the **Children (Scotland) Act 1995, the Adoption and Children (Scotland) Act 2007 and the Children's Hearings (Scotland) Act 2011** a local authority is empowered to apply to a sheriff court for a range of court orders to help the local authority fulfil its obligations in respect of children. These include:

- **child protection** orders;
- **child assessment** orders;
- **exclusion** orders; and
- **permanence** orders.

Under the 2011 Act hearings comprised of children's panels exist to deal with children under 16, who are in need of a compulsory supervision orders.

---

[492] 2011 Act s.156(2) and (3).
[493] 2011 Act s.156(1).
[494] 2011 Act s.131.
[495] 2011 Act s.132(2) and (3).
[496] 2011 Act s.83(7).

▼ CHAPTER SUMMARY

FAMILIES, MARRIAGE AND CIVIL PARTNERSHIP

1. Scots law no longer discriminates against children on the basis of whether or not 15–102 their parents are married:

   ➢ Law Reform (Parent and Child) (Scotland) Act 1986 s.1(1).

2. The legal consequences of marriage and civil partnership include: rights to property and support; parenthood; financial provisions on the termination of a relationship; and rights to intestate succession on the death of one of the spouses or civil partners.

3. Parties are free to marry or register a civil partnership provided there are no legal impediments:

   ➢ Marriage (Scotland) Act 1977 s.5(4);
   ➢ Civil Partnership Act 2004 s.86.

4. Marriage takes place between a man and a woman; civil partnership takes place between persons of the same sex.

5. Regular marriage may be either a religious or a civil marriage:

   ➢ Marriage (Scotland) Act 1977 s.8.

6. A civil marriage must be conducted by an authorised registrar, but there is no prescribed form of ceremony.

7. A religious marriage may be solemnised by a minister of the Church of Scotland, a minister, clergyman, pastor or priest of a religious body prescribed by the regulations, or other approved celebrant:

   ➢ Marriage (Scotland) Act 1977 s.8(1);
   ➢ Marriage (Prescription of Religious Bodies) (Scotland) Regulations 1977.

8. The registration of a civil partnership is a civil ceremony and cannot take place in religious premises.

9. The form of irregular marriage known as marriage by cohabitation with habit and repute has been abolished:
   Two exceptions:

   — The cohabitation began before the commencement of the Family Law (Scotland) Act 2006.
   — Where a marriage celebrated abroad is discovered to be invalid after the death of one of the parties.

PARENTS AND CHILDREN

1. Being identified as a parent in law has important legal consequences.
2. A woman who gives birth is regarded as the legal mother of the child, regardless of whether she is married to the child's father.
3. Acquiring the status of parentage does not automatically accord parental responsibilities and rights to a parent except where: that parent is the mother; or the father has married the child's mother; or the father has been registered as the child's father on or after 4th May 2006 when the Family Law (Scotland) Act 2006 came into force.

4. **Parental responsibilities and rights are now codified:**

   ➢ Children (Scotland) Act 1995.

5. **Where any major decision arises, those exercising parental responsibilities and rights or entrusted with the care and control of children, must have regard to the child's views (if the child wishes to express them) so far as is practicable:**

   ➢ Children (Scotland) Act 1995 s.6(1).

6. **A parent may appoint a "testamentary" guardian or guardians to act in the event of his or her death.**
7. **A child's welfare prevails over parental responsibilities and rights.**
8. **General rule—children under 16 have no legal capacity to enter into any transaction:**

   ➢ Age of Legal Capacity (Scotland) Act 1991 s.1(1).

PROPERTY DURING MARRIAGE, CIVIL PARTNERSHIP AND COHABITATION

1. **Property is generally subject to the separate property rule—a marriage or civil partnership shall not of itself affect the property rights of the spouses:**

   ➢ Family Law (Scotland) Act 1985 s.24.

2. **Most couples buying a home take title in joint names, but where they do not, it is only the person whose name is recorded in the Land Register who is treated as the owner in law.**
3. **Spouses and civil partners are obliged to aliment one another, to provide such support as is reasonable in the circumstances having regard to the needs and resources of the parties, their earning capacities, and all the circumstances of the case:**

   ➢ Family Law (Scotland) Act 1985 s.1(1)(a), (b) and (bb) and s.4.

4. **Children have a right to financial support from both parents, whether or not the parents are or have been married to one another and whether or not they live together or apart:**

   ➢ Family Law (Scotland) Act 1985 s.1(1)(c) and (d).

5. **There is an administrative scheme for assessing and enforcing maintenance owed by a parent to a "qualifying" child administered by the Child Maintenance and Enforcement Commission:**

   ➢ Child Support Act 1991, as amended.

6. **A maintenance calculation in respect of a child arises compulsorily.**

DOMESTIC VIOLENCE AND THE FAMILY HOME

1. **A spouse or civil partner has the right to occupy and to exclude a violent party from the matrimonial or family home. This is an exception to the general principle that marriage or civil partnership has no effect on the property rights of the spouses:**

   ➢ Matrimonial Homes (Family Protection) (Scotland) Act 1981;
   ➢ Civil Partnership Act 2004.

2. There is limited protection for "cohabiting couples" who must be a man and a woman who are living with each other as if they were man and wife, or two persons living together as if they were civil partners:

> Matrimonial Homes (Family Protection) (Scotland) Act 1981.

PROPERTY ON DIVORCE AND TERMINATION OF NON-MARITAL RELATIONSHIPS

1. Marriage or civil partnership cannot be terminated until death, except by divorce or dissolution.
2. A divorce or dissolution is granted on the irretrievable breakdown of marriage or civil partnership, where there has been: adultery (restricted to divorce); behaviour of such a kind that the other party cannot reasonably be expected to cohabit; non-cohabitation for a period of one year combined with consent; or non-cohabitation for a period of two years:

> Divorce (Scotland) Act 1976.
> Civil Partnership Act 2004 ss.117–122.

3. Matrimonial or partnership property includes all property acquired during the relevant period by either or both spouses or civil partners (subject to the stated exceptions).
4. Unmarried couples (whether opposite sex or same sex) can seek an award of financial provision on the breakdown of their relationship:

> Family Law (Scotland) Act 2006 under s.28.

PRIVATE ORDERING

1. Couples can make their own agreement as to child care, aliment and the distribution of property on the termination of a relationship. Where such agreements are made during the marriage or on or after divorce they are formally referred to in law as Minutes of Agreement.
2. Once made agreements are binding and enforceable in law (except possibly in the case of children).
3. Variation or reduction of such agreements may occur:

— with regard to children;
— where there are contractual grounds allowing for reduction or variation;
— where variation of periodical allowance to ex-spouse or civil partner or aliment for children is permitted; or
— following a statutory challenge under s.16 of the Family Law (Scotland) Act 1985 (Was it fair and reasonable? Did the parties have independent legal advice?—the mere fact that there has been an unequal division of assets between the parties by agreement does not of itself give rise to an inference of unfairness or unreasonableness.)

ADOPTION

1. Adoption creates a new legal family for the child.
2. An adoption order terminates the parental responsibilities and rights of the birth parent in respect of the child.
3. An adoption order cannot be made unless the birth parent consents or grounds exist to dispense with the parent's consent.
4. The welfare principle governs every stage of the adoption process.

STATE INTERVENTION IN THE LIVES OF CHILDREN: CARE AND PROTECTION

1. Three main institutions in Scotland involved where children are in need of care and protection are: the local authority; the courts; and the children's hearing system.
2. A local authority is empowered to apply to a sheriff court for a range of court orders to help the local authority fulfil its obligations in respect of children. These include: child protection orders; child assessment orders; exclusion orders; and permanence orders:

   ➤ Children (Scotland) Act 1995;
   ➤ Adoption and Children (Scotland) Act 2007;
   ➤ Children's Hearings (Scotland) Act 2011.

3. Hearings comprised of children's panels exist to deal with children under 16, who are in need of compulsory measures of supervision:

   ➤ Children's Hearings (Scotland) Act 2011.

4. The proceedings before children's hearings involve the determination of civil rights and obligations that are subject to the terms of art.6(1) of the European Convention on Human Rights dealing with the right to a fair trial:

   ➤ *S v Miller*, 2001 S.L.T. 531.

? QUICK QUIZ

FAMILY LAW

- Who can marry or enter a civil partnership?
- When is a man presumed to be the father of a child?
- Which exceptions are there to the "separate property" rule?
- What is aliment?
- When would a court make an exclusion order?
- Name the four conditions meeting the ground of "irretrievable breakdown of marriage"?
- Which Acts are framed around the rights to occupy and to exclude a violent party from the family home?
- What are the benefits of private ordering?
- When can the consent of a parent or guardian to an adoption order be dispensed with?
- What is the effect of a CPO?

📖 FURTHER READING

There are numerous sources for further information on family law in Scotland.

For more in depth analysis see the two Scottish Universities Law Institute's titles: Wilkinson and Norrie, *The Law Relating to Parent and Child in Scotland*, 2nd edn, by K.McK. Norrie (W. Green/SULI, 1999); and Clive, *The Law of Husband and Wife*, 4th edn (W. Green/SULI, 1997).

Numerous textbooks are also recommended, such as Edwards and Griffiths, *Family Law*, 2nd edn (W. Green, 2007); and Thomson, *Family Law in Scotland*, 6th edn (Tottel, 2011).

For a pre-examination guide see Sutherland, *Family LawBasics* (W. Green, 1999); and for a comprehensive collection of extracts see Mays, *Child and Family Law: Cases and Materials* (W. Green, 2001).

It is recommended that the following reports and white papers be referred to for discussion of the various contentious areas:

- Kilbrandon Committee, *Report on Children and Young Persons*, Scotland (1964), Cmnd.2306.
- Scottish Law Commission, *Report on Family Law* (1992), Scot. Law Com. No.135.
- Parents and Children: A White Paper on Scottish Family Law (2000).
- Scottish Law Commission, *Report on the Reform of the Ground for Divorce* (1989), Scot. Law Com. No.116.

🖱 RELEVANT WEB LINKS

General Registrar for Scotland—Getting Married in Scotland:
http://www.gro-scotland.gov.uk/regscot/getting-married-in-scotland/index.html
The Child Support Agency: *http://www.csa.gov.uk*
Children's Hearings Information on the Scottish Executive website:
http://www.childrens-hearings.co.uk
Children in Scotland. This is a is the national agency for voluntary, statutory and professional organisations and individuals working with children and their families in Scotland: *http://www.childreninscotland.org.uk*

Chapter 16   Civil Litigation

ROBERT SHIELS[1]

▶ CHAPTER OVERVIEW

16–01 The peaceful settlement of disputes might be conducted in a manner that avoids formal court hearings and appearances. These can include arbitration or other means of alternative dispute resolution. However popular these developments might be, there are still a large number of cases that go to the civil courts for a determination. The nature of civil procedure, and the manner in which a decision is reached, is radically different in detail for these civil cases. This chapter outlines these procedures and explains the different aspects of the civil procedure.

✓ OUTCOMES

16–02 At the end of the chapter you should have:

 ✓ an understanding of the nature of the Scottish civil courts;
 ✓ familiarity with the terminology of the civil process in the courts;
 ✓ an insight into the different procedures for each means of raising an action.

INTRODUCTION

16–03 It is wrong to think of all disputes as resulting in civil litigation. If the law is certain and, for example, the injury or harm done is admitted, then the matter may be resolved without litigation. The threat of civil litigation, which might involve expense and publicity, often helps to resolve that which may be in dispute.

A civil dispute may arise where two or more parties are at issue on a matter of fact or law, or both, which affects their relevant legal rights and duties. The compromise, agreement or arbitration, involved in the resolution of disputes is very much a matter of legal practice and is probably a universal part of lawyers' work throughout the world. What follows here, however, is a consideration of some of the civil proceedings that may be undertaken in Scotland to obtain a civil remedy.

The civil courts in Scotland provide a means of resolving disputes between individuals. In Scotland the Court of Session in Edinburgh is the senior court for civil cases, although much civil business is conducted in the local sheriff courts. The potential litigant—with or without legal aid—is presented with a wide variety of different means of getting his or her dispute, or problem, into court in order to obtain a redress. The decision, as to which

---

[1] Solicitor in Scotland.

possible option is to be selected in order to get into court, can be one of the most important decisions to be taken.

The remedies that are sought depend on the nature of the dispute: the classic phrase in this context is "what is the wrong? what is the remedy?" The pursuer requires to lead evidence, not necessarily with corroboration, in order to prove his or her case on the balance of probabilities. The rules to be applied in all the different types of actions are designed to give the other party fair notice of the evidence to be relied on and the nature of the dispute. While swift movement of the cases may be sought, the procedure also has to allow the defender time to meet the case against him. Appeals on the merits and awards are competent.

Remedies

A client may wish a particular result, but the lawyer must have regard to various **16–04** approaches in order to obtain the result. Civil remedies may be classified according to their purposes. The following list is not comprehensive, but includes the principal remedies.

- *Declaratory judgments*. By these decisions the court declares that particular rights do, or do not, exist. It does not follow that the court makes a further order as to consequential action.
- *Reduction*. A court will reduce, or set aside, a contract, will, decree or other writing which then becomes invalid.
- *Prevention*. By this remedy a court orders the cessation of a legal wrong, either actual or intended, before any harm or further harm is done to the pursuer. An interdict is a common remedy in this regard and equates broadly with the English injunction.
- *Performance*. The court may order something to be done, which ought otherwise to have been done under a legal duty. An example is an action of specific implement.
- *Damages*. The court may order financial compensation for loss, injury or harm caused by the failure to undertake a legal duty owed to the pursuer by the defender. Damages may be awarded in compensation for personal injuries sustained by the pursuer resulting from the defender's fault.
- *Matrimonial remedies*. Actions of judicial separation may relieve a spouse from legal duties that ought to follow from marriage. Actions of divorce will end a marriage. These are sometimes known as consistorial remedies.

Questions of law and fact

In the wide variety of circumstances giving rise to wrongs for which someone seeks a **16–05** remedy, the distinction between questions of fact and questions of law must be observed. There are seldom circumstances, which are exclusively matters of pure law. Equally, there are unlikely to be circumstances that are exclusively matters of fact. Most circumstances combine matters of fact and law.

It is said that in every set of circumstances there are four elements. First, there are rules of law and these are abstract and general. Secondly, there are facts and these are concrete and specific. Thirdly, there are human beings, who are complex and variable. Fourthly, there is the environment. This is to be seen in its broadest context and amounts to the background to the circumstances giving rise to a wrong. It is the accumulation of physical, social, cultural, intellectual, economic, political and industrial circumstances.

A question of fact concerns the existence, in the past or present, of some act or event or state of circumstances and these must be recognised or ascertained by human senses. A question of law concerns the existence or content, or applicability of some doctrine, principle or rule of the legal system.

The importance of the distinction is pre-eminent: disputed questions of fact must be alleged in the written pleadings and the dispute must be decided upon by the judge, or the jury if there is one, after hearing the evidence. Disputed questions of law must be raised by appropriate pleas-in-law and are decided by the judge after hearing legal argument. Disputed questions of mixed fact and law are determined by the judge after hearing evidence of fact, and legal argument as to the consequences of the evidence being interpreted in one way or another. It is not unknown for circumstances to allow a jury verdict that amounts to a decision of a mixed question of fact and law.

The value of extensive written pleadings in civil litigation is that the points of dispute become clear before the actual trial or proof, thus narrowing the issues. The resolution of the disputed issues takes a different approach according to whether they are facts or law.

A disputed question of fact has to be determined by proof by adducing evidence of the events, namely what happened, was said, seen, heard or done. A disputed question of law, by contrast, is determined not by evidence but by legal argument, giving in support previous relevant decisions, statutes and related material.

It should also be mentioned, in relation to disputed questions of fact, that reliance is often placed on other branches of knowledge. There is probably no science or body of knowledge outside law, which is not at some time relied on to explain or settle questions of facts in issue in a legal context. Of course, these practitioners from other disciplines do not themselves determine facts, but they do provide explanations, information and evidence on questions of fact to which principles of law can be applied. Some of these practitioners become experienced enough in court work to develop specialist titles, e.g. forensic odontologist (someone who does dental work for court cases, such as teeth impressions from the accused).

Facts can also be distinguished themselves into acts and events. An act is a happening brought about by human activity, positive (by acting) or negative (by abstaining or refraining from acting). An event is a happening, which occurs independently of human intervention. Moreover, a distinction is often drawn between fact and opinion. This is particularly so when an expert gives evidence. What a person has seen, heard or otherwise observed are facts. Guided by his or her professional knowledge he or she has then formed an opinion on the basis of these facts and that is a fact, but the substance, or content, of the opinion itself is not a fact, but a view reached by him or her.

These remedies that a court may provide, and the distinction between fact and law and the various consequences, apply to all civil actions in each of the courts. The emphasis varies, however, in each case because, to repeat a well-known legal principle, every case turns on its own facts and circumstances.

COURT OF SESSION

16–06 The Court of Session is the supreme civil court in Scotland and dates back more than 400 years. The court sits only in Edinburgh and it does not go out on circuit. Historically, all of the judges of the Court of Session sat as one court to hear cases, as was then the custom elsewhere in Europe. In time, the court split into two divisions of equal status where they sat together—or at least in a settled minimum number. Matters developed with judges in the Outer House sitting alone to hear cases and appeals were heard by a quorum of judges in the Inner House. The Inner House is itself now split into the First Division and Second Division. If the Court of Session wishes to change any of its rules or procedures it may do so by means of delegated legislation known as an Act of Sederunt.

The various forms of procedure in the Court of Session are:

- Ordinary Action;
- Petition Action;
- Commercial Cause;
- Judicial Review;
- Personal Injuries Procedure.

Prior to considering each of these forms of procedure, it is helpful to have a general description of the nature and extent of the Scottish system of written pleadings. These are often documents that are long and detailed and which encompass the case for the person starting the court case (pursuer) and the person from whom something is wanted in the case (defender). The purpose of the written pleadings is to narrow, as far as possible, the likely evidence that will be called by both sides and the extent to which that evidence is agreed or in dispute. The precise law applicable to the complaint is also identified. The result is that at any court hearing there is a high degree of predictability as to what each side will say and do—although not necessarily as to what decision a court will come to at the end.

Written pleadings

The papers, that constitute a civil case, are the written pleadings in which the facts are **16–07** alleged and the relevant law to be applied is identified. There has to be a conclusion, or a statement of what remedy it is that the action is intended to achieve. Proceedings are usually initiated in the Outer House by summons, although some actions commence by petition. A summons is a writ running in the name of the Queen and passed by the Signet, that is to say, it has been stamped to authenticate it.

A civil action is commenced by a pursuer and directed against a defender. The summons requires the defender, if there is any good reason why decree should not be pronounced, to appear in court to answer the allegations by the pursuer. The threat is that without an appearance the action may proceed without the defender and the pursuer will achieve the remedy sought.

The front page of the summons is a pre-printed form in which the parties are identified. This part is known as the instance. There is then the brief statement of the precise remedy claimed. This part is known as the conclusion.

The remainder of the summons is divided into two parts. The condescendence consists of numbered paragraphs of facts, which form the basis of the case. The number of paragraphs varies with the complexity of the circumstances. The pleas-in-law are the propositions of law upon which the pursuer bases his or her case.

A solicitor entitled to practice before the Court of Session and signeted, or authenticated, at the court office signs the summons. The defender is cited by having a copy of the summons served on him or her personally or by post. The defender is allowed a certain period of time to answer the summons. This is known as the induciae. After that period has passed the summons is called by being listed in the Rolls of Court. The bundle of court papers, known as the process, is lodged for use in court.

A defender has two options. He or she may do nothing in, which event the pursuer may take decree in absence against him. Alternatively, if the defender wishes to defend the case wholly or in part, he or she must enter appearance and then lodge defences. The defences are statements of fact, which answer each part of the pursuer's document. In drafting defences the summons must be considered line by line and indicate whether each fact is admitted, denied or simply not known about. The defender must also set out his or her pleas-in-law for the court to be able to identify, taking the summons and defences together, the precise issue in each case. It follows that a defender may defend on the facts, or on the law, or both together.

The summons and defences together make up the open record and this document reproduces the summons, conclusions, and the detailed condescendence with the precise answers by both sides and the pleas-in-law for each side. This document is then available for adjustment and that frequently requires to be done once each side becomes aware of the precise points made by the other. The ultimate aim is to adjust the written pleadings in order to give the other side fair warning of the grounds of the claim or defences, to identify the legal issues and to limit the evidence at any later hearing.

At the end of the period allowed for adjustments, the Lord Ordinary will pronounce an interlocutor closing the record. The final written pleadings then become the closed record, which incorporates the various adjustments made to the open record. It is competent (that is to say, it is within the power of the court) to grant summary decree at this stage. This would be decree in favour of the pursuer and allowing the remedy sought. The court can only do that, however, where it is satisfied from the written pleadings in the closed record that there is no defence to the claim or a part of it.

Debate

16–08 The procedure of debate, or discussion on the legal aspects, may be contrasted with proof, which is the hearing of evidence from witnesses. The parties may be at issue on both law and fact. If the parties are at issue on a question of fact alone, the court will order a proof where a judge alone sits to decide upon the evidence, or a jury trial so that the jury can decide the issues: Court of Session Act 1988 (the "1988 Act") ss.9 and 11. There are 12 persons in a civil jury: 1988 Act s.13. The case can also be sent to the procedure roll for a debate on whether a jury trial is appropriate.

If the parties wish to address a legal point, arising from the pleadings, the court will send the case to the procedure roll for a debate on the legal points raised by the pleas-in-law for the parties. When the case proceeds on that roll the debate proceeds on the law alone. The defender must at this stage accept for these purposes the pursuer's narration of the facts in the condescendence.

After the debate the judge may there and then give a decision, but with the complexity of the issues frequently raised it is usual to make *avizandum*. This means giving a decision later and in writing. The nature and extent of that decision depends to a great extent on the issues that have been debated.

If the point of law is decided in favour of the defender the case may be ended at this point, or restricted. If the point of law is decided in favour of the pursuer the case may then proceed to proof or to jury trial. A further option is proof before answer, which means in effect that the circumstances of the case are such that any legal issues are reserved until the evidence is heard.

Proof

16–09 There are no opening speeches for either side. The pursuer, or the lawyer for the pursuer, calls the witnesses in support of the case. The benefit of the extensive written pleadings is that there is no need to prove any matter of fact admitted in the closed record. Careful drafting is necessary because failure in the pleadings to deny an averment of fact within a party's knowledge, is to be construed as an admission of fact.

At proof each witness takes, or affirms, an oath and is then examined-in-chief by the party who called the witness. The witness is then cross-examined by the lawyer for the other party and then re-examined. The first stage determines the evidence of the witness, the second tests or challenges that evidence and allows the other party to explore such relevant matters as he chooses, and the third stage allows an opportunity to clear up any remaining matters of doubt. The judge may also intervene to clarify points of doubt. This procedure is undertaken for each witness called by each party.

The length of time that the proof takes depends on the facts and circumstances in issue, the need to prove them, the extent to which the parties agree evidence, the depth to which facts are explored and the intervention of the judge.

At the conclusion of all the evidence, the lawyers for the parties address the court and make their submissions on the evidence and on the inferences to be drawn from it. While the judge could give a decision, it is usual to make *avizandum*. Later the opinion of the judge is issued and motions heard on awards of expenses if this cannot be agreed on. Decree granting, or refusing, the remedy sought is contained in the interlocutor.

Summary trial

The parties to any dispute or question may present a petition in the Outer House setting **16–10** out the dispute or question, and asking that it may be decided by a particular Lord Ordinary: 1988 Act s.26. The case may be determined in chambers. The decree is final and not appealable: *Britain Steamship Co v Lithgows Ltd.*[2] Summary trial is a convenient, but rare means of obtaining a judicial construction of a deed or a writ: *Shaw v Shaw.*[3]

Jury trial

Jury trial is competent only in specified types of action, for example, an action of damages **16–11** for personal injuries: 1988 Act s.11. Even with these specified types of action, the court may be persuaded that special reasons exist for hearing the case by proof, rather than by jury trial: 1988 Act s.9 and see, e.g. *Meechan v McFarlane.*[4]

An issue is a question of fact formulated precisely in writing by the pursuer for the jury to answer. There may also be a counter-issue for the defender. These are designed to obtain an answer from the jury to the major matters of fact on which the parties are in dispute. There are opening speeches. The evidence is led in the same way as at a proof. At the conclusion of the evidence, the lawyers for the parties address the jury advocating their respective cases. The judge charges the jury on the law.

The verdict of the jury may be given unanimously or by a majority. The verdict is normally a general verdict by giving answers to the questions in the issue or in the counter-issue. A special verdict may follow if a specific question is put to a jury. The verdict is recorded and the jury discharged and the lawyer for the party for whom the jury have decided then moves the court to apply the verdict and this allows decree to be granted.

Reclaiming motions

Any party to a cause initiated in the Outer House either by a summons or a petition who is **16–12** dissatisfied with an interlocutor may reclaim (appeal to the Inner House) against that interlocutor: 1988 Act s.28. These appeals may challenge the Lord Ordinary's opinion on the law and one may also reclaim a decision on the facts, e.g. *Islip Pedigree Breeding Centre v Abercromby.*[5]

Any party who is dissatisfied with the verdict of the jury in any jury action may apply to

---

[2] 1975 S.C. 110.
[3] 1968 S.L.T. (Notes) 94.
[4] 1996 S.L.T. 208.
[5] 1959 S.L.T. 161.

the Inner House for a new trial on various statutory grounds, e.g. misdirection of the jury by the judge: 1988 Act s.29.

Appeals from the sheriff court are also heard by the Inner House and disposed of in the same way as reclaiming motions. These appeals (like reclaiming motions and applications for new trials) appear on the rolls of either Division of the Inner House and the judges have before them prints of the sheriff court record and interlocutors.

Petitions

16–13 Petitions may be presented to the Outer House. Petitions for judicial review of administrative actions are now competent. Some kinds of petitions, however, are presented directly to the Inner House. The petitions to the *nobile officium* of the Court of Session proceed to the Inner House, as they constitute a request for the exercise of an extraordinary equitable remedy where the law is otherwise silent as to the correction of a wrong.

Forms of procedure

Ordinary action

16–14 If a party wants to raise a matter as an ordinary action in the Court of Session then the instructed solicitor would draft a summons in accordance with the rules and practice described above. The summons would be lodged at the general department of the court for which a fee is payable. A summons requires to be signetted and that is the authority of the court to serve the summons on the defender. Service may be by post, Sheriff Officer or Messenger-at-Arms. The defender will be given by these means a service copy of the summons with a copy of the warrant and a form of citation.

The pursuer may lodge the principal summons with the clerk for the calling of the case. That is done after 21 days have passed since the service copy was served on the defender. The case calls in the Rolls of Court and these lists are published daily. Once the case has been lodged for calling and it appears on the calling list, the defender has three days in which to intimate formally to the clerk that he is entering an appearance in the action. The necessary details of such appearance are noted by the clerk on the principal summons after which the defender has seven days after calling to lodge written defences.

The written pleadings are as described above. Once the summons and the answers have been lodged then they are combined together and published as an open record. The case is published on the Adjustment Roll of the Court of Session and a period of eight weeks is allowed for adjustments to be made. Either side may make adjustments to their own pleadings in the context of what the other has written and amended. At the end of the adjustment period the record is closed. The closed record must be lodged with the clerk within four weeks of the expiry of the adjustment period.

At this procedural point there are four options:

    (a) the case may be sent to the procedural roll for a debate on a matter of law that arises from the written pleadings of the parties;

    (b) the court can fix a proof and that involves a hearing of the evidence on the disputed facts;

    (c) the court can set a hearing for a proof before answer, at which it is necessary to hear evidence from both parties before deciding any legal question that may have to be settled before making a final decision;

    (d) the court can fix a jury trial.

Petition action

As well as raising an action by means of a summons in the Court of Session, a party can **16–15** start a proceedings by way of a petition. This is an approach that involves a less formal procedure than a summons. In general terms, the object of a petition is to obtain from the Court of Session a power to do something, or to require something to be done which it is just and proper should be done, but which the person petitioning the court has no legal right to do or to require apart from with judicial authority.

Petitions to the Outer House include, for example, an application in relation to trusts. An application to the Inner House must be made under legislation relating to solicitors and notaries public. The rules of the court provide simplified procedures for the petitions to go before the court and for intimation of a copy of the petition to individuals specified in the petition.

Commercial cause

A general belief that the rules of procedure in an ordinary action were too formal, complex **16–16** and slow led to the establishment of a commercial action. The rules for commercial actions were intended to speed up court actions, although they were based on different ideas about efficiency and the resolution of disputes.

The terms or details of a summons for a commercial action may be less detailed than those of an ordinary summons. The summons will be served in the same way as service for an ordinary action and the defender will require to state an intention to defend the summons similarly.

The calling of a commercial action will take place on the commercial roll and the procedure will be at the discretion of the commercial judge who has been nominated for that type of work for a set period of time. The judge will be entitled to use discretion within the rules. There is emphasis on resolving disputes by means of a full disclosure of earlier attempts by the various parties to do so.

Judicial review

Judicial review is the mechanism for the Court of Session to scrutinise the manner by **16–17** which decision-making bodies have reached a particular decision. Only the Court of Session has such a regulatory or supervisory power and such a remedy is not available in the sheriff court. In deciding a matter of a judicial review the court is not sitting as an appeal court, nor is it merely substituting its decision for that of the decision-making body complained about. The court is concerned about the manner in which a decision has been reached rather than the decision itself.

An individual may apply for review by lodging a petition for judicial review in the form prescribed in the rules regulating the power of review. Documents or affidavits in support ought to be lodged at the same time. The petition is lodged at the petitions department of the Court of Session. When the petition calls before a judge submissions will be heard from the representative of the petitioner. The result will be a first order setting out the period of intimation of the petition, any documents that ought to be copied, a date for a first hearing and any interim order.

At the first hearing a judge should be enabled to ascertain the position of each of the parties and determine any outstanding matters that might be settled then. The nature of the problems complained about mean that there is seldom a proof or a hearing on the facts. Hearings are often for legal debate rather than listening to witnesses.

Personal injuries procedure

16–18 The procedure in personal injuries actions in the Court of Session differs from the other types: the written statement of the case is simpler than that required in an ordinary action. The summons will give an outline of the circumstances with an associated indication of the law applicable to the incident. The amount of money claimed should be stated, but not necessarily in the elements that make up the total. It is expected that in most cases the further procedure will be a proof or a jury trial.

HOUSE OF LORDS AND SUPREME COURT

16–19 Prior to 2009, an appeal against a decision of the Inner House of the Court of Session could have been taken to the Appellate Committee of the House of Lords: 1988 Act s.40. Appeals were competent (that is to say, allowable in law) on grounds of fact or law. Appeals on fact were difficult to contemplate because the Law Lords were not readily prepared to differ on an issue of fact from the view of the judge who saw and heard the witnesses: *Martinez v Grampian Health Board*.[6] An appeal from the Inner House is now competent and lies with the Supreme Court of the United Kingdom and may be from any order or judgment of a court in Scotland if an appeal lay from that court to the House of Lords at or immediately before the commencement of s.40 of the Constitutional Reform Act 2005.

An appeal to the House of Lords took the form of a petition and a joint statement of facts and issues, and an appendix must also be included with all the relevant court papers and the opinions of the judges in the other courts. The judgment of the House of Lords was returned to the Inner House, where that judgment was applied. The Supreme Court now has its own Directions which replace the various practice Directions and standing orders of the Appellate Committee of the House of Lords.

Scotland has a distinctive tradition of criminal law and procedure. The High Court of Justiciary, sitting as an Appeal Court, is the final court of appeal in Scottish criminal cases and its decisions are not subject to review by any court whatsoever. The only exception to that rule is in relation to "devolution issues" under the Scotland Act 1998. The Scotland Act 1998 creates a limited right of review for the Supreme Court in relation to criminal cases in which a devolution issue arises because it is said that an act which is or would be incompatible with community law or any of the Convention rights is proposed or is alleged to have occurred, or that legislation which the court is asked to apply is outside the legislative competence of the Scottish Parliament: Scotland Act 1998 Sch.6 para.13(a).

Section 29(2) of the Scotland Act 1998 provides that a provision in an Act of the Scottish Parliament is outside the Parliament's legislative competence if it is incompatible with any of the Convention rights or with EU law. Section 57(2) of the Scotland Act provides that a member of the Scottish Executive now the Scottish Government has no power to do any act so far as it is incompatible with any of the Convention rights or with EU law. From 1999 to 2009 the determination of all devolution cases was for the Judicial Committee of the Privy Council. The Supreme Court has taken over that responsibility: Constitutional Reform Act 2005 s.40(4)(b). For an example of a civil devolution case see *A v Scottish Ministers*.[7]

---

[6] 1996 S.C. (H.L.) 1.
[7] 2002 S.C. (P.C.) 63.

Sheriff Court

The sheriff courts are to be found throughout Scotland. There is a long history of the **16–20** growth of the sheriff court in Scots law, but it would be out of place to rehearse that here as much of it deals with the rules of procedure at different times and which would be irrelevant for this era. The modern sheriff courts were, for practical purposes, established by the Sheriff Courts (Scotland) Act 1907 and developed further by the Sheriff Courts (Scotland) Act 1971. One of the most striking changes was the introduction, by the Sheriff Courts (Scotland) Act 1971 s.33, of the Sheriff Court Rules Council, whose principal function is to keep under review the procedures and practices to be followed in civil proceedings in the Sheriff Court. Further, the Council is to prepare and submit to the Court of Session suggested draft rules for regulating Sheriff Court procedure and practice.

The various forms of procedure in the sheriff court are:

- Ordinary Actions;
- Summary Cause;
- Small Claim;
- Summary Application.

Ordinary Actions

The principles of written pleading and procedure in the Court of Session have been set out **16–21** at some length above. They apply in a generally similar way in the sheriff court, but with some variation. Most proceedings are governed by the Act of Sederunt (Sheriff Court Ordinary Cause Rules) 1993. Reform was necessary then, as there had been sustained complaints of delay, excessive formality and unnecessary complexity under the earlier procedure. It should be said that civil jury trial in the sheriff court was abolished in 1980.

An action is commenced by an initial writ, petition or summons and the relevant document requires a warrant from the Sheriff Clerk. The warrant is the authority of the court to serve a copy of the writ on the person who is to be the defender of the action. The defender thus receives a copy of the writ and also a copy of the warrant from the court. The defender has 21 days from the date of service of the writ on him or her in which to respond. The response is one of acceptance of the claim being made, or a rejection of some or all of it. If there is no response a pursuer may ask the court for decree in absence.

However, if the matter is to proceed then there are several dates of procedural importance after service and that which is the most important depends on whether the claim is accepted or rejected. For example, if the defender signifies that he or she intends to defend a claim then a notice is served on the defender and the important date is 14 days after service of that note: within that period the defender must lodge written defences.

Another significant date is that for the options hearing. This is a date not sooner than 10 weeks after the expiry of notice from the service of the writ. At an options hearing a sheriff might, amongst other things, fix a date for a proof so that the pursuer is allowed the opportunity to lead evidence on some or all of the case with the defender doing likewise for his or her case. A sheriff might set down a date for a legal debate, if it is thought that there is a particular matter of law that the parties wish decided before evidence is led.

In a defended action the pursuer must return the principal initial writ along with proof of the date when the writ was served on the defender. That must be done within seven days of the expiry of the period of notice. The defender may, and indeed should, lodge defences to the initial writ in the form of answers that correspond to the numbered paragraphs in the writ. Together, the initial writ and the defences should narrow the issues—that is to say give an indication of the contentious aspects of the case.

If a dispute proceeds all the way to a proof, then the Ordinary Cause Rules contain detailed provision for a wide range of particular matters such as the hearing of evidence in whole or in part, the citation of witnesses and the notices to admit facts.

Summary Causes

16–22 These actions are in essence for minor claims that consist of values more than £3000 but not exceeding £5,000 and other matters set out in s.35 of the Sheriff Courts (Scotland) Act 1971. They commence with the completion of a standard printed form, with an annexed statement of claims containing a statement of the facts, which constitute the ground of action. There are different forms for the different types of action that can be raised as summary causes. The Sheriff Clerk signs the summons. The summary nature of the procedure is emphasised by the absence of formal and highly detailed written pleadings, as would otherwise be required under ordinary actions.

The pursuer serves the proceedings by sending the defender a service copy of the principal summons. The service copy is on a pre-printed form and contains the same details as are on the first two pages of the principal summons. The service copy, however, has a tear off part that allows for the defender to respond simply to the claim made against him or her. A defender may choose to do nothing in which event a decree will be made against him or her. He or she may accept some or all of the details of claim depending on the circumstances. If the action is defended the defender must lodge a written note of the proposed defence and give that to the court when returning the form of response.

At the first calling of the case the court must, amongst other things, ascertain the factual basis of the action and any defences, and the legal basis on which the matter is proceeding. The court must also seek to negotiate and secure settlement of the action of the parties. The next stage of the case occurs only when the court concludes that there is no prospect that the dispute could be resolved at that point. If not, then the sheriff must identify and note issues of fact and law that are in dispute and note facts that are agreed.

The summary nature of the case is emphasised by the provision that if a sheriff considers there to be no good legal basis for the claim or any defence, he or she may hear argument and decide the case immediately. If there is a valid dispute then a date for a proof must be decided on for the hearing of evidence.

Small Claims

16–23 This is an even more expedited procedure. It is for a claim not exceeding £3000, or for an action brought to enforce the performance by the defender of an act other than the payment of money, or for the recovery of possession of moveable property where the value of the subject matter does not exceed £3000. The procedure is intended to be simple and flexible. The procedure is very similar to that under the Summary Cause Rules.

The Sheriff Clerk signs the printed form and, again, there are no written pleadings. The sums involved are often much lower than the maximum and the procedure is pragmatic; a claim, if incompetent, may be dismissed. However, a sheriff must seek to negotiate and secure settlement of the claim between parties if possible. If that cannot be done he or she is to identify the issues of fact and law that are in dispute and note these on the summons as well as noting the agreed facts. A decision on the whole dispute, on the basis of the information put before the court, then is required if possible. At a hearing of evidence the procedure is that which is considered by the sheriff to be fair, best suited to clarify and determine the issues before the court. There are rules allowing for the transfer of small claims to summary cause or ordinary cause and vice versa. The Sheriff Principal may hear an appeal on a point of law.

Summary Applications

Summary application is the general name given to a form of procedure available in the **16–24** sheriff court and that procedure can be used in a number of specific cases. The application may be made at common law, although many of the summary applications now made are for authority for something to be done under a particular statute. The application is set out in writing in the form of a writ and it ought to contain details of the factual background and the order that is being sought from the sheriff. The general form of the written pleadings is broadly the same as in an ordinary action. However, a court can set down a hearing immediately to be addressed on the merits of the application and the sheriff is given a very wide discretion as to the appropriate procedure to follow in summary applications.

Sheriff court appeals

Appeal is competent from the judgment of the sheriff, or sheriff principal, by means of a **16–25** note of appeal signed by the appellant. Thereafter, appeal may be competent to the Court of Session by note of appeal against final judgments of either sheriff or sheriff principal: see Sheriff Courts (Scotland) Act 1971 s.38.

▼ CHAPTER SUMMARY

INTRODUCTION

1. **The principal remedies available are declaratory judgments, reduction, prevention** **16–26** **performance, damages and matrimonial remedies.**
2. **There is an important distinction between questions of law and fact.**

COURT OF SESSION

1. **The Court of Session comprises the Inner House (First Division and Second Division) and the Outer House**
2. **Changes in rules of procedure in the Court of Session are made by Acts of Sederunt.**

WRITTEN PLEADINGS

1. **A civil action is commenced by a pursuer and directed against a defender.**
2. **A summons requires the defender to appear in court to answer the allegations by the pursuer. Parts of the summons include: the instance; the conclusion; the condescendence; and pleas-in-law.**
3. **The defender enters appearance and then lodges defences. A defender may defend on the facts, or on the law, or both together.**
4. **The summons and defences make up the open record. After a period of adjustment, the final written pleadings become the closed record.**

DEBATE

1. **A debate is a discussion of the legal points raised by the pleas-in-law.**
2. **Possible outcomes:**

   ➢ If the point of law is decided in favour of the defender the case may end.
   ➢ If the point of law is decided in favour of the pursuer the case may proceed to proof or to jury trial.
   ➢ Where the circumstances of the case are such that any legal issues are reserved until the evidence is heard, the case may proceed to a proof before answer

PROOF

1. **If the parties are at issue on a question of fact alone, the court will order a proof or a jury trial:**

   ➢ Court of Session Act 1988 ss.9 and 11.

2. **A proof is the hearing of evidence from witnesses. At proof each witness takes or affirms an oath and is examined-in-chief by the party who called the witness, cross-examined and then re-examined. At the conclusion of the evidence the lawyers address the court and make their submissions on the evidence and on the inferences to be drawn from it.**

SUMMARY TRIAL

1. **The parties to any dispute may present a petition in the Outer House setting out the dispute or question, and asking that it may be decided by a particular Lord Ordinary:**

   ➢ Court of Session Act 1988 s.26.

2. **The decree is final and not appealable:**

   ➢ *Britain Steamship Co v Lithgows Ltd* (1975).

JURY TRIAL

1. **There are 12 persons in a civil jury:**
   ➢ Court of Session Act 1988 s.13.

2. **Jury trial is competent only in specified types of action, e.g. an action of damages for personal injuries:**
   ➢ Court of Session Act 1988 s.11.

RECLAIMING MOTIONS

1. **Any party to a cause initiated in the Outer House, either by a summons or a petition, who is dissatisfied with an interlocutor may reclaim (appeal) to the Inner House against that interlocutor:**

   ➢ Court of Session Act 1988 s.28.

2. **Any party who is dissatisfied with the verdict of the jury in any jury action may apply to the Inner House for a new trial on various statutory grounds:**

   ➢ Court of Session Act 1988 s.29.

FORMS OF PROCEDURE

1. **The various forms of procedure in the Court of Session are: ordinary action; petition action; commercial cause; judicial review; and personal injuries procedure.**

SUPREME COURT

1. **An appeal against a decision of the Inner House may be taken to the Supreme Court of the United Kingdom:**

   ➢ Court of Session Act 1988 s.40 as amended.

SHERIFF COURT

1. **The modern sheriff courts were established and developed by:**

   ➢ Sheriff Courts (Scotland) Act 1907;
   ➢ Sheriff Courts (Scotland) 1971.

2. **The Sheriff Court Rules Council reviews the procedures and practices to be followed in civil proceedings in the sheriff court.**

SHERIFF COURT PROCEDURE

1. **Ordinary Actions:**

   (a) Most proceedings are governed by the Act of Sederunt (Sheriff Court Ordinary Cause Rules) 1993;
   (b) Civil jury trial in the sheriff court was abolished in 1980.

2. **Summary Causes—minor claims that if they relate to money exceed £3000 but do not exceed £5,000:**

   ➢ Sheriff Courts (Scotland) Act 1971 s.35.

3. **Small Claims:**
   A claim not exceeding £3000, or for an action brought to enforce the performance by the defender of an act other than the payment of money, or for the recovery of possession of moveable property where the value of the subject matter does not exceed £3000.

SHERIFF COURT APPEALS

1. **Appeal is competent from the judgment of the sheriff, or sheriff principal, by means of a note of appeal. Thereafter, appeal may be competent to the Court of Session by note of appeal against final judgments of either sheriff or sheriff principal:**

   ➤ Sheriff Courts (Scotland) Act 1971 s.38.

? QUICK QUIZ

CIVIL LITIGATION

- What are the principal civil remedies?
- What are the different procedures that are competent in the Court of Session?
- What is contained in a:

  (a) Condescendence?
  (b) Conclusion?
  (c) Plea in law?

- What is meant by the term *induciae*?
- What is the closed record?
- Explain what a debate is?
- What is meant by the term *Avizandum*?
- What is an examination in chief?
- What is a reclaiming motion?
- What is the difference between an ordinary action and a commercial cause in the Court of Session?
- What type of action is commenced by an initial writ?
- What kind of claims are summary causes?

📖 FURTHER READING

Charles Hennessy, *Civil Procedure and Practice*, 3rd edn (W. Green, 2008).
D.M. Walker, *The Scottish Legal System*, 8th edn (W. Green, 2001), Ch.8.

🖱 RELEVANT WEB LINKS

Scottish Court Service: *http://www.scotcourts.gov.uk*
Scottish Legal Aid Board: *http://www.slab.org.uk*
Consumer Focus Scotland: *http://www.consumerfocus.org.uk/scotland*
Supreme Court of the United Kingdom *http://www.supremecourt.gov.uk*

ROBERT SHIELS[1]

► CHAPTER OVERVIEW

This chapter concerns the administration of criminal justice in Scotland. It looks at public **17–01** prosecution. It then turns to examine the courts and procedures used to prosecute crime. The various elements of solemn and summary procedures are outlined. The chapter concludes with common law appeals and the laws of evidence.

✓ OUTCOMES

At the end of the chapter you should have: **17–02**

    ✓   an understanding of the nature of the Scottish criminal courts;
    ✓   familiarity with the terminology of the criminal process in the courts; and
    ✓   an insight into the different procedures for each prosecution.

INTRODUCTION

The administration of criminal justice in any legal system is dependent on several areas of **17–03** the law; the criminal law itself is central to the task and that law varies from one jurisdiction to another. A jurisdiction may be a particular geographical area but it may also be specialised in some other manner e.g. military law as applied to the army. The manner in which the administration is carried out is heavily dependent on the criminal procedure—the rules to be applied in and prior to court appearances, and the criminal law of evidence—the rules of how facts are to be proved or admitted. The attainment of justice is thus achieved by an intimate mixture of criminal law, evidence and procedure.

    The activities of lawyers in practice are determined by this law, evidence and procedure, and that is equally so for civil and criminal work. It must also be said that lawyers in practice deal with clients' legal problems without necessarily considering each of these areas individually and separately: the academic divisions of the law need not necessarily parallel law in practice.

    The High Court of Justiciary is the senior court for criminal business and it sits in the cities, and many of the major towns, throughout Scotland to deal with the most serious of cases. The huge bulk of the ordinary criminal business is, however, prosecuted in the sheriff courts and the justice of the peace courts.

    The system of public prosecution in Scotland means that there are, for most practical purposes, no private prosecutions in the High Court of Justiciary, and few in the sheriff

---

[1] Solicitor in Scotland.

court or the justice of the peace courts. The Crown must call corroborated evidence in order to prove a crime beyond reasonable doubt. The prosecutor often meets with the police to discuss cases and, for example, obtains warrants for the police, but the relationship is not that of solicitor and client. Appeals against either conviction or sentence, or both, are possible after a prosecution has concluded.

PUBLIC PROSECUTION

17–04 Private prosecution is competent (that is to say, possible in law) in Scotland and may result in trial by jury, e.g. *Sweeney v X*.[2] It may also bring about trial without jury, e.g. *Caven v Cumming*.[3] However, a principal feature of criminal proceedings is that public prosecution is the general rule and private prosecution is exceedingly rare.

The Lord Advocate is the supreme public prosecutor: see *Dumfries CC v Phyn*.[4] The Lord Advocate is assisted by the Solicitor-General for Scotland and by a number of Advocates Depute, known collectively as Crown Counsel. The Lord Advocate and the Solicitor General are appointed by the Government of the day. Crown Counsel work from the Crown Office in Edinburgh and there are a number of permanent officials there who, as civil servants, provide the continuity at the centre of the system.

The senior permanent official is the Crown Agent who is in the position of managing director of the department: the Deputy Crown Agent deals mainly with operational matters. The department is, in essence, the Procurator Fiscal Service. The permanent local public prosecutor is the procurator fiscal and each is appointed by the Lord Advocate and subject to direction as appropriate by Crown Counsel.

All prosecutions commenced in Scotland by the public prosecutors are done so in the public interest and there must be sufficient evidence for that to happen: a sufficiency of evidence, or corroboration, is central to the decision to prosecute. Public prosecutors also decide the forum, or court, in which a case is to proceed.

SOLEMN AND SUMMARY PROCEDURE

17–05 The decision as to forum is, essentially, a decision between solemn and summary procedure. Solemn procedure is trial on indictment before a judge at the High Court of Justiciary and a jury of 15 people, or before a sheriff principal or sheriff also with a jury of 15 people. Summary procedure is trial on summary complaint before a sheriff principal or a sheriff, or a stipendiary magistrate, or one or more justices of the peace, but without a jury.

The factors to which public prosecutors must have regard in deciding upon forum vary from case to case. First, the High Court of Justiciary has exclusive jurisdiction in cases of treason, murder, rape, incest, deforcement of messengers, breach of duty by magistrates, and certain cases of statutory offences. In practical terms the trials that proceed in the High Court of Justiciary do so because they are the most serious.

Secondly, as judges, sheriffs and justices of the peace have sentencing powers of varying degrees, the more serious a crime is, or appears to be, the more appropriate it becomes that a particular allegation should be tried in a higher court. It is a general rule, but not an invariable principle, that the more serious crimes attract the heaviest sentences.

Thirdly, many individuals who are to be tried have previous convictions that require to

---

[2] 1982 J.C. 70.
[3] 1998 S.L.T. 768.
[4] 1895 2 S.L.T. 580.

be taken into consideration on being sentenced for later criminal behaviour. Modest, or even trivial crimes, may be tried on indictment to allow greater powers of sentencing to the trial judge: a man may, for example, have been sentenced to a long period of imprisonment for supplying controlled drugs. To return to such unlawful activity on release may result in a prosecution in a higher forum than the later crime necessarily merits in itself.

Fourthly, the terms of a statute may require that a particular forum is envisaged: thus vandalism is an offence which can only be prosecuted summarily because no provision is made for sentence on indictment: Criminal Law (Consolidation) (Scotland) Act 1995 s.52(3). The point is narrow, for many statutory offences can easily be prosecuted as common law crimes to avoid such restrictions: vandalism may be charged as malicious damage.

Finally, there may be merit in many cases that have been reported in considering alternatives to prosecution, as these may achieve justice or a more practical result without a hearing in a criminal court. The last point is of special relevance where a very young accused is involved. The procurator fiscal is very likely to pass jurisdiction in such a case to the Reporter to the Children's Panel.

These decisions, and others, are taken by the Crown, the general name for the prosecution. As public prosecutors in Scotland are not police prosecutors the decisions are taken independently of the police. The police complete their investigations by submitting a report to the procurator fiscal for consideration. The interests of the public and the Crown are, or should be, consistent with each other but they are not identical. The police in Scotland do not prosecute in court.

The independent nature of the public prosecutor is emphasised further by the regular receipt by the procurator fiscal of reports for consideration for prosecution from many other agencies. Some 40 or so non-police agencies, such as the Scottish Environment Protection Agency or local authorities, submit reports and these are dealt with on the same principle as police cases.

One important difference ought to be noted. The police are required to make such reports to the procurator fiscal: Police (Scotland) Act 1967 s.17(1). The procurator fiscal has the power to direct the police: 1967 Act, proviso to s.17(3). The non-police reporting agencies, however, are not obliged to report matters to the procurator fiscal, who in turn has no power to direct the agencies.

Solemn procedure

Any crime or offence which is triable on indictment may be tried by the High Court of **17–06** Justiciary sitting at any place in Scotland: the Criminal Procedure (Scotland) Act 1995 (hereafter the "1995 Act") s.3(2). A judge in the High Court of Justiciary is a judge of the Supreme Court and he or she may thus impose any sentence, provided that the sentence is not in excess of the maximum competent sentence. A sheriff is not entitled, on the conviction on indictment of an accused, to pass a sentence of imprisonment for a term exceeding five years: 1995 Act s.3(3).

Petition

Solemn procedure is commenced with the procurator fiscal presenting a petition to a **17–07** sheriff. That petition identifies the accused, the charge under consideration and seeks a warrant to arrest the accused, to search him or her and the premises where the accused is found, and authority to cite witnesses for precognition.

The authority sought by such a warrant does not exclude any other common law or statutory power of arrest. The petition warrant is also separate from the warrant that may be sought for special inquiry, e.g. a warrant to take dental impressions: *Hay v HM Advocate.*[5] A warrant may be sought for a blood sample: *HM Advocate v Milford.*[6]

A petition for a warrant to arrest and commit a person suspected of, or charged with, a crime proceeds as set out in s.34 of the 1995 Act.

First appearance or first examination

17–08 On being arrested an accused person is entitled to have intimation of his or her detention, and the details of the place where he or she is being detained, sent to a solicitor and to one other person reasonably named by him or her without delay, or with minimum delay in the public interest: 1995 Act ss.15(1)(b) and 17. There are now statutory powers to take prints, and various samples: 1995 Act s.18.

As soon as possible after arrest, the accused is brought before a sheriff for examination and that should take place on the next lawful court day after arrest that is not a Saturday, Sunday or court holiday.

The first appearance on a petition warrant is normally brief and formal and in private. The accused may state a plea or make a declaration (a statement made in front of a sheriff), but in practice that is now rare.

A procurator fiscal may have an accused brought to court for judicial examination, that is the accused may be questioned by the prosecutor in so far as such questions are directed to eliciting any admission, denial, explanation, justification or comment: 1995 Act s.36. A judicial examination is not allowed to be a cross-examination of the accused. The accused's solicitor shall be entitled to be present: 1995 Act s.35. The record of the judicial examination may be put in evidence at a subsequent trial, e.g. *Moran v HM Advocate.*[7]

Second appearance or full committal

17–09 After the first appearance or first examination the accused may either be committed for further examination, or committed until liberated in due course of law (also committed for trial). The distinction is important, because if only the former happens then the prosecutor must ensure that the accused is in due course committed for trial unless he or she is released on bail. The length of time between first appearance or first examination and committal for trial is usually in practice about a week but it might be slightly longer; see *Dunbar, Petr.*[8] If an accused has been committed for further examination and then liberated on bail it is not necessary to commit him or her until liberated in due course of law: 1995 Act s.23(3).

These procedures are important for the timings of prosecutions. First, committal for further examination, after which an accused is released on bail requires that a subsequent trial be commenced within 12 months of the first appearance of the accused on petition: 1995 Act s.65(1). Secondly, committal until liberation in due course of law, with the accused remanded in custody, requires a trial to be commenced within 110 days of the date of that full committal and if that is not done then the accused is released on bail: 1995 Act s.65(4).

Any person accused on petition of a crime, which is by law bailable, is entitled immediately on the occasion on which he or she is brought before the sheriff prior to committal until liberation in due course of law, to apply to the sheriff for bail: 1995 Act s.23(1). All crimes and offences, except murder and treason, are bailable: 1995 Act s.24(1).

---

[5] 1968 J.C. 40.
[6] 1973 S.L.T. 12.
[7] 1990 J.C. 196.
[8] 1986 S.C.C.R. 602.

Investigation

All cases require preparation and the sages of the legal profession have always said that **17–10** the secret of success lies in the preparation. For some cases the preparation is mainly collecting together and checking all the productions, these being the items to be relied on in presenting a case such as a knife in an assault case.

However, in Scotland, the process of investigation is thorough and not necessarily the same as in the other jurisdictions of the United Kingdom. First, some of the investigation is actually carried out by others, because of the skill and knowledge required. Pathologists will examine a body or other medical specialists will look at a person in life in order to make an assessment. Forensic scientists will, under laboratory conditions, examine various items and offer a professional view about the item or the substance. These and other specialists will present their findings in the form of a report that may in the event of a prosecution be produced in a court as a production.

Secondly, a procurator fiscal may carry out investigations. That may take the form of a meeting with a skilled witness in order to obtain some understanding of a particular background to a case: forensic scientists may differ in their interpretation of an area of evidence and that has to be discussed and an accurate understanding of the nature of a problem established. Most often, however, a procurator fiscal would wish to obtain from a witness what is known as a precognition, that is, in essence, a précis of the intended evidence of a witness.

The police, or the non-police reporting agency, will have produced a witness statement but that does not in itself allow for an assessment of the credibility and reliability of a witness by a prosecutor and that may be an important element in the assessment of a case prior to taking decisions about prosecution. A meeting for a precognition is also important in allowing for an injury to be viewed, for example, where someone has been scarred in an assault that happened some months earlier.

The final result of the investigations of a procurator fiscal (often assisted by others who have been trained for the work) is a collection of precognitions and police statements. These, with an analysis of the case and consequential recommendations, are sent to the Crown Office for a decision to be taken by Crown Counsel. Once a decision is taken, the papers are returned to the procurator fiscal with an appropriate instruction and that is then implemented.

It has to be emphasised that a procurator fiscal acts in the public interest and assists where possible the defence, so that the process is not to be seen as some sort of competition—to use a sporting analogy. The procurator fiscal provides list of names and addresses of possible witnesses so that the defence are able to undertake their own precognitions. The procurator fiscal also provides copies of the police statements, so that the defence solicitors have full knowledge of the nature and extent of the case against their client. Precognitions, however, are regarded as confidential to the taker and are not copied for the other side.

The indictment

If after investigation Crown Counsel instruct that there is to be a trial by jury, an **17–11** indictment is prepared and signed. An accused has no right to choose how he or she is to be tried. The indictment is in the name of the Lord Advocate in the High Court or on the authority of the Lord Advocate in the sheriff court. The form of the indictment is set out in law: see the 1995 Act s.64(2) and Sch.2.

After the indictment is served on the accused, there must be a preliminary diet in a High Court case: 1995 Act s.72. There must also be a first diet in a sheriff court case: 1995 Act s.71. The essence of these diets is to consider preliminary points or to try to agree evidence and thus narrow the issues for trial.

Trial by jury

17–12 At the trial diet the accused is required to plead guilty or not guilty and a jury of 15 is balloted from the potential jurors present (the assize). Before a juror is sworn in, the prosecutor and the defence may excuse that juror from service without giving a reason: 1995 Act s.86(1). An objection may be stated with a reason: 1995 Act s.86(2).

There are no opening speeches by either side, that is to say there is no opening speech by the prosecutor at the start of the case, nor an opening speech at the start of the defence case. Trials usually commence with, for example, a victim in an assault, or a skilled witness—such as a photographer who took pictures of a particular and relevant place or person.

The evidence is taken from the prosecution witnesses by the prosecutor and the defence may test that evidence and explore other evidence in cross-examination. At the end of the Crown case it may be said by the defence that there is insufficient evidence to justify a conviction, that is to say, that there is no case to answer: 1995 Act s.97(1). If the case proceeds, the accused may give evidence but need not necessarily do so. In speeches to the jury the defence speaks last: 1995 Act s.98.

A special defence is a fact, which if established, must lead to the acquittal of the accused of the charge on the indictment: *Adam v Macneill.*[9] That defence is required to be stated timeously: 1995 Act s.78. The jury must be informed of the special defence: 1995 Act s.89. The special defences are alibi, insanity, incrimination and self-defence.

The verdict of the jury, given after the judge or sheriff has advised them of the law to be applied, is given orally by the foreman or forewoman: 1995 Act s.100(1). The three possible verdicts are guilty, not guilty and not proven. The accused may only be convicted if at least 8 of the 15 jurors have voted for guilty: *McPhelim v HM Advocate.*[10]

Appeals from solemn proceedings

17–13 A person convicted on indictment after trial by jury in the High Court of Justiciary, or the sheriff court, may appeal to the High Court of Justiciary sitting for the disposal of appeals and other proceedings: 1995 Act s.103. An appeal may be against conviction or sentence, or in regard to other orders of the court: 1995 Act s.106.

By an appeal (using a note of appeal) a person may bring under review of the High Court of Justiciary any alleged miscarriage of justice, which may include a miscarriage based on the existence and significance of evidence which was not heard at the original proceedings and the jury's having returned a verdict which no reasonable jury, properly directed by the judge or sheriff, could have returned: 1995 Act s.106(3).

The High Court of Justiciary may dispose of an appeal against conviction by affirming the verdict of the trial court, setting aside the verdict of the trial court and either quashing the conviction or substituting for it an amended verdict, or setting aside the verdict and granting authority for a new prosecution: 1995 Act s.118(1). There are similar powers in regard to appeals against sentence: 1995 Act s.118(3). In certain circumstances devolution issues arising from the Scotland Act 1998 may be referred to the Supreme Court of the United Kingdom in London for determination: see Constitutional Reform Act 2005 ss.23 to 60.

---

[9] 1972 J.C. 1.
[10] 1960 J.C. 17.

Summary procedure

All courts of criminal jurisdiction in Scotland, except the High Court of Justiciary, have a **17–14** summary procedure. Under this procedure a sheriff, a stipendiary magistrate or others sit without a jury to decide both matters of fact and points of law.

A sheriff sitting summarily has extensive powers of sentencing which, without prejudice to wider powers in other statutes, include a fine not exceeding £10,000, a requirement to find money (caution) or security for good behaviour for a period not exceeding 12 months, and to imprison for up to 3 months: 1995 Act s.5(2). Where a person is convicted by the sheriff of a second, or subsequent, offence inferring dishonest appropriation of property, or an attempt to do so, or a second or subsequent offence inferring personal violence, the court may imprison for up to six months: the 1995 Act s.5(3).

The sheriff court has jurisdiction to try all common law offences except murder, rape, incest and wilful fire-raising, and also statutory offences, except where jurisdiction is expressly or impliedly excluded: *Wilson v Hill.*[11]

A justice of the peace court, without prejudice to any other or wider powers in other statutes, is entitled on convicting of a common law offence to impose imprisonment for a period not exceeding 60 days or to impose a fine not exceeding £2,500: 1995 Act s.7(6). However, a justice of the peace court when constituted by a Stipendiary Magistrate has the *summary* criminal jurisdiction and powers of a sheriff: 1995 Act s.7(5).

These statutory powers impose a degree of constraint, but otherwise the decision as to which court a case is to proceed in lies with the Lord Advocate and the procurator fiscal. In Scotland the Crown prosecutes in the public interest and not for some narrow or vexatious purpose. The justice, or the merits, of some minor incident may suggest consideration of alternatives to prosecution. A warning letter may be sent, or a fixed penalty, in the form of a conditional offer, may be made. The latter allows for a payment within a period of time instead of prosecution: 1995 Act s.302. This, and other similar approaches, remove from the courts, cases at the lower end of seriousness.

Preparation

It is not usually the practice in Scotland to have the same detailed and lengthy investi- **17–15** gations for a summary case that is routinely undertaken for solemn matters. Of course, after a solemn case has been investigated fully, then a decision may be taken to reduce what was initially regarded as a solemn case to summary procedure, so that such investigation has been undertaken. That option is necessarily uncommon, but not rare. More likely is the decision to prosecute a case summarily and thereafter preparation for the trial is conducted, but with little of nothing of the detailed investigation routinely undertaken for solemn cases.

Summary complaint

Summary proceedings require the service of a summary complaint on the accused. In the **17–16** vast number of prosecutions the procurator fiscal is the complainer and the prosecution is carried out in the name of the procurator fiscal. Attached to a summary complaint there should be a schedule of any previous convictions, which is intended to be put before the court in the event of a plea of guilty or a finding of guilt by the court: see the 1995 Act Pt IX generally.

---

[11] 1943 J.C. 124.

Intermediate diet

17–17 An intermediate diet is required to be held before the actual trial. The purpose of the intermediate diet is to ascertain whether a trial is likely to proceed on the trial date and also to ascertain the state of preparation of the prosecutor and the accused, whether the accused still pleads not guilty and the extent to which evidence can be agreed as being not contentious: 1995 Act s.148.

Summary Trial

17–18 No part of a trial may take place outwith the presence of the accused: 1995 Act s.154. Once the trial has begun the prosecution calls witnesses in support of the charge and the witnesses may be cross-examined by the accused or his or her lawyer. The summary complaint may be amended so as to cure any error or defect in it, to meet any objection to it or to cure any discrepancy or variance between the complaint and the evidence: 1995 Act s.159. Immediately after the close of the evidence for the prosecution, the accused may submit that he or she has no case to answer: 1995 Act s.160.

Appeals from summary proceedings

17–19 Either party to a summary prosecution may, on the final determination, apply to the court to state a case for the opinion of the High Court of Justiciary. Such an appeal may be against conviction or sentence or in regard to other orders of the court: 1995 Act s.175.

By an appeal, a person may bring under review of the High Court of Justiciary any alleged miscarriage of justice, which may include a miscarriage based on the existence and significance of evidence which was not heard at the original proceedings: 1995 Act s.175(5).

The High Court of Justiciary may dispose of a stated case by (a) remitting the matter to the trial court with its opinion and any direction; (b) affirming the decision of the trial court; (c) setting aside the original verdict and either quashing the conviction or substituting their own verdict; or (d) setting aside the original verdict and granting authority to bring a new prosecution: 1995 Act s.183(1).

Appeals may be taken against sentence only, by means of a note of appeal: 1995 Act s.186(1). That and the other statutory means of appeal do not exclude other common law means of appeal such as Bills of Suspension or Advocation: 1995 Act s.191.

In certain circumstances devolution issues arising from the Scotland Act 1998 may be referred to the High Court of Justiciary and then on to the Judicial Committee of the Privy Council in London for determination: see the Scotland Act 1998 s.98 and Sch.6 paras 9 and 11.

COMMON LAW APPEALS

17–20 Suspension is the procedure whereby an illegal or improper warrant, conviction or judgment from a lower court, dealing with summary criminal procedures, may be reviewed and set aside by the High Court of Justiciary. This procedure is not available to trials on indictment: *Outram v Lees.*[12] Generally this is a remedy open only to a person accused or convicted and not to a prosecutor.

Advocation may be used by the accused, but it is normally used by the prosecutor:

---

[12] 1992 J.C. 17.

Macleod v Levitt.[13] In essence, an accused may present a Bill if there has been a funda-mental nullity or flagrant breach of fundamental principles of justice. The prosecution may proceed if there has been a serious mistake with the case at the court of first instance.

The *nobile officium* is the inherent equitable power of the High Court of Justiciary to deal with extraordinary or unforeseen circumstances, or where there is no other common law or statutory remedy: *Wan Ping Nam v German Minister of Justice*[14]; *Black v HM Advocate.*[15] A petition may also proceed where there is no other means of review, which appears competent or appropriate: *Anderson v HM Advocate.*[16]

LAW OF EVIDENCE

The rules of evidence are more strictly applied in criminal cases than they are in civil cases. **17–21** The Crown must prove the charge on indictment, or on summary complaint, beyond reasonable doubt. Moreover, there is always a question of sufficiency of evidence, which means in practice that every essential fact must be corroborated. By corroboration it is meant that the evidence must be supported by independent evidence from other sources. Corroboration amounts to an independent check on the evidence. Not every fact must be corroborated, only those facts that go to proving the commission of a crime and the identification of the accused as a person responsible for committing the crime charged. In civil cases the standard is a balance of probabilities and corroboration is not essential.

▼ CHAPTER SUMMARY

PUBLIC PROSECUTION

1. **Public prosecution is the general rule and private prosecution is exceedingly rare. 17–22
However, private prosecution is competent:**

   ➢ *X v Sweeney* (1982).

2. **The Lord Advocate is the supreme public prosecutor and is assisted by the Solicitor-General for Scotland and by a number of Advocates Depute, known collectively as Crown Counsel.**
3. **All public prosecutions are in the public interest and there must be sufficient evidence to proceed to prosecute.**
4. **Public prosecutors decide whether a case is to be tried under solemn or summary procedure and which court will hear a case.**
5. **An accused has no right to choose trial by jury.**
6. **Solemn procedure is trial on indictment before a judge and a jury of 15 people. Summary procedure is trial on summary complaint before a judge without a jury.**
7. **The public prosecutor is independent. The public prosecutor receive reports for consideration from the police and a wide range of non-police agencies.**

---

[13] 1969 J.C. 16.
[14] 1972 J.C. 43.
[15] 1991 S.C.C.R. 609.
[16] 1974 S.L.T. 239.

SOLEMN PROCEDURE

1. **Any crime or offence which is triable on indictment may be tried by the High Court of Justiciary sitting at any place in Scotland:**

   ➢ Criminal Procedure (Scotland) Act 1995 s.3(2).

2. **A judge in the High Court of Justiciary may impose any sentence provided that the sentence is not in excess of the maximum competent sentence.**

3. **A sheriff is not entitled on the conviction on indictment of an accused to pass a sentence of imprisonment for a term exceeding five years:**

   ➢ Criminal Procedure (Scotland) Act 1995 s.3(3).

4. **Solemn procedure is generally commenced with the procurator fiscal presenting a petition to a sheriff.**

5. **After the first appearance or first examination the accused may either be committed for further examination or committed until liberated in due course of law (also committed for trial).**

6. **Committal for further examination after which an accused is released on bail requires that a subsequent trial be commenced within 12 months of the first appearance of the accused on petition:**

   ➢ Criminal Procedure (Scotland) Act 1995 s.65(1).

7. **Committal until liberation in due course of law with the accused remanded in custody requires a trial to be commenced within 110 days of the date of that full committal. If this is not done the accused is released on bail:**

   ➢ Criminal Procedure (Scotland) Act 1995 s.65(4).

8. **All crimes and offences except murder and treason are bailable:**

   ➢ Criminal Procedure (Scotland) Act 1995 s.24(1).

TRIAL BY JURY

1. **At the trial diet the accused is required to plead guilty or not guilty and a jury of 15 is balloted from the potential jurors present (the assize).**
   Before a juror is sworn in, the prosecutor and the defence may excuse that juror from service without giving a reason:

   ➢ Criminal Procedure (Scotland) Act 1995 s.86(1).

2. **The evidence is taken from the prosecution witnesses by the prosecutor and the defence test that evidence and explore other evidence in cross-examination.**

3. **At the end of the Crown case, it may be said by the defence that there is insufficient evidence to justify a conviction, that is to say, that there is no case to answer:**

   ➢ Criminal Procedure (Scotland) Act 1995 s.97(1).

4. **A special defence is a fact which, if established, must lead to the acquittal of the accused of the charge on the indictment:**

   ➢ *Adam v McNeill* (1971).

5. **The special defences are alibi, insanity, incrimination and self-defence.**

6. The three possible verdicts are guilty, not guilty and not proven.
7. The accused may only be convicted if at least eight of the 15 jurors have voted for guilty

APPEALS FROM SOLEMN PROCEEDINGS

1. There is an appeal to the High Court of Justiciary sitting as an appeal court. An appeal may be against conviction or sentence:

   ➤ Criminal Procedure (Scotland) Act 1995 s.106.

2. The High Court of Justiciary may affirm the verdict, set aside the verdict and either quash the conviction or substitute an amended verdict, or set aside the verdict and grant authority for a new prosecution:

   ➤ Criminal Procedure (Scotland) Act 1995 s.118.

SUMMARY PROCEDURE

1. All courts of criminal jurisdiction in Scotland, except the High Court of Justiciary, have a summary procedure.
2. A judge sits without a jury to decide both matters of fact and points of law.
3. A sheriff's powers of sentencing include a fine not exceeding £10,000, a requirement to find money (known as caution) or security for good behaviour for a period not exceeding 12 months, and to imprison for up to 12 months.
4. The sheriff court has jurisdiction to try all common law offences except murder, rape and incest, and also statutory offences, except where jurisdiction is expressly or impliedly excluded.
5. A justice of the peace court can impose imprisonment for a period not exceeding 60 days or to impose a fine not exceeding £2,500. When the court is constituted by a stipendiary magistrate it has the summary criminal jurisdiction and powers of a sheriff.
6. Alternatives to prosecution include: a warning letter or a fixed penalty.

SUMMARY COMPLAINT

1. In the vast number of prosecutions the procurator fiscal is the complainer and the prosecution is carried out in the name of the procurator fiscal.

APPEALS FROM SUMMARY PROCEEDINGS

1. Either party to a summary prosecution may appeal against conviction or sentence:

   ➤ Criminal Procedure (Scotland) Act 1995 s.175.

2. The High Court of Justiciary may dispose of a stated case by: (a) remitting the matter to the trial court; (b) affirming the decision; (c) setting aside the original verdict and either quashing the conviction or substituting their own verdict; or (d) setting aside the original verdict and granting authority to bring a new prosecution:

   ➤ Criminal Procedure (Scotland) Act 1995 s.183(1).

COMMON LAW APPEALS

1. **Suspension is the procedure whereby an illegal or improper warrant, conviction or judgment from a lower court dealing with summary criminal procedures may be reviewed and set aside by the High Court of Justiciary. Generally this is a remedy open only to a person accused or convicted.**
2. **Advocation is normally used by the prosecutor. The prosecution may proceed if there has been a serious mistake with the case at the court of first instance.**
3. **The *nobile officium* is the inherent equitable power of the High Court of Justiciary to deal with extraordinary or unforeseen circumstances, or where there is no other common law or statutory remedy;:**
   - ➤ *Wan Ping Nam v German Minister of Justice* (1972);
   - ➤ *Black v HM Advocate* (1991).

LAW OF EVIDENCE

1. **The rules of evidence are more strictly applied in criminal cases than they are in civil cases.**
2. **The Crown must prove the charge beyond reasonable doubt.**
3. **Every essential fact must be corroborated.**

? QUICK QUIZ

CRIMINAL PROCEDURE

- Is private prosecution competent in Scotland?
- Who is the supreme public prosecutor in Scotland?
- Who decides which court a case is to be tried in?
- What factors are relevant to the decisions as to whether to use solemn or summary procedure?
- What is the difference between solemn and summary procedure?
- How many people sit on a criminal jury?
- Can a person convicted on indictment appeal against sentence?
- Can the sheriff court try a rape case?
- What is the purpose of an intermediate diet in summary procedure?
- Who can use the suspension procedure and what is it?
- What is the name given to the equitable power of the High Court of Justiciary?
- What is meant by corroboration?

📖 FURTHER READING

Renton and Brown Criminal Law, 6th edn (W. Green).
Renton and Brown Annotated Acts: Criminal Procedure Legislation, 11th edn (W. Green).

⌨ RELEVANT WEB LINKS

Crown Office and Procurator Fiscal Service: *http://www.copfs.gov.uk*
Scottish Environment Protection Agency: *http://www.sepa.org.uk*
Scottish Children's Reporter Administration: *http://www.scra.gov.uk*

Chapter 18   Legal Skills

Dr Nick McKerrell[1]

▶ CHAPTER OVERVIEW

18–01 Although law is fundamental to the way we live our lives, very few of us ever have to study it, or learn exactly how it works. The other chapters in this book deal with a variety of specific legal topics, covering a wide range of issues. As well as understanding the details of these subjects, you have to adapt to new methods of learning and feel comfortable referring to different types of sources.

This chapter is an attempt to help you with this. It introduces the two major legal sources: statutes and cases. You will see that these are continually referred to in the substantive chapters. By using examples of cases and statutes, this chapter will show you how to find, read and understand these materials.

Not only are the sources of law unfamiliar but, in some respects, so are the methods of assessing the law—problems, essays and exams. This chapter is also designed to provide guidance on your knowledge of these forms of assessment and uses examples to help you with your study of the topic.

UNDERSTANDING STATUTORY LAW

18–02 Acts of Parliament are written in a very formal style that is unlike other texts. The language is very precise and outlines exactly what situations the law is designed to cover. This is to minimise confusion, when the law is implemented, and to prevent any ambiguities. It also helps the courts in the process of statutory interpretation. Drafting legislation in this specific way is a skilled and specialised job carried out by trained "draftsmen".

All this means that reading Acts of Parliament is not straight forward and indeed not a pursuit that many people ever have to carry out! Yet, there are common structures for all Acts of Parliament which can aid the process of reading and understanding a statute.

Finding statutes

18–03 There are several different paper-based collections of statutes, one of which is *Current Law Statutes* (London: Sweet & Maxwell). All statutes are organised by year and by their short title.[2] These paper versions only have the Acts as they were when passed, i.e. they do not have subsequent amendments included. The official electronic source of statues is provided by the National Archives on behalf of HM Government. Their website at *http://www.legislation.gov.uk.* provides access to the full text of all legislation dating back to 1988 and many Acts passed prior to that. Much work has gone into this official (and free) statutory

---

[1] Lecturer in Law, Glasgow Caledonian University.
[2] See below at para.18–05.

database over the last few years. An Act on this website will appear either in its original format that is as it was when passed without subsequent amendment or the latest available version which incorporates any changes. The database aims to be up-to-date as possible, however there may be outstanding revisions to the legislation. Where this is the case the database will clearly indicate this. It is really important that you check that you are accessing the latest version particularly if you arrive at the legislation website from a search engine like Google.

The most regularly updated legal databases give a very accurate record of current legislation. Examples of updated electronic legal databases for all sources are *Westlaw* and *LexisNexis*. Alternatively, changes that have been made to statutes can be tracked by using the paper-based looseleaf *Current Law* (London: Sweet & Maxwell), *Current Law Legislation Citator*.

Once you have found a statute what are they liable to look like?

Understanding statutes—an Act of the UK Parliament

Excerpt 1 from the Identity Documents Act 2010: **18–04**

ELIZABETH II

[A] Identity Documents Act 2010

[B] **2010 CHAPTER 40**

[C] An Act to make provision for and in connection with the repeal of the Identity Cards Act 2006.

[D] [21st December 2010]

[E] Be it enacted by the Queen's most Excellent Majesty, by and with the advice and consent of the Lords Spiritual and Temporal, and Commons, in this present Parliament assembled, and by the authority of the same, as follows:—

Repeal of Identity Cards Act 2006

[F] **1 Repeal of Identity Cards Act 2006**
   (1) The Identity Cards Act 2006 is repealed.
   (2) But—
      (a) sections 25 and 26 of that Act (possession of false identity documents etc), and
      (b) section 38 of that Act (verifying information provided with passport applications etc),
   are re-enacted by this Act (with consequential amendments and, in the case of section 38, also with minor amendments).
   (3) In addition, the amendment of section 1 of the Consular Fees Act 1980 made by section 36 of the Identity Cards Act 2006 continues to have effect subject to a consequential amendment (see paragraph 2 of the Schedule to this Act).

2 Cancellation of ID cards etc

(1) No ID cards are to be issued by the Secretary of State at any time on or after the day on which this Act is passed.

(2) All ID cards that are valid immediately before that day are to be treated as cancelled by the Secretary of State at the end of the period of one month beginning with that day.

(3) As soon as reasonably practicable after that day, the Secretary of State must send a letter to every cardholder—

    (a) informing the cardholder that the cardholder's ID card is to be treated as cancelled as mentioned in subsection (2), and

    (b) providing the cardholder with such information about the consequences of its cancellation as the Secretary of State considers appropriate.

(4) A letter under subsection (3) must be sent to the address recorded (at the time it is sent) in the National Identity Register as the address of the cardholder's principal place of residence in the United Kingdom.

(5) For the purposes of this section a person is a "cardholder" if—

    (a) an ID card has been issued to the person, and

    (b) the ID card is valid immediately before the day on which this Act is passed.

(6) In this section "ID card" has the same meaning as in the Identity Cards Act 2006.

[A] The Short Title

18–05 All Acts of Parliament are indexed in any system of referencing by their short title. It gives a brief summary of the issue, which the Act covers, and tells the year in which it was passed. This Act clearly refers to the controversial issue of identity documents. This is how you should reference an Act of Parliament.

Tip: try not to add any words to the short title when discussing an Act in an essay—in particular "The" at the start.

[B] The "Chapter" No.

18–06 A further method of referencing, and one which differentiates UK Parliament legislation from Scottish Parliament legislation, is the chapter number. This tells us this was the fortieth Act passed by the Westminster Parliament in 2010. This may be shortened to 2010 c.40.

[C] The Long Title

18–07 The first paragraph in every Act of the Westminster Parliament provides a summary of the aims of the Act. Why is it being passed? What is it seeking to achieve? This is called the long title of the Act.

Here the long title tells us this Act was passed to *repeal* an earlier Act of Parliament the Identity Cards Act 2006. To repeal an Act means it will be overturned and no longer exist as law.

[D] Date of Royal Assent

18–08 This date at the end of the long title, is when a Bill has completed its journey through Parliament and becomes an Act.

Tip: this is not necessarily the date that the Act comes into force.

The Queen as the head of the British State must formally "assent" to all statutes that are passed by Westminster and the Scottish Parliament. The Queen has not had to grant the Assent in person since the nineteenth century. It can now be given in her absence by written consent under the process of letters patent. Once approved, the formal Royal Seal and Coat of Arms can appear on the Act.

This Act was granted Royal Assent on December 21, 2010.

[E] Standard enactment formula

This paragraph is contained in every Act passed at Westminster. It indicates that: **18–09**

- the proper Parliamentary processes have been carried out;
- that it has gone through both Houses of Parliament: the elected House of Commons and the unelected House of Lords—or "Lords Spiritual and Temporal"; and
- that it has been given assent by the monarch.

[F] Sections

All Acts of Parliament are organised by numbered sections. Numbered paragraphs within **18–10** each section are called "sub-sections". It is important to be accurate when referencing the statute. For each section there will normally be a heading or note in the margin to explain what it is meant to cover.

For example here s.2(1)—read as "section 2 subsection 1"— states plainly that the Secretary of State, a Government Minister will not issue ID cards at any time. This is a fairly short Act of Parliament with 14 sections, but there is wide variation in how long an Act of Parliament can be. The record for the longest Act was broken in 2006 by the Companies Act which has 1,300 sections.

A later excerpt, Excerpt 2 from the Identity Documents Act 2010:

[G]   8 Meaning of "personal information" **18–11**

(1) For the purposes of sections 4 and 5 "personal information", in relation to an individual ("A"), means—

(a) A's full name,

(b) other names by which A is or has previously been known,

(c) A's gender,

(d) A's date and place of birth,

(e) external characteristics of A that are capable of being used for identifying A,

(f) the address of A's principal place of residence in the United Kingdom,

(g) the address of every other place in the United Kingdom or elsewhere where A has a place of residence,

(h) where in the United Kingdom and elsewhere A has previously been resident,

(i) the times at which A was resident at different places in the United Kingdom or elsewhere,

(j) A's current residential status,

(k) residential statuses previously held by A, and

(l) information about numbers allocated to A for identification purposes and about the documents (including stamps or labels) to which they relate.

(2) In subsection (1) "residential status" means—

(a) A's nationality,

(b) A's entitlement to remain in the United Kingdom, and

(c) if that entitlement derives from a grant of leave to enter or remain in the United Kingdom, the terms and conditions of that leave.

9 Other definitions

(1) "Apparatus" includes any equipment, machinery or device and any wire or cable, together with any software used with it.

(2) In relation to England and Wales and Northern Ireland, an identity document is "false" only if it is false within the meaning of Part 1 of the Forgery and Counterfeiting Act 1981 (see section 9(1)).

(3) An identity document was "improperly obtained" if—

    (a) false information was provided in, or in connection with, the application for its issue to the person who issued it, or

    (b) false information was provided in, or in connection with, an application for its modification to a person entitled to modify it.

(4) In subsection (3)—

    (a) "false" information includes information containing any inaccuracy or omission that results in a tendency to mislead,

    (b) "information" includes documents (including stamps and labels) and records, and

    (c) the "issue" of a document includes its renewal, replacement or re-issue (with or without modifications).

(5) References to the making of a false identity document include the modification of an identity document so that it becomes false.

(6) This section applies for the purposes of sections 4 to 6.

[H] 14 Commencement, extent and short title

(1) Sections 2 and 3 and this section come into force on the day on which this Act is passed.

(2) The other provisions of this Act come into force at the end of the period of one month beginning with that day.

(3) Any amendment, repeal or revocation made by this Act has the same extent as the enactment to which it relates.

(4) Subject to that, this Act extends to England and Wales, Scotland and Northern Ireland.

(5) This Act may be cited as the Identity Documents Act 2010.

[G] Interpretation section

18–12 As has been mentioned, it is vital that a statute is clear in its intentions and not capable of being misapplied. To that end, each statute normally has an Interpretation section where key phrases used in the legislation are defined. The Interpretation section can be a useful starting point in the context of reading and understanding a statute. This Act has no specific Interpretation section but we can see that in s.8 and s.9 critical words are defined. For example, s.8(1) tells us what is meant by "personal information".

[H] Commencement and extent section

18–13 When referring to a statute, it is crucial to know whether the law is binding at the relevant time. That is, has the law come into force? The section that tells the reader this is known as the "Commencement Section".

Here we are told that implementation of the legislation is being carried out on two dates. That is s.14(1) tells us that s.2 and s.3 come into force on the date of Royal Assent which we know is December 21, 2010.[3] Then we are told in s.14(2) that the rest of the law will apply exactly one month after this—January 21, 2011.

Tip: an Act is passed on the date of Royal Assent—but does not necessarily come into force.

18–14 The part of this section labelled the "extent" section is a necessary element, because of the unique multi-national status of the UK Parliament. Although there is now a strong element of legislative devolution in Scotland, Wales and Northern Ireland, Acts of the Westminster Parliament can still be binding across the whole of the United Kingdom. To clarify the position, s.14(4) tells us to which parts of the United Kingdom this Act applies and we can see that it applies in all areas of the United Kingdom.

Tip: this section also confirms the short title of the Act.

---

[3] See para.18–08.

Repeals and amendments

No statute operates in a vacuum and its existence will have an impact on previous legis- **18–15** lation. It may overturn those laws (repeal) or change aspects of them (amend). Each statute will list the repeals and amendments it will make in an appendix to the statute. This is known as a Schedule. This statute is unusual because its overarching aim is to repeal one specific earlier statute: the Identity Cards Act 2006. Yet, this is not the only law it affects and there are other amendments listed in the Schedule to the Act.

When reading a statute it is necessary to know if there have been subsequent amendments and, indeed, if the statute is still valid law, as it may have been repealed. If you simply take the statute off the shelf in the library you will not get this information. To get the up-to-date text of a statute one can use an electronic database (*Westlaw* or *LexisNexis*), the free online service provided by the National Archive at *www.legislation.gov.uk*[4] or use a paper-based legislation citator.

Understanding statutes—an Act of the Scottish Parliament

Since 1999 the Scottish Parliament, created by the Scotland Act 1998, has had the power **18–16** to pass primary legislation. This power is limited by the 1998 Act and the Parliament cannot pass any legislation which deals with "reserved matters", breaches European law, or runs contrary to the European Convention of Human Rights.[5]

The Acts which are passed by the Scottish Parliament, have similarities in terms of layout with UK Parliament legislation.

Excerpt 1 from the Offensive Behaviour at Football and Threatening Communications **18–17** (Scotland) Act 2012:

| [I] | Offensive Behaviour at Football and Threatening Communications (Scotland) Act 2012 |

| [II] | **2012 asp 1** |

[III] The Bill for this Act of the Scottish Parliament was passed by the Parliament on 14th December 2011 and received Royal Assent on 19th January 2012

[IV] An Act of the Scottish Parliament to create offences concerning offensive behaviour in relation to certain football matches, and concerning the communication of certain threatening material.

Offensive behaviour at regulated football matches

[V] **1 Offensive behaviour at regulated football matches**
  (1) A person commits an offence if, in relation to a regulated football match—

---

[4] Although see limitations on this service outlined in para.18–03.
[5] Scotland Act 1998 s.29(1).

(a) the person engages in behaviour of a kind described in subsection (2), and
(b) the behaviour—
    (i) is likely to incite public disorder, or
    (ii) would be likely to incite public disorder.
(2) The behaviour is—
(a) expressing hatred of, or stirring up hatred against, a group of persons based on their membership (or presumed membership) of—
    (i) a religious group,
    (ii) a social or cultural group with a perceived religious affiliation,
    (iii) a group defined by reference to a thing mentioned in subsection (4),
(b) expressing hatred of, or stirring up hatred against, an individual based on the individual's membership (or presumed membership) of a group mentioned in any of sub-paragraphs (i) to (iii) of paragraph (a),
(c) behaviour that is motivated (wholly or partly) by hatred of a group mentioned in any of those sub-paragraphs,
(d) behaviour that is threatening, or
(e) other behaviour that a reasonable person would be likely to consider offensive.
(3) For the purposes of subsection (2)(a) and (b), it is irrelevant whether the hatred is also based (to any extent) on any other factor.
(4) The things referred to in subsection (2)(a)(iii) are—
(a) colour,
(b) race,
(c) nationality (including citizenship),
(d) ethnic or national origins,
(e) sexual orientation,
(f) transgender identity,
(g) disability.
(5) For the purposes of subsection (1)(b)(ii), behaviour would be likely to incite public disorder if public disorder would be likely to occur but for the fact that—
(a) measures are in place to prevent public disorder, or
(b) persons likely to be incited to public disorder are not present or are not present in sufficient numbers.
(6) A person guilty of an offence under subsection (1) is liable—
(a) on conviction on indictment, to imprisonment for a term not exceeding 5 years, or to a fine, or to both, or
(b) on summary conviction, to imprisonment for a term not exceeding 12 months, or to a fine not exceeding the statutory maximum, or to both.

[I] The Short Title

18–18 As with UK Acts, the short title is used to organise and reference Scottish statutes. Most Scottish statutes will have the word "Scotland" in the short title to differentiate them in a clear way from legislation passed by the UK Parliament. This applies here as we can see.

[II] Act of the Scottish Parliament (asp)

18–19 Another distinction in referencing, is the use of the acronym "asp" standing for Act of the Scottish Parliament. This is equivalent to the chapter number used in UK Parliament legislation.[6]

---

[6] See para.18–06.

[III] Relevant dates

Unlike UK Parliament legislation, Acts of the Scottish Parliament identify two dates in **18–20** their introductions. The date on which the Bill was passed by the Parliament (December 14, 2011) and the date when Royal Assent was received (January 19, 2012). This is done in a separate paragraph at the beginning of the Act. As with Westminster, Royal Assent is required for Scottish primary legislation.

There is a time delay between these two dates, normally of about four weeks. As the Scottish Parliament is limited by law, this time allows the British Government to monitor the legislation, to ensure that it is valid within the powers of the Scotland Act before Royal Assent is granted. From 1999 to the time of writing, the British Government has never intervened to prevent a piece of legislation gaining approval from the monarchy.

[IV] The Long Title

This paragraph outlines the purpose of the legislation and gives a guide to the reader. **18–21** However, the use of the long title is not as uniform as in UK Parliament legislation and occasionally there are no equivalent paragraphs in Scottish statutes. Here the long title is relatively brief and covers the controversial topic of creating new criminal offences that can be committed at football matches and on the internet.

[V] Sections

The Westminster tradition of utilising draftsmen is continued in Scotland, where legisla- **18–22** tion is also organised in sections and sub-sections. Section 1(1) outlines the specific offence that can be committed now at a "regulated football match".

A later excerpt, Excerpt 2 from the Offensive Behaviour at Football and Threatening Communications (Scotland) Act 2012:

[VI] **8 Section 6: interpretation**
    (1) Subsections (2) to (5) define expressions used in section 6.
    (2) "Communicates" means communicates by any means (other than by means of unrecorded speech); and related expressions are to be construed accordingly.
    (3) "Material" means anything that is capable of being read, looked at, watched or listened to, either directly or after conversion from data stored in another form.
    (4) "Hatred on religious grounds" means hatred against—
        (a) a group of persons based on their membership (or presumed membership) of—
            (i) a religious group (within the meaning given by section 74(7) of the Criminal Justice (Scotland) Act 2003 (asp 7)),
            (ii) a social or cultural group with a perceived religious affiliation, or
        (b) an individual based on the individual's membership (or presumed membership) of a group mentioned in either of sub-paragraphs (i) and (ii) of paragraph (a).
    (5) "Seriously violent act" means an act that would cause serious injury to, or the death of, a person.
    (6) In subsection (4)—
        (a) "membership", in relation to a group, includes association with members of that group, and
        (b) "presumed" means presumed by the person making the communication.

9 Power to modify sections 6(5)(b) and 8
    (1) The Scottish Ministers may by order—
        (a) modify section 6(5)(b) so as to—

        (i) add or remove a ground of hatred to or from those for the time being mentioned in that section,

        (ii) vary a ground of hatred for the time being mentioned in that section,

    (b) modify section 8 so as to—

        (i) add or remove a definition to or from those for the time being mentioned in that section in consequence of a modification made under paragraph (a),

        (ii) vary a definition that relates to a ground of hatred for the time being mentioned in section 6(5)(b).

(2) An order under subsection (1) may—

    (a) specify grounds of hatred by reference to hatred against groups of persons, or individuals, of specified descriptions,

    (b) specify such descriptions by reference to specified personal characteristics,

    (c) in relation to any ground added by the order, modify this Act so as to make such provision for the same or similar purposes as that in section 7 as the Scottish Ministers consider necessary or appropriate,

    (d) remove or vary any provision made under paragraph (c).

(3) An order under subsection (1)—

    (a) may make such consequential, transitional, transitory or saving provision as the Scottish Ministers consider appropriate,

    (b) may, for the purpose of making consequential provision under paragraph (a), modify this Act,

    (c) is subject to the affirmative procedure.

Offences outside Scotland

10 Sections 1(1) and 6(1): offences outside Scotland

(1) As well as applying to anything done in Scotland by any person, section 1(1) also applies to anything done outside Scotland by a person who is habitually resident in Scotland.

(2) As well as applying to anything done in Scotland by any person, section 6(1) also applies to a communication made by a person from outside Scotland if the person intends the material communicated to be read, looked at, watched or listened to primarily in Scotland.

(3) Where an offence under section 1(1) or 6(1) is committed outside Scotland, the person committing the offence may be prosecuted, tried and punished for the offence—

    (a) in any sheriff court district in which the person is apprehended or in custody, or

    (b) in such sheriff court district as the Lord Advocate may direct,

as if the offence had been committed in that district (and the offence is, for all purposes incidental to or consequential on the trial and punishment, deemed to have been committed in that district).

Report on operation of offences

11 Report on operation of offences

(1) The Scottish Ministers must lay before the Scottish Parliament—

    (a) a report on the operation of the offence in section 1(1) during the review period, and

    (b) a report on the operation of the offence in section 6(1) during the review period.

(2) Before preparing a report under subsection (1), the Scottish Ministers must consult such persons as they consider appropriate.

(3) A report under subsection (1) must be so laid no later than 12 months after the end of the review period.

(4) In subsections (1) and (3), "the review period" means the period—

    (a) beginning on the relevant day, and

    (b) ending 2 years after the 1 August next occurring after the relevant day.

(5) In subsection (4), "the relevant day" means—

    (a) in relation to a report under subsection (1)(a), the day on which section 1 comes into force,

(b) in relation to a report under subsection (1)(b), the day on which section 6 comes into force.

Commencement and short title

[VII] 12 Commencement
    (1) This section and section 13 come into force on the day of Royal Assent.
    (2) The other provisions of this Act come into force on such day as the Scottish Ministers may by order appoint.

13 Short title
    The short title of this Act is the Offensive Behaviour at Football and Threatening Communications (Scotland) Act 2012.

[VI] Interpretation section

As in UK Parliament legislation, the importance of precision in statutory language means **18–23** that Scottish Parliament Acts continue the tradition of using "Interpretation Sections" as a guide to those reading the law. Within this legislation there are key phrases defined throughout but s.8 brings many of them together. For example, s.8(2) defines the meaning of "communicates" and s.8(5) what a "serious violent act" amounts to in the context of this Act.

[VII] Commencement section

To confirm when a law comes into force, it is always necessary to look at the actual **18–24** statute. From this section we can see that there is reference to two dates. The Commencement Section s.12(1) tells us that the section itself comes into force on January 19, 2012, the date of Royal Assent.

However, s.12(2) tells us that the rest of the Act, the bulk of the law, comes into force on a date "as the Scottish Ministers may by order appoint".

To find out this information we would need to use an electronic database like *Westlaw* or *LexisNexis* or a paper-based journal called a citator.[7]

On searching these sources we can discover that the rest of this law came into force on March 1, 2012 with the passing of the Offensive Behaviour at Football and Threatening Communications (Scotland) Act 2012 (Commencement) Order 2012 (SSI 2012/20).[8]

Tip: there is also a reminder of the Short Title in s.13 but unlike Westminster there is no need for an extent section because the Scottish Parliament only has jurisdiction for Scotland.

Repeals and amendments

Any changes to prior legislation, including Acts of the UK Parliament, are listed in the **18–25** Schedules to the Act.

Subordinate/delegated legislation

Subordinate legislation has been discussed in Chapter 1. A large amount of subordinate **18–26** legislation is passed each year, e.g. in 2011, 3133 statutory instruments were passed. Specific statutory instruments, can be located in the legal databases such as *Westlaw* or *LexisNexis*, which contain their up-to-date versions. All statutory instruments issued at a

---

[7] See para.18–03.
[8] This was announced in the March 2012 edition of the Current Law Citator.

UK and Scottish level since 1987 and a selection from before that can be found on the National Archive site.[9]

UNDERSTANDING CASE LAW

18–27 Every day in Britain tens of thousands of cases are heard in civil and criminal courts, but only a fraction of these will be reported in "official law reports". Those that are reported, will generally cover an area of particular interest, apply a particular legal principle, or develop the law in some way.

Judicial precedent

18–28 The concept of judicial precedent has been discussed in Chapter 1. An important legal skill is being able to identify a precedent and explain what it means.

So, firstly how do you locate a case you are searching for?

Citation

18–29 If a case is reported it will have a citation. This tells us where the report was published and how to find it.

Starrs v Ruxton, 2000 S.L.T. 42
(a)   (b)   (c)

Here is a common example.

(a) Case name—two parties are nearly always named in a case. Although we are used to seeing the use of "versus" in the context of sporting events like football and boxing, it is also used in legal reporting.
(b) Year of reporting.
(c) Citation of report—the initials here stand for *Scots Law Times*, one of the more regularly cited law reports in Scotland. It is published on a weekly basis and, as well as case reports from all types of Scottish courts, it also publishes articles and announcements for the Scottish legal profession.

All law reports have their own citation, which is internationally recognised—thus, it is vital that you use the correct abbreviation. As you study law in more detail, you will become familiar with some of the more commonly referenced series of case reports.

Examples:

All E.R.—the All England Law Reports, are a very heavily utilised series covering the English jurisdiction.
I.R.L.R.—Industrial Relations Law Reports is a specialist series covering cases dealing with employment law issues.

---

[9] *http://www.legislation.gov.uk* [Accessed May 12, 2012].

If you do not recognise a citation, there is a useful resource: the *Cardiff Index of Legal Abbreviations* website can provide you with the name of the legal report if you type in the abbreviation.[10]

When you have identified the case and its citation, you can either find the case in hard copy in a law library, or utilise a legal database like *Westlaw* or *LexisNexis,* which offer access to many of the major law reports.

Tip: if you ever mention a case in a piece of written coursework, always use its correct citation.

Reading a case

If we examine a recently reported case in Scotland, we can identify the key elements in reading a case. This is a case from 2010. **18–30**

Headnote from *Russell v Dyer*[11]:

[A] RUSSELL v DYER

[B] No 21 Lord Carloway, [C]
26 November 2010 Lord Mackay of Drumadoon and
[2010] HCJAC 138 Lord Nimmo Smith

[D] RICHARD LANGLEY RUSSELL, Appellant—*LK Kennedy*
CATHERINE DYER (Procurator fiscal, Glasgow), Respondent—*Clancy QC, A-D*

[E] *Justiciary—Crime—Breach of the peace—Public element—Conduct severe enough to cause alarm to ordinary people and threaten serious disturbance to the community—Sending threatening letter to headmistress of primary school then appearing at school door at the start of the day—Whether breach of the peace*

[F] The appellant was convicted of a charge of conducting himself in a disorderly manner, repeatedly harassing M, the headmistress at his children's school, threatening M by means of a letter, entering the school playground, repeatedly failing to comply with requests to retreat from the teacher, placing M in a state of fear and alarm for her safety and committing a breach of the peace. The appellant applied for a stated case, but leave to appeal was refused at the sifts. The Scottish Criminal Cases Review Commission referred the case to the High Court of Justiciary on the grounds that the incidents did not support a charge of breach of the peace. The appellant argued that the letter was a private communication and could not have provoked a serious disturbance of the public peace, and his presence in the playground could not have caused alarm to ordinary people or threatened serious disturbance to the community. The Crown argued that each element of the charge on its own amounted to a breach of the peace, and if they did not amount to a breach of the peace individually, they did when taken together.

[G] *Held* that: (1) the sending of a threatening letter to the headmistress of a primary school followed by an appearance by the sender at the door of that school at the start of the day, when parents, teachers (including the headmistress) and children could be expected to be present, was conduct which satisfied the dual test in *Smith v Donnelly* and thus amounted to a breach of the peace, and the appropriate course was to look at the two episodes together (para 21); (2) the terms of the letter could reasonably be described as presenting a death threat by the appellant to M, the threat was regarded seriously by the solicitor and by M, and the

---

[10] *http://www.legalabbrevs.cardiff.ac.uk/* [Accessed May 12, 2012].
[11] 2011 J.C. 164.

background was communicated to the members of staff at the school and would be liable to be known to others, including parents (para 24); (3) the sheriff was entitled to hold that the appellant went to the playground on a pretext and to conclude that his real motive was to intimidate and provoke the complainer (para 25); (4) the appellant's behaviour would be genuinely alarming and disturbing and would threaten serious disturbance to the community (para 26); and appeal *refused*.

[H]   *Observed* it may be that where there is a Scottish Criminal Cases Review Commission reference in a summary conviction case which raises a different point of appeal from that originally tendered, the court should consider remitting that point to the sheriff for a report (paras 22, 23).

[I]   *Smith v Donnelly* 2002 JC 65 *applied.*

[J]   Richard Langley Russell was charged in the sheriffdom of Glasgow and Strathkelvin at Glasgow on a summary complaint at the instance of Catherine Dyer, Procurator fiscal there, the libel of which set forth a breach of the peace. The cause came to trial before a sheriff (DW Ferguson). On 12 March 2008 the appellant was convicted, and the sheriff imposed a fine of £350 and a 12-month non-harassment order. The appellant applied for a stated case, but leave to appeal was refused at both sifts. The appellant applied for a reference from the Scottish Criminal Cases Review Commission, which referred the case to the High Court of Justiciary.

[A] Name

18–31   This is how the case is referenced using the surnames of both parties to the case.

[B] Date and official citation

18–32   This gives us the day when judgment was given. Further the official or neutral citation[12] follows this [2010] HCJAC 138. These initials stand for the High Court of Justiciary (Appeal Court). Thus we can tell it is a **criminal appeal** case. This was the 138th case reported from this court in 2010.

[C] Judges

18–33   The list tells us that a group of High Court Judges heard this case, this is the norm for an appeal.

[D] Full case details

18–34   This lists the full name of the parties, their legal status and their legal representatives. The person who has brought the appeal Richard Russell (the appellant) was represented by advocate L.K. Kennedy. Only advocates have the right of appearance in the senior courts in Scotland. We are also informed that the other party Catherine Dyer was the Procurator Fiscal for Glasgow and was represented by a senior advocate, a Queens' Counsel.

[E] Key phrases

18–35   This list of key phrases identifies the most important legal elements of the case. The phrase "breach of the peace" tells us it concerns the criminal charge of that name. We can see that the legal question is to determine whether sending a threatening letter to a headmistress then appearing at the school amounts to that crime.

---

[12] Neutral citations were introduced by the Court Services—in Scotland in 2005 and England in 2001—to make it easier to locate as yet unreported cases.

These key words and phrases are very useful for indexing cases and showing exactly where they fit into the law of Scotland. For example, this case is referred to in the *Current Law Case Citator* as: Current Law May 2011 382: Breach of Peace *Russell v Dyer* [2010] HCJAC 138, note use of neutral citation.

You can also use the key words when using an electronic database to help you find cases in any named area of law.

[F] Facts

This paragraph outlines the most important facts of the case. Remember, every case will **18–36** have its own story. As it is an appeal case it also describes the legal history of the case, i.e. which other court has heard this case and what was its decision. What key facts can we gain from this paragraph?

Mr Russell was convicted of breach of the peace following a series of incidents involving the headmistress of his children's school. Some of these incidents took place at the school itself and others involved communication between Mr Russell and the headmistress.

Mr Russell applied for an appeal but this was refused. Then the official organisation the Scottish Criminal Case Review Commission intervened to argue that the incidents as reported did not amount to a breach of the peace.

This was because the communication between the two was private and his presence at the playground would not cause alarm nor did it threaten serious disturbance to the community.

The Crown, which prosecutes crime in Scotland, argued that each element amounted to a breach of the peace. Further that even if they did not individually, then taken together they did.

[G] Decision

The decision in a headnote always follows the word "Held". **18–37**
What then did the court decide?

- The High Court ruled that the sending of the letter plus the appearance at the school at the beginning of the day where many people (adults and children) were present amounted to a breach of the peace. In making this conclusion they referred to a "dual test" in an earlier case *Smith v Donnelly*. They also said that both episodes should be taken together.
- The letter—regarded as a death threat—was communicated to other members of staff and parents were likely to know as well.
- The visit to the school could have been fairly seen by the sheriff (the original judge) as an attempt to intimidate and provoke the headmistress,
- Thus Mr Russell's behaviour was "genuinely alarming and disturbing" and threatened "serious disturbance to the community".
- The appeal was refused.

[H] Observation

A separate paragraph at the end of the headnote begins with the phrase "Observed". This **18–38** tells us that the following is not a legally binding part of the judgment but rather a relevant comment on some of the related issues to the case. This one tells us that the High Court could ask the Sheriff who heard the original case for a report in some instances where the Scottish Criminal Cases Review Commission intervenes. This observation is formally known as an obiter dicta.

[I] Authority

18–39 An earlier case *Smith v Donnelly*[13] is mentioned here with the phrase *applied*. This means that the court is applying the law in *Smith* to this situation. That is, they are using the earlier case as a *precedent*. This follows the earlier mention of the case in the headnote. There are a number of phrases, which courts can use when discussing earlier precedents. For example:

Distinguished —this means the court are drawing a distinction with the precedent in a previous case and the current one.

Overruled—this is important to note, as it means that an older precedent is being overturned by the current case and is no longer legally binding.

[J] Procedural issues

18–40 These few paragraphs outline the legal process used to bring the criminal charges and appeal to the High Court. This tells us the charge was heard at Glasgow Sheriff Court by Sheriff Ferguson on a summary basis. This means the judge alone decides on the guilt of the accused without a jury. The trial was heard on March 12, 2008 Mr Reid was found guilty and fined £350 and faced a 12-month non-harassment order. We are also told that the Scottish Criminal Cases Review Commission referred the case to the High Court. This illustrates that a lot of information is to be found in a headnote and the reader might even be tempted to stop there. However, the headnote only summarises the issues and we cannot fully discover the precedent and significance of a case unless we read the judgment itself.

18–41 A further excerpt, Excerpt 2 from *Russell v Dyer*[14]:

OPINION OF THE COURT—

(1) Trial procedure

[1] The appellant appeared at Glasgow Sheriff Court on a summary complaint which libelled that:

'[B]etween 6 February 2007 and 8 March 2007 at the premises of Wright, Johnstone and MacKenzie, Solicitors ... Glasgow and at ... School, Glasgow you ... did conduct yourself in a disorderly manner repeatedly harass [M], a teacher at [the] School and did by means of a letter threaten said [M], enter the playground, repeatedly fail to comply with requests to retreat from the teacher, place said [M] in a state of fear and alarm for her safety and commit a breach of the peace'.

[2] After sundry procedure, the case called for trial on 22 February 2008. The appellant elected to represent himself. As the sheriff recorded events in the subsequent stated case, at the outset of the trial diet the appellant explained that he had been unable to find an agent to act for him. Four agents had declined to do so and a fifth had withdrawn from acting. The appellant sought an adjournment, not to secure the services of a sixth agent, but because he was of the view that there had not been full disclosure to him, notably in the form of a statement by PC Stephen Kay, the arresting officer, and the name of a procurator fiscal who, he said, had instructed his arrest. The appellant also wished a commissioner appointed to take the evidence of his six-year-old son. The purpose of that was said to be to avoid the child giving evidence in court.

[3] The sheriff refused the motion to adjourn, not being satisfied that there had been any

---

[13] 2002 J.C. 65.
[14] 2011 J.C. 164.

failure to disclose relevant material and having regard to the likelihood that the trial would be adjourned part-heard in any event. That was indeed what happened; the adjourned diets being 27 February, when the Crown case was closed and the defence began, and 12 March 2008, when the sheriff convicted the appellant, fined him £350 and made a 12-month non-harassment order.

[4] During the course of the trial, the playing of part of an audiotape of the appellant's police interview had been the subject of an objection by the appellant. The respondent had proposed to play only part of the tape, pursuant to an agreement reached with the appellant's previous agent, who had been concerned about extraneous prejudicial content. The objection raised was on the bases that: (1) the tape had been 'doctored' by the removal of a question about the appellant's religious beliefs; (2) the whole tape ought to be played; and (3) the police questioning had been unfair. The sheriff held a trial within a trial, although the appellant decided not to lead any evidence during that procedure. The sheriff repelled the objection, being satisfied that none of the bases for the objection had been made out.

(2) Findings in fact

[5] M was the headmistress of a primary school in Glasgow. She had raised interdict proceedings against the appellant. She was represented by a solicitor from Wright Johnstone and MacKenzie. The appellant appeared on his own behalf in that process too. On 6 February 2007, the solicitor received a handwritten letter dated 4 February requesting him to "give the note enclosed" to his client. The appellant had signed the letter, to which was attached a handwritten note. This note started with the sentence:

> 'In the name of Jesus, I am asking you to admit you have told evil lies about me.
> Admit that you have lied to your own lawyer and Council bosses'.

It urged M to admit all her sins so that she would be forgiven. It concluded:

> 'If you do not, then the Lord, King of Kings, Lord of Lords, will condemn you to solitude.
> If you do not tell the truth now, this letter and my voice, will be the last things you see and hear before being cast to Hell.
> In God's name, Amen [signature of the appellant]'.

Not surprisingly, the solicitor was alarmed by the note, the terms of which he immediately conveyed to M at the school over the telephone and then by fax. M was anxious, distressed, upset and placed in a state of fear and alarm. She had to stop work and go home. The police were called and the appellant was detained and interviewed. He admitted that it was possible that he had written the note.

[6] Some time prior to 8 March 2007, the appellant had been interdicted from approaching M, telephoning her, writing to her, approaching her at her place of work and placing her in a state of fear and alarm. However, it did not prohibit him from entering the playground of the school, apparently because he had children attending there. A white line had been painted across one end of the school playground, beyond which line parents were encouraged not to go, in order that the children could line up for class at the other end of the playground, some distance away. On 8 March, the appellant crossed that line with his youngest son and took him to the other end of the playground near to the door leading to the classrooms. The sheriff found in fact:

> '(20) This was under a pretext that the appellant wished to inform the said child's teacher that the child was not to go on a school trip that morning but should remain instead at school to do extra academic work'.

[7] The appellant, who was wearing dark sunglasses, spoke to the child's teacher near the door to the classrooms. The teacher was apprehensive and wary of the appellant's intentions as she knew of the terms of the interdict, as did other members of staff. At this point M arrived at the door. She became frightened upon seeing the appellant, felt intimidated and was placed in a state of fear and alarm. She asked him repeatedly to retreat behind the white line, but he ignored those requests, making M more anxious and distressed. The appellant then stopped

talking to the teacher, looked at M and walked slowly away across the playground. The police were called and arrested the appellant later at his home, purporting to use the power of arrest attached to the interim interdict.

[8] The sheriff observed in his note (stated case, p 16) that:

> 'I have no doubt that [the appellant's] mere presence was designed to intimidate [M] and was provocative. He went up to the school building on a pretext to speak to [the class teacher] about his son—it was quite unnecessary, a telephone call the day before would have sufficed. As indicated above, I was also entirely satisfied on the evidence that the appellant had written and posted or caused to have posted the note to [the solicitor] enclosing the letter to [M]. The Crown brought a single charge of breach of the peace referring to both "incidents" and the Crown in its closing submission was, in my view, correct to state that the two matters must be taken together. The complainer was apprehensive at the mere sight of the appellant on 8 March 2007 because of the events of 6 February 2007 and the granting of the intervening interim interdict'.

The judgment issued here is made in the name of the court as a whole, which means that all three judges were united in the decision itself.

These eight paragraphs outline more facts of the case which have been accepted by both parties and give details of the legal procedures that occurred during the criminal trial.

During the trial we see that Mr Russell represented himself after four "agents"—that is solicitors—declined and one other withdrew from acting. He also wanted to adjourn the hearing so he could discover more material—this was rejected by the sheriff. There was also a "trial within the trial" to determine whether a taped interview between Mr Russell and the police could be played as Mr Russell objected. The sheriff ruled it could be played.

Evidence is presented in the judgment including extracts from the threatening letter sent on February 6, 2007 to the headmistress's solicitors which finishes with the phrase: "this letter and my voice, will be the last things you see and hear before being cast to Hell". This caused the headmistress, who we see remains anonymous, to be extremely alarmed. She also sought her own legal remedy: an interdict which banned Mr Russell from making any contact with the headmistress although this did not prevent him taking his son to school.

We are shown how Mr Russell entered the playground wearing dark glasses despite parents being prohibited from doing so to speak to his child's teacher who was aware of the terms of the interdict. The headmistress then arrived at the door to the school and this again placed her in a state of fear and alarm. Mr Russell reluctantly left the school premises and was arrested later that day for breaching the interdict.

Thus the judgment in these introductory eight paragraphs separates the factual scenario from the legal reasoning. However, the facts that are highlighted are of relevance to the legal issues, as shall be shown.

18–42 A later excerpt, Excerpt 3 from *Russell v Dyer*[15]:

(5) Submissions

> [17] The appellant provided a helpful written outline submission. This, as amplified in oral argument, essentially followed the reasoning of the SCCRC to the effect that the sending of the letter could not have amounted to a breach of the peace. It was a private communication and could not have provoked a serious disturbance of the public peace (*Smith v Donnelly; Harris v HM Advocate; HM Advocate v Harris (No 2); cf Paterson v HM Advocate; Young v Heatly*). The nature of the note was unlikely to have caused persons to take the law into their own hands. At most, the solicitor could have been expected to have reported the content of the note

15 2011 J.C. 164.

to the police. The note did not enter the public realm nor was it intended that it should do so. There was no finding in fact to that effect or concerning the possibility of disturbance. No alternative verdict of 'uttering threats' should be substituted (*Buchanan v Hamilton*). The respondent had not suggested that at the trial and the threats had not been 'grave'.

[18] In the incident in the playground, it had been the complainer who had approached the appellant and initiated the conversation. The appellant had not even spoken to the appellant. He had, as the sheriff had found, simply ignored her. The white line rule had not been made of cast iron. The appellant had not refused to withdraw. He had withdrawn once he had finished his conversation. His behaviour, judged objectively, could not have caused alarm to ordinary people or threatened serious disturbance to the community. No explanation had been given by the sheriff for his use of the word 'pretext' in the context of the appellant's behaviour. Even if the sheriff had been correct in relation to the appellant's motive, the presence of a parent in a playground on a spring morning could not amount to a breach of the peace (*cf Raffaelli v Heatly*).

[19] The Advocate-depute argued that there had been two aspects to the charge and each element on its own amounted to a breach of the peace. The note had been sent using the public post and the solicitor was a member of the public. It was inevitable that he would pass on the terms of the letter to the complainer. It could be inferred that it would have been seen by others. It would thus enter the public domain. It was not essential that the conduct libelled required to amount to an unruly disturbance of the public peace. It was sufficient that alarm and annoyance were caused. Alternatively, a verdict of uttering threats could be substituted.

[20] If each event did not amount to a breach of the peace individually, they did when taken together. The conduct in the playground had been a deliberate act of provocation. It was reasonable to assume that the headmistress of a primary school would be in the vicinity of the playground at the start of the school day. There was a clear public element in the playground. The test of disturbance of the public peace was satisfied where it was established that the public had been seriously alarmed by what had occurred.

(6) Decision

[21] The court has no difficulty in holding that the sending of a threatening letter to the headmistress of a primary school followed by an appearance by the sender at the door of that school at the start of the day, when parents, teachers (including the headmistress) and children could be expected to be present, is conduct which satisfies the dual test in Smith v Donnelly and thus amounts to a breach of the peace. It is important to note that the Crown, no doubt advisedly, did not ultimately libel two separate episodes of breaching the peace but one episode consisting of conduct over a period of time. The sheriff was entitled, if not bound, to consider that conduct in the context of the charge as libelled. In this respect, the court does not consider that it is necessary, or desirable, to look at the two episodes separately and to decide whether one or other of them, taken in isolation, would amount to a breach of the peace. The appropriate course is to look at the two episodes together.

[22] Before doing that, it is worth making some comment on the problems which may arise on a SCCRC reference in a summary conviction case. The sheriff drafted a stated case which provided some information on events in the sheriff court. However, a stated case is a limited form of appeal, wherein a sheriff is asked to direct his or her mind to specific questions which an applicant wishes posed for consideration by the High Court. It is not a comprehensive report covering all issues raised at the trial diet. The application by this appellant was described by the sheriff as presenting 'in the same unfocussed, somewhat rambling, partially irrelevant and obsessive manner in which he conducted his own defence throughout' (stated case, p 17). Although there is some merit in that remark, it was possible for the sheriff to filter out from the application at least some potentially relevant points of appeal. These related to the refusal to allow an adjournment, the admissibility of the interview, the allowance of a commission and (para (c)) what appears to be a complaint about lack of corroboration. The application did not raise directly any issue of whether the proved conduct could amount to a breach of the peace in terms of the dual test in *Smith v Donnelly*. Although, following upon the reference, the note of appeal did raise that issue, the court does not have the sheriff's views on it as it would have had

in a solemn appeal where the ground in the note would normally have been remitted for comment.

[23] There is an additional problem. It is a fundamental part of the stated case procedure, which is not without its critics, that a sheriff's findings in fact must be taken as conclusive unless they are challenged by a specific question directed to their validity. In the stated case here, for example, the sheriff has found in fact that the appellant went to the school on a 'pretext' (finding 20); that is to say, the appellant's purported reason about speaking to the class teacher disguised his real purpose. This finding of fact was not challenged in the stated case and, accordingly, the sheriff has not had his attention drawn to any criticism of that finding. Accordingly, only a limited explanation has been given by the sheriff for his conclusion. Any comment about the lack of any 'factual basis' for this finding in fact must be seen in that context. It may be, therefore, that where there is a SCCRC reference in a summary conviction case, which raises a different point of appeal from that originally tendered and focused in a stated case, the court should consider remitting that point to the sheriff for a report.

[24] Returning to the merits of the appeal, the terms of the letter received by the complainer's solicitor on 6 February 2007 can reasonably be described as presenting a death threat by the appellant to M. That is the only meaning to be placed on the phrase that, if she did not tell what the appellant considered to be the truth, the letter and his voice would be the last things that she would see and hear before being cast into hell. This threat was regarded seriously, as it indeed it was bound to be, by the solicitor who immediately contacted the complainer. She too regarded it as serious. Where the headmistress of a primary school is threatened with death by a parent of children at the school and a relative interim interdict has been obtained, it is reasonable to assume, as was indeed the case, that the background would be communicated to the members of staff at the school. Indeed, knowledge of such an unusual occurrence would be liable to be known to others, including parents.

[25] The sheriff held that, having sent the letter and been interdicted from approaching the headmistress, the appellant went to the school playground on a 'pretext'. The court is unable to agree with the SCCRC that this finding can legitimately be criticised. The appellant would have known that it would be likely that the headmistress would be in the vicinity of the classroom door at the start of the school day. There was no legitimate reason for him to cross the white line and to approach the door. He could have communicated with the teacher by telephone or note. He did not do so and the sheriff was entitled to conclude that the appellant's real motive in acting as he did was to intimidate and provoke the complainer (stated case, p 16).

[26] The situation then was that a person, who was known to be interdicted from approaching a headmistress because of a previous death threat to her, was seen to walk across a line in the playground, beyond which parents were requested not to go, approach the door to the classrooms, where the headmistress might be expected to be, causing her fear and alarm. Using the dual test in *Smith v Donnelly*, this was behaviour which, looked at objectively, would be genuinely alarming and disturbing, in its context, to any reasonable person observing the scene as well as to those directly involved. It would threaten serious disturbance to the community, notably that of the staff of the school and any parents in the vicinity who might have been aware of the background. In short, this is a case where the appellant threatened the headmistress of his children's school with death. He then deliberately approached her place of work, where she and other persons could be expected to be congregating, with a view to intimidating her. That conduct is archetypal of behaviour calculated to cause a public commotion.

[27] This appeal is accordingly refused.

THE COURT refused the appeal.

McIntosh and MacLachlan—Crown Agent

Submissions and decisions

The concluding parts of the judgments have the sub-headings "Submissions" and **18–43** "Decisions". In here we will find the binding legal precedent of the case. Prior to that, the "Submissions" section briefly summarise the arguments of either side of the case.

The appellant has provided a submission in writing which was combined with the spoken argument of his representative. His argument centres around the contention that the letter was a private communication which did not enter the public realm. This means it did not have the necessary elements to be a breach of the peace. Also in the playground he did not approach the headmistress—she had approached him and asked him to leave. His behaviour there could not be said to "cause alarm to ordinary people" or "threaten serious disturbance"—thus again it could not be a breach of the peace.

On the other side the Crown representative known as the Advocate Depute stated that the letter was issued through the public post and sent not to the headmistress but her solicitor. Thus it had entered the public domain. Further, the behaviour in the playground was provocative and had taken place in a public place that is the playground.

The Court's Decision is outlined in the last six paragraphs of the judgment. This is where we find the precedent of this case. In many cases there are no such clear indicators over the binding part of the decision such as a subheading. Another phrase for the binding precedent in a case is the "ratio decidendi", literally the reason for the decision. When reading a case this is what you are looking for. This legal reason for the decision is the only part of a judgment which is binding.[16]

Paragraph 21 states the court's view clearly that they "have no difficulty" in holding that the two actions carried out by the accused amounts to a breach of the peace as outlined in the case *Smith v Donnelly*. Also that both episodes should be looked at together and not in isolation.

The next two paragraphs concern the observation discussed above on requesting a report from the original sheriff in some instances.

Then the court explains why it does not accept Mr Russell's argument. The letter can reasonably be seen as a death threat. That where a headmistress of a primary school receives a death threat from a parent it is reasonable to assume that other people would know in particular other teachers and perhaps some parents. Having sent this letter Mr Russell had then gone to the school and entered the playground when he could have used other means to contact his child's teacher. This can fairly be seen as a provocation. So taken together this behaviour "looked at objectively" would be genuinely alarming and could threaten disturbance to the school community. Indeed the court concludes by saying this is "archetypal of behaviour calculated to cause a public commotion".

What then is the ratio decidendi of the case?

In determining the binding legal reason of a case, it is necessary to think in terms of **18–44** general legal principles. Do not get mired in the particular facts of the case. This is difficult in this case, because the crime of breach of the peace depends so much on the particular factual situation. However, here we could say the ratio is that the crime of breach of the peace, either requires alarm to be felt by ordinary people, or to cause serious disturbance to a community as outlined previously in the *Smith v Donnelly* decision. The sending of a private letter to a public figure (like a primary school headmistress) when it contained

---

[16] As opposed to obiter dicta observations, see para.18–38.

extremely threatening language combined with taking one's child into their school play-ground and speaking to their teacher can fall into this category.

Is the case up to date?

18–45 As when examining statutes, the reader must be aware of whether the case they are looking at is still valid. Has it been overturned by later precedent? Clearly this information will not be given by the hard copy of the report taken off the shelf in the library. *Westlaw* and *LexisNexis* are regularly updated with information regarding the status of cases. This tells us if the case has been discussed in later decisions and if it is still valid law. The *Current Law Case Citator*, which is updated monthly, also provides this information.

STATUTORY INTERPRETATION

18–46 Issues of statutory interpretation arise, when the meaning of a section of an Act is dis-cussed by a judge in a court case. Parliament tries to ensure that its legislation is as clear and specific as possible,[17] yet it is not always possible to avoid ambiguity. Where this occurs, the judiciary adopt certain approaches and use legal tools to help them find the meaning of specific sections, or phrases within sections of a statute.

The starting point would be the Act of Parliament itself. The long title[18] gives guidance as to the aim of the entire statute. The interpretation section[19] of the Act will define key phrases within the legislation and as we have seen there may be other references to the definitions of significant phrases throughout the Act. The judges tend to view the statute as a whole and determine what the "purpose" of the Act is and interpret phrases with that in mind. This is called the "purposive" approach towards interpreting legislation.

There are also external guides, which the courts can use to help them determine the meaning of the statute including several other Acts of Parliament.

- Interpretation Act 1978
  This Act gives some definitions of phrases which are commonly used in statutory law. For example:

  - Schedule 1: " 'Writing' includes typing, printing, lithography, photography and other modes of representing or reproducing words in a visible form, and expressions referring to writing are construed accordingly."

- European Communities Act 1972
  When Britain entered the European Community on January 1, 1973 this Act indicated that all future legislation had to be interpreted in line with European laws:

  - Section 2(4): "Any enactment passed or to be passed ... shall be construed and have effect subject to the foregoing provisions of this section."

- Human Rights Act 1998
  This piece of legislation allowed Acts of the UK Parliament to be challenged, if they breached the European Convention of Human Rights. It also added a new dimension to judicial interpretation of legislation:

---

[17] This was seen when the content of an Act was examined above.
[18] See para.18–07.
[19] See para.18–12.

- Section 3(1): "So far as it is possible to do so primary legislation and sub-ordinate legislation must be read and given effect in a way which is compatible with Convention rights."

Thus, the courts must now try to interpret Acts of Parliament in such a way to ensure that they correspond with the European Convention of Human Rights.

PROBLEM SOLVING

When studying law, you will find that the use of problem scenarios is very common, **18–47** whether in seminar questions, exams or pieces of coursework. There are several reasons for this. All legal subjects have a practical dimension and knowing how they could work in the real world is essential to understanding the law. Problem questions can also be used to test applied knowledge, i.e. rather than simply repeating information learned off by heart, the knowledge can be "applied" to particular situations. Finally, all legal practitioners, or those who work in the world of legal advice, commonly deal with this type of scenario: an individual presents them with a problem and they have to provide some form of informed legal advice and a potential solution.

For all these reasons, knowing how to deal with legal problem questions is an important skill to develop. We shall go through a specific problem and examine the necessary steps to answer it effectively.

Example:

> Jim, who lives on the seventh floor in a block of flats, is so fed up with his dog's barking that he picks it up and throws it out of the window. The dog lands on the street below in front of Sid, who gets such a fright that he suffers a heart attack. An ambulance is called but is unfortunately involved in a serious accident whilst transporting Sid to hospital. Sid is killed in the crash. Can Sid's wife recover compensation for Sid's death from Jim?

1. Identify the general legal issues

An initial reaction may be "That's outrageous! Of course, she should get compensation". **18–48** However, legal problem solving means that the issues have to be examined in a systematic "legal" way. The first step is to identify the broad area of law this problem concerns?

Clearly, this deals with an individual suffering a loss at the hands of another—the death of a spouse. It could be seen that this has been caused by the actions of Jim. Thus, we can identify this problem concerns the Scots private law concept of delictual liability, or delict.

2. Identify relevant facts

Although every problem is a story, it is important that you do not get lost in the details. **18–49** You need to be clear about the most significant issues within the scenario.

Here we could see:

- Chain of events, which began with Jim throwing his dog from a window from a fairly significant height.
- Sid was not hit by the animal, but suffered a heart attack as a result of the sight—this may suggest he had a weak heart?

- This heart attack did not kill him.
- The ambulance crashed, which led to his death—do the ambulance crew now take responsibility? Thus can Sid's wife now sue them?

These facts clearly identify the issues of the problem presented to us, but if we left it there we would be failing in our task, because there is no legal content to this. An answer to a legal problem must balance its content with reference to relevant factual material and legal analysis.

3. Identify more specific legal issues

18–50 We have named the broad area of law, which is examined by this question, and broken down the scenario into key facts. We now need to drill beneath this to look at the specific dimensions of delict, that require to be examined in this problem.

How would you be able to identify these issues? This would depend on the context of the question. In an exam scenario, hopefully your revision strategy[20] will have paid dividends and you will remember the issues that you have studied. If, however, it is a seminar question, or a piece of course work, you will have the ability to reference materials to help you: lecture notes and text books, which should point you in the right direction.

Here there are several specific legal issues:

- *Duty of care and its breach*: this concept is fundamental to delict problems. Was a duty of care owed to Sid and, if so, was it breached by someone's negligence?
- *Reasonable foresee-ability*: one of the tests to determine if a duty has been breached is the application of the foreseeable nature of the harm caused by the individual's action. Were the consequences of Jim's action in throwing the dog foreseeable?
- *Egg-shell skull rule*—taking the victim as you find them. This is a delictual concept, which is relevant here because of Sid's potentially weak heart.
- *Causation*: what was the chain of causation that led to Sid's death? Does it go directly back to Jim's action, or did the intervention of the ambulance driver change the situation. This concerns another delictual concept: novus actus interveniens.

4. Identify appropriate legal sources

18–51 Merely listing the legal concepts in an answer would not be sufficient. You also need relevant sources of law, which support the legal points which are mentioned. The law of delict has mainly developed through common law reasoning: that is through court decisions. There are a number of statutes which deal with delictual issues, although none seem to be relevant here. Thus, we will have to identify cases that are appropriate. When using cases as a legal source it is important that we identify the ratio decidendi[21] of the case— that is the legally binding point of the decision.

- *Duty of care and its breach*: the legal source which laid down the concept of duty of care is *Donoghue v Stevenson*.[22] Lord Atkin's judgment created the neighbourhood principle, where people "closely and directly affected" by an act are seen as your neighbours to whom you owe a duty of care.
  This test for the duty of care has been developed in more recent decisions such as

---

[20] See para.18–81.
[21] See para.18–44.
[22] 1932 S.C. (H.L.) 31.

Caparo Industries plc v Dickman.[23] The ratio decidendi of this case laid down three elements to creating a duty of care: reasonable foresee-ability of harm, closeness between victim and individual carrying out the act and that the imposition of the duty is fair, just and reasonable.

- *Reasonable foresee-ability*: in some cases, the definition of reasonable foresee-ability must be examined to develop the understanding of the concepts. *Muir v Glasgow Corporation,*[24] stated that an individual was liable for the "reasonable and probable consequences of the failure to take care". This was not simply what the individual concerned thought could happen but what "the hypothetical reasonable person" could have foreseen.

  This was developed in the case *Hughes v Lord Advocate.*[25] This looked at the extent of injury caused by an accident and ruled that it was not necessary to foresee the extent of injuries, but simply that an injury would take place: "the fact that the features and developments of an accident may not reasonably have been foreseen does not mean that the accident itself was not foreseeable".

- *Egg-shell skull rule*: there is a lot of authority to support the principle that you take the victim as you find them. *McKillen v Barclay Curle & Co Ltd*[26] is the classical statement of this legal concept in Scots law. A more recent case, *Page v Smith*[27] is also good authority, as it expanded the concept to psychiatric as well as physical injury—although this is an English decision.

- *Causation*: there are two legal concepts of causation here *causa sine qua non* and *causa causans*.

- *Causa sine qua non*: is the factual cause of the injury. It is sometimes known as the "but for" cause, i.e. "but for" the initial incident the injury would not have occurred.

- *Causa causans*; is legal causation, that is, for an individual to be liable in delict, this also needs to be established.

  In most instances these two elements of causation would coincide, unless the chain of events is broken by another element. The legal name for this is novus actus interveniens. *Sayers v Harlow Urban District Council*[28] explained that a chain of causation will not be broken if the subsequent actions were reasonably foreseeable.

5. Apply the law (principles and sources) to the relevant facts of the case.

To illustrate your knowledge of the application of law in this question, it is necessary to **18–52** integrate the legal issues with the specific facts of this problem.

- Jim's action in throwing his dog out the window started the chain of events, which lead to the death of Sid. Throwing any object, particularly a dog (regardless of species!), out of a seven storey flat is a reckless negligent act. Using the neighbourhood test from *Donoghue v Stevenson*[29] it is fair to say that Jim owed Sid a duty of care, as someone who was "closely and directly" affected by his act. He

---

[23] 1990 1 All E.R. 568.
[24] 1944 S.L.T. 60.
[25] 1963 S.L.T. 150.
[26] 1967 S.L.T. 41.
[27] [1995] 2 All E.R. 736.
[28] [1958] 2 All E.R. 342.
[29] 1932 S.C. (H.L.) 31.

also fits the criteria of *Caparo Industries plc v Dickman*.[30] It is reasonably fore-seeable that his actions could cause harm to Sid, there was a proximity in their relationship, and it is fair, just and reasonable that a duty of care is imposed on Jim, as the action of throwing large objects out of your window should not be encouraged in society. In summary, Jim has breached his duty of care to Sid.

- The fact that Jim did not know that Sid would be outside his window is not relevant. As in *Muir v Glasgow Corporation*[31] the "hypothetical reasonable person" could have foreseen such an occurrence was likely when throwing a dog out of the window.

- The fact that it is surprising that Sid had a heart attack is not of importance. Using the ratio in *Hughes v Lord Advocate*[32] the unusual "feature" of this incident, i.e. Sid having a heart attack need not be foreseen, while it is necessary that "the accident itself was foreseeable".

- What if Sid had a particularly weak heart? This is also irrelevant. Applying the egg-shell skull rule, as discussed in the case of *McKillen v Barclay Curle & Co Ltd*[33] and *Page v Smith*,[34] you must take the victim as you find them. In summary, up until this point using the principles and authorities of the Scots law of delict, Jim is liable for the injuries to Sid.

- However, what of the intervention of the ambulance driver—does this mark a break in the change of causation, i.e. a *novus actus interveniens*? It has already been pointed out that Jim's actions were the *causa sine qua non* of this incident: "but for" Jim throwing the dog out of the window the accident would not have occurred. If this is not to also be seen as the *causa causans* (that is the legal cause of the accident) there must be a break in the chain of causation.

- In *Sayers v Harlow Urban District Council*,[35] an act was not seen as a novus actus interveniens if the subsequent actions were reasonably foreseeable. Using the test mentioned in *Muir v Glasgow Corporation*,[36] would the "hypothetical reasonable person" foresee a road accident involving an ambulance? Ambulances travel at high speeds, so perhaps it is not surprising that they could be involved in road accidents. Yet, they also have highly skilled drivers who are used to driving in this way—we also have an expectation of an ambulance driver having an enhanced understanding of safety. On balance, it would be quite difficult to foresee Sid's death in an ambulance accident. Thus, the argument could be made that the accident did amount to a novus actus interveniens, thus the chain has been broken.

- In conclusion, this means that if Sid's wife wants to bring a legal action she will have to sue the employers of the ambulance driver, because the novus actus interveniens has broken the chain of causation from the actions of Jim. Therefore, to answer the question, she cannot recover it from Jim.

We have concluded our informed examination of the legal issues in this problem with a clear answer. In doing this, we have balanced our examination of relevant facts from the scenario with the use of recognised legal sources and principles. This is the correct approach to adopt when dealing with legal problem questions.

---

[30] [1990] 1 All E.R. 568.
[31] 1944 S.L.T. 60.
[32] 1963 S.L.T. 150.
[33] 1967 S.L.T. 41.
[34] [1995] 2 All E.R. 736.
[35] [1958] 2 All E.R. 342.
[36] 1944 S.L.T. 60.

LEGAL COURSEWORK

Essay writing skills are necessary in any academic discipline. Writing legal essays has much **18–53** in common with completing coursework in any subject, yet there are some specific differences which you need to bear in mind when embarking on this task.

1. Type of question

Problem

We have examined how to tackle problem questions in general.[37] This approach should be **18–54** used for coursework, however, there are some details relating to the written structure which will be examined below.

Analytical

This type of question would require the student to examine an area of law critically. It **18–55** normally involves a degree of explanation and analysis. It may also involve the student's own opinions—backed by legal authority.

Example: The last decade has seen several major pieces of anti- terrorist legislation. Explain the main provisions of these laws and analyse how effective and fair you think they are.

Purely factual

It is rare, but you may get a piece of coursework that simply asks you to explain a specific **18–56** legal principle, or source. It is more common for this to be done in conjunction with another type of question

Example:

> *Scottish Farmer's Dairy Company v McGhee*, 1933 S.C. 148. Was the restrictive covenant in this case valid in the judgment of the Court of Session? What legal reasons did Lord Clyde give for his decision?

2. Structure

Unlike the time-limited frenzy of an exam, a student normally has weeks, or even months, **18–57** to prepare and complete a piece of coursework. As a result, more emphasis is placed on the style and structure of a piece of coursework.

Some key points to remember:

Go with the flow

There are many guides on how best to structure an essay, but there is one element that **18–58** overrides all others. The essay should be readable: the reader can understand what you are saying and the work has a coherent flow to it.

A common problem when students tackle their first pieces of legal coursework is jumble. A legal source is considered, then another one, then the writer goes back to the first one and repeats themselves and so on. There is no coherence to the work. This is understandable, as new students are tackling concepts and types of source materials that they

---

[37] See para.18–47.

will have never worked with before. However, clarity of structure helps to create an understanding of the work.

Know your limits

18–59 When you are embarking on writing an essay there will be some inbuilt limitations.

- Deadline
  Each piece of coursework will have a date for completion. This means you will know how much time you will have to devote to the work. This will dictate the amount of research you carry out for the essay.
- Word Count
  It is important to take care that your work falls within the requisite word limit. A fairly standard length for a piece of law coursework would be 1500–2000 words. The limit is given for a reason, as it determines the depth that the essay can have. It will also be a factor in the work you can put into writing it.

Notes

18–60 Before work can commence on the essay, preparation will come in the way of research. This will in general take the form of writing notes from legal sources. These could be primary sources, such as statutes and cases or secondary sources, e.g. text books and lecture notes. Many pieces of coursework will have a list of suggested reading—this is always a useful starting point.

This may be an appropriate example for the above question, on anti-terrorist laws.

Reading List

A v Secretary of State for the Home Department [2005] 3 All E.R. 169
David Feldman "Human Rights, Terrorism and risk: The roles of Politicians and Judges", 2006 Public Law, 364-384
Prevention of Terrorism Act 2005
Terrorism Act 2006

Key points from the sources should be noted down, as should the full details of the material looked at—this will be important when we come to referencing the work.[38]

Using quotations from sources, especially written texts, can be very effective as long as it is not over-done. When doing this the words must be reported accurately—so care is needed when taking notes. When you begin your first piece of legal coursework, you may feel you are overly reliant on one particular source. This could be a textbook, a specific case or even a statute. There is nothing wrong with this in principle, as long as the source is relevant, but as your knowledge of law develops you should broaden the amount of materials from which you take notes.

---

[38] See para.18–64.

Introduction

A good piece of coursework will always have a clear introduction. This should outline **18–61** what your objectives are in the essay and how you are going to achieve them. If you have clarity in this it will give the reader of the work confidence that you understand the issues and how you are going to discuss them.

If the essay begins with discussing the topic of the question immediately, with no introduction, it catches the reader off-guard. It also suggests that you have not had time to stand back from the topic and give an overview of exactly what you are attempting to achieve in the work. If you feel you are reaching the limits of the word count for the essay, your introduction need not be very long, but it should not be sacrificed completely.

Body of the work

The bulk of the coursework will be taken over by a discussion of the legal issues. As **18–62** explained above, these should be structured in a coherent way that is readable.

- Relevance
  The points must all be relevant. In a word-limited piece of work every phrase is critical, so do not waste them on material which you do not need. Alternatively, a strategy that a student may adopt if they are running out of things to say, or if they do not really understand the issues, is "padding". That is putting material in the essay which they know is not needed, but fills it out. An experienced marker of work though, can see through this approach very quickly.
- Repetition
  Repeating a key point in an answer can be effective, as it emphasises your findings and conclusions. But this is something else that can be over-done. Subtly rephrasing the point that you just made, several times throughout the work, can also be spotted by a marker. In this way, repetition adds very little to a piece of coursework.
- Problem questions—get the balance right.
  The tackling of problem questions has been examined above.[39] As explained, the use of legal sources is critical. In the essay format, though, one issue that often arises is that the discussion of the legal sources can become too abstract.
  Before you apply the law to the specific scenario, you may want to explain what the area of law is about, by discussing legal principles, or perhaps the ratio of a case. However, you need to be aware of where this fits into the overall structure. A common occurrence in essays, is that the student spends too long discussing the law in general and not relating it to the specific scenario. Remember, this is ultimately what a problem question is about; it is not a general discussion of legal issues. So, although there is a place for a broader explanation of issues you **must** balance this with applying the law to the problem.

Conclusion

As with the introduction, having a conclusion to your work is a good sign to the marker **18–63** that you have an overall coherence in your understanding of the topic. At the very least it shows that the essay has not tailed off and you just finished writing it when you ran out of words!

---

[39] See para.18–47.

The conclusion also allows you to bring together all the main points explored in the coursework—thus showing the power and not abuse of repetition. It also allows you to summarise your answer to the specific question in the coursework. For example, a problem question might end with the phrase:

> Advise Ann as to her legal obligations in this situation.

A conclusion could then begin with:

> So to conclude, my advice to Ann would be ...

3. Referencing

18–64 In our discussion of problem questions, the importance of using appropriate legal sources was emphasised.[40] This is particularly important in the context of coursework. As you have time to prepare any essay, you must show you are confident in referencing a variety of sources. This also illustrates that your work is informed and is not made up of general assertions, but is actually backed up by legal authority. Learning to reference, then, is an important part of developing legal coursework.

Plagiarism

18–65 There is also another, potentially more serious, reason for referencing work correctly. Plagiarism, or passing someone else's work off as your own, is a serious academic offence. In all educational institutions, serious penalties can be imposed on a student if they are found to have carried out this activity. Many universities are investing in high-tech software to detect this.

Copying whole essays, or chapters of books, from another source are clear examples of serious plagiarism, or to put it more plainly cheating. What a student should seek to avoid though is "plagiarism by accident". This may occur where a paragraph, or even a couple of sentences, are lifted from another work and there is no acknowledgement of where the material is taken from. This can be avoided by having a good system of referencing within your work.

Bibliography

18–66 In every piece of written coursework that you submit, there should be a list of all the source material you looked at when preparing and writing the work. This comprehensive list is called a bibliography and should be at the end of the essay. This is the starting point for any system of referencing, because it should mention every source that you utilise in your coursework. Different institutions have different requirements and you should check which bibliographic conventions are expected by your institution. The following are some general guidelines.

---

[40] See para.18–51.

Sections

Law uses a variety of source materials therefore it is important to have different sections **18–67** within the bibliography. This separates each category of material referred to in the work. Within this general definition of what a bibliography is there are several different styles but a uniform approach to each category must be adopted.

These categories could include:

Authored works

This includes textbooks, reports and legal journal articles. For written texts like this all **18–68** relevant information should be included in the bibliography:

- Author
- Title
- Edition Number
- Year
- Publisher
- Correct citation (if journal article)

This information should be taken from the text when you are researching the essay.

Websites

Increasingly used for academic work any web reference that you have used in work should **18–69** be listed in a section of bibliography.

Tip: there is no need to refer to Westlaw or LexisNexis—these are databases which are used as a tool to retrieve other legal sources.

Cases

All case reports referred to in the essay should be listed in a section of bibliography. These **18–70** should be listed alphabetically, by the initial of the first party to the legal action. Remember, you must always use the correct citation for a case, never put it in the bibliography simply as the two parties' names.

Statutes

Equally, there should be a list of statutes that are mentioned in the work. These can either **18–71** be listed alphabetically or chronologically. Remember, this is done with the short titles of the statutes.

Footnotes

For referencing to be complete, there needs to be a link from the bibliography to the text **18–72** of the coursework. At the point in your essay where are you using materials mentioned in the bibliography.

One way of linking these two is by using a system of footnotes. In some academic disciplines and journals, the Harvard system is utilised—this references the source by author in the body of the text.

Example:

> As a reflection of this at the higher levels of private practice the number of women enrolled as partners is significantly less. In the same time period of the large growth of women within practice there has been an increase in the number of female partners but at a much lower rate. In 1987/88 5.4 per cent of all partners were women, whereas in 2002/03 7.9 per cent were. Yet, if these figures are taken as a proportion of the total number of women practising law this has remained constant at 20% (MacMillan, McKerrell & McFadyen 2005, 23).

For most law essays this is not really an appropriate form, because you are using a variety of different sources—not only authored works, but cases and statutes. In this instance, a system of numbered footnotes can be more effective.

These numbered references identify within the text, when bibliographical details are used. They also give more specific details like page numbers.

Example:

> *Clancy v Caird* (1) was a significant case regarding Human Rights in Scotland. Himsworth states that the case was significant in its use of Canadian sources of law in making its judgment (2).
> (1) 2000 S.L.T. 546.
> (2) Himsworth & O'Neill (2004), p141.

If you have a comprehensive bibliography, you do not have to put all the details in the footnote. Rather, the reader can cross reference material and check which source you are mentioning in the bibliography.

LAW EXAMS

18–73 When preparing for examinations with a legal topic, is there any specific advice that can be given as opposed to general exam technique? This section identifies three areas that should be remembered when preparing for law-based exams. before some general issues on examinations are mentioned.

1. Sources of law

18–74 The use of legal sources in exams is critical; this factor above all else can determine how successful you are. In most situations, students can exhibit a general understanding of legal concepts and ideas. However, unless this can be coupled with appropriate legal authority it will be a weak answer. If proper sources are not utilised then the answer can have the air of uncertainty—"I'm not really sure what the law is ...".

In most instances, the difference in exam results between a higher and lower mark will be, to a large extent, determined by the use of legal sources. By sources, in general, we mean the two major ones we have identified in this work: statutes and cases.

When answering a question, you should review the sources by asking yourself a few of your own questions.

Cases

- Is there an appropriate case/s that I can discuss in the context of this question?   **18–75**
- How does this case's ratio apply to this situation?
- Can I remember the case name?

Tip: in a time limited unseen exam you do not need to recite the full citation of a case apart from the names of the parties.

Statutes

- Is this legal issue regulated by a statute?   **18–76**
- If so what is the "short title" of the Act?[41]
- Can I remember the relevant sections of the statute?

Tip: it can be difficult to recall a lot of specific sections of an Act of Parliament, but it can be advantageous if you remember the key ones.

Finally, when you have finished writing your answer read it over and ask:

- Are there any legal sources in this answer?
- If so are they appropriate?
- Have I referenced them correctly? In the context of cases that would mean the names of the parties and the correct short title when discussing an Act of Parliament.

2. Types of question

In law exams there are only three categories of questions that can be asked. This applies   **18–77** regardless of the specific law subject that is being assessed.

They are:

- (a) Problem questions.
- (b) Notes questions.
- (c) Discursive questions.

(a) Problem questions

We have looked at how to tackle problem questions above.[42] Essentially, the same method   **18–78** can be used for dealing with this style of question in an exam or piece of coursework. However, this task becomes much harder in an examination context.

First, the question will be, in most instances, unseen.[43] That is, the student must identify the significant legal issues and appropriate sources almost immediately. This is quite a difficult thing to do and will require a strong exam revision strategy.[44]

Secondly, you will be limited by time. This makes planning a structure and being thorough with your application of sources critical.

Both these issues and the general nature of problem questions make these quite challenging assessments in the context of an exam.

---

[41] See para.18–05.
[42] See para.18–47.
[43] Although some law departments have experimented with the use of giving out the problem scenario to students at some point prior to the exams.
[44] See para.18–81.

(b) Notes questions

18–79 This type of assessment is often used in exams. If problem questions are seen as "applied law" these assess "pure law".

Example:

> 1. This is a *compulsory* question. Attempt any **TWO** of the following:
> (a) Discuss the statutory provisions which may allow a person to have set aside, a contract which he entered into while aged 16 or 17. (5)
> (b) Explain the key statutory provisions which govern formality in contract and describe the circumstances in which a contract may be enforced despite not being properly executed (signed). (5)
> (c) Explain the statutory provisions which might protect a customer who is told that, because of a disclaimer notice on the counter, the dry cleaner will not compensate her for ruining her best party frock. (5)
> (d) With reference to case law, explain the circumstances in which an employer may enforce a contractual provision preventing an employee from going to work for a trade competitor. (5)

This notes question, deals with the law of contract in Scots law. It deals with four distinct areas and helps the student by identifying the legal sources they should look at in their answer. When tackling this sort of question, it is worthwhile to remember a couple of points.

Check how much each part is worth

Although notes questions can often come up in exams there can be a broad variation in the marks awarded and hence the amount of detail needed to get the maximum mark. If we look at the example given above, each part has the same weighting and would require equal time to be given to them.

Try not to answer notes with notes

The question may not be as lengthy as a problem scenario, but that should not mean that you are casual in your answer. Structure and paragraphs are as important here as in any other type of exam question. It does not allow you to utilise bullet points excessively in your answer.

It would not be appropriate to answer the question above in this way:

> 1. (a) The key statutory provisions which allow a 16 year old to set a contract aside are in Age of Legal Capacity (Scotland) Act 1991. They are
> - S1(1)(a) a person under age of 16 shall have no legal capacity
> - S1(1)(b) a person over the age of 16 shall have legal capacity
> - S2(1)... etc.

Although the correct legal source has been identified, in this case an Act of the UK Parliament, there is no structure to the answer. It reads more like notes taken from a lecture or from reading a text book.

Write all you know ... as long as it is relevant

You should be as comprehensive as possible when answering these questions, but always check the information is related to the questions. There can be a tendency to "open the floodgates" when dealing with this type of assessment and thus you want to write down, literally, everything you know about an area of law. Remember, it may not be relevant to the specific point asked about.

A bad way to approach writing one of the answers would be:

> 1. (c) When a customer puts a party frock into a dry cleaners she is entering into a contract. Contracts are legally binding obligations in Scots law. A contract is formed in Scotland if there is consensus between the parties—this means there must be an offer and acceptance. This is illustrated by the case of *Hunter v General Accident Fire and Life Assurance Ltd* where an advert in a diary was ruled to be an offer. You must have full capacity to make a contract, this means under the Age of Legal Capacity (Scotland) Act 1991 you must be at least 16. The dry cleaner is refusing to pay compensation because of a disclaimer notice this is similar to the case of *Olley v Marlborough Court Hotel.*

Here the answer is far too broad, and the student is trying to give a potted summary of everything they know about the law of contract. Also when they start to examine the specific question, they deal with a case whereas the question is specifically asking them to look at the relevant statute. In this case, it should be the Unfair Contract Terms Act 1977. Thus, although legal sources are used in this answer they are not appropriate to the question.

Discursive questions

These types of question are less common in many disciplines of law, but it is still important **18–80** to be aware of how to deal with them. Essentially, a discursive question is asking the student to advance different opinions on a subject and perhaps to put forward their own viewpoint.

> 3. (a) What does the defeat of Margo MacDonald's End of Life Assistance Bill in December 2010 tell us about the process of an individual MSP introducing a potential Act of the Scottish Parliament? (10 marks)
>
> (b) How does this compare with Westminster? (5 marks)
>
> (c) Does the Scottish Parliament listen to the "people" more? (5 marks)

This is a question examining the legal system in Scotland, in relation to the passing of legislation in both the Scottish Parliament and the UK Parliament. The first part, is a fairly straight forward examination of legal procedure on how a Member of the Scottish Parliament can propose a change in the law, although it requires a specific knowledge of the Members' Bill introduced by Margo MacDonald in the Parliament related to assisted suicide in Scotland.

It is in questions (b) and (c) that the discursive elements come through. In both parts the student is asked to put forward what they "think" about the legal issue. First, in a comparative setting by looking at the Westminster procedure and then on the validity of the proposition that the Scottish Parliament is a more inclusive people's parliament.

When answering the question remember:

A discursive question is not an excuse for a "law-free" answer.

When asked your opinion on a topic there can be a tendency to view the answer as one where there is no need to worry about the use of legal sources, which have been shown to be very important in other legal answers.

This might cause part of the above question to begin to be answered in the following way:

> 3. (c) I think the process in the Scottish Parliament is the better way and it shows we listen to the people. For too long we have been ruled by England and its Westminster ways. Since 1707 Scotland has been forced into a Union and had to give up elements of its legal situation. The Scottish Parliament allows the Scottish people to be free. including its own elected members. This means they can introduce laws in a way that they can't in the London dominated House of Commons.

This answer is certainly putting forward a strong opinion. That can be a good thing in the context of a discursive answer. However, this needs to be an informed opinion particularly by legal content. This should be relevant to the question. If not, then the answer can appear at best vague and at worst inaccurate.

Dealing with this question, an important source to examine would be the Scotland Act 1998 which created the Scottish Parliament. Also, successful pieces of Scottish legislation that have been passed after being introduced by individual Members of the Scottish Parliament could be scrutinised: for example, the Abolition of Poindings and Warrant Sales (Scotland) Act 2001 and the Property Factors (Scotland) Act 2011. Further, the specific procedures used in Holyrood should also be explored. The same should be done for the House of Commons' procedure.

This does not mean that you cannot have a clear opinion in questions like this, but you must still be aware of using legal materials in your answer.

These three types of questions, either on their own or in some form of combination, are the most common way that law is assessed in the context of an exam.

3. Revision strategy

18–81 When preparing for an unseen exam, the method you adopt when revising is critical. In law, given the importance of using appropriate legal sources in a relevant way, a strategy needs to be adopted where you can remember these in the appropriate context.

Historically, there tended to be a belief that revising for a law exam consisted of learning off by heart a long list of case names, which you could then write down during the exam. This was partly a myth, but it does highlight the importance of using legal sources.

Now, however, in most law exam settings such an approach would not be enough. It is important that you place a legal source, be it case law or statute, within its relevant subject.

Break the subject down

18–82 When you are revising from lecture notes or text books it is always a good idea to break the subjects of law down to manageable areas. When you have done this, you could attach relevant sources to them. So that when you are memorising sources you are doing it under the head of a topic.

For example, in the context of contract law the topic of formation of contract is a discrete area of that subject. You could begin to draw up a list of the key issues and legal

sources relevant to it. The summaries at the end of the chapters in this book could help
you with this.

It could begin:

Formation of Contract

- *Consensus in idem*
- Offer and Acceptance—need to match

    - *General Accident Fire and Life Assurance Ltd v Hunter*

- Offer v Invitation to treat

    - *Pharmaceutical Society of Great Britain v Boots Cash Chemists*

- Counter-Offer

    - *Wolf and Wolf v Forfar Potato Co...*

Here is the beginning of a list of the key concepts around the formation of contract and a
number of sources are attached to them. Thus, you are not learning these cases in isolation
but remembering them in a legal context.

Remembering cases

As explained[45] the binding and legally significant point of a case is its ratio decidendi. **18–83**
However, it can be difficult to remember what this is in isolation. In general in an exam
(and indeed in coursework) you should try to avoid simply telling the facts behind a case.
But you can turn this to your advantage in revision. The human memory tends to focus on
stories: histories of very old civilisations were often passed down as sagas. So knowing
some of the factual issues of a case can help you remember but you **must** attach them to the
ratio of the decision.

Let us use the example of one of the key sources listed above:

Pharmaceutical Society of Great Britain v Boots Cash Chemists
Overall Legal Issues

- Formation of Contract: Offer v Invitation to Treat

Facts

- Boots were taken to court by a regulatory body because they were displaying
products on open shelves. This was part of their shift to become a more self-
service style shop—quite pioneering for the time: 1953.
- These products required to be sold in the presence of a qualified pharmacist.
- The Pharmaceutical Society argued that a shop display was an offer and the
contract was formed when the customer picked the product off the shelf. This
was not done in the presence of a chemist, therefore, Boots were breaking the
rules.
- Boots argued that the shop display was an invitation to treat, showing what
was available in the shop. The offer was made by the customer when they
took the product to the counter and the contract was formed when the shop

---

[45] See para.18–44.

assistant accepted the offer. At the counter a chemist would be present, thus no rules were broken.

- The court sided with Boots, i.e. they agreed that Boots had not broken the rules.

Ratio

- A display of goods in a shop amounts only to an invitation to treat, not an offer. Thus, a contract cannot be formed by picking up goods from the shelf.

Useful Quote:
On self-service in Boots:

"is this to be regarded as a more organised way of doing what is already done in many types of shops—and a bookseller is perhaps the best example—namely, enabling customers to have free access to what is in the shop, to look at the different articles, and then, ultimately having got the ones which they wish to buy to come up to the assistant saying 'I want this'".

Lord Justice Somervell

Looking at the facts of this case in this way, helps us link in with the specific legal point on when a contract is formed and the contrast between an offer and an invitation to treat—both legal concepts. The facts are fairly easy to remember and deal with an activity that most people can relate to: shopping. Even the quote from the judge highlights this point.

This technique could be used for cases, which relate to the specific legal topic you are revising.

Remembering statutes

18–84 This can sometimes be a little more difficult to do than remembering cases. Some law exams allow the students to bring in copies of statutes to the exam room, but it would be rare for the same privilege to be given to case books.

There are several elements needed when revising a statute. What is its purpose and what are its key sections?

Using an example from contract law mentioned above:[46] Age of Legal Capacity(Scotland) Act 1991. This Act was passed to simplify the law relating to the capacity of young people to enter contracts.

Section 1: this sets the age of contractual capacity at 16. It also states that young people below that age cannot enter into contracts.

Section 2: this covers exceptions to this rule and states that young people can enter into contracts of a "kind commonly entered into" by someone of that age.

Section 3: this gives additional protection to 16 and 17 year olds. They have until the age of 21 to set a contract aside if it is a "prejudicial transaction" and it was entered into at that age.

Here, the key elements of this statute are highlighted and attached to the relevant section of the Act itself. This can be done here, as it is a fairly short statute with clear purpose. It is

---

[46] See para.18–79.

also difficult to have a word for word recognition of exactly what a statute states,[47] but it is important to remember key phrases from the Act of the Parliament.

General exam issues

General tips for exams are listed below: **18–85**

- **Use your time**
  Exams are normally a certain length of time for a purpose; the examiner believes that is the requisite time to deal with the question. A common reason for students to not perform well in exams is because they do not produce enough material. Use the full amount of time when answering your exam questions. This may not consist of constantly writing, taking a few minutes to think about your answers should also be encouraged.
  "Diving straight in" to a question may cause you difficulties. This is particularly true for problem questions, where you may have missed an element in your assessment of the problem or completely misunderstood it.
  Work out prior to the exam how much time you should devote to each question.

- **Read the question**
  Always look at the exam paper very closely. What exactly needs to be in the answer? In problem questions this is critical as a misreading of the relevant issues could result in an incorrect answer. There also needs to be clarity over which specific legal sources should be in the answer. These issues can be resolved by close reading of the questions.

- **Structure answers**
  Before you begin writing any answer, take a couple of minutes to think how the answer will be structured, what key points you are going to make and which legal sources you will use.
  It is easier to do this at the beginning of your time than trying to work it out as you go along. Although there is less emphasis in a time based exam, on absolute clarity of structure than there is in coursework,[48] it is still important that the answer is readable and makes sense.

---

[47] This is why many law exams allow students to bring in copies of the statute.
[48] See para.18–57.

Index